Early Records

HAMPSHIRE COUNTY VIRGINIA

Now West Virginia

Including at the start most of known Va. aside from Augusta District

—SYNOPSIS OF—

Wills from originals up to 1860

Grantee with acreage - location, wife's name and witnesses - Grantor
Deeds up to 1800 - Marriage records 1824-1828

and

Alphabetical arrangement of State Census 1782 and 1784

Revolutionary Soldiers Pensions residing in the County 1835

Privately Printed

CLARA McCORMACK SAGE and LAURA SAGE JONES

Delavan, Wisconsin

THE DELAVAN REPUBLICAN—PRINTERS & PUBLISHERS

Since 1863 — Delavan, Wis.

Printed, 1939

Notice

In many older books, foxing (or discoloration) occurs and, in some instances, print lightens with wear and age. Reprinted books, such as this, often duplicate these flaws, notwithstanding efforts to reduce or eliminate them. The pages of this reprint have been digitally enhanced and, where possible, the flaws eliminated in order to provide clarity of content and a pleasant reading experience.

Originally published:
Delavan, Wisconsin
1939

Reprinted by:

Janaway Publishing, Inc.
732 Kelsey Ct.
Santa Maria, California 93454
(805) 925-1038
www.JanawayGenealogy.com

2006, 2011

ISBN: 978-1-59641-081-7

Made in the United States of America

--PREFACE--

The Civil War as well as time took its toll in all counties of the South. The War of 1812 saw the destruction of the 1790 census of Virginia as well as of other states.

Many of the will books containing copied wills were burned but fortunately there remained many of the old original wills fast crumbling to dust.

The compilers of these records thought the gathering of the wills would be a benefit to geneology. In addition the deeds often supplied the names of wife, friends who witnessed and have location of the home in Virginia often earlier or later where there was no will. (Lacking Bible records, marriage records or wills, the deeds are the best proof of ancestry.)

By alphabetical arrangement of the 1782-84 census returns for the State, the originals of which are in Richmond, Va. in this volume, with markings to show in what neighborhood they were, as indicated by the census takers initials who had contiguous territory seemed to be a helpful aid to those trying to trace their families.

A few of the deeds often not recorded in the deed books where title was taken through tax sales or through confiscation of estates have also been included from Hampshire County History by Maxwell and Swischer.

The only marriage records that escaped destruction previous to 1866 are included with all names connected with the license and arranged alphabetically under both the man's and the woman's names.

The index has been carefully compiled and while all has been alphabeticaly arranged in the body of the book, every name appears in the index and in addition all married women are listed under maiden name as well as married name where this could be ascertained.

Different spellings of the same name in one document have led us to suggest in the index different names which are suggestive of the one indexed.

All has been done to make this book accessible quickly through the alphabetical arrangement and index for the searchers who, possibly as we, have had limited time for research. Often time the very meager or no index in a book that held out from its title hopes of family dates just had to be passed over because we did not have time to search page by page while well indexed books were at hand.

The compilers were in search of their Ross ancestry and the finding of the original will of Wm. Ross dated 1754 among the uncopied deeds led them to undertake the publishing of this book.

We are indebted to the officers and personel in Romney Court House for their helpful co-operation.

PUBLISHERS.

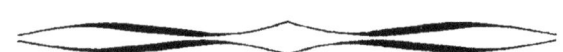

Table of Contents

	Page
Grantor Deeds	1
Grante Deeds	64
Census Virginia 1782 and 1784	88
Pensioners in Hampshire 1835	98
Marriage Records 1824 - 1828	99
Synopsis of Wills	106
Index of two Undestroyed Early Will Books	139
Miscellaneous Corrections	140

ALPHABETICAL INDEX OF

Deeds, Leases, Mortgages

and Other Instruments

GRANTOR-GRANTEE

—A—

| 1796 10-17 | ACTON, John of Hampshire Co. 54 a. on Allegany Mt.; rec. 10-17-1796. Wit.: None. | to Abraham Johnson of Hampshire Co. |

1796 4-14 ACTON, John (w. Mary) — to Jacob Barnick
of Hampshire Co. — of Hampshire Co.
112 a. on Allegany Mt., rec. 4-18-1796. Wit.: None.

1790 2-11 ACTON, Richard (w. Jemimah) — to Jesse Sharpleys
of Hampshire Co. — of Hampshire Co.
91 a. on Allegany Mt., rec. 2-11-1790. Wit.: None.

1792 8-28 ACTON, Richard (w. Jemimah) to Rawleigh Colstone,
of Hampshire Co. — Edward Smith,
110 a. on North Branch, rec. 8-28-179? — John Mitchell,
Wit.: None. — Alex. King,
William Janney,
Andrew Wodrow

1794 10-15 ACTON, Richard (w. Jemimah) to Andrew Smalley
of Hampshire Co. — of Hampshire Co.
170 a. on Montgomery's Run, rec. 10-15-1794. Wit.: None.

1794 10-15 ACTON, Richard (w. Jemimah) to John Acton
of Hampshire Co. — of Hampshire Co.
112 a. on Allegany Mt., rec. 10-15-1794. Wit.: None.

1795 6-10 EARSON, Jacob (w. Catherine) to Gustan Davis
of Hampshire Co. — of Hampshire Co.
100¼ a. near town of Springfield; rec. 7-20-1795.
Wit.: None.

1795 6-10 EARSON, Jacob (w. Catherine) to Richard Goffick
of Hampshire Co. — of Hampshire Co.
72 a. on South Br. R.; rec. 7-20-1795.
Wit.: None.

1796 4-16 EARSAM, Jacob (w. Catherine) to John Logan
of Hampshire Co. — of Hampshire Co.
142¾ a. on South Br. R.; rec. 4-18-1796.
Wit.: None.

1768 11-7 EARSHAM, Simon (w. Mary) to Mary Creymour
of Hampshire Co. (Mortgage) — of Hampshire Co.
385 a., South Branch; rec. 11-10-1768.
Wit.: John Lyne.

1769 3-6 EARSAM, Simon (w. Mary) to John Earson, his son
of Hampshire Co. — of Hampshire Co.
Part of Lot 35, So. Branch; rec. 3-14-1769.
Wit.: William Rannells, Susanna Earsam,
John Black.
(See IHRESOM also.)

1790 12-15 AHRSAM, Simeon, Sr. (w. Mary) to sons,
(See Earsom, Ihrsom, Ohrsom) Simeon Ahrsom, Jr.
of Hampshire Co. and John Ahrsom, dec'd
50 a. on South Branch R.;
rec. 12-16-1790.
Wit.: John Mitchell, Benj. Heale,
Robt. Rannels, Wm. Young.

1798 9-13 ALDERTON, Wm. (w. Margaret) to Henry Taylor
53 a. on Cacapeon R., rec. 9-17-1798.
Wit.: Francis White, Henry Hardy,
Andrew Wodrow, Matthew Lodge.

1761 12-18 ALEXANDER, James to Gabriel Jones
of Hampshire Co. (mtg.) of Augusta Co.
354 a. on Great Cape Capon, rec. 8-10-1762.
Wit.: Margaret Frogg, George Mallo, Henry Tyler.

1772 5-5 ALEXANDER, James to Thomas Littler
of Hampshire Co. (lease and release) of Hampshire Co.
138 a. on Cacapeon Creek, rec. 5-12-1772.
Wit.: William Hughes, John Hughes, Richard Mynatt.

1765 10-3 ALKIER, Maunis (w. Lydia) to Michael Thorn
of Hampshire Co. (lease and release) of Hampshire Co.
Wit.: Christian Bingamon, Peter Cutright,
Adam Brown.

1799 12-16 ALLEN, Jacob (w. Elizabeth) to Jacob Umpstott
of Hampshire Co. of Hampshire Co.
House and lot in Romney, rec. 12-16-1799. Wit.: None.

1794 10-14 ALLIN, Thomas to David Jones
of Frederick Co. of Hampshire Co.
67 a. on Patterson Creek, rec. 10-15-1794.
Wit.: John Jones, Sr., Aaron Jones,
Daniel Jones, Abel Emerson.

1779 3-1 ALT, Michael to David Welton
of Hampshire Co. of Hampshire Co.
78 a., Lot 43, on S. Branch; 24 a on S. Branch; rec. 3-9-1779.
Wit.: John Nevill, Jr., Abel Westfall,
Moses Hutten, Jonathan Heath.

1793 9-11 AMORY, Edward (w. Elizabeth) to Daniel Combs
of Hampshire Co. of Hampshire Co.
30 a. on Patterson Creek, rec. 9-11-1793.
Wit.: John Jones, John Reed, Abraham Johnson.

1768 5-6 ANDERSON, James to Henry Houglan
of Hampshire Co. Cornelius Conner
Personal property; rec. 5-11-1768.
Wit.: John Rousow.

1797 9-3 ANDERSON, Mena to Michael Fout
of Hampshire Co.
146 a. on New Creek, rec. 10-16-1797.
Wit.: James Clark, James O'Hara,
Notley Barnard, John Jones, Sr.

1794 8-20 ANDERSON, William to John Elliott
of Hampshire Co. of Hampshire Co.
205½ a. on road from Winchester to Romney; rec. 4-20-1795.
Wit.: James Carruthers, William Chisholm,
Michael Brady, Sam Dew, James Monroe, John Copsey.

1797 7-22 ANDERSON, Wm. (w. Margaret) to Thomas Anderson
of Hampshire Co. of Washington Co.
206 a. on North R.; rec. 9-18-1797.
Wit.: Rees Pritchard, William Crisholm,
James Monroe, Amy Day, Robert McKee.

1772 11-19 ANDERSON, Wm. (w. Rachel) to John Baker
of Hampshire Co. (lease and release) of Hampshire Co.
100 a. New Creek, rec. 11-10-1772. Wit.: None.

1787 9-17 ANDERSON, Wm. (w. Margaret) to James Molloy
of Hampshire Co. of Hampshire Co.
337 a. on Crooked Run, rec. 10-9-1793.
Wit.: John Lander, Ephraim Johnson,
Wm. Williamson, John Williamson, Andrew Wodrow.

1791 5-18 ANDERSON, Wm., Sr. to Thomas Anderson (son)
of Hampshire Co.
187 a. in state of Va.; 52 a. Allegany Co., Md.; rec. 10-13-1791.
Wit.: Joseph Mounts, Asa Mounts, William Anderson.

1797 10-10 ANDREWS, George (w. Margaret) to Benjamin Benan
271 a. on Little Cacapeon, rec. 10-16-1797. of Penna.
Wit.: None.

1779 11-9 ARCHER, John (w. Hannah) to John McBride
of Hampshire Co. of Hampshire Co.
149 a. on Little Cacapeon, rec. 11-9-1779. Wit.: None.

1794 10-17 ARMSTRONG, William (w. Ann) to John Gile
of Hampshire Co. of Alexandria
Parcel of land on Patterson Creek, rec. 2-16-1796.
Wit.: Charles Magill, Alex King, Edward Amory.

1796 10-1 ARMSTRONG, William (w. Ann) to John Gill
300 a. on Patterson Creek (Bill of Sale); rec. 10-17-1796.
Wit.: None.

1800 10-22 ARMSTRONG, William (w. Ann) to Jonah Thompson
of Hampshire Co. of Alexandria
Recorded 2-16-1801.
Wit.: Jacob Kiger, Isaac Birk, William Armstrong,
Charles Magill.

1771 3-22 ARNOLD, Andrew (w. Priscilla) to Levi Ashbrook
of Hampshire Co. (lease and release) of Hampshire Co.
400 a. on North R. of Cacapeon; rec. 4-9-1771. Wit.: None.

1771 4-8 ARNOLD, Andrew (w. Priscilla) to George Nixon
of Hampshire Co. (lease and release) of Hampshire Co.
170 a., south side of Cacapeon R., rec. 4-9-1771.
Wit.: Sam Dew.

1790 4-15 ARNOLD John (w. Hannah) to Thomas Pugh
of Hampshire Co. (lease and release) of Hampshire Co.
20 a. on Great Cacapeon; rec. 8-28-1792.
Wit.: Jesse Pugh, Elijah Davis, John Arnold George Beall.
Dedimus, June 8. 1792, rec. June 8, 1872; Elias Poston, George
Beall and James Monroe summoned to go examine Hannah
Arnold and see if she is willing to execute the deed, mentioned
before (she not being able to travel to the court).

1790 4-15 ARNOLD, John (w. Hannah) to Elijah Davis
of Hampshire Co. (lease and release) of Hampshire Co.
43 a. on Great Cacapeon; rec. 8-28-1792.
Wit.: Jesse Pugh, Thomas High, James Ress, John Arnold.
Dedimus, June 20, 1792; rec. July 2, 1792: George Beall, Elias
Poston and James Monroe summoned to go examine Hannah
Arnold and see if she is willing to execute the deed, mentioned
before (she not being able to travel to the court).

| GRANTOR-GRANTEE |

| 1792 6-20 | ARNOLD, John (w. Hannah) to George Spade of Hampshire Co. (lease and release) of Hampshire Co. 120 a. on Great Cacapeon; rec. 8-28-1792. Wit.: Elijah Davis, George Follis, William Hook. Dedimus, June 20, 1792; rec. July 2, 1792: George Beall, Elias Poston and James Monroe summoned to go examine Hannah Arnold and see if she is willing to execute the deed, mentioned before (she not being able to travel to the court). |

—B—

1800 2-17	BABBS, Beal (w. Deliverance) to William Fry of Hampshire Co. of Hampshire Co. Recorded 2-17-1800.
1799 11-20	BABBS, Beal to Alex Munroe of Berkeley Co. (lease) of Hampshire Co. Recorded 4-14-1800. Wit.: Elisha Beall, John Turner, John Doudall.
1792 6-20	ARNOLD, John (w. Hannah) to Andrew Arnold of Hampshire Co. of Hampshire Co. 231 a. on Great Cacapeon; rec. 8-28-1792. Wit.: Elijah Davis, George Sasollet, Thomas Megraw.
1800 4-20	BABBS, John (w. Rebecca) to Samuel Collins Recorded 5-19-1800. Wit.: Samuel Peters, Jacob Vanpelt, Abraham Pennington.
1771 8-13	ARNOLD, Jonathan (w. Sarah) to William Milbowen of Hampshire Co. (lease and release) of Hampshire Co. 400 a. on North River; rec. 8-14-1771. Wit.: George Brent, Sam Dew.
1800 4-14	BABBS, William to Benjamin Garritt of Hampshire Co. of Hampshire Co. Recorded 4-14-1800.
1773 3-10	ARNOLD, Joseph to George Nixon of Hampshire Co. (lease and release) of Hampshire Co. Parcer of land on Great Cacapeon; rec. 3-11-1773. Wit.: Sam Dew.
1800 4-14	BABBS, William Hamilton to Ben Garrart Recorded 4-14-1800. Wit.: George Horn, James Gibson.
1774 3-25	ARNOLD, Joseph to Moses Ashbrook of Hampshire Co. (lease and release) of Hampshire Co. 400 a. on North River of Great Cacapeon; rec. 3-14-1775. Wit.: Levi Ashbrook, John Prunty, Jonathan Pugh, Bean Pigman, Isaac Johns.
1779 9-4	BACORN, Job (w. Rhoda) to Moses Tichenall of Hampshire Co. of Morris Co. 400 a. on Cabbin Run; rec. 8-8-1780. Wit.: Abraham Johnson, Mary Wick.
1779 9-3	BACORN, Job (w. Rhoda) to Joseph Williams of Hampshire Co. of Washington Co. 307 a. on Cabbin Run; rec. 11-9-1779. Wit.: John Roussaw, Moses Wick, Mary Wick.
1799 4-15	ARNOLD, Samuel (w. Mary) to Zachariah Arnold of Hampshire Co. of Hampshire Co. 300 a. on Mill Creek; rec. 4-15-1799. Wit.: None.
1797 9-2	ASBERRY, Joseph to John Elliot and MONROE, James, of Hampshire Co. of Hampshire Co. 418 a. on Little Cacapeon R.; rec. 10-17-1796. Wit.: Andrew Wodrow.
1783 8-6	BACORN, Job (w. Rhoda) to Joseph Williams of Hampshire Co. of Washington Co. 100 a. on Patterson Creek; rec. 3-10-1784. Wit.: John Roussaw, Elijah Chenoweth, John Clinton.
1783 8-12	ASHBROOK, Aaron (w. Mary) to John Forman of Hampshire Co. (lease and release) of Hampshire Co. 110 a. on South Branch; rec. 8-12-1783. Wit.: None.
1784 1-23	BACORN, Job (w. Rhoda) to Thomas Martin of Hampshire Co. (lease and release) of Hampshire Co. 71 a. on Patterson Creek; rec. 3-10-1784. Wit.: Abraham Johnson, Samuel Martin, Thomas Holland.
1786 8-13	ASHBROOK, Aaron, to William McGuire (atty.) of Washington Co. of Hampshire Co. Authority to sell tract of land; rec. 2-13-1787. Wit.: James Murphy, Nicholas Casey, Elias Poston, Ralph Humphreys.
1787 6-13	BACORN, Job (w. Rhoda) to Valentine Purgett of Hampshire Co. of Hampshire Co. 400 a. on Patterson Creek; rec. 9-13-1787. Wit.: John Williams, Ezekiel Whitman, John Keller.
1777 3-10	ASHBROOK, Levi (w. Mary) to Elias Poston of Hampshire Co. (lease and release) of Hampshire Co. 200 a. on North River; rec. 3-11-1777. Wit.: None.
1779 1-27	ASHBROOK, Moses (w. Sarah) to Jacob Hubbard of Hampshire Co. (lease and release) of Hampshire Co. 400 a. on North R. of Cacapeon; rec. 3-9-1779. Wit.: Elias Poston, Wm. Milburn, James Smith.
1791 6-8	BACORN, Job (w. Rhoda) to Valentine Purgitt of Monongahela Co. of Hampshire Co. 115 a. on Patterson Creek; rec. 10-13-1791. Wit.: Solomon Jones, Ebenezer Williams, Aaron Jones.
1790 7-10	ASHBROOK, Thomas to Phillip Cool and CASEY, Nicholas, of Hampshire Co. Bond, 500 lbs. to sell 320 a. of land in Hamp Co.; rec. 9-11-1790 Wit.: None.
1794 1-9	BACORN, Job (w. Rhoda) to William Johnston, Jr. of Monongahela Co. of Monongahela Co. 22 a. on Patterson Creek; rec. 6-15-1795. Wit.: Isaac Johnson, Sam Martin, Henry Hazel, Abraham Johnston, Abraham Johnston, Jr.
1793 7-10	ASHBROOK, Thomas (w. Agnes) to Phillip Cool of Hampshire Co. of Hampshire Co. 325 a. on Branch Mt.; rec. 7-10-1793. Wit.: None.
1783 8-9	BAILEY, John (w. Grace) to Esac Morris of Fauquire Co. of Fauquire Co. 292 a. on Little Cacapeon; rec. 8-12-1783. Wit.: Eppa Timberlake, Francis Atwell, William Jones, Elias Hiett.
1800 9-16	ASHBROOK, Absolem (w. Rachel) to Levy Ashbrook of Hampshire Co. of Hampshire Co. Recorded 10-20-1800. Wit.: James Dailey, Thomas McCarthy, Phil P. Wilson, Andrew Wodrow.
1800 3-12	BAILEY, John (w. Ann) to Jacob Switzer of Berkeley Co. of Frederick Co. Recorded 4-14-1800. Wit.: Wm. Panabaker, Jacob Hamilton, Edward How.
1785 3-16	ASHBY, Martin to George Noble of Prince William Co. of Frederick Co. 424 a. on Looney's Creek; rec. Nov. 8, 1785. Wit.: Joseph Norris, Thomas Stroud, Thomas Smith, William Howell.
1791 12-23	BAKER, Henry (w. Mary Elizabeth) to Jacob Emmert of Frederick Co. of Hampshire Co. 153 a. on North R.; rec. 2-28-1792. Wit.: George Millslagle.
1799 3-1	BAKER, Henry (w. Marie) to Jacob Emmett of Frederick Co. of Hampshire Co. 114 a. on North River; rec. 4-15-1799. Wit.: Andrew Horn, Jacob Millslagle, Jacob Emmett, Jr.
1785 3-18	ASHBY, Martin to George Noble of Prince William Co. of Frederick Co. 104 a. on Little Cacapeon; rec. 11-8-1785. Wit.: Luke Metheany, Thos. Stroud, Thos. Smith, Joseph Norris, Thomas Noble.
1778 6-1	BAKER, Melcher to Henry Morse of Hampshire Co. of Hampshire Co. 82 a. on South Branch; rec. 8-11-1778. Wit.: Anthony Baker, Casper Hite, Abel Randall.
1787 5-1	ASHBY, Nathaniel (w. Peggy) to Andrew Redtruck of Frederick Co. of Hampshire Co. 188 a., Hampshire Co.; rec. 9-13-1787. Wit.: Buckner Thurston, Charles Magill, Robert White, Jr.
1799 11-27	BAKER, Patrick (w. Lucy) to Joseph Harford of Hampshire Co. of Hampshire Co. 400 a. on Little Cacapeon; rec. 12-16-1799. Wit.: Peter Williams, John Jack, Peter Parker.
1781 1-22	ASHBY, William to Samuel Hornback of Washington Co. of Hampshire Co. 45 a. on South Branch R.; rec. 2-13-1781. Wit.: Andrew Wodrow, Abraham Hite, Jesse Ashby, Garret Vanmeter.
1800 2-19	BAKER, Patrick (w. Lucy) to Charles Hauser Town of Romney (lease) Commonwealth of Virginia Guardians of children of Francis Taggart. Recorded 4-14-1800.
	ASHLEY, Ben to Jermiah Ashley of Hampshire Co. Recorded 2-17-1800. Wit.: Ebenezer Davis, James Abernethy, Lot Robinson.
1800 2-17	BAKER, William to The Court of Hampshire Co. (let of attorney) Recorded 2-17-1800. Wit.: None.
1772 9-14	ASHLEY, Thomas to John Foreman of Romney, Hampshire Co. of Hampshire Co. Personal property; rec. 11-12-1772. Wit.: Godfrey Lang, William Pool.
1785 10-21	BAKER, Samuel to James Smith of Hampshire Co. (mtg.) of Hampshire Co. 400 a. on Little Cacapeon; rec. 11-8-1785. Wit.: Sam Dew, James Barber, John Bosler, John Marly.
1798 4-15	ATHLEY, Thomas (w. Elizabeth) to Edward McCarty of Hampshire Co. of Hampshire Co. 106 a. on New Creek; rec. 4-16-1798. Wit.: None.
1779 5-11	AUGHNEY, Darby to Jacob Long of Hampshire Co. of Hampshire Co. 400 a. on So. Branch R.; rec. 5-11-1779. Wit.: Sam Dew.
1778 5-18	BALDWIN William (w. Jean) to George Beall of Berkeley Co. (lease and release) of Hampshire Co. 200 a. on North Br. of Cacapeon; rec. 11-10-1778. Wit.: George Rootes, Alex. White, John Magill.

GRANTOR-GRANTEE PAGE 3

1772 BANE, Joseph (w. Parthena) to **James Largent**
10-25 of Hampshire Co. (lease and release) of Hampshire Co.
125 a. on Great Cacapeon; rec. 11-10-1772.
Wit.: Sam Pritchard, Evan Hiett, James Cady.

1778 BARCLAY, Thomas to **Enoch Berry**
8-8 of Pennsylvania of Romney, Hampshire Co.
MAGILL, John, Attorney
Half acre in town of Romney; rec. 8-12-1778.
Wit.: None.

1787 BARCLAY, Thomas to **Enoch Berry**
11-1 of Philadelphia, Pa. (bill of sale) of Hampshire Co.
Half acre lot in town of Romney; rec. 1-10-1788.
Wit.: Andrew Wodrow, Charles Magill,
Robert White, Jr.

1798 BARKELOW, Johnson to **Joseph Briggs**
2-19 BARKELOW, Benjamin of Hampshire Co.
BARKELOW, Ruth
BARKELOW, Elizabeth
BARKELOW, Sarah
BEATTY, Charles
BEATTY, Eleanor
and POWELSON, Abraham and Mary
of Hampshire Co.
Gristmill, sawmill and 2 a. land, Hampshire Co.; rec. 9-17-1798.
Wit.: None.

1770 BARKLEY, John to **James Gelleson**
8-14 of Hampshire Co. and Daniel Richardson
Sheep, hogs; bill of sale; rec. 4-14-1771. of Hampshire Co.
Wit.: Thomas McCarty, Daniel McNeil.

1791 BARNHOUSE, John (w. Mary) to **Duncan McVicker**
9-15 of Hampshire Co. of Hampshire Co.
120 a. on Great Cacapeon; rec. 6-26-1792. Wit.: None

1793 BARNHOUSE, John (w. Mary) to **Thomas Mulledy**
10-9 of Hardy Co. of Hampshire Co.
287 a. on Alleghany Mt.; rec. 10-9-1793.
Wit.: William Baer, William Cochrane, John Forman.

1795 BARTON, Kimber (w. Elizabeth) to **Mary Burbridge**
4-14 of Hampshire Co. of Hampshire Co.
Parcel of land on Patterson Creek; rec. 4-20-1795.
Wit.: John Mitchell, Alex King, John McBride,
Thomas Hollenback.

1792 BATES, Edward (w. Sarah) to **Sampson Henderson**
11-18 of Fairfax Co. of Hampshire Co.
124 a. on North Branch; rec. 4-10-1793.
Wit.: James Carruthers, James Monroe, Joseph Asbury.

1792 BATES, Edward (w. Sarah) to **Thomas Bates**
11-23 150 a. on Maple Run; rec. 4-10-1793. of Prince William Co.
Wit.: James Carruthers, Joseph Asbury, John Higgins.

1793 BATES, Edward (w. Sarah) to **William Richards**
2-19 of Fairfax Co. of Fairfax Co.
200 a., Hampshire Co. rec. 6-12-1793.
Wit.: Thomas Bates, Jane Bates, George Richards.

1797 BATES, Thomas (w. Jane) to **William Adams**
10-21 of Hampshire Co. of Loudon Co.
150 a., Hampshire Co.; rec. 12-18-1797.
Wit.: None.

1774 BATTEN, Henry to **Friend Gray**
1-27 of Hampshire Co. (lease and release) of Hampshire Co.
100 a., South Branch; rec. 4-12-1774.
Wit.: Margaret Willeys, James Largent, Andrew Turke, James
McBride, Evan Hiett, Andrew Carlon.

1783 BATTIN, Simon to **Anderson Corbin**
10-7 of Chester Co. (lease and release) of Hampshire Co.
Parcel of land on Gibbon Run, a br. of North R. rec. 11-11-1783
Wit.: James Wearshall, Josiah Haines.

1761 BATTON, Henry to **John McMachan**
12-7 of Hampshire Co. (lease and release) of Frederick Co.
375 a., North River; rec. 12-8-1761.
Wit.: Ja. Keith, John Hayton, Gabriel Jones,
Cuthbert Bullett.

1778 BATTON, Henry (w. Margaret) to **James Largent**
2-23 of Hampshire Co. (lease and release) of Hampshire Co.
68 a. on Great Cacapeon; rec. 5-12-1778.
Wit.: Rees Pritchard, Hugh McKever,
Benj. Ely, Wm. Carlyle.

1778 BATTON, Henry (w. Margaret) to **James Largent**
2-23 of Hampshire Co. (lease and release) of Hampshire Co.
9½ a. on Great Cacapeon; rec. 5-12-1778.
Wit.: Rees Pritchard, Hugh McKever,
Benj. Ely, Wm. Carlyle.

1783 BATTON, Henry (w. Margaret) to **William Bills**
of Hampshire Co. (lease and release) of Hampshire Co.
77 a. on Great Cacapeon R.; rec. 5-13-1783.
Wit.: John Chenoweth, Enoch Enochs, William Largent.

1796 BAYLOS, Edward (w. Eleanor) to **Henry Miller**
7-18 of Hampshire Co. of Hampshire Co.
113 a. on Knobley Mt.; rec. 7-18-1796.
Wit.: None.

1778 BAYNTON, John to **Gasper Hirsman**
11-10 of Philadelphia, Pa. of Hampshire Co.
214 a. on Patterson Creek; rec. 11-11-1778.
Wit.: None.

1778 BEALE, Tavener (w. Betty) to **Isaac Zane**
11-24 of Shenandoah Co. (lease and release) of Frederick Co.
386 a. on Cacapeon R.; rec. 3-9-1779.
Wit.: Frances Ravenhill, John Magill,
Edwin Young, George Rootes, G. Jones, Peter Hog.

1796 BEALL, Eli to **Frederick Starkey**
10-17 of Hampshire Co. of Hampshire Co.
533 a. on North R.; rec. 10-17-1796.
Wit.: None.

1793 BEALL, George to **Eli Beall**
10-2 of Hampshire Co. of Hampshire Co.
100 a. on North River; rec. 10-9-1793.
Wit.: Elias Poston, Elisha Beall, John Parrill.

1793 BEALL, George to **Elisha Beall**
10-2 of Hampshire Co. of Hampshire Co.
77 a. on North River; rec. 10-9-1793.
Wit.: Elias Poston, Eli Beall, John Parill.

1776 BEALL, Isaac (w. Margery) to **Samuel Beall**
1-29 of Berkeley Co. (lease and release) of Frederick Co.
400 a. on New Creek; rec. 5-9-1780.
Wit.: Alex White, F. Peyton, Jr., Wm. Campbell,
Edward Keran.

1778 BEALL, Samuel to **Charles Lynch**
6-1 of Williamsburg of Hampshire Co.
212 a. on South Branch; rec. 8-8-1780.
Wit.: John Smith, John Cox, Abraham Hite,
Enoch Innis, William Booth.

1778 BEALL, Samuel to **Joseph Nevill**
5-29 of Williamsburg of Hampshire Co.
Power of atty.; authority to execute and convey to Hans Michael Miller, a tract of land on New Creek; rec. 8-11-1778.
John Cox, Abraham Hite, John Smith,
Enoch Innis.

1778 BEALL, Samuel to **Hanse Michael Miller**
8-11 of Williamsburg, Va. of Washington Co.
400 a. on New Creek; rec. 8-11-1778.
Wit.: Sam Dew.

1792 BEALL, Thomas to **Peter Putman**
6-26 of Alleghany Co. of Hampshire Co.
149 a. on North Br. of Potomac; rec. 6-26-1792.
Wit.: Andrew Wodrow.

1798 BEALL, Thomas (w. Malinda) to **Francis Deakins**
2-8 of Allegany Co. and Wm. Deakins, Jr.
352 a., Hampshire Co.; rec. 4-16-1798. of George Town, Md.
Wit.: John H. Bogard, John C. Beatty.

1770 BEAN, Joseph (w. Parthena) to **Henry Batton**
1-25 of Hampshire Co. (lease and release) of Hampshire Co.
125 a. on Mill Run; rec. 5-8-1770.
Wit.: Sam Pritchard, Rees Pritchard,
Thomas Edwards, William Lockhart.

1798 BEATTY (see Barkelow above)

1784 BEAVER, Matthew (w. Anne) to **James Fleming**
10-22 of Hampshire Co. (Bill of Sale) of Hampshire Co.
107 a., Hampshire Co.; rec. 11-9-1784.
Wit.: William Vause, Richard Sturman,
John Plumb, Richard Boyce.

1772 BEAVER, Peter to **Mathias Beaver (son)**
8-3 of Hampshire Co. of Hampshire Co.
107 a. in Hampshire Co.; rec. 8-11-1772.
Wit.: John Gillmer, Will Smith,
Elizabeth Beaver, Henry Heith.

1799 BEVER, John to **James Watson**
12-9 of Allegheny Co., Pa. of Berkeley Co.
Recorded 2-16-1801.
Wit.: William Littell, William Laughlin.

1782 BEVER, Peter (w. Elizabeth) to **Mathias Bever**
5-27 of Frederick Co. (bill of sale) of Hampshire Co.
107 a., Hampshire Co.; rec. 5-27-1782.
Wit.: None.

1784 BEAVER, Peter to **Henry Lighter**
3-13 of Hampshire Co. of Hampshire Co.
275 a. on Lick Run, a drain of Patterson's Creek; rec. 8-13-1770
Wit.: Sam Dew.

1790 BEAVOUR, Peter (w. Catherine) to **Jacob Hearsman**
4-15 of Hampshire Co. of Hampshire Co.
109 a., Hampshire Co.; rec. 4-15-1790.
Wit.: John H. Price.

1798 BECKNER, Peter to **John Kesler**
4-9 of Hampshire Co. of Hampshire Co.
130 a., Hampshire Co.; rec. 9-17-1798.
Wit.: Peter Bruner, John Matthew,
Henry Henderson, Jeremiah Thompson.

1796 BECKWITH, Marmaduke Brokenburrow, to **Moses Gill**
11-5 of Loudon Co. (Bill of Sale)
194 a. on Knobley Mt.; rec. 12-19-1796.
Wit.: James Leach, Thomas Jones,
Thomas Hogan, Anthony Buckner.

1798 BEEKMAN, Wm. (w. Sarah) to **Henry Powelson**
3-1 of Hampshire Co. of Hampshire Co.
Parcel of land on South Branch R.; rec. 4-16-1798.
Wit.: George Scott, Jacob Allen, Ann Conklin,
John J. Jacob.

1783 BEELER, Joseph to **John Moyers, Jr.**
9-15 of Westmoreland Co. (Bill of Sale) of Hampshire Co.
400 a. on New Creek; rec. 3-9-1784.
Wit.: James Reid, John Baker, Johannes Hess.

1770 10-15	BEGLY, Henry (w. Elizabeth) to Abraham Wise of Hampshire Co. (lease and release) of Hampshire Co. 100 a. on Patterson Creek; rec. 11-13-1770. Wit.: Sam Dew, Thomas Parsons, John Foreman, Elizabeth Heinzman.

1773 3-9	BELL, John (w. Agnes) to Okey Johnson of Hampshire Co. of Hampshire Co. 330 a.—Lot No. 11 on Patterson Creek; rec. 5-12-1773. Wit.: Abraham Johnson, Benjamin Parker.

1797 10-2	BELL, William (w. Margaret) to Richard Aires of Hampshire Co. (see PELL) of Hampshire Co. 402 a., Hampshire Co.; rec. 10-16-1797. Wit.: None.

1797 11-6	BELL, William (w. Margaret) to Henry Protzman of Hampshire Co. (see PELL) of Hampshire Co. 100 a. on Cabbin Run; rec. 12-18-1797. Wit.: John Snyder, A. King, Israel Stallcup, Arthur Allen, Robt. Allen, Thos. Allen, John Mitchell.

1797 10-12	BENAM, Benjamin (w. Sarah) to George Andrews of Pennsylvania of Hampshire Co. 271 a. on Little Cacapeon R.; rec. 10-17-1797. Wit.: John Higgins, George Laubinger, Francis Murphy.

1787 11-28	BERRY, Enoch (w. Elizabeth) to Thomas Barclay of Romney, Hampshire Co. (Bill of Sale) Lot in town of Romney; rec. 4-10-1788. Wit.: Andrew Wodrow, James Murphy, Samuel Murphy, Job Parker.

178- 	BERRY, Enoch (w. Elizabeth) to Andrew Wodrow of Hampshire Co. of Hampshire Co. Half acre lot in town of Romney; rec 1-10-1788. Wit.: Wm. Fox, John Murphy, Alex Ruthven, James Murphy.

1790 12-24	BERRY, Enoch (w. Elizabeth) to Andrew Wodrow of Hampshire Co. of Hampshire Co. 476 a. on Little Cacapaeon; rec. 2-10-1791. Wit.: None.

1790 12-28	BERRY, Enoch (w. Elizabeth) to Andrew Wodrow of Hampshire Co. of Hampshire Co. Half acre in town of Romney; rec. 2-10-1791. Wit.: None.

1784 5-7	BERRY, Reuben (w. Sarah) to Garret Vanmeter of Hampshire Co. (lease and release) of Hampshire Co. 173 a. on Mill Run; rec. 5-11-1784. Wit.: Abraham Hite, John Beall, Matthew Harrison, Abel Randall.

1780 4-9	BILLS, John (w. Ruth) to William Morgan of Hampshire Co. (lease and release) of Hampshire Co. 132 a. on Great Cacapeon; rec. 7-11-1786. Wit.: None.

1769 9-20	BILLS, William (w. Sarah) to Robert Rutherford of Hampshire Co. (lease and rel.) of Winchester, Frederick Co. 326 a. on Cacapeon River; rec. 5-9-1770. Wit.: James Chew, Joseph Wiley, Henry Lewis, Jr.

1770 3-14	BILLS, William (w. Sarah) to James Hamilton of Hampshire Co. lease and release) of Hampshire Co. 180 a. 4 mi. above the North River of Cacapeon; rec. 3-15-1770. Wit.: Sam Dew.

1786 7-9	BILLS, William (w. Sarah) to John Chenoweth, Jr. of Hampshire Co. (lease and release) of Hampshire Co. 102 a. on Great Cacapeon; rec. 7-11-1786. Wit.: None.

1789 4-17	BILLS, William (w. Sarah) to John Copsey of Hampshire Co of Hampshire Co. 81 a. on Great Cacapeon; rec. 4-17-1789. Wit.: None.

1800 10-10	BLACK, John to Francis White of Hampshire Co. DAILEY, James GAITHER, Elijah HEINSMAN, Henry MULLADY, Thomas Recorded 10-20-1800. Wit.: None.

1779 9-13	BLACKBURN, Edward (w. Mary) to Edward Bates of Fairfax Co. (lease and release) of Fairfax Co. 418 a. on North R. of Great Cacapeon; rec. 3-14-1780. Wit.: John Rhodes, William Blackburn, Sarah Goodwill, Nicholas Sebastian.

1779 9-30	BLACKBURN, Edward (w. Mary) to Edward Bates of Fairfax Co. (lease and release) of Fairfax Co. 408 a. on North River; rec. 3-14-1780. Wit.: John Rhodes, William Blackburn, Sarah Goodwill, Nicholas Sebastian.

1778 1-25	BLACKBURN, William (w. Sarah) to Okey Johnson of Hampshire Co. (lease and release) 100 a. on Patterson Creek; rec. 4-14-1778. Wit.: James Blackburn, James Flood, John Blackburn.

1779 8-10	BLACKBURN, William (w. Sarah) to Tasper Cather of Hampshire Co. (lease and release) of Hampshire Co. 67 a. on Patterson Creek; rec. 8-10-1779. Wit.: Andrew Fairley, John Fairly, Jacob Wolf.

1779 8-10	BLACKBURN, William (w. Sarah) to Jasper Cather 67 a. on Patterson Creek; rec. 8-13-1782. of Frederick Co. Wit.: None.

1795 11-11	BLOOMFIELD, Joseph (w. Mary) to Andrew Wodrow of Burlington, N. J. of Hampshire Co. McILVANE, William (w. Mary) 403 a. on South Branch; rec. 7-18,1796. Wit.: William Coxe, Jr., Charles Reed.

1770 8-13	BLUE, Abraham to Catherine Blue of Hampshire Co. widow of John Blue All claims or interest in father's estate (John Blue). Rec. 12-12-1770. Wit.: Abraham Johnson, Jacob Reasoner.

1783 10-9	BLUE, Abraham (w. Elizabeth) to Kimber Barton of Hampshire Co. of Hampshire Co. 94 a. on Patterson Creek; rec. 11-11-1783. Wit.: Abraham Johnson, David Jones, John Pearsall.

1794 3-20	BOARDMAN, Joseph (w. Elizabeth) to Peter Harsel of Hampshire Co. of Berkeley Co. 306 a. on Patterson Creek; rec. 4-9-1794. Wit.: John Dixon, Robt. Cowan, Lydia Cowan.

1784 4-10	BOGARD, Elizabeth to Joseph Petty of Hampshire Co. (Power of Attorney) of Hampshire Co. Authority to convey tract of land, 100 a., in Phila. Co., and all conveyances necessary. Rec. 4-12-1874. Wit.: Andrew Wodrow, Joseph Nevill, Jonathan Heath, Abel Randall.

1786 1-17	BOGARD, Jacob (w. Mary) to Okey Johnson of Hampshire Co. of Hampshire Co. 67 a. on Patterson Creek; rec. 9-12-1786. Wit.: Jacob Kimberlin, John Kimberlin, Abraham Johnson, Abraham Johnson, Jr., Thomas Holland.

1789 6-10	BOGARD, Jacob (w. Mary) to Jesse Kent of Hampshire Co. of Hampshire Co. 100 a. on Patterson Creek; rec. 10-15-1789. Wit.: Okey Johnson, Samuel Lewis, John Kent, William Ross.

1789 3-28	BOGGARD, Jacob to Abraham Johnson, Sr. of Pheatty Co., Pa. (Power of Attorney) of Hampshire Co. Authority to collect whatever due Jacob Boggard. Rec. 4-17-1789. Wit.: William Johnson, Jr., John Johnson.

1793 7-5	BOGELL, James (w. Mary) to Thomas Bogell of Hampshire Co. of Hampshire Co. 372 a. on New Creek; rec. 7-10-1793. Wit.: Sam Dew, J. Wheeler, Sam Dew, Jr., Mary Bogell.

1800 1-26	BOGLE, Andrew (w. Mary) to Peter Watters of Hampshire Co. of Frederick Co. Recorded 4-14-1800. Wit.: William Nanse, Michael Fout, Okey Johnston, Stephen Pilcher, George Miller.

1794 6-7	BOGLE, James (w. Mary) to Abraham Neff of Hampshire Co. of Hampshire Co. 48 a. on New Creek; rec. 9-10-1794. Wit.: J. G. Wheeler, Thos. Smart, Nathan Farrand, Wm. Vause, Okey Johnson.

1794 6-7	BOGLE, James (w. Mary) to Abraham Neff of Hampshire Co. of Hampshire Co. 68 a. on New Creek; rec. 9-10-1794. Wit.: Thomas Smart, Nathan Farrand, William Vause, Okey Johnson.

1769 3-13	BOND, Walter to Elizabeth Parker of Hampshire Co. (Bill of Sale) of Hampshire Co. Two ewes; rec. 8-9-1769. Wit.: Thomas Bon, James McDanyel.

1777 8-11	BONNETT, Samuel (w. Elizabeth) to David Myles of Hampshire Co. (lease and release) of Hampshire Co. 205 a. on Cedar Swamp; rec. 8-12-1777. Wit.: Isaac Parsons, Isaac Means.

1767 8-10	BORN, John to Mordecia Morgan GRAHAM, John, S. Carolina (Power of Atty.) Frederick Co., Va. Power to sell interest in two tracts of land in Hampshire Co.; rec. 8-8-1768. Wit.: Thomas Dixon, Joseph Pack.

1766	BOWEL, William to Bazel Bowel of Hampshire Co. (Deed of Gift) of Hampshire Co. 91 a. on Great Cape Cepon; rec 11-11-1766. Wit.: None.

1766	BOWEL, William to William Crecraft of Hampshire Co. (son-in-law) and Sarah, his wife (Deed of Gift) of Hampshire Co. Land on Great Cape Cepon; rec. 11-11-1766. Wit.: None.

1766	BOWEL, William to Joseph Crecraft of Hampshire Co. (son-in-law) and Margaret, his wife (Deed of Gift) of Hampshire Co. 92 a. on Great Cape Cepon; rec. 11-11-1766. Wit.: None.

1771 11-12	BOYCE, Richard to William Vandiver of Hampshire Co. of Hampshire Co. 529 a. on Patterson Creek; rec. 11-12-1771. Wit.: Sam Dew.

1772 8-10	BOYCE, Richard to Simon Doyle of Hampshire Co. (lease) of Hampshire Co. 208½ a. on Patterson Creek; rec. 8-10-1773. Wit.: Sam Dew, John Roussaw, Alex White, Peter Steenbergen,

GRANTOR-GRANTEE   PAGE 5

1791 BOYCE, Nicholas — to John Snyder
7-14 BOYCE, Sarah — of Hampshire Co.
Administrators of Rich. Boyce, dec'd
of Hampshire Co.   (lease)
625 a. on Patterson Creek; rec. 7-14-1791.
Wit.: None.

1795 BOYCE, Nicholas (w. Ann) — to Henry Landis
5-8 of Hampshire Co. — of Hampshire Co.
625 a. on Patterson Creek; rec. 7-20-1795.
Wit.: John Snyder, William Vause,
John Steerman, John Murphy.

1797 BOYCE, Nicholas — to William Sanford
10-14 PACK, Sarah — of Hampshire Co.
of Hampshire Co.
89½ a. on Mill Creek; rec. 12-18-1797.
Wit.: Henry Hawk, Frederick Hye.

1790 BOYD, Alexander (w. Sarah) — to Michael Brill
9-16 of Hampshire Co. — of Hampshire Co.
854 a. on Gibbons Run; rec. 9-16-1790.
Wit.: Jacob Combs, Henry Briel.

1790 BOYD, Alexander (w. Sarah) — to Jacob Grapes
9-16 of Hampshire Co. — of Hampshire Co.
225 a. on Gibbons Run; rec. 9-16-1790.
Wit.: Michael Briel, Phillipi Tabs.

1799 BRAHAN, John — to Griffin Taylor
7-12 of Frederick Co., Va. — of Frederick Co., Va.
Recorded 2-7-1800.
Wit.: Thomas Brock, Thomas Wolfe,
James Heard, Jno. Lefevre.

1797 BRANDENBURG, Aaron (w. Ann) — to Daniel Whoop
12-4 of Hampshire Co. — of Hampshire Co.
141½ a. on Beaver Run; rec. 12-18-1797.
Wit.: Andrew Wodrow, Okey Johnson,
John Umpstott, Daniel Arnold.

1789 BRANDENBURGER, Mathias — to Mathias Marsh
10-16 of Hampshire Co.   (lease) — of Hampshire Co.
48½ a. on Patterson Creek; rec. 9-15-1791.
Wit.: Rodham James, Abraham Johnson, Jr.,
William Hough.

1789 BRANNINGBURG, Mathias (w. Esther) — to Isaac Good
9-16 of Hampshire Co. — of Hampshire Co.
110¼ a. on Patterson Creek; rec. 10-15-1789.
Wit.: Arjalon Price, John H. Price,
Adam Neff, Mary Price, Okey Johnson.

1789 BRANDENBURG, Matthias — to George Hill
11-24 of Hampshire Co.   (Power of Attorney)
Authority to collect in lawful manner, anything due the said
Brandenburg; rec. 4-14-1791.
Wit.: John Birdman.

1772 BRAY, Henry — to Peter Peterson
4-13 of Hampshire Co.   (Bill of Sale) — of Hampshire Co.
Sheep, cows, heifers, two mares, hogs; rec. 5-13-1772.
Wit.: Richard Williams, Jonathan Ady,
John Roussaw.

1775 BREAK, Jacob (w. Catherine) — to John Wolf
5-8 of Hampshire Co.   (lease and release) — of Hampshire Co.
200 a. on mountain near South Branch; rec. 5-9-1775.
Wit.: None.

1795 BRELSFORD, Bernard (w. Naomi) — to Thomas Hughs
4-14 101 a. in Hampshire Co.; rec. 4-20-1795.
Wit.: James McBride, John Roseburgh,
Elisha Beall.

1795 BRELSFORD, Bernard (w. Naomi) — to Ellis George
4-18 316 a. on Dillons Run; rec. 4-20-1795.
Wit.: James McBride, John Roseburgh,
Elija Beall.

1765 BREWSTER, Ebenezer — to Nicholes McIntre
10-11 of Frederick Co.   (lease and release) — of Hampshire Co.
118 a. on Potomac River; rec. 6-10-1766.
Wit.: Thomas Sweaningen, Thomas Boydston,
Thomas Wiggins, Jr., Joseph Hastings.

1797 BRIGGS, Joseph (w. Abigail) — to Conrad Hoffman
5-16 of Hampshire Co. — of Hampshire Co.
75 a., Hampshire Co.; rec. 12-18-1797.
Wit.: Isaac Miller, Thomas Dean,
William Miller, Charity Hoffman.

1763 BRITAIN, Joseph — to William Baldwin
5-3 of Orange Co., N. C.   (lease and release) — of Frederick Co.
200 a., Hampshire Co.; rec. 2-15-1764.
Wit.: T. Carr, Gabriel Jones, Ja Keith, Pet Hog.

1770 BROMSEY, Mary — to Earhart Glaze
3-19 widow of Thomas Bromsey, — of Hampshire Co.
BROMSEY, Joshua (w. Mary)
(oldest son), of North Carolina   (lease and release)
416 a. on So. Branch; rec. 5-8-1770.
Wit.: Sam Dew, Isaac Van Meter,
Betty Dew, Hath Kuykendall.

1789 BROOKHART, Jacob — to Andrew Barthuff
9-10 of Hampshire Co.   (Bill of Sale) — of Hampshire Co.
¼ a. in town of Frankfort; rec. 9-10-1789.
Wit.: Andrew Wodrow.

1794 BROOKHART, Jacob — to Andrew Wodrow
3-24 of Hampshire Co. — of Hampshire Co.
126 a. on Patterson Creek; rec. 6-11-1794.
Wit.: Jacob Dunn, William Buffington,
Henry Heinzman, William Virdin.

1795 BROOKHART, Jacob (w. Catherine) — to Alex King
4-20 of Hampshire Co. — of Hampshire Co.
300 a. in Frankfort; rec. 4-20-1795.
Wit.: None.

1795 BROOKHART, Jacob — to Christian Musselman
4-20 of Hampshire Co. — of Frankfort
¼ a. in Frankfort; rec. 4-20-1795.
Wit.: None.

1797 BROOKHART, John — to Dennis Daniels
11-28 SWOBE, Barbara, of Hampshire Co. — of Hampshire Co.
2 a. in Frankfort; rec. 12-18-1797.
Wit.: John Mitchell, And. Bartruff,
Jacob Brookhart, Henry Protzman, John McMeekin.

1776 BROWN, Daniel — to daughter, Elizabeth Kuykendall
6-15 of West Augusta   and her husband, John Kuykendall
(Deed of Gift)
One negro woman, named Phyllis, and her two children, Kate
and Bob; rec. 3-10-1779.
Wit.: Sam Dew, Math. Kuykendall.

1773 BROWN, Daniel — to Joseph Nevill
10-11 of Hampshire Co.   (Mortgage) — of Hampshire Co.
Six negro slaves (Bob, Sam, Minney, Daphney, Tom and Guy).
Rec. 3-9-1774.
Wit.: Daniel McNeill, Richard Byrn,
Jonathan Heath.

1775 BROWN, John (w. Catherine) — to Robert Rutherford
8-12 of Frederick Co.   (lease and release) — of Frederick Co.
368 a. on Great Cacapeon; rec. 8-13-1776.
Wit.: Edward McGuire, Archibald Foster,
William Campbell, Samuel Beall, Alex White,
Will Mecrakin.

1795 BROWN, John (w Frances) — to Charles Magill
11-16 of Hampshire Co. — of Hampshire Co.
353 a. on South Br. R.; rec. 12-14-1795.
Wit.: None.

1793 BROWN, Nathan — to John Williamson
9-11 of Hampshire Co. — of Hampshire Co.
420 a. on Little Cacapeon; rec. 9-11-1793.
Wit.: None.

1795 BROWN, John — to Edward Smith
GAITER, Elijah
WODROW, Andrew
400 a. on Gibbons Run; rec. 2-15-1796.
Wit.: F. White, Ewd. Dyer, Ed McCarty,
John Jack, Henry Heinzman.

1785 BROWN, Thomas — to Abraham Hite
3-1 of Hampshire Co.   (Mortgage) — of Hampshire Co.
A negro slave boy, named George, age 2; rec. 8-9-1785.
Wit.: Richard Edwards, Reubin Berry.

1763 BRUEN (Bruin), Bryan — to John Keating
5-10 of Frederick Co.   (lease and release) — of Hampshire Co.
322 a., So. Branch; rec. 5-11-1763.
Wit.: Henry Heth, Luke Collins, John Collins.

1763 BRUEN, Bryan (w. Elizabeth) — to Owen Jones
8-2 of Frederick Co.   (Mortgage) — of Philadelphia, Pa.
2,000 a., Green Spring Valley; rec. 10-12-1763.
Wit.: Gabriel Jones, William Davis,
Pet Hog, Geo. Davis, Ja. Keith.

1765 BRUIN, Bryan (w. Elizabeth) — to John Ord
9-30 of Frederick Co.   lease and release) — of Philadelphia, Pa.
247 a. on Little Ca Capehon; rec. 10-8-1765.
Wit.: Ja. Keith, Gabriel Jones,
Angus McDonald Pet Hog, Edward McGuire.

1767 BRUEN, Bryan (w. Elizabeth) — to John Ord
4-29 of Winchester, Va.   (lease and release) — of Philadelphia, Pa.
26 a., Little Capon; rec. 9-17-1767.
Wit.: Angus McDonald, Edward McGuire
James Livingston.

1767 BRUEN, Bryan (w. Elizabeth) — to John Spone
9-3 of Frederick Co. Va. (lease and release) — of Lanchester Co., Pa.
195 a., L. Capon; rec. 11-9-1768.
Wit.: Pet Hog, Alex White, Gabriel Jones.

1767 BRUEN, Bryan (w. Elizabeth) — to John Spore
9-3 of Frederick Co. Va. (lease and release) — of Lanchester Co., Pa.
264 a., L. Capon; rec. 11-9-1768.
Wit.: Pet Hog, Alex White, Gabriel Jones.

1767 BRUEN, Bryan (w. Elizabeth) — to John Mitchel
9-14 of Frederick Co., Va.   (Mortgage) — of Fredericksburg, Va.
400 a., 304 a., 177 a., 400 a., 79 a., 288 a., 400 a., Green Spring
Valley; rec. 10-13-1767.
Wit.: Alexr. White, Ja. Keith, Pet Hog.

1767 BRUEN, Bryan (w. Elizabeth) — to Luke Collins
9-21 of Frederick Co., Va. — of Hampshire Co.
323 a., So. Branch; rec. 10-13-1767.
Wit.: Alexr. White, Henry Heth, Frederick Conrad,
Ja. Key, Edward McGuire, Daniel McNeel, and
G. Michl. Lawbinger.

1770 BRUIN, Bryan — to Charles Ridgely
11-13 of Winchester, Frederick Co. — John Ridgely
(Mortgage) — Charles Ridgely, Jr.
405 a. on Brocks Gap Run; rec. 12-12-1770. — of Baltimore, Md.
Wit.: Sam Dew.

1770 11-13	BRUIN, Bryan to Charles Ridgely of Winchester, Frederick Co. John Ridgely (Mortgage) Charles Ridgely, Jr. of Baltimore, Province of Maryland 425 a. on Stoney Branch of Little Cacapeon; rec. 11-13-1776. Wit.: Sam Dew.		3-13	of Hampshire Co. (Power of Atty) of Hampshire Co. Authority to convey parcel of land; rec. 4-15-1799. Wit.: Matthew Booge, Sam Gibbs, William Mannin, George Pierce.
1772 2-28	BRUIN, Bryan to Carson, Barclay & Mitchell of Winchester, Frederick Co. (lease and rel.) of Philadelphia 279 a. on Lick Branch on Tilehanzy's Branch; rec. 5-12-1772. Wit.: J. Watson, Edward McGuire, William Campbell, John Magill		1792 6-26	BUFFINGTON, Joel (w. Elizabeth) to Wm. Vandiver of Hampshire Co. of Hampshire Co. 150 a. on Abraham's Creek on Alleghany Mt.; rec. 6-26-1792. Wit.: None.
1774 3-12	BRUIN, Bryan to Patrick Keran of Winchester, Va. of Hampshire Co. 400 a. in Hampshire Co.; rec. 8-14-1775. Wit.: George Rootes, Peter Hog, Edward Keran.		1795 5-18	BUFFINGTON, Joel (w. Elizabeth) to John Johnston of Hampshire Co. of Hardy Co. 77 a. near South Br. R.; rec. 6-15-1795. Wit.: And. Wodrow, Isaac Miller. Okey Johnson, Henry Heinzman.
1775 3-8	BRUIN, Bryan to William Abernathy of Frederick Co. (lease and release) of Pennsylvania 67 a. on Mill Run; rec. 3-14-1775. Wit.: Edward McGuire, William Campbell, Alex White, Andrew Turk.		1795 5-18	BUFFINGTON, Joel (w. Elizabeth) to John Johnston of Hampshire Co. of Hardy Co. 200 a. on Alleganq Mt.; rec. 6-15-1795. Wit.: Isaac Miller, And. Wodrow, Okey Johnson, Henry Heinzman.
1776 10-11	BRUIN, Bryan to John Ashburner of Winchester, Va. (Mortgage) and Thomas Place of Baltimore, Md. 400 a. on Patterson Creek; 300 a. on Mill Creek; 400 a. on Patterson Creek, 396 a. on Patterson Creek; 1,122 a. near Pat- terson Creek; 456 a. on Patterson Creek; 996 a. on Plum Run; 448 a. on South Branch; 296 a. on Patterson Creek. Recorded 11-12-1776. Wit.: Alex White, John Magill, Wm. Campbell, George Rootes, G. Peyton, Jr., Thomas Collins.		1763 3-1	BUFFINGTON, William to Thomas, Lord Fairfax (w. Magdalena) of Hampshire Co. (lease and release) 3 a. 32 P. So. Branch.. rec. 5-10-1763. Wit.: Pet Hog, Ja. Keith, Gabriel Jones.
			1767	BUFFINGTON, William (see Collins, Luke)
			1779 8-10	BUFFINGTON, William (w. Mary) to Henry Nafe of Hampshire Co. of Hampshire Co. 100 a. on Patterson and Mill Creek; rec. 8-12-1779. Wit.: None.
1779 4-20	BRUIN, Bryan to Amos Dicken of Winchester, Va. (lease and release) of Washington Co. 110 a. on North Br. of Potomac; rec. 8-10-1779. Wit.: John Roussaw, John Magill, Alex White, George Rootes.		1773 11-10	BULLITT, Sarah to Abel Randall of Fauquier Co. (Deed of Trust) of Hampshire Co. One negro boy named Will (left her by her husband as part of her dower); rec. 11-11-1783. Wit.: Joseph Nevill, Robert Higgins, Abel Westfall.
1779 5-20	BRUIN, Bryan to Nicholas Deewald of Winchester, Va. (lease and release) of Hampshire Co. 300 a. on New Creek; rec. 8-10-1779. Wit.: None.		1796 6-11	BUMGARDNER, Rudolph to John Chenoweth, Jr. (w. Agnes) of Hampshire Co. of Hampshire Co. 421 a., Hampshire Co.; rec. 6-20-1796. Wit.: John Panill, Paul McKeever John Chenoweth.
1779 8-9	BRUIN, Bryan to Thomas Collins of Winchester, Va. (lease and release) of Hampshire Co. 175 a. on Patterson Creek; rec. 8-10-1779. Wit.: None.		1797 9-14	BUNN, Peter (w. Mary) to John Copsey of Hampshire Co. of Hampshire Co. 1034 a. on Little Cacapeon; rec. 4-16-1798. Wit.: William Richmond, James Carruthers, Elisha Beall.
1780 8-3	BRUIN, Bryan to Robert Buck of Winchester, Co. of Lancaster Co. 482 a., Hampshire Co.; 164 a., Hampshire Co.; rec. 8-9-1780. Wit.: None.		1799 10-17	BURACK, William (w. Ann) to Lewis Vandivear of Hampshire Co. of Hampshire Co. Recorded 2-7-1800. Wit.: William Vance, M. Pigman, John Mullin, Isaac Good, Jr.
1780 8-3	BRUIN, Bryan to William Buck of Winchester, Va. of Lancaster Co. 400 a., 79 a., 288 a., Hampshire Co.; rec. 8-9-1780. Wit.: None.		1779 11-4	BURGESS, William (w. Isabel) to William Chapman of Hampshire Co. (lease and release) of Hampshire Co. 80 a. on Little Cacapeon R.; rec. 11-9-1779. Wit.: John Stoker, Isaac Short.
1785 3-21	BRUIN, Bryan to Col. Peter Bryan Bruin of Winchester, Va. (lease and release) of Berkeley Co. 200 a. on Patterson Creek, 402 a. on Little Cacapeon R., 442 a. on North Branch, 421 a. on Patterson Creek; rec. 8-9-1785. Wit.: Alphius Gustin, Jr., Thomas Kelley, James Stuart.		1779 11-9	BURGESS, William (w. Isabel) to Isaac Short of Hampshire Co. of Hampsire Co. Parcel of land on Little Cacapeon; rec. 11-9-1779. Wit.: John Stoker, Enoch Berry.
1785 8-8	BRUIN, Charles (w. Margaret) to Thomas Dean of Hampshire Co. (lease and release) 400 a. on New Creek; rec. 8-9-1785. Wit.: None.		1777 4-13	BURK, Benjamin (w. Elizabeth) to Michael McKewn of Hampshire Co. of Berkeley Co. 400 a. on Captain John Run, br. of Potomac R.; rec. 11-9-1779. Wit.: Robert Cockburn, David Hunter, Daniel Brian.
1788 4-14	BRUIN, Peter Bryan to Messrs. Smith & Morcton of Berkeley Co. (Mortgage) of Baltimore Co. 200 a. on Patterson Creek, 402 a. on Little Cacapeon, 421 a. on Patterson Creek, 442 a. on North Branch; rec. 7-10-1788. Wit.: George Creamer, Robt. Nailer, Patrick Quenlly, Andrew Wodrow, James Murphy, Mary Ann Wodrow, Ralph Humphreys.		1796 4-26	BURK, John (w. Margaret) to Jonathan Nixon, Jr. of Hampshire Co. of Montgomery Co. 80 a. on Allegany Mt.; rec. 6-20-1796. Wit.: John Ravenscroft, Adam Whight, Sam. Ravenscroft.
1770 3-2	BRYAN, James (w. Mary) to Andrew Viney of Hampshire Co. (lease and release) of Hampshire Co. 270 a. near line of Frederick Co.; rec. 5-8-1770. Wit.: John Roussaw, William Baker.		1781 9-11	BURKIT, Simon to Jacob Burkit of Hampshire Co. (lease and release) of Hampshire Co. 120 a. on Patterson Creek; rec. 9-11-1781. Wit.: None.
1796 9-12	BUCK, John to Edward Coats of Hampshire Co. of Hampshire Co. 129 a. on Allegany Mts.; rec. 4-17-1797. Wit.: Andrew Wodrow, Henry Heinzman, William Verden, John Hansbrough.		1768 3-4	BURNS, John to Benj. Willett of South Carolina (lease and release) of Frederick Co., Va. GRAHAM, John of South Carolina HICKS, Samuel HICKS, Moses MORGAN, Mordecia of Virginia 161 a. on Potomac River; rec. 8-8-1768. Wit.: Cuth't McWilliam, James Magill.
1783 5-10	BUCK, Robert to Jeremiah Sullivan BUCK, William of Hampshire Co. of Hampshire Co. 80 a. in Green Spring Valley; rec. 5-13-1783. Wit.: James Donaldson, Anthony Buck.		1794 10-15	BURRIS, Henry (w. Rebecca) to Corenlius Ferree of Hampshire Co. of Hampshire Co. 376 a. on Great Cacapeon; rec. 10-15-1794. Wit.: And. Wodrow.
1785 11-9	BUCK, Robert to Robert Ross of Hampshire Co. of Hampshire Co. 482 a. on South Branch R.; rec. 3-15-1786. Wit.: Sam Dew, Robert Walker, C. Kuykendall, John VanSchaick, Betty Dew.		1782 8-13	BURROUGHS, Jeremiah to Col. Michael Crsap Apologizing to Mr. Cresap for accusing him of a crime, that he did not do. Rec. 8-14-1782. Wit.: None.
1783 3-10	BUCK, William to Anthony Buck of Hampshire Co. (lease) of Hampshire Co. 84 a. in Green Spring Valley; rec. 5-13-1783. Wit.: Jeremiah Sullivan, James Donaldson.		1799 11-25	BUSBY, John (w. Margaret) to Andrew Wodrow 146 a., Hampshire Co.; rec. 12-16-1799. of Hampshire Co. Wit.: Phil. Wilson, Jas. Dailey, Wm. Schrock.
1783 5-10	BUCK, William to James Donnalson of Hampshire Co. of Hampshire Co. 100 a. in Green Spring Valley; rec. 5-13-1783. Wit.: Jeremiah Sullivan, Anthony Buck.		1800 3-18	BUSBY, John (w. Margaret) to Andrew Wodrow of Hampshire Co. of Hampshire Co. Recorded 4-14-1800. Wit.: E. Gaither, P. P. Wilson, John W. Merridith, John Busby, Jr., Ab. Jenkins.
1799	BUFFINGTON, David to Francis White			

GRANTOR-GRANTEE

1800 BUSBY, John (w. Margaret) to **George Martin**
3-18 of Hampshire Co. of Hampshire Co.
Recorded 4-14-1800.
Wit.: Frd. White, Amery Day, George Martin, Esq.,
Andrew Wodrow, P. P. Wilson.

1801 BUSBY, John (w. Margaret) to **George Martin**
1-10 of Hampshire Co. of Hampshire Co.
Recorded 1-19-1801.

1801 BUSBY, John (w. Margaret) to **John Candy**
1-19 of Hampshire Co. of Hampshire Co.
Recorded 1-19-1801.

1773 BUSH, Phillip to **John Parrell**
8-2 of Frederick Co. (lease and release) of Hampshire Co.
219 a. on Dillion's Run; rec. 8-10-1773.
Wit.: Alex White Peter Hog, Abraham Hite,
Samuel Beall.

1772 BUSH, Phillip (w. Catherine) to **Dr. James Craike**
8-8 of Frederick Co. of Maryland
400 a. in Hampshire Co.; rec. 8-11-1772.
Wit.: James Sovervelle, Alex White, John Magill.

1794 BUSSEY, John (w. Eleanor) to **Loudon Roberts**
3-1 of Hampshire Co. of Hampshire Co.
20 a. on New Creek; rec. 4-9-1794.
Wit.: John Price, John Rawles, Thos. Buffington.

1794 BUSSEY, John (w. Eleanor) to **Andrew Smalley**
3-1 of Hampshire Co. of Hampshire Co.
112 a. on New Creek; rec. 4-9-1794.
Wit.: John Price, John Rawles, Thos. Buffington.

1797 BUSSY, John (w. Eleanor) to **Abraham Moore**
7-26 of Hampshire Co. of Maryland
112½ a., Hampshire Co.; rec. 12-18-1797.
Wit.: LeRoy Hill, Robt. Hill, Wm. Hill, Betty Hill.

1776 BYRN, Richard (w. Eleanor) to **Robert Fergerson**
5-13 of Hampshire Co. (lease and release) of Hampshire Co.
100 a. on South Branch; rec. 6-11-1776.
Wit.: John Roussaw, John Forman,
Robert Stephen, Jonathan Heath.

—C—

1795 CALVIN, Stephen to **William Fox**
10-8 of Hampshire Co. of Hampshire Co.
369 a. on South Br. R.; rec. 10-19-1795.
Wit.: Perez Drew, Samuel Ruckman, David Allen.

1775 CALVIN, Vincent to **Stephen Calvin**
5-19 of Augusta Co. (lease and release) of Hampshire Co.
869 a. on South Branch; rec. 6-11-1776.
Wit.: Nicholas Casey, Isaac Parsons,
William McGuire, Bauldin Parsons.

1794 CAMPBELL, Elizabeth to **Daniel Taylor**
12-10 CAMPBELL, John (w. Elizabeth)
CAMPBELL, Sarah
and PARKER, Robert and Sarah
489 a. on South Br.; rec. 12-10-1794.
Wit.: None.

1799 CAMPBELL, John (w. Elizabeth) to **Richard Sloan**
2-5 CAMPBELL, Runa of Hampshire Co.
CAMPBELL, Susanna
and CROSSLEY, Johanna
of Hampshire Co.
300 a. on Mill Creek; rec. 9-17-1799.
Wit.: Samuel Sage, Michael Dolohan, Henry Crossley,
Conrad Huffman, Phillip Cline, William Cooke,
William Richey, John Pembrook.

1794 CAMPBELL, Robert (w. Elizabeth) to **Samuel Berry**
4-9 of Hampshire Co. of Frederick Co.
345 a. on Spring Gap Run; rec. 4-9-1794.
Wit.: Jas. Dailey, John Copsey, Rees Pritchard.

1799 CAMPBELL, Rune (w. Susanna) to **Jacob Mouser, Sr.**
1-14 of Hampshire Co. of Hampshire Co.
One-half acre in Romney. Rec. 1-14-1799.
Wit.: None.

1784 CAMPBELL, William to **John Peyton**
12-27 of Hampshire Co. (mortgage) of Frederick Co.
332 a., S. Branch R.; rec. 8-9-1785.
Wit.: Robert Wood, David Deadrick, Simon Cray,
Absalom Hammond, John Magill, James Walker,
Robt. White, Jr.

1787 CAMPBELL, Wm. (w. Rosanna) to **Balson Shelhorn**
2-26 of Hampshire Co. (lease and release) of Hampshire Co.
332 a. on Patterson Creek; rec. 6-14-1787.
Wit.: Okey Johnson, Ralph Humphrey,
Jacob Slagle, John Schelhorn, James Wood.

1797 CANNON, John to **John Bailey, Sr.**
9-18 of Hampshire Co. of Berkeley Co.
121 a., Hampshire Co.; rec. 9-18-1797.
Wit.: None.

1770 CAPLINGER, John (w. Lydia) to **Thomas Lewis**
12-12 of Augusta Co., Va. (lease and release) of Frederick Co.
206 a., Lost River of Cacapeon; rec. 5-15-1771.
Wit.: Peter Hog, Phil Pendleton
Alex White, Joseph Heavill (Neavill)

1789 CARDER, John (w. Elizabeth) to **Henry Lighter**
3-31 of Green Co., N. C. of Hampshire Co.
361 a. on Patterson Creek; rec. 4-19-1789.
Wit.: Thomas Cooper, John Jack,
Joseph Keiser, William Jacob.

1791 CARDER, William to **Abbot Carder**
10-10 of Hampshire Co. (Bill of Sale) of Hampshire Co.
Livestock, personal property and crops; rec. 12-15-1791.
Wit.: Abraham Johnson, William Jacob.

1800 CARLYLE, William (w. Ann) to **William Glassell**
7-14 of Hampshire Co. of Spottsylvania
Recorded 7-11-1800.
Wit.: Charles Magill, John Brown, Henry Heinsman.

1792 CARDER, William (w. Sarah) to **William Hill**
4-13 of Hampshire Co. (mortgage) of Culpepper Co.
382 a. on Bartons Meadow Run; rec. 4-24-1792.
Wit.: Andrew Wodrow, John Herndon,
Francis Taggart.

1777 CARPENTER, John (w Ann) to **Thomas Holoback**
3-11 of Ohio Co., Virginia (lease and release) of Hampshire Co.
280 a.—Lot No. 9 on Patterson Creek; rec. 3-9-1779.
Wit.: Silas Hedges, William Scott.

1794 CARRUTHERS, James (w. Mary), to **Charles Tyler**
4-7 of Hampshire Co. of Hampshire Co.
392 a. on North River; rec. 4-9-1794.
Wit.: None.

1797 CARRUTHERS, James (w. Mary) to **John Higgins, Jr.**
10-1 of Hampshire Co. of Hampshire Co.
Wit.: None.
100 a. on North R.; rec. 4-16-1798.

1786 CARTWRIGHT, Peter to **John Hornback, Atty.**
5-9 of Fayette Co. (power of attorney)
Authority to make deeds of lease and release of a tract of
land in Hardy Co., of 86 a. to Moses Hutton. Rec. 2-13-1787.
Wit.: P. Patterson, Eli Clurland.

1785 CARTWRIGHT, Samuel to **Moses Hutton**
8-25 CARTWRIGHT, Peter of Hampshire Co.
CARTWRIGHT, Richard
of Hampshire Co.
86 a. on South Branch R.; rec. 11-8-1785.
Wit.: Andrew Wodrow, Peter Higgins, Jonathan Heath,
Abel Randall, Jacob Yoakman.

1785 CARTWRIGHT, Samuel to **Moses Hutton**
8-25 of Hampshire Co. of Hampshire Co.
187 a. on South Branch R.; rec. 11-8-1785.
Wit.: Andrew Wodrow, Peter Higgins,
Jonathan Heath, Abel Randall, Jacob Yoakum.

1786 CASEY, John
6-14 Age 87. Disabled while in service of U. S. To receive twelve
pounds yearly. (Certificate). Rec. 1-10-1788.

1795 CASEY, Nicholas (w. Grace) to **Isaac Parsons**
4-11 of Hampshire Co. of Hampshire Co.
119 a. on South Br.; rec. 4-20-1795.
Wit.: Isaac Miller, John Jack,
Stephen Calvin, George Fisher.

1797 CASEY, Nicholas to **Andrew Wodrow**
3-25 of Monongalia Co. of Hampshire Co.
94 a. on North R.; rec. 4-17-1797.
Wit.: Jas. Dailey, Joshua De Butts,
John McMeekin, John Jack.

1777 CASEY, Peter to **Benjamin Casey**
3-31 of Hampshire Co. (lease and release) of Hampshire Co.
400 a. on Patterson Creek; rec. 4-8-1777.
Wit.: Abraham Hite, Garret Vanmeter, Abel Randall.

1777 CASEY, Peter to **John Ryan**
4-1 of Hampshire Co. (lease and release) of Hampshire Co.
300 a. on Patterson Creek; rec. 4-8-1777.
Wit.: Abraham Hite, Garret Vanmeter, Abel Randall.

1778 CASEY, Peter (w. Mary) to **Nicholas Casey**
8-11 of Hampshire Co. (lease and release) of Hampshire Co.
356 a. on South Branch R.; rec 8-11-1778.
Wit.: None.

1781 CASEY, Peter, Jr. to **Jonathan Purcell**
9-26 of Hampshire Co. of Hampshire Co.
400 a. on Patterson Creek; rec. 11-13-1781.
Wit.: Andrew Wodrow, Abraham Hite, Isaac Vanmeter.

1787 CASEY, Peter to **Nicholas Casey**
9-26 of Mercer Co. (power of attorney) of Hampshire Co.
Authority to collect money or whatever due Peter Casey.
Rec. 4-10-1788.
Wit.: Andrew Wodrow, Chas. Lander, John Forman.

1800 CASEY, Nicholas to **Daniel Collins**
10-15 of Monongahalia Co., Va. of Hampshire Co.
Recorded 2-17-1800.
Wit.: James Parsons, Thomas Collins,
Michael Smith, Mary Collins.

1787 CASLER, Michael to **John Casler**
10-16 of Hampshire Co. (Bill of Sale) of Hampshire Co.
Livestock and household property; rec. 4-10-1788.
Wit.: I. W. Hewlings.

1787 CASLER, Michael to **John Casler**
10-14 of Hampshire Co. (lease and release) of Hampshire Co.
179 a. on Capt. John's Run; rec. 4-10-1788.
Wit.: Elizabeth Davis, I. W. Hewlings.

1759 CASSELLMAN, Ludwick to **David Cassellman**
3-12 (Castlemann) of Hampshire Co. (lease and rel.) of Frederick Co.
404 a., South Branch of Potomac; rec. 3-12-1760.
Wit.: Joseph Watson, Pet. Steinberger.

1759 CASSELLMAN, Ludwick to **Jacob Cassellman**
7-18 of Hampshire Co. (lease and release) of Frederick Co.
Lot 28—300 a., on South Branch of Potomac; rec. 3-12-1760.
Wit.: Job Pearsall, Thos. Bull, Charles Linzie.

1779 5-10	CASSELMAN, William (w. Margaret) to Simeon Earsom (see Ahrsom) of Hampshire Co. of Westmoreland Co. 400 a. on South Branch; rec. 8-4-1779. Wit.: Sam Dew, Robert Parker.

1779 5-10 CASSELMAN, William   to Simeon Earsom
(w. Margaret)   (see Ahrsom) of Hampshire Co.
of Westmoreland Co.
400 a. on South Branch; rec. 8-4-1779.
Wit.: Sam Dew, Robert Parker.

1762 8-9 CASTLEMAN, David   to Jacob Castleman
(w. Margaret)   of Hampshire Co.
of Frederick Co.   (lease and release)
119 a., So. Branch Lot No. 29; rec. 8-10-1762.
Wit.: William Calmes, Jas. Taaffe.

1762 9-2 CASTELEMAN, David   to William Calmes
(w. Margaret)   of Frederick Co.
of Frederick Co.   (lease and release)
275 a., So. Branch; rec. 8-10-1762.
Wit.: Jas. Taaffe, Nimrod Ashby.

1785 8-11 CASTLEMAN, Jacob   to William Smith
of Hampshire Co.   of Hampshire Co.
106 a. on South Branch R.; rec. 8-11-1785.
Wit.: Sam Dew.

1785 9-3 CASTLEMAN, Jacob   to William Fox
of Hampshire Co.   of Hampshire Co.
100 a. on South Branch; rec. 11-8-1785.
Wit.: Sam Dew, Priz. Drew, Enoch Berry,
David Corbin, Gabriel Fox.

1786 10-2 CASTLEMAN, Lewis   to Sam Dew (atty.)
of Hampshire Co. (power of attorney) of Hampshire Co.
Authority to collect all money and debts due Lewis Castleman.
Rec. 10-10-1786.
Wit.: Abraham Johnson, Abraham Johnson, Jr.

1786 10-2 CASTLEMAN, Lewis (w. Jemima) to John Dowden
of Hampshire Co.   of Hampshire Co.
150 a. on Patterson Creek; rec. 10-10-1786.
Wit.: Sam Dew, Abraham Johnson,
Okey Johnson, Abraham Johnson, Jr.

1782 6-1 CATHER, Jasper   to John Allen
of Frederick Co.   (Bill of Sale) of Frederick Co.
67 a. on Patterson Creek; rec. 8-13-1782.
Wit.: Andrew Wodrow, John Magill,
James Walker.

1798 11-26 CATHER, Jasper (w. Sarah)   to John Brahan
of Frederick Co.   of Frederick Co.
266 a. on Spring Gap Run; rec. 7-15-1799.
Wit.: Thomas Cather, John Cather, Sr.,
Elizabeth Dawson.

1793 10-9 CAVENDER, Garret (w. Janey) to Perez Drew
of Hampshire Co.   of Hampshire Co.
150 a. on Little Cacapeon; rec. 10-9-1793.
Wit.: William Bullitt, James Murphy.

1793 6-27 CHAMP, John   to Nathaniel Ferrand
of Botetourt Co.   of Hampshire Co.
132 a. on New Creek; rec. 4-9-1794.
Wit.: Sam Dew, Jas. Bogell, Mary Bogell,
Richard Ramsey, Chris Champ.

1789 4-15 CHENOWETH, John, Jr. (w. Mary) to John Copsey
of Hampshire Co. (lease and release) of Hampshire Co.
102 a. on Great Cacapeon; rec. 4-16-1789.
Wit.: None.

1791 4-14 CHENOWETH, John (w. Mary)   to John Copsey
of Hampshire Co.   of Hampshire Co.
9½ a. on Cacapeon R.; rec. 4-14-1791.
Wit.: William Richmond.

1794 2-12 CHENOWETH, John, Jr., (w. Mary) to Francis White
of Hampshire Co.   of Hampshire Co.
146 a. on North R.; rec. 2-12-1794.
Wit.: None.

1794 2-12 CHENOWETH, John, Jr.   to Ebenezer Williams
(w. Mary)   of Hampshire Co.
of Hampshire Co.
284 a. on Potomac R.; rec. 2-12-1794.
Wit.: None.

1784 8-3 CHINOWETH, John (w. Mary)   to Henry Enochs
of Hampshire Co. (lease and release) of Hampshire Co.
57 a. on North R. of Cacapeon; rec. 8-10-1784.
Wit.: None.

1771 11-26 CHENOWETH, William (w. Jane) to John Chenoweth
of Frederick Co. (lease and release) of Hampshire Co
124 a. on Great Cacapeon; rec. 5-12-1772.
Wit.: George Hickson, John Arnold, James Steward.

1768 7-9 CHESNUT, John   to James Chesnut
SUTTON, Jasper (power of attorney) Craven Co., S. C.
of Craven Co., South Carolina
Power to transact business in Frederick Co., Va.
Wit.: Thomas Jones, John Forman, Joseph Kerfham.

1771 5-7 CHESNUT, John   to Simon Taylor
Son and heir of Alexander Chestnut of Hampshire Co.
of Frederick Co.   (lease and release)
400 a. on South Branch; rec. 6-12-1771.
Wit.: James Chesnut, John Forman, William Boykin,
Daniel Richardson, Richard Sutton.

1778 2-26 CHEW, Benjamin   to William Holliday
GIBSON, John,   (lease and release) of Winchester, Va.
of Phaladelphia
247 a. on Little Cacapeon; rec. 5-12-1778.
Wit.: None.

1772 5-12 CHEW, Benjamin   to Moses Hutton
GIBSON, John, Philadelphia, Pa.   of Hampshire Co.
MAGILL, John, of Winchester, Frederick Co.
600 a. on South Branch; rec. 5-12-1772.
Wit.: Jonathan Heath, John Roussaw,
Daniel Richardson.

1788 6-11 CHISHOLM, Alexander (w. Mary) to Samuel Todd
of Hampshire Co. (lease and release) and John Todd
275 a. on S. Branch; rec. 6-12-1788.   of Loudon Co.
Wit.: None.

1785 11-1 CHISHOLM, Alexander (w. Mary) to Robert Lyle
of Hampshire Co.   (Mortgage)   of Fairfax Co.
403 a. on Gibbons Run; rec. 3-14-1786.
Wit.: Elias Poston, John Chenoweth, George Horn.

1789 10-15 CHISHOLM, Alexander (w. Mary) to John Chisholm
of Hampshire Co.   of Hampshire Co.
200 a. on Gibbins Run; rec. 10-15-1789.
Wit.: None.

1793 10-15 CHRISHOLM, Alex. (w. Mary) to Joseph Sevil
of Hampshire Co.   (Levil) (Nevil) of Berkeley Co.
118 a. on Gibbons Run; rec. 10-15-1794.
Wit.: None.

1794 10-15 CHRISHOLM, Alex (w. Mary) to Michael Brady
of Hampshire Co.   of Hampshire Co.
118 a. on Gibbons Run; rec. 10-15-1794.
Wit.: None.

1794 10-15 CHRISHOLM, Alex (w. Mary) to John Caswell
of Hampshire Co.   of Hampshire Co.
211 a. on Tearcoat Creek; rec. 10-15-1794.
Wit.: None.

1798 4-16 CHRISHOLM, Alexander (w. Mary) to Adam Haise
of Hampshire Co.   of Hampshire Co.
105 a., Hampshire Co... rec. 4-16-1798.
Wit.: None.

1798 4-2 CHRISHOLM, Alexander (w. Mary) to John Melick
of Hampshire Co.   of Hampshire Co.
576 a. on Tear Coat Creek; rec. 4-16-1798.
Wit.: None.

1769 4-7 CHRISMAN, Isaac (w. Jane)   to Joseph Claypoole
of Hampshire Co. (lease and release) of Hampshire Co.
36 a. on Lost River; rec. 8-8-1769.
Wit.: Stephen Ruddell, James Scott, Rebecca Chrisman.

1769 4-14 CHRISMAN, Isaac (w. Jane)   to Abraham Frye
of Hampshire Co. (lease and release) of Frederick Co., Va.
350 a. on Lost River; rec. 8-8-1769.
Wit.: Stephen Ruddell, James Scott, Rebecca Chrisman.

1763 5-9 CHRISMAN, Jacob, Jr.   to Thomas Perry
(w. Magdalena)   of Frederick Co.
of Hampshire Co. (lease and release)
400 a. on No. River; rec. 5-10-1763.
Wit.: Ga. Jones, Abraham Hite.

1794 12-15 CHRISMAN, Jacob   to Peter Beckner
of Hampshire Co.   of Hampshire Co.
130 a. Hampshire Co.; rec. 4-20-1795.
Wit.: None.

1795 4-10 CHRISMAN, Jacob   to Wm. Allender
of Hampshire Co   of Hampshire Co.
70 a., Hampshire Co.; rec. 4-20-1795.
Wit.: None.

1795 9-12 CRISMAN, Jacob (w. Mary)   to Angus McDonald
of Hampshire Co.   of Hampshire Co.
193 a., on Grindstone Mt.; rec 9-14-1795.
Wit.: None.

1795 9-12 CRISMAN, Jacob (w. Mary)   to Jacob Jenkins
of Hampshire Co.   of Hampshire Co.
169 a. in Hampshire Co.; rec. 9-14-1795.
Wit.: None.

1795 9-12 CRISMAN, Jacob (w. Mary)   to Wm. Baker
of Hampshire Co.   of Hampshire Co.
10 a. in Hampshire Co.; rec. 9-14-1795.
Wit.: None.

1773 3-6 CLARKE, Abraham   to Robert Cunningham
of Hampshire Co.   (Bill of Sale)   and Henry Clark
                                          of Hampshire Co.
Paid 50 pounds, 8 shillings, 1 penny; 2 cows, calves, 16 shoats,
carpenter tools, household furniture, etc.; rec. 3-10-1773.
Wit.: Mary Coberly, James Stell Coberly.

1784 11-3 CLARK, Abraham, Jr.   to Richard Seymour
of Hampshire Co.   of Hampshire Co.
136 a. on South Branch; rec. 11-9-1784.
Wit.: Abel Seymour, John Craige, Stephen Ratcliffe.

1785 1-19 CLARKE, Abraham   to Elias Sulard
of Hampshire Co. (lease)   (Lillard) of East New Jersey
412 a. on Looney's Creek; rec. 3-8-1785.
Wit.: None.

1792 6-26 CLARK, James   to Wm. Logan
of Hampshire Co.   (lease)   of Hampshire Co.
15 a. in Hampshire Co.; rec. 8-28-1792.
Wit.: John Dixon, David Walker.

1796 4-1 CLARK, James (w. Esther)   to Geo. Reed
of Hampshire Co.   of Frederick Co.
One-fourth a. in Frankfort; rec. 4-18-1796.
Wit.: None.

1792 10-30	CLARK, John (w. Massey) of Hampshire Co. 37 a. on Little Cacapeon; rec. 10-30-1792. Wit.: None.	to Thomas Birkhart and Thomas Pettit of Hampshire Co.	1785 3-8	COCHRAN, Simon (w. Susannah) to Suck Writing freeing this a negro woman slave negro woman; rec. 3-9-1785. Wit.: Sam Dew, Betty Dew.

1792 10-30 CLARK, John (w. Massey) to Thomas Birkhart
of Hampshire Co. and Thomas Pettit
37 a. on Little Cacapeon; rec. 10-30-1792. of Hampshire Co.
Wit.: None.

1779 8-11 CLARK, Robert to Cornelius Ward
of Hampshire Co. (lease) of Hampshire Co.
16 a. on South Branch; rec. 8-11-1779.
Wit.: None.

1785 3-7 CLARK, Stephen (w. Ruby) to Ajalon Price
of Hampshire Co. of Hampshire Co.
40 a., Hampshire Co.; rec. 3-9-1785.
Wit.: Abraham Hendricks, George Hill,
Matthias Brandenberg, Matthew Pigman, John Warner.

1784 8-20 CLARKE, Watson to Richard Seymour
of Hampshire Co. of Hampshire Co.
42 a. on Looney's Creek; rec. 11-9-1784.
Wit.: Abel Seymour, Thomas Seymour,
Henry Clarke, Stephen Ratchliffe.

1784 1-6 CLAYPOLE, Jeremiah to John Decker
of Hampshire Co. (Bill of Sale) of Ohio Co.
One negro woman named Rachel and Luke Decker
and her children, with their of Hampshire Co.
future increase; rec. 3-10-1784.
Wit.: Sam Dew, Robert Ferguson.

1798 4-9 CLAYPOLE, Jeremiah to Joseph Van Meter
(w. Blondius)
152 a. on S. Br. R.; rec. 4-16-1798.
Wit.: Francis White, Henry Heinzman,
John Jack, Jos. Harford, Andrew Wodrow.

1773 5-3 CLAYPOOLE, Joseph to James Claypoole, Sr.
(w. Abigail) of Hampshire Co.
of Hampshire Co. (lease and release)
174 a. on Lost River; rec. 5-11-1773.
Wit.: None.

1773 5-3 CLAYPOOLE, Joseph (w. Abigail) to Jacob Miller
of Hampshire Co. (lease and release) of Augusta Co.
36 a. on Lost River; rec. 5-11-1773.
Wit.: Benjamin Frye.

1787 10-11 CLAYTON, Thomas (w. Mary) to Tunis Peterson
of Hampshire Co. of Hampshire Co.
212 a., Hampshire Co.; rec. 10-11-1787.
Wit.: None.

1787 10-11 CLAYTON, Thomas (w. Mary) to Stephen Lee
of Hampshire Co. (See) of Hampshire Co.
212 a. on Tear Coat Creek; rec. 10-11-1787.
Wit.: None.

1793 1-29 CLEAVER, Peter to David Shin
of Berkeley Co. of Berkeley Co.
88 a. on Bear Garden Ridge; rec. 1-29-1793.
Wit.: None.

1791 9-2 CLEAVER, Sarah, executrix to Peter Cleaver
CLEAVER, Ezekiel of Berkeley Co.
CLEAVER, Ellis
Executors of will of Ezekiel Cleaver, dec'd, Montgomery Co.
88 a. on Bear Garden Ridge in Hampshire Co.; rec. 1-29-1793.
Wit.: Christian Dull, Aaron Scott.

1792 3-28 CLEISER, Joseph to Samuel Reed
of Hampshire Co. (lease) and James Cochran
of Hampshire Co.
One-half a. in town of Romney; rec. 4-24-1792.
Wit.: None.

1793 1-29 CLISER, Joseph to James Cochran
of Hampshire Co. of Hampshire Co.
One-half a. in Romney; rec. 1-29-1793.
Wit.: James Dailey.

1793 3-1 CLISHER, Joseph, (w. Elizabeth) to John Miller
of Hampshire Co. of Maryland
100 a. on Beaver Run; rec. 6-12-1793.
Wit.: Okey Johnson, Aaron Brandenbaugh.

1794 6-20 CLINTON, Charles to Benjamin Wiley
of Fayette Co. of Hampshire Co.
392 a. on Knobley Mt.; rec. 9-10-1794.
Wit.: Nathan Price, Able Wiley, John Boyd.

1795 6-9 CLINTON, Charles to Jacob Slagle
of Fayette Co. (lease) of Hampshire Co.
272 a. on North Branch; rec. 10-19-1795.
Wit.: John House, Chas. Longberry, John Collier.

1760 3-10 COBUN, Jonathan (w. Catherine) to John Kuykendall
of Hampshire Co. (lease and release) of Hampshire Co.
250 a.—Lot No. 6, on Great South Branch of Potomac.
Rec. 3-12-1760.
Wit.: Gabriel Jones.

1763 2-3 COBUN, Jonathan (w. Catherine) to Abraham Hite
of Hampshire Co. (lease and release) of Hampshir Co.
150 a. on Timber Ridge; rc. 5-10-1763.
Wit.: Sam Dew, Phil Ross, Jno. Douthit,
Peter Casey.

1794 11-10 COCHRAN, James (w. Mary) to Andrew Wodrow
of Hampshire Co. of Hampshire Co.
Half acre in town of Romney; rec. 12-10-1794.
Wit.: John Price, John Eansbrough, John Jack.

1779 4-14 COCHRAN, John to Robert Travis
of Hampshire Co. of Hampshire Co.
55 a.—Lot No. 70 on South Branch; rec. 4-14-1779.
Wit.: Sam Dew.

1785 3-8 COCHRAN, Simon (w. Susannah) to Suck
Writing freeing this a negro woman slave
negro woman; rec. 3-9-1785.
Wit.: Sam Dew, Betty Dew.

1774 2-16 COCKE, Christopher to Joseph Inskeep
(Cox) of Hampshire Co. of Hampshire Co.
133 a.—Lot No. 13, on So. Branch; rec. 4-14-1774.
Wit.: Joseph Neavill, Daniel McNeill,
James Gelison, Timothy Ryan, Abel Randall.

1796 9-20 COLLINS, Daniel to Thomas Collins
of Hampshire Co. (Deed of Mortgage) of Hampshire Co.
306 a. on South Br.; rec. 4-17-1797.
Wit.: None.

1797 2-20 COLLINS, Daniel to John Brown
of Hampshire Co. off Romney
Half acre in Romney; rec. 2-20-1797.
Wit.: None.

1798 4-23 COLLINS, Daniel to Thomas Collins
of Hampshire Co. of Hampshire Co.
158 a. in Hampshire Co.; rec. 9-18-1798.
Wit.: Jas. Dailey, Thos. Clark,
Chas. Vowles (Bowles), Mary Harvy.

1799 4-15 COLLINS, Daniel (w. Margaret) to Thomas Collins
of Hampshire Co. of Hampshire Co.
140 a. in Hampshire Co.; rec. 4-15-1799.
Wit.: None.

1791 6-16 COLLINS, Elisha (w. Jean) to John Mitchell
of Hampshire Co. of Frankfort
378 a. in Hampshire Co.; rec. 6-16-1791.
Wit.: None.

1765 3-10 COLLINS, John to John Keating
of Hampshire Co. (lease and release) of Hampshire Co.
133 a. on Little Ca Capehon; rec. 3-12-1765.
Wit.: William Dopson, Conrath Hofman.

1765 3-10 COLLINS, John to John Keating
of Hampshire Co. (lease and release) of Hampshire Co.
119 a., So. Branch; rec. 3-12-1765.
Wit.: William Dopson, Conrath Hofman.

1765 3-11 COLLINS, John to John Keating
of Hampshire Co. (Bill of Sale) of Hampshire Co.
Personal property; rec. 3-12-1765.
Wit.: William Dopson, Conrath Hofman.

1795 4-15 COLLINS, John (w. Hannah) to John Fry
of Hampshire Co. of Hampshire Co.
400 a. on Great Cacapeon; rec. 4-20-1795.
Wit.: None.

1758 6-19 COLLINS, Luke to William Cunninghan
of Hampshire Co. (lease and release) of King George Co.
400 a., Middle Fork of Pattersons Creek; rec. 12-13-1758.
Wit.: B. Johnston, Robt. Gregg,
Alexe Cunningham, Enoch Cornwell.

1759 5-7 COLLINS, Luke (w. Sarah) to William Cunningham
of Hampshire Co. (lease and release) Co. of King George
400 a., Pattersons Creek; rec. 5-8-1759.
Wit.: Cuthbt. Bullett, Willm. Gibson, Gabriel Jones.

1760 8-11 COLLINS, Luke (w. Sarah) to Stephen Ruddle
of Hampshire Co. (lease and release) of Hampshire Co.
386 a., on Lost River; rec. 8-14-1760.
Wit.: Gabriel Jones.

1763 12-12 COLLINS, Luke (w. Sarah) to William Ramsay
of Hampshire Co. (lease and release) of Alexandria, Va.
163 a. on Town Fort (Fork) Run; rec. 12-13-1763.
Wit.: None.

1763 12-12 COLLINS, Luke (w. Sarah) to William Ramsey
of Hampshire Co. (lease and release) of Alexandria, Va.
170 a. on So. Fork Luneys Creek; rec. 12-13-1763.
Wit.: None.

1764 2-9 COLLINS, Luke (w. Sarah) to Joseph Watson
of Hampshire Co. (lease and release) of Fairfax Co.
322 a., Hampshire Co.; rec. 2-15-1764.
Wit.: Pet. Hog, Ja Keith, Gabriel Jones.

1766 8-13 COLLINS, Luke (w. Sarah) to Thomas Barclay
of Hampshire Co. (lease and release) of Philadelphia, Pa.
Half acre in Rumney, Lot 47; rec. 8-30-1766.
Wit.: None.

1767 2-25 COLLINS, Luke to Lawrence Hass
BUFFINGTON, William, and Sarah Hass
DEW, Samuel (assignment of dower)
Sarah's dower interest in estate of former Luke Decker, deceased; rec. 4-15-1767.
Wit.: None.

1767 8-8 COLLINS, Luke to Thomas Lord Fairfax
of Hampshire Co. (mortgage) Proprietor Northern Neck of Va.
311 a., Mill Creek; rec. 8-11-1767.
Wit.: Samuel Pritchard, John McColloch,
Alexr. White, Bryan Bruen.

1768 8-2 COLLINS, Luke (w. Sarah) to Joseph Helm
of Hampshire Co. (mortgage) Frederick Co., Md.
311 a., Mill Creek; rec. 9-13-1768.
Wit.: Willm. McCleery, Isobel McCleery.

1768 8-3 COLLINS, Luke to Joseph Helm
of Hampshire Co. (mortgage) of Frederick Co., Md.
323 a. on South Branch; rec. 9-18-1768.
Wit.: Willm. McCleery, Isobel McCleery.

1770 3-13	COLLINS, Luke (w. Sarah) to Thomas Parsons of Hampshire Co. (lease and release) of Hampshire Co. 323 a. on South Branch; rec. 3-14-1770. Wit.: Sam Dew.
1772 8-11	COLLINS, Thomas to David Corbin of Hampshire Co. (lease and release) of Hampshire Co. 95 a. on Little Cacapeon; rec. 8-12-1772. Wit.: None.
1773 3-9	COLLINS, Thomas (w. Elizabeth) to Charles Prather of Hampshire Co. (lease and release) of Hampshire Co. 70 a. on North Branch of Potomac; rec. 3-11-1773. Wit.: William Dopson, John Forman, Humphrey Wostell, Benjamin Bowman.
1781 9-3	COLLINS, Thomas (w. Ruth) to Arsalon Price of Momongohela Co. of Hampshire Co. 175 a. in Hampshire Co.; rec. 11-13-1781. Wit.: Sam Dew, Isaac Miller, I. Price.
1794 5-20	COLLINS, Thomas to John S. Lehow of Stafford Co. (Bill of Sale) of Hampshire Co. One negro man, named Mordecai, age 24; rec. 7-9-1794. Wit.: Andrew Wodrow, John Reed, Perez Drew.
1800 8-20	COLLINS, Thomas to Henry Fleck of Hampshire Co. of Hampshire Co. Recorded 9-15-1800. Wit.: John Snyder, P. P. Wilson, Andrew Wodrow.
1788 1-12	COLLINS, Timothy (w. Catherine) to William Bell Dower of land of Catherine's (one-third part of a tract of land; rec. 6-12-1788. Wit.: Thos. Buffington.
1792 7-30	COLSON, Margaret to Robert Cowan Executrix of of Hampshire Co. COLSON, John of Hampshire Co. 100 a. on Patterson Creek; rec. 7-31-1792. Wit.: Abraham Johnson, John Snyder, Wm. Johnson.
1778 5-11	COLYER, Isaac (w. Mary) to James Martin of Washington Co. (lease and release) of Hampshire Co. 165 a. on North Br. of Potomac; rec. 5-12-1778. Wit.: None.
1795 8-12	COMBS, David to Daniel Fetter of Nelson Co., Ky. of Allegany Co. 400 a. on Little Cacapeon; rec. 4-17-1797. Wit.: Jas. Martin, Francis Murphy, John Critton.
1796 2-15	COMBS, John to William McPherson of Frederick Co. of Hampshire Co. 200 a., Hampshire Co.; rec. 2-15-1796. Wit.: None.
1798 6-13	COMBS, Joseph to Jonah Thompson of Mason Co., Ky. of Alexandria 35 a. on North R.; rec. 7-16-1798. Wit.: None.
1792 2-28	COMBS, Martha to Jonas Combs of Hampshire Co. of Hampshire Co. 205 a., on Lick Run; rec. 2-28-1792. Wit.: None.
1799 9-10	COMBS, Thomas to Robert Allan of Hampshire Co. of Hampshire Co. 83½ a., Hampshire Co.; rec. 9-16-1790. Wit.: None.
1798 10-30	CONKLIN, Annanias (w. Susanna) to Jacob Keizner of Hampshire Co. of Hampshire Co. House and lot in Romney; rec. 2-18-1799. Wit.: Peter Williams, John Jack, Francis White.
1798 11-22	CONKLIN, Jacob to Josiah Masters NIXON, John New York State WARDELL, John of New York City 5,000 a. on Great Cacapeon R.; rec. 2-18-1799. Wit.: Robert Wardell, Thomas Nixon, Alexander Mowatt
1763 5-10	CONNER, Cornelius (w. Margaret) to Bryan Bruen of Hampshire Co. (lease and release) of Frederick Co. 69 a. and 164 a. on Greepspring Run; rec. 5-11-1763. Wit.: Henry Heth, Edward McGuire, John Hayton.
1767 2-16	CONNER, Cornelius to John Forman of Hampshire Co. (Bill of Sale) of Hampshire Co. Personal property; rec. 4-14-1767. Wit.: John Keating, James Taaffe.
1785 5-5	CONRAD, Frederick to Jacob Clyne of Frederick Co. of Frederick Co. 816 a. on Great Cacapeon; rec. 11-8-1785. Wit.: None.
1783 8-10	CONRAD, James, Sr. (w. Jean) to James Conrad, Jr. of Hampshire Co. (lease and release) of Hampshire Co. 140 a. on Great Cacapeon R.; rec. 11-9-1784. Wit.: None.
1785 3-9	CONNARD, James to John Butcher of Hampshire Co. of Hampshire Co. Two tracts of land don Great Cacapeon; rec. 3-9-1785. Wit.: Sam Dew.
1791 10-10	CONNARD, James, Jr. (w. Hester) to Noah Larue of Hampshire Co. of Hampshire Co. 148 a. on Great Cacapeon R.; rec. 10-13-1791. Wit.: Peter Larue, John Larue, Abraham Larue. Dedimus: William Fox, James Monroe, Cornelius Free and John Mitchell, summoned to go and examine Hester Connrad, and find if she is willing to execute the said deed, she not being able to travel to the court. Witnesses: None.
1773 8-3	CONSTANT, John to Wm. Jackson of Hampshire Co. (lease and release) of Hampshire Co. 50 a. on Great Cacapeon; rec. 8-10-1773. Wit.: None.
1782 8-10	CONSTANT, John to Isaac Dawson of Hampshire Co. (Bill of Sale) of Hampshire Co. 200 a., Hampshire Co.; rec. 8-13-1782. Wit.: John Swain, William Jackson, John Morgain.
1789 4-14	CONSTANT, John to Jeremiah Thompson (w. Elizabeth) of Hampshire Co of Hampshire Co. (lease and release) 100 a. on Great Cacapeon; rec. 2-11-1790. Wit.: Daniel Newcomb, William Jackson, James Keele.
1790 2-8	CONSTANT, John (w. Elizabeth) to William Newcomb of Hampshire Co. (lease and release) of Hampshire Co. 84 a. on Great Cacapeon; rec. 2-11-1790. Wit.: Daniel Newcomb, William Jackson, George Keele.
1797 4-14	COOK, William (w. Alice) to Francis White of Hampshire Co. (Bill of Sale) of Hampshire Co. Half acre in town of Romney (No. 43); rec. 4-17-1797. Wit.: None.
1800 5-19	COOK, William (w. Alice) to Francis White of Hampshire Co. of Hampshire Co. Recorded 5-26-1800. Wit.: Andrew Wodrow.
1793 5-11	COOL, Phillip (w. Catherine) to Herbert Cool of Hampshire Co. of Hampshire Co. 200 a. on Little Cacapeon; rec. 6-12-1793. Wit.: None.
1796 11-11	COOPER, Andrew to Francis Deakins of Winchester. (Bill of Sale) William Deakins 265 a. in Hampshire Co.; rec. 12-19-1796. Wit.: Alex. White, Jas. McAlester, Arch. Magill.
1796 11-11	COOPER, Andrew to John Mitchell of Frederick Co., Va. of Hampshire Co. Six tracts of land in Hampshire Co., along road from Frankfort to Potomac River; rec. 2-20-1797. Wit.: Alexr. White, James McAlester, Archd. Magill, And. Wodrow.
1794 3-21	COOPER, George to William Babbs of Hampshire Co. of Hampshire Co. 3 7a., Hampshire Co.; rec. 4-9-1794. Wit.: Joseph Angell, Chas. Babb,, Israel Cunningham.
1786 8-6	COOPER, Joel to Andrew Smalley of Hampshire Co. (lease) of Hampshire Co. COOPER, Thomas 146 a. on Patterson Creek; rec. 9-12-1786. Wit.: Job Cowper, David Cooper, Joseph Cooper, Arjalon Price.
1795 6-15	COOPER, Thomas (w. Rebecca) to William Abernathy of Hampshire Co. of Hampshire Co. 50 a. on North Br. of Potomac; rec. 6-15-1795. Wit.: Redham James, Nicholas Miller, Timothy Corn.
1795 6-15	COOPER, Thomas (w. Rebecca) to William Junkan of Hampshire Co. Richard Junkan 67 a. on Allegany Mt.; rec. 6-15-1795. (Jenkin) Hampshire Co Wit.: Thos. Mulledy, Samuel Clarke, Wm. Donaldson.
1799 9-25	COOPER, Thomas, Sr. to Thomas Cooper, Jr. (w. Rebecca) of Hampshire Co. of Hampshire Co. 50⅝ a. on Allegany Mt.; rec. 10-14-1799. Wit.: Richard King, Thomas Shores, Thomas Fletcher.
1789 4-16	COPSEY, John (w. Sarah) to John Chenoweth of Hampshire Co. (release) of Hampshire Co. 184 a. on North R.; rec. 4-16-1789. Wit.: None.
1789 4-15	COPSEY, John to John Chenoweth of Hampshire Co. (lease) of Hampshire Co. 146 a. on North River; rec. 4-16-1789. Wit.: None.
1795 9-14	COPSEY, John (w. Sarah) to Geo. Crock of Hampshire Co. of Hampshire Co. 254 a. in Hampshire Co.; rec. 9-15-1795. Wit.: None.
1798 5-10	COPSEY, John (w. Sarah) to William Richmond of Hampshire Co. of Hampshire Co. 35 a. on Great Cacapeon R.; rec. 7-16-1798. Wit.: None.
1800 2-18	COPSEY, John (w. Sarah) to William Lockhart of Hampshire Co. of Hampshire Co. Recorded 5-19-1800. Wit.: James Higgins, John Kidwell, Benjamin Bauman, Andrew Wodrow, P. P. Wilson.
1787 5-10	CORBIN, Anderson to George Martin of Hampshire Co. (Bill of Sale) of Hampshire Co. 174 a. on Gibbins Run; rec. 6-14-1787. Wit.: Geo. Bealle, Isaac Hawk, Elijha Beall.
1794 2-8	CORBIN, Daniel (w. Jane) to William Grant of Hampshire Co. of Hampshire Co. 88 a. on Brushy Mt.; rec. 4-9-1794. Wit.: Wm. Day, James Dailey.

GRANTOR-GRANTEE — PAGE 11

1795 4-20 — CORBIN, Daniel (w. Jane) of Hampshire Co. — to Jacob Garrison of Hampshire Co.
145 a. on North R.; rec. 4-20-1795.
Wit.: None.

1791 10-13 — CORBIN, David (w. Bathsheba) of Hampshire Co. — to Alexander McBride of Hampshire Co.
109 a. in Hampshire Co.; rec. 10-13-1791.
Wit.: Geo. Beall, Wm. Buffington, Nathaniel Dyer, John McBride.

1791 10-13 — CORBAN, David of Hampshire Co. — to Robert McBride of Hampshire Co.
109 a. in Hampshire Co.; rec. 10-13-1791.
Wit.: Geo. Beall, Wm. Buffington, Nathaniel Dyer, John McBride.

1793 5-11 — CORBIN, David (w. Bathsheba) of Hampshire Co. — to Thomas Mason of Hampshire Co.
121 a. on North River; rec. 6-12-1793.
Wit.: None.

1793 5-10 — CORBIN, David (w. Bethsheba) of Hampshire Co. — to Phillip Cool of Hampshire Co.
400 a. on Little Cacapeon; rec. 6-12-1793.
Wit.: Sam Dew.

1793 5-11 — CORBIN, David (w. Bathsheba) of Hampshire Co. — to Michael Blue of Hampshire Co.
400 a. on Little Cacapeon; rec. 6-12-1793.
Wit.: None.

1794 1-15 — CORBIN, David (w. Bethsheba) of Hampshire Co. — to William Corbin of Hampshire Co.
130 a. on Little Cacapeon; rec. 1-15-1794.
Wit.: None.

1794 4-9 — CORBIN, David (w. Batesheba) of Hampshire Co. — to John Cannon of Hampshire Co.
121 a. in Hampshire Co.; rec. 4-9-1794.
Wit.: None.

1795 4-20 — CORBIN, David (w. Bersheba) of Hampshire Co. — to Joseph Garrison of Hampshire Co.
145 a. in Hampshire Co.; rec. 4-20-1795.
Wit.: None.

1798 12-8 — CORBIN, David (w. Barsheba) of Hampshire Co. — to Wm. Reeder, Sr. of Hampshire Co.
390 a. in Hampshire Co.; rec 12-17-1798.
Wit.: None.

1794 2-28 — CORBIN, William (w. Susanna) of Hampshire Co. — to Ferdinan Gulick of Loudon Co.
130 a. on Little Cacapeon; rec. 4-9-1794.
Wit.: Isaac Parsons, Nicholas Casey, Perez Drew, Francis Taggart.

1794 1-15 — CORBIN, William (w. Susanna) of Hampshire Co. — to David Corbin of Hampshire Co.
133 a. on Little Cacapeon; rec. 1-15-1794.
Wit.: None.

1773 4-16 — CORBLY, John of Monongahela River (lease and release) — to John Rice of Hampshire Co.
52 a. on Great Cacapeon; rec. 5-11-1773.
Wit.: Wm. Cracraft, Thomas Bowel, Bazel Bowel.

1775 8-7 — CORE, George (Cox?) of Hampshire Co. — to Andrew Pancake of Hampshire Co.
121 a. on South Br. R.; rec. 3-11-1777.
Wit.: Sam Dew, Wm. Ross, John Campbell.

1787 12-10 — CORN, William (w. Hannah) of Washington Co. — to Andrew Corn of Hampshire Co.
333 a. on Patterson Creek; rec. 6-12-1788.
Wit.: LeRoy Hill, Ann Hill, Arjalon Price, John Hill Price, Thomas Handy.

1755 5-15 — CORNWELL, Enoch of Hampshire Co. (lease and release) — to Roger Dyer of Augusta Co.
Lot No. 8—427 a. on So. Branch; rec. 6-11-1755.
Wit.: None.

1788 4-9 — CORY, Joseph of Hampshire Co. — to John McBride of Hampshire Co.
73 a. on Patterson Creek; rec. 4-10-1788.
Wit.: None.

1794 12-31 — COVERT, Bergen (w. Chirche) of Hampshire Co. — to George Gilpin and John Foster and Thomas Ricketts of Fairfax Co.
352 a., Hampshire Co.; rec. 2-16-1795.
Wit.: None.

1783 8-11 — COX, David of Hampshire Co. (lease and release) — to Isaac Hite of Frederick Co.
77½ a. on Potomac R.; rec. 5-14-1784.
Wit.: None.

1772 10-12 — COX, Friend of Hampshire Co. (lease) — to Isaac Hite of Frederick Co.
195 a. on South Branch; rec. 10-13-1772.
Wit.: None.

1772 10-12 — COX, Friend (w. Susannah) of Hampshire Co. (lease and release) — to Isaac Hite of Frederick Co.
240 a., just below mouth of Little Cacapeon; rec. 10-13-1772.
Wit.: None.

1767 4-8 — COX, Gabriel (w. Eleanor) of Hampshire Co. (lease and release) — to Enoch Innis of Hampshire Co.
162 a. North Branch; rec. 6-10-1767.
Wit.: John Hayes, Jonathan Hammer, George Martin, James Livingston, John Nicholas.

1776 3-11 — COX, Gabriel of Hampshire Co. (lease and release) — to Archabold McDonald of Hampshire Co.
168 a., Hampshire Co. Rec. 8-12-1776.
Wit.: None.

1779 3-10 — COX, Gabriel (w. Sarah) of Yochogany Co. — to David Mitchell of Washington Co.
143 a. on Cacapeon Creek; rec. 3-10-1779.
Wit.: None.

1779 3-10 — COX, Gabriel (w. Sarah) of Yochogany Co. (Dedimus) — to Archibald McDonald of Hampshire Co.
168 a. in Hampshire Co.; rec. 8-10-1779.
Wit.: None.

1775 — COX, George — to Andrew Pancake
(See CORE, George.)

1775 3-14 — COX, Isaac (w. Mary) of Hampshire Co. — to Archibald McDonald of Hampshire Co.
Parcel of land on South Branch; rec. 3-14-1775.
Wit.: None.

1776 11-12 — COX, John (w. Mary) of Hampshire Co. (lease and release) — to Paltzer Stoker of Hampshire Co.
80 a. on Little Cacapeon; rec. 11-13-1776.
Wit.: Sam Dew.

1771 3-8 — CRAIKE, James (w. Marianne) Charles Co., Md. (lease and release) — to Phillip Bush Winchester, Frederick Co.
219 a. on Dillons Run; rec. 8-11-1772.
Wit.: Peter Hog, G. Jones, John Magill, Alex White, Phil Pendleton.

1799 10-2 — CRAIK, James (w. Mary Anne) of Alexandria, Va. — to Francis White of Hampshire Co.
400 a. on North R.; rec. 10-14-1799.
Wit.: John Minor, Wm. Washington, Geo. Craik.

1795 2-10 — CRAM, John (w. Eleanor) of Hampshire Co. — to George Gilfin of Fairfax Co.
154 a. in Hampshire Co.; rec. 2-16-1795.
Wit.: John Mitchell, Alex. King, John McBride.

1761 9-8 — CREAMER, Mary of Hampshire Co. (lease and release) — to Abraham Wise of Hampshire Co.
203 a., Hampshire Co.; rec. 9-9-1761.
Wit.: Sam Dew, Silas Hedges, Ben Tutt.

1767 10-11 — CREAMER, Mary of Hampshire Co. (lease) — to Abraham Kuykendall of Hampshire Co.
Lot No. 35, 385 a., So. Branch; rec. 10-14-1767.
Wit.: John Lyne, Adam Obryan, John Black.

1778 4-20 — CREAMOUR, Mary of Hampshire Co. (mortgage) — to Simon Ahrsam wife, Mary Ahrsam of Hampshire Co.
385 a., S. Branch R.; rec. 5-12-1778.
Wit.: Samuel Cartwright, Sam Hornback, Simon Hornback.

1793 9-9 — CRECRAFT, Joseph (w. Eunice) of Hampshire Co. — to Henry Burris of Hampshire Co.
376 a. on Great Cacapeon; rec. 9-11-1793.
Wit.: John Hansbrough, James Connard, Jr., Thos. Hues.

1793 9-9 — CRECRAFT, Joseph (w. Eunice) of Hampshire Co. — to Thomas Williams of Hampshire Co.
340 a. on Great Cacapeon R.; rec. 9-11-1793.
Wit.: Cornelius Ferree, Joshua Ferree, Isaac Ferree.

1773 4-16 — CRACRAFT, William Westmoreland Co., Pa. (lease and release) — to John Keith of Hampshire Co.
38 a. on Great Cacapeon; rec. 5-11-1773.
Wit.: Joseph Cracraft, Thomas Bowel, Bazel Bowel.

1791 6-13 — CREETCHFIELD, Benj. (w. Mary) of Bedford Co. — to Jacob Fleck of Hampshire Co.
198 a. on Patterson Creek; rec. 6-16-1791.
Wit.: Cornelius Hoghland, Joseph Creetchfield, Christian Burn.

1777 6-9 — CRESAP, Daniel (w. Ruth) Washington Co., Md. (lease and release) — to Peter Haines Hampshire Co.
180 a. on South Branch; rec. 8-12-1777.
Wit.: Sam Dew, Thomas Collins, John Roussaw, Michael Cresap, Wm. Buffington, Enoch Berry.

1775 3-13 — CRESAP, Michael, Sr. (w. Mary) of Frederick Co. (lease and release) — to William Lockwood of Frederick Co.
40 a. on North Branch Potomac; rec. 3-14-1775.
Wit.: None.

1775 3-13 — CRESAP, Michael, Sr. (w. Mary) of Frederick Co., Md. (lease and release) — to David Mitchell Frederick Co., Md.
275 a. on South Branch; rec. 3-14-1775.
Wit.: None.

1763 2-15 — CRESAP, Thomas of Frederick Co., Md. (lease) — to William Haggard of Hampshire Co.
100 a. on So. Branch; rec. 5-10-1763.
Wit.: Enoch Innis, Teter Ebrod, Sarah Innis.

1763 3-10 — CRESAP, Thomas of Frederick Co., Md. (lease) — to William Young of Hampshire Co.
337 a. on So. Branch; rec. 5-10-1763.
Wit.: William Biggerstaff, Michael Cresap, Sarah Innis, Enoch Innis.

1777 8-8 — CRESAP, Thomas of Washington Co. (lease and release) — to Jacob Slagle of Hampshire Co.
150 a. on Patterson Creek; rec. 8-12-1777.
Wit.: Michael Cresap, James Tarpley, James Dale.

1777 8-9 — CRESAP, Thomas of Washington Co., Md. (lease) — to James Deale of Hampshire Co.
100 a. on South Branch; rec. 8-12-1777.
Wit.: Michael Cresap, James Tarpley, Jacob Slagle.

1779 12-8	CRESAP, Thomas (w. Margaret) to Michael Cresap of Washington Co. of Hampshire Co. 400 a. on North B. Potomac; rec. 8-8-1780. Wit.: Robert Wilson, Lawrence Hass, James Blue, T. Humphrey, Samuel Simeock, Enoch Innis.	4-1	of Hampshire Co. of Hampshire Co. Parcel of land in Hampshire Co.; rec. 4-9-1794. Wit.: Rod. James, Isaac Parsons, John Jack, George Newman.

1779
12-8 CRESAP, Thomas (w. Margaret) to Michael Cresap
      of Washington Co.   of Hampshire Co.
      400 a. on North B. Potomac; rec. 8-8-1780.
      Wit.: Robert Wilson, Lawrence Hass, James Blue,
      T. Humphrey, Samuel Simeock, Enoch Innis.

1784
5-11 CRESAP, Thomas   to Luther Martin
      of Baltimore, Md.   of Baltimore, Md.
      Parcel of land on South Branch; rec. 5-11-1784.
      Wit.: Michael Cresap, John J. Jacob,
      Charlotte Storddart.

1784
6-12 CRESAP, Thomas   to Michael Cresap
      of Washington Co.   of Washington Co.
      400 a. in Hampshire Co., near Skipton; rec. 8-10-1784.
      Wit.: John J. Jacobs, Michael Cresap,
      Charlotte Stoddart, Elizabeth Cresap.

1784
6-23 CRESAP, Col. Thomas   to William Young
      of Washington Co.   of Hampshire Co.
      Parcel of land on Potomac R.; rec. 8-10-1784.
      Wit.: Joseph Sprigg, Michael Cresap,
      John J. Jacobs, Elizabeth Cresap.

1786
7-23 CRESAP, Col. Thomas (w. Margaret) to Luther Martin
      of Hampshire Co.   of Baltimore Co.
      13 a. on Potomac River; rec. 4-12-1787.
      Wit.: Bazilla Clarke, Thomas Wells, John J. Jacob.

1774
11-5 CRIST, Jacob (w. Hannah)   to Okey Johnson
      of Hampshire Co. (lease and release) of Hampshire Co.
      167 a. on Patterson Creek; rec. 5-9-1775.
      Wit.: Abraham Johnson, Nicholas Carpenter,
      Mary Johnson.

1768
9-10 CRITTEN, John   to Isaac Cox
      of Hampshire Co. (lease and release) of Hampshire Co.
      214 a., Bakers Run; rec. 9-13-1768.
      Wit.: W. Hancher, Enoch Innis, Michael Cresap.

1788
10-16 CRITTEN, John, Jr.   to Thomas Healy
      of Hampshire Co. (lease)   of Hampshire Co.
      125 a. in Hampshire Co.; rec. 1-15-1789.
      Wit.: Andrew Wodrow, Jas. Carruthers,
      Fielding Calmes, Adam Hall, Sam Dew.

1792
6-25 CRITTON, John, Jr. (w. Barbara) to Robt. Gazaway
      of Hampshire Co. (lease and release) of Hampshire Co.
      250 a. on Bakers Run; rec. 6-26-1792.
      Wit.: Geo. Beall, Jas. Murphy,
      Richard Nelson, John Reed.

1791
4-9   CRITTON, William (w. Tatiska)   to John Downing
      of Hampshire Co. (lease and release) of Hampshire Co.
      150 a. in Hampshire Co.; rec. 4-14-1791.
      Wit.: John Critton, Jr., John Critton, Sr.,
      William Postlethwait.

1794
7-13 CROCK, George (w. Barbara)   to John Copsey
      of Hampshire Co.   of Hampshire Co.
      506 a. on Spring Gap Run; rec. 10-15-1794.
      Wit.: William Richmond, John Crock,
      Jas. Carruthers, F. White.

1795
9-14 CROCK, George (w. Barbara)   to George Gale
      of Hampshire Co.   of Berkeley Co.
      604 a. on Spring Gap Mt.; rec. 9-14-1795.
      Wit.: None.

1799 CROSSLEY, Johanna (see Campbell)

1795
11-27 CRUTCHLOW, John   to Valentine Purgitt
      of Hampshire Co.   of Hampshire Co.
      One-fourth acre in Frankfort; rec. 4-18-1796.
      Wit.: Christian Musselman, Wm. Armstrong,
      A. King, Israel Stallop, Thos. Emmerson.

1795
8-22 CUNDIFF, John (w. Sally)   to Joseph Jacobs
      of Hampshire Co.   of Hampshire Co.
      29¾ a. in Hampshire Co.; rec. 4-18-1796.
      Wit.: Geo. Hill, Robert Fuller, John Moore.

1785
3-9   CUNNARD, James (see Connard)   to John Butcher
      of Hampshire Co.   of Hampshire Co.
      Two tracts of land on Great Cacapeon; rec. 3-9-1785.
      Wit.: Sam Dew.

1792
2-28 CUNNINGHAM, John (w. Deborah) to William Babb
      200 a. on North R.; rec. 2-28-1792.
      Wit.: None.

1762
11-5 CUNNINGHAM, Wm. (w. Pheby) to Thomas Singleton
      of Hamphire Co. (lease and release) of Hampshire Co.
      430 a. on So. Branch; rec. 11-9-1762.
      Wit.: Garret Van Meter, Benj. Kuykendall,
      John McCulloch.

1772
8-10 CUNNINGHAM, William   to George Edington
      (Merchant) Co. of King George   of Hampshire Co.
      200 a. on North R. of Cacapeon; rec. 3-11-1773.
      Wit.: Peter Hog, Samuel Beall, John Magill.

1782
1-7   CUNNINGHAM, William, Sr. to Wm. Cunningham Jr.
      of Hampshire Co.   of Hampshire Co.
      242 a. on South Branch; rec. 8-13-1782.
      Wit.: Andrew Wodrow, Joseph Nevill,
      Vincent Williams.

1788
10-16 CUPPY, John, Jr. (w. Elizabeth) to Leonard Ludwick
      of Hampshire Co.   of Hampshire Co.
      100 a. on Mill Creek; rec. 10-16-1788.
      Wit.: Sam Dew, James Carruthers.

1790
9-16 CUPPY, John, Jr. (w. Elizabeth) to Leonard Ludwick
      of Hampshire Co.   of Hampshire Co.
      81 a. on Mill Creek; rec. 9-16-1790.
      Wit.: None.

1794 CUPPY, John (w. Margaret)   to Joseph Myers

1794
4-8   CUPPY, John (w. Margaret)   to Samuel Hague
      of Hampshire Co.   of Hampshire Co.
      260 a. on Mill Creek; rec. 4-9-1794.
      Wit.: None.

1777
8-11 CURLE, Jeremiah (w. Mary)   to Morris Thomas
      of Hampshire Co. (lease and release) of Hampshire Co.
      87 a. on Cedar Swamp; rec. 8-12-1777.
      Wit.: Isaac Parsons, Isaac Means.

—D—

1799
2-13 DAILEY, James (w. Elizabeth)   to Colby Chew
      of Hampshire Co.   of Hampshire Co.
      177 a., Hampshire Co.; rec. 2-18-1799.
      Wit.: Joseph Harmon, Samuel McClutuck,
      James Runnels.

1800 DAILEY, James   to Francis White
      See BLACK, John

1800
10-20 DAILEY, John   to James Dailey
      of Hampshire Co.   of Hampshire Co.
      Recorded 10-20-1800.
      Wit.: John Henderson, Richard Whiteman, John Sands.

1790
2-11 DANFORD, Peter   to Trustees of Frankfort
      of Hampshire Co.
      One-fourth acre in town of Frankfort; rec. 2-11-1790.
      Wit.: None.

1782
3-9   DASHER, Christian (w. Elizabeth) to Christian Simon
      of Hampshire Co.   of Hampshire Co.
      100 a. on South Branch.
      Wit.: None.

1782
3-9   DASHER, Christian (w. Elizabeth) to George Simon
      of Hampshire Co.   of Hampshire Co.
      200 a. on South Branch.
      Wit.: None.

1783
5-14 DAVIS, John (w. Ann)   to Job Bacorn
      of Hampshire Co.   of Hampshire Co.
      115 a. on Patterson Creek; rec. 5-14-1783.
      Wit.: John Jones, William Blackburn, David Jones.

1799
11-14 DAVIS, Samuel (w. Mary)   to George Beattie
      of Hunterdon, N. J.   of Hampshire Co.
      100 a. on South Br. R.; rec. 12-16-1799.
      Wit.: Phil. Wilson, Eli Davis, James Dailey,
      John Hansbrough.

1793
7-15 DAVIS, Thomas (w. Rachael)   to William Deakins
      of Fairfax Co.   of George Town
      151 a. on North River; rec. 6-11-1794.
      Wit.: Charles Simms, Baldwin Stith, Charles Lee,
      Charles Turner, Robert Jameson, John Abert.

1769
8-2   DAVIS, William (w. Alice)   to James Moore
      of Hampshire Co. (lease and release) of Hampshire Co.
      Parcel of land on Hughes' Run; rec. 8-8-81769.
      Wit.: Sam Pritchard, John Langley, Richard Mynatt.

1769 DAVISON, James   to Enoch Cornwell
      Personal property (bill of sale); rec. 6-13-1769.
      Wit.: Humphrey Spark, Leonard Arneft.

1779
3-20 DAVISON, Josiah (w. Edith)   to George Cowger
      of Rockingham Co.   of Hampshire Co.
      160 a. on South Branch; rec. 3-13-1781.
      Wit.: G. Jones, George Rootes, Peter Hog.

1779
3-20 DAVISON, Josiah (w. Edith)   to Georgie Trumbo
      of Rockingham Co.   of Hampshire Co.
      170 a. on South Branch; rec. 8-8-1780.
      Wit.: G. Jones, George Rootes, Peter Hog.

1783
9-27 DAWSON, David   to Jacob Dawson
      of Berkeley Co.   of Hampshire Co.
      150 a. on Great Cacapeon; rec. 10-14-1783.
      Wit.: John Prunty, Abraham Johnson, Thomas Collins.

1780
3-31 DAWSON, Mary   to Abraham Dawson
      DAWSON, David (w. Elizabeth)   of Hampshire Co.
      of Berkeley Co. (lease and release)
      161 a. on Cacapeon River; rec. 8-8-1780.
      Wit.: Joseph Crecraft.

1794
9-23 DAWSON, David (w. Elizabeth)   to Phillip Pendleton
      of Hampshire Co.   of Berkeley Co.
      270 a. on Cacapeon River; rec. 6-20-1796.
      Wit.: John Higgins, George Gale,
      Richard Sommerville, Cornelius Ferrew.

1790
10-8 DAWSON, Isaac (w. Sibyl)   to Christian Crumrine
      of Hampshire Co.   of Hampshire Co.
      267 a. on South Branch; rec. 10-14-1790.
      Wit.: Thomas Williams, Hannah Young,
      Cornelius Ferrell.

1792
9-25 DAWSON, James   to Thomas Bond
      of Alleghany Co.   of Hampshire Co.
      396¾ a. on North Branch; rec. 1-29-1793.
      496¾ a. on Noorth Branch; rec. 1-29-1793.
      Wit.: Andrew Wodrow, Thomas Collins,
      John Jack, Adam Hall.

1794 11-28	DAWSON, Thomas of Hampshire Co. 21 a., part of Swan Ponds; rec. 2-10-1795. Wit.: Daniel Collins, Thomas Peyton, John Purcell, E. Gaithers.	to Isaac Vanmeter and Abel Seymour of Hardy Co.
1791 5-2	DAY, Lewis of Hampshire Co. (Bill of Sale) Horse and personal property; rec. 9-15-1791. Wit.: Rodham James, Winny Day.	to William Johnson, Jr. of Hampshire Co.
1797 2-17	DAYTON, Isaac of Hampshire Co. (lease and release) 300 a. on South Branch R.; rec. 2-20-1797. Wit.: None.	to John Murphy
1791 2-10	DEADERICK, John DEADERICK, George Michael of Winchester, Va. 250 a. on North R.; 400 a. on North R.; rec. 4-14-1791. Wit.: Andrew Wedrow, James Carruthers, George Beall, William Corbin.	to Thomas Tucker of Hampshire Co.
1791 2-10	DEADERICK, John DEADERICK, George Michael of Winchester, Va. 200 a. on North River; rec. 4-14-1791. Wit.: Andrew Wodrow, George Beall, James Carruthers, William Corbin.	to Archibald Linthicum of Hampshire Co.
1791 2-10	DEADERICK, John DEADERICK, George Michael of Winchester, Va. 400 a. on North River; rec. 4-14-1791. Wit.: Andrew Wodrow, George Beall, James Carruthers, William Corbin.	to Joseph Tucker of Hampshire Co.
1798 1-31	DEAKINS, Francis DEAKINS, William, Jr. of Montgomery Co. Parcel of land on Allegany Mt.; rec. 9-17-1798. Wit.: Lloyd Beall.	to James Dunlap of Montgomery Co.
1790 4-9	DEAN, Thomas, Sr. of Hampshire Co. (Power of Attorney) Authority to recover all debts due Thomas Dean, Sr.; rec. 9-15-1791. Wit.: Jonathan Purcell, Jacob Kuykendall.	to Thomas Dean, Jr. of Hampshire Co.
1793 6-11	DEAN, Thomas, Sr. of Kentucky 400 a. on New Creek; rec. 6-11-1794. Wit.: None.	to Paul Sheridan of Hampshire Co.
1790 4-15	DEAN, Thomas, Jr., (w. Jane) of Hampshire Co. 401¼ a. on the Allegany Mt.; rec. 4-15-1790. Wit.: Sam Dew.	to Abraham Vanmeter of Hardy Co.
1793 10-9	DEATON, Isaac (w. Mary) of Hampshire Co. 100 a., Hampshire Co.; rec. 10-9-1793. Wit.: John Jones, Jr., John Bailey.	to Daniel McLoughlin of Hampshire Co.
1796 2-27	DEAVER, John (w. Mary) 150 a. on Mill Run; rec. 6-20-1796. Wit.: Martin Epple, Jonthon Deaver, George Deaver, Eli Beall.	to Amos Park
1763 5-4	DECKER, Garret (w. Cathran) of Hampshire Co. (lease and release) Lot No. 12—380 a. on So. Branch; rec. 5-10-1768. Wit.: Felix Seymour, Jonathan Heath, Jno. Creagh.	to Lawrence Hass of Hampshire Co.
1766 8-22	DECKER, John of Hampshire Co. (Bond) Bond, 900 pounds. Rec. 8-11-1767. Wit.: Sam Dew, Betty Dew.	to Abraham Kuykendall of Hampshire Co.
1767 5-12	DECKER, John (w. Diana) of Hampshire Co. (lease and release) 400 a. on South Branch. Wit.: None.	to Abraham Kuykendall of Hampshire Co.
1767 5-11	DECKER, John (w. Diana) of Hampshire Co. (lense and release) Lot No. 9—400 a., So. Branch; rec. 5-12-1767. Wit.: Sam Dew, Abrm. Hite, Abraham Johnson.	to Abraham Kuykendall of Hampshire Co.
1793 4-10	DECKER, John (w. Hannah) of Hampshire Co. Acting Trustees for the Parish of Hampshire Co. 420 a. on South Br. R.; rec. 4-10-1793. Wit.: None.	to John Pierceall Nicholas Casey Fielding Calmes
1793 4-10	DECKER, John (w. Hannah) of Hampshire Co. 70 a. on South Branch; rec. 4-10-1793. Wit.: None.	to Trustees of Hampshire County
1784 4-12	DECKER, Luke (w. Sarah) of Hampshire Co. 27 a. on South Branch R.; rec. 4-13-1784. Wit.: Sam Dew, Adam Harness, Nath. Kuykendall.	to John Kuykendall of Hampshire Co.
1794 9-9	DEMOSS, John (w. Martha), of Hampshire Co. 35 a. on Cacapcon R.; rec. 9-10-1794. Wit.: John Demoss, John Matthew, Catherine Demoss.	to Levi Matthew of Hampshire Co.
1794 9-10	DEMOSS, John (w. Martha) of Hampshire Co. 110 a., Hampshire Co.; rec. 9-10-1794. Wit.: Levi Matthew, George Tarvin, Elisha Cowgill, John S. Lehow.	to Elisha Cowgill of Hampshire Co.
1777 1-22	DEMOSS, William (w. Rachel) of Hampshire Co. (lease and release) 120 a. on Great Cacapeon; rec. 5-12-1778. Wit.: Thomas Bowel, John Demoss, Lewis Throckmorton.	to Jonah Leaman of Berkeley Co.
1777 1-22	DEMOSS, William (w. Rachel) of Hampshire Co. (lease and release) 99 a. on Great Cacapeon; rec. 5-12-1778. Wit.: Thomas Bowel, John Demoss, Lewis Throckmorton.	to Cornelius Hass of Berkeley Co.
1782 8-10	DEMOSE, William (DEMOSS) of Hampshire Co. 100 a. on Cacapeon R.; rec. 8-13-1782. Wit.: John Swain, William Jackson, John Morgan.	to Levi Matthews of Hampshire Co.
1783 3-8	DEMOSE, William (DEMOSS) of Hampshire Co. 99 a. on Great Cacapeon R.; rec. 8-12-1783. Wit.: James Connard, James Connard, Jr., Cornelius Hass, Jr.	to Cornelius Hass of Hampshire Co.
1790 4-12	DEMOSS, William of Hampshire Co. lease and release 58 a. on Great Cacapeon; rec. 4-16-1790. Wit.: None.	to Peter Larue of Hampshire Co.
1794 11-25	DEMOSS, William of Hampshire Co. 121 a. on Great Cacapeon; rec. 4-20-1795. Wit.: Robert Hastings, James Mason, William Broughton.	to John Vanmeter, Sr.
1795 9-14	DEMOSS, William of Hampshire Co. 176 a. on Great Cacapeon; rec. 9-14-1795.	to John Copsey of Hampshire Co.
1784 5-10	DENHAM, John of Hampshire Co. 60 a. on South Branch R.; rec. 5-11-1784. Wit.: Abraham Clarke, Salathiel Goff, James Tuckwell.	to Robert Cunningham of Hampshire Co.
1793 2-14	DENHAM, John (w. Guin) of Monongala Co. 154 a., Petterson Creek; rec. 9-18-1797. Wit.: John Jones, Jr., John Kimberline, Solomon Jones, John Mitchell, Jr.	to Abraham Peters of Hampshire Co.
1787 10-11	DENT, Thomas of Prince George Co. Lot of one-half a. in town of Romney; rec. 10-12-1787. Wit.: Andrew Wodrow.	to Perez Drew of Hampshire Co.
1780 11-10	DENTON, Jacob of Hampshire Co. 206 a. on Lost R. of Cacapeon; rec. 11-14-1780. Wit.: None.	to David Roberts of Hampshire Co.
1770 8-9	DENTON, John (w. Elizabeth) of Hampshire Co. 122 a. on Lost River; rec. 8-14-1770. Wit.: None.	to Thomas Denton of Hampshire Co.
1761 2-11	DENTON, Robert McBRIDE, Francis of Hampshire Co. 222 a., original tract on Lost River, is divided between the two above named men. rec. 2-11-1761. Wit.: George Hart, Ben Tutt, Patsy Linch.	Deed of Partition
1768 11-7	DENTON, Robert (w. Jane) of Hampshire Co. 122 a., Lost River; rec. 11-8-1768. Wit.: Stephen Ruddell, William Smith, Jacob Denton.	to John Denton of Hampshire Co.
1768 11-7	DENTON, Robert (w. Jane) of Hampshire Co. 116 a., Lost River; rec. 11-8-1768. Wit.: Stephen Ruddell, Thomas Denton, Wm. Smith.	to David Williams of Hampshire Co.
1768 11-7	DENTON, Robert (w. Jane) of Hampshire Co. 300 a., Lost River; rec. 11-8-1768. Wit.: Stephen Ruddell, William Smith, Jacob Denton.	to Thomas Denton of Hampshire Co.
1768 11-7	DENTON, Robert (w. Jane) of Hampshire Co. 179 a., Lost River; rec. 11-8-1768. Wit.: Stephen Ruddell, William Smith, Thomas Denton.	to Jacob Denton of Hampshire Co.
1768 11-7	DENTON, Robert (w. Jane) of Hampshire Co. 323 a., Lost River; rec. 11-8-1768. Wit.: Jacob Denton, Stephen Ruddell, William Smith.	to Joel Robinson of Augusta Co.
1770 8-8	DENTON, Thomas (w. Elizabeth) of Hampshire Co. (lease and release) 416 a. in Hampshire Co.; rec. 8-14-1770. Wit.: None.	to James Claypoole of Hampshire Co.
1775 8-7	DENTON, Thomas (w. Elizabeth) of Hampshire Co. (lease and release) 122 a., Hampshire Co.; rec. 8-8-1775. Wit.: None.	to John Claypoole of Hampshire Co.

1798	D'EVECMON (see Evecmon)	
1764 11-7	DEW, Samuel of Hampshire Co. (lease and release) 326 a. on So. Branch, 182 a. on South Branch; rec. 12-12-1764 Wit.: Cutht. Bullit.	to Thomas Wharton Joseph Wharton of Philadelphia
1767	DEW, Samuel (see Collins, Luke)	
1797 4-1	DICK, Elisha Cullen (w. Hannah) of Alexandria 326 a. on Allegany Mt.; rec. 9-18-1797. Wit.: Frederic Cuiso, Thomas Lemmes, John Burnill.	to John Sutton of Alexandria
1797 4-1	DICK, Elisha Cullen (w. Hannah) of Alexandria Parcel of land on North R.; rec. 9-18-1797. Wit.: Frederic Cuiso, John Burnill, Thomas Lemmis.	to John Sutton of Alexandria
1797 4-1	DICK, Elisha Cullen (w. Hannah) of Alexandria 211 a., Hampshire Co. (also some other tracts); rec. 9-18-1797. Wit.: Frederic Cuiso, Thomas Lemmes, John Burnill.	to John Sutton of Alexandria
1794 4-18	DIXON, John of Hampshire Co. (lease) Tract of land on the Swan Ponds; rec. 7-9-1794. Wit.: D. Welton, John Millet, George Harness, Jacob Fisher.	to Isaac Vanmeter of Hardy Co.
1786 10-9	DOBINS, Thomas (w. Elizabeth) of Hampshire Co. (lease and release) 222 a. on Cabbin Run; rec. 4-13-1787. Wit.: Abraham Johnson, William Johnson, Jr., John Turvey, John Johnson, Lewis Day.	to David Long of Hampshire Co.
1786 12-30	DOBSON, William of Hampshire Co. (lease) 100 a. in Hampshire Co.; rec. 6-14-1787. Wit.: Elizabeth Couchron, William Dostlethwait.	to Robert Jarvis of Hampshire Co.
1795 4-24	DOLAHAN, Daniel (w. Eleanor) of Bucks Co. 90½ a. on Mill Creek; rec. 6-15-1795. Wit.: Henry Heinzman, Henry Eckart, Jr., Andrew Wodrow, William Norman.	to Richard Sloan of Hampshire Co.
1798 4-16	DOLOHAN, Daniel of Hampshire Co. Tract of land in Hampshire Co.; rec. 4-16-1798. Wit.: None.	to James Ryan of Hardy Co.
1785 1-26	DONALDSON, Charles (w. Mary) of Monongalia Co. 300 a. in Monongalia Co.; rec. 5-10-1785. Wit.: John J. Jacob, Francis Pearpoint, Gabriel Jacob.	to Ezekiel Jacob of Prince George Co.
1784 8-10	DOUTHER, Thomas of Fauquier Co. 170 a. on North R.; rec. 8-11-1784. Wit.: Elias Poston, Cornelius Gard, James Hanshire.	to Enoch Enoch of Hampshire Co.
1774 3-12	DOUTHIT, John of Hampshire Co. (lease) 162 a. on Patterson Creek; rec. 5-12-1778. Wit.: None.	to John Koon of Hampshire Co.
1793 9-2	DOUTHIT, John Sr. (w. Margaret) of Hampshire Co. 150 a. on Patterson Creek; rec. 9-11-1793. Wit.: None.	to John Douthit Jr. of Hampshire Co.
1793 9-2	DOUTHIT, John Sr. (w. Margaret) of Hampshire Co. 150 a. on Patterson Creek; rec. 9-11-1793. Wit.: None.	to Solomon Douthit of Hampshire Co.
1797 4-1	DOUTHIT, Solomon (w. Mary) of Hampshire Co. 150 a., on Patterson Creek; rec. 4-17-1797. Wit.: John Snyder, John Dowden, James Parker, Andrew Armstrong.	to William Vause of Hampshire Co.
1795 5-19	DOUTHIT, Thomas (w. Mary) of Hampshire Co. 108 a., Hampshire Co.; rec. 6-15-1795. Wit.: Andrew Wodrow, Jonathan Purcell, Isaac Miller, John Douthit, Sr.	to William Roberts of Hampshire Co.
1793 4-10	DOUTHWARS, John (w. Margaret) of Hampshire Co. 251 a. on Mike's Run; rec. 4-10-1783. Wit.: None.	to John Primm of Stafford Co.
1797 6-19	DOVERIDGE, John (w. Mary) of Hampshire Co. 80 a. on Parkers Run; rec. 6-19-1797. Wit.: None.	to Thomas White of Hampshire Co.
1792 6-26	DOWDEN, John (w. Jean) of Hampshire Co. 337 a. on Patterson Creek; rec. 6-26-1792. Wit.: None.	to John Biggs Dowden of Hampshire Co.
1793 4-10	DOWDEN, John (w. Jane) of Hampshire Co. 120 a. on Patterson Creek; rec. 4-10-1793.	to John Filink of Hampshire Co.
1799 5-20	DOWDEN, John (w. Jane) of Hampshire Co. Quarter acre in Frankfort; rec. 9-16-1799. Wit.: John Burbridge, John Snyder, Elijah Greenwell.	to James Beard of Hampshire Co.
1800 12-15	DOWDEN, John B. (w. Sarah) of Hampshire Co. Recorded 1-19-1801.	to Thomas Ruchman of Hampshire Co.
1797 11-2	DOWDEN, Thomas of Hampshire Co. 120 a. on Patterson Creek; rec. 1-15-1798. Wit.: Ebenezer McKinley, Hendrick Roseboom.	to Hugh McKinley of Hampshire Co.
1797 2-20	DOWNING, John of Hampshire Co. (lease and release) 150 a. in Hampshire Co.; rec. 2-20-1797. Wit.: None.	to William Critton of Hampshire Co.
1796 11-1	DOYLE, Ference (w. Elizabeth) of Allegany Co. 325 a. on North Br. Potomac; rec. 9-18-1797. Wit.: John Mitchell, A. King, James Newman, John Lion, John McBride.	to Elisha Cullen Dick of Fairfax Co.
1798 1-6	DOYLE, Ferrance (w. Elizabeth) of Allegany Co. 306 a. on Allegany Mt.; rec. 2-20-1798. Wit.: William Armstrong, Richard Corbus, David Pringle, Abe Larjent, And. Pringle.	to William Burns of Allegany Co.
1774 4-12	DOYLE, Simon of Hampshire Co. (lease) 208½ a., on Patterson Creek; rec. 4-12-1774. Wit.: Sam Dew.	to John Lewis of Hampshire Co.
1781 1-4	DOYLE, Simon of Washington Co. (lease) 217 a. on Patterson Creek; rec. 5-13-1781. Wit.: William Vandivere, William Barber Lewis, William Howell.	to John Sturman of Hampshire Co.
1792 5-22	DREW, Perez of Romney (Mortgage) Half acre in Romney; rec. 6-26-1792. Wit.: James Cochran, W. Hackney.	to John Holmes of Baltimore, Md.
1792 9-18	DREW, Perez of Hampshire Co. Half acre in town of Romney; rec. 1-29-1793. Wit.: And. Wodrow, William Hackney, Abraham Tuly.	Edward McCarty of Hampshire Co.
1793 2-26	DREW, Perez (w. Mary) of Hampshire Co. 407 a. on Little Cacapeon; rec. 2-26-1793. Wit.: James Dailey, L. I. LeMonnier.	to James Sabes of Frederick Co.
1793 2-26	DREW, Perez (w. Mary) of Hampshire Co. 433 a. on Little Cacapeon; rec. 2-26-1793. Wit.: James Dailey, L. I. LeMonnier.	to James Sabes of Frederick Co.
1796 2-15	DREW, Perez (w. Mary) of Hampshire Co. Half acre in Romney; rec. 2-16-1796. Wit.: None.	to Andrew Wodrow of Hampshire Co.
1796 6-20	DREW, Perez (w. Mary) of Hampshire Co. Half acre in Romney; rec. 6-20-1796. Wit.: John Mitchell, Jr., Sam Dew, Jr.	to William Vandiver of Hampshire Co.
1800 3-17	DUGAN, Thomas of Hampshire Co. (bill of sale) Recorded 4-14-1800. Wit.: George Pancake, Sarah Boyd.	to William Welch of Hampshire Co.
1765 9-8	DUNBAR, John (w. Sarah) of Augusta Co. (lease and release) 412 a. on Lost R.; rec. 10-8-1765. Wit.: Jacob Crisman, Jr., John Keplinger, W. Millar, Jr.	to William Miller of Frederick Co.
1799 12-30	DUNCAN, William DUNCAN, Fr., (attorney) of Alexander Co. Recorded 5-19-1800. Wit.: James Paterson, William Ely, John Straw.	to Eder Thompson of Hampshire Co.
1799 12-30	DUNCAN, William DUNCAN, Fr., (attorney) of Culpepper Co. Recorded 5-19-1800. Wit.: James Patterson, William Ely, John Thompson.	to John Straw of Hampshire Co.
1797 11-4	DUNN, Thomas (w. Rosana) of Hampshire Co. 100 a. on Patterson Creek; rec. 4-17-1798. Wit.: John Jones, Sr., Ephraim Dunn, Christian Musselman.	to Abraham Eversole of Hampshire Co.
1797 11-15	DUNN, Thomas (w. Rosana) of Hampshire Co. 10½ a., Patterson Creek; rec. 4-17-1798. Wit.: John Jones, Sr., Ephraim Dunn, Abraham Eversole.	to Nicholas Crawlis of Hampshire Co.
1798 3-27	DUNN, Thomas (w. Rosanna) of Hampshire Co. 100 a. on Patterson Creek; rec. 9-17-1798. Wit.: A. King, Henry Protzman, John Dayton, John Jones.	to John Long of Hampshire Co.

1798 7-17	DUTTON, Kingsman (w. Mary) to John Boxell of Hampshire Co. of Frederick Co. 50 a. in Hampshire Co.: rec. 9-17-1798. Wit.: Benj. McDonald, Thomas Thrasher.		1761 9-8	ESSWICK, Rachel to John Keplinger (ELSWICK), executrix, and of Augusta Co. OLDACRE, Henry, executor of John Esswick of Hampshire Co. 206 a. on Lost River; rec 9-8-1761. Wit.: Peter Steenbergen, Petr. Hog, Joseph How, Sam Dew.
1796 9-19	DYER, Nathaniel (w. Susanna) to Henry Heinzman of Hampshire Co. of Hampshire Co. Half acre in Romney; rec. 9-19-1796. Wit.: None.		1778 8-12	ELSWISK, Thomas to son, Thomas Ellswick, Jr. of Hampshire Co. (deed of gift) of Hampshire Co. 406 a. on Lost River, 200 a. on South Branch; rec. 8-12-1778. Wit.: Sam Dew, David Wilson, Patrick Lynch.

—E—

1761 7-28	EARL, Samuel (w. Elizabeth) to Job Pearsal of Frederick Co. (lease and release) of Hampshire Co. Lot No. 16—823 a. on So. Branch; rec. 3-10-1762. Wit.: Max Ja. Keith, Gabriel Jones, Henry Begly.		1790 10-14	ELI, Benjamin (w. Mary) to Joshua Calvin of Hampshire Co. of Hampshire Co. 426 a., Hampshire Co.; rec. 10-14-1790. Wit.: Max Armstrong, John Thompson, Casper Littlemayer.
	EARSOM—See Ahrsam, Ihrsom, Ohrsom.		1792 10-30	ELY, Benjamin (w. Mary) to Paul Powelson of Barbin Co., Ky. of Hampshire Co. 96 a. on Little Cacapeon, 30 a. on Little Cacapeon; rec. 10-30-1792. Wit.: None.
1800 10-15	EARSOM, John to Ben Neil of Hampshire Co. of Hampshire Co. Recorded 10-20-1800. Wit.: Robert Rannels, ex.		1775 11-16	ELLIOTT, John (w. Annabelle) to Isaac Gray of Philadelphia, Pa. of Philadelphia, Pa. 400 a. on Potomac River; rec. 11-14-1780. Wit.: Samuel Elliott, Elijah Parker, Joseph Parker, Jas. Innis, Rawleigh Colston B. Wythe.
1800 6-4	EBERY, William (w. Elizabeth) to Henry Fleck of Frederick Co., heir of Ed Whitehead Hampshire Co. Recorded 1-19-1801. Wit.: James Dailey, Matthew Lodge, Chas. Magill, Arch Magill.		1770 11-6	ELMORE, Charity to John Martin Folkimer Widow of Mathias Elmore Mansfield Township, ELMORE, William (son) (Burlington Co.) ELMORE, Stephen (son) West New Jersey 400 a. on Dillons Run; rec. 12-11-1770. Wit.: Alex White, G. Jones, Peter Hog, John Magill.
1774 10-1	EDINGTON, George (w. Mary) to Levi Ashbrook of Hampshire Co. (lease and release) of Hampshire Co. 200 a. on North River of Cacapeon; rec. 3-14-1775. Wit.: Moses Pigman, Aaron Ashbrook, Isaac Johns.			
1765 10-23	EDWARDS, David (w. Abigail) to Peter Reeve of Hampshire Co. and Thomas Wharton (Lease and release) of Philadelphia, Pa. 412 a. on Great Cacapehon; rec. 4-14-1767. Wit.: Alex White, Edward McGuire, Samuel Pritchard, Henry Heth, Robert Gregg.		1793 11-29	ELSEY, Thomazier to Elias Poston of Fairfax Co. of Hampshire Co. 276 a. on Little Cacapeon R.; rec. 1-15-1794. Wit.: Jas. Machir, Jona. Parsons, Isaac Parsons, Fr. White.
1791 10-16	EDWARDS, Jesse to Isaac Newman of Hampshire Co. and George Newman (Deed of trust) of Hampshire Co. One negro wench, named Phillis, two negro girls, and livestock. Rec. 2-28-1792. Wit.: None.		1782 4-9	EMIT, George (w. Elizabeth) to Alexander McLintock of Hampshire Co. of Hampshire Co. 189 a. on Little Cacapeon; rec. 5-14-1782. Enoch Berry, John Prunty, William Corbin.
1794 4-1	EDWARDS, Jesse to Isaac Newman of Hampshire Co. and George Newman (Bill of sale) of Hampshire Co. Two negro girls, named Agnes and Flora; rec. 4-9-1794. Wit.: Daniel Collins, Thomas Collins, Frederick Hill.		1797 12-16	EMMERSON, Thomas (w. Mary) to Ann Sheetz of Hampshire Co. of Hampshire Co. One quarter acre in Frankfort; rec. 12-18-1797. Wit.: A. King, John Parril, Paul McKeever, Sam Bevan.
1761 12-3	EDWARDS, Joseph to Henry Batton of Hampshire Co. (lease and release) of Hampshire Co. 375 a. on North River; rec. 12-8-1761. Wit.: Ja. Keith, Cuthbt. Bullet, John Hayton, Gabriel Jones.		1798 9-13	EMMERSON, Thomas (w. Mary) to Frederick Sheetz of Hampshire Co. of Hampshire Co. 100 a. on Mill Creek; rec. 12-14-1795. Wit.: None.
1766 4-5	EDWARDS, Joseph to Samuel Pritchard of Hampshire Co. (lease) of Hampshire Co. Parcel of land on Cacapeon River; rec. 8-14-1770. Wit.: William Welton, Job Welton.		1795 10-15	ENGLE, Peter (w. Hannah) to Jacob Poiser of Hampshire Co. of Hampshire Co. One quarter acre in Frankfort; rec. 10-15-1798. Wit.: None.
1767 10-27	EDWARDS, Joseph to Joseph Saunders of Hampshire Co. (lease and release) of Philadelphia 150 a., Mills Branch; rec. 9-14-1768. Wit.: Robt. Pugh, Rachel McKeever, Mary Pugh, Ja. Keith, Edward McGuire, Samuel Prichard.		1800 1-29	ENGLE, William to Joseph Engle of Hampshire Co. of Hampshire Co. Recorded 7-14-1800. Wit.: Elias Poston, Joseph Yates, Rebekah Poston.
1787 1-30	EDWARDS, Samuel (w. Catherine) to Samuel Pugh of Hampshire Co. and Jesse Pugh (Bill of Sale) of Hampshire Co. 96 a. on Dillons Run, 69 a. on Dillons Run, 9 a. on Dillons Run; rec. 2-13-1787. Wit.: Robert Pugh, Geo. Beall, James Hiett.		1800 1-29	ENGLE, William to George Deaver of Hampshire Co. of Hampshire Co. Recorded 7-14-1800. Wit.: Elias Poston, Joseph Engle, Joseph Yates.
1787 2-13	EDWARDS, Samuel (w. Catherine) to Elias Poston of Hampshire Co. (bill of sale) of Hampshire Co. 200 a. on Great Cacapeon; rec. 2-13-1787. Wit.: Andrew Wodrow.		1788 7-25	ENOCH, Enoch (w. Rebecca) to James Largent of Hampshire Co. (lease and release) of Hampshire Co. 130 a. on Great Cacapeon; rec. 9-11-1788. Wit.: Sam Dew, Thomas Collins, Andrew Wodrow, James Murphy.
1789 10-11	EDWARDS, Samuel, (w. Catherine) to Elias Poston of Hampshire Co. of Hampshire Co. One a. and two poles on Great Cacapeon; rec. 10-15-1789. Wit.: None.		1762 8-9	ENOCH, Henry (w. Elizabeth) to George Untis of Hampshire Co. (lease and release) of Hampshire Co. 271 a. on Little Cacapeon; rec. 8-10-1762. Wit.: Cuthbt. Bullet.
1797 9-16	EDWARDS, Samuel to John Cheshire of Hampshire Co. of Hampshire Co. 88½ a. on Great Cacapeon; rec. 10-16-1797. Wit.: Elias Poston, Samuel Poston, James Candy.		1765 2-14	ENOCHS, Henry, Sr. to William Bowels, Sr. (w. Elizabeth) (lease and release) 100 a. on Great Cape Capin; rec. 11-11-1766. Wit.: William Crecraft, Henry Enochs, Jr. Jerh. York, Jno. Corbly.
1797 9-16	EDWARDS, Samuel to Samuel Gard of Hampshire Co. of Hampshire Co. 121½ a. on Great Cacapeon; rec. 9-18-1797. Wit.: Elias Poston, Samuel Poston, James Candy.		1765 2-14	ENOCHS, Henry, Sr. to William Bowels, Sr. (w. Elizabeth) (lease and release) 278 a. on Great Cape Capen; rec. 11-11-1766. Wit.: William Crecraft, Henry Enochs, Jr.
1786 4-26	EDWARDS, Thomas (w. Mary) to James McBride of Hampshire Co. (lease and release) of Hampshire Co. 600 a. on Cacapeon R.; rec. 7-11-1786. Wit.: Elias Poston, Jas. W. Ginnes, Thomas Edwards, William Alderton.		1779 5-10	ENOCH, Henry, Sr. (w. Mary) to Enoch Enochs of Hampshire Co. (lease and release) of Hampshire Co. 154 a. on Great Cacapeon; rec. 5-11-1779. Wit.: Daniel Newcomb, John Archer, John Royse.
1795 4-13	EDWARDS, Thomas (w. Martha) to Bernard Brelsford 206 a. on Great Cacapeon; rec. 4-20-1795. Wit.: Jas. McBride, Thos. Hughs, Elisha Beall.		1782 8-1	ENOCH, Henry (w. Elizabeth) to John Chinoth of Hampshire Co. (lease and release) of Hampshire Co. 57 a. in Enoch's Hollow, near North R.; rec. 11-12-1782. Wit.: Enoch Enochs, James Blue, Daniel Newcomb.
1800 7-14	EDWARDS, Thomas (w. Martha) to Thos. Nicholson of Hampshire Co. of Hampshire Co. Recorded 7-14-1800.		1784 5-10	ENOCHS, Henry (w. Elizabeth) to William Bills of Hampshire Co. (lease and release) of Hampshire Co. 104 a. on Big Cacapeon; rec. 5-11-1784. Wit.: John Largent, Wm. Morgan, John Bills.
1759 12-8	ELSWISK, John (w. Rachel) to son, Thomas Elswick of Hampshire Co. (deed of gift) 200 a. between Lost River and So. Branch Mt.; rec. 11-13-1759. Wit.: Joseph How, John Neeland, James Scott.			

1785 3-8	ENOCH, Henry, Sr. (w. Sarah) to John Minhur of Washington Co. (lease and release) of Hampshire Co. 308 a. on both sides of Hogs Path between Frenches and Little Cacapeon R.; rec. 8-8-1785. Wit.: None.
1789 1-11	ENOCH, Henry (w. Sarah) to John Burnfield of Washington Co. of Bartley Co. 57 a. in Enoch's Hollow of Cacapeon R.; rec. 9-16-1790. Wit.: Enoch Enochs, James Largent, William Bills, Stephen Danham, John Bills.
1790	ENOCH, Henry (w. Sarah) to James Largent of Washington Co. of Hampshire Co. 338 a. on Great Cacapeon; rec 9-16-1790. Wit.: None.
1794 2-12	EVANS, Caleb (w. Eve) to Daniel Rodrick of Hampshire Co. of Hampshire Co. 92 a. on Rorth River; rec. 2-12-1794. Wit.: None.
1794 2-12	EVANS, Caleb (w. Eve) to John Thompson of Hampshire Co. of Hampshire Co. 92 a. on North River; rec. 2-12-1794. Wit.: None.
1798 4-23	D' EVECMON, Peter (w. Hannah) to Isaac Polock of Allegany Co. of George Town, Md. Parcel of land on North Br. Potomac; rec. 5-14-1798. Wit.: None.
1798 4-23	D' EVERCMON, Peter (w. Hannah) to Isaac Polock of Allegany Co. of George Town, Md. Parcel of land on Allegany Mountain; rec. 5-14-1798. Wit.: None.
1795 5-27	EVERSAL, Abraham to Christian Musselman (w. Mary) of Hampshire Co. of Hampshire Co. 187 a. on Patterson Creek; rec. 6-15-1795. Wit.: John Mitchell, And. Wodrow, John Snyder, Alex King.
1800 9-6	EVERSOLE, Abraham (w. Mary) to Mose Rawlings of Hampshire Co. of Hampshire Co. Recorded 9-15-1800. Wit.: John J. Jacob, John Jones, Andrew Pope.
1798 10-24	EWELL, Bertram to James Welch of Prince William Co., Va. of Greenbrier Co. 353 a. on South Br.; rec. 12-17-1798. Wit.: Matthew Lodge, Ed. Dyer, Thos. Dowden, John Jack, John McMeekin.
1796 3-10	EWING, Tristram (w. Susannah) to William Linton of Allegany Co., Md. of Hampshire Co. 250 a. on Grind Stone Ridge; rec. 9-19-1796. Wit.: John Mitchel, A. King, Thos. Emmerson, Henry Protzman.
1796 2-10	EWING, Tristram to William Linton of Allegany Co. of Hampshire Co. 450 a. on South Branch; rec. 9-19-1796. Wit.: John Mitchell, A. King, Henry Protzman.

—F—

1791 9-17	FAIRFAX, Rev. Denny to Joseph Madden of Kent Co. (lease) of Hampshire Co. 186 a. on North River; rec. 4-24-1792. Wit.: Jas. Clark, Arthur O'Hara, Rich. Stafford.
1791 12-1	FAIRFAX, Denny to James Clark of Kent Co. (lease) of Hampshire Co. 46 a., part of Swan Ponds in Hampshire Co.; rec. 8-28-1792. Wit.: Thos. Dawson, Wm. Logan, G. Murray, John Dixon, James McCully, Abraham Monnett.
1791 12-1	FAIRFAX, Denny to Thomas Dawson of Kent Co. (a devisee and legatee named of Hampshire Co. in last will of Lord Fairfax, deceased) 36 a. on South Br.; rec. 8-28-1792. Wit.: Wm. Logan, Sylvester Tipton, G. Murray, John Nixon, James Muelly (McCully,) Abraham Monett, John Woodcock.
1791 12-1	FAIRFAX, Denny to Phillip Lewcas of Kent Co. of Campshire Co. 45 a. on South Br. R.; rec. 8-28-1792. Wit.: Thos. Dixon, Wm. Logan, G. Murray, John Dixon, James McCully, Abraham Monnett.
1791 12-1	FAIRFAX, Denny to Sylvester Tipton of Kent Co. (lease) of Hampshire Co. 30 a., part of the Swan Ponds in Hampshire Co.; rec. 8-28-1792. Wit.: Thos. Dixon, Wm. Logan, G. Murray, John Dixon, James McCully, Abraham Monnett.
1791 12-1	FAIRFAX, Denny to David Swanks of Kent Co. (lease) of Hampshire Co. 51 a., Hampshire Co., part of Swan Ponds; rec. 8-28-1792. Wit.: Thos. Dawson, Wm. Logan, Sylvester Tipton, Geo. Murray, John Dixon, Jas. McCully, John Woodcock, Abraham Monnett.
1791 12-12	FAIRFAX, Denny to Arthur O'Hara of Kent Co. (lease) of Hampshire Co. 129 a. on North Branch; rec. 4-24-1792. Wit.: Rich. Stafford, Patrick Rilly, John S. Woodcock, Andrew Wodrow.
1791 12-12	FAIRFAX, Denny to Richard Stafford of Kent Co. (lease) of Hampshire Co. 124 a. on North Br R.; rec. 4-24-1793. Wit.: Arthur O'Hara, Patrick Rilley, John Woodcock, Andrew Wodrow.
1791 12-29	FAIRFAX, Rev. Denny to Dickeson Limkins of Kent Co. (lease) of Maryland 40 a., part of Swan Ponds in Hampshire Co.; rec. 8-28-1792. Wit.: Silas Simkins, Sylvester Tipton, George Murray, John Woodcock, John Dixon, James McCully, Abraham Monnett.
1791 12-23	FAIRFAX, Denny to James Clarke of Kent Co. (lease) of Hampshire Co. 218 a., Hampshire Co., on North Branch; rec. 7-31-1792. Wit.: George Reed, John Woodcock, Andrew Wodrow.
1792 2-27	FAIRFAX, Rev. Denny to Abraham Monnett of Kent Co. (lease) of Hampshire Co. 46 a. in Hampshire Co.; rec. 8-28-1792. Wit.: John Woodcock, Jas. McCully, John Dixno, William Logan, William Hillery.
1792 4-16	FAIRFAX, Denny to Barton O'Neal of Kent Co. of Hampshire Co. 52 a., part of Swan Ponds; rec. 8-28-1794. Wit.: Wm. Hilley, Wm. Logan, Thos. Collins, And. Wodrow, Silas Simpkins, John O'Neal, Isaac Parsons.
1792 8-25	FAIRFAX, Denny to William Hillery of Kent Co. (lease) of Hampshire Co. 28 a. on North Branch; rec. 8-28-1792. Wit.: John Woodcock, Wm. Logan, Conrad Muma, Andrew Wodrow.
1792 8-25	FAIRFAX, Denny to Conrad Muma of Kent Co. (lease) of Hampshire Co. 13 a., Hampshire Co.; rec. 8-28-1792. Wit.: John Woodcock, Wm. Logan, William Hillery, Andrew Wodrow.
1748 5-21	FAIRFAX, Thomas, Lord to James Rutledge 500 a., drs. of So. Branch of Potomac. of Frederick Co. Rec. 12-14-1757. Reg. at proprietor's office—Book G, Fol. 56. JAMES RUTLEDGE to Henry Lanciscus (Obligation, dated July 30, 1749 and recorded Dec. 14, 1757)—Agrees to make deed on payment of 181 lbs. 9 shillings, together with two horses branded with "L. S." on their near buttock. Witnesses: Henry Van Metere, Andrew Noland.
1749 5-20	FAIRFAX, Thomas, Lord to Benjamin Forman Lot 22—300 a.. So. Branch. (Patent) of Hampshire Co. (Rec. June, 1755. Wit.: None.
1749 8-19	FAIRFAX, Thomas, Lord to John Cunningham Lot No. 38—430 a. on Wappacomo of Frederick Co. or Great South Branch of Potomac; rec. 12-13-1757. Reg. proprietor's office—Book G, Folio 285.
1749 9-29	FAIRFAX, Thomas, Lord to Conrad Hoffman Proprietor of Northern Neck of Va. of Frederick Co. 398 a. on South Branch; rec. 8-11-1773. Wit.: None.
1760 5-6	FAIRFAX, Thomas, Lord to Reuben Keyser Northern Neck of Va. (lease) of Hampshire Co. Lot 14—416 a. on So. Branch of Potomac; rec. 5-14-1760. Wit.: Cuthbt. Bullet, William Millar, Gabriel Jones, Ja. Keith.
1763 3-1	FAIRFAX, Thomas, Lord to William Buffington Northern Neck of Va. (lease and release) of Hampshire Co. 3 a., 21 p. on So. Branch; rec. 3-29-1768. Wit.: Pet. Hog, Jno, Greenfield, Gabriel Jones.
1763 3-3	FAIRFAX, Thomas, Lord to Benjamin Jones Northern Neck of Va. (lease) of Hampshire Co. 311 a. on Mill Creek; rec. 5-10-1763. Wit.: Pet. Hog, Jno, Greenfield, Gabriel Jones.
1766 3-10	FAIRFAX, Thomas, Lord to Darby Aughtney Northern Neck of Va. (lease) (Aughney) Hampshire Co. 400 a., South Branch. Anne Aughtney (Rec. 9-15-1768. Wm. Oldham Wit.: Pet. Hog, Alex White, Gabriel Jones. [Deed reads: "Ye term of time of ye natural lives of the sd. Darby Aughtney, his wife, Anne, and Wm. Oldham, and ye longest liver of them." Three grantees—Darby Aughtney, his wife, Anne, and Wm. Oldham.]
1766 11-6	FAIRFAX, Thomas, Lord to John Taylor Northern Neck of Va. (lease) of Hampshire Co. 416 a. on South Branch; rec. 8-13-1771. Wit.: Peter Hog, Alex White, G. Jones, Simon Taylor, Wm. Smith, Simon Taylor, Jr.
1767 9-18	FAIRFAX, Thomas, Lord to Benjamin Rutherford Northern Neck of Va. (lease) of Hampshire Co. Lot No. 4—529 a., Pattersons Creek; rec. 3-8-1768. Wit.: Ga. Jones, Pet Hog, Enoch Innis, Edward McGuire.
1767 9-14	FAIRFAX, Thomas, Lord to John Holliday Northern Neck of Va. of Philadelphia, Pa. 480 a. on Pattersons Creek; rec. 11-9-1768. Wit.: None.
1778 5-5	FAIRFAX, Thomas, Lord to George Carruthers Baron of Cameron, Scotland. of Hampshire Co. Proprietor of Northern Neck of Va. Lot 56, 238 a. on South Branch R.; rec. 5-12-1778. Wit.: Peter Hog, G. Jones.

1778 8-31	FAIRFAX, Thomas, Lord to Tapley Taylor Northern Neck of Va. (lease) of Hampshire Co. 349 a. on South Branch; rec. 11-10-1778. Wit.: Peter Hog, William Anderson.
1778 8-31	FAIRFAX, Thomas, Lord to John Rosseaw Northern Neck of Va. (lease) of Hampshire Co. 400 a. on New Creek; rec. 11-10-1778. Wit.: Peter Hog, William Anderson.
1778 8-31	FAIRFAX, Thomas, Lord to Mary Martin Northern Neck of Va. (lease) of Hampshire Co. 400 a. on South Branch River; rec. 11-10-1778. Wit.: Peter Hog, William Anderson.
1778 11-16	FAIRFAX, Thomas, Lord to Cornelius Hoghland Northern Neck of Va. (lease) of Hampshire Co. 328 a. on Patterson Creek; rec. 5-11-1779. Wit.: Peter Hog, Robert Stephen, G. Jones.
1779 3-9	FAIRFAX, Thomas, Lord to Robert Clark Northern Neck of Va. (lease) of Hampshire Co. 16 a. on South Branch River; rec 5-11-1779. Wit.: Peter Hog, G. Jones, Robert Stephen, Abraham Hite, Joseph Nevill, James Parsons, Garret Vanmeter, John Wilson.
1779 3-9	FAIRFAX, Thomas, Lord to Robert Cunningham Northern Neck of Va. (lease) of Hampshire Co. 254 a. on South Branch; rec. 5-11-1779. Wit.: Peter Hog, G. Jones, Robert Stephen, James Parsons, Abraham Hite, Garret Vanmeter, John Wilson.
1779 3-9	FAIRFAX, Thomas, Lord, to Christopher Ermintrout Northern Neck of Va. (lease) of Hampshire Co. 20 a. on South ranch; rec. 5-11-1779. (also Armintrout) Wit.: Peter Hog, G. Jones, Robert Stephen, Abraham Hite, Garret Vanmeter, John Liggett.
1779 3-9	FAIRFAX, Thomas, Lord to Matthew Gilmour Northern Neck of Va. (lease) of Hampshire Co. 155 a. o nSouth Branch; rec. 5-11-1779. Wit.: Peter Hog, G. Jones, Robert Stephen, Abraham Hite, Garret Vanmeter, John Liggett.
1779 3-1	FAIRFAX, Thomas, Lord to Henry Hamilton Northern Neck of Va. (lease) of Hampshire Co. 106 a. on South Branch; rec. 3-10-1779. W.ti: Peter Hog, G. Jones, Robert Stephen.
1779 3-9	FAIRFAX, Thomas, Lord to Christopher Hermantrout Northern Neck of Va. (lease) of Hampshire Co. (also Ermintraut, Armintraut) 120 a. on South Branch; rec. 5-11-1779. W.ti: Peter Hog, G. Jones, Robert Stephen.
1779 3-9	FAIRFAX, Thomas, Lord to Abraham Hite Northern Neck of Va. (lease) of Hampshire Co. 71 a. on South Branch R.; rec. 3-9-1779. W.ti: Peter Hog, G. Jones, Robert Stephen.
1779 3-9	FAIRFAX, Thomas, Lord to Abraham Hite Northern Neck of Va. (lease) of Hampshire Co. 128 a. on South Branch R.; rec. 3-9-1779. W.ti: Peter Hog, G. Jones, Robert Stephen.
1779 3-9	FAIRFAX, Thomas, Lord to Daniel Hole Northern Neck of Va. (lease) of Hampshire Co. 88 a. on South Branch; rec. 5-11-1779. W.ti: Peter Hog, G. Jones, Robert Stephen.
1779 3-9	FAIRFAX, Thomas, Lord to Christopher Hoffman Northern Neck of Va. (lease) of Hampshire Co. 6 a. on South Branch; rec. 5-11-1779. Wit.: Peter Hog, G. Jones, Robert Stephen, Abraham Hite, Abel Randall, Joseph Nevill.
1779 3-9	FAIRFAX, Thomas, Lord to John Legate 181 a. on South Branch. Francis Legate Rec. 5-11-1779. George Legate Wit.: Peter Hog, G. Jones, Robert Stephen, Abel Randall, Joseph Nevill.
1779 3-9	FAIRFAX, Thomas, Lord to Job Little Northern Neck of Va. (lease) of Hampshire Co. 60 a. on South Branch; rec. 5-11-1779. Wit.: Peter Hog G. Jones, Robert Stephen, Abraham Hite, Abel Randall, Joseph Nevill.
1779 3-9	FAIRFAX, Thomas, Lord to Robert Maxwell Northern Neck of Va. (lease) of Hampshire Co. 18 a. on South Branch; rec. 5-11-1779. Wit.: Peter Hog, G. Jones, Robert Stephen, Abraham Hite, James Parsons, Garret Vanmeter, John Wilson.
1779 3-9	FAIRFAX, Thomas, Lord to William Norman Northern Neck of Va. (lease) of Hampshire Co. 119 a. on South Branch; rec. 5-11-1779. Wit.: Peter Hog, G. Jones, Robert Stephen, Abraham Hite, Garret Vanmeter, Job Welton.
1779 3-9	FAIRFAX, Thomas, Lord to Thomas Parsons Northern Neck of Va. (lease) of Hampshire Co. 22 a. on South Branch; rec. 5-11-1779 Wit.: Peter Hog, G. Jones, Robert Stephen, Abraham Hite Garret Vanmeter, Job Welton.
1779 3-1	FAIRFAX, Thomas, Lord to William Renick Northern Neck of Va. (lease) of Hampshire Co. 108 a. on South Branch; rec. 3-10-1779. Wit.: Peter Hog, G. Jones, Robert Stephen.
1779 3-9	FAIRFAX, Thomas, Lord to Benjamin Robinson Northern Neck of Va. (lease) of Hampshire Co. 49 a. on South Branch; rec. 5-11-1779. Wit.: Peter Hog, G. Jones, Robert Stephen.
1779 3-9	FAIRFAX, Thomas, Lord to John Robinson Northern Neck of Va. (lease) of Hampshire Co. 48 a. on South Branch; rec. 5-11-1779. Wit.: Peter Hog, G. Jones, Robert Stephen, Abraham Hite, Garret Vanmeter, Peter Casey, Job Welton.
1779 3-9	FAIRFAX, Thomas, Lord to Benjamin Scott Northern Neck of Va. (lease) of Hampshire Co. 35 a. on South Branch; rec. 5-11-1779. Wit.: Peter Hog, G. Jones, Robert Stephen, Abraham Hite, Garret Vanmeter, Peter Casey, Job Welton.
1779 3-9	FAIRFAX, Thomas, Lord to Laurence Shuck Northern Neck of Va. (lease) (Schrick?) of Hampshire Co. 46 a. on South Branch; rec. 5-11-1779. Wit.: Peter Hog, G. Jones, Robert Stephen, Abraham Hite, Garret Vanmeter, Peter Casey, Job Welton.
1779 3-9	FAIRFAX, Thomas, Lord to Phillip Swank Northern Neck of Va. (lease) of Hampshire Co. 18 a. on South Branch R.; rec. 5-11-1779. Wit.: Peter Hog, G. Jones, Robert Stephen, Abraham Hite, Garret Vanmeter, Jonathan Heath, Abel Randall.
1779 3-9	FAIRFAX, Thomas, Lord to Cornelius Ward Northern Neck of Va. (lease) of Hampshire Co. 20½ a. on South Branch R.; rec. 5-11-1779. Wit.: Peter Hog, G. Jones, Robert Stephen, Abraham Hite.
1779 3-9	FAIRFAX, Thomas, Lord to Jesse Welton Northern Neck of Va. (lease) of Hampshire Co. 19 a. on South Branch R.; rec. 5-11-1779. Wit.: Peter Hog, G. Jones, Robert Stephen, Abraham Hite, Garret Vanmeter, Job Welton.
1779 3-9	FAIRFAX, Thomas, Lord to Job Welton Northern Neck of Va. (lease) of Hampshire Co. 172 a. on South Branch; rec. 5-12-1779. Wit.: Peter Hog, G. Jones, Robert Stephen.
1779 3-9	FAIRFAX, Thomas, Lord to George Whitman Northern Neck of Va. (lease) of Hampshire Co. 90 a. on Luney's Creek, part of the South Branch Manor. Rec. 5-11-1779. Wit.: Peter Hog, G. Jones, Robert Stephen, Abraham Hite, Garret Vanmeter, Abel Randall.
1779 3-9	FAIRFAX, Thomas, Lord to George Whiteman Northern Neck of Va. (lease) of Hampshire Co. 55 a. on South Branch R.; rec. 5-11-1779. Wit.: Peter Hog, G. Jones, Robert Stephen, Abraham Hite, Garret Vanmeter, Abel Randall.
1779 3-9	FAIRFAX, Thomas, Lord to John Wood Northern Neck of Va. (lease) of Hampshire Co. 9 a. on South Branch; rec. 5-11-1779. Wit.: Peter Hog, G. Jones, Robert Stephen, Abraham Hite, Garret Vanmeter, Peter Casey, Sylvester Ward.
1779 3-9	FAIRFAX, Thomas, Lord to John Wilson Northern Neck of Va. (lease) of Hampshire Co. 258 a. on Mill Creek; rec. 5-11-1779. Wit.: Peter Hog, G. Jones, Robert Stephen, Abraham Hite, Garret Vanmeter, Peter Casey, Sylvester Ward.
1780 3-6	FAIRFAX, Thomas, Lord to Michael Carr Northern Neck of Va. (lease) of Hampshire Co. 89 a. on South Branch; rec. 8-14-1780. Wit.: Robert Stephen, G. Jones, Andrew Wodrow, Job Welton, Michael Hornbeck.
1780 2-6	FAIRFAX, Thomas, Lord to Samuel Cutright Northern Neck of Va. (lease) of Hampshire Co. 137 a. on South Branch; rec. 3-14-1780. Wit.: Robt. Stephen, G. Jones, Andrew Wodrow.
1780 3-6	FAIRFAX, Thomas, Lord to Michael Hahn Northern Neck of Va. (lease) of Hampshire Co. 60 a. on South Branch; rec. 5-14-1782. Wit.: Robt. Stephen, G. Jones, Andrew Wodrow.
1780 3-6	FAIRFAX, Thomas, Lord to Jacob Helmick Northern Neck of Va. (lease) of Hampshire Co. 100 a. on South Branch; rec. 3-14-1780. Wit.: Robt. Stephen, G. Jones, Andrew Wodrow, Job Bacorn, John Bacorn.
1780 3-6	FAIRFAX, Thomas, Lord to Moses Hutton Northern Neck of Va. (lease) of Hampshire Co. 105 a. on South Branch; rec. 3-14-1780. Wit.: Robt. Stephen, G. Jones, Andrew Wodrow.
1780 3-6	FAIRFAX, Thomas, Lord to John Kimble Northern Neck of Va. (lease) of Hampshire Co. 60 a. on South Branch; rec. 3-14-1780. Wit.: Robt. Stephen, G. Jones, Andrew Wodrow, Abraham Hite, G. Vanmeter, Isaac Vanmeter.
1780 3-6	FAIRFAX, Thomas, Lord to James Parsons Northern Neck of Va. (lease) of Hampshire Co. 145 a. on South Branch; rec. 3-14-1780. Wit.: Robt. Stephen, G. Jones, Andrew Wodrow.

| 1780 3-6 | FAIRFAX, Thomas, Lord to George Reed
Northern Neck of Va. (lease) of Hampshire Co.
10 a. on South Branch; rec. 3-14-1780.
Wit.: Robt. Stephens, G. Jones, Andrew Wodrow, Abraham Hite, Abel Randall. |

| 1780 3-6 | FAIRFAX, Thomas, Lord to Garret Vanmeter
Northern Neck of Va. (lease) of Hampshire Co.
298 a. on South Branch; rec. 3-14-1780.
Wit.: Robt. Stephen, G. Jones, Andrew Wodrow. |

| 1780 3-6 | FAIRFAX, Thomas, Lord to Jacob Vanmeter
Northern Neck of Va. (lease) of Hampshire Co.
53 a. on South Branch; rec. 3-14-1780.
Wit.: Robt. Stephen, G. Jones, Andrew Wodrow. |

| 1780 3-6 | FAIRFAX, Thomas, Lord to Jacob Vanmeter
Northern Neck of Va. (lease) of Hampshire Co.
285 a. on Soouth Branch; rec. 3-14-1780.
Wit.: Robert Stephen, G. Jones, Andrew Wodrow, Peter Hog, Jacob Vanmeter. |

| 1780 3-6 | FAIRFAX, Thomas, Lord to Jacob Vanmeter
Northern Neck of Va. (lease) of Hampshire Co.
88 a. on South Branch; rec. 3-14-1780.
Wit.: Robt. Stephen, G. Jones, Andrew Wodrow. |

| 1780 3-6 | FAIRFAX, Thomas, Lord to John Yokum
Northern Neck of Va. (lease) of Hampshire Co.
119 a. on South Branch; rec. 3-14-1780.
Wit.: Robert Stephen, G. Jones, Andrew Wodrow, Abraham Hite, Garret Vanmeter, Abraham Clark. |

| 1795 10-17 | FAIRLEY, John (w. Elizabeth) to Ephraim Dunn
of Hampshire Co. of Hampshire Co.
106 a. on Patterson Creek; rec. 4-18-1796.
Wit.: Alex King, Thos. Dunn, Wm. Reddick, Sam Sheppherd, Benj. Sheppherd. |

| 1797 8-26 | FAIRLEY, John (w. Elizabeth) to Andrew Wodrow
of Hampshire Co. of Hampshire Co.
69 a. on Patterson Creek; rec. 9-18-17997.
Wit.: John Jones, Sr., Matthew Pigman, Henry Protzman, John Mitchell. |

| 1778 8-10 | FAIRLEY, Thomas to William Blackburn
of Hampshire Co. (lease an drelease) of Hampshire Co.
67 a. on Patterson Creek; rec. 8-11-1778.
Wit.: Andrew Fairley, John Fairley, Elisha Collings. |

| 1794 4-4 | FAKE, Adam to Benjamin Wiley
of Hampshire Co. of Hampshire Co.
96 a. on North Branch; rec. 4-9-1794.
Wit.: John House, Abel Wiley. |

| 1799 5-26 | FEARON, Robert to —— Vancouver
of Petersburg, Va.
Recorded 7-14-1800. |

| 1800 | FEARSON, Robert to Thomas Edwards
See FORECROFT, Judith |

| 1795 9-22 | FEATHER, Stephen to Thompson Pegg
of Hampshire Co. of Hampshire Co.
15 a. on Little Cacapeon; rec. 2-15-1796.
Wit.: Jacob Starn, Joseph Starn, James Meekens. |

| 1777 11-10 | FERGUSON, Robert (w. Frances) to Michael Hall
of Hampshire Co. (lease and release) of Hampshire Co.
100 a. on South Branch; rec. 11-11-1777.
Wit.: None. |

| 1797 3-10 | FERRALL, James to William Wilson
of Philadelphia of Berkeley Co.
260 a. on Allegany Mt.; rec. 4-17-1797.
Wit.: Wm. Burns, John Brown, Ewd. Dyer, John J. Jacob, Jacob Kuykendall. |

| 1797 10-16 | FERRALL, James to John Dunlap
of George Town, Md. of Alexandria
Parcel of land on New Creek; rec. 2-20-1798.
Wit.: Thomas Irwin, George Craik, Andrew Estrau. |

| 1794 9-10 | FERRAND, Nathaniel to Ernest Coulshine
of Hampshire Co. of Hampshire Co.
140 a. on New Creek; rec. 9-10-1794.
Wit.: Jas. Cochran. |

| 1796 9-15 | FERREE, Cornelius (w. Helena) to Jesse Harlow
of Hampshire Co. of Hampshire Co.
376 a. on Great Cacapeon; rec. 9-19-1796.
Wit.: None. |

| 1797 10-16 | FERRY, George, Sr. (w. Rachel) to son, Stephen Ferry
of Hampshire Co. of Hampshire Co.
206 a. on Patterson Creek; rec. 10-16-1797.
Wit.: None. |

| 1792 7-23 | FICHENAL, Moses (w. Margaret) to James Machir
of Hampshire Co. of Hardy Co.
180 a. on North Branch; rec. 7-31-1792.
Wit.: John Herndon. |

| 1794 12-10 | FIDLER, Elizabeth to Henry Purgitt
of Hampshire Co. of Hampshire Co.
137 a. on Mill Creek; rec. 12-10-1794.
Wit.: Benj. Hoffman, Jacob Fidler, Thos. Smart. |

| 1794 12-8 | FIDLER, Jacob to mother, Elizabeth Fidler
of Hampshire Co. of Hampshire Co.
137½ a. on Mill Creek; rec. 12-10-1794.
Wit.: Henry Purgitt, Benj. Hoffman. |

| 1796 3-4 | FIDLER, Jacob (w. Magdalene) to Christopher Shaffer
of Hampshire Co. of Frederick Co.
275 a. on Mill Creek; rec. 4-18-1796.
Wit.: Edward Dyer, Jost. Stimmell, William Baer, John Beizer. |

| 1794 12-27 | FIFE, John, (w. Margaret) to David Reese
of Allegany Co. of Bourbon Co., Ky.
352 a. on Patterson Creek; rec. 2-16-1795.
Wit.: Peter Barrett, Geo. Reese, Thomas Thompson. |

| 1791 9-10 | FINK, Frederick (w. Esther) to Thomas Leazenby
of Hampshire Co. of Hampshire Co.
117 a. on Middle Ridge; rec. 10-18-1791.
Wit.: John Hansbrough, Isaac Means. |

| 1791 9-10 | FINK, Frederick (w. Esther) to William Roberts
of Hampshire Co. of Hampshire Co.
181 a. on Middle Ridge; rec. 9-15-1791.
Wit.: None. |

| 1792 5-10 | FINK, Frederick (w. Esther) to James Watts
of Hampshire of Hampshire Co.
12½ a. on Beaver Run; rec. 6-26-1792.
Wit.: Peter Umstot, Henry Fink, Jacob Creagur. |

| 1795 5-19 | FINK, Frederick (w. Esther) to William Roberts
of Hampshire Co. of Hampshire Co.
131 a., Hampshire Co.; rec. 6-15-1795.
Wit.: None. |

| 1795 5-19 | FINK, Frederick (w. Esther) to Thomas Leasenby
of Hampshire Co. of Hampshire Co.
117 a., Hampshire Co.; rec. 6-15-1795.
Wit.: None. |

| 1796 6-20 | FINK, Frederick to Thomas Scardon
FINK, Eston of Hampshire Co.
of Hampshire Co.
50 a. on Beaver Run; rec. 6-20-1796.
Wit.: Archibald Watats, Jacob Geiger, James Watts. |

| 1796 6-20 | FINK, Frederick (w. Esther) to Thomas Scardon
of Hampshire Co. of Hampshire Co.
90 a. on Beaver Run; rec. 6-20-1796.
Wit.: Archibald Watats, Jacob Geiger, James Watts. |

| 1794 3-20 | FLECK, Jacob (w. Catherine) to Abraham Eversal
of Hampshire Co of Hampshire Co.
137 a. on Plum Run; rec. 9-10-1794.
Wit.: John Kimberlin, John Keller, Peter Eversal. |

| 1794 3-20 | FLECK, Jacob (w. Catherine) to Christian Musselman
of Hampshire Co. of Hampshire Co.
61 a. on Plum Run; rec. 9-10-1794.
Wit.: John Kimberline, John Keller, Peter Eversal. |

| 1793 6-12 | FLEMING, James (w. Ann) to Henry Miller
of Hampshire Co. of Frederick Co.
212 a. in Hampshire Co.; rec. 6-12-1793.
Wit.: None. |

| 1793 6-12 | FLEMING, James to William Branninburg
of Hampshire Co. of Hampshire Co.
141½ a. in Hampshire Co.; rec. 6-12-1793.
Wit.: None. |

| 1795 3-10 | FLEMING, James to Thomas Smoot
of Hampshire Co. of Hampshire Co.
30 a. on Mill Creek; rec. 4-20-1795.
Wit.: Jacob Piser, Peter Engle, John Piser. |

| 1795 9-21 | FLEMING, James to Michael Gillipsy
of Hampshire Co. of Cumberland Co.
Parcel of land on Beaver Run; rec. 6-20-1796.
Wit.: Rod. James, Denny Welch, Sylvester Welch. |

| 1795 9-21 | FLEMING, James (w. Ann) to Michael Gallaspy
of Hampshire Co. of Cumberland Co.
32½ a. on Knobley Mt.; rec. 6-20-1796.
Wit.: Rod. James, Denny Welch, Sylvester Welch. |

| 1800 9-15 | FORECROFT, Judith to James McBride
of Hampshire Co.
Recorded 9-15-1800.
Wit.: Thomas Dunn, William Vause. |

| 1800 9-15 | FORECROFT, Judith to Thomas Edwards
administratrix of John Forecroft, and Hampshire Co.
FEARSON, Robert, of London
Recorded 9-15-1800.
Wit.: Thomas Dunn, William Vause. |

| 1797 8-12 | FORMAN, Aaron to John Jack
of Bourbin Co., Ky. of Hampshire Co.
443 a. on South Branch R.; rec. 9-18-1797.
Wit.: Wm. Schrock, John Hansbrough, Soolomon Newman, Isaac Means, John J. Jacob. |

| 1798 12-15 | FORMAN, Aaron to Thomas Williams
of Hampshire Co. of Hampshire Co.
30 a. in Hampshire Co.; rec. 5-20-1795.
Wit.: Isaac Feree, Joshua Ferree, Cornelius Ferree. |

| 1754 7-22 | FORMAN, Benjamin to William Forman
of Hampshire Co. (lease and release) of Hampshire Co.
287½ a. on South Branch; rec. June, 1755.
Wit.: William Buffington, Benjamin Kuykendall, Abraham Kuykendall, Joshua Sutton. |

| 1755 5-25 | FORMAN, Benjamin to John Forman
of Hampshire Co. (lease and release) of Hampshire Co.
112½ a. on South Branch; rec. 6-17-1755.
Wit.: William Buffington, Benjamin Kuykendall, Abraham Kuykendall, Joshua Sutton. |

GRANTOR-GRANTEE — PAGE 19

1794 **FORMAN, Benjamin** to **William Vandiver**
11-15 of Mason Co., Ky. (power of attorney) of Hampshire Co.
Power to collect all debts for Benj. Forman; rec. 12-10-1794.
Wit.: None.

1780 **FORMAN, Catherine** to **John Williamson**
11-14 Relict of Wm. Forman, deceased of Hampshire Co.
FORMAN, John, son
of Hampshire Co.
200 a. on Little Cacapeon; rec. 11-14-1780.
Wit.: None.

1779 **FORMAN, Catherine** to **John Williamson**
5-11 of Hampshire Co. of Hampshire Co.
200 a. on Little Cacapeon; rec. 5-11-1779.
Wit.: Sam Dew, Andrew Wodrow.

1762 **FORMAN, James** to **John Forman**
3-9 Eldest son of Benjamin Forman **William Forman**
of Hampshire Co. (lease and release) of Hampshire Co.
Lot No. 22—300 a., South Branch; rec. 3-10-1762.
Wit.: Chas. Linch, Gabriel Joones, Ja. Keith.

1765 **FORMAN, John** (w. Mary) to **John Keating**
10-7 **FORMAN, William** (w. Catherine) of Hampshire Co.
of Hampshire Co. (lease and release)
150 a. on So. Branch; rec. 10-8-1765.
Wit.: Benjamin Kuykendall, Thomas Parsons.

1769 **FOREMAN, John** to **William Foreman**
6-22 GUPHILL, Edward (w. Elizabeth) of Hampshire Co.
of Craven Co., S. C. (lease and release)
400 a. on Great So. Branch; rec. 11-14-1769.
Wit.: Sam Dew, John Foreman,
James Chesnut, John Hougland.

1783 **FORMAN, John, Jr.** to **James Martin**
8-12 **FORMAN, Catherine** of Hampshire Co.
of Hampshire Co.
150 a. on North Branch of Potomac; rec. 8-12-1783.
Wit.: None.

1786 **FORMAN, John** (w. Mary) to **Samuel Rukman**
5-20 of Hampshire Co. of Hampshire Co.
120 a. on South Branch; rec. 7-11-1786.
Wit.: Wm. Forman, Ben Forman, Thomas Ruckman.

1790 **FORMAN, John, Sr.** (w. Mary) to **Abraham Inskeep**
9-15 of Hampshire Co. of Hardy Co.
400 a. on South Branch; rec. 9-16-1790.
Wit.: Nathaniel Dyer, Samuel Burn.
Tett Wodrow, Andrew Wodrow.

1790 **FORMAN, John** to **Joseph Forman**
10-23 of Hampshire Co. (power of attorney) of Berkeley Co.
Authority to collect all money due the said John Forman.
Rec. 2-10-1791.
Wit.: Wm. Fox, John Forman, Jr., Nicholas Boyce.

1791 **FORMAN, John, Jr.** to **William Forman, Jr.**
9-15 of Hampshire Co. of Hampshire Co.
190 a. on South Branch R.; rec. 9-15-1791
Wit.: Fielding Calmes, Isaac Parsons, Nicholas Casey,
Isaac Means, And. Wodrow, John Herndon,
John Mitchell

1791 **FORMAN, John, Jr.** to **Joseph Forman**
9-15 of Hampshire Co. of Hampshire Co.
173 a. on South Branch R.; rec. 9-15-1791.
Wit.: Fielding Calmes, Isaac Parsons, N. Casey,
Isaac Means. Andrew Wedrow, John Herndon,
John Mitchell

1791 **FORMAN, John** to **Ephraim Herriott**
4-14 of Hampshire Co. **David Allen**
195 a. on South Branch; rec. 4-14-1791. of Hampshire Co.
Wit.: None.

1795 **FORMAN, John** to **Joshua Colvin**
5-19 of Kentucky of Hampshire Co.
399 a., Hampshire Co.; rec. 6-15-1795.
Wit.: Andrew Wodrow, Wm. Johnson, John Blue,
Isaac Parsons.

1795 **FOREMAN, John** (w. Mary) to **John Brown**
5-19 of Kentucky of Virginia
353 a., South Branch R.; rec. 10-19-1795.
Wit.: Isaac Parsons, Isaac Means, John Blue,
Joel Buffington.

1797 **FORMAN, John** (w. Margaret) to **Joseph Forman**
2-18 of Hampshire Co. (bill of sale) of Hampshire Co.
297 a. on South Branch R.; rec. 2-20-1797.
Wit.: Wm. Inskeep, Francis White, John Jack.

1797 **FORMAN, John** (w. Margaret) to **William Forman**
2-18 of Hampshire Co. (bill of sale) of Hampshire Co.
356 a. on South Branch R.; rec. 2-20-1797.
Wit.: Wm. Inskeep, Francis White, John Jack.

1797 **FOREMAN, John** to **William Foreman**
3-2 of Hampshire Co. **Joseph Foreman**
Parcel of land on South Br. R; of Hampshire Co.
rec. 4-17-1797.
Wit.: Geo. Carruthers, Wm. Inskeep.

1797 **FORMAN, John** to **John Powelsosn**
9-9 of Bourbon Co., Ky. of Hampshire Co.
203 a. on Little Cacapeon; rec. 9-18-1797.
Wit.: Eli Davis, John Hansbrough, Wm. Linton.

1797 **FORMAN, John** to **John McMeekin**
9-9 of Bourbon Co., Ky. of Hampshire Co.
780 a. on South Br. R.; rec. 9-18-1797.
Wit.: Peter Williams, John Powelson, John Hansbrough.

1798 **FORMAN, Joseph** to **William Forman**
12-15 of Hampshire Co. of Hampshire Co.
297 a. on South Branch; rec. 12-17-1798.
Wit.: None.

1765 **FORMAN, William** (see Forman, John)

1796 **FORMAN, William** to **Thomas Pettet**
10-1 of Burboun Co., Ky. (bill of sale) of Hampshire Co.
345 a. on Little Cacapeon R.; rec. 12-19-1796.
Wit.: Robert Calvin, Ann Calvin, Daniel Laing

1796 **FORMAN, William** to **William Inskeep**
10-4 of Bourbcun Co., Ky. of Hampshire Co.
153 a. on South Branch R.; rec. 10-17-1796.
Wit.: Gabriel Fox, Geo. Scott, Henry Powelson.

1797 **FORMAN, William** to **William Inskeep**
6-19 of Hampshire Co. of Hampshire Co.
One acre, 6 poles, Hampshire Co.; rec. 6-19-1797.
Wit.: None.

1799 **FORMAN, William** (w. Elizabeth) to **William Inskeep**
2-18 of Hampshire Co. of Hampshire Co.
5¼ a. on South Branch River; rec. 2-18-1799.
Wit.: None.

1800 **FORMAN, William** (w. Elizabeth) to **William Inskeep**
4-14 of Hampshire Co. of Hampshire Co.
Recorded 4-14-1800.

1765 **FOSTER, Isaac** (w. Mary) to **John Parrell**
5-22 of Hampshire Co. (lease and release) of Hampshire Co.
413 a. on Dillcons Run; rec. 6-11-1765.
Wit.: John Lindsey, Humy. Wells, Joseph Wood.
David Ashby, Amos Richardson.

1791 **FOSTER, John** (w. Sarah) to **Robert Monroe**
6-16 of Allegany Co. of Hampshire Co.
100 a. on North Br. of Potomac; rec. 6-16-1791.
Wit.: None.

1796 **FOSTER, John** (w. Jane) to **John Thomas Ricketts**
3-17 of Alexandria of Alexandria
232 a., 419 a., 26 a., 50 a.. 72 a., 309 a., 569 a., in Hampshire
Co.; rec 6-20-1796.
Wit.: T. Lancaster, Wm. Paton, Jr.

1794 **FOSTER, Nathaniel** to **Richard Rounsovel**
9-10 SEBRING, John
ROGERS, John
91 a. on Furmans Run; rec. 9-10-1794.
Wit.: Jacob Doman, Jacob Starn.

1800 **FOUT, Michael** to **William Jacob**
10-21 of Hampshire Co. **Charlotte Fout**
Recorded 10-21-1800. of Hampshire Co.

1782 **FOX, Absalom** (w. Christian) to **Robert Calvin**
10-19 of Washington Co. (lease and release) of Hampshire Co.
276 a. on Branch Mt.; rec. 11-12-1782.
Wit.: John Ferman, Wm. Forman, Wm. Fox.

1797 **FOX, Gabriel** to **William Fox**
8-3 of Hampshire Co. of Hampshire Co.
400 a. in Hampshire Co.; rec. 12-18-1797.
Wit.: Wm. Inskeep, David Allen, Edward Ryan.

1793 **FOX, William** to **Andrew Wodrow**
10-22 MITCHELL, John (bill of sale) of Hampshire Co.
421 a. on Patterson Creek, 442 a. on North Branch R., 200 a
on Patterson Creek; rec. 12-11-1793.
Wit.: None.

1793 **FOX, William** to **Adam Hall**
10-29 MITCHELL, John of Hampshire Co.
SMITH, Edward
402 a. on Little Cacapeon; rec. 12-11-1793.
Wit.: Chas. Magill, And. Wodrow, J. McMeekin,
Ed. McCarty.

1776 **FOXCRAFT, John** to **John Morrel**
5-14 THOMPSON, Charles, Philadelphia, Pa. Dunmore, Va.
875 a. on North River, 24 a. on North River; rec. 11-12-1776.
Wit.: Sam Dew, Jonathan Heath, John Roussaw,
Robt. Stephen.

1778 **FOXCRAFT, John** to **Darby Aughney**
5-1 THOMPSON, Charles, Philadelphia, Pa. of Hampshire Co.
Bill of sale—168 a. on South Branch; rec. 9-11-1778.
Wit.: David Mitchell, Abraham Hite, Garret Vanmeter.

1778 **FOXCRAFT, John** to **George Newman**
5-1 THOMPSON, Charles **Isaac Newman**
of Philadelphia. Pa. (bill of sale) of Prince William Co.
352 a. on South Branch; rec. 5-13-1778.
Wit.: None.

1779 **FOXCRAFT, John** to **Joseph Nevill**
5-10 THOMPSON, Charles, Philadelphia, Pa. of Hampshire Co.
242 a. on South Branch; rec. 9-10-1779.
Wit.: None.

1788 **FOXCRAFT, John** to **Isaac Steer**
10-7 of New York of Frederick Co.
175 a. on Little Cacapeon; rec. 4-16-1789.
Wit.: Murs Fisher, Thomas Fisher, Jr.

1796 **FRANK, Henry** to **Osborn Sprigg**
12-1 **FRANK, George** of Hampshire Co.
Fayette Co., Pa.
157 a. in Hampshire Co.; rec. 12-19-1796.
Wit.: Samuel Beckwith, Michl. Cresap,
John J. Jacob, Thomas Cresap.

1789 FRANKFORT, Trustees of — to Jacob Brookhart
[Trustees of Frankfort are John Ettitchel, John Reed Lewis Dunn, Jacob Brookhart, and John Williams]
¼ a. in Frankfort; rec. 10-14-1790. of Hampshire Co.
Wit.: And. Wodrow, Solomon Jones, Abraham Jones, M. A. Wodrow.

1790 2-11 FRANKFORT, Trustees of — to John Pearsall
(Now Co. seat of Mineral Co. (bill of sale) of Hampshire Co.
One-quarter acre in Frankfort; rec. 2-11-1790.
Wit.: None.

1790 6-19 FRANKFORT, Trustees of — to John Adams
Hampshire Co. of Hampshire Co.
¼ a. in Frankfort; rec. 9-16-1790.
Wit.: And. Wodrow, Solomon Jones, Abraham Jones, M. A. Wodrow.

1790 6-19 FRANKFORT, Trustees of — to Michael Brookhart
¼ a. in Frankfort; rec. 10-14-1790. of Hampshire Co.
Wit.: And. Wodrow, Solomon Jones, Abraham Jones, M. A. Wodrow.

1790 6-19 FRANKFORT, Trustees of — to Michael Brookhart
¼ a. in Frankfort; rec. 10-14-1790. of Hampshire Co.
Wit.: And. Wodrow, Solomon Jones, Abraham Jones, M. A. Wodrow.

1790 6-19 FRANKFORT, Trustees of — to James Clark
¼ a. in Frankfort; rec. 10-14-1790. of Hampshire Co.
Wit.: And. Wodrow, Solomon Jones, Abraham Jones, M. A. Wodrow.

1790 6-19 FRANKFORT, Trustees of — to Michael Collier
One-fourth acre in Frankfort; rec. of Washington Co.
10-14-1790.
Wit.: Abraham Johnson, Andrew Wodrow, M. A. Wodrow.

1790 6-19 FRANKFORT, Trustees of — to Andrew Cooper
½ a. in Frankfort; rec. 10-14-1790. of Hampshire Co.
Wit.: And. Wodrow, Solomon Jones, Abraham Jones, M. A. Wodrow.

1790 6-19 FRANKFORT, Trustees of — to Nicholas Dick
¼ a. in Frankfort; rec. 10-14-1790. of Hampshire Co.
Wit.: And. Wodrow, Solomon Jones, Abraham Jones, M. A. Wodrow.

1790 6-19 FRANKFORT, Trustees of — to James Dougherty
¼ a. in Frankfort; rec. 10-14-1790. of Hampshire Co.
Wit.: And. Wodrow, Solomon Jones, Abraham Jones, M. A. Wodrow.

1790 6-19 FRANKFORT, Trustees of — to John Dowden
¼ a. in Frankfort; rec. 10-14-1790. of Hampshire Co.
Wit.: And. Wodrow, Solomon Jones, Abraham Jones, M. A. Wodrow.

1790 6-19 FRANKFORT, Trustees of — to James Grant
¼ a. in Frankfort; rec. 1-13-1791. of Hampshire Co.
Wit.: And. Wodrow, Solomon Jones, Abraham Jones, M. A. Wodrow.

1790 6-19 FRANKFORT, Trustees of — to Daniel Hollas
¼ a. in Frankfort; rec. 10-14-1790. of Hampshire Co.
Wit.: And. Wodrow, Solomon Jones, Abraham Jones, M. A. Wodrow.

1790 6-19 FRANKFORT, Trustees of — to Thomas Hollenback
¼ a. in Frankfort; rec. 10-14-1790. of Hampshire Co.
Wit.: And. Wodrow, Solomon Jones, Abraham Jones, M. A. Wodrow.

1789 FRANKFORT, Trustees of — to Abraham Johnson
¼ a. in Frankfort; rec. 10-14-1790. of Hampshire Co.
Wit.: And. Wodrow, Solomon Jones, Abraham Jones, M. A. Wodrow.

1790 6-19 FRANKFORT, Trustees of — to John Jones, Jr.
¼ a. in Frankfort; rec. 10-14-1790. of Hampshire Co.
Wit.: And. Wodrow, Solomon Jones, Abraham Jones, M. A. Wodrow.

1790 6-19 FRANKFORT, Trustees of — to Peter Jones, Sr.
¼ a. in Frankfort; rec. 10-14-1790. of Hampshire Co.
Wit.: And. Wodrow, Solomon Jones, Abraham Jones, M. A. Wodrow.

1790 6-19 FRANKFORT, Trustees of — to Solomon Jones
¼ a. in Frankfort; rec. 10-14-1790. of Hampshire Co.
Wit.: And. Wodrow, Solomon Jones, Abraham Jones, M. A. Wodrow.

1790 6-19 FRANKFORT, Trustees of — to Alexander King
¼ a. in Frankfort rec. 9-16-1790. of Hampshire Co.
Wit.: And. Wodrow, Solomon Jones, Abraham Jones, M. A. Wodrow.

1790 6-19 FRANKFORT, Trustees of — to John Miller
¼ a. in Frankfort; rec. 10-14-1790. of Hampshire Co.
Wit.: And. Wodrow, Solomon Jones, Abraham Jones, M. A. Wodrow.

1790 6-19 FRANKFORT, Trustees of — to John Mitchell
¼ a. in Frankfort; rec. 10-14-1790. of Hampshire Co.
Wit.: And. Wodrow, Solomon Jones, Abraham Jones, M. A. Wodrow.

1790 6-19 FRANKFORT, Trustees of — to Benjamin Parker
Oen-fourth acre in Frankfort. of Hampshire Co.
one-fourth acre in Frankfort; rec. 9-16-1790.
Wit.: Andrew Wodrow, Abraham Johnson, Solomon Jones, M. A. Wodrow.

1790 6-19 FRANKFORT, Trustees of — to Abraham Peters
¼ a. in Frankfort; rec. 10-14-1790. of Hampshire Co.
Wit.: And. Wodrow, Solomon Jones, Abraham Jones, M. A. Wodrow.

1790 6-19 FRANKFORT, Trustees of — to John Rannells
¼ a. in Frankfort; rec. 10-14-1790. of Hampshire Co.
Wit.: And. Wodrow, Solomon Jones, Abraham Jones, M. A. Wodrow.

1790 6-19 FRANKFORT, Trustees of — to John Reed
1 a. in Frankfort; rec. 9-16-1790. off Hampshire Co.
Wit.: And. Wodrow, Solomon Jones, Abraham Jones, M. A. Wodrow.

1790 6-19 FRANKFORT, Trustees of — to Robert Reynolds
¼ a. in Frankfort; rec. 10-14-1790. of Hampshire Co.
Wit.: And. Wodrow, Solomon Jones, Abraham Jones, M. A. Wodrow.

1790 6-19 FRANKFORT, Trustees of — to Berry Shepherd
¼ a. in Frankfort; rec. 10-14-1790. of Hampshire Co.
Wit.: And. Wodrow, Solomon Jones, Abraham Jones, M. A. Wodrow.

1790 6-19 FRANKFORT, Trustees of — to John Shepherd
¼ a. in Frankfort; rec. 10-14-1790. of Hampshire Co.
Wit.: And. Wodrow, Solomon Jones, Abraham Jones, M. A. Wodrow.

1790 6-19 FRANKFORT, Trustees of — to Benjamin Shepherd
¼ a. in Frankfort; rec. 10-14-1790. of Hampshire Co.
Wit.: And. Wodrow, Solomon Jones, Abraham Jones, M. A. Wodrow.

1790 6-19 FRANKFORT, Trustees of — to Nathan Smith
½ a. in Frankfort; rec. 10-14-1790. of Hampshire Co.
Wit.: And. Wodrow, Solomon Jones, Abraham Jones, M. A. Wodrow.

1790 6-19 FRANKFORT, Trustees of — to Jacob Staddler
¼ a. in Frankfort; rec. 10-14-1790. of Hampshire Co.
Wit.: And. Wodrow, Solomon Jones, Abraham Jones, M. A. Wodrow.

1790 6-19 FRANKFORT, Trustees of — to Richard Stafford
¼ a. in Frankfort; rec. 10-14-1790. of Hampshire Co.
Wit.: And. Wodrow, Solomon Jones, Abraham Jones, M. A. Wodrow.

1790 6-19 FRANKFORT, Trustees of — to Israel Stallcop
½ a. in Frankfort; rec. 10-14-1790. of Hampshire Co.
Wit.: And. Wodrow, Solomon Jones, Abraham Jones, M. A. Wodrow.

1790 6-19 FRANKFORT, Trustees of — to Peter Walker
¼ a. in Frankfort; rec. 10-14-1790. of Hampshire Co.
Wit.: And. Wodrow, Solomon Jones, Abraham Jones, M. A. Wodrow.

1790 6-19 FRANKFORT, Trustees of — to John Waters
¼ a. in Frankfort; rec. 1-15-1794. of Hampshire Co.
Wit.: Andrew Wodrow, John McMeekin, Morgan Wodrow.

1790 6-19 FRANKFORT, Trustees of — to John Williams
¼ a. in Frankfort; rec. 10-11-1790. of Hampshire Co.
Wit.: And. Wodrow, Solomon Jones, Abraham Jones, M. A. Wodrow.

1790 6-19 FRANKFORT, Trustees of — to Ebenezer Williams
¼ a. in Frankfort; rec. 10-14-1790. of Hampshire Co.
Wit.: And. Wodrow, Solomon Jones, Abraham Jones, M. A. Wodrow.

1790 6-19 FRANKFORT, Trustees of — to John Williams, Jr.
¼ a. in Frankfort; rec. 1-13-1791. of Hampshire Co.
Wit.: And. Wodrow, Solomon Jones, Abraham Jones, M. A. Wodrow.

1790 6-19 FRANKFORT, Trustees of — to Abraham Wise
¼ a. in Frankfort; rec. 10-14-1790. of Hampshire Co.
Wit.: And. Wodrow, Solomon Jones, Abraham Jones, M. A. Wodrow.

1792 5-19 FRANKFORT, Trustees of — to Frederick Sheetz
– a. in Frankfort; rec. 6-26-1792. of Hampshire Co.
Wit.: John Kimberline, And. Turk, Robert Ross, Andrew Wodrow.

1792 6-16 FRANKFORT, Trustees of — to Henry Sheetz
8 lots—2 a. in Frankfort; rec. 6-26-1792. of Hampshire Co
Wit.: John Kimberline, Edward Moore, Andrew Turk, Andrew Wodrow.

1792 5-19 FRANKFORT, Trustees of — to Tristman Ewin
¼ a. in Frankfort; rec. 6-26-1792. of Frederick Co.
Wit.: John Kimberline, Andrew Turk, Robert Ross, Andrew Wodrow.

1792 5-19 FRANKFORT, Trustees of — to William Reddick
½ a. in Frankfort; rec. 6-26-1792. of Hampshire Co.
Wit.: John Kimberline, Robt. Ross, John Keller, Andrew Wodrow.

1792 6-16 FRANKFORT, Trustees of — to James McQuilling
¼ a. in Frankfort; rec. 6-26-1792. of Hampshire Co.
Wit.: John Kimberline, Andrew Turk, Edward Moore, Andrew Wodrow.

1792 6-16 FRANKFORT, Trustees of — to Edward Moore
¼ a. in town of Frankfort; rec. 6-26-1792. of Hampshire Co.
Wit.: John Kimberline, Andrew Turk, John House, John Kimberline.

1792 6-16 FRANKFORT, Trustees of — to Andrew Fink
1 a. in Frankfort; rec 6-26-1792. of Hampshire Co.
Wit.: John Kimberline, John House, Edward Moore.

| GRANTOR-GRANTEE | | PAGE 21 |

1794 3-14	FRANKFORT, Trustees of to John Crutchlow ¼ a. in Frankfort; rec. 4-9-1794. Wit.: None.

1800 6-14	FRANKFORT, Trustees of to Richard Glover Recorded 9-15-1800. of Frederick Co. Wit.: Will Armstrong, Thomas Dunn, John Jones, Aaron Jones, Joshua Jones, John Reasoner, Angus McDonal, James Bailey.

| 1771
9-24 | FRENCH, Matthew (w. Sarah)   to John Foxcraft
of Frederick Co. (lease and release)   Charles Thompson
246 a. on So. Brasch; rec. 4-12-1774.   Philadelphia, Pa.
Wit.: Val. Crawford, Hugh Stephenson, J. Stephenson,
Marcus Stephenson, Stephen Ruddell, Thomas Lewis.
John Lewis, J. Watson. |

| 1794
8-7 | FRENCH, Robert   to William Buffington
of Hampshire Co. (bill of sale)   of Hampshire Co.
One negro woman named Minna; rec. 4-20-1795.
Wit.: Thos. Mulledy, Fras. Taggart. |

| 1801
2-15 | FRENCH, ROBERT   to Richard Nelson
of Hampshire Co.   of Hampshire Co.
Recorded 2-16-1801. |

| 1795
10-19 | FRENCH, William   to Robert French
225 a. on Little Cacapeon; rec. 10-19-1795.
Wit.: None. |

| 1797
5-27 | FRENCH, William   to Friend Gray
of Romney   of Hampshire Co.
One acre in Romney; rec. 9-18-1797.
Wit.: Thos. Fitzgerald, Thos. McGuire, Jacob Mouser, Jr. |

| 1793
10-25 | FRIEND, Andrew   to John Hartley
252 a. on So. Branch; rec. 1-15-1794.   of Hampshire Co.
Wit.: William Biggerstaff, Frederick Houghty,
Thos. Dutty. |

| 1796
3-10 | FRIEND, Gabriel (w. Jane)   to Jonathan Purcell
of Washington Co.   of Hampshire Co.
126 a. in Hampshire Co.; rec. 6-20-1796
Wit.: Isaac Parsons, James Dailey, Edw. Dyer,
Wm. Purcell. |

| 1765
8-9 | FRIEND, John (w. Carenhapech)   to Dennis Pursley
of Hampshire Co. (lease and release)   of Frederick Co.
194 a. on Potomac River; rec. 10-8-1765.
Wit.: John Johnson, Isaac Cox, Daniel Pursley. |

| 1789
3-14 | FRIEND, John   to Archibald McDonald
(w. Kerunhappuck)   of Hampshire Co.
of Washington Co. (bill of sale)
75 a. on Little Cacapeon R.; rec. 6-11-1789.
Wit.: John Crook, John Walker. |

| 1793
9-9 | FRIEND, John   to Luke Hass
(Lease and release)   of Hampshire Co.
Wit.: Abraham Hass, Joseph Flora, Angus McDonald. |

| 1800
9-27 | FRIEND, John   to Thomas Flora
of Hampshire Co.   of Hampshire Co.
Recorded 9-27-1800.
Wit.: Joseph Flora, Gabriel Friend,
Margaret Flora, Archibald Flora. |

| 1768
2-27 | FRIEND, Nicholas   to Lawrence Hass
of Hampshire Co. (lease and release)   of Hampshire Co.
142 a. on Little Capon; rec. 2-8-1768.
Wit.: Isaac Cox, David Cox, Nicholas Decker. |

| 1772
7-22 | FRY, Abraham   to Jacob Miller
of Frederick Co. (lease and release)   of Augusta Co.
350 a. on Lost River; rec. 8-11-1772.
Wit.: None. |

| 1763
5-9 | FRY, Benjamin   to Henry Fry
of Hampshire Co. (lease and release)   of Hampshire Co.
33 a. on Cape Capon Creek; rec. 5-10-1763.
Wit.: Sam Dew. |

| 1772
4-10 | FRY, Joseph   to Thomas Littler
of Frederick Co. (lease and release)   of Hampshire Co.
138 a. on Cacapeon River; rec. 8-11-1772.
Wit.: Henry Fry, James Alexander, John Littler. |

| 1800
9-15 | FRYE, William (w. Phoeby)   to John Keith
Wit.: Isaac Jenkins, Thomas McBride, Thomas Boyd.
of Hampshire Co.
Recorded 9-15-1800. |

—G—

| 1792
10-26 | GADDIS, Priscilla   to Frederick Buzzard
of Fayette Co.   of Hampshire Co.
421 a. on Mills Branch, a branch of Cacapeon; rec. 10-30-1792.
Wit.: John Herndon, Henry Heinzman,
Wm. Jacobs, Thos. Collins, Jas. Cochran. |

| 1799
12-9 | GAITHER, Elijah (w. Harriot)   to Andrew Wodrow
of Hampshire Co.   of Hampshire Co.
1 a. in Romney; rec. 12-16-1799.
Wit.: None. |

| 1795 | GAITER, Elijah   to Edward Smith
BROWN, John
WODROW, Andrew
400 a. on Gibbons Run; rec. 2-15-1796.
Wit.: F. White, Ewd. Dyer, Ed McCarty,
John Jack, Henry Heinzman. |

| 1797
10-17 | GAITHER, Elijah   to Alexander King
WODROW, Andrew
382 a. in Hampshire Co.; rec. 10-17-1797.
Wit.: None. |

| 1800 | GAITHER, Elijah   to Francis White
See BLACK, John |

| 1767
8-10 | GALLENT, James (w. Mary)   to John Boyton
of Frederick Co., Va.   Samuel Wharton
(Lease and release)   John Rheas
200 a., Tearcoat; rec. 8-12-1767.   David Rheas
Wit.: Sam Dew, G. Wilson.   Abraham Mitchell
    of Philadelphia |

| 1767
8-10 | GALLENT, James (w. Mary)   to John Boyton
of Frederick Co., Va.   Samuel Wharton
(Lease and release).   John Rheas
214 a. on Patterson's Creek;   David Rheas
rec. 8-12-1767.   Abraham Mitchel
Wit.: Sam Dew; G. Wilson.   of Philadelphia, Pa. |

| 1796
4-1 | GARD, Nathan   to Beel Babbs
of Hampshire Co.   of Hampshire Co.
100 a. in Hampshire Co. (on North R.); rec. 6-20-1796.
Wit.: Geo. Beall, Eli Beall, Chas. Babb. |

| 1795
4-20 | GARRISON, Joseph (w. Charity)   to William Lane
of Hampshire Co.
38 a. on South Br. Mt.; rec. 4-20-1795.
Wit.: None. |

| 1797
3-21 | GATEWOOD, John   to Elizabeth Amiger
of Hampshire Co. (deed of gift)
Personal property; rec. 4-17-1797.
Wit.: John Brittin, Joseph Lambert, Nathan Price. |

| 1799 | GAW, James   to Edw. Garrigues
See KENNEDY, William |

| 1776
5-23 | GEINITZ, John William   to Christopher Strather
(GEMITZ) of Hampshire Co.   of Hampshire Co.
51 a. on South Branch; rec. 6-11-1776.
Wit.: Sam Dew, Isaac Parsons, Enoch Berry. |

| 1768
99-12 | GIBONEY, Alexr. (w. Ann)   to Joseph Neavill, Jr.
of Hampshire Co. (lease and release)   of Hampshire Co.
200 a. on Patterson's Creek; rec. 9-18-1768.
Wit.: None. |

| | GIBSON, James   to Thomas Collins
of Hampshire Co. (bill of sale)   of Hampshire Co.
Wit.: Patrick Baker, Eli Davis. |

| 1772 | GIBSON, John   to Moses Hutton
See CHEW, Benjamin
MAGILL, John |

| 1778 | GIBSON, John   to William Holliday
See CHEW, Benjamin |

| 1762
3-6 | GIBSON, William   to Peter Stalker
of Hampshire Co. (mortgage)   Samuel Stalnaker
On personal propertp; rec. 12-13-1763.
Wit.: Sam Dew, Abrm. Hite. |

| 1780
10-12 | GILCHRIST, Robert   to Reuben Berry
SOMERVILLE, James   of Hampshire Co.
400 a. on Beaver Run; rec. 2-14-1788.
Wit.: Sam Dew, John Taylor, Abel Randall. |

| 1780
10-12 | GILCHRIST, Robert   to John Renick
of Port Royal   of Hampshire Co.
SOMERVILLE, James, of Fredericksburg
24 a. on South Branch; rec. 2-14-1788.
Wit.: Job Welton, Phil Pendleton. |

| 1780
10-12 | GILCHRIST, Robert   to Henry Litler
SOMERVILLE, James   of Hampshire Co.
256 a. on Beaver Run; rec. 2-14-1788.
Wit.: None. |

| 1787
11-20 | GILKINSON, Samuel   to Ralph Humphreys
of Washington Co. (lease and release)   of Hampshire Co.
131 a. on Tear Coat Creek; rec. 4-10-1788.
Wit.: James Murphy, Richard Holliday
Francis Taggart, Sam Murphy, Robt. French. |

| 1797
5-25 | GILL, John (w. Esther)   to Andrew Wodrow
of Alexandria   of Hampshire Co.
Parcel of land on Patterson Creek; rec. 10-16-1797.
Wit.: None. |

| 1774
10-4 | GILLMER, Margaret   to Matthias Brandenburgen
widow of John Gillmer
HOWELL, William, of Hampshire Co.
421 a. on Patterson Creek; rec. 8-13-1776.
Wit.: Wm. Barber, Lewis, Peter Hartman,
Adam Leser. |

| 1785
8-10 | GILLMOR, Arm   to Abraham Vanmeter
GILLMOR, Elizabeth   of Hampshire Co.
GILLMOR, Mary
GILLMORE, Jane
of Hampshire Co.
401 a. on Alleghany Mt.; rec. 9-10-1785.
Wit.: Andrew Wodrow. |

| 1761
10-5 | GLASS, Robert (w. Sarah)   to Jacob LaRue
of Frederick Co. (lease and release)   of Frederick Co.
285 a. on Great Cape Capon; rec. 3-10-1762.
Wit.: Gabriel Jones, Chas. Linch, Ja. Keith. |

1793 12-11	GLAZE, Andrew of Hampshire Co. (Kyger?) 418 a. on South Branch River; rec. 12-11-1793. Wit.: None.	to George Thyger of Hampshire Co.
1786 9-10	GLAZE, John (w. Elizabeth) of Hampshire Co. 300 a. on Mill Creek; rec. 9-12-1786. Wit.: Andrew Wodrow.	to John Campbell of Hampshire Co.
1779 8-10	GLAZE, Eve GLAZE, Lawrence of Hampshire Co. 119 9a. on South Branch R.; rec. 5-9-1780. Wit.: None.	to Nicholas Casey of Hampshire Co.
1780 5-9	GLAZE, Eve Widow of Earhart Glaze GLAZE, Lawrence, son of Hampshire Co. 133 a. on South Branch; rec. 5-9-1780. Wit.: Sam Dew, John Rannels.	to George Glaze of Hampshire Co.
1787 4-20	GLAZE, John (w. Elizabeth) of Hampshire Co. 131 a. on Mill Creek; rec. 9-18-1787. Wit.: Elias Poston, Enoch Berry, Geo. Berry.	to John Cuppy, Jr. of Hampshire Co.
1786 3-5	GLAZE, Lawrence (w. Mary) of Hampshire Co. (lease and release) 283 a. on South Branch; rec. 3-14-1786. Wit.: Geo. Glaze, John Vincent, Ralph Wilson, James Flaherty.	to Ralph Humphreys of Hampshire Co.
1795 4-16	GOFF, John of Hampshire Co. (power of attorney) Authority to collect all debts due John Goff; rec. 7-20-1795. Wit.: None.	to Abraham Kuykendall of Hampshire Co.
1791 4-14	GOOD, Abraham of Hampshire Co. 224 a. on Cabbin Run; rec. 4-14-1791. Wit.: None.	to Robert Irwine of Hampshire Co.
1786 3-9	GOOD, Isaac of Hampshire Co. 278 a. on Patterson Creek; rec. 7-11-1786. Wit.: Rodham James, Michael Miller, John H. Price.	to Andrew Smalley of Hampshire Co.
1799 12-20	GOOD, Isaac (w. Elizabeth) of Hampshire Co. Recorded 4-14-1800. Wit.: George Hill, Michael Miller, John A. Price, William House, Okey Johnstone, George Miller.	to Stephen Pitcher of Hampshire Co.
1782 5-14	GOOD, Jacob, dec'd, by PUTMAN, Peter, executor of will Hampshire Co. 278 a. on Patterson Creek; rec. 5-10-1785. Wit.: Sam Dew.	to Isaac Good of Hampshire Co.
1794 6-11	GOOSET, Peter (w. Eve) of Hampshire Co. 75 a. on Patterson Creek; rec. 6-11-1794. Wit.: Andrew Smalley, Jesse Kent, Wm. Purcell.	to Thomas Greenwell of Hampshire Co.
1793 3-29	GOSSICK, Richard of Frederick Co. (bill of sale) Personal property; rec. 10-9-1793. Wit.: John McCoole, Elinor McCoole.	to Jacob Earsam of Hampshire Co.
17994 6-10	GRAFF, Andrew of Lancaster Co. (release of a mortgage) Two tracts of land on Little Cacapeon; rec. 6-11-1794. Wit.: None.	to John Meesby
1796 4-16	GRAGG, Robert (Gregg?) of Washington Co. 20 a. on Potomac River; rec. 4-18-1796. Wit.: Jas. Martin, John Critton, Wm. Young.	to Daniel McDonald of Hampshire Co.
1768	GRAHAM, John See BURNS, John HICKS, Moses HICKS, Samuel	to Benj. Willett
1776 8-12	GRAY, Friend (w. Sarah) of Hampshire Co. (lease and release) 100 a. in Hampshire Co.; rec. 8-13-1776. Wit.: James Largent, Samuel Parker, Andreas Michlschlegel.	to David Forman of Berkley Co.
17799 11-15	GRAY, Isaac (w. Mary) of Philadelphia, Pa. 400 a. on South Branch; rec. 11-14-1780. Wit.: Isaac Howell, John Elliott, Plun Fleeson.	to Benjamin Wynkoop of Philadelphia, Pa.
1772 9-10	GREATHOUSE, Harman (w. Mary) of Hampshire Co. (lease and release) 275 a., 249 a., on Potomac River; rec. 9-11-1772. Wit.: None.	to Michael Cresap of Frederick Co.
1762 11-19	GREGG, Robert (see Gragg) of Patterson Creek (bill of sale) One negro child; rec. 5-11-1763. Wit.: Samuel Poe, Thomas Bull.	to Power Hazell of Hampshire Co.
1777 3-7	GREGG, Robert (w. Margaret) of Washington Co. (lease and release) 100 a. on Patterson Creek; rec. 9-11-1778. Wit.: Sam Dew, Wm. Buffington, Isaac Parsons.	to Benjamin Parker of Hampshire Co.
1763 5-3	GREENFIELD, John (w. Mary) of Frederick Co. (lease and release) 149 a., Spreen Gap (Spring Gap) Mt.; rec. 5-10-1763. Wit.: Thom. Dent, Germ. Keyes, Bryan Bruen, Geo. Hoge, Tho. Rutherford.	to John Royce of Frederick Co.
1763 5-	GREENFIELD, John (w. Mary) of Frederick Co. (lease and release) 23 a., Hampshire Co.; rec. 5-10-1763. Wit.: Thom. Dent, Germ. Keyes, Bryan Bruen, Tho. Rutherford.	to John Royce of Frederick Co.
1767 8-4	GREENFIELD, John of Frederick Co., Va. (lease and release) LIVINGSTON, John, of Frederick Co., Md. 143 a. on Little Capon; rec. 8-12-1767. Wit.: Alexr. White, Thos. Edmondson, Peter Stalker, Angus McDonald, Luke Collins, John Lyne, John Hardin.	to Isaac Cox of Hampshire Co.
1767 9-2	GREENFIELD, John of Frederick Co., Va. (lease and release) 200 a. on Patterson Creek; rec. 10-13-1767. Wit.: Henry Heth, Bryan Bruen, Edward McGuire, Alexr. Wodrow, John Lyne, Ja. Keith, Alexr. White.	to Alexr. Gibbony of Hampshire Co.
1771 11-3	GREENFIELD, John, dec'd, by McDONALD, Angus WHITE, Alexander Executors, and LIVINGSTON, Mayor James 149 a. on Little Cacapeon; rec. 9-13-1772. Wit.: John Magill, Abraham Hite, Phil Pendleton.	to Peter Hog Attorney, of Augusta Co.
1798 2-19	GREENWELL, Elijah of Hampshire Co. 86 a. on Patterson Creek; rec. 2-19-1798. Wit.: Arjalon Price, Timothy Corn, David Wolfe.	to William Reasoner of Hampshire Co.
1791 9-12	GREENWELL, Thomas of Hampshire Co. (mortgage) 100 a. on Patterson Creek; rec. 9-15-1791. Wit.: None.	to William Johnson of Hampshire Co.
1796 10-14	GREENWELL, Thomas (w. Anna) of Hampshire Co. 122 a. on Patterson Creek; rec. 10-14-1796. Wit.: None.	to Jacob Shobe of Hampshire Co.
1796 10-14	GREENWELL, Thomas (w. Anna) of Hampshire Co. 50 a. in Hampshire Co.; rec. 10-17-1796. Wit.: None.	to Jacob Shobe of Hampshire Co.
1798 4-16	GREENWELL, Thomas (w. Ann) of Hardy Co. 100 a., Hampshire Co., 75 a., Hampshire Co.; rec. 4-16-1798. Wit.: None.	to Elijah Greenwell of Hampshire Co.
1799 4-15	GREENWELL, Thomas of Hampshire Co. 337 a., 50 a., on Potomac River; rec. 4-15-1799. Wit.: None.	to William Young of Hampshire Co.
1792 6-20	GREENWOOD, Thomas of Washington Co. 400 a. on Patterson Creek; rec. 6-26-1792. Wit.: Andrew Wodrow.	to John Murphy of Hampshire Co.
1797 5-17	GROVE, Henry (w. Charlotte) of Hampshire Co. 58 a. on Great Cacapeon River; rec. 99-18-1797. Wit.: Rees Pritchard, John Arnold, Morris Ellis.	to John Brown of Hampshire Co.
1797 5-17	GROVE, Henry (w. Charlotte) of Hampshire Co. 120 a. on Timber Ridge; rec. 9-18-1797. Wit.: Rees Pritchard, John Arnold, Morris Ellis.	to John Brown of Hampshire Co.
1797 5-17	GROVE, Henry (w. Charlotte) of Hampshire Co. 159 a. on Great Cacapeon River; rec. 9-18-1797. Wit.: Rees Pritchard, John Arnold, Morris Ellis.	to John Brown of Hampshire Co.
1761 6-8	GUM, Jacob (w. Sarah) of Augusta Co. (lease and release) 330 a. on Lost River; rec. 6-9-1761. Wit.: None.	to James Claypool of Hampshire Co.
1769	GUPHILL, Edward (w. Elizabeth) See FOREMAN, John	to Wm. Foreman
1792 4-2	GUSTIN, John of Barkley Co. 225 a. on South Branch; rec. 6-26-1792. Wit.: Nath. Dyer, Christian Shank, John Hunter, Wm. Smith, And. Wodrow, John Herndon.	to Alpheus Gustin, Jr. of Barkley Co.

—H—

1782 8-13	HAHN, Michael of Hampshire Co. 6 0a. on Mill Creek; rec. 8-13-1782. Wit.: None.	to Matthias Hite of Hampshire Co.
1795 2-15	HAINES, Peter of Allegany Co. 180 a., 48 a., in Hampshire Co.; rec. 2-16-1795. Wit.: None.	to Daniel Mitchell John Mitchell of Allegany Co.
1796 12-22	HAINES, Peter (w. Lenah) of Bedford Co. Bill of Sale. 134 a. on North Branch of Potomac; rec. 1-16-1797. Wit.: Murdock, Hanson Briscoe.	to Francis Deakins William Deakins of Montgomery Co., Md.

GRANTOR-GRANTEE PAGE 23

1771 HALDEMAN, Peter (Holderman) to **Joseph Mitchell**
3-21 of Frederick Co. of Frederick Co.
260 a. on Great Cacapeon River; rec. 11-11-1772.
Wit: Wm. Mcleery, Pat Allison, John Shelby,
Angus McDonald, Moses Hunter, James Piggot.

1778 HALL, Michael to **Cornelius Ward**
1-29 of Hampshire Co. (lease and release) of Hampshire Co.
10 0a. on South Branch; rec. 3-10-1778.
Wit.: None.

1787 HALLOWELL, Thomas to **Caleb Foulke**
3-31 of Philadelphia Co. Jeremiah Parker
247 a. on Mill Branch, a of Philadelphia, Pa.
branch of Cacapeon; rec. 9-13-1787.
Wit.: William Parker, Rich. Jones, Rich. Gardiner.

1779 HAMILTON, Henry (w. Mary) to **William Morgan**
7-11 of Hampshire Co. (lease and release) of Hampshire Co.
280 a., 4 miles above North R. of Cacapeon R.; rec. 8-10-1779.
Wit.: John Stoker, John Largent, Clothem Brown,
John Archer, Daniel Newcomb.

1781 HAMILTON, Henry to **George Bathas**
11-20 of Hampshire Co. of Hampshire Co.
106 a. on South Branch; rec. 2-12-1782.
Wit.: Joseph Nevill, Andrew Wodrow, Abraham Hite,
Thomas McCarty, Vincent Williams.

1795 HAMILTON, Henry to **Basil Lucas**
4-10 SMALLEY, Christian of Hampshire Co.
of Hampshire Co.
Parcel of land on New Creek; rec. 4-20-1795.
Wit.: Jacob Beck, Thos. Cooper, Evan Turner,
John D. Lucas.

1761 HAMLIN, Joseph to **Henry Bagley**
6-8 of Hampshire Co. (lease and release) of Hampshire Co.
50 a. on Patterson's Creek; rec. 6-9-1761.

1793 HAMMOND, William to **David McMechen**
4-24 of Baltimore Co. of Baltimore Co.
Three tracts of land in Hampshire Co.; rec. 6-12-1793.
Wit.: James Dailcy, Wm. McMechen.

1788 HAMPSHIRE Co. Commissioners to Hampshire Co.
4-8 Report of the Commissioners for running and Hardy Co.
the division line between Hampshire
and Hardy counties. Rec. 12-11-1788.
(Signed by) THOS. COLLINS.
JOHN FOLEY.
JOS. NEVILL.
Commissioners of Hampshire Co.

1792 HAMPSHIRE CO., Trustees of to **James Donaldson**
8-18 79 a. on Green Spring Run; rec. 4-10-1793.
Wit.: John Mitchell, John Rannels, John Donaldson,
William Donaldson, Anthony Buck.

1792 HAMPSHIRE Co., Trustees of, to **Thos. Holloback, Sr.**
12-1 400 a. on a drain of Patterson Creek; rec. 6-12-1793.
Wit.: And. Wodrow, Francis Taggart, John Mitchell,
John Murphy, Thos. Mulledy, John Lehow.

1792 HAMPSHIRE CO., Trustees of to **Daniel Jones**
12-1 400 a. on Patterson Creek; rec. 6-12-1793 Hampshire Co.
Wit.: And. Wodrow, John Mitchell, Francis Taggart,
John Murphy, Thos. Mulledy, John Lehow.

1792 HAMPSHIRE CO., Trustees of to **John Mitchell**
12-1 322 a. on Patterson Creek; rec. 6-12-1793. Hampshire Co.
Wit.: And. Wodrow, John Murphy, Francis Taggart,
Thos. Mulledy, John Sehow, Perez Drew,
Edward Dyer, John McMeckin.

1793 HAMPSHIRE CO., Trustees of to **Robert Buck**
4-1 164 a. on North Branch; rec. 6-12-1793.
Wit.: John Murphy, Francis Taggart, John Mitchell,
And. Wodrow, John Lehow, Thos. Mulledy.

1784 HANKS, Joseph (Hawks?) to **Peter Putman**
3-9 of Hampshire Co. (mortgage) of Hampshire Co.
108 a. on Patterson Creek; rec. 11-9-1784.
Wit.: Samuel Dew, Betty Dew, Phillip Baker, Henry Nuff.

1796 HANSBROUGH, John to **Edward Dyer**
6-20 of Hampshire Co. (bill of sale)
Personal property; rec. 6-20-1796.
Wit.: Wm. Buffington, Geo. Smith, Jacob Lavender.

1798 HANSBROUGH, John (w. Mary) to **Edward Dyer**
9-17 of Hampshire Co. of Hampshire Co.
Parts of real estate; rec. 9-17-1798.
Wit.: E. Gaither, Wm. French, Wm. Cook.

1771 HARDIN, John to **Thomas Farely**
3-9 of Cumberland Co., Pa. (lease and release) of York Co., Pa.
106 a. on Drains of Patterson Creek; rec. 5-14-1771.
Wit.: John Forman, Wm. Forman, Nathaniel Parker,
John Jones.

1773 HARDIN, John to **Mark Hardin**
3-8 of Bedford Co., Pa. (lease and release) of Hampshire Co.
126 a. on Patterson Creek; rec. 5-11-1773.
Wit.: John Jones, Andrew Farley, Jacob Wolf,
John Hartley, Peter Jones.

1773 HARDIN, John (w. Catherine) to **William Blackburn**
10-6 of Westmoreland Co., Pa. (lease and release) of Hampshire Co.
327 a. on Patterson Creek; rec. 3-8-1774.
Wit.: Joseph Heavill, Wm. Campbell, Daniel Brown,
Alex White, Peter Hog.

1774 HARDIN, John to **William Blackburn**
3-3 (Lease and release)
100 a. on Patterson Creek; rec. 3-8-1774.
Wit.: Alex White, Wm. Campbell, George Rootes,
Peter Hog, Abraham Hite.

1780 HARDIN, John, Sr. (w. Catherine) to **Joseph House**
5-9 of Monongala Co. (lease and release) of Hampshire Co.
211 a. on Birds Run, a branch of North Branch of Potomac.
Rev. 5-9-1780.
Wit.: None.

1789 HARDIN, Mark (w. Ann) to **Jacob Brookhart**
8-17 of Hampshire Co. of Hampshire Co.
126 a. on Patterson Creek; rec. 2-11-1790.
Wit.: John Mitchell, And. Cooper, Ezekiel Whiteman.

1772 HARMAN, Thomas to **Abraham Hite**
8-15 of Hampshire Co. (power off atty.) of Hampshire Co. (atty.)
Authority to convey tract of land on Mill Creek; rec. 5-11-1773.
Wit.: Sam Dew, Garret Vanmeter, Hathel Manning,
I. Hite.

1788 HARNESS, Adam (w. Sarah) to **Leonard Harness**
4-13 KUYKENDALL, Abraham (w. Catherine) of Hampshire Co.
of Hampshire Co. (lease and release)
202 a. on Looney's Creek; rec. 4-14-1778.
Wit.: Stephen Ruddell, Joel Berry, Ann Jennings.

1799 HARNESS, Adam (w. Sarah) to **Henry Heinzman**
4-15 of Hampshire Co. of Hampshire Co.
337 a. on South Branch R.; rec. 4-15-1799.
Wit.: None.

1794 HARNESS, George, Jr. to **Adam Harness Jr.**
7-22 (w. Rebecca) of Hampshire Co.
of Hardy Co.
456 a. on Patterson Creek; rec. 10-15-1794.
Wit.: Adam See, El Dyer, And. Wodrow,
J. I. Demonnier.

1795 HARNESS, George (w. Rebecca) to **Adam Harness, Jr.**
1-2 Bill of sale, 450 a. in Hampshire Co.
Wit.: None.

1780 HARNESS, Leonard to **Daniel Richardson**
11-4 of Hampshire Co. of Hampshire Co.
140 a. on South Branch; rec. 5-14-1782.
Wit.: Job Welton, McKenney Robinson,
Abel Randall, Andrew Wodrow.

1784 HARNESS, Leonard to **Jacob Harness**
8-10 of Hampshire Co. (bill of sale) of Hampshire Co.
202 a. on Looney's Creek; rec. 8-10-1784.
Wit.: None.

1780 HARNESS, Michael, Sr. to **Jacob Harness (son)**
12-23 of Hampshire Co. (deed of gift) of Hampshire Co.
249 a. on South Branch; rec. 3-13-1781.
Wit.: Andrew Wodrow, Solomon Vanmeter,
Jacob Vanmeter, John Wilson.

1798 HARRE, John (w. Phoebe) to **Marjoram Brelsford**
12-17 of Hampshire Co. of Hampshire Co.
5 a. in Hampshire Co.; rec. 12-17-1798.
Wit.: None.

1788 HARRIS, Nehemiah (w. Margaret) to **Abel Emereson**
9-11 of Hardy Co. of Hampshire Co.
336 a. on Patterson Creek; rec. 9-12-1788.
Wit.: John McBride, Malign Pugh.

1769 HARRISON, Matthew to **Thomas Carson**
3-2 of Augusta Co. of Alexandria, Va. (Fairfax Co.
Mortgage. Henry Mitchell
Parcel of land on Green Spring of Fredericksburg, Va.
Branch; rec. 3-6-1769.
Wit.: Bryan Bruin, William Scott,
Alexander White, John I. Collins.

1773 HARRISON, Matthew to **George Mitchell**
8-3 of Augusta Co. (Mortgage) Neil McCoull
300 a. and 100 a. of Spotsylvania, Va.
in Hampshire Co., joining land of James Bryan; rec. 8-10-1773.
Wit.: Phil Pendleton, Alex White, Robert Stephen,
John Magill, James Somerville, Peter Hog, Abraham Hite.

1777 HARTLEY, John to **Thomas Fearly**
3-10 of Hampshire Co. (lease and release) of Hampshire Co.
67 a. on Patterson Creek; rec. 3-11-1777.
Wit.: Wm. Blackburn, John Farley, Elisha Collins.

1793 HARTLY, John to **Samuel Hague**
9-10 of Hampshire Co. of Hampshire Co.
160 a. on Mill Creek; rec. 9-11-1793.
Wit.: None.

1797 HARTSHORNE, William to **Timothy Smith**
6-7 (w. Susanna) of Hampshire Co.
of Fairfax Co.
412 a. on Elk Horn Run; rec. 10-14-1799.
Wit.: None.

1792 HASS, Abraham (w. Sarah) to **Noah Larue**
6-26 of Hampshire Co. of Hampshire Co.
279 a. on Great Cacapeon; rec. 6-26-1792.
Wit.: None.

1796 HASS, Abraham to **Archibald McDonald**
4-18 of Hampshire Co. of Hampshire Co.
Parcel of land on Little Cacapeon; rec. 4-18-1796.
Wit.: None.

1765 10-8	**HASS, Lawrence** (w. Sarah) of Hampshire Co. (lease and release) Lot 12, 380 a. on South Branch; rec. 10-9-1765. Wit.: Gabriel Jones.	to **Samuel Dew** of Hampshire Co.	1797 10-16	**HEALY, Thomas** of Hampshire Co. 100 a. in Hampshire Co.; rec. 10-16-1797. Wit.: None.	to **William Chapman** of Hampshire Co.

1765 10-8 HASS, Lawrence (w. Sarah) to Samuel Dew
of Hampshire Co. (lease and release) of Hampshire Co.
Lot 12, 380 a. on South Branch; rec. 10-9-1765.
Wit.: Gabriel Jones.

1769 6-17 HASS, Lawrence to Samuel Dew
of Hampshire Co. (mortgage) of Hampshire Co.
142 a. on Potomack River; rec. 8-8-1769.
Wit.: John Holliday, James Lewis, Joanna Farrow.

1772 5-12 HASS, Lawrence (w. Sarah) to John Decker
of Hampshire Co. of Hampshire Co.
Parcel of land on South Branch; rec. 8-11-1772.
Wit.: Sam Dew.

1794 4-8 HASS, Luke to Abraham Hass
of Hampshire Co. (lease and release) of Hampshire Co.
75 a. in Hampshire Co.; rec. 4-9-1794.
Wit.: Wm. Twilly, Elisha Cowgill, Angus McDonald,
George Tarvin, Wm. Wheeley.

1763 5-5 HAAS, Peter to Jacob Brechtel
of Hampshire Co. (lease and release) of Hampshire Co.
Lot No. 1, 680 a. on South Branch; rec. 5-10-1763.
Wit.: Sam Dew.

1767 6-10 HASS, Peter to George Wilson
of Hampshire Co. (mortgage) of Hampshire Co.
Personal property; rec. 6-10-1767.
Wit.: Samuel Dew, Peter Hog.

1796 4-12 HAWK, Isaac (w. Mary) to John Fry
of Bath Co. of Hampshire Co.
180 a. in Hampshire Co.; rec. 919-1796.
Wit.: None.

1792 4-24 HAWK, John (w. Christian) to Andrew Tivault
of Hardy Co. of Hampshire Co.
128 a. on North R. Mt.; rec. 4-24-1792.
Wit.: None.

1791 5-7 HAYDON, William (w. Lydia) to Belemus Haydon
of Hampshire Co. of Hampshire Co.
800 a. in Hampshire Co.; rec. 4-9-1794.
Wit.: Edward McGinnis, Samuel McGinnis, Abigail O'Dell.

1793 4-10 HAYDON, William to William Hook
of Hampshire Co. (bill of sale) of Hampshire Co.
30 a. in Hampshire Co.; rec. 4-10-1793.
Wit.: John Arnold, John Chenoweth, Elijah Davis.

1794 4-? HAYDON, William to Henry Groves
of Hampshire Co. of Hampshire Co.
468 a. in Hampshire Co.; rec. 4-9-1794.
Wit.: Kingman Dutton, Mary Dutton, Richard Lyon.

1794 9-22 HAYDON, William to Henry Grove
of Hampshire Co. of Hampshire Co.
600 a. in Hampshire Co.; rec. 10-15-1794.
Wit.: John Chenoweth, John Purcell, John Arnold.

1795 6-13 HAYDON, William (w. Lydia) to William Hook
of Hampshire Co. of Hampshire Co.
140 a. on Cacapeon; rec. 6-15-1795.
Wit.: Richard Arnold, John Chenoweth, Morris Ellis.

1795 8-11 HAYDON, William to Elias Poston
of Hampshire Co. of Hampshire Co.
520 a. on Great Cacapeon River; rec. 4-18-1796.
Wit.: John Chenoweth, Cornelius Gard, Morris Ellis.
Wm. Gossett.

1795 11-10 HAYDON, William to John Hobbs
of Hampshire Co. (bill of sale) of Hampshire Co.
50 a. in Hampshire Co.; rec. 4-18-1796.
Wit.: Strausbury Long, Henry Groves, Chas. Groves.

1795 11-24 HAYDON, William to Strausbury Long
of Hampshire Co. of Hampshire Co.
130 a. in Hampshire Co.; rec. 4-18-1796.
Wit.: Chas. Groves, Kingsman Dutton, Henry Groves.

1795 11-24 HAYDON, William to Henry Groves
of Hampshire Co. (bill of sale) of Hampshire Co.
120 a. in Hampshire Co.; rec. 4-18-1796.
Wit.: Kingsman Dutton, Strausbury Long.

1796 4-13 HAYDON, William to Kingman Dutton
of Hampshire Co. of Hampshire Co.
50 a. in Hampshire Co.; rec. 4-18-1796.
Wit.: Strausbury Long, Henry Groves, Chas. Groves.

1791 6-7 HAZELL, Henry (w. Sarah) to Arjalon Price
of Monongahela Co. of Hampshire Co.
228 a. on Patterson Creek; rec. 6-16-1791.
Wit.: Abraham Johnson, Abraham Johnson, Jr.,
Okey Johnson, Wm. Dennon.

1798 7-26 HAZELL, Henry (w. Sarah) to Arjalon Price
of Mongalia Co. of Hampshire Co.
228 a. on Patterson Creek; rec. 9-17-1798.
Wit.: Geo. Pierce, Henry Protzman, A. King,
John Mitchell.

1796 12-28 HAZLE, Henry (w. Sarah) to Ellis Chandler
of Mongala Co. Rachel Rinehart
328 a. on Patterson Creek; Sarah Chandler
rec. 2-20-1797. Elizabeth Chandler
Wit.: John Snyder, Wm. Johnson, of Hampshire Co.
Abraham Johnson, Jr., Abraham Johnson.

1795 10-14 HEALY, Thomas to Wilmor Mail
of Hampshire Co. of Hampshire Co.
150 a. in Hampshire Co.; rec. 12-14-1795.
Wit.: Jas. Martin, Wm. Young, Daniel McDonald.

1797 10-16 HEALY, Thomas to William Chapman
of Hampshire Co. of Hampshire Co.
100 a. in Hampshire Co.; rec. 10-16-1797.
Wit.: None.

1797 10-16 HEALY, Thomas to William Chapman
of Hampshire Co. of Hampshire Co.
150 a. on Potomac River; rec. 10-16-1797.
Wit.: None.

1781 3-10 HEARSMAN, Gasper to Christopher Hearsman
(w. Anne) of Hampshire Co.
of Hampshire Co.
107 a. on Beaver Run; rec. 3-13-1781.
Wit.: None.

1783 8-12 HARSMAN, Casper (w. Agnes) to George Ut
of Hampshire Co. of Hampshire Co.
248 a. on Beaver Run; rec. 8-12-1783.
Wit.: None.

1785 3-19 HIERSMAN, Casper to John Pierce
of Hampshire Co. of Berkeley Co.
107 a. on Patterson Creek; rec. 5-10-1785.
Wit.: Ben. Parker, James Parker,
Absalom Parker, Edward Cowper.

1791 11-19 HERSMAN, Casper (w. Mary) to Peter Umstot
of Hampshire Co. of Hampshire Co.
100 a. on Beaver Run; rec. 6-26-1792.
Wit.: Thos. Leazenby, Christopher Hersman, James Watts.

HERSMAN (see Heisman)

1792 6-10 HERSMAN, Casper (w. Mary) to Cornelius Peyat
of Hampshire Co. of Hampshire Co.
50 a. on Beaver Run; rec. 6-26-1792.
Wit.: Thos. Leazenby, James Watts. Frederick Fink.

1793 12-11 HERSMAN, George (w. Barbara) to William Linn
of Hampshire Co. of Hampshire Co.
20½ a. on Patterson Creek; rec. 12-11-1793.
Wit.: None.

1779 5-11 HEARSMAN, Mathias Ulrick to George Hearsman
(w. Eve) of Hampshire Co.
of Hampshire Co.
143 a. on Patterson Creek; rec. 5-11-1779.
Wit.: None.

1779 5-11 HERSMAN, Mathias U. (w. Eve) to Phillip Hearsman
of Hampshire Co. of Hampshire Co.
160 a. on Patterson Creek; rec. 5-11-1779.
Wit.: None.

1783 8-12 HARSMAN, Matthias Ulrick to George Beard
of Hampshire Co. of Hampshire Co.
160 a. on Patterson Creek; rec. 9-12-1783.
Wit.: None.

1781 4-13 HARSMAN, Phillip to Matthias Ulrick Harsman
(w. Hannah) of Hampshire Co.
of Hampshire Co. (lease)
160 a. on Patterson Creek; rec. 5-14-1782.
Wit.: Abraham Johnson, Lewis Casselman, George Hersman.

1799 1-29 HEATH, Agnes to Andrew Wodrow
HEATH, William of Hampshire Co.
258 a., on Mill Creek; 400 a. on Little Creek; rec. 9-16-1799.
Wit.: Matthew Lodge, Henry Heinzman, Edward Dyer,
William Naylor, Phillip Wilson

1764 2-8 HEATH, Henry (w. Agnes) to Joseph Watson
of Winchester, Va. of Alexandria, Va.
161 a. on North River; rec. 2-15-1764.
Wit.: Pet. Hog, Ja. Keith, Gabriel Jones.

1764 2-8 HEATH, Henry (w. Agnes) to Joseph Watson
of Winchester, Va. (lease and release) of Alexandria, Va.
115 a. on North River; rec. 2-15-1764.
Wit.: Pet. Hog, Ja. Keith, Gabriel Jones.

1764 12-6 HEATH, Henry (w. Agnes) to Wodrow & Neilson
of Frederick Co. (lease and release) of King George Co.
246 a. on North River; rec. 12-12-1764.
Wit.: Thom. Dent, Luke Collins, Ja. Keith.

1784 7-1 HEATH, Henry to James Murphy
of Pennsylvania (lease and release) of Hampshire Co.
206 a. on North River; rec. 3-9-1785.
Wit.: Simon Taylor, George Glaze
Sam. Murphy, John Rannells.

1773 3-10 HEATH, Jonathan to Robert Walker
Sheriff of Hampshire Co. of Cumberland Co., Pa.
400 a. in Green Spring Valley; rec. 3-9-1773.
Wit.: None.

1774 3-8 HEATH, Jonathan (Sheriff) to George Meade
of Hampshire Co. of Philadelphia, Pa.
400 a. on North Branch of Potomac; rec. 5-11-1774.
Wit.: None.

1775 3-14 HEATH, Jonathan to James Sommerville
Sheriff, Hampshire Co. of Fredericksburg
400 a. in Green Spring Valley; rec. 3-14-1775.
Wit.: None.

1775 11-13 HEATH, Jonathan to Hugh Walker
Sheriff of Hampshire Co. of Middlesex Co.
416 a. on Capt. John's Run; rec. 11-14-1782.
Wit.: None.

GRANTOR-GRANTEE — PAGE 25

1779 **HEATH, Jonathan** to **Enoch Hayden**
11-9   HUTTON, Moses   of Hampshire Co.
     RANDALL, Abel
     VANMETER, Garret
     Trustees of the Town of Moorefield, Hampshire Co. (now county seat, Hardy Co.).
     Half acre lot in town of Moorefield; rec. 3-14-1780.
     Wit.: None.

1761 **HEDGES, Silas** to **Jacob Douthit**
9-8   of Hampshire Co. (lease and release)   of Hampshire Co.
     800 a. on Pattersons Creek; rec. 9-9-1761.
     Wit.: Sam. Dew, Ben Tutt, William Ashmore.

1760 **HEDGES, Solomon** (w. Rebecca) to **Peter Steenbergen**
8-1   of Hampshire Co. (lease and release)   of Hampshire Co.
     320 a. on New Creek; rec. 8-13-1760.
     Wit.: Gabriel Jones.

1789 **HEDGES, Solomon** to **Thomas Dean**
6-11   of Ohio Co. (bill of sale)   of Hampshire Co.
     250 a. on New Creek; rec. 6-11-1789.
     Wit.: None.

1799 **HEINZMAN, Henry** to **Cochran & Thursby**
9-26   of Hampshire Co.   of Philadelphia, Pa.
     337 a. on South Branch River; rec. 12-16-1799.
     Wit.: John Wickins, Wm. Naylor, Chas. Magill.

1800 **HEINZMAN, Henry** (w. Elizabeth) to **Charles Magil**
9-15   of Hampshire Co.   of Winchester, Frederick Co.
     Recorded 2-16-1801.
     Wit.: Frd. White, Wm. Taylor, Wm. Vause, John Parsons.

1800 **HEINSMAN, Henry** to **Francis White**
     See BLACK, John

1800 **HEINSMAN, Jacob** (w. Catherine) to **Wm. Leazenby**
9-22   of Hampshire Co.   of Hampshire Co.
     Recorded 12-15-1800.
     Wit.: John Jack, P. P. Wilson, J. J. Jacob,
     Thomas Leazenby, George Carruthers, Jr., James Gibson.

1800 **HEINSMAN, Jacob** (w. Catherine) to **Wm. Leazenby**
9-22   of Hampshire Co.   of Hampshire Co.
     Recorded 12-16-1800.
     Wit.: John Jack, P. P. Wilson, John J. Jack,
     Thomas Leazenby, James Gibson, George Carruthers.

1795 **HEISMAN, George** (w. Barbara) to **Thomas Greenwell**
4-10   of Hampshire Co.   of Hampshire Co.
     122 a. on Patterson Creek; rec. 4-20-1795.
     Wit.: Abraham Johnson, John Dowden,
     Okey Johnson, Peter Harsel.

1795 **HEISMAN, George** (w. Barbara) to **Thomas Greenwell**
4-10   of Hampshire Co.   of Hampshire Co.
     50 a. on Patterson Creek; rec. 4-20-1795.
     Wit.: Abraham Johnson, John Dowden,
     Okey Johnson, Peter Harsel.

HEISMAN (see Hersman)

1799 **HENDERY, Alexander** (w. Scythe) to **Plunket Phillips**
3-8   of Hampshire Co.   of Hampshire Co.
     149 a. on Capt. John's Run; rec. 7-15-1799.
     Wit.: Virgil McCrackin, Cornelius Ferree,
     David Simpson, Thomas Williams.

1792 **HENRY, John** (w. Elizabeth) to **Henry Enoch, Sr.**
11-3   of Fayette Co.   of Washington Co.
     77 a. on South Branch; rec. 7-9-1794.
     Wit.: James Trotter, Henry Enoch, Jr.

1799 **HENWOOD, William** to **Sarah Fox**
4-15   of Hampshire Co.   of Hampshire Co.
     Bill of sale, personal property; rec. 4-20-1799.
     Wit.: Phillip Horn, John Thomas.

1773 **HERMAN, Thomas** to **Isaac Van Meter**
5-8   of Hampshire Co. (lease and release)   of Hampshire Co.
     100 a. on Drains of Mill Creek (a drain of the So. Branch).
     Rec. 5-11-1773.
     Wit.: Sam Dew.

1772 **HEW, Peter** to **John Stag**
8-11   of Hampshire Co.   of Hampshire Co.
     185 a. on Patterson's Creek; rec. 8-11-1772.
     Wit.: None.

1785 **HEWES, Caleb** to **Moses Hutton, Atty.**
7-19   of Montgomery Co. (power of attorney)   of Hampshire Co.
     Authority to obtain deeds to six tracts of land on Patterson Creek; rec. 8-9-1785.
     Wit.: Abraham Hite, James Parsons, Andrew Wodrow,
     Chas. Lynch, Abel Randall.

1760 **HIATT, George** (Hiett?) to **John Hiatt, Sr.**
4-28   of Rowan Co., N. C. (lease and lelease)   of Rowan Co., N. C.
     272 a. on Davids Run, branch of North River; rec. 11-11-1760.
     Wit.: Thomas Edwards, Mary Edwards, Jeremiah Ham.

1768 **HICKS, Samuel** to **Mordecia Morgan**
2-22   HICKS, Moses   of Frederick Co.
     of Frederick Co. (power of attorney)
     Power to sell interest in two tracts of land in Hampshire Co.
     Rec. 3-8-1768.
     Wit.: Joseph Pack, Cuth't McWilliam, William Carlyle.

1768 **HICKS, Samuel** to **Benj. Willett**
     HICKS, Moses
     See BURNS, John
         GRAHAM, John
         MORGAN, Mordecia

1772 **HIETT, Evan** to **James Largent**
10-25   of Hampshire Co. (lease and release)   of Hampshire Co.
     233 a. on Great Cacapeon; rec. 11-10-1772.
     Wit.: Som Pritchard.

1798 **HIETT, Evan** (w. Sarah) to **John Slane**
12-15   of Hampshire Co.   of Hampshire Co.
     154 a. on Knob Mt.; rec. 12-17-1798.
     Wit.: Geo. Barber, Joseph Hiett.

1790 **HIETT, James** (w. Lucresia) to **Evan Hiett**
4-14   of Hampshire Co.   of Hampshire Co.
     50 a. on road from Winchester to Romney; rec. 4-14-1791.
     Wit.: John Slane, James Largent.

1790 **HIETT, James** (w. Lucretia) to **James Largent**
4-14   of Hampshire Co.   of Hampshire Co.
     194 a. on road from Winchester to Romney; rec. 4-14-1791.
     Wit.: John Slane, Evan Hiett.

1795 **HIETT, James** (w. Lucy) to **William Alderton**
4-18   53 a. on Cacapeon R.; rec. 4-20-1795.
     Wit.: None.

1795 **HIETT, James** (w. Lucy) to **Francis White**
4-18   142 a. on Cacapeon River; rec. 4-20-1795.
     Wit.: None.

1795 **HIGGING, John, Jr.** (w. Sarah) to **Joshua Johnson**
3-15   of Hampshire Co.   of Washington Co.
     122 a. on Potomac River; rec. 1-18-1796.
     Wit.: And. Wodrow, Thos. Dowden,
     Thos. Mulledy, John J. Jacob, Jr.

1796 **HIGGINS, John** (w. Jane) to **Joshua Johnson**
3-15   of Hampshire Co.   of Washington Co.
     115 a. on Potomac River; rec. 4-18-1796.
     Wit.: And. Wodrow, E. Gaither, John J. Jacob, Jr.

1799 **HIGGINS, John** (w. Sally) to **James Briant**
7-14   of Hampshire Co.   of Hampshire Co.
     150 a. on South Branch R.; rec. 7-15-1799.
     Wit.: None.

1796 **HIGGINS, Metilda** (wid. of Judiah) to **Charles Osman**
11-1   of Hampshire Co. (power of attorney)
     Power to rent lands, etc., belonging to her husband, Judiah Higgins, deceased; rec. 6-19-1798.
     Wit.: Ovid Mecrakin, Alexr. Sutherland, John Williams,
     G. Washington Williams, John Higgins.

1785 **HIGGINS, Robert** (w. Hannah) to **Major Cade**
2-2   of Hampshire Co. (lease and release)   of Hampshire Co.
     100 a. on Vanmeter's Run; rec. 9-9-1785.
     Wit.: John Renick, Christopher Snyder, Matthew Busby.

1785 **HIGGINS, Robert** (w. Hannah) to **Peter Umstot**
11-7   of Hampshire Co.   of Hampshire Co.
     240 a. in Hampshire Co.; rec. 11-10-1785.
     Wit.: Robt. Higgins, John Higgins, Andrew Wodrow.

1795 **HIGH, John** (w. Elizabeth) to **Molly Fidler**
1-19   of Hampshire Co. (deed of gift)   (daughter)
1-19   of Hampshire Co. (deed of gift)
     Sheep, personal property; rec. 2-16-1795.
     Wit.: And. Wodrow, Wm. Bullitt, Jr., Sam Dew, Jr.

1796 **HIGH, John** (w. Elizabeth) to **Henry Hawk**
10-25   of Hampshire Co. (bill of sale)   of Hampshire Co.
     400 a. on Mill Creek; rec. 12-19-1796.
     Wit.: None.

1797 **HIGH, John** (w. Elizabeth) to **Henry Hawk**
1-7   of Hampshire Co. (bill of sale)   of Hampshire Co.
     400 a. in Hampshire Co.; rec. 2-20-1797.
     Wit.: None.

1797 **HIGH, John** (w. Elizabeth) to **James Fleming**
8-26   of Hampshire Co.
     84 a. in Hampshire Co.; rec. 9-18-1797.
     Wit.: Okey Johnson, Wm. Vause, Geo. Hill, Henry Liller.

1799 **HIGH, John** to **Henry High**
1-4   of Hampshire Co.   of Hampshire Co.
     400 a. on Mill Creek; rec. 2-18-1799.
     Wit.: John Foley, John Foley, Jr.

1799 **HIGH, John** to **Henry High**
1-4   of Hampshire Co.   of Hampshire Co.
     100 a. on Mill Creek; rec. 2-18-1799.
     Wit.: John Foley, John Foley, Jr., Daniel Ellor.

1799 **HIGH, John** to **John High, Jr.**
1-4   of Hampshire Co.   of Hampshire Co.
     213 a. on Mill Creek; rec. 2-18-1799.
     Wit.: John Foley, John Foley, Jr., Daniel Ellor.

1784 **HIGHLEY, Rubin** to **Charlotta Highley**
4-6   of Hampshire Co.   Sarah Highley
     Deed of Gift.   (daughters)
     Bay horse, 3 sheep, 2 hogs (Charlotte); 1 bay mare, 2 sheep, 3 hogs (Sarah); rec. 5-11-1784.
     Wit.: None.

1792 **HILL, George** to **Okey Johnson**
11-1   of Hampshire Co.   of Hampshire Co.
     133 a. on Knobley Mt.; rec. 7-10-1793.
     Wit.: J. Wheeler, Geo. Staggs, John Dowden, LeRoy Hill.

1783 **HILL, Joseph** to **James Stone**
3-10   of Hampshire Co. (lease and release)   of Hampshire Co.
     150 a. on Little Cacapeon; rec. 3-11-1783.
     Wit.: David Collins, Daniel Hill, George Lewis.

1783 **HILL, Joseph** to **Daniel Hill**
3-10   of Hampshire Co. (lease and release)   of Hampshire Co.
     73 a. on Little Cacapeon R.; rec. 3-11-1783.
     Wit.: James Stone, George Lewis, David Collins.

1796 10-7	HILL, LeRoy (w. Ann) of Hampshire Co. 200 a., Hampshire Co.; rec. 10-17-1796. Wit.: None.	to Isaac Welch of Hampshire Co.		1800 3-4	HOGELAND, Cornelius of Wood Co. Recorded 5-19-1800. Wit.: A. King, John Mitchell, John Keller, Henry Schart, Jr.	to Isiah Beall of Hampshire Co.	

1780 4-10 HIMELWRIGHT, Joseph — to Andrew Reidt
Philadelphia Co., Pa. (lease & release) Philadelphia Co., Pa.
267½ a. on North R. of Great Cacapeon; rec. 5-9-1780.
Wit.: None.

1780 4-10 HIMELWRIGHT, Joseph — to Andrew Reidt
Philadelphia Co., Pa. (lease & release) Philadelphia Co., Pa.
198 a. on North Mt.; rec. 5-9-1780.
Wit.: None.

1799 5-15 HINES, Joseph — to Capt. John Blue
of Hampshire Co. of Hampshire Co.
150 a. in Hampshire Co.; rec. 5-20-1799.
Wit.: Henry Hines, John Blue, Jr., Barnet Blue.

1781 4-24 HIRE, Rudolph — to Martin Shobe
of Hampshire Co. of Hampshire Co.
165 a. on South Branch; rec. 11-13-1781.
Wit.: Phillip Swank, Jacob Peterson, Alexander Simpson.

1762 11-9 HITE, Major Abraham — to James Keith
of Hampshire Co. (lease and release) of Frederick Co.
110 a. on So. Branch; rec. 11-10-1762.
Wit.: Sam Dew.

1780 3-9 HITE, Abraham (w. Rebekah) — to John High
of Hampshire Co. of Hampshire Co.
400 a. on Mill Creek; rec. 5-9-1781.
Wit.: None.

1782 1-10 HITE, Abraham (w. Rebecca) — to Vincent Williams
of Hampshire Co. (lease and release) of Hampshire Co.
398 a. on head drains of Hiccory Bottom Run; rec. 2-12-1782.
Wit.: Andrew Wodrow, Peter Casey, Wm. Vause,
Abraham Hite, Jr.

1785 8-1 HITE, Abraham (w. Rebecca) — to Rudolph Buzzard
of Hampshire Co. (lease and release) of Hampshire Co.
110 a. on South Branch; rec. 11-8-1785.
Wit.: None.

1787 3-2 HITE, Abraham (w. Rebecca) — to Benjamin Hoffman
of Hampshire Co. (bill of sale) of Hampshire Co.
24 a. on Mill Creek; rec. 6-12-1788.
Wit.: Jacob Parker, Ben. Norman, Wm. Carder.

1787 3-21 HITE, Abraham (w. Rebecca) — to Ezekiel Smalley
of Hardy Co. (bill of sale) of Loudon Co.
200 a. in Hampshire Co.; rec. 4-13-1787.
Wit.: Andrew Smalley, Wm. Norman, Henry Hawk.

1787 3-21 HITE, Abraham (w. Rebecca) — to Andrew Smalley
of Hardy Co. (bill of sale) of Hampshire Co.
200 a. on South Branch; rec. 4-13-1787.
Wit.: Wm. Norman, Jacob High, Henry Hawk, John High.

1783 5-8 HITE, Isaac (w. Eleanor) — to Jonathan Clark
of Frederick Co. of Spotsylvania
435 a. on Little Cacapeon; rec. 5-13-1783.
Wit.: Phil Pendleton, John Magill, Alex White,
James Walker.

1762 10-8 HITE, John (w. Sarah) — to William Bowell
of Frederick Co. (lease and release) of Frederick Co., Md.
207 a. in Hampshire Co.; rec. 11-10-1762.
Wit.: Pet. Hog, Ja. Keith, Ga. Jones.

1767 4-8 HITE, John (w. Sarah) — to Simon Taylor
of Frederick Co. (lease and release) of Hampshire Co.
400 a. on South Branch, Lot No. 52; rec. 4-14-1767.
Wit.: David Deitrick, Cornelius Thompson,
John Hite, Jr., Ja. Keith, Pet. Hog, Alex White.

1767 10-5 HITE, John (w. Sarah) — to John Foxcroft
of Frederick Co., Va. Charles Thompson
(Lease and release) of Philadelphia, Pa.
363 a. on Capon; rec. 5-10-1768.
Wit.: Samuel Pritchard, Alex White, Bryan Bruen,
Pet. Hog, Ja. Keith.

1775 3-14 HITE, Matthias — to Magdalena Hart
of Dunmore Co. of Hampshire Co.
50 a. on South Branch; rec. 3-14-1775.
Wit.: Sam Dew.

1798 3-16 HODDY, Richard (w. Mary) — to Cornelius Devore
of Hampshire Co. of Bedford Co.
100 a. on Patterson Creek; rec. 4-16-1798.
Wit.: Jacob Purgitt, John Bord, Wm. Reed.

1792 6-1 HOFFMAN, Benjamin (w. Sarah) — to James Barkelow
of Hampshire Co. of Hampshire Co.
Parcel of land on South Branch, for the erection of a grist mill
and water mill; rec. 6-26-1792.
Wit.: Andrew Wodrow, Francis Taggart, Wm. Jacob.

1789 6-10 HOFFMAN, Henry (w. Agnes) — to Abraham Good
of Hampshire Co. of Hampshire Co.
210 a. on Cabbin Run; rec. 9-16-1790.
Wit.: Okey Johnson, Geo. Miller, Peter Good.

1793 4-10 HOFFMAN, John (w. Catherine) — to John Mantell
of Hampshire Co. (Montell?) of Hampshire Co.
100 a. on Beaver Run; rec. 4-10-1793.
Wit.: John Plumb, Okey Johnson, Aaron Brandenbaugh,
Christian Muselinan.

1763 7-8 HOGE, George (w. Elizabeth) — to Col John Hite
of Hampshire Co. (lease and release) of Frederick Co.
400 a. on So. Branch; rec. 12-12-1764.
Wit.: Jno. Greenfield, Ja. Keith, Edward McGuire,
Briyan Bruin, Chs. Smith, Angus McDonald.

1794 4-9 HOGUE, Samuel (Hague?) — to Leonard Carnend
(w. Eleanor) of Hampshire Co.
of Hampshire Co.
42 a. on Mill Creek; rec. 4-9-1794.
Wit.: None.

1794 4-9 HOGUE, Samuel (w. Eleanor) — to Leonard Carnend
of Hampshire Co. of Hampshire Co.
157 a. on Mill Creek; rec. 4-9-1794.
Wit.: None.

1794 6-10 HOGUE, Samuel (w. Eleanor) — to John Cuppy
of Hampshire Co. of Hampshire Co.
260½ a. on Mill Creek; rec. 6-11-1794.
Wit.: None.

1795 4-24 HOGUE, Samuel (w. Eleanor) — to Daniel Dolohan
of Hampshire Co. of Buck Co., Pa.
200½ a. in Hampshire Co.; rec. 6-15-1795.
Wit.: And. Wodrow, Richard Sloan, Wm. Norman.

1768 9-27 HOLLIDAY, John, — to William Turner
of Hampshire Co. of Hampshire Co.
480 a. on Patterson's Creek; rec. 11-9-1768.
Wit.: Abrm. Hite, Luke Collins, Sam Dew.

1782 3-9 HOLLIDAY, John (w. Jane) — to John Thompson
of Winchester, Va. (lease and release) of Lancaster Co.
247 a. on Little Cacapeon; rec. 11-12-1782.
Wit.: Andrew Wodrow, James Walker, John Magill.

1797 3-30 HOLTERMAN, Abram (w. Noney) — to Francis Deakins
(see Halterman) of Alegany Co., Ml. William Deakins
250 a. on Clover Lick Run, of Montgomery Co., Md.
222 a. on Patterson's Creek, 78 a. on
Patterson's Creek; rec. 4-17-1797.
Wit.: John Mitchel, John Keller, Dan MacAllister,
A. King.

1799 4-6 HOOVER, Henry — to Jacob Hoover
of Washington Co. of Lancaster Co.
270 a. on Patterson's Creek; rec. 5-20-1799.
Wit.: And. Wodrow, Thos. Collins, Jas. Dailey,
Sam Gibbs.

1762 9-7 HOPKINS, John — to Job Pearsall
of North Carolina (power of attorney) of Hampshire Co.
Gives Job Pearsall authority to sell land to Thomas Cresap.
Rec. 12-13-1763.
Wit.: Enoch Floyd, Lambeth Hopkins, Enoch Innis.

1794 2-11 HOPPY, Christopher John — to David Hoppy
of Hampshire Co. (bil of sale)
Personal property; rec. 2-12-1794.
Wit.: Roger Hartley.

1797 10-17 HORN, Andrew (w. Catherine) — to Marjarom Brelsford
of Hampshire Co. of Hampshire Co.
Parcel o fland on North R. Mt.; rec. 10-17-1797.
Wit.: Arjalon Price.

1796 2-13 HORN, George, Sr. (w. Mary) — to Daniel Belsford
191 a. on Dillons Run; rec. 2-15-1796.
Wit.: And. Horn, Henry Horn, Phillip Horn.

1798 12-15 HORN, George, Jr. (w. Elizabeth) — to Wm. Williamson
50 a. on Tear Coat Creek; rec. 12-17-1798.
Wit.: Robert Young, Philip Horn.

1796 2-15 HORN, Henry — to Andrew Horn
of Hampshire Co. of Hampshire Co.
102 a. on North R. Mt.; rec. 2-15-1795.
Wit.: Jas. McBride, Jas. Carruthers.

1783 9-17 HORNBACK, Abraham — to Samuel Hornback
of Hampshire Co. of Hampshire Co.
17 a. on South Br. R.; rec. 11-11-1783.
Wit.: Joseph Nevill, Samuel Curtright, Charles Myers,
Daniel McNeill, John Obannan, Abel Randall.

1785 8-6 HORNBACK, Isaac — to Edward Williams
of Hampshire Co. of Hampshire Co.
235 a. on South Branch; rec. 11-8-1785.
Wit.: Andrew Wodrow, Abel Randall, Job Welton,
Peter Higgins, Moses Hutton, M. W. Hite.

1785 9-20 HORNBACK, Isaac (w. Elizabeth) — to Edward Williams
of Hampshire Co. of Hampshire Co.
222 a. on South Branch; rec. 11-8-1785.
Wit.: Andrew Wodrow, Job Welton, Abel Randall,
Peter Higgins, Moses Hutton, M. W. Hite.

1785 9-20 HORNBACK, James — to Samuel Hornback
of Hampshire Co. of Hampshire Co.
9½ a. on South Branch; rec. 11-8-1785.
Wit.: Martin Leonard, Edward Williams, And. Wodrow,
Abel Randall, Jonathan Heath.

1761 3-27 HORNER, George (w. Elizabeth) — to John Woodson
Lease and release.
350 a. on North River; rec. 9-9-1761.
Wit.: John Arnold, George Nickson, Rudy Bumgarner,

1761 3-30 HORNER, George — to John Owens
OWENS, Ann (son-in-law of George Horner)
of Hampshire Co. of Hampshire Co.
50 a. on North River; rec. 9-9-1761.
Wit.: John Arnold, George Nickson, Rudy Bumgarner,
John Thomas, George Hoge, William Hoge.

GRANTOR-GRANTEE

1774 **HORNER, Stephen** to **John Prunty**
11-7 of Chester Co. (lease and release) of Hampshire Co.
146 a. on North River; rec. 11-12-1776.
Wit.: Thomas Keeran, Jonathan Pugh, Bethel Pugh,
Hugh Sidwell, Morris Rees.

1774 **HORNER, Stephen** to **Hugh Sidwell**
11-7 of Chester Co. Pa. (lease and release) of Chester Co.
146 a. on North River; rec. 3-12-1776.
Wit.: Thomas Heerman, Jonathan Pugh, Bethel Pugh,
Morris Rees, John Prunty.

1772 **HOTTINGHAM, Thomas** to **Abraham Cantien**
6-2 (Nottingham?) (w. Susannah) of Marble Town, N. Y.
of Marble Town, N. Y.
400 a. on South Branch; rec. 10-13-1772.
Wit.: Daniel Graham, Charles D'Witt, Stephen Hottingham,
Jr., Richard Brodhead, Jacob Lametter.

1773 **HOTZENBEHLER, Jacob** to **Stephen Hotzenbehler**
4-23 (w. Elizabeth) of Frederick Co.
of Hampshire Co. (lease and release)
100 a. on Cacapeon Creek; rec. 11-9-1773.
Wit.: None.

1779 **HOTSINBILLER, Jacob** to **Jacob Hoover**
5-3 (w. Elizabeth) of Hampshire Co.
of Frederick Co. (lease and release)
294 a. on Cacapeon River; rec. 5-11-1779.
Wit.: James Walker, Alex. White,
George Rootoes, John Magill.

HOTSINPILLER, Jacob to **Jacob Hoover**
(w. Elizabeth)
of Frederick Co. (Dedimus for taking acknowledgement.)
Rec. 9-17-1788.
Wit.: None.

1788 **HOTZINPILLER, Jacob** to **Jacob Hoover**
8-20 Receipt. Received of Jacob Hoover full satisfaction all bonds,
notes, debts due and demands from the beginning of the world
till this day I say received by
Rec. 4-9-1794. —Jacob Hotzinpoller.
Wit.: None.

1761 **HOTSENBELLA, Stephen** to **Valentin Switzer**
3-19 Attorney in fact for of Frederick Co.
ROBINSON, Nicholas (lease and release)
of Frederick Co.
400 a. on Great Cape Capon; rec. 6-10-1761.
Wit.: William Millar, Job Pearsall, Abram Kuykendall,
John Collins, H. Churchill, Babriel Jones.

1761 **HOTSENBELLA, Stephen,** to **Jacob Hotsenbella (son)**
5-1 (w. Elizabeth) of Frederick Co.
of Frederick Co. (lease and release)
394 a. on Cape Capon; rec. 6-10-1761.
Wit.: Cuthbt. Bullet, Ja. Keith, Ga. Jones.

1779 **HOTSINBILLER, Stephen** to **John Winterton**
5-10 of Frederick Co. (lease and release) of Hampshire Co.
68½ a. on Great Cacapeon; rec. 5-11-1779.
Wit.: None.

1797 **HOUGH, John (w. Hannah)** to **Richard Hunter**
4-14 of Hampshire Co. of Hampshire Co.
91 a. in Hampshire Co.; rec. 4-17-1797.
Wit.: John Mitchell, A. King, John Jones, Sr.,
John Keller.

1762 **HOUGLAND, Richard (w. Elizabeth)** to **John Foxman**
8-12 of Frederick Co. (lease and release) of Hampshire Co.
Lot No. 23, 260 a. on So. Branch; rec. 11-10-1762.
Wit.: Gabriel Jones, Phil Ross, Abrm. Hite, Sam Dew.

1779 **HOUGLAND, Richard, dec'd, by** to **Wm. Vandivear**
6-9 REED, John, his executor (lease and release) Hampshire Co.
180 a. on New Creek; rec. 9-16-1790.
Wit.: Andrew Wodrow, John Herndon,
Alex Ruthven, J. Darlinton, Wm. Jacob.

1790 **HOUGLAND, Richard, dec'd, by** to **Uriah Blew**
6-9 REED John, his executor (lease and release) Hampshire Co.
200 a. on South Branch; rec. 12-16-1790.
Wit.: Andrew Wodrow, John Herndon,
Alex Ruthven, J. Darlinton, Wm. Jacob.

1793 **HOUSE, Andrew (w. Catherine)** to **Charles Clinton**
3-21 of Fayette Co. (lease and release) of Fayette Co.
173 a. on Knobley Mt.; rec. 9-11-1793.
Wit.: John Clinton, Mary Clinton., Jas, Murphy,
Fras Taggart, John Jack, Daniel Collins, Wm. Fingle.

1794 **HOUSE, Joseph (w. Catherine)** to **George Gilpin**
12-31 of Hampshire Co. **John Foster**
419 a. on Plum Run; rec. 2-16-1795. **John Ricketts**
Wit.: A. Brown, John Mitchell, Alex. King,
Abraham Johnson.

1798 **HOUSE, Joseph (w. Catherine)** to **Jacob Slagle**
2-14 of Hampshire Co. of Hampshire Co.
166 a. on North Br., Potomac River; rec. 2-19-1798.
Wit.: A. King, Wm. Hough, Jacob Stottler,
Henry Protzman.

1793 **HOUSE, William (w. Elizabeth)** to **George Bethel**
1-19 of Jefferson Co., Ohio of Hampshire Co.
Parcel of land in Hampshire Co.; rec. 6-12-1793.
Wit.: Elias Poston, Wm. Carlyle, Chas. Carlyle.

1767 **HOW, Joseph (w. Eleanor)** to **William Smith**
8-6 of Augusta Co., Va. (lease and release) of Philadelphia, Pa.
386 a., Lost River; rec. 8-11-1767.
Wit.: Ja. Keith, Pet. Hog, Luke Collins,
W. Rannells, John Lyne.

1800 **HOWARD (Honore?), Francis Maurice** to **Jas. Dailey**
2-3 (w. Louisa Genovera) of Hampshire Co.
and Francis Maurice Howard as guardian to
LEMMONEIRS, Alex Lewis
LEMMONIERS, Lewis, Victor,
LEMMONIERS, Valentine Louisa
MALOPEAN, Alexander Joseph,
curator to Valentine Louisa Lemmoniers
PEYROUET, John Baptist, and his wife,
Adelaide Louisa
All of France.
Recorded 7-14-1800.
Wit.: Thomas Clark, Edw. Dyer.

1775 **HOWARD, Reason (w. Esther)** to **Aaron Ashbrook**
1-20 of Hampshire Co. of Hampshire Co.
Parcel of land on North R. of Cacapeon; rec. 3-14-1775.
Wit.: Sam Pritchard, Jas. Carruthers,, Thomas Essex.

1779 **HOWARD, Reason (w. Esther)** to **John Jones**
11-8 of Hampshire Co. (lease and release) of Hampshire Co.
241 a. on Gibbins Run; rec. 11-9-1779.
Wit.: None.

1779 **HOWARD, Reason (w. Esther)** to **William Lineger**
11-8 of Hampshire Co. (lease and release) of Hampshire Co.
200 a. on Gibbins Run; rec. 11-9-1779.
Wit.: None.

1795 **HOWARD, Reason (w. Esther)** to **Thomas Henderson**
4-20 of Hampshire Co. of Hampshire Co.
89 a. on road from Winchester to Romney; rec. 4-20-1795.
Wit.: Rees Pritchard, Barthama Pritchard,
John Howard, Abigail Warner.

1797 **HOWARD, Reason (w. Esther)** to **George Martin, Jr.**
2-20 of Hampshire Co.
441 a. on road from Romney to Winchester; rec. 2-20-1797.
Wit.: Michael Miers, Eli Martin, Moses Jones.

1787 **HOWELL, Jemima**
1-25 Widow of George Howell, a private in the army and died in
the service of the U. S. Is entitled to 10 pounds yearly.
Certificate; recorded 9-13-1787.
Wit.: None.

1774 **HOWELL, William** to **Mathias Brandenburgen**
See GILLMER, Margaret

1798 **HOYE, William** to **Paul Hoye**
10-1 of Allegany Co. of Washington Co.
555 a. on North Br. Potomac; rec. 10-15-1798.
Wit.: John Bayard, Jesse Comlinson,.

1785 **HUBBARD, Jacob (w. Catherine)** to **James Smith**
3-14 of Hampshire Co. of Hampshire Co.
89½ a. on North River; rec. 3-14-1786.
Wit.: None.

1799 **HUBBARD, Jacob (w. Catherine)** to **John Monroe**
9-9 40 a. on North R., 311 a. on North R.; rec. 9-16-1799.
Wit.: Geo. Horn, Jr., Stephen Leigh, Tunis Petters.

1796 **HUFFMAN, Benjamin (Hoffman)** to **Conrad Huffman**
12-12 of Hampshire Co. (bill of sale)
104 a. on South Br. R.; rec. 12-19-1796.
Wit.: And. Wodrow, Richard Sloan,
John Hansbrough, John Jack.

1785 **HUGHES, Caleb** (see HEWES)

1772 **HUGHES, Ellis (w. Jane)** to **Samuel Baker**
12-4 of Hampshire Co. (lease and release) of Hampshire Co.
Parcel of land on Cacapeon Creek; rec. 3-9-1773.
Wit: James Stell Coberly, Moses Hutton, Henry Fry.

1759 **HUGHES, Hugh (w. Susanna)** to **Benjamin Fry**
2-12 of Hampshire Co. (lease and release) of Frederick Co.
33 a., 105 poles. along Cape Capon Creek; rec. 2-13-1759.
Wit.: H. Churchill, James Ireson, Peter Casey.

1771 **HUGHES, Hugh** to **William Hughes**
12-10 of Hampshire Co. (lease and release) of Hampshire Co.
40 a. in Hampshire Co.; rec. 3-10-1772.
Wit.: Ellis Hughes, Wm. Hughes, Christian Powell.

1772 **HUGHES, Hugh** to **Henry Fry**
3-9 of Hampshire Co. (lease and release) of Hampshire Co.
170 a. on Hughes's Run on Cacapeon; rec. 3-10-1772.
Wit.: Thomas Elswick, David Hughes, Richard Mynatt.

1759 **HUGHES, Thomas (w. Susannah)** to **Henry Fry**
2-12 of Hampshire Co. (lease and release) of Frederick Co.
219 a. on Great Cape Capon; rec. 2-13-1759.
Wit.: James Ireson, H. Churchill, Peter Casy.

1761 **HUGHES, Thomas (w. Susannah)** to **Henry Fry**
6-8 of Hampshire Co. (lease and release) of Hampshire Co.
219 a. on Great Cape Capon; rec. 12-8-1761.
Wit.: Sam Dew.

1763 **HUGHES, Thomas (w. Susannah)** to **Henry Fry**
5-9 of Hampshire Co. (lease and release) of Hampshire Co.
200 a. on Great Cape Capon; rec. 5-10-1763.
Wit.: Gabriel Jones.

1797 **HUGHS, Thomas (w. Jane)** to **John Athy**
9-4 of Hampshire Co. of Berkeley Co.
132 a., Hampshire Co.; rec. 9-18-1797.
Wit.: Job Curtis, Peter Laren,, Abraham Larue,
Jacob Larue.

1772 12-3	HUGHES, William (w. Mary) to Henry Fry of Hampshire Co. of Hampshire Co. 460 a., on Cacapeon Creek; rec. 3-9-1773. Wit.: James Stell Coberly, Moses Samuel Baker.
1763 5-6	HUGHES, Susanna, widow, and to Benjamin Fry HUGHES, William, of Hampshire Co. Eldest son of Hugh Hughes of Hampshire Co. 33 a. on Cape Capon Creek; rec. 5-10-1768. Lease and release. Wit.: Sam Dew.
1784 2-28	HULSE, Henry to Thomas Williams of Washington Co. of Washington Co. 104 a. on Great Cacapeon R.; rec. 3-9-1784. Wit.: Wm. Neely, Richard Hule, Abraham Dawson, William Blyth, Conrad Cristman.
1788 4-15	HUMPHREYS, Ralph (w. Agnes) to Andrew Wodrow of Hampshire Co. (lease an drelease) of Hampshire Co. 131 a. on Tear Coat Creek; rec. 7-10-1788. Wit.: James Murphy, Mary Murphy, Mary Drew.
1788 4-17	HUMPHREYS, Ralph (w. Agnes) to Osburn Sprigg of Washington Co. 456 a. on South Branch; rec. 7-10-1788. Wit.: Andrew Wodrow, James Murphy, Mary Wodrow, Mary Murphy.
1788 8-1	HUMPHREYS, Ralph to Andrew Wodrow of Hampshire Co. of Hampshire Co. 283 a. on South Branch R.; rec. 9-11-1788. Wit.: James Murphy, Wm. Fox, Wm. Jacob, Isaac Means.
1799 12-2	HURFORD, Joseph to Runa Campbell of Hampshire Co. John Crossley Parcel of land on Mill Creek; of Hampshire Co. rec. 12-16-1799. Wit.: And. Wodrow, Phil Wilson
1779	HUTTON, Moses to Enoch Hayden See HEATH, Jonathan RANDALL, Abel VANMETER, Garrett

—I—

1764 3-19	ICE, Frederick to Robert Gregg of Hampshir Co. (lease and release) of Hampshire Co. 100 a. on Patterson Creek; rec. 8-14-1765. Wit.: Wm. Dopson, John Forman, Humphrey Wastell, David Gregg.
1765 10-25	ICE, Frederick (w. Eleanor) to John Greenfield of Frederick Co. Md. (lease and release) Frederick Co., Va. 187 a. on Pattersons Creek; rec. 4-14-1767. Wit.: Bryan Bruen, Robt. Gregg, John Lyne, Jno. Moffett, Henry Heth, Thos. Wood.
1791 1-31	ICE, Frederick (w. Elanor) to Robert Kile of Monongahela Co. (lease and release) of Hampshire Co. 187 a. on Patterson Creek; rec. 2-10-1791. Wit.: Addom Isac, Hensom Bright, Michael Cain.
	IHRESOM (see Ahrsom, Earsom, Ohrsom)
1766 8-12	INGRAM, Samuel (w. Anne) to Joseph Pritchard of Hampshire Co. (lease and release) of Hampshire Co. 260 a. on Hughs Run; rec. 8-13-1766. Wit.: None.
1781 12-27	INNIS, Enoch to John Haynes of Hampshire Co. of Bedford Co. 134 a. on North Branch of Potomac; rec. 5-14-1782. Wit.: John Roussau, Joseph Haynes, Joseph Williams, Joseph Nicholas.
1778 11-19	INNIS, Enoch (w. Sarah) to Michael Heter of Hampshire Co. (lease and release) of Washington Co. 162 a. on North Branch of Potomac, 128 a. on North Branch of Potomac; rec. 11-11-1778. Wit.: None.
1781 3-15	INNIS, Enoch (Atty.) to Francis Perpoint LIVINGSTON, James of Hampshire Co. of Hampshire Co. 191 a. on North Branch of Potomac; rec. 5-8-1781. Wit.: Sam Dew, James Scott, William Price.
1796 8-13	INSKEEP, Abraham to William Inskeep of Hardy Co. of Hampshire Co. 400 a., 26 a., on South Branch R.; rec. 9-19-1796. Wit.: And. Wodrow, John Jack, Nathaniel Dyer, William Burns.
1782 3-7	IRONTON, Ritchard (w. Lydia) to Jacob Keysner of Hampshire Co. (lease and release) of Frederick Co. 200 a. on Tear Coat Creek; rec. 3-12-1782. Wit.: None.
1793 2-19	IRWIN, Robert (w. Margaret) to LeRoy Hill of Hampshire Co. of Hampshire Co. 224 a. on Cabbin Run; rec. 9-11-1793. Wit.: George Hill, Wm. Howell, David Cottel, John H. Price.

—J—

1796 4-18	JACK, John (w. Rebecca) to William Vandiver of Romney of Hampshire Co. 1 a. in Hampshire Co.; rec. 4-18-1796. Wit.: None.
1797 6-24	JACK, John to Patrick Delany of Romney,, by of Philadelphia MAHONY, Jeremiah, his attorney 300 a. on South Branch R.; rec. 12-18-1797. Wit.: James DeBaufre, Blaise Cenas, Hilary Baker.
1798 5-14	JACK, John to Jacob Umpstot of Romney of Hampshire Co. Half acre in Romney; rec. 5-14-1798. Wit.: None.
1800 5-19	JACK, John to Isaac Parsons of Hampshire Co. of Hampshire Co. Recorded 5-19-1800.
1780 5-1	JACKSON, William (w. Elizabeth) to John Swim of Hampshire Co. (lease and release) of Hampshire Co. 50 a. on Cacapeon R.; rec. 5-9-1780. Wit.: William Forman, John Forman, Benjamin Forman.
1797 2-18	JACKSON, William (w. Elizabeth) to Moses Dimmitt of Hampshire Co. of Hampshire Co. 342 a. on Great Cacapeon; rec. 2-20-1797. Wit.: Peter Bruner, Levi Matthew, John Matthew, Sam. Treakel.
1797 2-18	JACKSON, William (w. Elizabeth) to Peter Bruner of Hampshire Co. of Washington Co. 92 a., 894 a., on Great Cacapeon; rec. 2-20-1797. Wit.: Moses Dimmitt, Levi Matthew, John Matthew, Samuel Treakel.
1787 9-26	JACOB, Jeremiah to Slaves of Hampshire Co. Freeing of his slaves: Peter, Banjamin, Charles, Johanna, Andrew, Harry, Letty, female child of Johanna, Mary, female child of Johanna, Hansan, and parents, Joseph and Mima, George (no last name given), to be freed from his services forever. Recorded 4-10-1788. Wit.: Sam Dew, Betty Dew.
1788 4-10	JACOB, John Jeremiah to Slaves of Hampshire Co. Betty and Priscilla, negro women Freed, with the conditions that they stay with his wife during natural life, as hired servants, to receive annual wages of 16 Spanish mill'd dollars. Rec. 4-10-1788. Wit.: None.
1789 5-15	JACOB, John Jeremiah to Pompey of Hampshire Co. a negro man Discharged from his service. Wit.: None.
1791 5-21	JACOB, John Jeremiah (w. Mary) to Luther Martin (Executrix of Michael Cresap, dec'd) of Frederick Co. All lands and tenements and real property Ozburn Sprigg of every kind in Hampshire Co. and of Hampshire Co. Alleghany Co. Rec. 6-16-1791. Lenox Martin Wit.: John Mitchell, James Prather, of Frederick Co. Daniel Cresap, Jr.
1794 1-23	JACOB, John Jeremiah to Slaves of Hampshire Co. Freeing of three negro children from his services. Rec. 4-9-1794. Wit.: Thomas Cresap, Benj. Foste, Benj. Whitehead.
1799 10-5	JACOBS, Joseph (w. Elizabeth) to LeRoy Hill of Hampshire Co. of Hampshire Co. 50 a. on Patterson Creek; rec. 10-14-1799. Wit.: Thomas Shores, Thomas Fletcher.
1800 11-1	JAMES, William (w. Elizabeth) to John Feater of Randolph Co. of Hampshire Co. Recorded 4-14-1800. Wit.: Jno. Discon, William Duling, Thomas Athey.
1800 6-10	JENKINS, Jacob to David Barrett of Hampshire Co. of Frederick Co. Recorded 9-15-1800.
	JOHNSON—See Johnston, Johnstone.
1784 1-28	JOHNSON, Abraham, Sr. (w. Rachel) to Jacob Bogard of Hampshire Co. of Hampshire Co. 46 a. on Cabbin Run; rec. 3-9-1784. Wit.: Gabriel Wright, William Hough, Abraham Johnson, Jr.
1789 4-16	JOHNSON, Abraham, Jr. to Robert Cowens (w. Abigail) William McClellen of Hampshire Co. of Barkley Co. 275 a. on Patterson Creek; rec. 4-16-1789. Wit.: James Daugherty, Andrew Hurne, William Johnson, Jr.
1790 6-9	JOHNSON, Abraham (w. Abigail) to William Reese of Hampshire Co. of Barkley Co. 219 a. on Patterson Creek; rec. 6-10-1790. Wit.: None.
1790 9-13	JOHNSON, Abraham to William Johnson of Hampshire Co. of Hampshire Co. 169 a. on Patterson Creek; rec. 9-16-1790. Wit.: None.
1792 7-20	JOHNSON, Abraham (w. Rachel) to John Snyder of Hampshire Co. of Hampshire Co. 133 a. on Patterson Creek; rec. 8-28-1792. Wit.: None.
1796 2-15	JOHNSON, Abraham, Jr. (w. Abigail) to John Snyder of Hampshire Co. of Hampshire Co. 206 a. on Patterson Creek; rec. 2-15-1796. Wit.: None.

GRANTOR-GRANTEE — PAGE 29

1797 / 11-6 JOHNSON, Abraham (w. Hannah) to Robert Allen, Thomas Allen, Arthur Allen
of Hampshire Co. — of Hampshire Co.
Parcel of land on Patterson Creek.
Rec. 4-16-1798.
Wit.: Israel Stalcup, Henry Protzman, Adam Morrow, Richard Hunter, John Snyder.

1797 / 11-6 JOHNSON, Abraham (w. Hannah) to Israel Stalcup
of Hampshire Co. — of Hampshire Co.
Quarter acre in Frankfort; rec. 4-16-1798.
Wit.: A. King, Richard Hunter, Thos. Dunn, Abraham Jones, Arthur Allen, John Snyder.

1789 / 12-9 JOHNSON, Ephraim to Jacob Mouser
of Hampshire Co. (lease and release) of Hampshire Co.
337 a. on Crooked Run; rec. 12-10-1789.
Wit.: Andrew Wodrow.

1765 / 8-13 JOHNSON, John to Daniel McGlolin (McLaughlin, no doubt)
of Hampshire Co. — of Hampshire Co.
134 a. on Little Cape Capepon.
Rec. 8-13-1765.
Wit.: None.

1769 / 11-13 JOHNSON, John (w. Elizabeth) to Christian Croose
of Hampshire Co. (lease and release) of Augusta Co.
250 a. on Patterson's Creek; rec. 11-14-1769.
Wit.: None.

1779 / 3-8 JOHNSON, John (w. Dinah) to William Chapman
of Hampshire Co. — of Hampshire Co.
134 a. on Little Cacapeon Creek; rec. 5-11-1779.
Wit.: David Mitchell, James Tarpley, Benjamin Reeve.

1797 / 6-3 JOHNSON, John (w. Rachel) to Wm. Vandiver
of Hampshire Co.
176 a. on Allegany Mt.; rec. 6-19-1797.
Wit.: Okey Johnson, William Vause, Michael Miller.

1791 / 9-15 JOHNSON, Joseph (w. Eleanor) to Daniel Royce
of Hampshire Co. — of Hampshire Co.
70 a. on Great Cacapeon R.; rec. 9-15-1791.
Wit.: None.

1794 / 4-9 JOHNSON, Joseph (w. Eleanor) to Joseph Autraw
of Hampshire Co. — of Hampshire Co.
31½ a. on Great Cacapeon; rec. 4-9-1794.
Wit.: None.

1794 / 4-9 JOHNSON, Joseph (w. Eleanor) to John Johnson
of Hampshire Co. — of Hampshire Co.
121 a. in Hampshire Co.; rec. 4-9-1794.
Wit.: Rees Pritchard, John Royse.

1774 / 11-8 JOHNSON, Okey (w. Catherine) to Louis Casselman
of Hampshire Co. (lease and release) of Hampshire Co.
150 a. on Patterson Creek; rec. 5-9-1775.
Wit.: Michael Leard.

1775 / 3-14 JOHNSON, Okey (w. Margaret) to Simon Purgatt
of Hampshire Co. (lease and release) of Hampshire Co.
200 a. on Patterson Creek; rec. 3-14-1775.
Wit.: T. Collins, Ezekiel Totten, John Allinton.

1777 / 4-23 JOHNSON, Okey (w. Catherine) to Job Bacorn
of Hampshire Co. (lease & release) Morris Co., West Jersey
200 a. on Patterson Creek; rec. 11-11-1777.
Wit.: Abraham Johnson, Garret Reasoner, Gabriel Wright.

1779 / 4-12 JOHNSON, Okey (w. Catherine) to Joseph Corey
of Hampshire Co. (lease and release) of Hampshire Co.
73 a. on Patterson Creek; rec. 5-11-1779.
Wit.: John Kimberlin, Abraham Blue, Ruth Kimberlin.

1779 / 4-12 JOHNSON, Okey (w. Catherine) to Abraham Blue
of Hampshire Co. (lease and release) of Hampshire Co.
94 a. on Patterson Creek; rec. 5-11-1779.
Wit.: John Kimberlin, Joseph Cory, Ruth Kimberlin.

1784 / 8-10 JOHNSON, Okey to Nicholas Leatherman
of Hampshire Co. — of Hampshire Co.
130 a. on Patterson Creek; rec. 8-10-1784.
Wit.: Sam Dew.

1794 / 4-8 JOHNSON, Okey to Samuel Hague
of Hampshire Co. — of Hampshire Co.
157 a. on Mill Creek; rec. 4-9-1794.
Wit.: None.

1794 / 4-8 JOHNSON, Okey to Thomas Smoot
of Hampshire Co. — of Hampshire Co.
100 a. on Mill Creek; rec. 4-9-1794.
Wit.: None.

1774 / 8-9 JOHNSON, William to Ezekiel Totten
of Hampshire Co. (lease) of Hampshire Co.
295 a. on Patterson Creek; rec. 8-9-1774.
Wit.: None.

1791 / 9-12 JOHNSON, William (w. Charity) to Thomas Greenwell
of Hampshire Co. — of Hampshire Co.
100 a., 75 a., on Patterson Creek; rec. 9-15-1791.
Wit.: None.

1792 / 7-20 JOHNSON, William (w. Charity) to John Snyder
of Hampshire Co. — of Hampshire Co.
40 a. on Patterson Creek; rec. 8-23-1792.
Wit.: None.

1792 / 8-20 JOHNSON, William (w. Charity) to Alex Randall
of Hampshire Co. — of Hardy Co.
256 a. on Patterson Creek; rec. 8-20-1792.
Wit.: And. Wodrow.

1792 / 10-27 JOHNSON, William (w. Charity) to Peter Gooset
of Hampshire Co. — of Hampshire Co.
75 a. on Patterson Creek; rec. 10-30-1792.
Wit.: Abraham Johnson, John Snyder, Wheny Day, John Dowden.

1795 / 4-13 JOHNSON, William to Thomas Greenwell
of Mason Co., Ky. — of Hampshire Co.
175 a. on Patterson Creek; rec. 4-20-1795.
Wit.: And. Wodrow, John Jack, Wm. French, John Dowden, Okey Johnson.

1797 / 11-18 JOHNSON, Thomas to John Matthew
of Washington Co., Va. — of Hampshire Co.
34 a., 205 a., on Great Cacapeon River; rec. 4-16-1798.
Wit.: Levi Matthew, Daniel Royse, John Johnson, Jas. Butcher, John Butcher, Jeremiah Thompson, Jas. Matthew.

JOHNSTON—See Johnson, Johnstone.

1799 / 3-4 JOHNSTON, Abraham to Thomas Buffington
of Hampshire Co. — of Hampshire Co.
275 a. on Patterson Creek.
Wit.: John Snyder, Wm. Johnson, Okey Johnson, Jacob Burkett, Abraham Brook.

JOHNSTONE—See Johnson, Johnston.

1800 / 4-7 JOHNSTONE, Ephrem to John Caun
of Hampshire Co. — of Hampshire Co.
by MATTHEWS, Levi, attorney
Recorded 4-14-1800.
Wit.: Thomas Offord, Thomas Haines, John Matthews, Edward Treable.

1800 / 4-7 JOHNSTONE, Ephrem to John Matthews
of Hampshire Co. — of Hampshire Co.
by MATTHEWS, Levi, attorney
Recorded 4-14-1800.

1799 / 4-13 JONES, Abraham (w. Mary) to Isaac Vanmeter, Able Semore
of Hampshire Co. — of Hampshire Co.
421 a. on Patterson Creek; rec. 4-15-1799.
Wit.: None.

1764 / 12-11 JONES, Benjamin to Joseph Watson
of Hampshire Co. (lease and release) Fairfax Co., Va.
320 a. on Pattersons Creek; rec. 12-12-1764.
Wit.: Luke Collins, John McColloch, Chas. Linch, Saml. Pritchard, Jno. Greenfield.

1764 / 3-9 JONES, Benjamin to Joseph Watson
of Hampshire Co. (lease and release) of Fairfax Co.
400 a. on Patterson Creek; rec. 12-12-1764.
Wit.: Luke Collins, John McCulloch, Chas. Linch, Saml. Pritchard, Jno. Greenfield.

1767 / 6-27 JONES, Benjamin (w. Mary) to Luke Collins
of Hampshire Co. — of Hampshire Co.
311 a., So. Branch; rec. 10-13-1767.
Wit.: Sam Dew, William Buffington, Benj. Kuykendall, Charles Martin, William McGuire.

1794 / 12-5 JONES, Daniel (w. Rosanah) to Henry Flich
of Hampshire Co. — of Hampshire Co.
483 a. on Cabbin Run; rec. 12-10-1794.
Wit.: Alex King, John Mitchell, Wm. Johnson, John Kimberline.

1794 / 12-31 JONES, Daniel (w. Rosannah) to Francis Deakins, William Deakins of Maryland, George Gilpin of Alexandria, Va.
of Hampshire Co.
400 a. in Hampshire Co.
Rec. 2-16-1795.
Wit.: John Mitchell, A. Brown, Abraham Johnson.

1795 / 5-21 JONES, DANIEL, McGUIRE, William to Henry Lee, Elisha C. Dick
211 a. in Hampshire Co.; rec. 9-18-1799.
Wit.: Vincent Gray, Charles Young, Jr.

1795 / 5-21 JONES, DANIEL, McGUIRE, William to Henry Lee, Elisha Cullen Dick
Parcel of land in Hampshire Co.; rec. 9-18-1797.
Wit.: Frederic Cuiso, Thomas Lemmes., John Burnill.

1798 / 2-19 JONES, Daniel to David Jones, Isaac Jones, John Jones, Moses Jones
of Hampshire Co.
360 a. on Patterson Creek.
Rec. 2-20-1798.
Wit.: Arjalon Price, G. W. Price, Will Armstrong, Hamp. Co. Thos. Emerson.

1798 / 7-13 JONES, Daniel (w. Rosanna) to Alexander King
of Hampshire Co. — of Hampshire Co.
360 a. on Patterson Creek; rec. 9-17-1798.
Wit.: Abraham Johnson, William Armstrong, John Mitchell, David Jones, John Keller.

1798 / 7-28 JONES, Daniel (w. Rosanna) to Leonard Eckstine
of Hampshire Co. — of Hampshire Co.
50 square perches adjoining the town of Frankfort.
Wit.: John Snyder, Henry Protzman, A. King,
Rec. 2-18-1799.
John Mitchell, John McMeekin, John Keller.

1799 / 4-1 JONES, Daniel (w. Rosanna) to Frederick Purgett
of Hampshire Co. — of Hampshire Co.
112 a. on Patterson Creek; rec. 9-16-1799.
Wit.: Eli Davis, Thos. Fitzgerald, James Dailey.

1799 6-17	JONES, Daniel (w. Rosannah) of Hampshire Co. 400 a. on Patterson Creek; rec. 2-17-1800. Wit.: John Jones, Thos. Dunn,, Wm. Johnston, John Keller, Leonard Eckstine.	to William O'Neal of Prince George Co., Md.		

1799 6-17 JONES, Daniel (w. Rosannah) to William O'Neal
of Hampshire Co. of Prince George Co., Md.
400 a. on Patterson Creek; rec. 2-17-1800.
Wit.: John Jones, Thos. Dunn,, Wm. Johnston,
John Keller, Leonard Eckstine.

1800 6-17 JONES, Daniel (w. Rosanna) to William O'Neal
of Hampshire Co. of Prince George Co.
Recorded 2-17-1800.
Wit.: John Jones, Thomas Dunn,
William Johnston, John Keller, Leonard Eckstine.

1798 1-29 JONES, David (w. Sarah) to Daniel Jones
JONES, Isaac (w. Elizabeth) of Hampshire Co.
JONES, John (w. Isabella)
JONES, Moses
JONES, Catherine
345 a., 44 a., 29 a., on Patterson Creek; rec. 2-19-1798.
Wit.: Arjalon Price, Will Armstrong, Thos Emmerson,
Geo. W. Price, John Jones, Sr., James Clark,
John Mitchell.

1798 3-9 JONES, David to Daniel Jones
of Hampshire Co. of Hampshire Co.
Lot in Frankfort; rec. 5-14-1798.
Wit.: John Jones, Sr., Aaron Jones,, David Jones, Jr.,
Abraham Jones.

1800 6-10 JONES, David (w. Rosannah) to Thomas Allen
of Hampshire Co. Robert Allen
Recorded 9-15-1800. Arthur Allen
Wit.: A. King, John Jones, of Hampshire Co.
George W. Long, John Keller, Daniel Miller,
William McGowan.

1757 12-9 JONES, Gabriel (w. Margaret) to George Hoge
of Cty. of Augusta (lease and release) of Cty. of Hampshire
Lot No. 52—200 acres, upon Wappocomo, or Great South
Branch of Potomac; rec. 12-13-1757.
Wit.: Ja. Keith, H. Churchill.

1760 3-11 JONES, Gabriel (w. Margaret) to Henry Kuykendall
of Augusta Co. (lease and release) of Hampshire Co.
250 a., Lot 58, on So. Branch of Potomac; rec. 5-16-1760.
Wit.: None.

1772 8-31 JONES, Gabriel to James Alexander
of Augusta Co. (release) of Hampshire Co.
354 a. on Great Cacapeon.
Wit.: Alex Keith, Peter Hog, John Magill.

1771 6-19 JONES, James (w. Susanna) to Jacob Brake
of New Castle Co., Pa. (lease & release) of Hampshire Co.
200 a. on Fork of South Branch; rec. 11-12-1771.
Wit.: Chas. Lynch, Moses Hutton, Humphrey Sparks.

1770 5-9 JONES, John to Michael Tebolt
of Hampshire Co. (mortgage) of Hampshire Co.
170 a. on Drains of Patterson Creek, joining Lots 15 and 16.
Rec. 5-9-1770.
Wit.: Sam Dew.

1780 8-8 JONES, John (w. Elizabeth) to Reason Howard
of Faquier Co. (lease and release) of Hampshire Co.
241 a. on Gibbins Run; rec. 8-9-1780.
Wit.: None.

1777 12-1 JONES, Joseph (w. Eleanor) to Martin Roller
of Frederick Co. (lease and release) of Dunmore Co.
69 a. on Hugh's Run; rec. 5-12-1778.
Wit.: Alex White, John Magill, George Cale.

1798 10- JONES, Moses to George Sharff
of Hampshire Co. (bil lof sale) of Hampshire Co.
10 a. in Hampshire Co.; rec. 2-18-1799.
Wit.: Rees Pritchard, John Candy.

1767 10-28 JONES, Owen to Bryan Bruen
WISTER, Daniel (mortgage) of Winchester, Va.
of Philadelphia, Pa.
400 a., 204 a., 177 a., 400 a., 79 a., 288 a., 400 a., Green Spring
Valley; rec. 5-10-1768.
Wit.: Jno. Greenfield, John Holliday, G. Mich, Laubinger,
Alexr. White, William Scott, Frederick Conrad.

1795 6-15 JONES, Peter to Thomas Emmerson
of Hampshire Co. James Clarke
10 a., Hampshire Co.; rec. 6-15-1795. of Hampshire Co.
Wit.: None.

1796 4-18 JONES, Samuel (w. Esther) to Thomas Hogan
of Hampshire Co. of Fauquier Co.
144 a. on Knobley Mt.; rec. 4-18-1796.
Wit.: John Candift, Joseph Jacobs.

—K—

1798 4-14 KARNES, Patrick, Sr. to James Galloway
of Hampshire Co. of Hampshire Co.
200 a. on Tear Coat Creek; rec. 4-16-1798.
Wit.: Thos. Leazenby, Bryan Keran.

1782 2-20 KAY, John to Isaac Parsons
of Hampshire Co. (mortgage) Robert Ferguson
Five negro slaves—Willis, Bob, of Hampshire Co.
Charles, Jude and George. Rec. 3-13-1782.
Wit.: Sam Dew, Betty Dew.

1782 7-22 KAY, John to Nathaniel Kuykendall
of Hampshire Co. (bill of sale) of Hampshire Co.
Horse, cows and personal property; rec. 8-13-1782.
Wit.: Joel Berry, Wm. McGuire, Isaac Means.

1763 12-12 KEATING, John (w. Jane) to Luke Collins
Lot No. 37, 322 a., on South Branch; rec. 12-13-1763.
Wit.: Sam Dew.

1766 6-10 KEATING, John (w. Jane) to Hugh Murphy
of Hampshire Co. (lease and release) of Hampshire Co.
133 a. in Hampshire Co.; rec. 6-11-1766.
Wit.: None.

1767 6-10 KEATING, John to Mary Keating
One negro boy named Bobb; rec. 6-10-1767. his daughter
Wit.: Garrat Van Meter, John Collins.

1767 8-11 KEATING, John (w. Joan) to John Boyton
of Hampshire Co. (lease and release) Samuel Wharton
406 a., Little Capon. John Rheas
Rec. 8-12-1767. David Rheas
Wit.: John Hord, John Quirk, Abraham Mitchel
John Lyne. of Philadelphia, Pa.

1767 11-29 KEATING, John (w. Jane) to Thomas Wharton
of Hampshire Co. (lease and release) Joseph Wharton
400 a., So. Branch Mt.; rec. 3-9-1768.
Wit.: John Hayton, John Quirk, Henry Bagley,
John Lyne, Pet. Steenbergen.

1768 2-24 KEATING, John (w. Jane) to George Wilson
of Hampshire Co. (lease and releaase) of Hampshire Co.
Half acre, Lot No. 57, Romney; rec. 3-9-1768.
Wit.: Benj. Kuykendall, Edward McGuire,
Nich's Seaver, John Lyne.

1768 7-7 KEATING, John (w. Jane) to Earhart Glaze
of Hampshire Co. (lease and release) of Hampshire Co.
219 a., 150 a., South Branch; rec. 9-13-1768.
Wit.: Peter Steenbergen, Phillip Ross, John Collins.

1795 6-14 KEEDER, William (w. Jemima) to John Millison
of Hampshire Co. of Prince William Co.
150 a. in Hampshire Co.; rec. 6-15-1795.
Wit.: None.

1789 10-14 KELSO, James to William Hammond
of Annarundale Co. of Baltimore Co.
WILSON, James (w. Susannah), of Berkeley Co.
400 a., 463 a., on Great Cacapeon; rec. 10-14-1789.
Wit.: Wm. Williams, Hugh Holmes, John Slaughter.

1764 2-17 KEITH, James to Abraham Hite
of Frederick Co. (lease and release) of Hampshire Co.
110 a. on So. Branch; rec. 12-11-1764.
Wit.: Tho. Keith, Tho. Harmon, Garret Van Meter.

1778 10-1 KEITH, James (w. Elizabeth) to Moses Pigman
of Berkeley Co. (lease and release) of Hampshire Co.
228 a. on New Creek; rec. 3-9-1779.
Wit.: G. Jones, Alex. White, John Magill.

1777 11-1 KEITH, John (w. Mary) to James Conrad
of Monongala Co., Va. (lease and release) of Hampshire Co.
209 a. on Great Cacapeon; rec. 11-11-1777.
Wit.: None.

1777 11-10 KEITH, John (w. Mary) to James Conrad
of Monongalia Co. (lease and release) of Hampshire Co.
38 a. on Great Cacapeon; rec. 11-11-1777.
Wit.: None.

1799 7-15 KEIZNER, Jacob (w. Martha) to Thomas Edwards
of Hampshire Co. of Hampshire Co.
Half acre in Romney; rec. 7-15-1799.
Wit.: None.

1799 10-11 KEIZNER, Jacob (w. Judy) to Catherine Fry
of Hampshire Co. of Hampshire Co.
192 a. on Crooked Run; rec. 10-14-1799.
Wit.: None.

1800 4-30 KEIZNER, John to Thomas Edwards
of Hampshire Co. of Hampshire Co.
Recorded 5-19-1800.
Wit.: Silas Price, Sam Brown, John W. Merridith.

1786 2-16 KELLER, John to Richard Staford
of Hampshire Co. of Hampshire Co.
Lot of ground in New Frankford, town in Hampshire Co., on
Patterson Creek, containing 99 square feet. Rec. 3-14-1786.
Wit.: None.

1788 4-10 KELLER, John to Peter Danford
of Hampshire Co. of Hampshire Co.
Quarter acre in town of Frankfort; rec. 4-10-1788.
Wit.: None.

1788 4-10 KELLER, John to Thomas Emberson
of Hampshire Co. of Hampshire Co
One half acre, 10 acres, in town of Frankfort; rec. 4-10-1788.
Wit.: None.

1788 4-10 KELLER, John to John Mitchell
of Hampshire Co. of Hampshire Co
Quarter acre in Frankfort; rec. 9-11-1788.
Wit.: None.

1788 4-10 KELLER, John to John Mitchell
of Hampshire Co. of Hampshire Co
Quarter acre in Frankfort; rec. 9-11-1788.
Wit.: None,

1788 4-10 KELLER, John to Christian Stephens
of Hampshire Co. of Hampshire Co
Quarter acre in Frankfort; rec. 9-11-1788.
Wit.: None.

GRANTOR-GRANTEE — PAGE 31

1788 4-10 KELLER, John — of Hampshire Co. — to Andrew Cooper of Hampshire Co.
Quarter acre in Frankfort; rec. 6-12-1788.
Wit.: None.

1788 4-10 KELLER, John — of Hampshire Co. — to John Waters of Frederick Co.
Quarter acre in town of Frankfort; rec. 6-12-1788.
Wit.: None.

1788 5-11 KELLER, John — of Hampshire Co. — to James Gathrop of Hampshire Co.
Quarter acre in town of Frankfort; rec. 6-12-1788.
Wit.: None.

1788 5-11 KELLER, John — of Hampshire Co. — to James Rennells of Hampshire Co.
Quarter acre in town of Frankfort; rec. 6-12-1788.
Wit.: None.

1788 6-12 KELLER, John — of Hampshire Co. (bill of sale) — to John Swobe of Hampshire Co.
22 a. and 23 perches, in Frankfort; rec. 6-12-1788.
Wit.: None.

1788 6-12 KELLER, John — of Hampshire Co. (bill of sale) — to James Daugherty of Hampshire Co.
Quarter acre in town of Frankfort; rec. 6-12-1788.
Wit.: None.

1788 6-12 KELLER, John — of Hampshire Co. — to Thomas Thompson of Hampshire Co.
Quarter acre in Frankfort; rec. 6-12-1788.
Wit.: None.

1788 12-30 KELLER, John — of Hampshire Co. (bill of sale) — to Ezekiel Whiteman of Hampshire Co.
1½ a. in Frankfort; rec. 6-11-1789.
Wit.: James Clark, Rich. Stafford, John Mitchell, Andrew Wodrow.

1788 12-31 KELLER, John — of Hampshire Co. — to Phillip Brookhart of Hampshire Co.
Quarter acre in Frankfort; rec. 6-11-1789.
Wit.: James Clark, Ezekiel Whitman, John Mitchell, Andrew Wodrow.

1788 12-31 KELLER, John — of Hampshire Co. — to Jacob Stotter of Hampshire Co.
Quarter acre in Frankfort; rec. 6-11-1789.
Wit.: James Clark, Ezekiel Whitman, John Mitchell, Andrew Wodrow.

1788 12-31 KELLER, John — of Hampshire Co. — to Richard Stafford of Hampshire Co.
2 acres in Frankfort; rec. 6-11-1789.
Wit.: James Clark, Ezekiel Whiteman, John Mitchell, Andrew Wodrow.

1788 12-31 KELLER, John — of Hampshire Co. — to Jacob Brookhart of Hampshire Co.
Quarter acre in Frankfort; rec. 6-11-1789.
Wit.: James Clark, Ezekiel Whiteman, John Mitchell, Andrew Wodrow.

1788 12-31 KELLER, John — of Hampshire Co. — to Peter Jones of Hampshire Co.
Half acre in Frankfort; rec. 6-11-1789.
Wit.: James Clark, Richard Hofford, Ezekiel Whitman, Andrew Wodrow.

1789 9-16 KELLER, John (w. Ann) — of Hampshire Co. — to Aaron Mercer of Frederick Co.
Quarter acre, 4 acres, in Frankfort; rec. 9-16-1790.
Wit.: Chas. Magill.

1789 9-16 KELLER, John (w. Ann) — of Hampshire Co. — to John Showp of Hampshire Co.
Quarter acre in Frankfort; rec. 9-16-1790.
Wit.: Chas. Magill.

1790 6-19 KELLER, John — of Hampshire Co. — to John Williams, Sr. of Hampshire Co.
Quarter acre in Frankfort; rec. 1-18-1791.
Wit.: Lewis Dunn, And. Wodrow, John Mitchell, Abraham Johnson.

1790 6-19 KELLER, John — of Hampshire Co. — to Joseph Williams of Hampshire Co.
Quarter acre in Frankffort; rec. 1-18-1791.
Wit.: Lewis Dunn, Abraham Johnson, Andrew Wodrow, John Mitchell.

1790 6-19 KELLER, John — of Hampshire Co. — to John Williams, Jr. of Hampshire Co.
Quarter acre in Frankfort; rec. 1-18-1791.
Wit.: Lewis Dunn, Abraham Johnson, Andrew Wodrow, John Mitchell.

1790 9-16 KELLER, John (w. Ann) — of Hampshire Co. — to Christian Musselman of Hampshire Co.
Half acre, 2 acres, in Frankfort; rec. 9-16-1790.
Wit.: None.

1791 10-6 KELLER, John (w. Ann) — of Frankfort — to John Adams, Sr. of Frankfort
Two quarter-acre parcels in Frankfort; rec. 10-18-1791.
Wit.: None.

1791 10-3 KELLER, John (w. Ann) — of Frankfort, Hampshire Co. — to Mahlon Hough of Loudon Co.
Quarter acre in town of Frankfort; rec. 10-18-1791.
Wit.: Alex King, John Shannon, John Williams.

1792 3-12 KELLER, John (w. Ann) — of Frankfort — to Abraham Faw of Montgomery Co.
Half acre in town of Frankfort; rec. 4-24-1792.
Wit.: John Mitchell, John Reed, Alex King.

1794 4-9 KELLER, John (w. Ann) — of Hampshire Co. — to John Kimberline of Hampshire Co.
Quarter acre, half acre, in town of Frankfort; rec. 6-11-1794.
Wit.: Alex King, Thomas Emereson, Robert Kile, John McGlumphy, Thos. Cromwell.

1794 6-21 KELLER, John (w. Ann) — of Hampshire Co. — to John McMeekin of Hampshire Co.
Quarter acre in town of Frankfort; rec. 12-10-1794.
Wit.: John Brown, John Mitchell, Will Armstrong, Alex King.

1794 9-10 KELLER, John (w. Ann) — of Hampshire Co. — to Alexander King of Hampshire Co.
Quarter acre, 2 acres, in Frankfort; rec. 9-10-1794.
Wit.: None.

1794 9-10 KELLER, John (w. Ann) — of Hampshire Co. — to Christian Musselman of Hampshire Co.
7 a., half a., in Frankfort; rec. 9-10-1794.
Wit.: None.

1795 12-30 KELLER, John (w. Ann) — of Hampshire Co. — to John Mitchell of Hampshire Co.
Half acre in Frankfort; rec. 2-15-1796.
Wit.: John Jones Sr., Abrm. Johnson, Alex King, Job Sheppherd, John Snyder.

1797 1-26 KELLER, John (w. Ann) — of Hampshire Co. — to Daniel Hollenback of Hampshire Co.
Quarter acre in Frankfort; rec. 9-13-1797.
Wit.: Alex King, John Mitchell, Daniel Jones, Henry Protzman.

1799 3-11 KELLER, John (w. Ann) — of Hampshire Co. — to John McMeekin of Hampshire Co.
Half acre in Frankfort; rec. 4-15-1799.
Wit.: John Mitchell, Thos. Dowden, Frederick Sheetz.

1788 10-16 KENNEDY, Samuel (w. Jane) — of Hampshire Co. — to Malichi Yother of Montgomery Co.
408 a., Hampshire Co.; rec. 10-16-1788.
Wit.: None.

1797 4-11 KENNEDY, Thomas — of Hampshire Co. — to James Craig of Fairfax Co.
297 a. in Hampshire Co.; rec. 9-18-1797.
Wit.: Elias Poston, Sam Edwards, Sam Poston.

1800 9-8 KENNEDY, Thomas (w. Elizabeth) — of Hampshire Co. — to John Kidwell of Hampshire Co.
Recorded 2-15-1801.
Wit.: John Hawkins, Philip Wolfe, John Hawkins, Jr.

1799 3-28 KENNEDY, William — of Frederick Co. — to Edw. Garrigues
GAW, James
McGUIRE, Edward
McGUIRE, Dowdell
Recorded 5-19-1800.
Wit.: Jane Crawford, William Russell, Margaret Russell, Emilia Russell, R. Whitehead, A. Byerly.

1773 8-6 KENNISON, Edward (w. Matilda) — of Boteowet Co., Va. (lease and release) — to Adam Schried of Hampshire Co.
400 a. on Cacapeon Creek; rec. 8-10-1773.
Wit.: None.

1796 4-18 KENT, Jesse — of Hampshire Co. — to Okey Johnson of Hampshire Co.
100 a. on Patterson Creek; rec. 4-18-1796.
Wit.: None.

1790 6-10 KERAN, Patrick — 329 a. on Tear Coat Creek; 6-10-1790. — to John Peters of Loudon Co.Rec.
Wit.: None.

1799 10-13 KERAN, Patrick — (Curran?) of Hampshire Co. (lease and release) — to Geo. Whitteberry Hampshire Co.
200 a. on North River; rec. 12-16-1790.
Wit.: Rees Pritchard, James Murphy, Robt. French.

1791 4-14 KERAN, Patrick — of Hampshire Co. — to son, William Keran of Hampshire Co.
256 a. on Tear Coat Creek; rec. 4-14-1791.
Wit.: Rees Pritchard.

1798 10-15 KERAN, Patrick (w. Rebecca) — of Hampshire Co. — to John Arnold
57 a. on road from Winchester to Romney; rec. 10-15-1798.
Wit.: None.

1799 7-3 KERAN, Patrick (w. Sarah) — of Monongalia Co. — to James Powell of Hampshire Co.
200 a., Hrampshire Co.; rec. 7-15-1799.
Wit.: And. Wodrow, Wm. Fox, Isaac Miller, Phillip Wilson.

1799 7-3 KERAN, Patrick (w. Sarah) — to James Galloway
200 a. in Hampshire Co.; rec. 7-15-1799.
Wit.: None.

1763 5-14 KESTER, Frederick (w. Hanner) — of Augusta Co. (lease and release) — to James Seers of Hampshire Co.
427 a., Lot No. 8 on South Branch; rec. 12-13-1763.
Wit.: Felix Seymour, Jas. Simpson, Thomas Parsons, Michael Stump, Jonathan Cobun.

| 1791 3-6 | KEYES, Francis of Berkeley Co. (lease) 123 a. on North R. Mt.; rec. 2-28-1792. Wit.: John Redding, George Millslagle. | to Francis Myres of Hampshire Co. |

| 1791 4-15 | KEYES, Francis (w. Anne) of Berkeley Co. 213 a. on Tear Coat Creek; rec. 9-15-1791. Wit.: Thos. Bennett, Thos. Mattock, Sarah Newcomb, John Redding, Wm. Murphy, Geo. Millslagle | to George Cooper of Maryland |

| 1792 11-20 | KEYES, Francis of Berkeley Co. 100 a. on North River; rec. 4-10-1793. Wit.: Geo. Millslagle, Jacob Paulsgrove Henry Crompton. | to William Murphy of Hampshire Co. |

| 1792 11-20 | KEYES, Francis of Berkeley Co. 100 a. in Hampshire Co.; rec. 4-9-1794. Wit.: None. | to William Murphy of Hampshire Co. |

| 1778 11-14 | KEYES, Humphrey (w. Sarah) of Berkeley Co. 170a. on South Branch R.; rec. 5-11-1779. Wit.: John Keyes, R. Rutherford, Thomas Rutherford, Reuben Rutherford, Peter Hog, G. Jones, Alex White, George Rootes, John Magill. | to Isaac Zane of Frederick Co. |

| 1785 10-28 | KEYSAR, Phillip of Hampshire Co. (power of attorney) Authority to collect all debts due Phillip Keysar. Recorded 11-8-1785. Wit.: Joseph Nevill, W. Hackney, Stephen Ashby. | to Adam Moses Attorney. |

| 1797 5-30 | KILEX, Robert See PUTMAN, Peter. | to Mary Putman |

| 1795 2-14 | KIMBERLINE, John (w. Ruth) of Hampshire Co. Quarter acre in Frankfort; rec. 9-14-1795. Wit.: Christian Musselman, Alex King, Daniel Jones. | to Thomas Emmerson of Hampshire Co. |

| 1797 1-20 | KIMBERLINE, John (w. Ruth) of Hampshire Co. Quarter acre 3 lots, ¼ a. each, in Frankfort; rec. 9-18-1797. Wit.: John Newman, Henry Brinker, John Mason, Henry Protzman, Daniel Macalister,, John Jones, Sr., John Keller, John Pierce, Aaron Jones, John Mitchell, Jr. | to Thomas Emmerson of Hampshire Co. |

| 1762 8-9 | KIMZEY, William (w. Elizabeth) (KUNZEY, KINZEY?) of Hampshire Co. (lease and release) 270 a. near Frederick Co. line; rec. 8-10-1762. Wit.: Gabriel Jones, Sam Dew. | to James Bryan of Hampshire Co. |

| 1792 12-20 | KINCHELOE, John (w. Milly) of Prince William Co. 338 a. on Spring Gap Mountain; rec. 6-12-1793. Wit.: None. | to Moses Cock of Prince William Co. |

| 1797 6-12 | KINCHELOW, John (w. Milly) of Prince William Co. 788 a. on Great Cacapeon R.; rec. 2-20-1798. Wit.: Jas. R. Dermott, Geo. W. Lindsay, A. Thompson, Henry Suttle. | to Lund Washington of Washington |

| 1796 5-1 | KING, Alexander (w. Sarah) of Hampshire Co. (bill of sale) Quarter acre in Frankfort; rec. 10-17-1796. Wit.: John Lyle, John Mitchell, Christian Stevens. | to Dennis Daniels of Hampshire Co. |

| 1798 5-14 | KING, Alexander (w. Sarah) of Hampshire Co. Quarter acre in Frankfort; rec. 5-14-1798. Wit.: None. | to John McKinn, Jr. Wm. Cochrane of Baltimore |

| 1800 1-15 | KING, Alex (w. Sarah) of Hampshire Co. Recorded 1-20-1800. Wit.: None. | to William Jenny of Hampshire Co. |

| 1800 1-18 | KING, Alexander (w. Sarah) of Hampshire Co. 1200 a. in Hampshire Co.; rec. 1-20-1800. Wit.: None. | to William Jenny of Hampshire Co. |

| 1790 9-13 | KING, James McLAUGHLIN, Mrs. Rachel of Hampshire Co. Parcel of land on South Branch; rec. 4-14-1791. Wit.: James Martin, David Williams, John Offord. | to Daniel McLaughlin of Hampshire Co. |

| 1798 9-17 | KING, Valentine (w. Sophia) 802 a. on Potomac R.; rec. 9-17-1798. Wit.: None. | to James Malcolm |

| 1794 6-10 | KING, Valentine (w. Sophia) of Hampshire Co. 12¾ a. on Bakers Run; rec. 9-10-1794. Wit.: None. | to Isaac Short of Hampshire Co. |

| 1788 5-2 | KINKADE, Samuel (w. Elizabeth) of Fayette Co. (lease and release) Half acre in Romney; rec. 7-10-1788. Wit.: Alexander French, Sarah Wilson, Ralph Humphreys, John Prunty. | to Andrew Wodrow of Hampshire Co. |

| 1798 11-14 | KIRK, Thomas of Hampshire Co. Parts of real estate; rec. 12-17-1798. Wit.: Patrick Baker, Wm. Cook, Thos. Wood. | to Edward Dyer of Hampshire Co. |

| 1790 2-8 | KIZNER, Jacob (w. Hannah) of Hampshire Co. 200 a. on Cabbin Run, a branch of North R.; rec. 6-16-1791. Wit.: John Dowden, Rees Pritchard Patrick Keran. | to John Stutzman of Hampshire Co. |

| 1779 12-3 | KNOTT, John (w. Hannah) of Frederick Co. 258 a. on Alleghany Mt. Rec. 8-8-1780. Wit.: None. | to John Peter Teskin Henry Wiser Christopher Frinkle of Frederick Co. |

| 1791 12-15 | KNOTT, John (w. Betsy) of Frederick Co. 248 a. on Spring Gap Run, a drain of North R.; rec. 12-15-1791. Wit.: None. | to George Sly of Hampshire Co. |

| 1774 5-4 | KNOTT, Robert Hundred Co., New Castle, Pa. (power of atty.) Authority to sign, seal, execute and acknowledge all deeds, and conveyances, as necessary, in conveying a tract of land., 100 a. on Tear Coat Creek; rec. 3-14-1775. Wit.: Edward Keran, Bryan Keran, James Dunshaw. | to Bryan Bruin Winchester, Va. |

| 1784 3-10 | KOON, John of Hampshire Co. (lease) 162 a. on Patterson Creek; rec. 3-10-1784. Wit.: None. | to William Vause of Hampshire Co. |

| 1768 3-8 | KUYKENDALL, Abraham (w. Catherine) of Hampshire Co. (lease and release) 385 a. on South Branch; rec. 3-9-1768. Wit.: John Black John Lyne. | to Simeon Iresham (See Ahrsam) of Hampshire Co. |

| 1777 3-10 | KUYKENDALL, Abraham (w. Catherine) of Hampshire Co. (lease and release) 337 a. on South Branch; rec. 3-11-1777. Wit.: Sam Dew, Robert Stephen Nath. Kuykendall. | to Adam Harness of Hampshire Co. |

| 1777 8-28 | KUYKENDALL, Abraham (w. Catherine) of Hampshire Co. (lease and release) 125 a. on Looney's Creek; rec. 4-14-1778. Wit.: William Jennings, Ann Jennings, Mary Hass. | to Adam Harness George Harness of Hampshire Co. |

| 1778 11-7 | KUYKENDALL, Abraham Bill of sale. A negro wench named Rachel. Rec. 3-14-1781. Wit.: Sam Dew. | to John Decker |

| 1778 1-20 | KUYKENDALL, Benjamin (w. Sarah) of Yohogany Co., Va. (lease and release) 217 a. on South Branch; rec. 3-10-1778. Wit.: Wm. Buffington, John Campbell, Henry Kuykendall, Samuel Jacobs. | to Isaac Parsons of Hampshire Co. |

| 1783 11-13 | KUYKENDALL, Benjamin (w. Sarah) of Vokogania Co., Va. 400 a. on South Branch R.; rec. 11-13-1783. Wit.: Sam Dew, Andrew Wodrow. | to John Glaze of Hampshire Co. |

| 1781 9-20 | KUYKENDALL, Henry of Hampshire Co. 251 a. on South Branch; rec. 3-13-1782. Wit.: Isaac Parsons, Robt. Ferguson, Wm. McGuire. | to James Murphy of Hampshire Co. |

| 1781 9-20 | KUYKENDALL, Henry of Hampshire Co. 111 a. on South Branch; rec. 3-13-1782. Wit.: Isaac Parsons, Robt. Ferguson Wm. McGuire. | to James Murphy of Hampshire Co. |

| 1785 11-8 | KUYKENDALL, Henry of Hampshire Co. Agreement to erect a grist mill near South Branch. Rec. 11-9-1785. Wit.: Jonathan Chenoweth, Abel Crosley, David Coone. | to John Hoffman of Hampshire Co. |

| 1786 10-30 | KUYKENDALL, Henry of Hampshire Co. Parcel of land on South Branch R.; rec. 2-13-1787. Wit.: And. Wodrow Isaac Parsons, James Murphy. | to Jesse Tomlinson of Washington Co. |

| 1787 6-14 | KUYKENDALL, Henry of Hampshire Co. 448 a. on South Branch; rec. 6-14-1787. Wit.: Andrew Wodrow, Sam Dew. | to Jacob Kuykendall |

| 1792 11-15 | KUYKENDALL, Henry of Hampshire Co. (power of attorney) Authority to use legal course in collecting debts due Henry Kuykendall. Recorded 1-29-1793. Wit.: John Herndon, Wm. Jacob, James Cochran. | to Andrew Wodrow of Hampshire Co. |

| 1793 4-10 | KUYKENDALL, Henry of Hampshire Co. 266¼ a. on South Branch; rec. 4-10-1793. Wit.: None. | to John Decker of Hampshire Co. |

| 1793 4-10 | KUYKENDALL, Henry of Hampshire Co. 71 a., 23 a., on Buffalo Run; 400 on Saw Mill Run; near South Branch; rec. 4-10-1793. Wit.: None. | to John Decker of Hampshire Co. |

| 1771 2-26 | KUYKENDALL, Jacob of Hampshire Co. One negro woman named Lyd, and one child named Dine; rec. 5-14-1771. Wit.: None. | to Eve Ramsey, Wife of Andrew Ramsey of Hampshire Co. |

GRANTOR-GRANTEE PAGE 33

1773 2-19	KUYKENDALL, Jacob to Barbara Decker Kuykendall Divorce. Intermarried with James Colvin. Rec. 8-10-1773. Wit.: Sam Dew, James Sullivan.

1793 KUYKENDALL, Jacob (w. Mary) to John Decker
4-10   224 a. on South Br.; rec. 6-12-1793.
       Wit.: Isaac Miller, Isaac Parsons,
       Iared Davis, Isaac Van Meter.

1782 KUYKENDALL, John to John Kuykendall, Jr.
1-22   of Hampshire Co.   of Hampshire Co.
       250 a. on South Branch; rec. 3-12-1782.
       Wit.: Abel Crosley, John Huffman, Daniel Brown.

1786 KUYKENDALL, John to Nathaniel Kuykendall
5-8   of Hampshire Co. (mortgage)   of Hampshire Co.
       250 a. on South Branch; rec. 9-12-1786.
       Wit.: Sam Dew, Andrew Wodrow, Betty Dew.

1788 KUYKENDALL, John to Joseph Briggs
4-9   of Hampshire Co. (lease and release) of Hampshire Co.
       250 a. on South Branch; rec. 7-10-1788.
       Wit.: Sam Dew, Isaac Miller, Adam Harness,
       Frederick Claypoole.

1788 KUYKENDALL, John to Joseph Briggs
5-9   of Hampshire Co.   of Hampshire Co.
       27 a. on South Branch; rec. 7-10-1788.
       Wit.: Sam Dew, Isaac Miller,
       Adam Harness, Jeremiah Claypoole.

1791 KUYKENDALL, Nathaniel to Joseph Briggs
6-22   of Hampshire Co. (release)   of Hampshire Co.
       Parcel of land on South Branch; rec. 7-14-1791.
       Wit.: Isaac Kuykendall, George Fisher, Jacob Kuykendall.

1795 KYGER, George to Basil Brall
8-10   Freeing him from his services. a negro man
       Wit.: John Dixon, Jacob Dunkle, Geo. Kyger, Jr.

1783 KYGER, John (w. Hannah) to William Odle
8-12   of Hampshire Co.   of Hampshire Co.
       280 a. on Alleghany Mt.; rec. 8-12-1783.
       Wit.: Edward McCarty, Edward Amory.

1783 KYGER, John (w. Hannah) to William Odle
8-12   of Hampshire Co.   of Hampshire Co.
       173 a. on Alleghany Mt.; rec. 8-12-1783.
       Wit.: Edward Amory, Edward McCarty

1786 KYGER, John (w. Hannah) to Abraham Inskeep
5-15   of Hampshire Co.   of Hardy Co.
       MILLER, Michael, of Franklin Co.
       400 a. on New Creek; rec. 7-11-1786.
       Wit.: Arjalin Price, William Vause, Jemima Vause,
       Rachel Vause, Theadosia Vause.

—L—

1795 LABES, James to C. Ratien
6-16   of Frederick Co.   Nicholas Konecke
       433 a. on Little Cacapeon; rec. 7-20-1795. of Baltimore
       Wit.: And. Wodrow, John Lehow, Henry Heinzman,
       Nathan Dyer.

1795 LABES, James to Henry Schroder
6-15   of Frederick Co.   of Baltimore
       407 a. on Little Cacapeon; rec. 7-20-1795.
       Wit.: And. Wodrow, John Lehow, Henry Heinzman,
       Nathan Dyer, Henry Eckhart, Jr., E. Dyer.

1790 LACOCK, David (w. Rachel) to Joseph Garrison
9-16   of Hampshire Co.   of Hampshire Co.
       38 a. on South Branch Mountain; rec. 6-16-1791.
       Wit.: None.

LAKUE—See LaRue

1788 LAKUE, Isaac (w. Phoebe) to Jacob Starn
5-10   of Frederick Co. (lease and release) of Hampshire Co.
       209 a. on South Branch; rec. 6-12-1788.
       Wit.: Wm. Williamson, John McBride, John Starn,
       Joseph Starn, George Smith.

1788 LAKUE, Isaac (w. Phoebe) to Jacob Starn
5-10   of Frederick Co. (lease and release) of Hampshire Co.
       47 a. on South Branch; rec. 6-12-1788.
       Wit.: Wm. Williamson, John McBride, Joseph Starn,
       Joseph Starn, George Smith.

1797 LAME, Daniel (w. Elizabeth) to Jesse Edwards
11-12 of Hampshire Co.   Mason Co., Ky.
       200 a. on Branch Mt.; rec. 2-19-1797.
       Wit.: John Timbrook, Isaac Newman, Christopher Newman.

1793 LANDER, Henry (w. Hannah) to Andrew Millslagle
2-26   of Hampshire Co.   of Hampshire Co.
       121 a. on North R. of Cacapeon; rec. 2-26-1793.
       Wit.: None.

1794 LANDER, Henry (w. Hannah) to John Peters
4-9   of Hampshire Co.   of Loudon Co.
       294 a. on Tear Coat Creek; rec. 4-9-1794.
       Wit.: None.

1791 LANDER, John (w. Sarah) to John Chenoweth
9-15   of Hampshire Co.   of Hampshire Co.
       284 a. on Potomac River; rec. 9-15-1791.
       Wit.: None.

1783 LANDERS, Michael (w. Jane) to Jacob Neale
8-13   of Hampshire Co.   of Hampshire Co.
       90 a. on New Creek; rec. 8-13-1783.
       Wit.: John Forman, John Lewis, Alex Gibboney.

1784 LANDERS, Michael (w. Jane) to William Janney
3-9   of Hampshire Co.   of Hampshire Co.
       NEAL, Jacob (w. Nancy) of Hampshire Co.
       400 a. on New Creek; rec. 3-9-1784.
       Wit.: None.

1783 LANDERS, Michael (w. Jane) to Aaron Royce
8-13   of Hampshire Co.   of Hampshire Co.
       168 a. on North Branch of Potomac; rec. 8-13-1783.
       Wit.: John Forman, John Lewis, Alex Gibboney.

1771 LANE, William (w. Ann) to Garret Vanmeter
9-13   of Hampshire Co. (lease and release) of Hampshire Co.
       209 a. on South Branch; rec. 11-12-1771.
       Wit.: Abraham Hite, T. B. Bowen, T. Hite,
       John Sibly, Abraham Hite, Jr., James Gellisen.

1775 LANGE, Godfrey to John Foreman
4-1   Bill of sale.   of Hampshire Co.
       Personal property (hogs, table, etc.); rec. 8-8-1775.
       Wit.: Enoch Berry.

1772 LANSISCUS, Henry to Valentine Power
12-16 of Augusta Co., Va. (lease and release) of Hampshire Co.
       500 a. on South Branch; rec. 3-9-1773
       Wit.: Joseph Keavill, Wm. Welton, John Reid.

1794 LAPP, George (w. Christiana) to John J. Jacob
6-12   of Allegany Co.   of Hampshire Co.
       76 a. in Hampshire Co.
       Wit.: Gabriel Jacob, James Prather.

1788 LARGENT, James (w. Margaret) to John Copsey
4-9   of Hampshire Co. (lease and release) of Hampshire Co.
       146 a. on North River; rec. 4-10-1788.
       Wit.: None.

1799 LARGENT, James (w. Margaret) to John Chenoweth
12-17 of Hampshire Co.   of Hampshire Co.
       9½ a. on Cacapeon River; rec. 4-14-1791.
       Wit.: John Slane, Joseph Yates, John Hawkins.

1791 LARGENT, James (w. Margaret) to James Hiett
2-27   of Hampshire Co.   of Hampshire Co.
       233 a. on mouth of Mill Run; rec. 4-14-1791.
       Wit.: John Slane, Daniel Slane, James Candy.

1796 LARGENT, James (w. Margaret) to Daniel Loy
6-20   of Hampshire Co.   of Hampshire Co.
       102 a. on Sandy Lick Branch; rec. 6-20-1796.
       Wit.: Arjalon Price, John Pancake, John Pancake.

1798 LARGENT, James (w. Margaret) to Anne Slane
4-10   of Hampshire Co.   Thomas Slane
       280 a. Hampshire Co.; rec. 4-16-1798. Benjamin Slane
       Wit.: William Cuthbert, John Thomas, James Slane
       Elias Poston.

LA RUE—See Lakue.

1773 LA RUE, Jacob to Jacob Locke
1-3   of Frederick Co. (lease and release) of Hampshire Co.
       72 a. on Cacapeon; rec. 11-9-1773.
       Wit.: John LaRue, Joseph Carman, Richard Hutchings,
       Samuel Larew

1792 LARUE, Isaac to Thomas Johnson, Jr.
11-5   34 a. on Great Cacapeon; rec. 1-29-1793. Hampshire Co.
       Wit.: Geo. Whiteberry, Levi Matthew, Elijah Johnson,
       Peter Larue, Isaac Larue, Abraham Larue.

1791 LARUE, John (w. Hannah) to Noah Larue
10-13 of Hampshire Co.   of Hampshire Co.
       19 a. on Great Cacapeon; rec. 10-13-1791.
       Wit.: None.
       DEDIMUS: Authority to William Fox, James Monroe, John
       Mitchell, Virgil Meckrakin, to go and examine Hannah Larue
       privately, to see if she is willing to execute the deed mentioned
       before (she not being able to travel to the court house).

1779 LAREW, John to William Jackson
1-6   of Frederick Co.   of Hampshire Co.
       137 a. on Cacapeon River; rec. 8-10-1779.
       Wit.: Thomas Bowel, John Constant,
       George Tarvin, Thomas Morgan, John Constant.

1778 LAUBINGER, George Michael to Martin Roller
4-7   (w. Barbara)   of Dunmore Co.
       of Frederick Co. (lease and release)
       800 a. on Cacapeon River; rec. 5-12-1778.
       Wit.: John Magill, Wm. Campbell, George Rootes.

1785 LAWRENCE, Michael to Christopher Fry
10-4   of Hampshire Co. (lease)   of Winchester, Va.
       80 a. on Great Cacapeon.
       Wit.: John Magill, J. Peyton, Robt. White, Jr.

1789 LAWSON, James (w. Sophia) to John Wagoner
4-4   of Hampshire Co.   of Hampshire Co.
       400 a. on Patterson Creek; rec. 4-4-1789.
       Wit.: John Mitchell, James Daugherty, Christian Museluman.

1789 LAWSON, James (w. Sophia) to John Wagoner
4-4   of Hampshire Co. (dedimus)   of Hampshire Co.
       400 a. on Patterson Creek; rec. 4-16-1789.
       Wit.: None.

1797 LAWSON, Thomas to 2 negroes, Monday and Clem
10-29 Free from his services forever; rec. 2-16-1796.
       Wit.: John Newman, Margaret Newman.

1796 6-20	**LEASONBY, Thos. (w. Elizabeth)** to **Archibald Watts** of Hampshire Co. of Hampshire Co. 117 a. in Hampshire Co.; rec. 6-20-1796. Wit.: None.	
1796 6-20	**LEASENBY, Thos. (w. Elizabeth)** to **Archibald Watts** of Hampshire Co. of Hampshire Co. 50 a. on South Branch River; rec. 6-20-1796. Wit.: None.	
1798 4-16	**LEAZENBY, Thos. (w. Elizabeth)** to **Archibald Watts** of Hampshire Co. of Hampshire Co. 50 a. in Hampshire Co.; rec. 4-16-1798. Wit.: None.	
1780 8-4	**LEAVER, Nicholas, Sr.** to **John Ravenscraft** (Seaver?) of Hampshire Co. of Hampshire Co. 200 a. on North Branch; rec. 8-8-1780. Wit.: None.	
1796 4-18	**LEAVERS, Nicholas (w. Elizabeth)** to **Edward McCarty** (Seaver) of Hampshire Co. of Hampshire Co. 27 a. on North Br. R. of Potomac; rec. 6-20-1796. Wit.: None.	
1798 8-13	**LEE (or See), Richard Bland** to **William Vallandghom** of Fairfax Co. of Fairfax Co. 226 a. on North River; rec. 10-15-1798. Wit.: None.	
1798 10-11	**LEE, Solomon (w. Nancy)** to **John McBride** of Hampshire Co. 268a. on Patterson Creek; rec. 10-15-1798. Wit.: John Mitchell, Henry Protzman, John Lewis, John McMeekin.	
1794 9-15	**LEESON, Richard (w. Elizabeth)** to **Solomon Lee** of Hampshire Co. of Hampshire Co. 268 a. on Patterson Creek; rec. 10-15-1794. Wit.: Arjalin Price, Okey Johnson, Wm. Hoddy, Thos. Carder.	
1794 10-18	**LEASON, Thomas (Leeson)** to **Margaret** Deed of emancipation; free from a negro woman his service; rec. 12-10-1794. Wit.: Daniel Jones, Israel Stallcup.	
1800	**LEMMONEIRS, Alex Lewis** to **James Dailey** **LEMMONIERS, Lewis Victor** **LEMMONIERS, Valentine Louisa** See HOWARD (HONORE?), Francis Maurice	
1773 5-25	**LEONARD, Enoch (w. Phoebe)** to **John Carlyle** of Berkeley Co. **John Dalton** Lease and release. of Alexandria 150 a. on South Branch; rec. 11-9-1773. Wit.: Wm. Little, Ronald Roy, Charles Murray, Alexander Burnett, John Magill, Bryan Bruin, Wm. Campbell, Alex White.	
1798 6-11	**LEVIN, John (w. Jane)** to **Abraham Vanorsdel** of Mason Co., Ky. **Cornelius Vanorsdel** Parcel of land, 514 a., in Hampshire Co. Hampshire Co. Rec. 9-17-1798. Wit.: None.	
1771 5-8	**LEWIS, John** to **Samuel Pritchard** of Hampshire Co. Request for Sam Pritchard to make deed to his son, Thomas Lewis. Recorded 5-14-1771. Wit.: John Wood, Samuel McHenry, Thomas Denton.	
1774 5-3	**LEWIS, John** to **Simon Doyle** of Hampshire Co. (mortgage) of Hampshire Co. Two negro men and one woman, named James, Henry and Rebecca; personal property. Recorded 8-9-1774. Wit.: Ezekiel Totten, Wm. Barber Lewis.	
1782 5-28	**LEWIS, John** to **Wm. Barber Lewis** of Hampshire Co. (power of attorney) of Hampshire Co. Authority to collect sums of money or anything owing to him. Rec. 9-10-1782. Wit.: Samuel Lewis, John Lenox, John H. Price.	
1782 6-1	**LEWIS, John** to **William Harding** of Hampshire Co. (power of attorney) Northumberland Co. Authority to collect all money, slaves, lands and whatever owing to John Lewis. Recorded 11-13-1782. Wit.: None.	
1785 11-8	**LEWIS, John (w. Hannah)** to **George Harness** of Hampshire Co. of Hampshire Co. 456 a. on Patterson Creek; rec. 11-8-1785. Wit.: None.	
1787 8-16	**LEWIS, John** to **George Miller** Eldest son of Fielding Lewis, deceased, Hampshire Co. Fredericksburg Party of third part MERCER, James, of Fredericksburg 260 a. on Patterson Creek; rec. 12-10-1789. Wit.: Abraham Johnson, Jr., Isaac Parsons, Isaac Means, Andrew Wodrow.	
1790 3-1	**LEWIS, John** to **Wm. Barber Lewis** of Hampshire Co. (power of attorney) of Hampshire Co. Authority to collect in any way what is due John Lewis. Recorded 10-11-1790. Wit.: John Lewis, Jr., Samuel Lewis, Samuel Harding Lewis, Andrew Wodrow, John Herndon.	
1790 3-8	**LEWIS, John (w. Hannah)** to **Adam Hider** of Hampshire Co. (lease) of Hampshire Co. 625 a. on Patterson Creek; rec. 9-16-1790. Wit.: I. Wheeler, Arjalon Price, John H. Price, George Hill.	
1771 5-14	**LEWIS, Thomas** to **Samuel Pritchard** of Frederick Co. (lease and release) of Hampshire Co. 206 a. on Lost River of Cacapeon; rec. 5-15-1771. Wit.: None.	
1773 3-29	**LEWIS, Thomas** to **Samuel Pritchard** of Hampshire Co. (lease and release) of Hampshire Co. 206 a. on Lost River; rec. 3-9-1774. Wit.: John Wood, Robert Wood, Thomas Campbell, Bryan Bruin, Thomas Wood, Achibald Foster.	
1787 4-12	**LIGHTER, Henry** to **James Fleming** of Hampshire Co. of Hampshire Co. 32 a. on Patterson Creek; rec. 8-13-1787. Wit.: None.	
1793 4-10	**LIGHTER, Henry (w. Catherine)** to **Samuel Thomas** of Hampshire Co. (see Litner) of Frederick Co. 61½ a. on Beaver Run; rec. 4-10-1793. Wit.: None.	
1793 4-10	**LIGHTER, Henry (w. Catherine)** to **Samuel Thomas** of Hampshire Co. of Frederick Co. 192 a. on Patterson Creek; rec. 4-10-1793. Wit.: None.	
1793 4-10	**LIGHTER, Henry (w. Catherine)** to **Samuel Thomas** of Hampshire Co. of Frederick Co. 361¾ a. on Beaver Run; rec. 4-10-1793. Wit.: None.	
1798 2-9	**LIGHTOR, Henry** to **Samuel Thomas** of Kentucky of Hampshire Co. 15 a. on Beaver Run; rec. 4-16-1798. Wit.: None.	
1779 9-20	**LIGGATE, Alexander** to **Jacob May** of Hampshire Co. (lease) of Hampshire Co. 175 a. on South Branch; rec. 8-13-1782. Wit.: R. Maxwell Adam Fisher, Nicholas Mace.	
1779 9-13	**LIGGET, Alexander,** to **Michael Hahn** of Hampshire Co. of Hampshire Co. 175 a. on South Branch; rec. 8-13-1782. Wit.: R. Maxwell, Robt. Cunningham, Jesse Cunningham.	
1779 9-20	**LIGGET, Alexander** to **Nicholas Mace** of Hampshire Co. of Hampshire Co. 32 a. on South Branch; rec. 8-13-1782. Wit.: R. Maxwell, Adam Fisher, Jacob May.	
1766 11-10	**LINCH, Charles (w. Nelle)** to **Joseph Ogden** of Hampshire Co. (lease and release) **Josiah Hews** 229 a. on Pattersons Creek; rec. 11-11-1766. of Philadelphia Wit.: Sam Dew.	
1766 11-10	**LINCH, Charles (w. Mille)** to **Joseph Ogden** of Hampshire Co. (lease and release) **Josiah Hews** 154 a. on New Creek Mt.; rec. 11-11-1766. of Philadelphia Wit.: Sam Dew.	
1763 10-8	**LINDSEY, Edmond** to **Thomas Speake** of Frederick Co. (lease and release) of Frederick Co. 108 a. on Little Ca Capehon; rec. 10-12-1763. Wit.: Ja. Keith, Pet. Hog, Gabriel Jones.	
1788 10-20	**LINDSEY, James** to **James Patterson** of Hampshire Co. (lease and release) of Hampshire Co. 250 a. in Hampshire Co.; rec. 2-12-1789. Wit.: John Starn, Joseph Starn, Jacob Starn.	
1762 11-4	**LINDSEY, John** to **Humphrey Wells** of Frederick Co. (lease and release) of Hampshire Co. 400 a. on New Creek; rec. 11-4-1762. Wit.: Ja. Keith, Gabriel Jones, Pet. Hog.	
1763 12-11	**LINDSEY, John (w. Alice)** to **Bryan Bruin** of Frederick Co. (lease and release) of Winchester, Va. 264 a. on Little Ca Capehon; recorded 2-15-1764. Wit.: Ja. Keith, Gabriel Jones, Pet. Hog.	
1763 12-11	**LINDSEY, John (w. Alice)** to **Bryan Bruin** of Frederick Co. (lease and release) of Winchester, Va. 195 a. on Great Ca Capehon; rec. 2-15-1764. Wit.: Ja. Keith, Gabriel Jones, Pet. Hog.	
1791 9-14	**LINEGAR, William (w. Hester)** to **Alexander Brown** of Hampshire Co. of Frederick Co. 223 a. on North River; rec. 9-15-1791. Wit.: Rees Pritchard, Wm. Neill.	
1790 1-9	**LINTON, William** to **John Williams** of Hampshire Co. ((mortgage) of Hampshire Co. 232 a. on South Branch; rec. 6-10-1790. Wit.: And. Wodrow, Peter Williams, John Hansbrough.	
1796 4-18	**LINTON, William (w. Mary)** to **John Pancake, Jr.** of Hampshire Co. of Hampshire Co. 232 a. on South Branch River; rec. 4-18-1796. Wit.: None.	
1798 10-3	**LINTON, William (w. Mary)** to **Peter Williams** 413 a. on the South Branch; rec. 10-15-1798. Wit.: None.	
1798 10-10	**LINTON, William (w. Mary)** to **Peter Williams** 450 a. on South Branch River; rec. 10-18-1798. Wit.: None.	

1798 10-10	**LINTON, William** (w. Mary) **to Peter Williams** 150 a. in Hampshire Co.; rec. 10-15-1798. Wit.: None.		1762 5-11	**LONG, Christian** (w. Elizabeth **to John Reno** of Carlyle Co., Pa. (lease and release) of Hampshire Co. 160 a., Pattersons Creek; rec. 5-12-1762. Wit.: Tho. Wood, Benj. Kuykendall, Charles Seaver. DEDIMUS: Writing of authority from Gabriel Jones, Clerk of County Court of Hampshire County, to Benjamin Kuykendall, Jonathan Heath and Robert Parker, to determine if Elizabeth Long, wife of Christian Long, willingly sign the deed.
1790 6-10	**LITNER, Henry** (w. Catherine) **to Joseph Clisher** (See Lighter) of Hampshire Co. of Hampshire Co. 100 a. on Beaver Run; rec. 6-10-1790. Wit.: None.			
1790 6-10	**LITNER, Henry** (w. Catherine) **to John Huffman** of Hampshire Co. of Hampshire Co. 100 a. on Beaver Run; rec. 6-10-1790. Wit.: None.		1782 7-14	**LONG, Jacob** **to Andrew Glaze** of Hampshire Co. of Hampshire Co. 158 a. on South Branch; rec. 8-13-1782. Wit.: Sam Dew.
1783 6-2	**LITTLE, Job** **to John Denham** of Hampshire Co. of Hampshire Co. 60 a. on South Branch River; rec. 8-12-1783. Wit.: Abraham Clark, Andrew Wodrow, John Wilson.		1797 4-5	**LONG, Pompey** **to Benjamin Bellford** of Hardy Co. of Hampshire Co. Half acre in Romney; rec. 4-17-1797. Wit.: Andrew Wodrow, Eli Davis, John Jack.
1783 12-24	**LITTLE, Michael** **to John Shobe** of Hampshire Co. of Hampshire Co. 282 a. on North Branch of Potomac; rec. 3-9-1784. Wit.: Patrick Oryley, Job Bacorn, Jacob Kimberline.		1792 10-12	**LOVE, Neilson** **to Andrew Wodrow** NEILSON, Isabel (power of attorney) of Hampshire Co. Glasglow, Eng. Authority to sell all lands and lots belonging to Isabel Neilson and Nielson Love. Recorded 9-11-1793. Wit.: John Maxwell, John Maxwell, Jr., Wm. Wingat.
1794 4-9	**LITTLER, Thomas** (w. Magdalene) **to Nicholas Casey** of Hardy Co. of Hampshire Co. 94 a. on North River; rec. 4-9-1794. Wit.: None.		1792 10-12	**LOVE, Neilson** **to Andrew Wodrow** NEILSON, Isabel of Hampshire Co. Glasglow, Eng. 314 a., 250 a., on North River; 114 a. on Great Cacapeon; 388 a. on Middle Ridge. Recorded 9-11-1793. Wit.: John Maxwell, John Maxwell, Jr., Wm. Wingat.
1767 9-7	**LIVINGSTON, James** **to Enoch Innis** of Frederick Co., Md. (power of atty.) of Hampshire Co. Power to sell land in Virginia and Pennsylvania. Rec. 3-9-1768. Wit.: David Cox, John Nicholas, Jonathan Hammar, Thos. Spencer, Joseph Tomblinson, Jr., John Pierpoint.			
			1799 2-16	**LOY, Daniel** (w. Christiana) **to John Loy** of Hampshire Co. of Hampshire Co. 5 a. on Cacapeon River; rec. 2-18-1799. Wit.: Wm. McPherson, Geo. Barker, John Thomas.
1768 9-12	**LIVINGSTON, James** **to Daniel Cresap** of Frederick Co., Md. (lease & release) Frederick Co., Md. 158 a. on North Branch of Potomac; rec. 9-13-1768. Wit.: Bryan Bruen, W. Hancher, John Lyne, John Keating.		1799 2-16	**LOY, Daniel** (w. Christiana) **to John Loy** of Hampshire Co. of Hampshire Co. 169½ a. on Cacapeon River; rec. 2-18-1799. Wit.: Wm. McPherson, Geo. Barker, John Thomas.
1771	**LIVINGSTON, Mayor James** **to Peter Hog** See GREENFIELD, John McDONALD, Augus WHITE, Alexander		1795 3-1	**LUPTON, Isaac** (w. Elizabeth) **to Asa Lupton** of Hampshire Co. of Hampshire Co. 226 a. on Dillon's Run; rec. 4-20-1795. Wit.: Thos. Hughs, James George, Richard Barrett.
1767	**LIVINGSTON, John** **to Isaac Cox** See GREENFIELD, John		1795 1-19	**LUPTON, John** (w. Ann) **to Ellis George** of Frederick Co. of Hampshire Co. 286 a. on Dillon's Run; rec. 4-20-1795. Wit.: Richard Barrett, James George Joshua Lupton.
1781	**LIVINGSTON, John** **to Francis Perpoint** See INNIS, Enoch		1764 8-31	**LYNCH, Charles** (see Linch) **to Mathias Bush** of Hampshire Co. (mortgage) of Philadelphia, Pa. 112 a., Pattersons Creek, 165 a., South Branch, 2 more tracts on South Branch; rec. 12-12-1764. Wit.: Ja. Keith, Bryan Bruin, Edward McGuire.
1793 12-2	**LNICK, Benjamin** (Lynch?) **to William Linton** LNICK, Monaca of Hampshire Co. of Hampshire Co. 150 a. in Hampshire Co.; rec. 7-9-1794. Wit.: John Mitchell, Alex King, John Kimberline, John Adams.		1773 3-15	**LYNCH, Charles** **to Abraham Hite** of Hampshire Co. (power of atty.) of Hampshire Co. (Atty.) Authority to lease for three years a tract of land, 116 a., on South Branch. Recorded 11-9-1773. Wit.: Daniel McNeill, John Reid, John Westfall.
1795 9-14	**LOCK, Abraham** **to Jacob Zailor** of Washington Co. of Berkeley Co. 72 a. on Cacapeon River; rec. 12-14-1795. Wit.: John Bailey, Thos. Bailey, Michael Widmeyer, Charles Yost.		1779 2-11	**LYNCH, Charles** (w. Mille) **to Daniel McNeal** of Hampshire Co. of Hampshire Co. 116 a., Lot No. 23, on South Branch; rec. 3-9-1779. Wit.: None.
1772 11-11	**LOCKHART, John** **to William Stewart** Bill of sale. of Hampshire Co. 52 bushels Indian corn, fodder in a log house, 6 acres wheat and rye, 1 turnip patch, 1 churn, 1 linen wheel, etc. (paid 15 pounds). Recorded 3-9-1773. Wit.: Wm. Carlyle, Aaron Royse.		1780 11-14	**LYNCH, Charles** (w. Milly) **to John Plumb** of Hampshire Co. of Hampshire Co. 112 a., on Patterson Creek; rec. 10-4-1781. Wit.: Andrew Wodrow, Abraham Hite, Abraham Johnson.
1794 2-12	**LOCKHART, Robert** **to John Myers** of Frederick Co. of Hampshire Co. 10 a. on Hogg Run; rec. 6-11-1794. Wit.: And. Wodrow, Geo. Beall, Henry Heinzman, John Pierce.		1781 10-4	**LYNCH, Charles** (w. Milly) **to Joseph Ogden** of Hampshire Co. Josiah Hughs 116 a. on Patterson Creek; rec. 11-13-1781. Wit.: Andrew Wodrow, Abel Randall, Michael Stump.
1796 10-6	**LOCKHART, Robert** **to William Lanford** of Frederick Co. (lease) of Hampshire Co. 227 a. on Mill Creek; rec. 12-19-1796. Wit.: John Brown, Abel Seymour, Arch. Magill, Alex. White, Eli Davis, And. Wodrow.		1785 8-16	**LYNCH, Charles** (w. Milley) **to Andrew Wodrow** of Hampshire Co. of Hampshire Co. 317 a. on Cornwell's Run; rec. 11-9-1785. Wit.: Henry Marrs, Alex Randall, Jonathan Heath, Abel Randall, Peter Higgins, Moses Hutton, Jacob Yoakum.
1797 1-1	**LOCKHART, Robert** **to George Hill** of Frederick Co. (lease) of Hampshire Co. 233 2/3 a. on Patterson Creek; rec. 7-16-1798. Wit.: And. Wodrow, John McMeekin, Matthew Lodge, Henry Hardy.		1785 8-16	**LYNCH, Charles** (w. Milley) **to Andrew Wodrow** of Hampshire Co. of Hampshire Co. 212 a. on South Branch; rec. 11-9-1785. Wit.: Henry Marrs, Alex Randall, Jonathan Heath, Abel Randall, Peter Higgins, Moses Hutton, Jacob Yoakum.
1798 1-1	**LOCKHART, Robert** **to Thomas Jaco** of Frederick Co. (lease) of Hampshire Co. 188 a. on Patterson Creek; rec. 7-16-1798. Wit.: And. Wodrow, John McMeekin, Matthew Lodge, Henry Hardey.		1793 10-12	**LYONS, Joseph** (w. Mary) **to Elias Browning** of Hampshire Co. Stephin Lewis 336 a. on Allegany Mt.; rec. 6-11-1794. Wit.: Sol. Ravenscroft, Lewis Vandiver, J. G. Wheeler, John Ravenscroft.
1789 11-14	**LOCKWOOD, William** **to Aquila Johns** of Hampshire Co. (bill of sale) Baltimore Co. One negro woman named Cloe, one negro girl named Sharlat, and one negro boy named James; livestock and household goods. Recorded 12-10-1789. Wit.: John Pritchard, Christopher Wagner.		1786 1-9	**LYON, Mary,** relict of **William Lyon** **Certificate** deceased, who was a private in the 7th Virginia Regiment, and killed in the service of the Continent, is entitled to the sum of 18 pounds yearly. Recorded 4-13-1787. Wit.: None.
1799 12-16	**LOGAN, John** (w. Elizabeth) **to John Claton** of Hampshire Co. of Hampshire Co. Lot in town of Springfield; rec. 1-20-1800. Wit.: William Donaldson, William Parks, George Fouty.			

—M—

1799 9-16	**McALLISTER, James** (w. Sarah) **to George Crock** of Hampshire Co. of Hampshire Co. 96 a. on road from Romney to Winchester; rec. 9-16-1799. Wit.: John Mitchell, John Jones, Benoni Peirce, James O'Hara, David Jones.
1761 3-25	**LONG, Christian** (w. Elizabeth) **to John Reno** of Hampshire Co. (lease and release) of Hampshire Co. Lot No. 2, 203 a., Pattersons Creek; rec. 6-9-1761. Wit.: Benj. Kuykendall, Benjamin Parker, Isaac Green, William Reno.
1761	**McBRIDE, Francis** **Deed of Partition** See DENTON, Robert

1761 2-9	McBRIDE, Francis (w. Mary) of Augusta Co. (lease and release) 270 a. near Frederick Co. line, known as Three Springs. Rec. 2-11-1761. Wit.: Gabriel Jones.	to William Kinsley of Hampshire Co.
1761 2-9	McBRIDE, Francis (w. Mary) of Augusta Co. (lease and release) 386 a. on Lost River; rec. 2-11-1761. Wit.: Gabriel Jones.	to Isaac Chrisman of Hampshire Co.
1761 2-9	McBRIDE, Francis (w. Mary) of Augusta Co. (lease and release) 385 a. on Lost River; rec. 2-11-1761. Wit.: Gabriel Jones.	to William Smith of Hampshire Co.
1761 2-9	McBRIDE, Francis (w. Mary) of Augusta Co. (lease and release) 122 a. on Lost River; rec. 2-11-1761. Wit.: Gabriel Jones.	to John Claypole of Hampshire Co.
1761 5-2	McBRIDE, Francis (w. Mary) of Augusta Co. (lease and release) 330 a. on Lost River; rec. 6-9-1761. Wit.: James Claypole, Jr., James Thomas, Nathaniel Baley, John Dunbar.	to Jacob Gum of Hampshire Co.
1786 3-14	McBRIDE, James (w. Sarah) of Hampshire Co. 329 a. on Spring Gap Mt.; rec. 3-14-1786. Wit.: Rees Pritchard, Jacob Hubbard.	to Henry Davis of Frederick Co.
1796 9-19	McBRIDE, James of Hampshire Co. 104 a. on Bear Garden Mt.; rec. 9-19-1796. Wit.: None.	to William Carlyle of Hampshire Co.
1794 12-10	McBRIDE, John of Hampshire Co. Quarter acre in town of Springfield; rec. 12-10-1794. Wit.: None.	to John Roberts of Fauquier Co.
1799 12-25	McBRIDE, John (w. Elizabeth) of Hampshire Co. Recorded 4-14-1800.	to John Mollison of Hampshire Co.
1796 6-23	McCARROLL, Thomas of Green Co., S. C. 174 a. on South Branch; rec. 2-20-1797. Wit.: Isaac Cloud, Jas. Scott, Andrew Wells.	to Reese Pritchard of Hampshire Co.
1788 3-14	McCARTNEY, John of Hampshire Co. (mortgage) 200 a. on South Branch; rec. 7-10-1788. Wit.: Timothy Corn, Sam Dew, John Marby.	to Perez Drew of Romney
1800 9-15	McCARTNEY, —— of Hampshire Co. Recorded 9-15-1800. Wit.: John McCartney.	to John Newman of Hampshire Co.
1796 6-20	McCARTY, Edward (w. Elizabeth) of Hampshire Co. Half acre in Romney; rec. 6-20-1796. Wit.: None.	to Perez Drew of Hampshire Co.
1798 12-15	McCARTY, Edward of Hampshire Co. 200 a. on New Creek; rec. 12-17-1798. Wit.: None.	to James Dall Samuel McKean John Pleasants of Baltimore, Md.
1798 12-15	McCARTY, Edward of Hampshire Co. 106 a. on New Creek; rec. 12-17-1798. Wit.: None.	to James Dall Samuel McKean John Pleasants of Baltimore, Md.
1798 12-17	McCARTY, Edward of Hampshire Co. 100 a., 25 a., in Hampshire Co.; rec.12-17-1798. Wit.: Andrew Wodrow	to James Dall Samuel McKean John Pleasants of Baltimore, Md.
1766 8-9	McCULLOCH, John of Hampshire Co. (mortgage) 450 a., So. Branch, and one negro slave named Berry. Rec. 4-15-1767. Wit.: Felix Seymour, Peter Hog.	to George Wilson of Hampshire Co.
1788 12-23	McCULLOUGH, John Mortgage. Livestock; rec. 4-17-1789. Wit.: William Jacob, Gabriel Jacob.	to Nathan Gregg Thomas Gregg of Washington Co.
1768 9-14	McCOLLOUGH, George McCOLLOUGH, John of Hampshire Co. (bill of sale) 400 a. on South Branch; rec. 11-8-1768. Wit.: Chas. Linch, Philip Ross, G. Jones.	to Abraham White Garret Vanmetere of Hampshire Co.
1769 ?-6	McCRACKEN, Jane McCRACKEN, Margaret RUTHERFORD, Benjamin (w. Elizabeth) WORTHINGTON, Robert (w. Ann) of Frederick Co., Va. 306 a., Patterson's Creek; rec. 3-14-1769. Wit.: Ja. Keith, Edward McGuire, Alex White, Pet. Hog.	to John Harden of Hampshire Co.
1768	McCRACKEN, Margaret RUTHERFORD, Benjamin (w. Elizabeth) WORTHINGTON, Robert (w. Ann) of Frederick Co. (lease and release) 201 a., 306 a., Pattersons Creek; rec. 3-8-1768. Wit.: Ja. Keith, Enoch Innis, Rich'd Hougland, Job Pearsall.	to John Hardin of Hampshire Co.
1793 11-18	McCRAKIN, Seneca of Woodford Co., Ky. 69 a. on Potomac River; rec. 4-9-1794. Wit.: John Higgins, Virgil McCrakin, John Weatherinton.	to Ovid McCrakin of Allegany Co.
1799 11-10	McCRACKIN, Virgil of Hampshire Co. Freeing slave; recorded 9-15-1800. Wit.: John Newman, James McGarrety.	to a slave, Frank
1793 10-9	McDEVIT, James (w. Mary) of Hardy Co. 60 a., Hampshire Co.; rec. 10-9-1793. Wit.: None.	to Samuel Jones of Hampshire Co.
1771	McDONALD, ANGUS, Executor See GREENFIELD, John LIVINGSTON, Mayor James WHITE, Alexander	to Peter Hog
1776 7-13	McDONALD, Angus WHITE, Alexander, (Executors of John Greenfield) Winchester, Va. 425 a. on Little Cacapeon; rec. 5-9-1781. Wit.: Wm. Campbell, John Parrill, James Walker, Patrick Kirks.	to Bryan Bruin of Winchester, Va.
1800 9-12	McDONALD, Angus (w. Anne) of Hampshire Co. Recorded 9-16-1800. Wit.: Joseph Flora, Archibald Flora, Margaret Flora.	to Francis White of Hampshire Co.
1796 4-16	McDONALD, Daniel of Hampshire Co. Parcel of land in Hampshire Co.; rec. 4-18-1796. Wit.: Jas. Martin, John Critton, Wm. Young.	to George McDonald of Hampshire Co.
1795 9-14	McDONALD, Donald (w. Hannah) of Hampshire Co. Quarter acre in Springfield; rec. 10-19-1795. Wit.: None.	to John Dailey of Hampshire Co.
1779 5-10	McDONALD, John (w. Elizabeth) of Hampshire Co. ((lease and release) 225 a. on Great Cacapeon; rec. 5-11-1779. Wit.: Levi Ashbrook, Jacob Pugh, Valentine Switzer.	to Nicholas Swisher of Loudon Co.
1796 11-13	McDONALD, John (w. Elizabeth) of Hampshire Co. (bill of sale) 91 a. on Little Cacapeon; rec. 12-19-1796. Wit.: None.	to Wm. Williamson of Hampshire Co.
1797 10-12	McDONALD, John (w. Elizabeth) of Hampshire Co. 191 a. on Little Cacapeon; rec. 10-16-1797. Wit.: John Hansbrough, William Linton, John Jack, John Jacob, Jr.	to Andrew Wodrow of Hampshire Co.
1798 10-10	McDONALD, Peter (w. Jemima) 100 a. on Middle Ridge; rec. 10-15-1798. Wit.: None.	to Peter Williams
1774 4-11	McGLOUHGLAN, Daniel (w. Anne) Hampshire Co. (see McLoughlin) (lease & rel.) 134 a. on Little Cacapeon Creek. Wit.: Sam Dew.	to John Royse Hampshire Co.
1764 6-5	McGUIRE, Edward (w. Susannah) of Frederick Co. (mortgage) Lot No. 49—346; rec. 12-12-1764. Wit.: Ja. Keith, Bryan Bruin, Luke Collins, Thom. Dent, John Lagabede.	to Richard Parker of Philadelphia, Pa.
1764 7-25	McGUIRE, Edward (w. Susannah) Mortgage. 393a., 100 a., 200 a., 352 a., Mill Creek; rec. 12-12-1764. Wit.: Ja. Keith, Luke Collins, Bryan Bruin, Thom. Dent.	to Mathias Bush of Philadelphia, Pa.
1765 10-1	McGUIRE, Edward (w. Susannah) of Frederick Co. (mortgage) 403 a., 85 a., on Pattersons Creek; rec. 10-8-1765. Wit.: Gabriel Jones, Ja. Keith, Alex White.	to William Ball of Philadelphia, Pa.
1774 5-6	McGUIRE, Edward of Winchester, Va. 393 a., 100 a., 200 a., on Patterson Creek; 352 a. on Mill Creek; rec. 5-10-1774. Wit.: Peter Hog, Gabriel Jones, George Rootes, D. Reno.	to Matthias Bush of Philadelphia, Pa.
1777 5-12	McGUIRE, Edward (w. Melicent) of Winchester, Va. (lease and release) 346 a. on South Branch; rec. 5-13-1777. Wit.: John Magill, Charles Lynch, Andrew Turk.	to Conrad Glaze of Hampshire Co.
1777 5-13	McGUIRE, Edward (w. Melicent) of Winchester, Va. 346 a. on South Branch R.; rec. 8-12-1777. Wit.: None.	to Conrad Glaze of Hampshire Co.
1779 8-7	McGUIRE, Edward of Winchester, Va. (lease and release) 307 a. on Patterson Creek; rec. 8-10-1779. Wit.: John Magill, Bryan Bruin, James Walker.	to Job Bacorn of Hampshire Co.

GRANTOR-GRANTEE — PAGE 37

1791 McGUIRE, Edward (w. Millicent) to **Daniel Jones**
3-16 of Winchester, Va. (lease and release) of Hampshire Co.
400 a. on Patterson Creek; rec. 4-14-1791.
Wit.: John Keller, John Reed, Alex King.

1791 McGUIRE, Edward (w. Millicent) to **Aaron Jones**
3-16 of Winchester, Va. (lease and release) of Hampshire Co.
400 a. on Patterson Creek; rec. 4-14-1791.
Wit.: John Keller, John Reed, Alex King.

1791 McGUIRE, Edward (w. Millicent) to **David Jones**
3-16 of Winchester, Va. (lease and release) of Hampshire Co.
400 a. on Patterson Creek; rec. 4-14-1791.
Wit.: John Keller, John Reed, Alex King.

1791 McGUIRE, Edward (w. Millicent) to **Abraham Jones**
3-16 of Winchester, Va. (lease and release) of Hampshire Co.
421 a. on Patterson Creek; rec. 4-14-1791.
Wit.: John Keller, John Reed, Alex King.

1797 McGUIRE, Edward (w. Mellicent) to **James Meekins**
10-8 of Frederick Co. of Hampshire Co.
400 a. on Little Cacapeon River; rec. 5-14-1798.
Wit.: None.

1799 McGUIRE, Edward to **Edw. Garrigues**
McGUIRE, Dowdell
See KENNEDY, William

1797 McGUIRE, James to **Thomas Hogan**
1-4 of Hampshire Co. of Hampshire Co.
296 a. on Carns Run; rec. 6-17-1797.
Wit.: Thos. Jones, Saml. Jones, Wm. Jones, Robt. Jones.

1800 McGUIRE, John to **Hendrick Roseboom**
12-15 of Hampshire Co., Va. (bill of sale) of Hampshire Co.
Recorded 12-15-1800.
Wit.: Thomas Emberson, Jacob Putman, George Young.

1765 McGUIRE, Thomas (w. Elizabeth) to **Robert Parker**
6-12 PARKER, Elizabeth, **Richard Parker**
wife of John Parker, deceased **Nathaniel Parker**
113 a., 350 a., So. Branch; **Aaron Parker**
312 a., Patterson's Creek; **William Foxman**
350 a., 150 a., N Branch; (Forman) (w. Catherine
200 a., Little Ca Caphon; **John Nall**
1,459 a., Culpepper Co.. Rec. 6-12-1765. (w. Elizabeth)
Wit.: None.

1792 McGUIRE, Thomas (w. Hannah) to **Edward Baylep**
12-20 of Hampshire Co. (Bayless?) Hampshire Co.
113 a. on Knobley Mt., between Patterson Creek and New
Creek; rec. 4-10-1793.
Wit.: Ed McCarty, John Savage,
Francis Ravenscroft, Wm. Ravenscroft.

1795 McGUIRE, William to **Henry Lee**
5-21 JONES, Daniel **Elisha C. Dick**
211 a. in Hampshire Co.; rec. 9-18-1799.
Wit.: Vincent Gray, Chas. Young, Jr.

1795 McGUIRE, William to **Henry Lee**
5-21 JONES, Daniel **Elisha Cullen Dick**
a parcel of land in Hampshire Co.; rec. 9-18-1797.
Wit.: Frederic Cuiso, Thomas Lemmes, John Burnill.

1773 McHENDRY, John (w. Susannah) to **George Lewis**
8-10 of Hampshire Co. (lease and release) of Hampshire Co.
58 a. on Lost River; rec. 8-11-1773.
Wit.: Joseph Fawcett, Robert Gregg.

1754 McHENDRY, Samuel to **Stephen Ruddell**
10-1 of Hampshire Co. (lease and release) of Hampshire Co.
400 a. on Lost River; rec. June,1755.
Wit.: William Millar, William Baker,
Joseph Carroll, John Stackhouse.

1770 McINTYRE, Nicholas (w. Abigail) to **John Williams**
8-14 of Frederick Co. (lease and release) of Frederick Co.
118 a. in Hampshire Co.; rec. 8-15-1770.
Wit.: Sam Dew.

1795 McILVANE, William (w. Mary) to **Andrew Wodrow**
10-10 of Burlington, N. J. of Hampshire Co.
403 a. on South Branch River; rec. 7-18-1796.
Wit.: Charles Reed, Wm. Coxe, Jr.

1795 McILVANE, William (w. Mary) to **Andrew Wodrow**
10-11 of Burlington, N. J. of Hampshire Co.
BLOOMFIELD, Joseph (w. Mary), Burlington, N. J.
403 a. on South Branch; rec. 7-18-1796.
Wit.: Charles Reed, Wm. Coxe, Jr.

1770 McKEVER, Paul to **Frederick Conrad**
10-7 of Hampshire Co. (lease and release) of Winchester
315 a. on Great Cacapeon; rec. 12-11-1770. Frederick Co.
Wit.: Alex White, Thomas Heill, John Wood,
Wm. Campbell, Edward McGuire, G. Laubinger.

1779 McKEWN, Michael to **Thomas Russell**
9-14 of Berkeley Co. of Baltimore, Md.
400 a. on Captain John's Run, a branch of the Potomac River.
Rec. 11-9-1779.
Wit.: Robert Cockburn, John Higgins, Alex White,
Judiah Higgins, David Hunter, John Magill,
George Rootes.

1789 McKIERNAN, Michael to **Patrick McKiernan**
5-15 of Washington Co. (bill of sale) of Washington Co.
118 a. on South Branch; rec. 6-11-1789.
Wit.: John Dixon, James Murphy,
William Jacob, William Fox.

1798 McKINLEY, Hugh to **John Dowden, Jr.**
7-21 of Hampshire Co. of Hampshire Co.
120 a. on Patterson Creek; rec. 1-14-1799.
Wit.: John H. Price, Michael Miller, Adam Hider.

1800 McKINLEY, Ebenezer to **Mathias Jones**
4-5 of Hampshire Co. (bill of sale) of Hampshire Co.
Wit.: Christopher Hershman, Sam Steele,
Phil P. Wilson, Andrew Wodrow.

1786 McLAUGHLIN, Daniel, Sr. to **Daniel McLaughlin**
10-9 (w. Rachel) (see McGloughlin) of Hampshire Co.
100 a. on South Branch; rec. 10-10-1786.
Wit.: Ralph Humphreys, Baryn Keran, Simon Fields.

1790 McLAUGHLIN, Mrs. Rachel to **Daniel McLaughlin**
9-13 KING, James of Hampshire Co.
of Hampshire Co.
Parcel of land on South Branch; rec. 4-14-1791.
Wit.: James Martin, David Williams, John Offord.

1782 McLINTOCK, Alexander (w. Mary) to **John Pan-cake**
3-11 of Hampshire Co. of Hampshire Co.
189 a. on North Fork of Little Cacapeon; rec. 3-11-1783.
Wit.: None.

1771 McMACHAN, William (w. Christian) to **John Nevill**
3-13 of Hampshire Co. (mortgage) of Frederick Co.
416 a. in Hampshire Co., joining Lord Fairfax' land, which
includes Warm Springs, in Frederick Co. and Hampshire Co.
Recorded 4-9-1771.
Wit.: Joseph Mitchell, Edward McGuire,
Alex White, John Magill.

1765 McMAHAN, John (w. Izabella) to **John Foxcraft**
8-2 of Frederick Co. (lease and release) **Charles Thompson**
375 a. on North River; rec. 8-14-1765. of Philadelphia, Pa.
Wit.: Edward McGuire, Joseph Neavill, Jr.,
Samuel Pritchard, Bryan Bruin, John McColloch.

1793 McMEEKIN, John (w. Ann) to **Thomas Williams**
11-29 of Frankfort **Joseph Cary**
126 a., Hampshire Co., ¼ a. in Frankfort. of Alexandria
Recorded 12-11-1793.
Wit.: Chas. Magill, Wm. Armstrong,
Thos. Dowden, Andrew Turk, Edward Moore.

1794 McMEEKIN, John (w. Nancy) to **William Davey**
6-21 of Hampshire Co.
Quarter acre in Frankfort; rec. 12-10-1794.
Wit.: John Brown, And. Wodrow, John Mitchell.

1796 McMEEKIN, John to **Robert Sinclair**
2-11 438 a. on Patterson Creek of Allegony Co.
Rec. 4-18-1796. **John Kingan**
Wit.: Alex King, John Mitchell, John Reasoner. of Virginia

1796 McMEEKIN, John to **Nancy Fisher**
5-21 Release from slavery; rec. 7-18-1796. a slave
Wit.: John Brown, David Parsons.

1799 McMEEKIN, John (w. Ann) to **Patrick Baker**
4-13 of Hampshire Co. of Hampshire Co.
180 a. in Hampshire Co.; rec. 4-15-1799.
Wit.: None.

1784 McNEAL, John to **John Barnhouse**
2-26 of Green Brier Co. (lease and release) of Hampshire Co.
120 a. on Great Cacapeon; rec. 3-9-1784.
Wit.: Alex Monroe, John Chenoweth, Paul McKeever.

1784 McNEAL, John to **John Barnhouse**
2-27 of Greenbrier Co. (bond) of Hampshire Co.
Bond—110 pounds; rec 3-9-1784.
Wit.: Alex Monroe, Joseph Chenoweth, Paul McKeever.

1790 McNEILL, Daniel to **Jonathan Purcell**
4-10 of Hardy Co. of Hampshire Co.
400 a. on Patterson Creek; rec. 4-14-1791.
Wit.: John Dixon, Abel Randall, Isaac Parsons,
William Fox.

1795 McPHERESON, William to **John Combs**
6-16 of Hampshire Co. of Frederick Co.
200 a. on Beans Run; rec. 2-15-1796.
Wit.: Elias Poston, Thomas White,
Andrew Wodrow, James Candy.

1795 MADDEN, Joseph to **Abraham Monett**
9-12 of Hampshire Co. of Hampshire Co.
118., Hampshire Co.; rec. 9-14-1795.
Wit.: Andrew Wodrow, E. Gaither, Francis Taggart,
Nath. Dyer.

1796 MADDEN, Joseph to **Barton O'Neal**
9-15 of Hampshire Co. of Hampshire Co.
186 a. in Hampshire Co.; rec. 9-19-1796.
Wit.: Andrew Wodrow, Nath. Dyer,
Henry Hines, Wm. Schrock.

1796 MADDEN, Michael to **Christopher Parrott**
11-11 RAMSEY, Dennis of Berkeley Co.
of Fairfax Co. (bill of sale)
400 a. on New Creek; rec. 1-16-1797.
Wit.: Joseph Luearinger, N. Henry, John Baker, Jr.,
E. Laughan.

PAGE 38 — GRANTOR-GRANTEE

1796 MADDEN, Michael   to **Thomas Turner**
11-11   RAMSEY, Dennis   of Berkeley Co.
of Fairfax Co. (bill of sale)
102 a. on New Creek; rec. 12-19-1796.
Wit.: Joseph Luearinger, Henry Bedinger, N. Henry, John Baker, Jr., E. Laughan.

1796 MADDEN, Michael   to **Thomas Turner**
11-11   RAMSEY, Dennis   of Berkeley Co.
of Fairfax Co. (bill of sale)
400 a. on New Creek; rec. 1-16-1797.
Wit.: Joseph Luearinger, Henry Bedinger, N. Henry, John Baker, Jr., E. Laughan.

1796 MADDEN, Michael   to **Thomas Turner**
11-11   RAMSEY, Dennis   of Berkeley Co.
of Fairfax Co. ((bill of sale)
320 a. on New Creek; rec. 1-16-1797.
Wit.: Joseph Luearinger, Henry Bedinger, N. Henry, John Baker, Jr., E. Laughan.

1792 MAGILL, Charles   to **Samuel Dinnett**
8-18   SMITH, Edward
THURSTON, Charles Mynn
WAGGENER, Andrew
400 a. on Patterson Creek; rec. 8-28-1792.
Wit.: Alex King, And. Hume, Robert Buck, John Mitchell, Daniel Jones.

1794 MAGILL, Charles   to **James McAlster**
9-5   SMITH, Edward   of Hampshire Co.
THURSTON, Charles Mynn
WAGGONER, Andrew
67 a. on South Branch River; rec. 9-10-1794.
Wit.: Andrew Wodrow, Abraham Johnson, William Fox, John Mitchell.

1796 MAGILL, Charles (w. Mary)   to **John Brown**
10-17   353 a. on South Branch River; rec. 10-17-1796.
Wit.: None.

1796 MAGILL, Charles (w. Mary)   to **Samuel Ruckman**
11-15   Bill of sale.
406 a. on Little Cacapeon; rec. 12-19-1796.
Wit.: Jas. Dailey, Enos Davis, John McMeekin, And. Purcell.

1772 MAGILL, John   to **Moses Hutton**
See CHEW, Benjamin
GIBSON, John

1774 MAGILL, John (Atty.)   to **Andrew Graff**
11-11   of Philadelphia, Pa. (assignment)   of Lancaster, Pa.
Two tracts of land, 264 a., on Little Cacapeon; rec. 5-9-1775.
Wit.: None.

1797 MAHONY, Jeremiah, atty. for   to **Patrick Delany**
(See) JACK, John

1792 MALIN, Isaac (w. Susanna)   to **Philip Grove**
11-1   of Nelson Co.,   of Hampshire Co.
355 a. in Hampshire Co.; rec. 4-24-1792.
Wit.: John Herndon, Andrew Wodrow, John Millett.

1798 MAIRHEAD, George (w. Martha)   to **Daniel Corbin**
4-13   of Harrison Co., Va.   of Hampshire Co.
158 a. on Tear Coat Creek; rec. 12-17-1798.
Wit.: John Bartlett, Isaac Anderson, Geo. Mairheid, Jr.

1800 MALOPEAN, Alexander Joseph   to **James Dailey**
See HOWARD (HONORE?), Francis Maurice

1798 MANNIN, William   to **Robert Shepherd**
6-19   of Hampshire Co. (bill of sale)   of Hampshire Co.
Personal property; rec. 7-16-1798.
Wit.: Thos. Duggan, Pat Carrole.

1794 MANTILL, John (w. Mary)   to **David Miller**
4-5   of Hampshire Co.   of Hampshire Co.
100 a. on Beaver Run; rec. 4-9-1794.
Wit.: None.

1793 MARQUIS, Richard   to **Ambrose Clark**
11-14   of Allegany Co.   of Berkeley Co.
206 a. on South Branch; rec. 12-11-1793.
Wit.: And. Wodrow, John Jack, Wm. Fox, John Mitchell.

1793 MARQUIS, Richard (w. Ann)   to **Samuel Barrett**
11-15   of Alleghany Co.   of Hampshire Co.
200 a. in Hampshire Co.; rec. 12-11-1793.
Wit.: And. Wodrow, John Jack, Wm. Fox, John Mitchell.

1793 MARQUIS, Richard (w. Ann)   to **Alexander Henry**
11-15   of Alleghany Co.   of Hampshire Co.
149 a. on Capt. John's Run; rec. 12-11-1793.
Wit.: And. Wodrow, John Jack, Wm. Fox, John Mitchell.

1793 MARQUIS, Richard (w. Ann)   to **Thomas Bennett**
11-15   of Alleghany Co.   of Hampshire Co.
199 a. on Capt. John's Run; rec. 12-11-1793.
Wit.: And. Wodrow, John Jack, Wm. Fox, John Mitchell.

1784 MARSH, Henry   to **John Conrad**
9-7   of Hampshire Co.   of Hampshire Co.
137 a. on South Branch; rec. 11-9-1784.
Wit.: None.

1784 MARSH, Henry   to **David Welton**
11-9   of Hampshire Co.   of Hampshire Co.
Two 21 acre tracts on South Branch; rec. 11-9-1784.
Wit.: None.

1784 MARSH, Henry   to **David Welton**
11-9   of Hampshire Co.   of Hampshire Co.
82 a. on South Branch; rec. 11-9-1784.
Wit.: None.

1799 MARSHALL, Christopher   to **Alex White**
7-26   WILLIAMS, Ben (Letters of admin.)   of Hampshire Co.
WILLIAMS, Charles
WILLIAMS, Daniel
of Philadelphia
Recorded 10-20-1800.
Wit.: Frank Baker, Joseph Field.

1800 MARSHALL, Christopher   to **Abraham White**
9-13   MARSHALL, Charles   of Woodvill, Va.
of Philadelphia
Recorded 10-20-1800.
Wit.: Arch Magill, Obed White, James Sumwalt, Thomas McKennard, Robert Yates, Elia Magill, Andrew Wodrow.

1799 MARSHALL, James (w. Hester)   to **David Parsons**
2-16   of Winchester, Va.   of Hampshire Co.
250 a. on South Branch River; rec. 4-15-1799.
Wit.: Archibald Magill, Henry Morris, Eliza Murphy, Matthew Lodge, E. Gaither, John Brown.

1799 MARSHALL, James   to **Joseph Hurford**
4-1   of Winchester (lease)   of Hampshire Co.
Parcel of land on Mill Creek; rec. 10-14-1799.
Wit.: Andrew Wodrow, E. Gaither, John Brown, Matthew Lodge, Phil Wilson.

1799 MARSHALL, James (w. Hatty)   to **James Machir**
5-15   of Winchester, Va.   of Moorefield
311 a. on Mill Creek; rec. 12-16-1799.
Wit.: E. Gaither, And. Wodrow, Wm. Naylor, Chas. Magill, Phil Wilson.

1799 MARSHALL, James M. (w. Hester)   to **John Higgins**
6-1   of Winchester, Va.   of Hampshire Co.
238 a. on South Branch River; rec. 7-15-1799.
Wit.: None.

1799 MARSHALL, James M. (w. Hester)   to **John Taylor, Jr.**
8-18   of Winchester, Va.   of Hampshire Co.
400 a. on South Branch River; rec. 9-16-1799.
Wit.: Chas. Magill, Andrew Wodrow, Phillip Wilson.

1799 MARSHALL, James M. (w. Hester)   to **James Parsons**
8-23   of Hampshire Co.
16 a. in Hampshire Co.; rec. 9-16-1799.
Wit.: And. Wodrow, Phillip Wilson, Fr. White, E. Gaither.

1799 MARSHALL, James (w. Hester)   to **Peyton Skipwith**
8-14   of Mecklenburg Co., Va.
314 a., Hampshire Co.; rec. 12-16-1799.
Wit.: Chas. Magill, Daniel Conrad, Edward Conrad, Arch Magill, Elisha Boyd, John Hill, And. Wodrow, Phil Wilson, Edward Dyer.

1799 MARSHALL, James (w. Hatty)   to **James Machir**
11-19   of Winchester, Va.   of Moorefield
497 a. on South Branch; rec. 12-16-1799.
Wit.: Andrew Wodrow, Phil Wilson, John Hansbrough, E. Gaither.

1799 MARSHALL, James (w. Hetty)   to **John Higgins**
11-19   of Hampshire Co.   of Hampshire Co.
Recorded 2-17-1800.
Wit.: Robert Mackey, Dan Conrad.

1795 MARTIN, Christopher (w. Elizabeth)   to **Benj. Norman**
7-20   of Hardy Co.   of Hampshire Co.
412 a. on Mill Creek; rec. 9-14-1795.
Wit.: None.

1792 MARTIN, George, Sr. (w. Ann)   to **Benjamin Stone**
8-1   of Hampshire Co.   of Hampshire Co.
180 a., about 4 miles above North River of Cacapeon; rec. 8-28-1792.
Wit.: Geo. Beall, John Arnold, Thomas Clayton, Joseph Asbury.

1795 MARTIN, George, Jr. (w. Ann)   to **George Martin, Sr.**
10-5   of Hampshire Co.   of Hampshire Co.
174 a. on Gibbons Run; rec. 10-19-1795.
Wit.: Jas. Dailey, Wm. Day, Adam Harness.

1796 MARTIN, George (w. Ann)   to **John Wolford**
4-18   of Hampshire Co.
174 a. in Hampshire Co.; rec. 4-18-1796.
Wit.: John Hanson, Jacob Emmert, Absalom Ashbrook.

1790 MARTIN, James   to **Peter Putman**
3-18   of Hampshire Co. (bill of sale)   off Hampshire Co.
Livestock and grain; rec. 9-16-1790.
Wit.: Rod. James, Abraham Johnson, Jr., Abraham Johnson.

1792 MARTIN, Luther   to **Luther Martin, Jr.**
7-17   of Baltimore, Md.   of Hampshire Co.
5 a. on South Branch; rec. 1-29-1793.
Wit.: John J. Jacob, Jas. Martin, John William, Jr.

1792 MARTIN, Luther, Jr.   to **Maria Martin**
7-17   of Hampshire Co.   of Baltimore, Md.
Land in Ann Arundel Co.; rec. 1-29-1793.
Wit.: James Prather, John J. Jacob, James Martin, John Williams, Jr.

1773 MARTIN, Nehemiah (w. Margaret)   to **Edward Martin**
11-8   of Hampshire Co. (lease and release)   of Hampshire Co.
150 a. on South Branch; rec. 11-9-1773.
Wit.: None.

1771 5-14	MARTIN, Phillip	to	Richard Boyce

1771 5-14 MARTIN, Phillip   to Richard Boyce
Captain stationed at Newfoundland (lease) of Hampshire Co.
625 a.—Lot No. 3, on Patterson Creek; rec. 5-15-1771.
Wit.: Peter Hog, John Magill, George Brent, Phil Pendleton.

1771 5-14 MARTIN, Phillip   to Andrew Corn
Captain stationed at Newfoundland (lease) of Hampshire Co.
335 a.—Lot No. 7, on Patterson Creek; rec. 5-15-1771.
Wit.: Peter Hog, John Magill, George Brent, Phil Pendleton.

1771 5-14 MARTIN, Phillip   to John Gilmore
Captain stationed at Newfoundland (lease) of Hampshire Co.
421 a., Lot No. 6, on Patterson Creek; rec. 5-15-1771.
Wit.: Peter Hog, John Magill, George Brent, Phil Pendleton.

1771 5-14 MARTIN, Phillip   to George Miller
Captain of Royal Arttillery of Hampshire Co.
stationed at Newfoendland (lease)
280 a.—Lot No. 8, on Patterson Creek; rec. 5-15-1771.
Wit.: Peter Hog, John Magill, George Brent, Phil Pendleton.

1771 5-14 MARTIN, Phillip   to John Parker
Captain stationed at Newfoundland (lease) of Hampshire Co.
295 a.—Lot No. 10, on Patterson Creek; rec. 5-15-1771.
Wit.: Peter Hog, John Magill, George Brent, Phil Pendleton.

1771 5-14 MARTIN, Philip   to John Ramsey
Captain stationed at Newfoundland (lease) of Hampshire Co.
278 a.—Lot No. 9, on Patterson Creek; rec. 5-15-1771.
Wit.: Peter Hog, John Magill, George Brent, Phil Pendleton.

1771 5-15 MARTIN, Phillip   to William Vause
Captain stationed at Newfoundland (lease) of Hampshire Co.
299 a. — Lot No. 2, on Patterson Creek; rec. 5-15-1771.
Wit.: Peter Hog, John Magill, George Brent, Phil Pendleton.

1771 8-13 MARTIN, Phillip   to Robert Bell
Captain stationed at Newfoundland of Hampshire Co.
MARTIN, Thomas Bryan
of Frederick Co. (lease)
330 a. on Patterson Creek; rec. 8-13-1771.
Wit.: G. Jones, Peter Hog, J. Watson, Robert Stephen.

1771 8-13 MARTIN, Phillip   to John Douthit
Captain stationed at Newfoundland of Hampshire Co.
MARTIN, Thomas Bryan
of Frederick Co. (lease)
162½ a. on Patterson's Creek; rec. 8-13-1771.
Wit.: G. Jones, Peter Hog, J. Watson, Robert Stephen.

1771 8-13 MARTIN, Phillip   to Peter Heaw
Captain stationed at Newfoundland of Hampshire Co.
MARTIN, Thomas Bryan
of Frederick Co. (lease)
371 a. on Patterson Creek; rec. 8-14-1771.
Wit.: G. Jones, Peter Hog, J. Watson, Robert Stephen.

1772 8-6 MARTIN, Phillip   to Thomas Cooper
Captain at Newfoundland (lease) of Hampshire Co.
295½ a. on Patterson Creek; rec. 11-10-1772.
Wit.: Peter Hog, John Magill, G. Jones, Alexander White.

1778 8-5 MARTIN, Phillip   to Michael Vanbuskirk
Captain at Newfoundland (lease) of Hampshire Co.
206 a.—Lot No. 18, on Patterson Creek; rec. 8-11-1778.
Wit.: George Rootes, Alex White, G. Jones, Peter Hog.

1778 8-5 MARTIN, Phillip   to Simon Doyle
Captain at Newfoundland (lease) of Washington Co.
217 a.—Lot No. 16, on Patterson Creek; rec. 3-10-1779.
Wit.: George Rootes, Alex White, G. Jones, Peter Hog.

1760 8-5 MARTIN, Thomas Bryan   to Thomas, Lord Fairfax
of Greenaway Court, Va. (lease & rel.) North'n Neck of Va.
Lot No. 13—191 a., South Branch of Potomac; rec. 8-12-1760.
Wit.: Cuthbt. Bullet, Ja. Keith, H. Churchill, Ga. Jones.

1768 9-4 MARTIN, Thomas Bryan   to Thomas, Lord Fairfax
of Greenway Co., Va. (lease and release)
1,550 a., South Branch; rec. 3-15-1769.
Wit.: Peter Hog, Gabriel Jones, John Lagarde, Byran Bruen, William Scott, Alex White, Edward McGuire.

1768 4-4 MARTIN, Thomas Bryan   to Lord Fairfax
Greenaway Ct., Va. (lease and release)
54,596 a., South Branch; rec. 3-15-1769.
Wit.: Peter Hog, Gabriel Jones, Bryan Bruen, William Scott, Alex White, Edward McGuire, Jno. Lagarde.

1769 8-8 MARTIN, Phillip   to John Hartley
Captain stationed in Newfoundland (lease) of Hampshire Co.
283 a. on Patterson's Creek; rec. 8-9-1769.
Wit.: Peter Hog, Alex White, Gabriel Jones.

1777 11-2 MARTIN, Thomas Bryan   to Thomas, Lord Fairfax
of Frederick Co. Cameron, Scotland
641 a. on South Branch River; rec. 5-12-1778.
Wit.: George Rootes, Will Drew, Phil Pendleton, D. Drew, John Magill, Alex White.

1785 4-21 MARTIN, Thomas (w. Charlotte) to Wm. Johnson, Jr.
of Hampshire Co. of Hampshire Co.
71 a. on Patterson Creek; rec. 5-10-1785.
Wit.: Abraham Johnson, Jr., Jacob Bogard, John Dixon.

1793 8-4 MASON, John (w. Ann)   to Christian Slonaker
of Hampshire Co. of Hampshire Co.
156 a. on Timber Ridge; rec. 9-11-1793.
Wit.: Elias Poston, Samuel Cheshire.

1795 4-4 MASON, John (w. Ann)   to Joseph Gile
of Hampshire Co. of Berkeley Co.
239 a. on Great Cacapeon; rec. 6-15-1795.
Wit.: Thos. McLarn, Solomon Silkwood,, John Robinson.

1795 4-20 MASON, John   to Adam Snyder
of Hampshire Co. of Hampshire Co.
402 a. in Hampshire Co.; rec. 4-21-1795.
Wit.: None.

1795 6-6 MASON, John   to Jacob Kerns
of Hampshire Co. of Hampshire Co.
72 a. in Hampshire Co.; rec. 6-15-1795.
Wit.: None.

1774 6-7 MASON, Phillip   to Anthony Baker
of Hampshire Co. of Hampshire Co.
82 a. on South Branch River; rec. 5-9-1775.
Wit.: Jonathan Heath, Moses Hutten, Wm. Heath.

1783 1-1 MASON, Samuel   to James Kelso
of Washington Co. James Wilson
180 a. in Hampshire Co.; rec. 9-17-1796. Berkeley Co.
Wit.: None.

1799 4-17 MASTORS, Josiah (w. Lucy)   to John Atkinson
of New York of New York
Recorded 9-15-1800.
Wit.: William Johnson, John Hall, Abel Atkins, William Shelton, George Beal.
(latter two witnessed Lucy Masters signature.)

1794 12-10 MATHEW, Jonathan (w. Huldah)   to John Bland
of Hampshire Co. of Hampshire Co.
171 a. on Mill Run; rec. 12-10-1794.
Wit.: None.

1800 MATTHEWS, Levi   to John Caun
See JOHNSTONE, Ephrem

1800 MATTHEWS, Levi   to John Matthews
See JOHNSTONE, Ephrem

1770 7-4 MATLOCK, Thomas (w. Rebecca)   to John Constant
of Hampshire Co. (lease and release) of Hampshire Co.
100 a. on Great Cacapeon; rec. 5-14-1771.
Wit.: J. Watson, Charles Cracraft, Wm. Demsoe, John Morgan.

1770 7-4 MATLOCK, Thomas (w. Rebecca) to William Jackson
of Hampshire Co. (lease and release) of Hampshire Co.
92 a. on Cacapeon River; rec. 5-14-1771.
Wit.: J. Watson, Charles Cracraft, John Morgan, William Demose.

1782 8-13 MAY, Jacob   to Mathias Hite
of Hampshire Co. of Hampshire Co.
175 a. on South Branch; rec. 8-18-1782.
Wit.: None.

1779 11-9 MEANS, Isaac (w. Ann)   to John Norman
of Hampshire Co. of Hampshire Co.
400 a. on Mill Creek; rec. 11-9-1779.
Wit.: Sam Dew.

1787 10-10 MEANS, Isaac (w. Ann)   to Hugh Balentine
of Hampshire Co. (lease and release) of Frederick Co.
321 a. on Mill Creek; rec. 10-11-1787.
Wit.: None.

1794 10-31 MEDLEY, John, Jr.   to Henry Horn
of Patrick Co., Va. of Hampshire Co.
102 a. on North R. Mt.; rec. 12-10-1794.
Wit.: Geo. Horn, Jr., And. Horn.

1782 10-14 MENIFEE, Henry (w. Elizabeth)   to Joseph Asbury
Lease and release. of Hampshire Co.
333a. on Maple Branch; rec. 11-12-1782.
Wit.: James Monroe, Alex Monroe, John Corbin.

1787 8-13 MERCER, James   to John Lewis
of Fredericksburg of Fredericksburg
Parcel of land on Patterson Creek; rec. 6-12-1793.
Wit.: And. Wodrow, Isaac Vanmeter, Peter Higgins, Abel Seymour, J. Wheeler, Robert Higgins, Joseph O'Cannon.

1787 8-16 MERCER, Hon. James   to John Lewis
of Fredericksburg of Hampshire Co.
354 a. on South Branch; rec. 8-28-1792.
Wit.: Isaac Means, Isaac Parsons, John Lewis, Jr., Andrew Wodrow.

1787 MERCER, James   to George Miller
See LEWIS, John

1789 9-4 MERCER, James   to Perez Drew
of Fredericksburg of Hampshire Co.
Half acre in town of Romney; rec. 9-15-1791.
Wit.: Robert Mercer, John Mercer, Robert Chew, John Herndon.

1790 12-20 MERCER, James   to William Vandiver
of Spotsylvania Co. (lease) of Hampshire Co.
561 a. on Patterson Creek; rec. 9-15-1791.
Wit.: Robert Mercer, John Mercer,, Robert Chew, Charles Yates, James Somerville.

1791 1-22	**MERCER, James** of Spotsylvania Co. 206 a. on Mill Creek; rec. 9-15-1791. Wit.: Robert Mercer, John Mercer.	**to Abraham Kuykendall** of Hampshire Co.	
1799 12-16	**MERRIDITH, John W.** (w. Elizabeth) of Hampshire Co. Half acre in Romney; rec. 12-16-1799. Wit.: None.	**to John Busby** of Hampshire Co.	
1785 1-6	**MESHIA, Christian** of Lancaster Co. 195 a. on Little Cacapeon; rec. 5-12-1785. Wit.: Peter Kratzer, William Smith.	**to Daniel Miller** of Lancaster Co.	
1785 3-25	**MESHIA, John** of Lancaster Co. 264 a. on Cacapeon River; rec. 5-12-1785. Wit.: Jacob Evhart.	**to Christian Mumma** of Lancaster Co.	
1797 4-5	**MIERS, John** of Hampshire Co. 10 a. on Mill Creek; rec. 4-17-1797. Wit.: Andrew Wodrow, John McMeekin, Samuel DeButts, Perez Drew.	**to William Sanford** of Hampshire Co.	
1796 10-17	**MILLER, Daniel** of Hampshire Co. (bill of sale) 195 a. on Little Cacapeon; rec. 10-17-1796. Wit.: None.	**to Peter Bunn** of Berkeley Co.	
1795 4-20	**MILLER, David** of Hampshire Co. 100 a. on Beaver Run; rec. 4-20-1795. Wit.: None.	**to Lookey Possilman** of Hampshire Co.	
1793 12-10	**MILLER, Henry** (w. Sintly, Sinthy) of Hampshire Co. 198 a. in Hampshire Co.; rec. 12-11-1793. Wit.: John Price, George Hill, Michael Miller.	**to Robert Fuller** of Hampshire Co.	
1768 5-4	**MILLER, John** (w. Hannah) of Augusta Co. (lease and release) 380 a. on Lost River; rec. 5-10-1768. Wit.: Samuel McHendry, William Smith, John Osburn.	**to George Osburn** of Hampshire Co.	
1768 5-4	**MILLER, John** (w. Hannah) of Augusta Co. (lease and release) 184 a. on Lost River; rec. 5-10-1768. Wit.: Samuel McHendry, George Osburn, William Smith.	**to John Osburn** of Hampshire Co.	
1786	**MILLER, Michael** See KYGER, John	**to Abraham Inskeep**	
1758 2-15	**MILLER, William** of Frederick Co. (bill of sale) 400 a., South Branch of Potomac, 2 miles above Trough. Recorded 2-15-1758. Wit.: Saml. Dew, John McColloch.	**to Lieut. John King** Va. Regiment	
1768 5-9	**MILLS, Jacob** of Hampshire Co. (lease and release) 87 a. on Cedar Swamp, Hampshire Co.; rec. 5-10-1768. Wit.: None.	**to Joseph Yagar** of Hampshire Co.	
1779 2-15	**MINIFEE, Garrard** (w. Agnes) of Montgomery Co. 227 a. in Hampshire Co.; rec. 11-12-1782. Wit.: Reuben Strother, Daniel Brown, Wm. Strother.	**to James Strother** of Fauquier Co.	
1793	**MITCHELL, John** See FOX, William	**to Andrew Wodrow**	
1793	**MITCHELL, John** See FOX, William SMITH, Edward	**to Adam Hall**	
1794 11-12	**MITCHELL, John** WODROW, Andrew of Hampshire Co. 296 a. on Patterson Creek; rec. 12-10-1794. Wit.: None.	**to William Johnson** of Hampshire Co.	
1794 11-12	**MITCHELL, John** WODROW, Andrew of Hampshire Co. 312 a. near New Creek; rec. 12-10-1794. Wit.: None.	**to Edward McCarty** of Hampshire Co.	
1795 2-6	**MITCHELL, John** (w. Eliza) of Hampshire Co. 322 a. on Patterson Creek. Rec. 2-16-1795. Wit.: None.	**to George Gilpin** of Fairfax Co. Francis Deakins William Deakins of Maryland	
1797 2-10	**MITCHELL, John** (w. Elizabeth) of Frankfort Quarter acre in Frankfort. Wit.: A. King, Henry Protzman, Chas. Magill, Joshua Jones, Edward Amory, John Mitchell, Jr.	**to George Pierce** of Hampshire Co.	
1799 9-14	**MITCHELL, John** (w. Eliza) of Hampshire Co. 340 a. on Great Cacapeon; rec. 10-14-1799. Wit.: None.	**to Will Sterrett** of Hampshire Co.	
1799 9-14	**MITCHELL, John** (w. Eliza) of Hampshire Co. 192 a. on New Creek; rec. 12-16-1799. Wit.: None.	**to Matthew Pigmaer** of Hampshire Co.	
1800 2-3	**MITCHELL, John** (w. Elizabeth) of Hampshire Co. Recorded 2-17-1800.	**to William Sarrett** of Hampshire Co.	
1800 4-14	**MITCHELL, John** of Hampshire Co. Recorded 4-14-1800.	**to Rawleigh Colston** of Frederick Co.	
1800 10-10	**MITCHELL, John** (w. Elizabeth) of Hampshire Co. Recorded 10-20-1800.	**to Gabriel Wood** of Baltimore	
1800 10-14	**MITCHELL, John** (w. Eliza) of Hampshire Co. Recorded 10-20-1800.	**to James Craig** of London	
1773 7-23	**MITCHELL, Joseph** (w. Martha) of Berkeley Co., Va. (lease and release) 400 a. on Little Cacapeon; rec. 11-10-1773. Wit.: Phil Pendleton, Joseph Holmes, Moses Hunter Samuel Craig.	**to Robert Walker** Cumberland Co., Pa.	
1773 7-23	**MITCHELL, Joseph** (w. Martha) of Berkeley Co., Va. (lease and release) 263 a. on Little Cacapeon; rec. 11-10-1773. Wit.: Phil Pendleton, Joseph Holmes, Moses Hunter Samuel Craig.	**to Robert Walker** Cumberland Co., Pa.	
1773 7-23	**MITCHELL, Joseph** (w. Martha) of Berkeley Co., Va. (lease and release) 266 a. on Great Cacapeon; rec. 11-10-1773. Wit.: Phil Pendleton, Joseph Holmes, Moses Hunter Samuel Craig.	**to Robert Walker** Cumberland Co., Pa.	
"14th yr. of our reign" 11-10	**MITCHELL, Joseph** (w. Martha) Deed of lease and release. 266 a. in Hampshire Co.; rec. 3-10-1778. Wit.: None.	**to Robert Walker** of Cumberland Co.	
"14th yr. of our reign" 11-10	**MITCHELL, Joseph** (w. Martha) Deed of lease and release. 400 a. in Hampshire Co.; rec. 3-10-1778. Wit.: None.	**to Robert Walker** of Cumberland Co.	
1788 5-12	**MITSCAW, Eve** widow of Valentine Mitscaw (bill of sale) **MITSCAW, Nicholas, son** of Hampshire Co. 130 a. on Mill Creek; rec. 8-11-1778. Wit.: Sam Dew.	**to Joshua Hill** of Hampshire Co.	
1785 2-23	**MOFFETT, John** of Fauquier Co. 157 a. on Mill Creek; rec. 3-9-1785. Wit.: Richard Sturman, George Hill, John Lewis, Ezekiel Fotten, John Sturman, Wm. Barbar Lewis, Nicholas Boyce.	**to Richard Boyce** of Hampshire Co.	
1785 2-24	**MOFFETT, John** (w. Lydia) of Fauquier Co. 400 a. on Mill Creek; rec. 3-9-1785. Wit.: John Wilkinson, Lucritia Wilkinson, Nicholas Boyce, Richard Sturman, George Hill, John Sturman, Ezekiel Fotten, John Lewis, Wm. Barber Lewis.	**to Richard Boyce** of Hampshire Co.	
1785 2-24	**MOFFETT, John** of Fauquier Co. 325 a. on Patterson Creek; rec. 3-9-1785. Wit.: Richard Sturman, Richard Herman, Ezekiel Fotten, John Lewis, John Sturman, Wm. Barber Lewis, Nicholas Boyce.	**to John Wilkinson** of Prince William Co.	
1787 10-10	**MOLLOY, James** (w. Rachel) of Hampshire Co. (lease and release) 337 a. on Crooked Run; rec. 10-11-1787. Wit.: None.	**to Ephraim Johnson** of Hampshire Co.	
1795 2-25	**MONNETT, Abraham** of Hampshire Co. 45 a., part of Swan Pond tract; rec. 4-20-1795. Wit.: Andrew Wodrow, Isaac Means, John Mitchell, Benj. O'Neal, John Snyder.	**to Isaac Vanmeter** Abel Seymour	
1800 2-17	**MONROE, Jacob** (w. Christinia) of Hampshire Co. Recorded 4-17-1800. Wit.: Jacob Monroe, Jr.	**to Francis White** of Hampshire Co.	
1790 9-16	**MONROE, James** (w. Sinney) of Hampshire Co. 24 a. on North River; rec. 9-16-1790. Wit.: None.	**to Joseph Asbury** of Hampshire Co.	
1797 9-2	**MONROE, James** ASBERRY, Joseph of Hampshire Co. 418 a. on Little Cacapeon River; rec. 9-18-1797. Wit.: And. Wodrow.	**to John Elliott** of Hampshire Co.	
1799 9-9	**MONROE, John** of Hampshire Co. Recorded 2-17-1800. Wit.: George Horn, Stephen Leigh, Tunis Petters.	**to Jacob Hubbard** of Hampshire Co.	
1796 7-18	**MONTGOMERY, Matthew** (w. Elizabeth) of Romney Half acre in Romney; rec. 7-18-1796. Wit.: None.	**to William H. Burns** of Romney	
1793 8-30	**MOORE, Edward** of Hampshire Co. Quarter acre in Frankfort; rec. 12-11-1793. Wit.: Andrew Wodrow, Wm. Schrock, Mary Ann Wodrow.	**to Moses Wind** of Hampshire Co.	

GRANTOR-GRANTEE   PAGE 41

1783 MOORE, Henry (w. Katherine)   to Andrew Cherry
3-12   of Frederick Co. (lease and release)   of Hampshire Co.
       304 a. on Oldacres Run; rec. 3-11-1783.
       Wit.: None.

1787 MOORE, John   to Eneas Moore
3-10   of Hampshire Co. (bill of sale)
       Personal property; rec. 4-13-1787.
       Wit.: Edward McCarty, John Miller.

1799 MOORE, John (w. Lydia)   to Elijah Greenwell
4-12   of Hampshire Co.   of Hampshire Co.
       480 a. in Hampshire Co.; rec. 7-15-1799.
       Wit.: John Reasoner, Peter Reasoner,
       Jonathan Parker.

1788 MOORE, Joseph (w. Rebecca)   to John Rogers
6-12   of Hampshire Co.   of Hampshire Co.
       55 a. on Little Cacapeon; rec. 6-12-1788.
       Wit.: None.

1788 MOORE, Joseph (w. Rebecca)   to James Slack
6-12   of Hampshire Co.   of Hampshire Co.
       73 a. on Little Cacapeon; rec. 6-12-1788.
       Wit.: None.

1793 MOORE, Joseph   to Thomas Birket
9-10   of Barbor Co., Ky.   Thomas Pettit
       328 a. on Little Cacapeon; rec. 9-11-1793.   Hampshire Co.
       Wit.: None.

1790 MOORE, Joseph (w. Rebecca)   to Garret Cavender
9-16   of Hampshire Co.   of Frederick Co.
       250 a. on Little Cacapeon; rec. 9-16-1790.
       Wit.: None.

1790 MOORE, Joseph (w. Rebecca)   to John Clarke
9-16   of Hampshire Co.   of Hampshire Co.
       37 a. on Little Cacapeon; rec. 9-16-1790.
       Wit.: None.

1790 MOORE, Joseph (w. Rebecca)   to Thomas Combs
9-16   of Hampshire Co.   of Hampshire Co.
       100 a. on Little Cacapeon; rec. 9-16-1790.
       Wit.: None.

1790 MOORE, Joseph (w. Rebecca)   to David Laycock
9-16   of Hampshire Co.   of Hampshire Co.
       38 a. on South Branch Mountain; rec 9-16-1790.
       Wit.: None.

1790 MOORE, Joseph (w. Rebecca) to George Whetetebary
9-16   of Hampshire Co.   of Hampshire Co.
       200 a. on Little Cacapeon; rec. 9-16-1790.
       Wit.: None.

       MOORE, Michael   to Phillip Moore
       of Hampshire Co. (bill of sale)   of Hampshire Co.
       Hogs, cows, heifers, personal property; rec. 5-10-1774.
       Wit.: Abraham Hite, John Spohr,
       Abraham Hite, Jr.

1764 MOORE, Philip, Sr.   to Michael Moore
7-30   of Hampshire Co. (lease and release)   of Hampshire Co.
       138 a. on South Branch; rec. 12-12-1764.
       Wit.: Jonathan Heith, George Hart,
       Thos. Douthit, Sam Dew, Thos. Keith.

1784 MOOREFIELD, Trustees of   to Leonard Exkstine
7-24   Hampshire Co. (bill of sale)   of Frederick Co.
       Lot of one-half acre in Moorefield; rec. 8-10-1785.
       Wit.: Andrew Wodrow, Robert Higgins,
       William Bullitt.

1784 MOOREFIELD, Trustees of   to Isaac Hite
7-24   Hampshire Co.   of Lincoln Co.
       Half acre in town of Moorefield; rec. 8-10-1784.
       Wit.: Andrew Wodrow, Robert Higgins,
       William Bullitt.

1784 MOOREFIELD, Trustees of   to Mary Manning
7-24   Hampshire Co.   of Berkeley Co.
       Quantity of land in Moorefield, to be laid off in lots of one-
       half acre each; rec. 8-10-1784.
       Wit.: Andrew Wodrow, Robert Higgins,
       William Bullitt.

       MOOREFIELD, Trustees of   to Joseph Neavill
                                      Andrew Wodrow
       Pursuant to the act of Assembly for establishing the town of
       Moorefield in the County of Hampshire, sundry freeholders of
       the town of Moorefield, in said county, having assembled in
       the house of William Bullitt, in Moorefield, proceeded to elect
       two trustees for the said town in the room of Jacob Reed and
       George Renick, deceased — when Joseph Neavill and Andrew
       Wodrow were duly and legally elected.
       Recorded 8-10-1784.
       Wit.: None.

1784 MOOREFIELD, Trustees of   to Joseph Baker
8-10   Hampshire Co. (bill of sale)   Frederick Co.
       Lot of one-half acre in town of Moorefield; rec. 8-9-1785.
       Wit.: None.
       [Trustees of Moorefield were Garret Vanmeter,
       Abel Randall, Moses Hutton, Jonathan Heath,
       and Daniel McNeill]

1784 MOOREFIELD, Trustees of   to William Bullitt
8-10   Hampshire Co. (bill of sale)   of Hampshire Co.
       Lot No. 11, 8½ a. in Moorefield; rec. 8-10-1784.
       Wit.: Andrew Wodrow, Jonathan Heath,
       Moses Hutton, Joseph Nevill.
       [These trustees were Andrew Wodrow, Abel Ran-
       dall, Moses Hutton, Jonathan Heath, and Joseph
       Nevill.]

1785 MORGAN, John (w. Martha)   to John Aikman
4-18   of Hampshire Co. (lease and release)   of Hampshire Co.
       308 a. on Bennett's Run; rec. 5-10-1785.
       Wit.: John Constant, Jonathan Morgan,
       James Stuart.

1785 MORGAN, John (w. Martha)   to Jonathan Morgan
5-9   of Hampshire Co. (lease&release) (brother) of Hampshire Co.
       100 a. on Big Cacapeon; rec. 5-10-1785.
       Wit.: John Swain, Wm. Jackson, James Stuart.

1785 MORGAN, John (w. Martha)   to John Bills
8-8   of Hampshire Co. (lease and release)   of Hampshire Co.
       132 a. on Great Cacapeon; rec. 8-7-1785.
       Wit.: Daniel Royse, Solomon Royse, Aaron Royse.

1797 MORGAN, Jonathan (w. Mary) to John Cann
3-8   of Hampshire Co. (bill of sale)   of Frederick Co., Va.
       100 a. on Cacapehon River; rec. 4-17-1797.
       Wit.: Job Curtis, Peter Larew, F (?) White,
       John Copsey, And. Wodrow, E. Gaither.

1768 MORGAN, Mordecia   to Benj. Willett
       See BURNS, John
           GRAHAM, John
           HICKS, Samuel, and Moses

1784 MORGAN, William (w. Elizabeth) to George Martin
5-10   of Hampshire Co. (lease and release)   of Hampshire Co.
       180 a. on North River of Cacapeon; rec. 5-11-1784.
       Wit.: John Largent, William Bills,
       John Bills, John Prunty.

1793 MORGAN, William (w. Elizabeth) to Thomas Hughs
10-5   of Hampshire Co.   of Hampshire Co.
       132 a. in Hampshire Co.; rec. 10-9-1793.
       Wit.: John Jack, Geo. Beall, Thos. Greenville.

1778 MORRELL, John (w. Martha)   to Jonathan Pugh
10-23 of Hampshire Co.   of Hampshire Co.
       375 a., 24 a., on North River of Cacapeon; rec. 11-10-1778.
       Wit.: John Keyes, George Martin, Ezekiel Thomas,
       Jas. Carruthers, Reason Howard.

1786 MORRIS, Esack   to Frances Taggart
4-25   of Hampshire Co.   of Hampshire Co.
       292 a. on Little Cacapeon; rec. 9-12-1786.
       Wit.: Wm. Corbin, Hugh Murphy,, Samuel Murphy,
       Jacob Humphreys.

1772 MORRIS, Robert   to Archibald Wigg
8-11   of Hampshire Co.   (Wiggins?) of Hampshire Co.
       63 a., one mile above Great Cacapeon River; rec. 8-11-1772.
       Wit.: None.

1769 MORRISON, John   to James White
8-9   of Hampshire Co. (power of attorney)   of Philadelphia, Pa.
       Authority to sell lots in Philadelphia; rec. 8-9-1769.
       Wit.: None.

1791 MOSLEY, Abraham (w. Lary)   to James Fleming
1-10   of Hampshire Co.   of Hampshire Co.
       80 a. on Mill Creek; rec. 2-10-1791.
       Wit.: And. Smalley, Andrew Redtruck, And. Wodrow,
       Isaac Miller, Wm. Fox, John Mitchell.

1791 MOSLEY, Abraham   to Andrew Smalley
9-15   of Hampshire Co.   of Hampshire Co.
       100 a. on Mill Creek; rec. 2-10-1791.
       Wit.: None.

1793 MOUSER, Jacob (w. Catherine) to Joseph Reeder
2-12   of Hampshire Co.   of Hampshire Co.
       100 a. in Hampshire Co.; rec. 2-12-1794.
       Wit.: Elisha Beall, John McBride.

1794 MOUSER, Jacob (w. Catherine) to Thomas Johnson
3-1   of Hampshire Co.   of Hampshire Co.
       337 a. on Crooked Run; rec. 4-9-1794.
       Wit.: None.

1794 MOUZER, Jacob (w. Katherine) to Jacob Mouzer
6-11   of Hampshire Co.   of Hampshire Co.
       100 a. on Crooked Run; rec. 6-11-1794.
       Wit.: None.

1798 MOUSER, Jacob, Sr. (w. Catherine) to Henry Hoffman
4-16   of Hampshire Co.   (w. Catherine)
       Parcel of land on Little   Herbert Humes
       Cacapeon River; rec. 4-12-1798.   (w. Margaret)
       Wit.: Andrew Wodrow.   George Hoffman
                                                (w. Juliana)
                                                Peter Fry
                                                (w. Susanna)
1798 MOUSER, Jacob, Jr.   to Hugh O'Dannel
2-19   (w. Christiana)   of Hampshire Co.
       of Hampshire Co.
       Half acre in Romney; rec. 2-19-1798.
       Wit.: None.

GRANTOR-GRANTEE

1799 MOUSER, Jacob, Jr. (w. Christina) **to Jacob Umpstot**
2-18 of Romney   of Hampshire Co.
100 a. on Crooked Run; rec. 2-18-1799.
Wit.: None.

1780 MOXLEY, John (w. Ann) **to Conrad Myre**
10-28 of Montgomery Co.   of Montgomery Co.
405 a. on Patterson Creek; rec. 9-13-1787.
Wit.: Wm. Campbell, Rub. Smith, John Macberry, Samuel Biggs.

1784 MOYERS, John **to Henry Marsh**
9-9 of Hampshire Co.   of Hampshire Co.
400 a. on New Creek; rec. 11-9-1784.
Wit.: Andrew Wodrow, Wm. Bullett, Joseph Nevill, Abel Randall.

1799 MULLIN, Charles **to John Jack**
4-6 of Hampshire Co. (power of attorney)   of Hampshire Co.
Authority to sell and convey tract of land on Little Cacapeon River; rec. 4-15-1799.
Wit.: And. Armstrong, Wm. Schrock, Tacobas Hines, Sam Gibbs, Peter Williams, James Gibson.

1801 MULLINS, Charles **to William Beard**
2-15 of Hampshire Co.   (w. Elizabeth), Hampshire Co.
Recorded 2-16-1701.

1797 MULLEDY, Thomas (w. Mary) **to James Ferrall**
2-1 of Hampshire Co. (bill of sale)   of Philadelphia, Pa.
287 a. on Allegany Mountain; rec. 2-20-1797.
Wit.: Edward Dyer, John Hansbrough, James Hamson.

1800 MULLADY, Thomas **to Francis White**
See BLACK, John

1788 MUMMA, Christian (w. Nancy) **to Daniel Miller**
6-12 of Hampshire Co.   of Hampshire Co.
46 a. on Little Cacapeon; rec. 6-12-1788.
Wit.: None.

1794 MUMA, Christian **to Daniel Weller**
4-9 of Hampshire Co.   of Hampshire Co.
205 a. on Little Cacapeon; rec. 4-9-1794.
Wit.: John McBride, John Keener, John Rogers.

1793 MUMA, Christian **to John Kenner**
6-10 of Hampshire Co.   of Hampshire Co.
12¼ a. on Little Cacapeon; rec. 6-12-1793.
Wit.: Perez Drew, John Kenner, John Jones, Jr.

1760 MURPHEW, Hugh **to Thomas Cresap**
8-8 of Hampshire Co.   of Frederick, Md.
Lot No. 62 on So. Branch; rec. 3-10-1762.
Wit.: Sam Dew.

1800 MURPHY, Francis **to John Higgins**
8-19 of Hampshire Co.   of Hampshire Co.
Recorded 9-16-1800.
Wit.: James Dailey, Thomas Clark, William French.

1768 MURPHY, Hugh **to Edward McGuire**
3-6 of Hampshire Co. (bill of sale)   Bryan Bruen
Personal property; rec. 3-10-1768.   of Frederick Co., Va.
Wit.: Jno. Lyne, Chas. Linch, Jno. Collins.

1769 MURPHY, Hugh **to Angus McDonald**
6-12 of Hampshire Co. (lease and release)   Alexander White
297 a. on Little Cacapeon and North River; rec. 6-13-1769.   of Frederick Co.
Wit.: None.

1769 MURPHY, Hugh **to Angus McDonald**
6-12 of Hampshire Co. (lease and release)   Alexander White
Lease and release.   Executors of John Greenfield
425 a. on Little Cacapeon R.; rec. 6-13-1769.   of Frederick Co.
Wit.: None.

1777 MURPHY, Hugh **to William Corbin**
5-13 of Hampshire Co. (lease)   of Hampshire Co.
Parcel of land on Little Cacapeon; rec. 5-13-1777.
Wit.: None.

1778 MURPHY, Hugh **to John Spenser**
5-11 of Hampshire Co. (lease and release)   of Hampshire Co.
315 a. on George's Run; rec. 8-11-1778.
Wit.: William Johnson, Wm. Blackburn, John Thompson.

1779 MURPHY, Hugh **to John Cryder**
5-11 of Hampshire Co. (lease and release)   of Philadelphia, Pa.
339 a.—on both sides of main road from Winchester to Romney; rec. 5-11-1779.
Wit.: James Murphy, Valentine Switzer, Jacob Pugh.

1779 MURPHY, Hugh **to William Corbin**
8-23 of Hampshire Co.   of Hampshire Co.
133 a. on Little Cacapeon; rec. 3-14-1780.
Wit.: Andrew Wodrow, John Roussaw, William McGuire, Abel Randall.

1786 MURPHY, Hugh **to Thomas Greenwood**
12-20 of Hampshire Co. (lease)   of Washington Co.
400 a. on Patterson Creek; rec. 2-13-1787.
Wit.: Andrew Wodrow.

1788 MURPHY, Hugh **to John Murphy**
7-9 of Hampshire Co. (lease and release)   of Hampshire Co.
400 a. on Patterson Creek; rec. 7-10-1788.
Wit.: None.

1788 MURPHY, Hugh **to Joshua Calvin**
10-15 of Hampshire Co. (lease and release)   of Hampshire Co.
103 a. on Little Cacapeon; rec. 2-12-1789.
Wit.: John Lander, John Blue.

1790 MURPHY, Hugh **to John Lyon**
9-10 of Hampshire Co.   Joseph Lyon
375 a. on Patterson Creek; rec. 9-16-1790.
Wit.: Andrew Wodrow, John Herndon, Elijah Newman.

1791 MURPHY, Hugh **to John Jack**
9-15 of Hampshire Co.   of Hampshire Co.
800 a. in Hampshire Co.; rec. 2-28-1792.
Wit.: Geo. Newman, Wm. Newman, Wm. Jacob.

1791 MURPHY, Hugh, Sr. **to Hugh Murphy, Jr.**
12-15 of Hampshire Co.   of Hampshire Co.
161 a., 27 a., 420 a., 77a., Little Cacapeon; rec. 12-15-1791.
Wit.: Alex King, John Jack.

1791 MURPHY, Hugh, Jr. **to Francis Taggart**
12-29 of Hampshire Co.   Daniel Taggart (son)
100 a. on Little Cacapeon; rec. 7-31-1792.
Wit.: John Buck, John Murphy, William Jacob, Andrew Wodrow.

1792 MURPHY, Hugh **to Alexander McBride, Jr.**
2-27 of Hampshire C.o   of Hampshire Co.
153 a. on North River; rec. 2-28-1792.
Wit.: John Jack, Francis Murphy.

1792 MURPHY, Hugh (w. Lender) **to Richard Nelson**
4-24 of Hampshire Co.   of Hampshire Co.
200 a. on Little Cacapeon; rec. 4-24-1792.
Wit.: Robt. French, Francis Murphy, James Neson.

1793 MURPHY, Hugh, Jr. (w. Lender) **to Richard Nelson**
2-26 of Hampshire Co.   of Hampshire Co.
100 a. on Little Cacapeon; rec. 2-26-1793.
Wit.: None.

1793 MURPHY, Hugh, Jr. **to Francis Taggart**
2-26 of Hampshire Co.   Daniel Taggart (son)
100 a. on Little Cacapeon; rec. 2-26-1793.
Wit.: None.

1793 MURPHY, Hugh, Jr. (w. Lender) **to Francis Taggart**
4-10 of Hampshire Co.   of Hampshire Co.
27 a., 20 a., on Little Cacapeon; rec. 4-10-1793.
Wit.: None.

MURPHY, James **to Samuel Dew**
PARSONS, Isaac   Thomas Buffington
Agreement to pay 500 pounds more for land bought, if not paid at date stated. Rec. 3-13-1782.
Wit.: None.

1783 MURPHY, James **to Isaac Parsons**
11-7 of Hampshire Co. (power of attorney)
Authority to take charge of collecting all moneys and whatever due James Murphy. Recorded 5-12-1784.
Wit.: William McGuire.

1786 MURPHY, James **to Ralph Humphries**
3-15 of Hampshire Co.   of Hampshire Co.
114 a. on South Branch River; rec. 3-15-1786.
Wit.: None.

1788 MURPHY, James (w. Mary) **to Andrew Wodrow**
9-10 of Hampshire Co.   of Hampshire Co.
112½ a. on South Branch; rec. 9-11-1788.
Wit.: None.

1791 MURPHY, James (w. Mary) **to Andrew Wodrow**
4-14 of Hampshire Co.   of Hampshire Co.
Half acre in Romney; rec. 4-14-1791.
Wit.: None.

1792 MURPHY, James **to Simon Taylor**
12-30 of Hampshire Co.   of Hampshire Co.
218 a. on South Branch; rec. 1-29-1793.
Wit.: None.

1794 MURPHY, James (w. Mary) **to Sarah Dowden**
12-10 of Hampshire Co.   of Montgomery Co.
418 a. on Little Cacapeon River; rec. 7-20-1795.
Wit.: John Jack, N. Casey, Edward Dyer.

1796 MURPHY, James (w. Mary) **to James Carruthers**
2-15 of Hampshire Co.   of Hampshire Co.
206 a. on North River; rec. 2-15-1796.
Wit.: None.

1796 MURPHY, James (w. Mary) **to Francis Murphy**
8-15 of Hampshire Co. (bill of sale)   of Hampshire Co.
251 a. on South Branch; rec. 1-16-1797.
Wit.: John Brown, Matthew Montgomery, John Cullins, James Dailey, Chas. Queen, Thomas Mulleday.

1798 MURPHY, James (w. Mary) **to John Higgins**
11-20 of Hampshire Co.   of Hampshire Co.
150 a. on South Branch River; rec. 12-17-1798.
Wit.: Thos. Mulledy, Thomas Couther, Eli Davis.

1801 MURPHY, John (w. Mary) **to Isaac Dayton**
2-9 of Hampshire Co.   (w. Mary), Hampshire Co.
Recorded 2-16-1801.

1796 MURPHY, William **to Beal Babbs**
12-20 of Hampshire Co.   of Hampshire Co.
Land in Hampshire Co. (amount not given); rec. 6-19-1797.
Wit.: Frs. Keys, Chas. Babbs, Thos. Watson.

GRANTOR-GRANTEE   PAGE 43

1797 11-4	MUSSELMAN, Christian of Hampshire Co. 137 a. on Patterson Creek; rec. 12-18-1797. Wit.: John Jones, Sr., Ephriam Dunn, Abraham Eversole.	to Thomas Dunn of Hampshire Co.

1798 7-2 MUSSELMAN, Christian (w. Susanna)   to John Pearceall of Hampshire Co.
of Hampshire Co.
Quarter acre in Frankfort; rec. 9-17-1798.
Wit.: John Mitchell, John Keller, A. King, Henry Protzman.

1798 7-2 MUSSELMAN, Christian (w. Susanna)   to John Pearceall of Hampshire Co.
of Hampshire Co.
Half acre in Frankfort; rec. 9-17-1798.
Wit.: John Mitchell, John Keller, A. King, Henry Protzman.

1798 7-2 MUSSELMAN, Christian (w. Susanna)   to Joseph Frazer of Hampshire Co.
of Hampshire Co.
2 acres in Frankfort; rec. 9-17-1798.
Wit.: John Mitchell, John Keller, A. King, Henry Protzman.

1787 9-10 MYRE, Conrad (w. Elizabeth   to Hezekaiah Beall of George Co.
of Montgomery Co.
405 a. on Patterson Creek; rec. 9-11-1788.
Wit.: Andrew Campbell, John Maclary, Christopher Reed, Lawrence O'Neal.

1792 10-27 MYERS, Francis   to Okey Johnson of Hampshire Co.
205 a. in Hampshire Co.; rec. 10-30-1792.
Wit.: P. Devecmon, Moses Ticheval, Wm. Jary, J. Wheeler, Peter New, Jacob New.

1794 5-12 MYERS, John   to Robert Lockhart of Frederick Co.
of Hampshire Co.
4¼ a. on Hogg Run; rec. 10-15-1794.
Wit.: None.

1794 4-2 MYERS, Joseph (w. Anna)   to Peter Engle of Hampshire Co.
of Hampshire Co.
100 a. on Mill Creek; rec. 4-9-1794.
Wit.: Jacob Biser, John Biser, Hendrick Roseboom, Isaac Parsons.

1794 4-2 MYERS, Joseph (w. Anna)   to Joseph Stemmell of Hampshire Co.
of Hampshire Co.
250 a. on Mill Creek; rec. 4-9-1794.
Wit.: Jacob Biser, John Biser, Hendrick Roseboom, Peter Engle.

—N—

1784 8-10 NEACE, Peter (NEACI, NEAW or NEW)   to Nicholas Leatherman of Hampshire Co.
of Hampshire Co. (bill of sale)
185 a. on Patterson Creek; rec. 8-10-1784.
Wit.: Sam Dew.

1784 3-9 NEAL, Jacob (w. Nancy)   to William Janney
See LANDERS, Michael

1796 9-14 NEAW, Jacob (w. Mary)   to Edward McCarty of Hampshire Co.
of Hampshire Co.
182 a. on New Creek; rec. 9-19-1796.
Wit.: None.

1794 4-8 NEFF, Abraham   to Samuel Hague of Hampshire Co.
of Hampshire Co.
42 a. on Mill Creek; rec. 4-9-1794.
Wit.: None.

1787 11-16 NEFF, Christina   to Sylvester Neff of Hampshire Co.
NEFF, Adam (son)
NEFF, Catherine
NEFF, Esther
(daughters of Christina Neff and Henry Neff, dec'd.)
SMOOT, Thomas Barton
420 a. on Patterson Creek; rec. 4-10-1788.
Wit.: Eam Dew, Isaac Miller, Job Parker, Isaac Welch.

1787 3-7 NEFF, Henry   to Sylvester Welch of Fauquier Co.
of Hampshire Co. (Bond)
304 pounds and 16 shillings; rec. 4-10-1788.
Wit.: Thomas Smoot, Adam Neff, Samuel Jones.

1799 8-1 NEFF, Henry (w. Elizabeth)   to Jonas Smoot of Hampshire Co.
of Hampshire Co.
Parcel of land in Hampshire Co.; rec. 9-16-1799.
Wit.: Wm. Fox, Wm. Vause, Abraham Neff, Henry Eckhart, Andrew Armstrong, Chas. Heinzman.

1792 NEILSON, Isabel   to Andrew Wodrow
See LOVE, Neilson

1800 1-20 NELSON, James   to Richard Nelson of Hampshire Co.
of Hampshire Co.
300 a. on Tear Coat Creek; rec. 1-20-1800.
Wit.: E. Gaither

1800 1-20 NELSON, James   to Richard Nelson of Hampshire Co.
of Hampshire Co.
Recorded 1-20-1800.
Wit.: None.

1793 2-26 NELSON, Richard (w. Elizabeth   to Herbert Cool of Hampshire Co.
of Hampshire Co.
200 a. on Little Cacapeon; rec. 2-26-1793. Wit.: None.

1793 2-28 NEILSON, Richard (Nelson)   to Robert French of Hampshire Co.
of Hampshire Co. (bill of sale)
One negro woman, one negro boy, livestock, personal property and 515 acres of land in Rudolph Co.; rec 9-11-1793.
Wit.: John Corbin, Sr., William Corbin.

1775 3-13 NEVILL, Joseph (w. Agnes)   to Okey Johnson of Hampshire Co.
of Hampshire Co. (lease and release)
200 a. on Patterson Creek; rec. 8-14-1775.
Wit.: None.

1792 8-20 NEWCOMB, William (w. Jean)   to John Constant of Hampshire Co.
of Hampshire Co.
84 a. in Hampshire Co.; rec. 8-28-1792.
Wit.: Wm. Jackson, John Ewain, Jeremiah Thompson.

1794 9-3 NEWMAN, David (w. Anna)   to William Beekman of Hampshire Co.
of Hampshire Co.
101 a. on South Branch; rec. 12-10-1794.
Wit.: William Cane, Edward Moore.

1791 2-10 NEWMAN, Isaac (w. Margaret)   to John Wallis of Washington Co.
WILLIAMSON, William
of Hampshire Co.
288 a. in Hampshire Co.; rec. 4-14-1791.
Wit.: None.

1795 4-19 NEWMAN, Isaac (w. Margaret)   to Henry Powelson of Hampshire Co.
of Hampshire Co.
198 a. on South Branch River; rec. 10-19-1795.
Wit.: None.

1790 4-14 NEWMAN, John (w. Hannah)   to Perez Drew of Hampshire Co.
of Hampshire Co.
180 a. on South Branch; rec. 4-15-1790.
Wit.: Joseph Darlinton, Alex Ruthvan.

1790 10-25 NEWMAN, John (w. Hannah)   to Isaac Newman of Hampshire Co.
of Hampshire Co.
114 a. on South Branch; rec. 10-13-1791.
Wit.: David Long, Geo. Newman, Christopher Newman.

1790 10-25 NEWMAN, John (w. Hannah)   to Isaac Newman of Hampshire Co.
of Hampshire Co.
198 a. on South Branch R.; rec. 10-13-1791.
Wit.: David Long, Geo. Newman, Christopher Newman.

1796 9-23 NICHOLAS, Amos (w. Margaret)   to John Forman of Hampshire Co.
of Berkeley Co.
357 a. on Cacapeon River; rec. 9-18-1797.
Wit.: None.

1769 10-2 NICHOLAS, John   to Joseph McHenry (w. Hannah)
of Frederick Co., Va.
Parcel of land on Patterson's Creek; rec. 11-14-1769.
Wit.: John Hartly, Richard Harrison, Enoch Innis.

1798 NIXON, John   to Josiah Masters
See CONKLIN, Jacob
WARDELL, John

1790 9-4 NOBLE, Thomas   to Daniel Henry of Baltimore Co.
of Barkeley Co.
144½ a. on Cacapeon River; rec. 1-13-1791.
Wit.: James Murphy, Isaac Means, Wm. Buffington.

1793 10-4 NOBLE, Thomas   to John Mason of Hampshire Co.
of Berkeley Co.
100 a. on Great Cacapeon; rec. 10-9-1793.
Wit.: Daniel Carmichael.

1793 10-9 NOBLE, Thomas   to Solomon Silkwood
of Berkeley Co.
315 a. on Great Cacapeon; rec. 10-9-1793.
Wit.: None.

1796 10-19 NOBLE, Thomas   to William James of Hampshire Co.
of Frederick Co., Va. (bill of sale)
Attorney for Ignatius Wheeler
of Kentucky.
157¾ a. on New Creek; rec. 12-19-1796.
Wit.: John Mitchel, A. King, John Mitchel, Jr., Richard Whiteman.

1787 12-17 NOEL, Peter   to Conrad Doll of Frederick Co.
of Hampshire Co. (bill of sale)
Livestock; rec. 2-14-1788.
Wit.: Andrew Wodrow, Jacob Doll.

1783 8-11 NORMAN, Benjamin   to William Norman
(w. Margaret   John Norman
of Hampshire Co.
300¼ a. on Mill Creek; rec. 8-12-1783.
Wit.: Andrew Wodrow, Samuel Dew.

1788 10-14 NORMAN, Benjamin   to Christopher Martin of Hampshire Co.
of Hampshire Co. (lease and release)
4 a. on South Branch River; rec. 10-15-1789.
Wit.: None.

1795 7-20 NORMAN, Benjamin (w. Margaret) to Daniel Dolohan of Hampshire Co.
of Hampshire Co.
100 a. on Mill Creek; rec. 9-14-1795.
Wit.: None.

1795 10-19 NORMAN, Benjamin (w. Margaret) to Daniel Dolohan of Hampshire Co.
of Hampshire Co.
412 a. on Mill Creek; rec. 10-19-1795.
Wit.: None.

1796 NORMAN, William (w. Mary)   to Daniel Dolohon

GRANTOR-GRANTEE

2-24 of Hampshire Co.
154 a. in Hampshire Co.; rec. 4-18-1796.
Wit.: And. Wodrow, John Jack, A. Eckhart,
Nath. Dyer, H. Heinzman, Wm. Buffington.

1797 NOURSE, Gabriel (w. Ann) to Walter Roe
1-23 of Berkeley Co. of Baltimore
281 a., 247 a., in Hampshire Co.; rec. 9-18-1797.
Wit.: Phil Pendleton, John Davis,
John Buff, Thomas Hammond.

—O—

1775 O'BRYAN, Adam to James Stell Coberly
3-21 of Hampshire Co. of Hampshire Co.
85 a. on South Branch; rec. 5-9-1775.
Wit.: Sam Dew, Joseph Siston, Mary Waters.

1798 O'DONNELL, Hugh (w. Elizabeth) to William French
8-4 of Hampshire Co. of Hampshire Co.
Half acre in Romney; rec. 9-18-1798. Wit.: None.

1797 O'HAVER, Christopher (w. Mary) to Jacob Michael
10-13 of Hampshire Co. George Michael
144 a. in Hampshire Co.; rec. 10-16-1797. Hampshire Co.
Wit.: None.

1790 OHRSOM (see Ahrsam, Ihresam, Earsom)

1762 OLDACRE, Henry (w. Elinor) to Samuel Ingram
5-10 Yeoman, Hampshire Co. (lease &rel.) yeoman, Hampshire Co.
260 a. in Hampshire Co.; rec. 5-11-1762.
Wit.: None.

1761 OLDACRE, Henry, executor to John Keplinger
9-3 ESSWICK, Rachel, executrix of Augusta Co.
of John Esswick (Elswick), deceased, of Hampshire Co.
206 a. on Lost River; rec. 9-8-1761.
Wit.: Peter Steenbergen, Peter Hog, Joseph How, Sam Dew.

1764 OLDACRE, Elinor
2- DEDIMUS: Authority from court to Michael Stump, Thomas
Parsons and Joseph How to examine Elinor Oldacre.
Recorded 12-11-1764.

1766 OLDAKERS, Henry (w. Helenore) to Edward Snickers
4-7 of Loudoun Co. (lease and release) of Frederick Co.
347 a. on Lost River; rec. 4-14-1767.
Wit.: Peter Hog, Gabriel Jones, Alex White.

1795 O'NEAL, Barton to Isaac Vanmeter
2-25 of Hampshire Co. Abel Seymour
52 a., part of Swan Ponds; rec. 4-20-1795.
Wit.: John Snyder, Isaac Means, John Mitchell,
Benj. Neal, Andrew Wodrow.

1765 OSBORN, George, (w. Hannah) to Christopher Leek
6-11 of Hampshire Co. (lease and release) of Hampshire Co.
93 a. on Mill Creek; rec. 6-11-1765.
Wit.: None.

1765 OSBORN, George (w. Hannah) to Jacob Reed
6-11 of Hampshire Co. (lease and release) of Hampshire Co.
Lot No. 18 on South Fork, 396 acres; rec. 6-11-1765.
Wit.: None.

1767 OSBORNE, Isaac to William McCrackin
6-8 of Hampshire Co. (lease and release) of Frederick Co., Md.
270 on Potomac River; rec. 6-10-1767.
Wit.: Thomas Cresap, Michael Cresap.

1775 OSBORN, John (w. Betty) to James Claypoole, Jr.
8-7 of Hampshire Co. (lease and release) of Hampshire Co.
184 a. on Lost River; rec. 8-8-1775.
Wit.: None.

1785 OZBURN, Jeremiah to James Davis
3-29 220 a. on South Branch River; rec. 8-9-1785.
Wit.: None.

1797 OSMAN, Samuel to Charles Osman
2-20 of Allegany Co. of Hampshire Co.
168 a. on Potomac River; rec. 2-20-1797.
Wit.: None.

1797 OSMAN, Samuel (w. Comfort) to James O'Quin
2-20 of Allegany Co. of Barkley Co.
182 a. on Potomac River; rec. 2-20-1797.
Wit.: None.

1796 OVERLEY, Peter to John Howard
9-12 of Alligania (Allegany) Co., Md. of Hampshire Co.
130 a. in Hampshire Co.; rec. 4171797.
Wit.: Jeremiah Thompson, Samuel Todd, John Todd,
William Quinn, Esther Thompson, Rebekah Todd.

1777 OWEN, Robert to Moses Hutton
11-11 of Frederick Co. of Hampshire Co.
100 a. on South Branch; rec. 11-11-1777.
Wit.: Sam Dew.

1761 OWENS, John to Benjamin Suten
4-4 of Hampshire Co. of Frederick Co.
Assignment of land deeded him by George Horner and
Ann Owens. 50 acres on North River.
Wit.: Nathaniel Bell, Edward Dodd, Thos. Berry.

—P—

1797 PACK (PARK), Sarah to William Sanford
10-14 BOYCE, Nicholas of Hampshire Co.
of Hampshire Co.
89½ a. on Mill Creek; rec. 12-18-1797.
Wit.: Henry Hawk, Frederick Hye.

1792 PAINTER, Benjamin (w. Susanna) to William Duling
11-2 of Hampshire Co. of Hampshire Co.
279 a. on New Creek; rec. 1-29-1793.
Wit.: Jas. Dailey, And. Wodrow, Jas. Cochran,
L. I. Monnier, Wm. Jacob.

1770 PANCAKE, Andrew to Felix Seymour
3-3 PANCAKE, John Abraham Hite
of Hampshire Co. (mortgage) of Hampshire Co.
Plantation and tract of land in Manor of Lord Fairfax, on
South Branch of Potomac; rec. 8-14-1770.
Wit.: Joseph Heavill (Neville?) Peter Sternberger.

1776 PANCAKE, Andrew to Adam Hider
9-14 of Hampshire Co. of Hampshire Co.
121 a. on South Branch; rec. 2-11-1777.
Wit.: Sam Dew, John Pancake,, George Fidler,
Betty Dew.

1777 PANCAKE, Andrew to Daniel McNeill
3-11 of Hampshire Co. of Hampshire Co.
164 a. on South Branch R.; rec. 8-11-1777.
Wit.: Sam Dew.

1777 PANCAKE, John to Andrew Pancake
3-11 of Hampshire Co. of Hampshire Co.
90 a. on South Branch; rec. 8-11-1777.
Wit.: Sam Dew.

1781 PANCAKE, John to Andrew Pancake
3-14 of Hampshire Co. of Hampshire Co.
52 a. on South Branch; rec. 3-14-1781.
Wit.: John Roussaw, Sam Dew.

1785 PANCAKE, John (w. Susannah) to John Yeizear
5-11 of Hampshire Co. of Baltimore, Md.
189 a. on North Fork of Little Cacapeon; rec. 5-10-1785.
Wit.: None.

1787 PANCAKE, John (w. Susanna) to Robert Alexander
10-11 of Hampshire Co. of Fairfax Co.
482 a. on South Branch R.; rec. 10-11-1787.
Wit.: Sam Dew, Stephen Calvin, George Beall.

1796 PANCAKE, John, Jr. to William Linton
4-18 of Hampshire Co. of Hampshire Co.
132 a. on South Branch; rec. 4-18-1796.
Wit.: None.

1796 PANCAKE, John (w. Susanna) to Nicholas Baker
10-17 of Hampshire Co. (bill of sale) of Hampshire Co.
213¼ a. on Little Cacapeon R.; recorded 10-17-1796.
Robert Parker, Jas. Flaherty.
Wit.: None.

1796 PANCAKE, John (w. Susanna) to Joseph Starn
10-17 of Hampshire Co. of Hampshire Co.
154½ a. on Little Cacapeon; rec. 10-17-1796.
Wit.: None.

1797 PANCAKE, John (w. Susanna) to Jacob Hinds
7-7 of Hampshire Co. of Hampshire Co.
234 a. on South Br. R.; rec. 2-19-1798.
Wit.: E. Gaither, Arthur Richardson, Eli Davis.

1799 PANCAKE, John, Jr. to James Dailey
8-20 of Hampshire Co. of Romney
232 a. on South Branch R.; rec. 12-16-1799.
Wit.: Thos. Clarke, Jas. Parsons, John Hansbrough.

1800 PANCAKE, John (w. Susannah) to Mich Blue
10-11 PANCAKE, Simon of Hampshire Co.
of Hampshire Co.
Recorded 10-20-1800.
Wit.: Andrew Wodrow, Thomas Collins,
Edw. Dyer, Phil P. Wilson.

1801 PANCAKE, John (w. Catherine) to John McNeill
2-16 of Hampshire Co. of Hardy Co.
Recorded 2-16-1801.
Wit.: John Pancake.

1796 PARELL, Edward (w. Rachel) to Ashbrook Heirs
6-20 of Hampshire Co.
Parcel of land in Hampshire Co.; rec. 6-20-1796.
Wit.: None.

1796 PARISH, John to John Hammock
4-18 of Hampshire Co. of Hampshire Co.
203 a. on Dillons Run; rec. 4-18-1796.
Wit.: None.

1774 PARK, John (w. Susannah) to Andrew Park
4-10 of Hampshire Co. (lease and release) of Hampshire Co.
182 a. on Edwards Mill Branch; rec. 4-13-1774.
Wit.: None.

1783 PARK, John (w. Sarah) to George Horn
8-11 of Hampshire Co. (lease and release) of Hampshire Co.
135 a. on Mill Run, a branch of Cacapeon; rec. 11-11-1783.
Wit.: None.

1771 PARKE, George (w. Lydia) to Daniel Wood
11-12 of Botetowet Co., Va (lease and release) of Hampshire Co.
400 a. on Great Cacapeon; rec. 11-18-1771.
Wit.: Sam Dew.

1760 PARKER, Ann (spinster) to Benjamin Parker
11-1 of Hampshire Co. (lease and release) of Hampshire Co.
20 0a. on Pattersons Creek; rec. 11-18-1760.
Wit.: Gabriel Jones.

GRANTOR-GRANTEE PAGE 45

| 1760 11-3 | PARKER, Benjamin to Ann Parker
of Hampshire Co. of Hampshire Co.
Lease paying rent yearly of one peppercorn upon the Feast Day of St. Michael, the Archangel; rec. 11-18-1760.
Wit.: Gabriel Jones. |

1766
6-9
PARKER, Benjamin (w. Margaret) to James Gallant
of Hampshire Co. (lease and release) of Frederick Co.
214 a. on Pattersons Creek; rec. 6-10-1766.
Wit.: Sam Dew.

1766
6-9
PARKER, Benjamin (w. Margaret) to John Cuppy
of Hampshire Co. (lease and release) of Hampshire Co.
227 a. on Mill Creek; rec. 6-10-1766.
Wit.: Sam Dew.

1782
PARKER, Benjamin (w. Margaret) to George Taylor
of Hampshire Co.
120 a. on Pattersons Creek; rec. 3-9-1785;
Wit.: None.

1783
PARKER, Benjamin to James Parker (son)
of Hampshire Co. of Hampshire Co.
100 a. on Patterson Creek; rec. 3-10-1784.
Wit.: None.

1789
4-16
PARKER. Benjamin to Abraham Parker
of Hampshire Co. (deed of gift) of Hampshire Co.
119 a. on Patterson Creek; rec. 4-16-1789.
Wit.: None.

1790
PARKER, Benjamin (w. Margaret) to David Wolfe
of Hampshire Co. of Hampshire Co.
78 a. on Patterson Creek; rec. 4-14-1791.
Wit.: Jas. Parker, Wm. Rees, Gesse Bane.

1791
4-10
PARKER, Benjamin to Archable Campbell
(w. Margaret) of Hampshire Co.
of Hampshire Co.
80 a. on Patterson Creek; rec. 4-14-1791.
Wit.: Jas. Parker, Wm. Rees, Gesse Bane.

1793
10-9
PARKER, Benj. to William Linn
of Hampshire Co. of Hampshire Co.
24 a. on Patterson Creek; rec. 12-11-1793.
Wit.: None.

1765
PARKER, Elizabeth (w. of John) to Robert Parker
See McGUIRE, Thomas and others

1798
1-23
PARKER, Isaias to Rees Pritchard
of Mecklenburg Co., N. C. of Hampshire Co.
129 a. on Cacapeon R.; rec. 4-16-1798.
Wit.: Sam Bowman, Andrew Henderson, Cornes Henderson, Robert Parks.

1768
9-12
PARKER, John (w. Mary) to Bryan Bruen
of Hampshire Co. (lease and release) of Frederick Co., Va.
300 a., on New Creek; rec. 9-13-1768.
Wit.: Sam Dew.

1772
2-13
PARKER, John (w. Mary) to John Gillmer
of Hampshire Co. (lease and release) of Hampshire Co.
401 a. on waters of Smeries hunting camp run, a branch of Brams Creek on the Allegany Mt.; rec. 5-13-1772.
Wit.: Michael Leard, Richard Boyce, John Powers, Elinor Gillmer.

1772
3-9
PARKER, John to William Johnson
of Hampshire Co. of Hampshire Co.
295 a. on Patterson Creek.
Wit.: None.

1775
11-14
PARKER, John to Peter Puttman
of Hampshire Co. (lease) of Hampshire Co.
147 a. on Patterson Creek; rec. 11-14-1775.
Wit.: Michael Leard, Mathias Brandinburger, Henry Leiter, Michael Miller.

1799
7-15
PARKER, John (w. Mary) to Jacob Vanmeter, Sr.
of Hampshire Co. of Hardy Co.
209 a. on Allegany Mt.; rec. 7-15-1799.
Wit.: Edw. McCarty, John Ravenscroft, Sam Ravenscroft, Wm. Ravenscroft, John Daton, Jean Daton.

1791
3-3
PARKER, Nathaniel to David Jones, Jr.
of Hampshire Co. of Hampshire Co.
29 a. on Patterson Creek; rec. 4-14-1791.
Wit.: John Reed, John Jones, Jr., Abraham Johnson.

1792
3-1
PARKER, Nathaniel to William Armstrong
of Hampshire Co. of Hampshire Co.
502½ a. on Patterson Creek; rec. 10-13-1792.
Wit.: John Mitchell, Wm. Johnson, John Reed.

1792
3-1
PARKER, Nathaniel to William Armstrong
of Hampshire Co. of Hampshire Co.
800 a. on Patterson Creek; rec. 10-30-1792.
Wit.: John Mitchell, Wm. Johnson, John Reed.

1800
11-14
PARKER, Nathaniel to Thomas Parker
of Hampshire Co. (letters of administration)
Recorded 2-16-1801.
Wit.: None.

176?
PARKER, Robert (w. Hannah) to Christopher Smith
of Hampshire Co. (lease and release) of Hampshire Co.
72 a. on Little Capon; rec. 5-11-1768.
Wit.: Richard Hougland, John Forman.

1776
3-12
PARKER, Robert, Sheriff to John Foxcraft
of Hampshire Co. of Philadelphia, Pa.
247 a., 126 a., on Cacapeon River; rec. 3-12-1776.
Wit.: None.

1791
4-14
PARKER, Robert to Jacob Neaw
WILLIAMS, John of Hampshire Co.
of Hampshire Co.
182 a. on New Creek; rec. 10-13-1791.
Wit.: None.

1794
PARKER, Robert to Daniel Taylor
PARKER, Sarah
See CAMPBELL, Elizabeth, John, Sarah

1794
10-13
PARKER, Robert (w. Mary) to James Hiett
of Hampshire Co. of Hampshire Co.
96 a. on Great Cacapeon; rec. 4-20-1795.
Wit.: John Slane, Wm. Olderton, Elizabeth Parker.

1796
10-10
PARKER, Robert to John Williams
of Hampshire Co. of Hampshire Co.
232 a. on South Br.; rec. 10-17-1796.
Wit.: None.

1796
5-28
PARKER, Sarah to Reese Pritchard
of North Carolina (bill of sale) of Hampshire Co.
237 a. on North River; rec. 2-20-1797.
Wit.: Thos. Alexander, Wm. B. Alexander.

1793
12-29
PARKER, William to Luther Martin
of Alleghany Co.   Mary Martin
350 a. on North Br. of Potomac.   Ozburn Sprigg
Rec. 1.29-1793.   Sarah Sprigg
Wit.: None.   Lenox Martin
     Elizabeth Martin

1776
4-2
PARKINS, Isaac (w. Mary) to Godfrey Wilkins
of Frederick Co. (lease and release) of Dunmore Co.
206 a. on Lost R., of Cacapeon R.; 16 a. on Lost R. of Cacapeon R.; rec. 11-12-1776.
Wit.: F. Peyton, Jr., Alex White Wm. Campbell, Geo. Rootes.

1798
10-13
PARRILL, John (w. Christina) to William Layfottet
of Hampshire Co. (Lafollet) of hampshire Co.
Parcel of land on Cacapeon R.; rec. 10-15-1798.
Wit.: None.

1798
11-4
PARRILL, John (w. Christina) to William Layfottet
(Lafollet)
Bill of sale.
159¾ a. in Hampshire Co.; rec. 12-17-1798.
Wit.: None.

1776
3-11
PARSONS, Baulden (w. Rachel) to Isaac Parsons
of Hampshire Co. (lease and release) of Hampshire Co.
161 a. on South Branch; rec. 3-11-1776.
Wit.: Robert Gregg, Wm. Foreman, William Buffington, John Campbell.

1793
2-15
PARSONS, Baldwin to John, a negro servant
of Ohio Co.
Freeing him from his service forever; rec. 2-26-1793.
Wit.: James Dailey, Perez Drew.

1799
2-26
PARSONS, David (w. Catherine) to James Marshall
of Hampshire Co. of Winchester, Va.
217 a. on South Branch R.; rec. 4-15-1799.
Wit.: Wm. Naylor, John Snyder, Isaac Miller, Okey Johnson.

PARSONS, Isaac to Samuel Dew
MURPHY, James   Thomas Buffington
Agreement to pay 500 pounds more for land bought, if not paid at date stated. Rec. 3-13-1782.
Wit.: None.

1792
8-28
PARSONS, Isaac to James Machir
WODROW, Andrew of Hardy Co.
of Hampshire Co.
404 a. on North Branch; rec. 8-28-1792.
Wit.: None.

1797
9-16
PARSONS, James to Mary Parsons
PARSONS, David of Hampshire Co.
of Hampshire Co.
Two plantations in Hampshire Co.; rec. 9-18-1797.
Wit.: E. Gaither, John Jack, Edward Dyer.

1761
9-8
PARSONS, Thomas, Exor. to Henry Vanmetre
RICHARDSON, Daniel (lease and release) of Hampshire Co.
465 a. on Mill Creek; rec. 9-9-1761.
Wit.: Ga. Jones.

1777
3-10
PARSONS, Thomas to Richard Troutten
PARSONS, James of Hampshire Co.
(Executors of Thomas Parsons)
of Hampshire Co. (lease and release)
400 a. on Tear Coat Creek; rec. 3-11-1777.
Wit.: Sam Dew.

1778
1-14
PARSONS, Thomas to Hybert Brink
PARSONS, James of Hampshire Co.
of Hampshire Co. (lease and release)
200 a. on Mill Creek; rec. 11-10-1778.
Wit.: Abel Randall Job Welton.

1773
11-8
PATTEN, John to James McIlhany
of Kent Co., Pa (lease and release) of Loudon Co.
(Heir of James Patten, deceased)
157 a. on Mill Creek; rec. 11-9-1773.

1790
8-16
PATTERSON, James (w. Jean) to John Wallis
of Hampshire Co. of Washington Co.
127 a. in Hampshire Co.; rec. 9-16-1790.
Wit.: None.

GRANTOR-GRANTEE

1796 PEARCE, Henry — to George Miller
See RELFE, John, and Richard

1797 PEARCE, Henry W. (w. Rachael) — to John Copsey
2-20   of Philadelphia   of Hampshire Co.
15 a. on Cacapeon River; rec. 2-20-1797.
Wit.: None.

1797 PEARCE, Henry Ward — to John Slane
6-19   of Cecil Co., Md.   of Hampshire Co.
PEARCE, Rachel, his wife
(widow of Jno. Relfe [Rolfe] of Philadelphia)
RELFE, John
RELFE, Richard
315 a. on North River; rec. 6-19-1797.
Wit.: None.

PEARCEALL (see Pearsoll, Pearsal, Pearsel, Purcel, Piercell, Pursel).

1774 PEARCEALL, John (w. Hannah) to Leonard Tipsord
3-12   of Hampshire Co. (lease and release)   of Hampshire Co.
174 a. on North Branch of Potomac; rec. 3-14-1775.
Wit.: Elias Poston, Okey Johnson, Nath. Kuykendall, Simon Doyle.

1762 PEARSAL, Job (w. Bithia) — to Bryan Bruen
3-10   of Hampshire Co. (mortgage)   Merchant, of Winchester,
328 a. on South Branch; rec. 8-11-1762.   Frederick Co.
Wit.: Sam Dew.

PEARCE (see Pierce)

1797 PEARSAL, John — to Peter Williams
11-14   of Hampshire Co.   of Hampshire Co.
Half acre in Romney; rec. 12-18-1797.
Wit.: And. Wedrow, Wm. Linton, Eli Davis, James Gibson.

1766 PEARSALL, Job — to Luke Collins
11-10   of Hampshire Co.   of Hampshire Co.
328 a. on South Branch; rec. 11-12-1766.
Wit.: None.

1797 PEARSALL, John — to Mary Putman
See PUTMAN, Peter

1763 PEARSOLL, Job (lease and release) to Thomas Cresap
12-12   of Hampshire Co.   of Frederick Co., Md.
Lot No. 64, 310 a. on South Branch; rec. 12-13-1763.
Wit.: Sam Dew, Enoch Innis.

1785 PEERPOINT, Francis — to Thomas Beall
5-11   of Hampshire Co.   of Washington Co.
391 a. on North Branch; rec. 11-9-1785.
Wit.: Asa Mounts, Joseph Anderson, Joseph Mounts.

1794 PEPPER, John — to John Pepper, Jr.
3-29   of Frederick Co.   of Frederick Co.
352 a. on North River; rec. 2-16-1795.
Wit.: Jacob Young, Wm. Luckett, Jonathan Pugh, David Pugh, Jacob Emmert.

1767 PERSEL, Daniel (w. Kesiah) — to William McCrakin
6-8   of Frederick Co., Md. (lease and release)   of Hampshire Co.
130 a. on Potomac, survey by Geo. Washington; rec. 6-10-1767.
Wit.: None.

1798 PEIRCE, Bononie — to Thomas Dunn
10-13   (Pierce, Pearce) of Hampshire Co.   of Hampshire Co.
Bill of sale, personal property; rec. 10-15-1798.
Wit.: None.

1770 PERRY, Daniel (w. Maudlen) — to Abraham Hite
4-27   of Hampshire Co. (lease and release)   of Hampshire Co.
276 a. on Drains of Walnut Bottom River, Hampshire Co.; rec. 5-8-1770.
Wit.: I. Hite, Solomon Hedges, Garret VanMeter, Peter Casey.

1765 PERRY, Samuel — to John Relfe (Rolfe)
8-6   of Shippensburg, Pa. (lease and release)   of Philadelphia, Pa.
315 a. on North River; rec. 8-13-1765.
Wit.: Edward McGuire, Alexr. White, James Anderson, Luke Collins.

1793 PETERS, Abraham (w. Marian) to Jonathan Shepherd
11-29   of Hampshire Co.   of Hampshire Co.
126 a. in Hampshire Co.; rec. 12-11-1793.
Wit.: Chas. Magill, Andrew Turk, Edward Moore, Thomas Dowden.

1801 PETERS, Abraham (w. Mariam) to Thomas Dunn
1-8   of Rolfe, W. T.   of Hampshire Co.
Recorded 1-19-1801.
Wit.: Lewis Dunn, David Griffith, John Keller, Ephm. Dunn.

1772 PETERS, Peter — to Richard Williams
7-23   of Hampshire Co. (lease and release)   of Hampshire Co.
232 a. on South Branch; rec. 8-11-1772.
Wit.: Wm. Forman, Jacob Cassalman, Humprey Worstell, Stephen Calvin.

1777 PETERS, Peter — to Edward Peters
3-13   of Culpepper Co., Va. (lease and release)   of Hampshire Co.
214 a. on South Branch; rec. 5-13-1777.
Wit.: Sam Dew, John Forman, Enoch Berry, William Forman.

1789 PETERS, Peter — to Robert Wright
1-1   of Hampshire Co. (lease and release)   of Loudon Co.
214 a. on South Branch; rec. 2-12-1789.
Wit.: None.

1766 PETTER, John (w. Catherine) — to Robert Parker
9-1   of Hampshire Co. (lease and release)   of Hampshire Co.
Lot 42, 270 a. on South Branch; rec. 11-11-1766.
Wit.: Sam Dew.

1797 PETTET, Thomas (w. Elizabeth) — to Thomas Burkett
4-17   of Hampshire Co.   of Hampshire Co.
37 a. on Little Cacapeon; rec. 4-17-1797.
Wit.: None.

17997 PETTET, Thomas (w. Elizabeth) — to Thomas Burket
4-17   of Hampshire Co. (bill of sale)   of Hampshire Co.
328 a. on Town Hill; rec. 4-17-1797.
Wit.: None.

1796 PEYAT, Cornelius (w. Elizabeth) — to Peter Umstott
8-20   of Hampshire Co.   of Hampshire Co.
50 a. on Beaver Run; rec. 6-20-1796.
Wit.: None.

1800 PEYROUET, John Baptist — to James Dailey
(w.) Adelaide Louisa)
See HOWARD (HONORE?), Francis Maurice

1786 PEYTON, John — to William Campbell
10-20   of Winchester, Va. (bill of sale)   of Hampshire Co.
332 a. on South Branch; rec. 4-18-1787.
Wit.: James Walker, Andrew Wodrow, Chas. Magill, Robert White, Jr.

1794 PHILLIPS, John (w. Ann) — to Benjamin Thomas
10-11   of Hampshire Co.   of Hampshire Co.
92 a. in Hampshire Co.; rec. 2-16-1795.
Wit.: John Mitchel, John Snyder, Alex King, Joseph House, Thos. Allen.

1760 PHIPPS, Benjamin — to Samuel Pritchard
12-15   of North Carolina (lease and release)   of Frederick Co.
400 a. on North River; rec. 9-8-1761.
Wit.: Ja. Keith, Alexr. Wodrow, Luke Collins, George Nickson.

PIERCE—See Pearce, Peirce.

1798 PIERCE, George — to Peter Walker
11-1   of Hampshire Co.   of Hampshire Co.
Quarter acre in Frankfort; rec. 4-15-1799.
Wit.: Wm. French, John Wilkins, Wm. Schrock.

1798 PIERCE, George C. — to John Pierce
11-1   of Hampshire Co.   of Hampshire Co.
Quarter acre in Frankfort; rec. 5-20-1799.
Wit.: None.

1797 PIERCE, Henry (w. Rachael) — to Francis White
10-17   of Cecil Co., Md.   of Hampshire Co.
233 a. on North River; rec. 5-14-1798.
Wit.: None.

1797 PIERCE, Henry Ward (w. Rachel) to James Malcom
11-20   of Cecil Co., Md.   of Hampshire Co.
158 a. near Cox's Ferry, on Potomac; rec. 1-15-1798.
Wit.: Arjalon Price, E. Gaither, And. Wedrow, John Brown.

1798 PIERCE, Henry (w. Rachael) — to John Copsey
7-27   of Cecil Co., Md.   of Hampshire Co.
156 a. on Cacapeon R.; rec. 10-15-1798.
Wit.: John Higgins, Archibald Magill, F. White, And. Wodrow.

1797 PIERCE, James (w. Frances Ann) — to Edward Dyer
2-20   of Romney   of Romney
Half acre in Romney; rec. 2-20-1797.
Wit.: Richard Sloan, Pat Dolon, Thomas Mulledy.
Wit.: None.

1797 PIERCE, James (w. Frances Ann) to William French
3-7   of Romney   of Romney
One acre in Romney; rec. 9-18-1797.
Wit.: Eli Davis, John Hansbrough, John McMeekin.

1797 PIERCE, John — to Arthur Richardson
6-10   of Hampshire Co.   of Hampshire Co.
Half acre in Romney; rec. 10-16-1797.
Wit.: None.

1799 PIERCEALL, John (w. Hannah) to Ebenezer McNary
4-14   of Hampshire Co.   (w. Meony), Hampshire Co.
Recorded 4-14-1800.

PIERCELL (see Pearceall, etc.)

1780 PIGMAN, Moses — to Mena Barnard
8-8   of Hampshire Co.   of Hampshire Co.
146 a. on New Creek; rec. 11-12-1782.
Wit.: None.

1789 PIGMAN, Moses (w. Margaret) — to Henry Gaither
11-13   of Hampshire Co. (lease and release)   of Montgomery Co.
373 a., 390 a., 420 a. on Tear Coat Creek; rec. 11-12-1782.
Wit.: Elias Poston, Thomas Collins, James Carruthers, William Engle, James Mackdevit.

1796 PLOUGH, Jacob (w. Lydia) — to Noah Bishop
9-19   of Hampshire Co.   Joseph Ward
386 a. on South Br. R.; rec. 9-19-1796.   of Hampshire Co.
Wit.: Thos. Mulledy, John McDonald, David Coone.

1773 PLUMB, Elizabeth — to Samuel Worthington, Jr.
10-8   (Relict of Samuel Plumb, dec'd)   of Barkley Co., Va.
of Frederick Co. (lease and release)
160 a. on North Br. of Potomac; rec. 11-10-1773.
Wit.: John Hartley, Francis Burrell, Minard Johnston, John Vanboskirk.

1800 4-7	POPE, Robert (w. Lidia) of Hampshire Co. Recorded 9-15-1800. Wit.: John Lyle, George M. Lanberger, Joseph Hienes, Daniel Black.	to Anthony Buck of Hampshire Co.		1797 2-20	PRITCHARD, Rees (w. Barthama) of Hampshire Co. 174 a. on South Branch; rec. 2-20-1797. Wit.: None.	to Daniel Reeder of Hampshire Co.

1800 4-7 **POPE, Robert** (w. Lidia) **to Anthony Buck**
of Hampshire Co.   of Hampshire Co.
Recorded 9-15-1800.
Wit.: John Lyle, George M. Lanberger, Joseph Hienes, Daniel Black.

1762 3-10 **POULSON, Anderson** **to William Dopson**
(POWELSON) Hampshire Co. (lease and rel.)   Hampshire Co
200 a. on North Branch; rec. 3-11-1762.
Wit.: Sam Dew.

1794 3-1 **POWELL, Abraham** (w. Ann) **to Jesse Lupton**
of Hampshire Co.   of Frederick Co.
429 a. on Dillons Run; rec. 6-11-1794.
Wit.: Perez Drew, John Reed, Thos. Collins, Isaac Parsons.

1798 2-19 **POWELSON, Abraham** (w. Mary) **to Joseph Briggs**
BARKELOW, Johnson   of Hampshire Co.
BARKELOW, Benjamin
BARKELOW, Ruth
BARKELOW, Sarah
BARKELOW, Elizabeth
BEATTY, Charles
BEATTY, Eleanor
of Hampshire Co.
Grist mill, saw mill and 2 a. of land in Hampshire Co.; rec. 9-17-1798.
Wit.: None.

1799 5-29 **POWELSON, John** **to Charles Powelson**
of Hampshire Co.   of Hampshire Co.
200 a. on Little Cacapeon; rec. 7-15-1799.
Wit.: None.

1795 2-2 **PRATHER, Charles** (w. Ruth) **to John Shellhorn**
of Charles Town   of Allegany Co.
Parcel of land on North Branch R.; rec. 4-20-1795.
Wit.: None.

1791 2-7 **PRICE, Arjalon** (w. Catey) **to LeRoy Hill**
of Hardy Co.   of Hampshire Co.
289 a. on Mill Run; rec. 6-16-1791.
Wit.: None.

1791 2-7 **PRICE, Arjalon** (w. Catey) **to LeRoy Hill**
of Hardy Co.   of Hampshire Co.
175 a., 40 a., in Hampshire Co.; rec. 6-16-1791.
Wit.: None.

1794 10-15 **PRICE, Arjalon** (w. Kate) **to James Smith, Sr.**
of Hampshire Co.   of Hampshire Co.
246 a. on North River; rec. 10-15-1794.
Wit.: None.

1795 6-15 **PRICE, John** (w. Mary) **to Timothy Corn**
of Hampshire Co.   of Hampshire Co.
333 a. on Patterson Creek; rec. 7-20-1795.
Wit.: None.

1768 8-5 **PRICE, Phillip** (w. Frances) **to Thomas Parsons**
of Frederick Co., Va. (lease and release)   of Hampshire Co.
400 a. on Tear Coat; rec. 9-13-1768.
Wit.: Angus McDonald, John Greenfield.

1775 2-4 **PRICE, Thomas** **to William Thickson**
of Hampshire Co. (bill of sale)   of Hampshire Co.
Parcel of land on South Br. R.; rec. 8-11-1779.
Wit.: William Neilson, Elizabeth Camell.

1790 9-21 **PRITCHARD, Rees** (w. Barthama) **to Henry Horn**
of Hampshire Co.   of Hampshire Co.
174 a. on Tear Coat Creek; rec. 12-16-1790.
Wit.: Phillip Horn, Andrew Horn.

1790 9-21 **PRITCHARD, Rees** (w. Barthama) **to George Horn Jr.**
of Hampshire Co.   of Hampshire Co.
128 a. on Tear Coat Creek; rec. 12-16-1790.
Wit.: Henry Horn, Phillip Horn, Andrew Horn.

1790 **PRITCHARD, Rees** (w. Barthama) **to John Smoot**
of Hampshire Co.   of Hampshire Co.
202 a. on Great Cacapeon; rec. 4-15-1790.
Wit.: None.

1791 6-3 **PRITCHARD, Rees** (w. Barthama) **to William Reader**
of Hampshire Co.   of Hampshire Co.
400½ a. on Little Cacapeon; rec. 9-15-1791.
Wit.: Joseph Johnson, George Whiteberry, Daniel Royse.

1794 4-18 **PRITCHARD, Rees** (w. Barthama) **to Thos. Kennedy**
of Hampshire Co.   of Hampshire Co.
4 a. on North River; rec. 4-20-1794.
Wit.: John Howard, Thos. Henderson.

1794 7-8 **PRITCHARD, Rees** (w. Barthamy) **to John Smoot**
of Hampshire Co.   of Hampshire Co.
202 a. on Gibbons Run, a branch of North River; rec. 7-9-1794.
Wit.: None.

1794 7-12 **PRITCHARD, Rees** (w. Barthamy) **to John Gusler**
of Hampshire Co.   of Hampshire Co.
83 a. on road from Winchester to Romney; rec. 9-10-1794.
Wit.: Wm. Day, John Biggins,.

1794 9-10 **PRITCHARD, Rees** (w. Barthamy) **to John Torrence**
of Hampshire Co.   of Berkeley Co.
67 a. on Gibbons Run; rec. 9-10-1794.
Wit.: None.

1796 1-23 **PRITCHARD, Rees** (w. Barthama) **to John Hawkins**
of Hampshire Co.   of Hampshire Co.
219 a. on North River; rec. 2-20-1797.
Wit.: Wm. Carlyle, Wm. Reeder.

1797 2-20 **PRITCHARD, Rees** (w. Barthama) **to Daniel Reeder**
of Hampshire Co.   of Hampshire Co.
174 a. on South Branch; rec. 2-20-1797.
Wit.: None.

1798 4-16 **PRITCHARD, Rees** (w. Barthama) **to George Scharf**
of Hampshire Co.   of Hampshire Co.
28 7a. on Great Cacapeon River; rec. 4-16-1798.
Wit.: None.

1800 10-13 **PRITCHARD, Ross** (Rees?) **to Alex White**
(w. Barbara) of Hampshire Co.   of Hampshire Co.
Recorded 10-20-1800.
Wit.: None.

1755 6-23 **PRITCHARD, Robert** **to Thomas Parker**
of Hampshire Co. (mortgage)   of Hampshire Co.
237 a. on North River; rec. 6-11-1765.
Wit.: Thos. Bry. Martin, Archd. Wager, Geo. Parkes, Joseph Edwards, William Mullen, Robert Pugh, Joseph Tudor, William Smith.

1798 2-20 **PRITCHARD, Robert** **to Rees Pritchard**
of North Carolina   of Hampshire Co.
237 a. on North River; rec. 4-16-1798.
Wit.: John Black Iuart, I. Caldwell, Reynold Allen.

1767 8-6 **PRITCHARD, Samuel** **to Humphrey Keys**
(w. Margaret)   of Frederick Co.
of Frederick Co., Va. (lease and release)
400 a. on North River; rec. 8-11-1767.
Wit.: Edward McGuire, Luke Collins, Alex White, Jacob Ford, Jr., John Lyne.

1770 2-1 **PRITCHARD, Samuel** **to John Foxcraft**
(w. Margaret)   of Philadelphia, Pa.
of Hampshire Co. (mortgage)
Two plantations, 611 a., on Mills Run; rec. 5-9-1770.
Wit.: William Campbell, Jacob Sowers, John Magill.

1773 4-9 **PRITCHARD, Samuel** **to Isaac Perkins**
of Hampshire Co.   Bryan Bruin
Mortgage.   of Frederick Co.
206 a., 16 a., on Lost River of Cacapeon; 1¼ a. on Lost River.
Rec. 5-11-1773.
Wit.: Thomas Wood, Wm. Campbell, Thomas Ratheil, Peter Hog, G. Jones, John Nevill, J. Skelding, John Magill, Alex White.

1773 8-24 **PRITCHARD, Samuel** (w. Margaret) **to Rees Pritchard**
of Hampshire Co.
Bond, one thousand pounds; rec. 11-10-1773.
Wit.: James Carruthers, James McBride, Charles Farrell.

1773 11-10 **PRITCHARD, Samuel** **to Thomas Campbell**
of Hampshire Co. (bill of sale)   of Winchester, Va.
One servant man named Wm. Todd, Mary, his wife, two horses, personal property; rec. 11-11-1783.
Wit.: George Brent, John Roussaw, Richard Byrn.

1773 12-3 **PRITCHARD, Samuel** **to Rees Pritchard**
of Hampshire Co. (bill of sale)
Personal property, two servants, Wm. Todd and Mary, his wife; rec. 4-13-1774.
Wit.: W. Broughton, John Park, John Prunty.

1774 3-27 **PRITCHARD, Samuel** (w. Margaret) **to Isaac Perkins**
of Hampshire Co. (lease and release)   of Frederick Co.
206 a. on Lost River of Cacapeon; rec. 4-12-1774.
Wit.: Wm. Campbell, Joseph Reid, Thomas Campbell, Alex White.

1775 5-8 **PRITCHARD, Samuel** **to Peter Hog**
of Hampshire Co. (power of attorney)   of Augusta Co.
Authority to settle controversy between Samuel Pritchard and Humphrey Keys concerning a sum of money due on a bill.
Rec. 5-9-1775.
Wit.: Alex. White, Elias Poston, Friend Gray, James Carruthers.

1768 11-14 **PRICHARD, Stephen** **to Alice Prichard**
of Fauquier Co., Va. (release)
Releasing estate of Joseph Prichard. Legacy of 15 pounds in Joseph Pritchard's will. Rec. 11-8-1768.
Wit.: Jacob Pugh, Joseph Powell, Wm. McFadin, Richard Mynatt.

1785 5-9 **PRUNTY, John** (w. Mary) **to James Largent**
of Harrison Co. (lease and release)   of Hampshire Co.
146 a. on North River; rec. 5-10-1785.
Wit.: None.

1797 10-16 **PRUNTY, John** (w. Mary) **to John Brown**
of Harrison Co., Va.   of Hardy Co.
403 a. on Tear Coat Creek; rec. 12-18-1797.
Wit.: Jas. Dailey, Wm. Cooke, Wm. French, And. Wodrow, E. Gaither.

1789 7-31 **PUGH, Bethuel** (w. Rebecca) **to George Martin**
of Hampshire Co. (lease and release)   of Hampshire Co.
111 a. on North River; rec. 8-3-1789.
Wit.: Elias Poston, Henry Lander, John Prunty.

1794 4-9 **PUGH, Daniel** (w. Sally) **to Francis Taggart**
of Hampshire Co.   of Hampshire Co.
34 a. on North River; rec. 4-9-1794.
Wit.: None.

1799 9-16 **PUGH, David** (w. Jane) **to Beall Babbs**
of Hampshire Co.   of Hampshire Co.
154 a. on North River; rec. 9-16-1799.
Wit.: None.

1764 2-10	PUGH, Evan, Jr. to Jonathan Pugh of Hampshire Co. (lease and release) of Hampshire Co. 160 a. on Great Cacapeon; rec. 8-13-1765. Wit.: Geo. Nickson, John Arnold, Nathaniel Brittain, Elizabeth Nickson.		PURSEAL (see Pearceall, etc.)
		1782	PUTMAN, Peter, executor to Isaac Good See GOOD, Jacob
1794 5-19	PUGH, Evan to Joseph Pugh of Darlington Co., S. C. of Hampshire Co. 129 a. between Great Cacapeon and North River; rec. 9-10-1794. Wit.: Wm. Zimmerman, Benj. Wright, John King.	1790 11-5	PUTMAN, Peter (w. Mary) to John Cundiff of Hampshire Co. of Hampshire Co. 200 a. in Hampshire Co.; rec. 10-18-1791. Wit.: LeRoy Hill, S. Liller, Isaac Welch.
1787	PUGH, Jesse—See Samuel Pugh.	1790 11-5	PUTMAN, Peter (w. Mary) to Henry Liller of Hampshire Co. of Hampshire Co. 200 a. in Hampshire Co.; rec. 10-18-1791. Wit.: LeRoy Hill, Isaac Welch, Geo. Hill, John Cundiff.
1794 10-6	PUGH, Jesse to George Deaver of Hampshire Co. of Hampshire Co. 55¾ a. on Dillons Run; rec. 10-15-1794. Wit.: None.		
1770 11-3	PUGH, John to Bethuel Pugh of Orange Co., N. C. (lease and release) of Hampshire Co. 175 a. on North River of Cacapeon; rec. 12-11-1770. Wit.: James Alexander, John Collins, Levi Ashbrook, Jacob Pugh.	1790 11-7	PUTMAN, Peter to James Bosley of Hampshire Co. of Frederick Co. 147 a. on Patterson Creek; rec. 4-14-1791. Wit.: John Cundiff, Henry Liller, Geo. Hill.

1774 11-7	PUGH, Jonathan (w. Margaret) to Andrew Millslagle
	of Hampshire Co. (lease and release) of Hampshire Co.
	160 a. on Great Cacapeon; rec. 3-14-1775.
	Wit.: None.
		1797 5-30	PUTMAN, Peter, dec'd to Mary Putman
			through RANDOLPH, John widow of Peter
			          PEARSALL, John
			          KILEX, Robert
			Division of land. Assignment of dower interest of estate of Peter Putman to Mary Putman. Recorded 6-19-1797.
			Wit.: None.

1790 4-15	PUGH, Jonathan (w. Margaret) to John Peppers of Hampshire Co. of Frederick Co. 352 a. on North River of Cacapeon; rec. 4-15-1790. Wit.: None.		—R—
1793 11-11	PUGH, Jonathan (w. Margaret) to William Myers of Hampshire Co. of Hampshire Co. 200 a. on North River; rec. 12-11-1793. Wit.: Rees Pritchard, Joseph Angell, David Pugh.	1784 6-2	RAGAN, Jacob (w. Mary) to Valentine Cooper of Hampshire Co. (bill of sale) of Hampshire Co. 93 a. on Mill Creek; rec. 8-10-1784. Wit.: Andrew Wodrow, Abel Randall, John Westfall, John Wilson.
1799 1-14	PUGH, Joseph (w. Mary) to George Cooper of Hampshire Co. of Hampshire Co. 129 9a. on Cacapeon River; rec. 2-18-1799. Wit.: None.	1796 5-12	RALSTON, Robert to William Reese of Philadelphia of Hampshire Co. 185 a. on Patterson Creek; rec. 9-19-1796. Wit.: R. Grahame, John McIlhenney.
1787 1-30	PUGH, Samuel (w. Sarah) to Samuel Edwards PUGH, Jesse (w. Sarah) of Hampshire Co. of Hampshire Co. (bill of sale) 400 a. on Great Cacpneon River; rec. 2-18-1787. Wit.: Robert Pugh, Geo. Beatty, James Hiett.	1788 6-6	RAMBO, Peter to John Williams of Dauphin Co. of Hampshire Co. 182 a. on South Branch; rec. 6-12-1788. Wit.: Henry Prizer, Ezekiel Rambo, Robt. Parker.
1798 9-18	PUGH, Samuel (w. Sarah) to William Carlisle of Hampshire Co. of Hampshire Co. 67 a. on Dillons Run, a branch of Great Cacapcon; rec. 2-18-1799. Wit.: Jesse Pugh, Joseph Pugh, Mary Pugh.	1794 10-15	RAMSEVIL, Richard to Joel Wolverton of Hampshire Co. of Hunterdon Co., N. J. 10 a. in Hampshire Co.; rec. 10-15-1794. Wit.: None.
1795 4-18	PUGH, Thomas to Jesse Pugh of Hampshire Co. of Winchester, Va. 20 a. on Great Cacapeon; rec. 4-20-1795. Wit.: Malin Pugh, John Cohoon, Eli Pugh.	1761 9-7	RAMSAY, John (w. Margaret) to William Ramsay of Hampshire Co. (lease and release) (Merchant), Alexandria, 400 a. on New Creek; rec. 9-8-1761. Fairfax Co., Va. Wit.: Gabriel Jones.
1781 11-13	PURCELL, Jonathan (w. Catherine) to Daniel McNeal of Hampshire Co. (mortgage) of Hampshire Co. 400 a. on Patterson Creek; rec. 3-12-1782. Wit.: Andrew Wodrow, Abraham Hite, Peter Casey, Jr., Garret Vanmeter.	1773 10-16	RAMSEY, Andrew (w. Eve) to Henry Hitfe of Hampshire Co. (lease and release) of Hampshire Co. 429½ a. on Patterson Creek; rec. 11-9-1773. Wit.: Michael Leard, George Parker, John Ramsey, Gilbert Hearsman.
1791 9-15	PURCELL, Jonathan (w. Catherine) to David Welton of Hampshire Co. of Hardy Co. 400 a. on Patterson Creek; rec. 9-15-1791. Wit.: None.	1796 11-11	RAMSEY, Dennis to Christopher Parrot MADDEN, Michael of Berkeley Co. of Fairfax Co. (bill of sale) 400 a. on New Creek; rec. 1-16-1797. Wit.: Joseph Luearinger, N. Henry, John Baker, Jr., E. Loughan.
1797 4-4	PURCELL, Jonathan to James Cunningham (w. Catherine) of Hardy Co. of Hampshire Co. 126 a. on Allegany Mt.; rec. 4-17-1797. Wit.: And. Wodrow, Jas. Dailey, Francis White, John Jack.	1796 11-11	RAMSEY, Dennis to Thomas Turner MADDEN, Michael of Berkeley Co. of Fairfax Co. (bill of sale) 102 a. on New Creek; rec. 12-19-1796. Wit.: Joseph Luearinger, Henry Bedinger, N. Henry, John Baker, Jr., E. Loughan.
1768 11-5	PURSEL, Dennis (w. Susanna) to Lawrence Hass of Hampshire Co. (lease and release) of Hampshire Co. 194 a. on Potomac River; rec. 11-9-1768. Wit.: Daniel Pursel, Lawrence Hass, Jr., Geo. Cox.	1796 11-11	RAMSEY, Dennis to Thomas Turner MADDEN, Michael of Berkeley Co. of Fairfax Co. (bill of sale) 400 a. on New Creek; rec. 1-16-1797. Wit.: Joseph Luearinger, Henry Bedinger, N. Henry, John Baker, Jr., E. Loughan.
1772 8-10	PURSELL, Daniel (w. Keziah) to Isaac Osmun of Frederick Co. (lease and release) of Hampshire Co. 100 a. on Potomac River; rec. 8-11-1772. Wit.: None.	1796 11-11	RAMSEY, Dennis to Thomas Turner MADDEN, Michael of Berkeley Co. of Fairfax Co. (bill of sale) 320 a. on New Creek; rec. 1-16-1797. Wit.: Joseph Luearinger, Henry Bedinger, N. Henry, John Baker, Jr., E. Loughan.
1794 4-22	PURGITT, Fetty (w. Magdalene) to Daniel Jones of Hampshire Co. of Hampshire Co. 400 a. on Cabbin Run; rec. 7-9-1794. Wit.: John McMeekin, John Kimberline, Christian Musselman, Alex King.	1773 8-9	RAMSEY, John to Jacob Good of Hampshire Co. (lease) of Frederick Co. 278 a. on Patterson Creek; rec. 8-10-1773. Wit.: John Parker, Jacob Doll, Jean Leard.
1782 8-13	PURGET, Valentine (w. Madelana) to John Davis of Washington Co. (lease and release) of Hampshire Co. 115 a. on Patterson Creek; rec. 8-14-1782. Wit.: None.	1764 12-11	RANDALL, Abel (w. Catherine) to Alexander Wodrow of Hampshire Co. (lease and release) of King George Co., Va. 100 a. on Cornwell Run; rec. 12-12-1764. Wit.: Sam Dew.

1795 9-14	PURGETT, Valentine (w. Mary) to Jacob Purgitt
	of Hampshire Co. of Hampshire Co.
	40 a. on Patterson Creek; rec. 9-14-1795.
	Wit.: Arjalon Price.
		1779	RANDALL, Abel to Enoch Hayden
			See HEATH, Jonathan
			      HUTTON, Moses
			      VANMETER, Garrett

1796 12-19	PURGETT, Valentine (w. Madaline) to Jacob Purgett of Hampshire Co. (bill of sale) of Hampshire Co. 115 a. on Patterson Creek; rec. 12-19-1796. Wit.: None.	1797 8-18	RANDALL, Alexander to John Snyder of Hardy Co. of Hampshire Co.
1797 7-3	PURGETT, Valentine to George C. Pierce (w. Magdaline) of Hampshire Co. of Hampshire Co. Quarter acre in Frankfort; rec. 2-19-1798. Wit.: A. King, John Mitchell, Henry Protzman, Patrick Rogers, John Magaw.		RANDALL, Felix (w. Linda) of Harrison Co. 256 a. on Patterson Creek; rec. 4-17-1798. Wit.: John Prunty, James Simpson, Wm. Haymond, Thos. Haymond, Geo. Roby, James Clark, Okey Johnson, Geo. Miller, And. Wodrow.

GRANTOR-GRANTEE — PAGE 49

1797 RANDOLPH, John — to Mary Putman
See PUTMAN, Peter

1798 2-1 RANDOLPH, John — to Thomas Hollenback
(w. Elizabeth) — of Hampshire Co.
of Hampshire Co.
150 a. in Hampshire Co.; rec. 2-19-1798.
Wit.: John Mitchell, Henry Protzman, A. King, John Pierce, Thos. Emmerson, John Dunbar.

1793 4-10 RAVENSCROFT, Samuel — to Denny Welch
(w. Priscilla) — of Hampshire Co.
of Hampshire Co.
150 a. on Alleghany Mt.; rec. 4-10-1793.
Wit.: Timothy Corn, Wm. Vause, Michael Miller.

1793 9-7 RAVENSCROFT, Samuel — to Loudon Roberts
of Hampshire Co. — of Hampshire Co.
114 a. on the Allegany Mt.; rec. 4-9-1794.
Wit.: None.

1795 10-15 RAVENSCROFT, Samuel — to Francis Deakins
(w. Priscilla) — William Deakins, Jr.
of Hampshire Co. — of Montgomery Co.
27 a. on North Branch River; rec. 10-19-1795.
Wit.: None.

1790 6-16 RAWLES, John — to William Vandiver
of Hampshire Co. — of Hampshire Co.
142 a. on Alleghany Mt.; rec. 6-16-1791.
Wit.: None.

1794 9-10 RAWLES, John — to John Williamson
of Hampshire Co. — of Hampshire Co.
232 a. on New Creek; rec. 9-10-1794.
Wit.: None.

1794 9-10 RAWLES, John — to John Dixon
of Hampshire Co. — of Hampshire Co.
129 a. on New Creek; rec. 9-28-1794.
Wit.: None.

1794 9-10 RAWLES, John — to Samuel Canby
of Hampshire Co. — of Hampshire Co.
82 a. on New Creek; rec. 9-10-1794.
Wit.: None.

1796 4-20 RAWLINGS, Moses
of Hampshire Co.
Certificate showing that a number (9) of his slaves had not been imported from Africa or the West India Islands since Nov. 1, 1778. Rec. 6-20-1796.
Wit.: None.

1780 8-7 REAGER, Jacob — to Mathews George
(Son of Anthony Reager, dec'd) — of Hampshire Co.
SHOOK, Herman
275 a. on South Branch River; rec. 8-8-1780.
Wit.: Andrew Wodrow, Abraham Hite, Solomon Vanmeter.

1784 8-9 REASONER, Garret (w. Kisiah) to William Johnson
of Hampshire Co. (lease and release) — of Hampshire Co.
277 a. on Patterson Creek; rec. 8-10-1784.
Wit.: None.

1772 6-18 REASONER, Peter (w. Mary) — to Garret Reasoner
of Cumberland Co., Pa. (lease and release) — of Hampshire Co.
277 a. on Patterson Creek; rec. 8-11-1772.
Wit.: Abraham Kuykendall, John Rutan, Abraham Frye, Frederick Harman, Jacob Reasoner.

1772 6-19 REASONER, Peter (w. Mary) — to Jacob Reasoner
of Cumberland Co., Pa. (lease and release) — of Hampshire Co.
277 a. on Patterson Creek; rec. 8-11-1772.
Wit.: Abraham Kuykendall, John Rutan, Abraham Frye, Frederick Harman, Garret Reasoner.

1798 2-19 REASONER, William — to Elijah Greenwell
(w. Jeremiah [probably Jemimiah]) — Hampshire Co.
of Hampshire Co.
86 a. on Patterson Creek; rec. 2-19-1798.
Wit.: Timothy Corn, David Wolfe, Arjalon Price.

1796 2-13 REDDICK, William (w. Margaret) to Alexander King
of Frankfort — of Frankfort
Quarter acre in Frankfort; rec. 2-15-1796.
Wit.: John Snyder, Abrm. Johnson, John Mitchell.

1793 9-27 REED, Eleanor — to 2 Negro Slaves
of Hampshire Co. — Grace, 15; Joshua, 11
Freeing them from her services; rec. 9-17-1799.
Wit.: Jas. Cochran, Thos. Collins, Daniel Collins.

1763 12-9 REED, John (w. Elizabeth) — to Abel Randal
of Hampshire Co. (lease and release) — of Hampshire Co.
100 a. on South Branch; rec. 12-14-1763.
Wit.: None.

1791 4-1 REED, John — to John Johnson
of Hampshire Co. — of Hampshire Co.
Quarter acre in Frankfort; rec. 4-14-1791.
Wit.: None.

1793 11-25 REED, John — to Henry Miller
of Hampshire Co.
198 a. on Patterson Creek; rec. 12-11-1793.
Wit.: Michael Miller, David Cotrel, Henry Franks.

1779 9-30 REED, Solomon (w. Elizabeth) — to Michael Neiff
of Hampshire Co. — of Hampshire Co.
396 a. on South Branch; rec. 11-9-1779.
Wit.: Joseph Nevill, Abel Randall, William Row, Henry Shepler.

1798 12-8 REEDER, Joseph (w. Hannah) — to John Robinson
of Hampshire Co. — of Hampshire Co.
100 a. in Hampshire Co.; rec. 12-17-1798.
Wit.: None.

1787 6-1 REEDER, Joseph — to William Reeder
of Hampshire Co. (bill of sale) — of Hampshire Co.
Livestock and household furniture; rec. 9-13-1787.
Wit.: Joseph Reeder, Jr., Sarah Reeder.

1800 4-14 REEDER, Joseph (w. Hannah) — to William Reeder
of Hampshire Co. — of Hampshire Co.
Recorded 4-14-1800.
Wit.: John Millison, James Monroe, Joseph Asbury.

1800 9-15 REEDER, William — to John Crock
of Hampshire Co. — of Hampshire Co.
Recorded 9-15-1800.

1798 5-13 REEDER, William (w. Jemima) to William Richmond
of Hampshire Co. — of Hampshire Co.
29 a. on Great Cacapeon River; rec. 7-16-1798.
Wit.: None.

1798 12-3 REEDER, William, Sr. (w. Jemima) to Joseph Reeder
of Hampshire Co. — of Hampshire Co.
18½ a. on Crooked Run; rec. 12-17-1798.
Wit.: Wm. Reeder, Jas. Carruthers, James Monroe.

1798 12-13 REEDER, William, Sr. — to William Reeder, Jr.
(w. Jemima) — of Hampshire Co.
15½ a. on Little Cacapeon River; rec. 12-17-1798.
Wit.: James Monroe, James Carruthers, Joseph Reeder.

1782 10-5 REEL, David (w. Margaret) — to Henry Rule
of Hampshire Co. (bill of sale) — of Hampshire Co.
110 a. on Mill Creek; rec. 11-18-1782.
Wit.: Andrew Wodrow, Abel Randall, James Cunningham, Michael Stump.

1795 1-17 REESE, George — to John Daton
of Hampshire Co.
352 a. on Johnson's Run; rec. 2-16-1795.
Wit.: John Ravenscroft, John Miller, Edward McCarthy.

1792 3-27 REEVES, Benjamin (w. Sibbey) — to Isaac Parsons
of Hampshire Co. — of Hampshire Co.
Parcel of land on South Branch River; rec. 4-24-1792.
Wit.: Chas. Magill, Perez Drew, Nicholas Carey, Wm. Hackney.

1792 3-27 REEVES, Benjamin (w. Sibbey) — to Isaac Parsons
of Hampshire Co. — of Hampshire Co.
400 a. on South Branch; rec. 4-24-1792.
Wit.: Chas. Magill, Perez Drew, Nicholas Casey, Wm. Hackney, John Purcell.

1778 8-3 REEVE, Peter (w. Mary) — to Patrick Murray
WHARTON, Thomas (w. Rachel) — of Winchester, Va.
of Philadelphia, Pa. (release)
412 a., 200 a., on Great Cacapeon; rec. 8-10-1779.
Wit.: David Kennedy, John Conrad, John Thurston, Isaac Wharton, Miers Fisher.

1800 6-26 REEVE, Peter — to Charles Vancouver
of Philadelphia (let of atty.) — of Hampshire Co.
Recorded 9-21-1800.
Wit.: Joseph S. Lewis, Robert Lewis, Joseph S. Coates.

1797 RELFE, John — to John Slane
RELFE, Richard
See PEARCE, Henry Ward

1767 6-19 RELFE, John (see Relse, Rolfe) — to John Largent
of Philadelphia, Pa. — William Cook
350 a.—196 a.—400 a.—204 a. — George Aufere
—191 a.—202 a.—447 a.—316 — Christopher Chambers
a.—123 a.—285 a.—154 a.—
212 a.—88 a.—337 a.—161 a. — of London, England
—195 a.—125 a.—70 a.—in Hampshire Co., Lot 85 in Town of Romney. Recorded 3-9-1769.
Wit.: Tench Tilghman, William Gallagher, David Kennedy.

1796 12-19 RELFE, John (Rolfe) — to George Miller
of Ohio Co. — of Hampshire Co.
RELFE, Richard, of Philadelphia
PEARCE, Henry, of Cecil Co., Md. (bill of sale)
Wit.: None.

1791 12-16 RELSE, John (Kelse?) — to Andrew Wodrow
of Washington Co. (power of attorney) — of Romney
Authority to dispose of or convey tracts of land lying in Hampshire Co.; rec. 4-24-1792.
Wit.: Moses Chapline, Henry Purviance, David Shepherd.

1792 4-16 RELSE, John — to Samuel Arnold
of Washington Co. — of Hampshire Co.
150 a. on Mill Creek; rec. 4-24-1792.
Wit.: John Herndon.

1792 1-14 RELSE, Richard — to Samuel Arnold
150 a., 408 a., on Mill Creek; rec. 4-24-1792. Frederick Co.
Wit.: Daniel Arnold, Jacob Ludwig, Jacob Young.

1763 5-10 RENICK, George — to John Petter
eldest son of Thomas Renick — of Hampshire Co.
of Hampshire Co. (lease and release)
Lot No. 42, 270 a. on South Branch; rec. 5-11-1763.
Wit.: Sam Dew.

1766 11-11	RENNICK, George (w. Mary) of Hampshire Co. (lease and release) 208 a. on Drain Luneys Creek; rec. 11-11-1766. Wit.: Silas Hedges, Benj. Kuykendall.	to Felix Seymour of Hampshire Co.		

1766 11-11 **RENNICK, George** (w. Mary) — to **Felix Seymour**
of Hampshire Co. (lease and release)   of Hampshire Co.
208 a. on Drain Luneys Creek; rec. 11-11-1766.
Wit.: Silas Hedges, Benj. Kuykendall.

1767 12-1 **RENNOCK, George** (w. Mary) — to **Joseph Watson**
(RENICK) Hampshire Co. (lease and release)   Fairfax Co., Va.
200 a. in Hampshire Co.; rec. 5-10-1768.
Wit.: Joseph Neavill, Joseph McCarty, William Neton, Joseph Inskeep.

1771 11-11 **RENICK, George** (w. Mary) — to **Felix Seymour**
of Hampshire Co. (lease and release)   of Hampshire Co.
406 a. on a drain of Looney's Creek; rec. 11-12-1771.
Wit.: Sam Dew.

1764 11-1 **RENO, John** — to **James Douglas**
of Hampshire Co. (lease and release)   Prince William Co., Va.
600 a. on Pattersons Creek; rec. 12-11-1764.
Wit.: None.

1770 12-11 **RENO, John, Sr.** (w. Susanah) — to **Okey Johnson**
of Hampshire Co. (lease and release)   of Hampshire Co.
105 a. on western side of Patterson Creek; rec. 12-11-1770.
Wit.: Wm. Johnson, Henry Heazell.

1771 10-22 **RENO, John** — to **Mathias Hearsman**
of Hampshire Co. (lease and release)   of Frederick Co.
298 a. on Patterson Creek; rec. 11-13-1771.
Wit.: Abraham Johnson, Garret Reasner, Michael Leard, Phillip Hearsman.

1771 10-22 **RENO, John** — to **Mathias Hearsman**
of Hampshire Co. (lease and release)   of Frederick Co.
160 a. on Patterson Creek; rec. 11-13-1771.
Wit.: Abraham Johnson, Garret Reasner, Michael Leard, Phillip Hearsman.

1795 11-2 **RHODES, Tholemiah** — to **John Park**
of Berkeley Co.   of Hampshire Co.
400 a. on Little Cacapeon; rec. 4-1-1796.
Wit.: Henry Horn, Sam Park, Geo. Park.

1798 11-13 **RHODES, Thomas** — to **Daniel Fetter**
of Hampshire Co. (bill of sale)   of Allegany Co.
Livestock and crops; rec. 4-15-1799.
Wit.: Geo. Fetter, Dunkin McCoy, John J. Jacobs.

1772 1-13 **RICHARDSON, Abraham** — to **Daniel Richardson**
of Granvill Co., S. C. (power of attorney)   Attorney
Authority to collect all sums of money due Abraham Richardson.
Rec. 5-10-1774.
Wit.: Richard Tutt, Jr., Ben Tutt.

1761 **RICHARDSON, Daniel** (dec'd) — to **Henry Van Metere**
by (see) PARSONS, Thomas, executor

1797 5-6 **RICKETTS, John Thomas** (w. Mary) — to **Amos Alexander, William Newton**
of Fairfax Co.   of Fairfax Co.
352 a. in Hampshire Co.; rec. 10-16-1797.
Wit.: L. Cooke, Francis Peyton, Jacob Wiremiller.

1777 3-15 **RIGHT, John** (Kight?) — to **Barnet Johnson**
of Berkeley Co.   of Frederick Co.
100 a. on South Branch; rec. 8-11-1778.
Wit.: Geo. Brent, Wm. Johnson, Thos. Ridout, Charity Brent, George Campbell.

1765 10-1 **RINKER, Casper** (w. Mary) — to **George Michael Loubinger**
of Frederick Co. (lease and release)   of Frederick Co.
800 a. on Dillons Run; rec. 10-8-1765.
Wit.: Ja. Keith, Peter Hog, Gabriel Jones.

1795 5-19 **ROBERTS, William** (w. Elizabeth) — to **Archibald Watts**
131 a. in Hampshire Co.; rec. 6-15-1795.
Wit.: Andrew Wodrow, Jonathan Purcell, Isaac Miller, David Collins.

1783 5-24 **ROBINSON, Benjamin** — to **Benjamin Bean**
of Hampshire Co.   of Hampshire Co.
49 a. on South Branch River; rec. 11-11-1783.
Wit.: Andrew Wodrow, Henry Cartright, Sylvester Ward.

1779 5-9 **ROBINSON, Joel** (w. Margaret) — to **Thomas Slater**
of Hampshire Co.   of Hampshire Co.
323 a. on Thorn Bottom, branch of Great Cacapeon; rec. 5-11-1779.
Wit.: Aaron Ashbrook, Wm. Renick, Jacob Denton.

1781 8-10 **ROBINSON, John** — to **McKenney Robinson**
of Hampshire Co.   of Hampshire Co.
114 a. on South Branch; rec. 11-13-1781.
Wit.: Jos. Nevill, Sylvester Ward, Job Welton.

1773 10-29 **ROBINSON, Joseph** — to **William Campbell**
of Frederick Co. (lease and release)   of Frederick Co.
332 a. on Patterson Creek; rec. 11-9-1773.
Wit.: George Rootes, Samuel Beall, Alex White, Bryan Bruin.

1783 11-10 **ROBINSON, McKenney** — to **Benjamin Bean**
of Augusta Co.   of Hampshire Co.
114 a. on South Branch River; rec. 11-11-1783.
Wit.: Henry McMarro, Jacob Ragan, Abraham Clarke.

1761 3-19 **ROBINSON, Nicholas** — to **Valentin Switzer**
of Frederick Co., by (lease and release)   Frederick Co.
HOTSENBELLA, Stephen, attorney in fact for above
400 a. on Great Cape Capon; rec. 6-10-1761.
Wit.: William Miller, Job Pearsall, Abram Kuykendall, John Collins, H. Churchill, Gabriel Jones.

RODGERS—See Rogers, Roogers.

1771 3-24 **RODGERS, James** (w. Martha) — to **Nathaniel Parker**
of Hampshire Co. (lease and release)   of Hampshire Co.
220 a. on Patterson Creek; rec. 5-14-1771.
Wit.: None.

1772 10-12 **RODGERS, James** (w. Martha) — to **Peter Jones**
of Hampshire Co. (lease and release)   of Hampshire Co.
44 a. on Patterson Creek; rec. 11-10-1772.
Wit.: Wm. Rodgers, David Jones, Adam Wise, John Jones.

1778 5-11 **RODGERS, William** (w. Sarah) — to **Valentine Burket**
of Hampshire Co. (lease and release)   of Hampshire Co.
51 a. on Patterson Creek; rec. 5-12-1778.
Wit.: None.

1799 4-15 **RODROCK, Andrew** (w. Eave) — to **Jacob Sudwick**
of Hampshire Co.   of Hampshire Co.
Recorded 10-20-1800.

1797 9-12 **RODRICK, Daniel** (w. Elizabeth) — to **Samuel Davis**
of Hampshire Co.   of Hardy Co.
92 a. on North River; rec. 9-18-1797.
Wit.: None.

ROGERS—See Rodgers, Roogers.

1791 6-15 **ROGERS, Ezekiel** — to **Baptist & Presbyterian Churches**
of Hampshire Co.   of Hampshire Co.
2½ a. in Hampshire Co.; rec. 6-16-1791.
Wit.: None.

1793 12-11 **RODGERS, Ezekiel** (w. Mary) — to **Stephen Feather**
of Hampshire Co.   of Hampshire Co.
15 a. on Little Cacapeon; rec. 12-11-1793.
Wit.: None.

1793 12-11 **RODGERS, Ezekiel** (w. Mary) — to **Richard Rounsoser**
of Hampshire Co.   of Hampshire Co.
10 a. on Little Cacapeon; rec. 12-11-1793.
Wit.: None.

1794 6-9 **ROGERS, Ezekiel** (w. Mary) — to **James Slack**
of Hampshire Co.   of Hampshire Co.
10 a. on Little Cacapeon; rec. 6-11-1794.
Wit.: None.

1794 6-11 **ROGERS, Ezekiel** — to **Samuel Stephenson**
of Hampshire Co.   of Hampshire Co.
117½ a. on Little Cacapeon; rec. 6-11-1794.
Wit.: None.

1794 6-11 **ROGERS, Ezekiel** — to **Elizabeth Allen**
of Hampshire Co.   of Hampshire Co.
250 a. on Little Cacapeon; rec. 6-11-1794.
Wit.: None.

1794 6-11 **ROGERS, Ezekiel** — to **John Rogers**
of Hampshire Co.   of Hampshire Co.
21 a. on Little Cacapeon; rec. 6-11-1794.
Wit.: None.

1794 9-10 **ROGERS, George** — to **Jacob Doman**
of Hampshire Co.   of Lancaster Co.
193 a. on Branch Mt.; rec. 9-10-1794.
Wit.: Jonathan Parker, Isaac Newman.

1794 **ROGERS, John** — to **Richard Rounsovel**
(See FOSTER, Nathaniel, and SEBRING, John)

1799 9-1 **ROGERS, John** — to **Stephen Ganno**
of Hampshire Co.   of Hampshire Co.
212 a. in Hampshire Co.; rec. 10-14-1799.
Wit.: None.

1799 10-14 **ROGERS, John** (w. Deiadamia) — to **Nathan Huddlerton**
of Hampshire Co.   of Hampshire Co.
55 a. on Little Cacapeon River; rec. 10-14-1799.
Wit.: None.

1799 10-14 **ROGERS, John** (w. Diedamia) — to **Nathan Huddlerton**
of Hampshire Co.   of Hampshire Co.
167 a. on Little Cacapeon; rec. 10-14-1799.
Wit.: None.

1772 8-3 **RODGERS, Jonathan** — to **Peter Jones**
of Hampshire Co. (lease and release)   of Hampshire Co.
115 a. on Patterson Creek; rec. 8-11-1772.
Wit.: Sam Dew, Abraham Johnson, Abraham Kuykendall.

1799 3-11 **ROGERS, Patrick** (w. Mary) — to **Thomas Mulledy**
of Hampshire Co.   of Hampshire Co.
4 a. in Frankfort; rec. 7-15-1799.
Wit.: F. Calmes, John Jones, Jr., Will Armstrong.

1767 4-13 **ROGERS, William** (w. Sarah) — to **James Rogers**
of Hampshire Co.   of Hampshire Co.
264 a. on Pattersons Creek; rec. 4-14-1767.
Wit.: None.

1778 11-3 **ROLLER, Martin** (w. Priscilla) — to **James Smith**
of Sharrando Co., Va. (lease and release)   of Hampshire Co.
800 a. on Dillon's Run; rec. 11-10-1778.
Wit.: Alex White, John Chenoweth, John Magill.

1796 10-17 **ROMNEY, Trustees of** — to **Jacob Allen**
(Bill of sale)   of Hampshire Co.
Half acre in Romney; rec. 10-17-1796.
Wit.: None.

1795 7-21 **ROMNEY, Trustees of** — to **Levi Beatty**
    of Hampshire Co.
Half acre in Romney; rec. 9-14-1795.
Wit.: None.

| GRANTOR-GRANTEE | PAGE 51 |

1795	ROMNEY, Trustees of	to John Brown
7-25	Half acre in Romney; rec. 9-14-1795.	of Hampshire Co.
	Wit.: None.	

1795 ROMNEY, Trustees of — to William Buffington
10-17 One acre in Romney; rec. 10-19-1795. of Hampshire Co.
Wit.: None.

1795 ROMNEY, Trustees of — ot John Burns
9-10 Half acre in Romney; rec. 9-14-1795. of Hampshire Co.
Wit.: None.

1795 ROMNEY, Trustees of — to William Cook
7-25 Half acre in Romney; rec. 9-14-1795. of Hampshire Co.
Wit.: None.

1799 ROMNEY, Trustees of — to William Cook
4-15 Half acre in Romney; rec. 4-15-1799. of Hampshire Co.
Wit.: None.

1795 ROMNEY, Trustees of — to Annanias Conklin
7-1 Half acre in town of Romney; rec. 7-20-1795. Hampshire Co.
Wit.: None.

1795 ROMNEY, Trustees of — to Runey Campbell
10-19 Half facre in Romney; rec. 10-19-1795. of Hampshire Co.
Wit.: None.

1796 ROMNEY, Trustees of — to James Dailey
6-20 Half acre in Romney; Lewis James
rec. 6-20-1796. James Lemonier
Wit.: None.

1796 ROMNEY, Trustees of — to Perez Drew
2-1 Half acre in Romney; rec. 2-16-1796. of Hampshire Co.
Wit.: None.

1795 ROMNEY, Trustees of — to Edward Dyer
7-1 Half acre in town of Romney; rec. 7-20-1795. Hampshire Co.
Wit.: None.

1795 ROMNEY, Trustees of — to Nathaniel Dyer
7-1 Hampshire Co. of Hampshire Co.
Half acre in town of Romney; rec. 7-20-1795.
Wit.: None.

1795 ROMNEY, Trustees of — to Thomas Fitzgerald
7-1 One acre in Romney; rec. 7-20-1795. of Hampshire Co.
Wit.: None.

1796 ROMNEY, Trustees of — to Henry Heinzman
2-15 Half acre in Romney; rec. 2-15-1796. of Hampshire Co.
Wit.: None.

1796 ROMNEY, Trustees of — to Henry Heinzman
2-15 Half acre in Romney; rec. 2-15-1796. of Hampshire Co.
Wit.: None.

1796 ROMNEY, Trustees of — to Henry Heinzman
2-15 Half acre in Romney; rec. 2-15-1796. of Hampshire Co.
Wit.: None.

1796 ROMNEY, Trustees of — to Henry Heinzman
2-15 Half acre in Romney; rec. 2-15-1796. of Hampshire Co.
Wit.: None.

1795 ROMNEY, Trustees of — to Frederick Hilley
7-21 Half acre in Romney; rec. 9-14-1795. of Hampshire Co
Wit.: None.

1795 ROMNEY, Trustees of — to Frederick Hilley
7-21 Half acre in Romney; rec. 9-14-1795. of Hampshire Co
Wit.: None.

1795 ROMNEY, Trustees of — to John Jack
7-1 Half acre in Romney; rec. 7-20-1795. of Hampshire Co.
Wit.: None.

1795 ROMNEY, Trustees of — to John Jack
7-1 Half acre in Romney; rec. 7-20-1795. of Hampshire Co.
Wit.: None.

1795 ROMNEY, Trustees of — to John Jack
10-15 One acre in Romney; rec. 10-19-1795. of Hampshire Co.
Wit.: None.

1796 ROMNEY, Trustees of — to Abraham Johnson
10-15 One acre in Romney; rec. 10-17-1795. of Hampshire Co.
Wit.: None.

1796 ROMNEY, Trustees of — to Lewis James Lemonier
2-15 Half acre in Romney; rec. 2-15-1795. of Hampshire Co.
Wit.: None.

1795 ROMNEY, Trustees of — to Pompey Long
7-20 Half acre in Romney; rec. 7-20-1795. of Hampshire Co.
Wit.: None.

1799 ROMNEY, Trustees of — to John W. Merridith
10-14 Half acre in Romney; rec. 10-14-1799. of Hampshire Co.
Wit.: None.

1799 ROMNEY, Trustees of — to John W. Merridith
10-14 Half acre in Romney; Lot 21; rec. 10-14-1799. Hampshire Co.
Wit.: None.

1795 ROMNEY, Trustees of — to Jacob Mouser
7-21 Half acre in Romney; rec. 9-14-1795. of Hampshire Co.
Wit.: None.

1795 ROMNEY, Trustees of — to Matthew Montgomery
7-21 Half acre in Romney; rec. 9-14-1795. of Hampshire Co
Wit.: None.

1795 ROMNEY, Trustees of — to Matthew Montgomery
7-21 Half acre in Romney; rec. 9-14-1795. of Hampshire Co.
Wit.: None.

1795 ROMNEY, Trustees of — to Mary Moore
7-20 Half acre in Romney; rec. 7-20-1795. of Hampshire Co.
Wit.: None.

1795 ROMNEY, Trustees of — to Thomas Mulledy
9-1 One acre in Romney; rec. 9-14-1795. of Hampshire Co.
Wit.: None.

1795 ROMNEY, Trustees of — to James Pierce
9-14 Half acre in Romney; rec. 9-14-1795. of Hampshire Co.
Wit.: None.

1796 ROMNEY, Trustees of — to James Pierce
6-20 Half acre in Romney; rec. 6-20-1796. of Hampshire Co.
Wit.: None.

1795 ROMNEY, Trustees of — to James Pierce
12-14 Half acre in Romney; rec. 2-15-1796. of Hampshire Co.
Wit.: None.

1795 ROMNEY, Trustees of — to John Pierce
9-1 Half acre in Romney; rec. 9-14-1795. of Hampshire Co.
Wit.: None.

1797 ROMNEY, Trustees of — to William Schrock
8-16 Lot in Romney; rec. 10-16-1797. of Hampshire Co.
Wit.: None.

1795 ROMNEY, Trustees of — to Francis Taggart
9-14 Half acre in Romney; rec. 9-14-1795. of Hampshire Co.
Wit.: None.

1797 ROMNEY, Trustees of — to Isaac Vanmeter
4-10 Half acre in Romney; rec. 4-17-1797. of Hampshire Co.
Wit.: None.

1795 ROMNEY, Trustees of — to Peter Williams
7-20 Half acre in Romney; rec. 7-20-1795. of Hampshire Co.
Wit.: None.

1797 ROMNEY, Trustees of — to Francis White
4-14 Half acre in Romney; rec. 4-17-1797. of Hampshire Co.
Wit.: None.

1797 ROMNEY, Trustees of — to John Wilkins
1-16 Bill of sale. of Hampshire Co.
Half acre in Romney; rec. 1-16-1797.
Wit.: None.

1797 ROMNEY, Trustees of — to Peter Williams
12-18 Lot in Romney; rec. 12-18-1797. of Hampshire Co.
Wit.: None.

1795 ROMNEY, Trustees of — to Andrew Wodrow
7-1 Half acre in Romney; rec. 7-20-1795. of Hampshire Co.
Wit.: None.

1795 ROMNEY, Trustees of — to Andrew Wodrow
7-1 Half acre in Romney; rec. 7-20-1795. of Hampshire Co.
Wit.: None.

ROOGERS—See Rodgers, Rogers.

1769 ROOGERS, William (Rogers?) to Jonathan Roogers
3-14 of Hampshire Co. (lease and release) (Rogers) Hampshire Co.
115 a. on Patterson's Creek; rec. 3-13-1770.
Wit.: None.

1770 ROOGERS, William — to Matthew Roogers
3-14 of Hampshire Co. (lease and release) (Rogers) Hampshire Co.
115 a. on Patterson's Creek; rec. 3-13-1770.
Wit.: None.

1782 ROSS, Arminilla — to Lawrence Ross
4-30 (widow of Wm. Ross) Hampshire Co. (son of Wm. Ross)
446 a. in Hampshire Co. (No. 55—land mentioned in
Wm. Ross' will); rec. 8-13-1782.
Wit.: Geo. Carruthers, Wm. Ross, Winyfrite Ross.

1762 ROSS, John — to Bryan Bruen
1-4 of North Carolina (lease and rel.) Winchester, Frederick Co.
322 a. on South Branch; rec. 5-11-1763.
Wit.: Jn. Keith, Geo. Hoge, Cornelius Conner.

1762 ROSS, John (w. Barbary) — to Benjamin Reeve
11-9 (Heir of Francis Ross) of Hampshire Co.
of Hampshire Co. (lease and release)
Lot 54—400 a. on South Branch; rec. 11-10-1762.
Wit.: Sam Dew.

1763 ROSS, John (w. Barbary) — to Thomas Lawson
5-10 of Hampshire Co. (lease and release) of Pennsylvania
Lot No. 46—236 a. on South Branch; rec. 5-11-1763.
Wit.: None.

1766 ROSS, John (w. Barbara) — to William Reynals
10-29 Mecklenburg Co., N. C. (lease & rel.) Mecklenburg Co., N. C.
400 a on South Branch; rec. 3-9-1768.
Wit.: Alex. White, John Neaville, Henry Heth.

1784 ROSS, John — to James Murphy
5-7 of Westmoreland Co. (lease and release) of Hampshire Co.
100 a. on South Branch; rec. 5-12-1784.
Wit.: David Long, Phin Mixer
Robert Parker James Flauherty.

1784 ROSS, John — to James Murphy
5-7 of Westmoreland Co. (lease and release) of Hampshire Co.
160 a. on Little Cacapeon; rec. 5-12-1784.
Wit.: None.

1769 ROSS, Phillip (w. Elizabeth) — to Michael Cresap
3-14 of Hampshire Co. (lease and release) of Frederick Co., Md.
408 a. on North Branch of Potomac; rec. 3-15-1796.
Wit.: None.

GRANTOR-GRANTEE

1771 ROSS, Phillip (w. Elizabeth) to John Reed
8-13 of Hampshire Co. (lease and release) of Hampshire Co.
150 a. on South Branch; rec. 9-14-1771.
Wit.: None.

1787 ROSS, Robert (w. Letty) to John Pancake
10-11 of Hampshire Co. of Hampshire Co.
482 a. on South Branch R.; rec. 10-11-1787.
Wit.: Sam Dew, Stephen Calvin, Geo. Beall.

1799 ROSS, Robert (w. Lettice) to Benjamin Neil
12-3 of Hampshire Co. of Hampshire Co.
Recorded 2-17-1800.
Wit.: John Newman, John Henderson,
Dennis Warner, George M. Laubinger.

1799 ROSS, Robert to Henry Brinker
12-10 of Hampshire Co. of Hampshire Co.
Recorded 2-17-1800.
Wit.: John Newman, John Henderson,
Dennis Warner, Benj. Neals.

1780 ROUSSAW, John to Cornelius Ward
8-8 of Hampshire Co. (lease) of Hampshire Co.
400 a. on New Creek; rec. 8-8-1780.
Wit.: None.

1791 ROYSE, Frederick to Robert Campbell
10-6 of Fayette Co of Hampshire Co.
345 a. on Spring Gap Run; rec. 12-15-1791.
Wit.: John Lander, Daniel Royse, Jas. Largent,
Geo. Crock, John Crock, David Crock,
Jos. Screachfield, John Johnson.

1773 ROYSE, John (w. Hannah) to Daniel M'Gloughlan
11-8 of Hampshire Co. (lease & rel.) (McLoughlin) Hampshire Co.
228 a. on South Branch; rec. 11-9-1773.
Wit.: Sam Dew.

1775 ROYSE, John to William Chapman
11-13 of Hampshire Co. (lease) of Hampshire Co.
134 a. on Little Cacapeon River; rec. 11-14-1775.
Wit.: None.

1787 ROYCE, John (w. Hannah) to George Crock
2-10 of Hampshire Co. of Hampshire Co.
254 a. on Spring Gap Mt.; rec. 2-13-1787.
Wit.: John Lander, Sarah Rannels.

1788 ROYSE, John (w. Hannah) to Joseph Johnson
10-13 of Hampshire Co. (lease and release) of Hampshire Co.
264 a. on Little Cacapeon; rec. 10-16-1788.
Wit.: None.

1791 ROYSE, John, Sr. to Daniel Royse
12-14 of Hampshire Co. of Hampshire Co.
52 a., 142 a. on Great Cacapeon; rec. 12-15-1791.
Wit.: John Rannels, Joseph Long, David Long.

1790 ROYENER, Gedivn (w. Eve) to James Fleming
4-15 of Hampshire Co. of Hampshire Co.
116 a. in Hampshire Co.; rec. 4-15-1790.
Wit.: None.

1761 RUDDEL, Stephen (w. Mary) to Daniel Wood
12-7 of Hampshire Co. of Hampshire Co.
300 a. on Lost River; rec. 12-8-1761.
Wit.: Joseph How, Jas. ——, Samuel Baker.

1761 RUDDELL, Stephen (w. Mary) to Robert Denton
8-15 of Hampshire Co. of Hampshire Co.
416¼ a. on Lost River; rec. 9-8-1761.
Wit.: Joseph How, William Baker, James Sears.

1792 RUSH, John (w. Leah) to John Bussey
10-27 of Hampshire Co. of Hampshire Co.
242 a. on New Creek; rec. 10-30-1792.
Wit.: Ed McCarty, Sam Ravenscroft, J. Wheeler.

1788 RUSSELL, Thomas to James Ryan
4-9 of Baltimore (deed trust) of Baltimore
Lot No. 5 in Baltimore and 400 a. on South Br.; rec. 4-9-1788.
Wit.: Joseph Prater, Chas. Madiria.

1789 RUSSELL, Rebecca to James Ryan
12-30 (widow of Thomas Russell) Baltimore of Baltimore
400 a. on Captain John's Run; rec. 9-16-1790.
Wit.: Samuel Chase, Jr., Samuel Moale.

1770 RUTAN, John (w. Catherine) to Abraham Johnson
12-4 of Hampshire Co. (lease and release) of Hampshire Co.
60 a. on Patterson's Creek; rec. 5-14-1771.
Wit.: Michael Leardd, Wm. Johnson, Okey Johnson.

1774 RUTAN, John (w. Catherine) to William Johnson
4-11 of Hampshire Co. (lease and release) of Hampshire Co.
294 a. on Patterson Creek; rec. 4-12-1774.
Wit.: Okey Johnson, Jacob Resonner,
John Thompson, Robt. Gregg.

1762 RUTHERFORD, Benjamin to John Hardin
11-8 of Frederick Co. (lease and release) of Frederick Co.
83 a. on Patterson Creek; rec. 11-9-1762.
Wit.: None.

1768 RUTHERFORD, Benjamin (w. Elizabeth) to John Hardin
See McCRACKEN, Margaret
WORTHINGTON, Robert

1769 RUTHERFORD, Benjamin (w. Elizabeth) to John Harden
See McCRACKEN, Jane, and Margaret
WORTHINGTON, Robert

1769 RUTHERFORD, Benjamin to Richard Boyce
11-15 of Frederick Co. of Frederick Co.
529 a. on Patterson's Creek; rec. 11-16-1769.
Wit.: Solomn Hedges, Edward E. Corn,
Richard Hougland, J. M. Offett.

1772 RUTHERFORD, Robert (w. Mary) to John Royse
8-5 of Winchester, Frederick Co. (lease & rel.) Hampshire Co.
231 a. on South Branch; rec. 3-11-1773.
Wit.: Alex White, John Magill, Samuel Beall,
Edward McGuire, Bryan Bruin.

1779 RUTHERFORD, Robert (w. Mary) to Isaac Zane
4-7 of Berkeley Co. of Marlbro Iron Works, Frederick Co.
252 a. on Enoch's Run, 368 a. on Reason's Run, 860 a. on Cacapeon, 400 a. on Enoch's Run, 208 a. on Cacapeon River.
Rec. 5-11-1779.
Wit.: Alex White, George Rootes, John Magill,
James Walker, James Hutchinson, Bryan Bruin,
Ben Rutherford.

1763 RUTHERFORD, Thomas to Abraham Hite
6-7 of Frederick Co. (lease and release) of Hampshire Co.
400 a. on Mill Creek; rec. 10-12-1763.
Wit.: Ja. Keith, Gabriel Jones, Peter Hog.

1799 RUTHERFORD, Thomas to William McPhereson
7-20 (w. Drusilla) of Hampshire Co.
of Berkeley Co.
152 a. on Bean Br. R.; rec. 9-17-1799.
Wit.: Van. Rutherford, Edward Christian,
Samuel Offutt, Thomas White.

1749 RUTLEDGE, James to Henery Lanciscus
7-30 (Obligation). Agrees to make deed on payment of 131 pounds, nine shillings, together with two horses branded with "L. S." on their near buttock. Recorded 12-14-1757.
Wit.: Henry Van Metere, Andrew Noland.

1769 RYAN, James (w. Mary) to Peter Casey
6-13 Lease and release of Hampshire Co.
300 a. on Petersons Creek; rec. 6-13-1769.
Wit.: None.

1789 RYAN, James to Samuel Barrett
12-12 of Baltimore of Baltimore
400 a. on Capt. John's Run; rec. 9-16-1790.
Wit.: Jacob Small, James Calhoun, Jr.

1795 RYAN, John (w. Sarah) to David Welton
2-16 of Hampshire Co. of Hardy Co.
300 a. on Patterson Creek; rec. 2-16-1795.
Wit.: None.

—S—

1790 SANDS, Othniel to John Stotts
9-16 Lease.
215 a. on North Branch of Potomac; rec. 9-16-1790.
Wit.: John Ohara, Nathaniel Dyer, Adam Hall.

1800 SAVAGE, John to Edward McCarty
12-15 of Hampshire Co. of Hampshire Co.
Recorded 12-15-1800.
Wit.: None.

1773 SCHRIED, Adam to Edward Kennison
8-6 of Hampshire Co. (mortgage) of Boutetourt Co.
400 a. on Cacapeon Creek; rec. 8-10-1773.
Wit.: Henry Fry, John Collins, R. Mynatt.

1778 SCHULLAR, Benjamin to John Cornman
11-2 (w. Katherine) (lease and release) of Philadelphia
of Philadelphia, Pa.
208 a. at foot of North Mt., near head of Tarrington Branch.
Rec. 11-10-1778.
Wit.: Henry Fry, John McDonald, Thos. Littlar.

1771 SCOTT, Edward (w. Susanna) to John Carpenter
9-18 of Hampshire Co. (lease and release) of Hampshire Co.
280 a. on Patterson Creek; rec. 8-11-1772.
Wit.: John Forman, Abraham Johnson, Wm. Rodgers.

1771 SCOTT, James (Jane) to John Wood
5-13 of Hampshire Co. of Hampshire Co.
386 a. on Lost River of Cacapeon; rec. 5-15-1771.
Wit.: Peter Steenbarger, Thos. Branan, Lawrence Hass.

1774 SCOTT, James to William Wilson
5-9 of Hampshire Co. (lease and release) of Hampshire Co.
437 a. on Lost River; rec. 5-10-1774.
Wit.: Joseph Fawcet, William Blackburn.

1775 SCOTT, James (w. Elizabeth) to Felix Seymour
8-16 of Augusta Co. (lease and release) of Hampshire Co.
400 a. on Looney's Creek; rec. 11-14-1775.
Wit.: George Rennick, Charles Hammond, Sam Dew,
Abraham Hite, Garret Vanmeter.

1775 SCOTT, James (w. Elizabeth) to David Scott
8-16 Heir-at-law of Adonijah Scott (lease & rel.) Augusta Co.
400 a. on Looney's Creek; rec. 11-14-1775.
Wit.: George Rennick, Charles Hammond, Sam Dew,
Abraham Hite, Garret Vanmeter.

1799 SCOTT, Patrick to Henry Eckhart
10-14 of Monongalia Co., Va. of Hampshire Co.
Recorded 12-16-1799.
Wit.: John Sturman, Isaac Good, Jr.,
Benjamin Thrasher, Andrew Wodrow, P. P. Wilson.

GRANTOR-GRANTEE　　　　　　　　　　　　　　　　　　　PAGE 53

1779 SCOTT, Robert　　　　　　　　to John Johnson
3-16　　of Fauquier Co., Va. (lease and release)　of Hampshire Co.
　　　180 a. on Patterson Creek; rec. 4-14-1779.
　　　Wit.: Sam Dew, William Buffington, Paul Haggarty,
　　　Uriah Blue.

1780 SCOTT, Robert　　　　　　　　to Samuel Jones
6-1　　of Fauquier Co.　　　　　　　of Fauquier Co.
　　　151 a. on Patterson Creek; rec. 11-14-1780.
　　　Wit.: None.

1780 SCOTT, Robert　　　　　　　　to John Prim
9-23　　of Fauquier Co.　　　　　　　of Fauquier Co.
　　　235 a. on Patterson Creek; rec. 11-14-1780.
　　　Wit.: Thomas Hog, John Cantwell, John Elliott,
　　　Silvester Welch.

1780 SCOTT, Robert　　　　　　　　to Thomas Doughtie
11-3　　of Fauquier Co.　　　　　　　of Fauquier Co.
　　　170 a. on North River Mt.; rec. 11-14-1780.
　　　Wit.: William Nall, William Nall, Jr.

1780 SCOTT, Robert　　　　　　　　to William Nall
11-3　　of Fauquier Co. (bill of sale)　of Fauquier Co.
　　　400 a. on Little Cacapeon Mt.; rec. 11-14-1780.
　　　Wit.: James Lawler, Wm. Nall, Jr., Thomas Doughty,
　　　Samuel Jones.

1780 SCOTT, Robert　　　　　　　　to John Bailie
11-7　　of Fauquier Co.　　　　　　　of Fauquier Co.
　　　292 a. on Little Cacapeon; rec. 11-14-1780.
　　　Wit.: Wm. Nall, Samuel Jones, Kimber Barton,
　　　James Lawler, Joseph Russell, Andrew Gilchrist.

1780 SCOTT, Robert　　　　　　　　to Thelomiah Rhodes
11-10　of Fauquier Co.　　　　　　　of Loudon Co.
　　　400 a. on Little Cacapeon; rec. 11-14-1780.
　　　Wit.: John Prim, Samuel Jones, Thomas Doughtie, Wm. Nall.

1794 SEBRING, John　　　　　　　　to Richard Rounsovel
　　　See FOSTER, Nathaniel
　　　ROGERS, John

1763 SEERS, James (w. Sarah)　　to Michael Stump
5-16　　of Hampshire Co. (mortgage)　of Hampshire Co.
　　　427 a. on South Branch; rec. 12-13-1763.
　　　Wit.: None.

1773 SEYMOUR, Felix　　　　　　　to George Renick
11-8　　of Hampshire Co.　　　　　　of Hampshire Co.
　　　250 a. on South Branch; rec. 11-9-1773.
　　　Wit.: None.

1773 SEYMOUR, Felix　　　　　　　to David Welton
11-8　　of Hampshire Co.　　　　　　of Hampshire Co.
　　　200 a. on South Branch; rec. 11-9-1773.
　　　Wit.: None.

1799 SHANHOLTZER, Peter　　　　to John Smoot
6-29　　of Hampshire Co. (bill of sale)　of Hampshire Co.
　　　Horse, two cows, wagon; rec. 12-16-1799.
　　　Wit.: James Monroe, James Carruthers.

1790 SHANTON, Abraham　　　　　to Joseph Shanton
2-10　　of Hampshire Co. (power of attorney)　(brother)
　　　Authority to use lawful ways in collecting whatever due
　　　Abraham Shanton. Recorded 2-10-1791.
　　　Wit.: None.

1770 SHAUGHAN, Daniel　　　　to son, Darby Shaughan
11-13　of Hampshire Co. (deed of gift)　of Hampshire Co.
　　　Personal property; rec. 11-13-1770.
　　　Wit.: Thomas Branan, John Douthit.

1794 SHELLHORN, Balser (w. Mary) to Peter Eversal
3-24　　of Maryland　　　　　　　　of Hampshire Co.
　　　199 a. on Patterson Creek; rec. 9-10-1794.
　　　Wit.: John Kimberline, John Mitchell, John Keller,
　　　Alex King.

1794 SHELLHORN, Balser (w. Mary) to Abraham Eversal
3-24　　of Maryland　　　　　　　　of Hampshire Co.
　　　178 a. on Patterson Creek; rec. 9-10-1794.
　　　Wit.: John Kimberline, John Mitchell, John Keller,
　　　Alex King.

1794 SHELLHORN, Balser (w. Mary) to Abraham Eversal
10-14　of Allegany Co.　　　　　　　of Hampshire Co.
　　　239 a. in Hampshire Co.; rec. 10-15-1794.
　　　Wit.: John Mitchell, Wm. Johnson,
　　　John Jones, Jr., Abraham Brookhart.

1798 SHEPHERD, Benjamin (w. Catherine) to Lewis Dunn
10-19　of Hampshire Co.　　　　　　of Hampshire Co.
　　　Quarter acre in Frankfort; rec. 5-20-1799.
　　　Wit.: John Mitchell, A. King, Israel Clawson, Geo. Young.

1793 SHEPHERD, Jonathan (w. Rachel) to John McMeekin
11-29　of Hampshire Co.　　　　　　of Hampshire Co.
　　　126 a. in Hampshire Co.; rec. 12-11-1793.
　　　Wit.: Thomas Dowden, Charles Magill,
　　　Andrew Turk, Edward Moore.

1782 SHEPLER, Henry (w. Catherine) to Robert Higgins
5-14　　of Hampshire Co.　　　　　　of Hampshire Co.
　　　Parcel of land on South Branch; rec. 5-14-1782.
　　　Wit.: Joseph Nevill, Charles Lynch, Abel Randall.

1775 SHIPLER, Henry　　　　　　　to William Row
6-11　　of Hampshire Co. (lease and release)　of Hampshire Co.
　　　138 a. on South Branch River; rec. 3-12-1775.
　　　Wit.: Peter Steenburgen, John Welton
　　　Abraham Hoornbeeck, John Shipler, John Hedger.

1780 SHOOK, Herman　　　　　　　to Mathews George
　　　See REAGER, Jacob

1784 SHORT, Jacob (w. Mary)　　　to William Critton
5-11　　of Hampshire Co. (lease and release)　of Hampshire Co.
　　　278 a. on Baker's Run; rec. 5-11-1784.
　　　Wit.: John Stoker, Daniel Newcomb, John Critton, Jr.

1784 SIBLEY, John　　　　　　　　to Garret Vanmeter
4-14　　of Hampshire Co. (mortgage)　of Hampshire Co.
　　　187 a. on South Branch River; rec. 5-11-1785.
　　　Wit.: Abraham Hite, Rubin Berry, Isaac Vanmeter.

1783 SIDWELL, Hugh　　　　　　　to John Busby
10-14　of Chester Co. (lease and release)　of Hampshire Co.
　　　140 a. on North River; rec. 5-11-1784.
　　　Wit.: George Beall, Jas. Carruthers,
　　　Jonathan Pugh, William Murphy.

1799 SIMCOCK, Samuel (w. Elizabeth) to Conrad Pusinger
1-23　　of Brooke Co., Va.　　　　　of Hampshire Co.
　　　107 a. on Potomac River; rec. 5-20-1799.
　　　Wit.: Charles Prather, John Relfe, John Prather.

1779 SIMMONDS, Thomas (w. Agnes) to Charles Clinton
8-9　　of Hampshire Co. (lease and release)　of Washington Co.
　　　199 a. on North Branch of Potomac; rec. 8-10-1779.
　　　Wit.: None.

1757 SIMPSON, James　　　　　　　to Thomas Waggener
7-1　　of Hampshire Co.　　　　　　of Hampshire Co.
　　　100 a. in county of Hampshire, on South Fork of South
　　　Branch of Potomac. Recorded 12-14-1757.
　　　Wit.: William Woodford, Robt. Johnston, Jas. Ta—?

1763 SIMPSON, James　　　　　　　to Benjamin Beall
10-3　　of Hampshire Co. (lease and release)　of Hampshire Co.
　　　Lot No. 4—400 a. on South Branch; rec. 10-12-1763.
　　　Wit.: Richard Young, William Halle, Sam Dew,
　　　Abraham Hite, John McColloch, William Darling.

　　　SIMPSON, James　　　　　　　to Benjamin Beall
　　　of Hampshire Co.　　　　　　of Hampshire Co.
　　　Bond. Need not pay interest on purchase price. Rec. 10-12-1763.
　　　Wit.: Abraham Hite, Richard Yancey, Sam Dew.

1793 SINGLETON, John　　　　　　to George Newman
9-9　　of Hardy Co.　　　　　　　　Isaac Newman
　　　430 a. on South Branch; rec. 9-11-1793.
　　　Wit.: Adam Lee, William Bullitt, James Cochran.

1794 SLAUGHTER, James　　　　　to Joseph Cravine
6-21　　of Hampshire Co.　　　　　　of Hampshire Co.
　　　505 a. on Crooked Run; rec. 9-10-1794.
　　　Wit.: Andrew Wodrow, Henry Heinzman,
　　　Nathaniel Dyer, James Cochran.

179) SLONAKER, Christian (w. Mary) to Jacob Haauver
8-4　　of Hampshire Co. (HOOVER) of Hampshire Co.
　　　111½ a. in Hampshire Co. rec. 10-9-1793.
　　　Wit.: Elias Poston, John Mason.

1789 SMALLEY, Andrew　　　　　　to Isaac Miller
3-31　　of Hampshire Co.　　　　　　of Hampshire Co.
　　　139 a. on Patterson Creek; rec. 4-16-1789.
　　　Wit.: John Unger, Alex Ruthven, William Jacob.

1791 SMALLEY, Andrew　　　　　　to Henry Rosebroom
10-23　of Hampshire Co. (lease)　　　of Hampshire Co.
　　　146 a. on Patterson Creek; rec. 10-13-1791.
　　　Wit.: None.

1795 SMALLEY, Andrew (w. Christina) to Henry Hamilton
2-20　　of Hampshire Co.　　　　　　of Hardy Co.
　　　Parcel of land on New Creek; rec. 4-20-1795.
　　　Wit.: Basil Lucas, Richard Patton, John Hooker,
　　　John Lucas.

1796 SMALLEY, Andrew (w. Christiana) to Ed McCarty
2-20　　of Hampshire Co.　　　　　　of Hampshire Co.
　　　Parcel of land on New Creek; rec. 4-18-1796.
　　　Wit.: Basil Lucas, Rd. Patton, John Hooker,
　　　John D. Lucas.

1796 SMALLEY, Andrew　　　　　　to Basil Lucas
3-7　　of Hampshire Co.　　　　　　of Hampshire Co.
　　　170 a. on Allegany Mt.; rec. 4-18-1796.
　　　Wit.: Ed McCarty, Wm. Vause, John Hooker,
　　　John D. Lucas.

1796 SMALLEY, Andrew　　　　　　to John High
10-25　of Loudon Co. (bill of sale)　of Hampshire Co.
　　　SMALLEY, Ezekiel
　　　of Hampshire Co.
　　　400 a. on Mill Creek; rec. 12-19-1796.
　　　Wit.: Vincent Williams, Henry Hawk,
　　　Isaac Williams, Edward Williams, Jr.

1797 SMALLEY, Andrew　　　　　　to Adam White
3-20　　of Hampshire Co.　　　　　　of Hampshire Co.
　　　112½ a. on Abraham Gapp Run; rec. 6-19-1797.
　　　Wit.: Okey Johnson, Hendrick Roseboom, —? Johnson.

1797 SMALLEY, Azariah (w. Rebecca) to Gassedg Simkins
4-16　　of Hampshire Co.　　　　　　of Hampshire Co.
　　　270 a. on North River; rec. 4-17-1797.
　　　Wit.: None.

1795 SMALLEY, Christian　　　　　to Basil Lucas
　　　See HAMILTON, Henry

1798 9-15	SMILEY, Elizabeth to Thomas Smiley of Cumberland Co., Pa. of Carlisle Co., Pa. 219 a. on South Branch River; rec. 12-17-1798. Wit.: William Irvine, John Jordan.
1762 12-11	SMITH, Charles (w. Rebecca) to Bryan Bruin of Winchester, Va. (lease and release) of Winchester, Va. 57 a. on Ca Capehon; rec. 2-15-1764. Wit.: Peter Hog, Ja. Keith, Gabriel Jones.
1770 3-12	SMITH, Charles (w. Rebecca) to William Bills of Frederick Co. (lease and release) of Hampshire Co. 180 a., about four miles above North River of Cacapeon. Recorded 3-15-1770. Wit.: John Goodwine, Ralph Bradruck, Joseph Wiley.
1771 12-27	SMITH, Charles (w. Rebecca) to Robert Rutherford Frederick Co. (lease and release) Winchester, Frederick Co. 252 a. on Enoch's Run, near forks of Cacapeon; rec. 3-10-1772. Wit.: Phil Pendleton, Angus McDonald, Thomas Swearinger, Thos. Rutherford, Bryan Bruin, Alex White, John Magill.
1785 8-9	SMITH, Charles to Stephen Miller of Hampshire Co. of Cumberland Co. 155 a. on South Branch; rec. 8-9-1785. Wit.: None.

1792	SMITH, Edward to Samuel Dinnett
	See MAGILL, Charles
	      THURSTON, Charles Mynn
	      WAGGENER, Andrew

1793	SMITH, Edward to Adam Hall See FOX, William MITCHELL, John

1794	SMITH, Edward to James McAlster
	See MAGILL, Charles
	      THURSTON, Charles Mynn
	      WAGGONER, Andrew

1791 6-16	SMITH, George (w. Elizabeth) to Michael Smith of Hampshire Co. (deed of gift) of Hampshire Co. 402 a. on waters of Marle Bottom, a branch of North River. Rec. 6-16-1791. Wit.: None.
1780 11-7	SMITH, James (w. Mary) to Abraham Powell of Hampshire Co. lease and release) of Hampshire Co. 429 a. on Dillon's Run; rec. 11-14-1780. Wit.: None.
1785 11-8	SMITH, James (w. Mary) to Isaac Lupton of Hampshire Co. of Hampshire Co. 371 a. on Dillons Run; rec. 11-8-1785. Wit.: Isaac Parsons, John Bosler, Abraham Powitt.
1790 9-10	SMITH, James to Samuel Baker of Hampshire Co. (release of mortgage) of Hardy Co. 400 a. in Hampshire Co.; rec. 9-16-1790. Wit.: Andrew Wodrow.
1796 7-18	SMITH, James, Sr. to Thomas Tucker, Jr. SMITH, Mary of Hampshire Co. of Hampshire Co. 246 a. on South Branch; rec. 7-18-1796. Wit.: None.
1798 9-14	SMITH, James (w. Rachael) to Michael Buck of Washington Co. of Hampshire Co. 238 a. on Great Cacapeon Mt.; rec. 9-17-1798. Wit.: Cornelius Ferree, Geo. Smith, Isaac Ferree.
1772 11-9	SMITH, John to Michael Cresap of Hampshire Co. (lease and release) of Frederick, Md. 40 a. on North Branch of Potomac; rec. 11-12-1772. Wit.: Michael Cresap, Jr., Joseph Stibbs, Thomas Humphres, B. Ashby.
1793 7-10	SMITH, Michael to William Williamson of Hampshire Co. of Hampshire Co. 402 a. on North River; rec. 9-14-1795. Wit.: None.
1791 6-11	SMITH, Nathaniel to Nathan Price of Hampshire Co. (lease) of Allegany Co. Parcel of land on Knobley Mt., and Plum Run; rec. 9-15-1791. Wit.: Alex Argos, Micady Argo.
1795 6-23	SMITH, Nathaniel to Robert Monroe of Hampshire Co. of Hampshire Co. 40 a. on Knobley Mt.; rec. 6-23-1795. Wit.: Alex King, Daniel Jones, John Mitchell, Will Armstrong.
1795 6-23	SMITH, Nathaniel to Robert Monroe of Hampshire Co. of Hampshire Co. 141 a. on Knobley Mt.; rec. 9-14-1795. Wit.: Alex King, Daniel Jones, John Mitchell, Will Armstrong.
1770 11-17	SMITH, Richard to Bryan Bruin of Hampshire Co. (mortgage) Winchester, Frederick Co. 400 a on Capt. John's Branch; rec. 12-11-1770. Wit.: Edward McGuire, Wm. Scott, G. Michael Laubinger, Thomas Wess, Thomas Edmonson.
1780 11-14	SMITH, Thomas to Thomas Littler of Hampshire Co. of Hampshire Co. 94 a. on North River; rec. 11-14-1780. Wit.: None.
1762 8-2	SMITH, William (w. Mary) to John Claypoole of Hampshire Co. (lease and release) of Hampshire Co. 100 a. on Lost River; rec. 8-10-1762. Wit.: None.
1764 12-11	SMITH, William to William Anderson of Hampshire Co. (lease and release) of Hampshire Co. 100 a. in Hampshire Co.; rec. 12-12-1764. Wit.: Sam Dew.
1768 3-31	SMITH, William (w. Anne) to Bryan Bruen of Hampshire Co. (lease and release) of Frederick Co., Va. 400 a. on South Branch; rec. 9-18-1768. Wit.: None.
1779 9-6	SMITH, William (w. Mary) to Cornelius Vanteventer of Hampshire Co (lease and release) of Loudon Co. 286¼ a. on Lost River of Cacapeon; rec. 5-9-1780. Wit.: Stephen Ruddell, Levi Ashbrook, Thomas Slaten.
1787	SMOOT, Thomas Barton to Sylvester Neff See NEFF, Christina, Adam, Catherine, Esther.
1795 3-10	SMOOT, Thomas (w. Catherine) to Daniel Ellor of Hampshire Co. of Hampshire Co. 21 a. on Mill Creek; rec. 4-20-1795. Wit.: Jas. Fleming, John Piser, Peter Engle.
1795 3-12	SMOOT, Thomas (w. Catherine) to Jacob Piser of Hampshire Co. of Hampshire Co. 160 a. on Mill Creek; rec. 4-200-1795. Wit.: Jas. Fleming, John Piser, Peter Engle.
1779 8-6	SNIKERS, Edward to Joseph Hill of Frederick Co. (lease and release) of Hampshire Co. 223 a. on North River of Cacapeon; rec. 5-9-1780. Wit.: John Oldakers, Samuel Barkley, William Harris, Daniel Harris, Henry Oldaker.
1779 8-10	SNICKERS, Edward to William Oldakers of Frederick Co. (lease and release) of Hampshire Co. 347 a. between the meanders that divide Lost River from Ca- capeon; rec. 5-9-1780. Wit.: Daniel Harris, John Oldakers, Henry Oldakers, Samuel Barklay, William Harris.
1784 3-2	SNICKERS, Edward to George Beatty of Frederick Co. of Hampshire Co. 90 a. on South Branch; rec. 5-11-1784. Wit.: A. Waggener, Elias Poston.
1792 7-31	SNYDER, John (w. Letitia) to Nicholas Boyce of Hampshire Co. (lease) of Hampshire Co. 625 a. on Patterson Creek; rec. 7-31-1792. Wit.: None.
1774 8-2	SOMMERVILLE, James to William Abernethy of Fredericksburg 400 a . onSouth Branch; rec. 3-12-1775. Wit.: Bryan Bruin, Alex White, George Rootes, Thos. Campbell, Peter Bruin, Wm. Campbell, Wm. Clancy, Ben. Grubb.
1780	SOMERVILLE, James to Reuben Berry See GILCHRIST, Robert
1780	SOMERVILLE, James to John Renick See GILCHRIST, Robert
1780	SOMERVILLE, James to Henry Litler See GILCHRIST, Robert
1794 2-8	SPENCER, John, Sr. (w. Joice) to John Spencer, Jr. of Hampshire Co. of Hampshire Co. 372 a. on Cabbin Run; rec. 6-11-1794. Wit.: Daniel Combs, Stephen Cooper, John Metts.
1799 8-29	SPENCER, John (w. Sarah) to Robert Williams of Hampshire Co. of Hampshire Co. Two acres on Patterson Creek; rec. 10-14-1799. Wit.: None.
1791 10-30	SPIKER, Jacob to Benjamin Rollins of Washington Co. of Hampshire Co. 260 a. on Middle Run; rec. 10-30-1792. Wit.: None.
1772 8-15	SPORE, John (w. Mary) to Bryan Bruin Winchester, Fred'k Co. (lease & rel.) Winchester, Fred'k Co. 264 a. on Little Cacapeon River; rec. 11-10-1772. Wit.: John Magill, Edward McGuire,, Wm. Campbell, Robert Wood, Alex White.
1772 9-28	SPOHR, John (w. Mary) to Christopher Marshall of Winchester, (mortgage) Charles Marshall Frederick County Benjamin Marshall 195 a. on Little Cacapeon; Daniel Williams Rec. 11-10-1772. of Philadelphia, Pa. Wit.: Edward McGuire, John Magill, Wm. Campbell.
1780 3-14	SPOHRE, John Ulrick (w. Judith) to John Rennock of Hampshire Co. of Hampshire Co. 215 a. on South Branch River; rec. 5-9-1780. Wit.: None.
1779 12-14	SPORE, John (w. Mary) to Benjamin Meshy of Lancaster Co., Pa. of Lancaster Co. 410 a. in Hampshire Co.; rec. 2-18-1799. Wit.: Christian Petrid.
1800 10-20	SPRIGG, Osborn to James Parsons of Hampshire Co. David Parsons Recorded 10-20-1800. of Hampshire Co.

1777 3-25	**SPRINGER, Anne** of Hampshire Co.	to **Jacob Larue** of Hampshire Co.	

SPRINGER, Zadock
of Monongala Co. (bond)
Bond—Fifteen hundred pounds; rec 11-11-1777.
Wit.: Wm. Hendshaw, James Dosten, Thomas Dosten, John Larue.

1792 4-24 **SPRINGFIELD, Trustees of** Hampshire Co. to **Joseph Williams** of Hampshire Co.
Quarter acre in Springfield; rec. 4-24-1792.
Wit.: None.
[Trustees of Springfield were: William Campbell, Robert Rannells, Jacob Earson, John Pancake, and John Taylor.]

1792 4-24 **SPRINGFIELD, Trustees of** Hampshire Co. to **William Williamson** of Hampshire Co.
Half acre in Springfield; rec. 4-24-1792.
Wit.: None.

1792 4-24 **SPRINGFIELD, Trustees of** Hampshire Co. to **John Williamson** of Hampshire Co.
Quarter acre in Springfield; rec. 4-24-1792.
Wit.: None.

1792 4-24 **SPRINGFIELD, Trustees of** Hampshire Co. to **Robert Ross** of Hampshire Co.
Quarter acre in Springfield; rec. 4-24-1792.
Wit.: None.

1792 4-24 **SPRINGFIELD, Trustees of** Hampshire Co. to **Joseph Pancake** of Hampshire Co.
Quarter acre in Springfield; rec. 4-24-1792.
Wit.: None.

1792 4-24 **SPRINGFIELD, Trustees of** Hampshire Co. to **John McBride** of Hampshire Co.
Two quarter-acre tracts in Springfield; rec. 4-24-1792.
Wit.: None.

1792 4-24 **SPRINGFIELD, Trustees of** Hampshire Co. to **James McAtester** of Springfield
Quarter acre in Springfield; rec. 4-24-1792.
Wit.: None.

1792 4-24 **SPRINGFIELD, Trustees of** Hampshire Co. to **John Logan** of Hampshire Co.
Quarter acre in Springfield; rec. 4-24-1792.
Wit.: None.

1792 4-24 **SPRINGFIELD, Trustees of** Hampshire Co. to **John Donaldson** of Hampshire Co.
Quarter acre in Springfield; rec. 4-24-1792.
Wit.: None.

1792 4-24 **SPRINGFIELD, Trustees of** to **John Dixon**
Quarter acre in Springfield; rec. 4-24-1792.
Wit.: None.

1792 4-24 **SPRINGFIELD, Trustees of** Hampshire Co. to **Francis Combs** of Hampshire Co.
Quarter acre in Springfield; rec. 4-24-1792.
Wit.: None.

1792 4-24 **SPRINGFIELD, Trustees of** Hampshire Co. to **Robert Buck** of Hampshire Co.
Quarter acre in Springfield; rec. 4-24-1792.
Wit.: None.

1792 4-24 **SPRINGFIELD, Trustees of** Hampshire Co. to **Jacob Ahrsam** of Hampshire Co.
Quarter acre in town of Springfield; rec. 4-24-1792.
Wit.: None.

1799 12-1 **SPRINGFIELD, Trustees of** Hampshire Co. to **Joseph Harman** of Hampshire Co.
Recorded 2-17-1800.
Wit.: John Taylor, Andrew Haines, Jacob Earsom, John Pancake, William Campbell.

1800 2-17 **SPRINGFIELD, Trustees of** Hampshire Co. to **William Newell** of Hampshire Co.
Recorded 2-17-1800.
Wit.: John Taylor, Andrew Haines, Jacob Earsom, Robert Rannels, John Pancake, William Campbell

1794 6-21 **STADLOR, Jacob (w. Hannah)** to **John McMeekin**
One acre in Frankfort; rec. 12-10-1794.
Wit.: John Brown, John Mitchell, Alex King, Will Armstrong.

1791 8-16 **STAFFORD, Richard (w. Catherine)** of Frankfort to **John Littlejohn** of Leesburg, Va.
Quarter acre in town of Frankfort; rec. 12-15-1791.
Wit.: John Mitchell, Solomon Jones, Alex King.

1797 1-21 **STAGG, John** of Hampshire Co. to **Thomas Dowden** of Hampshire Co.
185 a. on Patterson Creek; rec. 2-20-1797.
Wit.: None.

1797 10-16 **STALLMAN, Lewis (w. Mary)** of Hampshire Co. to **Jacob Boft** of Frederick Co.
130 a. on Patterson Creek; rec. 10-16-1797.
Wit.: Thomas Lory, Archibald Watts, John Heinsman.

1795 9-14 **STOLLMAN, Lewis (w. Mary)** of Hampshire Co. to **John Doveridge** of Hampshire Co.
80 a. on Patterson Creek; rec. 9-14-1795.
Wit.: Andrew Wodrow.

1791 **STARN, Jacob (w. Catherine)** of Hampshire Co. to **John Starn** of Hampshire Co.
100 a. on Little Cacapeon; rec. 6-16-1791.
Wit.: None.

1791 6-16 **STARN, Jacob (w. Catherine)** of Hampshire Co. to **Joseph Starn** of Hampshire Co.
85 a. on Little Cacapeon; rec. 6-16-1791.
Wit.: None.

1800 10-20 **STARR, James (w. Nancy)** of Hampshire Co. to **Abraham Jones** of Hampshire Co.
Recorded 10-20-1800.

1801 2-5 **STARR, John** of Hampshire Co. to **John McBride** of Hampshire Co.
Recorded 2-16-1801.

1792 8-25 **STATTECOP, Israel (Stallcop?)** of Frankfort to **George Rollins** of Frankfort
Half acre in town of Frankfort; rec. 8-28-1792.
Wit.: John Reed, John Kimberline, Solomon Jones.

STEATHER—See Strether, Strother.

1767 4-14 **STEATHER, John** of Hampshire Co. (bill of sale) to **Capt. John Welton**
Three cows; rec. 4-14-1767.
Wit.: Peter Hog.

1790 1-13 **STEED, Aaron** to **Phillip Crisman**
Bill of sale.
111 a. in Hampshire Co.; rec. 6-16-1791.
Wit.: John Critton, Balser Stoker, Cornelius Ferrel.

1796 4-18 **STEED, Aaron (w. Eleanor)** of Hampshire Co. to **John Critton** of Hampshire Co.
400 a. on Potomac River; rec. 4-18-1796.
Wit.: None.

1767 11-10 **STEEL, John** Cumberland Co., Pa. (lease & rel.) to **Joseph Steel** Cumberland Co., Pa.
390 a on Great Capon; rec. 11-11-1767.
Wit.: Abraham Hite, Simon Taylor, Sam Dew.

1790 9-13 **STEEL, John** of Cumberland Co. to **Robert Parviance** of Baltimore
111 a., 235 a., 275 a., 333 a., 363 a., on Little Cacapeon.
Rec. 2-28-1792.
Wit.: Thomas Foster, Jas. Hamilton, Steel Semple.

1794 1-27 **STEEL, Joseph** of Cumberland Co. to **John Perril** of Hampshire Co.
390 a. on Great Cacapeon River; rec. 2-12-1794.
Wit.: Elisha Beall, Joseph Perril, George Beall, John Perril, Jr.

1761 2-9 **STEENBERGEN, Peter** of Hampshire Co. (lease and release) to **William Ramsay** of Alexandria, Fairfax Co., Va.
320 a., New Creek; rec. 2-10-1761.
Wit.: None.

1763 6-13 **STEENBERGEN, Peter** of Hampshire Co. (mortgage) to **William Fowler**
Personal property; rec. 12-13-1763.
Wit.: Samuel Dew, Phil Ross.

1774 3-3 **STEPHENS, Adam** of Frederick Co. (lease and release) to **Angus McDonald** of Frederick Co.
542 a. in Hampshire Co.; rec. 3-8-1774.
Wit.: Edward McGuire, Wm. Scott, John Lowry, Phil Pndleton, Robert Stephens, Samuel Beall, Alex White, George Rootes, James Somerville.

1796 6-20 **STEPHENS, Christian (w. Elizabeth)** of Hampshire Co. (bill of sale) to **Patrick Rogers** of Hampshire Co.
Quarter acre and 4 acres in Frankfort Town; rec. 2-20-1797.
Wit.: John Mitchell, A. King, Joshua Jones, Benoni Pierce, John Mitchel, Jr.

1798 11-6 **STEPHENS, Christian** of Northwestern Territory to **Thomas Dunn** of Hampshire Co.
326 a. on Patterson Creek; rec. 5-20-1799.
Wit.: Henry Protzman, John Mitchell, Lewis Dunn.

1765 9-3 **STEPHENS, Peter (w. Mary)** of Frederick Co. (lease and release) to **Thomas Perry** of Frederick Co.
206 a. on North River; rec. 10-8-1765.
Wit.: James Wood, James Ireson, Ja. Keith, Peter Hog, Alex White, Gabriel Jones.

1768 8-19 **STEPHENS, William (w. Mary)** of Hampshire Co. (lease and release) to **Joseph Ogden** / **Josiah Hughes** of Philadelphia
354 a. on Patterson Creek; rec. 9-13-1768.
Wit.: Joseph Neaville, Patrick Linch, Charles Linch.

1794 6-11 **STEPHENSON, Samuel** of Hampshire Co. to **Thomas Rogers** of Hampshire Co.
117 a. on Little Cacapeon; rec. 6-11-1794.
Wit.: John Rogers, Stephen Feattier, Jacob Starn.

1795 10-19 **STEPHENSON, Samuel** of Hampshire Co. to **Moses Henderson** / **David Henderson** of Hampshire Co.
117 a. in Hampshire Co.; rec. 10-19-1795.
Wit.: Thompson Pegg, John Stuard.

GRANTOR-GRANTEE

1789 STEER, Isaac — from Jury
4-17 Summons to the Sheroff of Hampshire Co. to summon 12 men to meet on land of Isaac Steer's, to review the land where the said Mr. Steer intends to erect a water grist mill and saw mill, and report whether this erection will affect the property of other neighbors.
Permission was given him to erect the mill.
The jury: James McBride, John Critton, Aaron Rise, Henry Miller, Edward McCarthy, William Day, William McGuire, John House, James Largent, Daniel Newcomb, William Milburn, and John Pursell.

1779 STOKER, Babzer (w. Eve) (lease and release) — to John Stoker
5-11 of Hampshire Co. of Hampshire Co.
100 a. on Little Cacapeon River; rec. 11-9-1779.
Wit.: Isaac Short, John Johnson, William Chapman, Samuel Shivers.

1792 STONE, Benj. (w. Anna) — to Cornelius Williamson
8-1 of Hampshire Co. of Hampshire Co.
152½ a. on North River; rec. 8-28-1792.
Wit.: George Beall, John Arnold, Thomas Clayton, Joseph Asbury.

1792 STONE, Benjamin (w. Ann) — to William Martin
8-24 of Hampshire Co. (mortgage) of Hampshire Co.
120 a., four miles above North River; rec. 8-28-1792.
Wit.: George Beall, John Arnold, Thomas Clayton, Joseph Asbury.

1794 STONE, Benj. (w. Ann) — to Samuel Williamson
4-7 of Hampshire Co. of Hampshire Co.
172 a. on North River; rec. 6-11-1794.
Wit.: Joseph Asbury, Mary Asbury.

1794 STONE, Benj. (w. Ann) — to Henry Asberry
4-7 of Hampshire Co.
721¾ a. on North River.
Wit.: Joseph Asbury, Mary Asbury.

1794 STONE, Benj. (w. Anna) — to Azariah Smalley
11-10 of Hampshire Co. of Hampshire Co.
270 a. on North River; rec. 12-10-1794.
Wit.: Joseph Asbury, Henry Asbury, Alex Brown.

1794 STONE, Benj. (w. Anna) — to William Martin
11-10 of Hampshire Co. of Harrison Co.
180 a. on North River; rec. 12-10-1794.
Wit.: Joseph Asbury, Henry Asbury, Alex Brown.

1801 STONE, Joseph — to Barton Smoot
2-5 of Hampshire Co. of Hampshire Co.
Recorded 2-16-1801.
Wit.: None.

1767 STRAIDER, Frances — to Hugh Murphy
5-12 of Hampshire Co. (bill of sale) of Hampshire Co.
Personal property; rec. 5-12-1767.
Wit.: John Keating.

STRETHER—See Steather, Strother.

1767 STRETHER, John — to Frances Strether
4-24 of Hampshire Co. of Hampshire Co.
22 hogs; rec. 4-15-1767.
Wit.: E. Pelly.

1775 STRICKER, George (lease and release) — to Garret Vanmeter
1-16 of Frederick Co. of Hampshire Co.
195 a. on Mill Run; rec. 3-14-1775.
Wit.: Abraham Hite, Abraham Hite, Jr., John Sibley, Isaac Vanmeter.

1795 STRODE, Margaret — to Edward Strode
10-14 of Berkeley Co. of Hampshire Co.
121 a. on Potomac River; rec. 10-26-1795.
Wit.: Joseph Forman, Amos Nicholas, John Strode.

STROTHER—See Steather, Strether.

1782 STROTHER, James (w. Jane) — to James Monroe
11-13 of Fauquier Co. of Culpepper Co.
227 a. in Hampshire Co.; rec. 5-13-1783.
Wit.: Alex Monroe, John Chenoweth, Reason Howard.

1765 STUMP, Michael, Sr. — to Michael Stump, Jr.
10-7 (w. Catherine) of Hampshire Co.
of Hampshire Co. ((lease and release)
Lot No. 2—400 a., on South Branch; rec. 10-8-1765.
Wit.: None.

1797 STUTZMAN, John (w. Mary) — to Patrick Keran
9-4 of Hampshire Co. of Hampshire Co.
57 a. on road from Winchester to Romney; rec. 10-16-1797.
Wit.: None.

1758 SULLIVAN, Giles — to Nathaniel Kuykendall
7-4 Co. of Creaven, N. C. (lease & rel.) of Hampshire Co.
415 a., on South Branch of Potomaac; rec. 5-13-1760.
Wit.: William Millar, Geo. Hart, Thomas Chester, Thomas Spicer.

1766 SUTTON, Benjamin — to Samuel Woodson
10-30 East New Jersey, Somerset Co. Hampshire Co
Bond—100 pounds; rec. 5-10-1770.
Wit.: Sam Pritchard, Isaac Sutton.

1768 SUTTON, Jasper — to James Chesnut
6-9 CHESNUT, John Craven Co., S. C.
Craven Co., S. C. (power of attorney)
Power to transact business in Frederick Co., Va.
Wit.: Thomas Jones, John Forman, Joseph Kerfham.

1771 SUTTON, Jasper (lease & rel.) — to Simon Taylor
5-7 CHESNUT, John, son and heir of Hampshire Co.
Alexander Chesnut, Frederick Co.
400 a. on South Branch; rec. 6-12-1771.
Wit.: James Chesnut, John Forman, Wm. Boykin, Daniel Richardson, Richard Sutton.

1782 SWANK, Phillip — to Valentine Forst
2-23 of Hampshire Co. of Hampshire Co.
60 a. on South Branch; rec. 5-14-1782.
Wit.: Job Welton, Christopher Ermantrout, Martin Shobe.

1782 SWANK, Phillip — to Valentine Post
2-23 of Hampshire Co. of Hampshire Co.
18 a. on South Branch; rec. 5-14-1782.
Wit.: Job Welton, Christopher Ermantrout, Martin Shobe.

1797 SWOBE, Barbara — to Dennis Daniels
See BROOKHART, John.

1796 SWOBE, John (w. Barbara) — to John Mitchell
2-15 Quarter acre in Frankfort; rec. 2-15-1796.
Wit.: Alex King, Abraham Johnson, John Snyder.

—T—

1785 TAGGART, Francis (w. Lucy) — to Thomas Combs
8-9 of Hampshire Co. of Hampshire Co.
425 a. on Drains of Palmer Run; rec. 8-9-1785.
Wit.: Sam Dew, Andrew Wodrow.

1786 TAGGART, Francis (w. Lucy) — to Thomas Rukman
9-12 of Hampshire Co. of Hampshire Co.
292 a. on Little Cacapeon; rec. 9-12-1786.
Wit.: None.

1793 TAGGART, Francis (w. Lucy) — to Joseph Tidbal
12-11 of Romney of Winchester
428 a. on Little Cacapeon; rec. 11-25-1798.
Wit.: None.

1800 TAGGART, Children of Francis — to Charles Hauser
by BAKER, Patrick (w. Lucy), guardians.

1784 TARPLEY, James (w. Elizabeth) — to Robert Gregg
5-11 of Hampshire Co. of Washington Co.
20 a. on South Branch River; rec. 5-11-1784.
Wit.: John Stoker, Daniel Newcomb, John Critten, Jr.

1794 TARPLEY, James (w. Elizabeth) — to John J. Jacob
4-3 of Mason Co., Ky. (power of attorney) of Hampshire Co.
To convey trace of land on South Branch River; rec. 4-3-1794.
Wit.: None.

1794 TARPLEY, James — to James Martin
12-10 120 a. near forks of North and South Branch Rivers.
Rec. 2-16-1795.
Wit.: Michael Cresap, James Cresap, Thomas Cresap.

1794 TARVIN, George — to John McCormick, Sr.
9-10 of Hampshire Co. of Berkeley Co.
103 a. in Hampshire Co.; rec. 9-10-1794.
Wit.: Andrew Wodrow, John Reed.

1794 TARVIN, George (w. Sarah) — to John Easton
10-18 of Hampshire Co. of Hampshire Co.
417 a. about one mile from Potomac River; rec. 12-10-1794.
Wit.: Lewis Throckmorton, Henry Beckner, Jacob Chrisman, Charles McCracken.

1798 TARVIN, George — to John Easter
9-17 of Mason Co., Ky. of Hampshire Co.
110 a. on Potomac River; rec. 9-15-1798.
Wit.: None.

1797 TAYLOR, Henry (w. Mary) — to Valentine Switzer
10-15 of Hampshire Co. of Hampshire Co.
285 a. on Great Cacapeon; rec. 12-18-1797.
Wit.: George Deer, John Chenoweth, Cornelius Gard.

1799 TAYLOR, John (w. Lettie) — to Edward Cochran
2-16 of Hampshire Co. of Hampshire Co.
100 a. on North R. Mt.; rec. 2-18-1799.
Wit.: None.

1798 TAYLOR, Richard — to Joseph Taylor
4-16 of Hampshire Co. of Hampshire Co.
119 a. on Little Cacapeon River; rec. 4-16-1798.
Wit.: None.

1765 TEGARDEN, Abraham — to Thomas Allen
2-17 of Frederick Co. (lease and release) of Frederick Co.
200 a. on Cabin Run; rec. 11-12-1766.
Wit.: Luke Collins, Bryan Bruin, James Anderson, Benjamin Parker.

1769 TEPOLT, Michael — to John Jones
11-14 of Hampshire Co. (lease and release) of Hampshire Co.
170 a. on drain of Patterson Creek; rec. 11-15-1769.
Wit.: John Roussaw, John Reno.

1787 TERNAY, Matthew (w. Phoebe) — to James Murphy
9-3 of Hampshire Co. of Hampshire Co.
Half-acre lot in town of Romney; rec. 9-13-1787.
Wit.: Alex Ruthven, Rub. Holliday, Ralph Humphreys, John Murphy.

1800 TERRY, George (w. Mary Ann) — to Stephen Terry
8-15 of Hampshire Co. of Hampshire Co.
Recorded 8-15-1800.
Wit.: Zachariah Linton, John Primm, Betty Primm.

GRANTOR-GRANTEE   PAGE 57

1799 12-16	TEVAULT, Nicholas to George King of Mercer Co., Ky. of Hampshire Co. 387 a. on New Creek; rec. 12-16-1799. Wit.: None.	1797 10-16	THOMPSON, John (w. Elizabeth) to John Taylor of Hampshire Co. of Hampshire Co. 100 a. on North R. Mt.; rec. 10-16-1797. Wit.: None.
1795 9-14	THOMAS, Enoch, Sr. (w. Anna) to Enoch Thomas, Jr. of Hampshire Co. of Hampshire Co. 219 a. on Mill Creek; rec. 9-14-1795. Wit.: Andrew Wodrow.	1800 4-11	THOMPSON, John (w. Martha) to Byansa Powelson of Hampshire Co. of Hampshire Co. Recorded 4-14-1800. Wit.: John Thompson, Betty Thompson.
1796 4-30	THOMAS, Enoch to Stephen Thomas 219 a. in Hampshire Co.; rec. 6-20-1796. Wit.: Andrew Wodrow, Edward Dyer, John J. Jacob Jr., James Dailey.	1800 10-18	THOMPSON, John (w. Ann) to Frederick Wise of Hampshire Co. of Hampshire Co. Recorded 10-20-1800. Wit.: James Thompson, George Nelson, Elisha Thompson.
1798 9-19	THOMAS, Enoch to Jacob High of Hampshire Co. of Hampshire Co. THOMAS, Stephen 219 a. on Mill Creek; rec. 10-15-1798. Wit.: John Foley, William Foley, Phillip Kline, Ann Thomas.	1762 3-22	THOMPSON, Moses to Henry Philips of Hampshire Co. of Hampshire Co. Mortgage on Personal property; rec. 5-11-1762. Wit.: Jonathan Cobun, George Hart.
1797 11-14	THOMAS, Hugh to Peter Putman of Chester Co. of Hampshire Co. 829 a. on Patterson Creek; rec. 4-16-1798. Wit.: Andrew Wodrow, James Dailey, Peter Williams, William Linton.	1791 3-29	THOMPSON, William (w. Mary) to Caleb Evans of Hampshire Co. (lease and release) of Hampshire Co. 229 a. on North River; rec. 4-14-1791. Wit.: Levi Ashbrook, Joseph Tucker, William Milburn, Joseph Thompson.
1797 11-14	THOMAS, Hugh to Cornelius Devore of Chester Co., S. C. of Bedford Co. 204 a. in Hampshire Co.; rec. 12-18-1797 Wit.: Andrew Wodrow, James Dailey, Peter Williams, William Linton.	1774 8-1	THORN, Michael, (w. Catherine) to Leonard Naff (THOM?) Hampshire Co. (lease & rel.) of Hampshire Co. 202 a. on South Branch; rec. 3-14-1775. Wit.: Henry Shibler, Jacob Reed, Phillip Moore.
1797 11-14	THOMAS, Hugh to John Bowman of Chester Co. of Hampshire Co. 204 a. in Hampshire Co.; rec. 12-18-1797. Wit.: Andrew Wodrow, James Dailey, Peter Williams, William Linton.	1774 8-1	THORN, Michael, (w. Catherine) to Leonard Naff (THOM?) Hampshire Co. (lease & rel.) of Hampshire Co. 203 a. on South Branch; rec. 3-14-1775. Wit.: Henry Shibler, Jacob Reed, Phillip Moore.
1761 5-11	THOMAS, James (w. Sarah) to James Claypole, Sr. of Augusta Co. (lease and release) of Hampshire Co. 187½ a. on Lost River; rec. 9-8-1761. Wit.: Joseph Row, Andrew Sadowski, Thomas Bull.	1792 7-20	THORNTON, John to Daniel McNeil of King George Co. of Hardy Co. 371 a. on North Branch of Potomac; rec. 8-28-1792. Wit.: Will Steenberger, Daniel McNeil, Jr., William Renick, John McNeil.
1797 10-23	THOMAS, Johannah to James Fillit Thomas of Chester Co., S. C. (power of atty.) Chester Co., S. C. Authority to collect money or whatever due Johannah Thomas. Recorded 12-18-1797. Wit.: Luis Morris, James Murphy.	1798 9-25	THROCKMORTON, Daniel (w. Mary) to John Morrow of Hampshire Co. of Hampshire Co. Recorded 9-25-1798. Wit.: Patrick Boyle, Patrick O'Harra, Lewis Demors.
1760 7-4	THOMAS, John to James Craik of Hampshire Co. (lease and release) 400 a. along North River; rec. 11-11-1760. Wit.: Ja. Keith, Thomas Rutherford, John Hogg, Ezekiel Thomas.	1795 4-13	THROCKMORTON, Lewis to Thomas Flora of Hampshire Co. of Hampshire Co. 37½ a. in Hampshire Co.; rec. 9-14-1795. Wit.: Jacob Flora, Jacob Chrisman, Mary Chrisman.
1794 8-29	THOMAS, Moses to Ignatius Wheeler of Hampshire Co. of Hampshire Co. 166 a. on New Creek; rec. 12-10-1794. Wit.: Joseph Jacobs, John Bland, Sam Davis, William Hogan.	1797 9-16	THROGMORTON, Lewis (w. Rachel) to Robt. Rogers of Hampshire Co. of Hampshire Co. 37½ a. on Potomac River; rec. 9-18-1797. Wit.: Andrew Wodrow.
1797 4-17	THOMAS, Moses (w. Sophia) to John Godfrey of Hampshire Co. of Hampshire Co. 84 a. on New Creek; rec. 4-17-1797. Wit.: None.	1797 9-18	THROGMORTON, Lewis (w. Rachel) to Chas. Bevins of Hampshire Co. of Hampshire Co. 361 a. near Potomac River; rec. 9-18-1797. Wit.: Andrew Wodrow.
1793 4-11	THOMAS, Samuel to Henry Lighter of Frederick Co. (mortgage) of Hampshire Co. 615¼ a. on Beaver Run; rec. 4-11-1793. Wit.: Andrew Wodrow.	1792	THURSTON, Charles Mynn to Samuel Dinnett See MAGILL, Charles SMITH, Edward WAGGENER, Andrew
1798 4-13	THOMAS, Samuel (w. Magdalene) to Daniel Arnold of Hampshire Co. of Hampshire Co. 270 a. on Beaver Run; rec. 5-14-1798. Wit.: None.	1794	THURSTON, Charles Mynn to James McAlster See MAGILL, Charles SMITH, Edward WAGGONER, Andrew
1776	THOMPSON, Charles to John Morrell See FOXCRAFT, John	1783 1-14	TICHENAL, Moses (w. Margaret) to Job Beacorn of Washington Co. of Hampshire Co. 200 a. on Cabbin Run; rec. 1-14-1783. Wit.: None.
1778	THOMPSON, Charles to Derby Aughney See FOXCRAFT, John	1795 5-12	TIERMAN, Patrick to Michael Tierman, Jr. (w. Margaret) of Washington Co. of Fayette Co. 118 a. in Hampshire Co.; rec. 2-15-1796. Wit.: Joseph Wells, John Pottenger.
1778	THOMPSON, Charles to George and Isaac Newman See FOXCRAFT, John	1790 9-26	TIPSORD, Leonard (w. Pashinsh) to Thomas Green of Monongalia Co. of Hampshire Co. 174 a. on South Branch; rec. 12-16-1790. Wit.: Benj. Thrasher, B. McCarty, William Daton.
1779	THOMPSON, Charles to Jacob Nevill See FOXCRAFT, John	1800 10-20	TOMS, Abraham to James Starr of Hampshire Co. of Hampshire Co. Recorded 10-20-1800.
1790 2-1	THOMPSON, David (w. Elizabeth) to Jacob Reasoner of Hampshire Co. of Hampshire Co. 312 a. on Patterson Creek; rec. 4-15-1790. Wit.: Abraham Thompsin, William Thompson, Abraham Johnson, John Dixon, William Johnson.	1775 3-14	TOTTEN, Ezekiel to Okey Johnson of Hampshire Co. (lease) of Hampshire Co. 295 a. on Patterson Creek; rec. 3-14-1775. Wit.: T. Collins, John Pearsall, John Savidg.
1796 1-13	THOMPSON, George to Jacob Conklin of Philadelphia John Nixon 5,000 a. on Great Cacapeon. John Wardell Rec. 2-18-1799. of New York City Wit.: Benjamin Chambers, Abraham Thomaker.	1787 11-15	TOTTEN, Ezekiel to William Howell of Hampshire Co. of Hampshire Co. Parcel of land in State of East Jersey; rec. 6-12-1788. Wit.: Andrew Wodrow, John Marley, Samuel Dayley.
1798 2-24	THOMPSON, Jeremiah (w. Esther) to Israel Hoge of Hampshire Co. of Hampshire Co. 93 a. on Great Cacapeon River; rec. 9-17-1798. Wit.: Eleanor Eakman, Levi Matthew, John Matthew, Samuel Todd, John Todd.	1794 4-16	TRACY, Archibald to Walter Davis of Hampshire Co. (bill of sale) of Hampshire Co. Horse and calf; rec. 9-10-1794. Wit.: Nathan Price, Sophia King.
1800 9-1	THOMPSON, Jeremiah (w. Esther) to Henry Bruner of Hampshire Co. of Hampshire Co. Recorded 99-16-1800. Wit.: Peter Bruner, William Jackson, William Quinn, Elizabeth Todd, Martha Vanarsdal.	1780 4-24	TRAVIS, Robert to Job Welton of Hampshire Co. of Hampshire Co. 55 a. on South Branch River; rec. 5-9-1780. Wit.: Samuel Thompson, Garret Van Meter, Abraham Hite, Joseph Hite.

1785 4-5	**TRINKLE, Christopher** (w. Elizabeth) **to Henry Wiser** of Frederick Co. of Frederick Co. 258 a. on Alleghany Mt.; rec. 5-10-1785. Wit.: John Magill, Phil Pendleton, Andrew Wodrow.
1765 8-5	**TRIPLETT, Thomas** (w. Elizabeth) **to John Relfe** of Hampshire Co. (lease and release) of Philadelphia, Pa. 233 a. on North River; rec. 11-12-1766. Wit.: Gabriel Jones, Alex White, Joseph Watson, Bryan Bruin, George Wilson, John McColloch.
1799 5-16	**TRIPLETT, Thomas** **to James Coudin** (w. Betsy Hedgman) of Hampshire Co. of Harrison Co. 245 a. in Hampshire Co.; rec. 5-20-1799. Wit.: None.
1781 8-22	**TRUMBO, Andrew** (w. Margaret) **to Peter Harness** of Hampshire Co. (lease and release) of Hampshire Co. 232 a. on South Branch; rec. 9-11-1781. Wit.: None.
1800 4-14	**TUCKER, Joseph** (w. Lucey) **to Examus Tucker** of Hampshire Co. of Hampshire Co. Recorded 4-14-1800.

1796
6-20
	TUCKER, Thomas (w. Phoebe) **to Elizabeth Ashbrook**
	Parcel of land in Hampshire Co. Aaron Ashbrook
	Recorded 6-20-1796. Absalom Ashbrook
	Wit.: None. Eli Ashbrook
	    Mary Ashbrook
	    Rody Ashbrook
	    Amilia Ashbrook
	    William Ashbrook
	    Thomas Ashbrook
	(All children and heirs of Levy Ashbrook, deceased.)

1783 4-15	**TURK, Andrew** (w. Jean) **to William Adams** of Berkeley Co. (lease and release) of Hampshire Co. 160 a. on Mills Branch; rec. 5-14-1783. and Frederick Co. Wit.: Phil Pendleton, John Magill.
1790 5-1	**TURNER, William** **to Abraham Halderman** of Hampshire Co.; 250 a. and 203 a. in Hampshire Co., 178 a. near Nobley Mt.; rec. 6-10-1790. Wit.: Andrew Wodrow, John Herndon, William Jacob.
1792 8-21	**TURNER, William** **to Andrew Wodrow** of Hampshire Co. (power of attorney) of Hampshire Co. Authority to prosecute, sue and recover all debts due William Turner. Recorded 9-28-1792. Wit.: John Herndon.
1795 3-14	**TURNER, William** **to John Moores** of Hampshire Co. (lease) (wife, Lydia—not named as 480 a. in Hampshire Co.; grantee, but mentioned in rec. 4-17-1797. writing.) Wit.: Abrm. Johnson, William Johnson, William Hough.
1798 10-10	**TYLER, Charles** **to Robert Rogers** of Hampshire Co. of Hampshire Co. 392 a. on North River; rec. 10-15-1798. Wit.: Andrew Wodrow, Matthew Lodge.

—U—

1799 2-18	**UMPSTOT, Jacob** (w. Catherine) **to Jacob Mouser, Jr.** of Romney of Hampshire Co. Half acre in Romney; rec. 2-18-1799. Wit.: None.
1799 9-16	**UMPSTOTT, Jacob** (w. Catherine) **to Daniel Stover** of Romney of Hampshire Co. Half acre in Romney; rec. 9-16-1799. Wit.: None.
1768 10-7	**UPP, Frederick** **to Henry Danmetere** of Hampshire Co. (bill of sale) of Hampshire Co. Personal property; rec. 11-8-1768. Wit.: Alex. Farrow, John Fife.
1788 6-9	**UTT, George** (w. Catherine) **to Frederick Fink** of Hampshire Co. of Hampshire Co. 50 a. in Hampshire Co.; rec. 9-11-1788. Wit.: Christian Long.

—V—

1779 8-10	**VANBUSKIRK, Michael** **to Michael Waxler** of Hampshire Co. of Hampshire Co. 206 a. on Patterson Creek; rec. 8-10-1779. Wit.: Sam Dew.
1783 4-8	**VANCE, Joseph** (w. Sarah) **to John Lewis** of Frederick Co. of Hampshire Co. 456 a. on Patterson Creek; rec. 5-18-1783. Wit.: Sam Dew, William Barber Lewis, Isaac Parsons, Enoch Berry, William Fox.
1774 4-13	**VANMETER, Garret** **to David Rodgers** of Hampshire Co. of Hampshire Co. 400 a., known by the name of "Gum Spring" Tract, in Hampshire Co.; rec. 4-13-1774. Wit.: Sam Dew.

1779	**VANMETER, Garret** **to Enoch Hayden**
	See HEATH, Jonathan
	       HUTTON, Moses
	       RANDALL, Abel

1782 2-9	**VANMETER, Garret** (w. Ann) **to Isaac Vanmeter** of Hampshire Co. (lease and release) of Hampshire Co. 89 a. on Patterson Creek; rec. 2-12-1782. Wit.: Andrew Wodrow, Joseph Kayser, Abraham Hite, Abel Randall.
1767 6-2	**VAN METER, Henry** **to Samuel Dew** of Hampshire Co. (mortgage) Conrad Hoffman Lot No. 2. So. Branch; rec. 10-13-1767. Wit.: G. Wilson, Richard Byrn, Cornelius Conner.
1784 8-10	**VANMETER, Jacob** **to Negro Slaves** of Hampshire Co. (freeing of slaves Gudge and Judith "Said slaves shall be discharged and become free from further service to me or my heirs." Recorded 8-10-1784. Wit.: Betty Dew, Elizabeth Forman, Ann Forman.
1796 9-25	**VANMETER, John, Sr.** **to Jeremiah Thompsin** of Berkeley Co. of Hampshire Co. 121 a. on Great Cacapeon; rec. 10-17-1796.
1779 4-10	**VANPELT, Jacob** (w. Sarah) **to James Dailey** of Hampshire Co. of Hampshire Co. 86 a. on Sandy Ridge; rec. 4-15-1779. Wit.: None.
1779 9-6	**VESTALL, William** (w. Hannah) **to Jacob Sibert** (Westfall?) of Berkeley Co. (lease and release) Frederick Co. 250 a. on Cacapeon River; rec. 5-9-1780. Wit.: Andrew Wodrow, John Magill, Bryan Bruin, James Walker.
1770 5-7	**VINEY, Andrew** (w. Susan) **to William Wilson** of Hampshire Co. (lease and release) of Hampshire Co. 386 a. on Lost River; rec. 5-8-1770. Wit.: None.

—W—

1773 3-3	**WAGGENER, Andrew** **to Robert Owens** of Frederick Co. of Frederick Co. 100 a. on South Branch. Wit.: Alex White, John Magill, Peter Hog.

1792	**WAGGENER, Andrew** **to Samuel Dinnett**
	See MAGILL, Charles
	       SMITH, Edward
	       THURSTON, Charles Mynn

1794	**WAGGONER, Andrew** **to James McAlster**
	See MAGILL, Charles
	       SMITH, Edward
	       THURSTON, Charles Mynn

1775 9-12	**WAITES, John, Sr.** (w. Ann) **to John McDonald** of Hampshire Co. (lease and release) of Hampshire Co. 225 a. on Great Cacapeon; rec. 8-12-1777. Wit.: James Taasse, James Hughs, Jacob Pugh.
1775 8-12	**WALKER, John, Sr.** **to Thomas Walker** of Hampshire Co. (lease and release) of Hampshire Co. 33 a. on North Branch of Potomac; rec. 8-13-1776. Wit.: None.
1784 8-10	**WALKER, John, Sr.** **to John Jeremiah Jacob** (w. Mary) Hampshire Co. (bill of sale) Hampshire Co. of Hampshire Co. 200 a., 150 a., on North Branch; rec. 8-10-1784. Wit.: None.
1790 4-3	**WALKER, Peter** **to Robert Williams** of Hampshire Co. of Hampshire Co. Quarter acre in Frankfort; rec. 9-16-1790. Wit.: James Murphy, Andrew Wodrow, Benj. Wright, James Martin.
1796 3-9	**WALKER, Peter** (w. Phoebe) **to John Jones, Sr.** Half acre in Frankfort; rec. 4-18-1796. Hampshire Co. Wit.: John Mitchell, A. King, Nath. Evans, Richard Whiteman.
1781 6-21	**WALKER, Robert** (w. Jean) **to James Kelso** of Cumberland Co., Pa. James Wilson 400 a. on Little Cacapeon, 463 a., 266 a., Berkeley Co. on Great Cacapeon; rec. 8-13-1782. Wit.: Joseph Mitchell, I. Irwin, James Walker.
1785 11-22	**WALKER, Robert** **to John Walker** of Hampshire Co. (bill of sale) Samuel Walker Livestock and household property. of Hampshire Co. Recorded 3-15-1786. Wit.: Robert Buck, Anthony Buck, John Donaldson.
1789 6-3	**WALKER, Robert** **to Elizabeth Savage** of Franklin Co. of Hampshire Co. 152 a. in Green Spring Valley; rec. 4-15-1790. Wit.: John Walker, Robert Walker, Andrew Walker.
1792 1-10	**WALKER, Robert** **to James Walker** of Franklin Co. Andrew Walker 400 a. in Green Spring Valley. Robert Walker Rec. 1-29-1793. Wit.: Thomas Dowell, Andrew Walker.
1784 8-10	**WALKER, Thomas** **to James Prather** of Hampshire Co. (bill of sale) of Washington Co. 33 a., 62½ a. on North Branch; rec. 8-10-1784. Wit.: None.
1786 8-8	**WALLACE, Robert** **to James Donaldson** of Hampshire Co. of Hampshire Co. 127 a. in Green Spring Valley; rec. 4-13-1787. Wit.: Jeremiah Sullivan, Robt. Walker, Anthony Buck.

1769 11-14	**WALTER, Ephraim** (w. Mary) of Frederick Co. (lease and release) 238 a. on Fatterson's Creek; rec. 11-15-1769. Wit.: John Roussaw, John Reno.	**to John Jones** of Frederick Co.	1764 12-11	**WATSON, Joseph** to **Thomas Wharton** of Fairfax Co. (lease and release) **Joseph Wharton** 340 a. on North Branch; rec. 12-12-1764. Philadelphia, Pa. Wit.: None.

1769 11-14 WALTER, Ephraim (w. Mary) to John Jones
of Frederick Co. (lease and release) of Frederick Co.
238 a. on Fatterson's Creek; rec. 11-15-1769.
Wit.: John Roussaw, John Reno.

1800 9-16 WALTERS, John (w. Mary) to Samuel Bevin
of Frederick Co. of Hampshire Co.
Recorded 9-15-1800.
Wit.: Charles Magill, William Armstrong, Owen Rodgers,
George Newman, Abram Johnstone, Andrew Wodrow.

1785 8-9 WARD, Cornelius to Adam Fisher
of Hampshire Co. (lease) of Hampshire Co.
20 a. on South Branch River; rec. 8-10-1785.
Wit.: Robert Maxwell, George Ferguson.

1785 8-9 WARD, Cornelius to Adam Fisher
of Hampshire Co. of Hampshire Co.
16 a. on South Branch; rec. 8-10-1785.
Wit.: Robert Maxwell, George Ferguson.

1798 11-21 WARDELL, John to Josiah Masters
See CONKLIN, Jacob, and NIXON, John.

1773 8-7 WARDEN, Elizabeth to Peter Tatfe
of Hampshire Co. (deed of gift) of Hampshire Co.
Cow, heifer; rec. 8-11-1773.
Wit.: John McHendry, George Lewis.

1772 11-7 WARDEN, James to Peter Hog
Cumberland Co., Pa. (power of attorney) Attorney at Law,
Authority to convey and make over in the Hampshire Co.
usual form and manner, "all my estate, right, title, interest,
claim and demand, whatsoever, of, in and to a certain tract of
land on Lost River. Authority to any conveyances necessary."
Recorded 3-10-1773.
Wit.: James Chew, Robert Ferral.

1794 8-9 WART, Joseph (w. Mary) to Thomas Dunn
of Hampshire Co. of Hampshire Co.
100 a. in Hampshire Co.; rec. 2-16-1795.
Wit.: Abrm. Eversold, Jacob Straddler, Peter Eversold.

1797 10-18 WASHINGTON, Lund (w. Susanna) to Robt. T. Hooe
of Washington of Alexandria
788 a. on Great Cacapeon River; rec. 2-20-1798.
Wit.: Elisha Dick, George Gilpin.

1791 12-14 WATERMAN, James (w. Leah) to John Rush
of Hampshire Co of Hampshire Co.
342 a. on New Creek; rec. 12-15-1791.
Wit.: None.

1792 10-20 WATERMAN, James (w. Leah) to Henry Franks
of Hampshire Co. of Hampshire Co.
100 a. on New Creek; rec. 10-30-1792.
Wit.: Ed McCarthy, Samuel Ravenscroft, J. Wheeler.

1794 3-21 WATERS, John (w. Ann) to Enoch Thomas
of Hampshire Co. of Hardy Co.
219 a. on Mill Creek; rec. 6-11-1794.
Wit.: Andrew Wodrow, Isaac Parsons, John Jack,
Robert Beatty.

1772 8-7 WATERS, Philemon (w. Catherine) to James Scott
of Frederick Co. (lease and release) of Hampshire Co.
437 a. on Lost River; rec. 8-10-1773.
Wit.: None.

1762 11-4 WATKINS, Moses to John Steel
Frederick Co. (lease and release) Trader, of Frederick Co.
390 a. on Great Cape Capon; rec. 5-10-1763.
Wit.: Ga. Jones.

1796 1-18 WATSON, James to John Bever
of Allegany Co. of George Town Co.
Parcel of land on Potomac River; rec. 4-18-1796.
Wit.: None.

1800 2-26 WATSON, James to Phil Penniston
of Allegheny Co., Pa. of Berkeley Co.
Recorded 10-28-1800.
Wit.: Elisha Boyd, A. Waggener,
Phil C. Penniston, David Hunter.

1800 6-17 WATSON, James (w. Mary) to Mathias Hook
of Allegheny Co., Pa. of Allegheny Co., Pa.
Recorded 2-16-1801.
Wit.: Joseph Calwell, Noah Roth.

1764 2-9 WATSON, Joseph to John Ralfe
of Alexandria (lease and release) of Philadelphia
115 a. on North River; rec. 2-15-1764.
Wit.: Peter Hog, Gabriel Jones, Ja. Keith.

1764 2-9 WATSON, Joseph to John Ralfe
of Alexandria (lease and release) of Philadelphia
161 a. on North River; rec. 2-15-1764.
Wit.: Peter Hog, Gabriel Jones, Ja. Keith.

1764 2-9 WATSON, Joseph to John Ralfe
of Alexandria (lease and release) of Philadelphia
400 a. on Pattersons Creek; rec. 2-15-1764.
Wit.: Peter Hog, Gabriel Jones, Ja. Keith.

1764 12-11 WATSON, Joseph to Thomas Wharton
of Fairfax Co. (lease and release) Joseph Wharton
400 a. on Patterson Creek; rec. 12-12-1764. Philadelphia, Pa.
Wit.: None.

1764 12-11 WATSON, Joseph to Thomas Wharton
of Fairfax Co. (lease and release) Joseph Wharton
320 a. on Pattersons Creek; rec. 12-12-1764. Philadelphia, Pa.
Wit.: None.

1764 12-11 WATSON, Joseph to Thomas Wharton
of Fairfax Co. (lease and release) Joseph Wharton
340 a. on North Branch; rec. 12-12-1764. Philadelphia, Pa.
Wit.: None.

1765 6-28 WATSON, Joseph to John Relfe
of Fairfax Co., Va. of Philadelphia, Pa.
70 a. on North River; rec. 10-8-1765.
Wit.: Charles Thompson, John Foxcraft, Thos. Foxcraft,
George Wilson, John McColloch, Samuel Prichard.

1765 8-5 WATSON, Joseph to John Foxcraft
of Alexandra, Va. (lease and release) Charles Thompson
322 a. on So. Branch; rec. 8-14-1765. Philadelphia, Pa.
Wit.: George Wilson, Edward McGuire, John Reno,
Bryan Bruin.

1767 3-17 WATSON, Joseph to John Foxcraft
of Fairfax Co. Charles Thompson
163 a., 242 a., on South Branch; of Philadelphia, Pa.
rec. 6-9-1767.
Wit.: Thomas FoxCraft, Thomas Tillyer.

1771 7-20 WATSON, Joseph to John Foxcraft
of Fairfax Co. (lease and release) Charles Thompson
424 a. on Mill Run; rec. 8-14-1771. of Philadelphia
Wit.: None.

1771 9-24 WATSON, Joseph to David Roberts
of Fairfax Co. (bond) of Hampshire Co.
Bond of 135 pounds. Sold to Roberts, 400 a. on Lost River;
Recorded 8-8-1780.
Wit.: John Wood.

1772 1-4 WATSON, Joseph to John Foxcraft
of Fairfax Co. Charles Thompson
430 a. on South Branch; rec. 5-14-1773. of Philadelphia
Wit.: Alex White, Edward McGuire,
G. Michael Laubinger, William Scott, John Magill.

1761 1-13 WATSON, William to Benjamin Kuykendall
of Frederick Co. (lease and release) of Hampshire Co.
Lot 17—217 a. on South Branch; rec. 2-10-1761.
Wit.: Felix Seymour, Michael Stump, Aron Ashbrook,
JohnWestfall.

1791 10-29 WATTS, James (w. Susannah) to James Fleming
of Hampshire Co. (bill of sale) of Hampshire Co.
120 a. on Middle Ridge; rec. 6-26-1792.
Wit.: Frederick Fink, Christopher Hershman,
Isaiah Scott, Andrew Wodrow, John Herndon.

1792 5-10 WATTS, James (w. Susannah) to Jacob Creagur
of Hampshire Co. of Hampshire Co.
42½ a. on Beaver Run; rec. 6-26-1792.
Wit.: Peter Umstot, Frederick Fink, Henry Fink.

1792 5-10 WATTS, James (w. Susannah) to Henry Fink
of Hampshire Co. of Hampshire Co.
45 a. on Beaver Run; rec. 6-26-1792.
Wit.: Peter Umstat, Frederick Fink, Jacob Creagur.

1798 10-15 WATTS, James (w. Susanna) to Christian Hilky
of Hampshire Co. of Hampshire Co.
225 a. in Hampshire Co.; rec. 10-15-1798.
Wit.: None.

1798 10-15 WATTS, James (w. Susanna) to Archibald Watts
of Hampshire Co. of Hampshire Co.
50 a. on Beaver Run; rec. 10-15-1798.
Wit.: None.

1781 1-9 WAXLER, Michael to Samuel Lewis
of Hampshire Co. of Hampshire Co.
205 a. on Patterson Creek; rec. 3-13-1781.
Wit.: Wm. Barber Lewis, John Vandiver, John Lewis.

1779 3-4 WEIDNAR, Jacob (w. Sally) to Thomas Smith
of Hampshire Co. (lease and release) of Hampshire Co.
94 a. on North River of Cacapeon; rec. 3-9-1779.
Wit.: Aaron Ashbrook, John McDonald, Abraham Powell.

1798 9-17 WELCH, Demsey to Daniel Stover
of Hampshire Co. of Hampshire Co.
150 a. on Allegany Mountain; rec. 9-17-1798.
Wit.: Isaac James, Rod. James.

1772 11-20 WELLS, Humphrey to Isaac Beall
of Frederick Co. (lease and release) of Berkeley Co.
400 a. on New Creek; rec. 3-10-1773.
Wit.: William Campbell, Alex White, James Wood,
Ach. Foster, Sam Beall, John Magill, Edward McGuire.

WELTON—See Wetton.

1758 2-14 WELTON, John to William Westfall
of Hampshire Co. (lease) of Hampshire Co.
400 a. in Hampshire Co., on a branch of the Great South
Branch of the Potomac called Mill Creek; rec. 2-15-1758.
Wit.: William Cunningham, David Ward.

1764 2-13 WELTON, John (w. Jane) to Joseph Watson
of Hampshire Co. (lease and release) of Alexandria, Va.
340 a. on North River; rec. 2-15-1764.
Wit.: Sam Dew.

1764 2-14 WELTON, John to Job Welton
of Hampshire Co. (lease and release) of Hampshire Co.
Lot No. 31—243 a., on South Branch; rec. 2-16-1764.
Wit.: Peter Hog, Sam Dew.

1779 9-13	**WELTON, John** (w. Susannah) of Hampshire Co. 400 a. on Mill Creek; rec. 5-9-1780. Wit.: Abraham Hite, Abel Randall, James Parsons, William Welton.	to **Isaac Means** of Hampshire Co.	1778 8-8	**WHITE, Alexander** (Atty.) (w. Elizabeth) of Frederick Co. (bill of sale) 149 a. on Little Cacapeon; rec. 9-8-1778. Wit.: None.	to **John Archer, Jr.** of Frederick Co.
1780 6-21	**WELTON, John** of Hampshire Co. 244 a. on Looney's Creek; rec. 11-16-1780. Wit.: Joseph Nevill, Jonathan Purcell, Abel Randall, Job Welton.	to **David Welton** of Hampshire Co.	1790 10-30	**WHITE, Alexander** Executor of John Greenfield, deceased 400 a. on Castleman's Run; rec. 12-16-1790. Wm. McGuire, Max. Armstrong, John Dixon.	to **David Bookless** of Hampshire Co.
1772 8-10	**WELTON, Solomon** of Hampshire Co. (lease and release) 412 a. on Looney's Creek; rec. 8-10-1772. Wit.: None.	to **Abel Randal** of Hampshire Co.	1796 6-10	**WHITE, Alexander** of Frederick Co. 204 aa. on Patterson Creek; rec. 6-20-1796. Wit.: Alex White III, Charles Magill, Archibald Magill.	to **James Fleming** of Hampshire Co.
1769 3-10	**WELTON, William** (w. Ann) of Hampshire Co. (lease) 354 a. on Cape Capon; rec. 3-12-1760. Wit.: H. Churchill, Henry Redman, Eliza Westfall.	to **James Alexander** of Hampshire Co.	1799 10-10	**WHITE, Alex** of Frederick Co. Recorded 10-14-1799. Wit.: John Copsey, Arch Magill, Charles Magill, Elisha Boyd.	to **James Higgins** of Hampshire Co.
1760 3-10	**WELTON, William** (w. Ann) of Hampshire Co. (release) 354 a. on Cape Capon; rec. 3-12-1760. Wit.: H. Churchill, David Scott, William Fowler.	to **James Alexander** of Hampshire Co.	1796 9-19	**WHITE, Francis** (w. Margaret) of Hampshire Co. 146 a. on North River; rec. 2-20-1797. Wit.: None.	to **John Candy**
	WETTON—See Welton.		1796 12-20	**WHITE, Francis** of Hampshire Co. Parcel of land on Cacapeon River; rec. 2-20-1797. Wit.: Andrew Wodrow, Alex White III, John Mitchell.	to **James McBride**
1771 11-11	**WETTON (Welton), David** of Hampshire Co. (lease and release) 373 a. on Looney's Creek at the Flats; rec. 11-13-1771. Wit.: Sam Dew.	to **Felix Seymour** of Hampshire Co.	1798 4-16	**WHITE, Francis** (w. Margaret) of Hampshire Co. 233 a. on North River; rec'd 7-16-1798. Wit.: None.	to **John Copsey** of Hampshire Co.
1770 8-14	**WETTON (Welton), Job** (w. Mary) of Hampshire Co. (lease) 243 a. on South Branch; rec. 8-14-1770. Wit.: Sam Dew.	to **John Blue** of Hampshire Co.	1799 10-3	**WHITE, Francis** (w. Margaret) of Hampshire Co. 400 a. on Little Cacapeon River. Rec. 10-14-1799. Wit.: John Minor, William Washington, Geo. Craik.	to **James Keith Samuel Craig** Alexandria, Va.
1760 5-19	**WERBEL, John** of Hampshire Co. Mortgage on personal property—To secure Jonathan Coban and Peter Steenbergen their money for going his bail, to release John Werbel from jail. Wit.: John Greenfield, Peter Statler, Sam Dew.	to **Jonathan Coban Peter Steenbergen**	1800 5-20	**WHITE, Francis** (w. Margaret) of Hampshire Co. Recorded 5-20-1800.	to **Jacob Monroe** of Hampshire Co.
1800 4-11	**WESTELL, Humphrey** of Hampshire Co. by DIXON, Jno., attorney in fact Recorded 4-14-1800.	to **Thomas Allen** of Hampshire Co.	1791 9-14	**WHITEBERRY, George** of Hampshire Co. (lease and release) 200 a. on North River; rec. 9-15-1791. Wit.: None.	to **Martin Shaver** of Frederick Co.
1761 11-23	**WESTFALL, Cornelius** of Essex Co., Montague Township, New East Jersey. (lease and release) Lot No. 9—400 a., on South Branch; rec. 12-8-1761. Wit.: Felix Seymour, Thomas Singleton, George Osborn, Iseak Hoornbeck.	to **George See** of Hampshire Co.	1793 4-9	**WHITEBERRY, George** (w. Nancy) of Hampshire Co. 100 aa. on Little Cacapeon; rec. 6-12-1793. Wit.: None.	to **James Slack** of Hampshire Co.
1764 12-4	**WESTFALL, Jacob** (w. Judith) of Hampshire Co. (lease and release) 140 a. on Luney's Creek; rec. 3-12-1765. Wit.: David Scott, William Westfall, Benjamin Scott, Mathew Kuykendall.	to **Peter Reeves** of Philadelphia, Pa.	1793 10-7	**WHITEBERRY, George** (w. Mary) of Hampshire Co. 35 a. on Little Cacapeon; rec. 10-9-1793. Wit.: None.	to **William Starky** of Hampshire Co.
1784 3-9	**WESTFALL, John** of Hampshire Co. 42 a. on Looney's Creek; rec. 3-9-1784. Wit.: None.	to **Watson Clark** of Hampshire Co.	1795 9-17	**WHITEMAN, Ezekiel** (w. Dorcas) of Hampshire Co. Quarter acre in Frankfort; rec. 2-15-1796. Wit.: Job Sheppherd, Nath. Evans, John Williams, And. Smalley, John Mitchell, Jr., John Mitchell, Christiana Stephens, John Snyder.	to **Alex King** of Hampshire Co.
1760 3-10	**WESTFALL, Wm.** (w. Elizabeth) of Hampshire Co. (lease and release) (See Vestfall) 400 a. on Mill Creek; rec. 3-12-1760. Wit.: Gabriel Jones.	to **John Welton, Jr.** of Hampshire Co.	1791 4-25	**WHITEMAN, John** of Washington Co. 146 a. on Alleghany Mt.; rec. 10-13-1791. Wit.: Andrew Smalley, Henry New, Wm. Daton, John Rush.	to **Edward McCarty** of Hampshire Co.
1773 4-1	**WHARTON, Joseph, Jr.** of Philadelphia 409 a. on Patterson Creek; rec. 8-11-1773. Wit.: Robert Stephen, Will Parr.	to **Thomas Wharton** of Philadelphia	1790 12-14	**WIGGING, Archibald** (w. Mary) of Hampshire Co. 63 a. on Cacapeon River; rec. 6-16-1791. Wit.: William Florane, G. Creamer, Cornelius Ferrel.	to **Thomas Williams** of Hampshire Co.
1795 3-2	**WHARTON, Thomas** of Philadelphia (power of attorney) Authority to sell land on Patterson Creek; rec. 4-20-1795. Wit.: John Wharton, Abraham Shoemaker.	to **Joseph Neville** of Hardy Co.	1795 2-10	**WIGGINS, Archibald** (w. Mary) of Hampshire Co. 219 a. on Potomac River; rec. 2-16-1795. Wit.: Thomas Wiggins, Ezekiel Dimmitt, Cornelius Ferree, Sam Dew, Andrew Wodrow.	to **John Dimmitt Moses Dimmitt** Berkeley Co.
1789 9-20	**WHEELER, Ignatious** of Hampshire Co. 300 a. on New Creek; rec. 10-15-1789. Wit.: Andrew Wodrow.	to **William Taney** (JANEY?) Hampshire Co.	1795 2-10	**WIGGINS, Archibald** (w. Mary) of Hampshire Co. 400 a. on Potomac River; rec. 2-16-1795. Wit.: Ezekiel Dimmitt, Thos. Wiggins, Cornelius Ferree, Andrew Wodrow, William Bullitt, Sam Dew.	to **John Dimmitt Moses Dimmitt** Berkeley Co.
1794 8-29	**WHEELER, Ignatius** of Hampshire Co. 94 a. on New Creek; rec. 4-7-1795. Wit.: John Rawles, William Hogan, Paul Sheridan William Duling, Joseph Jacobs, John Bland, Samuel Davis.	to **Moses Thomas** of Hampshire Co.	1790 6-7	**WIGGINS, Philip** of Hampshire Co. 250 a. on South Branch; rec. 6-10-1790. Wit.: Rueben Smith, Thomas Wiggins, Joseph Wiggins.	to **Archibald Wiggins** of Hampshire Co.
1794 11-11	**WHEELER, Ignatius** of Kentucky (power of attorney) To sell tract of land containing 150 a., in Hampshire Co. Recorded 6-20-1796. Wit.: Sam Davis, John Dixon, William Duling.	to **Thomas Noble** of Frederick Co.	1790 6-7	**WIGGINS, Phillip** of Hampshire Co. 80 a. on South Branch; rec. 6-10-1790. Wit.: Reuben Smith, Thomas Wiggins, Metilda Wiggins, Joseph Wiggins.	to **Henry Fawver** of Washington Co.
1796	**WHEELER, Ignatious** by atty., see NOBLE, Thomas	to **William James**	1768 9-13	**WIGGINS, Thomas, Sr.** of Hampshire Co. 100 a. on Great Capon; rec. 9-13-1768. Wit.: W. Hancher, Richard Byrn.	to **Thomas Wiggins, Jr.** of Hampshire Co.
1771	**WHITE, Alexander, Executor** See GREENFIELD, John LIVINGSTON, Mayor James McDONALD, Angus	to **Peter Hog**	1768 9-13	**WIGGINS, Thomas, Sr.** of Hampshire Co. 150 a. on Great Capon; rec. 9-13-1768. Wit.: W. Hancher, Richard Byrn.	to **Phillip Wiggins** of Hampshire Co.
1776	**WHITE, Alexander** See McDONALD, Angus	to **Bryan Bruin**			

GRANTOR-GRANTEE — PAGE 61

1789 9-26 **WIGGINS, Thomas** — to **Phillip Wiggins**
of Washington Co. — of Hampshire Co.
100 a. on Potomac River (surveyed by George Washington).
Recorded 6-10-1790.
Wit.: Arch. Wiggins, Francis Harvey, William Flora, Mary Wiggins.

1794 12-31 **WILLEY, Benjamin (w. Ann)** — to **George Gilfin, John Foster, John Ricketts**
of Hampshire Co. of Alexandria
252 a. on North Branch River.
Recorded 2-16-1795.
Wit.: John Mitchell, Alex King, A. Brown, Abraham ——?

1796 10-26 **WILLIAM, Ebenezer (w. Catherine)** — to **John Mitchell, Alex King**
of Allegany Co. (bill of sale) — Hampshire Co.
168 a. in Hampshire Co.; rec. 12-19-1796.
Wit.: John Lyle, Job Shepherd, Nath. Evans, Christian Stevens, John Snyder, Jonathan Purcell, John Mitchell, Jr.

1799 **WILLIAMS, Ben** — to **Alex White**
WILLIAMS, Charles
WILLIAMS, Daniel
See MARSHALL, Christopher

1771 8-7 **WILLIAMS, David (w. Sarah)** — to **William Wilson**
of Hampshire Co. — of Hampshire Co.
116 a. on Lost River of Great Cacapeon; rec. 8-13-1771.
Wit.: Peter Steenberger, John Roussaw, Joseph Heavill.

1774 4-11 **WILLIAMS, John** — to **Patrick Lynch**
of Augusta Co. (power of attorney) — of Hampshire Co.
Authority to convey and sign a deed for tract of land at head of Fort Pleasant, Mill Run—350 acres; rec. 11-15-1775.
Wit.: John Allenton, Joel Berry, Cornelius Lynch, Evan James.

1775 11-14 **WILLIAMS, John** — to **Mrs. Joseph Ogden, Josiah Hughs**
of Augusta Co. (lease and release) — of Philadelphia, Pa.
350 a. at head of Fort Pleasant, Mill Run; rec. 11-15-1775.
Wit.: None.

1779 8-10 **WILLIAMS, John (w. Prudence)** — to **George Fiddler**
of Fauquier Co. — of Hampshire Co.
145 a. on Mill Creek; rec. 8-10-1779.
Wit.: Samuel Atchison, Sillas Atchison, William Atchison.

1780 8-3 **WILLIAMS, John** — to **Michael McThiernan**
of Hampshire Co. (lease and release) — of Washington Co.
270 a. on South Branch; rec. 8-8-1780.
Wit.: Arch. Wiggins, Will McCrackin, John Black.

1780 8-8 **WILLIAMS, John** — to **Michael McThiernan, Sr.**
of Hampshire Co. (lease and release) — of Washington Co.
118 a. on South Branch; rec. 8-8-1780.
Wit.: Arch. Wiggins, Will McCrackin, John Black.

1790 1-8 **WILLIAMS, John** — to **William Linton**
Eldest son of Richard Williams, dec'd — Hampshire Co.
of Hampshire Co.
232 a. on South Branch; rec. 1-10-1790.
Wit.: Andrew Wodrow, Peter Williams, John Hansbrough.

1791 4-14 **WILLIAMS, John** — to **Jacob Neaw**
See PARKER, Robert

1794 10-1 **WILLIAMS, John (w. Martha)** — to **Stacy Brown**
of Loudon Co. — of Hampshire Co.
206 a. on Enochs Run; rec. 9-14-1795.
Wit.: None.

1796 10-10 **WILLIAMS, John** — to **William Linton**
of Hampshire Co. (bill of sale) — of Hampshire Co.
232 a. on South Branch; rec. 10-17-1796.
Wit.: None.

1796 10-10 **WILLIAMS, John** — to **William Linton**
of Hampshire Co. (bill of sale) — of Hampshire Co.
413 a. on South Branch River; rec. 10-17-1796.
Wit.: None.

1784 10-28 **WILLIAMS, Joseph (w. Elizabeth)** — to **Jacob Bogard**
of Hampshire Co. — of Hampshire Co.
100 a. on Patterson Creek; rec. 11-9-1784.
Wit.: Abraham Johnson, Sr., Wm. Johnson, Nathaniel Williams, John Dixon.

1784 11-8 **WILLIAMS, Joseph (w. Elizabeth)** — to **Moses Williams**
of Hampshire Co. — of Hampshire Co.
157 a. on Cabbin Run of Patterson Creek; rec. 11-9-1784.
Wit.: Jacob Bogard, Gabriel Wright, John Dixon, Thomas Holland.

1793 8-9 **WILLIAMS, Joseph (w. Elizabeth)** — to **John Kent**
of Washington Co. — of Hampshire Co.
150 a. on Patterson Creek; rec. 8-12-1793.
Wit.: Burnit Williams, Nathaniel Williams, Mary Wick.

1779 7-31 **WILLIAMS, Martha** — to **Garret Vanmeter**
Bill of sale.
Place on which she lived, for 500 pounds, one bushel salt, two bushels corn, and one and one-half bushels wheat; rec. 8-10-1779.
Wit.: Jacob Vanmeter, Noah Williams.

1770 11-8 **WILLIAMS, Mary** — to **Thomas McCarty**
of Hampshire Co. — of Hampshire Co.
Parcel of land on South Branch; rec. 11-12-1770.
Wit.: Joseph Heavill (Neavill), Alex Keith, Daniel McHeil.

1791 10-13 **WILLIAMS, Moses (w. Ruth)** — to **Samuel Hatten**
of Hampshire Co. — of Washington Co.
45 a. on Cabbin Run, a drain of Patterson Creek; rec. 10-13-1791.
Wit.: Ed McCarty, John Daton, Henry New.

1797 4-29 **WILLIAMS, Peter** — to **Elijah Gaither**
of Hampshire Co. — Town of Romney
Lots 45 and 55 in Town of Romney; rec. 6-19-1797.
Wit.: Perez Drew, Arthur Richardson, William Linton, Eli Davis.

1799 4-11 **WILLIAMS, Peter** — to **James Gibson, Harry Myers**
of Hampshire Co. (lease) — of Hampshire Co.
Half acre in Romney; rec. 7-15-1799.
Wit.: Samuel Gibbs, Patrick Baker, Thomas Coulter.

1799 11-16 **WILLIAMS, Peter** — to **William Linton**
of Hampshire Co. — of Hampshire Co.
Recorded 7-14-1800.

1799 12-23 **WILLIAMS, Peter (w. Ann)** — to **John Pierceall, John Jack, Henry Heinsmann, James Dailey**
of Hampshire Co., Va. — of Hampshire Co.
Recorded 1-20-1800.
Wit.: Patrick Baker, Charles D. Houser, Henry Myers, Henry Hines.

1799 12-23 **WILLIAMS, Peter (w. Ann)** — to **John Purcell, John Jack, Henry Heinsman, James Dailey**
of Hampshire Co. — of Hampshire Co.
Half acre in Romney.
Recorded 1-20-1800.
Wit.: Patrick Baker, Charles D. Houser, Henry Myers, Henry Hines.

1765 4-4 **WILLIAMS, Providence** — to **Richard Williams**
of Berkeley Co., S. C. (power of attorney)
Power to sell 200 a. of land on Potomac River; rec. 8-14-1765.
Wit.: Edward Musgrove, James Williams, James McFadden.

1766 8-1 **WILLIAMS, Providence** — to **Daniel Cresap**
Berkeley Co., S. C. (lease and rel.) — of Hampshire Co.
180 a. on Potomac River; rec. 8-12-1766.
Wit.: Ja. Keith.

1772 7-25 **WILLIAMS, Richard** — to **Peter Peters**
of Hampshire Co. (mortgage) — of Hampshire Co.
232 a. on South Branch; rec. 8-11-1772.
Wit.: William Foreman, Jacob Cassalman, Humphrey Worstell, Stephen Calvin.

1786 12-19 **WILLIAMS, Robert** — Certificate
Age 80, being disabled while in the service of the United States, is entitled to the sum of 15 pounds yearly. Rec. 4-13-1787.
Wit.: None.

1798 12-15 **WILLIAMS, Thomas** — to **Aaron Forman**
of Hampshire Co. — of Hampshire Co.
20 a. in Hampshire Co.; rec. 5-20-1799.
Wit.: Cornelius Ferree, Isaac Ferree, Joshua Ferree.

1771 4-8 **WILLIAMS, Vincent** — to **Peter Casey**
son of Vincent Williams, dec'd — of Hampshire Co.
(w. Elizabeth Van Meter)
of Hampshire Co. (lease and release)
400 a. on Patterson Creek; rec. 4-10-1771.
Wit.: None.

1761 9-7 **WILLIAMS, William** — to **Robert Rose**
of Frederick Co. (lease and release) — of Hampshire Co.
181 a. on Potomac River; rec. 9-8-1761.
Wit.: Cuthbert Bullet, Jonathan Heath, Sam Dew, Ben Tutt.

1793 4-25 **WILLIAMS, William (w. Sabinah)** — to **Margaret Strode**
of Hampshire Co. — of Berkeley Co.
121 a. in Hampshire Co.; rec. 10-16-1797.
Wit.: Virgil McCrakin, Peter Shriver, Cornelius Ferree.

1794 9-10 **WILLIAMSON, Cornelius** — to **Henry Compston**
(w. Rodey) — of Hampshire Co.
of Hampshire Co.
132½ a. on North River; rec. 9-10-1794.
Wit.: Jacob Starn George Beall, John Starn.

1794 6-11 **WILLIAMSON, John** — to **John Bryan, Thomas Baker**
of Hampshire Co. — Hampshire Co.
300 a. on Little Cacapeon; rec. 6-11-1794.
Wit.: Jacob Starn, Cornelius Williamson.

1793 12-11 **WILLIAMSON, Samuel** — to **Richard Taylor**
of Hampshire Co. — of Hampshire Co.
119 a. on Little Cacapeon; rec. 12-11-1793.
Wit.: None.

1798 9-17 **WILLIAMSON, Samuel** — to **Richard Taylor**
of Hampshire Co. — of Hampshire Co.
100 a. on Little Cacapeon River; rec. 9-17-1798.
Wit.: None.

1795 9-14 **WILLIAMSON, Thomas** — to **James Patterson**
of Hampshire Co. — of Hampshire Co.
92 a. on Little Cacapeon; rec. 9-14-1795.
Wit.: James Dailey, John Cullins, Alex McBride.

1796 12-10 **WILLIAMSON, Thomas** — to **Abraham Pugh**
of Hampshire Co. — of Hampshire Co.
70 a. in Hampshire Co.; rec. 4-17-1797.
Wit.: None.

1791 **WILLIAMSON, William** — to **John Wallis**
See NEWMAN, Isaac

1795 4-16	**WILLIAMSON, William** (w. Elizabeth) to **John Bailey** Parcel of land in Hampshire Co. of Hampshire Co. Recorded 4-20-1795. Wit.: Andrew Wodrow, Perez Drew.	1794 12-10	**WODROW, Andrew** (w. Mary Ann) to **John Michell** of Hampshire Co. of Hampshire Co. 381 a. on Abraham's Ridge; rec. 2-16-1795. Wit.: None.
1799 9-16	**WILLIAMSON, William** to **Thompson Pegg** of Hampshire Co. of Hampshire Co. 168 a. on Little Cacapeon; rec. 9-16-1799. Wit.: None.	1795 2-2	**WODROW, Andrew** to **Edward Smith** of Hampshire Co. of Hampshire Co. 110 a. on North Branch River; rec. 2-16-1795. Wit.: None.
1789	**WILSON, James** to **William Hammond** See KELSO, James	1795 4-19	**WODROW, Andrew** to **Alexander McBride** of Hampshire Co. of Hampshire Co. 128 a. on Little Cacapeon; rec. 4-20-1795. Wit.: None.
1799 8-17	**WILSON, James** to **William McMahon** of Hampshire Co. (bill of sale) of Allegaany Co. Personal property; rec. 9-16-1799. Wit.: David Jones, James Dailey, A. King.	1795 10-19	**WODROW, Andrew** to **Thomas Ruckman** of Hampshire Co. of Hampshire Co. 71 a. on Little Cacapeon River; rec. 10-19-1795. Wit.: None.
1779 5-11	**WILSON, John** (w. Priscilla) to **Enoch Berry** of Hampshire Co. of Hampshire Co. Lot No. 46 in town of Romney; rec. 5-11-1779. Wit.: None.	1795 10-22	**WODROW, Andrew** to **Aaron Forman** of Hampshire Co. of Hampshire Co. 114 a. on Great Cacapeon; rec. 4-18-1796. Wit.: Isaac Parsons, Michael Miller, Benj. Neale.
1770 8-14	**WISE, Abraham** (w. Margret) to **William Turner** of Hampshire Co. (lease and release) of Hampshire Co. 203 a. in Hampshire Co.; rec. 8-15-1770. Wit.: Sam Dew.	1795 12-14	**WODROW, Andrew** to **Edward Smith** See BROWN, John, and GAITER, Elijah
1795 4-16	**WISE, Abraham** to **William Armstrong** of Hampshire Co. of Hampshire Co. Quarter acre in Frankfort; rec. 4-18-1796. Wit.: Abrm. Johnson, Wm. Johnson, Christian Stephens, Alex King.	1796 4-18	**WODROW, Andrew** to **Richard Hunter** of Hampshire Co. of Hampshire Co. 200 a. on Patterson Creek; rec. 4-18-1796. Wit.: None.
1795 4-16	**WISE, Abraham** to **William Armstrong** of Hampshire Co. of Hampshire Co. 100 a. on Patterson Creek; rec. 12-14-1795. Wit.: Abrm. Johnson, Wm. Johnson, Christian Stephens, Alex King.	1796 6-20	**WODROW, Andrew** to **Negro Slaves** of Hampshire Co. Pompey, and Sylvia, his wife Freeing these negroes from his service; rec. 6-20-1796. Wit.: None.
1796 10-17	**WISE, Adam** (w. Catherine) to **John Randolph** of Hampshire Co. (bill of sale) of Hampshire Co. 50 aa. on Patterson Creek; rec. 10-17-1796. Wit.: A. King, John Mitchell, Daniel Jones, John Mitchell, Jr.	1797 4-14	**WODROW, Andrew** (w. Mary) to **Francis White** of Hampshire Co., Va. (bill of sale) of Hampshire Co., Va. Half acre lot in Town of Romney (No. 46); rec. 4-17-1797. Wit.: None.
1779 11-1	**WODROW, Andrew** to **George Reed** of Hampshire Co. of Hampshire Co. 100 a. on South Branch; rec. 11-9-1779. Wit.: None.	1797 9-2	**WODROW, Andrew** (w. Mary) to **Edward McCarty** of Hampshire Co. of Hampshire Co. 420 a. on North Branch of Potomac; rec. 9-18-1797. Wit.: None.
1783 4-8	**WODROW, Andrew** to **Isaac Hite** of Hampshire Co. (power of attorney) of Lincoln Co. Authority to make assignment of a certain military land warrant for 2,000 acres; rec. 5-14-1783. Wit.: William Forman, Abel Randall, Samuel Dew.	1797 9-2	**WODROW, Andrew** (w. Mary) to **Francis Deakins** of Hampshire Co. **William Deakins** 400 a. on Patterson Creek. of George Town, Md. Recorded 9-18-1797. Wit.: None.
1788 12-10	**WODROW, Andrew** (w. Mary Ann) to **Joseph Cleizer** of Hampshire Co. (lease and release) of Hampshire Co. Half acre in Romney; rec. 12-11-1788. Wit.: None.	1797 10-17	**WODROW, Andrew** to **Alexander King** See GAITHER, Elijah
1792	**WODROW, Andrew** to **James Machir** See PARSONS, Isaac	1798 10-10	**WODROW, Andrew** (w. Mary) to **Edward McCarty** of Hampshire Co. of Hampshire Co. 442 a. on New Creek; rec. 12-17-1798. Wit.: None.
1792 1-22	**WODROW, Andrew** (w. Mary Ann) to **John Jack** of Hampshire Co. of Hampshire Co. Half acre in town of Romney; rec. 1-29-1793. Wit.: John Lehow.	1799 2-28	**WODROW, Andrew** to **William Heath** of Hampshire Co. of Henrico Co. 400 a. on Little Cacapeon River; rec. 9-16-1799. Wit.: Matthew Lodge, Henry Heinzman, Edward Dyer, William Naylor.
1792 4-24	**WODROW, Andrew** (w. MaryAnn) to **Francis Taggart** of Hampshire Co. of Hampshire Co. Half acre in town of Romney; rec. 4-24-1792. Wit.: None.	1799 12-16	**WODROW, Andrew** (w. Mary) to **Elijah Gaither** of Hampshire Co. of Hampshire Co. Half acre in Romney; rec. 12-16-1799. Wit.: None.
1792 9-1	**WODROW, Andrew** to **Henry Heinzman** (w. Mary Ann) of Hampshire Co. of Hampshire Co. Half acre in town of Romney; rec. 4-10-1793. Wit.: None.	1800 10-8	**WODROW, Andrew** (w. Mary) to **John Lyons** of Hampshire Co. of Hampshire Co. Recorded 10-20-1800. Wit.: None.
1793 1-18	**WODROW, Andrew** (w. Mary Ann) to **James Cochran** of Hampshire Co. of Hampshire Co. Half acre in town of Romney; rec. 1-29-1793. Wit.: John Lehow.	1800 10-6	**WODROW, Andrew** (w. Mary) to **James Mitchell** of Hampshire Co. of Hampshire Co. Recorded 10-20-1800.
1793 4-10	**WODROW, Andrew** (w. Mary Ann) to **John Plumb** of Hampshire Co. of Hampshire Co. 400 acres on Patterson Creek; rec. 4-10-1793. Wit.: None.	1800 4-16	**WODROW, Andrew** (w. Mary) to **George Bishop** of Hampshire Co. of Hardy Co. Recorded 9-15-1800.
1793 9-12	**WODROW, Andrew** to **Samuel Ravenscroft** of Hampshire Co. (lease) of Hampshire Co. 420 a. on North Branch; rec. 12-11-1793. Wit.: Nicholas Seavers, Newman Beckwith.	1784 4-24	**WOLFE, George** to **Abraham Johnson, Jr.** of Hampshire Co. (mortgage) of Hampshire Co. 200 a. on Patterson Creek; rec. 3-9-1785. Wit.: Abraham Johnson, Wm. Hough, Thomas Holenback.
1793 10-1	**WODROW, Andrew** to **Henry Heizman** (w. Mary Ann) of Hampshire Co. of Hampshire Co. Half acre in town of Romney; rec. 10-9-1793. Wit.: None.	1766 8-7	**WOLFE, Mary** to **John Collins** Widow of Michael Wolfe, of Frederick Co. formerly known as Mary Nisewanger of Frederick Co. (lease and release) 400 a. in Hampshire Co.; rec. 8-12-1766. Wit.: Peter Hog, Job Pearsall, Ja. Keith, Angus McDonald.
1794	**WODROW, Andrew** to **William Johnson** See MITCHELL, John	1800 4-10	**WOLVERTON, Isaac** (w. Elizabeth) to **Joshua Peters** of Hampshire Co. **Phil Peters** Recorded 5-19-1800. of Hampshire Co. Wit.: Andrew Wodrow, Edw. Dyer, William Naylor, Phil P. Wilson.
1794	**WODROW, Andrew** to **Edward McCarty** See MITCHELL, John	1771 8-13	**WOOD, Daniel** (w. Margret) to **Joel Robinson** of Hampshire Co. of Augusta Co. 300 a. on Lost River; rec. 8-13-1771. Wit.: Peter Steenberger, Jacob Cassalman, David Williams.
1794 4-9	**WODROW, Andrew** (w. Mary Ann) to **Samuel Park** of Hampshire Co. of Hampshire Co. 131 a. on Tear Coat Creek; rec. 4-9-1794. Wit.: None.	1779 3-9	**WOOD, Daniel** (w. Margret) to **George Cale** of Hampshire Co. of Hampshire Co. 400 a. on Great Cacapeon; rec. 3-9-1779. Wit.: Rees Pritchard, Wm. Hayden, Wm. Johnson.
1794 12-10	**WODROW, Andrew** (w. Mary Ann) to **John Michell** of Hampshire Co. of Hampshire Co. 121 a. on Patterson Creek; rec. 2-16-1795. Wit.: None.		

1775 10-24	WOOD, John of Hampshire Co. (lease and release) 386 a. on Cacapeon River; rec. 11-15-1775. Wit.: Enoch Innis, Elias Poston, F. Peyton, Jr., Thomas Edmondson, Henry Heth.	to Tavener Beall of Dunmore Co.		

1775 10-24 WOOD, John to Tavener Beall
of Hampshire Co. (lease and release) of Dunmore Co.
386 a. on Cacapeon River; rec. 11-15-1775.
Wit.: Enoch Innis, Elias Poston, F. Peyton, Jr., Thomas Edmondson, Henry Heth.

1772 3-2 WOOD, Thomas (w. Mary) to John Blue
of Frederick Co., Va. (lease and release) of Hampshire Co
212 a. on South Branch; rec. 3-9-1773.
Wit.: Samuel Beall, David Welton, Daniel McHeal.

1761 9-3 WOODSON, John to Rudy Bombgardner
of Hampshire Co. (lease and release) of Hampshire Co.
316 a. on Great Cacapeon; rec. 9-10-1761.
Wit., Gabriel Jones.

1770 5-9 WOODSON, Samuel (w. Elizabeth) to Jonathan Pugh
of Hampshire Co. (lease and release) of Hampshire Co.
400 a. on North River of Cacapeon; rec. 8-14-1770.
Wit.: Alex White, John Rousaw, Sam Dew, Sam Pritchard, G. Wilson, Alex Keith, Joseph Heavill.

1796 6-15 WOODSON, Samuel to John Woodson
of Hampshire Co. Mary Woodson
Deed of gift. Nicholas Woodson
Personal property, one negro slave, Betty Woodson
named Tanter. Rec. 6-15-1769. Thomas Woodson
Wit.: Sam Dew, John Rousaw.

1768 WORTHINGTON, Robert to John Hardin
See McCRACKEN, Margaret
RUTHERFORD, Benjamin

1769 WORTHINGTON, Robert to John Harden
See McCRACKEN, Jane, and Margaret
RUTHERFORD, Benjamin

1773 5-10 WORTHINGTON, Samuel, Jr. to John Vanbuskirk
(w. Elizabeth) of Hampshire Co.
of Barkley Co. (lease and release)
291 a. near Patterson Creek, on Burds Run; rec. 5-10-1774.
Wit.: John Hartley, Francis Burrell, Minard Johnston.

1773 11-5 WORTHINGTON, Samuel, Jr. to John Vanbuskirk
of Hampshire Co. (lease and release) of Hampshire Co.
160 a. on North Branch of Potomac; rec. 5-10-1774.
Wit.: None.

1795 10-17 WOSTEL, Humphry to John Dixon
of Fayette Co. of Hampshire Co.
112 a. on Cabbin Run; rec. 4-18-1796.
Wit.: Robert Allen, Nathan Allen, Thomas Allen.

1790 9-16 WYECOFF, Peter to John Sebring
of Hampshire Co. of Hampshire Co.
426 a. on Little Cacapeon; rec. 9-17-1790.
Wit.: None.

—Y—

1772 8-24 YAGAR, Joseph (w. Catherine) to Jeremiah Ewel
of Hampshire Co. (lease and release) Hampshire Co.
87 a. on drains of Sedar Swamp; rec. 3-9-1773.
Wit.: Abraham Hite, Jonathan Heath, Henry Marsh, I. Hite.

1796 3-19 YEISER, John (w. Elizabeth) to John Pancake
of Baltimore of Hampshire Co.
130 a. on Little Cacapeon; rec. 6-20-1796.
Wit.: John Pancake, Jr., Thomas Dugan.

1788 3-13 YETTER, Peter (w. Elizabeth) to John Hartley
of Hampshire Co.
160 a. on Mill Creek; rec. 4-10-1788.
Wit.: Abraham Johnson, Perez Drew, Nicholas Casey.

1799 1-11 YOUNG, Robert to Bertrand Ewell
of Alexandria, Va. of Prince William Co.
780 a. on South Branch River; rec. 9-16-1799.
Wit.: George Young, Charles Alexander, Jr., John Abart, Walter Jones, Jr.

1799 4-15 YOUNG, William to Thomas Greenwell
of Hampshire Co. of Hampshire Co.
337 a. on Potomac River; rec. 4-15-1799.
Wit.: Andrew Wodrow.

Surveys on Wappacomo---South Branch of Potomac

These surveys, numbered by Lord Fairfax from 1 to 66, beginning at the source and numbering toward the Potomac, the author has found, were held at some time by the following, and are mentioned in the wills or deeds by number (Lot No.)

1	Michael Stump	25	William Foreman and Benjamin Foreman	46	John Ross, Thomas Lawson
2	Michael Stump	26	William and John Foreman	47	John Marshall and George Gale
3	Michael Stump	27	Uriah Blue and Richard Blue	48	Thomas Bromsey heirs, E. Glaze J. Fred Fields
4		28		49	—— McGuire
5		29		50	Simon Taylor and W. F. Taylor
6	John Rosseau	30	Welton and Blue	51	Mary Martin and W. F. Taylor
7		31	John Welton and Job Welton	52	Hoge and Taylor
8	James Seavers, Michael Stump	32	John Wright, George Washington, and R. M. Marsh	53	Darby Aughney, Ann Aughney, Wm. Oldham and W. F. J. Taylor
9	John Decker, Abraham Kuykendall	33	John Pancake, Jr., and John Pancake, Sr.	54	
10	Sam Dew, Lawrence Haff			55	William Ross and heirs, Lawrence Ross, James and David Parsons, and Osbourn Spriggs
11		34	John Pancake, Jr.		
12		35			
13	Michael Stump, Christopher Cocke, and Joseph Inskeep	36	John Keating, Luke Collins, and William Castleman	56	William Ross, John Ross, George Carruthers
14	W. B. Stump	37	John Keating, Luke Collins, and William Castleman	57	
15	A. V. Parker and brothers (includes island)	38	John Cunningham and others	58	
16	Job Pearsol and Sam Earl	39	Simon Earsom	59	
17	Benjamin Kuykendall, Wm. Watson	40	Tarpley Taylor	60	John Coles, Griffen Taylor
18	S. H. Williams	41	Robert Ross	61	
19		42		62	
20	Cornelius Hoagland	43	Robert Parker	63	John Coles, Griffin Taylor
21	Michael Cresap and Peter Casey	44		64	Job Pearsoll, Thomas Cresap
22	Benjamin Forman	45		65	
23	John Forman and Richard Howland			66	
24					

Grantee-Grantor

(Grantor - Grantee pages only indexed for all names.)

—A—

1774 Abernathy, William, from James Sommerville
1775 Abernathy, William, from Bryan Bruin
1795 Abernathy, William, from Thomas Cooper and wife
1794 Acton, John, from Richard Acton and wife
1790 Adams, John, from Trustees of Frankfort
1791 Adams, John, Sr., from John Keller and wife
1783 Adams, William, from Andrew Turk and wife
1797 Adams, William, from Thomas Bates and wife
Ahrsam—See Earsom, Earson, Ihreeom, Ohrsam
1792 Ahrsam, Jacob, from Trustees of Springfield
1790 Ahrsam, John, from Simeon Ahrsam, Sr., and wife
1790 Ahrsam, Simeon, Jr., from Simeon Ahrsam Sr., and w.
1778 Ahrsam, Simeon (w. Mary) from Mary Creamour
1785 Aikman, John, from John Morgan and wife
1797 Aires, Richard, from William Pell and wife
1795 Alderton, William, from James Hiett and wife
1797 Alexander, Amos, from John Thomas Ricketts and wf.
1760 Alexander, James, from William Welton and wife
1760 Alexander, James, from William Welton and wife
1772 Alexander, James, from Gabriel Jones
1787 Alexander, Robert, from John Pancake and wife
1790 Allan, Robert, from Thomas Coombs
1797 Allen, Arthur, from Abraham Johnson and wife
1800 Allen, Arthur, from David Jones and wife
1791 Allen, David, from John Forman
1794 Allen, Elizabeth, from Ezekiel Rogers
1796 Allen, Jacob, from Trustees of Romney
1782 Allen, John, from Jasper Cather and wife
1797 Allen, Robert, from Abraham Johnson and wife
1800 Allen, Robert, from David Jones and wife
1765 Allen, Thomas, from Abraham Tegarden and wife
1797 Allen, Thomas, from Abraham Johnson and wife
1800 Allen, Thomas, from David Jones and wife
1800 Allen, Thomas, from Humphrey Westell
1795 Allender, William, from Jacob Christman
1797 Amiger, Elizabeth, from John Gatewood
1791 Anderson, Thomas, from William Anderson, Sr.
1797 Anderson, Thomas, from William Anderson and wife
1764 Anderson, William, from William Smith
1797 Andrews, George, from Benjamin Benam and wife
1794 Antrau, John, from Joseph Johnson and wife
See Autraw)
1778 Archer, John, Jr., from Alexander White and wife
1792 Armstrong, William, from Nathaniel Parker
1792 Armstrong, William, from Nathaniel Parker
1795 Armstrong, William, from Abraham Wise
1795 Armstrong, William, from Abraham Wise
1792 Arnold, Andrew, from John Arnold and wife
1798 Arnold, Daniel, from Samuel Thomas and wife
1798 Arnold, John, from Patrick Kern and wife
1792 Arnold, Samuel, from Richard Relse (or Kelse)
1792 Arnold, Samuel, from John Relse (or Kelse)
1799 Arnold, Zachariah, from Samuel Arnold and wife
1794 Asbury, Henry, from Benjamin Stone and wife
1782 Asbury, Joseph, from Henry Menifee and wife
1790 Asbury, Joseph, from James Monroe and wife
1796 Ashbrook, Absalom, from Thomas Tucker and wife
1775 Ashbrook, Aaron, from Aeason Howard and wife

1796 Ashbrook, Aaron, from Thomas Tucker and wife
1796 Ashbrook, Eli, from Thomas Tucker and wife
1796 Ashbrook, Elizabeth, from Thomas Tucker aed wife
1796 Ashbrook Heirs, from Thomas Tucker and wife
1796 Ashbrook Heirs, from Edward Parell and wife
1771 Ashbrook, Levi, from Andrew Arnold and wife
1774 Ashbrook, Levi, from George Edington and wfe
1800 Ashbrook, Levy, from Absolem Ashbrook and wife
1774 Ashbrook, Moses, from Joseph Arnold and wife
1776 Ashburner, John, from Bryan Bruin
1800 Ashley, Jermiah, from Ben Ashley
1797 Athy, John, from Thomas Hughs and wife
1799 Atkinson, John, from Josiah Mastors and wife
1767 Aufere, George, from John Relfe
1766 Aughtney, Darby, from Thomas Lord Fairfax
1766 Aughtney, Ann, from Thomas, Lord Fairfax
1778 Aughney, Derby, from John Foxcraft, Chas. Thompson
1794 Autraw, John, from Joseph Johnson and wife
See Antrau

—B—

1796 Babbs, Beel, from Nathan Gard
1799 Babbs, Beall, from David Pugh and wife
1792 Babb, William, from John Cunningham and wife
1794 Babbs, William, from George Cooper
1777 Bacorn, Job, from Okey Johnson and wife
1779 Bacorn, Job, from Edward McGuire
1783 Bacorn, Job, from John Davis and wife
1761 Bagley, Henry, from Joseph Hamlin
1780 Bailie, John, from Robert Scott
1795 Bailey, John, from William Williamson and wife
1797 Bailey, John, Sr., from John Cannon
1774 Baker, Anthony, from Phillip Mason
1772 Baker, John, from William Anderson
1784 Baker, Joseph, from Trustees of Moorefield
1796 Baker, Nicholas, from John Pancake and wife
1799 Baker, Patrick, from John McMeekin and wife
1772 Baker, Samuel, from Ellis Hughes and wife
1790 Baker, Samuel, from James Smith
1794 Baker, Thomas, from John Williamson
1795 Baker, William, from Jacob Crisman and wife
1763 Baldwin, William, from Joseph Britain
1787 Balentine, Hugh, from Isaac Means and wife
1765 Ball, William, from Edward McGuire and wife
1791 Baptist Church, Hampshire Co., from Ezekiel Rogers
1772 Barclay, Carson & Mitchell, from Bryan Bruin
1766 Barclay, Thomas, from Luke Collins and wife
1787 Barclay, Thomas, from Enoch Berry and wife
1792 Barkelow, James, from Benjamin Hoffman and wife
1780 Barnard, Mena, from Moses Pigman
1784 Barnhouse, John, from John McNeal
1784 Barnhouse, John, from John McNeal
1796 Barnick, Jacob, from John Acton and wife
1800 Barret, David, from Jacob Jenkins
1789 Barrett, Samuel, from James Ryan
1793 Barrett, Samuel, from Richard Marquis and wife
1789 Barthuff, Andrew, from Jacob Brookhart and wife
1783 Barton, Kimber, from Abraham Blue and wife

GRANTEE-GRANTOR   PAGE 65

1779	Bates, Edward, from Edward Blackburn and wife	1800	Blue, Mich, from John Pancake, w., and Simon Pancake
1779	Bates, Edward, from Edward Blackburn and wife	1797	Boft, Jacob, from Lewis Stallman and wife
1792	Bates, Thomas, from Edward Bates and wife	1784	Bogard, Jacob, from Abraham Johnson, Sr., and wife
1781	Bathas, George, from Henry Hamilton	1784	Bogard, Jacob, from Joseph Williams and wife
1761	Batton, Henry, from Joseph Edwards	1793	Bogell, Thomas, from James Bogell and wife
1770	Batton, Henry, from Joseph Bean and wife	1761	Bombgardner, Rudy, from John Woodson
1792	Bayless, Edward, from Thomas McGuire and wife	1792	Bond, Thomas, from James Dawson and wife
1783	Beacorn, Job, from Moses Tichenal and wife	1790	Bookless, David, from John Greenfield, (by adm.)
1763	Beall, Benjamin, from James Simpson	1790	Bosley, James, from Peter Putman
1763	Beall, Benjamin, from James Simpson	1766	Bowel, Bazel, from William Bowel
1793	Beall, Eli, from George Beall	1762	Bowell, William, from John Hite and wife
1793	Beall, Elisha, from George Beall	1765	Bowels, William, Sr., from Henry Enochs, Sr. and w.
1778	Beall, George, from William Baldwin and wife	1765	Bowels, William, Sr., from Henry Enochs, Sr. and w.
1792	Beall, George, dedimus from Hampshire Co. Court	1797	Bowman, John, from Hugh Thomas
1787	Beall, Hezekaiah, from Conrad Myre and wife	1798	Boxell, John, from Kingsman Dutton and wife
1772	Beall, Isaac, from Humphrey Wells	1792	Boyce, Nicholas, from John Snyder and wife
1800	Beall, Isiah, from Cornelius Hogeland	1769	Boyce, Richard, from Benjamin Rutherford
1776	Beall, Samuel, from Isaac Beall and wife	1771	Boyce, Richard, from Phillip Martin
1775	Beall, Tavener, from John Wood	1785	Boyce, Richard, from John Moffett and wife
1785	Beall, Thomas, from Francis Pearpoint	1785	Boyce, Richard, from John Moffett
1783	Bean, Benjamin, from Benjamin Robinson and wife	1767	Boyton, John, from John Keating and wife
1783	Bean, Benjamin, from McKennery Robinson	1767	Boyton, John, from James Gallent and wife
1783	Beard, George, from Matthias Ulrick Harsman	1767	Boyton, John, from James Gallent and wife
1799	Beard, James, from John Dowden and wife	1794	Brady, Michael, from Alex Chrisholm and wife
1801	Beard, William (w. Elizabeth), from Charles Mullins	1798	Brahan, John, from Jasper Cather and wife
1799	Beattie, George, from Samuel Davis and wife	1795	Brall, Basil, a negro man, from George Kyger
1784	Beatty, George, from Edward Snickers	1774	Brandenburger, Matthias, from Margaret Gillmer et al
1795	Beatty, Levi, from Trustees of Romney	1793	Branninburg, William, from James Fleming
1772	Beaver, Mathias, from Peter Beaver	1771	Brake, Jacob, from James Jones and wife
1794	Beckner, Peter, from Jacob Chrisman	1763	Brechtel, Jacob, from Peter Haas
1794	Beekman, William, from David Newman and wife	1795	Brelsford, Bernard, from Thomas Edwards and wife
1771	Bell, Robert, from Phillip Martin, Thos. Bryan Martin	1798	Brelsford, Marjoram, from John Harre and wife
1788	Bell, William, from Timothy Collins and wife	1797	Brelsford, Marjoram, from Andrew Horn and wife
1797	Bellford, Benjamin, from Pompey Long	1799	Briant, James, from John Higgins and wife
1796	Belsford, Daniel, from George Horn, Sr., and wife	1788	Briggs, Joseph, from John Kuykendall
1797	Benan, Benjamin, from George Andrews and wife	1788	Briggs, Joseph, from John Kuykendall
1793	Bennett, Thomas, from Richard Marquis and wife	1791	Briggs, Joseph, from Nathaniel Kuykendall
1778	Berry, Enoch, from Thomas Barclay and John Magill	1798	Briggs, Joseph, from Barkelow, Powelson, Beatty etc.
1779	Berry, Enoch, from John Wilson and wife	1790	Brill, Michael, from Alexander Boyd and wife
1787	Berry, Enoch, from Thomas Barclay	1778	Brink, Hybert, from James and Thomas Parsons
1780	Berry, Reuben, from Robt. Gilchrist, Jas. Somerville	1799	Brinker, Henry, from Robert Ross
1794	Berry, Samuel, from Robert Campbell and wife	1788	Brookhart, Jacob, from John Keller
1793	Bethel, George, from William House and wife	1789	Brookhart, Jacob, from Mark Hardin and wife
1794	Bevan, Stacy, from John William and wife	1789	Brookhart, Jacob, from Trustees of Frankfort
1796	Bever, John, from James Watson	1790	Brookhart, Michael, from Trustees of Frankfort
1782	Bever, Matthias, from Peter Bever and wife	1790	Brookhart, Michael, from Trustees of Frankfort
1797	Bevins, Charles, from Lewis Throgmorton and wife	1788	Brookhard, Phillip, from John Keller
1800	Bevins, Samuel, from John Walters and wife	1791	Brown, Alexander, from William Linegar and wife
1785	Bills, John, from John Morgan and wife	1795	Brown, John, from John Foreman and wife
1770	Bills, William, from Charles Smith and wife	1795	Brown, John, from Trustees of Romney
1783	Bills, William, from Henry Batton and wife	1796	Brown, John, from Charles Magill and wife
1784	Bills, William, from Henry Enochs and wife	1797	Brown, John, from Daniel Collins
1793	Birket, Thomas, from Joseph Moore	1797	Brown, John, from Henry Grove and wife
1792	Birkhart, Thomas, from John Clark and wife	1797	Brown, John, from Henry Grove and wife
1800	Bishop, George, from Andrew Wodrow and wife	1797	Brown, John, from Henry Grove and wife
1796	Bishop, Noah, from Jacob Plough and wife	1797	Brown, John, from John Prunty and wife
1773	Blackburn, William, from John Hardin and wife	1793	Browning, Elias, from Joseph Lyons and wife
1774	Blackburn, William, from John Hardin	1762	Bruan, Bryan, from Job Pearsal and wife
1778	Blackburn, William, from Thomas Fairley	1762	Bruen, Bryan, from John Ross
1794	Bland, John, from Jonathan Mathew and wife	1763	Bruen, Bryan, from Cornelius Conner and wife
1790	Blew, Uriah, from Richard Hougland, by John Reed	1767	Bruen, Bryan, from Owen Jones and Daniel Wister
1779	Blue, Abraham from Okey Johnson and wife	1768	Bruen, Bryan, from William Smith and wife
1770	Blue, Catherine, from Abraham Blue	1768	Bruen, Bryan, from John Parker and wife
1770	Blue, John, from Job Welton and wife	1768	Bruen, Bryan, from Hugh Murphy
1772	Blue, John, from Thomas Wood and wife	1763	Bruin, Bryan, from Charles Smith and wife
1799	Blue, Capt. John, from Jacob Hines	1763	Bruin, Bryan, from John Lindsey and wife
1793	Blue, Michael, from David Corbin and wife	1763	Bruin, Bryan, from John Lindsey and wife

1770	Bruin, Bryan, from Richard Smith	1772	Cantien, Abraham, from Thomas Hottingham and wife
1772	Bruin, Bryan, from John Spore and wife	1791	Carder, Abbot, from William Carder
1773	Bruin, Bryan, from Samuel Pritchard	1798	Carlisle, William, from Samuel Pugh and wife
1776	Bruin, Bryan, from John Greenfield (by executors)	1773	Carlyle, John, from Enoch Leonord and wife
1774	Bruin, Bryan, from Robert Knott	1796	Carlyle, William, from James McBride
1785	Bruin, Col. Peter Bryan, from Bryan Bruin	1794	Carnend, Leonard, from Samuel Hague and wife
1800	Bruner, Henry, from Jermiah Thompson and wife	1794	Carnend, Leonard, from Samuel Hague and wife
1797	Bruner, Peter, frfom William Jackson and wife	1771	Carpenter, John, from Edward Scott and wife
1762	Bryan, James, from William Kimzey and wife	1780	Carr, Michael, from Thomas Lord Fairfax
1794	Bryan, John, from John Williamson	1780	Carruthers, George, from Thomas Lord Fairfax
1783	Buck, Anthony, from William Buck	1796	Carruthers, James, from James Murphy and wife
1800	Buck, Anthony, from Robert Pope and wife	1772	Carson, Barclay & Mitchell, from Bryan Bruin
1798	Buck, Michael, from James Smith and wife	1769	Carson, Thomas, from Matthew Harrison
1780	Buck, Robert, from Bryan Bruin	1793	Cary, Joseph, from John McMeekin and wife
1792	Buck, Robert, from Trustees of Springfield	1777	Casey, Benjamin, from Peter Casey
1793	Buck, Robert, from Turstees of Hampshire Co.	1786	Casey, John—Certificate from U. S. government
1780	Buck, William, from Bryan Bruin	1778	Casey, Nicholas, from Peter Casey and wife
1782	Buffington, Thomas, from Isaac Parsons, Jas. Murphy	1779	Casey, Nicholas, from Eve and Lawrence Glaze
1799	Buffington, Thomas, from Abraham Johnston	1787	Casey, Nicholas, from Peter Casey
1763	Buffington, William, from Thomas Lord Fairfax	1793	Casey, Nicholas, from John Decker and wife
1794	Buffington, William, from Robert French	1794	Casey, Nicholas, from Thomas Littler and wife
1795	Buffington, William, from Trustees of Romney	1769	Casey, Peter, from James Ryan and wife
1784	Bullitt, William, from Trustees of Morefield	1771	Casey, Peter, from Vincent Williams and wife
1796	Bunn, Peter, from Daniel Miller	1787	Casler, John, from Michael Casler
1795	Burbridge, Mary, from Kimber Barton and wife	1787	Casler, John, from Michael Casler
1797	Burket, Thomas, from Thomas Pettet and wife	1759	Cassellman, David, from Ludwick Cassellman
1778	Burket, Valentine, from William Rodgers and wife	1759	Cassellman, Jacob, from Ludwick Cassellman
1797	Burkett, Thomas, from Thomas Pettet and wife	1762	Castleman, Jacob, from David Castleman and wife
1781	Burkit, Jacob, from Simon Burkit	1774	Casselman, Lewis, from Okey Johnson and wife
1789	Burnfield, John, from Henry Enoch and wife	1794	Caswell, John, from Alex Christholm and wife
1795	Burns, John, from Trustees of Romney	1779	Cather, Jasper, from William Blackburn and wife
1796	Burns, William H., from Matthew Montgomery and w.	1779	Cather, Jasper, from William Blackburn and wife
1798	Burns, William, from Ferrance Doyle and wife	1800	Caun, John, from Ephrem Johnstone by Levi Matthews
1793	Burris, Henry, from Joseph Crecraft and wife	1790	Cavender, Garret, from Joseph Moore and wife
1783	Busby, John, from Hugh Sidwell	1767	Chambers, Christopher, from John Relfe
1799	Busby, John, from John W. Merridith and wife	1796	Chandler, Ellis, from Henry Hazle and wife
1764	Bush, Mathias, from Charles Lynch (or Linch)	1796	Chandler, Elizabeth, from Henry Hazle and wife
1764	Bush, Matthias, from Edward McGuire and wife	1796	Chandler, Sarah, from Henry Hazle and wife
1774	Bush, Matthias, from Edward McGuire	1775	Chapman, William, from John Royse
1771	Bush, Phillip, from James Craike and wife	1779	Chapman, William, from William Burgess and wife
1792	Bussey, John, from John Rush and wife	1779	Chapman, William, from John Johnson and wife
1785	Butcher, John, from James Cunnard (Connard?)	1797	Chapman, William, from Thomas Healy
1792	Buzzard, Frederick, from Priscilla Gaddis	1797	Chapman, William, from Thomas Healy
1785	Buzzard, Rudolph, from Abraham Hite and wife	1771	Chenoweth, John, from William Chenoweth and wife
		1786	Chenoweth, John, Jr., from William Bills and wife
	—C—	1789	Chenoweth, John, from John Copsey
1785	Cade, Major, from Robert Higgins and wife	1789	Chenoweth, John, from John Copsey and wife
1793	Calmes, Fielding, from John Decker and wife	1790	Chenoweth, John, from James Largent and wife
1762	Calmes, William, from David Castleman and wife	1791	Chenoweth, John, from John Lander and wife
1788	Calvin, Joshua, from Hugh Murphy	1796	Chenoweth, John, Jr., from Rudolph Bungardner & w.
1790	Calvin, Joshua, from Benjamin Eli and wife	1783	Cherry, Andrew, from Henry Moore and wife
1782	Calvin, Robert, from Absalom Fox and wife	1797	Cheshire, John, from Samuel Edwards
1775	Calvin, Stephen, from Vincent Calvin	1768	Chesnut, James, from John Chesnut, Jasper Sutton
1791	Campbell, Archable, from Benjamin Parker and wife	1799	Chew, Colby, from James Dailey and wife
1786	Campbell, John, from John Glaze and wife	1782	Chinoth, John, from Henry Enoch and wife
1791	Campbell, Robert, from Frederick Royse	1789	Chisholm, John, from Alexander Chisholm and wife
1795	Campbell, Robert, from Trustees of Romney	1761	Chrisman, Isaac, from Francis McBride and wife
1795	Campbell, Runey, from Trustees of Romney	1793	Clark, Ambrose, from Richard Marquis
1799	Campbell, Runa, from Joseph Hurford	1773	Clark, Henry, from Abraham Clarke
1773	Campbell, Thomas, from Samuel Pritchard	1790	Clark, James, from Trustees of Frankfort
1773	Campbell, William, from Joseph Robinson	1791	Clark, James, from Denny Fairfax
1786	Campbell, William, from John Peyton	1791	Clarke, James, from Denny Fairfax
1794	Canby, Samuel, from John Rawles	1795	Clarke, James, from Peter Jones
1796	Candy, John, from Francis White and wife	1783	Clark, Jonathan, from Isaac Hite and wife
1801	Candy, John, from John Busby and wife	1790	Clarke, John, from Joseph Moore and wife
1797	Cann, John, from Jonathan Morgan and wife	1779	Clark, Robert, from Thomas Lord Fairfax
1794	Cannon, John, from David Corbin and wife	1784	Clark, Watson, from John Westfall

1799	Claton, John, from John Logan and wife	1793	Cool, Phillip, from David Corbin and wife
1761	Claypole, James, Sr., from James Thomas and wife	1793	Cool, Phillip, from Thomas Ashbrook
1761	Claypole, John, from Francis McBride and wife	1788	Cooper, Andrew, from John Keller
1761	Claypool, James, from Jacob Gum and wife	1790	Cooper, Andrew, from Trustees of Frankfort
1770	Claypoole, James, from Thomas Denton and wife	1791	Cooper, George, from Francis Keyes and wife
1773	Claypoole, James, Sr., from Joseph Claypools and w.	1799	Cooper, George, from Joseph Pugh and wife
1775	Claypoole, James, Jr., from John Osborn and wife	1772	Cooper, Thomas, from Phillip Martin
1762	Claypoole, John, from William Smith and wife	1799	Cooper, Thomas, Jr., from Thomas Cooper, Sr., and w.
1775	Claypoole, John, from Thomas Denton and wife	1784	Cooper, Valentine, from Jacob Ragan and wife
1769	Claypoole, Joseph, from Isaac Chrisman and wife	1788	Copsey, John, from James Largent and wife
1791	Cleaver, Peter, from Ezelkiel Cleaver, by executors	1789	Copsey, John, from John Chenoweth, Jr., and wife
1788	Cleizer, Joseph, from Andrew Wodrow and wife	1789	Copsey, John, from William Bills and wife
1779	Clinton, Charles, from Thomas Simmonds and wife	1791	Copsey, John, from John Chenoweth and wife
1793	Clinton, Charles, from Andrew House and wife	1794	Copsey, John, from George Crock and wife
1790	Clisher, Joseph, from Henry Litner and wife	1795	Copsey, John, from William Demoss
1785	Clyne, Jacob, from Frederick Conrad	1797	Copsey, John, from Henry W. Pearce and wife
1796	Coats, Edward, from John Buck	1797	Copsey, John, from Peter Bunn and wife
1760	Coban, Jonathan, from John Werbel	1798	Copsey, John, from Henry Pierce and wife
1775	Coberly, James Stell, from Adam O'Bryan	1798	Copsey, John, from Francis White and wife
1799	Cochran & Thursby, from Henry Heinzman	1783	Corbin, Anderson, from Simon Battin
1799	Cochran, Edward, from John Taylor and wife	1798	Corbin, Daniel, from George Mairheid and wife
1792	Cochran, James, from Joseph Cleiser	1772	Corbin, David, from Thomas Collins
1793	Cochran, James, from Andrew Wodrow and wife	1794	Corbin, David, from William Corbin and wife
1793	Cochran, James, from Joseph Cliser	1777	Corbin, William, from Hugh Murphy.
1785	Cochran, Suck, negro slave, from Simon Cochran & w.	1779	Corbin, William, from Hugh Murphy
1798	Cochran, William, from Alexander King and wife	1794	Corbin, William, from David Corbin and wife
1792	Cock, Moses, from John Kincheloe and wife	1779	Corey, Joseph, from Okey Johnson and wife
1779	Cole, George, from Daniel Wood and wife	1771	Corn, Andrew, from Phillip Martin
1790	Collier, Michael, from Trustees of Frankfort	1787	Corn, Andrew, from William Corn and wife
1766	Collins, John, from Mary (Nisewanger) Wolfe	1795	Corn, Timothy, from John Price and wife
1766	Collins, Luke, from John Keating and wife	1778	Cornman, John, from Benjamin Schullar and wife
1766	Collins, Luke, from Job Pearsall	1769	Cornwell, Enoch, from James Davison
1767	Collins, Luke, from Benjamin Jones and wife	1799	Coudin, James, from Thomas Triplett and wife
1799	Collins, Daniel, from Nicholas Casey	1794	Coulshine, Ernest, from Nathaniel Ferrand
1767	Collins, Luke, from Bryan Bruin and wife	1792	Cowan, Robert, from John Colson (by executrix)
1800	Collins, Samuel, from John Babbs and wife	1789	Cowens, Robert, from Abraham Johnson, Jr., and wife
	Collins, Thomas, from James Gibson	1779	Cowger, George, from Josiah and Edith Davison
1779	Collins, Thomas, from Bryan Bruin	1794	Cowgill, Elisha, from John Demoss and wife
1796	Collins, Thomas, from Daniel Collins	1767	Cox, Isaac, from John Greenfield, John Livingston
1798	Collins, Thomas, from Daniel Collins	1768	Cox, Isaac, from John Critten
1799	Collins, Thomas, from Daniel Collins and wife	1797	Craig, James, from Thomas Kennedy
1792	Colstone, Rawleigh, from Richard Acton and wife	1800	Craig, James, from John Mitchell and wife
1800	Colston, Rawleigh, from John Mitchell	1799	Craig, Samuel, from Francis White and wife
1795	Colvin, Joshua, from John Forman	1760	Craik, James, from John Thomas and wife
1793	Combs, Daniel, from Edward Amory and wife	1772	Craike, Dr. James Craike, from Phillip Bush and wife
1792	Combs, Francis, from Trustees of Springfield	1794	Cravine, from James Slaughter
1795	Combs, John, from William McPhereson	1797	Crawlis, Nicholas, from Thomas Dunn and wife
1792	Combs, Jonas, from Martha Combs	1792	Creagur, Jacob, from James Watts and wife
1785	Combs, Thomas, from Francis Taggart and wife	1766	Crecraft, Joseph (w. Margaret) from William Bowel
1790	Combs, Thomas, from Joseph Moore and wife	1766	Crecraft, William (w. Sarah) from William Bowel
1794	Compston, Henry, from Cornelius Williamson and w.	1766	Cresap, Daniel, from Providence Williams
1795	Conklin, Annanias, from Trustees of Romney	1768	Cresap, Daniel, from James Livingston
1796	Conklin, Jacob, from George Thopmson	1769	Cresap, Michael, from Phillip Ross and wife
1768	Conner, Cornelius, from James Anderson	1722	Cresap, Michael, from Harman Great House and wife
1770	Conrad, Frederick, from Paul McKever	1772	Cresap, Michael, from John Smith
1777	Conrad, James, from John Keith and wife	1779	Cresap, Michael, from Thomas Cresap and wife
1777	Conrad, James, from John Keith and wife	1782	Crsap, Col. Michael, from Jeremiah Burroughs
1783	Conrad, James, Jr., from James Conrad, Sr., and wife	1784	Cresap, Michael, from Thomas Cresap
1784	Conrad, John, from Henry Marsh	1760	Cresap, Thomas, from Hugh Murphew
1792	Constant, John, from William Newcomb and wife	1763	Cresap, Thomas, from Job Pearsoll (Pearsall)
1770	Constart, John, from Thomas Mattock and wife	1768	Creymour, Mary, from Simon Earsham and wife
1767	Cook, William, from John Relfe	1790	Crisman, Phillip, from Aaron Steed
1795	Cook, William, from Trustees of Romney	1796	Critton, John, from Aaron Steed and wife
1799	Cook, William, from Trustees of Romney	1784	Critton, William, from Jacob Short and wife
1793	Cool, Herbert, from Richard Nelson and wife	1797	Critton, William, from John Downing
1793	Cool, Herbert, from Phillip Cool and wife	1787	Crock, George, from John Royce and wife
1790	Cool, Phillip, from Thomas Ashbrook, Nicholas Casey	1795	Crock, George, from John Copsey and wife

Year	Entry
1799	Crock, George, from James McAllister and wife
1800	Crock, John, from William Reeder
1769	Croose, Christian, from John Johnson and wife
1799	Crossley, from Joseph Hurford
1790	Crumrine, Christian, from Isaac Dawson and wife
1794	Crutchlow, John, from Trustees of Frankfort
1779	Cryder, John, from Hugh Murphy.
1790	Cundiff, John, from Peter Putman and wife
1797	Cunningham, James, from Jonathan Purcell and wife
1749	Cunningham, John, from Thomas Lord Fairfax
1773	Cunningham, Robert, from Abraham Clarke
1779	Cunningham, Robert, from Thomas Lord Fairfax
1784	Cunningham, Robert, from John Denham
1758	Cunningham, William, from Luke Collins
1759	Cunningham, William, from Luke Collins and wife
1782	Cunningham, William, Jr., from Wm. Cunningham, Sr.
1766	Cuppy, John, from Benjamin Parker and wife
1787	Cuppy, John, Jr., from John Glaze and wife
1794	Cuppy, John, from Samuel Hague and wife
1780	Cutright, Samuel, from Thomas Lord Fairfax

—D—

Year	Entry
1796	Dailey, James, from Trustees of Romney
1799	Dailey, James, from John Pancake, Jr.
1799	Dailey, James, from Peter Williams and wife
1799	Dailey, James, from Peter Williams and wife
1799	Dailey, James, from Jacob Vanpelt and wife
1800	Dailey, James, from Francis Maurice Howard et al
1800	Dailey, James, from John Dailey
1795	Dailey, John, from Donald McDonald
1798	Dall, James, from Edward McCarty
1798	Dall, James, from Edward McCarty
1798	Dall, James, from Edward McCarty
1773	Dalton, John, from Enoch Leonard and wife
1788	Danford, Peter, from John Keller
1796	Daniels, Dennis, from Alexander King and wife
1797	Daniels, Dennis, from John Brookhart, Barbara Swobe
1795	Daton, John, from George Reese
1788	Daugherty, James, from John Keller
1794	Davey, William, from John McMeekin and wife
1790	Davis, Elijah, from John Arnold and wife
1795	Davis, Gustan, from Jacob Earson and wife
1786	Davis, Henry, from James McBride and wife
1785	Davis, James, from Jeremiah Ozburn
1782	Davis, John, from Valentine Purget and wife
1797	Davis, Samuel, from Daniel Rodrick and wife
1794	Davis, Walter, from Archibald Tracy
1780	Dawson, Abraham, from Mary and David Dawson & w.
1782	Dawson, Isaac, from John Constant
1783	Dawson, Jacob, from David Dawson
1791	Dawson, Thomas, from Denny Fairfax
1801	Dayton, Isaac, from John Murphy and wife
1794	Deakins, Francis, from Daniel Jones and wife
1795	Deakins, Francis, from John Mitchel and wife
1795	Deakins, Francis, from Samuel Ravenscroft and wife
1796	Deakins, Francis, from John Haines and wife
1796	Deakins, Francis, from Andrew Cooper
1797	Deakins, Francis, from Abram Halterman and wife
1797	Deakins, Francis, from Andrew Wodrow and wife
1798	Deakins, Francis, from Thomas Beall and wife
1794	Deakins, William, from Daniel Jones and wife
1795	Deakins, William, from John Mitchel and wife
1795	Deakins, William, from Samuel Ravenscroft and wife
1796	Deakins, William, from John Haines and wife
1796	Deakins, William, from Andrew Cooper
1797	Deakins, William, from Abram Halterman and wife
1797	Deakins, William, from Andrew Wodrow and wife
1798	Deakins, William, from Thomas Beall and wife
1777	Deale, James, from Thomas Cresap
1785	Dean, Thomas, from Charles Bruin and wife
1789	Dean, Thomas, from Solomon Hedges
1790	Dean, Thomas, Jr., from Thomas Dean, Sr.
1794	Deaver, George, from Jesse Pugh
1800	Deaver, George, from William Engle
1773	Decker (Barbara Decker Kuykendall) divorce from Jacob Kuykendall
1772	Decker, John, from Lawrence Hass and wife
1778	Decker, John, from Abraham Kuykendall
1784	Decker, John, from Jeremiah Claypole
1793	Decker, John, from Henry Kuykendall
1793	Decker, John, from Henry Kuykendall
1793	Decker, John, from Jacob Kuykendall
1784	Decker, Luke, from Jeremiah Claypole
1779	Deewald, Nicholas, from Bryan Bruin
1797	Delany, Patrick, from John Jack (by Jeremiah Mahony, attorney)
1783	Denham, John, from Job Little
1768	Denton, Jacob, from Robert Denton and wife
1768	Denton, John, from Robert Denton and wife
1761	Denton, Robert, from Stephen Ruddell and wife
1768	Denton, Thomas, from Robert Denton and wife
1770	Denton, Thomas, from John Denton and wife
1797	Devore, Cornelius, from Hugh Thomas
1798	Devore, Cornelius, from Richard Hoddy and wife
1765	Dew, Samuel, from Lawrence Hass and wife
1767	Dew, Samuel, from Henry Van Meter
1769	Dew, Samuel, from Lawrence Hass
1782	Dew, Samuel, from Isaac Parsons, James Murphy
1786	Dew, Samuel, from Lewis Castleman
1795	Dick, Elisha C., from William McGuire, Daniel Jones
1795	Dick, Elisha Cullen, from Wm. McGuire, Daniel Jones
1796	Dick, Elisha Cullen, from Ference Doyle and wife
1790	Dick, Nicholas, from Trustees of Frankfort
1779	Dicken, Amos, from Bryan Bruin
1795	Dimmitt, John, from Archibald Wiggins and wife
1795	Dimmitt, John, from Archibald Wiggins and wife
1795	Dimmit, Moses, from Archibald Wiggins and wife
1795	Dimmit, Moses, from Archibald Wiggins and wife
1797	Dimmit, Moses, from William Jackson and wife
1792	Dinnett, Samuel, from Charles Magill et al
1792	Dixon, John, from Trustees of Springfield
1794	Dixon, John, from John Rawles
1795	Dixon, John, from Humphry Wostel
1787	Doll, Conrad, from Peter Noll
1795	Dolohan, Daniel, from Samuel Hague and wife
1795	Dolohan, Daniel, from Benjamin Norman and wife
1795	Dolohan, Daniel, from Benjamin Norman and wife
1796	Dolohan, Daniel, from William Norman and wife
1794	Doman, Jacob, from George Rogers
1783	Donnalson, James, from William Buck
1786	Donaldson, James, from Robert Wallace
1792	Donaldson, James, from Trustees of Hampshire Co.
1792	Donaldson, John, from Trustees of Springfield
1762	Dopson, William, from Anderson Poulson (Powelson)
1790	Dougherty, James, from Trustees of Frankfort
1761	Douthit, John, from Silas Hedges
1771	Douthit, John, from Phillip Martin, Thos. B. Martin
1793	Douthit, John, Jr., from John Douthit, Sr., and wife
1793	Douthit, Solomon, from John Douthit, Sr., and wife
1780	Doughtie, Thomas, from Robert Scott
1764	Douglas, James, from John Reno
1795	Doveridge, John, from Lewis Stollman and wife
1786	Dowden, John, from Lewis Castleman and wife
1790	Dowden, John, from Trustees of Frankfort

1792	Dowden, John Biggs, from John Dowden and wife		1792	Enoch, Henry, Sr., from John Henry and wife
1798	Dowden, John, Jr., from Hugh McKinley		1779	Ermintrout, Christopher, from Thomas Lord Fairfax
1794	Dowden, Sarah, from James Murphy and wife		1791	Evans, Caleb, from William Thompson and wife
1797	Dowden, Thomas, from John Stagg		1794	Eversal, Abraham, from Jacob Fleck and wife
1791	Downing, John, from William Critton and wife		1794	Eversal, Abraham, from Balser Shellhorn and wife
1772	Doyle, Simon, from Richard Boyce		1794	Eversal, Abraham, from Balser Shellhorn and wife
1774	Doyle, Simon, from John Lewis		1797	Eversole, Abraham, from Thomas Dunn and wife
1778	Doyle, Simon, from Phillip Martin		1794	Eversal, Peter, from Balser Shellhorn and wife
1787	Drew, Perez, from Thomas Dent		1799	Ewell, Bertrand, from Robert Young
1788	Drew, Perry, from John McCartney		1772	Ewell, Jeremiah, from Joseph Yagar and wife
1789	Drew, Perez, from James Mercer		1792	Ewin, Tristman, from Trustees of Frankfort
1790	Drew, Perez, from John Newman and wife			Extine—see Eckstine
1793	Drew, Perez, from Garret Cavender and wife		1784	Extine, Leonard, from Trustees of Moorefield.

—F—

1796	Drew, Perez, from Trustees of Romney		1760	Fairfax, Thomas, Lord, from Thomas Bryan Martin
1796	Drew, Perez, from Edward McCarty and wife		1763	Fairfax, Thomas, Lord, from Wm. Buffington and w.
1792	Duling, William, from Benjamin Painter and wife		1767	Fairfax, Thomas, Lord, from Luke Collins
1798	Dunlap, James, from Francis and William Deakins		1768	Fairfax, Thomas, Lord, from Thomas Bryan Martin
1797	Dunlap, John, from James Ferrall		1768	Fairfax, Thomas, Lord, from Thomas Bryan Martin
1795	Dunn, Ephraim, from John Fairley and wife		1777	Fairfax, Thomas, Lord, from Thomas Bryan Martin
1798	Dunn, Lewis, from Benjamin Shepherd and wife		1771	Farely, Thomas, from John Hardin
1794	Dunn, Thomas, from Joseph Wart and wife		1792	Faw, Abraham, from John Keller and wife
1797	Dunn, Thomas, from Christian Musselman		1790	Fawver, Henry, from Phillip Wiggins
1798	Dunn, Thomas, from Bononie Peirce		1777	Fearly, Thomas, from John Hartley
1798	Dunn, Thomas, from Christian Stephens		1799	Feater, John, from William James and wife
1801	Dunn, Thomas, from Abraham Peters and wife		1793	Feather, Stephen, from Ezekiel Rodgers and wife
1796	Dutton, Kingman, from William Haydon		1776	Fergerson, Robert, from Richard Byrn and wife
1755	Dyer, Roger, from Enoch Cornwell		1782	Ferguson, Robert, from John Kay
1795	Dyer, Edward, from Trustees of Romney		1797	Ferrall, James, from Thomas Mulledy and wife
1796	Dyer, Edward, from John Hansbrough		1793	Ferrand, Nathaniel, from John Champ
1797	Dyer, Edward, from James Pierce and wife		1794	Ferree, Cornelius, from Henry Burris and wife
1798	Dyer, Edward, from John Hansbrough and wife		1797	Ferry, Stephen, from George Ferry, Sr., and wife
1798	Dyer, Edward, from Thomas Kirk		1795	Fetter, Daniel, from David Combs
1795	Dyer, Nathaniel, from Trustees of Romney		1798	Fetter, Daniel, from Thomas Rhodes

—E—

	Earsam—See Ahrsam, Ihresom, Ohrsom		1779	Fiddler, George, from John Williams and wife
1793	Earsam, Jacob, from Richard Gossick		1794	Fidler, Elizabeth, from Jacob Fidler
1769	Earson, John, from Simon Earsam and wife		1795	Fidler, Molly, from John High and wife
1779	Earsom, Simon, from William Casselman and wife		1793	Filink, John, from John Dowden and wife
1798	Easter, John, from George Tarvin		1792	Fink, Andrew, from Trustees of Frankfofrt
1794	Easton, John, from George Tarvin and wife		1788	Fink, Frederick, from George Utt and wife
1799	Eckhart, Henry, from Patrick Scott		1792	Fink, Henry, from James Watts and wife
	Eckstine—see Extine		1785	Fisher, Adam, from Cornelius Ward
1798	Eckstine, Leonard, from Daniel Jones and wife		1785	Fisher, Adam, from Cornelius Ward
1772	Edington, George, from William Cunningham		1796	Fisher, Nancy (slave), from John McMeekin
1797	Edwards, Jesse, from Daniel Lame and wife		1795	Fitzgerald, Thomas, from Trustees of Romney
1787	Edwards, Samuel, from Sam'l and Jesse Pugh and wvs.		1800	Fleck, Henry, from Wm. Frederick Ebery and wife
1799	Edwards, Thomas, from Jacob Keizner		1800	Fleck, Henry, from Thomas Collins
1800	Edwards, Thomas, from Forecroft, Judith, executrix		1791	Fleck, Jacob, from Benjamin Creetchfield and wife
1800	Edwards, Thomas, from John Keizner		1784	Fleming, James, from Matthew Beaver and wife
1794	Elliott, John, from William Anderson		1787	Fleming, James, from Henry Lighter
1797	Elliott, John, from James Monroe, Joseph Asberry		1790	Fleming, James, from Gedivn Royener and wife
1795	Ellor, Daniel, from Thomas Smoot and wife		1791	Fleming, James, from Abraham Mosley and wife
1778	Elswick, Thomas, Jr., from Thomas Elswick		1791	Fleming, James, from James Watts and wife
1759	Elswick, Thomas, from John and Rachel Elswick		1796	Fleming, James, from Alexander White
1788	Emberson, Thomas, from John Keller		1797	Fleming, James, from John High and wife
1788	Emereson, Abel, from Nehemiah Harris and wife		1794	Flich, Henry, from Daniel Jones and wife
1795	Emmerson, Thomas, from Peter Jones		1795	Flora, Thomas, from Lewis Throckmorton
1795	Emmerson, Thomas, from John Kimberline and wife		1800	Flora, Thomas, from John Friend
1797	Emmerson, Thomas, from John Kimberline and wife		1770	Folkimer, John Martin, from Charity Elmore, et al
1799	Emmett, Jacob, from Henry Baker and wife		1795	Forman, Aaron, from Andrew Wodrow
1791	Emmert, Jacob, from Henry Baker and wife		1798	Forman, Aaron, from Thomas Williams
1800	Engle, Joseph, from William Engle		1749	Forman, Benjamin, from Thomas Lord Fairfax
1794	Engle, Peter, from Joseph Myers and wife		1776	Forman, David, from Friend Gray and wife
1779	Enochs, Enoch, from Henry Enoch, Sr., and wife		1755	Forman, John, from Benjamin Forman
1784	Enoch, Enoch, from Thomas Douther		1762	Forman, John, from James Forman
1784	Enochs, Henry, from John Chinoweth and wife		1762	Forman, John, from Richard Hougland and wife

Year	Entry
1767	Forman, John, from Cornelius Conner
1772	Foreman, John, from Thomas Ashley
1775	Foreman, John, from Godfrey Lange
1783	Forman, John, from Aaron Ashbrook and wife
1796	Forman, John, from Amos Nicholas and wife
1790	Forman, Joseph, from John Forman
1791	Forman, Joseph, from John Forman, Jr.
1797	Forman, Joseph, from John Forman and wife
1797	Foreman, Joseph, from John Foreman
1754	Forman, William, from Benjamin Forman
1762	Forman, William, from James Forman
1765	Forman, William, from Thomas McGuire et al
1765	Forman, William, and wife, from Thos. McGuire et al
1769	Foreman, Wm., from John Foreman, Edw. Guphill & w.
1791	Forman, William, Jr., from John Forman, Jr.
1797	Foreman, William, from John Foreman
1797	Forman, William, from John Forman and wife
1798	Forman, William, from Joseph Forman
1782	Forst, Valentine, from Phillip Swank
1794	Foster, John, from Bergen Covert and wife
1794	Foster John, from Joseph House and wife
1794	Foster, John, from Benjamin Willey and wife
1794	Foster, John, from Joseph House and wife
1787	Foulke, Caleb, from Thomas Hallowell
1800	Fout, Charlotte, from Michael Fout
1800	Fout, Jacob, from Michael Fout
1797	Fout, Michael, from Mena Anderson
1800	Fout, William (or Jacob, William), from Michael Fout
1763	Fowler, William, from Peter Steenbergen
1799	Fox, Sarah, from William Henwood
1785	Fox, William, from Jacob Castleman
1791	Fox, William, dedimus from Hampshire Co. Court
1791	Fox, William, dedimus from Hampshire Co. Court
1795	Fox, William, from Stephen Calvin
1797	Fox, William, from Gabriel Fox
1765	Foxcraft, John, from John McMahan and wife
1765	Foxcraft, John, from Joseph Watson
1767	Foxcraft, John, from Joseph Watson
1767	Foxcraft, John, from John Hite and wife
1770	Foxcraft, John, from Samuel Pritchard and wife
1771	Foxcraft, John, from Joseph Watson
1771	Foxcraft, John, from Joseph Watson
1771	Foxcraft, John, from Matthew French and wife
1772	Foxcraft, John, from Joseph Watson
1776	Foxcraft, John, from Robert Parker, sheriff
1790	Frankfort, Trustees of, from Peter Danford
1792	Franks, Henry, from James Waterman and wife
1798	Frazer, Joseph, from Christian Musselman and wife
1791	Free, Cornelius, dedimus from Hampshire Co. Court
1779	Frinkle, Christopher, from John Knott and wife
1769	Frye, Abraham, from Isaac Chrisman and wife
1759	Fry, Benjamin, from Hugh Hughes and wife
1763	Fry, Benjamin, from Susanna and William Hughes
1799	Fry, Catherine, from Jacob Keizner and wife
1785	Fry, Christopher, from Michael Lawrence
1759	Fry, Henry, from Thomas Hughes and wife
1761	Fry, Henry, from Thomas Hughes and wife
1763	Fry, Henry, from Benjamin Fry
1763	Fry, Henry, from Thomas Hughes and wife
1772	Fry, Henry, from William Hughes and wife
1772	Fry, Henry, from Hugh Hughes
1795	Fry, John, from John Collins
1796	Fry, John, from Isaac Hawk and wife
1798	Fry, Peter, from Jacob Mouser, Sr., and wife
1800	Fry, William, from Beal Babs and wife
1793	French, Robert, from Richard Neilson (or Nelson)
1795	French, Robert, from William French
1797	French, William, from James Pierce and wife
1798	French, William, from Hugh O'Donnell and wife
1793	Fuller, Robert, from Henry Miller and wife

— G —

Year	Entry
1797	Gaither, Elijah, from Peter Williams
1799	Gaither, Elijah, from Andrew Wodrow and wife
1780	Gaither, Henry, from Moses Pigman and wife
1795	Gale, George, from George Crock and wife
1766	Gallant, James, from Benjamin Parker and wife
1795	Gallaspy, Michael, from James Fleming and wife
1798	Galloway, James, from Patrick Karnes, Sr.
1799	Galloway, James, from Patrick Keran and wife
1799	Ganno, Stephen, from John Rogers
1797	Gard, Samuel, from Samuel Edwards
1799	Garrigues, Edw., from William Kennedy et al
1790	Garrison, Joseph, from David Lacock and wife
1795	Garrison, Joseph, from Daniel Corbin and wife
1795	Garrison, Joseph, from David Corbin and wife
1800	Garrart, Ben, from William Hamilton Babbs
1800	Garritt, Benjamin, from William Babbs
1788	Gathrop, James, from John Keller
1792	Gazaway, Robert, from John Critton, Jr. and wife
1770	Gelleson, James, from John Barkley
1795	George, Ellis, from John Lupton and wife
1795	George, Ellis, from Bernard Brelsford and wife
1780	George, Mathews, from Jacob Reager, Herman Shook
1767	Gibbony, Alexander, from John Greenfield
1799	Gibson, James, from Peter Williams
1794	Gile, John, from William Armstrong
1795	Gile, Joseph, from John Mason and wife
1796	Gill, John, from William Armstrong and wife
1796	Gill, Moses, from Marmaduke Brokenburrow Beckwith
1795	Gillipsy, Michael, from James Fleming
1772	Gillmer, John, from John Parker and wife
1771	Gilmore, John, from Phillip Martin
1779	Gilmour, Matthew, from Thomas Lord Fairfax
1794	Gilpin, George, from Bergen Covert and wife
1794	Gilpin, George, from Joseph House and wife
1794	Gilpin, George, from Daniel Jones and wife
1794	Gilfin, George, from Benj. Willey and wife
1795	Gilfin, George, from John Cram and wife
1795	Gilpin, George, from John Mitchel and wife
1800	Glassell, William, from William Carlyle and wife
1782	Glaze, Andrew, from Jacob Long
1777	Glaze, Conrad, from Edward McGuire and wife
1777	Glaze, Conrad, from Edward McGuire and wife
1768	Glaze, Earhart, from John Kenting and wife
1770	Glaze, Earhart, from Mary and Joshua Bromsey & wf.
1780	Glaze, George, from Eve and Lawrence Glaze
1783	Glaze, John, from Benjamin Kuykendall
1800	Glover, Richard, from Trustees of Frankfort
1797	Godfrey, John, from Moses Thomas and wife
1795	Goffick, Richard, from Jacob Earson
1789	Good, Abraham, from Henry Hoffman and wife
1782	Good, Isaac, from Jacob Good, by Peter Putman, ex.
1789	Good, Isaac, from Mathias Branningburg
1773	Good, Jacob, from John Ramsey
1792	Gooset, Peter, from William Johnson and wife
1774	Graff, Andrew, from John Magill, attorney
1790	Grant, James, from Trustees of Frankfort
1794	Grant, William, from Daniel Corbin and wife
1790	Grapes, Jacob, from Alexander Boyd and wife
1774	Gray, Friend, from Henry Batten
1797	Gray, Friend, from William French
1775	Gray, Isaac, from John Elliott and wife
1788	Gregg, Nathan, from John McCullough

| GRANTEE-GRANTOR | | PAGE 71 |

Year	Entry
1764	Gregg, Robert, from Frederick Ice
1784	Gregg, Robert, from James Tarpley and wife
1788	Gregg, Thomas, from John McCullough
1790	Green, Thomas, from Leonard Tipsord and wife
1765	Greenfield, John, from Frederick Ice and wife
1798	Greenwell, Elijah, from William Reasoner and wife
1798	Greenwell, Elijah, from Thomas Greenwell and wife
1799	Greenwell, Elijah, from John Moore and wife
1791	Greenwell, Thomas, from William Johnson and wife
1794	Greenwell, Thomas, from Peter Gooset and wife
1795	Greenwell, Thomas, from George Heisman and wife
1795	Greenwell, Thomas, from William Johnson
1795	Greenwell, Thomas, from George Heisman and wife
1799	Greenwell, Thomas, from William Young
1786	Greenwood, Thomas, from Hugh Murphy
1794	Grove, Henry, from William Haydon
1794	Groves, Henry, from William Haydon
1795	Groves, Henry, from William Haydon
1792	Grove, Phillip, from Isaac Malin and wife
1794	Gulick, Fardinan, from William Corbin and wife
1761	Gum, Jacob, from Francis McBride and wife
1794	Gusler, John, from Rees Pritchard and wife
1792	Gustin, Alpheus, Jr., from John Gustin

—H—

Year	Entry
1763	Haggard, William, from Thomas Cresap
1794	Hague, Samuel, from Abraham Neff
1794	Hague, Samuel, from Okey Johnson
1793	Hague, Samuel, from John Hartly
1794	Hague, Samuel, from John Cupy and wife
1779	Hahn, Michael, from Alexander Ligget
1780	Hahn, Michael, from Thomas Lord Fairfax
1798	Haise, Adam, from Alexander Chrisholm and wife
1796	Hammock, John, from John Parich
1777	Haines, Peter, from Daniel Cresap and wife
1790	Halderman, Abraham, from William Turner
1793	Hall, Adam, from William Fox et al
1777	Hall, Michael, from Robert Ferguson and wife
1770	Hamilton, James, from William Bills and wife
1789	Hammond, Wm., from James Kelso, James Wilson & w.
1779	Hamilton, Henry, from Thomas Lord Fairfax
1795	Hamilton, Henry, from Andrew Smalley and wife
1788	Hampshire Co., from Hampshire Co. Commissioners
1793	Hampshire Co., Trustees of, from John Decker and wf.
1762	Hardin, John, from Benjamin Rutherford
1773	Hardin, Mark, from John Hardin
1782	Harding, William, from John Lewis
1797	Harford, Joseph, from Patrick Baker and wife
1796	Harlow, Jesse, from Cornelius Ferree and wife
1799	Harman, Joseph, from Trustees of Springfield
1768	Hardin, John, from Margaret McCrackin et al
1769	Harden, John, from Margaret McCracken, et al
1788	Hardy Co., from Hampshire Co. Commissioners
1777	Harness, Adam, from Abraham Kuykendall and wife
1777	Harness, Adam, from Abraham Kuykendall and wife
1794	Harness, Adam, Jr., from George Harness, Jr., and wf.
1795	Harness, Adam, Jr., from George Harness and wife
1777	Harness, George, from Abraham Kuykendall and wife
1785	Harness, George, from John Lewis and wife
1780	Harness, Jacob, from Michael Harness, Sr.
1784	Harness, Jacob, from Leonard Harness
1778	Harness, Leonard, from Adam Harness et al
1781	Harness, Peter, from Andrew Trumbo and wife
1794	Harsel, Peter, from Joseph Boardman and wife
1775	Hart, Magdalena, from Matthias Hite
1769	Hartley, John, from Phillip Martin
1788	Hartley, John, from Peter Yetter and wife
1793	Hartley, John, from Andrew Friend
1794	Hass, Abraham, from Luke Hass
1777	Hass, Cornelius, from William Demoss and wife
1783	Hass, Cornelius, from William Demose (Demoss)
1767	Hass, Lawrence, from Luke Collins, et al
1768	Hass, Lawrence, from Dennis Pursel and wife
1768	Hass, Lawrence, from Nicholas Friend
1763	Hass, Leonard, from Garret Decker and wife
1793	Hass, Luke, from John Friend
1767	Hass, Sarah, from Luke Collins, et al
1791	Hatten, Samuel, from Moses Williams and wife
1800	Hauser, Charles, from Patrick Baker and wife, gdns.
1796	Hawk, Henry, from John High and wife
1797	Hawk, Henry, from John High and wife
1796	Hawkins, John, from Rees Pritchard and wife
1779	Hayden, Enoch, from Trustees of Moorefield
1791	Haydon, Belimus, from William Haydon and wife
1781	Haynes, John, from Enoch Innis
1762	Hazell, Power, from Robert Gregg
1788	Healy, Thomas, from John Critten, Jr.
1781	Hearsman, Christopher, from Gasper Hearsman and w.
1779	Hearsman, Geo., from Matthias Ulrick Hearsman & w.
1790	Hearsman, Jacob, from Peter Beavour and wife
1771	Hearsman, Mathias, from John Reno
1771	Hearsman, Mathias, from John Reno
1779	Hearsman, Phillip, from Mathias U. Hersman and w.
1762	Heath, Jonathan, dedimus from Hampshire Co. Court
1799	Heath, William, from Andrew Wodrow
1771	Heaw, Peter, from Philip Martin, Thos. Bryan Martin
1779	Heinzman, Henry, from Adam Harness and wife
1792	Heinzman, Henry, from Andrew Wodrow and wife
1793	Heinzman, Henry, from Andrew Wodrow and wife
1796	Heinzmann, Henry, from Trustees of Romney
1796	Heinzman, Henry, from Trustees of Romney
1796	Heinzman, Henry, from Trustees of Romney
1796	Heinzman, Henry, from Trustees of Romney
1796	Heinzman, Henry, from Nathaniel Dyer and wife
1799	Heinsman, Henry, from Peter Williams and wife
1799	Heinsmann, Henry, from Peter Williams and wife
1790	Hellmick, Jacob, from Thomas Lord Fairfax
1768	Helm, Joseph, from Luke Collins
1768	Helm, Joseph, from Luke Collins and wife
1795	Henderson, David, from Samuel Stephenson
1795	Henderson, Moses, from Samuel Stephenson
1792	Henderson, Sampson, from Edward Bates and wife
1795	Henderson, Thomas, from Reason Howard and wife
1793	Henry, Alexander, from Richard Marquis and wife
1790	Henry, Daniel, from Thomas Noble
1779	Hermantrout from Thomas Lord Fairfax (Ermintraut, Armintraut)
1791	Herriott, Ephraim, from John Forman
1778	Heter, Michael, from Enoch Innis and wife
	Hews—see Hughes, Hughs
1766	Hews, Josiah, from Charles Linch and wife
1766	Hews, Josiah, from Charles Linch and wife
1760	Hiatt, John, Sr., from George Hiatt
1776	Hider, Adam, from Andrew Pancake
1790	Hider, Adam, from John Lewis and wife
1790	Hiett, Evan, from James Hiett and wife
1791	Hiett, James, from James Largent and wife
1794	Hiett, James, from Robert Parker and wife
1799	Higgins, James, from Alex White
1797	Higgins, John, Jr., from James Carruthers and wife
1798	Higgins, John, from James Murphy and wife
1799	Higgins, John, from James M. Marshall and wife
1799	Higgins, John, from James Marshall and wife
1800	Higgins, John, from Francis Murphy

1782	Higgins, Robert, from Henry Shepler and wife	1778	Holliday, William, from John Gibson, Benjamin Chew
1798	High, Jacob, from Enoch and Stephen Thomas	1792	Holmes, John, from Perez Drew
1799	High, Henry, from John High	1777	Holoback, Thomas, from John Carpenter and wife
1799	High, Henry, from John High	1797	Hooe, Robert T., from Lund Washington and wife
1780	High, John, from Abraham Hite and wife	1800	Hook, Mathias, from James Watson and wife
1796	High, John, from Andrew and Ezckiel Smalley	1793	Hook, William, from William Haydon
1799	High, John, Jr., from John High	1795	Hook, William, from William Hayden an dwife
1784	Highley, Charlota, from Rubin Highley	1779	Hoover, Jacob, from Jacob Hotsinbiller and wife
1784	Highley, Sarah, from Rubin Highley	1788	Hoover, Jacob, from Jacob Hotzinpiller
1798	Hilky, Christian, from James Watts and wife	1788	Hoover, Jacob, from Jacob Hotsinpiller and wife
1783	Hill, Daniel, from Joseph Hill	1799	Hoover, Jacob, from Henry Hoover
1789	Hill, George, from Matthias Brandenburg	1793	Hauver, Jacob, from Christian Slonaker and wife
1797	Hill, George, from Robert Lockhart	1794	Hoppy, David, from Christian John Hoppy
1779	Hill, Joseph, from Edward Snikers	1796	Horn, Andrew, from Henry Horn
1778	Hill, Joshua, from Eve and Nicholas Mitscaw	1783	Horn, George, from John Park and wife
1791	Hill, LeRoy, from Arjalon Price and wife	1790	Horn, George, Jr., from Rees Pritchard and wife
1791	Hill, LeRoy, from Arjalon Price and wife	1790	Horn, Henry, from Rees Pritchard and wife
1793	Hill, LeRoy, from Robert Irwin and wife	1794	Horn, Henry, from John Medley, Jr.
1799	Hill, LeRoy, from Joseph Jacobs and wife	1786	Hornback, John, from Peter Cartwright
1792	Hill, William, from William Carder and wife	1781	Hornback, Samuel, from William Ashby
1792	Hillery, William, from Denny Fairfax	1783	Hornback, Samuel, from Abraham Hornback
1795	Hilley, Frederick, from Trustees of Romney	1785	Hornback, Samuel, from James Hornback
1795	Hilley, Frederick, from Trustees of Romney	1781	Harsman, Matthias Ulrick, from Philip Harsman & w.
1797	Hinds, Jacob, from John Pancake and wife	1761	Hotsenbella, Jacob, from Stephen Hotsenbella and w.
1778	Hirsman, Gasper, from John Baynton	1773	Hotzenbehler, Stephen, from Jacob Hotzenbehler & w.
1763	Hite, Abraham, from Jonathan Cobun and wife	1791	Hough, Mahlon, from John Keller and wife
1763	Hite, Abraham, from Thomas Rutherford	1768	Houglan, Henry, from James Anderson
1764	Hite, Abraham, from James Keith	1780	House, Joseph, from John Hardin, Sr., and wife
1770	Hite, Abraham, from Daniel Perry and wife	1764	How, Joseph, dedimus from Hampshire Co. Court
1770	Hite, Abraham, from Andrew and John Pancake	1796	Howard, John, from Peter Overley
1772	Hite, Abraham, from Thomas Harman	1780	Howard, Reason, from John Jones and wife
1773	Hite, Abraham, from Charles Lynch	1787	Howell, Jemima, from United States Government
1779	Hite, Abraham, from Thomas Lord Fairfax	1787	Howell, William, from Ezekiel Totten
1779	Hite, Abraham, from Thomas Lord Fairfax	1798	Hoye, Paul, from William Hoye
1785	Hite, Abraham, from Thomas Brown	1779	Hubbard, Jacob, from Moses Ashbrook and wife
1772	Hite, Isaac, from Friend Cox	1799	Hubbard, Jacob, from John Monroe
1772	Hite, Isaac, from Friend Cox and wife	1799	Huddlerton, Nathan, from John Rogers and wife
1784	Hite, Isaac, from Trustees of Morefield	1779	Huffman, Christopher, from Thomas Lord Fairfax
1784	Hite, Isaac, from Andrew Wodrow	1796	Huffman, Conrad, from Benjamin Huffman
1793	Hite, Isaac, from David Cox	1790	Huffman, John, from Henry Litner and wife
1763	Hite, Col. John, from George Hoge and wife		Hughes, Hughs—see Hews
1782	Hite, Matthias, from Michael Hahn	1768	Hughes, Josiah, from William Stephens and wife
1782	Hite, Mathias, from Jacob May	1775	Hughs, Josiah, from John Williams
1773	Hitfe, Henry, from Andrew Ramsey	1781	Hughs, Josiah, from Charles Lynch and wife
1795	Hobbs, John, from William Haydon	1793	Hughs, Thomas, from William Morgan and wife
1787	Hoffman, Benjamin, from Abraham Hite and wife	1795	Hughs, Thomas, from Bernard Brelsford and wife
1749	Hoffman, Conrad, from Thomas Lord Fairfax	1771	Hughes, William, from Hugh Hughes
1767	Hoffman, Conrad, from Henry Van Meter	1798	Humes, Herbert, from Jacob Mouser, Sr., and wife
1797	Hoffman, Conrad, from Joseph Briggs and wife	1786	Humphreys, Ralph, from Lawrence Glaze and wife
1798	Hoffman, George, from Jacob Mouser, Sr., and wife	1786	Humphries, Ralph, from James Murphy
1798	Hoffman, Henry, from Jacob Mouser, Jr., and wife	1787	Humphreys, Ralph, from Samuel Gilkinson
1785	Hoffman, John, from Henry Kuykendall	1796	Hunter, Richard, from Andrew Wodrow
1757	Hoge, George, from Gabriel Jones and wife	1797	Hunter, Richard, from John Hough and wife
1798	Hoge, Isaac, from Jeremiah Thompson and wife	1799	Hurford, Joseph, from James Marshall
1771	Hog, Peter, from John Greenfield et al	1772	Hutton, Moses, from Benjamin Chew, et al
1772	Hog, Peter, from James Warden	1777	Hutton, Moses, from Robert Owen
1775	Hog, Peter, from Samuel Pritchard	1780	Hutton, Moses, from Thomas Lord Fairfax
1796	Hogan, Thomas, from Samuel Jones and wife	1785	Hutton, Moses, from Caleb Hewes (or Hughes)
1797	Hogan, Thomas, from James McGuire	1785	Hutton, Moses, from Samuel, Peter, Rich'd Cartwright
1778	Hoghland, Cornelius, from Thomas Lord Fairfax	1785	Hutton, Moses, from Samuel Cartwright
1779	Hole, Daniel, from Thomas Lord Fairfax		
1790	Hollas, Daniel, from Trustees of Frankfort		—I—
1767	Holliday, John, from Thomas Lord Fairfax		
1790	Hollenbeck, Thomas, from Trustees of Frankfort	1762	Ingram, Samuel, from Henry Oldacre and wife
1797	Hollenbeck, Daniel, from John Keller and wife	1767	Innis, Enoch, from Gabriel Cox and wife
1792	Holloback, Thomas, Sr., from Trustees of Hamp. Co.	1767	Innis, Enoch, from James Livingston
1798	Hollenback, Thomas, from John Randolph and wife	1786	Inskeep, Abraham, from John Kyger et al
		1790	Inskeep, Abraham, from John Foreman, Sr. and wife

1774	Inskeep, Joseph, from Christopher Cocke (Cox)
1796	Inskeep, William, from William Forman
1797	Inskeep, William, from William Forman
1799	Inskeep, William, from William Forman
1800	Inskeep, William, from William Forman and wife
1796	Inskeep, William, from Abraham Inskeep
1768	Iresham, Simon, from Abraham Kuykendall and wife (See Ahrsam, Earsam, Ohrsom)
1791	Irwine, Robert, from Abraham Good

—J—

1791	Jack, John, from Hugh Murphy
1792	Jack, John, from Andrew Wodrow and wife
1795	Jack, John, from Trustees of Romney
1795	Jack, John, from Trustees of Romney
1795	Jack, John, from Trustees of Romney
1797	Jack, John, from Aaron Forman
1799	Jack, John, from Charles Mullin
1799	Jack, John, from Peter Williams and wife
1799	Jack, John, from Peter Williams and wife
1770	Jackson, William, from Thomas Matlock and wife
1773	Jackson, William, from John Constant
1779	Jackson, William, from John Larew (LaRue)
1798	Jaco, Thomas, from Robert Lockhart
1788	Jacob, Betty and Priscilla, (negro slaves freed) from John Jeremiah Jacob
1785	Jacob, Ezekiel, from Charles Donaldson and wife
1784	Jacob, John Jeremiah, from John Walker, Sr., and wf.
1794	Jacob, John J., from George Lapp and wife
1794	Jacob, John, Jr., from James Tarpley and wife
1795	Jacobs, Joseph, from John Cundiff
1787	Jacob (negro slaves freed) from John Jeremiah Jacob
1789	Jacob, Pompey, (negro slave freed) from John Jeremiah Jacob
1794	Jacob (3 negro children freed) from John Jeremiah Jacob
1800	Jacob, William, from Michael Fout
1796	James, Lewis, from Trustees of Romney
1796	James, Wm., from Thomas Noble, atty. for I. Wheeler
1784	Janney, William, from Michael Landers et al
1792	Janney, William, from Richard Acton and wife
1786	Jarvis, Robert, from William Dobson
1795	Jenkins, Jacob, from Jacob Crisman and wife
1800	Jenny, William, from Alexander King and wife
1800	Jenny, William, from Alexander King and wife
1789	Johns, Aquila, from William Lockwood
1770	Johnson, Abraham, from John Rutan and wife
1784	Johnson, Abraham, Jr., from George Wolfe
1789	Johnson, Abraham, Sr., from Jacob Boggard
1789	Johnson, Abraham, from Trustees of Frankfort
1796	Johnson, Abraham, from Trustees of Romney
1796	Johnson, Abraham, from John Acton
1777	Johnson, Barnet, from John Right (or Kight)
1787	Johnson, Ephriam, from James Molloy and wife
1779	Johnson, John, from Robert Scott
1791	Johnson, John, from John Reed
1794	Johnson, John, from Joseph Johnson
1795	Johnston, John, from Joel Buffington and wife
1795	Johnston, John from Joel Buffington and wife
1788	Johnson, Joseph, from John Royse and wife
1795	Johnson, Joshua, from John Higgins, Jr., and wife
1796	Johnson, Joshua, from John Higgins and wife
1770	Johnson, Okey, from John Reno, Sr., and wife
1773	Johnson, Okey, from John and Agnes Bell
1774	Johnson, Okey, from Jacob Crist and wife
1775	Johnson, Okey, from Joseph Nevill and wife
1775	Johnson, Okey, from Ezekiel Totten
1778	Johnson, Okey, from William Blackburn and wife
1786	Johnson, Okey, from Jacob Bogard and wife
1792	Johnson, Okey, from George Hill
1792	Johnson, Okey, from Francis Myers
1796	Johnson, Okey, from Jesse Kent
1792	Johnson, Thomas, Jr., from Isaac Larue
1794	Johnson, Thomas, from Jacob Mouser and wife
1772	Johnson, William, from John Parker
1774	Johnson, William, from John Rutan and wife
1784	Johnson, William, from Garret Reasoner and wife
1785	Johnson, William, Jr., from Thomas Martin and wife
1790	Johnson, William, from Abraham Johnson
1791	Johnson, William, from Thomas Greenwell
1791	Johnson, William, Jr., from Lewis Day
1794	Johnson, Wm., from Andrew Wodrow, John Mitchell
1794	Johnston, William, Jr., from Job Bacorn and wife
1791	Jones, Aaron, from Edward McGuire and wife
1791	Jones, Abraham, from Edward McGuire and wife
1800	Jones, Abraham, from James Starr and wife
1763	Jones, Benjamin, from Thomas Lord Fairfax
1791	Jones, Daniel, from Edward McGuire and wife
1792	Jones, Daniel, from Trustees of Hampshire Co.
1794	Jones, Daniel, from Fetty Purgitt and wife
1798	Jones, Daniel, from David Jones et al
1798	Jones, Daniel, from David Jones
1791	Jones, David, from Edward McGuire and wife
1791	Jones, David, Jr., from Nathaniel Parker
1794	Jones, David, from Thomas Allin
1798	Jones, David, from Daniel Jones
1761	Jones, Gabriel, from James Alexander
1798	Jones, Isaac, from Daniel Jones
1769	Jones, John, from Michael Tepolt and wife
1769	Jones, John, from Ephraim Walter and wife
1779	Jones, John, from Reason Howard and wife
1790	Jones, John, Jr., from Trustees of Frankfort
1796	Jones, John, Sr., from Peter Walker and wife
1798	Jones, John, from Daniel Jones
1800	Jones, Mathias, from Ebenezer McKinley
1798	Jones, Moses, from Daniel Jones
1763	Jones, Owen, from Bryan Bruen and wife
1772	Jones, Peter, from Jonathan Rodgers
1772	Jones, Peter, from James Rodgers and wife
1788	Jones, Peter, from John Keller
1790	Jones, Peter, Sr., from Trustees of Frankfort
1780	Jones, Samuel, from Robert Scott
1793	Jones, Samuel, from James McDevit and wife
1790	Jones, Solomon, from Trustees of Frankfort
1795	Junkan, Richard, from Thomas Cooper and wife
1795	Junkan, William, from Thomas Cooper and wife

—K—

1763	Keating, John, from Bruen
1765	Keating, John, from John Forman et al
1765	Keating, John, from John Collins
1765	Keating, John, from John Collins
1765	Keating, John, from John Collins
1767	Keating, Mary, from John Keating
1762	Keith, James, from Major Abraham Hite
1799	Keith, James, from Francis White and wife
1773	Keith, John, from William Cracraft
1800	Keith, John, from William Frye and wife
1798	Keizner, Jacob, from Annanias Conklin and wife
1781	Kelso, James, from Robert Walker and wife
1783	Kelso, James, from Samuel Mason
1793	Kenner, John, from Christian Muma
1789	Kent, Jesse, from Jacob Bogard and wife
1783	Kent, John, from Joseph Williams and wife
1794	Kennedy, Thomas, from Rees Pritchard and wife
1773	Kennison, Edward, from Adam Schried
1761	Keplinger, John, from Rachel Esswick, exec., et al

1774 Keran, Patrick, from Bryan Bruin
1797 Keran, Patrick, from John Stutzman and wife
1791 Keran, William, from Patrick Keran
1795 Kerns, Jacob, from John Mason
1798 Kesler, John, from Peter Beckner
1767 Keys, Humphrey, from Samuel Pritchard and wife
1760 Keyser, Reuben, from Thomas Lord Fairfax
1782 Keysner, Jacob, from Richard Ironton and wife
1800 Kidwell, John, from Thomas Kennedy and wife
1791 Kile, Robers, from Frederick Ice and wife
1794 Kimberline, John, from John Keller and wife
1790 Kimble, John, from Thomas Lord Fairfax
1790 King, Alexander, from Trustees of Frankfort
1792 King, Alex, from Richard Acton and wife
1794 King, Alexander, from John Keller and wife
1795 King, Alex, from Jacob Brookhart and wife
1795 King, Alex, from Ezekiel Whiteman and wife
1796 King, Alexander, from William Reddick and wife
1797 King, Alexander, from Andrew Wodrow, Elijah Gaither
1798 King, Alexander, from Daniel Jones and wife
1799 King, George, from Nicholas Tevault
1758 King, Lieut. John, from William Miller
1796 Kingan, John, from John McMeekin
1761 Kinsley, William, from Francis McBride and wife
1795 Konecke, Nicholas, from James Labes
1774 Koon, John, from John Douthit
1766 Kuykendall, Abraham, from John Decker
1767 Kuykendall, Abraham, from John Decker and wife
1767 Kuykendall, Abraham, from John Decker and wife
1767 Kuykendall, Abraham, from Mary Creamer
1791 Kuykendall, Abraham, from James Mercer
1795 Kuykendall, Abraham, from John Goff
1773 Kuykendall, Barbara Decker, from Jacob Kuykendall (divorce)
1761 Kuykendall, Benjamin, from William Watson
1762 Kuykendall, Benjamin, dedimus from Hamp. Co. Court
1776 Kuykendall, Elizabeth, from Daniel Brown
1760 Kuykendall, Henry, from Gabriel Jones and wife
1787 Kuykendall, Jacob, from Henry Kuykendall
1760 Kuykendall, John, from Jonathan Cobun and wife
1776 Kuykendall, John, from Daniel Brown
1782 Kuykendall, John, Jr., from John Kuykendall
1784 Kuykendall, John, from Luke Decker and wife
1758 Kuykendall, Nathaniel, from Giles Sullivan
1782 Kuykendall, Nathaniel, from John Kay
1786 Kuykendall, Nathaniel, from John Kuykendall
1793 Kyger, George, (see Thyger) from Andrew Glaze

—L—

1793 Labes, John, from Perez Drew and wife
1793 Labes, John, from Perez Drew and wife
1749 Lanciscus, Henery, from James Rutledge
1795 Landis, Henry, from Nicholas Boyce and wife
1795 Lane, William, from Joseph Garrison and wife
1796 Lanford, William, from Robert Lockhart
1772 Largent, James, from Joseph Bane and wife
1772 Largent, James, from Evan Hiett
1778 Largent, James, from Henry Batton and wife
1778 Largent, James, from Henry Batton and wife
1785 Largent, James, from John Prunty and wife
1788 Largent, James, from Enoch Enoch and wife
1790 Largent, James, from Henry Enoch and wife
1790 Largent, James, from James Hiett and wife
1767 Largent, John, from John Relfe
1761 LaRue, Jacob, from Robert Glass and wife
1777 Larue, Jacob, from Ann and Zadock Springer
1791 Larue, Noah, from James Connard, Jr., and wife
1791 Larue, Noah, from John Larue and wife

1792 Larue, Noah, from Abraham Hass and wife
1790 Larue, Peter, from William Demoss
1794 Lawson, Monday and Clem, slaves, from Thos. Lawson
1763 Lawson, Thomas, from John Ross and wife
1790 Laycock, David, from Joseph Moore
1798 Layfottet, William, from John Parrill and wife
1798 Layfottet, William, from John Parrill and wife
1777 Leaman, Jonah, from William Demoss
1794 Leason, Margaret, negro woman, from Thos. Leeson
1784 Leatherman, Nicholas, frof Peter Neau (Neace)
1784 Leatherman, Nicholas, from Okey Johnson
1791 Leazenby, Thomas, from Frederick Fink and wife
1795 Leasenby, Thomas, from Frederick Fink and wife
1800 Leazenby, William, from Jacob Heinsman and wife
1800 Leazenby, William, from Jacob Heinsman and wife
1761 Lee, George, from Cornelius Westfall
1795 Lee, Henry, from William McGuire, Daniel Jones
1795 Lee, Henry, from William McGuire, Daniel Jones
1794 Lee, Solomon, from Richard Leeson and wife
1787 Lee, Stephen, from Thomas Clayton and wife
1765 Leek, Christopher, from George Osborn and wife
1779 Legate, Francis, from Thomas Lord Fairfax
1779 Legate, George, from Thomas Lord Fairfax
1779 Legate, John, from Thomas Lord Fairfax
1794 Lehow, John S., from Thomas Collins
1795 Lemonier, Lewis James, from Trustees of Romney
1796 Lemonier, James, from Trustees of Romney
1793 Levil, Joseph, from Alex Chrisholm and wife (See Nevil, Sevil)
1791 Lewcas, Phillip, from Denny Fairfax
1773 Lewis, George, from John McHenrry and wife
1774 Lewis, John, from Simon Doyle
1787 Lewis, John, from James Mercer
1787 Lewis, John, from Hon. James Mercer
1783 Lewis, John, from Joseph Vance and wife
1781 Lewis, Samuel, from Michael Waxler
1793 Lewis, Stephin, from Joseph Lyons and wife
1770 Lewis, Thomas, from John Caplinger and wife
1782 Lewis, William Barber, from John Lewis
1790 Lewis, William Barber, from John Lewis
1770 Lighter, Henry, from Peter Beaver
1789 Lighter, Henry, from John Carder
1793 Lighter, Henry, from Samuel Thomas
1790 Liller, Henry, from Peter Putman and wife
1791 Limkins, Dickeson, from Rev. Denny Fairfax
1779 Linegar, William, from Reason Howard and wife
1793 Linn, William, from Benjamin Parker
1793 Linn, William, from George Hersman and wife
1791 Linthicum, Archibald, from John Deaderick et al
1790 Linton, William, from John Williams
1793 Linton, William, from Benjamin and Monaca Lnick
1796 Linton, William, from Tristam Ewing
1796 Linton, William, from Tristram Ewing and wife
1796 Linton William, from John Pancake, Jr.
1796 Linton, William (or Sinton), from John Williams
1796 Linton, William (or Sinton), from John Williams
1799 Linton, William, from Peter Williams
1780 Litler, Henry, from Robert Gilchrist et al
1779 Little, Job, from Thomas Lord Fairfax
1791 Littlejohn,, John, from Richard Stafford and wife
1772 Littler, Thomas, from James Alexander
1772 Littler, Thomas, from Joseph Fry
1780 Littler, Thomas, from Thomas Smith
1773 Locke, Jacob, from Jacob LaRue
1794 Lockhart, Robert, from John Myers
1800 Lockhart, William, from John Copsey and wife
1775 Lockwood, William, from Michael Cresap, Sr., and wf.
1792 Logan, John, from Trustees of Springfield

GRANTEE-GRANTOR   PAGE 75

1796 Logan, John, from Jacob Earsam and wife
1792 Logan, William, from James Clark
1786 Long, David, from Thomas Dobins and wife
1779 Long, Jacob, from Darby Aughney
1798 Long, John, from Thomas Dunn and wife
1795 Long, Pompey, from Trustees of Romney
1795 Long, Strausbury, from William Heydon
1765 Loubinger, George Michael, from Casper Rinwer & wf.
1796 Loy, David, from James Largent and wife
1799 Loy, John, from Daniel Loy and wife
1799 Loy, John, from Daniel Loy and wife
1796 Lucas, Basil, from Andrew Smalley
1795 Lucas, Basil, from Henry Hamilton et al
1799 Ludwick, Jacob, from Andrew Rodrock and wife
1788 Ludwick, Leonard, from John Cuppy, Jr., and wife
1790 Ludwig, Leonard, from John Cuppy, Jr., and wife
1785 Lulard, Elias (or Sulard), from Abraham Clarke
1795 Lupton, Asa, from Isaac Lupton and wife
1785 Lupton, Isaac, from James Smith and wife
1794 Lupton, Jacob, from Abraham Powell and wife
1785 Lyle, Robert, from Alexander Chisholm and wife
1778 Lynch, Charles, from Samuel Beall
1774 Lynch, Patrick, from John Williams
1790 Lyon, John, from Hugh Murphy
1800 Lyons, John, from Andrew Wodrow and wife
1790 Lyon, Joseph, from Hugh Murphy.
1786 Lyon, Mary, from United States Government

—M—

1794 McAlester, James, from Charles Magill et al
1792 McAtester, James, from Trustees of Springfield
1791 McBride, Alexander, from David Corbin and wife
1792 McBride, Alexander, Jr., from Hugh Murphy
1795 McBride, Alexander, from Andrew Wodrow
1761 McBride, Francis, from Robert Denton
1786 McBride, James, from Thomas Edwards and wife
1796 McBride, James, from Francis White
1800 McBride, James, from Judith Forecroft
1779 McBride, John, from John Archer and wife
1788 McBride, John, from Joseph Cory
1792 McBride, John, from Trustees of Springfield
1798 McBride, John, from Solomon Lee and wife
1801 McBride, John, from John Starr
1791 McBride, Robert, from David Corban
1791 McCarty, Edward, from John Whiteman
1792 McCarty, Edward, from Perez Drew
1794 McCarty, Edward, from John Mitchell et al
1796 McCarty, Ed, from Andrew Smalley and wife
1796 McCarty, Edward, from Nicholas Leavers and wife
1796 McCarty, Edward, from Jacob Neaw and wife
1797 McCarty, Edward, from Andrew Wodrow and wife
1798 McCarty, Edward, from Thomas Athly and wife
1798 McCarty, Edward, from Andrew Wodrow and wife
1800 McCarty, Edward, from John Savage and wife
1770 McCarty, Thomas, from Mary Williams
1789 McClellen, Wm., from Abraham Johnson and wife
1773 McCoull, Neil, from Matthew Harrison
1800 McCrackin, Frank (slave), from Virgil McCrackin
1793 McCrakin, Ovid, from Seneca McCrakin
1797 McCrackin, William, from Isaac Osborne
1767 McCrackin, William, from Daniel Persel and wife
1794 McCormick, John, Sr., from George Tarvin
1769 McDonald, Augus, from Hugh Murphy
1769 McDonald, Angus, from Hugh Murphy
      (as executor of John Greenfield)
1774 McDonald, Augus, from Adam Stephens
1795 McDonald, Augus, from Jacob Crisman and wife
1775 McDonald, Archibald, from Isaac Cox

1776 McDonald, Archabold, from Gabriel Cox
1779 McDonald, Archibald, from Gabriel Cox and wife
1789 McDonald, Archibald, from John Friend and wife
1796 McDonald, Archibald, from Abraham Hass
1796 McDonald, Daniel, from Robert Gragg (or Gregg)
1796 McDonald, George, from Daniel McDonald
1775 McDonald, John, from John Waites, Sr., and wife
1765 McGlolin, Daniel (McLaughlin), from John Johnson
1773 McGlaughlan, Daniel (McLaughlin),
                                from John Royse and wife
1768 McGuire, Edward, from Hugh Murphy
1786 McGuire, William, from Aaron Ashbrook
1769 McHenry, Joseph, and wife, from John Nicholas
1773 McIlhany, James, from John Patten
1765 McIntire, Nicholas, from Ebenezer Brewster
1798 McKean, Samuel, from Edward McCarty
1798 McKean, Samuel, from Edward McCarty
1798 McKean, Samuel, from Edward McCarty
1777 McKewn, Michael, from Benjamin Burk and wife
1789 McKiernan, Patrick, from Michael McKiernan
1797 McKinley, Hugh, from Thomas Dowden
1798 McKinn, John, Jr., from Alexander King and wife
1786 McLaughlin, Daniel, from Daniel McLaughlin, Sr. & w.
      (See McGlaughlan McLolin)
1790 McLaughlin, Daniel, from James King, et al
1793 McLoughlin, Daniel, from Isaac Deaton and wife
1782 McLintock, Alexander, from George Emit and wife
1761 McMachan, John, from Henry Batton
1799 McMahon, William, from James Wilson
1793 McMechen, David, from William Hammond
1793 McMeekin, John, from Jonathan Shepherd and wife
1794 McMeekin, John, from Jacob Stadlor and wife
1797 McMeekin, John, from John Forman
1799 McMeekin, John, from John Keller and wife
1794 McMeekin, John, from John Keller and wife
1799 McNary, Ebenezer, and w., from John Pierceall and w.
1779 McNeal, Daniel, from Charles Lynch and wife
1781 McNeal, Daniel, from Jonathan Purcell and wife
1792 McNeil, Daniel, from John Thornton
1777 McNeill, Daniel, from Andrew Pancake
1801 McNeill, John, from John Pancake and wife
1796 McPhereson, William, from John Combs
1799 McPhereson, William, from Thomas Rutherford & w.
1792 McQuilling, James, from Trustees of Frankfort
1780 McThiernan, Michael, from John Williams
1780 McThiernan, Michael, from John Williams
1791 McVicker, Duncan, from John Barnhouse and wife
1779 Mace, Nicholas, from Alexander Ligget
1792 Machir, James, from Isaac Parsons, Andrew Wodrow
1792 Machir, James, from Moses Fichenal and wife
1799 Machir, James, from James Marshall and wife
1799 Machir, James, from James Marshall and wife
1791 Madden, Joseph, from Rev. Denny Fairfax
1795 Magill, Charles, from John Brown and wife
1800 Magill, Charles, from Henry Heinzman and wife
1795 Mail, Wilmor, from Thomas Healy
1798 Malcolm, James, from Valentine King and wife
1797 Malcom, James, from Henry Ward Pierce and wife
1784 Manning, Mary, from Trustees of Moorefield
1793 Mantett, John, from John Hoffman and wife
1784 Marsh, Henry, from John Moyers
1789 Marsh, Mathias, from Mathias Brandenburger
1772 Marshall, Benjamin, from John Spohr and wife
1772 Marshall, Charles, from John Spohr and wife
1772 Marshall, Christopher, from John Spohr and wife
1779 Marshall, James, from David Parsons and wife
1788 Martin, Christopher, from Benjamin Norman
1773 Martin, Edward, from Nehemiah Martin and wife

Year	Entry
1780	Martin, George, from Bethuel Pugh and wife
1784	Martin, George, from William Morgan and wife
1787	Martin, George, from Anderson Corbin
1795	Martin, George, Sr., from George Martin Jr. and wife
1797	Martin, George, Jr., from Reason Howard and wife
1800	Martin, George, from John Busby and wife
1801	Martin, George, from John Musby and wife
1778	Martin, James, from Isaac Colyer and wife
1783	Martin, James, from Catherine and John Forman, Jr.
1794	Martin, James, from James Tarpley
1791	Martin, Lenox, from John Jeremiah Jacob and wife
1793	Martin, Lenox, and wife, from William Parker
1784	Martin, Luther, from Thomas Cresap
1786	Martin, Luther, from Col. Thomas Cresap and wife
1791	Martin, Luther, from John Jeremiah Jacob and wife
1792	Martin, Luther, Jr., from Luther Martin
1793	Martin, Luther, and wife, from William Parker
1792	Martin, Maria, from Luther Martin, Jr.
1778	Martin, Mary, from Thomas Lord Fairfax
1784	Martin, Thomas, from Job Bacorn and wife
1792	Martin, William, from Benjamin Stone and wife
1794	Martin, William, from Benjamin Stone and wife
1793	Mason, John, from Thomas Noble
1793	Mason, Thomas, from David Corbin and wife
1798	Masters, Josiah, from Jacob Conklin et al
1782	Matthews, Levi, from William Demose
1794	Matthew, Levi, from John Demoss and wife
1797	Matthew, John, from Thomas Johnson
1800	Matthews, John, from Ephrem Johnstone (by Levi Matthews, attorney)
1779	Maxwell, Robert, from Thomas Lord Fairfax
1779	May, Jacob, from Alexander Liggate
1774	Meade, George, from Jonathan Heath, sheriff
1779	Means, Isaac, from John Welton and wife
1791	Meckrakin, Virgil, dedimus from Hampshire Co. Court
1794	Meesby, John, from Andrew Graff
1797	Meekins, James, from Edward McGuire and wife
1798	Melick, John, from Alexander Chrisholm and wife
1789	Mercer, Aaron, from John Keller and wife
1799	Merridith, John, from Trustees of Romney
1799	Merridith, John W., from Trusteesof Romney
1779	Meshy, Benjamin, from John Spore and wife
1797	Michael, George, from Christopher O'Haver and wife
1797	Michael, Jacob, from Christopher O'Haver and wife
1771	Milbower, William, from Jonathan Arnold and wife
1785	Miller, Daniel, from Christian Meshia
1788	Miller, Daniel, from Christian Mumma and wife
1794	Miller, Daniel, from John Mantill and wife
1771	Miller, George, from Phillip Martin
1787	Miller, George, from John Lewis, James Mercer
1796	Miller, George, from Henry Pearce et al
1778	Miller, Hanse Michael, from Samuel Beall
1793	Miller, Henry, from James Fleming and wife
1793	Miller, Henry, from John Reed
1796	Miller, Henry, from Edward Baylos and wife
1789	Miller, Isaac, from Andrew Smalley
1772	Miller, Jacob, from Abraham Fry
1773	Miller, Jacob, from Joseph Claypoole and wife
1790	Miller, John, from Trustees of Frankfort
1793	Miller, John, from Joseph Clisher and wife
1785	Miller, Stephen, from Charles Smith
1765	Miller, William, from John Dunbar and wife
1795	Millison, John, from William Keeder and wife
1774	Millslagle, Andrew, from Jonathan Pugh and wife
1793	Millslagle, Andrew, from Henry Lander and wife
1785	Minhur, John, from Henry Enoch, Sr., and wife
1767	Mitchel, Abraham, from James Gallent and wife
1767	Mitchel, Abraham, from James Gallent and wife
1767	Mitchel, Abraham, from John Keating and wife
1795	Mitchell, Daniel, from Peter Haines
1775	Mitchell, David, from Michael Cresap, Jr. and wife
1779	Mitchell, David, from Gabriel Cox and wife
1773	Mitchell, George, from Matthew Harrison
1769	Mitchell, Henry, from Matthew Harrison
1800	Mitchell, James, from Andrew Wodrow and wife
1767	Mitchel, John, from Bryan Bruen and wife
1796	Mitchel, John, from Andrew Cooper
1788	Mitchell, John, from John Keller
1788	Mitchell, John, from John Keller
1790	Mitchell, John, from Trustees of Frankfort
1791	Mitchell, John, from Elisha Collins and wife
1791	Mitchell, John, dedimus from Hampshire Co. Court
1791	Mitchell, John, dedimus from Hampshire Co. Court
1792	Mitchell, John, from Richard Acton and wife
1792	Mitchell, John, from Trustees of Hampshire Co.
1794	Mitchell, John, from Andrew Wodrow and wife
1794	Mitchell, John, from Andrew Wodrow and wife
1795	Mitchell, John, from Peter Haines
1795	Mitchell, John, from John Keller and wife
1796	Mitchell, John, from John Swobe and wife
1796	Mitchell, John, from Ebenezer Williams and wife
1771	Mitchell, Joseph, from Peter Haldeman (Holderman)
1772	Mitchell, Carson & Barclay, from Bryan Bruin
1799	Mollison, John, from John McBride and wife
1787	Molloy, James, from William Anderson and wife
1792	Monnett, Abraham, from Rev. Denny Fairfax
1795	Monett, Abraham, from Joseph Madden
1795	Montgomery, Matthew, from Trustees of Romney
1795	Montgomery, Matthew, from Trustees of Romney
1800	Monroe, Jacob, from Francis White and wife
1782	Monroe, James, from James Strother and wife
1791	Monroe, James, dedimus from Hampshire Co. Court
1791	Monroe, James, dedimus from Hampshire Co. Court
1792	Monroe, James, dedimus from Hampshire Co. Court
1799	Monroe, John, from Jacob Hubbard and wife
1791	Monroe, Robert, from John Foster and wife
1795	Monroe, Robert, from Nathaniel Smith
1795	Monroe, Robert, from Nathaniel Smith
1797	Moore, Abraham, from John Bussy and wife
1792	Moore, Edward, from Trustees of Frankfort
1787	Moore Eneas, from John Moore
1769	Moore, James, from William Davis and wife
1795	Moores, John, and wife, from William Turner
1795	Moore, Mary, from Trustees of Romney
1764	Moore, Michael, from Philip Moore, Sr.
1774	Moore, Philip, from Michael Moore
1788	Morcton (Messrs. Smith & Morcton) from Peter Bryan Bruin
1785	Morgan, Jonathan, from John Morgan and wife
1767	Morgan, Mordecia, from John Born, John Graham
1768	Morgan, Mordecia, from Moses and Samuel Hicks
1779	Morgan, William, from James Hamilton and wife
1780	Morgan, William, from John Bills and wife
1776	Morrel, John, from John Foxcraft, Charles Thompson
1783	Morris, Esac, from John Bailey and wife
1798	Morrow, John, from Daniel Throckmorton and wife
1778	Morse, Henry, from Melcher Baker
1785	Moses, Adam, from Phillip Keysar
1789	Mouser, Jacob, from Ephraim Johnson
1794	Mouzer, Jacob, from Jacob Mouzer and wife
1795	Mouser, Jacob, from Trustees of Romney
1799	Mouser, Jacob, Sr., from Rune Campbell and wife
1799	Mouser, Jacob, Jr., from Jacob Umpstot and wife
1783	Moyers, John, Jr., from Joseph Beeler
1793	Mulledy, Thomas, from John Barnhouse and wife
1795	Mulledy, Thomas, from Trustees of Romney

GRANTEE-GRANTOR   PAGE 77

1799 Mulledy, Thomas, from Patrick Rogers and wife
1792 Muma, Conrad, from Denny Fairfax
1785 Mumma, Christian, from John Meshia
1799 Munroe, Alex, from Beall Dabbs
1796 Murphy, Francis, from James Murphy and wife
1766 Murphy, Hugh, from John Keating and wife
1767 Murphy, Hugh, from Frances Straider
1791 Murphy, Hugh, Jr., from Hugh Murphy, Sr.
1781 Murphy, James, from Henry Kuykendall
1781 Murphy, James, from Henry Kuykendall
1784 Murphy, James, from John Ross
1784 Murphy, James, from John Ross
1784 Murphy, James, from Henry Heath
1787 Murphy, James, from Matthew Ternay and wife
1788 Murphy, John, from Hugh Murphy
1792 Murphy, John, from Thomas Greenwood
1797 Murphy, John, from Isaac Dayton
1792 Murphy, William, from Francis Keyes
1792 Murphy, William, from Francis Keyes
1778 Murray, Patrick, from Peter Reeve et al
1790 Musselman, Christian, from John Keller and wife
1794 Musselman, Christian, from Jacob Fleck and wife
1794 Musselman, Christian, from John Keller and wife
1795 Musselman, Christian, from Abraham Eversal and wf.
1795 Musselman, Christian, from Jacob Brookhart and wife
1777 Myles, David, from Samuel Bonnett and wife
1799 Myers, Harry, from Peter Williams
1794 Myers, John, from Robert Lockhart
1794 Myers, Joseph, from John Cuppy and wife
1793 Myers, William, from Jonathan Pugh and wife
1780 Myre, Conrad, from John Moxley
1791 Myres, Francis, from Francis Keyes

—N—

1774 Naff, Leonard, from Michael Thom (Thorn) and wife
1774 Naff, Leonard, from Michael Thom (Thorn) and wife
1779 Nafe, Henry, from William Buffington and wife
1765 Nall, John, and wife, from Thomas McGuire et al
1780 Nall, William, from Robert Scott
1791 Neaw, Jacob, from John Williams, Robert Parker
1794 Neff, Abraham, from James Bogle and wife
1794 Neff, Abraham, from James Bogle and wife
1787 Neff, Sylvester, from Christina Neff et al
1779 Neiff, Michael, from Soloman Reed and wife
1783 Neale, Jacob, from Michael Landers and wife
1800 Neil, Ben, from John Earsom
1799 Neil, Benjamin, from Robert Ross and wife
1764 Neilson, & Wodrow, from Henry Heath and wife
1792 Nelson, Richard, from Hugh Murphy and wife
1793 Nelson, Richard, from Hugh Murphy, Jr., and wife
1800 Nelson, Richard, from James Nelson
1800 Nelson, Richard, from James Nelson
1801 Nelson, Richard, from Robert French
1771 Nevill, John, from William McMachan and wife
1768 Neavill, Joseph, Jr., from Alexr. Giboney and wife
1773 Nevill, Joseph, from Daniel Brown
1778 Nevill, Joseph, from Samuel Beall
1779 Nevill, Joseph, from John Foxcraft, Charles Thompson
1784 Neavill, Joseph, from Freeholders, Town of Moorefield
1793 Nevil, Joseph, from Alex Chrisholm and wife
    (See Levil, Sevil)
1795 Neville, Joseph, from Thomas Wharton
1790 Newcomb, William, from John Constant and wife
1800 Newell, William, from Trustees of Springfiled
1778 Newman, George, from John Foxcraft et al
1791 Newman, George, from Jesse Edwards
1793 Newman, George, from John Singleton
1794 Newman, George, from Jesse Edwards

1778 Newman, Isaac, frfom John Foxcraft et al
1790 Newman, Isaac, from John Newman and wife
1790 Newman, Isaac, from John Newman and wife
1791 Newman, Isaac, from Jesse Edwards
1793 Newman, Isaac, from John Singleton
1794 Newman, Isaac, from Jesse Edwards
1800 Newman, John, from —— McCartney
1797 Newton, William, from John Thomas Ricketts and wf.
1800 Nicholson, Thomas, from Thomas Edwards and wife
1771 Nixon, George, from Andrew Arnold and wife
1773 Nixon, George, from Joseph Arnold
1796 Nixon, John, from George Thompson
1796 Nixon, Jonathan, Jr., from John Burk and wife
1785 Noble, George, from Martin Ashby
1785 Noble, George, from Martin Ashby
1794 Noble, Thomas, from Ignatius Wheeler
1795 Norman, Benjamin, from Christopher Martin and wife
1779 Norman, John, from Isaac Means and wife
1783 Norman, John, from Benjamin Norman and wife
1779 Norman, William, from Thomas Lord Fairfax
1783 Norman, William, from Benjamin Norman and wife

—O—

1798 O'Dannel, Hugh, from Jacob Mouser, Jr., and wife
1783 Odle, William, from John Kyger and wife
1783 Odle, William, from John Kyger and wife
1766 Ogden, Joseph, from Charles Linch and wife
1766 Ogden, Joseph, from Charles Linch and wife
1768 Ogden, Joseph, from William Stephens and wife
1781 Ogden, Joseph, from Charles Lynch and wife
1785 Ogden, Mrs. Joseph, from John Williams
1791 O'Hara, Arthur, from Denny Fairfax
1779 Oldakers, William, from Edward Snickers
1766 Oldham, William, from Thomas Lord Fairfax
1792 O'Neal, Barton, from Denny Fairfax
1796 O'Neal, Barton, from Joseph Madden
1799 O'Neal, William, from Daniel Jones and wife
1799 O'Neale, William, from Daniel Jones and wife
1797 O'Quin, James, from Samuel Osman and wife
1705 Ord, John, from Bryan Bruin and wife
1767 Ord, John, from Bryan Bruen and wife
1768 Osburn, George, from John Miller and wife
1768 Osburn, John, from John Miller and wife
1796 Osman, Charles, from Matilda Higgins
1797 Osman, Charles, from Samuel Osman
1772 Osmun, Isaac, from Daniel Pursell and wife
1761 Owens, John, from George Horner and Ann Owens
1773 Owens, Robert, from Andrew Waggener

—P—

1775 Pancake, Andrew, from George Core (or Cox)
1777 Pancake, Andrew, from John Pancake
1781 Pancake, Andrew, from John Pancake
1782 Pancake, John, from Alexander McLintock and wife
1787 Pancake, John, from Robert Ross and wife
1796 Pancake, John, from John Yeiser and wife
1796 Pancake, John, Jr., from William Linton
1792 Pancake, Joseph, from Trustees of Springfield
1796 Park, Amos, from John Deaver and wife
1774 Park, Andrew, from John Park and wife
1795 Park, John, from Tholemiah Rhodes
1794 Park, Samuel, from Andrew Wodrow and wife
1765 Parker, Aaron, from Thomas McGuire et al
1789 Parker, Abraham, from Benjamin Parker
1760 Parker, Ann, from Benjamin Parker
1760 Parker, Benjamin, from Ann Parker
1777 Parker, Benjamin, from Robert Gregg and wife
1790 Parker, Benjamin, from Trustees of Frankfort

1760 Parker, Elizabeth, from Walter Bond	1792 Pettit, Thomas, from John Clark and wife
1783 Parker, James, from Benjamin Parker	1793 Pettit, Thomas, from Joseph Moore
1787 Parker, Jeremiah, from Thomas Hallowell	1796 Pettet, Thomas, from William Forman
1771 Parker, John, from Phillip Martin	1784 Petty, Joseph, from Elizabeth Bogard
1765 Parker, Nathaniel, from Thomas McGuire, et al	1792 Peyat, Cornelius, from Casper Hersman and wife
1771 Parker, Nathaniel, from James Rodgersand wife	1784 Peyton, John, from William Campbell
1764 Parker, Richard, from Edward McGuire and wife	1762 Philips, Henry, from Moses Thompson
1765 Parker, Richard, from Thomas McGuire et al	1799 Phillips, Plunket, from Anexander Hendery and wife
1762 Parker, Robert, dedimus from Hapmshire Co. Court	1797 Pierce, George, from Valentine Purgett and wife
1765 Parker, Robert, from Thomas McGuire et al	1797 Pierce, George, from John Mitchell and wife
1766 Parker, Robert, from John Petter and wife	1795 Pierce, James, from Trustees of Romney
1755 Parker, Thomas, from Robert Pritchard	1795 Pierce, James, from Trustees of Romney
1800 Parker, Thomas, from Nathaniel Parker	1796 Pierce, James, from Trustees of Romney
1773 Perkins, Isaac, from Samuel Pritchard	1785 Pierce, John, from Casper Hiersman
1765 Parrell, John, from Isaac Foster and wife	1795 Pierce, John, from Trustees of Romney
1773 Parrell, John, from Phillip Bush	1798 Pierce, John, from George C. Pierce
1796 Parrot, Christopher, from Michael Madden et al	1793 Pierceall, John, from John Decker and wife
1799 Parsons, David, from James Marshall and wife	1799 Pierceall, John, from Peter Williams and wife
1800 Parsons, David, from Osborn Sprigg	1799 Pigmaer, Matthew, from John Mitchell
1780 Parsons, James, from Thomas Lord Fairfax	1778 Pigman, Moses, from James Keith and wife
1799 Parsons, James, from James M. Marshall and wife	1795 Piser, Jacob, from Thomas Smoot and wife
1800 Parsons, James, from Osborn Sprigg	1799 Pitcher, Stephen, from Isaac Good and wife
1793 Parsons, John, negro slave, from Baldwin Parsons	1776 Place, Thomas, from Bryan Bruin
1776 Parsons, Isaac, from Baulden Parsons and wife	1798 Pleasants, John, from Edward McCarty
1778 Parsons, Isaac, from Benjamin Kuykendall and wife	1798 Pleasants, John, from Edward McCarty
1782 Parsons, Isaac, from John Kay	1798 Pleasants, John, from Edward McCarty
1783 Parsons, Isaac, from James Murphy	1790 Plumb, John, from Charles Lynch and wife
1792 Parsons, Isaac, from Benjamin Reeves and wife	1793 Plumb, John, from Andrew Wodrow and wife
1792 Parsons, Isaac, from Benjamin Reeves and wife	1795 Poiser, Jacob, from Peter Engle and wife
1795 Parsons, Isaac, from Nicholas Casey and wife	1798 Polock, Isaac, from Peter D'Evercmon and wife
1800 Parsons, Isaac, from John Jack	1798 Polock, Isaac, from Peter D'Evecmon and wife
1797 Parsons, Mary, from David and James Parsons	1795 Possilman, Lookey, from David Miller
1764 Parsons, Thomas, dedimus from Hampshire Co. Court	1782 Post, Valentine, from Phillip Swank
1768 Parsons, Thomas, from Phillip Price and wife	1777 Poston, Elias, from Levi Ashbrook and wife
1770 Parsons, Thomas, from Luke Collins and wife	1787 Poston, Elias, from Samuel Edwards and wife
1779 Parsons, Thomas, from Thomas Lord Fairfax	1789 Poston, Elias, from Samuel Edwards and wife
1790 Parviance, Robert, from John Steel	1792 Poston, Elias, dedimus from Hampshire Co. Court
1788 Patterson, James, from James Lindsey	1793 Poston, Elias, from Thomazier Elsey
1795 Patterson, James, from Thomas Williamson	1795 Poston, Elias, from William Haydon
1761 Pearsal, Job, from Samuel Earl and wife	1780 Powell, Abraham, from James Smith and wife
1762 Pearsall, Job, from John Hopkins	1799 Powell, James, from Patrick Keran and wife
1790 Pearsall, John, from Trustees of Frankfort	1800 Powelson, Byansa, from John Thompson and wife
1798 Pearceall, John, from Christian Musselman and wife	1799 Powelson, Charles, from John Powelson
1798 Pearceall, John, from Christian Musselman and wife	1795 Powelson, Henry, from Isaac Newman and wife
1795 Pegg, Thompson, from Stephen Feather	1798 Powelson, Henry, from William Beekman and wife
1779 Pegg, Thompson, from William Williamson	1797 Powelson, John, from John Forman
1794 Pendleton, Phillip, from David Dawson and wife	1792 Powelson, Paul, from Benjamin Ely and wife
1800 Penniston, Phil, from Watson, James	1772 Power, Valentine, from Henry Lansiscus
1790 Peppers, John, from Jonathan Pugh and wife	1773 Prather, Charles, from Thomas Collins and wife
1794 Pepper, John, Jr., from John Pepper	1784 Prather, James, from Thomas Walker
1781 Perpoint, Francis, from James Livingston (by Enoch Innes, attorney)	1791 Presbyterian Church, Hamp. Co., from Ezekiel Rogers
1794 Perril, John, from Joseph Steel	1781 Price, Arjalon, from Thomas Collins and wife
1763 Perry, Thomas, from Jacob Chrisman, Jr., and wife	1785 Price, Ajalon, from Stephen Clark and wife
1765 Perry, Thomas, from Peter Stephens and wife	1791 Price, Arjalon, from Henry Hazell and wife
1790 Peters, Abraham, from Trustees of Frankfort	1798 Price, Arjalon, from Henry Hazell
1793 Peters, Abraham, from John Denham and wife	1791 Price, Nathan, from Nathaniel Smith
1777 Peters, Edward, from Peter Peters	1768 Prichard, Alice, from Stephen Prichard
1790 Peters, John, from Peter Keran	1766 Pritchard, Joseph, from Samuel Ingram and wife
1794 Peters, John, from Henry Lander and wife	1773 Pritchard, Rees, from Samuel and Margaret Pritchard
1800 Peters, Joshua, from Isaac Wolverton and wife	1773 Pritchard, Rees, from Samuel Pritchard
1772 Peters, Peter, from Richard Williams	1796 Pritchard, Reese, from Sarah Parker
1800 Peters, Phil, from Isaac Wolverton and wife	1796 Pritchard, Reese, from Thomas McCarroll
1772 Peterson, Peter, from Henry Bray	1798 Pritchard, Rees, from Isaias Parker
1787 Peterson, Tunis, from Thomas Clayton and wife	1798 Pritchard, Rees, from Robert Pritchard
1774 Perkins, Isaac, from Samuel Pritchard and wife	1760 Pritchard, Samuel, from Benjamin Phipps
1763 Petter, John, from George Renick	1766 Pritchard, Samuel, from Joseph Edwards
	1771 Pritchard, Samuel, from John Lewis

GRANTEE-GRANTOR

1771 Pritchard, Samuel, from Thomas Lewis
1773 Pritchard, Samuel, from Thomas Lewis
1780 Prim, John, from Robert Scott
1793 Primm, John, from John Douthwars and wife
1797 Protzman, Henry, from William Pell (Bell?) and wife
1774 Prunty, John, from Stephen Horner
1796 Pugh, Abraham, from Thomas Williamson
1770 Pugh, Bethuel, from John Pugh
1795 Purgitt, Jacob, from Valentine Purgett and wife
1795 Pugh, James, from Thomas Pugh
1787 Pugh, Jesse, from Samuel Edwards and wife
1764 Pugh, Jonathan, from Evan Pugh, Jr.
1770 Pugh, Jonathan, from Samuel Woodson and wife
1778 Pugh, Jonathan, from John Morrell and wife
1794 Pugh, Joseph, from Evan Pugh
1787 Pugh, Samuel, from Samuel Edwards and wife
1790 Pugh, Thomas, from John Arnold and wife
1799 Purcell, John, from Peter Williams and wife
1781 Purcell, Jonathan, from Peter Casey, Jr.
1790 Purcell, Jonathan, from Daniel McNeill
1796 Purcell, Jonathan, from Gabriel Friend and wife
1799 Purgett, Frederick, from Daniel Jones and wife
1794 Purgitt, Henry, from Elizabeth Fidler
1796 Purgett, Jacob, from Valentine Purgett and wife
1775 Purgatt, Simon, from Okey Johnson and wife
1787 Purgett, Valentine, from Joh Bacorn and wife
1791 Purgitt, Valentine, from Joh Bacorn and wife
1795 Purgitt, Valentine, from John Crutchlow
1765 Pursley, Dennis, from John Friend and wife
1799 Pusinger, Conrad, from Samuel Simcock and wife
1797 Putman, Mary, from Peter Putman, dec'd, through Robert Kilex, John Pearsall and John Randolph
1775 Puttman, Peter, from John Parker
1784 Putman, Peter, from Joseph Hanks
1799 Putman, Peter, from James Martin
1792 Putman, Peter, from Thomas Beall
1797 Putman, Peter, from Hugh Thomas

—R—

1771 Ramsey, Eve, from Jacob Kuykendall
1771 Ramsey, John, from Philip Martin
1761 Ramsay, William, from Peter Steenbergen
1761 Ramsay, William, from John Ramsay and wife
1763 Ramsay, William, from Luke Collins and wife
1763 Ramsay, William, from Luke Collins and wife
1763 Randal, Abel, from John Reed and wife
1772 Randel, Abel, from Solomon Welton
1773 Randall, Abel, from Sarah Bullitt
1792 Randall, Alex, from William Johnson
1796 Randolph, John, from Adam Wise and wife
1790 Rannells, John, from Trustees of Frankfort
1795 Ratien, C., from James Labes
1780 Ravenscraft, John, from Nicholas Leaver (Seaver) Sr.
1793 Ravenscraft, Samuel, from Andrew Wodrow
1800 Rawlings, Mose, from Abraham Eversole and wife
1772 Reasoner, Garret, from Peter Reasoner and wife
1772 Reasoner, Jacob, from Peter Reasoner
1790 Reasoner, Jacob, from David Thompson and wife
1798 Reasoner, William, from Elijah Greenwell
1792 Reddick, William, from Trustees of Frankfort
1787 Redtruck, Andrew, from Nathanial Ashby and wife
1779 Reed, George, from Andrew Wodrow
1780 Reed, George, from Thomas Lord Fairfax
1793 Reed, Grace and Joshua, slaves, from Eleanor Reed
1796 Reed, George, from James Clark and wife
1765 Reed, Jacob, from George Osborn and wife
1771 Reed, John, from Phillip Ross and wife
1790 Reed, John, from Trustees of Frankfort

1792 Reed, Samuel, from Joseph Cleiser
1797 Reeder, Daniel, from Rees Pritchard and wife
1793 Reeder, Joseph, from Jacob Mouser and wife
1798 Reeder, Joseph, from William Reeder, Sr., and wife
1787 Reeder, William, from Joseph Reeder
1791 Reader, William, from Rees Pritchard and wife
1798 Reeder, William, Sr., from David Corbin and wife
1798 Reeder, William, Jr., from William Reeder, Sr., and w.
1800 Reeder, William, from Joseph Reeder and wife
1794 Reese, David, from John Fife and wife
1790 Reese, William, from Abraham Johnson and wife
1796 Reese, William, from Robert Ralston
1762 Reeve, Benjamin, from John Ross and wife
1764 Reeves, Peter, from Jacob Westfall (Vestfall) and wf.
1765 Reeve, Peter, from David Edwards and wife
1780 Reidt, Andrew, from Joseph Himelwright
1780 Reidt, Andrew, from Joseph Himelwright
1765 Relfe, John, from Joseph Watson
1765 Relfe, John, from Thomas Triplett and wife
1765 Relfe, John, from Samuel Perry
1773 Renick, George, from Felix Seymour
1780 Renick, John, from Robert Gilchrist, Jas. Somerville
1779 Renick, William, from Thomas Lord Fairfax
1788 Rennells, James, from John Keller
1780 Rennock, John, from John Ulrick Spohre and wife
1761 Reno, John, from Christian Long and wife
1762 Reno, John, from Christian Long and wife
1790 Reynolds, Robert, from Trustees of Frankfort
1766 Reynals, William, from John Ross and wife
1767 Rheas, David, from John Keating and wife
1767 Rheas, David, from James Gallent and wife
1767 Rheas, David, from James Gallent and wife
1767 Rheas, John, from James Gallent and wife
1767 Rheas, John, from James Gallent and wife
1767 Rheas, John, from John Keating and wife
1780 Rhodes, Thelomiah, from Robert Scott
1773 Rice, John, from John Corbly
1793 Richards, William, from Edward Bates and wife
1797 Richardson, Arthur, from John Pierce
1770 Richardson, Daniel, from John Barkley
1772 Richardson, Daniel, from Abraham Rihcardson
1780 Richardson, Daniel, from Leonard Harness
1798 Richmond, William, from John Copsey
1798 Richmond, William, from William Reeder and wife
1794 Ricketts, John, from Joseph House and wife
1794 Ricketts, John, from Benjamin Willey and wife
1796 Ricketts, John Thomas, from John Foster and wife
1794 Ricketts, Thomas, from Bergen Covert and wife
1770 Ridgely, Charles, from Bryan Bruin
1770 Ridgely, Charles, from Bryan Bruin
1770 Ridgely, Charles, Jr., from Bryan Bruin
1770 Ridgely, Charles, Jr., from Bryan Bruin
1770 Ridgely, John, from Bryan Bruin
1770 Ridgely, John, from Bryan Bruin
1796 Rinehart, Rachael, from Henry Hazle and wife
1771 Roberts, David, from Joseph Watson
1780 Roberts, David, from Jacob Denton
1794 Roberts, John, from John McBride
1793 Roberts, Loudon, from Samuel Ravenscroft
1794 Roberts, Loudon, from John Bussey and wife
1791 Roberts, William, from Frederick Fink and wife
1795 Roberts, William, from Thomas Douthit and wife
1795 Roberts, William, from Frederick Fink and wife
1779 Robinson, Benjamin, from Thomas Lord Fairfax
1779 Robinson, Benjamin, from Thomas Lord Fairfax
1771 Robinson, Joel, from Daniel Wood and wife
1768 Robinson, Joel, from Robert Denton and wife

1798	Robinson, John, from Joseph Reeder and wife	1797	Schrock, William, from Trustees of Romney
1781	Robinson, McKenney, from John Robinson	1705	Schroder, Henry, from James Labes
1794	Rodrick, Daniel, from Caleb Evans and wife	1779	Scott, Benjamin, from Thomas Lord Fairfax
1797	Roe, Walter, from Gabriel Nourse and wife	1775	Scott, David, from James Scott and wife
1774	Rodgers, David, from Garret Vanmeter	1772	Scott, James, from Philemon Waters and wife
1767	Rogers, James, from William Rogers and wife	1790	Sebring, John, from Peter Wyecoff
1788	Rogers, John, from Joseph Moore and wife	1763	Seers, James, from Frederick Kester and wife
1794	Rogers, John, from Ezekiel Rogers	1793	Sevil, Joseph, from Alex Chrisholm and life (See Levil, Nevil)
1769	Roogers, Jonathan, from William Roogers		
1770	Roogers, Matthew, from William Roogers	1794	Seymour, Abel, from Thomas Dawson
1796	Rogers, Patrick, from Christian Stephens and wife	1795	Seymour, Abel, from Barton O'Neal
1797	Rogers, Robert, from Lewis Throgmorton and wife	1795	Seymour, Abel, from Abraham Monnett
1798	Rogers, Robert, from Charles Tyler	1766	Seymour, Felix, from George Rennick and wife
1794	Rogers, Thomas, from Samuel Stephenson	1770	Seymour, Felix, from Andrew and John Pancake
1777	Roller, Martin, from Joseph Jones and wife	1771	Seymour, Felix, from George Renick and wife
1778	Roller, Martin, from George Michael Laubinger and w.	1771	Seymour, Felix, from David Welton
1792	Rollins, George, from Israel Stattecop	1775	Seymour, Felix, from James Scott and wife
1792	Rollins, Benjamin, from Jacob Spiker	1784	Seymour, Richard, from Watson Clarke
1764	Rolfe, John, from Joseph Watson	1784	Seymour, Richard, from Abraham Clark, Jr.
1764	Rolfe, John, from Joseph Watson	1796	Shaffer, Christopher, from Jacob Fidler and wife
1764	Rolfe, John, from Joseph Watson	1790	Shanton, Joseph, from Abraham Shanton
1761	Rose, Robert, from William Williams	1798	Sharf, George, from Rees Pritchard and wife
1800	Rosebroom, Frederick, from John McGuire	1798	Sharff, George, from Moses Jones
1791	Rosebroom, Henry, from Andrew Smalley	1790	Sharpleys, Jesse, from Richard Acton and wife
1782	Ross, Lawrence, from Arminilla Ross	1770	Shaughan, Darby, from Daniel Shaughan
1785	Ross, Robert, from Robert Buck	1791	Shaver, Martin, from George Whiteberry
1792	Ross, Robert, from Trustees of Springfield	1797	Sheetz, Ann, from Thomas Emmerson and wife
1778	Rosseaw, John, from Thomas, Lord Fairfax	1792	Sheetz, Frederick, from Trustees of Frankfort
1794	Rounsovel, Richard, from Nathaniel Foster et al	1798	Sheetz, Fdererick, from Thomas Emmerson and wife
1793	Rounsover, Richard, from Ezekiel Rodgers	1792	Sheetz, Henry, from Trustees of Frankfort
1775	Row, William, from Henry Shipler	1787	Shelhorn, Balson, from William Campbell and wife
1783	Royce, Aaron, from Michael Landers and wife	1795	Shellhorn, John, from Charles Prather and wife
1791	Royse, Daniel, from John Royse, Sr.	1790	Shepherd, Benjamin, from Trustees of Frankfort
1791	Royce, David, from Joseph Johnson and wife	1790	Shepherd, Berry, from Trustees of Frankfort
1763	Royce, John, from John Greenfield and wife	1799	Shepherd, John, from Trustees of Frankfort
1763	Royce, John, from John Greenfield and wife	1793	Shepherd, Jonathan, from Abraham Peters and wife
1772	Royse, John, from Robert Rutherford and wife	1798	Shepherd, Robert, from William Mannin
1774	Royce, John, from Daniel McGlaughlan and wife	1793	Sheridan, Paul, from Thomas Dean, Sr.
1786	Rukman, Samuel, from John Forman and wife	1793	Shin, David, from Peter Cleaver
1796	Ruckman, Samuel, from Cahrles Magill and wife	1799	Shipwith, Peyton, from James Marshall
1786	Ruckman, Thomas, from Francis Taggart	1796	Shobe, Jacob, from Thomas Greenwell and wife
1795	Ruckman, Thomas, from Andrew Wodrow	1796	Shobe, Jacob, from Thomas Greenwell and wife
1800	Ruchman, Thomas, from John B. Dowden and wife	1783	Shobe, John, from Michael Little
1754	Ruddell, Stephen, from Samuel McHendry	1781	Shobe, Martin, from Rudolph Hire
1760	Ruddle, Stephen, from Luke Collins and wife	1779	Short, Isaac, from William Burgess and wife
1748	Rutledge, James, from Thomas Lord Fairfax	1794	Short, Isaac, from Valentine King and wife
1748	Rutledge, James, from Thomas Lord Fairfax	1789	Showp, John, from John Keller and wife
1782	Rule, Henry, from David Reel and wife	1779	Shuck, Lawrence, from Thomas Lord Fairfax
1791	Rush, John, from James Waterman and wife	1779	Sibert, Jacob, from William Vestall and wife
1779	Russell, Thomas, from Nichael McKewn	1774	Sidwell, Hugh, from Stephen Horner
1767	Rutherford, Benjamin, from Thomas Lord Fairfax	1793	Silkwood, Solomon, from Thomas Noble
1769	Rutherford, Robert, from William Bills and wife	1797	Simkins, Gassedg, from Azariah Smalley
1775	Rutherford, Robert, from John Brown and wife	1782	Simon, Christian, from Christian Dasher
1771	Rutherford, Robert, from Charles Smith and wife	1782	Simon, George, frfom Christian Dasher and wife
1788	Ryan, James, from Thomas Russell	1796	Sinclair, Robert, from John McBeekin
1789	Ryan, James, from Rebecca Russell	1762	Singleton, Thomas, from William Cunningham and w.
1798	Ryan, James, from Daniel Dolohan	1788	Slack, James, from Joseph Moore and wife
1777	Ryan, John, from Peter Casey	1793	Slack, James, from George Whiteberry and wife
	—S—	1794	Slack, James, from Ezekiel Rogers and wife
1797	Sanford, William, from John Miers	1777	Slagle, Jacob, from Thomas Cresap
1797	Sanford, William, from Nicholas Boice, Sarah Pack	1795	Slagle, Jacob, from Charles Clinton
1800	Sarrett, William, from John Mitchell and wife	1798	Slagle, Jacob, from Joseph House and wife
1767	Saunders, Joseph, from Joseph Edwards	1798	Slane, Anne, from James Largent and wife
1789	Savage (or Lavage), Elizabeth, from Robert Walker	1798	Slane, Benjamin, from James Largent and wife
1796	Scardon, Thomas, from Frederick Fink and wife	1797	Slane, James, from Henry Ward Pearce et al
1796	Scardon, Thomas, from Frederick and Eston Fink	1798	Slane, James, from James Largent and wife
1773	Schried, Adam, from Edward Kennison and wife	1798	Slane, John, from Evan Hiett and wife

1798 Slane, Thomas, from James Largent and wife	1788 Starn, Jacob, from Isaac Lakue and wife
1779 Slater, Thomas, from Joel Robinson and wife	1791 Starn, John, from Jacob Starn and wife
1795 Sloan, Richard, from Daniel Dolohan and wife	1791 Starn, Joseph, from Jacob Starn and wife
1799 Sloan, Richard, from John Campbell et al	1796 Starn, Joseph, from John Pancake and wife
1793 Slonaker, Christian, from John Mason and wife	1800 Starr, James, from Abraham Toms
1791 Sly, George, from John Knott and wife	1762 Steel, John, from Moses Watkins
1794 Smalley, Agariah, from Benjamin Stone and wife	1767 Steel, Joseph, from John Steel
1786 Smalley, Andrew, from Isaac Good	1760 Steenbergen, Peter, from John Werbel
1786 Smalley, Andrew, from Joel and Thomas Cooper	1760 Steenbergen, Peter, from Solomon Hedges and wife
1787 Smalley, Andrew, from Abraham Hite and wife	1788 Steer, Isaac, from John Foxcraft
1791 Smalley, Andrew, from Abraham Mosley	1789 Steer, Isaac, from Jury
1794 Smalley, Andrew, from John Bussy and wife	1794 Stemmell, Joseph, from Joseph Myers
1794 Smalley, Andrew, from Richard Acton and wife	1788 Stephens, Christian, from John Keller
1787 Smalley, Ezekiel, from Abraham Hite and wife	1794 Stephenson, Samuel, from Ezekiel Rogers
1798 Smiley, Thomas, from Elizabeth Smiley	1799 Sterrett, Will, from John Mitchell and wife
1768 Smith, Christopher, from Robert Parker and wife	1772 Stewart, William, from John Lockhart
1792 Smith, Edward, from Richard Acton and wife	1779 Stoker, John, from Balzer Stoker and wife
1795 Smith, Edward, from Andrew Wodrow	1776 Stoker, Paltzer, from John Cox and wife
1795 Smith, Edward, from Elijah Gaiter et al	1762 Stalker, Peter, from William Gibson
1778 Smith, James, from Martin Roller and wife	1762 Stalnaker, Samuel, from William Gibson
1785 Smith, James, from Jacob Hubbard and wife	1792 Stone, Benjamin, from George Martin, Sr., and wife
1785 Smith, James, from Samuel Baker	1783 Stone, James, from Joseph Hill
1794 Smith, James, Jr., from Arjalon Price and wife	1788 Stotter, Jacob, from John Keller
1791 Smith, Michael, from George Smith and wife	1790 Stotts, John, from Othniel Sands
1790 Smith, Nathan, from Trustees of Frankfort	1798 Stover, Daniel, from Demsey Welch
1779 Smith, Thomas, from Jacob Weidnar and wife	1799 Stover, Daniel, from Jacob Umpstott and wife
1797 Smith, Timothy, from William Hartshorne and wife	1776 Strather, Christopher, from John William Geinitz
1761 Smith, William, from Francis McBride and wife	1799 Straw, John, from Wm. Duncan, by Fr. Duncan, atty.
1767 Smith, William, from Joseph How and wife	1767 Strether, Frances, from John Strether (Strother)
1785 Smith, William, from Jacob Castleman	1795 Strode, Edward, from Margaret Strode
1788 Smith & Morcton, Messrs., from Peter Bryan Bruin	1793 Strode, Margaret, from William Williams and wife
1801 Smoot, Barton, from Joseph Stone	1779 Strother, James, from Garrard Menifee and wife
1790 Smoot, John, from Rees Pritchard and wife	1763 Stump, Michael, from James Seers and wife
1794 Smoot, John, from Rees Pritchard and wife	1764 Stump, Michael, dedimus from Hampshire Co. Court
1799 Smoot, John, from Peter Shanholtzer	1765 Stump, Michael, Jr., from Michael Stump, Sr., and w.
1799 Smoot, Jonas, from Henry Neff and wife	1781 Sturman, John, from Simon Doyle
1794 Smoot, Thomas, from Okey Johnson	1790 Stutzman, John, from Jacob Kinzer and wife
1795 Smoot, William, from James Fleming	1761 Suten, Benjamin, from John Owens
1766 Snickers, Edward, from Henry Oldakers and wife	1797 Sutton, John, from Elisha Cullen Dick and wife
1795 Snyder, Adam, from John Mason	1797 Sutton, John, from Elisha Cullen Dick and wife
1791 Snyder, John, from Nicholas and Sarah Boyce	1797 Sutton, John, from Elisha Cullen Dick and wife
1792 Snyder, John, from Abraham Johnson and wife	1783 Sullivan, Jeremiah, from Robert and William Buck
1792 Snyder, John, from William Johnson and wife	1791 Swanks, David, from Denny Fairfax
1796 Snyder, John, from Abraham Johnson, Jr., and wife	1779 Swank, Phillip, from Thomas Lord Fairfax
1797 Snyder, John, from Alexander Randall et al	1780 Swim, John, from William Jackson and wife
1775 Sommerville, James, from Jonathan Heath	1800 Switzer, Jacob, from John Bailey and wife
1763 Speake, Thomas, from Edmond Lindsey	1779 Swisher, Nicholas, from John McDonald and wife
1778 Spenser, John, from Hugh Murphy	1761 Switzer, Valentin, from Stephen Hotsenbella, et al
1794 Spencer, John, Jr., from John Spencer, Sr., and wife	1797 Switzer, Valentine, from Henry Taylor and wife
1792 Spode, George, from John Arnold and wife	1788 Swobe, John, from John Keller
1767 Spore, John, from Bryan Bruen and wife	—T—
1767 Spore, John, from Bryan Bruen and wife	1793 Taggart, Daniel, from Hugh Murphy, Jr.
1788 Sprigg, Asburn, from Ralph Humphreys and wife	1793 Taggart, Daniel, from Hugh Murphy, Jr.
1791 Sprigg, Azburn, from John Jeremiah Jacob and wife	1791 Taggart, Daniel, from Hugh Murphy, Jr.
1793 Sprigg, Ozburn, and wife, from William Parker	1786 Taggart, Frances, from Esack Morris
1796 Sprigg, Osborn, from George and Henry Frank	1792 Taggart, Francis, from Andrew Wodrow and wife
1790 Staddler, Jacob, from Trustees of Frankfort	1793 Taggart, Francis, from Hugh Murphy, Jr.
1786 Staford, Richard, from John Keller	1793 Taggart, Francis, from Hugh Murphy, Jr., and wife
1788 Stafford, Richard, from John Keller	1794 Taggart, Francis, from Daniel Pugh and wife
1790 Stafford, Richard, from Trustees of Frankfort	1795 Taggart, Francis, from Trustees of Romney
1791 Stafford, Richard, from Denny Fairfax	1789 Taney, William, from Ignatious Wheeler
1772 Stag, John, from Peter Hew	1773 Tatfe, Peter, from Elizabeth Warden
1797 Stalecup, Israel, from Abraham Johnson and wife	1794 Taylor, Daniel, from Elizabeth & John Campbell et al
1790 Stallcop, Israel, from Trustees of Frankfort	1782 Taylor, George, from Benjamin Parker and wife
1796 Starkey, Frederick, from Eli Beall	1799 Taylor, Griffin, from John Brahan
1793 Starky, William, from George Whiteberry and wife	1798 Taylor, Henry, from William Alderton and wife
1788 Starn, Jacob, from Isaak Lekue and wife	1766 Taylor, John, from Thomas Lord Fairfax

1797	Taylor, John, from John Thompson and wife	1799	Umpstot Jacob, from Jacob Mouser, Jr., and wife
1799	Taylor, John, Jr., from James M. Marshall and wife	1799	Umpstott, Jacob, from Jacob Allen and wife
1798	Taylor, Joseph, from Richard Taylor	1791	Umstot, Peter, from Casper Hersman and wife
1793	Taylor, Richard, from Samuel Williamson	1785	Umstot, Peter, from Robert Higgins and wife
1798	Taylor, Richard, from Samuel Williamson	1796	Umstott, Peter, from Cornelius Peyat and wife
1767	Taylor, Simon, from John Hite and wife	1762	Untis, George, from Henry Enoch and wife
1771	Taylor, Simon, from John Chesnut et al	1783	Ut, George, from Casper Harsman and wife
1792	Taylor, Simon, from James Murphy		—V—
1778	Taylor, Taply, from Thomas Lord Fairfax	1798	Vallandghom, William, from Richard Bland Lee
1770	Tebolt, Michael, from John Jones	1798	Vanarsdal, Abraham, from John Levin and wife
1800	Terry, Stephen, from George Terry and wife	1798	Vanarsdal, Cornelius, from John Levin and wife
1779	Teskin, John Peter, from John Knott and wife	1773	Vanbuskirk, John, from Samuel Worthington, Jr., & w.
1775	Thickson, William, from Thomas Price	1773	Vanbuskirk, John, from Samuel Worthington, Jr.
1794	Thomas, Benjamin, from John Phillips and wife	1778	Vanbuskirk, Michael, from Phillip Martin
1794	Thomas, Enoch, from John Waters and wife	1799	Vancouver, ——, from Robert Fearon
1795	Thomas, Enoch, Jr., from Enoch Thomas, Sr., and wife	1800	Vancouver, Charles from Peter Reeve
1797	Thomas, Jas. Fillit, from Johannah Thomas	1799	Vandivear, Lewis, from William Burack and wife
1777	Thomas, Morris, from Jeremiah Curle and wife	1771	Vandiver, William, from Richard Boyce
1794	Thomas, Moses, from Ignatius Wheeler	1779	Vandivear, William, from John Reed, executor of Richard Hougland, deceased
1793	Thomas, Samuel, from Henry Lighter and wife	1790	Vandiver, William, from John Rawles
1793	Thomas, Samuel, from Henry Lighter and wife	1790	Vandiver, William, from James Mercer
1793	Thomas, Samuel, from Henry Lighter and wife	1792	Vandiver, William, from Joel Buffington and wife
1798	Thomas, Samuel, from Henry Lightor	1794	Vandiver, William, from Benjamin Forman
1796	Thomas, Stephen, from Enoch D. Thomas	1796	Vandiver William, from Perez Drew and wife
1765	Thompson, Charles, from Joseph Watson	1796	Vandiver, William, from John Jack and wife
1765	Thompson, Charles, from John McMahan and wife	1797	Vandiver, William, from John Johnson and wife
1767	Thompson, Charles, from Joseph Watson	1785	Vanmeter, Abraham, from Arm Gillmor et al
1767	Thompson, Charles, from John Hite and wife	1790	Vanmeter, Abraham, from Thomas Dean, Jr., and wf.
1771	Thompson, Charles, from Joseph Watson	1768	Vanmetere, Garret, from George and John McCollough
1771	Thompson, Charles, from Matthew French and wife	1771	Vanmeter, Garret, from William Lane and wife
1772	Thompson, Charles, from Joseph Watson	1775	Vanmeter, Garret, from George Stricker
1799	Thompson, Eder, from Wm. Duncan, by Fr. Duncan	1779	Vanmeter, Garret, from Martha Williams
1789	Thompson, Jeremiah, from John Constant and wife	1780	Vanmeter, Garret, from Thomas Lord Fairfax
1796	Thompson, Jeremiah, from John Vanmeter, Sr.	1784	Vanmeter, Garret, from John Sibley
1782	Thompson, John, from William Holliday and wife	1784	Vanmeter, Garret, from Reuben Berry and wife
1794	Thompson, John, from Caleb Evans and wife	1761	Vanmetere, Henry, from Thomas Parsons et al
1798	Thompson, Jonah, from Joseph Combs	1768	Vanmeters, Henry (Danmeters), from Frederick Upp
1901	Thompson, Jonah, from William Armstrong and wife	1773	Van Meter, Isaac, from Thomas Herman
1788	Thompson, Thomas, from John Keller	1782	Vanmeter, Isaac, from Garret Vanmeter and wife
1765	Thorn, Michael (or Thom), from Maunis Alkier and w.	1794	Vanmeter, Isaac from John Dixon
1793	Thyger, George (see Kyger) from Andrew Glaze	1794	Vanmeter, Isaac, from Thomas Dawson
1779	Tichenall, Moses, from Job Bacorn and wife	1795	Vanmeter, Isaac, from Barton O'Neal
1793	Tidbal, Joseph, from Francis Taggart and wife	1795	Vanmeter, Isaac, from Abraham Monnett
1795	Tierman, Michael, Jr., from Patrick Tierman and wife	1797	Vanmeter, Isaac, from Trustees of Romney
1774	Tipsord, Leonard, from John Pearceall and wife	1799	Vanmeter Isaac, from Abraham Jones and wife
1791	Tipton, Sylvester, from Denny Fairfax	1780	Vanmeter, Jacob, from Thomas Lord Fairfax
1792	Tivault, Andrew, from John Hawk	1780	Vanmeter, Jacob, from Thomas Lord Fairfax
1788	Todd, John, from Alexander Chisolm and wife	1780	Vanmeter, Jacob, from Thomas Lord Fairfax
1788	Todd, Samuel, from Alexander Chisolm and wife	1799	Vanmeter, Jacob Sr., from John Parker and wife
1786	Tomlinson, Jesse, from Henry Kuykendall	1794	Vanmeter, John, Sr., from William Demoss
1794	Torrence, John, from Rees Pritchard and wife	1798	Van Meter, Joseph, from Jeremiah Claypole and wife
1774	Totton, Ezekiel, from William Johnson	1784	Vanmeter, Gudge and Judith, (negro slaves) from Jacob Vanmeter
1779	Travis, Robert, from John Cochran	1779	Vanteventer, Cornelius, from William Smith and wife
1777	Troutten, Richard, from James and Thomas Parsons	1771	Vause, William, from Phillip Martin
1779	Trumbo, Georgie, from Josiah Davison and wife	1784	Vause, William, from John Koon
1800	Tucker, Examus, from Joseph Tucker and wife	1797	Vause, William, from Solomon Douthit and wife
1791	Tucker, Joseph, from John and George M. Deaderick	1770	Viney, Andrew, from James Bryan and wife
1791	Tucker, Joseph, from John and George M. Deaderick		—W—
1796	Tucker, Thomas, Jr., from James Jr. and Mary Smith	1757	Waggener, Thomas, from James Simpson
1796	Turner, Thomas, fr. Michael Madden, Dennis Ramsey	1789	Wagoner, John, from James Lawson and wife
1796	Turner, Thomas, fr. Michael Madden, Dennis Ramsey	1789	Wagoner, John, from James Lawson and wife
1796	Turner, Thomas, fr. Michael Madden, Dennis Ramsey	1792	Walker, Andrew, from Robert Walker
1768	Turner, William, from John Holliday	1782	Walker, Hugh, from Jonathan Heath
1770	Turner, William, from Abraham Wise and wife	1792	Walker James, from Robert Walker
1794	Tyler, Charles, from James Carruthers and wife	1786	Walker, John, from Robert Walker
	—U—		
1798	Umpstott, Jacob, from John Jack		

1790	Walker, Peter, from Trustees of Frankfort	1764	Wharton, Thomas, from Joseph Watson
1798	Walker, Peter, from George Pierce	1764	Wharton, Thomas, from Joseph Watson
1773	Walker, Robert, from Joseph Mitchell and wife	1764	Wharton, Thomas, from Joseph Watson
1773	Walker, Robert, from Joseph Mitchell and wife	1765	Wharton, Thomas, from David Edwards and wife
1773	Walker, Robert, from Jonathan Heath	1773	Wharton, Thomas, from Joseph Wharton Jr.
1773	Walker, Robert, from Joseph Mitchell and wife	1767	Wharton, Joseph, from John Keating and wife
1778	Walker, Robert, from Joseph Mitchell and wife	1767	Wharton, Thomas, from John Keating and wife
1778	Walker, Robert, from Joseph Mitchell and wife	1768	White, Abraham, from George and John McCollough
1792	Walker, Robert, from Robert Walker	1800	White, Abraham, from Christopher and Chas. Marshall
1785	Walker, Samuel, from Robert Walker	1797	White, Adam, from Andrew Smalley
1775	Walker, Thomas, from John Walker, Sr.	1769	White, Alexander, from Hugh Murphy
1790	Wallis, John, from James Patterson and wife	1769	White, Alexander, from Hugh Murphy (as executor of John Greenfield)
1791	Wallis, John, from Isaac Newman, Wm. Williamson	1799	White, Alex, from Charles Marshall et al
1778	Ward, Cornelius, from Michael Hall	1800	White, Alex, from Rees Pritchard and wife
1779	Ward, Cornelius, from Thomas Lord Fairfax	1794	White, Francis, from John Chenoweth Jr., and wife
1779	Ward, Cornelius from Robert Clark	1795	White, Francis, from James Hiett and wife
1780	Ward, Cornelius, from John Roussaw	1797	White, Francis, from William Cook and wife
1796	Ward, Joseph, from Jacob Plough and wife	1797	White, Francis from Trustees of Romney
1796	Wardell, John, from George Thompson	1797	White, Francis, from Henry Pierce and wife
1797	Washington, Lund, from John Kinchelow and wife	1797	White, Francis, from Andrew Wodrow and wife
1788	Waters, John, from John Keller	1799	White, Francis, from David Buffington
1790	Waters, John, from Trustees of Frankfort	1799	White, Francis, from James Craike and wife
1800	Watters, Peter (or Walters) from Andrew Bogle & w.	1800	White, Francis, from Jacob Monroe and wife
1799	Watson, James, from John Bever	1800	White, Francis, from William Cook and wife
1764	Watson, Joseph, from John Welton and wife	1800	White, Francis, from Angus McDonald and wife
1764	Watson, Joseph, from Henry Heath and wife	1800	White, Francis, from John Black et al
1764	Watson, Joseph, from Henry Heath and wife	1769	White, James, from John Morrison
1764	Watson, Joseph, from Luke Collins and wife	1797	White, Thomas, from John Doveridge and wife
1764	Watson, Joseph, from Benjamin Jones	1788	Whiteman, Ezekiel, from John Keller
1764	Watson, Joseph, from Benjamin Jones	1779	Whitman, George, from Thomas Lord Fairfax
1767	Watson, Joseph, from George Rennock and wife	1779	Whiteman, George, from Thomas Lord Fairfax
1795	Watts, Archibald, from William Roberts and wife	1790	Whetetebary, George, from Joseph Moore and wife
1796	Watts, Archibald, from Thomas Leasonby and wife	1790	Whitteberry, George from Patrick Keran
1796	Watts, Archibald, from Thomas Leasonby and wife	1794	Wheeler, Ignatius, from Moses Thomas
1798	Watts, Archibald, from Thomas Leazenby and wife	1797	Whoop, Daniel, from Aaron Brandenburg and wife
1798	Watts, Archibald, from James Watts and wife	1772	Wigg, Archibald (Wiggins), from Robert Morris
1792	Watts, James, from Frederick Fink and wife	1768	Wiggins, Phillip, from Thomas Wiggins, Sr.
1779	Waxler, Michael, from Michael Vanbuskirk	1789	Wiggins, Phillip, from Thomas Wiggins
1793	Welch, Denny, from Samuel Ravenscroft and wife	1790	Wiggins, Phillip, from Archibald Wiggins
1796	Welch Isaac, from LeRoy Hill and wife	1768	Wiggins, Thomas, Jr., from Thomas Wiggins, Sr.
1798	Welch, James, from Bertram Ewell	1794	Wiley, Benjamin, from Adam Fake
1800	Welch, William, from Thomas Dugan	1794	Wiley, Benjamin, from Charles Clinton
1794	Weller, Daniel, from Christian Muma	1776	Wilkins, Godfrey, from Isaac Perkins and wife
1787	Welsh, Sylvester, from Henry Neff	1797	Wilkins, John, from Trustees of Romney
1762	Wells, Humphry, from John Lindsey	1785	Wilkinson, John, from John Moffett
1773	Welton David, from Felix Seymour	1768	Willett, Benjamin, from John Burns et al
1779	Welton, David from Michael Alt	1772	Williams, Daniel, from John Spohr and wife
1780	Welton, David, from John Welton	1768	Williams, David, from Robert Denton and wife
1784	Welton, David, from Henry Marsh	1790	Williams, Ebinezer, from Trustees of Frankfort
1784	Welton, David, from Henry Marsh	1794	Williams, Ebenezer, from John Chenoweth, Jr., and w.
1791	Welton, David, from Jonathan Purcell and wife	1785	Williams, Isaac from Isaac Hornback
1795	Welton, David, from John Ryan and wife	1785	Williams, Isaac from Isaac Hornback
1760	Welton, John, Jr., from William Westfall and wife	1770	Williams, John, from Nicholas McIntyre and wife
1767	Welton, Capt. John, from John Steather	1788	Williams, John, from Peter Rambo
1779	Welton, Jesse, from Thomas Lord Fairfax	1790	Williams, John, from William Linton
1764	Welton, Job, from John Welton	1790	Williams, John, from Trustees of Frankfort
1779	Welton, Job, from Thomas Lord Fairfax	1790	Williams, John, Sr., from John Keller
1780	Welton, Job, from Robert Travis	1790	Williams, John, Jr., from Trustees of Frankfort
1758	Westfall, William, from John Welton	1790	Williams, John, Jr., from John Keller
1764	Wharton, Joseph, from Joseph Watson	1796	Williams, John, from Robert Parker
1764	Wharton, Joseph, from Joseph Watson	1779	Williams, Joseph, from Job Bacorn and wife
1764	Wharton, Joseph, from Joseph Watson	1783	Williams, Joseph, from Job Bacorn and wife
1764	Wharton, Joseph, from Samuel Dew	1790	Williams, Joseph, from John Keller
1767	Wharton, Samuel, from John Keating and wife	1792	Williams, Joseph, from Trustees of Springfield
1767	Wharton, Samuel, from James Gallent and wife	1784	Williams, Moses, from Joseph Williams and wife
1767	Wharton, Samuel, from James Gallent and wife	1795	Williams Peter, from Trustees of Romney
1764	Wharton, Thomas, from Samuel Dew		

Year	Entry
1797	Williams, Peter, from John Pearsal
1797	Williams, Peter, from Trustees of Romney
1798	Williams, Peter, from William Linton and wife
1798	Williams, Peter, from William Linton and wife
1798	Williams, Peter, from William Linton and wife
1798	Williams, Peter, from Peter McDonald and wife
1765	Williams, Richard, from Providence Williams
1772	Williams, Richard, from Peter Peters
1786	Williams, Robert, from United States Government
1790	Williams, Robert, from Peter Walker
1799	Williams, Robert, from John Spencer
1784	Williams, Thomas, from Henry Hulse
1790	Williams, Thomas, from Archibald Wiggins and wife
1793	Williams, Thomas, from Joseph Crecraft and wife
1793	Williams, Thomas, from John McMeekin and wife
1798	Williams, Thomas, from Aaron Forman
1782	Williams, Vincent, from Abraham Hite
1792	Williamson, Cornelius, from Benjamin Stone and wife
1779	Williamson, John, from Catherine Forman
1780	Williamson, John, from Catherine Forman et al
1792	Williamson, John, from Trustees of Springfield
1793	Williamson, John, from Nathan Brown
1794	Williamson, John, from John Rawles
1794	Williamson, Samuel, from Benjamin Stone and wife
1792	Williamson, William, from Trustees of Springfield
1793	Williamson, William, from Michael Smith
1796	Williamson, William, from John McDonald and wife
1798	Williamson, William, from George Horn, Jr., and wife
1766	Wilson, George, from John McCulloch
1767	Wilson, George, from Peter Hass
1768	Wilson, George, from John Keating and wife
1781	Wilson, James, from Robert Walker and wife
1783	Wilson, James, from Samuel Mason
1779	Wilson, John, from Thomas Lord Fairfax
1770	Wilson, William, from Andrew Viney and wife
1771	Wilson, William, from David Williams and wife
1774	Wilson, William, from James Scott
1797	Wilson, William, from James Ferrall
1793	Wind, Moses, from Edward Moore
1779	Winterton, John, from Stephen Hotsinbiller
1761	Wise, Abraham, from Mary Creamer
1770	Wise, Abraham, from Henry Begly and wife
1790	Wise, Abraham, from Trustees of Frankfort
1800	Wise, Frederick from John Thompson and wife
1779	Wiser, Henry, from John Knott and wife
1795	Wiser, Henry, from Christopher Trinkle and wife
1764	Wodrow, Alexander, from Abel Randell and wife
1784	Wodrow, Andrew, fr. Freeholders, Town of Moorefield
1785	Wodrow, Andrew, from Charles Lynch and wife
1785	Wodrow, Andrew, from Charles Lynch and wife
1788	Wodrow, Andrew, from Enoch Berry and wife
1788	Wodrow, Andrew, from Ralph Humphreys and wife
1788	Wodrow, Andrew, from Samuel Kinkade and wife
1788	Wodrow, Andrew from Ralph Humphreys
1788	Wodrow, Andrew, from James Murphy and wife
1790	Wodrow, Andrew, from Enoch Berry and wife
1790	Wodrow, Andrew, from Enoch Berry and wife
1791	Wodrow, Andrew, from James Murphy and wife
1791	Wodrow, Andrew, from John Relse (Kelse, Relfe?)
1792	Wodrow, Andrew, from Richard Acton and wife
1792	Wodrow, Andrew, from William Turner
1792	Wodrow, Andrew, from Neilson Love et al
1792	Wodrow, Andrew, from Neilson Love et al
1792	Wodrow, Andrew, from Henry Kuykendall
1793	Wodrow Andrew, from Wm. Fox, John Mitchell
1764	Wodrow & Neilson, from Henry Heath and wife
1794	Wodrow, Andrew, from Jacob Brookhart and wife
1794	Wodrow, Andrew, from James Cochran and wife
1795	Wodrow, Andrew, from Trustees of Romney
1795	Wodrow, Andrew, from Trustees of Romney
1795	Wodrow, Andrew, from William McIlvane and wife
1705	Wodrow, Andrew, from Joseph Bloomfield et al
1796	Wodrow, Andrew from Perez Drew and wife
1797	Wodrow, Andrew, from Nicholas Casey
1797	Wodrow, Andrew, from John Gill and wife
1797	Wodrow, Andrew, from John Fairley and wife
1797	Wodrow, Andrew, from John McDonald and wife
1799	Wodrow, Andrew, from Agnes and William Heath
1799	Wodrow, Andrew, from John Busby and wife
1799	Wodrow, Andrew from Elijah Gaither and wife
1800	Wodrow, Andrew, from John Busby and wife
1796	Wodrow, Pompey and Sylvia (negro slaves freed) from Andrew Wodrow
1761	Wood, Daniel, from Stephen Ruddel and wife
1771	Wood, Daniel, from George Parke and wife
1800	Wood, Gabriel, from John Mitchell and wife
1771	Wood, John, from James Scott and wife
1779	Wood John, from Thomas Lord Fairfax
1769	Woodson, Betty, from Samuel Woodson
1761	Woodson, John, from George Horner and wife
1769	Woodson, John, from Samuel Woodson
1769	Woodson, Mary, from Samuel Woodson
1769	Woodson, Nicholas, from Samuel Woodson
1766	Woodson, Samuel, from Benjamin Sutton
1769	Woodson, Thomas, from Samuel Woodson
1775	Wolf, John, from Jacob Break and wife
1790	Wolfe, David, from Benjamin Parker and wife
1796	Wolford, John, from George Martin and wife
1794	Wolverton, Joel, from Richard Ramsevil
1773	Worthington, Samuel, Jr., from Elizabeth Plumb
1789	Wright, Robert, from Peter Peters
1779	Wynkoop, Benjamin, from Isaac Gray and wife

—Y—

Year	Entry
1768	Yagar, Joseph, from Jacob Mills
1785	Yeizear John, from John Pancake and wife
1780	Yokum, John, from Thomas Lord Fairfax
1788	Yother, Malichi, from Samuel Kennedy and wife
1763	Young, William, from Thomas Cresap
1784	Young, William, from Col. Thomas Cresap
1799	Young, William, from Thomas Greenwell

—Z—

Year	Entry
1795	Zailor, Jacob, from Abraham Lock
1778	Zane, Isaac, from Tavener Beale and wife
1778	Zane, Isaac, from Humphrey Keyes and wife
1779	Zane, Isaac, from Robert Rutherford and wife

Fairfax Lands Taken Up---1788-1800

Fairfax lands were taken up by the state, and many were sold from 1788 to 1810, for taxes. Maxwell & Swisher History of Hampshire County states that 1,986 land entries were made in the years 1788 to 1819, exclusive of the years 1804 to 1808, for which the entries are missing. By this time, Hardy County had been cut out (1785), as also had Morgan County (1787). In the state land office at Richmond, Va., may be found many entries not embodied in the county records. Andrew Cooper was the largest land holder in Hampshire County. Many of those whose names appear in the records were speculators who did not reside in the county. Here are a few of the entries and locations as given up to 1800:

1788

James Machan—400 acres on Knobley, adjoining Lawrence Washington.
John Danson—80 acres on North Branch.
Andrew Cooper—100 acres on Painter's Run.
David Hunter—79 acres on North Branch.
William Bel—120 acres on Patterson's Creek.
Tom Collins—800 acres on North Branch.
Hugh Malone—300 acres on waters of Mill Creek.
Thomas Bryan Martin—400 acres on South Branch.
Thomas Whittecher—150 acres on Knobby.
Marvin McGraw—300 acres on Capon.
Reese Pritchard—400 acres on North Run.
Isaac Means—400 acres, Mill Creek Gap.
William Adams—400 acres on Patterson's Creek.
Sam Boyd—20 acres on North Branch.
Sam Boyd—800 acres on Capon.
Nathaniel Parker—300 acres on Patterson's Creek.
Henry Hawk—400 acres, waters of Mill Creek.
William Armstrong—400 acres on North Branch, adjoining Michael Cresap.
Andrew Wodrow—100 acres on Capon.
William Keeder—100 acres on Capon.
John Jones—50 acres on Patterson's Creek.
Even Williams—300 acres on Patterson's Creek.
Ezekiel Whitman—150 acres on Cat-Tail Run.
Ezekiel Whitman—180 acres at head of Great Spring Valley.
Richard Stafford—400 acres near crossroads on S. Branch.
Fred Metheny—100 acres on Limestone Run.
Adam Hall—150 acres on South Branch at Halls Mill.
Elisha Collins—300 acres on Clay Lick Run.
Joseph Bute—100 acres on Buck Island Run.
William Young—50 acres on South Branch.
David Holmes—2,400 acres on waters of Capon.
David Holmes—900 acres on Lost River.
David Williams—100 acres on Patterson's Creek.
Henry Kuykendall—91 acres on Buffalo Run.
John Peyton—115 acres on Capt. John's Run.
John Payton—319 acres at foot of Sidelong Hill.
John Peyton—800 acres on Watt Run.
John Wolleston—400 acres on Capon.
John Wolleston—100 acres on Capon.
Abraham Jhnson—100 acres on Patterson Creek.
Abraham Johnson—200 acres on Cabin Run.
Joseph Mitchel—405 acres on waters of Patterson's Creek.
James Fleming—150 acres on Mill Creek.
James Fleming—500 acres on Lick Run.
Joshua Calvin—400 acres on Little Capon.
John J. Jacob—212 acres on South Branch Mountain.
Joseph Steers—50 acres on Bloomery Run.
Moses Starr—300 acres on Middle Ridge.
Peter McDonald—100 acres on Middle Ridge.

1789

Ebenezer McKinley—150 acres on Mill Creek.
John Hugh—200 acres on Thompson's Run.
Arch Magill—500 acres on Mill Creek.
John Kellar—400 acres on Patterson's Creek Ridge.
John Wilkins—92 acres on Saw Mill Run.
Benjamin Stone—50 acres on Maple Run.
Richard Huff—130 acres on North Run.
John Bishop—400 acres on Mill Creek.
Jesse Pugh—4 acres on South Branch.
James Keys—50 acres at foot of Dillons Mountain.

1790

George Wolf—350 acres on Lick Run.
Robert Ross—400 acres on Morgan's Run.
Dan Slain—170 acres on Sandy Ridge.
James Hiatt—200 acres on Sandy Ridge.
James Forman—780 acres on Sugar Run.
Lewis Stallman—250 acres on Stagg Run.
John Chenoweth—50 acres on North River.
Thomas Williamson—400 acres, headwaters of Little Capon.
Jacob Miller—150 acres on Hazel Run.
William Fox—300 acres on Middle Ridge.
Jacob Short—100 acres on Spring Run.
William Russell—50 acres on Capon.
William Smith—200 acres on South Branch.
Valentine Swisher—222 acres on Capon.
Alex King—800 acres on North Branch.

1791

Fred High—610 acres on Mill Creek.
Thomas Morgan—50 acres on White Oak Bottom.
Ephraim Johnson—150 acres on Sugar Tree Bottom.
William Jeney—500 acres on Deep River.
Robert McFarland—100 acres on Town Hill.
John Hough—100 acres on Pargatt's Run.
Richard Neilsen—234 acres on Tearcoat.
Peter Kizer—100 acres on Town Hill.
William Chapman—25 acres on Clay Lick Ridge.
Dan Pugh—9,600 acres, each side of Patterson Creek, which included most of Phillip Martin Manor.
Isaac Means—50 acres on Mill Creek.
Moses Thomas—100 acres on Cray's Run.

1792

John Goff—25 acres on Kuykendall Saw Mill Run.
Hugh Murphy—50 acres on Little Capon.
John Blue—300 acres on South Branch, below Hanging Rick.
Robert French—260 acres on Little Capon.
Benjamin Ayres—200 acres on Patterson's Creek.
Peter Larew—100 acres on Capon.
Dan Newcomb—160 acres on Sidelong Hill.
Isaac Daton—200 acres on South Branch.

Michael Boyce—400 acres on Mill Creek.
George Bowman—100 acres on George's Run.
John High—137 acres on Mill Creek.
Thomas Hailey (Dailey?)—50 acres on Spring Gap Mt.
William Jackson—200 acres on Capon.
William Carlyle—15 acres on High Top Mountain.
Jonathan Pursell—100 acres on South Branch.
Jacob Doll—50 acres on Knobly.

1793
Newman Beckwith—300 acres near Davis Mill.
John Butcher—50 acres on Capon Mountain.
Jesse Barnett—100 acres on New Creek.
John Seaburn—30 acres on Little Capon.
Abraham Reinhart—200 acres on Edwards Run.
Peter Putman—25 acres on Knobley Mountain.
James Jamison—100 acres on Little Mountain.
Thomas Fry—100 acres on Capon.
Virgil Graybill—100 acres on Potomac, adjoining General Washington's land.
William Scott—50 acres on Sidelong Hill.
Jacob Jerkins—25 acres near and including the meeting house.
Joseph Lang—100 acres on meadow of Gilmer's Run, nearby Mud Lick.
Jacob Purget—50 acres at foot of Knobly.
Francis and William Deakins—12,000 acres between Patterson's Creek and New Creek, next to North Branch.
Virgil McCracken—100 acres adjoining Washington's survey.
Moses Ashbrook—300 acres on Maple Run.

1794
James Carruthers—4 acres on Capon.
James Largent—100 acres on Chimney Tract.
Isaac Lupton—28 acres on Sandy Ridge.
Jacob Baker—175 acres on North River.
Perez Drew—8 2acres on Little Capon.
John Walles—100 acres on Little Capon.
Job Shepherd—65 acres an Wiggins' Run.
Abraham Neff—100 acres on Mld. Meadow Run.
Jacob Umstott—50 acres on Mill Creek.
Jacob Hoover—100 acres on North Mountain.
John Stokes—100 acres on Spring Gap Mountain.
George Phebus—100 acres near Phobey's Gap.
Dan Stephens—100 acres on Capon.
George Chambers—64,544 acres near Hardy County line, Patterson Creek Mountain, and North Branch.
George Gilpin—14,000 acres on Knogly and along Hardy County line.

1795
Jacob Kisner—80 acres on North River.
John Plumb—100 acres on Mill Creek.
Simon Taylor—200 acres on South Branch.
Isaac Parsons—100 acres on South Branch.
Phil Pendleton—1,000 acres on Great Capon Mountain.
John Jack—100 acres on Road between Romney and Winchester.
Sam Chesshire—69 acres on Tear Coat.
Elisha C. Dick—40,000 acres along Alley Mountain and New Creek, North River; 2,400 acres in other locations.
John and Joseph Swan—10,000 acres, Spring Gap and Little Capon.
Aaron Steed—100 acres on Hopkins Run.
Joseph Billings—727 acres on North Branch ,etc.
John Randolph—300 acres on Abraham's Creek.

1796
Peter Good—50 acres on Dry Run.
John Pancake—50 acres on South Branch.
William Winterton—50 acres on Capon.

1797
Joseph Baker—100 acres on Capon.
Fred Gulick—50 acres on Little Capon.
Fred Haus—64 acres on South Branch.
Gabriel Throckmorton—600 acres on Capon.
Robert Gustin—100 acres on Capon.
Sam Dobbin—100 acres on Cabbin Run.
David Parsons—300 acres on South Branch.

1798
Sam Howard—50 acres on Capon.
Charles Dowles—1,500 acres on road, Romney to Winchester
John Pearsall—100 acres on Patterson's Creek.
John Wolf—40 acres on Capon.
Jacob Bowes—50 acres on Dilling's Mountain.
John Lay—20 acres on Knobly Mountain.
Dan Duggan—50 acres on North River.
John Stwitzer—190 acres on Dillinger's Run.
Luther and Sam Colvin—100 acres on waters of S. Branch.
William Reeder—40 acres on Crooked Run.

1799
John Templeton—300 acres on North Branch.
Adam Hider—4 acres on Shrub Mountain.
John Foley—300 acres on Long Ridge.
Thomas Parker—50 acres on Green Spring Run.
John Abernathy—5 acres on Pine Swamp Run.
Norman Bruce—100 acres on Potomac.
Notley Robey—100 acres on Mill Creek.
John Jones—115 acres on North River.
Phil Pendleton—9,500 acres on Branch Mountain ,etc.
Dan Hopwood—100 acres on Knobley.
William Gray—50 acres on Potomac.

1800
William Buffington—100 acres on South Branch.
Francis White—20 acres on North River.
George Harris—50 acres on Mill Creek.
James Larramore—225 acres on South Branch.
Henry Hartman—139 acres on Mill Creek.
Jacob Millslagle—150 acres on Timber Ridge.
Alex Monroe—300 acres on North River.
Alex Monroe—1,700 acres on Patterson's Creek.
Jeremiah Ashby—300 acres on North Branch.

1801
James Slack—16 acres on South Branch.
John Casper—50 acres on North River.
David Bookless—80 acres on Castleman's Run.
John Moore—50 acres on Myker Run.
Schautzenbach Kisler—100 acres on Sidelong Hill.
Andrew Bogle—100 acres on New Creek.
Robert Rogers—100 acres on Potomac.
William Naylor—50 acres on Town Run.
Thomas Carscaddon—250 acres on Stagg Run.
Richard Holliday—5 acres on Spring Run.
John Griffin—83 acres on Horse Camp Run
William Stemmelt—500 acres on Spring Gap Mountain.
John Poland—41 acres on Kuykendall Run.

1802
Andrew Walker—100 acres on Green Spring Run.
Solomon Hoge—25 acres on South Branch Mountain.
George Beatty—139 acres on Mill Creek.
Daniel Lutz—50 acres in Green Spring Valley.
Robert Gustin—73 acres on Rock Gap Run.
James Caudy—50 acres on Mill Creek.

FAIRFAX LANDS TAKEN UP

1803
John Selby—50 acres on North River Mountain.
Eli Ashbrook—100 acres on Tear Coat.
Jacob Jenkes—50 acres, Bear Garden.

1804
William Florence—200 acres on Cabin Run.

1808
Lewis Vandever—279 acres on Patterson's Creek.
William Armstrong—1 00acres on Patterson's Creek.
Michael Widmire—70 acres on Capon.
Henry Dangerfield—20 acres on Capon.

1809
Peter Bruner—25 acres on Capon.
Jacob Stuckslagle—6 acres on Potomac.
Nathan Sutton—148 acres on High Gap Mountain.
Fred Buzzard—10 acres on Mill Branch.
John Swisher—50 acres on Hughs Run.
Jacob Leopard—30 0acres on North Branch.
Henry Heitzman—600 acres on South Branch.
John Wolford—25 acres on North River.
James Glum—25 acres an Bennet's Run.
Thomas Youngley—84 acres on North River Mountain.

ALPHABETICAL ARRANGEMENT OF

The State Census

of

HAMPSHIRE COUNTY, VIRGINIA

—o—O—o—

1782 *and* 1784

—o—O—o—

THE Federal Census of 1790 for Virginia was destroyed in the War of 1812. The State Census of 1782 and 1784 for Hampshire County remained intact, and is now in the hands of the Virginia Historical Society at Richmond, Va. In 1790 there were in Hampshire County 7,346 souls, of which 1,662 were free white males above 16 years of age; 1,956 were free white males under 16; 3,261 were free white females, and 454 were slaves.

For the sake of those working on genealogy, there is included here a copy of these Hampshire County census returns, alphabetically arranged. It is suggested that if in 1782 a man and his family are listed, but are gone in 1784, that the 1790 census for Pennsylvania be consulted, and the counties in the western part—Alleghany, Bedford, Fayette, Washington and Westmoreland—be especially noted. It is quite likely that the names will be found there.

The census takers had contiguous territory, therefore the same initials following two names indicates that those families were neighbors. The names of these men, and the initials used, are as follows:

JhW—John Wilson; JbW—Job Welton; MC—Michael Cresap; MqC—Marquis Calmes ('84 only); LA—Levi Ashbrook ('82 only); VW—Vincent Williams; WV—William Vause; AH—Abraham Hite; DM—David Mitchell; AJ—Abraham Johnson; OJ—Okey Johnson; MS—Michael Stump; ST—Simon Taylor; AR—Abel Randall; WB—William Buffington ('82 only); SR—Stephen Ruddle; EP—Elias Posten ('84 only).

In 1782, census figures following names indicate free whites; sl denotes slaves. In the 1784 census, the first figure is free whites, the second, dwellings, and the third, other buildings.

— A —

Albin, James (not in '82) — (ER) 3-0-1.
Abman, John (see Alman) — (SR) 8-1-2
Acton, Richard (WV) 9 — (gone in '84)
Ahrsam, John (not in '82) — (ST) 9-1-5
Ahrsam, Simon — (ST) 2-1-1
(for '82 see Earsom)
Alfree, Joseph (WV) 3 — (gone in '84)
Algier, Hermanous (MS) 12
— (MS) 10-1-2
Algier, John (JhW) 7 — (MS) 3
Algier, Michael (JhW) 6 — (JhW) 7-1-2
Algier, William (MS) 3 — (MS) 4-1-1
Allan, David (WB) 4 — (MqC) 5-1-1
Allen, Eliza (MC) 2 — (gone in '84)
Allenton, David (not in '82) — (MS) 2-1
Alexander, Robert (not in '82 — (ST) 5
Alman, John (SR) 9 — see Abman
Anderson, Henry (not in '82)—(ST) 3-1-1
Anderson, James (WB) 3 — (EP) 3-0-1
Anderson, John (AR) 8 — (AR) 9-1

Anderson, Thomas (OJ) 10 — (OJ) 9-1-1
Anderson, William (OJ) 5 — (OJ) 1-1
Anderson, William (ST) 3 — (EP) 5-1-2
Andrews, George (ST) 10 — (ST) 10-1-4
Archer, Benj. (OJ) 3 — (gone in '84)
Archer, John (OJ) 5 — (gone in '84)
Armintraut, Christopher — (JhW) 9-1-4
(for '82 see Ermintraut)
Arnold, Andrew (not in '82)—(EP) 3-1-1
Arnold, John (LA) 9 — (EP) 9-1-3
Arnold, Moses (VW) 10 — (gone in '84)
Asberry, Joseph (LA) 2-2sl —(EP) 5-1-3
Ashbrook, Aaron (LA) 9-1sl—(gone, '84)
Ashbrook, Levi (LA) 13 — (EP) 12-1-2
Ashby, Benj. (WV) 4-2sl — (WV) 6-2
Ashby, Henry (not in '82) — (AH) 7-1-4
Ashby, Jesse (AH) 6 — (AH) 7-1-1
Ashby, Peter (AH) 5 — (AH) 7-1-4
Ashby, Stephen (AH) 9-3 sl.
— (AH) 10-1-5

Ashby, Thomas (AH) 7 — (gone in '84)
Atcason, William — (MqC) 6-1
(for '82 see Atchison)
Atchison, Sam (see Etchason)
Atchison, William, 8 — (MS) 10-1-2
Atchison, William, Jr. (JhW) 12
(for '84 see Atcason)
Atchison, William (WB) 5-1sl
(for '84 see Atcason)
Aughney, Darby (MC) 4-3sl.
— (MC) 5-1-3

— B —

Bacorn, Job (AJ) 3 — (AJ) 3-1-5
Badgley, Anthony (JbW) 7
— (JbW) 11-2-3
Badgley, David — (JbW) 10-1-3
(not in '82)
Bailey, Ann (AH) 2 — (gone in '84)
Bailey, William (JhW) 7 — (gone in '84)
Baker, Anthony (AR) 8 — (AR) 8-1-3
Baker, Jacob (SR) 5 — (SR) 5-1-2

HAMPSHIRE CO. CENSUS—1782-1784

Baker, James (SR) 8 — (SR) 9-1-1
Baker, John (WV) 8 — (WV) 7-1-3
Baker, John (OJ) 2 — (gone in '84)
Baker, Sam (SR) 10-1sl — (gone in '84)
Baker, William (SR) 8 — (SR) 7-1-1
Ball, James (ST) 6 — (MqC) 7
Balthas, George (AH) 7 — (gone in '84)
Barber, James (WB) 11 — (MqC) 7-1-1
Barger, Jacob (MS) 4 — (gone in '84)
Barnes, Elijah (not in '82) — (MS) 6-1
Barnet, Mainy (WV) 7 — (WV) 5-2
  (or Mene)
Barnhouse, John (LA) 8 — (EP) 11-0-2
Barton, Kimber (not in '82)—(AJ) 7-1-0
Batman, John (not in '82)—(AH) 11-1-0
Batson, Mordecai (AH) 5 — (AH) 5-1-2
Batson, Mordecai, Jr. (AH) 3
            — (AH) 5-1-2
Batten, Henry (ST) 6 — (gone in '84)
Baughman, Andrew   — (SR) 5-1
  (not in '82)
Beagle, Jonathan (DM) 2 — (gone, '84)
Beale, Benjamin (DM) 6 — (gone in '84)
Beale, George (not in '82) — (EP) 6-1-2
  see Bell, (possibly Beall)
Bean, Benj. (not in '82) — (JbW) 6-1-2
Bean, John (WB) 2 — (gone in '84)
Beard, George (not in '82) — (AJ) 8-1-2
Beatty, Robert (WB) 3 — (MqC) 4-
Beattis, George (WB) — (MqC) 8-1-1
  (probably Beatty) not in '82
Beaver, Matthias (AJ) 6 — (gone, '84)
Beaver, Michael (AJ) 6 — (gone in '84)
Beeler, Charles (AJ) 3-2sl — (AJ) 5-1-3
Belew, John (DM) 10   —(see Blue)
Belford, Barnett (LA) 4 — see below
Belford, Barnaba (not in '82)—(EP) 4-1-3
Bell, George (LA) 5 — (see Beale)
Bell, William   — (MC) 2-1-0
  see Bill, Beal or Beale
Bell, Zephaniah   (MqC) 11-1-1
  (not in '82)
Benat, Robert (see Bennet)—(MC) 6-1-1
Benet, Thomas (not in '82) — (DM) 4-1-0
Benkit, Jacob (AJ) 7 — (gone in '84)
Bennet, Robert (see Benat)—(MC) 6-1-1
Berry, Enoch (WB) 4 — MqC) 5-1-2
Berry, George (AH) 4-2sl — (gone, '84)
Berry, Joel (WB) 4 — (MqC) 7-1-2
Berry, Joel (JhW) 5 — (gone in '84)
Berry, Reuben (AH) 7 — (AH) 8-1-3
Berry, William (WB) 4 — (gone in '84)
Best, Hannah (not in '82) — (MS) 3-1
Best, Jacob (not in '82) — (AH) 4-1
Beverley, John (AJ) 5 — (AJ) 5
Bezley, Jesse (not in '82) — (WV) 2-1-0
Bible, Christian (MS) 6 — (MS) 7-1-3
Bickerstaff—see Biggerstaff
Bickerstaff, John (DM) 8 — (DM) 7-1
Bickerstaff, Wm., Sr. (DM) 3 —
Bickerstaff, Wm., Jr.   — (DM) 7-1
Biggerstaff, Wm., Jr.   —(DM) 3-1
Bickerstaff, Wm.   — (DM) 7-1
Bierly, John (WB) 5 — (MqC) 5
Bigam, Hugh (DM) 5 — (gone in '84)
Bills, John (ST) 3 — (EP) 3-0-1
Bills, William (ST) 6 — (EP) 6-1-2
  possibly Bell
Black, John (ST) 4 — (gone in '84)
Blackburn, William (AH) 3 — (AH) 4-2

Blackburn, William (AJ) 11
            — (ST) 9-1-2
Blair, William (AR) 6 — (gone in '84)
Blew—see Blue and Belew.
Blith, William (DM) 6 — (gone in '84)
Blue, Abraham (AJ) 6 — (gone in '84)
Blue, Garret (not in '82) — (MqC) 2-1
                 (Blew)
Blue, James (ST) 10-3sl — (EP) 9-0-9
                 (Blew)
Blue, John (see Belew) —(MqC) 12-1-2
Blue, John, Sr. (ST) 12 — (gone, '84)
Blue, John, Jr. (ST) 10 — (MqC) 8-1-2
Blue, Michael (ST) 6-1sl — (gone, '84)
Blue, Uriah (WB) 7-1sl — (MqC) 7-1
                 (Blew)
Boa(r)dman, Joseph (WB) 4-1sl
            — (gone in '84)
Bodkin, Richard (not in '82)—(JbW) 7-1
Bogard, Jacob (AJ) 5 — (AJ) 5-1-2
Boggard, Ezekiel (AR) 9 — (AR) 8-1-2
Bogle, James (WV) 7 — (WV) 8-1-1
Bond, Thomas (WV) 2 — (WV) 6-1-4
Bonefield, Sam (not in '82) — (AJ) 4-1
Bonham, Hezekiah (WB) 8—(AH) 10-1-1
Bonner, William (not in '82)—(JbW) 6-1
Bonnet, Henry (not in '82)—(AH) 2-1-1
  see Bennett
Bonnet, Sam (not in '82) —(AR) 10-1-1
Book, Anthony (see Buck)—(MC) 3-1-1
Book, Robert (see Buck) — (MC) 8-1-1
Booker, Phil (not in '82) — (AJ) 8-1-1
Boots, George (not in '82) — (JhW) 4-1-2
Borah, Charles (Borrer?) — (JhW) 5-1
Borrer, Charles (JhW) 3 — (Borah?)
Borrer, Jacob (not in '82 — (AR) 2-1
Borrer, Thomas (not in '82)—(JbW) 10-1
Borrer, Widow (AR) 4 — (gone in '84)
Bosler, John (not in '82) — (MqC) 3-1
Boulger, John (JbW) 4 — (gone in '84)
Bowman, Charles (not in '82)—(MC) 4-1
Boyce, Richard (not in '82) — (AJ) 9-1-7
Bradford, John (AH) 5 — (AH) 5-1
Brake, Jacob, Sr. (MS) 8 — (MS) 9-1-4
Brake, Jacob, Jr. (MS) 4 — (MS) 4-1-1
Brake, John (MS) 3 — (MS) 3-1
Brandenburg, Matthias (AJ) 12
            — (AJ) 12-1-2
Branson, Amos (AH) 7 — (AH) 8-1-2
Brechen, William (not in '82)—(MqC) 3-1
Bremegen, Wm. (not in '82) — (ST) 3
Bright, John (LA) 8 — (gone in '84)
Brink, Ursulla (AR) 9 — (AR) 9-1-2
Brody, James (LA) 4 — (gone in '84)
Brookes, James (WB) 3 — gone in '84)
Brookes, Richard (not in '82) —(JhW) 2
Broughton, William (AH) 8 — (SR) 8
Brown, Dan (not in '82) — MqC 5
Brown, James (not in '82) — (AR) 5-1
Brown, John (ST) 3 — (AR) 5-1-1
Brown, John (not in '82) — (EP) 6-1-2
Brown, Thomas (AR) 10 — (AR) 8-1-2
Brown, Thomas   —(AH) 9-1
Brown, Thomas (not in '82) — (AH) 5-1
Bruce, Charles (WV) 7 — (WV) 4-1-2
Bruce, Joseph (DM) 5 — (gone in '84)
Buck, Anthony (MC) 2 — see Book
Buck, Robert (MC) 6 — see Book
Buck, William (MC) 7 — (gone in '84)

Buckridge, James (MC) 8 — (gone, '82)
Buffington, David (not in '82)—(MqC) 2-1
Buffington, Joel (WB) 7 —(MqC) 8-1-1
Buffington, Mary   — (MqC) 9-1-5
  (not in '82)
Buffington, Peter   — (JbW) 6-1
  (not in '82)
Buffington, Thomas (AJ) 4-1sl
            — (gone in '84)
Buffington, Wm. (WB) 12 — (see Mary)
Bullett, Wm. (MS) 6-2sl — (AH) 8-1-3
Bumgarner, Rudy (LA) 10 — see below
Bumgarner, Rudolph   —(EP) 8-1-3
Burgit, Jacob (not in '82) — (AJ) 8-1-3
Burk, Jonathan (not in '82) — (DM) 2-1
Burkit, Fred (not in '82) — (AJ) 3-1
Burkit, Henry (WB) 3 — gone in '84
Burns, John (WB) 3 — see Byrnes
Busby, John (see Buzby) — (EP) 9-0-2
Bush, Henry (not in '82) — (AH) 2
Bush, John (WB) 5 — (gone in '84)
Bush, Lewis (WV) 3 — gone in '84)
Butcher, Eve (JhW) 3 — gone in '84)
Butcher, John (DM) 7 — (DM) 7-1-2
Butcher, Paul(sen) (JhW) 7
            — (JhW) 6-1
Buttler, Richard (LA) 6 — (EP) 7-0-1
Buzby, John (WB) 9 — see Busby
Buzzard, Henry (JhW) 11
            — (JhW) 12-1-2
Buzzard, John (AR) 5 — (AR) 2-1-1
Buzzard, Rudolph (not in '82)—(AH 2-1
Byrn(e)s, Barnet (WB) 1 — gone, '84)
Byrnes, John (see Burns) — (EP) 5-0-2
Byrnes, Phillip (JbW) 8 — (JbW 6-1

— C —

Cade, Major (AH) 10 — (AH) 12-2-1
Calahan, Charles (MS) 8 — (gone, '84)
Calerman, Dan (not in '82) —(JhW) 5-1-2
Calf, James M. (see Metcalf)—(SR) 4-1
Calmes, Marquis (ST) 2-12sl
            — (MqC) 5-1-4
Calvin, Stephen (WB) 8-1sl
            — (gone in '84)
Campbell, John (WB) 7 — (MqC) 4-1-5
Campbell, John (see Jr.) — (MqC) 3-1
Campbell, John, Jr. (WB) 2 —see above
Campbell, Wm. (not in '82) —(OJ) 4-1-2
Canada—see Kanada
Candy, David (LA) 9 — (gone in '84)
Candy, Martha (not in '82)—(EP) 8-1-1
Cann, Michael (see Carr)—(JhW) 3-1
Cannon, Thomas (AJ) 7 — (AJ) 7-1-1
Canter, Henry (AH) 8 — (see Carter)
Cantrell, Christopher (JhW) 6
            — (MS) 8-1-0
Capell, Littleton (AJ) 9 — (gone, '84)
Caplinger, Jacob   — (JhW) 7-1-1
  (not in '82)
Caplinger, John (JhW) 7 — (JbW) 8-1-2
Car, Henry Sr. (not in '82)—(JbW) 7-1-3
Carabaugh, Peter (not in '82)—(MqC 3-1
Carder, William (WB) 9 — see Carter
Carlin(e), Andrew (ST) 6 — (EP) 7-0-2
Carlin(e), Andrew (MC) 3 (gone, '84)
Carlyle, Ann (LA) 5 — (gone in '84)
Carlyle, William (not in '82)—(EP) 7-0-1

PAGE 89

Carpender, Conrod — (JhW) 7-1
(not in '82)
Carpender, Jacob (JhW) 7 — (JhW) 6-1
Carr, Conrod (not in '82)—(JhW) 7-1-1
Carr, John (AH) 5 — (AH) 6-1-1
Carr, Michael (see Cann) — (JbW) 3-1
Carr, William (not in '82)—(AH) 4-1-2
Carroll, John (not in '82) — (MS) 5
Carruthers, James (LA) 6 — (EP) 6-0-2
Carruthers, Geo. (not in '82) — (MC) 7-1-2
Carter, Henry (MC) 9 — (MC) 10-1-2
Carter, William (MS) 5 — see Carder
Casey, Nicholas (WB) 7-1sl—(MqC) 8-2-8
Casey, Peter (AH) 8-2sl — (gone, '84)
Casler, Michael (DM) 4 — (DM) 2-1-1
Casner, John (not in '82) —(JhW) 6-1-4
Casselman, Jacob (MC) 8 — gone, '84
Cassellman, Lewis (AJ) 9—(see below)
Castleman, Lewis (see above)—(AJ) 8-1-4
Caufman, Adam (MS) 3 — (MS) 5-1
(Kaufman?)
Champ, Thomas (WV) 12 — (gone, '84)
Champ, William (not in '82)—(WV) 3-1
Chapman, Luke (MC) 7-1 — (MC) 5-1-3
Chapman, William (ST) 5 — (gone, '84)
Cherry, Andrew (LA) 6 — (SR) 8-1-3
Cheshire, Ann (LA) 3 — (EP) 3-0-1
Cheshire, Sam (LA) 5 — (EP) 6-0-1
Chesterton, John (SR) 5 — (gone, '84)
Chilcott, Eber (SR) 2 — (SR) 2-1-2
Chilcott, Eli (not in '82) — (SR) 4-1
Chilcott, Joel (not in '82) — (SR) 3-1
Chilcott, Mary (SR) 4 — (gone in '84)
Childers, Wm. (JbW) 5 — (JbW) 8-1
Chitton, John (not in '82) —(OJ) 4-1-1
(Critton?)
Chinowith, Arthur (LA) 7 — (gone, '84)
Chinoweth, John, Sr. (LA) 13 —(below)
Chinoweth, John (above) —(EP) 11-1-6
Chinoweth, John, Jr. (LA) 5
— (EP) 5-1-1
Chinoweth, Jonathan — JbW 6-1
(not in '82)
C(h)risman, Adam (DM) 6 — (DM) 6-1
C(h)risman, Conrad (DM) 3—(DM) 4-1
C(h)risman, Jacob (DM) 3 —(AJ) 3-1-1
C(h)risman, Jacob (SR) 8-1sl
— (SR) 8-1-4
C(h)risman, Phil (DM) 2 — (AJ) 2-1
(Phil, Jr., in '84)
C(h)risman, Phil, Sr. (DM) 4
— (DM) 4-1-1
Christie, James (not in '82) —(JbW) 4-1
Clark(e), Abraham (JbW) 7
— (JbW) 4-1-2
Clark(e), Abraham, Jr. —(JbW) 2-1-1
(not in '82)
Clark, Henry (JbW) 7 — (JbW) 8-1-2
Clark, John (not in '82) — (JbW) 5-1
Clark, Robert (not in '82) — (JbW) 8-1
Clark, Stephen (AJ) 9 — (AJ) 9-1-1
Clark, Watson (JbW) 4 — (JbW) 5-1-1
Claypoole, Abr. (not in '82) —
Claypoole, George (SR) 3 — (gone, '84)
Claypoole, James (SR) 11 —(SR) 11-1-4
Claypoole, James, Sr. — (SR) 1-1-3
(not in '82)
Claypoole, Jeremiah (WB) 3-1sl
— (MqC) 6-1-2

Claypoole, Jesse (SR) 7 — (SR) 7
Claypoole, John (SR) 15 — (SR) 15-1-3
Clayton, Thomas (LA) 8 — (EP) 8-0-4
(Claton in '84)
Clifford, James (not in '82) — (AR) 7-0-1
Clintock, Robert M. —(ST) 3-1-2
for '82 see McLintock)
Clutter, Jacob (LA) 11 — (EP) 12-1
Cochran, Simon (not in '82)—(MS) 8-1-2
Cockran, Susanna (not in '82) — (MC) 6-1
Cole, Francis (not in '82) — (MC) 6-1
Collens, Elisha (OJ) 5 — (OJ) 6-1
see Collins, Cullins
Collins, Thomas (WB) 6-3sl—(MqC) 6-1
Colvin, Robert (WB) 4 — (ST) 5-1-1
(Calvin.)
Combs, Frances (MS) 6-1sl—(gone, '84)
Combs, Thomas (not in '82)—(ST) 8-1-1
Connard, James Sr. (DM) 4—(Cunnard)
Connard, James Jr. (DM) 5—(Cunnard)
Connor, Thomas (AJ) 7 — (gone, '84)
Connor, Dan (AH) 8 — (gone in '84)
Conrod, John (not in '82) — (AR) 1-1-3
Constant, John (DM) 8 — (DM) 6-1-4
Coon(s)—see Koons, Kuhu(s)
Coon(s), David (VW) 4 — (gone, '84)
Coon(s), Joseph (JhW) 4 — (gone, '84)
Coon(s), Lorry (not in '82) —(JhW) 3-1
Coon(s), Peter (JhW) 5 — (JhW) 5
Cooper, Job (not in '82) — (AJ) 3-1
Cooper, Joel (AJ) 11 — (AJ) 11-1-1
Cooper, Thomas (AJ) 10 — (AJ) 10-1-1
Cooper, Valentine (JhW) 7 — 8-3-1
Corbin, Ann (LA) 6 — (EP) 4-1-3
Corbin, Charles (not in '82)—(EP) 3-0-1
Corbin, David (ST) 6 — (gone in '84)
Corbin, Wm. (not in '82 — (MqC) 6-1-1
Corbin, Wm. (not in '82) — (MqC) 6-1-2
Corn, Andrew (AJ) 4 — (AJ) 4-1-2
Cory, Joseph (AJ) 5 — (gone in '84)
Cosgrove—see Posgrove
Cotrall, Eliz. (LA) 5 — (gone in '84)
Couden, James, Sr. — (EP) 9-0-4
(not in '82)
Couden, James, Jr. — (EP) 5-1-1
(not in '82)
Coulson, John (AJ) 3-7sl — (gone, '84)
Coulson, Margaret — (AJ) 3-1-9
(not in '82)
Coutzman, Adam (MS) 3 — (MS) 3-2
Cowfelt, Henry (not in '82) — (MS) 2
Cowfelt, Phil (MS) 9 — (MS) 8-1
Cowger, George (MS) 4 — (MS) 6-1-5
Craig, David (not in '82) — (JbW) 3-1-1
(Craike—Craige)
Crawford, Wm. (LA) 3 — (EP) 5-0-1
Craycraft, Joseph (DM) 9 —(DM) 8-1-2
Cracraft, Thos. (not in '82) — (DM) 7-1
see Crecraft or Craycraft
Crecraft, Thos. (DM) 7 — (see above)
Cresap, Michael (MC) 6-3sl—(MC) 5-1-5
Crites, Jacob (JhW) 6 — (gone in '84)
Crites, Phil, Sr. (JhW) 4 — (JhW) 3-1-1
Crites, Phil, Jr. (JhW) 3 — (JhW) 4-1-1
Critchelow—see Crutchlow
Critton, John, Sr. (ST) 11 — (ST) 9-1-3
Critton, John (ST) '—(ST) 6-1-2 (Jr.)
(John, Jr. in '84)
Critton, Wm. (not in '82) — (ST) 1-1-2

Crock, George (ST) 6 — (EP) 6-1-2
Crosley, Abel (WB) 6 — (MqC) 6-1
Cross, Christian (VW) 11 — (gone, '84)
Crow, David (not in '82) — (JbW) 2-1-2
Crutchlow, Wm. (OJ) 8 — (OJ) 9
Cubberly, James (not in '82) — (JbW) 8-1
Cudding, John (AH) 4 — (gone in '84)
Cunnard, James — (DM) 4-1-4
(for '84 see Connard)
Cunnard, James, Jr. — (DM) 5-1-2
(for '84 see Connard)
Cunningham, James (JhW) 8-3sl
— (JhW) 8-1-5
Cunningham, John (AJ) 5 — (EJ) 7-0-1
Cunningham, John —(AJ) 6-1-0
(not in '82)
Cunningham, Robert (AR) 9-10sl
(JhR) 8-6-7
Cunningham, Wm. (see Sr.) (AR) 2-1-2
Cunningham, Wm. (see Jr.) (JhW) 8-1-2
Cunningham, Wm., Sr. (AR) 2-4sl
— (gone in '84)
Cunningham, Wm., Jr. (AR) 5-8sl
— (gone in '84)
Cullins, John (see Collins) — (MqC) 3-1
Cuppy, John (WB) 8 — (MqC) 5-1-2
Cuppy, John (WB) 7 — (MqC) 5-1-2
Curle, Jeremiah (JbW) 8 — (JbW) 10-1
Curle, Wm. (not in '82) — (JbW) 7-1-3
Cutrack, John (JhW) 5 — (gone in '84)
Cutrack, Henry (JhW) 7 —(JhW) 8-1-1
Cutrack, Sam (not in '82) — (AR) 7-1-1
Cutright, Sam (AR) 6 — (gone in '84)

— D —

Daily, Wm. (see Dayley) — (MqC) 3-1
Daniels, Mary (not in '82) — (EP) 8-0-1
Daniels, William (ST) 9 — (gone, '84)
Darling, Wm. (not in '82)—(AH) 6-1-5
Darling, Wm. Jr. (not in '82)—(AH) 5-1-2
Dasher, Christian (MS) 7 — (MS) 7-1-2
Davis, Augustus (not in '82) — (ST) 7-1
Davis, Elijah (not in '82) — (EP) 5-0-1
Davis, John (JhW) 8 — (gone in '84)
Davis, Sam (SR) 9 — (SR) 9-1-0
Davis, Theophilus (not in '82)—(JhW) 6-1
Davis, Thomas (AH) 3 — (JbW) 6-1
Davis, Thomas (LA) 3 — (gone in '84)
Davison, Abr. (DM) 4-1sl —(DM) 5-1-2
Davison, David (DM) 12 — (gone, '84)
Davison, Isaac (DM) 4 — (DM) 5-1
Davison, Jacob (not in '82) — (DM) 6-1-3
Day, Leonard (not in '82)—(JbW) 6-61-1
Dayley, Wm. (WB) 2 — (see Dailey)
Dayton, Susannah (not in '82)—(AH) 5-1
Dean, Dan (not in '82 — (OJ) 4-1
Dean, Joshua (not in '82) — (SR) 8-1
Dean, Susannah (SR) 10 — (gone, '84)
Dean, Thos. (not in '82) — (AH) 12-1-2
Deaton, Isaac (ST) 5 — (see Dayton)
Decker, John (WB) 5-1sl —(MqC) 7-1-3
Delm, John (not in '82) — (AH) 2-1
Delonga, John (see below) —(AH) 7-1-2
Delozea, John (AH) 8 — (see above)
Demoss, John (DM) 6 — (gone in '84)
Demoss, Mary (DM) 8 — (gone in '84)
Demoss, Thomas (DM) 9 — (DM) 10-1
Demoss, William (DM) 7 — (gone, '84)
(Demose,)
Denham, John (MC) 9 — (gone in '84)

Denham, John (OJ) 9 — (gone in '84)
Denton, Jacob (SR) 11 — (SR) 9-1-4
Denton, Jane (SR) 2-2sl — (SR) 2-1-1
Denton, Thomas (SR) 8 — (SR) 8-1-0
Devear, John (LA) 10 — (see below)
Devoe, John (see above) —(EP) 11-0-4
Devore, David (not in '82) — (MqC) 7-1
Devore, John (WB) 2 — (EP) 3-0-1
Devore, William (WB) 3 — (gone, '84)
Dew, Sam (WB) 9-2sl — (MqC) 10-1-9
Dewit, Peter (WV) 5 — (gone in '84)
Deyea, Charles Sr. (not in '82)—(OJ) 2-1
Deyea, Charles Jr. (not in '82)—(DM) 2-1
Dickson, George (see Dixon)—(DM) 3-1
Dicki(n)son, Jacob (MS) 8 —(MS) 8-1-3
Dicki(n)son, John (not in '82)—(MS) 3-1
Dixon, John (WB) 4 — (AH) 7-1-1
Dixon, Thomas (LA) 7 — (SR) 8-1
Dobbins, Thomas (AJ) 5 —(gone in '84)
Dobson, William (MC) 3 —(see Dopson)
Dobson, ? (not in '82) — (JhW) 4-1
Doe, John (MC) 4 — (gone in '84)
Donaldson, James (MC) 9 —(see below)
Donelsol, James (above) — (MC) 9-1-1
Donnelly, Elizabeth (LA) 4—(gone, '84)
Dopson, Wm. (see Dobson)—(MC) 3-1-3
Doran, Felix (VW) 11 — (gone in '84)
Dougherty, James (OJ) 1 — (gone in '84)
Douthait, John (VW) 14—(gone in '84)
Douthait, Thomas (VW) 3—(gone, '84)
Downing, Dillon (LA) 3 — (gone, '84)
Doyal, Frances (MS) 6 — (gone in '84)
(Doyle?)
Doyle, Torrance (WV) 3 — (gone, '84)
Dudley, William (MC) 4 — (see Dutly)
Duffil, William (DM) 4 — (gone in '84)
Duggan, Alex (AH) 4 — (gone in '84)
Dugan, William (LA) 4 — (gone in '84)
Duging, Pat (not in '82) — (AJ) 3-1
Dunbar, John (SR) 6 — (gone in '84)
Dunham, John (OJ) 9 — (gone in '84)
Durgan, John (OJ) 6 — (gone in '84)
Dutly, Thomas (DM) 5 — (see Dudley)

— E —

Ealy, Isaac (ST) 2 — (see Ely)
Early, Thomas (OJ) 9 — (gone in '84)
Earsom, Simon (ST) 2 — (see Ahrsam)
Earsom, Jacob (ST) 7 — (ST) 6-1-4
Earson, John (ST) 8 — (see Ahrsam)
Eaton, Benj. (JbW) 3 — (JbW) 3-1
Eaton, Joseph (JbW) 4 — (JbW) 5-1
Eaton, Thomas (JbW) 8 — (JbW) 9-1-1
Edwards, Sam (LA) 6 — (EP) 6-1-1
Edwards, Sarah (LA) 5 — (gone, '84)
Edwards, Thos. (not in '82)—(EP) 8-1-2
Eldridge, David (MS) 2 — (gone, '84)
Ellis, Phillip (SR) 10 — (SR) 11-1-1
Elswick, Thomas (SR) 6 — (gone, '84)
Elswick, Thomas, Sr. —(SR) 7-1-2
(not in '82)
Ely, Benjamin (see Ealy) — (ST) 8-1-2
Ely, Isaac (see Ealy) — (ST) 3-1-1
Emberson, Able (not in '82) — (EP) 4-1
Emberson, Thos. (not in '82) —(EP) 7-0-3
Emmery, John (LA) 6 — (gone in '84)
Emery, Edw. (not in '82) — (AJ) 4-1-2
Emmett, Jacob (LA) 8 — (EP) 1-0-2

Engle, Wm., Sr. (LA) 5 — (gone, '84)
Engle, Wm. (not in '82) — (EP) 1-0-1
Engle, Wm., Jr. (LA) 5 — gone, '84)
English, William (not in '82) — (OJ) 2
Enoch(s), Eliz. (not in '82) — (EP) 1-1
Enoch(s), Enoch (ST) 13 —(EP) 13-1-2
Enoch(s), Henry (ST) 2 —(gone in '84)
Ermintraut, Christopher (JhW) 9
  (for '84 see Armintraut)
Etchason, Sam (not in '82) —(MqC) 2
  see Atchison, Atcason
Euldy, Thos. (not in '82) — (AH) 2-1-0
Everman, Michael (JbW) 12
  — (JbW) 11-1-1
Extine, Leonard (not in '82) — (AH) 1

— F —

Fairly, John (OJ) 3 — (gone in '84)
Fairly, David (OJ) 9 — (gone in '84)
Farce, Cornelius —(ST) 12-1-5
  (not in '82 — Ferree?)
Farley, Jane (not in '82) — (OJ) 2-1
Fearend, Isaac (AJ) 8 — (AJ) 10-1-1
  (Ferrand)
Ferguson, James (not in '82)—(MqC) 2
Ferguson, Robert (WB) 8-4sl
  — (MqC) 8-1-3
Ferrall, Pat (DM) 4-1sl — (gone, '84)
Feut, George (not in '82)—(JhW) 2-1
  (Fout—Kent?)
Fiddler, Edw. (AH) 3 — (gone in '84)
Fiddler, George (WB) 3 — (MqC) 3
Fiddler, Jacob (not in '82) — (MqC) 1
Fields, Simon (MC) 3 — (gone in '84)
Fisher, Adam (not in '82) — (AR) 7-1-1
Fisher, Adam Sr. (AR) 9-2sl—(gone '84)
Fisher, Adam, Jr. (AR) 5 —(gone, '84)
Fisher, Christiana — (AR) 4-1-1
  (not in '82)
Fisher, Dan (not in '82) — (MC) 2-1
Fisher, Geo. (JhW) 10 — (JhW) 10-1-3
Fisher, Jacob (not in '82) —(EP) 12-1-5
Fisher, John (not in '82) — (AR) 2-1-1
Fitzpatrick, Anthony (SR) 6—(gone '84)
Flarty, James — (MC) 5-1
  (for '82 see Flougherty)
Fleming, James (not in '82)—(AJ) 9-1-2
Fleming, James (not in '82)—(JbW) 4-1
Fletcher, Joseph (not in '82)—(EP) 4-0-1
Flora, Abijah (not in '82)—(DM) 3-1-0
  (Flore)
Flora, Thomas (DM) 13 — (DM) 10-1-1
Flora, William (DM) 7 — (DM) 7-1-1
Flougherty, James (ST) 5 — see Flarty
Foley, John (AH) 8 — (AH) 9-1-2
Forman, Benj. (WB) 6 — (gone in '84)
Forman, David (LA) 9 — (EP) 11-1-3
Forman, John (WB) 7-6sl
  — (MqC) 10-1-2
Forman, John, Jr. (WB) 8-9sl
  — (MqC) 7-2-7
Forman, William (WB) 4-1sl
  — (MqC) 8-1-3
Forshey, John (OJ) 8-3sl — (gone, '84)
Fowler, John (AH) 7 — (gone in '85)
Fox, Gabriel (WB) 4 — (MqC) 6-1-5
Frazier, Dan (not in '82) — (OJ) 4
Freeman, Rosanna (not in '82) —(AH) 9-1
Friback, George (ST) 2 — (gone in '84)
Fry, Henry (LA) 8-1sl — (SR) 9-1-7
Fryback, John (MC) 4 — (gone in '84)

Fultz, Phillip (not in '82) —(JhW) 6-1-3
Funk, Adam (MS) 5 — (gone in '84)
Furst, Valentine (not in '82)—(JhW) 9-1-2

— G —

Gard, Cornelius (LA) 9 — (gone, '84)
Garrison, John (SR) 7 — (gone in '84)
Garvis, Robt. (not in '82) — (MC) 6-1-1
George, Joseph (VW) 3 — (gone, '84)
  see Gouge
George, Susannah (MS) 7-6sl—(gone '84)
Gibbony, Alex Sr. (WV) 3-1sl
  — (gone in '84)
Gibbony, Alex Jr. (WV) 6-1sl
  — (gone in '84)
Gibbony, Robert (AH) 5 — (AH) 4-1
Giddens, James (not in '82)—(WV) 6-1
Gilmore, Sarah (not in '82) —(JbW) 6-1-1
Glass, Sam (LA) 6 — (gone in '84)
Glaze, Andrew (MC) 1 — (MC) 5-1-2
Glaze, Conrod (MC) 6 — (MC) 7-1-4
Glaze, Earhart (MC) 1 — (gone in '84)
Glaze, George (ST) 5 — (MqC) 6-1-4
Glaze, John (WB) 4 — (MqC) 5-1-3
Godfrey, Edw. (AH) 10 — (AH) 10-1-3
Godfrey, William (AH) 4 — (AH) 5-1-2
Goff, Thomas (AR) 3-6sl — (AR) 4-1-1
Good, Isaac (AJ) 6 — (gone in '84)
Good, Peter (AJ) 3 — (gone in '84)
Goodman, Ignatious (not in '82)—(OJ) 5-1
Goodwine, Solomon (MS) 2 — (MS) 2-1
Gordon, George (DM) 6 — (gone in '84)
Gouge, Chas. (not in '82) — (JbW) 12-1
  see George
Gray, Friend (not in '82) —(MqC) 6-1-0
Green, Henry (AH) 7 — (gone in '84)
Green, Lewis (AH) 4 — (AH) 5-1
Grim, Balsar (not in '82) — (MqC) 5
Guset, Peter (not in '82) — (AJ) 6-1
Gustin, Adolphus (DM) 8 — (gone, '84)

— H —

Haden, Webb (not in '82) — (EP) 3-0-2
Haff, Cornelius (DM) 7 — (DM) 6-1-2
  (Hass?)
Haff, Lawrence (DM) 7-1sl—(gone, '84)
Haff, Luke (not in '82) — (DM) 5-1-3
Haff, Peter (WB) 5 — (gone in '84)
Haff, Richard (DM) 6 — (gone in '84)
Hagarty, John (ST) 5 — (see Hogarty)
Hagler, Bastion (JhW) 9 —(JhW) 9-1-3
Hagler, William (not in '82)—(JhW) 5-1
Hahn, John (see Haun) — (JhW) 7
Haines, Rudolph (DM) — (DM) 5-1
Haines, Joseph (MC) 5 — (see Hanes)
Hall, Joseph (not in '82) — (WV) 4-1
Hall, Peter (not in '82) — (EP) 7-0-2
Hall, Thomas (MS) 7 — (MS) 6-1
Hambler, William — (ST) 5-1-1
  (for '82 see Humbler)
Hamilton, Henry (LA) 3 — (SR) 5-1-1
Hamilton, Thomas (ST) 6 — (gone '84)
Hammory, John (LA) 5 — (gone, '84)
Hanks, Joseph (LA) 11 — (see Hawk)
Hanson, Thomas (AJ) 4 — (gone, '84)
Hanes, Joseph — (MC) 5-1-2
  see Haines
Hardin, Evanglist — (AH) 6-1-3
  (for '82 see Vanglist Hardin)
Hardin, Mark (OJ) 11 — (OJ) 10-1

Hardin, Vanglist (AH) 5
  (for '84 see Evanglist Hardin)
Hardin, Wm. (not in '82) — (EP) 4-1-3
Hargis, William (MC) 7 — (MC) 8-1
Harness, Adam (WB) 7 — (gone in '84)
Harness, George (AR) 6-2sl
  — (AR) 6-1-2
Harness, John (AR) 14-2sl —(AR) 12-1-2
Harness, John (not in '82) — (MqC) 6-1-3
Harness, Leonard (MS) 6 — (MS) 7-1-0
Harness, Leonard (not in '82)—(MS) 7-1
Harness, Michael, Sr. (AR) 3-12sl
  — (AR) 3-1-3
Harness, Michael, Jr. (AR) 5
  (AR) 9-1-1
Harness, Peter (MS) 6-1sl —(MS) 7-1-1
Harod, Ephraim (not in '82)—(MqC) 8-1
Harper, Adam (not in '82—(JbW) 8-1-1
Harpole, Adam (not in '82)—(JhW) 5-1-1
Harpole, Adam, Jr. (JhW) 4
  — (JhW) 3-1-2
Harris, John (SR) 8 — (EP) 8-1-1
Harris, John (AH) 10 — (gone in '84)
Harris, John (LA) 6 — (gone in '84)
Harris, Thomas (not in '82)—(EP) 8-1-1
Harrison, John (not in '82)—(SR) 6-1-2
Harrison, Simeon (not in '82)—(SR) 2-1
Harsher, Thomas (LA) 7 — (gone, '84)
Hartley, Hugh (AJ) 5 — (AH) 6-1
Hartley, John (DM) 7 — (DM) 6-1
Hartley, Thomas (DM) 6 — (gone, '84)
Hartman, Peter (WB) 5 — (gone, '84)
Hase, Thomas (not in '82) — (EP) 2-1
Hathaway, Eliezer (WB) 10—(ST) 11-1-1
Haun, Michael (JhW) 7 — (see Hahn)
Haver—see O'Haver
Hawk, Catherine — (JbW) 6-1-3
  (for '82 see Hock)
Hawk, Henry (AH) 7 — (MqC) 8-2-2
Hawk, John (LA) 5 — (SR) 6-1-3
Hawk, Isaac (LA) 9 — (EP) 10-1-2
Hawkins, John (not in '82) —(EP) 6-0-1
Hayden, William (LA) 3 —(see Haden)
Hays, John (MS) 3 — (MS) 2-1
Hazle, Henry (AJ) 8-2sl — (AJ) 9-1-2
  (Hazell)
Hearsman—see Her(r)sman, Hiersman,
  Hirsman, Hoarsman
Hearsman, Philip — (AJ) 5-1
  (not in '82)
Heath, Azakel (AR) 6 — (gone in '84)
Heath, Jonathan (AR) 4-7sl
  — (AR) 9-2-2
Heater, Michael (OJ) 9 — (gone, '84)
Hedger, John (MS) 7 — (MS) 7
Helmick, Jacob (AR) 7 — (AR) 8-2
Helmick, John (not in '82) — (AR) 5-1
Henderson, Sampson — (EP) 3-0-1
  (not in '82)
Hendricks, Abraham (AJ) 3 —(AJ) 3-1
Hennery, John (not in '82) — (WV) 7-1
Henkle, Barbara — (JhW) 6-1-3
  (for '82 see Widow Henkle, or Hinkle?)
Henkle, Mose (JhW) 5 — (gone in '84)
Henkle, Widow (JhW) 7 — see Barbara
Henry, Michael (WB) 8-1sl —(Hennery)
Henwood, William (ST) 3 — (gone, '84)
Herriott, Ephraim (WB) 8 — (gone '84)
Herrsman, Cristopher (WB) 4
  —(gone '84)
Hersman, George (AJ) 2 — (gone, '84)

Hersman, Matthias (AJ) 2 —(gone '84)
Hess, Henry (WV) 10 — (gone in '84)
Hicks, Thomas (JhW) 3 — (MS) 4-1-2
Hider, Adam (AH) 10-2sl—(AH) 12-1-6
Hier, John (JhW) 5 — (JhW) 6-1-2
Hier, Leonard, Sr. (JhW) 1
  — (JhW) 5-1-4
Hier, Leonard, Jr. (JhW) 4
  — (JhW) 5-1-2
Hier, Lewis (not in '82 — (JhW) 3-1-1
Hiett, Evan (LA) 8 — (see Hyett)
Higgins, John (DM) 9 — (gone in '84)
Higgins, John (AH) 10-4sl
  — (AH) 3-1-8
Higgins, Peter — (AH) 5-2-2
  (not in '82)
Higgins, Robt. (AH) 11-10 —(MS) 6-1-6
High, John (WB) 9 — (gone in '84)
Hiley, Rudolph (not in '82) — (ST) 3-1
Hill, Dan (SR) 1 — (SR) 2-1-1
Hill, Gasper (see Hite) — (MqC) 5-1
Hill, Joseph (SR) 9 — (SR) 10-1-2
Hill, William (LA) 4 — (gone in '84)
Hirsman, Casper (AJ) 8 — (gone, '84)
Hite, Abraham (AH) 5-7sl
  — (AH) 8-1-15
Hite, Casper (AR) 6 — (AR) 8-0-2
Hite, Matthias (AR) 5 — (gone in '84)
Hoarsman, Stephen —(MqC) 5-1
  see Hearsman, Hiersman
Hock, Catherine (JbW) 6 —(see Hawk)
Hodger, Reuben — (MqC) 2
  (not in '82)
Hoff, Peter (not in '82) — (MqC) 5-1
Hoffman, Conrad — (MqC) 7-2-1
  see Huffman
Hog, Aaron (MS) 9 — (gone in '84)
Hogbine, John — (JhW) 5-1-2
  (not in '82)
Hoge, John (not in '82) — (MqC) 9-1-3
Hoge, John (not in '82) — (EP) 4-0-2
Hoge, Moses (not in '82) (AR) 3-1-2
Hogerty, John (Hagerty) —(EP) 5-0-2
Hogeland, Cornelius (OJ) 10
  — (OJ) 9-1-1
Hobbs—see Hubs, Hubbs
Hole or Hall, Dan (JbW) 5 —(JbW) 6-2
Holland, Thomas (AJ) 2 — (gone, '84)
Hol(l)oback, Thomas (AJ) 11
  (AJ) 12-1
Homan, Jacob (SR) 8 — (SR) 8-1-2
Hook, William (LA) 2 — (gone, '84)
Hoover, Jacob (LA) 13 — (gone in '84)
Horebaugh, Phillip (AH) 8 —(gone '84)
Horn, George (LA) 7 — (EP) 6-0-3
Hornback, Abraham (AR) 6 —(gone '84)
Hornback, James (AR) 3 — (AR) 5-1-1
Hornback, Isaac (AR) 10-3sl
  — (AR) 7-1-3
Hornback, Magdalena — (AR) 8-1
  (not in '82)
Hornback, Michael (JbW) 8
  — (JbW) 8-1-3
Hornback, Sam (AR) 6-1sl
  — (AR) 7-1-2
Hornback, Simon (AR) 12 —(AR) 13-1-2
Horse, Peter (not in '82) — (JbW) 4-1
Horst, William, Sr. (JhW) 5
  — (gone in '84)
Horst, George — (JhW) 3-1-3
  (not in '82)
Horsman, Jacob (not in '82) — (AJ) 8-1

House, Jacob (MS) 5 — (MS) 6-1-1
House, John (ST) 3 — (gone in '84)
House, John (OJ) 6 — (OJ) 7-1-0
House, Joseph (OJ) 3 — (gone in '84)
Howard, Parson — (EP) 6-0-2
  (not in '82)
Howard, Resin (LA) 6 — (gone in '84)
Howell, Jonathan (not in '82) — (AJ) 4
Howell, William (AJ) 6-1sl
  — (AJ) 7-1-2
Howman, Stithman — (JbW) 5-1-2
  (not in '82)
Hubbard, John, Sr. (LA) 3
  — (EP) 3-1-3
Hubbard, John, Jr. (LA) 4-1sl
  — (EP) 6-1-3
Hubbard, Jacob (Hubbert)—(EP) 8-1-2
Hubs, Thomas (ST) 3 — (gone in '84)
Hubbs, Thomas, Sr. — (ST) 3-1
  (not in '82)
Hubbert, Jacob (LA) 5-1sl —(Hubbard)
Huber, Jacob (not in '82) — (EP) 14-1-1
  see Hubbard — Hubbert
Hudson, John (not in '82) — (JhW) 3-0
Hudson, David (not in '82) — (JbW) 8-1
Huffman—see Huffmans, Hoffman
Huffman, Benjamin (WB) 3 (gone '84)
Huffman, Catherine (MS) 6—(gone '84)
Huffman, Conrod (WB) 12-1sl
Huffman, Christopher — (JbW) 9-1-3
  (not in '82)
Huffman, Henry —(MqC) 4-1-2
  (not in '82)
Huffman, Henry (AJ) 6 — (AJ) 5-1
Huffman, Phillip — (MS) 5-1-0
  (not in '82)
Hughes—see Hews, Hewes, Hughs
Hugh(e)s, James (LA) 8 —(SR) 10-1-3
Hugh(e)s, Jonathan (LA) 4
  — (SR) 4-1-2
Hughs, John (DM) 4 — (gone in '84)
Hughs, Susanna (LA) 4 — (gone, '84)
Hughs, Thomas (DM) 5 — (gone '84)
Humbler, Adam (ST) 6 — see Hambler
Humes, Andrew (ST) 3 — (gone in '84)
Humphreys, Ralph (ST) 7-10sl
  —(ST) 5-3-2
Hunter, Thomas (not in '82) — (SR) 3
Hunter, William (AH) 3 — gone in '84)
Hutson, David (JbW) 8 — see Hudson
Hutson, John (JbW) 3 — see Hudson
Hutton, Isaac (AR) 2 — (AR) 9-2-2
Hutton, Jacob (not in '82) — (AR) 3-1
Hutton, Moses (AR) 9-12 — (AR) 9-1-9
Hyett, James (see Hiett) — (EP) 3-0-2
Hyett, Evan (see Hiett) — (EP) 8-1-4

— I —

Inskeep, Abraham (AR) 11
  — (AR) 11-1-5

— J —

Jackson, Thomas (not in '82)—(DM) 3-1
Jackson, Wm. (not in '82)—(DM) 8-1-2
Jacobs, John J. — (MC) 0-1-3
  (not in '82)
Jacobs, Sam (WV) 3 — (gone in '84)
Jane—see Bane, Zane
Jane, Joseph (not in '82) — (JbW) 7-1
Jefferson, Luke (MS) 4 — (MS) 4-1
Jenkins, Ann (not in '82) — (EP) 7-0-4
Jenkins, Evan (DM) 4 — (EP) 6-0-3

HAMPSHIRE CO. CENSUS—1782-1784   PAGE 93

Jenkins, Jacob — (EP) 8-1-1
 (not in '82)
Jenny, William (AR) 6-1sl —(AR) 6-1-2
 (Janny)
Johns, Isaac (LA) 8 — (gone in '84)
Johnson, Abraham Sr. (AJ) 2—(AJ) 3-1
Johnson, Abraham Jr. (AJ) 6 — (AJ) 7-1-4
Johnson, Elisha (AR) 6 — (gone in '84)
Johnson, John Sr. (ST) 3 — (gone, '84)
Johnson, John (VW) 12 — (ST) 3-1-3
Johns(t)on, John — (WV) 8-1
Johns(t)on, John, Jr — (ST) 3-1-1
 (not in '82)
Johnson, Joseph (ST) 4 — (ST) 5-1-1
Johnson, Okey (AJ) 6 — (AJ) 6-1-2
Johnson, Okey (OJ) 8 — (OJ) 9-1-3
Johnson, William (AJ) 9 — (AJ) 9-1-2
Johnson, William, Jr. (AJ) 2-1sl
Johnson, William Sr. (DM) 8 — (gone in '84)
Johnson, William (OJ) 7 — (gone, '84)
Johnson, (?) —(AJ) 3-1
Jones, David (AJ) 5 — (AJ) 6-1-1
Jones, John (AJ) 10 — (AJ) 10-1-2
Jones, Peter (AJ) 4 — (AJ) 4-1-0
Jones, Peter (AJ) 11 — (gone in '84)
Jones, Solomon (AJ) 2 — (AJ) 3-1-0
Jones, Sam (not in '82) — (AJ) 11-1-1
Jordan, Julius (JbW) 3 — (gone in '84)
Jordan, Katherine (MS) 3 — (gone '84)
Jordan, Mark (OJ) 5 — (gone in '84)
Judy, Henry (JhW) 7 — (JhW) 6-1-2
Judy, Margaret (JbW) 8 —(JbW) 8-1-1
Judy, Martin (not in '82) —(JhW) 2-1
Judy, Nicholas (JhW) 7 — (JhW) 6-1-3

— K —

Kail (Kale), John (LA) 3 — (EP) 4-1
Kail, George (LA) 6 — (EP) 7-1-3
Kail, Peter (LA) 5 — (gone in '84)
Kanada, Thos. (not in '82) —(EP) 7-0-2
 See Canada, Kennedy
Kayser, Joseph (AH) 7 — (gone in '84)
Kearen, Barnard (MC) 3 — (gone, '84)
Kellar, George — (JhW) 5-1-2
 (not in '82)
Kelly, Patrick (DM) 3 — (gone in '84)
Kelly, Sam (VW) 10 — (gone in '84)
Kennedy, Thomas (LA) 7—(see Kanada)
Kent, Isabel (MS) 3 — (gone in '84)
Kent, John (AJ) 11 — (AJ) 9-1-0
Keran, Peter (WB) 1 — (gone in '84)
Keran, Pat (ST) 9 — (EP) 10-0-2
Kersman ? (JhW) 6 — (gone in '84)
Key (Kee), Sarah (MC) 3 — (MC) 5-1
Keys, James (LA) 5 — (gone in '84)
Kezoil, Michael (not in '82)—(EP) 6-0-1
Kidner, George (SR) 7 — (SR) 7-1-3
Kiger, John (WV) 2 — (see Kyger)
Kimberlin, Abr. (AJ) 6 — (gone in '84)
Kimberlin, Jacob (OJ) 8 —(OJ) 10-1-10
Kimberlin, John (AJ) 5 — (gone in '84)
Kimberly, Michael (MC) 7 —(gone, '84)
Kimball, Adam (not in '82) — (AR) 2
Kimble, Lambert (AR) 5 — (AR) 5-1
Kimble, John (AR) 10 — (AR) 8-1-1
King, Henry (JhW) 2 — (gone in '84)
Kiser, John (MC) 10 — (gone in '84)
Kisner, Jacob (not in '82) —(EP) 8-0-1

Kite, Henry (not in '82) — (WV) 2-1-0
Kite, Sam (WV) 4 — (WV) 3-1
Kittle, Abraham (AR) 10 —(gone, '84)
Koon, John (VW) 15 — (see Coon)
Kuykendall, Cath (WB) 2-1sl — (gone in '84)
Kuykendall, Henry (WB) 7-3sl — (MqC) 6-2-1
Kuykendall, Jane — (JhW) 9-1-1
 (not in '82)
Kuykendall, John (WB) 6-6sl — (MqC) 6-1-2
Kuykendall, Nathaniel (WB) 7-7sl — (MqC) 7-1-8
Kyger, George (WV) 9 — (WV) 9-1-1
Kyger, John (WV) 8 — (see Kiger)
Kyger, Thomas — (WV) 6-1-4
 (not in '82)
Kyger, Wm. (not in '82) —(MqC) 8-1

— L —

Lacefield, Elias (see below)—(MS) 6-1
Lacewell, Elias (MS) 6 — (see above)
Laird—see Lard, Leard
Laird, Michael (ST) 7 — (see Lard)
Lamaster, Isaac (DM) 5 — gone, '84)
Lamaster, Joseph (DM) 4—(gone, '84)
Lambert, Barnabas — (JhW) 7-1
 (not in '82)
Landen, Charles (WB) 3-1sl—(gone '84)
Lander, Henry (LA) 9 — (gone, '84)
Lander, Jacob (LA) 4 — (EP) 5-1-3
Lander, Michael (WV) 7 — (gone, '84)
Lansisko, Henry — (JbW) 10-1-3
 (not in '82)
Lard, Michael (WB) 5 — (see Leard)
Largent, James (LA) 7 — (EP) 7-1-4
 (see Sargent)
Largent, John Sr. (DM) 10—(see Largin)
Largent, John Jr. (ST) 8 — (gone, '84)
Largent, William (ST) 7—(gone, '84)
Largin, John (see Largent) — (DM) 10-1-3
Larue—see La Rue, Lerew
Larue, Jacob (DM) 5 — (gone, '84)
Larue, John (DM) 6 —(DM) 7-1-4
Lashby, Wm. (not in '82) — (EP) 6-0-1
Laughlin, Jas. (see McLaughlin)—(SR) 1
Laurence, John (not in '82)—(AH) 10-1-2
Lawrence, Michael — (EP) 7-0-2
 (not in '82)
Lawson, Jacob (not in '82) — (ST) 1
Lawson, James (not in '82)—(OJ) 2
Lawson, Moses (not in '82) —(OJ) 3-1
Lawson, Richard (not in '82) — (OJ) 4-1
Lawson, Thos. (OJ) 12-15sl—(OJ) 10-1-1
Leaphart, Augusteen (LA) 8—(gone '84)
Leard, Michael (see Laird)—(MC) 5
Leary, Dennis (AR) 4 — (AR) 7-1
Leason, Richard (ST) 5 — (gone in '84)
Lee, George (see See)—(MS) 8-1-5
Lee, Michael (see Sea)—(AR) 9-1-2
Lee, Peter (OJ) 7 — (gone '84)
Lee, William (VW) 9 — (gone, '84)
Leg, Ambrose (SR) 6 — (gone, '84)
Leonard, Martin (MS) 7 — (AR) 8-1
Lerew, Noah (not in '84) — (DM) 3-1-6
Lerew, Peter (DM) 9 — (DM) 10-1-4
Lewis, Amos (SR) 8 — (gone, '84)
Lewis, David (not in '82) — (EP) 6
Lewis, George (SR) 9 — (gone, '84)

Lewis, John (MS) 5 — (EP) 4-1
Lewis, John (VW) 9-1sl — (gone, '84)
Lewis, Sam (VW) 7-7sl — (gone, '84)
Liggett, John (JhW) 4 — (gone, '84)
Lighter Henry (AJ) 7 — (see Liter)
Lightholse, John (not in '82— (JhW) 4-1-1
Likens, John (JhW) 7 — (JhW) 7-1
Likings, Richard (not in '82)—(AH) 4-1
Lilly, David (AH) 5 — (AR) 5-1-1
Lineger, William (LA) 4 — (EP) 1-0-2
Linore, John (not in '82) (OJ) 4-1-0
Liter, Henry (see Lighter)—(AJ) 8-1-2
Little, Josiah (JbW) 7 — (gone, '84)
Little, Thomas (LA) 9 — (gone, '84)
Littler, Thos. (not in '82) — (SR) 11-1-5
Lion, John (see Lyons) — (OJ) 10-1
Lions, Mary (see Lyons) — (ST) 4-1
Lock, Jacob (DM) 7 — (DM) 7-1-2
Lockhart, Bird (ST) 5 — (gone, '84)
Lockwood, Wm. (not in '82)—(MC) 4-1-2
Logan, David (AH) 6 — (AH) 5-1-3
Long, Christian (MC) 8 — (gone, '84)
Long, David (ST) 8 — (ST) 9-1
Long, Jacob (MC) 9 — (MC) 9-1-3
Long, Rosanna (AH) 6 — (gone, '84)
Longworth, Thomas (AR) 3 — (AR) 4-1
 (Longwith)
Lorrentz, John (AH) 12 — (gone, '84)
Louther, Geo. (not in '82) — (JhW) 5-1
Lowrie, Adam (SR) 8 — (SR) 8-1
Lowry, Sam (not in '82) — (SR) 2-1-1
Lupton, Isaac (not in '82) — (EP) 6-0-2
Lynch—see Linch
Lynch, Charles (MS) 4 — (MS) 9-1-4
Lynch, Pat (AH) 2-2sl — (AH) 2-1-2
Lymes, John (not in '82) — (JhW) 5-1-1
Lyon, Charles (MS) 4 — (MS) 4
Lyon, Ezekiel (OJ) 6 — (see Lion)
Lyon, Michael (LA) 5-1sl — (gone, '84)

— M —

McBride, Frances (SR) 3 — (SR) 3-1
McBride, James (LA) 7 — (gone, '84)
McBride, John (ST) 6 — (ST) 5-1-2
McBride, John (not in '82) — (EP) 9-0-3
McBride, John (AJ) 7 — (AJ) 7-1
McCabe, Terrance (DM) 3 — (gone, '84)
McCarny, James (not in '82)—(AH) 4-1-1
McCarty, Chas. (not in '82) — (OJ) 6-1
McCarty, Edw. (WV) 5 — (WV) 6-1-3
McCarty, Thos. (AH) 5-1sl—(AH) 6-1-5
McCave, Ross (not in '82)—(JbW) 6-1-1
McClintock—see McLintock, Lintock
McCord, John (LA) 6 — (gone, '84)
McCormack, John (LA) 3 — (gone, '84)
McCracken, Ovid — (DM) 9-1-4
 (for '82 see Mecrakin)
McDade, James (WV) 4 — (gone, '84)
McDavid, James (not in '82) — (AH) 5-1
McDaniel, Arch (see below) — (DM) 7-1-5
McDonald, Archibald (DM) 8-1sl
 (for '84 see McDaniel, above)
McDonald, Dan (MC) 4 — (gone, '84)
McDonald, Neil (DM) 8 — gone, '84)
McDougal, James (not in '82) —(ST) 7-1
 (McDewgal)
McFarlane, Thomas (SR) 8—(gone, '84)
McFarling, Thos. (not in '82)—(SR) 7-1-1
McFerson, Wm. (not in '82)—(EP) 1-0-1

McGlolan—see McLaughlin, McLaughlin
McGloughlan, Dan (MC) 2 —(MC) 2-1-2
McGloughlan, Dan, Jr. (MC) 5
 — (MC) 5-1-2
McGraw, Morris (see Magraw)
 — (EP) 6-0-3
McGuire, Wm. (WB) 9-3sl—(MqC)10-1-1
McHendry, Wm. (SR) 10 — (SR) 10-1-1
McIlhaney, Felix (JhW) 5-1sl
 — (gone, '84)
McIver, Paul (LA) 9 — (see McKeever)
McKever, Paul (see McIver) (?) 10-1-4
McKenny, John (AH) 3 — (AH) 4-1-1
McLamore, John (not in '82) —(AH) 8-1
McLamore, Phil (not in '82) —(AH) 9-1
McLintock, Alex (ST) 8—
 (see McClintock—Clintock)
McLintock, John (ST) 3 — (gone, '84)
McLintock, Robert (ST) 3-1-2
 (fofr '82 see Lintock)
McMahan, Barnard (AR) 7-1-1
 (not in '82)
McMahan, Wm. (DM) 7 — (DM) 7-1
McNamarr, Joseph — (AH) 9-1
 (not in '82)
McNeal, Dan (AH) 9-4sl—(AH) 9-1-6
McNeal, John (AH) 6-1sl—(AH) 6-1-3
McNees, John (SR) 6 — (see Nees)
Mace, Ann (MS) 5 — (gone, '84)
Mace, Issac (AR) 4 — (JbW) 4-1
Mace, John (MS) 7 — (JhW) 6-1
Mace, Nicholas (JhW) 7 — (JhW) 9-1-3
Mace, Nicholas (MS) 3 — (gone, '84)
Made—see Maid
Made, John (not in '82) — (MC) 2-1-2
Magraw, Morris (LA) 8 —(see McGraw)
Mahan, James (OJ) 8 — (OJ) 9-1-3
Mahan, William (OJ) 10 — (OJ) 9-1-3
Mahuren, Ebenezer (MS) 3—(gone, '84)
Maid, John (MC) 2 — (ST) 2-1-3
Majors, John (JbW) 9 — (gone, '84)
Malcolm, James (DM) 2—(gone, '84)
Male, Wilmer Sr. (not in '82) —(EP)2-0-1
Male, Wilmer (ST) 11 — (EP) 10-0-2
Mallow, Adam (JhW) 6 —(JhW) 6-1-3
Mallow, Henry (JhW) 3 — (JhW) 4-1-1
Maloy, James (not in '82) — (EP) 5-0-1
Manear, Abraham (not in '82)—(ST) 2
Mann, Christopher (not in '82—(MC) 7-1
March, Henry (AR) 12-2sl—(W.V) 10-3-4
 (Marsh)
Marquis, And (DM) 6 — (DM) 7-1-1
Marquis, Christopher — (DM) 2-1-1
 (not in '82)
Marquis, Richard (DM) 10 —(DM) 9-1-2
Marrs, Barnabas (MS) 4 — (MS) 3-1
Marrs, Henry M. (AR) 6-1sl
 —(AR) 5-1-1
Marsh—see March
Marshall, Benj. (MS) 3-1sl—(MS) 4-1
Martin, David (DM) 5 — (gone, '84)
Martin, Edmund (OJ) 8 — (OJ) 8-1
Martin, Euria (see Uriah)—(MC) 4-1-4
Martin, George (LA) 10 —(EP) 11-0-4
Martin, James (MC) 7 — (MC) 7-1-0
Martin, Janes (not in '82)—(MC) 8-1-0
Martin, John (LA) 6 — (EP) 7-1-2
Martin, John (DM) 8 — (DM) 8-1-2
Martin, Sam (AJ) 3 — (AJ) 5-1
Martin, Sam (not in '82) — (MC) 2-1

Martin, Thomas (AJ) 3 — (gone, '84)
Martin, Uriah (MC) 5 — (see Euria)
Mator, Phil (not in '82) — (MC) 7-1-1
Matthews, Jonathan (not in '82)—(WV) 6
Matthews, Lewis (Lew) (DM) 6
 (DM) 7-1-7
Maxwell, Robt. (AR) 5 — (AR) 5-1-2
May, John (not in '82) — (EP) 5-1-1
Means, Isaac (WB) 9 — (MqC) 11-1-1
Mecrakin, Ann (DM) 2—(see McCrakin)
Mecrakin, Ovid (DM)11—(see McCrakin)
Melone, John (not in '82) (ST) 4-1
Menear, John (not in '82) — (ST) 5-1-4
Metcalf—see James M. Calf
Metcalf, James (SR) 5 — (gone, '84)
Miars, George (LA) 8 — (see Myers)
Miers, Frances (not in '82)—(MC) 5-1
Miers, John, Sr. (WV) 2 — (see Myers)
Miers, John (WV) 4 — (see Myers)
Michael, George (LA) 9 — (SR) 11-1-2
Milaw, James (ST) 4 —(gone in '84)
Miles, David (AR) 6 — (AR) 6-1-3
Miles, James (not in '82) — (ST) 3-1-4
Mil(l)burn, Andrew (LA) 5—(gone, '84)
Mil(l)burn, Joseph — (EP) 6-0-1
 (not in '82)
Mil(l)burn, William (LA) 6 — (EP) 2
Mil(l)burn, William, Jr. — (EP) 6-1-2
 (not in '82)
Miller, Abraham (WB) 6—(MqC) 6-1-1
Miller, Anthony (not in '82)—(SR) 7-1-2
Miller, Catherine (AH) 5 — (gone, '84)
Miller, George (JbW) 5—(JbW) 5-1-1
Miller, George (AJ) 8 — (gone, '84)
Miller, Henry (WV) 5 — (WV) 4-1-1
Miller, Isaac (WB) 5-2sl—(MqC) 6-1-3
Miller, Jacob (SR) 5-2sl — (SR) 4-1-4
Miller, John (AR) 7 — (AR) 6-1
Miller, John, Jr. (WB) 4 — (gone, '84)
Miller, John (WB) 11 — (gone, '84)
Miller, John Henry (WB) 9—(MqC) 8-1
Miller, Leonard (not in '82)—(JbW) 2
Miller, Michael (JbW) 7 — (JbW) 4-1
Miller, Michael (AJ) 6 — (AJ) 7-1-3
Miller, Michael (not in '82)—(JhW) 10
Miller, Phillip (MC) 8 — (gone, '84)
Miller, Thomas (JbW) 5 — (gone, '84)
Miller, William (not in '82)—(ST) 4-1-0
Millslagle, And. (LA) 7 — (EP) 6-1-2
Millslagle, George (LA) 3 — (EP) 3-1-0
Mitchar, Nicholas (MS) 9 — (MS) 11-1
Mitchell, David (DM) 1-6sl—(DM) 1-1-4
Mitchell, John (MS) 4 — (gone, '84)
Mitts, Adam (not in '82) — (MS) 3-1-1
 (Mills)
Moak, Henry (AR) 3 — (AR) 5-1-1
Monks, John (AH) 4 — (gone, '84)
Money, Bryan (see Moonie)—(SR) 4-1-2
Monroe, Alex (LA) 2 — (gone, '84)
Moonie, Bryan (LA) 4 — (see Money)
Moor(e), Anthony (MS) 9 —(MS) 8-1-1
Moor(e), Conrad —(AH) 5-1-3
Moor(e), James (LA) 12 — (SR) 13-1-4
Moor, John (WV) 6 — (WV) 5-1
Moor, Joseph (not in '82) — ST) 5-1
Morehead, George (LA) 5 — (gone, '84)
Morgan, Jonathan (DM) 5—(DM) 4-1-2
Morgan, John (DM) 9 — (DM) 10-1-1

Morgan, Thomas (DM) 8 — (DM) 6-1-2
Morgan, William ST) 7 — (EP) 7-0-1
Morris, John (not in '82) — (JbW) 7-1-1
Morrow, James (MS) 7 — (MS) 7-1-3
Morrow, Ralph (JhW) 2 — (JhW) 2-1-1
Moses, Adam (JhW) 7 — (JhW) 11-1-3
Mouse, Dan (not in '82) — (JbW) 9-1-1
 (Muse)
Murphy, Hugh (WB) 4 — (gone, '84)
Murphy, Gabriel (not in '82)—(MqC) 2-1
Murph(e)y, James (MC) 6-2sl
 — (MC) 9-1-3
Murphy, Wm. (AH) 8-1sl —(EP) 5-0-2
Murphy, Wm. (MC) 4 — (OJ) 4-1
Muse, George (MC) 3 — (gone, '82)
Myers, Francis (WV) 8 — (WV) 10
Myers, Frances (MC) 4 — see Miers)
Myers, John (see Miers) — (WV) 2
Myers, Geo. (see Miars) — (EP) 8-0-2

— N —

Naaf—(see Nave, Neff, Neiff)
Naaf, Geo. (MS) 6-1sl — (MS) 5-1-4
Naaff, Henry (MS) 6 — (MS) 7-1-2
Naaff, Michael (MS) 8 — (MS) 8-1-1
 (Nave)
Nailor, William (SR) 6 — (gone, '84)
Nave, Henry (AJ) 10 —(see Neiff)
Neal, Edw. (see O'Neal) — (AH) 4-1-3
Neel, Benj. (see O'Neal) — (SR) 5-1
Neel, Jacob (WV) 8 — (gone, '84)
Neale, Thos. (not in '82) — (AH) 4-1-3
Neale, William (ST) 4 — (gone, '84)
Nees, John M. (see McNees) (SR) 6-1-7
Neil, John (AH) 7 — (AH) 8-1-1
 (Neale)
Neiff, Henry (see Nave) — (AJ) 10-1-2
Nevill, Joseph (AH) 2-9sl — (gone, '84)
Nevill, Joseph, Jr. (AH) 13-7sl
 (for '84 see Newell)
New, Peter (AJ) 7 — (WV) 7-1-3
Newcomb, Dan (ST) 8 — (EP) 9
Newell, John (not in '82) — (ST) 3-1
Newell, Joseph (OJ) 1 — (gone in '84)
Newell, Joseph, "gent." —(AH) 19-1-4
 (for '82 see Nevill)
Newman, David (ST) 4 — (ST) 4-1
Newman, George (ST) 11 — (ST) 12-1
Newman, Isaac (ST) 4 — (ST) 4-1
Newman, John (ST) 2 — (ST) 3-1-1
Newman, John (not in '82) — (ST) 8-1-1
Newman, Solomon (not in '82) — (ST) 8
Nixon, George (LA) 3-2 — (EP) 3-2-2
Nixon, Marey (LA) 5 — (gone, '84)
Noel, Peter (AJ) 5 — (gone, '84)
Norman, Benj. (WB) 2 — (MqC) 4-1
Norman, George (ST) 4 — (ST) 4-1-2
Norman, John (WB) 9 — (gone, '84)
Norman, Sarah (not in '82) —(MqC) 9-2
Norman, William (JbW) 6 — (gone, 84)
Noteman, Jane (not in '82) — (ST) 4-1
Notman, James (ST) 6 — (gone, '84)
Nut, John (WV) 4 —(gone in '84)

— O —

Obannion, Joseph (AH) 2 — (AH) 6-1-8
O'Bryan, Tallent (WB) 5 —(see Bryan)
O'Conner, Dan (not in '83)—(AH) 7-1-1
Oddle, William (WV) 11—(gone, '84)

O'Haver, Cornelius (LA) 2 — (SR) 4-1
O'Haver, Christopher (LA) 9—(SR) 4-1-1
Ogin, Peter (not in '82) — (EP) 9-0-2
Oldacre, Isaac (SR) 6 — (SR) 7-1-2
Oldacre, Isaac (LA) 5 — (gone, '84)
O'Neal, Benj. (SR) 5 — (see Neal)
O'Neal, Edw. (AH) 11 — (AH) 12-1-1
Orahood, Alex (not in '82)—(JbW) 9-1
Orr, James (not in '82) — (AR) 6-1
Orton, Robert (LA) 10) — (SR) 11-1-3
Osmun, Sam (see Ozmund)—(DM) 3-1-4
Ours, Stithman (JhW) 4 —(JhW) 5-1-7
Outs, George (not in '82) — (AJ) 4-1
Ozburn, George (SR) 10 — (gone, '84)
Ozburn, Isaac (SR) 4 — (gone, '84)
Ozburn, Jeremiah (MS) 10 —(MS) 7-1-4
Ozburn, Josiah (SR) 4
Ozmund, Isaac (DM) 4 —(see Osman)
Ozmund, Jabez (DM) 10—(see Osman)
Ozmund, Sam (DM) 3—(see Osman)

— P —

Pain, Evan (see Payne) — (AH) 3-1
Painter, Benj. (WV) 6 — (WV) 7-1-1
Pancake, And. (AH) 10 — (AH) 8-1-3
Pancake, Catherine (AR) 3-1-1
  (not in '82)
Pancake, John (not in '82)—(AH) 3-1-1
Pancake, John (ST) 8 — (ST) 9-1-2
Pancake, Joseph (AR) 4 — (gone, '84)
Parell—see Parill, Perrill
Parell, John (LA) 8 — (EP) 9-1-2
Parish, Joseph (not in '82) — (EP) 8-0-3
Park(e)(s), Andrew (LA) 5—(EP) 4-1-4
Park(e)s, Job (WB) 7 — (see Parker)
Park(e)(s), John (not in '82)—(EP) 3-1
Park(e)(s), John (LA) 11—(EP) 12-1-7
Park(e)s, Samuel (LA) 6—(EP) 6-1-0
Parker, Benj. (AJ) 7 — (gone, '84)
Parker, Benj. (AJ) 6 — (AJ) 5-1-2
Parker, George (AJ) 6 —(gone, '84)
Parker, James (AJ) 3 — (AJ) 3-2
Parker, Job (see Parke)—(MqC) 6-1-2
Parker, John (WV) 4 — (WV) 3-1-4
Parker, Nathaniel, Sr. (OJ) 3-3sl
  — (gone, '84)
Parker, Nathaniel (AJ) 10-5sl
  — (AJ) 10-1-6
Parker, Robert (ST) 7-10sl —(ST) 7-1-9
Parsons, Alex (not in '82) — (SR) 8-5-1
Parsons, Isaac (WB) 4-6sl—(MqC) 4-1-3
Parsons, James (AH) 8-13sl—(AH) 8-1-6
Parker, Thos. (AR) 11-7—(AR) 10-1-2
Paugh, John (AJ) 7 — (gone, '84)
Payne—(see Pain)
Payne, David (SR) 4 — (gone, '84)
Payne, John (SR) 6 — (gone, '84)
Pearsall—(see Piersell, Purceal)
Pearsall, John (see Piersall)—(AJ) 4-1-3
Pearrson, David (not in '82)—(EP) 3-0-1
Peck, George (not in '82) — (JbW) 6-1-1
Pendleton, John (JhW) 5 — (gone, '84)
Pendleton, Richard (not in '82)—(JhW) 6
Pepper, Joshua, Sr. — (SR) 5-1-1
  (not in '82)
Pepper, Joshua Jr. (not in '82)—(SR) 5-1
  (not in '82)
Perrell, John (LA) 8 — (see Parill)
Perrin, Thomas (DM) 9 — (JhW 6

Person, Alex (LA) 4 — (gone, '84)
Peters, John (not in '82) — (EP) 7-1-0
Peterson, Jacob, Sr. (JhW) 6—see below
Peterson, Jacob, Sr. (JhW) 8—see below
Peterson, Jacob (not in '82)—(JhW) 8-1-2
Peterson, Margaret — (JhW) 5-1-1
  (not in '82)
Peterson, Martin (JhW) 8—(JhW) 8-1-2
Peterson, Michael (JhW) 6—(JbW) 7-1-1
Peterson, Peter (ST) 5 — (MqC) 6-1-3
Petro, Leonard (JhW) 5—(JhW) 5-1
Petty, Joseph (AR) 13 — (AR) 9-1-4
Pickle, Jacob (JhW) 9 — (gone, '84)
Pierse—see Pearce, Pierce
Pierse, Benj. (MC) 3 — (gone, '84)
Pierce, Dan (MC) 2 — (gone, '84)
Piersall, John (AJ) 3-5sl—(see Pearsall)
Pigman, Moses (AJ) 7 — (WV) 7-1-2
Pillman, Peter (not in '82)—(AJ) 11-1-1
Plank, Fredrick (not in '82)—(MC) 8-1
Plough, Jacob (WB) 5 — (MqC) 7-1
Plow, Alder(t) (WB) 8—(MqC) 9-1-1
  (Plough)
Plumb, John (WV) 6 — (gone, '84)
Poague, Robert (JhW) 2—(JhW) 4-1-2
Popejoy, Terrance — (MqC) 5-1
  (not in '82)
Popejoy, John (WV) 2 — (MqC) 4-1
Porter, Eli (not in '82)—(EP) 4-0-2
Porter, Elias (ST) 4 — (gone, '84)
Porter, Phil (not in '82) — (EP) 9-0-2
Porter, Robert (JhW) 5 — (JhW) 6-1-4
Porter, William (ST) 8 — (gone, '84)
Posgrove —(EP) 6-0-1
  (for '82 see Cosgrove)
Post, Valentine (JhW) 6 — (gone, '84)
Posten, Elias (LA) 5-3sl — (EP) 7-1-3
Powell, Abraham (LA) 4 — (EP) 5-0-4
Powell, Caleb (AR) 7 — (gone, '84)
Powell, Caleb (JbW) 8 — (gone, '82)
Powell, Sam (LA) 1 — (SR) 2-1-1
Powell, William (AJ) 8 — (gone, '84)
Power(s), Martin (JhW) 9—(JhW) 9-2-2
Power(s), Valentine —(JbW) 10-1-3
  (not in '82)
Price, Arjalon (AJ) 8-6sl — (AJ) 9-2-2
Price, Lewellen (not in '82) — (ST) 1
Price, William (WB) 7 — (gone, '84)
Pritcherd, Margaret — (EP) 2-0-2
  (not in '82)
Pritchard, Reese (LA) 7 — (EP) 7-1-5
Pritchard, Reese (ST) 4 — (gone, '84)
Prunty, John (LA) 8-2sl — (EP) 6-1-5
Pugh, Bethuel (LA) 8 — (EP) 9-0-2
Pugh, Dan (not in '82) — (EP) 2-1-1
Pugh, Jacob (LA) 9 — (gone, '84)
Pugh, Jesse (not in '82) — (EP) 2
Pugh, Jonathan (LA) 11-2sl—(EP) 9-1-3
Pugh, Robert (LA) 11 — (EP) 9-1-4
Pugh, Samuel (LA) 3 — (EP) 4-0-3
Pugh, Thomas (LA) 6 — (EP) 5-0-1
Purgit, Henry (not in '82)—(MqC) 3-1-1
Purcell, Edw. (VW) 5 — (gone, '84)
Purcell, Jonathan (VW) 6 — (gone, '84)
Purcell, William (VW) 6 — (gone, '84)
Putman, Peter (AJ) 12 —(gone in '84)

— Q —

Quehan, Paul (SR) 3 — (gone, '84)

Queen, Charles (AJ) 7 —(gone in '84)

— R —

Radcliff, Benj. (AH) 5 — (AH) 6-1-2
Radcliff, Richard (JbW) 7 — (AR) 8-1
Radcliff, Stephen — (JbW) 7-1-1
  (not in '82)
Randell, Abel (AR) 10 — (AR) 11-1-3
Rannels, John (ST) 4 — (ST) 6-1
Rannels, Jeremiah (OJ) 5 — (gone, '84)
Rannels, William (ST) 6-4sl—(ST) 6-1-6
Rasner, Gideon (not in '82)—(AJ) 3-1
Ravenscraft, John (WV) 7—(WV) 6-1-2
Ravenscraft, Samuel — (WV) 8-1-1
  (not in '82)
Ravenscraft, William — (WV) 2-1-0
  (not in '82)
Rawl(e)s, John (WV) 7 — (WV) 5-1-1
Ray, Joseph (OJ) 3 — (see Roy)
Read, Mrs. (MC) 2 —(see Reed, Reid)
Reasoner, Jacob (AJ) 9-1sl—(AJ) 10-1-3
Reasoner, Garrett (AJ) 2-2sl—(gone '84)
Reaves, Austin (not in '82)—(MC) 4-1-1
  (Reeve(s)
Reaves, Benj. (MC) 15 — (MC) 9-1-3
Reaves, Richard (DM) 5 — (DM) 6-1-1
Rector, Charles (MC) 2 — (gone, '84)
Rector, Dan (MC) 9 — (gone, '84)
Redman, William (AJ) 4 — (gone, '84)
Redsleeves, Jacob (SR) 3 —(gone, '84)
Reed, Eliz. (not in '82) — (AH) 4-1-2
Reed„ George (LA) 4 — (AH) 6-1-2
Reed, John (not in '82) — (AH) 7-1-2
Regar, Anthony (MS) 1 — (JhW) 10-2-1
Regar, Jacob (MS) 11 — (JbW) 10-1-1
Regar, John (MS) 4 — (MS) 5-1-1
Reel, David (JhW) 7 — (JbW) 7-1
Reel, David (not in '82) — (MS) 4-1
Reel, Nicholas (MS) 5 — (MS) 6
Reid, George (see Read) — (EP) 8-1-2
Reid, James (WV) 3 — (gone, '84)
Reid, Jeremiah (LA) 8 — (EP) 9-0-3
Reilly, Patrick (OJ) 3 — (gone, '84)
Rending, Reuben (not in '82)—(WV) 3-1
Rennick, Eliz. (AH) 5 — (AH) 5-1-2
  (Rennock?)
Rennick, John (AH) 10 — (AH) 10-1-5
Rennick, Wm. (AH) 12-1sl—(AH) 11-1-8
Revnals, William (LA) 4 — (gone, '84)
Rhodes, Henry (see Roads)—(MS) 6-1
Rhodes, John (MC) 2 — (gone, '84)
Rhodes, Thomas (MC) 5 — (MC) 5-1-1
Richards, Isaac (DM) 6 — (MC) 5-0-1
Richards, Wm. (not in '82)—(EP) 5-0-1
Richardson, Dan (AR) 6-1sl—(AR) 6-1-1
Richardson, Richard (LA) 6—(gone, '84)
Richardson, Jonathan (JbW) 7
  — (JbW) 7-1
Richardson, Joseph (JbW) 5—(gone '84)
Richison, Wm. (not in '82)—(SR) 6-1-1
Riding, Joseph (AJ) 8 — (gone, '84)
Risley, Dan (DM) 5 — (gone, '84)
Ritchards, John —(EP) 10-5-1
  (Pritchards?)
Roads, Henry (MS) 5 — (see Rhodes)
Roberts, David, Sr. (SR) 7—(gone, '84)
Roberts, David, Jr. — (SR) 4-1-3
  (not in '82)
Roberts, Thomas (SR) 4 —(SR) 5-1-2
Robinson, Joel (SR) 9 — (SR) 9-1-3

Robinson, John (not in '82)—(DM) 2-1-0
Robinson, John (not in '82)—(JbW) 7-1-3
Robinson, Roger (WV) 4 — (WV) 5-1
Roby, Benj. (WB) 4 — (gone, '84)
Roby, David, Sr. (not in '82) — (SR) 6-1-2
Roby, Peter (AH) 9 — (AH) 9-1-4
Roby, Prior (not in '82) — (JbW) 8-1-1
Roby, Thomas (WB) 8 — (JbW) 8-1-1
Roby, William (not in '82) — (SR) 4-1
Roby, William (not in '82)—(JbW) 3-1-1
Rodebaugh, Adam (MS) 9
  (for '84 see Rudybaugh)
Rodebaugh, Henry (JhW) 8
  (for '84 see Rorebaugh)
Rodgers, William (AJ) 10 —(AJ) 11-1-2
Rorebaugh, Henry — (JhW) 10-1-1
  (for '82 see Rodebaugh)
Rorebaugh, John (MS) 11 —(MS) 11-1-2
Rose, Jacob (DM) 4 — (gone, '84)
Rose, John (LA) 5 — (see Ross)
Rosencrantz, Henry (JhW) 4—(gone '84)
Ross, John (not in '82) — (ST) 9-1
Ross, John (see Rose) — (DM) 5-1-2
Ross, Lawrence (AJ) 10-12sl—(gone '84)
Ross, Robert, Sr. (ST) 4 — (gone, '84)
Ross, Robert (ST) 8 — (MC) 9-1
Ross, Stephen (VW) 9 — (gone, '84)
Rousevell, Benj. (SR) 6 — (SR) 6-1-4
Row, William (MS) 5 — (MS) 6-1
Roy, Abraham (MC) 3-2sl —(MC) 3-1-1
  (see Ray)
Roy, James (MC) 6-3sl — (see Ray)
Roy, Joseph (see Ray) — (JbW) 10-1-1
Roy, Thomas (MS) 5 — (MC) 6-1-2
Royce, Aaron (not in '82) — (WV) 7-1
  (Royse)
Royce, John (not in '82) —(EP) 2-1-2
Ruddle, Stephen (SR) 6 — (SR) 12-1-4
Ruder, Joseph (not in '84) — (EP) 9-0-1
Rudybaugh, Adam — (MS) 8-1-3
  for '82 see Rodebaugh)
Rule, Henry (not in '82) — (JhW) 6-1
Rule, Henry, Sr. (JhW) 11—(gone, '84)
Rule, Henry, Jr. (JhW) 5 — (gone, '84)
Rush, Lewis (not in '82)—(WV) 5-1
Rust, Jacob (not in '82) — (SR) 3-1-1
Ryan, James (VW) 12 — (gone, '84)
Ryan, John (VW) 8 — (gone, '84)

— S —

Sadowski, Jacob (AR) 4 — (gone, '84)
Sadowski, Sam (not in '82) — (JbW) 9-1-1
Sage, William (VW) 13 — (AH) 11-1-1
Salts, Thomas (LA) 3 — (SR) 3-1-1
Sanders, Chas. (not in '82)—(MqC) 4-1-2
Sanders, Henry (not in '82) — (EP) 8-1-3
Saturly, Samuel (not in '82)—(AH) 7-1
Savage, John (WV) 7 — (WV) 6-1-1
Schreid, Charity (LA) 4 —(EP) 4-0-1
  (Schraid)
Schoonover, Benj (JhW) 5—(JbW) 8-1-1
Scoals, John (DM) 6 — (gone, '84)
Scott, Alex. (JbW) 3 — (JbW) 6-1-1
Scott, Benj. (JbW) 6-1sl—(gone, '84)
Scott, Benj. Sr. (not in '82)—(JbW) 7-1-2
Scott, Benj. Jr. (not in '82)—(JbW) 7-1-1
Scott, James (WB) 8 — (gone, '84)
Scott, John (MC) 7—(MC) 9-1-1 (Scoot)
Scott, Joseph (MS) 1 — (MS) 5-1
Sea—see See, Lee, Lea

Sea, George (MS) 8-3sl—(see See)
Sea, Michael (AR) 9-1sl — (AR) 9-1-2
Sears, James (MS) 3 — (gone, '84)
Sears, John (MS) 8 — (MS) 9-1-2
Sears, Sarah (not in '82) — (MS) 1-1
Sears, William (MS) 10 — (MS) 10-1-1
Seavers, Nicholas (WV) 2—(WV) 8-1-4
Seavers, Nicholas, Jr. (WV) 4
  — (gone, '84)
Sellars, Fredrick (not in '82)—(AR) 4-1-2
Sellars, John (MS) 5 — (MS) 5-1-0
Seymour, Abel (not in '82)—(JbW) 1-0-2
Seymour, Felix (not in '82)—(JbW) 9-1-4
Seymour, Geo. (not in '82)—(JbW) 1-0-2
Seymour, Richard — (JbW) 3-1-2
  (not in '82)
Seymour, Thos. (not in '82)—(JbW) 4-1-1
Shadd, George (AR) 7 — (gone, '84)
Shadd, George (MS) 9 — (gone, '84)
Shade, George (not in '82) —(EP) 3-2
Shanklin, Richard (AR) 4 — (gone, '84)
Shanklin, Robert (AR) 5 — (gone, '84)
Shanks, Joseph (not in '82) —(EP) 5-0-2
Shannon, Hugh (LA) 4 — (gone, '84)
Shannon, Ruth (not in '82) —(EP) 4-0-2
Shanton, Raymond — (WV) 4-1-1
  (not in '82)
Shares, Michael (AH) 4 — (gone, '84)
Sharp, Andrew (LA) 3 — (gone, '84)
Sharpless, Joseph (not in '82)—(WV) 6-1
Shepard, James (not in '82) —(AH) 3-1
Shepard, John (AH) 10 — (AH) 9-1-2
Sheplar, Henry (MS) 5 — (MS) 6-1
Shevelear, Anthony (JbW) 5—(gone '84)
Shields, Peter (not in '82) —(JhW) 4-1
Shill, George (not in '82)—(JbW) 3-1
Shinear, George (MS) 8 — (gone, '84)
Shipley, Richard (AH) 4 — (AR) 3-1
Shobe, Jacob (JhW) 8—(JhW) 6-1-2
Shobe, Martin (JhW) 6 — (JhW) 8-1-3
Shobe, Rudolph (JhW) 3 — (JhW) 8-1-3
Shobe, Ridely (JhW) 6 —(gone in '84)
Shobe, Rudy (not in '82) — (JhW) 4-1-2
Shoemaker, Peter (LA) 4 — (SR) 5-1-2
Sholder, Conrad (not in '82)—(MC) 8-1
Shook, David (not in '82) — (MS) 3-1
Shook, Harman (MS) 6 — (MS) 3-1-3
  (Harman, Sr., in '84)
Shook, Harman Jr. (not in '82)—(MS) 3-1
Shook, Jacob (JbW) 3 — (gone, '84)
Shook, John (MS) 3 — (MS) 4-1-1
Shook, Jonas (not in '82) — (MS) 6-1-1
Shook, Laurence (JbW) 8— (JbW) 8-1-3
Shock, Peter (MS) 7 — (MS) 7-1
Shook, William (MS) 12 — (MS) 13-1
Shorebaugh, David (not in '82) —(SR) 2
Short, Isaac (ST) 10 — (gone, '84)
Short, Jacob (ST) 2 — (ST) 3-1
Shrodes, John (not in '82) —(MC) 3-1
Shrote, Peter (AH) 8 — (AH) 7-1
  (Shrobe)
Shrout, Samuel (not in '82) —(ST) 3-1
Shultz, Andrew (JhW) 4 — (gone, '84)
Shumate, James (not in '82)—(AH) 8-1-1
Sibley, John (AH) 4 — (AH) 5-1-2
Simond, Christian (MS) 4 — (gone, '84)
Simon(d), George (MS) 9 — (MS) 8-1-1
Simon(d), John (not in '82) — (DM) 3-1-0

Simon(d), Leonard (MS) 3 — (MS) 4-1-0
Simon(d), Phillip — (MS) 3-1-2
  (not in '82)
Simmons, Henry —(MC) 2-1
Simpson, Alex (not in '82)—(JbW) 7-1-2
Simpson, Jonathan — (JbW) 7-1-1
  (not in '82)
Sims, John, Jr. (JhW) 2 — (gone, '84)
Sims, William (not in '82)—(JbW) 5-1
Sinks, Jacob (not in '82) — (WV) 10-1-0
Sisler, William (MC) 5 — (gone, '84)
Skidmer, Mary (not in '82) — (MC) 2-1
Sit(e)s, George (JhW) 7 —(JhW) 10-1-3
Slagle, Jacob (OJ) 8-3sl — (OJ) 10-1-1
Slater, Richard (not in '82) — (WV) 2
Sleith, Alex (JhW) 3 — (gone, '84)
Sloan, John (LA) 6—(EP) 7-0-2 (Slone)
Slone, Daniel (not in '82) —(EP) 8-1-1
Slone, James (SR) 9 — (SR) 9-1-2
Sly, David (not in '82) — (SR) 1
Sly, George (not in '82) — (EP) 7-0-2
Smalley, And. (WB) 6 — (gone, '84)
Smith, Charles (MS) 12 — (MS) 10-1-9
Smith, David (AR) 7 — (JhW) 7
Smith, David (VW) 10 — (ST) 10-1
Smith, Jacob (AR) 9 — (gone, '84)
Smith, James (LA) 9 — (EP) 8-1-4
Smith, John (AH) 2 — (WV) 6-2-4
Smith, John (not in '82) —(EP) 10-0-1
Smith, John (DM) 3 — (JhW) 4-1
Smith, Michael (MS) 3 — (MS) 3-1
Smith, Nathaniel (not in '82) —(OJ) 7-1
Smith, Richard (DM) 6 — (DM) 6-1-1
Smith, Robert (not in '82)—(JbW) 9-1-2
Smith, Thomas (LA) 7 — (gone, '84)
Smith, William (JbW) 7 — (JbW) 8-1-0
Smith, William (not in '82)—(MqC) 5-1-1
Smith, Yokle (not in '82)—(JhW) 10-1-1
Smock, Jacob (WB) 4 — (MqC) 5-1
Snall, William (AH) 2 — (AH) 4-1-2
Snyder, Christopher (AH) 8—(AH) 8-1-5
Sommett, Jacob (LA) 2 — (gone, '54)
Spealman—see Spillman
Spealman, Wm. (not in '82)—(ST) 5-1-0
Spelman, Robt. (not in '82) —(MC) 4-1-1
Spencer, John (AJ) 7 — (AJ) 8-1
Sperry, Peter (not in '82 — (SR) 3-1-2
Spilman, James (not in '82)—(ST) 4-1
Spillman, John (MS) 6 —(JhW) 7-1
Spillman, John (ST) 6 —(gone in '84)
Spillman, William (ST) 4
  (for '84 see Spealman)
Spore, John W. (MS) 10—(MS) 9-1-1
  (Spoar)
Stacey, Thomas (not in '82)—(JbW) 3-1
Stackhouse, Isaac (MS) 4—(gone, '84)
Stackhouse, Isaac (LA) 4—(gone, '84)
Stagg, John (AJ) 8 — (AJ) 5-1-4
Stallcup, John (not in '82) —(OJ) 11-1-1
Stambaugh, Phil (not in '82)—(JhW) 8-1
Starkey, Fred (LA) 6 — (EP) 6-0-2
Starr, Catherine (AR) 8 — (gone, '84)
Steed, Aaron (DM) 4 — (gone, '84)
Steel, Henry (AR) 8 — (AR) 7-1-1
Steel, John (AR) 2 — (AR) 3-1
Stephenson, James (MS) 7 —(MS) 8-1-3
Stettler, John (not in '82) —(JhW) 3-1
Stevenson, Edw. (DM) 2 — (gone, '84)
Steward, James (LA) 10 — (SR) 9-1

Steward, Joseph (not in '82) — (SR) 1
Stinglee, Jacob (JhW) 5 — (JbW) 5-1-2
Stocker, Bolser (ST) 2 — (gone, '84)
Stoddard, James (not in '82)—(MC) 5-1-1
Stoker, Basser (not in '82)—(ST) 2-1-4
Stoker, John (ST) 6 — (ST) 7-1-3
Stookey, Abraham (JhW) 6—(gone, '84)
Stookey, Magdalen (JhW) 4
    — (JhW) 10-1-3
Stotts, Abraham (AR) 6 — (gone, '84)
Strader, Christopher (JhW) 9
    — (JhW) 10-1-3
Straley, Christian (JhW) 6—(JhW) 7-1-1
Strett, John (not in '82) — (AJ) 4-1
Stritchfield, Joshua (OJ) 3—(gone, '84)
Stroud, Adam (not in '82)—(JbW) 10-1
Stump, Catherine (not in '82)—(MS) 1-1
Stump, George (MS) 8-2sl — (MS) 9-1-2
Stump, Leonard (MS) 7 — (MS) 6-1-3
Stump, Michael (MS) 7-1sl—(MS) 8-1-4
Sturman, John (VW) 6 — (gone, '84)
Suffolk, John (AH) 4 — (AH) 5-1
Sullivan, Jeremiah (MC) 4 —(MC) 6-1-1
Sutherland W. (not in '82)—(DM) 3-1
Suttles, Henry (AH) 6 — (AH) 6-1
Swank, Phillip (JhW) 5 — (gone, '84)
Swim, John (DM) 3 — (DM) 3-1
Swim, Lasler (DM) 4 —(gone in '84)
Swisher, John (LA) 8 — (EP) 11-0-1
Swisher, Nicholas (LA) 5 — (SR) 8-1-2
Swisher, Valentine (LA) 5—(EP) 10-1-4

— T —

Taaff, Elizabeth (SR) 3 — (SR) 2-1-1
Taaff, James (SR) 1-1sl — (gone, '84)
Talbott, Thomas (AH) 5 — (AH) 6-1
Tarvin, Geo. (see Tervin)—(DM) 11-2-3
Tarpley, James (MC) 4 — (MC) 3-1-2
Taylor, George (AJ) 4 — (AJ) 5-1-1
Taylor, John (AJ) 1 — (ST) 3-1-4
Taylor, Libbey (not in '82—(ST) 6-1-2
Taylor, Marg. (ST) 9 — (gone, '84)
Taylor, Richard (ST) 2 — (gone, '84)
Taylor, Robert (WB) 8 — (gone, '84)
Taylor, Simon (MC) 5 — (gone, '84)
Taylor, Simon (ST) 6-21sl—(ST) 5-1-10
Taylor, Tarpley (ST) 6 — (gone, '84)
Terry, Geo. Sr. (VW) 3 — (gone, '84)
Terry, Geo. Jr. (VW) 5 — (gone, '84)
Tervin, George (DM) 10 — (see Tarvin)
Tevault, Andrew (LA) 1 — (SR) 9-1-1
Tevault, John, Sr.   — (SR) 10-1-2
(not in '82)
Tevault, John (not in '82) —(SR) 8-1-3
Tevault, Nicholas (WV) 6 —(WV) 9-1-3
(see Tivault)
Thickstone, Thos. (JbW) 8—(see below)
Thixton, Thos. (see above)—(JbW) 7-1-1
Thomas, David (SR) 2 — (gone, '84)
Thomas, Enoch David (AH) 8
    — (AH) 9-1-2
Thomas, Ezekial (LA) 10 — (gone '84)
Thomas, James (SR) 8 — (SR) 7-1-3
Thomas, Morris (AR) 10 — (AR) 9-1-1
Thompson, David (AJ) 5 — (AJ) 5-1-1
Thompson, Frances (AJ) 1 —(AJ) 2-1-1
Thompson, Jeremiah   —(DM) 5-1-1
(not in '82)   (Thomson)

Thompson, John (AJ) 6 — (AJ) 7-1-1
Thomson, Jethro (not in '82)—(JbW) 8-1
Thomson, John (AJ) 6 — (AJ) 7-1-1
Thomson, Joseph (LA) 4 — (gone, '84)
Thomson, Sam (AJ) 4 — (gone, '84)
Thomson, Wm. (not in '82) — (EP) 2-1-1
Thomson, Wm. Sr. (LA) 2—(gone, '84)
Thomson, Wm. Jr. (LA) 8—(gone, '84)
Thorn, Fred (not in '82) — (JhW) 7-1
Thorn, Peter (AH) 3 — (gone, '84)
Thorn, Valentine (JhW) 7 — (gone, '84)
Thorp, William (not in '82) —(SR) 4-1-1
Throgmorton, Lewis (DM) 10
    — (DM) 10-1-1
Thursby, Hannah (AR) 6 — (gone, '84)
Timmons, John (AJ) 7 — (gone, '85)
Timmons, Sam (AR) 10 — (AH) 11-1-3
Titzord, Isaac (AJ) 3 — (gone, '84)
Tilford, Isaac (not in '82) — (AJ) 3-1
Tivault, John (LA) 11 — (gone, '84)
(see Tevault)
Tivebaugh, Dan (MS) 8-2sl
    — (MS) 8-1-2
Toopes, John (not in '82)—(JhW) 7-1-1
Toselwright, William   — (MC) 5-1-1
(not in '82)
Totten, Ezekiel (AJ) 9 — (AJ) 9-1-1
Trace, Jacob (MS) 7 — (see Traise)
Tracy, Archibald (not in '82)—(EP) 2-1-1
Traise, Jacob (see Trace)—(MS) 8-1-1
Trouten, Richard (ST) 3 — (gone, '84)
Trumbo, Andrew (MS) 8 — (MS) 9-1-1
Trumbo, George (MS) 7-1sl—(MS) 8-1-3
Tucker, Jacob (AH) 11 — (AH) 11-1-3
Tucker, William (VW) 8 —(gone, '84)
Turner, Solomon (not in '82)—(JhW) 3
Tweey, Dan (not in '82)—(AH) 6-1-1
Tweey, John (not in '82)—(AH) 2-1-0
Twilley, William (MC) 5 — (gone, '84)
Tygart, Frances (not in '82)—(ST) 3-1-2

— U —

Umstott, Peter (AJ) 7 — (AJ) 8-1-2

— V —

Vancehock, John (not in '82)—(MqC) 5
Vandevander, Peter (not in '82)—(SR) 3
Vandeventer, Jacob (SR) 7 —(SR) 8-1-2
(see Vantiventer)
Vandivear, John (AJ) 2 — (gone, '84)
Vandiver, Wm. (AJ) 12-5sl—(AJ) 14-1-4
Vandivere, George (OJ) 7 — (gone, '84)
Vanmeter, Abr. (VW) 4-3sl—(gone, '84)
Vanmeter, Garrett (AH) 8-16sl
    — (AH) 7-1
Vanmeter, Isaac (WB) 9-4sl
    — (MqC) 7-1-4
Vanmeter, Isaac (not in '82) —(AH) 5-1-4
Vanmeter, Istac (not in '82) —(AH) 4-1-3
Vanmeter, Jacob (AH) 8-1sl—(AH) 7-1-3
Vanmeter, Joseph (AH) 6-10sl
    — (AH) 9-1-7
Vantiventer, Janely (SR) 7-3sl
    —(gone, '84)
Vause, Wm. (WV) 10-1sl—(WV) 11-1-6
Vestfall—see Westfall.
Vincent, John (OJ) 4 — (gone, '84)
Viney, Stephen (not in '82) —(SR) 3-1-2
Viney, Susannah (SR) 4 — (gone, '84)

— W —

Wagonner, John (AH) 4—(gone, '84)
Walker, James (MC) 5 — (gone, '84)
Walker, John (MC) 7 — (gone, '84)
Walker, Robert (MC) 8 — (MC) 9-1-3
Walker, Thomas (MC) 8 — (gone, '84)
Ward, George (not in '82) — (JbW) 3-1
Ward, Joseph (not in '82)—(AH) 6-1
Ward, Israel (AR) 2 — (gone, '84)
Ward, Stephen (MC) 8 — (MC) 8-1
Ward, Sylvester (not in '82)—(MC) 8-1
Warden, William (SR) 7 — (SR) 5-1-3
Waterman, James (WV) 11—(WV) 7-1-2
Waterman, John (not in '82)—(WV) 2
Watters, John (WB) 8 — (MqC) 10-1
    (Waters)
Watts, Jonathan (JbW) 4 — (JbW) 5-1
Watts, Thomas (MS) 6 — (JbW) 6-1
Wayler, Micheal (not in '82)—(AJ) 3-1-2
Weatherington, John   — (DM) 8-1-2
(for '82 see Worthington)
Weaver, George — (AR) 5 — (AR) 6-1
Weaze, Adam, Sr. (JhW) 13
    — (JhW) 14-1-2
Weaze, Adam, Jr. (JhW) 15—(JhW) 6-1
Weaze, Jacob (JhW) 5 — (JhW) 7-1-2
Weaze, John (JhW) 6 — (JhW) 6-1-1
Weaze, Michael (not in '82)—(JhW) 2
Weaze, Michael (JhW) 2—(JhW) 3-1
Weidener, Jacob (AH) 5 — (AH) 6-1-1
Weitmiller, John   —(MS) 4-1-5
(for '82 see Wertmiller)
Wells, Phineas (AR) 6 — (gone, '84)
Welton, David (AR) 7-3sl—(AR) 8-1-2
Welton, Jesse (not in '82) — (JbW) 9-1-2
Welton, Job (JbW) 10-6sl—(JbW) 11-1-5
Wertmiller, Jacob (MS) 6
(for '84 see Weitmiller)
Westfall, Daniel (JhW) 11—(gone, '84)
Westfall, Cornelius (AR) 2—(gone, '84)
Westfall, Eleanor (AR) 2—(gone, '84)
Westfafll, Henry (AR) 8 — (AR) 7-1
Westfall, Isaac (AR) 2 — (AR) 4-1
Westfall, Jacob (AR) 6 — (AR) 7-1-2
Westfall, John, Sr. (AR) 8-2sl
    — (AR) 14-1-3
Westfall, John Jr. (AR) 7—(gone '84)
Wheeler, Ignatius   — (WV) 9-2-4
(not in '82)
Whetstone, George (JhW) 7—(JhW) 8-1
White, Charles (AH) 3 — (AH) 4-1
White, Ebenezer (JhW) 7—(JbW) 8-1
Whitecotton, James (JhW) 9—(JhW) 9-2
Whitman, Geo. (not in '82)—(JbW) 7-1-2
Whitman, John (WV) 3 — (gone, '84)
Wickham, Matthew (LA) 6—(OJ) 5-1
Wilkins, George (SR) 6 — (SR) 6-1-2
Wilkins, Matthias (SR) 9 — (SR) 11-1-5
Williams, Ebenezer (OJ) 2 — (gone, '84)
Williams, Edw. (VW) 4 — (gone, '84)
Williams, Geo. (not in '82)—(OJ) 8-1-2
Williams, James (WV) 7 — (gone, '84)
Williams, Moses (not in '82) — (AJ) 3
Williams, Nathaniel   — (MqC) 6-1
(not in '82)
William, Rememberance (ST) 2
    — (gone, '84)
Williams, Richard, Sr. (ST) 10
    — (gone, '84)

Williams, Richard (WB) 9 — (MqC) 10-1-6
Williams, Thos (not in '82)—(EP) 5-0-1
Williams, Thos. (LA) 5 — (SR) 2
Williams, Thos. (DM) 9 — (DM) 9-1-4
Williams, Vincent (VW) 10-2sl — (gone, '84)
Williams, Wm. (DM 12 — (DM) 9-1-2
Williamson, John (ST) 3 — (gone, '84)
Williamson, Sam (ST) 9 — (MqC) 9-1
Williamson, Thos. (ST) 2 — (ST) 3-1
Williamson, Wm. (ST 10—(EP) 10-1-3
Willowby, Benj. (MS) 10 — (gone, '84)
Wilson, Charles (MS) 5 — (MS) 7-1-1
Wilson, David (MS) 7 — (gone, '84)
Wilson, David (SR) 4 — (SR) 5-1-4
Wilson, Henry (not in '82) — (SR) 8-1-1
Wilson, John (JhW) 9-9sl—(JhW) 8-5-3
Wilson, John (MS) 2 — (gone, '84)
Wilson, John (SR) 5 — (gone, '84)
Wilson, Mary (not in '82) — (OJ) 5-2
Wilson, Robert (MC) 4 — (gone, '84)
Wilson, Wm. (not in '82) — (SR) 6-1-4

Wilson, Wm. Sr. (LA) 6-3sl—(gone, '84)
Wilson, Wm. Jr. (LA) 3 — (gone, '84)
Winterton, John (not in '82)—(EP) 8-1-1
Wiggins, Archibald (DM) 11 — (DM) 10-1-5
Wiggins, Phillip (ST) 2 — (gone, '84)
Wiggins, Phillip (DM) 11—(DM) 11-1-3
Wirey, Robert (not in '82)—JhW) 5-1
Wise, Adam (AJ) 6 — (AJ) 6-1-3
Wise, Bastian (not in '82)—(JhW) 2-1
Wise, Christopher (SR) 10 —(SR) 9-1-3
Wise, Jacob (JhW) 5 — (JhW) 6-1-2
Wise, John Sr. (JhW) 8—(JhW) 8-1-4
Wise, John Jr. (JhW) 5 — (JhW) 5-1
Wise, Martin (not in '82 — (JhW) 2-1
Wodrow, And. (not in '82) —(AR) 3-1-3
Wolf, David (not in'82) — (AJ) 2-1
Wolf, George (AJ) 8 — (AJ) 8-1-1
Wolf, John (JhW) 8 — (JbW) 9-1
Wood, Bethia (LA) 3 — (gone, '84)
Wood, Ebenezer (AH) 3 — (AH) 5-1-1
Wood, Joseph (JhW) 3 — (gone, '84)
Wood, Peter (not in '82) — (MS) 5-1

Wood, Richard (VW) 4 — (gone, '84)
Wood, Thomas (not in '82)—(MqC) 6-1
Worley, Michael (AR) 6 — (gone, '54)
Worthington, John (DM) 8
  (for '84 see Weatherington)
Wright, Gabriel (AJ) 8 — (AJ) 9-1-1
Wycoff, Jeter (not in '82) — (ST) 7-1-2

— X Y Z —

Y(e)azle, Jacob (JhW) 3 — (SR) 4-1
Yeater, Peter (WB) 6 — (gone, '84)
Yoakim, Eliz. (not in '82) —(AH) 5-1-2
Yoakim, George (MS) 4 — (gone, '84)
Yoakim, Jacob (AR) 6-2sl—(AR) 9-1-1
Yoakim, John (AR) 4 — (AR) 6-1-1
Yoakim, Michael (AH) 3 — (AH) 4-1
Yoakum, Phil Paul (AR) 6-1sl — AR) 1-1-3
Young, Henry (not in '82) — (MC) 4-1
Young, John (LA) 3 — (SR) 4-1
Young, William (MC) 12 — (gone, '84)
Zane, Joseph — (JbW) 7-1
  (see Bane or Jane)

PENSIONERS IN HAMPSHIRE COUNTY — 1835

—o—O—o—

Henry Brinker, 73 (lieutenant).
John Brown, 72 (sergeant).
William Berry, 90.
John Cundiff, 75.
Henry Cump, 77.
Sam B. Davis, 77.
Spencer Davis, 73 (Pennsylvania state trooper.
William Herin, 72.
John Hinkens, 84.
John Harrisburg, 72.
Christian Haas, 78.
William Hook, 75.
Siras Hamrick, 81.

Isaac James, 72.
George Little, 79.
John Malick, 72 (New Jersey).
John Peters, 80.
James Parker, 74.
Henry Purgett, 81.
Henry Powelson, 76.
John Queen, 79 (South Carolina).
John Rosenborough, 90 (Pennsylvania).
Asa Simmons, 75.
Daniel Taylor, 76.
Thomas Taylor, 74.
William Vandever, 72.

Marriage Bonds
1824 to 1828

—o—O—o—

This is the only marriage bond book that has been preserved. Indexed here for both male and female—complete record after male only. Where consent (con) was given and witnesses' (wit.) names, these are entered. Abbreviations: apm. means age of male vouched for; apf. means age of female vouched for; apb. means age of both vouched for. Bd., bondsman; con., consent; wit., witness or witnesses.

—o—O—o—

—A—

ABERNATHY, Elizabeth, to Phillip Good.
ABERNATHY, William, to Elizabeth D. W. Stump, dau John. Smith T. Price, bd. 1-8-1825.
ALLEN, James, to Sarah Hiett, dau John, bd. 2-20-1826.
ALLEN, William, to Sarah Case. Samuel Larrimore, bd; apb. 6-25-1824.
ALLENDER, Mary, to Amos Johnson.
ALLER, Isabella, to Stephen Hannas.
ALLOWAY, Hiram, to Rebecca Unglesby. Ebenezer Collins, bd; apb. 3-29-1827.
ARNHOLT, Andrew, to Alice Bosley. La. James Murphy, bd. 7-3-1824.
ARNOLD, Archibald, to Mary Groves, dau Jacob. Con. Frederick Spaid, wit. William Groves, bd and wit. 8-22-1827.
ARNOLD, Catherine, to Harrison Watkins.
ARNOLD, Joseph, to Elizabeth Sloan, dau Richard, bd. (John Sloan name in place of Richard, scratched. 1-20-1827.
ARNOLD, Michael, to Sarah Sloan, dau Richard, bd. 2-16-1828.
ARRENT (or Anent), Frederick, to Sarah Hacok. David Ludwick, bd; apm. 4-19-1824.
ASBURY, Mary, to William Shearer.
ATHEY, Elizabeth, to Isaac Critton.

—B—

BAILEY, Eleanor, to John Kelly.
BAKER, Elenor, to Levi Prickett.
BAKER, Jesse, to Rachel Marshall, dau John. Con. Samuel P. White, bd. 4-11-1826.
BAKER, John, to Parthenia McCauley, wid. Thomas B. White, bd. 12-4-1826.
BAKER, Lucy, to William Short.
BAKER, Rachel, to John Culp.
BAKER, Richard, to Mary Martin. John Martin bd, 3-7-1825.
BANE, Abner, to Elizabeth Whip. La. James Hamilton, bd. Apb. 2-21-1826.

BANE, George, to Margaret Thrash. La. William Stagg, bd. Apb. 6-23-1828.
BARNES, Deliah, to Robert Powelson.
BARNETT, Samuel, to Milly Slone. La. James Largent, bd. Apb. 8-23-1825.
BARRETT, Eleanor, to Michael Slonaker.
BARRETT, Rhoda, to John Shivens.
BEAN, Bennett III, to Ann Marshall, dau John, Elizabeth Carlisle apf; Bennett Bean II, bd, apm. 9-15-1827.
BEAN, Elizabeth, to James Burgess.
BEAN, Mary, to John C. Bosley.
BENNETT, John, to Catherine Grapes. La. Peter Shafer, bd. Apf. 12-19-1826.
BENNETT, Maria, to John Grapes.
BENNETT, William, to Isabel Wolford, dau John, bd. Apm. 12-19-1827.
BERRY, James, to Rachel Larrimore, dau William, bd. 10-1-1827.
BERRY, Samuel, to Elizabeth Larrimore, dau William, bd. 7-18-1825.
BERRY, William, Jr., to Mary Williamson, dau Cornelius con; William Berry, Sr., con. Samuel Hott and Alexander McBride, witnesses. 12-20-1827.
BETTERTON, Margaret, to Thomas Smoot.
BIZER, Mary, to James Stewart.
BLACK, John, to Betsy White, dau James, bd. 9-27-1825.
BLACKMAN, David, to Rebecca Sloan. Thomas Sloan, bd. 1-25-1825.
BLUE, Zachariah, to Mary Ann Ruckman, dau Richard, bd. 2-20-1826.
BOBO, Rebecca, to John Summers.
BONHAM, Samuel, to Maude Malcom, dau William, con. Alfred Anderson, bd., wit. James Malcom, wit. Apm. 12-25-1827.
BOSLEY, Alice, to Andrew Arnholt.
BOSLEY, John C., to Mary Bean. La. John Roberts, bd. Apb. 3-16-1827.
BOWMAN, Andrew, to Margaret McBride, dau Robert, bd. 3-22-1827.
BOWMAN, George, to Rachel Peatt. Thomas Leize, bd, and Daniel Hollenbeck, apb. 3-13-1827.

BRANDT, John, to Catherine Doman, dau William, bd. Jacob Chopper, apm. 1-10-1825.
BRILL, Eleanor, to Bartholomew LaFollette.
BRILL, Isaac, to Catherine Riggle, wid of Elijah. Walter Carr, bd. 3-21-1825.
BRILL, Isaac, to Jane Kelso, dau of James bd. Apb. 5-20-1825.
BROOKHART, Rhody, to Joseph Trevett.
BROWN, Ann M., to John Hansbrough, Jr.
BROWN, John Jr., to Parthenia Taylor. John Sloan, bd; apf. 9-13-1828.
BRUNER, George, to Maria Reede, dau John, bd. Apm. 4-30-1827.
BULL, Mary, to Jacob Stockslager.
BURGESS, James, to Elizabeth Bean. Andrew Bean, bd. Apf. 6-25-1824. (name may be Buyness).
BURKETT, John, to Maria Smoot, day Barton, bd. 1-19-1824.
BURKETT, Rachel, to Henry Dowsman.
BURNS, Morgan, to Sarah Steinbeck, wid of Frederick. Warner Throckmorton, bd. 7-20-1824.
BURNS, Ruth, to Thomas Starn.
BUSBY, Ann, to John N. Shutten.

—C—

CACKLEY, Margaret, to Christy Sine.
CARDER, Ann, to George Parke. (name may be Corder).
CARDER, Charlotte, to William Ely.
CARDER, Elizabeth, to Joel Wolverton.
CARDER, George, to Maria Hansborough, dau John, bd; and Albert Carter, bd. 6-9-1825.
CARDER, Mary, to John Poland.
CARLYLE, William, Jr., to Rebecca More, dau Alexander B. William Carlyle, Sr., bd. 3-20-1826.
CARPENTER, William, to Hannah McBride. William Gore, bd. 2-16-1825.
CARTER, Albert, to Mary Thompson, dau James, con. John G. Thompson, bd. and wit. James S. Thompson, wit. 6-6-1825.

CARTER, Robert, to Sophia Peppers, dau John, bd. 6-6-1825.
CANN, Jacob, to Jane Doyle, dau of James. John Doyle, bd. Apb. 11-22-1828.
CARMICHAEL, Hannah, to William Doran.
CASE, Sarah, to William Allen.
CAUDY, Margaret, to Peter Stump.
CAUDY, Sarah, to Ezra Pugh.
CHESHIRE, Deliah, to Benjamin Slane.
CHESHIRE, John, to Mary Dicks, dau Peter. Jacob Emmert, bd. Apm. Jacob Emmert, Sr., Febe McNemason, wit. 12-31-1828.
CHESHIRE, Samuel, to Delila Posten, dau Alexander, con. Branson Posten, bd. and wit. William Posten, wit. 11-29-1824.
CESSNA, Samuel, to Margaret H. Groves, dau Sam H. Groves. Apb. Joseph Welch, bd. 10-22-1825.
CLINE—See Kline.
COE, Wesley, to Jane Hook. La. Malachi Pugh, bd. John W. Winterton, Apb.
CONKENOW, Henry, to Catherine Swisher. La. John Swisher. Apm. 8-19-1827.
COLLINS, Moses, to Margaret Tytus, dau Tunis. Apb. Guy M. Collins, bd. 1-4-1826.
COMBS, Sarah, to Fredrick Starkey.
COOL, Catherine, to Elisha Hamilton.
COOPER, Catherine, to John Hinkle.
COOPER, Jacob, to Anna Park, dau Amos, bd. 2-7-1825.
CORBIN, Cornelius, to Parthenia White. John Corbin, Apm. Peter W. Jones, bd. 8-29-1825.
CORBIN, David, to Catherine Swier, dau Jacob, con. David Swier, wit., John Swier, wit. and bd. (Benjamin Corbin written in and scratched out on bond.) 2-7-1826.
CORBIN, Winney, to Mathew Doyle.
CRAMPTON, Jane, to Archibald Linthicum.
CRITTON, Issac, to Elizabeth Athey, dau Bazil, con. George Moreland, bd. and wit. 8-25-1826.
CULP, John, Jr., to Rachel Baker, dau. Micheal, bd. 6-12-1826.
CULP, Maria, to John D. Ravenscraft.
CUNDIFF, Catherine Nash, to John Page.
CUNDIFF, Elizabeth, to Jacob Hull.
CUNDIFF, Nancy, to William Werman.
CUNDIFF, Henry, to Milly Cundiff, ward of Wm. Welch, bd. 4-19-1824.
CUNDIFF, Milly, to Henry Cundiff.
CURLETT, Christiana, to David Long.
CURLETT, Mary, to James G. Parsons.
CURRY, Jane, to Leonard Heizer.

—D—

DAVIS, Felix, to Sarah C. Smith. Peter Peters, bd. Apf. 7-25-1825.
DAVIS, James, to Eleanor Yates. La. Gabriel Yates, Apf, bd. 4-26-1825.
DAY, William, to Ann Pug. JJacob Pugh, bd. Elijah Warfield, Apm. 6-14-1824.
DEANE, Anne, to Elijah Duling.
DICKS, Mary, to John Cheshire.
DOLL, Abraham, to Jane Thomas, dau Sophria Thomas, mo. con. Jacob Doll, fa., con. Moses and Aaron Sherrard, John Dye and Abr. Doll, wit. John Dye and Aaron Thomas, bd. 6-11-1827.
DOMAN, Catherine, to John Brat (or Brandt).
DORAN, Joseph, to Lucy G. Frye, dau Benjamin and Mary, con. James H. Frye, bd. and wit. Jesse P. Frye, wit. 9-22-1827.
DORAN, Sarah, to Thomas Moore.
DORAN, William, to Hannah Carmichael, wid. of Richard. Samuel Guard (Gard?), bd. 5-2-1825.
DOUSMAN, Henry, to Rachel Burkett, dau Thomas, bd. 4-30-1825.
DOYLE, Jane, to Jacob Cann.
DOYLE, Matthew, to Winney Corbin. La. Benjamin Corbin, bd. Apf. 6-16-1828.
DULING, Elijah, to Anne Deane. William Duling, bd. 2-7-1824.
DULING, Nancy, to Jacob Knabenschue.
DUVER, Richard, to Susan Duver, dau Thos. Largent, bd. 5-25-18244. (name may be Deever, Devore, or Seever.)
DUVER, Susan, to Richard Duver.

—E—

EASTER, HENRY, to Nancy Fleming. La. Lander Shores, bd. Apf. 4-12-1825.
EDMONSTON, Elizabeth, to James W. Hancher.
EDWARDS, Martha, to David Scott.
EDWARDS, Ann, to John Powell.
EDWARDS, Robert, to Eve Hawkins. La. James Slane, bd, apf. William Edwards, con. James Slane and Alex Beane, wit. 11-27-1826.
ELY, Benjamin, to Rosannah Powelson, dau Ryneay (Rinear), bd, apb. 3-29-1828.
ELY, William, to Charlotte Carder, dau George, bd. Benjamin Ely, bd. and apm. 3-7-1828.
EMMERSON, James, to Hannah Reese, wid. of William. Ashford Parker, bd. 9-12-1827.
ELEFRITZ, Sarah, to Henry Liller.
ELLIS, David, to Sarah Jane Farmer, dau Francis, apf. Thomas B. White, bd. Samuel Farmer and Alice Seaton, wit. 9-29-1828.
ELLIS, Eliza, to Franklin Weaver.
ENGLE, Hiram, to Amelia Groves, dau Peter. William Groves, bd. 8-28-1824.
ENTLER, Nancy, to Jacob Smith.
ENTLER, William, to Sally Race, ward of Issac Kuykendall, bd. 6-3-1826.
EVANS, Alexander, son of Caleb, to Ann Thorp, dau John, bd. Caleb Evans, fa., bd. 1-2-1826.
EVERETT, Enos, to Sarah Pettit, dau Moses, bd. 4-19-1824.

—F—

FAHS, Leah, to George Martin.
FAHS, Joseph, to Maria Slane, dau Thomas, bd. 4-2-1827.
FAIRFAX, Louisa, to Newton Tapscott.
FARMER, Sarah Jane, to David Ellis.
FERRYMAN, Francis, to Lydia Shockey, dau Joseph, bd. 10-29-1827.
FERRYMAN, Rebecca, to James McDonald.
FITZGERALD, Nancy, to John Plumb.
FITZGERALD, Mariah, to Joseph D. Wilson.
FLEEK, Peter, to Rachel Spencer, dau John, Sr., bd. Apm. 1-29-1828.
FLEMING, Anne, to Lazurus Shurley.
FLEMING, Nancy, to Henry Easter.
FLETCHER, Elijah, to Elizabeth Queen, dau John, bd. Benjamin Wilson, bd. George Fletcher, fa. con. John Smith, wit. 1-20-1826.
FLICK, Madgeline, to Jacob Putman. (may be Fleek.)
FOGEL, Charlotte, to Benjamin Kervey (Harvey?).
FOLEY, Milley, to Solomon Moore.
FOUT, Ann, to Isaac Lillas.
FOUT, Mary, to Benjamin Grayson.
FRAZIN, Eleanor, to Jacob Probasco.
FRENCH, William, to Susan Taylor, ward of William F. Taylor, bd. 5-28-1825.
FRIDDLE, Henry, to Betsy Ann Kirk. La. John Friddle, bd. 5-10-1824.
FRIDDLE, John, Jr., to Lydia Peters, ward of Peter Peters, bd. John Friddle, Sr., bd. 1-11-1827.
FRYE, James H., to Nancy Frye, ch. of Benjamin and Thomas Frye, bd. 5-8-1826.
FRYE, Lucy G., to Joseph Doran.
FRYE, Nancy T., to James H. Frye.

—G—

GANOE, Margaret, to Elisha Kearns.
GANOE, Elizabeth, to John Smith 1st
GEORGE, Silas, to Nancy Wasson, ward of Silas George. Jesse Lupton, bd. 7-19-1824.
GOOD, Phillip, to Elizabeth Abernathy. La. William Abernathy. Apb. 12-10-1825.
GRAPES, Catherine, to John Bennett.
GRAPES, John, to Maria Bennett. La. William Bennett, bd. Apf. 12-13-1828.

GRAYSON, Benjamin, to Mary Fout. La. William Fout, bd. Apb. 4-30-1827.
GROVES, Amelia, to Hiram Engle.
GROVES, Margaret H., to Samuel Cessna.
GROVES, Mary, to Archibald Arnold.
GROVES, Phillip, to Mary Lafollett. Jacob Kale, bd. Apf. Francis R. Armstrong, wit. 10-7-1825.
GROVES, William, to Barbara Kline, dau Phillip. James Groves, bd. 6-16-1828.
GRYMMS, Elizabeth, to John Ward.
GUARD, Sarah, to John Pugh. (name may be Gard.)

—H—

HACOK, Sarah, to Frederick Arrent.
HAINES, Eliza, to Abraham Saville.
HAINES, Rachel, to Thomas Larrimore.
HAMILTON, Elisha, to Catherine Cool, dau Harbert, bd. 6-17-1825.
HAMILTON, Samuel, to Hannah Shafer. La. George Shafer, bd. Apf. 9-29-1825.
HANCHER, James W., to Elizabeth Edmonton, dau Thomas Edmiston, bd. William Edmindson, bd. 6-16-1825.
HANNAS, Charity, to Wilson Ruckman.
HANNAS, Stephen, to Isabelle Aller, dau Peter, bd. William Hannas, fa., bd. 3-14-1825.
HANSBOROUGH, John, Jr., to Ann M. Brown. James Hansborough, bd. Apb. 8-2-1828.
HANSBOROUGH, Maria, to George Carder.
HARE, Matthew, to Margaret Powelson, dau Charles, bd. 11-12-1825.
HARRISON, Orpha, to John Head.
HARTMAN, Margaret, to Joseph Shokey.
HARVEY—See Kervey.
HASS, Catherine, to Israel Mayberry.
HAWK, Issac, to Jane High, dau of Henry, con. George High, bd. 6-10-1826.
HAWKINS, David, to Mary Kidwell. James Sloane, bd. Apb. 10-1-1825.
HAWKINS, Eve, to Robert Edwards.
HAYNES, John, to Nancy Larrimore, dau John, bd. Apm. 4-13-1825.
HAYS, Rebecca, to Mathew Stollaberger.
HEAD, John, to Orpha Harrison. La., dau Jo, con. Robert Harrison, bd. Nathaniel Harrison, wit. 5-7-1825.
HEARN, John L., to Eliza Powellson, dau Rynear, bd. Matthew Hearn. Apm. 10-20-1828.
HEIZER, Leonard John, to Jean Curry, wid. John Hein and John Snyder, bd. 1-11-1825.
HEIZER, Mary Ann, to Caleb Levings (Evans?).

HERRIOTT, Ephraim, to Eliza Reese, dau William. John Reese, bd. Apb. 11-10-1827.
HICKLE, Elizabeth, to Isaac Moore.
HIETT, Sarah, to James Allen. (name may be Hutt).
HIGGINS, Patsy, to Charles S. Taylor.
HIGH, Mary, to George Ludwick.
HIGH, Jane, to Isaac Hawk.
HINKLE, John, to Catherine Cooper, dau Martin, bd. 4-4-1825.
HINES, Thomas, to Nancy McBride, dau Robert, bd. 11-25-1825.
HOBSON, Jane, to Sylvester Monroe.
HOFFMAN, Elizabeth, to Samuel Smoot.
HOFFMAN, Sarah, to Henry Swisher.
HOLLIDAY, Angus, M. D., to Susan Vandiver. La. Samuel Vandiver, bd. Apf. 12-20-1824.
HOOK, Jane, to Wesley Coe.
HOOVER, Sarah, to George Stern.
HORN, Elizabeth, to William King.
HOUSE, Amon, to Catherine Lawson. La. Samuel House, bd. Apb. 8-26-1827.
HOUSE, Samuel, to Nancy Lawson. La. Jacob Adams, bd. Apf. 4-16-1827.
HOUSEHOLDER, Mary, to Moses Jones.
HUNZMAN, Elizabeth, widow, to Adam Sea (or Lea).
HUMES, Nancy, to William Rannels.
HULL, Jacob, to Elizabeth Cundiff, dau John, con. Henry Cundiff, bd. and wit. Oliver Cundiff, wit. 5-15-1827.

—I—

INSKEEP, Isaac A., to Margaret V. King. La. Thomas B. White, bd. 12-12-1825.

—J—

JENKINS, Mary, wid., to James L. Powell.
JENKINS, Mary, to George Tasker.
JOHNSON, Amos, to Mary Alender, dau. James, bd. Apm. 5-5-1828.
JOHNSON, Bazel, to Jane McVicker, dau Archibald, bd. 6-13-1826.
JOHNSON, Benjamin, to Mariah Means, ward of John Vance, bd. 2-21-1826.
JOHNSON, William, to Abigail Ward. Henry Ward, bd. 1-17-1825.
JONES, Moses, to Mary Householder. La. Easter, mo. con, Apf. Moses Jones, Sr., con. Abraham Sear, wit. 3-3-1825.

—K—

KAIL, Christiana, to Elijah Thompson.
KAIL, Elizabeth, to Robert Taylor.
KEARNS, Elisha, to Margaret Ganoe. La. William Critton, bd. John S. Keslar, bd. Apb. 1-8-1827.

KEIZER—See Heizer.
KELLAR, Charles, to Elmira Price, ward of Ephraim Dunn. Charles H. Clark, bd. 1-28-1826.
KELLY, Isabelle, to Alexander Riley.
KELLY, John, to Eleanor Bailey. La. Benjamin Bailey, bd. Apf. 8-20-1827.
KELSO, Jane, to Isaac Brill.
KERVEY, Benjamin, to Charlotte Fogel. Henry Fogel, bd. Apb. 9-4-1826.
KIDWELL, Mary, to David Hawkins.
KING, John, to Lucy Norman, ward of Samuel Probasco, bd. Apb. Oct. or Nov., 1825.
KING, Margaret V., to Isaac Inskeep.
KING, William, to Elizabeth Horn. John Horn, bd. Apb. 4-3-1824.
KIRK, Betsy Ann, to Henry Friddle.
KLINE, Barbara, to William Groves.
KLINE—See Cline.
KLINE, Phillip, to Elizabeth Spaid, dau of Fred, con. David Gibson, bd. John Kline, William Groves and George Spaid, wit. 2-14-1827.
KNABENSHUE, Jacob, to Nancy Duling. La. John Smith, bd. 10-16-1824.
KUYKENDALL, Luke, to Elizabeth Welch, dau Denny, ward of William McDonald, con. Thomas B. White, bd. 11-10-1828.
LaFOLLETTE, Bartholomew, to Eleanor Brill, dau Henry & Eleanor, mo con. Phillip Grove, bd. Jane and Michael Brill, wit. 11-14-1825.
LaFOLLETTE, Mary, to Phillip Groves.

—L—

LANHAM, Dennis, to Nancy Nixon, dau. George, bd. Apm. 11-6-1826.
LARRIMORE, Elizabeth, to Samuel Berry.
LAURIMORE, Nancy, to John Haynes (Haines).
LARRIMORE, Rachel, to James Berry.
LARRIMORE, Thomas, to Rachel Haines, dau Isaac, bd. 8-6-1825.
LAWSON, Catherine, to Amon House.
LAWSON, Nancy, to Samuel House.
LEAPLEY, John, to Elizabeth McDonald, dau Charles and Jemima, con. John McDonald, wit.
LEATHERMAN, Benjamin, to Elizabeth Rannel, dau James, bd. and wit. Elisha Karnes, bd. and wit. 2-6-1826.
LEATHERMAN, Polly, to Benjamin Roberts.
LEATHERMAN, Susannah, to James Long.
LEITH, Sarah, to William Mauzee.
LEVINGS, Caleb, to Mary Ann Jones, ward of John L. Heizer, bd. Apm. 10-25-1827.
LILLAS, Isaac, to Ann Fout. Thomas Grayson. Apf. (bond torn out). 8-19-1827.

LILLER, Henry, to Sarah Elefritz. William Clark, bd. Apf. 5-22-1826.

LINTHICUM, Archibald, to Jane Crampton, ward of Joseph Clutter, bd. 9-18-1826.

LOCKHART, Elizabeth to John Pugh.

LONG, David, to Christiana Curlett, dau William, bd. 7-17-1827.

LONG, Eliza Jane, to Benjamin Parker.

LONG, James, to Susannah Leatherman, dau Daniel, bd. James Randall, Apm. 11-13-1826.

LOOS, Sarah, to Martin Whitefield. (name may be Loar, Loan).

LOY, Samuel, to Lea Martin. La. William Loy, bd. Apb. 6-9-1828.

LUDWICK, George, to Mary High, dau Henry, bd. 8-20-1825.

LUDWICK, Joseph, to Ann Taylor, dau. Thomas, con. George Sloan, bd. and wit. Isaac Hawk, wit. 9-10-1825.

LUSE, Thomas, to Sibble Sthrechfield. La. Israel Stalcup, bd. Apb. (Lee, Leize?). 5-28-1827.

LYON, John, to Mary Smith, dau of Timothy, bd. Apf. 3-12-1827.

—Mc—

McBRIDE, Hannah, to William Carpenter.

McBRIDE, Louisa, to Davis Sweir.

McBRIDE, Lydia, to Ezra Pugh.

McBRIDE, Margaret, to Andrew Bowman.

McBRIDE, Matilda, to Robert Nowell White.

McBRIDE, Nancy, to Robert McBride.

McBRIDE, Nancy, to Thomas Hines.

McBRIDE, Nancy, to Samuel Patterson.

McBRIDE, Martha, to George Short.

McBRIDE, Robert, to Nancy, wid. Thomas. Jacob Buzzard, bd. 1-8-1825.

McCAULEY, George, to Julianna Pepper, ward of George McCauley. Henry Peppers, bd. 8-20-1827.

McCAULEY, Parthinia, wid., to John Baker.

McCAULEY, Rebecca, to John Simpson.

McDONALD, Angus W., to Lucy Ann Naylor, dau of William. James N. Stevens and C. Tapscott, bd. 1-11-1827.

McDonald, Elizabeth, to John Leapley.

McDONALD, George, to Mary Miller, both wards of Absalom Miler, bd. 7-14-1828.

McDONALD, James, to Rebecca Ferryman, dau Stephen, con. Henry Ferryman, wit. William McDonald, fa., con. Ebenezer Collins, bd. and wit. Nancy McDonald, wit. 11-13-1828.

McDONALD, Millicent S., to William Sherrard.

McDONALD, Susan, to John Powell.

McFARLAND, Catherine, to John Sickafos (Sigapoos).

McGRAW, Samuel, to Margaret Shores. Thomas Shores, bd. Apb. 1-6-1826.

McNEILL, Sydney, to Hannibal Page.

McVICKERS, Isabelle to John Posten.

McVICKERS, Jane, to to Bazel Johnson.

McVICKERS, Mary, to Ashford Posten.

—M—

MALCOLM, James, to Jane Watson, dau James, con. Samuel Bonham, bd. 10-14-1828.

MALCOLM, Maude, to Samuel Bonham.

MARSHALL, Ann, to Bennett Bean, III.

MARSHALL, Rachel, to Jesse Baker.

MARTIN, George, to Leah Fahs. La. Joseph Fahs, bd. Apf. 4-28-1827.

MARTIN, John, to Ellen Thompson, dau James. Alexander Beall (Deavis, Deaver, Dunn?), bd. 2-19-1827.

MARTIN, Lea, to Samuel Loy.

MARTIN, Mary, to Richard Baker.

MARTIN, Sarah, to John J. Pownall.

MAUZEY, John, Jr., to Elizabeth Powell, dau Robert M., con. Elisha Powell, bd. and wit. 1-11-1825.

MAUZEE, William, to Sarah Leith, dau James, bd. Apm. 6-18-1827.

MAYBERRY, Israel, to Catherine Hass, dau Peter. John Myers, bd. 3-27-1827.

MEANS, Mariah to Benjamin Thompson.

MEDCALF, Fenton, to Lucy Ann Wolf, dau Jacob, bd. Asa Metcalf, fa, con. James Metcalf and James M. Wolf, wit. 10-28-1826.

MILLER, James, to Susannah Morehead, ward of Absalom Miller, bd. Apb. 11-19-1827.

MILLER, Mary, to George McDonald.

MILLER, Peter, to Julia Ann Spencer, dau John. 2-21-1824.

MILLESON, Martha, to Benjamin Williamson.

MILLESON, Silas, ward of Thomas Sloan, to Harriet Sloan, dau of Thomas, bd. 2-19-1827.

MILLSLAGLE, Hannah, to James Pennington.

MEYERS, Elizabeth, wid of Jacob, to Sylvester Welch.

MONROE, James, to Margaret Pugh, dau Robert, con, John and James Pugh, wit. John Pugh, bd. 11-8-1827.

MONROE, Sylvester, to Jane Hobson. La. Benjamin B. Thornton, bd., apf. Alexander Monroe, apm. 12-15-1828.

MORED, Rebecca, to William Carlyle.

MOREHEAD, Sarah, to James Miller.

MORELAND, Mary, to Stephen Queen.

MORELAND, Mary, to Robert M. Powell.

MOORE, Abraham, to Sarah Stump, dau Joseh, con. Alex Deavers, wit. John Stump, wit. and bd., apm. 10-1-1828.

MOORE, Isaac, to Elizabeth Hickle (Hinkle), dau Steven, con. Thomas Moore, fa, con. Timothy, Joseph and Stephen Hickle, wit. 9-25-1826.

MOORE, Solomon, to Milley Foley. La. Larkin C. Kelley bd. 12-10-1828.

MOORE, Thomas, to Sarah Doran, dau Alexander, bd. 10-4-1824.

MULLIDAY, Milly, to David Parsons.

MUTTE, Archibold, to Susan Wingfield. Elijah Wingfield, bd, apf. 4-18-1826.

—N—

NAYLOR, Jane, to Chichester Tapicott.

NAYLOR, Lucy Ann, to Angus W. McDonald.

NEWMAN, Catsby, to Sarah Reed, dau George, bd. 9-3-1824.

NICHOLSON, Elizabeth, to George Young.

NIXON, Nancy, to Dennis Lanahan.

NORMAN, Lucy, to John King.

—O—

OFFUT, Ann, to Jonathan Pugh, Jr.

OFFUTT, Sarah, to John Pugh.

—P—

PAGE, Hannibal, to Sydney McNeil. La. John Kern, Jr., bd. 7-29-1828.

PAGE, John, to Catherine Nash Cundiff, dau John, bd. James Cundiff, bd. 12-19-1825.

PANCAKE, John McNeill, to Parthenia Parsons, dau James, bd. 2-13-1826.

PARISH, Adam, to Mary Ruckman, dau John, bd. William Parish, apm. 5-31-1824.

PARK Anna, to Jacob Cooper.

PARK, Elizabeth, to Sam Park, Jr.

PARKE, George, to Anna Carder, dau George, bd. Enoch Parke, apm. 1-8-1827.

PARK, John, to Mary Amon. George Park, fa., bd. Apf. 8-18-1828.

PARK, Samuel, Jr., to Elizabeth Park, dau George. George Horn, bd. Mar. or Apr., 1824.

PARKER, Benjamin, to Eliza Jane Long, dau David, bd. 12-18-1828.

PARKER, John, to Mary Ann Whiteman, ward of John Piper, bd. 2-11-1826.

PARROTT, Dennis M., to Louisa Price, dau Arjalon. John Kelly, bd. 10-14-1824.

PARSONS, David, to Milly Mulliday, dau Thomas, bd. 1-11-1827.

PARSONS, James G., to Mary Curlett, dau William. Walter Curlett, bd. 3-22-1825.

PARSONS, Parthena, to John McNeill Pancake.

MARRIAGE BONDS

PATTERSON, Samuel, to Nancy McBride. Thomas McBride, apf. Thomas Patterson, bd, apm. 11-24-1825.

PEATT, Rachel, to George Bowman.

PENNINGTON, James, to Hannah Milslagle, dau John. Samuel Milslagle, bd. 5-14-1825.

PEPPER, Frederick, to Deborah Slocum, ward of John Wolford, con. John Pugh, bd., wit., apm. Isabel Wolford, wit. 1-13-1827.

PEPPERS, Juliana, to George McCauley.

PEPPERS, Sophiah, to Robert Carter.

PETERS, Lydia, to John Friddle.

PETTIT, Sarah, to Enos Everett.

PICKERING, Hiram, to Sarah Ann Posey. William Posey, bd. Apb. 8-17-1828.

PILES, Elizabeth, to John Williams.

PILES, John H., to Elizabeth Ruckman, ward of Susannah Ruckman, bd. John Williams, apf. 3-13-1824.

PLUMB, John, to Nancy Fitzgerald, ward of John Fitzgerald. John Singleton, bd. 11-22-1826.

POLAND, John, to Mary Carder, dau Abbott, bd. 3-9-1825.

POSEY, Sarah Ann, to Hiram Pickering.

POSTEN, Ashford, to Mary McVicker, ward of John Posten, bd. Apb. 11-19-1827.

POSTEN, Deliah, to Samuel Cheshire.

POSTEN, John, to Isabelle McVickers. Ashford Posten, apm. Charles Capper, bd, apf. 1-31-1825.

POWELL, Elizabeth, to John Mauzey, Jr.

POWELL, James L., to Mary Jenkins, wid of Jacob. Dade Powell, bd. 5-13-1824.

POWELL, Joanna W., to Thornton F. Powell.

POWELL, John, to Ann Edwards, ward of Robert Sherrard. Elisha Powel, bd, apm. 4-5-1824.

POWELL, John, to Susan McDonald. La. Thomas Slane, apb. 8-16-1828.

POWELL, Robert M., to Mary Moreland. James R. Powell, apf. (Bond torn out.) 1-15-1827.

POWELL, Thornton F., to Joanna W. W. Powell. Horatio N. Powell, bd., apb. 9-22-1827.

POWELSON, Eliza, to John L. Hearn.

POWELSON, Margaret, to Mathew Hare.

POWELLSON, Robert, to Delilah Barnes, dau Francis, bd. Charles Powelson, fa., bd. 6-15-1825.

POWELSON, Rosannah, to Benjamin Ely.

POWNAL, John J., to Sarah Martin La. Joseph Ruckman, bd., apf. 4-8-1828.

PRICE, Elmira, to Charles Keller.

PRICE, Louisa, to Dennis Parott.

PRICKETT, Levi, to Eleanor Baker, dau Thomas, bd. Apm. 10-22-1824.

PROBASCO, Elijah, to Margaret Probasco, wid Francis T. Jacob Probasco, bd. 12-10-1828.

PROBASCO, Jacob, to Eleonar Frazin. Samuel Probasco, bd., apf. 7-7-1825.

PROBASCO, Margaret, to Elijah Probasco.

PUGH, Ann, to William Day.

PUGH, Ezra, to Lydia McBride, ward of Jessie Pugh, bd., apf. 1-15-1827.

PUGH, Ezra., to Sarah Caudy, ward of William Nixon, con. Robert Pugh, fa., con. Jesse and Darius Pugh, wit. 6-13-1826.

PUGH, Jonathan, Jr., to Ann Offutt, dau Solomon, bd. 6-9-1827.

PUGH, John, to Sarah Guard (Gard), dau Samuel, bd. George Horn, apm. 8-16-1824.

PUGH, John, to Elizabeth Lockhart, dau William, bd. Jacob Pugh, fa., bd. 1-1-1825.

PUGH, John, to Sarah Offutt, dau Solomon, con. Owen Offut, bd., wit. Joseph Offutt, wit. 2-18-1828.

PUGH, Margaret, to James Monroe.

PURGIT, Rachel, to Henry Shultzer.

PUTMAN, Jacob, to Magdalene Flick (Fleek), dau Adam, bd. Apm. 3-24-1824. (David Long says Putman on muster roll 4 years ago.)

—Q—

QUEEN, Elizabeth to Elijah Fletcher

QUEEN, Stephen, to Mary Moreland, dau Richard, con. Steven Queen, bd., fa con. Sarah Queen, wit. 1-29-1827.

—R—

RACE, Sally, to William Entler.

RANDALL, Thomas, to Priscilla Stewart, dau John, bd., apf. 6-24-1824.

RANNELS, Elizabeth, to Benjamin Leatherman.

RANNELS, Mary, to John Wallace.

RANNELS, William, to Nancy Humes. Samuel Humes, bd., apf. 8-20-1824.

RAVENSCRAFT, John D., to Maria Culp, dau John, bd. James Ravenscraft, apm. 12-17-1827.

REED, Mariah, to George Bruner (or Brunar).

REED, Sarah, to Catsby Newman.

REESE, Eliza, to Ephraim Herriott.

REESE, Hannah, wid of William, to James Emmerson.

REESE, Lydia, to John Rogers.

REES, Thomas, Sen., to Catherine Umpstott, wid of Jacob. John Lambert, bd. 12-26-1827.

RIGGLE, Catherine, to Isaac Brill.

RILEY, Alexander, to Isabelle Kelly. La. John Kelley, bd. 3-19-1837.

RILEY, Jane, to Josiah Smoot.

ROBERTS, Benjamin, to Polly Leatherman. Joseph Leatherman, bd., apf. 12-28-1825.

ROBERTS, Martha, to Solomon Smith.

ROBINSON, Solomon, to Hannah Ruckman. La. Wilson Ruckman, bd., apf. 2-7-1825.

ROGERS, John, to Lydia Reese. La. Thomas Welch, bd., apf. 11-20-1828.

ROGERS, Martha Ann, to Daniel Taylor.

RUCKMAN, Elizabeth, to John H. Piles.

RUCKMAN, Eliza, to William L. Trentor.

RUCKMAN, Elizabeth, to Solomon Ruckman.

RUCKMAN, Mary, to Adam Parish.

RUCKMAN, Mary Ann, to Zachariah Blue.

RUCKMAN, Sam, to Elizabeth Watkins. John Timbrook, bd., apm. Zachariah Piles, apf. 9-8-1824.

RUNNELS, Jacob, to Sarah Young. William B. Young, bd., apf. 12-31-1824.

RUCKMAN, Wilson, to Charity Hannas. La. William Timbrook, bd., apb. 10-14-1828.

—S—

SAVILLE, Abraham, to Eliza Haines. La. David Haines, bd. Apb. 6-9-1827.

SCOTT, David, to Martha Edwards. Thomas Edwards, bd. 4-17-1826.

SEA, Adam. to Elizabeth Hunzman, wid of Henry. John B. White, bd. 1-6-1825 (name may be Lea).

SEEVER, Susan—See Duver.

SHAFER, Hannah, to Samuel Hamilton.

SHANNON, Andrew, to Rebecca Smith. La. John B. White, bd. 12-21-1826.

SHEARER, William, to Mary Asbury, dau Jeremiah H., bd. Peter Peters, bd., apf. 3-1-1824.

SHERRARD, William, to Millicent S. McDonald. Joseph Sherrard, bd. 5-24-1825.

SHIVENS, John, to Rhoda Barrott, ward of Jonathan Barrott, bd. 1-17-1825.

SHO(C)KEY, Joseph, to Margaret Hartman. Peter Hartman, bd., apf. 11-3-1828.

SHOCKEY, Lydia, to Francis Ferryman.

SHOPE, Elias, to Margaret Stiff. Stephen Stiff, bd. 4-5-1824.

SHORES, Margaret, to Samuel McGraw.

SHORT, George, to Martha McBride, ward of John Smith, bd. 12-29-1828.

SHORT, Isaac, to Mary Vandergriff, dau Christopher, con. William Powell (or Pownall), bd. and wit. Richard Short, wit. Edward Trickle, apm. 1-24-1827.

SHORT, William, to Lucy Baker. La. dau Perry, bd. 7-31-1827.

SHULTZER, Henry, to Rachel Purgit. William S. Feley, apb. Leonard Bumrotz, bd. 8-15-1825.

SHURLEY, Lazarus, to Anne Fleming, dau Patrick, bd. 3-14-1825.
SHUTEN, John N., to Ann Busby. James Busby, apf., bd. 10-29-1828.
SIGAPOOS, John, Jr., to Catherine McFarland, dau John, bd., apf. (bond mutilated). 7-26-1826.
SIMPSON, Jane, to Joseph Spotz.
SIMPSON, John, to Rebecca McCauley. La. George Emmert (Emmit), apf., bd. 12-11-1826.
SINE, Christy, to Margaret Cackley, dau Abraham, bd. 4-27-1825.
SLANE, Benjamin, to Deliah Cheshire. dau John, bd. 6-7-1824.
SLANE, Mariah, to Joseph Fahs.
SLANE, Nancy, to Phillip Winckelbeck.
SLOAN, Elizabeth, to Joseph Arnold.
SLONAKER, Michael, to Eleanor Barrett, ward of Johnathan Barrett, bd. Apb. 4-16-1827.
SLOANE, Harriet, to Silas Milleson.
SLOAN, Rebecca, to David Blackburn.
SLOAN, Sarah, to Michael Arnold.
SLOCUM, Deborah, to Frederick Peppers.
SLONE, Milly, to Samuel Barnett.
SMITH, Abraham I., to Sarah White, dau James, bd. Apm. 10-3-1825.
SMITH, Jacob, to Nancy Entler, dau John, bd. 9-17-1828.
SMITH, John 1st, to Elizabeth Gamoe, ward of John Smith 2nd, bd., Apm. 12-15-1828.
SMITH, Mary, to John Lyon.
SMITH, Rebecca, to Andrew Shannon.
SMITH, Sarah C., to Felix Davis.
SMITH, Solomon, to Martha Roberts. La. Daniel Hollenbeck, apb., bd. 8-18 1825.
SMOOT, Josiah, to Jane Riley. La., dau Alexander, bd. 2-19-1827.
SMOOT, Maria, to John Burkett.
SMOOT, Samuel, to Elizabeth Hoffman, dau Aaron, bd. 5-24-1825.
SMOOT, Thomas Norman, to Margaret Betterton, ward of Daniel Mytinger, bd. 8-16-1825.
SNAPP, Mariah, to Isaac Woolverton.
SNYDER, Harriet, to Alanzo Welton.
SPAID, Elizabeth, to Phillip Kline.
SPENCER, JuliaAnn, to Peter Miller.
SPENCER, John, to Mary Miller, dau Jacob. Peter Miller, bd. 11-10-1824.
SPENCER, Rachel, to Peter Fleek.
SPOTZ, Joseph, to Jane Simpson. La. John Simpson, bd., apb. 11-13-1828.
STAGG, William, to Mary Thrash. La. John Thrash, bd., apb 1-7-1828.
STARKEY, Frederick, Jr., to Sarah Combs, dau James. Frederick Starkey, Sr., bd. 1-?-1824.
STARN, Thomas, to Ruth Burns. Amat (Arnat) Day, bd., apf. 12-27-1824.
STEINBECK, Sarah, to Morgan Burns.

STERN, George, to Sarah Hoover. John Hoover, bd. John Heister, apm. 9-2-1828.
STEWART, James, to Mary Bizer. La. Jacob Bizer, apf. Jacob Arnold, bd. 6-23-1826.
STEWART, Priscilla, to Thomas Randall
STRECHFIELD, Sibble, to Thomas Luse (Lees, Leize?).
STIFF, Margaret, to Elias Shope.
STILEY, Jacob, to Elen Wilson, dau John. James Stevens, bd., apm 4-13-1824.
STOCKSLAGER, Jacob, to Mary Bull. John Bull, apf., bd. 11-3-1826. (name may be Stockslayer).
STOLLEBERGER, Matthew, to Rebecca Hays. Isaac Hull, bd., apf. 12-18-1826.
STUMP, Elizabeth D. W., to William Abernathy.
STUMP, Peter, to Margaret Caudy. David Caudy, bd., apf. 5-3-1827.
STUMP, Sarah, to Abraham Moore.
STUMP, Rebecca, to William Stump.
STUMP, William, to Rebecca Stump. La. Peter Stump, bd., apb. 7-17-1826.
SUMMERS, John, to Rebecca Bobo, dau William, bd. John Summers' mo., Rebecca Fuller, apm. 2-18-1828.
SWEIR, David, to Louisa McBride, ward of Thomas M. McBride, bd. 9-15-1828.
SWIER, Catherine, to David Corbin.
SWISHER, Catherine, to Henry Cokenow.
SWISHER, Henry, to Sarah Hoffman, dau Joseph, bd. 2-12-1827.

—T—

TAPPISCOTT, Chichester, to Jane Naylor, dau William Naylor, Esq. Alfred T. Magill, bd. 8-6-1825.
TAPPISCOTT, Newton, to Louisa W. Fairfax, ward of Thomas Ragland, bd. 3-3-1825.
TASKER, George, to Mary Jenkins. La. John Jenkins, bd., apf. 9-26-1825.
TAYLOR, Ann, to Joseph Ludwick.
TAYLOR, Charles S., to Patsy Higgins, dau John. John Piper, bd. 6-10-1826.
TAYLOR, Daniel, to Martha Ann Rogers, dau John, bd. Apm. 10-25-1824.
TAYLOR, Parthenia, to John Brown, Jr.
TAYLOR, Robert, to Elizabeth Kail, dau George, con. John Kail, wit., bd., apm. 1-30-1825.
TAYLOR, Susan, to William French.
THOMAS, Jane, to Abraham Doll.
THOMPSON, Elijah, to Christiana Kail, dau George of Capeapeon, con. John G. Thompson, wit., bd. John Kail, wit. 4-4-1825.
THOMPSON, Mary, to Albert Carter.
THOMPSON, Ellen, to John Martin.

THORP, Ann to Alexander Evans.
THRASH, Margaret, to George Bane.
THRASH, Mary, to William Stagg.
THRUSH, Michael, to Catherine Umstott. Jacob Fleck, bd., apf. 3-1-1824.
TRENTOR, William L. to Eliza Ruckman, dau Richard, bd., apf. 3-14-1825.
TREVETT, Joseph, to Rhody Brookhart. Samuel Richards, bd., apf. 9-9-1825.
TYTUS, Margaret, to Moses Collins. (or Titus?)

—U—

UNGLESBY, Rebecca, to Hiram Alloway.
UMPSTOTT, Catherine, to Michael Thrush.
UPSTOTT, Catherine, wid of Jacob, to Thomas Reese, Sr.

—V—

VANCE, James, to Catherine Heiskell,, wid of Jacob. John B. White, bd. 7-31-1826.
VANDERGRIFF, Mary, to Isaac Short.
VANDIVER, Susan, to Angus Holliday, M. D.

—W—

WALLACE, John, to Mary Rannels. La. William Rannels, bd., apf. 11-3-1828.
WARD, Abigail, to William Johnson.
WARD, John, to Elizabeth Grymes, dau George, con. John H. Grymes, bd. John W. Grymes, wit. 11-25-1825.
WASSON, Nancy, to Silas George.
WATKINS, Elizabeth, to Samuel Ruckman.
WATKINS, Harrison, to Catherine Arnold, dau John, bd. 4-23-1824.
WATSON, Jane, to James Malcom.
WEAVER, Franklin, to Eliza Ellis, dau David Ellis, bd., apm. 4-7-1828.
WELCH, Elizabeth, to Luke Kuykendall.
WELSH, Sylvester, to Elizabeth Myers, wid of Jacob. Thomas B. White, bd. 12-4-1826.
WELTON, ALANZO, to Harriet Snyder. Andrew Wodrow, bd. 2-21-1825.
WERMAN, William, to Nancy Cundiff, dau John, bd. Thomas Werman, apm. 4-2-1825. (name may be Worman)
WHIP, Elizabeth, to Abner Bane.
WHITE, Betsy, to John Black.
WHITE, Parthenia, to Cornelius Corbin.
WHITE, Nowell, to Matilda McBride. John B. White, bd. 2-13-1824.
WHITE, Sarah, to Abraham Smith.

MARRIAGE BONDS

WHITEFIELD, Martin, to Sarah Loos (Loar, Loan?), dau Nathan, bd. 12-8-1828. (This is not bound in, but a yellowed slip of paper).

WHITEMAN, Mary Ann, to John Parker.

WILLIAMS, John, to Elizabeth Piles, dau Zachariah, bd. John H. Williams, bd. 2-25-1824.

WILLIAMSON, Benjamin, to Martha Milleson, dau Isaac, bd. 11-21-1827.

WILLIAMSON, Mary, to William Berry.

WILSON, Alexander, to Margaret Yost. John Yost, bd., apf. 4-26-1827.

WILSON, Elen, to Jacob Stiley.

WILSON, Joseph D., to Mariah Fitzgerald, ward of Angus McDonald, bd. 9-15-1826.

WINGFIELD, Susannah, to Archibald Mutte.

WINCKELBECK, Phillip, to Nancy Slane. La. James McDonald, bd. Apb. 12-25-1826.

WOLF, Lucy Ann, to Fenton (Phenton) Medcalf (Metcalf).

WOLFORD, Isabel, to William Bennett.

WOLVERTON, Isaac, to Maria Snapp, dau Joseph, bd. 5-16-1826.

WOLVERTON, Joel, ward of Jacob Wolverton, to Elizabeth Carder, dau George, bd. 3-5-1825.

—Y—

YATES, Elenor, to James Davis.

YOST, Margaret, to Alexander Wilson.

YOUNG, George, to Elizabeth Nicholson, dau Thomas, bd. 3-4-1824.

YOUNG, Sarah, to Jacob Runnels.

AN ALPHABETICALLY ARRANGED

Synopsis of Wills

BOOKS I to XXI

MANY FOUND ONLY IN THE ORIGINAL

ROMNEY, HAMPSHIRE COUNTY, VIRGINIA
(now West Virginia)

—o—:o—o—

ABBREVIATIONS USED: pr., date will presented to court. Exec., executor named in will or appointed by court. Sec., security. Wit., witnesses. W., wife. Fa., father. M., mother. S-i-l, son-in-law or sister-in-law. Nep., nephew. Nc., niece. Nm., names mentioned, not necessarily legatees. Ch., children. Hus., husband. Dau., daughter. Bro., brother.

—A—

ABERNATHY, John Sr.—12-29-1829; pr. 1-18-1830. W. Hannah. 9 ch., 1-William, 2-John, 3-Thomas, 4-Robert, 5-James, 6-Eleanor, 7-Marget, 8-Martha, 9-Hannah. Exec., wife. Sec., Nat. Kuykendall, William Abernathy. Wit., John Jenkins, George and Benj. Tasker.

ABERNATHY, Nancy—10-4-1856; pr. 6-28-1859. Sister, Harriet. Exec., sister, Harriet. No sec. Wit.: William Donaldson, David Gibson.

ABERNATHY, Samuel—4-24-1835; pr. 3-23-1840. Wife, but not named. 7 ch., 1-Samuel, 2-William (land adj. Springfield) [he is the son of "this wife"], 3-John, 4-James, 5-Elisabeth Patterson, 6-Eleanor Chisler, 7-Susan Lee. Evidently 2 sets of children. Exec., William Abernathy. Sec., William Abernathy. Wit., William Abernathy and John Brady.

ABERNATHY, William—3-1-1854; pr. 1-22-1855. W., but not named; no ch. Sisters, Harriet and Nancy; has others, dec'd. Exec., Charles S. Taylor, who dies; David Gibson appointed. Sec., George W. Washington. Wit.: Jacob Daley, James Abernathy.

ADAMS, Catherine, of Frankfort, Va.—3-16-1807; pr. 4-20-1807. 3 ch., 1-Jacob (has all land), 2-Catherine (hus. Dennis Daniels), 3-Rachel. Exec., Dennis Daniels. Wit., Frederick Sheets, John Hollinback, Michael Sheets.

ADAMS, Lydia—8-5-1831; pr. 12-22-1834. 2 ch., 1-William (in suit against mother; land in Frederick County adj. Isaac and Thomas Adams), 2-Rachel (hus. Jacob Adams); John Adams, son of William, who is suing. Exec., Jacob Adams, s-i-l. Sec., Jacob Stackslager, Washington Adams. Wit. Thos. Ruse, Isac Beal, A. King.

ADAMS, William—7-10-1828; pr. 8-18-1828. W., Eleanor. Son, George; "other children who may be living." Exec.: John Millason. Sec., William Vance and John Martin. Wit.: C. Heiskell, Ann Day, Sarenah McDonald, John Martin, William Henderson, George Short.

AIKMAN, John—9-11-1802; pr. 4-14-1806. W., Mary. 1 ch. Wife to get 100 acres John Howman improved; son, Adam, 200 acres (son Adam Boyd Eakman). Exec., wife. Wit.: Benj. Foreman, John Bodine, Cornelius Powelson.

ALEXANDER, James—8-11-1768; pr. 5-11-1773. W. Sarah; dau., ———, w. of Thomas Littler; Martha Nash, relationship not shown; sisters, Jane Laurener, Elizabeth Laurener; two sons of brother, William, not named. Exec., Thomas Littler and Henry Fry. Wit.: William and Elis Hughes and Richard Mynatt.

ALLEN, James—1-28-1857. W., Catherine; ch. not named. "4 youngest boys to have as good education as elder children." Exec., Angus McDonald, Jr. Sec., David Gibson and William A. Vance. Wit.: John Johnson and William D. Rees.

ALLEN, Robert—3-8-1816; pr. 3-18-1816. W., Isabelle. Ch., Samuel, Wilum and Ivey; "other children," but not named. Exec., Samuel Alan. Sec., Adam Haire. Wit., Adam Heare and Daniel McCabe.

ALLEN, Samuel—9-2-1842; pr. 8-28-1843. Sarah, widow of William, gets Robert Allen's land. Nep., Isaac Gano. Sisters, Margaret Col (Colvin?) (hus. S.), Elizabeth Burket (hus. Thomas); Anna Vandagrift (hus. Christopher), Mary Cunningham (hus. Israel); nc., Eva McCabe (hus. Daniel); her mother, Jane Ganoe (Jane Ganoe now the widow of Stephen Ganoe). Exec., James Latimore. Sec., John Rannels. Wit., Isaiah Powell, Sam Larrimore, Sam Sneathen, Arthur Combs.

ALLEN, Thomas—6-4-1853; pr. 7-25-1853. W., but not named. 9 ch., James, Jane (hus. Davis T. Dunn of Frankfort), Thomas M., Robert, Elizabeth, Arthur (and "his children"), John, Rhona Greenwade, Lepah Rinehart. Land bought of William Cull, adjoining Abr. Reinhart. Exec., John Allen. Sec., James and Robert Allen, John Arnold. Wit.: John Arnold, Arthur Fleek, Simon Unstot, Thomas Dunn.

ALLEN, William—1:30-1830; pr. 2-15-1830. Verbal will; W. not named; no ch. Brother, Samuel, to have all except widow's support. Exec. and sec., Samuel Allen and William Vance. Wit., James and Naomi Larremore and Jonathan Pownell.

ALLENDER, William—5-6-1807; pr. 6-14-1813. W., Christine. Ch., Jorge (eldest), William, Jacob, James, (who has a wife, Cristine). Exec., son, James. Sec., William Alderton and John McBride. Wit., Job Curtis, William and John Alderton.

ALLOWAY, William—10-28-1828; pr. 12-18-1829. No wife. Ch., Jane Hines, Hannah, "my daughter's children," Eben Colens and Cathern Ferman (daughter dec'd); Lucy Simpson and "my daughter Lidy Simpson's children (daughter dec'd). Evidently two dec'd; speaks of dividing into four parts. Exec., sheriff. Wit.: John L. Heare, John Powelson, Thomas Hines.

SYNOPSIS OF WILLS

ANDERSON, Thomas—3-22-1856; pr. 4-28-1856. W., Elizabeth. 2 ch., Sarah Angeline, and Margaret Eleanor. "My father, Thomas." Father-in-law, Bartholomew La Follette. Mention is made of James La Follette, who is to buy land wife got of father. Exec., Henry W. La Follette. Sec., Samuel Millslagle. Wit.: John N. Hannam (or Hannan), Elias La Follette, H. W. La Follette, Amos A. McKee.

ANDERSON, William—9-10-1786; pr. 4-9-1794. W., but not named. 6 ch., 1-Nancy, 2-Rachel, 3-Sarah, 4-Catherine, 5-Hannah, and 6-Thomas, "my only son." Exec., Thomas Anderson. Sec., Arthur O'Hara, John House. Wit., Evan Gwynne, Henry Haines, Arthur O'Hara.

ANDERSON, William—12-8-1810; pr. 6-19-1815. W., Marget. No ch. William J. Phillips (relationship not shown) to get property after wife's death. Exec., wife, who refused to serve, and Sylvanus Bennett, who died; John Anderson of Little Capon appointed. Sec., Richard Robertson. Wit., Richard and Elsa Robertson, and Frd. Bennet.

ARNOLD, Andrew—3-20-1838; pr. 4-22-1844. W. Mary. 8 ch., Archibald, Elias, William, John, Lettice, Sarah, Rebecca, and Mary; land adjoining David Pugh, William Hooks and John Spaid. 3 gr. s., Amos, Tilbury and William Arnold; gr. d., Evaline Arnold (ch. of William, dec'd, widow alive). Exec., wife, who refuses to serve; Archibald Arnold appointed. Sec., David Pugh. Wit.: Azariah Pugh, Jacob McKeever, Phillip Kline.

ARNOLD, Archibald—11-14-1854; pr. 10-27-1856. W. Mary. 9 ch., Louiza Jane, Rebecca, Frances Eggleson, Mary Catherine, Lewis, Elias, Andrew Jackson, Lemuel Smith, Joseph Earley. Exec., David Pugh. Sec., Phillip Kline and George Spaid. Wit.: Phillip Kline, George Spaid.

ARNOLD, Daniel—5-25-1848; pr. 9-24-1849. W. Elizabeth; 14 ch., 1-Solomon, 2-Sam (evidently dec'd; has 4 ch.), 3-Christiana Miler, 4-Emmanuel, 5-Daniel (has sons, Daniel and John), 6-Ann Smoot, 7-Michael, 8-Catherine Wine, 9-Lydia Carrey (has ch., Michael and Catherine Carrey), 10-Elizabeth, 11-Magdalena Sloan, 12-Susan Flanigan (hus. Daniel), 13-John, 14-—— Leatherman (hus. Benjamin). Nm—Benjamin Arnold, Nicholas Bizer. Exec., Peter Arnold, nep. Sec., Solomon and Zechariah Arnold and Nicholas Bizer. Wit., Thomas Clarkson, Nicholas Bizer, Jacob Bizer.

ARNOLD, Jacob—1-14-1828; pr. 2-18-1828. W., Sarah. 7 ch., Samuel and Barbary, by first wife; Mary, Susan, Catherine, William, Lydia (evidently 12 years old). Sister-in-law, Elizabeth Agg. Exec., John Sloan. Sec., Richard Sloan. Wit.: John Vance, William Welch and Daniel Arnold.

ARNOLD, Rev. John (Baptist) — 8-6-1850; pr. 10-28-1850. (will and codicil.) W., Rosanna; 8 ch., 1-George W., land; 2-Joshua, land; 3-William F., land; 4-Angeline, land; 5-Eleanor Bowman (evidently dec'd, had 10 ch.); 6-Catherine Watkins (hus. Harrison Watkins) dec'd, 4 ch., Jane, John A, William and James Watkins); 7-dau., —— Pownall (evidently dec'd, 4 ch., John A, Isaac J., Mahala and Elizabeth Pownall); 8-Elizabeth McBride. Names mentioned, no relationship shown: Joseph Garrison, David Corbin, William Grant, Thomas Mason, Peter and Jacob Sweirs, Joshua and William Pownall. Exec., sons, Joshua and George Arnold. Sec., William Vance, John McBride, John Carter. Wit., Aaron Malick, John J. Pownall (also sec.), Isaac Saville, A. Munroe and John Ambley.

PAGE 107

ARNOLD, John — 6-16-1816; pr. 6-14-1819. W., Hannah. 8 ch., Sarah Hart, Phoebe Groves, Amelia Wall, Andrew (eldest), John Monroe, Richard, Levi, Hannah Pugh (evidently dec'd; these are her children: Catherine Pugh, Sarah Trowbridge, Jesse, Michael, Phebe, Mary and Hannah Pugh). Exec., sons, Andrew and John Monroe. Sec., Abraham Cresswell. Wit.: Abraham Cresswell, Michael Pugh, and Jesse Pugh.

ARNOLD, Richard—9-24-1758; pr. 12-12-1758. 4 ch., Elizabeth (hus. George Nixon), Andrew, Nimrod, younger son, John; gr. s. Joseph Arnold; s-i-l. Sarah Davis. Exec., Jesse Pugh and George Nixon. Wit.: Roger Parke, James Cody, John Ashbrook.

ARRENTS, Sarah—12-24-1856; pr. 2-23-1857. Bro., Henry Hawk, Jr., dec'd, left her farm; nm., Joseph Ludwick and w., Ann (who gave her care and attention); their heirs, Sarah Jane, Mary Ann Ludwick, Katherine Ann Arnold, Henry Ludwick (his uncle is Henry Hawk). Adm., Henry M. High. Sec., Elijah High. Wit., Elijah and Henry High.

ASBURY, Jeremiah—4-22-1826; pr. 9-18-1826. W., Ruth. Ch., Joseph, one-half, and "to my other children," balance of uncle Joe Asbury's estate. Exec., widow, who dies and Joseph Asbury is appointed. Wit.: Samuel Williamson, Joseph Storm and Jesse Fryer.

ASHBY, Benjamin—9-29-1779; pr. 9-17-1804. W., Hannah. 3 ch. Wife to get one-third during life, then to son, Jeremiah, and daughters, Lottie and Elizabeth Ashby. Exec., Thomas Neel, Abraham Vanmeter. Wit.: Nicholas Seaver, Jr., Nicholas Seaver, Sr., John Ravenscroft.

ATHEY, Thomas—2-20-1826; pr. 10-16-1826 (codicil dated same date. 11 ch., 1-Samuel, 2-Nancy, 3-Martha, 4-Joseph ("these 4 by this wife"), 5-Sarah Elizabeth, 6-Walter, 7-Thomas, 8-Emma, 9-Susan, 10-Virtuity, 11-Mary. Exec., Henry Smith of Hardy Co. Sec., Reuben Davis. Wit.: William M. Tanney, Samuel and Reuben Davis.

AUGHNEY, Ann—11-17-1795; pr. 4-18-1796. "My grandson, Samuel Bray," slaves; son, Samuel Oldham, 1 shilling; daughters as follows, each 1 shilling: Winefford Nevil, Abigail Lyal, Susannah Ross, Mary Ann Kirkpatrick, Nancy Rector; "to my two grandchildren, Sam Bray and Nancy Rector." Exec., Conway Rector and Sam Bray. Wit.: George Carruthers, Daniel McLaughlin, William Young, John Higgins.

AUGHNEY, Darby—5-16-1795; pr. 10-19-1795. Wf. Ann; no children. Land to wf. during life, then half each to Sam Bray and Conway Rector, Rector to take half of "lower end where he now lives"; 5 shillings each to brothers and sisters if they should come to claim it; also currency to the folowing: Sam Oldham, Mary Ann Kirkpatrick, Wineford Nevil, Sussanah Ross, Abigal Lyal, Samuel Bray. Exec., Conway Rector and John J. Jacob. Wit.: John Higgins, Sam Beckwith, Wm. Taylor.

—B—

BAILEY, Benjamin—5-29-1829; pr. 4-19-1830. W., Mary. 3 ch., Elizabeth Wilkey (hus. John), William Bailey (w. Elizabeth), Edw. Bailey (w. Mary). Exec., Thomas Cascaddon and John Kelley. Sec., John Kelley and William Reese. Wit.: Isaac Flick, Abraham Lemmon and George Abrell. Mentions James Sturman, John Kelley, and heirs of Hendrix by Mary Bailey, evidently heirs.

BAILEY, Edward — 4-25-1825; pr. 6-18-1828. No wife. 8 ch., Eleanor, John (from whom he had not heard for years), Edward, Elizabeth Hilkey, Benjamin, William, Alice Stearman, and Mary Clark. Exec., John Kelley. Sec., Francis Kelley and Samuel Vandiver. Wit.: Francis Kelley, Noah Liller, Reuben Davis.

BAKER, James—11-7-1856; pr. 2-22-1858. W., Rebecca. 5 ch., Isaac Newton, Virginia Catherine (25 dollars for schooling), John William, Sarah Elizabeth, and Henry Frederick (eldest). Mentions Joseph Carlisle land sold to Isaac Carlyle by White (relationship not shown). Exec., wife, and Evan Hiett. Sec., James Alkire. Wit.: Sydnor McDonald, Uriah Millslagle, Spencer Gray.

BAKER, John Y.—1-12-1860; pr. 2-27-1860. W., Mary. 4 ch., Andrew, William, John R., Elizabeth Taggart. Exec., son, Andrew. Sec., William Donaldson, George W. Washington and Henry Hoffman. Wit.: Alen McGlathery and Jacob Grace.

BAKER, Joseph—1-26-1846; pr. 4-26-1847. W. not named. 1 ch., Rebecca Witt, given extra land for care of father and mother. Nm., William Duling, Thomas Segull. Exec., John M. Wilt. Sec., George G. Tucker. Wit.: William Welch, Hamilton Mills.

BAKER, Sarah (of Frederick County, Va.)—7-8-1842; pr. 2-28-1853. 2 ch., d., Elizabeth Yeider (hus. John), of Frederick Co., s., Lewis. Gr. ch., Joseph McQuad and Elizabeth Yeider ("children of my daughter"). Mentions John Fenton, Daniel and Lorenzo Oats. Exec., William Wood, Frederick Co., and Andrew Emmett, of Hampshire Co. Sec., Charles Blue. Wit.: Charles Levi Baker, Daniel C. Little, Charles Blue.

BAKER, Thomas—11-14-1843; pr. 2-26-1844. No wife. 7 ch., "3 sons, 4 daughters," John, Nancy, William, dec'd; Thomas; others not named. John gets bible. Exec., William P. Slump. Sec., John Meyers. Wit.: Thomas Walker, Davis Kinnison.

BANE, Alexander—12-18-1856; pr. 1-26-1857. W., Heste. 3 ch., James, Robert and Zimri. Exec., James and Robert. Sec., James Sheetz, Sam Davis, Thomas and Zimri Bane. Wit.: William Trout, George Bank, James Sheetz.

BANE, Jesse—2-21-1830; pr. 19-17-1831 and 11-26-1832. Wife not mentioned. Ch., Alexander, Jesse, George, Nancy Chamberlin's heirs. Exec., Alexander and George Bane. Sec., Thomas Carskaddon. Wit.: Fredrick Sheetz and Samuel Cockerell.

BARKLOO, James—8-20-1796; pr. 9-19-1796. W., Elizabeth. 6 ch., Benjamin, Johnson, Sarah, Mary Powelson (hus. Abraham), Leanah Bealy (hus. Charles), Anne Stout (hus. St. Ledger). Exec., sons, Benjamin and Johnson. Wit.: Isaac Miller, John Decker, Thomas Taylor, George Beaty. See will of Elizabeth Bartlow, 1811.

BARNHOUSE, John—3-23-1848; pr. 1-28-1850. W., Rachel. 7 ch., Fielding A., William, Andrew, John, Mathew, Marium Tasker, Elizabeth Green. Fielding received land on New Creek. Exec., Samuel Arnold. Wit.: Joseph Frazier, John Barrick, James W. Carter.

BARR, John—7-12-1814; pr. 12-14-1818 and 1-18-1819. W. Sarah. If no heir, goes to Adam Barr (relationship not shown). Sister, Sarah Racy, and her son, John. Exec., wife, and Michael Pugh. Sec., William Heron. Wit.: Thomas Davis, William Lafollette, John Barr.

BARRETT, John—10-24-1823; pr. 12-15-1825. W., Rhoda. 3 ch., Jonathan, Edith and David. Brother, David (dec'd, left widow). Exec., brother, Benjamin. Wit., Thomas Barrett, Benj. Pickering.

BARRICK, George—1-26-1841; pr. 2-22-1841. W., Catherine. All to wife until youngest child is 21. Children not named. Exec., Thomas Carskaddon. Sec., John Sloan, Samuel Davis. Wit.: Jacob Knabenshine, William Welch and Achilles and William Duling.

BARTLOW, Elizabeth—5-15-1811 and 5-9-1812 (will had two dates); pr. 3-16-1818. 2 ch., 1-Sarah Bartlow, 2-Leanor Beatty (d.). Sister, Rachel Srawders (leaves her her dower). S-i-l, Charles Baley. Bro, Cornelius Johnson. Exec., Sarah Bartlow. Sec., James Beaty. Wit.: William Donaldson, Thomas Walis, James Savage. (See will of James Barkloo.)

BARTON, William G.—4-26-1855; pr. 7-28-1865. Wife not named; no children. Exec., wife. Sec., William Nixon. Wit.: Samuel Cooper, E. P. Cooper.

BEALL, Benjamin (of Frederick County, Md)—3-2-1765; pr. 4-1-1765. W., Mary. 4 ch., Lloyd, Nenian, Cephas, and Nancy. Wit., Jos. Beal, John Beale, Robert Beale, Thos. Simms. (This is probated in Hampshire County, for he owned land there.)

BEALES, George—6-27-1797; pr. 8-18-1797. W., Prudence. 3 ch., Ann Thompson, Elisha, Elizabeth. (Prudence was evidently his second wife, and a widow when he married her. Exec., John Parrell, Sr., and John Thompson. Sec., Archibald Linthicum and George Spade. Wit.: John Higgins, Joseph Johnson and Sam Blue.
Land in Hardy County. Mentions Jacob Swamley of Barkley County, James Smith of Hampshire, Nicholas Sperry and Doctor Craikes of North River.

BEARD, George V.—7-28-1821; pr. 9-17-1821. No wife. One ch., Martha Thompson. Thomas Reed (or Rese). Exec., Martha Thompson and William Naylor. Wit., William Ely, William and Clark Powell.

BERRY, Joseph—10-8-1802; pr. 10-18-1802. W., Sarah. 2 ch., Evin, Amasia. If wife is pregnant, that child to share with others. Exec., Jacob, Sr., and John Jenkins of Hampshire Co., William Wilson of Berkley Co. Sec., Joseph Asberry, Evan Jenkins, Robert Rogers. Wit.: Nicholas Dick, Peter Tallman. Some land in Belmont Co., N. W. Territory, and Steubenville.

BETHELL, George—5-3-1810; pr. 8-15-1814. W., Jane. 7 ch., Joshua (youngest son), George, Mary Ann Engle, Edward, Nancy, Mary, Ruth Asbury. Wit.: Robt. Wynn, Richard George, John Barrett, Henry George, Henry Meyers.

BIGGERSTAFF, Will—3-22-1807; pr. 5-15-1809. W., Rachel. 9 ch. named, Frend and Hugh, land; Nancy, Mary, Rachael Johnson, Sarah, Alice and Susana, personal property; Plesent, cash. Mentions Frederick Foutley and George Malee, cash bequest (relationship not shown). Exec., wife. Wit., Philip and Salome Longstreth, James Follery, Ann Biggerstaff. (See Bickerstaff.)

BIGGERSTAFF, William—7-20-1802; pr. 4-18-1803. No w. 5 ch., 1-John (dec'd, has 2 sons, William and John), land; 2-William; 3-Samuel (dec'd, w., Ann, land; 3 sons, Isaac, William and Sam); 4-Hugh; 5-Rebecca Hartley (dau., Susan). John Hartley (think hus. of Rebecca) and Thomas, son; Dennis Parsley, Drousilla Throgmorton. Wit., John Mitchell, Sr., John Mitchell, Jr., Thomas Davis, Thomas Mitchell.

BLACKS, Edmund E.—7-10-1860; pr. 8-29-1860. W., Helen. 27 acres, Ferebee Place. Exec., wife; no sec. Wit.: John Marshall, William Cling (McClung?).

BLUE, Garrett—8-30-1832; pr. 3-23-1835. W., Mary. 3 ch., Eleanor (hus. Jesse Monroe); Hannah (hus. Daniel Maglaulin, probably McLaughlin; he evidently out of favor); Nancy Chambers. Exec., Jesse Monroe, and nep, Garrett W. Blue. Sec., Jesse Monroe and Richard Blue. Wit.: Michael, Uriah, Garret J. and Uriah Blue.

BLUE, John—7-20-1770; pr. 8-14-1770. W., Cattron. 4 ch., John, Abraham, Uriah, Mical. Exec., wife and son, Abraham. Sec., Garrat Reasum and John Reasun. Wit.: Garret Rusum, John Rutan, Sarah Johnson.

BLUE, John, Sr.—10-16-1790; pr. 4-14-1791. W., Margaret. 12 ch., Uriah, Abraham, Peter, John, Elizabeth, Jacob, David, Michael, Benjamin, William, Jesse, Garrat, Margaret, Hannah. Exec., Uriah and John Blue. Sec., David Forman and Stephen Calvin. Wit., David Long, William Linton, Isaac Daton. Mentions Job Welton—land he bought.

BLUE, Michael—10-27-1840; pr. 3-28-1842. Wife not named (see will of Hannah Lawson). 7 ch., Michael, Thomas, John, Hannah (hus. James Kuykendall); Lawson, Charity, Garrett. Exec., Thomas and Michael Blue. Sec., Garrett W. Blue and John Donaldson. Wit.: John Earsons, John and Thomas Walker.

BLUE, Richard—3-12-1844; pr. 3-24-1851. No wife. 8 ch., Susannah (hus. William Barnes); Ivea (hus. William Gulick), 60 acres; Zachariah, Richard, Hannah (hus. John Forman Inskeep); Louisa (hus. Silas Lewis); James, and John. Gr. s., John Trenton. Bro., Garrett Blue. Exec., son John, and Garrett Blue. Sec., Sam D. Brady, James Parsons. Wit.: John B. White, John Kern, Jr., and John P. Tapscott. Mentions Richard Horen, John Pownell and Levi Baker—land in Monongalia and Tyler Co.

BOGART, Gaisbert (Gysbert)—2-14-1776; pr. 5-12-1778 and 8-11-1778. W., Elizabeth. 6 ch., Cornelius, Ezekill, Hannah Bresst, Phebe More, Charity Riche, Grizena Lee. Gr. s. Gysbert Bogart, s. of Cornelius. Bro., Warner Bogart. Exec., Felix Symer, Capt. John Harness, Mr. George Lee. Wit., R. Maxwell, Isaac Hornbeck, Hybert Brink.

BOND, Thomas—6-8-1813; pr. 4-8 & 5-15-1814. W., Spelman. 6 ch., John, Thomas, Anne Dawson, Winnifred, Mary and Elizabeth. Exec., wife. Wit.: Thomas Dawson, James Ravenscraft, Ellonder Mabbry.

BONHAM, Jeremiah—8-23-1852; pr. 6-14-1861. No wife. Ch., John and Benjamin (both dec'd; 5 gr. ch. share theirs), Sarah (hus. Jacob) Fouty, Samuel. Gr. s., Wesley Bonham. Mentions Adam and David Berry, Jacob Penceor, Halls lines, Robert Pool tract, Methodist Episcopal church. Exec., son, Samuel. Sec., Henry and Thomas Burkett. Wit.: Thomas A. Burkett, David Swisher, Jacob Pence.

BORER, Jacob (of Commonwealth of Virginia)—10-19-1778; pr. 11-10-1778. W., Barbary. 8 ch., Barbary, Charles, Mary, Jacob, Elizabeth, Thomas, Martin, and Rosanna. Exec., wife, and Jacob Haukle and John Wilson. Sec., Christopher Ermintrout and Henry Judy. Wit.: Jacob Helmick, Jaco Ross and Chas. Bower (Borrer?).

BOSLEY, Elizabeth—3-19-1846; pr. 2-28-1853. Ch., Robert, w., Jemima. Henry Bosley and w. Hannah (Henry Bosley's relationship with dec'd not shown; he was son of William Bosley; his wife, Hannah, was sister of Robert Bosley; it would indicate Bosley marrying Bosley). Mary Bosley, daughter of Robert, gets Bible. Sister, Mary Roberts, Eleanore Bosley, Anna Burgess. Brothers, James, Joseph, John, Levin and William. Sisters, Priscilla Evans and Arabella Arnholt. Exec., Henry Bosley. Sec., John Ward and Abraham Parker. Wit.: John Ward, Norman Smoot, John W. Ward.

BOSLEY, James (of New Creek)—4-2-1832; pr. 3-24-1834. No wife. 10 ch., John, $5; Eleanor, $5; Elizabeth, James, William, Arabella Arenholt (her ch., Andrew and Ann Arenholt); Jacob, Priscilla Evans (her ch., Nancy and Ellenor Evans); Mary Roberts, Anna (hus. Thomas Burgess, and d., Priscilla Burgess). Exec., friend, Jeremiah Moon, and son, Jacob Bosley, John Vandiver and William Bosley (last two appointed when Jacob refused to serve). Sec., William Vandiver, Jesse Davis, Enoch Baker. Wit., J. Moon, William Fout, B. Welch.

BOSLEY—John, Elk Garden, Alleghany Mts.—6-22-1852; pr. 7-28-1856. No w. Brothers, William, James, Jacob. Sisters, Elizabeth, Mary Roberts, Priscilla Evans, Annabel Arbholt. Mentions Joseph Bosley, w. Mary (rel. not shown) to get money due. Mentions John G. Grant. Exec., William Jenkins. Sec., John Jenkins. Wit.: William and John Dixon, John Green.

BOSLEY, Nelly (near Elkgarden)—4-22-1847; pr. 3-24-1856. Brother, John Bosley, land. Sisters, Polly Roberts, Betsy Barclay, Priscilla Evans, Arbella Aronhatt. Brothers, James, William and Jacob Bosley. Mentions James Frazier. Wit.: Jas Frazier of Alleghany Co., Md., Andrew Bogle, Jr.

BOURK, Michael, (of Capt. John's Run)—2-16-1811; pr. 11-18-1811. W., Elizabeth. Gr. d., Elizabeth Johnson. Wife to have land for 7 years, then as a child if she remains his widow. Child not mentioned by name. Exec., widow, Elizabeth. Wit., Richard Smith, John Johnson, P. Phillips.

BOWMAN, Andrew—1-24-1847; pr. 2-22-2847 and 7-1-1875. W., Nelly. Ch. not mentioned by name "hers and mine." Wife "everything, that she may be able to raise her children and mine." Exec., William E. Larimore. Wit.: Isaiah and Isaac J. Powell, James Larimore. Mentions Isaih Pownall.

BOYCE, Richard—9-3-1790; pr. 9-3-1790. W., Sarah. 6 ch., Richard, Green River Cantucky Co. part of Geo. Berry's Cont. Survey, Nicholas, John, Robert, James, Ann. (John Robert and James to be bound out to learn trades. Exec., Isaac Parsons, Thomas Hogan, and Isaac Miller. Sec., Joseph Neville and Thomas Collins. Wit.: Thomas Douthit, Mary Douthit, Christina and Richard Sturman.

BRANSON, Joseph — 7-10-1780; pr. 8-9-1780. No wife son, John, Bible; rest to be divided between Barbarry, Fredick, Cathran and Susan Sellers (relationship not shown). Exec., Fred. Sellers. Wit.: Jonathan Heath.

BREEZE, Margaret — 9-30-1797; pr. 10-19-1807. Sister, Mary Knight, half of her property of every kind; Methodist Church, chartered fund; "Sister and her children," not named. Exec., John Jeremiah Jacob of Hampshire Co. Sec., John Mitchel. Wit.: John and William Thompson and Martin Hull.

BRELESFORD, Bernard—1-12-1843; pr. 8-26-1844. No wife. 11 ch., 1-Jesse, 2-David (dec'd, left ch., Jesse and Thomas); 3-Elizabeth Higgins, 4-Mary Harper, 5-Leah Stevens, 6-Rachel, 7-Sarah, 8-Phoeba, 9-Margaret, 10-Ann, 11-Mahaly. Mentions Charles Gill, Abrill heirs. Wit., Nash Offut, Robert Mildrum, Robert Harrison.

BRELSFORD—Eve—9-7-1852; pr. 1-28-1856. Son, John. Mentions Mary Sewart, housekeeper. Exec., S. A. Kidwell and Benjamin F. Largent. Sec., Lorenzo Kidwell. Wit.: S. A. Kidwell, Benj. F. Largent, and Nath. Offut.

BRELSFORD, Marjoram—2-1-1841; pr. 8-23-1847. W. Eve. Son, John. Exec., Robert Carmichael and William Heiskell. Sec., Joseph Smith. Wit., Townsend Clayton, William King, Sr., C. Heiskell.

BRIGGS, Joseph, (of Ross Co., Ohio)—3-17-1820; pr. 8-18-1823. W., Villetta. 2 ch., 1-Ann Crabbe, dec'd (her 5 ch., Joseph, Nancy, Abagail, Isaac, Johnaan Crabbe) gr. s., Joseph and Thomas, sons of 2-Walter, dec'd. Exec., John McLene of Ross Co., Ohio; William Naylor, Hampshire Co. Sec., James Dailey. Mentions Jacob Hotsenpillar of Ross Co., Clerk Humphrey Fullerton of Ross Co., O.

BRINK, Hybert—4-20-1778; pr. 5-12-1778. W., Huselty. 6 ch., Phillip, Isaac, Hybert, John, Huselty and Mary. (wife pregnant; child to share). Exec., wife and Robert Maxwell and John Westfall, Sr. Sec., Joseph Petty, Abraham Kuykendall, Henry Marsh. Wit., Joseph Petty, Barnet Simms, R. Maxwell. Mill Creek land.

BRINKER, Henry—12-13-1837; pr. 3-27-1838. To John Brady for use and benefit of Hannah Laubinger, wife of George, "during her coverture" (relationship not shown). Exec., John Brady. Sec., Christopher Heiskell. Wit.: David Kinnison, R. G. Piper, James M. Brady.

BROWN, Alexander—8-14-1816; pr. 9-16-1816. Wife not named, but mentioned. 10 ch., Adam, Samuel, Isaac, Jane Brown Pugh, Polly Brown Claton, Elizabeth, Matthew, John, David, Nancy Brown Day. Gr. s., William Day, smith tools. Exec., George Sharf, Daniel Carmichael, John Candy. Sec., John Sargent. Wit.: John Malick, John and William Forrence. Has Thomas Lewis bonds.

BROWN, Daniel—12-19-1777; pr. 5-1-1780. W. Frances. 5 ch., Daniel, Sarah, Ann, Mary, Thomas. Exec., son, Thomas, and Joseph Nevil. Wit.: Andrew Arnold, Daniel Carmichael, Sarah Arnold. Land on Ohio, 40 miles below Fort Pitt, to be sold and money divided between first four children mentioned.

BRUCE, Andrew, of Allegheny Co., Md.—3-18-1814; pr. Md. 4-1-1815; Hampshire, 10-22-1832. No w. 8 ch., 1-Susannah, of Frederick Co., 400 acres in Hardy Co.; 2-William (dec'd, to his sons, Daniel, Andrew and George, 250 acres in Hardy Co); 3-Helen, 4-Norman Murdock, 5-Bruce, 6-George, 7-Charles, 8-Andrew. Exec., George, Charles, Helen and Andrew. Wit., John and Margaret Combs, John Workman.

BRYAN, Thomas—This will, an early one, is missing, but cover shows there was one.

BUBBERS (BUPORS), Sambred—2-10-1774; pr. 5-10-1774. W., Catherine. (Part of will destroyed). Mentions Hummel and Juda Buzzard, daughters of Eva Buzzard. Exec., wife. Wit.: Charles Meyers, John Buzzard, John Harness.

BUCKWALTER, Madeline, widow, of Schuylkill Twp., Chester Co., Pa.—6-21-1849; pr. Chester Co., 1853; Hampshire Co., 1854. 6 ch., David (w. Sarah), land in Chester Co.; Sarah B. Richards, land in Hampshire County; Anthony, Jacob, Mary Morgan, John. Mentions ch. of Anthony, who lives on Hampshire farm. Exec., Jacob B. Morgan. Wit.: Jacob Buckwalter, Matthey (called Matthias) Pennypacker and w., Elizabeth.

BUFFINGTON, Richard—5-23-1811; pr. 6-14-1819. No wife. Father, William, dec'd; farm left Richard and William, adj. David Parsons. Sister Mary's 7 ch., Catherine, Richard, William, Edward, Eliza, Thomas and Mary Elen Fitzgerald); bro. David's 3 ch., Richard, Mary and William. Exec., Christopher Heiskell, William Naylor. Sec., James Dailey. Wit.: James Gibson, Jno. Temple, Jno. McDonald.

BUFFINGTON, William, Sr.—3-13-1784; pr. 3-23-1784 and 3-25-1784 (codicil). W., Mary. 9 ch., Thomas, William, Joel, David, Jonathan, Richard, Ruth Collins, Susannah Sullivan, Mary. Gr. s., Richard and William, sons of William. Mentions William Sullavin, orphans of Christopher Smith, Capt. John Savage, and Bryan Bruin. Exec., wife and sons, Thomas and William. Sec., Isaac Miller, John Decker, Thomas Collins, John Campbell. Wit., Samuel Dew, Joseph Hall, William Carder, Christena Andrews. Widow remarried McCartney.

BUFFINGTON, William—8-2-1824; pr. 6-20-1825. No wife named. Br., David, has sons, John, Peter, William, and daughters, Rebecca Fitzgerald and Susanna Mouser. Sister, Mary Black (hus. Johnathan—1st hus. Thomas Fitzgerald; She had 7 ch. by Fitzgerald; 2 by Black, Rebecca and Sarah Black). Brother, Thomas' sons and daughters, $1.00 each. Brother, Joel's 5 ch., William, Joseph, Abraham, Phillip, and a daughter whose name he does not recall. Exec., John Jack and James Gibson. Sec., Isaac Kuykendall, John B. White, John Singleton. Wit.: John Snyder, William Parker, Matthew Yost, Job Fitzgerald. Land in Hampshire and Hardy Counties.

BUMEROTZ, Leonard—4-9-1827; pr. 9-17-1827. W., Elliner. (step-daughter George Hoke). Ch., William, George, Mary High, Elliner Huniman, John, Leonard, Jr. Exec., Thomas Welch. Sec., Leonard Bumerots. Wit.: Issas Hide, Nicholas Leatherman, Mary Harress (Judge Elliner not the mother of children).

BUMEROTZ, William—7-30-1859; pr. 8-26-1850. No wife. 8 ch., Landron, John, Eliza Ann (hus. David Arnold); Catherine (hus. Steven Davy); George (bound to Vance); Sarah Ann, Julian, Mortimore (youngest son). Wit.: John Stratton and Luke High.

BUMGARDNER, Rudolph—9-16-1805; pr. 12-16-1805. W., Agnes. Names 2 ch., Reuben, to have land after death of wife, 50 acres, east side of Cacapon; Rebecca, 100 from Reuben after wife's death; balance to be divided between "other children," equally "except Reuben." Exec., John and Benj. Fry. Sec., John Winterton and Jacob Mouser. Wit., John Winterton, Jacob Moober, Sr., Thomas Littler. Mentions Gabriel Throckmorton.

BUMGARNER, Sam—4-6-1864; pr. 9-3-1866. W. Elenor (of Shenandoah Co. probate). Sis. Hannah's heirs (she was Godlin); daughters, Jemima, Rachel and Susan. Exec., app. Rev. Peter Miller and Henry Frye; court app. Aaron McKee exec. for Hampshire. (This is a circuit court deed.)

BUSBEY, John—3-15-1808; pr. 11-19-1810. W., Margaret. 7 ch., Elizabeth Meridith. William, lot in Romney; Mathew, $20; John, $1; Samuel, land; Benjamin and Hamilton minors. Exec., Samuel Busbey, John Caudy, Daniel Carmichael. Wit.: Adam Brown, John and Joseph Martin.

BUZZARD, Fredrick—7-11-1812; pr. 1-18-1816. Wife not mentioned. 8 ch., Elizabeth Mouser (hus. Peter), Magdalene (Molly) Ragan, Barbary Lutrell, Esther Keiter hus. George), Susan Cowgill, John (dec'd, house clock; he left family, no will), Frederick, Jacob. Exec., son, Frederick, and son-in-law, Peter Mouser. Wit., Robert Sherrard, Abraham Weaver.

BUZZARD, Jacob—7-21-1851; pr. 7-28-1851. No wife. 4 ch., Everline Haines (gets loom and tackle), John, Susannah, Eliza. Exec., Col. George Warfield, friend and neighbor. Sec., James Albin and Joshua Arnold. Wit.: Jacob McCauley and Aaron Malick.

BYSER, Jacob—6-2-1823; pr. 8-18-1823. W., Elizabeth. Children mentioned, but not named. Exec., wife, and John Sloan. Wit.: Jacob Byser, Richard Sloan, John Arnold, John Sloan.

—C—

CALDWELL, Charles—undated; pr. 12-28-1840. W. mentioned but not named. 1 ch., Sam. Not witnessed; proved by Thos. Chaskadon and Sam Caldwell, both exec.

CALMES, Fielding—1-7-1804; pr. 5-14-1804. No w. or ch. Sister, Isabella Beneon. Nm., Collo Andrew Wodrow, John Cram, Abendego Burton. Exec., William Helm, Jr. and Meredith Helm, Jr. Sec., John Lyle, Edw. Dyer, Phillip Grace. Wit., John Lyle, Edw. Dyer, Phillip Grace, Joseph Kirkpatrick, Isaac Br——.

CALMES, George (of Alleghany Co., Md.)—3-12-1822; pr. 12-22-1824. 3 ch., 1-Lucy Perry, 2-Mary Hoye (Hoge), 3-Isabella Rogers. Mentions grandchildren, but not by name. Exec., "good friend," John Hoye (Hoge), and s-i-l, John Rogers. Wit., Alpheus and Richard Beall, William Armstrong, Isaac McCarty, Sarah White and William McMahon.

CALMES, William (of Alleghany Co., Md.)—10-10-1848; pr. 12-24-1849. W. Catherine sole heir. Land bought of David Castleman and John Hendrixon. Power of attorney given to Angus McDonald and John K—— Jr., of Romney, by widow. Wit., Nathan Wilson, Dan C. and Margaret Bruce.

CAMPBELL, Elizabeth (of Romney)—1 ch., Henry Heinzman; 4 gr. sons, ch. of Henry—Samuel, Henry, Jr., Andrew F. and John Heinzman. Exec., son, Henry Heinzman. Wit., Sam McGuire, Frederick Steinbeck.

CARMICHEAL, Daniel — 6-1-1844; pr. 8-26-1844. No w. 4 ch., 1-Ann Carmichael, 2-Robert, 3-Franklin, 4-John; gr. dau. Nancy Ruckman. Wit., Sam Stump, Jonathan Hiett, Basil Moreland.

CARRUTHERS, Mary Ann — 1-25-1845; pr. 8-27-1849. Mary Ann Rayer (Roger), relationship not shown; sister-in-law, Mary, widow of James Carruthers, dec'd; Richard B. Gulick, relationship not shown. Wit., Garrett Blue, James H. Inskeep, John Connelly.

CARRUTHERS, Mary—3-27-1855; pr. 6-29-1856. Jane Gulick, rel. not shown; Isabel Lewis, w. of Mahlon Lewis, rel. not shown; Mary Lewis, dau. of above; Lorena Bell, "a woman of color." Wit., Garrett W. and Garrett I. Blue.

CARSKADON, Thomas — 3-22-1856; pr. 4-28-1856. No. w. 7 ch., 1-James, 2-William, 3-Issac H., 4-Thomas R. (B) 5-John Robert, 6-Catherine Shutz, 7-Elizabeth I. Head (Hear). Exec., sons. Wit., James Shutz, Alexander Bane.

CARSWELL, John—4-25-1807; pr. 7-20-1807. W., Abigail. 2 stepsons, Robert and John Slocum. Exec., Robert Slocum, Adam Hare. Wit., John and Philip Malick, Phillip Fash.

CARTER, Eleanor—11-27-1843; pr. 5-26-1865. 1 ch., Hannah. Exec., friend, Jonathan Hiett. Wit., Christopher Kurtz and Evan Hiett.

CARTER, George—5-20-1841; pr. 8-12-1841. W., Elizabeth or Bettsy (dau. of Benj. Grayson). 3 ch., 1-George, 2-Benjamin, 3-Grayson. Bro., John Tasker Carter. Wit., James Lufborough, Richard Grayson, William Lack.

CASLER, Michael (of Capt. John Run)—1-30-1810; pr. 3-19-1810. No w. 2 ch., 1-John, 2-Sarah Johnson; gr. son, Thomas —— (gets shotgun); John and James Casler. Sec., Jesse Harland. Exec., gr. son, James Casler. Wit., —— Phillips, Johnathan and Mary Howard.

CAUDY, James—12-2-1783; pr. 3-9-1784. No w. 5 ch., 1-David (dec'd, wid., Martha, and ch.); 2-Ann Dulain; 3-Margaret Wood (hus., Daniel); 4-Mary Kinman; 5-Sarah Hancher (hus. John). Gr. son, John, 100 acres adj. Robert Pugh; gr. son, Evin, land Eliz. Danley lives on; gr. son, James. Exec., Robert Pugh and Evan Hiett. Wit., Elias Posten, John Hancher, Samuel Edwards, Samuel Cheshire, Hugh Slane.

CAUDY, Rebecca—Pr. 1-26-1866. 1 ch., Rebecca Stump (hus. Sam); 3 gr. dau., Margaret Elizabeth, Rebecca and Sarah Jane Stump. Sam Stump "to pay each of his three daughters $50.00 out of what he owes me." Wit., Jane (or James) Pugh, Jonathan Hirt.

CHAPMAN, William—11-3-1795; pr. 2-15-1796. W. Cattran. 4 ch., 1-William (only son; 240-plus acres on Town Hill); 2-Feby (little land Cape Cape); 3-Elizabeth (173 acres on Little Cape); 4-Dorety. Wit., Henry Frazee, John Johnson, Sr., John Johnson, Jr.

CHENOWITH, John—4-19-1811; pr. 9-14-1812. W. Eleanor. 9 ch., 1-William (one-tenth part of his grandfather's legacy); 2-Absolom, 3-John, 4-James, 5-Elias, 6-Elizabeth Monroe, 7-Eleanor Ashbrook, 8-Mary Ashbrook, 9—Rachael Ashbrook. Exec., Elias Chenowith, John Monroe. Sec., Francis White, Joseph Nixon. Wit., Abraham Cresswell, George Cole, William and Joseph Nixon, Thomas Meguire.

CHESHIRE, Barbary — 3-11-1828; pr. 10-19-1829. 8 ch.; 1-Uriah, 2-Obadiah, 3-Sam, 4-Joel, 5-Nancy Emmarts (hus. John, 6-Axhsa Millslagle (hus. George), 7-Sarah Kisner (hus. Jacob), 8-Rebecca Emmart (hus. Henry). One-eighth of piece of land on Tearcoat husband had given to son, Joel. Exec., Henry Emmart. Wit., William Doran, Thomas Robertson, John Horn.

CHESHIER, Obidiah — 12-29-1860. W. Sarah. 3 ch., 1-William, 2-Maris, 3-Maria. Wit., Aaron Malick and Sam Cheshire.

CHESHIRE, Uriah—4-6-1850; pr. 10-26-1857. W. Mary Ann. 15 ch., ("several children"—1-William, 2-Perry, 3-John, 4-Sam, 5-Elias, 6-Delilah Swartz (hus. John), 7-Nancy Cross (hus. Washington); 8-Mary McCarty or McCauly (hus. Jacob); 9-Juliet Ann Robeson or Robertson (hus. Benjamin); 10-Catherine Ann Powelson (hus. James); 11-Rachel, 12-James, 13-Franklin, 14-Barbara, 15-Uriah. Exec., William A. Vance. Wit., James McDonald, William C. Clayton.

CLINE (Kline), Abraham—8-14-1854; pr. 3-12-1866. W., ? 13 ch., 1-Phillip, 2-Jacob, 3-Joseph, 4-John, 5-Stephen, 6-Michael, 7-James, 8-Abraham, 9-Rebecca, 10-Elizabeth, 11-Mary, 12-Sarah, 13-Anthony (dec'd; dau. Mary Jane). Exec., Phillip and Joseph Kline.

CLUTTER, Jos. P.—9-18-1852; pr. 11-28-1853. W., Ann. 10 ch., 1-Peggy Ann, 2-Mary, 3-Harriett Rozanne, 4-Nancy, 5-Rebecca C., 6-Margaret J., 7-Sarah, 8-Eliza F., 9-Caroline, 10-Joseph. Exec., "friend and neighbor," Jesse Lupton. Wit., Sam W. Hawkins, Adam Wolford, Michtel C. Wolford.

COCKSWELL, Samuel — 12-22-1841; pr. 6-24-1842. No wife, no children. Nephew, William S. Cockewell, of Ohio; young friend, Sam Shutz (or Sheetz); sister, Susan, Sam Lain's dau., Catherine Stwewart, dau. of Geo. Whaley; bros., Thomas and Spencer; nep., Charles A. Jonley (Tonley), dec'd sister, Jane Thornton, has dau., Jane Thornton Williams, is dead, left ch., Lucy, by her hus., Dr. Martin Williams. Exec., friends Fred. Shutz and John Sloan.

COLLINS, Tom, Sr.—6-3-1820; pr. 2-16-1821. W., Elizabeth. 5 ch., 1-Daniel, 2-John, 3-Thomas, Jr., 4-Jenny Jones, 5-Cassandra Callehan. 4 Callahan ch., John, Jenny, Charity, Cassandra. Exec., son, Daniel. Wit., Joseph Cresap, Samuel Wells, Benjamin Whitehead.

COLSTON, John—4-15-1784; pr. 8-10-1784. W., Margaret. No ch. Legatees, relationship not shown: Thomas Hampton, son of George of Frederick Co., dec'd; John Colston, son of Jacob, gets Sowers land; Charles Beeler, exec.; John Meentner, son of Jacob; John Beeler, son of Charles Beeler. Wit., Abraham and John Thompson, John Beverly.

COMBS, Thomas—9-17-1791; pr. 10-13-1791. W., Martha. 9 ch., 1-Jonas, elder son, 2-Jonathan (one-ninth), 3-Mary White (hus. Joseph, of Hunterton Co., "West New Gersies"), 4-David, 5-Daniel, 6-Francis, 7-Thomas, 8-Moses, 9-John (last two minors). Exec., Joseph White and Joshua Calvin; they refuse, and Joseph White is of New Jersey, so Joseph Asbery and widow are appointed executors. Sec., Isaac Newman, Joshua Calvin. Wit., William Corbin, Peter Bilber, Nathaniel Foster.

CONLEY, Margaret (of Nelson Co., Ky.) — 8-4-1850; pr. 2-26-1851. Nm—Patrick Jewel, Mary Whelen, Amy Larner, Mary Daulton. Exec., friend, Patrick Jewel. Wit., Amy Larner, Mary Whelen.

CONNARDS, James — 10-17-1795; pr. 4-18-1796. 1 ch., James (5 shillings only); s-i-l, John Butcher. Exec., s-i-l, John Butcher. Wit., John Offord, Jacob Larew, Jonath Romain.

CONNELLY, Catherine (from Harrison Co., Ohio)—2-28-1844; pr. 1847. Sister, Margaret; cousins, John Patrick Connelly and Mary Denanna (hus. Patrick). Exec., Sam Thompson. Wit., Sam Thompson, John Cheney, Susan Cowerden.

COOL, Harbot—5-10-1833; pr. 6-23-1836. 6 ch., 1-Herbert 2-William, 3-Nancy, 4-Polly Posten (hus. Richard), 5-Rebecca Pettit (Pellit), 6-Catherine Hamilton (evidently dead. 3 gr. ch., John, Mary and Elizabeth Hamilton; gr. dau., Rebecca Park; "my father, Phillip Cool." Speaks of land bought of Isaac Brown, Richard Nelson, James and John Gloid, William Vance, Phillip Horn, Stephen and John Lee, Mrs. Thompson and Richard Posten on land. Land in Frederick Co. Exec., son, Herbert. Wit., Clark D. and Julia D. Powell, Amery C. Powell.

COOL, Philip — 11-29-1793; pr. 4-20-1795. W., Catherine. 5 ch., 1-Paul, 2-Jacob, 3-Phillip, 4-Herbert, 5-Lydia. Land in Harrison Co. Nm—Jacob Nelson, who lives next to Herbert. Exec., sons, Jacob and Herbert. Wit., Joshua and Samuel Calvin.

COOPER, Adam—1-11-1854; pr. 3-26-1855. 4 ch., 1-Charles, 2-Sam, 3-Sarah Engle, 4-Mary Carter. Exec., Sam Ruckman, w. Catherine, and son, Charles. Wit., Charles Blue, Elias Lupton (he has gone to McLean Co., Ill.).

COOPER, George — 6-29-1808; pr. 6-19-1809. W., Mary. 6 ch., 1-John (land bought of Joseph Pugh), 2-Christian, 3-Adam, 4-Elizabeth Milslagle, 5-Caty, 6-Jacob Rutman. Exec., Jacob Rutman and son, Christian. Sec., Lawrence Parke and Sam Posten. Wit., John Malick, John Wolford, Phillip Malick.

COOPER, Joel—3-26-1858; pr. 4-26-1858. No w., no ch. "Beloved mother and sister Margaret" get most of his property during their lives. Sisters, Catherine Horn and Mary Simmons; Rachel Rudolph. Mentions nieces and nephews, but not by name. Exec., brother, Jacob. Wit., John Pugh, Elias McCanley, Charles Blue.

COOPER, John—8-24-1848; pr. 11-24-1848. W., Mary. 7 ch., 1-Joel, 2-Solomon (dec'd, believes he left 1 dau. and 5 sons, names not known), 4-Margaret, 5-Rachel Rudolph, 6-Cathenie Horn, 7-Mary Simmons. Wit., George McConley, Abr. Millslagle, John Darby, Jr., Nathan Offut.

COOPER, Thomas—6-2-1799; pr. 12-16-1799. W., Rebecca. Ch., 1-Joseph, 2-Mary, 3-Reachel, 4-Margaret, 5-Elender, 6-Joul, 7-Elizabeth, 8-Thomas. Boys to pay Kety, Sally and Rebecky 25 pounds each from plantation (evidently children). Exec., wife, and Edw. Emery. Sec., Micheal Miller, John Douthitt. Wit., William McChisney, Richard Junkin, John Douthit.

COPSEY, John—6-28-1867. No w. 4 ch., 1-Sally D. Daugherty (hus. E. E.), 2-Ann D. Milton, 3-Lucindy Martin, 4-Mary (married first Francis Murphy, who died, left 2 ch., Sally, who married — Myers, and a son, Francis Murphy). These gr. ch. left out of the will because of their dissatisfaction with John Copsey's handling of their father's estate (see Mary Rector will). Gr. ch., James Vance Daugherty, Patsy Hosman, John William Melton. "My grandchildren children of E. E. Daugherty, and James Higgins and John Melton and B. Martin. A gr. son, Martin Copsey, also John Vanburen Copsey; Montgomery P. Higgins (evidently a gr. son), "a saddle." Dodd Martin, James Higins, Jr., of Kentucky, "my watch." Bank stock to gr. sons, J. W. Melton, James Vance Daugherty and Copsey D. Martin. Exec., James Higgins, who went to Missouri, so Peter Vanorsdall was appointed in his place with Sam D. Brady. Land adjoining John Largent. Wit., John M. and Thos. B. White, Stephen B. Wheeler. Codicil Wit., Robert Pownell, Peter and Hiett Loy.

CORBIN, Amelia—6-2-1851; pr. 6-25-1851. "Dear sister," Alsy Corbin; friend, Susan Hines. Exec., nep., Joseph Hines. Wit., Jacob Lunt, Dan Shannon, Janeny Hall.

CORBIN, David—8-11-1824; pr. 4-14-1828. W., Bathsheba. 6 ch., 1-Alsy, 2-Mildred, 3-Humphery, 4-Israel, 5-Daniel, 6-Elizabeth Powelson. Land adj. Robert French and William M. Powell. Exec., John Arnold. Wit., Clark and Joseph Powell, Robert French.

CORDER, George, Jr.—12-15-1829; pr. 1-19-1830. W., Betsy (Letyts?). 4 ch., 1-William, 2-Judith, 3-Charlotty, 4-Ann. Nm—William Vance, John Meyers. Exec, William Ely, Jr. Wit., William Ely, Jr., Martin Hardy.

CORDER, George, Jr.—10-19-1829; pr. 9-19-1831. W. Mary Ann. No ch. mentioned. Exec., wife. Wit., William Vance and John Meyers.

COULSHIRE, Earnest—undated; pr. 4-18-1796. W. Elizabeth. 3 ch., 1-Henry, 2-John, 3-Lotty (and if wife has another, it shares). Exec., Michael Fout, with widow. Wit., William James, Moses Thomas.

COWAN, Robert (Conan?)—6-6-1795; pr. 9-14-1795. W. Lydia. Son, William (if wife pregnant, that child shares with William). Exec., wife. Sec., Peter Hasel, Ed Baylis. Wit., John Reasener, Arjalon Price, Sr., Arjalon Price, Jr., Lydia Lesse.

COX, John A.—4-11-1859. W., Hannah. Ch., but not named. —— Bowen, dau., has son, Uriah Bowen, whose w. is Lucy Ann. "Thos. Coxe's children"; Peter Bowen, $1.00. Wit., George Moreland, John Hall, James M. Grant.

CRESAP, Michael (of Frederick Co., Md.)—6-28-1774; pr. Maryland, 11-24-1775; Hampshire Co., 6-16-1791. W., Mary. 3 ch., 1-Mary Elizabeth, 2-Sarah, 3-James, land in Maryland, Frederick Co., Seven Springs. Also speaks of land in Skipton. Exec., wife and Michael Cresap. Wit., Thomas Cresap, Enoch Ennis, P. Warring, Thomas Humphries. Wife refuses to abide by will; takes one-third. Wit. to codicil of same date, Thomas Bowler, dep. com., David Mitchel, Thomas French. Court appointed John Jeremiah Jacob, and w., Mary, "late Mary Cresap" as executors. Will mentions Issac and Gabriel Cox.

CROCK, George — 6-4-1802; pr. 7-19-1802. W., Barbary. 1 dau., Ann Elizabeth. Exec., wife, and William Donaldson. Wit.: John Henderson, Andrew Haines, Benjamin Neale. Sec., Andrew Haines and William Donaldson.

CROSSLEY, Abel—4-9-1793; pr. 10-11-1793. W., Joanna. 1 ch. plus., 1-John (land held with John Ruynon in Mongolia Co.); other children; Mill Creek land to wife for children's support. Wit., Andrew Smalley, William Norman.

SYNOPSIS OF WILLS

CULP, Ann — 3-22-1852; pr. 6-28-1852. 2 ch., 1-Amos, 2-Elizabeth Nutter (hus. Thomas C.); gr. son, Garrett Culp; gr. dau., Clara Isabel. Exec, son, Amos. Wit., John Crossley, Thomas Daniels, Dennis Culp.

CULP, John, Sr.—7-27-1843; pr. 8-28-1843—W., but not named. 11 ch., 1-Sally Dawson, 2-Elizabeth James, 3-Maria Ravenscraft, 4-Nancy, 5-William, 6-George, 7-Elijah, 8-James, 9-Randle, 10-Edward, 11-John. Exec., sons, John and James. Wit., John Crossley, Thomas Daniels, Dennis Culp.

CUNDIFF, Benjamin—4-6-1819; pr. 12-16-1822. W., Alley (Allender). "Divided among my children." Exec., Alex Cundiff. Wit., Ruth Holliday, Sylvester Moelt, Casper Fitsmiller. Sec., John Cundiff.

CUNDIFF, Layton S. — 11-28-1846; pr. 1-25-1847. W., Hannah (exec. in Buchannan Co., Mo., property). No ch. Wife is to pay Charlie Ross. No family mentioned. John Ward is exec. in Virginia. Wit., Henry Trout, Hiram Murphy, A. Hendrickson (Amaria Henderson proves will).

CURLATT, Mary—8-14-1841; pr. 1-4-1850. 3 ch., 1-Catherine Cain, 2-Elizabeth Curlatt, 3-John (who has died since her husband's will was probated.) Exec., s-i-l, Leve Cain. Wit., M. Blue, George W. Washington.

CURLETT, William — 10-3-1832; pr. 11-26-1832. Wife, Marey. 6 children, 1-Catherine, 2-Elizabeth, 3-John, four orphaned children of dec'd daughter, 4-Margaret Newman, 3 gr ch. of dau., 5-Mary Parsons (hus. James), s-i-l, David Long, and his wife, 6-Christiana. Wife is sole exec. Wit., Mr. H. Maxwell, Jacob Daley, John Earsom.

—D—

DAILEY, Samuel—6-15-1790; pr. 4-14-1791. No w. or ch. Bro., Hugh Dailey. Exec., John Rolls (he has bought land in Allegania Mts. of dec'd.). Wit. Friend Gray, James Scott, James Cunningham.

DALEY, Jacob—7-4-1854; pr. 1-15-1868. W., Jane. Son, John, exec. "Other children who remain with wife."

DANIELS, Dennis—3-15-1849; pr. 3-26-1849. W., Catherine. 4 ch., 1-Rachel Ward (hus. Alex) 2-John, 3-Thomas, 4-Jacob P. Exec. sons. Wit., A. J. Haines, Lewis T. Dunn.

DAVIS, Elijah—5-27-1813; pr. 11-15-1813. W., Ann. 10 ch., 1-Thomas, "eldest son"; 2-John, "2nd"; 3-Elizabeth Hellyer, "eldest daughter"; 4-Ann Siramons, 5-Meriam Secrest, 6-Absalom, 7-Attelia, 8-Sarah, "youngest daughter"; 9-David, 10-Elijah, "2 young sons." Exec., wife and "friend," Thomas Davis. Wit., Henry and Stephen Hickle and John Reed.

DAVIS, Sam B., Sr.—11-19-1835; pr. 5-25-1840. W., Ann "last wife." 10 ch., 1-Nancy, 2-Sarah Matilda, 3-Granville and 4-Jethrow, "four youngest"; 5-Alfred, 6-Mary Barker, 7-Eliza Ann, 8-Jane, 9-Joseph Warters, 10-Nancy Baker. Children by first wife taken care of. Exec., Reuben Davis, and friend Nath. Kuykendall. Wit., Thomas Jones, Thomas Carnell, R. Davis.

DAWSON, Abraham—11-30-1804; pr. 2-18-1805. No wife. 6 ch., 1-Isaac, 2-Israel, 3-Abraham, 4-Ary, 5-Teeny, 6-Betsy. Isaac, eldest, got land, Hampshire Co., on Capeon Creek and Round Bottom Creek. Israel and Abraham divide 200 a. in Hampshire Co. Nm—John Constent, Jeremiah Thompson, John and James Matthews, William Catlitt, and Capt. Isaac Bell (suit against them over land). Exec., sons Isaac and Abraham. Sec., John Critton, Lewis McCool, Levi Matthews. Wit., Thomas and John Williams, Peter Hardie, Micheal Widmeyer.

DEAKINS, Francis (of Georgetown, D. C.)—9-4-1804; pr. 3-11-1833; pr. later, Hampshire Co., 11-27-1843. No w. or ch. Bro., Leonard, has sons, William Francis and Francis Deakins. "A William Deakins" estate and lands. Exec., nep., John Hoge (Hoye?), and bro., Leonard M., and Paul Hoge. Wit., William Uham, Clement Smith, William D. Beall.

DEAN, Thomas (of New Creek)—3-9-1809; pr. 4-17-1809. W., Jane, "alias Jane Bilmore." 11 ch., 1-John, one-eleventh; 2-Elizabeth, 3-Thomas, 4-Henry, 5-William, 6-Daniel, 7-Nathan, 8-Mary, 9-Margaret, 10-Eleanor, 11-Ann. Exec., William Voss (Vause), Jacob Dull; refused to act, court appointed wife, and son, John Dean. Wit., Edmond Duling, Isaac James, Adam Aronholt and Andrew Boyd.

DENTON, Robert — 10-16-1777; pr. 5-12-1778. W., Jane. 6 ch., 1-Jacob (Robert is Jacob's eldest son); 2-John, 3-Thomas, 4-—— Robinson (hus. Joel); 5-—— Crow, (hus. John); 6-—— Williams (hus. David). Exec., son, Jacob, and Joel Robinson. Wit., Steven Ruddlee, John McNees, George Claypool.

DEVOLT, Elizabeth ("wider")—11-20-1815; pr. 11-20-1816. 4 ch., 1-Eliza Huffman (hus. Joseph); 2-Rebecca, 3-Caty Constable; 4-Andrew. Wit., John Seely, Caleb Evans, Joseph Martin.

DEW, Betty Ann—8-17-1827; pr. 8-20-1827. A verbal will. "My mother," sisters, Sarah and Susannah ("weakly"). Wit., Elizabeth Wrenn and Judith Carter.

DEW, Sam—2-14-1827; pr. 7-19-1827. No wife. 3-plus ch., 1-Betsy Ann, "youngest"; 2-Susan, 3-William Harrison, "other older children." Exec., Samuel Cockewell, John B. White, Sam Park. Wit., George Park, Robert Riordan, Elisha Pownall.

DOBBINS, Samuel — 1-8-1844; pr. 3-23-1846. W., Sarah. 9 ch., 1-John, 2-Thomas, 3-Vance, 4-Johnson, 5-Jackson, 6-Martin, 7-William, 8-Elizabeth Spencer, 9-Sarah Ann Long (evidently dec'd, her ch). Exec., sons, Vance, William and Johnson Dobbins. Sec., William Vandiver and Thomas Carichadon. Wit. of will, John B. White, Thos. Carzkahadon, William J. Armstrong. Wit. of codicil, John Kern, Jr., Alf Taylor, George Varm (Vance?).

DOBBINS, Thomas — 3-20-1802; pr. 9-17-1804. No wife. 6 ch., 1-Thomas, Jr., land, but pays 20 lbs. a year to 2-Esable Means; 3-Samuel, 4-John, 5-Ann Wolf ("Nancy" of Thos. Jr., will), and 6-Mary Hutson (dec'd, her ch). Exec., sons, Thomas and Samuel. Sec., Thomas Dunn and Sam Hatter. Wit., David Long, Thomas Means and William Long.

DOBBINS, Thomas, Jr.—1-23-1806; pr. 9-15-1806. No w., no ch. Bro., Samuel, land (father left him) now lives on, and land on Sciota-Walnut Creek, in Ohio. Sister, Ezabel; bro., John; nc., July; nep., Thomas Thompson. Nm—Nancy Wolf (relationship not stated, but evidently a sister, called "Ann" in will of Thomas S. Dobbins. Exec., bro., Samuel. Sec., Sam and Phil Hatten. Wit., Sam and Phil Hatten, John Hough.

DOLL, Catherine—6-7-1848; pr. 3-28-1849 (widow of Jacob, a Baptist). 2 ch., 1-George W., land she bought of Aaron Thomas; 2-Daniel (has daughters, Susannah and Sarah). George remained and took care of her and other children, $1.00 each. Wit., B. J. Gregg, John Ruckman and Elijah Ruckman. An affidavit filed from Shelby Co., Mo., in 1859.

DOLL, Jacob (blacksmith)—5-9-1836; pr. 5-23-1836. W., Catherine. 9 ch., 1-Abraham, 2-Phillip, 3-Jacob, 4-Catherine Davis (2 3 and 4 gone to Illinois); 5-Mary, 6-Margaret Thomas, 7-Daniel, 8-George, 9-Anna. One-ninth part of Hardy Co. land now in possession of Christopher Martin heirs, conveyed to me by Abraham Doll." Exec., Isac Bly, John Vance (Vause). Wit., Hannah and Thomas Dye, Reuben Davis, Elias McNemar.

DONALDSON, James — 12-21-1840; pr. 2-22-1841. Bro., Robert; sister, Peggy. Exec., nep., Daniel McEnally. Wit., Jacob and Fred Waggoner and George Smith.

DONALDSON, John—11-5-1847 (circuit court will). All to nephew, William Donaldson. App. him and William Stump exec. Says he is entitled to $5,216 in division of family in court action vs. Uriah Blue and w., Elizabeth, Isaac Parsons and w., Susan.

DONALDSON, Margaret—11-10-1846; pr. 3-11-1847.. Of Allegheny Co., Md., now late of Hampshire Co. Nep., Daniel McEnally; bro., Richard, died in May. Wit., Andrew Bruce, George Armstrong.

DONALDSON, Mary—11-5-1847; pr. 2-25-1849. Bro., Robert (has 2 ch., William and Mary; William gets real estate); 3 dec'd brothers, James, Anthony and William. Exec., William P. Stump. Wit., Henry Forte, William Walker, Moses Raymond.

DOPSON, William—9-15-1798; pr. 10-15-1798. W., Margret (Martha?). 3 ch., 1-Margaret, 2-dau., —— Hargis, 3-dah. —— Parker. Gr. sons, William Hargis, Thomas Parker, Nathaniel Parker, William Parker. Exec., William Donaldson, Jeremiah Sullivan. Wit., Robert and Andrew Walker, Samuel McAttee.

DORAN, Alex—9-21-1841; pr. 5-27-1850. W., —— Reed; his mother-in-law, Sarah Reed. 7 ch., 1-William, 2-Sarah Moore, 3-Elizabeth Smith (hus. ..Joseph.), 4-James, 5-Joseph, 6-Peter, 7-John (dec'd, his ch. get their father's share, names—William, Elizabeth, Jesse, Mary Anne, Sarah Jane, Evadne, James Alexander). Exec., William Doran and Joseph Smith, s-i-l. Wit., John Seville, Jacob Pepper, Addison McCauley.

DOWMAN, Jacob—undated and unsigned, but pr. 5-15-1815. W., Margaret, 9 ch., 1-Sarah, 2-John, gets 2 shares, 3-Wm., 1½ shares; 4-Anna, 5-Jacob, 6-Margaret, 7-Mary evidently w. of Gabriel Cane); 8-Catherine, 9-Rachel. Wit., Simon Taylor, William Ely. See Bowman.

DOUTHIT, John—9-26-1803; pr. 12-19-1803. W., Margaret. 12 ch., 1-Thomas, 2-John, 3-Silas, 4-Solomon, 5-Caleb (5 shillings earlier provision); 6-David and 7-Daniel, 200 acres; 8-Rebecca Cooper, 9-Catherine Tuncle, 10-Mary, 11-Sarah, 12-Christena. Widow, land in Canawa Co., on Ohio. Exec., wife, and William Vause. Sec., Lewis Vandiver, Stephen Pilcher. Wit., John Michel, Richard Holliday and Thomas Vause.

DREW, Perez (of Romney)—8-8-1797; pr. 9-18-1797. W., Mary. No ch. Elisabeth Egan (hus. James), bro. Sylvanus' sons; to Samuel Delano's sons; to James Southward's sons; to all their daughters. Bro. Sylvanus gets land in Plymouth, Mass. Friend, James Dailey. Exec., James Dailey. Wit., And. Woodrow, John McMicklin, Thomas Mulledy, William Fox.

DULING, William, Sr.—10-18-1831 (codicil 10-13-1839); pr. 11-25-1839. 9 ch., 1-William Collin, 2-Edmond, 3-Sarah Ann Dean, 4-Achilles, 5-Elijah, 6-Nancy Knabenshue (hus., Jacob), 7-Ruth Dean, 8-Eliza James (dec'd, her ch.), 9-Zecheriah (dec'd, has dau., Elizabeth). Exec., son, Achilles, and Jacob Knabenshue. ..Sec., Silas Reese and George Barrick. Wit., William Welch, John and George Barrick. Wit. to codicil, Thomas Carshaddon, John and George Barrick.

DULING, William, Sr.—7-7-1854; pr. 11-24-1856. Harriet R., "my present wife." 11 ch., 1-Virginia, 2-Rebecca Frances, 3-Margaret Maranda, 4-Philadelphia, 5-Harriet Eliza, 6- Sarah Jane Welch, 7-Anna Dew (hus., John L.), 8-Mary Davis (hus., Joseph), 9-James S. Duling, 10-David Gibson Duling, 11-William Duling. Two nieces, Adelaide Caroline Missouri Wineow and Margaret Catherine Wincow; their mother, Catherine Wineow. Exec., James Carskaddon. Sec., John M. Pancake, William French, Silas Reese. Wit., Achilles Duling and Ruben Davis. Widow refuses will and claims her one-half dower right. Wit., Achilles Duling and William H. Barrick.

DUNN, Ephraim—12-17-1841; pr. 6-26-1843. Bro., Jacob; Sisters, Rosanna, Rebecca and Mary; neps., William and Ephraim Jefferson Dunn; to Ephraim Conner, Ephraim Thrasher, Ephraim Caid and Ephraim Millat, namesakes. Exec., William Dunn and Jacob and John Donaldson.

DUNN, Rosannah—not dated; proved 11-27-1843. 4 ch., 1-Drusilla, 2-Louisa, 3-Sophiean, 4-Lewis T. Bro., Ephraim Kelso. Exec., son, and friend Dan Dunn. Wit., James Abernathy, Thomas Dunn, Charles Kellar.

DYE, John — 3-17-1854; pr. 3-27-1854. W., Rebecca. 1 ch., Mary Evline. Exec., friend, John Wart. Wit., Elijah Ruckman and Hugh Parrill.

DYE, Thomas, Sr.—12-13-1837; pr. 11-25-1844. W., Anna. 8 ch., 1- James, one-eighth; 2- William, one-eighth; 3-John, one-eighth of two-thirds; 4-Thomas, one-eighth of two-thirds; 5-George, one-eighth of two-thirds; 6-David, one-eighth of two-thirds; 7-Anna Cundiff and her children, one-eighth; and 8- Anna Maria McNemar, one-eighth of two-thirds. After wife's death, one-third of estate divided among ch. and gr. ch. Exec., John and George Dye. Wit., Abr. Doll, Thomas Carnell, Joe Harrison.

—E—

EARSOM, Jane—6-20-1850; pr. 4-23-1855. 9 ch., 1- Mary M., 2-Simon, 3-Samuel, 4-William, 5-James, 6-Nancy Rizer, 7-Sarah Bellmire, 8-Harriet Ann Taylor, 9-Sidney Grace (hus. Ephraim M.). Exec., Ephraim M. Grace. Wit., John and Jacob Grace.

EARSOM, John—7-7-1847; pr. 8-23-1847. W. not mentioned by name (see Jane Earsom's will) 8 ch., 1-Simon, 2- James, 3-William, 4-Nancy Ryer, 5-Ann Taylor, 6-Sarah, 7-Mary, land got of Colby Chew; 8-Sidney Grace (hus. Ephraim), Humes place. Exec., son, William. Wit., Levi Cain, Jacob Darby, John Brady.

EARSOM(N), John—1-18-1790; pr. 4-15-1790. W. Christiana. Ch., 6 plus, 1-Simon, 2-Barbara, 3-John, 4-Mary, 5-Susannah, 6-——Rannels (hus. Robert). "My younger children," evidently others. Exec., "my friend, Robert Parker, Sr., and my son-in-law, Robert Rannels." Sec., Andrew Hume, David Long. Wit., Lewis Dunn, Dvaid Long, Robert Rannels.

EARSOM, Mary—1-10-1859. No hus. or ch. mentioned. Nep., John E. Ridger and John Billmore; brother-in-law, Ephraim M. Grace (w. Sidney). Wit., Stephen and Jacob Grace.

EARSOM(N), Simon—6-20-1795; pr. 6-20-1795; codicil, 9-8-1795; pr. 6-20-1796. No wife. 3 ch., 1-John (dec'd, his heirs, Simon and John—see his will); 2-Jacob, 450 a. for life, then to his sons, Jacob and John; Jacob's w., Catherine, to have her third during life; 3-Susannah Pancake, land during life, then it goes to Simon and John Pancake (presumably her sons). Exec., Rebert Parker, Sr., and Robert Parker, Jr. Wit., of will, John Newman, Benjamin Neale, Henry Hines, Richard Guffick. Wit. of codicil, James Rannels, William Buck, John Newman.

ECKSTINE, Leonard—3-4-1796; pr. 4-14-1800. Ch., 5-plus, 1-Magdalene, 2-Margaret Stip (or Stafter, hus., Peter); 3-Mary, 4-Elizabeth, 5-Rosanna. "Two children begotten of my wife after separation and consequent divorce in state of Pennsylvania, bearing name of Nancy and City, illegitimate." Wit., A. King, John Jones, Sr., John Kellar, Richard Stafford, George Price.

EDWARDS, Joseph—4-10-1781; pr. 5-14-1782. No wife. 4 ch., 1-David, 2-Joseph, 3-Thomas, 4-Mary Pugh (hus. Robert). Gr. sons, Samuel and Jesse Pugh, sons of Robert Pugh, land on Gr. Capehon. Gr. son, Samuel Edwards, son of David. Exec., Robert and Jesse Pugh. Sec., Elias Posten, Levi Ashbrook. Wit.: Timothy Hiett, Cornelius Gard, David Candy, Joel Cheshire, William Carlyle.

SYNOPSIS OF WILLS

EDWARDS, Martha (widow of Thomas)—10-8-1827; pr. 12-17-1827. Dau., Ann Powell, gets all for care of her. "Loves all my children" (rest not named. Exec., s-i-l, John Powell, and Zebulon Sheets. Wit., Eli Beall, Benjamin Slane and William H. Topper.

EDWARDS, Thomas—2-8-1786; pr. 7-14-1791. W., Mary. 6 ch., 1-Thomas, 2-David (dec'd, left ch., Jesse, Andrew and David); 3-Sarah Ann, 4-Naomi, 5-Margaret, 6-Hannah (dec'd, her ch. have her share). Exec., bro.-in-law, Even Hiett, and w. Wit., John Slane, David Sonnen, Evan Jenkins.

ELLIS, Joel—10-30-1845; pr. 2-23-1846. Dec's bro., Dudley Brown Ellis, late of Kentucky; rel. and friend, William Dunlap of Kentucky; neps, John and Nelson W. Ellis, also nep., Ira Elis, of Texas; dec'd niece, Mahala Clift. Exec., Sam Baumgarner. Wit.: Nath Offutt, Michael C. Woolford.

ELSWICK, John — 1-12-1754; pr. 11-13-1759. W., Rachel. 3 ch., 1-Thomas, 2-John (dec'd), 3-Rachel. Gr. dau., Rachel. Exec., w. and Henry Oldaker. Wit., Joseph How and James Scott.

ELY, Isaac—11-1-1792; pr. 2-7-1796. W., Sarah. "Only son," Benjamin, mentioned in will. Exec., w. and gr.son, William. Wit., John Thompson, Robert Alexander, Jacob Starn.

ELY, Sarah—7-12-1848; pr. 8-25-1848. 7 ch., 1-Jean or Janie, 2-Benjamin, 3-Joshua, 4-Elizabeth Powell, 5-Margaret (Miler?), 6-William, 7-James. Money in hands of Matthew Hare after settling her husband, William Ely's estate. Wit., Martin Hardy, Robert Patterson, Adam Hidner.

ELY, William—5-2-1844; pr. 7-22-1844. W., Sarah. 8 ch., 1-Joshua, 2-Isaac, 3-Elizabeth, 4-Benjamin, 5-Margaret Blake, 6-William, 7-James, 8-Jane. (2-Isaac, and 3-Elizabeth Powell evidently older ch., possibly of earlier marriage.) Exec., s. Joshua, and friend, John L. Heare. Wit., Martin Hardy, Matthew Heare, George Thompson.

EMMERT, Andrew—2-1-1855; pr. 3-29-1855. W., Elizabeth. 10 ch., 1-Jacob, 2-Mirianna, 3-Elizabeth, 4-Catherine, 5-Washington, 6-Hannah, 7-Eliza, 8-Benjamin F., 9-Eliza Jane, 10-Isaac N. Son, George Washington. Wit., Jacob Peppe, Joseph S. Kline.

EMMERT, George—7-14-1851; pr. 9-22-1851. Nep., Isaac Newton Emmert, son of his bro., Andrew.

EMMERT, Jacob—3-29-1819; pr. 4-19-1819. W., but not named. 8 ch., 1-Mary, 2-Catherine Horn, 3-Elizabeth Fleming, 4-Christina Cleishers, 5-John Henry, 6-Phillip, 7-Andrew, 8-Jacob. Exec., son, Jacob Emmert, and Jacob Millslagle. Wit., James Pugh, John Barker.

ENGLE, Peter (of Frederick Co., Md.)—8-7-1790; pr. 11-2-1792. W. Elizabeth. 6 ch., 1-Justinius, (eldest son), 2-Peter, 3-Charlotte, 4, 5 and 6, daus., wives of Adam Wasser, John Nicholas Warner and Abraham Yangling, respectively. Speaks of bonds of Justinian Engle of York Co., Pa. Wit., Dan Beesar, George Shoff, William Loos.

ENTLER, John—10-2-1842. W. and ch. mentioned, but not by name. Will proved but not witnessed by John Kern, Jr., Dan Maloney, Edw. M. Armstrong. Exec., William Davis and Henry Entler.

ENTLER, William, Sr.—9-20-1843. W., Margaret. Married daughters men but not named. Gr. dau. Isabella, to figure as a child. Sons, William and Jeptha. Exec., sons and David Gates. Wit., Jno. Kern, Jr., Tow Clayton, George Y. Hanson.

EVANS, Abel—9-11-1858; pr. 3-28-1859. W., Elizabeth. "To John Olover and garet Evlilner, William, Sarah and James, nothing at tall." Exec., John Evans. No wit.

EVERETT, Darius—7-8-1821; pr. 1823. W., Sarah. 8 ch., 1-Moses, 2-Asa, 3-Enos, 4-Elizabeth, "youngest dau.," 5-Sarah, "infirm dau.," 6-Fanny, 7-Ezekiel, 8-Dan. Will speaks of "all my sons and sons-in-law." He was of Kingwood twp., N. J. Speaks of Ruckman survey. Has estate in Hunterdon Co., N. J., as well as in Hampshire Co. Exec., George Wanamaker. Wit., John Waterhouse, Henry Snyder, Stacey B. Bancroft.

—F—

FAIRFAX, Miss Mary Martin—12-16-1825; pr. 1-16-1826. Sister, Eliza C. Ragland; 2 nieces, Virginia Carey and Louisa Craig Ragland. Exec., John B. White and Wm. C. Wodrow. Wit., R. Newman and And. Wodrow. Land in Jefferson county, Virginia.

FARLEY, Thomas— Pr. 5-14-1782. W., Jane. 5 ch., 1-John, 2-David, 3-Mary, 4-Margaret, 5-Elinor, 6-Andrew. Exec., Okey Johnson and Thos. Lasson. Wit., Okey Johnson and Wm. Blackburn.

FARMER, Frances—7-1-1835; pr. 4-5-1835. 3 ch., 1-Sarah Ellis (hus., David), 2-Samuel Farmer, 3-Alice Fletcher (dec'd, her 3 minor ch., Harriet Elizabeth, Frances and George W.; David Ellis, guardian). Exec., David Ellis. Wit., George A. Smith, James W. Ellis, James Burnett and Nathan B. Brelsford.

FILLING, Catherine—11-23-1820 pr. 2-19-1821, and again 3-18-1822. 4 ch., 1-Susannah and 2-Barbara (both married), 3-Elizabeth, 4-Nancy (lame). Gr son, Samuel, $50 from his grandfather's estate (her father's). Exec., Thos. Carshadon. Wit., James Parker, Joseph Long.

FINK, Fred—9-18-1835; pr. 12-25-1837. No w. 3 ch plus. 1-Sam, 2-Catherine. Divide between "all my children"; evidently more. Exec., son, 3-Dan. Wit., John Sloan, Christian Huffman, John Hurness (Harness).

FISHER, Adam (blacksmith)—5-14-1778; pr. 3-11-1783. W., Christina. 8 ch., 1-Adam, 2-Jacob, 3-John, 4-George, 5-Michael, 6-Solomon, 2 dau., 7-Elizabeth and 8-Catherine. Exec., w., John Westfall, Sr., and Michael Sea (or Lea). Wit., Robert Maxwell, William Cunningham, — Rottle (?), — Poelze (?), Samuel Brink. (Some names signed in German).

FITZGERALD, Edward—1-16-1789; pr. 6-12-1793. W., Ann. 1 ch., Maria, when of age to get home in Morganstown which he owns with Jeremiah Mahony. Exec., w. and Patrick Campbell of Chambersburg, Pa. Sec., James Murphy. Wit., Wm. McGuire, James Murphy, Flor Mahony.

FLEEKS, Henry, Sr.—7-31-1816; pr. 12-19-1820. W., Susannah. 3 sons named, 1- Henry, 2-Solomon (indebted to him), and 3-John; "all my sons"; gr. dau., Susannah Fleek. Exec., sons, John and Henry. Wit., John Spencer, Geo. Unce, Fred Wiltz, Abr. Crookhart.

FLEMING, Patrick—9-27-1838; pr. 10-22-1838. No w. 6 ch., 1-James, 2-Ann Shirley (Shinley?); gr son, Thos. Shirley; gr dau., Elizabeth Shirley; 3-John, 4-Edward, 5-Catherine. One-fifth part of land occupied by Wm. S. Kline "to James Fleming, my son, in trust for daughter, 6-Christina Kline (hus. Wm. S.). Wit., Josiah Smoot, Benjamin Arnold.

FLOOD, John — 1-14-1821; pr. 4-18-1828. 10 ch., 1-John, (use of property, then to gr. ch., his ch.,) has son, John; 2-Elizabeth, 3-Sarah, 4-Mary, 5-Eloner, 6-Mary Rachen, 7-Ann, 8-Sarah Elizabeth, 9-Phoby, 10-Charles O, who has sons, Washington and John; they are to have land after paying off the mother and grandmother of Charles' sons. A gr. son, William, Eleonor's ch., by John Raukin, dec'd. Does not say "my wife," but speaks of "the mother of these children." Exec., Ephraim Dunn.

FORMAN, Christene—9-9-1778. Says she is 67 years old. No children. "Beloved brother," Samuel (w. Anna), sister, Margaret; nep., James Forman; niece, Sarah Jane Shunholtz; Moses and Henry Forman, "who had a part of my money" (relationship not shown). Wit., Nath. Offut, Stephen Miller, William Largent.

FORMAN, Sarah—3-4-1851; pr. 5-2-1851. 4 gr. ch., Amos, Catherine, Sarah and Susan Hollenbeck. Land to be divided between Thos. M. Allen and Dan Hollenbeck, heirs. Exec., Abr. Renihart. Wit., Elijah Rinehart, Wm. D. Rees

FOX, Gabriel—2-26-1798; pr. 12-15-1799. W., but not named. Son, William, carpenter tools; gr sons, Wm. and John Allen; gr dau., Margaret Allen; gr dau., Ivea Fox. W. has care of Malen Lewis to school him, evidently a bound boy. Wit., Edw. Ryan, James Clark, Richard Jenking, David Allen. Sec., And. Wodrow, Sam Parsons.

FRENCH, James — 10-14-1773; pr. 11-9-1773. W., Mary. 2 ch., 1-Robert, 2-William. Land, "Lower Blue" adj. Hugh Murphy. Exec., W. and Robert Parker. Wit., T. Collins (Thomas Collins), Hugh Murphy and David Corban.

FRENCH, John—9-25-1830; pr. 11-15-1830. W., but not named. 5 ch., evidently young; John Arnold, guardian. Wit., Isaac Staler (Stater?), Enos Hoak, Esq.

FRENCH, Robert—3-26-1829. W., Eleanor. 8 ch., 1-William, 2-Nancy Corbin, 3-James, 4-John, 5-Eliza Maria, 6-Sarah, 7-Katherine, 8-Robert. Exec., friend, John Arnold. Wit., John McBride, Joshua Arnold and John Arnold. Sec., John McBride, John Robinson.

FRENCH, Thomas—9-3-1859; pr. 11-28-1859. W., Ann Elizabeth.

FRIDDLE, John — 3-3-1842; pr. 3-28-1842. W., Mary. "Between all my children." Wit., John Kern, Robert Newman, Rebecca Valentine.

FRY, Benjamin—8-31-1839; pr. 2-24-1840. W., Mary. 11 ch., sons, 1-Henry, 2-Abr. W., 3-Benj. P., 4-Isaac L., dau., 5-Nancy A., 6-Susan Setler (or Leller), 7-Lucy I. Doran, (hus. Joseph), 8-Fanny More, 9-Jane Elizabeth Fry, 10-Sarah M. Fry. Jackson Fry, son of dec'd dau., Mary Ann Moore. Will contested as of unsound mind; lost. Exec., sons. Wit., Jared J. Williams, Samuel Frye, and Hugh McKiver.

FULKAMORE, John Martin — 6-18-1821; pr. 10-11-1821. No w. 4 ch., 1-Asa, land in Ohio; 2-John; 3-Tasey, dec'd dau., ch. by her, Leah gets no land, rest get Ohio land; 4-Unity Barrett, dec'd dau., her ch. get land in Ohio; gr. son, Joseph, second son of Asa. Exec., Jonathan Pugh. Wit., Jesse Lupton, Erasmus Unglesley (?)

—G—

GADDIS, William—10-11-1772; pr. 3-9-1775. W. Persila. Son, John. Exec., w., and son, John. Sec., Jonathan Pugh and John Largent. Wit., Jacob Jenkins, John Largent and Owen Rogers.

GALASPY, Michael (Gillespie) — 3-8-1803; pr. 5-16-1805. W., Catherine (formerly Catherine Moore). 3 ch., 1-Henry, 2-James "when Henry is of age," 3-Mary; Nancy Moore, dau. of w. Exec., w., and John Jack. Wit., John J. Jacob, Archibald Watts, Andrew Gibson, Jr.

GANOE, Jane (widow of Stephen)—1-2-1854; pr. 1-23-1854. 5 living ch.; Abigail McBride mentioned, relationship not stated. Exec., nep., John Cunningham, son of sister, Mary. Wit., James Moreland, Arthur T. Pugh, Edgar W. Canfield.

GANOE, Stephen—4-30-1809. W., but not named. Ch and representatives. Son, Stephen. Names, Moses Henderson, David Henderson, William Williams, William Harnass (Hannas); gr. sons, Stephen; William and Peter Bird; dau., long since dec'd. Exec., s-i-l, David Henderson, and friend, Wm. Ely. Wit., John Higgins, William Doman, Jonas Combs.

GASSAWAYS, Robert—12-16-1805. W., Sarah. 8 ch., 1-Nicholas, 2-Nance, 3-Miriam, 4-Robert, 5-Benjamin, 6-Liddey, 7-Nelly, 8-Sally. William Critton, land laid off by John Michael (relationship not shown). Sole exec., son, Robert. Wit., Richard Short, Robert Calvin, John Johnson, Jr., William Critton.

GEORGE, Ellis—12-20-1805; pr. 4-16-1810. W., Lydia. 5 ch., 1-James, 2-Rich (land bought of John Lupton, George Myers land; "to all my friends the members of Hopewell Monthly Meeting, a burying place," land bought of Bernard Brelsford near Dillon's Run; 3-Sarah Barrett (hus., Richard); 4-Rebecka Lupton (hus., Jesse), 5-Rachel Barrett (hus., Jonathan). Exec., James and Richard George, sons. Wit., Henry and Lydia George, Jr.

GEORGE, Matthew—12-7-1781; pr. 5-14-1782. W., Susannah Ch., 4 plus, 1-James, 2-King, 3-George, 4-Matthew; "rest of my children." Exec., George See, George Stump and w. Sec., Sam Dew and Joseph Neville for w. Wit., James Sears and David Shook. Land on South Branch Fork.

GEORGE, Richard—8-27-1818; pr. 9-20-1824. W., Mary. 8 ch., 1-Henry, "eldest son," 2-Evan, 3-Richard, 4-John, 5-Mary Lydia, "eldest daughter," 6-Ruth, 7-Rachel, 8-Sarah. "Land willed me by by father, Ellis George." Wit., James and Silas George.

GILMER, John (on Patterson's Manor)—8-10-1773; pr. 11-9-1792. W., Margaret. 6 ch., 1-Margaret, 2-Eleanor, bound to John Warren, 410 acres; 3-Elizabeth, 4-Mary Groves, of Ireland; 5-Ann, 6-Jane. Names mentinoed, William Parks and William Carroll, his free-servants; Michael Leard, cloth for coat (he relinquishes legacy). Exec., w., and Michael Leard. Sec., John Parker, William Howell, Ezek Totten. Wit., Michael Leard, Eleanor Gillmer, Ammey York.

GILMER, Henry —

GLASS, Sarah Ann, of Frederick Co., dau. of Rev. Joseph Glass, his estate—9-13-1837; cod. 9-14-1837; pr. ?-1837. Seven sisters, 1-Mary, 2-Hester Sophia, 3-Emaline Marshall, 4-Ann McAllister Glass; niece, Ann Watterman Foote, dau. of Rev. William Henry Foote, hus. of Sarah Ann Glass' sister, 5-Eliza; 6-Susan Emily Baker; 7-Sidney O. McDowell. Land bought of Joseph Jones. Wit., John B. White and William Henry Foote.

GLAZE, Conrad—5-17-1831; pr. 6-21-1831. 7 ch., 1-Andrew, 2-Nancy Belinger, dec'd; 3-Polly Long, 4-Peggy Wallace, 5-Sally Taylor, 6-Conrad, 7-Hannah (dec'd, her dau., Elizabeth Cather). Mentions Thomas Wallace, John Long, Thomas Cather, heirs. Exec., son, Conrad. Wit., William Donaldson, Robert Buck, Benj. Martin. Sec., John Brady and John Donaldson.

GOOD, Abraham—12-28-1833; pr. 9-27-1840. W., Sarah; her sister, Ann Smith; bro., Peter. Exec., Thomas Welch. Sec., Luke and Nath. Kuykendall. Wit., Joseph Crossley, John Saulters, John Crossley.

GOOD, Jacob—4-1-1780; pr. 5-9-1780. W., Susannah. 3 ch., 1-Peter, 2-Abraham, 3-Isaac. Exec., Peter Putnam. Wit., Micheal Miller, Henry Lightner, William Bell.

GOOD, Phillip—2-5-1827; pr. 3-19-1828. W., Elizabeth. 4 ch., 1-John, 2-Phillip, 3-Elizabeth, 4-Mary. Wit., George R. and George G. Tasker, James McCormack.

GOOD, Sarah—9-18-1854; pr. 10-22-1855. German O. Homan, Almona K. Homan, sister, Susanner Hogan. Exec., Henry Homan. Sec., John Ward, Hugh Parrell, Elijah Ruckman. Wit., John Ward, Joseph B. Chamberlin.

GRANT, William—3-13-1837; pr. 11-2-1841. Codicil 8-29-'39. W., Hannah. 2 gr. sons, William Smoot (Bible) and William "Herrios." 2 gr. sons, George and William Shank; gr. dau., Lucinda Buzzard (late Smoot); s-i-l, Jacob Shank. Exec., friend, John Arnold. Sec., John Parker and John J. Pownall Wit., John McBride and Joshua Arnold. Codicil revokes land given to Jacob Shank.

GRAYSON, Ambrose—1-4-1816; pr. 6-19-1816. W., Sarah. 10 ch., 1-Thomson, 2-Catherine, 3-Benjamin, 4-Lidday, 5-Nancy, 6-Elizabeth, 7-William, 8-Mariah, 9-Felix, 10-Rhubin. Exec. and sec., wife. Wit., John Cundiff, Jr., Thomas Hogans, Robert Jones.

GRAYSON, Sarah—3-30-1848; pr. 5-28-1849. 10 ch., 1-William, 2-Reuben (land), 3-Catherine, 4-Lydia, 5-Benjamin, gr. dau., Ann (evidently living with them), 6-dau., Nancy Liller, 7-Maria Hendrickson, 8-Felix Grayson, 9-Thomazen, son (dec'd, his heirs), 10-Elizabeth Liller. Exec., sons, William and Reuben. Sec., son, Benjamin. Wit., Silas Rees William Fout, William A. Duling.

GRAYSON, Thomazen—11-20-1843; pr. 1-22-1844. W., Margaret A. 4 ch., 1-Benjamin, 2-John (left to John Ravenscroft), 3-Clary, 4-Sanford (minor). Exec., wife and Benjamin Grayson. Sec., John Vandiver and Joseph Frazin. Wit., John Green, M. Harrison.

GREENEWELL, Elijah—10-24-1825; pr. 10-16-1826. W., Catherine. Elizabeth Page (hus., Thomas), Hetty Brown ("who lives with my wife—no rel."); "my half-sister, Mary Reasoner (hus., Peter), and children. Suit in chancery at Winchester with William Rees. Sec., Sam Cockerell and Okey Johnson. Wit., Sam Cockerell, Thomas Caskaden, Frederick Sheets.

GROVES, Jacob—11-3-1827; pr. 11-19-1827. W., Elizabeth. 11 ch., nine named: 1-Catherine Keller, elder dau.; 2-Anna Kale, 3-Polly Arnold, 4-Eliza, 5-Jacob, 6-Jackson, 7-John, 8-Elizabeth Ann, 9-Phillip, eldest son; "3 youngest" minors. Wit., John Spaid, Philip Kline, Fred Spaid. Sec., Philip Kline.

GULICK, Fred (of Pickway, O.)—10-6-1831; pr. 3-8-1837. No w. named. 4 ch. He lives with dau., 1-Polly; 2-Amos, 3-Elisha, 4-Stephen, "youngest son." "All my children," evidently others. Wit., George Ambrose, John Ritchart.

—H—

HAFF, Cornelius—6-29-1786; pr. 9-12-1786. W., Elizabeth. 4 ch., 1-Cornelius and 2-John, land; 3-Elizabeth, 4-Rachel. Exec., son, John, and John Larew. Sec., Peter Larew. Wit., Richard Haff, Peter Larew, Abraham Larew.

HAFF, Cornelius—6-4-1795; pr. 7-20-1795. W., Elizabeth. 5 ch., 1-Andrew, 2-John, 3-Jacob, 4-Catherine, 5-Hannah. Exec., w., and friend, Conrad Ronomus. Wit., Levi Matthew, Hannah Leren, Christopher Ponemus, Ann Hardy.

HAFF, Laurence—11-11-1778; pr. 5-3-1783. W., Sarah. 4 ch., 1-Laurence, 1 silver spoon, 1 gold ring, silver snuff box; 2-Paul, 2 silver spoons and gold ring (he has dau., Sarah); 3-Luke, land he lives on; 4-Abraham, land where house stands. Exec., wife and John Deckar. Sec., John Westfall and Jonathan Purcell. Wit., Joseph Nevill, Peter Hog, Dan McNeil, Alex White.

HAINES, John (Harrison Co., O.)—9-13-1824; pr. Hampshire Co., 11-16-1824. W., Rachel, 160 a. during life. 4 ch., 1-Sarah, 2-Samuel, 3-Israel, 4-Leweza. Farm to Samuel and Israel. Hampshire Co. land to be sold. Exec., son, Israel. Wit., Joseph Fry, Benj. and Robt. Paisley.

HALL, Joseph—2-6-1785; pr. 3-9-1785. W., Mary. No ch. Sarah McDaniel gets land, has dau., Mary, 200 acres. James Scott, "son of my wife," land; Mary Scott, "dau. of my wife," land. Exec., John Baker. Sec., Nicholas Tewalt. Wit., John Rowles and Nicholas Tewalt.

HALL, Richard—1-31-1850; pr. 1-27-1853. W., Winney. 10 ch., 1-William, 2-Amanda Holland (hus. Norris), 3-Elijah, 4-Sydner (is trustee for ch. of Boolys Hall in Ky.), 5-Boales (or Beales), 6-Norman, 7-Emily Thompson (hus. John), 8-Catherine Frazier (hus. Thomas), 9-Lucy Blakley (hus. Charles), 10-James. Exec., William Hall, father, and son-in-law, Joseph Thompson. Sec., James Parsons, William Hall, William A. Vance, Norman Urton and Benj. F. Richards. Wit., William Vance and James McDonald. Wit. to codicil, Phillip B. Sheet and Norman Urton.

HAMMACK, John—8-7-1852; pr. 4-24-1854. W., Catherine. 5 ch., 1-Abraham, 2-Jacob, 3-Samuel, 4-Sarah Secrist, 5-Rebecca Yonley. Land patented to him and Thomas Yonley. Exec., son, Abraham. Sec., Joseph Smith and James Baker. Wit., Spencer R. Gray, John McCauley.

HAMMACK, Samuel—7-30-1832; pr. 8-27-1832. W., Jane. 4 ch., 1-William Thornton Hammack, a minor, 2-Harriet Ann, 3-Mary, 4-Catherine. Exec., Thomas Caskhadon and William Welch. Sec., Samuel Cockrill, Thomas Carskhadon, Richard Davis, Sam Vandiver. Wit., William Welch, Moses McClintic.

HAMRICK, Siras—6-9-1835; pr. 11-23-1835. W. dec'd. To Jacob Doll, real and personal estate forever. Exec., Phillip Doll. Sec., Reuben Davis. Wit., Thomas and Reuben Davis and Phillip Doll.

HANNAS, William—12-31-1836; pr. 3-27-1837. Son, Daniel, gets all; other children had left him. Exec., son, Daniel. Wit., William Vance, John Hannas, Samuel Hains.

HANSBROUGH, John—6-19-1844; pr. 6-22-1846. W., but not named, step-mother of John; she had paid $400 on land. 2 ch., 1-John, 2-Eveline Cherry. Wit., Wesley B. McNemer and Jonathan Pownell.

HEAD (or Hard), Mary Magdalene — 4-5-1775; pr. 3-12-1776. Daughter, Sovia Elizabeth Heard. Exec., Henry Marige. Wit., Anthony Baker, Micheal Alt, John Kinnle (Kimle?).

HARNESS (or Herness), Michael (of South Branch) — 1779; pr. 3-8-1785. W., Elizabeth. Nine ch., 1-Jacob, "youngest son," 2-John, 3-George, 4-Leonard, 5-Peter, 6-Elizabeth Yoakum, 7-Barbara Zee, 8-Dorothy Hornbeck, 9-Margaret Trumbo; gr. son, Michael, and sister; gr. dau., Elizabeth Robinson, sister of above Michael Harness; gr. dau., Barbara Zee. Exec., John Harness and s-i-l, Samuel Hornbeck. Sec., Dan Tieverbaugh. Wit., Anthon Baker, Joseph Petty and Jacob Yoakum. The above will was filed under "E" but think from the body that it is "H."

HARRIS, William—12-31-1831; pr. 1-16-1832. To Elizabeth Harris and dau., Sharloty; to Geo. Hill and son, John W. Exec., friend, George Moreland. Sec., Fred Ker. Wit., Benjamin Taylor and Josiah Calos.

HARRISON, Elizabeth—Pr. 10-15-1804. Divided between 3 ch. (Andrew, Jr., Craig, and Emily Wodrow) of my sister, Mary, and her husband, Andrew Wodrow. Exec., br.-in-law, Andrew Wodrow. Wit., William Taylor, Betsy Dailey and Elizabeth Heinzman.

HARRISON, Elizabeth—7-7-1854; pr. 3-22-1859. Bro., Theodore; niece, Melvina, dau. of Robert; bro., Robert; bro., George D. Exec., George D. Harrison. Wit., John W. Earhart, later in Marion Co., Mo;. Harrison Goyas, later in Shelby Co., Mo.; A. W. Roberts.

HARRISON, Mary—9-24-1836; pr. 2-23-1852. Land in St. Mary's Co., Md. 11 ch., 1-Pricy, 2-Betsy, 3-Rebecca, 4-Margaret Davis, 5-Theodore (trustee for Ann Harrison, widow of son, 6-James); 7-Henry (dec'd, his widow); 8-Amy's dau., Betsy, 9-John, 10-Robert, 11-George D. Exec., George D. Harrison. Wit., Thomazen and Benj. Grayson, Jr., Dency Welch.

HARTLEY, John—6-5-1783; pr. 3-9-1784. W. dec'd. 6 ch., 1-Elizabeth, 2-Ann Harden, 3-Hannah Pearsall, 4-Eleanor Houghland's 8 ch., Mary, Henry, Hannah, Cornelius, Macey, Margaret, Eleanor and Ann Houghland; 5-Mary Wilson, 4 ch., Dan, William, James and Ruth Wilson; 6-Margaret. Exec., Cornelius Houghland and gr. son, Dan Wilson, son of Mary Wilson. Wit., Jacob Slagle, Joseph House, James Dougherty.

HARTMAN, Henry—no date; pr. 6-16-1823. W., Mary. 6 ch., 1-Peter, 2-Antony, 3-Daniel, 4-Caty and 5-Margaret and "their first children"; 6-Phillip (or Sam), dec'd. Exec., Isaac Kuykendall; James Dailey and A. Kuykendall, ex. app. Wit., John Temple, Abraham Plumb, Henry and Fred High.

HASS, Peter—11-8-1858; pr. 1-14-1867. W. not mentioned. 6 ch., 1-Abraham, 2-William, 3-Nancy Stump, 4-Susan Pancake, 4-Sarah Ach, 6-Elizabeth Cann; gr. ch., Thomas, Francis, Peter and Sarah Mayberry, and Mary Smith.

HAWK, Henry—4-30-1856; pr. 8-25-1856. "Advanced in years." To Isaac Hawk's 2 ch., interest in bro. Joseph's estate in Illinois; sister, Sarah, gets land and balance of property divided among Nancy Meguire, Peter Miers, Everline and Jeremiah Oats, Thomas Dudwick, Catherine Arnold, Henry M., Ailsa C., William H., Sarah Jane, Mary A. and Esdras Ludwick, Mary, John, Richard and Solo. Brown, Warner T. High, Margaret A. Taylor and Elizabeth High Slone. Exec., Warner T. High. Wit., Henry Kelley, Henry M., and Elijah High. Sec., Henry M. and Elijah High.

HEARSHMAN, Christopher—3-4-1843; pr. 2-26-1844. Sell and divide 7 parts; 7 ch., 1-Eve Stagg's ch. and she, one-seventh; 2-Margaret Leatherman, dec'd; 3-Abraham and his ch. (Mark, Marguerite, and Christopher), one-seventh; 4-Mark, one-seventh; 5-Susannah Ludwick, one-seventh; 6-Jemz, one-seventh; 7-George, one-seventh. Nep., Solo. Arnold. Exec., Thomas Carskadon. Sec., Dan Clark. Wit., Thomas Carskadon, Dan Arnold, Dan Clark and Roland Dayton.

HEATOR, Micheal—5-13-1781; pr. 4-18-1796. W., Marey. 5 ch., 1-Solomon, 2-Phillip, 3-Micheal, 4-Barbara, 5-Marget. Exec., w., and Lemuel Barret and Jacob Slagle. Wit., John Vanbuskirk, William and Richard Chenoweth.

HEFFELBOWER, David—1113-1859; pr. 9-12-1864. W., Elizabeth. 5 ch., 1-Mary Ann Morris (dec'd; hus., Pythagoras; ch., John David Morris and Frances C. Remheart, [hus., John W.], Ersram, David H., and Bushrod); 2-Daniel F.; 3-Sarah Jane Offut (hus. Samuel); 4-Mary Eliza, 5-Edmond.

HEISKELL, Adam—7-22-1822; pr. 8-19-1822. No w. 6 ch., 1-Susanna O'Harra, 2-John, 3-Christopher, 4-Samuel (has ch.), 5-Isaac, 6-Jacob (dec'd, wid. Catherine). Exec., sons, John and Christopher. Sec., William Vance, John B. White, William Naylor. Wit., Adam Heiskell Warner Throckmorton, Robert Newman.

HENDERSON, Thomas—11-6-1815; pr. 4-30-1818. W., Nancy (evidently nee Day, dec'd). 4 ch., 1-Larkin Day, 2-William Day, 3-John Day (sons of Nancy Day); "my son, 4-John Grant. Land bought of William and John Henderson. Nm., —— Peppers, Baldwin Conners, Daniel Tucker, Scharff line. Exec., Larkin Day. Wit., John Hiett, Adam Brown, Amey Day, David Brown.

HERRIN, William—9-17-1846; pr. 6-24-1848. No w. Bro., Isaac, of Ky; balance divided between the following, relationship not shown: Julius Waddle, Julia A. Smith, Emaly R. Delany; neps., William, James, Isaac, Thomas Duval (land in Ohio); Henry Shackelford, William Ross of Culpepper Co., Va.; George Herrin. Exec., Julius Waddle, James Duval and Samuel Bumgarner. Wit., Solo- Funkhouser, Isaac L. Frye, John Barr.

HERRIOT, Ephraim, Sr.—5-3-1800; pr. 7-14-1800. No W. 6 ch., 1-William, 60 acres adj. Cavid Cookley; 2-John, and 3-Ephraim, balance of land; 4-Ursela Wicuf, 5-Sarah Blue, 6-Isabella Blue. Exec., sons, William and John. Sec., Hugh Ballentine and William Foreman. Wit., William Fox, John Parker, David Alen, Jos. Inskeep.

HETH, William, of Henderson Co., Ky.—9-11-1819; pr. 5-22-1820. W., Elizabeth T., land in Romney, Mill Creek. 5 ch., 1-William Henry, gets land with wife; 2-Andrew Thomas, 3-John Thaddeus; 4-Sam Pleasants, 5-w. pregnant, if child is born, shares equally. Exec., wife. Wit., Talifero S. Howard, James M. Clay. Widow has married Lazarus Powell, and he, with James Powell as sec., is appointed guardian of his 3 stepsons, Andrew T., John T. and Sam P. Heth.

HIETT, Evan—8-1-1809; pr. 2-9-1815. W., Sarah. 10 ch., 1-Joseph, 2-John, 3——Jonathan, 4-Jeremiah, "land adj. Hugh Slanes"; 5-Margaret, 6-Elizabeth, 7-Ann, 8-Sarah, 9-Martha, 10-Mary. Exec., "four sons." Sec., Thomas Athey, James Caudy, John Baker. Wit., James and Evan Caudy, Sam Gard, Thomas Allen.

HIETT, Jeremiah—4-16-1860; pr. 9-23-1861. W., Lucinda. 14 ch., 1-Elizabeth Little, 2-Jonathan, 3-John, 4-Asa, 5-Sam Patton, 6-Evan, 7- Frances Cowgill, 8-James S., 9-Sarah, 10-Lucinda Deaver, 11-William, 12-Jeremiah, 13-Joseph, 14-Robert. Itemizes day he gave each legacy. Wit., John S. Kidwell, James W. Foreman, James Walter Hiett.

HIETT, Jonathan—4-15-1843. W., Hannah (died '65 or '66). 8 ch., 1-Evan, 2-James, 3-Jonathan, 4-Jeremiah, 5-Margaret, 6-Sarah, 7-Jane, 8-Eliza.

HIETT, Jno.—2-23-1856; pr. 1-28-1857. 5 ch., 1-Joseph S., land got of father, called Craig tract; 2-Arthur T. Hiett (dec'd; left heirs), John Allen land; 3-Lydia Ann Monroe, 4-Lucy Monroe, 5-Elizabeth Capper. Gr sons, Arthur Melancthon Hiett, Charles Hiett; gr. dau., Susan Hiett. Mentions George Scharf's heirs. Exec., son, Joseph S. Wit., Joseph Caudy, T. J. Stump.

HIETT, Susannah (Suzanny)—5-16-1846; pr. 6-22-1846. All to sister, Fanny Hansbrough, widow of John. Wit., Wesley B. McMemar and John Hansbrough.

HIGGINS, James (of Lafayette Co., Mo.)—9-18-1843; pr. 10-19-1843. 8 ch., 1-Sarah Y. Mills, gets land (gr. ch., James H. and Elizabeth Mary Mills); 2-Montgomery Pike Higgins gr. ch., Martha Ellen, John Copsey, Justinian Higgins); 3-James, 4-Bushrod W., 5-John M., 6-Martha V. Horsman, 7-Joseph C., 8-dau., —— Parker (hus., William P.); gr. son, James H. Parker. Nm., Joseph Mills (in Lewis Co., Mo.). Exec., Montgomery Pike Higgins and William P. Parker. Wit., Francis Weems, Alex K. Bishop, John Welch.

HIGGINS, John, Sr.—1-9-1806; pr. 4-20-1807. W., Jane "Ione". 10 ch., 1-James, 2-Joseph, 3 -Hetty French, 4-Mary Rickets, 5-Ann Plummer, 6-Rachel Springer, 7-John, 8-Thomas, 9-Jonathan, 10-Martha Williams. Exec., sons, James and John. Wit., Paul Sommers, William Garrett, Peter Johnson.

SYNOPSIS OF WILLS

HIGGINS, Major John—5-19-1827; pr. 2-10-1829. W. not mentioned in will.. W., Sarah 2-11-1829 asks to have John Brady named ex. Wit., William French, Jr., and James Higgins. Dau., Patsy Taylor, and Maria Abernathy (hus. Dr. James). Nm., John Burridge, John Copsey, Frances Murphy. Wit., John Brady, William Sommerville, J. F. Chadwick.

HIGGINS, Sarah—2-24-1847; pr. 7-26-1852. 2 ch., 1-Maria M. Abernathy, 2-Matty Taylor; gr. son, John William Taylor; gr. son, Charles M. Taylor. Exec., William P. Stump. Sec., Charles S. Taylor.

HIGGINS, Joseph—2-17-1823; pr. 8-15-1825. 2 ch., Joseph and Sarah Howell (does not call her daughter). Land sold to Moreses Gorden and Joseph Phenicia Ontang. Robert Sherrard. Sec., William Vance. Wit., Benjamin, Evan and James McDonald, J. W. and Sally Carlisle.

HIGGINS, Judiah—5-11-1795 pr. 6-20-1796. W., Matilda. 2 ch., 1-Sarah, 2-Archibald; a sister, Kewsiah Osborne; brother John; Maj. John Higgins (relationship not stated). Lot 117, town of Bath. Exec., wife, and bro. and Charles Ozmond (Osborne?). Sec., John Higgins, Sr., and Cornelius Fence (Feree?) Wit., John Higgins, Sr., John George, Jane Munchen.

HIGGINS, Thomas—4-10-1762; pr. 5-21-1762. 7 ch., "3 well beloved sons," 1-Thomas, 2-Joshua, and 3-James; 4-Edy Laurence, 5-Rachel, 6-Mary, 7-Judiah. Exec., son, Judiah, and Matthias Swim. Wit., William Swim, Barbary Williams, George Wright.

HIGH, Fred—3-22-1843; pr. 7-27-1844. W., Christiana. 6 ch., 1-Elijah, land; gr. dau., Ann Maria; 2-Catherine, 3-Margaret Statlers (or Statlin) (hus., Jacob); 4-Anna Hufman (hus., Daniel); 5-John; 6-Frederick. Elizabeth Frazin (hus. Joseph) and —— Ludwick (hus. Andrew), probably daughters. Exec., son, Elijah, and John Sloan. Wit., Fred and Henry High, Daniel Thompson and Randolph S. Welch.

HIGH, Henry—11-20-1833; pr. 2-24-1834. W., Susannah. 10 ch., 1-George, 2-Jonathan, 3-Jacob, youngest, 4-Elizabeth, 5-Mary Ludwick, 6-Emily, 7-Catherine Ludwick, 8-Henry M., 9-Sarah Ann, 10-Nancy. Gr. dau., Elizabeth Jane Hawk. Mentions Henry Friddle, Thomas Sloan, Henry Hawk High, Elijah High. Exec., George High and John Sloan. Sec., Dan and John Ludwick and Jonathan High.

HOGAN, Thomas—1-22-1832; pr. 4-18-1833. W. not named. 2 ch., 1- Mary, 2-Susannah. Mentions state of Ga., "legisee." Dempsey Welch, Jr., "to have some of my clothes." Exec., John Dye. Sec., William and Thomas Welch and Vincent Vandiver. Wit., John Dye, Denny Welch, Jr.

HOGE, Israel—7-31-1802; pr. 9-20-1802. W., Ruth. 3 ch., 1-Ann, 2-Ester, 3-Elizabeth, Exec., w., friend, Jacob Jenkins, and bro., Asa Hoge. Wit., William Hoge and William Hoge, Jr.

HOGE, Moses—10-31-1860; pr. 10-10-1865. W. not named. 4 ch., 1-Maria Wilson, 2-Sarah James, 3-Eliza Rees, 4-G. Wilson. Niece, Catherine Peacemaker; gr. ch., Melie, Edward and Sam. Mentions Adam Peacemaker, Amos Janney, Edw. Janney, William Griffin, Barton Griffin; 2 daughters in Indiana. Exec., William J. Grove.

HOLLENBACK, Dan—4-29-1836; pr. 3-23-1836. W., but not named. Stepson, Warner "Kirckram," land, Patterson Creek; dau., Caroline; bro., Isaac, Dan Smith, son of Solomon Smith; gr. dau., Mary Ann Lorence shares equally with daughter. Brother, Isaac guardian of dau., Caroline. Exec., Thomas Allen. Sec., Thomas Allen and Abraham Rinehart. Wit., Sam Cockewell, John Inskeep, Nimrod McNary.

HOOFMAN, Christopher—7-2-1803; pr. 4-20-1807. W., not mentioned. 2 ch., 1-Joseph, 2-Mary Harris; gr. son, Lawson, eldest son of dau., and other gr ch. Wit., Cabel Evans, Thomas A. Tucker.

HOOK, William—5-18-1825; pr. 5-24-1837. W., Mary. 9 ch., 1-Thomas, 2-William, 3-Samuel, 4-Joseph, 5-Josiah (minor), 6-Robert (minor), 7-Elizabeth Newbanks, 8-Hetty Pugh (minor), 9-Mary (minor). Exec., Robert Hook. Sec., James Kelso, Michael Pugh. Wit., Malachi Pugh, Michael Pugh, G. Gibbons.

HOOKERS, Susanna—7-5-1854; pr. 10-11-1865. To grandniece, Phoebe, w. of Edmond Murphy, and then to grandnephew, Thomas Newton Murphy.

HORN, George, Sr.—1-11-1800; pr. 4-14-1800. W., Mary. 5 ch., 1-Andrew, 338 acres; 2-George, 3-Phillip, 4-Eve Brelesford (see her will); 5-Henry. Gr. dau., Betsy Liller, dau. of Eve. Exec., sons, George and Phillip. Sec., James Moroe and Jos. Asberry. Wit., Andrew Millslagle, Jason Hartt, "Oiborosorm," "Hrinsardt."

HORNBECK, Daniel—3-3-1778; pr. 3-10-1778. W., Magdelene. 3 ch., 1-Abraham, 2-James, 3-Solomon. To Abraham Coffman; Elizabeth Anderson, w. of John, and their dau.; to Thomas Leary's ch., Daniel, Dennis and one dau.; to John Anderson's 3 ch., Mary, Thomas and Margaret. Exec., wife, and William Hornback. Wit., Simon Hornback, Charles Myers, Sam C. Curtright.

HORNBECK, John—8-4-1766; pr. 3-8-1768. W., Husselty. 6 ch., 1-Daniel, 2-Isaac, 3-Samuel, land; 4-Benjamin, 5-Richard, 6-dau., Eleanor Cutter (hus. Cornelius). Exec., son, Samuel. Sec., William Cunningham and Henry Shipler. Wit., Daniel, Isaac and Michael Hornbeck, John Tuckwell

HORSMAN, Matthias Alrick—4-8-1797; pr. 5-8-1801. W., Eve. 6 ch., 1-Christian, 2-Casper, 3-Jacob, 4-Phillip, 5-Christopher, 6-George. Exec., w. Wit., Abraham Johnson, Samuel Landers, Arjalon Price, another in German script.

HOTZINPELER, Henry (of Augusta Co.)—3-31-1819; pr. 4-19-1819. W., Christina. Levi is to get nothing; other children. Exec., Michael Swisher, br.-in-law. Sec., H. D. March (Machir?) and Stephen Swisher. Wit., Edw. Keenan, Stephen and Joseph Swisher.

HOTZENBELER, Peter—no date; pr. 5-2-1782. W., Ann. 4 ch., 1-John, land, 2-Henery, land, 3-Jacob, land, 4-Abraham land. Sec., Rudolph Bumgardner and Valentine Switzer. Exec., son, Abraham, John Cooper and Jacob Keckley. Wit., William Crawford, Rudolph Bumgardner, Valentine Switzer.

HOWARD, Sarah M.—4-26-1836; pr. 12-22-1837. Sister, Evelina Pugh, a widow. Exec., John C. Heiskell. Sec., Francis Murphy, John Hansbrough, H. K. Hoffman, James D. Armstrong, Robert White. Wit., James D. Armstrong, Felix Heiskell.

HOWARD, Jane Elizabeth—4-23-1861; pr. 1-15-1868. Niece, Susan Pugh and Elizabeth Pugh; Mary P. Heiskell; dec'd sister, Eveline Pugh's other ch., Robert J. and William E.; Roger Perry, nephew, son of dec'd sister, Susan Perry. Ex., John C. Heiskell. Wit., Jacob Kern and John Myers.

HOWARD, William—7-18-1849; pr. 19-22-1849. No wife. 4 sisters, 1-Mary Frances, 2-Margaret, 3-Elizabeth, 4-Lucy, Uncle, John Myers (exec). Sec., Dan Gibson, Thomas Carskadon, Vause Fox. Wit.. J. B. White, Robert W. Dailey.

HOWELL, Jemima—5-5-1828; pr. 9-20-1830. 3 ch., 1-Hannah Anderson, 2-Lucreasy Anderson, and Anna Johnson. Gr. ch., Anna and Jammima Anderson and George Warfield (exec.). Sec., Phil. Fahs and Daniel Haynes. Wit., William Torrance, Peter Shaffer, Jesse Warfield.

HOWZAR, Lewis—1840. No w. 7 ch., 1-Thomas Offut, 2-John, 3-Jacob, 4-Lysander, 5-Charlotte, 6-Cassandra, 7-Mary Pritchet Edmondston (hus. William), is dau., I believe.

HUFFMAN, Christian (of Hardy Co.)—1-6-1835; 2-23-1835. W., Elizabeth. 2 ch., 1-Dan, land; 2-Christian, has dau., Elizabeth. Exec., son, Dan; Sec., John High, George High of Henry. Wit., Henry and David Vanmeter.

HUGHES, Hugh—1-9-1762; pr. 5-10-1763. W., Susannah. 5 ch., 1-William, 2-James, 3-Hugh; 4-Evan and 5-Jonathan put to learn trade. Exec., son, William, and Joseph Powell. Wit., Joseph How, James Sears.

HUGHES, William—12-31-1762; pr. 6-9-1767. No w. 7 ch., 1-Hugh, 2-Thomas, 3-William, 4-Evan, 5-Mary Anderson, 6-Sudrah Carpenter, 7-Sarah Baker. Exec., Ellis Hughes. Sec., James Alexander and William Wilson. Wit., Joseph Howe, James Alexander, Henry Frey.

HULL, Benjamin—9-8-1800; pr. 9-18-1809. W., Jemimah. 10 ch., 1-Jacob, youngest son, 2-Martin, 3-Silas, 4-Benjamin, 5-Stephen, 6-Isaac, 7-William, 8-Elizabeth Barnes, 9-Mary Moon, 10-Ann. Exec., w. Sec., Jacob Moon and Johnathan Nixon. Wit., John and Magdalene Dixon (may be Nixon?) and Jacob Moon.

HUTTA, Christian—6-25-1834; pr. 7-28-1834. W., but not named. 3 ch., 1-Catherine, gets land with mother; 2-Christian, 100 acres bought of Richard Holladay; 3-Elizabeth and her ch., land; she has son, John. Abraham Tead. Exec., John T. Hickman. Wit., Sam B. Davis, Jr., Abraham Doll and Joseph Leatherman.

—I—

INGLE, Matthias—3-20-1815; pr. 8-14-1815. W., Christian. 5 ch., 1-Matthias, land in Harrison Co.; 2-Margaret, 3-Eve, 4-Rachel, 5-Elizabeth. Exec., Christan Engle, wife. Sec., Peter Bruner and Thomas Oare. Wit., Michael McKiernan, Adam Bartmess, Willam Redburn.

INNES, Enoch—2-10-1778; pr. 8-12-1783. W., Sarah; no ch. Father and mother alive; bro., James, and sister, not named. Names mentioned, W. Casper, land; James Livingston, land in Georgetown, Md. Sec., Daniel Cresap, Tom Collins, Abram Jackson. Wit., Abraham Johnson, Jonathan Heath, John Rosseau, Andrew Lurke, Sam Dew.

INSKEEP, Anna — 8-31-1836; pr. 2-24-1837. "My children, William Foreman, James Henry, Sarah W., Catherine, John Foreman (has dau., Hannah Elizabeth); Mary Ann Keller (hus., Thos. A.); Rebecca Blue (hus., Uriah); Scioto Blue (?—relationship not clear). Exec., Henry M. Inskeep, relative and neighbor, refuses, so son, James H., appointed. Sec., Isaac Parsons and Henry M. Inskeep. Wit., William Vance and William Bond. (was first wife of William Inskeep, no doubt).

INSKEEP, Elizabeth—9-4-1848; pr. 1-23-1854. Dau., Sarah Mytinger (hus. Daniel). Exec., s-i-l. Names mentioned —David Griffeth (dead 1854), John B. White, John Z. Moreland, who had left state.

INSKEEP, James—4-27-1843; pr. 6-28 and 8-28-1848. W., Sarah; 5 ch., 1-Abraham W. and 2-David (both had ch.; will just released these sons' debts to their father); 3-William Vance (had son, William Foreman Inskeep); 4-Joseph (had following 5 ch., Elizabeth Wilson, Samuel Inskeep, Rachel Shrock, John Inskeep, James Goldsmith); 5-Samuel. Exec., bro., Abraham, and friends, —Vance and Gabriel Fox. Wit., John B. White, William J. Armstrong, John W. Kern, William Davis, and Thomas Welch. Widow refuses will; wit., Jno. Myers and C. Heiskell.

INSKEEP, John—1-20-1824; pr. 2-16-1824. W., Sarah. 3 ch., (1) "my natural son, John Inskeep," 2-dau., Susan Vance Inskeep, 3-son, Henry Mackin Inskeep. Exec., bro., Jeremiah Inskeep, and a friend, Warren Throckmorton. Sec., William Inskeep, Sam Kercheval. Wit., John Temple, William Inskeep.

INSKEEP, Joseph, Jr.—5-21-1837; pr. 5-22-1837. Exec., Garrett Vanmeter, br. in law. Wit., Moses McClintic, David Gibson, Sam P. Smith.

INSKEEP, Sarah—10-1-1841; pr. 10-23-1843. Dau., Susan V. McClintick; son, Henry M. Estate; slaves. Wit., Garrett W. Blue, Garrett J. Blue, Uriah Blue.

INSKEEP, Sarah—5-7-1853; pr. 5-25-1853. Father (dec'd), William Inskeep, bro., (dec'd), stepmother, Elizabeth brother, Foreman; brother, William (had children); sister, Rebecca Blue (deceased); father, Uriah Blue, of these children, Frances Lawson Blue and William Inskeep Blue. Exec., friend, Abraham Inskeep of Hardy County appointed, but Foreman Inskeep becomes exec. Sec., Edw. M. Armstrong and James Parsons. Wit., Foster Pratt, Henry M. Inskeep, Daniel Gibson.

INSKEEP, William—6-5-1839; pr. 11-24-1845. W., Elizabeth (she gets her property, see her will); 6 ch., 1-Elizabeth (dec'd; hus., — Fox); 2-Isaac (lives in Ohio); 3-Foreman; 4-Sarah ("Sally"—see her will); 5-Rebecca Susan Blue; 6-William, Jr. (see his will 1853). Gr. ch., John I. and Susan Fox. ch. of dau., Elizabeth, dec'd; also ch. of 7-Catherine Throckmorton. Exec., son, Foreman. Wit., John B. White, Dan Mytinger, William Harper. Widow refuses will in a paper dated 11-15-1865, witnessed by John B. White, Pressley Rector, Jno. Kern, Jr.

INSKEEP, Wm., (Tippecanoe Co., Ind.)—10-1-1851; pr. 10-16-1851. Fa. was William, left son a slave. Exec., bro, Foreman Inskeep of Hampshire Co. Wit. Turman Seavny and Jethro Neville.

IRONTON, Richard—10-4-1798; pr. 12-17-1798. W., Lidias. No ch. Bro., Thomas, of Armough Co., Ireland; Elizabeth Young, a bound girl. Exec., Tunis Petters and Joseph Asbury. Wit., William Richmond, James and Ulary Carruthers, and Jeremiah Asbury.

—J—

JACK, John, of Romney—8-6-1837; pr. 10-23-1837. W., Rebecca. 1 ch., son, Robert Y. Jack, dec'd ch., Frances Rebecca Jack. Exec., friend, Daniel Gibson. Sec., John Myers. Wit, W. J. Naylor, Sam Kercheval, Jr.

JACK, Mrs. Rebecca B.—3-16-1846; pr. 7-28-1846. 5 ch., 1-Mary Magruder, 2-John G., 3-Edw. Wilson, 4-Judith, 5-Carter T. Exec., son, Edw. or Daniel Gibson. Sec., John B. Kercheval and Andrew McDowell. Wit., John B. White, Edw. Armstrong, William H. Kuykendall.

JACKSON, Benjamin—5-22-1855; pr. 11-26-1855. No w. 4 ch., sons, 1-Ebenezar and 2-Samuel A.; 3-William (deceased; left heirs.) 4-Elizabeth Anderson (her hus., Joshua, dec'd); she has a daughter. "To Christiana Tavener, $5.00" (relationship not shown). Exec., a Mrs. Watkins appointed, refuses to serve, so son, Samuel A., appointed. Sec., Mrs. Watkins. Wit., Daniel F. and Esron Hefelbonn.

JACOB, John J. (aged 76)—8-7-1833; pr. 5-27-1833. W., Susan. 2 ch., John Jeremiah, and Julia Ann. Names mentioned in will: friend, Gerard Morgan, Sam'l Ditty, Methodist preacher. Exec., James Prather of Alleghany Co., Md., and William Donnelson of Hampshire. Wife renounces will presented by Isaac Baker and William Naylor. Wit., Isaac Baker, P. Cresap, Sam B. Davis.

SYNOPSIS OF WILLS

JAMES, Issac—11-22-1830; pr. 8-28-1843. W., Elizabeth. 10 ch., 1-Sarah Harris, 2-Martha Athey, 3-Jemima Bosley, 4-Mary Anderson, 5-George C., 6-William C., 7-John Culp James, 8-James Lawson James, 9-Elizabeth Ann, 10-Isaac N. "My younger children under 21." Wit., John Culp, Sr., Reuben Davs, Thomas Daniels.

JAMES, Rodham—7-23-1802; pr. 5-19-1806. W., Huldah. 2 ch., 1-Thornton Bosley, 2-Elizabeth. Exec., w., and John Snyder. Wit., Solomon Newman, James Clark.

JENKINS, Jacob—1785; pr. 9-14-1795. W., Elizabeth. 8 ch., 1-Evan, w., Ann, land on which he now lives; 2-Ruth, 3-Micheal, 4-Jacob, 5-John, 6-Mary Hoge, 7-Sarah Ann Gaddis (called both Sarah and Ann); 8-Jonathan (dec'd, had ch., Mary, Israel, Jacob); Susannah, Elizabeth and Rachel Jenkins, nieces and nephews. Exec., sons, Evan and Michael Jenkins. Sec., Jacob McCoole, who marked land. Wit., Robert Rogers, John Lewis, John McCool.

JENKINS, Jacob—11-18-1823; pr. 12-15-1823. W., Mary. 6 ch., 1-Frederick, 2-John, 3-George, 4-Betsy Ann, 5-Susan Mariah, 6-Mary Eveline; father-in-law, Frederick Buzzard, Sr.; farm on Great Road; house a tavern, "Allen Place"; "Mr Mason the potter." Exec., wife and John Pratzman. Sec., George Sharfe, Robert Powell. Wit., Robert Powell, Joseph Scott, Jacob Hawkins.

JENKINS, William—1-3-1815; pr. 4-14-1817. W. not named. 5 ch., 1-James, 2-Joseph, 3-William, 4-John, 5-Benjamin. Sisterinlaw, Mary. Exec., James Jenkins. Sec., Elias Browning. Wit., Elias Browning, James Inskeep, Joseph Inskeep.

JENNINGS, William—4-4-1778; pr. 4-14-1778. W., Ann. Ch., Mary Jennings "grandchild by law." Exec., Sam Dew. Sec., Abraham Kuykendall, William Johnson. Wit., Adam Harness, Joseph Hall, Joel Berry.

JOHNSON, John, Sr.—11-10-1809; pr. 12-18-1809. W., Dinah. 3 ch., 1-Mary House, 2-James, 3-John. Exec., son, John. Sec., Christopher Erret, John Stoker, Sr. Wit., John Stokes, Sr., Luther Calvin, Jr., Christopher Erret.

JOHNSON, Joseph—12-12-1809; pr. 2-19-1819. W., Nance. 6 ch., 1-Deborah Pool, 2-Joseph, 3-William, 4-John, 5-Nancy, 6-James. Exec., son, William, or wife. Sec., Christopher Arrett, James Larrimore. Wit., Abraham Pennington, Richard Short, John A .Cox.

JOHNSON, Okey—will not dated; pr. 10-16-1788. W. and ch, but not named. Sons get land; "everything to wife and children." Exec., wife. Wit., Peter Jones, John Jones, William Rogers.

JOHNSON, Okey—3-27-1815; pr. 4-14-1815. W., not named. 5 ch., 1-Jonathan, 2-Abraham, 3-Nathaniel, land; 4-dau., —Carruthers, 5-dau., — Jacobs. Sons-in-in-law, George Carruthers and John Jacobs. Exec., sons, Jonathan and Abraham. Sec., Sam Cockerill and Thomas Collins. Wit., John Synder, John Miller, Peter Leatherman.

JOHNSON, Thomas (of Capt. John's Run)—4-27-1810; pr. 4-15-1811. W., Susannah. 6 ch., only one, Debra, mentioned by name. Exec., wife. Sec., Hugh Smith, William Johnson, Abraham Vanorsdol.

JOHNSON, William (gentleman)—9-8-1794; pr. 12-8-1794. W., Elizabeth. 7 ch., 1-William, 300 acres; 2-John, 100 acres; 3-Thomas, 80 acres adjoining Barnet's; 4-Elizabeth, 20 acres; 5-Mary, 6-Abigail, 7-Nancy. Exec., son, William. Wit., James and William Smith.

JONES, Elias (a surveyor)—5-16-1848; pr. 7-24-1848. Sister, Nancy Neal; nephews, Robert and Daniel D. Neal; sister, Sarah Darling; nephew, Robert Darling. "What Robert Jones left me." Lucy Harrison's heirs (6)—as follows: Elizabeth, Sarah M., Percy J., Elinor, Caroline, and Eliza Harrison. Nm., Dan Jones' heirs; Carlton S. Jones (gets surveyor's instruments); Louise E. Jones; Dan Hendricson on his land; Thomas Jones. Exec., John Ward. Sec., James Parsons, William Harrison. Wit., John R. Henderson, William Grayson; pr. by Jeremiah Cooper, also.

JONES, John—5-14-1792; pr. 10-15-1794 W., Catherine. 11 ch., 1-Peter, 2-Abel, 3-Samuel, 4-Kesiah, 5-David, 6-Solomon, 7-Aaron, 8-Abraham, 9-Daniel, 10-John, 11-Joshua. Gr. ch., Septamous, Catherine and Nancy Lawson; Margaret and Matty Rogers. Exec., sons, David and Solomon. Sec., William Rogers and John Thiller. Wit., John Dixon, David and Isaac Jones.

JONES, Peter—5-14-1792; pr. 10-19-1795. W., Catherine. 10 ch., 1-David, 2-Isaac, 3-John, 4-Moses, 5-Peter, 6-Aron and 7-Jacob (latter two under 16); 8-Susannah, 9-Ruth, 10-Sarah. Exec., sons, David and Peter. Wit., John Dixon, Aaron, John and David Jones.

JONES, Robert—5-18-1835. Sister, Lucy Harrison; sister, Nancy Neal of Champaign Co., Ohio, her sons, Robert and Daniel; sister, Sarah Darling of Nox Co., Ohio, son, Robert Darling; bro., Daniel Jones of Warren Co., Ky.; bro., William Jones; bro., Elias Jones of Hampshire Co. Wit., Michael Musselter, William H. Pool. Apparently Capt. Robert Jones, from the will.)

JUDY, Martin—4-7-1786; pr. 8-9-1785. W., Rosanna. 7 ch., 1-Martin (dec'd; his sons, Martin and Jacob, land North Fork; sons under 15; his widow to have possession of land until youngest reaches age of 15); 2-Henry, 3-Nicholas ("shall provide for my wife"); 4-Elizabeth, 5-Margaret, and two youngest daus., evidently others; dau., 6- — Borer (hus., Jacob, his heirs); 7-John, eldest son, "if he be yet alive and shall ever appear to demand it." Exec., son, Nicholas. Sec., Martin Shobe. Wit., Robert Prage, Adam Moses, Jacob Caplenor, Henry Melloc, Charles Borah, Geeorge Fisher, James Cunningham and Jacob Castleman.

—K—

KABUCK, Mrs. Sarah—est. 1830. Father, John Thompson, her guardian was Martha Thompson; her husband, Peter Kabuck.

KACKLEY, Joseph—9-8-1860; pr. 11-7-1860. W. not named. 6 ch., 1-Cephas, dec'd; 2-James Addison; 3-Joseph Ira; 4-Mary Elizabeth; 5-Lydia Turner. Farm Elias Kackley now lives on, 183 acres. Exec., wife. Sec., Sam Hook. Wit., Nath. and Jesse Ofut, Sam Hook.

KAIL, George—6-15-1797; pr. 9-10-1797 (will and codicil). W., Elizabeth. 5 ch., 3 sons, Peter, John and George, get land; one daughter alive and one dead, left ch., daus. not named. Widow renounced her rights under will. Exec., George Spade and Phillip Cline, "trusty friends." Sec., John Flye, Sr., and John Hammar. Wit., William Carlyle, John and Absolom Chenoweth.

KEENER, George—3-25-1801; pr. 10-19-1801. W., Elizabeth. 4 ch., 1-Mary, 2-Elizabeth, 3-George, 4-Caty. Sec., John McBride, Dan O'Laughlin.

KEENER, John—3-25-1801; pr. 10-19-1801. Wife, Elizabeth. 4 children, Mary, Elizabeth, George and Katy. Exec., wife refuses, appoint John McBride and Daniel McLaughlin. Wit., Robert Young, William Throckmorton and Henry Bunn.

KELSO, Anna (wid. of James)—4-10-1857; pr. 10-25-1858. 5 ch., 1-Joseph A., 2- — Pennington (has dau., Catherine V. Pennington); 3-Eliza, 4-James F., 5-John W. Exec., James Cather of Frederick. Sec., James Morrison. Wit., James Cather, B. F. Eaton, Sam Garvin.

KELSO, James — 5-26-1854; pr. 9-25-1854. Wife, Anna. 11 children, 1-Ellen, 2-Robert, 3-William, 4-Mary Dollson, 5-Elise, 6-Joseph A., 7-James F. ("my watch"); 8-John Wesley, 9-Isaac Bull, 10-dau., — Hook (hus., Robert); 11- — Pennington. Exec., James Cather of Frederick. Sec., Edw. Muse Robert T. Lockhart. and Aaron Dunlavy.

KERCHEVAL, Samuel, Jr., of Romney—9-9-1837; pr. 7-27-1840. Second wife, Jean. 4 children, 1-John Belfield, 2-deceased son, not named, 3-Andrew Wodrow, land in Brown Co., Ohio; 4-Mary Susan. Exec., bro., Robert C. Kercheval. Sec., John Brady, William Vance, Thomas Carshaddon, Vause Fox, Sam D. Brady. Wit., Angus W. McDonald, John B. White.

KERN, Elias, of Frankfort—2-16-1849; pr. 3-26-1849. Body of will missing. Exec., Isaac Hollenbeck, refuses; Sam Brady appointed. Sec., Thos. Carshaddon and Jacob Daniels. Wit., Lewis Kline and James G. Lash.

KERN, John—9-6-1843; pr. 11-27-1845. W., Elizabeth. 14 ch., 1-Issac, 2-Elizabeth, 3-Jacob, 4-Frederick, 5-William, 6-John, 7-Elisha, 8-Sarah Foley, 9-Henry, 10-Lewis, 11-Mary, 12-Catherine Cowgile, 13-Phillip, 14-Hannah McDonald. John Abdells mentioned. Wit., Nath Ofutt, Thomas and Jesse Brelsford.

KEYES, Frances—2-6-1799; pr. 2-15-1802. W., Ann P. 6 ch., 1-Horace (Horatio), 2-Clemm (Charles), 3-Alex, 4-Frances, 5-Janet (hus., Charles Frizel); 6-Ann. Exec., wife, and Alex White. Sec., Francis White. Wit., Alex Sanderson, William Payne, William and Clem (or Charles) Keyes.

KINSAY, William—5-8-1781; pr. 2-9-1799. W., Elizabeth. No ch. Bro., Benjamin (has son, Benjamin); wife's bro., James Cunningham (has eldest dau., Sarah). Exec., wife and George Stump. Wit., Stephen Ruddle, William M. Hendry.

KISNER, Jacob—6-21-1856; pr. 8-25-1856. No w. or ch mentioned. "Divide between lawful heirs." Exec., Sam Davis and Sam Millslagle. Sec., William Nixon. Wit., Charles W. Frank, Jesse Chilcott.

KLINE—Abraham (see Cline).

KLINE, Adam—5-?-1847; pr. 1-25-1847. 7 ch., 1-Jacob, land; 2-John, 3-Henry, 4-Mary Magdalene, 5-Christene, 6-Eve, 7-Rebecca, dec'd. Exec., son, Jacob, and John Switzer. Sec., Henry Bull (Brill?), Phillip Kline and Archibald Arnold. Wit., Simeon Ward, Jacob Ligner(?), Archibald Arnold.

KLINE, Mary—12-3-1855; pr. 1-25-1856. Bro., Jacob. Bro., Henry, who is in Ohio; sister, Elizabeth Swisher; sister, Eve. Exec., Sam Davis, who gets balance of estate and buries her. Wit., Michael Brill and David W. Kline.

KUMP, Henry—9-13-1840; pr. 3-25-1850. No w. 5 ch., 1-Henry, 2-Jacob, 3-Andrew, 4-Rebecca, and 5-Fred. Exec., son, Jacob. Wit., Sam Baumgarner, Abraham Secrest, Valentine Secrest.

KUYKENDAL, Abraham—2-20-1777; pr. 1-12-1779. W., Catherine. Stepson, Jeremiah Claypool; stepson, Isaac Harness (my wife his mother); stepdau., Sarah Harness, land on South Branch, lot in Ft. Pitt. Abraham Kuykendal, son of Nath.; Abraham Kuykendal, son of Henry. My mother, Sarah. Exec., wife, and Sam Dew and Henury Kuykendall. Sec., Nath. and Henry Kuykendall. Wit., Peter Sternberger, John Devore, Thomas Schoonhaven, Enoch Barry, William Cunningham, Adam Harness.

KUYKENDALL, Abraham—7-22-1781. Widow, Catherine land he purchased from John Decker. Mentions Nath. and Jeremiah Claypool. Estate division made by Isaac Miller, William Bufington, John Campbell, Sam Dew. Not a will, but filed with wills. Kuykendall C., estate papers.

KUYKENDALL, Isaac—10-1-1844; pr. 4-25-1845. W., but not named. 6 ch., 1-James, watch; 2-Nath, 3-Issac Taylor (minor), 4-Susan, 5-William, 6-Luke. Gr. son, Jacob. Exec., son, James. Sec., Sam D. Bodly, Sam Davis, Luke Kuykendall. Wit, David Gibson, John B. White.

KYGER, George—10-28-1795; pr. 5-14-1798. W., Mary. 6 ch., 1-George, 2-Benjamin, 3-John, 4-Catherine, 5-Mary, 6-Elizabeth. Boys get land in Kentucky and Hampshire County. Exec., wife, and son, George. Wit., David Long, John Dowden, Thomas Long.

—L—

LAFOLLET, Bartholomew—10-10-1836; pr. 2-27-1837. W., Eleanor. "My children." Exec., Henry Brill. Wit., Sam Burngame, John Brill, Lewis Racey.

LAFOLLETT, William—8-16-1853; pr. 1-25-1858. W., Jane. 9 ch., 1-Silas, 2-Elizabeth (hus., Michael Capper); 3-Mary (hus., Phillip Groves); 4-Margaret (hus., Hiram Spaid); 5-John, dec'd, 6-Bartholomew, dec'd, 7-James, 8-Amos, 9-Anna (hus., William McKee). Exec., Hiram Spaid in will, but son, Amos, appointed. Sec., H. W. Lafollett, David Pugh. Wit., I. I. Read, H. W. Lafollett, A. A. McKee.

LAMBERT, John — 11-6-1843; pr. 7-24-1845. W., Keziah. John Flanagan, w. and ch., get Totten farm; bro., William, in Germantown, Hunterton Co., N. J.; sister's ch., "in Ohio, so far as I know at present." John Blue, "the boy I raised." Exec., Thomas Carskadon. Wit., Archibald Vandiver, James Parker, Roland S. Daton.

LARGENT, James—5-14-1810; pr. 4-19-1813. W., Margery. 3 ch., 1-John, land conveyed by Enoch and Henry Enoch and James Slone or Slane; 2-Mary Slane (hus., Hugh), note of James Slane given her, returned to him; 3-Margrate. Exec., son, John, and friend, John Hiet. Sec., George Sharp and Francis White. Wit., Francis, Robert N. and Sam P. White.

LARGENT, John—12-15-1816; pr. 10-5-1831. W., Sarah. 7 ch., 1-William, 2-James, 3-John Washington, 4-Peggy, 5-Mary, 6-Betsy, 7-Milly. Exec., William Largent and John Hiett (refused; court appointed James Slane). Wit., Robert Sherrard, John Hiett, Nath. Offut and James Slane.

LARGENT, Thomas — 2-25-1829; pr. 9-18-1831. 9 ch., 1-Lewis, 2-Samuel, 3-Randle, 4-Thomas, 5-Jane, 6-Susan Dew, 7-Nancy Grace, 8-Sarah, 9-Ellender. Wit., Silas Prather.

LARUE, Jacob—10-20-1778; pr. 11-19-1784. W., Ann. 5 ch., 1-Peter, 117 acres on Big Capcapon; 2-John, where he lives, adj. Peter; 3-Noah, youngest, residue of land; 4-Sarah, 5-Abigail. Exec., sons. Wit., Thomas Bowel, George Tarvin, Thomas Morgan.

LARUE, Noah—12-27-1826; pr. 9-17-1827. W., Rachel. 4 ch., 1-Rachel, 2-Jacob, 3-Hannah, 4-Peter. Exec., Moses Hoge, Zebulon Streetz, Jacob Larue. Sec., Robert Sherrard, Jan Cockwill. Wit., Robert Sherrard, John B. Miller, David Ellis.

LAWSON, Halloras (Hannah?)—12-1-1810; pr. 12-17-1810. Daus., Ann Walker, Hannah Williams, Margaret Beeton, Fanny Blue. Gr. dau., Susan Connor; gr. son, Thomas Williams. Exec., Michael Blue. Wit., James Creegan, George Gale, James Lenosa (?).

SYNOPSIS OF WILLS

LAWSON, Thomas—9-15-1795; pr. 2-15-1796. W., Hannah. 14 ch., 1-William, 2-John, 3-Jacob, 4-Thomas, 5-Mary Johnson, 6-Jane Johnson, 7-Elizabeth Conner, 8-Ann, 9-Hannah McQuillen, 10-Sarah Williams, 11-Peggy, 12-Fanny, youngest dau., 13-James, 14-Catherine. "My 8 daughters." Thomas, John and Fanny are three youngest children. Gr. son, Thomas Cowkick. Land on S. Branch and Pattersons Creek. Exec., John Newman, John Taylor, Jr. Wit., Richard Whiteman and James McQuillen.

LEATHERMAN, John—4-17-1851; pr. 5-6-1856. No w. 3 ch., 1-Christiana, 100 acres; 2-Frederick, pays $1.00 to Christiana Hoffman and $3.00 to dau., Ann; 3-Ann, "her several children." Wit., Frederick Ludwick, Nicholas Leatherman, Jr.

LEE—or See.

LEE, Andrew — date unknown; pr. 5-20-1816. W., Catherine. 4 children, 1-Jacob, 2-Elizabeth, 3-George, 4-William. Exec., wife, and son, Jacob. Wit., John C. Newman, George Reinhart, Abraham Reinhart.

LEE, Margaret (Mary?)—3-28-1757; pr. 2-14-1758. 8 ch., 1-Frederick, eldest son; 2-George, 3-Micheal, 4-Letty Yakehan(?) (hus., Jacob); 5-Madline, 6-Barbara, 7-Mary, 8-Jacob. Exec., George Lee. Sec., Haress and William Cunningham and Micheal Lee. Wit., James Focsh(?—in German), David Crage.

LEEK, Christopher—2-2-1778; pr. 3-10-1780. W., Sofia. Sister, Catrika; to Jacob Ragun's eldest daughter, relationship not shown. Exec., Jacob Hankle and Martin Shobe. Sec., Mauris Algire, Abraham Kuykendall, Jacob Ragan. Wit., Samuel Brink, Robert Porter, — Mase(?).

LEEPER, Eliza—10-10-1823; pr. 12-15-1823 (she died 11-21-1823). Sisters, Martha Walker, Elloner Swaney, Rebecca Stewart. Nm., Issac Swaney. Exec., Isaac Swaney of Adams Co., Pa. Wit., Thomas Walker, John Walles. Sec., Robert Walker.

LEICHTER, George—6-14-1865; pr. 1-9-1866. 1st w., Catherine ———; 2nd w., Ann Stalcop. 11 ch., 1-Rebecca James, 2-Delilah Gsiner, 3-Margaret Abelman, 4-Nancy Cronfin, 5-Elizabeth Stafford, 6-Ann Lagstoo, 7-John Corbin, 8-Susan, 9-Elmira, 10-Daniel, 11-Emma (latter 5 "Annie's children." Mentions Christina Robeson, Lucretia Pelton, Andrew G. Leichter, Emma Stalcoop, Sr. and Jr.; Hiram Alkere, Samuel House, John Haye, Geo. Smith and Geo. Malone. Exec., Jacob P. Daniels.

LEWIS, David—3-7-1844; pr. 9-23-1844. W., Patsy. 8 ch., 1-Daniel, 2-Alfred, 3-Aney Bird, 4-Rosannah Combs, 5-Mary Barnes, 6-Elizabeth, 7-Oliver, 8-Silas. Exec., friend, Garrett W. Blue. Sec., William Vance, William P. Slump. Wit., Sam Lawson, John I. Hardy, William E. Larimore.

LEWIS, Henry—5-9-1774; pr. 11-14-1775. W., Mary, one-third. 7 ch., 1-Henry, 2-Sam, and 3-Evan (these three, land on Sleepy Creek, Frederick Co., Va.; 4-John, 5-Sidney Rees, 6-Elinor McCool, 7-Elizabeth Lewis. Exec., w. and son Sam. Sec., John Royse and John Largent. Wit., Owen Rogers, Lydia Rogers, William Pickering.

LINTHICUM, Sarah—3-4-1815; pr. 5-18-1828. Unmarried. Her mother, Mary, land during life; sister, Margaret Lyons; sister, Ann Linthicum; bros., Joseph and Hezekiah Linthicum. Exec., Timothy Smith. Wit., Elijah, Timothy and Joseph Smith.

LOCKS, Jacob—4-3-1785; pr. 5-8-1785. No w., 5 ch., Abraham, Thomas, and three daus., unnamed. Exec., William Jackson. Sec., John Morgan, Joseph Johnson. Wit., John Swan, John Constant, Richard Haff.

PAGE 123

LONG, David—1807; pr. 10-11-1811. W., but not named. 11 ch., 1-Joseph, 2-George, 3-Thomas, 4-David, 5-William, 6-Mary Miers, 7-Ruth Crackey, 8-Sarah, 9-Ann, 10-Rebeccah, 11-Elizabeth. Exec., son, Joseph. Wit., Andrew Hoskinson, Lucian Patrick, Elijah Rawlings.

LONG, Jacob—7-22-1810; pr. 11-19-1810. W. not mentioned. 4 ch., 1-Mary Ann, 2-Sam, 3-William, 4-David. Exec., Simon Taylor. Wit., Peter Parker, Robert Rannels, Jacob Earsom, Solomon Robinson.

LONG, Mary Ann—2-15-1820; pr. 8-20-1821. 7 ch., 1-David, 2-Jacob (dec'd, left ch.); 3-John 4-Sam, 5-William, 6-Elizabeth Taylor, 7-Sarah Smith. Exec., son, David, and Jacob Smith. Sec., Simon Taylor and John Long. Wit., Thomas Buck, John Rannels, Mary Rannels.

LONG, Sarah—5-16-1815; pr. 9-18-1815. Unmarried. Mother, Elizabeth Long; sister, Nancy Shrock; sister, Rebecca; bro., Thomas. Exec., Maj. Issac Means. Wit., Joseph Long, Mary Ann Riley, Mary Ann Means.

LUDWICK, Jacob—10-21-1841; pr. 11-25-1844. No w. 7 ch., 1-Daniel (his son, Isaac, gets eight-day clock); 2-John (has children); 3-William, 4-George, 5-Polly Parker, 6-Elizabeth Liller, 7-Catherine Clark. Gr. ch., Jacob, Margaret A., Mary E., Nancy, ch. of Daniel. Exec., Peter Arnold. Sec., John Carmell. Wit. to will, John Leatherman, Jr., Peter Arnold, Thomas Sloan, Zech Arnold. Wit. to codicil, Thomas Sloan, Jacob Bizer, Andrew Ludwick. Codicil dated 10-1-1844.

LUNNSFORD, Lewis—2-20-1823. Oral in Muskingum Co., Ohio, where he died at the home of John Smith on the Salt Section. Estate divided between two full sisters and one half-sister. A full sister, w. of John Smith, who gets money, William Moody has land; James Taylor of Zanesville now has. John Smith, sole exec. Wit. of John Smith's statement, Job Stanberry and James Currie.

LUNNSFORD, William—1-8-1850; pr. 11-22-1858. W., Catherine P. 7 ch. 4 by first w., Nancy; 3 by second w.), 1-Nancy, 2-Catherine, 3-Mary Susannah, 4-Simon P., 5-Martha Cinnamon, 6-Elizabeth Stockdale, 7- — Ball (hus., James). Exec., his son-in-law, James Ball, and wife's son, William G. Mathews. Sec., G. W. Maddox, John Kenyon. Wit., James F. Wilson and John Clayton who died 1858. Will probated in Oldham County.

LUPTON, Asa — 4-25-1807; pr. 10-20-1807. W., Hannah. 7 ch., 1-David, 2-Daniel, not 21; 3-Edith, 4-Hannah, 5-Margaret, 6-Ruth, 7-Anna. Exec., wife and Richard George. Wit., James George, William Horseman, Joseph Carter.

LUPTON, Hannah — 7-12-1807; pr. 12-?-1810. 6 children, son, 1-David, Bible when 21; daus., 2-Edith, 3-Hannah, 4-Margaret, 5-Ruth, 6-Ann. David's w., Ann, to have care of three younger girls. Exec., Richard George and David Lupton. Wit., James and Henry George and Isaac Lupton.

LUPTON, Jesse (bl'ksmith)—4-10-1839; pr. 6-24-1841. 8 ch., 1-Wm., eldest son, land formerly Issac's (rel not stated); 2-Jesse, fulling mill adj. Martin Fulkamores; 3-Ellis, land purchased of George Sharkey, also "Ben Knob" Edington Mountain, adj. Benj. Johnson's; 4-Jonah, home land bought of Benj. Cheshire; 5-Lydia Horseman, 6-Rebecca Yonley, "my daughter"; 7-Sarah, and 8-Rachel, Isaac's land where John White lives. Massey Pickering's ch., relationship not shown. Exec., William Horseman, and son, Ellis Lupton. Sec., Joseph Hofman, Adam Cooper. Wit., Lewis Smith, James Scarff, Issac Lochmiller.

LUTTS, Conrad—(verbal will)—1-27-1770; pr. 11-13-1770. W., Agnes. 2 ch., "my daughter, 1-Barbara Lutts," dau., 2-—— Green (hus., John). Stepsons, John and Peter Waggonner; stepdaus., Elizabeth and Barbara Waggoner. Will proved by oaths of Andrew Young, John Lorance, Phillip Mason. Wit., Thomas Barth Bowen, Charles Meyers. Sec., Henry Skiploe and Micheal Thorn.

LYLE, John—6-26-1807; pr. 7-20-1807. W., Sarah. 8 ch., 1-John Newton, 2-Eliza, 3-Daniel, 4-Jane, 5-John, 6-Wilberforce, 7-Sarah, 8-Joseph Glass Lyle. Wife has two-ninths. Exec., wife, Samuel Glass and Joseph Glass. Wit., Phillip Grace, Charles Beatty Sam Abernathy, Thomas Shannon. N. land near Anthony Buck, also lots in Springfield. Codicil relates to a slave.

LYONS, Elijah—10-9-1848; pr. 11-27-1848. W., Margaret 8 ch., 1-John, land he is on; 2-Archibald; 3-Joseph F. (Hildier), Lyons home; 4-Noah; 5-Greenwell, 6-Ellen Spencer; 7-Julyann Lease; 8-Bruce. Gr. dau., Margaret Ann Lyons. Exec., son, John. Wit., A. J. Hams, Vance Dunn.

—Mc—

McALESTER, James—4-30-1804; pr. 10-19-1807. W., Mary. 3 ch. 1-Mary Chambers, 2-Elizabeth Bush, 3-Sarah King. Gr. sons, James McAlester Bush, John Chambers, John McAlester. Exec., Henry Bush, Alex King, William Donaldson. Sec., Andrew Wodrow and Lewis Vandiver and Frederick Sheats. Wit., Isaac Brown, John Newman and James Gray.

McBRIDE, Alexander—11-3-1794; pr. 4-21-1795. W., Margaret. 6 ch., 1-John, 2-Alex, 3-Robert, 4-Thomas, 5-Jean, 6-Mary. Exec., son, John, and Jacob Starn. Wit., Peter McBride, Jacob Starn, James Patterson.

McBRIDE—Elizabeth—7-11-1824 pr. 8-18-1824. No ch. Bro., Stephen McBride; he has dau., Rachel; bro., James, wife Nance; bro., Thomas. Dec'd left ch. sisters, Marjery Hiett dec'd, Sarah Chenoweth, Eleanor Lyon, Mary Keats, Hannah and Elizabeth. Ncs., Marjory Yeats, Sarah Hiett. Exec., John Hiett. Wit., John Fahs (also Sec.), Geo. Hiett and George Sharp.

McBRIDE, James—5-20-1817; pr. 3-15-1818. W., Mary. 8 ch., 1-Stephen, 2-James, 3-Thomas, 4-Hannah, 5-Elizabeth, 6-Mary Yeats, 7-Eleanor Lyon, 8-Sarah Chenoweth. Gr. ch., Sarah and James W. Hiatt. Exec., John Hiatt, James McBride (son). Sec., Lewis Smith Nm., Richard Lyons, Thomas Edwards, Thomas Allen, Milburn Smith. Wit., Timothy, Simeon and Lewis Smith.

McBRIDE, John—1-21-1826; pr., 7-20-1829. 10 ch., no W., 1-Samuel, 2-Elijah, 3-John, 4-Adonorim, 5-Sarah James; dec'd left 3 ch.; 6-Rhoda (exec.), 7-Eliza, 8-Maria, 9-Matilda White, 10-Gelpha R. Exec., Fredrick Sheetz (also wit.). Sec., Sam Cockerell; wit., Robert K. Sheetz and Joshua Johnson.

McCARTY, Edw. of Alleghany Co., Md.—1-11-1842; pr. 8-23-1852. W., Ruth. 7 ch., 1-James, 2-Joseph, 3-John, 4-Rebecca Cresap (hus., Daniel), 5-Sally (hus., William, of Missouri.) 6-Elizabeth Susan McCarty, 7-Aquila Brown McCarty. Bro., Isaac exec. Wit., Leo W. Devrecmon, John Shepherd or Lephart, H. B. Wolfe.

McCORMAC, James—4-13-1847, pr. 7-23-1849. W., Ailsy, 5 ch., 1-John, 2-Rebecca Dayton, 3-Sarah Layman, 4-James, 5-Nancy Kight; gr. son, Geo. McCormac. Exec., W. and Geo. Tasker but court appointed Thos. Dixon, Jr., Benjamin Short, Jenkins W. and J. B. Harvey (also wit.) Sec., James W. and Robert Abernathy and Wm. Vandiver. Wit., John Sherill.

McCRACKEN, William—8-4-1778; pr. 5-1-1782. W., Sarah. 8 ch., 1-Ovid, land Hermits Retreat, 400 acres in Maryland on Devil's Alley, branch of Potomas, Hermit's Retreat; 4-Jane Flint; 5-Sarah Lancaster, 6-Seneca, land, Sugar Camp; 7-William, land in Bath; 8-Isaac. Exec., son, Ovid. Sec., William Jackson, Jabez Ozmun. Wit., Jabez Ozmun, Isaac Ozmun, John Gammage. Will mentions Daniel Pursel.

McDONALD, Benjamin—5-21-1856 ;pr. 7-28-1856. No w. 10 ch., 1-Evan 2-Benjamin, 3-James, 4-Sarah McClure, (mother of 3 ch., Rebecca, dec'd, and 2 living sons); 5-Elizabeth, 6-Margaret Brelsford, 7-Ann Farmer, 8-Mary Fens, 9-Phoebe Milleson, 10-Catherine Taylor. Exec., son, James, and S. J. Stump. Wit., Robert Carmichael, Asa Hiett and S. J. Stump. Sec., Silas Milleson and Ben D. Stump.

McDONALD, Daniel—Exec., Mr. Mathias Beau, J. M. and Mr. John Mitchell. Wit., John Stokes and Joseph Murphy and John Abbe Cox. Sec., John Gritton and Angus McDonald.

MacDONALD, George (of Maryland)—8-15-1803, pr., 4-6-1805. James Malcolm, Jennet and Catherine Malcolm. Exec., William Malcolm, son of James Dalis. Wit., Benton Jacques, John Heatherington and Henry Otto.

McDOUGAL, Peter (McDonald?)—verbal will 8-11-1790 ;pr. 1796. Bro., Alexander; two sisters, not named. Proved by Angus and Archibald McDonald. George McDonald only one present at his death. Dec'd wished certain Angus to be executor. Peter Malcom mentioned. Evidently some difficulty in division of property.

McDOWELL, John—2-10-1853; pr. 2-26-1855. W., Matilda. 6 ch., 1-William, 2-H. C., 3-John, gr. dau., Matilda Wodrow McDowell, 4-Sarah Matilda McDowell, 5-Mary Slaughter, 6-Jane Trimble. Exec., w., and son, John. Nm. Colo. Wodrow and Dr. Robert Newman. Wit., John B. White, David Gibson, John C. Heiskell, John Wathey and S. J. Bowles.

McDUGLE, Mary—Pr. 5-17-1824, will undated. Dau., Margaret Olly, who has son, James. Son-in-law, Joseph Shepherd. Exec., Thos. Carscaden. Wit., John Rankin and Daniel Fink.

McELWEE, David—3-22-1805; pr. 4-15-1805. Verbal will, written by James McBride. William Parrell, Samuel Beckwith, Jacob Clutter (sister's husband). Will spoken 3-16-1805; he died 3-17.

McGUIRE, Elizabeth—5-21-1771; pr. 9-17-1786. Stepson, William McGuire, gets land which was the estate of John Parker, and which she now possesses. Wit., Tom Collins, Vincent and Stephen Calvin.

McGUIRE, Millicent—2-25-1835; pr. 8-15-1835. Friend, Charity Johnson, — Williams; dau., Susan Naylor, and her ch., Edward, Millicent, James, John and Samuel Nayler. Wit., John B. White, David Gibson. Sec., Wm. Naylor, Angus McDonald.

McGUIRE, Rachel—6-14-1793; pr. 7-10-1793. 6 ch., 1-Margaret, 2-Mary, 3-Anna, 4-James, 5-Francis, 6-Robert. Exec., Nicholas Casey. Wit., Thomas McGuire and Isaac Means. Sec., Wm. Vause.

McGUIRE, William—12-2-1789; pr. 2-11-1790. W., Rachel. 4 sons, Robert, Francis, Thomas and James. Land So. Branch; Stradled's Meadows and New Creek. Exec., Job Welton and w., Rachel. Sec., Tom Collins and Stephen Calvin. Wit., John O'Brien, Barney McMongle.

McKEEVER, Margaret — 1-6-1857; pr. 9-28-1857. Heirs mentioned, but not named. Exec., Hugh McKeever, in place of two named, David Pugh and Samuel Bumgarner. Wit., James Lafollette, Michael Brill and Hiram Spaid. Sec., Phillip Kline, Aaron Chilcott.

SYNOPSIS OF WILLS

McKEEVER, Paul—3-9-1828; pr. 5-19-1828. W., Margaret. 9 ch., 1-Margaret, 2-Christina, 3-Sally, 4-Elizabeth, 5-Julian, 6-Eleanor, 7-Paul, 8-Hugh, 9-Moses. Names mentioned, Reuben Bumgardener, John Swisher, John W. McKeever, Isaac McNeel, John Hoover and w., William Richardson, William Pennington and w., Benj Coakley, Thomas Pennington and w., Enoch Pennington and w. Exec., David Ogden, Esq., John Swisher, Hugh McKeever. Wit., Abr., Phillip and John Kline and Isaac Ogden. Sec., Phillip Kline and Charles Capper.

McLAUGHLIN, Daniel—6-21-1829; pr., 2-15-1830. No. w. 6 ch., 1-David, 2-William, 3-Benjamin, 4-Anner, 5-Elizabeth Chapman, 6-Mary Collons. Exec., son, William. Wit., William Donaldson, Solomon Parker, William Taylor, Simon Taylor. Sec., Solomon Parker and Wm. F. Taylor.

McNARY, Ebenezer—10-1-1824; pr. 6-16-1828. W. not named. 3 ch., 1-William, 2-Nimrod, 3-Susan Reese. Exec., w., and William McNary. Nm. John Piercall, Peter Thrasher. Wit., Garret Seymour, Ephraim Dunn, Alex. King. Court appoints exec., Wm. and Nimrod McNary and Ashford Rees.

McPHERSON, William—6-27-1798; pr. 12-15-1800. James McPherson, James Caudy, his ch., Michael, David and Mary Elizabeth Caudy; Martha Pugh relationship not shown; brother, David, and his son, Angus; brother, Angus, and his son, William. Nm. James Fairley. Exec., James Caudy, Daniel Carmichael. Wit., Peter "Ongan," John McGinnis of Montgomery Co., Ky. Sec., Sam Park, James McBride.

McVICKER, William—5-2-1815; pr. 6-19-1815. W., Dianna. Ch. mentioned but not named. "All my daughters to have $30 when of age." Wit., John Clutter, Fredrick Kump. Exec., Stephen Hickle, John Reed.

—M—

MACHIR, Elizabeth—1-6-1830; pr. 8-27-1832. (of Washington, Mason Co., Ky.). Neph., John Brough, exec. Nc., Nancy Richie; bro., John Machir; ncs., Lillian Kennedy, Rachel Machir; nephs., Franklin and Charles M. Brough; sisters, Jane Brough and Maria Mitchell. Will mentions Mr. William Kennedy, David N. Richey, Joseph Foreman, M. W. Owens, Elijah Berry, Lawrence Butler, Angus W. McDonald. Wit., Sally Rannels, B. W. Wood. Estate Scotland dec'd brother, John.

MALCOM, James—5-13-1823; pr. 11-17-1823. No w. 5 ch., 1-Peter, 2-William, 3-James, 4-Catherine Longstrach, sec., 5-Jane Chrisman. Names mentioned, Isaac Short. Exec., son, Peter. Wit., Richard Short, James Taylor, William Malcom, Jr. Sec., Richard Short and Loyed Deever.

MALICK, John—9-16-1839; pr. 3-25-1844. W., dec'd. 8 ch., 1-Margaret 2-Martha Horsman (hus., Joseph), 3-Mary Shaffer (hus., David), 4-Phillip, 5-John, 6-Aaron, 7-David, 8-Uriah. Exec., Philip Fahs, Jr. Wit., Isaac Slocum, Fredrick Pepper, Henry Wolford. Sec., Daniel Wayung and John Rannels. Family burying ground 1 acre on Aarons land.

MANNING. Rev. Nathaniel—1-12-1774. pr., 1-1-1777. W., Mary. No. ch. W. gets land in Bergeley Co., purchased of Jacob Hite. Exec., w., Col. Abraham Hite of Hampshire, Mr. Thomas Hite of Berkeley. Sec., Abel Randell. Wit., Abraham Hite, Sr. and Jr., and I. Hite, 2nd.

MARSH, Matthias—4-4-1797. W., Elizabeth. 6 ch., 1-Ezekiel, 2-Vincent, 3-Mathias, 4-Cyrus, 5-Lemuel, 6-Hannah Loopry?. Exec., Rodham James, Ezekel Marsh, Marsh. Wit., Huldah, Isaac and Rodham James. Sec., Rodham and Isaac James.

PAGE 125

MARTCH, Henry—12-5-1786; pr. 4-13-1787. W., Christena; dau., Mary Smith has ch.; dau., Christena. Exec., Job Cheese, William Vanse or Vance, Esq., Anthony Baker, dau., Christena. Sec., Edw. McCarthy, Nicholas Seaver. Wit., William and John Odle, Jacob Sinks, William Vance, Anthony Baker.

MARTIN, Edw. (state of Ohio)—8-6-1796; pr. 1-19-1807. W., Catherine. Her son is John Martin. "To John Martin, son of Catherine Miller" land bought of Edw. Martin. Bro., Urias Martin. Dec'd. Exec., w., and John Martin. Sec., Benj. Hull. Wit., John Dixon (1807 in Belmont Co., Ohio), John Kerkbride and Benj. Hull.

MARTIN, George—10-27-1806; pr. 4-20-1807. W., Ann. 10 ch., 1-William, 2-George, 3-Joshua, 4-Job, 5-Jesse, 6-Eli, 7-Levy, 8-John, 9-Joseph, 10-Ann Slocomb. Exec., son, John and Daniel Carmichael. Nm. Bethuel Pugh, King and Holmes, John Busby. Wit., Jonathan Pugh, Jonathan Hiett, Samuel Busby.

MARTIN, John, Sr.—1-24-1831; pr. 5-16-1831. W. but not not named. 5 ch., 1-John, Jr., 2-— Devore (hus., Jacob), 3-— Ravenscraft (hus. Nicholas). 4-— Dawson (hus. Thomas), 5-Mary Baker (hus., Richard). Exec., son, John, Jr., Thomas Dunn, Sr., and Mason heirs. Court appoints Richard Baker, exec. Nep., Joseph Martin. Sec., Ephraim Dunn. Father, John Martin, dec'd. Wit., Geo. Gilbert, John N. Ravenscraft, Thos. J. Hooper.

MARTIN, John—11-11-1848; pr. 11-27-1848. No wife. 5 ch., 1-John, 2-Joseph, 3-Frances, 4-Mary, 5-Hannah. Exec., son, John. Wit., Edw. McCarty, Wm. Hull or Hills, Jr. and C. S. Ravenscraft. Sec., John Vandiver, Frances and Joseph Martin, Edward Gilpin and James Ravenscraft.

MARTIN, Mary—10-6-1818; pr. 11-17-1818. Neph., Henry Ward; ncs., Abigail and Cassey Ward; sister, Sarah Ward; (hus. Jesse) their mother. Wit., Susanna, Isaac and William Johnson and James Higgins.

MAUZY, John—318-1830; pr. 6-23-1846. Bro., Peter; neph., John, son of Peter. Exec., John, Peter and Henry Mauzy. Mentions Charles Carlyle, Thomas H. Fairdain, or Fairfax, Moses Hoge, Henry Huromonus (?), Rich Ridgeways, heirs, James Summerville. Will has 2 codicils. Sec., Sam Hook. Wit., Nath. Affut, Presley Rector, Robert Sherrard and David S. Hook.

MAUZY, Peter Sr.—12-20-1834; pr. 8-25-1835. W., Elizabeth. 9 ch., 1-Henry, 2-Peter, 3-John, 4-George, 5-William, 6-Polly, 7-Susan, 8-Nance Allen, 9-Elizabeth Sommerville. Exec., John Keiter, and sons, George and Henry. Wit., Nath. Offutt and James Vance. Names mentioned, John R. Williams, Hoge, Buzzard, Carlyle, Fairtairn (or Fairdown).

MAYHALL, Stephen—9-7-1799; pr. 9-15-1800. W., Ellender. No children. Exec., wife. Wit., Archibald Linthicum, Peter Switzer.

MEANS, Isaac—8-9-1817; pr. 4-20-1818. W., Nancy. 7 ch. 1-Robert, 2-Ephraim, 3-Isaac, 4-Sally Myers, 5-Betsy Myers, 6-Margaret Taylor (hus., Edward), 7-Jane Schrock, has dau., Betsy Schrock. Exec., son, Robert, and Thomas Mulledy. Wit., Edward Taylor and Jonas Douglas. Jacob Parker (3rd witness.) Nm. Hugh Ballentine.

McCRACKIN—See McCRACKEN, Wm. 1778.

MEEKINS, James—1-22-1829; pr. 11-15-1838. W., Tamer. 3 ch., 1-Joseph T., 2-James, 3-Milley Hulick. James Taylor mentioned. Wit., John H. and Absolom Maxwell.

MICHAEL, Mary Ann 5-31-1850; pr. 9-26-1853. Jacob Frye's two sons, George Washington and James Madison Frye, and dau., Sarah Ann (relationship not shown). Exec., Moses Rosenbrock (Rosenbrough). Wit., James, Jesse L. and Solomon Rosebrough.

MILLER, Elizabeth, "relist of Wm."—3-5-1816; pr. 2-17-1817. 2 ch., 1-William, 2-dau., — Rogers (has son, George Rogers). He gets money "Wm. owes on account of his grandfather's estate." Exec., son, William. Wit., James Slack, Jr., and Jno. Higgins.

MILLER, Isaac—9-30-1794; pr. 6-11-1794. Bro., George, has son, Wendel; bros., Henry and Michael, execs. Nm. John Burbridge of Hardy Co. Wit., John Snyder, Rodham James, Fred. Fink. Sec., Thos. Cooper and Timothy Corn.

MILLER, Isaac—9-16-1810; pr. 5-20-1816. W., but not named. 6 ch., 1-Michael, 2-Isaac, 3-Adam, 4-William, 5-Catherine Persons (hus., David), 6-Elizabeth. Exec., sons, Michael and William. Wit., Isaac Kuykendall, also sec.), Isaac Decker, Adam Bowman. Nm. Conrad Huffman. Adam, minor, now gets land E. side of Scioto Pickway Co., Ohio land son Wm.

MILLER, John Henry—1-30-1792; pr. 10-30-1792. (Verbal will). W., Elizabeth; eldest dau., Mary Harlman; sons, Jacob, Reuben and William. Will proved by widow, John Decker and Benjamin Hoffman. Exec., wife. Sec., John Cuppy.

MILLER, Michael—1866. Son, John D.; dau., Sarah Murphy, Fairfax grant, 398 acres, including island South Branch; dau., Elizabeth; son, William; gr. son, James Parsons. Names mentioned—Isaac Miller (patent 1789), Conrad Huffman and his heirs, Michael Miller, Lot 5. Exec., James Parsons. Wit., Joseph Pancake, Isaac N. Heiskele.

MILLER, Peter—2-7-1819; pr. 11-15-1819. W., but not named. 10 ch., 1-Peter, 2-Jacob, 3-John, 4-Elizabeth Wood, 5-Catherine, 6-Margaret Throush. 7-Polly Greawater, 8-Susannah Stump, 9-Adam, 10-Michael. Exec., Michael Miller. Wit., John Cundiff, Sr., Samuel Lillers. Sec., Henry Lelear.

MILLISON, Benj. 9-26-1826; pr. 10-16-1826. W., Phoebe. 3 ch., 1-John, 2-Silas, 3-Hannah Snapp (hus., John), has dau., Margarette. Exec., George Sharf and John Hiett, later Isaac Wolverton. Sec., Christopher Heeskell, Wm. Vance, Jonathan Pugh and John Martin. Wit., Isaac Milleson and Wm. Bennett.

MILLESON, Phoebe—5-24-1834; pr. 11-24-1834. 3 ch., 1-Hannah Snapp, 2-Silas, 3-John; dau.in-law, Harriet Milleson. Exec., son, Silas. Wit., Henry Spicer, son John evidently incompetent, Walker Louther and Joseph Snapp, Jr.

MINNEAR, John—6-13-1796; pr. 9-19-1796. W., Mary. 4 ch., 1-Isaac, 2-William, 3-Abraham, 4-Mary Glaze. Exec., son, Isaac. Wit., Jacob Blue, Henry Frazee, James Johnson (also sec.); John Higgins. Sec., Daniel McDonald.

MITCHELL, James—3-7-1820; pr. 9-16-1822. No w., 5 ch., 1-Izsabella Hatten (dec'd, has dau., Rebeckah), 2-James, Jr., 3-Sarah Dobbins, 4-Ann Palmer, 5-John Mitchell (has dau., Elizabeth.) Mt. Thornton B. James, and Abraham Reinhart. Exec., Daniel Hollenbeck.

MONROE, Jesse—5-11-1857. W., Eleanor. Dau., Elizabeth Blue (hus., John L.), son, John G., 2 gr. ch., John M. and Mary E. Taylor.

MONROE, John—6-13-1822; pr. 9-20-1824. W., Lucy. 10 ch., 1-James, 2-William, 3-Alexander (dec'd), 4-John, 5-Isse, 6-George, 7-Marcus, 8-Molley Ambler, 9-Ann, 10-Eliza Arnold. John Ambler and Derna Cunningham get Molley's estate. Son of No. 4. Elias Wood, gr. son, Sidney Monroe. Wit., Levi Arnold, Adam Cresswell and Joseph Nixon. Sec., John Martin. Refers to son, James, as exceptional. Son, John, left 6 ch., 1 born 4 days after his death.

MOORE, Elizabeth—2-16-1818; pr. 4-19-1819. Widow of James, Sr. 10 ch., 1-John, 2-Benjamin, 3-Thomas, 4-Elizabeth, 5-Mary, 6-Rebekah, 7-Catherine, 8-Peggy, 9-Sary, 10-James Moore. Wit., Benj Frye, Elizabeth and Frederick Michael (also sec.) Exec., son, James, Jr., and John Littler.

MOORE, James—2-6-1801; pr. 10-15-1804. W., Elizabeth. 10 ch., 1-Benjamin, 2-Thomas, 3-John, 4-James, 5-Sary (Sarah) Moore, 6-Elizabeth Smith, 7-Mary Secrist, 8-Catherine, 9-Rebecca, 10-Margaret. Exec., sons, Benjamin and Thomas. Sec., Archibald Linthicum and Fred Michael. Wit., Fredrick and Phillip Michael.

MOORE, Phillip—2-18-1774; pr. 3-10-1778. W., Mary. 6 ch., 1-Anthony, 2-Phillip, 3-Jacob, 4-Margaret, 5-Elizabeth, 6-Susannah. Exec., Charles Lynch and Capt. Jacob Reed (latter dead 1778). Wit., George Reed, Bernhart Mayer. Sec., Patrick Lynch and Wm. Welton.

MOORE, Reese — 6-15-1830; pr. 9-25-1830. W., Frances. Exec., William Torrance. Wit., Conrad Menser, Thos. Spicer and John Wolford (also sec.)

MORE, Samuel—11-13-1823. W., Elizabeth. 2 ch., Jeremiah and Ann. Exec., Jeremiah. Wit., John Vandivear, Richard Sturman, Joseph Parrott.

MORELAND, Richard—8-26-1845; pr. 9-22-1865. W., Elizabeth, 9 ch., 1-Margaret, 2-Mary Queen (hus., Stephen). has dau., Chloe; 3-John, 4-James, 5-William, 6-George, 7-Richard, 8-Jacob, 9-Bazil. Exec., Stephen Queen and William (son.) Wit., William P. Heiskell, John and Geo. Milleson.

MORRISON, James (of Alleghany Co., Md.)—5-20-1823; pr. 2-15-1825. W., Agnes. 6 ch., 1-Jen (Jane?) Ingman (hus., Henry), eldest dau.; gr dau., Nancy Ingman, their dau., and James their son; 2-Mary Hamil (hus., Patrick), her dau., Nancy, and son, James Hamil (Mary is dec'd); 3-John 4-James Morrison, Jr., dec'd; 5-Ruth Dawson died left dau. 6-Nancy Morrison. Exec., son, John. Nm. John Poland and Cartie John Hays and Jeremiah Ashby. Wit., Jere. Tripleman, Jacob Legler, Geo. Layman. Sec., John Brady.

MOTTS, Randolph—3-24-1847; pr. 5-24-1867. W. and ch., mentioned but not named; parents and sisters mentioned but not named. Exec., Henry Trout. Wit., Arthur F. Grim, Wm. H. Pool and W. H. Raflin. Sec., Wm. Pool and Henry Markwood.

MOUSER, Jacob, Sr.—10-5-1801; pr. 12-?-1801. W., Catherine. Ch. mentioned but not named. Exec., wife. Wit., James Delham, Michael More, Thomas Mulledy (also sec., with Jacob Mouser.)

MULLEDY, Thomas—4-30-1849; pr. 8-22-1853. No w. 7 ch., 1-Robert, 2-Alfred, 3-Thomas F., 4-Samuel, 5-Sarah Jarboe, 6-Mary, 7-Mildred Parsons. Exec., Robert and Alfred Mulledy. Wit., Thomas B. and John B. White and John Kern.

MURPHY, Mary—1-19-1815; pr. 6-17-1823. Wid. of **James Murphy**; (earlier w. of James French, d. 1773). 5 ch., 1-**William French**, 2-**Robert French**, 3-**Sally Higgins** has., John); 4-**Frances**, dec'd, 5-dau., **Collins**; gr. daus., **Maria** and **Patsy Higgins**; gr. dau., **Nancy Collins**; gr. daus., **Sally Ann** and **Francis** (ch. of Francis, dec'd.). See Mary Rector will. Annuity due 4-1-1813 paid by John Copsey. Exec., **John Higgins**. Sec., **James Gibson**. Wit., **William Miller, Aaron Hughes, George Rogers**.

MYERS, John—2-1-1854; pr. 2-27-1856. W., **Sarah**. 2 ch., 1-**Francis (Frak)**, 2-**Florence** (minor), (Jos. R. Armstrong, her guardian). Exec., **Jos. D. Armstrong**. Deposition taken of Chas. S. Taylor, ill, and Abrah Hass mt. Sec., **Edw. M. Armstrong, John C. Heiskell, Wm. Stump, John Singleton, James P. Heiskell**.

MYERS, Peter—4-29-1818; pr. 6-15-1818. W., **Sarrah**; dau., **Susan**. Exec., **Christopher Heiskell**. Wit., **Wm. Vance** and **Peter Heiskell**.

—N—

NAVE, Leonard—3-16-1778; pr. 5-12-1778. W., but not 6 ch., 1-**Henry**, 2-**Michael**, land bought of Thom; 3-**George**, a minor, land; 4-**Jacob**, a minor; 5 and 6- two daughters, not named; gr. son, **John**, son of Leonard Nave, deceased. Wit., **James Sears, Herman Shook**. Sec., **James Sears, Herman Shook, George Lee**.

NESBIT, John—5-18-1823; pr. 6-16-1823. W., **Elizabeth**. No ch. Bro., **Nathaniel**, who has son, **John**. Exec., w. Wit., **George Staggs Franklin Staggs** and one other, "Leatzfrit Babruch."

NEWBANKS, John——8-14-1826; pr. 4-8-1846. W., **Elizabeth**. Ch. mentioned but not named. Exec., w. and **Joseph Hook**. Wit., **Samuel Hook, Frederick** and **John Spaid**.

NEWMAN, John—5-22-1823; pr. 8-15-1826. W., **Elizabeth**, former w. mentioned but not named. 3 ch., 1-**Michael Piper**, 2-**James Meekin**, 3-dau., — **Piper** (hus., John). Exec., w. Wit., **Joseph Stump** and **William Stump**.

NEWMAN, Ralph—7-19-1852; pr. 3-28-1855. W., **Sally**. 4 ch., 1- **William C.**, 2-**Mary Ann Babb** (or Babbs), 3-**Elizabeth**, 4-**John**. Will mentions John C. Heiskell, John Newman, his father, Elizabeth, stepmother; Nancy Ann Baker, Hannah, Charles Wesley and Ralph Perrin, ch., of Upton Perrin and gr ch. of Sally, w. of Ralph. John Y. Baker was exec. of Nancy Baker, 1852. Wit., **Henry K. Hoffman, John Daily** and **Jacob Z. Chadwick**.

NIXON, George—2-15-1793; pr. 4-?-1793. W., **Rachel**, 7 ch., 1-**George**, land adj. John Gard and on Dillenger Mt., 82 acres; 2-**Joseph**, land, Lick Run home; 3-**William** (dec'd, his heirs—speaks of "my three sons"); 4-**Jonathan**, 5-**Elizabeth Web**; 6-**Hannah**, 7-**Nancy**. Gr. dau., **Rhoda Thomas**; gr. dau., **Molly**, dau. of Jonathan. Gr. sons, **George** and **Levi Nixon** (evidently sons of William). 79 acres.: Will mentions John Chenoweth, John Newbanks and Morris Ellis. Exec., w and **John Arnold**. Sec., **John Chenoweth** and **Joseph Asbury**. Wit., **Peter Kale, Francis White, John Sloan**.

—O—

OATS, George—1-20-1844; pr. 2-26-1844. W., **Catherine**. 5 ch., 1-**Peter**, "afflicted son," 2-**Christopher**, 3-**Jonathan**, 4-**Michel**, 5-**Margaret**. Exec., son **Christopher**. Wit., **Leonard Pugh, John Shivers**. Sec., **Wm. Lupton, Micheal Slonmaker** (also wit.), **Joseph Clutter**. Foreman farm to Peter.

OBAR, Peter—3-12-1782; verbal will; pr. 11-11-1783. Will much torn. Left all to his son, Capt. **William Vause** or **Vance**. Pr. by Samuel Decker. Exec., **William Vance**. Sec., **Alex Wodrow, Sol Van Meter**. Wit., **John** and **Simon Harris**.

OFFUT, Solomon—9-25-1834; pr. 3-27-1849. W., **Elizabeth**. 9 ch., 1-**Owen**, 2-**Joseph**, 3-**Zepheniah**, 4-**Nancy Pugh**, 5-**Sarah Pugh**, 6-**Rachel Die**, 7-**Hester**, 8-**Harriet**, 9-**Thornton**, youngest son. Exec., sons **Owen** and **Joseph**. Wit., **Nath. Offut, Martin Holtz, Reuben Holtz**.

O'HARRA, Daniel—3-29-1821; pr. 7-17-1821. W., **Susan**. No ch. Exec., w. and **James Gibson**. Sec., **John B. White, James Daily**. Wit., **John B. White, N. Kuykendall, R. Newman**.

O'NEALS, ARTHUR—("now of Hampshire") 5-25-1761; pr. 12-8-1761. Bro., **Daniel**, dec'd, he inherits his land and now wills it. Sister, **Ann Conlon** (hus., James), living in Ireland. Exec., **Nicholas Seaver**, friend, and **Patrick McCarthy**. Sec., **John Duckodd** and **Peter Cossy**. Wit., **Sam McMury, Isaac Green, Ann Purcoll**. In case Anna or children fail to come from Ireland, land to go to Nicholas Seaver.

ORCHARD, Nancy (a free woman of color)—11-28-1835; pr. 10-29-1842. Mentions William Naylor, John Jack, Mrs. Ward, Mrs. Galloway, John B. White, William Armstrong, William Vause (Vance?). Exec., **John Kern, Jr.**, and **David Gibson**. Wit., **James Busbey** and **Joseph Poling**.

OSBORNS, George—7-21-1783; pr. 1783. W., **Hannah**, gets one-third. 4 ch., 1-**Josiah**, 220 acres; 2-**Isaac** and 3-**Solomon**, get 160 acres on Raccoon Creek; 4-**Frances**. Gr. son, **George**. Ch. under age to be bound out. Exec., son,**Josiah**. ..Wit., **John Harras, Simeon Harras, Phoebe Harras**.

OSMAN, Elizabeth — 9-8-1784. 4 ch., 1-**Sam**, 2-**Rebecca**, gr. son, **Isaac**, to have jacket of broadcloth in the house; 3-dau., **Rodey Daley**, 4-**Catherine Lafferty**. Says to "divide equally between all my daughters." Wit., **Ovid Mccracken** and **Charles Osman**.

OSMON, Isaac—4-24-1783; pr. 11-9-1784. W., **Elizabeth**. Son, **Sam**. Wit., **Ovid Mecrackin, Virgil Mecrackin, Mecracken** and **Charles Osman**.

—P—

PALMER, Mary (of Patterson's Creek, Frederick Co.) — 10-15-1752; pr. 2-14-1758. 3 ch., 1-**Ann Miller**, 2-**Sofia Johnson**, 3-**Andrew Sadowsk**. Exec., **Sofia Darling** (hus., William Darling, sec.). Sec., **John Ryan, Luke Collins**. Wit., **John Douthit, Davis Rutter**.

PANCAKE, Andrew (Hardy Co.)—10-23-1786; pr. 9-11-1793. W., **Elizabeth** (pregnant). 8 ch., 1-**John**, 2-**Hannah**, 3-**Joseph**, farm; 4-**Agnes**, 5-**Isaac**, 6-**Mary**, 7-**Abraham**, 8-**George** (latter 5 minors) Exec., sons **John** and **Joseph**. Sec., **John Pancake, Sr., John Rannels**. Wit., wife, **Elizabeth, Thomas Talbot, John Shephard**.

PARK, Amos—4-26-1844; pr. 1-27-1845. No w. 8 ch., 1-**Evan**, 2-**Ann Cooper**, 3-**Amy McDonald**, 4-**Lydia Gragg**, 5-**Emily Hiett**, 6-**Griffith**, 7-**Samuel**, 8-**Amos Harvey**. Gr. dau., **Harriet Ann Hiett**. Exec., son, **Amos**. Sec., **Robert Carmichael, Joseph P. Simth**. Wit., **Nath. Offut, Isaac Heiskell, Stephen Miller**. Nm. **John Deaver, Geo. Horn, D. Foreman, John Barrett**. Sec. **Robert Carmichael, Paul** and **Joseph Smith**.

PARKE, Andrew—3-19-1789; pr. 4-15-1790. No w. 7 ch., 1-**Sam**, 2-**John**, 3-**Ruth Patten**, 4-**Rachel Nickson** (or Neckson), 5-**Sarah Shire**, 6-**Hannah Thomas**, 7-**Amos**. Exec., sons **John** and **Amos**. Sec., **Elias Posten**. Wit., **John Parrill, John Landis, Jesse Mosley**.

PARK, John—4-20-1816; pr. 11-19-1816. No w. 6 ch., 1-Amos, 2-George, 3-Samuel, 4-Joanna Dew, 5-Sarah Coe, 6-Solomon (dec'd; left 4 ch., Malinda, Maria, Wina and Solomon Park, Jr.) Exec., sons, Amos, Sec., John Barrott, George Park. Wit., John Barrott and Francis White.

PARKE, Roger—7-13-1773; pr. 11-9-1773. W., Hannah. Dau., Hannah Arnold (hus., John), exec. Sec., John Arnold, John Park, James Largent, Robert Pugh. Wit., John Chenoweth, David Wood, Elijah David.

PARKE, Samuel—4-3-1845; pr. 4-26-1852. W., Susannah. 11 ch., 1-Timothy, 2-Elizabeth Myers (hus., Jacob), 3-Amos, 4-Alfred, 5-Samuel, 6-Rhoda Burket (hus., William), 7-Westley, 8-Jefferson, 9-Washington, 10-Anne, 11-Susannah. Mentions David Reed. Exec., sons, Westley, Jefferson and Washington. Sec., James D. Albin, John C. Heiskell, Benjamin F. Richards. Wit., Nath. Offut, Harbart Park, Samuel Park, William Orendorf, George W. Smaltz.

PARKER, Benjamin—2-23-1808; pr. 9-19-1808. W., Margaret. 4 ch., 1-George, 2-James, 3-Absalom, 4-Elizabeth Wolfe. Gr. son, Thornton Parker. Exec., wife and son, James. Sec., Thomas Carskadden. Wit., Hendrick Roseboom, John Snyder, Thomas Carskadden (also sec.)

PARKER, George—2-27-1757; pr. 12-13-1758. W., Ann. Son, Benjamin. Mentions John Funk. Land on Patterson Creek; Fairfax grants. Sec., James Irison (Griscom?), Thomas McGuire, Nicholas Seaver. Wit., James Young and Daniel McFeron.

PARKER, Jacob—11-10-1834; pr. 12-22-1834. W., Sarah. Ch., Susanna (youngest), and Abraham; other ch. not named. Exec., friend, John Arnold, of Little Cacaphon, and son, Abraham Parker. Sec., Thomas and George Sloan. Wit., Edw. Taylor, Alfred Taylor, John Parker and Sam Kercheval, Jr.

PARKER, James—12-14-1833; pr. 9-19-1843. W., Rebecca. 10 ch., 1-George, 2-Thornton, 3-Elizabeth Johnson, 4-Mary Johnson, 5-David, 6-James, 7-Ashford, 8-Hannah Emmerson, 9-Benjamin, land; 10-Isabella Shutz. Gr. daus., Elizabeth Ann Long and Rebecca Johnson. Exec., son, Benjamin, and Thomas Carskadden. Wit., William H. Metcalf, John Hamilton, Abraham Shokey, George Bane.

NOTE. In Chancery 1843. Martha R. and Mary I. Parker, infant heirs of Benj. dec'd, and Eliza Jane, his widow.
vs.
Rebecca, widow of James; Geo. Parker, Jacob Johnson, wf., Mary, David Parker, James Johnson, wf., Elizabeth; James Parker, James Emmerson, wf., Hannah; John Sheets, wf., Isabella; Abner Bane, wf., Elizabeth (late Elizabeth Ann Long) ; Okey Johnson, wf., Rebecca (late Long), children of Joseph and Margaret Parker Long, dec., dau. of James Parker, dec.; Mary Jane, Thos. and Eliza Parker, ch. of Thornton Parker, dec'd; James T., John M., Mary E., children of Ashford Parker, dec'd.

PARKER, John—9-28-1760; pr. 11-11-1760. W., Elizabeth. Each child to share equally; gr. son, Thomas, equal part with rest. Exec., son, Robert. Sec., William Foreman, Benjamin Kuykendall. Wit., William Smith, John Ross.

PARKER, Robert—5-28-1808; pr. 2-20-1809. W., Grace. 3 ch., 1-John, 2-William, 3-Mary. John Parker, son of John Parker; John Frazer, son of Alex Frazier; Nobel Parker, son of William Parker. Exec., Joseph and John Hergot. Wit., James Gray, Thomas White.

PARKER, Robert—9-13-1805; pr. 12-16-1816. W., Margaret. 3 ch., 1-Catreen Johnson, 2-Solomon, 3-Peter. Land in Kentucky. Exec., son, Solomon. Sec., William Miller, Richard Blue. Wit., Joseph Lessman, Henry L. Wilson, Solomon Parker, William Miller.

PARKER, Sarah—7-22-1858; pr. 6-27-1859. 6 ch., 1-Robert W., 2-Joseph ("aflicted son), 3-Isaac (evidently dead, his unmarried children get his share); 4-Harriet, 5-Mary, 6-Sarah (dec'd, left ch.). Exec., son, Robert W. Sec., James Carskadden and David Mytinger. Wit., George W. Washington and Henry K. Hoffman.

PARKINSON, Eliza—4-20-1847; pr. 6-29-1849. (nee Cross, father, Gassaway C., dec'd intestate, late of Morgan Co.) Hus., Christopher, exec. Wit., Dan Mytinger, And. Helphinstine, John Kern, Jr.

PARRILL, Edward—3-10-1826; pr. 7-17-1826. W., Rachel nee Ashbrook.) Property divided between brothers and sisters; nc., Jane Crumpton. Anna Bell, "who I wish to come in for a child's part." Elijah Dolby mentioned. Exec., Joseph Parrell and Eli Bell. Wit., John Hammock, Sr. and Jr., and Robert Wynn.

PARRILL, John—5-8-1809; pr. 8-19-1811. W., Elizabeth. 5 ch., 1-Edward, 2-William, land; 3-Ann Beal, 4-Jane Crumpton (dec'd recently, has dau., Jane C.); 5-Joseph, land. Mentions Jonathan Lovett, John Newton, Paul McKeever. Exec., sons, Edward and William, and Archibald Linthicum. Wit., John Hammock, Joseph Clutter.

PARRELL, Rachel—3-10-1841; pr. 4-25-1846. No ch. Wid. of Edward; nee Ashbrook. Jane Linthicum (hus., Archibald), their sons, Edward Perrell Linthicum, land, and Charles Masterson Linthicum. Sarah Brown (late Beal). 9 brothers and sisters, 1-Aron Ashbrook, 2-Eli Ashbrook, 3-Thomas Ashbrook, dec'd, left ch.; 4-John Ashbrook, 5-William Ashbrook, 6-Absolom Ashbrook, 7-Phoebe Tucker, 8-Roda Williams, 9-Maria B. Peters. Mary Chiswell gets a stove. Nc., Rachel Crawford. Mentions Joseph P. Clutter, Ruth Moses and Peter Evans. Exec., bro., Ely Ashbrook of Ohio, or Aron or Thomas. Wit., David Pugh, John and James Cresswell.

PARROTT, Christopher — 9-28-1820; pr. 11-20-1820. W., Martha. 4 ch., 1-Dennis, 2-Joseph, 3-Margaret Lynch, 4-Nancy Davis. Exec., wife, and son, Joseph. Sec., William Vance, Samuel and Jacob Vandiver. Wit., Thomas Slane, Wheeler Gillett, Jacob Pugh.

PARSONS, James, Jr. (will and codicil)—11-27-1846; pr. 2-25-1867. 10 ch., 1-James, 2-Isaac, 3-Dana, 4-Elizabeth Shobe, 5-Rebecca Fairfax (hus., Buckner); 6-Sarah A. Blue (hus., Thomas); 7-dau. — Stump (hus., Adam); 8-dau., — Brady (hus., Samuel D.); 9-dau., — Jacobs (hus., R—); 10-dau, — Pancake (hus., John M.). Gr. ch., Isaac, John and Sarah Pancake, minors. Mentions Widow Dailey and John Park. Exec., sons, James and Isaac. Wit., David Ream, Dan Mytinger, R. M. Varden, Robert W. Dailey.

PARSONS, Mary E—9-22-1854; pr. 10-23-1854. Mother, Mary Parsons; gr. fa., William Curlatt; sis., Margaret (Rebecca) Parsons; bro., William. Exec., friend, William P. Stump. Wit., John C. Newman, George W. Washington.

PARSONS, Thomas—5-7-1771; pr. 3-10-1722. 7 ch., 1-Isaac, 2-Baldwin, 3-Elizabeth (wid. of Dr. Henry Heinsman), 4-Thomas, 5-James, 6-Agnes, 7-Prudence. Sons-in-law, William Welton and Robert Cunningham. Exec., sons, Thomas and James. Sec., George Wilson, William Buffington. Wit., Sam Dew, John Rosseau, Richard Byrn.

PATTERSON, James—7-29-1811; pr. 5-18-1812. W., Jennet. 9 ch., 1-John, land; 2-James, land, liberal education; 3-Alex, land; 4-Robert, land; 5-Thomas, 6-Betsy McVicker, 7-Peggy, 8-Mary, 9-Jane. Exec., sons, John and Robert. ..Wit., Adam and James Heare; John (or Johnston) Malick, Sr.

PATTERSON, John—7-13-1828; pr. 8-19-1828. 11 ch., 1-Samuel, 2-John, 3-James, 4-Thomas, 5-Robert, 6-Joseph, 7-Richard, 8-William, 9-Margaret, 10-Mary Ann, 11-Martha Jane. Exec., Zebulon Sheets, and son Samuel Patterson. Wit., Joseph Scott, William Torrence, John Grapes.

PATTERSON, Thomas—8-6-1850; pr. 5-26-1851. W., Sarah. 9 ch., 1-Nancy, 2-James Henry, 3-Robert, 4-Thomas, 5-John, 6-Sarah, 7-Margaret, 8-Isobel, 9-Jane. Nep., James Patterson. Exec., son, James Henry, and nep., James Patterson. Sec., Samuel Bethel, Peter Alkire, George Thompson. Wit., Robert Monroe, Anna Pattrson.

PEACEMAKER, David—4-4-1850; pr. 5-27-1850. W. not named. Bro., Adam; ch. mentioned not named. Exec., John C. Smith, Jacob Peacemaker, Jr. Sec., Jacob W. Peacemaker. Wit., Major Hoge, George, Jacob W. and William Peacemaker.

PEAR, Sarah—6-25-1860; pr. 7-23-1860. Son, Joseph. John O. Wilson's eldest son, Aquilla P.; S .S. Wilson, Thomas Dobson, Harrison Anderson of Charlestown. Exec., John Racy refuses; Alf. A. Brill appointed. Wit., M. F. Harmon, John H. Himelwright, Jacob Fishell.

PENNINGTON, Elijah (of Crawford Co., Ohio)—5-4-1832; pr. 5-25-1835. 14 ch., 1-John, 2-William, 3-Thomas, 4-James, 5-Enoch, 6-Adam, 7-Isaac, 8-Levy, 9-Henry, 10-Charlotte Caughney, 11-Feaby Miller, 12-Nancy, 13-Elizabeth Emmitt, 14-Faney Lefolet. Land in Harrison Co., Indiana, Warren and Putnam counties, Illinois. Exec., John Gibson of Seneca Co., and son, Adam. Wit., Calvin and Barnabas Rogers, John Gibson.

PENNINGTON, Hannah—11-12-1852; pr. 12-27-1852. Sister, Eady Ann Milslagle; bro., Elias Millslagle (exec.). Wit., Henry Brill, Alfred Brill.

PENNINGTON, James—3-24-1843; pr. 9-25-1843. W., Hannah. Exec., wife and Jacob Kump. Sec., Abraham Secrist. Wit., John Reed, Amos Anderson, Sam Milslager.

PENNINGTON, Thomas—2-4-1857; pr. 5-25-1857. W. not named. 5 ch., 1-Julius G., 2-William Paul, 3-Isaac J., 4-Sarah, 5-Mary Catherine; gr. son., Alfred Anderson. Wit., Joseph and George Spaid, Abraham Creswell.

PETERS, John—314-1840; pr. 2-26-1849. 7 ch., 1-John, 2-James, 3-Hester Ann, 4-Caty Cunningham, 5-Cherese Rogers (hus., Aaron), 6-Asenath Roberson, 7-Permelia Ann. Exec., Joseph L. Smith, Jacob Hammach. Sec., Stephen Smith, George Wolf, Wesley B. McNemar. Wit., Harbert Park, Aaron Rogers, James W. Allen.

PETERS, Peter—10-17-1772; pr. 3-9-1773. 3 daus., 1-Mary Rambo (hus., Peter); 2-Susannah Williams (hus., Richard); 3-Hannah Parker (hus., Robert). 2 gr. sons, Edw. and Peter Peters. Exec., Richard Williams, Robert Parker. Wit., Jacob Castleman, Stephen Calvin, Thomas Branan, William Buffington, Darby Aughney.

PETTIT, John—1-9-1839; pr. 10-11-1865. W., Rebecca.

PETTIT, John—12-18-1854; pr. 1-22-1855. W., Rebecca, exec. Estate divided between her and his heirs. Wit., John Kern, Jr., John M. Snyder.

PIERSALL (or Pursall), John—2-13-1809; pr. 11-18-1811. W., Hannah. Eleanor Lyons, Amee Kearfoot, daus. of Cornelius Hoagland, dec'd. Sister, Rachel Mooney; bro., Benjamin; sister, Margaret Jackson; sister, Eleanor Hall or Hill. Sis., Rachel has 7 ch., Rachel, Isaac, Edmund and David Mooney; also Mordecai, Elijah and John Berkley (Barkley). Benjamin has ch. Nm. probably nieces and nephews. Kesiah Hill, Hannah Kelley, sister?) Naomy McNary, (hus., Ebenezer), her children to get Alleg. Co., Md., land. Exec., Wm. Vause and John Snyder. Wit., Alex King, Wm. Fox, Vincent Williams, Lewis Dunn.

PIERSALL, Hannah—1-22-1812; pr. 8-19-1822. (Widow of John). Niece, Eleanor Lyons; relatives, John Piersall Kearfoot, Ami McNary, Anna Kearfoot. Exec., Ebenezer McNary. Wit., John McBride, Ephraim Dunn, William Fox.

POLAND, Nancy—11-14-1857; pr. 1-25-1858. Friend, William Haines, w., Elizabeth, their dau., Elizabeth, friend, Jackson Carder.: Exec., John B. Sherrard. Wit., William A. Kuykendall, Robert White.

POOL, William—10-11-1808; pr. 12-19-1808. W., Easter. 15 ch., 1-Henery, 2-George, 3-Robert, 4-Asby, 5-Haner (these five get home place); 6-William, 7-Sarah, 8-John, 9-Sufier, 10-Susannah, 11-Rhoda, 12-Elizabeth, 13-Ann, 14-Benjamin, 15-Mary (these to get 107 acres, in Berkley Co.). Wit., Richard Short, Joseph Johnson, also sec., with John Stoker and Richard Deever.

POSTEN, Elias—6-20-1802 (cod. 7-4-1802); pr. 9-20-1802. W. Rebecka, exec. and cod. 4 ch., 1-Sam (exec), 2-Catherine Nixon (hus., George); 3-William (exec.); 4-Delila Slane (hus., Benjamin.) Friend, James McBride, also exec. Sec., Francis White, George Horn, Joseph Thompson. Wit., Walter and Susannah Murphy, John Cheshire, and John Parker.

POWELL, Joseph—5-6-177-; pr. 11-12-1771. W., Christian. 5 ch., 1-Abraham, 2-Sam, 3-Joseph, 4-John, 5-Stephen. Exec., wife and Henry Fry. Sec., James Moore, James Alexander. Wit., Richard Mynatt, James Moore James Alexander. Latter two also sec.

POWELL, Robert M.—10-3-1842; pr. 9-11-1854. 9 ch., 1-Dade, deed of land 1829, and Bible; 2-James, 3-Nancy (Seaton) 4-Mary Leith, 5-Robert M., 6-Susanna Mauzey, 7-Elisha, 8-Elizabeth Mausy, 9-Sarah Ann Kenney. Exec., George Keiter, Jr., (gets land in trust), and Nath. Offutt. Wit., William Brown, Robert Powell, John J. Offutt.

POWELL, Sarah—10-3-1830; pr. 12-25-1830. Nc., Elizabeth B. Powell, dau. of bro., Joseph; nep., Thornton F. (has dau., Sarah B. Wit., Julia D. Powell, Jonah Corbin and Charles Powelson.

POWELSON, Cloann—6-28-1851; pr. 7-28-1851. Relationship not shown of Henry Powelson, James Powelson, Paul Powelson, Thomas Powelson, John Powelson, Ann Watkins and Rebecca Watkins. "4 brothers of Henry." Wit., Daniel Shomad, Uriah Cheshire, Wm. G. Shaub.

POWELSON, Cornelius—9-25-1837; pr. 12-25-1837. W., Elizabeth. Wit., John Powelson, Joseph Powell., Jr., and William F. Arnold.

POWELSON, Eve—12-29-1812; pr. 1-18-1813. Conrad, "my only son" to have my "right and title to one-twelfth part of plantation of Paul Powelson, dec'd." (relation not stated). Wit., Thos. and Alex McBride and John Powelson.

POWELSON, Henry—4-26-1845; pr. 8-25-1845. W. not even mentioned, but relinquishes her rights as ex. Exec., William Vance. Sec., Robert C. Kercheval. Nm. Wm. Merritt, S. I. Powelson, Isaac Newman. Wit., John Thompson, John J. Hardy.

POWELSON, Rinere—1-4-1838; pr. 5-28-1838. W., Elizabeth. 4 ch., 1-John R., 2-Rinear, 3-Eliza, 4-Rosannah; s-i-l, John L. Heare. Wit., Cloanne, Powell and Thomas Powelson.

POWNELL, Elisha—3-19-1833; pr. 8-28-1837. W., Abigail. 8 ch., 1-Isaiah, 2-Jonathan, 3-Ruben, 4-Martha, 5-Rachel, 6-Levina, 7-Abigail, 8-Sarah. Wit., William Powell, Isaac Ely, John Baker, Jr., Billy (or Bilby) Combs, And. Bowman, Geo. Carder. Exec., son, Isaiah and Philip Fahs.

PRATHER, James—2-10-1816; pr. 2-19-1821 (of Allegany Co., Maryland). 8 ch., 1-Charles, 2-James, 3-Basil, 4-Elizabeth, 5-Mary, 6-Martha, 7-Caty, 8-Ruth. Charles evidently away; must claim his in 2 years. Nm. Conrad Pusinger and Nancy Jackson. Exec., son, James, and Daniel Colliss. Wit., Samuel McBride, George W. Glaze, Nathan Burress.

PRATHER, Silas—6-13-1848; pr. 11-28-1869. W., Ann H. 8 ch., 1-Socratoris (dec'd), 2-Van, 3-Silas, 4-Laban A., 5-William B., 6-Theodoris W., 7-Ann M., 8-Martha M. Expects 160 acres from United States, also treasury draft. Wit., George Haggerty (d. 1869), John A. Hammaker, Sam H. Brady and George Millison.

PRINGLE, Henry (of Muskingum Co., Ohio, Zanesville twp.)—8-20-1818; pr. 1-19-1824. W., Mary. 10 ch., 1-Jedidiah, 2-Adaiah, 3———?, 4-Marget, 5-Elizabeth, 6-Mary, 7-Malinda, 8-William, 9-John, 10-George W. Exec., wife and William Cooksey. Sec., Warner Throckmorton. Wit., Daniel Jett and Minor McQueen.

PRITCHARD, Joseph—2-1-1768; pr. 3-8-1768. W., Alse. To bro., Rees' son, Stephen; bro, Sam; Rees Pritchard's dau., Hannah; Joseph and John James, sister's sons, and others. Wit., John Waite, William Hews, Ellis Hews. Sec., Luke Collins, William McFadian.

PUGH, Bethel—11-3-1821; pr. 1-14-1822. W., Rebecca. Son, Jacob. Bro. and sis. not named. Wit., Jonathan Pugh, John Fleming.

PUGH, Daniel—5-26-1794; pr. 9-11-1794. W., Sarah. 3 ch., 1-Hannibal, 2-Amy, 3-Juliana. Suit against James Parsons in Frederick Co. over negroes. Exec., Isaac and Jonathan Parsons, Hezekiah Davidson and John Prunty. Wit., Edw. Dyer, Jno. Brown, Francis Taggart.

PUGH, Jesse—3-18-1830; pr. 9-30-1830. W. not named. 5 ch., 1-Harriot, 2-Alfred, 3-Hannah, 4-Mahlon 5-Elizabeth. Exec., Gen. Josiah Lockhard. Sec., Thomas Hook, Azariah Pugh, Charles Capper. Wit., Azariah Pugh, James Thomas, William Gard.

PUGH, Jonathan—9-20-1794; pr. 10-15-1794. W., Margaret. 7 ch., 1-Jonathan, 2-David, 3-Jesse, 4-Amos, 5-John, 6-Lucy Taggart (hus., Francis , 7-Daniel, dec'd. Exec., son, Jonathan and son-in-law, Francis Taggart. Wit., Fr. Keyes, Jacob Emmert, John Pepper. Sec., Francis Keyes and James Carruthers. Nm. Wm., Bab and John McCoole, Wm. Myers, Lord Dunmore.

PUGH, Jonathan, Jr.—12-15-1831; pr. 3-26-1832. W., Anne. "My two little sons." Exec., Solomon Offut. Sec., John Pugh. Wit., John Martin, Henry Pepper, Jonathan Hiett.

PUGH, Jonathan—8-21-1834; pr. 10-27-1834. W. not named. 2 daus., Lucy and Maria, and son, John; 2 gr. sons, Arthur and Solomon Pugh. Exec., son, John, and John Hiett. Wit., John Martin, Uriah Cheshire, Moses McClintic.

PUGH, Michael—1-15-1838; pr. 9-?-1838. W., Margaret. Ch., Malachi, David, Margaret, Ann Dunlap, and others. Wit., James Cresswell, James Monroe and David Pugh of Joseph; Simon Ward and Sam Creswell. Gr. ch., Ferdinand I. and Mary Ann Dunlap. Nm. Robert Albin. Sec., Christopher Heiskell, Wm. Vance.

PUGH, Robert—11-23-1801; pr. 1-18-1808. W., Mary. 6 ch., 1-Sam, 2-Joseph, 3-Mishall, 4-Robert, 5-Jesse (he has 6 ch.); 6-Hannah Horn's 4 ch. Wit., James McBride, James Caudy, Sam Grand, John and Absolem Chenoweth. Joseph and Robert, exec.

PUGH, Robert—4-15-1846; 1-28-1850. W., Ann. "Mentions "my 7 children; lists Eleanor, Robert, Benjamin, James and Monroe. Exec., sons, Benjamin and Monroe. Sec., David, Malichi and Jesse Pugh. Wit., David and Malachi Pugh and Joseph Karkley.

PURGET, Henry Sen—2-4-1835; pr. 3-27-1837. W., Elizabeth. Ch., 1-William, 2-Frederick, 3-Henry, 4-George, 5-Mary Recer, 6-Elizabeth Shoemaker, 7-Rachel Suber, and "six other children"? Wit., Thomas Sloan, John and Thomas Ludwick, John High.

PULTZ, Michael—1857; pr. 1858. W. not named. 6 ch., 1-Katherine, 2-Jacob, 3-Michael (dec'd.), 4-Mary France, 5-Elizabeth, 6-Nancy Freman. Exec., George Warfield.

PUTMAN, Jacob—6-27-1833; pr. 8-26-1833. W., Rachel. Jacob, not yet 16, only ch. Exec., Thomas Daniels. Sec., Jacob Fleck, Dennis Daniels, John Stewart, Chas. Kellar, Lewis Dunn. Wit., Augustine and John Burham, John Stewart and John Singleton.

—Q—

QUEEN, Martha—8-18-1834; pr. 11-24-1835. Bro., John; nc., Sarah Queen Smoot; nc., Martha Queen Holt, her son, Absolom; nep., John Queen, Jr. Exec., John Queen, Jr. Sec., C. Heiskell and W. Shearer. Wit., Joseph Pugh, C. Heiskell, W. Shearer.

—R—

RACEY, John—3-15-1831; pr. 6-20-1831. W., Rebecca. Mentions "my children," but does not name them. Exec., John Reed. Sec., John Spaid. Wit., Chhisty Sine, John Reed and William Racey.

RACEY, Sarah—8-30-1819; pr. 9-20-1819. Son, John, use of land during life, then to Hugh and Adam Barr children. Exec., William Racey; sec., Fred Buzzard and Elias Posten. Wit., Mishack Pugh and William Racey.

RACEY, Thomas—5-30-1822; pr. 9-16-1822. W., Margaret. Divided between "legal rep," does not say children. Wit., Joel Ellis, William Bane.

RANNELS, Jane—8-5-1797; pr. 10-16-1797. 9 ch., 1-Mary, 2-Nancy, 3-Peggy, 4-John, 5-David, 6-William, 7-Samuel, 8-James, 9-Robert. Exec., James and Robert Rannels. Wit., Jeremiah Sullivan, Edw. Riley, Daniel Murray.

RANNELS, Mary—8-11-1844; pr. 8-24-1846. Dau., Christeny Glaze (or Grace); son, John, "and all my children.-' Exec., John Rannels. Sec., Philip Fahs, Jacob Grace. Wit., John Brady, Jacob Grace.

RANNELS, Robert—1-14-1819; pr. 5-18-1819. W., Mary. 3 ch., 1-John, 2-Christiana, 3-Jan (latter two married). Exec., William Donaldson, Esq. Sec., John Piper, Edw. Taylor. Wit., John Newman, Jacob Smith, Simon Earson.

SYNOPSIS OF WILLS

RANNELS, William—8-3-1794; pr. 10-15-1794. W., Jane. 7 ch., 1-James, land adjoining Calmes; 2-Sam; 3-John Robert; 4-Nancy Humes, Washington Co., Pa., land; 5-William; 6-David; 7-Margaret Earsom. Gr. dau., Jane Becket, to share as ch. Exec., Fielding Calmes, John Taylor. Wit., Fielding Calmes, Samuel Abernathy, and John Long.

RAWLINGS, Moses (will and codicil)—9-15-1807; pr. 5-11-1809. 3 ch., 1-Lloyd and 2-Moses, "2 little sons begotten of Elizabeth McMahon; 3-Ann (mentioned in codicil). Nancy Rawlings, dau. of Richard; Susan Jacob, dau. of G. Jacob; Moses R. Hurst, Mrs. Ann Jacques. Exec., Roger Perry of Cumberland. Sec., Alex King and Adam Heiskell. Wit., Joseph Slagle, Jeremiah Monett, George W. Price, George Timberlake, Adam Hider.

REASNER, Jacob—9-26-1795; pr. 2-20-1797. W. not mentioned. 7 ch., 1-Susannah, 2-Peter, 3-Rebecca, 4-Mary, 5-William, 6-John, 4 younger ch. Land, Patterson Creek and Cabbin Run Hill. John Murphy land adj. William Rees' shop. Exec., son, John. Wit., William Johnson, Arjalon Price, George Rollings, Thomas S. Dowden and John B. Dowden.

RECTOR, Mary—5-20-1838; pr. 3-25-1839. (See John Copsey, Mary Murphy wills). 6 ch., Sarah Murphy Myers, and Frances Murphy, have had their father's property and her father's; Aveline, Maria and Harriet Ann; son, James Nelson Rector. Exec., James Higgins and William Parker; John Myers appointed. Sec., David Gibson, John Bendy. Wit, Montgomery P. Higgins, Joseph C. Higgins, Elizabeth A. Parker.

NOTE: She was second wife of Conway Rector. Francis Murphy, son of James; her first husband died 1807.

REED—REID—READ.

REED, George—1-17-1800; pr. 2-17-1800. W., Hannah. His father, Jeremiah, gave him land, appointed exec., refused. 3 ch., 1-William, 2-John (minor), 3-Elizabeth. Exec., John Parrill, and George Reed of Frederick Co. Sec., John Collins. Wit., John Chenoweth, Absalom Ashbrook and Joseph C. Clutter.

READ, Jeremiah—9-18-1819; pr. 6-17-1822. W., Elizabeth. 7 ch., 1-Jane Wilberforce, 2-Ann Wilson, 3-Elizabeth McKee, 4-Rikey Heiskell; 5-George (has 2 sons he just deeded land to); 6-John, 7-Jeremiah, 8-dau., Clutter, dec'd. Exec., George Reed, a friend, of Winchester, refused; John Reed was appointed. Sec., Sam Park. Wit., Priscilla Capper and George Reed.

REID, Jeremiah—12-29-1851; pr. 2-23-1852. W., Nancy. 8 ch., 1-Jeremiah I., 2-Sarah Malinda, 3-Priscilla Ann Hook (hus., William. W); 4-Harriet Racey (hus., William); 5-Elizabeth R. Thomas (hus., Hiram); 6-Mary Ann George (hus., Joel); 7-Rhuan Sample (hus., Levi); 8-Margaret Jane Rinker (hus., Levi). Exec., son, Jeremiah, and William Racey. Wit., C. Kackley, H. W. and Elizabeth Lafollette.

REID, John——3-24-1853; pr. 7-24-1854. W., Mary Ann. 18 ch., 1-Martin V., 2-Francis V. A., 3-Smith, 4-Austin T. P., 5-Azariah P, 6-Alwilda, 7-Elizabeth Ann, 8-Lavina (has 2 ch.); 9-William (has ch.); 10-James, 11-John, 12-Monah, 13-Josiah; 14-Tilberry, 15-George, 16-Morgan, 17-Dorcey, 18-Theophelos P. There are "6 small children." Exec., Silvester Rudolph, refuses, and widow asks to asks to have Jesse S. Pugh appointed. Wit., Elias Milslagle and Henry W. Lafollett.

READ, John M—12-22-1823; pr. 2-16-1824. (Of Allegany Co., Md.) W., Mary Anne. "Our children," but not named. Exec., wife, Charles Wilson of Maryland, and Archibald McNeill of Hampshire Co. Sec., Jacob Zimmerman. Wit. Robert Swan, Thomas Thistle, David Lynn.

REED, James—12-17-1810; pr. 12-16-1811. W., Nancy. Nep., James and Charles Reed. Exec., friend, William Naylor. Wit., Thomas Mulledy, Andrew and Mary Wodrow, Peter Davis.

REED, Jacob—2-23-1778; pr. 4-14-1778. W., Ann. 4 ch., 1-Solomon, 2-Charles, 3-James, 4-Mary Knave (Nave?). Exec., wife, and Anthony Baker. Sec., David Welton. Wit., Benjamin Ratcliff, Charles Lynch, George Reed, Peter Thom. (Thorn.).

REED, Nancy—7-16-1778; pr. 3-19-1779. 4 ch., 1-Solomon, 2-Charles, 3-James, 4-Mary Nave, To Maryan Willis. Has Henry Marsh bonds. Exec., Anthony Baker. Wit., Ludwig F——, Abraham Powell, Jane Cherry.

REGAR, Anthony—11-4-1769; pr. 1770. W. not named; her lawful one-third. All to son, Anthony. Exec., son, and Herman Shuck. Wit., James Sears or Seacrist, Herman Shuck.

REGAR, Anthony—10-27-1775; pr. ?. W. not named, but one recorded in second will. 2 sons, Antony and Martin, youngest son;" 3 girls, one Maddenline. Exec., wife, and Hearmon Shuck. Wit., James Secrist and Thomas Powell. Land on South Fork.

RENNICK, George—3-16-1778; pr. 4-14-1778. W., Mary. 4 ch., 1-William, 2-Millia, 3-Jenny, 4-George. Exec., w., and Job Welton and William Renick. Sec., William and David Welton. Wit., David and Solomon Welton, and Charles Myers.

REES, Ashford—7-19-1833; pr. 8-26-1833. W., Susanna. 5 ch., 1-John McNary, 2-Harriet Ann, 3-William Davis, 4-Eleonor Naomia, 5-Susanna Matilda. Exec., Thomas Cascaden. Sec., Okey Johnson, William Rees, JJohn Vandiver. Wit., Okey Johnson, Thomas Allen, Abraham Rinehart.

REESE, Thomas, Jr.—6-9-1832; pr. 7-23-1832. W., Margaret. 10 ch., 1-Elizabeth, 2-John, 3-William, 4-Martha, 5-George, 6-Thomas, 7-Ellen, 8-Margaret, 9-Ashford, 10-Samuel (5 youngest are minors.) Exec., bro., Ashford Reese, and guardian. Wit., C. Heiskell, Joseph S. Wheat, William Gephart.

REYNOLDS, Cornelius—8-4-1810; pr. 8-20-1810. W., Elizabeth. 3 ch., 1-John, 2-Cornelius, 3-dau., —— Rogers (hus., Rhodom). Exec., David Long, Jr., gets land Harrison Ca. Wit., John Snyder Thomas and Joseph Long, Isaac Means.

REINHART, Abraham—5-17-1815; pr. 10-20-1817. W., Margaret. 10 ch., 1-Andrew, 2-George, 3-John, 4-Abraham, 5-Mary Cooper, 6-Catherine Ferman, 7-Susan Griffith, 8-Sarah, 9-Rachel, 10-Hannah. Exec., sons, George and Abraham. Sec., John Singleton, Charles King. Wit., David Foreman, Amos Park, Joel Ward.

REINHART, Abraham—8-29-1845; 4-26-1867. No. w. 8 ch., 1-Joel, 2-Anthony, 3-James, 4-Abner, 5-David, 6-John W., 7-Sary Baker, 8-Susannah Boath. Exec., sons, James and David. Wit., John Shiners, Joel Ward, David Rinehart.

RINEHART, Rachel—3-10-1849; pr. 11-27-1843. Dau., Sarah gets land. Wit., Susan M. Davis, Fred Sheets, Robert White, Jr.

RICHARD, Henry—2-26-1847; pr. 3-22-1847. W. but not named. 5 ch., 1-Rachel Ann, 2-Sarah Jane, 3-Henry Secris, 4-Benjamin Fry, 5-John W. Exec., Benjamin Fry. Sec., Herbert Park, Jackson McBride, James W. Albin, George W. Albin, Anson V. Porter, William Doran, Wesley M. McNemar, Branson Peters, Joseph Clutter, David Pugh. Wit., Lewis Smith, Jackson McBride, Joseph Smith.

RIDGELYS, Nicholas G. (of Baltimore, Md.; will and codicil) 6-13-1820; pr. 1-18-1830. No w. Dau., Eliza, (unmarried. Sisters, Sarah —, Elizabeth Griffith; bro., Richard (dec'd, left son, Edward, and wid., Matilda); "4 sisters of my late wife," Maria, Juliann, Elenor and Henrietta, daus. of Martin Eichelberger. Letter of instructions and money to Charles Burrell, late of Baltimore, now of Goshen, N. Y. Exec., Alex McDonald also legatee. Wit., Jno. Henderson, Jacob Small, Thomas Grundy, Thomas Whelan, P. Thierman, William Whelan.

RIGGS, John—7-3-1772; pr. 11-10-1772. (Will and codicil.) W., Rebecky. "Wife 1 shilling, for she has eloped from me." Legatees, relationship not shown: Laser and James Jackson, Abraham Bagley, Anthony Bagley, Jr., Anthony Bagley, Sr., Jean Savage, John Savage; Simeon Riggs, "nephew in the Gersies." Exec., John Savage. Wit., John and Lydia Savage, Nicholas and Ann Seaver, John Ravenscraft, Alex Gibboney, Alex Gibboney, Jr.

ROBERTS, Louden—2-15-1790; pr. 4-16-1790. W., Mary Elender. 2 ch., 1-Sary, 2-Kisey. Half brother and sister get property if his heirs die before he does. M. Finney, during life of his wife, land. Exec., Fred Metheny, William Baker. Wit., William James, William Duling, Priscilla Baker.

ROCK, Fridel—7-2-1799; pr. 9-15-1800. Of. Allegany Co., Md. W., Katherine. Son, John; son, Henry, "younger children. Wit., Thomas Frons, Daniel Frazer, John McDonald.

ROBINSON, John—11-18-1816; pr. 10-20-1817. No w. 3 ch., 1-Lidia, 2-Phebe; gr. son, James, son of 3-Richard. Sec., Barney Kerns. Wit., William Torrence, William Phillips, William Spicer, Barney Kerns.

ROGERS, Aaron—4-19-1850; pr. 9-23-1850. W., Cherise. 3 ch., 1-Lewiza Polin, 2-dau, — Ludwick (dec'd, evidently left ch., James W. and William B. Ludwick); 3-Catherine Yost. Branson Peters. Sec., Sam and Gibson Ruckman. Wit., John Peters, Gibson Ruckman, Joseph Smith.

ROGERS, Owen—7-11-1807; pr. 2-18-1811. W., Mary. 5 ch., 1-Robert, 2-Owen, 3-Evan (insane), 4-Lydia Bevan (has dau., Mary), 5-Robert. Wit., John McCool, William Beall, John Rogers, Stephen C. Powers.

ROSS, William (of Frederick Co.)—3-11-1754; pr. 9-11-1759. W., Arminella. 8 ch., 1-John (Fairfax grant No. 56); 2-Lawrence, 3-Robert, 4-William, 5-Tavener (these latter four, Lot 55, Fairfax grant; William gets part with house and gardens); 6-Hanna, 7-Elizabeth, 8-Arminella. Gr. ch., John and Cornelius Miller, (minors). Exec., wife. Sec., Thomas McGuire, Hugh Murphy. Wit., John Hammer, Jr., and John J. Ross, George Hog.

NOTE BY PUBLISHERS OF RECORD: John Ross m. Deborah Jane Johnson. Was her father, John and mother, Deborah Hood Johnson of Northern Liberties, Phil. Co., Pa.?
Laurence Ross, m. Susan Oldham, dau. of (John?) dead 1766. and Ann Conway Oldham (?) who, a widow by 1766, married Darby Aughney.
Robert Ross m. first Nancy Reeves, dau. of Benjamin Reeves, and sister of Austin Smith Reeves. Second, Elizabeth ———.
Wilham Ross m. Winifred Rector, dau. of Dan, sister of Conway and Charles Rector.
Tavener Ross m. first Indian wife. Second, Aphia Ward.
Hannah m. Miller; sons, John and Cornelius.
Elizabeth m. (Henry ?) Enoch.
Arminella m. .... Wood. Sold land Bracken Co., Ky., 1803.
Cornelius Miller killed by Indians, Cum., O., 1792 or 1793.

ROSENBERGER, John—11-9-1830; pr. 11-14-1831. W., Elizabeth. 2 ch., 1-Asamus and 2-Elizabeth. Nm.—And. S. Hieronimus, Nancy Slonaker, Martin Houseman, Nathan Keadsy (?).

ROYSE, John—9-15-1803; pr. 7-18-1808. Son, Daniel, had sons, Jacob and Fredrick. Exec., son, and Jacob Larue. Wit., Cornelius and Jesse Larue, and John Offord.

RUCKMAN, Sam—2-5-1819; pr. 1-16-1826. No w. 5 ch., 1-Richard, 2-John, 3-Wilson, 4-Samuel (dec'd, left 5 ch., Hannah, Samuel, Watson, Sarah and John); 5-Mary. Exec., son, Richard. Sec., William French and Uriah Cheshire. Wit., Enos and Sarah Everett.

—S—

SAVAGE, John—4-24-1787 (codicil 4-28-1788); pr. 10-13-1791. W., Lydia. 6 ch., 1-John, land; 2-Nicholas, land; 3-Ann, 4-Jean, 5-Ester, 6-Sary. Exec., wife and Edw. McCarty. Wit., Nicholas Savage, John Daton, Henr. Githens, Hutson Hammon, William Daton.

SAVAGE, Patrick—2-14-1819; pr. 4-7-1820. W., Elizabeth. 1 ch., Jane Curry; gr. dau., Betsy Harmon. Exec., wife. Sec., William Donaldson. Wit., John Lyon, James and William Donaldson.

SAVELLE, John—9-8-1817; pr. 9-16-1817. W., Susannah. To Isaac Kuykendall, all after w. dies. Exec., Isaac Kuykendall. Sec., James Dailey. Wit., John B. White, John Inskeep, Thompson McDonald.

SAVILLE, Joseph—2-28-1826; pr. 9-17-1827. W., Lydia. 4 ch., 1-Oliver, land; 2-Martha, 3-Elizabeth, 4-Nancy Poland. Exec., son, Oliver. Sec., Michael Putze. Wit., David Shaffer, William Torrence, John Patterson.

SAVILLE, Oliver—6-28-1855; pr. 11-26-1855. W. not named. 11 ch., 1-Joseph, 2-Abraham, 3-Isaac, 4-Jacob, 5-Peter, 7-George, 7-Phillip, 8-John, 9-Oliver, 10-Catherine, 11-Mary. Exec., sons, Phillip and John. Sec., Thomas Wells, George W. Gore, John G. Pultz. Wit., Aaron Malick, Jacob Pultz.

SCARFF, Tacey—7-3-1841; pr. 9-27-1841. Hus., James, alive. Samuel W. Brady gets land after husband dies, "because it was willed to me by my father." Wit., Jesse Lupton, Jr., and Ellis Lupton, neighbors.

SCOTT, William—9-22-1767; pr. 3-8-1768. W., Sarah. Dau., Marey, and w. each get one-half. Exec., wife. Sec., William Buffington, Benjamin Kuykendall. Wit., Isaac Ely, Samuel Williamson, John Munise.

SEATON, Alley—11-9-1830; pr. 11-15-1830. Hus., John, dec'd. 6 ch., 1-Hiram, 2-George, 3-William, 4-James, 5-Frankey Farmer (has son, Samuel); 6-Lydia Race. Bro., Reuben Murray; David Ellis gets $50; gr. ch. mentioned but not named; Caleb Rector. Exec., Robert Sherrard. Wit., Elizabeth Barker, Michael Mahony, Jacob Alabaugh.

SEARS, James—7-10-1782; pr. 8-12-1783. W. but not named. 3 ch., 1-John, 2-William (he has dau., Catherine Hook or Shook; 3-Mary Milleson. Exec., sons. Wit., Hermanous Shook, Stephen Hedger.

SEAVER, Nicholas, Sr.—5-20-1780; pr. 8-10-1784. W., Elizabeth. 3 ch., 1-Nicholas, Jr., 2-Lydia Savage (hus., John); 3-Prudence (Lendora?) has dau., Ann. Gr. son, John Seaver. Sis., Ann Gibbony (hus., Alex, Sr.). Gr. dau., Mary Cynthia McCarthy. Daniel O'Neal, dec'd; Arthur O'Neal proved himself heir. Exec., wife and son. Wit., Thomas and Elizabeth Bond; John and Sarah Whitman.

SEBRING, Elizabeth—5-7-1810; pr. 4-18-1816. 4 ch., 1-Peter Oller, land she bought of Ezekiel Rogers; 2-Ann Cool (hus., Herbert); 3-Elizabeth Cool (hus., Jacob); 4-Catherine Stephenson (hus., Samuel). Exec., son, and Jacob Cool. Sec., James Dailey, John McBride. Wit., Ezekiel Rogers, William F. Casey, James Dailey.

SECRIST, Fred—1833; pr. 1834. W., Rebecca. Son, Abraham (exec.), other ch. Sec., Jacob Rudolph, Jacob Fishel, John Sweir. Wit., Henry Brill, Jacob Fishell.

SHAFFER, Jacob—11-7-1834; pr. 11-24-1834. W., Gemima. Son, William, exec. Sec., Richard Baker. Wit., Richard Baker, Thomas J. Hooper.

SHANK, Jacob—6-4-1855; pr. 2-23-1857. W., Margaret. 8 ch., 1-George, 2-William G., 3-Ann, 4-Hannah, 5-Elizabeth, 6-Sarah Pownell, 7-Louisa I. Goings, 8-Mary Haines. Exec., A. Monroe and Joshua S. Arnold (he refuses). Sec., William G. Shanks, Martin Tutwiler, John Marline, George W. Gore. Wit., George W. and John J. Arnold.

SHANNON, Hugh — 12-7-1783; pr. 3-9-1794. W., Rachel. 2 ch., 1-Ruth Albin, 2-Esther Clark (dau. of Rachel). Stepson-in-law, Derby McKeever, John McKeever, heir. Gr. daus, Jean Clark and Jean Fugate. Exec., Jeremiah Reid, Paul McKeever. Wit., Alex Monroe, John Arnold, John Harris.

SHARP, George—5-23-1845; pr. 7-22-1850. W., Anna. No ch. Geo. S. Williams gets land after w. dies. Personal property w. had at marriage to her. Nc., Mary Johnson (has 6 ch.); nc., Elizabeth Miller; nep., Robert Miller. Fred B. Jenkins gets $100; George W. Johnson gets land (relationship of these legatees not stated. Nm., John Engle, John Orr. Exec., neighbors, Robert Carmichael and Samuel P. Stump. Sec., Jonathan Hickle, John Martin. Wit., Nathaniel Offut, Fred W. Heiskell, John Cunningham.

SHEETS, Fred, Sr.—6-10-1856; pr. 2-25-1861. No w. Will and 2 codicils. 9 ch., 1-James, 2-Robert K. (dec'd, has sons, George F. and Robert K.); 3-Fred, Jr., 4-Nancy Johnson (dec'd; hus., Joshua); 5-Henry T., 6-Elizabeth Yount (dec'd in 1858, left son, James S. Parker of Oxford, Ind.); 7-Susan M. Davis, dec'd (hus., Sam); 8-Margaret Johnson, dec'd (daus, Susan Harriett and Mary Jane); 9-Mary Ann Allen, dec'd (ch., Mary Virginia, Fred S., Thomas E.). Exec., John Johnson, gr. son, but son, James, appointed in codicil. Sec., Sam Davis, Okey Johnson. Wit., C. S., Alex, and J. B. White, Jr., Henry Head, William D. Rees.

SHEPLAR, Henry—12-1-1777; pr. 3-?-1778. W., Elizabeth. 3 ch., 1-John, 2-Henry, 3-Margaret. Exec., Randle and William Welton. Wit., Lewis Green, Marvis Alkier.

SHEPLER, William—3-17-1778; pr. ? W., Susanne. Debt of bro., Henry; debt of Henry Van Meter. Exec., William Welton. Sec., Daniel McNeill, Daniel Tivebaugh. Wit., Casper Hite, Valentine Thorn.

SHERRARD, Robert—2-14-1845; pr. 6-26-1848. W. not named. 5 ch., 1-Mary W. Stewart (hus., John); 2-Elizabeth Morton Sherrard (minor); 3-Robert B., 4-John B., 5-Frank Dixon. William Shearer and Nicholas Harris get land. Exec., James Carr Baker. Sec., John S. Magill, Robert J. Glass, Robert W. Sherrard, Charles Blew, William Vance. Wit., Sam H. Alexander, Robert B. Sherrard, John N. Stewart, William H. Street, John N. Bell.

SHERARD, William (of Romney)—9-7-1831; pr. 1-17-1832. W., Millicent. "My mother, Mary Abernathy"; nep., William Sherrard of Winchester, son of bro., Joseph H.; nep., Robert Sherrard; sis., Mary Myers, land in Morgan Co. Exec., Ed. C. McDonald, and bro., Joseph H. Sherrard. Wit., H. Chew.

SHINN, David—3-7-1815; pr. 4-17-1815. W., Mary. 2 ch., 1-Sam, 2-Lydia. S-i-l, Samuel Busbee. Exec., son, Sam, and Samuel Busbee. Sec., James Caudy. Wit., Richard George and John Barrett, George Meyers.

SHOBE, Jacob—9-16-1771; pr. 3-10-1772. W., Barbara. 8 ch., 1-Jacob, 2-Rudolph, 3-Martin, 4-Abraham, 5-Elizabeth, 6-Flore, 7-Barbara, 8-Eve. Exec., son, Martin. Wit., Christopher Ermintraut, Martin Shobe. Sec., Christopher Ermintraut, Jonathan Simpson. Will in high Dutch, translated by Abraham Hite.

SHORT, Isaac—3-1-1823; pr. 3-20-1826. W., Martha. 3 ch., 1-John, 2-William, 3-Richart. Exec., William and Richard. Wit., William Malcom, Jr., John Copsey, Peter Malcom.

SHRIDE, Adam — 1-28-1791; pr. 4-14-1791. W., Charity. Dau., Elizabeth Pennington (hus., Elijah); Valentine Swisher gets land, evidently an heir; step-daus., Juliet Cump and Mary Harbus. Nm. William Crawford. Exec., wife. Sec., John Switzer, Adam Given, Jacob Clutter. Wit., Jacob Schlagle, Gabriel Throckmorton, Jacob Clutter.

SHUMAN, John—4-10-1778; pr. 5-12-1778. Son, George, lot in Morefield. Exec., Anthony Baker. Sec., Henry Morse. Wit., Charles Lynch, Jonathan Purcell, John Denoze.

SIMMONS, Simon—1-23-1830; pr. 6-25-1831. W., Susannah. Two eldest sons, William and Josiah, named; other small ch. mentioned. Sec., Sam Cockerell, John Dye. Wit., Joseph Dixon, Edw. L. Blackburn.

SINCLAIR, Robert—2-14-1831; pr. 4-18-1831. W., Nancy. 8 ch., 1-Hugh, 2-Daniel, 3-Marjarh King, 4-Alex, 5-Robert, 6-Hector, 7-Jane, 8-Nancy. Exec., wife. Sec., Sam Cockewell. Wit., William and Thomas Abernathy, John Jenkins.

SINGLETON, John—3-24-1840; pr. 2-28-1842. W., Mary. 6 ch., 1-James (youngest); 2-Susan McCarty, 3-Mary Ann, 4-Rebecca Lynn, 5-John T., 6-Aaron. Exec., son, John T., and David Gibson. Sec., Arch. Vandiver, John F. and Aaron Singleton, Alfred Taylor, John Vance, Nath. Kuykendall, Christopher Heiskell. Wit., A. W. McDonald, John B. White, Washington Mosley and James Singleton.

SINGLETON, Martha—11-16-1858; pr. 6-25-1860. 2 sons, 1-Jonathan (land); 2-William (land; has w. Gracy and Matilda Hare (relationship not stated); John Singleton; gr. son, Tobe Singleton. Exec., son, William. Wit., Jonathan Purcell and George Loy.

SIX, George—11-6-1816; pr. 8-14-1820. W., Mary. 5 ch., 1-William, 2-Phillip, 3-John, 4-Conrad, 5-Elizabeth Johnson (has 2 daus., Money and Mary Ann). Exec., son, William. Wit., Jonathan Dixon, James Davis, and John Kelley.

SLACK, James—4-18-1822; pr. 5-20-1822. W. not named. 8 ch., 1-Henry, 2-Jane Ruckman, 3-Betsey Hartley, 4-Mary Huddleston, 5-George, 6-James, 7-John, 8-Jonathan land in Va.. Gr. son, Abraham Slack. Exec., son, Jonathan, and Peter Allen; court appointed David Pascall. Sec., Barton Smoot, Nath. Huddleston. Wit., Sam Larrimore, David Pascall.

SLAGLE, Conrad—2-8-1782; pr. 2-12-1782. No w. 5 ch., 1-John, left to Adam Couchman to learn smith trade; 2-Christiana (to John Yoakum); 3-Jacob, 4-Elizabeth, 5-"a young daughter." Nm., John Giling. Exec., Daniel Teverbaugh. Sec., Henry Sheplar. Wit., Edw. Purcell, Henry Sheplar, Thomas Longwith.

SLAGLER, Jacob—11-29-1800; pr. 12-15-1800. W., Hannah. 7 ch., 1-John, 2-Jacob, 3-Joseph, 4-Statia, 5-Elenor, 6-Ales, 7-Amy. Nm., Asa and Jesse Mounts, Michael Collier, James Martin, John O'Hara. Exec., son, Joseph, and Col. Moses Rawlings. Sec., Alex King, Andrew Wodrow. Wit., Moses Rawlings, Alex King, George Fouke.

SLOANE, Ann—11-9-1808; pr. 8-17-1829. Hus., Daniel, dec'd. Son, Benjamin, gets what her hus. left her. Exec., son, Benjamin. Sec., John Slane, Dan Carmichael. Wit., Francis, John B. and Thomas B. White.

SLANE, Benjamin—8-28-1841; pr. 10-24-1842. W., Delilah. 11 ch., 1-Benjamin, 2-Elias, 3-Daniel, 4-Samuel, 5-Thomas, 6-John, 7-Hugh, 8-James, 9-Catherine Bineger, 10-Mary, 11-Rebecca. Exec., son, James; w. asks court to appoint William C. Nixon. Wit., James and Dan Slane, Benjamin F. Largent.

SLANE, Dan—No date; pr. 4-20-1795. W., Ann. 6 ch., 1-Thomas, 2-Benjamin, 3-James, 4-John (Ohio land), 5-Hugh, 6-Jane. Exec., Evan Hiett. Wit., Elias Posten, James McBride, Robert Parker.

SLOAN, John—2-24-1852; pr. 4-25-1853. Bros., George, Thomas, Richard and James (latter is married). Sec., Thomas and Richard Sloan. Wit., Fred. and Solomon Biser, George Gilbert, Roberson A. Roberson.

SLOAN, Richard—4-21-1831; pr. 6-28-1831. W., Charlotte. "All my children." Gr. dau., Charlotte Arnold, dau. of Michael; Mary Arnold (hus., David); Elizabeth Arnald (hus., Joseph.) Son, John (exec). Wit., John B. White, Emily High, Thomas and William Mulleday.

SMITH, Anna—4-1-1853; pr. 5-25-1853. Nc., Mary Wolford; bros., James, Elijah Lewis and Joseph Smith; sis., Mary Lyons (dec'd), 3 ch., Daniel P., Noah and Margaret Ann Lyons. Exec., bro., Joseph. Sec., bro., Lewis. Wit., W. B. Kimball, Isaac Slocum, George Wolf.

SMITH, George (of Cacaphon) — 7-14-1798; pr. 9-17-1798. W., Elizabeth. 4 ch., 1-Margaret, 2-Michael, 3-William, 4-John. Exec., wife, and John McBride and James Powell, both of Cacapheon. Wit., John Higgins, John Keener, Charles Anderson.

SMITH, Jacob—1-3-1859; pr. 4-23-1860. Rachel, "present wife," (nee Rinehart. She has ch. "Children by my first wife." No names. Wit., S. S. Stump, Josiah Wolford.

SMITH, James—10-10-1845; pr. 10-27-1865. No w. 3 ch., 1-Sarah, 2-Abraham, 3-Isaac (has ch.). To Sam Gloyd's ch. (relationship not stated). Gr. ch., Lavinia, Elizabeth and Sarah McCauley. Exec., Charles Blue. Sec., Robert Carmichael, William Vance. Wit., Isaac N. Wilson, Lewis and Sam D. Smith.

SMITH, James—6-5-1815; pr. 5-15-1819. W., Mary. 9 ch., 1-Elizabeth Shinn (hus., Levi); 2-Ann Powell (hus., Abraham); 3-Sarah Lupton (hus., Samuel); 4-Rhody Fry (hus., Joseph); 5-Phebe Fry (hus., William); 6-Ruth Moor (hus., James); 7-Aaron, 8-James, and 9-Timothy. Gr., dau., Rhody Fry. Exec., sons, Aaron and James. Sec., Jesse Lupton, Samuel Park. Wit., Benj. Wilson, John and William Wilkinson, John Reynolds, Sam H. Morris.

SMITH, Richard, Sr.—7-13-1788; pr. 4-16-1789. W., Mary. 4 ch., 1-James, land, part of original tract; 2-Richard, Jr., home land; 3-George, land in Hardy Co.; 4-Fanny Buckingham, land in Hardy Co. Land in Smithfield, Md., now Middleton, and Berkley Co., Va. Exec., son, James. Sec., George Beale, James Carruthers. Wit., Michael Casler, William Johnson, Joseph W. Hewlings. Richard Smith and Andrew Pearce located much land together. Nm. Christopher Brayfall, Sam McGruder, Peter Beaver, George Creamer, Michael McCune, Michael Michael, Nicholas Tripp.

SMITH, Timothy—1-22-1848; pr. 4-14-1869. Will and codicill, a copy. W., Ann. 9 ch., 1-Joseph, 2-Lewis, 3-Simeon, 4-Elijah, 5-James, 6-Stephen, 7-Mary Lyon, 8-Anna. Nm. John Wolford, Owen Williams, Alex Posten, Charles Magill, —— Henderson. Exec., sons, Joseph and Stephen; court appointed Robert Carmichael. Sec., sons, Joseph and Stephen. Wit., William Doran, Abraham Emmart, Jacob Pepper.

SMITH—William—11-22-1771. Verbal will gives all to John Chenoweth (exec.) Sec., Levi Ashbrook. Wit. by Jacob and Catherine Pritchard.

SMOOT, Jane (nee Riley)—2-26-1858; pr. 3-22-1858. Bro., Alex Riley (has dau., Jane Arnold); bro., George Riley (has dau.,Sarah Jane); bro., Sam Riley (has son, William, who has dau., Jane. Exec., John T. Arnold. Sec., Peter Arnold, George Sloan. Wit., Peter and Zecheriah Arnold, John Leatherman.

SMOOT, John—12-11-1807; pr. 4-?-1898. W. not named, one-third. 12 ch., 1-Bartin (eldest); 2-Solomon, 3-Nancy Cornet, 4-Susan "Haize", 5-Lucrecy, 6-Charity, 7-Priscilla, 8-William, 9-Jacob, 10-Joshua, 11-Joseph, 12-James (dec'd, left heirs). Exec., son, Jacob, and Sylvanus Bennett. Sec., John Starn, Nathan Huddleston. Wit., Alex Chisholm, Joseph Saville, James Haggerty.

SMOOT, Josiah—9-17-1830; pr. 4-26-1847. W., Jane (she received her father's land back). 2 ch., 1-Samuel, and 2-Thomas; land bought of Abr. Rodrick; note of Thomas Wilson. Exec., John Sloan, Esq. Sec., Thomas and George Sloan, David Arnold. Wit., R. Newman (dec'd 1847), and Peter Arnold. Proved by John B. White and Robert Kercheval.

SMOOT, Lucrecy—4-10-1815; pr. 6-19-1815. Sam Colvin app. exec., gets all. Wit. & sec., Elizabeth Timbrook and Luther Calvin. Wit., John Calvin.

SNAPP, Joseph—3-16-1846; pr. 12-27-1847. W., Margaret. 9 ch. 1-James Cravens, exec., 2-Cynthia, 3-Diana Allin. 4-John, 5-Robert, 6-Wm. C., 7-Rhoda, 8-Joseph, exec., 9-Maria. Nm. Adam Smith, land in Fredrick Hampshire Co. Wit., Wm. and Nancy Waters, Thos. Spicer, David Henderson, John Cunningham.

SNAPP, Margaret—2-26-1848; pr. 4-27-1850. Wid. of Joseph. 3 ch. 1-James C., 2-Cynthia Jane, 3-Joseph, exec. Gr. ch., Margaret Wolverton. Wit., Wm. Heiskell, David Henderson, A. Monroe, Jas. Cunningham.

SNYDER, Dr. John—4-24-1815; pr. 6-19-1815. 6 ch., 1-Charles, 2-William, 3-John, 4-Elizabeth, 5-Harriet, 6-Samuel. Ky. land and on Tennessee river and Patterson creek. Exec., Col. William Fox, John Inskeep. Sec., Edw. McCarty, William Inskeep, Warner Throckmorton. Wit., James Dailey, William Naylor, Henry Cookes.

SPENCER, John, Jr.—3-1-1845; pr. 8-25-1857. W., Sarah (once Ray). 12 ch., 1-Ayese McKinney, 2-Joseph, 3-Nancy Fleek, 4-Susanna Urie (dec'd, has 2 ch.); 5-Arthur M., 6-Ruth Shoff, 7-William, 8-Juliann Miller (dec'd, has ch.); 9-Rachel Fleek, 10-Mary Fleek, 11-Elizabeth Fleek, 12-John, 13-Alex, 14-Othio H. Exec., "Okey Johnson of Okey Greenwell Johnson of Okey Johnson of Abraham Okey." Wit., Henry Flick, John Umstott, William Randall.

SPICER, Thomas—7-8-1850; pr. 8-26-1850. 5 children, 1-"Luezer," 2-"Luizer," 3-Maria, 4-Henry, 5-Thomas. S-i-l, Sam A. Topper (has ch.). Exec., Henry Spicer. Wit., George Milleson, John Flory, John Kuykendall. Sec., George Milleson, John Flory.

SYNOPSIS OF WILLS

SPILMAN, Williams—8-10-1816; pr. 10-20-1817. W., Sarah. 7 ch., 1-John, 2-James, 3-Polly, 4-Charles, 5-Rebekah, 6-Sarah, 7-Elizabeth. Exec., son, Charles. Sec., John Brady, Simon Earsom. Wit., Milly Jarviss, John C. Newman, Rachel Dixon.

STAGG, George—11-8-1844; pr. 2-24-1845. Will and codicil. No w. 10 ch., 1-Margaret, 2-Martha, 3-Elizabeth Leatherman, 4-Mary Mudey, 5-Abraham, 6-Christopher, 7-Franklin G., 8-George, Jr. (has dau., Elizabeth Ann); 9-John (his ch. get land); 10-William. Gr. ch. James H. and Catherine Stagg, ch. of John. Exec., sons, Franklin G. and George, Jr., and William Vandiver. Sec., Thomas Carskaden, Fred and Sam Fink. Wit., Mary Greenwalt, Fred and Dan Fink, James Long. "Any legacy left me in the western country at my father's decease."

STALLCUP, Emmor—7-25-1859; pr. 8-22-1859. 3 ch., 1-Israel, 2-Emmer, Jr. (has ch., John Quincy and Elizabeth); 3-Anne Lichteter. Exec., Hiram Alkire (trustee for Israel). Wit., Solomon Alkire, J. B. Young.

STAFFORD, Catherine — 7-23-1810; pr. ?. 2 ch., 1-Washington, 2-Sarah. Exec., Daniel Collins, William Bruce. Wit., Daniel Collins, John F. and Joseph S. Stafford, Joseph Cresap, Nicholas Durbin.

STARN, Jacob — 9-18-1796; pr. 4-17-1797. W., Kathryn. 2 ch., 1-Frederick (gets his gr. fa., Frederick's fowling piece); 2-Jacob. Exec., bros., John and Joseph Starn. Wit., Richard Taylor, John Wallis.

STARKEY, Fred—5-24-1803; pr. 7-19-1803. W., Mary. 6 ch., 1-Elizabeth, 2-Fred, Jr., 3-George, 4-Edward, 5-Mary, 6-Catiren. Exec., Joseph Parrell. Sec., Sam Posten, George Myers. Wit., Edw. and John Parrell, John Hammock.

STEINBECK, John C.—9-1-1818; pr. 1-3-1821. Of Baltimore, Md. W., Anna Dorothea, gets all and is exec. Wit., Joseph A. Strischka, John Hurd Wulff, John J. Salzwedel.

STERMAN, John—1-30-1822; pr. 4-16-1822. W., Hannah Christener. 6 ch., 1-John, 2-James, 3-Richard, 4-Ann, 5-Rachel, 6-Rebecca. Gr. ch., Elizabeth Wilson, Catherine Jenney, William Ginney, Daniel Geney (gr. ch. mentioned first). Ex., wife, and Dennis Parrott. Wit., William Beaver, Nathan Head, George Kine, Greenberry Kine.

STIMME(L), Jost (Stimble?), blacksmith — 11-3-1805; pr. 2-17-1806. W., Hannah Magdalanah. 9 ch., 1-Michael, 2-Peter, 3-Daniel, 4-Jacob, 5-Hannah Magdalena, 6-Elizabeth, 7-Catherine (a cripple), 8-Mary, 9-Ann. Exec., wife. Wit., Jacob Bizer, Dan and Zach Arnold.

STOVER, Daniel—8-2-1805. pr. 4-10-1806. W., Elizabeth. 5 ch. 1-Daniel, Jr., 2-Christopher, 3-Elizabeth Leatherman, 4-Nancy Good, 5-Mary. Wit., Okey Johnson, Jacob Vandiver, Denny Welch. Nm. Sam Bornfeald.

STUMP, John—3-22-1850; pr. 5-27-1850. No. W. 6 ch. 1-Samuel J., and 2-Wm. P., execs., 3-Benj. D., 4-Julia Ann Hiett, 5-Lucy J. McMachin, 6-A. J. Nm. John More and Wm. Abernathy as legatees. Sec., John Martin, Jonathan Hiett. Wit., Joseph and Abraham Moore, Charles Taylor.

STUMP, Michael, of S. Branch—7-2-1767; pr. 3-8-1768. W., Catherine, exec. 6 ch. 1-Geo., exec., land Fairfax grant Lot No. 13, 2-Leonard, Lot No. 3, 3-Michael, eldest, Lot No. 2, he has a son Michael 4, 5, 6 unnamed daughters. Wit., Felix Seymour, Leonard Huff.

STUMP, Peter (Baptist) — 7-22-1815; pr. 8-14-1815. W., Catherine. 6 or 7 ch. 1-Joseph, 2-Benj., 3-John, execs., 4-Rebecca, 5-Mary, 6-Peter, Betsy Moore. Nm. Col. Wm. Sterrett, Geo. Sharp, Esq., John Jenkins, John Shearwood. Sec., James Meekins, Sr., Lewis Lunsford.

STUMP, Wm. P., (of Springfield)—2-28-1855; pr. 3-26-1855. W., Harriet Ann. Ch., but not named. Bro., Benjamin. Exec., Henry K. Hoffman and brother, Sam J. Sec., Geo. W. Washington, Wm. Donaldson (also mt.) Wit., B. D. Stump, Benj. Shannon.

SWEARINGIN, Eli (of Alleg. Co., Md.) 12-1-1843; pr. 1-26-1846. No. w. 2 ch. 1-Charles, dec'd widow Sarah with children, 2-Franklin. Gr. ch., James Scott and Deborah Ann. Exec., John Galloway Lynn. Sec., Noah Noble. Wit., Thos. I. McKaig, John Black, A. G. Withers.

SWISHER, John—7-26-1844; pr. 9-28-1846. W., Elizabeth. 14 ch. 1-Catherine, 2-Isaac, 3-Adam, 4-Michael, 5-Rebecca, 6-Stephen, 7-John, 8-Elizabeth, 9-Christina, 10-Jacob, 11-Anthony, 12-Maria, 13-Henry F., 14-David. Exec., friend, Abraham Sechrist. Sec., Jacob Kemp, Valentine Sechrist, Enoch Pennington. Wit., John and Valentine Sechrist and Wm. Davis.

SWITZER, Valentine—11-7-1809; pr. 5-19-1817. No W., 8 ch. 1-Peter, 2-Philip, 3-John, 4-Abraham, 5-Henry, dec'd widow and two children by him, 6-Valentine, 7-Nicholas, 8-Catherine. Exec., bro., John, Phillip Hooker and Frederick Secrist. Sec. and Wit., Phillip Fishall, Wm. Parrill and Henry Secrist.

SWEIR, Jacob—8-23-1828; pr. 5-17-1830. W., Mary Ann. 10 ch. 1-David, 2-John, 3-Jacob, 4-George, 5-Martin, 6-Samuel, 7-Elizabeth, 8-Catherine Corbin, 9-Mary Ann Barbary, 10-Sarah. Gr. ch., Susan Maria Sweir, dau. of 8. Exec., Geo. Sweir. Sec., James Gibson and Wm. Sherrard. Wit., James R. Powell, Samuel Hott, Wm. French.

—T—

TAPSCOTT, Chichester, Esq.—1-30-1829; pr. 2-16-1829. W., Jane. Young children. Br. Baker. Wit., Comfort Dailey, Thos. Rutherford, Wm. C. Woodson, Thos. Allen Tidbale. Nm. Rev. Wm. Hill and wife, Mrs. Tidbale. Exec., Angus McDonald refuses and J. B. White appointed. Sec., Isaac Kuykendall.

TAPSCOTT, Newton—1-17-1826; pr. 6-19-1828. W., not named. Bros., Chichester and Baker. Sis., Caroline. Bro.-in-law, John B. White. Nm. Major Hickman.

TASKER, George R.—8-23-1833; pr. 1-22-1838. W., Katherine, exec. 3 ch., 1-Geo. G., exec., 2-Benjamin, 3-Christina. Nm. Newman Beckwith and Hezekiah Nalley. Wit., John and James McCormack.

TAYLOR, Edward—1-7-1839; pr. 5-27-1839. W., Margaret. 6 ch. 1-Warner, 2-Alfred, 3-Jacob, 4-Parsons, 5-Leacy Ann, 6-Eliza. Exec., John Sloan, Esq. Sec., David Gibson, James Parsons, Jr., John M. Pancake. Wit., John B. White and Thomas Mulledy.

TAYLOR, Simon—3-10-1784; pr. 3-14-1786. W., Mary. 5 ch. or 6. 1-John, eldest, exec., land South Branch No. 50, 2-James, youngest, 3-Simon, No. 52, 4-Rebecca Lee, 5-Mary Ann, Elizabeth Dudley probably dau. Nm. John Chestnut, Geo. Hoge, Elias Posten. Exec., Nath Kuykendall, Nicholas Casey, and Wodrow. Wit. Absolom Hammond, Austin Smith Reeve, Simon Field, Henry Carter, Simon Taylor, son of George.

TAYLOR, Simon—10-18-1847; pr. 6-23-1851. No W. 5 ch. 1-James, 2-William, 3-Isaac, dec'd widow Susan has 2 sons, Simon D. and Isaac, Jr., 4-John, dec'd, Brooks children get one-ninth of his land, his daughter, Nancy Brooks (hus., Thos. D.) has 3 ch., Thos. Brooks, Elizabeth Ann Brooks Taylor, Mary Ellen Price, 5-Jacob, dec'd, left children. Nm. Mary Parker (hus., Solomon) and John Parker. Exec., son Wm. Sec., Thos. T. Brooks, Wm. P. Stump, also wit. with Thos. Blue, David Arnold.

TAYLOR, Tarpley—10-22-1780; pr. 5-11-1784. W., Libia or Sibia. 4 ch. 1-Geo., 2-Wm., 3-John, 4-Nancy, (believe later son Tarpley, Jr.) Exec., Simon Taylor, Sr. James Tarpley. Wit., Joseph Kent, David Long, James Patterson, Simon Taylor.

TAYLOR, Thomas—3-14-1840; pr. 10-27-1851. No w. 12 ch. 1-John, 2-Thos., 3-Wm., 4-Joseph, 5-Daniel "my reputed son of Penna", 6-Parthenia Brown, 7-Mary High, 8-Ann Ludwick, 9-Sarah Thopmson, 10-Margaret Thompson, 11-Zulemma Thompson, 12-Hannah. Nm. Joh J. Powell. Wit., Thos. Sloan and Elizabeth Liller (in 1825 she is Elizabeth White).

TEMPLE, Wm. F. (of Coahoma Co., Miss.)—10-23-1846; pr. 3-28-1857. Bros., Solomon J. and John T., sis., Jane and Mary E. Exec., Aaron Shelby.

THOMAS, Moses—2-27-1817; pr. 12-10-1817. W., Sophia. "All my children except my two laughters, Mary and Jinny Thomas." Exec., Joseph and Moses Thomas. Sec., James Davis. Wit., Reuben Davis, Adam (E) Arnholt, Andrew Boyle.

THOMAS, Samuel—12-20-1815; pr. 11-15-1819. No w. 6 ch. 1-Jacob, 2-Elizabeth Arnold (hus., Daniel), 3-Magdelene Moser (hus. Jacob), 4-Mary Landers (hus. Fredrick), 5-Christina Landers (hus., Felix), 6-Samuel, 7-Barbary Landers (hus., Joseph), 8-Susannah Mash (hus., Ezekiel), has 5 ch., Elizabeth, Edw., Nancy, Magdelene and Scibi Mash. Exec., Daniel Arnold. Sec., Zacheriah Arnold, also wit., with Fred Sheets.

THOMPSON, Elisha—2-3-1844; pr. 7-24-1848. W., Elizabeth, exec. 5 ch. 1-Louisa Hayden, 2-Mary Thompson, 3-Sarah Jane Flury, 4-Peter Sperry, 5-Isaac Newton. Nm. A. B. Hayden. Sec., Isaac N. and Peter Thompson. Wit., Isaac N. Wilson and John Coffman.

THOMPSON, James—9-27-1841; pr. 8-26-1844. W., Elizabeth. 5 ch. 1-Rebecca, 2-Isaac, 3-John, 4-Abraham, 5-James. Nm. Rhoda Stone and Sarah Johnson, rel. not stated. Gr. ch., Sarah Ann Linthicum, Tempa Harris and Mary Carter. Exec., Albert Carter and Wm. Hersman. Sec., Wm. Doran, Isaac H. Thompson and Wm. J. Monroe. Wit., Lydia Stonsman, Amos and Joseph Huffman.

THOMPSON, Jeremiah—8-20-1808; pr. 9-19-1808. W., Esther, exec., gr. son, Jeremiah "my rifle," Billy Biggerstaff, Jr., a colt. Exec., friend Peter Bruner. Sec., James Reed and Benj. Moore (wit.) Wit., Michael Widmeyer, John Athey, Jacob Zilor Sr. and Jr.

THOMPSON, John (of Patterson's Creek)—10-9-1807; pr. 2-14-1807. W., Mary. 4 ch. 1-Wm., exec., 2-Geo. (minor), 3-Peggey, 4-Sarah. "All my unmarried children," property divided 1830. Nm. Richard Blue. Wit., John Grooms, Thos. Long, John Snyder.

THORP, Elizabeth—6-24-1843; pr. 8-28-1863. 5 ch. 1-John Thorp, Jr., dec'd. (Elizabeth Ann, Mary Braxton, Nancy, Isaac and Solomon). 1-Ann Evans, dec'd dau., who has children, John, Emily, Wm., Rhoda, Jemima Evans. 3-Elizabeth, 4-Isaac, 5-Solomon, exec., with Simon Taylor. Sec., Sam C. and Thomas Ruckman. Wit., Bennett Bean, James Davidson, Jr., Joseph Tucker.

THORNTON, B. B.—9-20-1810; pr. 1-28-1833. W., Hannah. No. ch. Came to Hampshire county after 1810; reaffirms will 2-14-1823. Sec., Jesse Monroe. Wit., Sam Park, Enoch Park, John Peters.

THROCKMORTON, Catherine — 6-27-1827; pr. 5-19-1828, widow, ch. not named. Exec., Samuel Kercheval, Jr. Sec. and wit., Wm. Inskeep, wit., Foreman Inskeep.

THROCKMORTON, Warner—2-22-1826; pr. 3-20-1826. W. not named. 5 ch. 1-Wm. Inskeep, "my oldest son will be 21 in 8 years, my interest in Armstrong property." "My five children." Nm. Wm. Armstrong, James Gibson and Wm. Kercheval. Sec., Wm. and Abr. Inskeep. Wit., David Gibson, John A. Thompson, Wm. L. Dyer.

TROWBRIDGE, John—6-5-1822; pr. 11-17-1823. No w. 4 ch. 1-Mary, 2-Catherine, 3-Elizabeth Nail (hus., John), 4-John. Gr. ch., Lucinda, Bery and Ellen, ch. of 3. Exec., Thos. Carskaddon, Thornton Parker. Sec., Sam Cockerill. Wit., Elizabeth Parker and Fred Sheets.

TOTTEN, Sam—4-1-1834; pr. 5-23-1836. No w. 2 ch. 1-James, 2-John. Exec. and wit., John Lambert. Wit., Peter Horsal, Jr., Joseph Palmer.

TUCKER, Erasmus—4-4-1826; pr. 5-15-1826. W., Mary. 5 ch. 1-Milley, 2-Asa, 3-Ruth, 4-Josephine, 5-Abraham. Exec. refuses, Nathan Tucker app. "My first children and her children" "my father's estate not settled." Sec., Marqus Monroe. Wit., Benj. Marshall, Samuel Cheses, Gideon Hutton, Sylvester McBride.

TUCKER, Joseph—7-1-1816; pr. 9-16-1816. W., Lucy. 3 ch. 1-John, 2-Nathan, and 3-Erasmus, exec., "the rest of my children." Wit., Josephus Tucker (sec.), George Bishop, Thomas Smith.

TUCKWELL, John—3-16-1769; pr. 6-13-1769. No W. 2 ch. 1-James, 2-Israel. Friend, Felix Seymour, gets horses if he gives son, James, one at 21. Wit., Ja. Keith, Abrm. Hite, Jonathan Heath.

TURK, Mary—12-29-1802; pr. 5-16-1803. Wid. of Andrew; sister, Margaret Ross. Samuel Turk, son of Andrew, has ch., Isaac and Betsy. Nm. Widows Campbell and Goldsberry. Exec., A. King, V. Frances and Frances F. M. Hilton. Wit., James Nelson, Dennis Danlels and Jacob Zimmerman.

TURNER, Charles—6-2-1803; pr. 9-19-1803. No w. 4 ch. 1-Daniel, exec., and 2-Plummer, have ch., 3-Solomon, 4-Evin. "My several children." Bros., Wm. and James. Wit., Peggy and John Turner, Elizabeth Andrews, Horatio Keyes.

TWIG, James (of Alleg. Co., Md.)—8-9-1854; pr. 2-26-1865. W., Catherine. 10 ch. 1-Amanda, 2-Rebecca, 3-Evelina. 4-Ovleire (?), 5-Wm., 6-Margaret, 7-Luvenia, 8-James Ross, 9-Ann Virginia, 10-Pearce. Nm. James Prater. Exec., John Hartley. Wit., John D. Kelley, Michael Crabtree, Eli Twigg.

—U—

URIES, Samuel—3-27-1855; pr. 2-23-1857. W., Phoebe. W. gets all. Exec., Chas. Uries. Sec., Thos. Daniels, Elisha Rhinehart. Wit., Thos. Daniels, Amos Culp, Newton Biser, Jr.

—V—

VANDEVANTER, Cornelius—7-9-1782; pr. 11-12-1782. W., Jannetee, exec. 5 ch. 1-Nicholas, 2-Peter, exec., 3-John, 4-Cornelius, 5-Molly. Sec., Stephen Ruddle, Jacob Miller also wit. with John Philips, Peter Vandeventer.

SYNOPSIS OF WILLS

VANDIVER, Elizabeth—12-4-1846; pr. 8-26-1850. A widow, legatees rel. not shown. Wm. Hiett and his dau., Mary Virginia; Sylvester Welch, wife, Betsy, Henry Trout, dau., Sarah, sons, James H., Wm. D.; Samuel Myers, dau., Margaret; Betsy, sister of Henry Trout; W. James Howard dec'd, daus., Elizabeth and Lucy; James B. Pugh, wife Evelina, dau., Ann, sons, Robert, James, Wm. and Edw. Pugh; Samuel Chinn, children, Susan, Helen, Walter McInskeep, wife Susan Ann, dau., Mary E.; Mary Howard, dau., of Michael Viser; Wm. Hull, dau., Mary V. Exec., Henry Trout. Sec., Wm. Vance, Wm. Vandiver, Wm. Perry. Wit., David and Benj. Pugh.

VANDIVER, John—10-13-1853; pr. 1-23-1854. W., Nancy. 2 ch. 1-Mary Elizabeth; 2-Elmira Jane. Bro., Wm., has son, John Wm., sisters, Matilda Riggs, Elizabeth Holliday and Sophia Henderson, dead and Sally Ann Priest. bro. i-1-Edwin L. Blackburn. Exec., John Thompson Pierce. Wit., John Kern, Jr., Isaac Kuykendall, Jacob Thomas.

VANDOSAL, Jeremiah—2-13-1851; pr. 3-24-1851. All to bro., Cornelius. Sec., John Heiskell and Josiah Constable. Wit., Thornton and John W. Johnston, Henry England (English.)

VANMETER, Henry—2-16-1778; pr. 5-11-1778. W., Rebecca. 5 ch. 1-Isaac, 2-Jacob, 3-Joseph, 4-Solomon, 5-Abraham. sons 2-4-5, exec. Sec., Abel Randall, Daniel McNeill. Nm. Robert and Thomas Parsons and Abr. Hite. Wit., Garrett and Isaac Van Meter, Morris Thomas.

VAN METER, Isaac—2-15-1754; pr. 12-14-1757. W., Annah. 7 ch. 1-Henry and 2-Jacob and 3-Garrett, exec., 4-Sarah Richman, 5-Catherine, 6-Rebecca (hus., Abr. Hite), 7-Hellita. Nm. Jonathan Heath, Garrett Decker, Michael Hider, Thos. Nottingham, land in New Jersey, "Penna money." Sec., Abel Randall, Thos. Parsons. Wit., Ebenezer Holmes, Abel Randall, Joseph Carroll.

VANMETER, Issac (of Hardy Co.)—3-16-1837; pr. 1-1-1838. No. W. 7 ch. 1-David, has ch. Betsy Ann and Wm. C., 2-Garrett, 3-John J., gets Ohio land, 4-Jacob, 5-Sally Cunningham, ch. Elizabeth J. Vanmeter, Isaac, Jesse and David Cunningham, 6-Anna M. Gibson, 7-Elizabeth Inskeep. Nm. Joseph Dixon, Solomon Heator, Joseph and John Sleagle, John House, Geo. Harness, James Higgins, David Cokeley. Ex-Sons 1-2-5.

VINEY, Andrew—7-12-1780; pr. 5-14 1782. W., Susannah, exec. 7 or 8 ch. 1-Stephen, 2-Margaret, 3-Ann Fitzgerald, 4-John, 5-Andrew, 6-Mary Bryan, 7-Elizabeth McHendry, 8-Susannah McHenry. Gr. dau., Drusilla Viney. Geo. Lewis, exec. Sec. and wit., Wm. Warden, Joseph Hill and James Stout.

—W—

WAGGONER, John M.—8-1-1834; pr. 5-22-1837. W. not named. 12 ch. 1-Elizabeth, exec., 2-Sally, 3-Catherine, 4-Henry L., 5-Fredrick, 6-Jacob, 7-Joseph, 8-Rosanna, 9-Mary, 10-Hannah, 11-Rachel, 12-Nancy. Gr. dau., Ruth. Nm. Thos. Dunn, Jacob Adams, James Lawson. Wit., Ephraim Dunn.

WALKER, Andrew—8-3-1802; pr. 5-14-1810. No. W., no ch. bros., James and Robert, sisters, Hannah Shannon, Jane Newell, Ann, Rebecca, Margaret and Sarah. His father alive, his grandfather was Robert. Exec., brothers. Sec., Robert Walker. Wit., John and Wm. Donaldson, Isaac Johnson.

WALKER, Thomas—10-6-1846; pr. 10-25-1847. No W. Bro., Wm. W., Andrew, sis., Isabella, Sally Raymond, nieces, Susan and Isabella Raymond. Exec., Sam Raymond. Wit., W. P. Stump, Benj. and James C. Shannon.

WARD, Israel (of Hardy Co.)—4-16-1779; pr. 11-9-1779. W., Susannah, 2 ch. 1-Israel, 2-Sylvester, exec. Gr. son, David Ward and friend Thos. Brown. Sec., Michael Hornbeck and Charles Lynch. Wit., Joseph and Anny Reding, Thos. Thieten, David Miles, John Hogbine, Sarah Hiles.

WARD, John—2-24-1807; pr. 2-20-1815. W., Mary. 7 ch. 1-Joel, exec., 2-Elizabeth Butler (hus., John), 3-John, exec., 4-Mary Rhinehart (hus., Abraham), 5-Lydia, 6-Hannah, 7-Sarah Barrett (hus., Benjamin, exec.) Gr. dau., Ruth, who lives with them "as a child." Wit., Amos Park Sr. and Jr., John Barrett.

WARD, John—2-12-1823; pr. 7-18-1825. W., Elizabeth. 7 ch. 1-John, 2-Jesse, 3-Edward, 4-Joel, 5-Sarah, 6-Elizabeth Jones, 7-Hester. Wit.,Wesley and John Sr., and Sally Cundiff, Robert Jones.

WASSON, James—8-23-1838; pr. 9-24-1838. No W. 11 ch. 1-Ann, 2-Polly, 3-Sally, 4-Isabella, 5-Jane, 6-Hannah, 7-Elizabeth, 8-Catherine, 9-Martha, 10-Dorcas, 11-Mary. Gr. ch., James Jackson and Harrit Lupton, also "Mary White's oldest child." Exec., Jesse Lupton, Jr. Sec., Wm. Lupton and Isaac Wolverton. Wit., Wm. Lupton and Wm. Walker.

WATSON, James— 11-2-1846; pr. 8-23-1867. W., Mary. 9 ch. 1-James, 2-Robert, 3-John, 4-William, 5-Mary Martin, 6-Jean Malcolm, 7-Rebecca Meriman, 8-Margaret Martin, 9-Martha Smoot. "To my five daughters' children." Wit., Robert Monroe, John M. Domar.

WATTS, James—3-14-1820; pr. 4-17-1820. W., Susannah, exec., 2 ch., 1-Isabella, 2-Susannah. Gr. son, James Smith. Exec., neph., Thos. Carskaden and Wm. Smith. Sec., Jesse Bane. Wit., Benj. David and Ashford Parker and Thos. Carskaden.

WATTS, Thomas—8 11-1758; pr. 12-12-1758. n. m. Prudence Savour, Patrick McCarthy, exec., relation not shown. Sec., Peter Casey. Wit., David Wilfred, Job Pearsell Thos. Bull.

WATTERMAN, John—7-23-1785; pr. 8-10-1785. W., Mary, one third, no ch. Father app. exec. and gets two-thirds. John Rush, exec. Sec., Moses Pigman. Wit., Sam Kennedy, Jared Irwin.

WEASE, Michael—6-15-1780; pr. 9-8-1780. W., Mary. 3 ch. 1-Henry, 2-Solomon, 3-Margaret, and others not named. 1 and 2 minors. Nm. David Tivebaugh. Exec., John Wilson. Sec., Elias Posten. Wit., Chas. C. Borer and Jacob Wease. These notes were on the body of the original will: "Henry was born 4-4-1776. Solomon 3 years old, coming November, Margaret, born 4-4-1779."

WELCH, Denny (Dency)—12-14-1831; pr. 11-26-1832. No. W. 2 ch. 1-Susan, 2-Elizabeth Kuykendall. Exec., Luke Kuykendall, Wm. Vandiver, Jr. Sec., Wm. Vance, Nathaniel Kuykendall, John Meyers. Wit., Wm. Welch, Nath. Heard, James Inskeep.

WELCH, SYLVESTER—9-30-1800; pr. 2-19-1810. W., Jemima, exec. 9 ch. 1-Dency, 2-Sylvester, 3-Benjamin, 4-Isaac, 5-Susanna, 6-Nancy Smith, 7-Elizabeth Henning, 8,Mary Mott dec'd, 9-Sarah Good. Gr. ch., Reuben, Jemima and Dorcas Smith-Sylvester, Sarah, Lucey and Jemima Mott. Sec., Jacob Vandiver. Wit., Joseph Davis, Jonas Smoot, Rodham James.

WELTON, John—4-16-1764; pr. 6-9-1767. W., Jan., exec. 7 ch. 1-Jesse, 2-David, 3-Solomon, 4-Job, 5-Wm., 6-Mary Jane, 7-Martha. Nm. Col. Carrol Semore. Sec., Garrett Vanmeter, Thos. Lawson, Moses Hutton also wit. with Felix Seymour, Benj. Beal.

WELTON, Solomon—3-20-1778; pr. 4-14-1778. W., Mary Magdalene. 3 ch. 1-John, 2-Michael, 3-Jonathan. If another born to share equally. Exec., Job and Jesse Welton. Sec., Wm. Welton and Wm. Rennick. Wit., Wm. and David Welton.

WESTABERGER, George—7-10-1802; pr. 7-20-1806. No W. 3 ch. 1-Barbara High (hus., Jacob), 2-Mary Cline, 3-Katy Cline (hus., Phillip). Gr. Son Geo. Liller, Minor, N. M., Geo. Hufman. Exec., Phillip Cline and John Plumsone. Wit., Geo. Hill, Mary Fidler.

WESTFALL, Cornelius—2-8-1781; pr. 3-11-1783. W., Magdalene in will, 1783 Eleanor. 5 ch. 1-Jacob, exec., 2-John, 3-Isaac, 4-Zechariah, 5-Cornelius, 6-Mary. "If Cornelius and John should not return." Exec., Samuel Hornbeck. Sec., Nath. Kuykendall. Wit., Stephen Rungels and Phineas Wells.

WHEATLY, Thos. (of Alleg. Co. Md., and Lewis Co., Va.)— 7-25-1859; pr. 3-29-1860. John, son of Thos. W. Morgan, land in Lewis Co. Anthony McGowan, legatee, rel. not shown. Exec.,Thos. Morgan. Wit., Josiah I. Fenton, Wm. McNally, P. I. Thrasher.

WHITE, Frances—10-1-1826; pr. 11-25-1826. No. W. 5 ch. 1-Sam P., 2-John A., 3-Robert N., and 4-Frances M., execs., 5-Thos. B. John White, exec. Wit., John Combs, Zebulon Sheets, Adam Loy, Thomas Nicholson.

WIGGINS, Thomas—8-6-1776; pr. 2-12-1778. W., but not named. 4 ch. 1-Archibald, exec. 2-Comfort Sabbaret, 3-Thomas, 4-Phillip, exec. Sec., Elias Posten and Jacob Pugh. Wit.,Wm. Sheplar, Joseph Crecraft and Thos. Conoway.

WILEY, Benjamin (of Alleg. Co., Md.)—7-2-1832; pr. 8-23-1833. W., Fanny. 2 ch., 1-Betsy Beven has sons Benj. Wiley and John Wiley Bevan, 2-Laban, he has sons Benjamin and Asahel Wiley. Exec., Dr. Samuel P. Smith. Wit., Jacob Snyder, Jonathan Witt, Lorenzen McGruder.

WILEY, Zail—11-10-1855; pr. 11-26-1855. W., Sarah (Laura) Jane. 5 ch. 1-John, 2-Edward, 3-Laban, 4-Elizabeth Ann, 5-Eliza Jane. Exec., Joseph W. Pollock of Alleg. Co. Sec., David Gibson. Wit.,J. B. Widmer, P. H. Healey, John J. Bruce.

WILLIAMS, Edward (of South Branch)—9-17-1754; pr. 9-8-1761. W., Mary. 7 ch. 1-Venson (Vincent, 2-James, 3-Edward, 4-Sarah, 5-Phillip, 6-Mary. 7-William, exec. Sec., Micheal Thorn, Samuel Stalnaker. Wit., Wm. Miller, Jonathan Cobron, Geo. Hart.

WILLIAMS, John (of Frankfort)—8-1-1795; pr. 2-19-1798. W., Martha. 8 ch. 1-John, 2-Benj., 3-Ebenezer, 4-Joseph, 5-Ephraim, 6-Sarah Painter, 7-Elizabeth Garrett, 8-Dorcas Whitman. Nm. Christian Stephens, Micheal Brookhart, Dr. John Ganthorp, Charis Alley (Olley), John Kelley, Stephen Alley. Exec., sons 1 and 2. Sec., John Jones and Robert Rannels. Wit., Job Shepard, John Mitchell, John Lyle.

WILLIAMS, Richard—3-3-1788; pr. 6-12-1788. No W. No ch. Father, John Williams, exec., refuses; Ezekiel Whitman, bro. -i-l app. "to brothers and sisters." Wit., Isaac Loan, John Kimberlin, Richard Stafford. Sec., John Kellar, John Williams.

WILLIAMS, Thomas—10-21-1816; pr. 11-19-1816. W., Elizabeth. 11 ch. 1-Isaac, 2-Benj., 3-John, 4-Thos., 5-William, 6-Zedekiah, 7 to 11 "to my five daughters and their children." Nm. John Constant, Jacob and Isaac Dawson, John Summerson. Exec., Abraham Dawson. Sec., Peter Bruner, Joseph Stone. Wit., Wm. Neeley, John A. Hamilton, James Smith, Isaac Williams, Elizabeth and Wm. Dawson.

WILSON, Isaac N.—12-29-1855; pr. 3-24-1856. W., Rachel. 3 ch. 1-Lucinda, 2-Eliza Jane, 3-Julianna Painter (hus. Israel, exec., Wit., A. B. Haden, W. B. E. Hayden. Lewis Smith.

WILSON, Jonathan (of Alleg. Co., Md.)—1-24-1855; pr. 5-27-1861. W., Elizabeth. 7 ch. 1-Abraham, exec., 2-Sarah F. Baker, 3-Elizabeth Welch, 4-Jonathan, exec., 5-Susan V. Davis, 6-Rachel, 7-Hester Ann. Nm. Garrett V. Dixon, minor, lives with him, Thos. Wilson's Mills, John Timkens. Wit., Henry Hammel, Benj. Tasker, Wm. Lower.

WILSON, William—12-18-1817; pr. 12-17-1821. W., Wilinda. 4 ch. 1-Alex, 2-Tacey Ann, 3-Elizabeth, 4-Susan Ann Mason. Wit., John Kearns, Robert and Wm. French, Wm. Galloway, John Arnold.

WINTERTON, John—3-28-1821; pr. 6-21-1821. W., Mary. 1 ch. Gr. son, Moses Rosenbrough, exec., with John Cleaver. 1-Mary Rosenbrough (hus., John). Sec., James Kelso, Stephen Hickle also wit. with John Barr, Jesse Leekins.

WODROW, 10-14-1813; pr. 9-16-1814. Will and codicil, W., Mary, 5 ch. "3 ch. of present wife" get estate of Elizabeth Harrison, dec'd. 1-Andrew Jr., 2-Wm., 3-Emily, 4-Elizabeth Dailey (hus., James, exec.), 5-Matilda McDowell. n. m., friend, Obed Waite of Martinsburg. Sec. James Dailey and John McDowell. Wit., Wm. Naylor and Ignatius Price. Exec., Andrew, Jr.

WOLFORD, John—11-14-1849; pr. 11-26-1849. No. W. 10 ch. 1-Henry, 2-Martin, 3-Jacob, 4-Elizabeth, 5-Phoebe, 6-Ann, she gets one-third of farm he lives on, then it goes to her daughters, Lucinda and Deborah, 7-Adam, 8-John, 9-Rosanna Crim, 10-Isabella Bennett. Exec., Christopher and Frederick Heiskell. Sec., Henry and Martin Wolford, Josiah Constable. Wit., Phil Fahs, Perry A. Stewart.

WOOD, Mary—10-1762; pr. 11-9-1762. Ch. Son, Jonathan, exec., John Reed, "divide equally between my children." Sec., Garrett Vanmeter, Wit., Andrew Sadowski, Benj. Tutt, Stephen Ross.

WORLEY, Micheal—9-4-1784; pr. 5-10-1785. W., Margaret, exec. 2 ch. 1-Jude Carr (hus., James, exec.), 2-John. Wit., Jonathan Head, Fredrick Sellars, Wm. Dooley.

WREN, John—12-21-1829, pr. 8-19-1830. W., Hannah. 4 ch. 1-Wm., has dau., Angeline, 2-Lucinda Wiatt (hus., James) has dau., Mary, 3-Turner, 4-Margaret Carr (hus., Wm.). Nm. James Wren and wife Elizabeth, Sarah and Elizabeth Harris, Fanny Harrison, rel. not shown. Wit., Christopher and John Vandergrift, Isaac Pownall.

WRIGHT, Robert—2-28-1803; pr. 9-19-1803. W., Margaret. 8 ch. 1-Elizabeth Allen, 2-Fanny Allen, 3-Anna Herriott, 4-Pegga, 5-Sallie, 6-Wm., exec., 7-John, exec., 8-Joseph. Wit., Nancy Blue, sec., Wm. Fox and James Reed.

—Y—

YOAKAM, Jacob—8-17-1780; pr. 11-14-1780. W., Elizabeth. 8 ch. 1-Michael, 2-Elizabeth, 3-George, 4-Millia, 5-Jacob, 6-Solomon, 7-Matthias, 8-Isaac. Exec.,Geo. and Micheal Lee or See. Sec., Samuel Hornback, Abel Randall. Wit., Chas. Meyers, Jonathan Purcell, Henry Green.

ESTATES REFERRED TO IN INDEX OF BOOK 2

Herewith are given early estates, with date before which the person died. Some have interesting data, as buyers in a sale bill and items in inventories. These are all early, and no wills appear.

ALLEN, John—Inventory, 2-6-1784.

ASHBROOK, John—Division of his land; his widow (1780) had married a Howard. His heirs mentioned, Gemima Baker (hus. Jacob), Mary Blackburn (hus. William), Aaron Baker.

BRUCE, Joseph, est., before 1783. Ovid Mecracken, ex.

CASEY, Benjamin—Peter Casey, Jr., administrator.

CAUDY, David, before 1784, James Caudy, ex.

CAUDY, James, before 1784.

CLAYPOLE, Geo., 1782. "Abraham Kuykendall who intermarried with Tramey or Fanny Claypool."

CRESAP, Col. Thomas, est., 10-11-1787.

CRITCHFIELD, Amos. Dec'd before 1778.

CUNNINGHAM, Jesse—Many names. Widow Rebecca?

DARLINGTON, Meredith., est., involved in Jonathan Jenkins'.

GEORGE, Matthew, 1782.

GILMORE, Matthew, 1787.

GILMORE, Michael, 1783. Ex., Benj. Casey and Peter Casey, Jr.

HAGGERTY, John, est., 1787.

HENKLE, Jacob, died 5-26-1779. Speaks of Moses and Paul Henkle.

INSKEEP, Joseph—Dec. before 1779; Ex., Abraham Inskeep.

JENKINS, Jonathan — Before 8-5-1784.

KIRKENDALL, John—5-13-1783.

McBRIDE, Archibald—1781.

MAHEN, William, est., 1787.

MILLER, Thos., inventory Thos. Humphrey, Simon Taylor and James Tarpley, appraisers.

MOORE, Phillip, est. Joseph Nevill and Abel Randall, ex.

NIXON, William, inventory, 1782.

NOTEMAN, James—Before 1784.

PARKE, Daniel—1782.

PAUGH, Nicholas — Michael Paugh, adm., 1785.

PETERSON, Peter, est. 1773. Richard Williams and Robert Parker, ex. Large estate, notes and mortgages.

PRICE, William—5-10-1785.

PURCELL, Edward—Before 1782.

RATCHLIFF, David — Before 11-17-1784.

REED, John—1777-1785.

RENNICK, George, est, 1786.

ROGERS, David, est. appraised 7-19-1783 by Simon Taylor, William Dopson and Thomas Humphrey.

SCHUMAN, John—ex. Anthony Baker. 5-9-1780.

SINGLETON, Thomas, est., 1787.

SKIDMORE, William—A bound child hired by Peter Peters until 6-14-1778, then to Isaac Daton. Witnesses are Michael Leard and Susanna Williams.

SMITH, Christopher, est., 1787. In account with Mary McCartney, late Mary Smith. George Smith an heir. Indication here that the widow of William Buffington was this Mary McCartney.

TAFFEE, James—Died 11-29-1782.

TAYLOR, Septimus—1782. William Mecrackin, Archibald Wiggins, John Constant, John Irwin, appraisers.

THOMPSON, David, est. Widow, Mary, ex, and John Thompson. Evidently these are heirs: David, Frances, Abraham and Jacob Reasner, William Blackburn, James Daugherty and Nathaniel Parker.

WEAVER, George, est. He died 9-26-1785.

WERTMILLER, Jacob—Before 1784.

WISE, Abraham, 1780. Est. Left widow.

ESTATES REFERRED TO IN INDEX OF BOOK 5

BUZZARD, John—1813.

BREEZE, Margaret—1807

BUMGARDNER, Rudolph—1810.

BURTON, Meshak—1811.

CHAPMAN, Wm., 1797.

CHESHIRE, Samuel—1810.

DAWSON, Abraham—1805.

DEAN, Thomas—1809.

DEVAULT, Andrew—1814.

DEVER, William—1812.

ERRETT, Christopher—1812.

FOREMAN, John. Daus., Nancy and Catherine; guardian, Daniel Collins.

FRY, Henry—1812.

JONES, John—1810.

HUME, Andrew—1810.

HERRIOT, William—1810.

HAMILTON, Harry, est. settled 1810.

KISNER, Jacob—1810.

KELLER, John—1805.

KLINE, Mrs. Isabella—1808.

KILES, Hannah—Guardian appointed 1814.

KILES, Robert—Guardian appointed 1813.

LA RUE, John—1797. Hannah, ex.

LINTHICUM, Archibald—1812.

MILLER, George, est., 1809.

MURPHY, Frances—1807; John Copsey, administrator.

MURPHY, John—1810.

MURPHY, James—1810.

McCRACKEN, Catherine, orphan, 1807; guardian, Conway Rector.

McDONALD, Donald—Sale bill; Ann and Sarah McDonald buy.

PANCAKE, James—1814.

PARKER, Benjamin—1813.

PRITCHARD, John—1813.

O'QUEEN, James—1809.

PIERCALL, John—1812.

PRICE, Silas—1814. Large estate.

POWNALL, Isaac—1813.

RANNELS, James—1807. Left orphans.

RAWLINGS, Benjamin—1814.

RUCKMAN, Thomas—1809.

SAVAGE, James—1814.

SEBRING, Eliz., estate.

SHANNON, Thomas—1812.

SIMPKONS, Gassedgin—1809.

SIXE, Henry—(Father, George). Dec. 1814.

SMITH, William—1813.

SMOOT, John—1809.

SOUTHAN, George—1813. His orphan.

SQUIRE, Michael—1808.

STAFFORD, Richard—1809.

STARNS, Fred—1813.

STARKEY, Fredrick Sr. Ex., Fred Starkey, Jr. 1806.

STEM, Isabella—1808.

TAYLOR, Elizabeth, guardian John Taylor's orphans, Mary, Elizabeth, Rebecca, Joseph Susanna and John. 1810.

TAYLOR, John—1809. William Taylor, administrator.

THOMPSON, Jeremiah—1809. Huge estate; many names.

THOMPSON, John—1812.

WEADLE, Peter—1811.

WILKINS, Jno.—1808.

Miscellaneous Corrections and Additions to Census

Baiorn-Bacorn
Baker, Sam—1784 (S.R.) 7-1-1
Barnard, Edward—1782 (V.W.) 4
Beaver, Peter—1782 (A.J.) 4
Blackman not Blackburn to Rebecca Sloan, page 104
Bodkin, Richard—1782 (JbW) 7
Bonner, William—1782 (JbW) 6
Boulger, Micheal—1782 (JbW) 8
Broom, John—1782 (S.T.) 2 (Brown?)
Buffinberry, Peter—1782 (JbW) 5—error Buffington—1784 (JbW) 6-1-1
Calvin-Colvin
Calvin, Robert—1784 (S.T.) 5-1-1
Candy is Caudy
Campbell, Eliz. Will page 111, date 1-16-1812, proved 6-16-1812
Carn, Andrew—1782 (A.J.) 4 (Corn)
Carr, Henry, Sr.—1782 (JbW) 9
Carr, Conrad—1782 (JbW) 9
Carr, Joseph—1782 (JbW) 6
Caterman, Daniel—1784 (Jhw) 5-1-2 see Calerman 1782
Caulson (Coulson), Margaret
Chinoth, Jonathan—1782 (JbW) 4
Claton-Clayton
Clark(e), Dan—1782 (JbW) 4
Clark(e), John—1782 (JbW) 4
Clark(e), Robert—1782 (JbW) 8
Coberly, James—1782 (JbW) 9 see Cubberly
Combs, Francis Ignatious
Coones, Lovey not Lorry
Crack, George—1782 (JbW) (Crock)
Craig, David—1782 (JbW) 3-1
Critchlow, William—1782 (O.J.) 8
Crites, Jacob—1784 (JhW) 7-1
Crosby, Abel—1784 (MqC) 6-1
Crosley—1782
Cubberly, Thos.—1782 (JbW) 3
Cuppy, John—1782 (W.B.) 7
Cuppy, John, Jr.—1782 (W.B.) 4
Curle, Wm.—1782 (JbW) 5
Davis, Joseph—1784 (S.T.) 8-1-0
Davis, Thomas—1784 (A.H.) 4-1-3
Davison error for Dawson
Dawson, Abraham—1782 (D.M.) 4-1
Dawson, David—1782 (D.M.) 12
Dawson, Isaac—1782 (D.M.) 4-1
Dever (not Devoe) E. P.
Ely, Benjamin—1782 (JbW) 8
Farpley, James—1784 9-1-3 (Tarpley)
Fearis, James—1782 (JbW) 7
Fent (Feut) see Fout
Finley, Patrick—1782 (JbW) 3
Fleming, James—1782 (JbW) 3
Foy, Gabriel see Fox—1782
Gilmore, Sarah—1782 (JbW) 6-3
Goodwin not Goodman
Hael, Peter—1784 (S.T.) 7-0-2 not Hall
Haines, Rudolph—(D.M.) 4
Haines, John—1782 (JhW) 14-2
Hale, James—1784 (JbW) 6-2 not Hole
Hanes, Joseph—1784 (M.C.) 5-1-2
Hansom not Hanson, Thos.—(A.J.) 7
Hargis-Hargus
Harness, Adam—1784 (MqC) 8-1
Harpole, Adam—1782 (JbW) 8

Harsman, Jacob—1784 (A.J.) 8-1
Hartman, Henry (not Peter)—1782 (W.B.) 5
Heath, Asabel not Azakel
Hier, Jacob—1784 (JbW) 3-1
Hiss, Henry—1782 (W.V.) 10
Hornback, James—1782 (JhW) 9
Hornback, Anthony—1782 (M.S.) 8
Hornback, Anthony—1784 (M.S.) 10-1
Horse, Peter—1782 (JbW) 3
Hoghland-Houghland
Hubs, Thos.—1782 (JbW) 3 (Hobbs)
Hudson, John—1784 (JbW) 3-1 not Hutson
Huffman, Christopher—1782 (JbW) 9
Jackson, Wm.—1782 (D.M.) 11
Jane, Joseph—1782 (JbW) 7
Jenny not Jinney, Wm.—1782
Johnson, William—(A.J.) 3-1
Jones, Mary in place of Mary Ann Heizer, page 101 to Caleb Levings date 10-25-1828
Keener, John not Geo. wills
Keller-Kellar, Geo.
Kezoil not Kerzoil
Kersman, John—1782 (JhW) 6
Kyger, John—1784 (W.V.) 7-1-2 see Kiger 1782, Thyger
Lander not Landen—1782
Lanisisko, Henry—1782 (JbW) 12
Largent, James see Sargent
Larue-La Rue--Lerew
Lawson, Moses—1784 (O.J.) 3-1
Lawson, Richard—1784 (O.J.) 4-1
Lawrence, John—1784 (A.H.) 10-1-2
Lewis, George—1784 (S.R.) 10-1-3
Ligget, Frances—1784 (JhW) 5-1-2
Little, Job—1782 (JbW) 6
Mc Dewgle, James—1784 (S.T.) 7-1
McKave, Ross—1782 (JbW) 5 (McCave 1784)
Mace, Isaac—1782 (A.R.) 4
Marsh, Henry—1784 (W.V.) 10-3-4 March 1782
Martin, George—1782 (L.A.) 10
Matthews, Levi—1782 (D.M.) 6
Milaw not Milan
Miller, Henry—1782 (JbW) 2
  There are 2 Henry Millers
Morehead Sarah, not Susannah p. 102
Mouse, Daniel—1782 (JbW) 8
Nave, George—1784 (M.S.) 5-1-4
Nave, John—1784 (M.S.) 4-1-1
Nave, Micheal—1784 (M.S.) 8-1-1
Neale, John—1784 (A.H.) 8-1-1
Newill (Neville), Joseph, Sr.—3-1-2
Nut, John—1782 (W.V.) 4
O'Neal, Edward—1784
Orahood, Alex—1782 (JbW) 6
Osborne not Ozburn, Josiah
Panter, Benj.—1784 7-1-1 Painter—1782
Parker, Thomas—1782 & 1784 error Parsons, Thos.
Parsons, Sarah (hus. Wm.) under Edw. McCarty Will, page 124
Peck, George—1782 (JbW) 7
Pugh, Jacob—1784 (S.R.) 8-1-3

(Ratchliff and Ratcliff)
Reaves-Reeves
Redsleeves not Redsteeves
Reed-Reid-Read
Regan, Jacob—1784 (JbW) 10-1-1 not Regar
Reuding, not Rending
Reynals not Revnals see Ronnels
Riley, Alux. to Isabelle Kelley, date is 3-19-1827
Ritchar, John—1784 (E.P.) 10-0-1
Roberts, David. Sr.—1784 (S.R.) 6-1
Robey, Prior—1782 (Jbw) 9
Robinson, John—1782 (JbW) 6
Rodgers, Ezekiel—1784 (S.T.) 7-1-4
Roders, James—1784 (M.S.) 8
Rogeds, Owen—1782 (E.P.) 7-1-4
Rogers, Wm.—1782 (A.J.) 10
Ronnels, Jeremiah—1782 (O.J.) 5
Rose (not Jacob), John—(D.M.) 4
Rosencrantz (not Henry), Hezekiah—1782
Royce (Royse), John—1784 (E.P.) 2-1-1
Ruchman, Hannah to Solomon Robinson in place of Ruckman, Eliz. to Solomon Ruckman, page 103
Sadouskie, Samuel—1782 (JbW) 8
Sargent (Largent), James—1784 (E.P.) 7-1-4
Scott, Benj., Sr.—1782 (JbW) 6-1
Scott, Benj.—1782 (JbW) 6
Scritchfield, Joshua—1782 (O.J.) 3
See(Lee), George—1784 (M.S.) 8-1-5
Seymour, Felix—1782 (JbW) 12-3
Seymour, Thomas—1782 (JbW) 2
Shrodes not Srobes
Shook, Jonas—1782 (JbW) 5
Simon, Christian—1784 (M.S.) 6-1
Sims, John, Sr.—1782 (M.S.) 7
Simson, Alex—1782 (JbW) 1 Simpson
Simson, Jonathan—1782 (JbW) 8
Sits not Sites
Smith, Robert—1782 (JbW) 9
Spealman, Wm.—1784 (S.T.) 5-1
Stacey, Thomas—1782 (JbW) 3
Statts, Elijah—(JbW) 1
Stone (Slone-Sloan), James—1782 (S.R.) 9
Stone, James—1784 (S.R.) 9-1-2
Street not Strett
Stroud, Adam—1782 (JbW) 7
Tarpley see Farpley 84
Tevalt-Tevault-Tivalt
Tharp, Andrew—1784 (S.R.) 4-1-1
Thomson, Jethro—1782 (JbW) 6
Thompson, John—1784 (E.P.) 6-0-3
Thompson, John in place of John Johnson to Maria Means, page 101
Thompson, Joseph—1784 (E.P.) 5-2
Titford not Tilford
Tivebaugh, Dan (not Dean)
Vause-Vanse-Vance
Wamsley, David—1782 (JbW) 4
Ward, Syl—1782 (JbW) 11-3
Ward, Slyl—1784 (JbW) 12-1-3
Wease-Weaze
Welton, Jesse—1782 (JbW) 8-2
Whitman, George—1782 (JbW) 7
Woolf, John not Wolf

INDEX

ABART (Abert)
John 12, 68
ABERNATHY (Abernethy)
Eleanor 106(2)
Elizabeth 99, 100, 106
Elizabeth, Mrs. 99
Hannah 106(2)
Harriet 106(2)
James 2,106(3), 114
Dr. James 119
James W. 124
John 86,106(2)
John, Sr. 106
Marget 106
Maria 119
Martha 106
Mary 133
Nancy 106(2)
Robert 106, 124
Samuel 106,124, 131
Susan 106
Thomas 106, 133
William 6, 10, 54, 64(3), 99, 100, 104, 106(6), 133, 135
ABDELL
John 122
ABELMAN
Margaret 123
ABMAN see Alman
John 88
ABRELL (Abrill
George 107
Heirs 109
ACH
Sarah 118
ACHESON see Atchison
ACTON
Jemimah 1(4)
John 1(8), 64
Mary 1
Richard 1(4), 88
ADAMS
Catherine 106
Eleanor 106
George 106
Isaac 106
Jacob 101, 106(3), 137
John 20, 35, 64, 106
John, Sr. 31, 64
Lydia 106
Rachel 106(2)
Thomas 106
Washington 106
William 3, 58, 64(2), 85, 106(2)
ADY
John 5
AFFUT (Offut)
Nath. 125
AGG
Elizabeth 107
AHRSON see Earsam, Earson, Earsham, Ihrson
Jacob 55, 64
John 1, 64, 88
Mary 1, 11, 64
Simeon 11, 64, 88
Simeon, Jr. 1, 64
Simeon, Sr. 1
AIKINS
Abel 39
AIKMAN (see Eakman)
Adan Boyd 106
John 41, 64, 106
Mary 106
AIRES (see Ayres)
Richard 4, 64
ALABAUGH
Jacob 132
ALAN (see Allen, Allin)
David 88
Robert 64
Samuel 106
ALBIN
George W. 131
James 88, 110
James D. 128
James W. 131
Robert T. 130
Ruth 133
ALDERTON
John 106
Margaret 1
Wm. 1, 15, 25, 64, 106(2)
ALEN (see Allen)
David 118
ALENDER (see Allender)
James 101
Mary 101
ALEXANDER - Alexandry
Amos 50, 64
Charles, Jr. 63
Elizabeth 106
James 1(2), 2, 30, 48, 60 (2), 64(8), 106, 120(2), 129(2)

Jane 106
Robert 44, 64, 88, 115
Samuel H. 133
Sarah 106
Thomas 45
William B. 45, 106
ALFREE
Joseph 88
ALGIER (see Alkier - Algier)
Hermanous 88
John 88
Mauris 123
Micheal 88
William 88
ALKIER (see Algier and Alkire - Alkere)
Hiram 122, 123, 135
James 108
Lydia 1
Mauris 1
Marvis 133
Peter 129
Solomon 135
ALLEN (see Alan - Allan and Allin and Alin)
Allen Place 121
Anna 106
Arthur 4, 7, 29, 30, 64(2), 106
Catherine 106
David 7, 19, 64, 88, 116
Diana 134
Eliz. 1, 50, 64, 106(2), 138
Eliza 88
Fanny 138
Fred S. 133
Isabelle 106
Ivey 106
Jacob 1, 3, 50, 64
James 99, 101, 106
James W. 129
Jane 106(3)
John S. 64, 106, 116, 118, 139
Lepah 106(2)
Margaret 106, 116
Mary 106
Mary Ann 133
Mary Virginia 133
Nance 125
Nathan 69
Peter
Reynold 47
Rhona 106
Robert 4, 10, 29, 30, 63, 64 (3), 106(3)
Samuel 106(5)
Sarah 46, 56, 106
Sarah, Mrs. 99(2)
Thomas 1, 4, 6, 7, 29, 30, 46, 56, 60, 63, 64(4), 118 (2), 119, 124, 131
Thomas E. 133
Thomas M. 106, 116
Wilum 106
Wm. 99, 100, 104, 106(2), 116
ALLENDER (see Alender)
Christine 106(2)
Jacob 106
James 21, 30, 101, 106
Mary 99, 101
William 64, 106
ALLENTON
David 88
John 29
ALLER (see Oller)
Isabella 99, 101
Peter 101
ALLEY
Stephen 138
ALLINGTON see Allenton
David 88
John 61
ALLISON
Patrick 23
ALLOWAY
Hannah 106
Hiram 99, 104
Jane 106
Lidy 106
Rebecca, Mrs. 99
William 106
ALMAN see Abman
John 88
ALT
Micheal 1. 117
AMBLER
John 126
Molley 126
AMBLEY
John 107
AMBROSE
George 117
AMIGER
Elizabeth 1, 21, 64

AMON
Mary 102
AmORY perhaps Emory
Edward 1(2), 38(2), 40
Elizabeth 1
ANDERSON
Alfred 99, 129
Amos 129
Ann 120
Catherine 107
Charles 184
Eliza 126
Elizabeth 107, 119, 120
Hannah 107, 119, 120
Harrison 129
Henry 88
Isaac 38
James 1, 46, 56, 88
Jemima 120
John 88, 107, 119(2)
Joseph 46, 120
Joshua 120
Lucresay 120
Margaret 1(2), 107, 119
Marget 107
Margaret Eleanore 107
Mary 119, 120, 121
Mena 1
Nancy 107
Rachel 1, 107
Sarah 107
Sarah Angeline 107
Thomas 1(2), 64(2), 88, 107(3), 119
William 1(5), 17, 54, 64, 88 (2), 107(2)
William, Sr. 1, 64
ANDREWS
Christena 110
Elizabeth 136
George 1, 64, 88
Margaret 1
ANENT see Arrent
ANGELL
Joseph 10, 48
ANTRAU see Autraw
John 64
ARBHOLT error for Arnholt
Annabella 109
ARCHER
Benjamin 88
Hannah 1
John 1, 15, 23, 88
John, Jr. 60, 64
ARENHOLT see Arnholt
Adam 113
Andrew 109
Ann 109
Arabella 109
ARGOS
Alex 54
Michady 54
ARMINTRAUT see Erimintraut
Christopher 88
ARMSTRONG
Andrew 14, 42, 43
Ann 1(3)
Edward 120
Edward M. 115, 127
Frances R. 101
George 114
James D. 119(2)
Joseph D. 127
Joseph R. 127
Max 15, 60
William 1(8), 12, 14, 21, 29(2), 30, 31, 37, 45, 50, 54(2), 59, 62(2), 64(4), 85, 87, 111, 127, 136
William, Jr. 113, 120
ARNEST probably Harness
Leonard 12
ARNHOLT see Aranholt - Aronholt - Aranhatt - Aronhatt
Adam E. 136
Ann 109
Alice, Mrs. 99
Andrew 99(2), 100
Ann 109
Annabella 109
Arrabella 109
ARNOLD (Arnald)
A. Monroe 133
Amelia 107
Amos 107
Andrew 1(2), 2, 64, 88, 107 (2), 110
Andrew Jackson 107
Angeline 107
Ann 107, 110
Archibald 99, 101, 104, 107 (3), 122(2)
Barbary 107
Benjamin 107, 115

Catherine 99, 104, 107(8), 118
Charlotte 134
Christina 107
Daniel 5, 49, 57, 64, 107(3), 110, 118, 135, 136(2)
David 110, 134(2), 135
Eleanore 107
Elias 107(2)
Eliza 126
Eliza Ann 110
Eliz. 107(4), 110, 134, 136
Elizabeth, Mrs. 99
Emmanuel 107
Evaline 107
Francis 107
George 107(2)
George W. 107, 133
Hannah 1(4), 2(3)
Jacob 104, 107(2), 128
Jane 107, 184
John 1(4), 2(2), 22(8), 24 (2), 26(2), 31, 88, 48, 56 (2), 64, 88, 104, 106(2), 107, 110, 112, 116(3), 117, 127, 126(2), 133, 138
Rev. John 107
John J. 133
John Monroe 107(2)
John T. 134
Jonathan 2
Joseph 2(2), 99, 104, 107, 134(2)
Joseph Early 107
Josh. 107(2), 110, 116, 117
Joshua S. 133
Katherine Ann 107
Lemuel Smith 107
Lettie 107
Levi 107, 126
Lewis 107
Louiza June 107
Lydia 107(2)
Magdalena 107
Mary 2, 107(8), 134
Mary, Mrs. 99
Mary Catherine 107
Micheal 99, 104, 107, 134
Moses 88
Nimrod 107
Peter 107, 134
Phoebe 107
Polly 117
Priscilla 1(2)
Rebecca 107(2)
Rosanna 107
Richard 24, 107
Samuel 2, 49(2), 64, 107 (2), 108
Sarah, 2, 107(3), 110
Sarah, Mrs. 99
Solomon 107(2), 118
Susan 107
Susan Catherine 107
Tillbury 107
William 107(4)
William F. 107, 129
Zachariah 2, 64, 107, 123, 134, 135, 136
ARONHOLT (see Arnholt)
Adam 113
Arabella 109
ARRETT (see Errett)
ARRENTS
Fredrick 99, 101
Sarah 107
Sarah, Mrs. 99
ASBERRY see Asbury
Henry 56
Joseph 2, 40, 88, 99, 108, 112, 119
ASBURY see Asberry
Henry 56(2), 64
Jeremiah 107, 120
Jeremiah H. 103
Joe 107, 109
Joseph 3(2), 38, 40, 49, 56 (6), 64(2), 107(2), 120, 127
Mary 99, 103
Ruth 107, 108
ASHBROOK
Aaron 2(2), 15, 27, 50, 58, 59(2), 64(2), 88, 128
Absolem 2, 38, 58, 64, 122, 131
Agnes 2
Amilia 58
Eleanor 111
Eli 58, 64, 87, 128
Elizabeth 58, 64
Ely 128
Heirs. 44, 64
John 107, 128, 139
Levi 1, 2, 15, 48, 54, 57, 58, 64(2), 88(2), 114, 134

Levy 2, 64
Maria B. 128
Mary 2(2), 58, 111
Moses 2, 64, 86
Phoebe 128
Rachel 2, 128(2)
Roda 128
Rody 58
Sarah 2
Thomas 2(2), 58, 128
William 58, 128
ASHBURNER
John 6, 64
ASHBY see Ashley
B. 54
Benjamin 2, 88, 107
Elizabeth 107
Hannah 107
Henry 88
Jeremiah 2, 64, 86, 107, 126
Jesse 2, 88
Lottie 107
Martin 2(2)
Nathaniel 2
Nimrod 8
Peggy 2
Peter 88
Stephen 32, 88
Thomas 88
William 2
ASHLEY
Benjamin 2
Jeremiah 2, 64
Thomas 2
ASHMORE
William 25
ATCASON see Atkinson Etchason
William 88
ATCHISON - Atkinson Atcheson
John 39, 61
Sam 88
Silas 61
William 61, 88(2)
William, Jr. 88
ATHEY
Bazil 100
Elizabeth 99, 100
Emma 107
John 136
Joseph 107
Martha 107, 121
Mary 107
Nancy 107
Samuel 107
Sarah Elizabeth 107
Susan 107
Thomas 28, 107, 118
Virtuity 107
Walter 107
ATHLEY
Elizabeth 2
Thomas 2
ATHY
John 27, 64
ATKINSON
John 64
ATWELL
Frances 2
AUFERE
George 49, 64
AUGHNEY (Aughtney)
Ann 16, 63, 107, 132
Darby 2, 16, 19, 57, 63, 64, 129, 132
AUGHTNEY (Aughney)
Ann 16(3), 64
Darby 16(3), 64
AUTRAW see Antrau
John 29, 64
AYRES see Aires
Benjamin 85
BAB
William 130
BABBS
Beal (Beele) 2(2), 21, 64 (2), 42, 47
Charles 10, 21(2), 21, 42
Deliverance 2
John 2
Mary Ann 127
Rebecca 2
William 2, 10, 12, 64(2)
William Hamilton 2
"BABRUCH"
Leazfrite 127
BACORN (Beacorn - Baicorn) 140
Job 1, 2(7), 12, 17, 29, 35, 36(2), 57, 64(3), 88
John 17
Rhoda 2(7)
BADGLEY (Bagley - Begley)

BADGLEY
Abraham 132
Anthony 88
Anthony, Sr. 132
Anthony, Jr. 132
David 88
Henry 23, 30, 64
BAER
William 3, 18
BAGLEY see Badgley
BAILIE
John 64, 58
BAILEY (see Boley and Hailey)
Ann 2, 88
Alice 107
Benjamin 101, 107
Edward 107(2)
Eleanor 99, 101, 107
Elizabeth 107(3)
Grace 2
James 21
John 2(2), 13, 35, 62, 64, 107
John, Sr. 7, 64
Mary 107(4)
Thomas 35
William 88, 107(2)
BAKER
Aaron 139
Andrew 108(2)
Anthony 2, 89, 64, 88, 117, 125(2), 131(3), 133, 139
Charles Levi 108
Ele(a)nor 99, 103
Elizabeth 108(2)
Enoch 109
Frank 38
Gemima 139
Henry 2(2)
Henry Fredrick 108
Hilary 28
Isaac 120(2)
Isaac Newton 108
Jacob 86, 88, 139(2)
James 89, 108, 117
James Carr 133
Jesse 99, 102
John 1, 3, 64, 89(2), 99, 102, 108(2), 117, 118
John, Jr. 27(4), 48(4), 130
John R. 108
John William 108
John Y. 108, 117, 127
Joseph 41, 64, 86, 108
Levi 109
Lewis 108
Lucy 2(2), 66, 99, 108
Marie 2
Mary 108, 125
Mary, Mrs. 99
Mary Elizabeth 2
Melcher 2
Micheal 100
Moses Samuel 28
Nancy 108, 113, 127
Nancy Ann 127
Nicholas 44, 64
Parthenia, Mrs. 99
Patrick 2(2), 21, 32, 37, 56, 61(3), 64
Perry 105
Philip 23
Priscilla 132
Rachel 99, 100
Rachel, Mrs. 99
Rebecca 108(2)
Richard 99, 102, 125(2), 133(2)
Samuel 2, 27, 52, 54, 64(2), 89, 108, 140
Sarah 120
Sarah Elizabeth 108
Sarah F. 138
Sary 131
Susan Emily 116
Thomas 61, 64, 103, 108
Virginia Catherine 108
William 2, 6, 8, 37, 52, 64, 89, 108(2), 132
BALDWIN
Jean 2
William 2, 5, 64
BALENTINE (Ballintyne)
Hugh 89, 64, 118, 125
BALEY (Boley)
Charles 108
Nathaniel 36
BALL (Bell)
James 89, 123(2)
William 36, 64
BALTHAS (Bathas)
George 89
BANCROFT
Stacy B. 115
BANE
Abner 99, 104, 128
Alexander 108(2), 111
Elizabeth, Mrs. 99
Elizabeth Ann 128
George 99, 104, 108(2), 128

Gesse 45(2)
Heste 108
James 108(2)
Jesse 108, 137
Joseph 8
Margaret, Mrs. 99
Nancy 108
Parthena 3
Robert 108(2)
Thomas 108
William 130
Zimri 108(2)
BANK
George 108
BAPTIST
Baptist Church 50, 64, 78
BARBER (Barbour)
George 25
BARCLAY (Berkley and Barkley)
Betsy 109
Carson, Barclay & Mitchell 8, 64
John 3
Samuel 54(2)
Thomas 3(2), 4, 9, 64(2)
BARGER
Jacob 89
BARKER
Elizabeth 132
George 35(2)
John 115
Mary 113
BARKLOO (same as Barlow & Bartlow)
Ann 108
Benjamin 3, 47, 108(2)
Eleanor (Leanor) 108(2)
Elizabeth 3, 47, 108(2)
James 26, 64, 108
Johnson 3, 47, 108(2)
Leanor (Lenah) 108(2)
Mary 108
Ruth 3, 47
Sarah 3, 47, 108(2)
BARKLEY (see Barclay & Berkley)
BARKLOW (see Barkloo)
BARNARD
Edw. 140
Mena 46, 64
Noltey 1
BARNES
Deliah 99, 103
Elijah 89
Elizabeth 120
Frances 103
Mary 123
Susannah 109
William 109
BARNET (Barnett)
Jesse 86
Mainy 89
Mene 89
Milly, Mrs. 99
Samuel 99, 104
BARNHOUSE
Andrew 108
Elizabeth 108
Fielding A. 108(2)
John 3(2), 37(2), 64(2), 89, 108
Marium 108
Mary 8(2)
Mathew 108
William 108
BARNICK
Jacob 1, 64
BARR
Adam 108, 130
Hugh 130
John 108, 118, 138
Sarah 108(2), 130
BARRET (Barrott-Baret)
Benjamin 108, 137
David 28, 108(2)
Edith 108
Eleanor 99, 104
George 128(2), 133
John 108, 127, 133, 137
Jonathan 103, 104, 108, 116
Lemuel 113
Peter 18
Rachel 116
Rhoda 99, 103, 108
Richard 35(2), 116
Samuel 38, 52, 64(2)
Sarah 116, 137
Thomas 108
Unity 116
BARRICK
Catherine 108
George 114(3)
John 108, 114
William H. 114
BARRY (Berry)
Enoch 122
BARTHOFF
Andrew 5(2), 64

BARTLETT
John 38
BARTMESS
Adam 120
BARTLOW (see Barkloo)
BARTON
Elizabeth 8
Kimber 3, 4, 53, 64, 89
William G. 108
BATES
Edward 3(3), 4(2), 65(2)
Jane 3(2)
Sarah 3(3)
Thomas 3(8)
BATHAS (see Mathes also Balthas)
George 23, 65
BATMAN
John 89
BATSON
Mordacai 89
Mordacai, Jr. 89
BATTEN (Batton & Battin)
Henry 1, 3(5), 15, 65(2), 89
Margaret 3(3)
Simon 3
BAUGHMAN (probably Bowman) see Bauman
Andrew 89
Benjamin 10
BAUMGARNER (see Bumgarner or gardner)
Sam 112, 115, 118, 122
BAYARD
John 27
BAYLESS (Baylis - Bayloss-Ballep)
Edward 3, 37, 112, 65
Eleanor 3
BAYNTON
John 3
BEACORN (Bacorn)
Job 65
BEAGLE
Jonathan 89
BEALL (Beale - Beales - Beal)
Alexander 102
Alpheus 111
Ann 108, 128
Benjamin 53(2), 65, 89, 108, 138
Betty 3
Cephas 108
Eli 3(2), 13, 21, 65, 115
Elijah 5, 10
Elisha 2, 3(2), 5, 6, 15, 41, 55, 65, 108
Elizabeth 108
George 1(3), 2(2), 3(2), 10, 11(2), 12, 13(3), 15, 21, 35, 36, 39, 41, 44, 52, 53, 55, 56(2), 61, 65(2), 89, 134
Hezekiah 43, 65
Isaac 3, 59, 65, 106
Isaiah 26, 65
John 4, 108
Joseph 108
Lloyd 13, 108
Malinda 3
Margery 3
Mary 108
Nancy 108
Nenian (Ninian) 108
Prudence 108(2)
Richard 111
Robert 108
Samuel 3(4), 5, 7, 12, 50, 52, 55, 59, 63, 65
Sarah 128
Tavener 3, 63, 65
Thomas 3(2), 46, 65
William 132
William D. 113
BEALY (Bailey - Beaty)
Lenah 108
BEAN (Beane)
Alex 100
Andrew 99
Ann, Mrs. 99
Benjamin 50(2), 65(2), 89
Bennet 136
Bennet Second 99
Bennet Third 99, 102
Elizabeth 99(2)
John 89
Joseph 3
Mary 99(2)
Parthenia 3
BEARD
Elizabeth 42
George 24, 65, 89
George V. 108
James 14, 65
Martha 108(2)
William 42, 65
BEATTY (Beattie - Baty - see Bealey)
Charles 3, 47, 124
Eleanor 3, 47, 108

George 12, 48, 54, 86, 89, 65, 108
James 108
John C. 3
Lenah -08(2)
Levi 50, 65
Robert 59, 89
BEAU
Matthias 124
BEAVER (Bever - Beavour)
Anne 3
Catherine 3
Elizabeth 3(2)
John 3, 59, 65
Matthias 3(2), 65, 89
Matthew 3
Micheal 89
Peter 3(3), 134, 140
William 135
BECK
Jacob 3
BECKET
Jane 131
BECKNER
Henry 56
Peter 3, 8, 65
BECKWITH
Marmaduke Brokenburrow 3
Newman 62, 86, 135
Samuel 107, 124
BEDINGER
Henry 38(3), 48(3)
BEEKMAN
Sarah 3
William 3, 48, 65
BEELER
Charles 89, 111(2)
John 111
Joseph 3, 65
BEESAR
Dan. 115
BEETON
Margaret 122
BEGLEY (Badgley & Bagley)
Eliz. 4
Henry 4, 15
BEISER (Beizer - see Biser and Byser)
John 18
BEL (probably Bell)
William 85
BELEW (Blue)
John 80
BELFORD (Bellford - Brelsford)
Barnaba 89
Barnet 89
Benjamin 35, 65
Daniel 26, 65
BELINGER
Nancy 116
BELL (see Bel - Beele and Bills - Beal)
Agnes 4
Anna 128
Eli 128
George 89
Isaac, Capt. 113
John 4
John N. 133
Lorena 111
Margaret 4(2)
Nathaniel 44
Robert 39, 65
Wm. 4(2), 10, 65, 89, 116
Zephaniah 89
BELLMIRE (Belmyre)
Sarah 114
BELSFORE (see Belford)
BENAN (Benam)
Benjamin 4, 65
Sarah 4
BENAT (see Bennet and Benet)
Robert 89
BENDY
John 131
BENET
Thomas 80
BENKIT
Jacob 89
BENNET (Bennett - Bennit - see Benat & Benit)
Catherine, Mrs. 99
Fred 107
Isabella 138
Isabella, Mrs. 99
John 99, 100
Maria 99, 100
Robert 89
Sylvanus 107, 134
Thomas 32, 38, 65, 89
William 99, 105, 126
BENON
Isabella 111
BERKLEY (see Barclay & Barkley)
Elijah 129
John 129
Mordecai 129

BERRY (see Barry)
Adam 109
Amasia 108
David 109
Elijah 125
Elizabeth 4(4)
Elizabeth, Mrs. 99
Enoch 3(2), 4(4), 6, 8, 11, 15, 21, 22, 33, 46, 58, 62, 65(3), 89, 122
Evin 108
George 22, 89, 109
James 99, 101
Joel 23, 30, 61, 65(2), 89(2), 121
Joseph 103
Mary, Mrs. 99
Reuben (Rubin) 4, 5, 21, 53, 54, 65, 89
Rachel, Mrs. 99
Samuel 7, 65, 99, 101
Sarah 4, 108
Thomas 44
William 89, 98
William, Sr. 99
William, Jr. 99, 105
BEST (see Brest)
Hannah 89
Jacob 89
BETHEL (Bethell)
George 27, 65, 108
Edward 108
Jane 108
Joshua 108
Mary 108
Mary Ann 108
Nancy 108
Ruth 108
Samuel 129
BETTERTON
Margaret 99, 104
BEVAN (Bevins - Beven)
Benjamin Wiley 138
Betsy 138
Charles 57, 65
John Wiley 138
Lydia 132
Mary 132
Samuel 15, 59, 65
Stacy 65
BEVER (see Beaver)
BEVERLY
John 89, 111
BEZELY
Jesse 89
BIBLE
Christian 80
BICKERSTAFF (Biggerstaff)
John 89
William 89
William, Jr. 87, 89
BIERLY
John 89
BIGAM (Bigham)
Hugh 89
BIGGERSTAFF (Bickerstaff)
Alice 108(2)
Ann 108
Billy, Jr. 136
Frend. 108
Hugh 108(2)
Isaac 108
John 89, 108(2)
Mary 108
Nancy 108
Pleasant 108
Rachel 108(2)
Rebecca 108(2)
Samuel 108(2)
Sarah 108
Susana 108
Wm. 3, 2, 11, 21, 89, 108(2)
William, Sr. 89
William, Jr. 89
BIGGS
Samuel 42
BIGGINS
John 47
BILBER
Peter 112
BILLINGS
Joseph 86
BILLS (see Bell & Beall)
John 4, 15, 16, 41(2), 65, 89
Ruth 4
Sarah 4(4)
William 4(4), 15, 16, 41, 54, 65(3), 89
BILMORE (Billmore and Bellmire)
Jane 113
John 114
BINEGAR
Catherine 134
BINGAMON
Christian 1
BIRD (Byrd)
Aney 128
Peter 116

INDEX PAGE 143

Stephen 116
William 116
BIRDMAN
John 5
BIRK
Isaac 1
BIRKET (Burket-Burkit)
Thomas 65
BIRKHART (Burkhart)
Thomas 9, 65
BISER (see Byser & Byser)
Fred 134
Jacob 43(2)
John 43(2)
Newton, Jr. 136
Solomon 134
BISHOP
Alex K. 118
George 62, 65, 136
John 85
Noah 46, 65
BIZER (Beizer - Biser)
Elizabeth 110
Jacob 104, 107, 123, 136
John 1, 18
Mary 99, 104
Nicholas 107(8)
Newton, Jr. 136
Solomon 134
BLACK (Blacks)
Betsy, Mrs. 99
Daniel 47
Edmond E. 108
Helen 108
John 4, 11, 12, 21, 25, 32, 42, 61(2), 89, 99, 104, 135
Jonathan 110
Mary 110
Rebecca 110
Sarah 110
BLACKBURN
Edward 4(2)
Edward L. 37, 133, 137
James 4
John 4
Mary 4(2), 139
Sarah 4(8)
William 4(5), 12, 18, 23(3), 42, 52, 65(8), 115, 139
BLACKMAN
David 99, 104
Rebecca, Mrs. 99, 140
BLAIR
William 89
BLAKE
Margaret 115
BLAKELEY
Charles 117
Lucy 117
BLAND
John 39, 57, 60, 65
BLEW (see Blue & Belew)
Charles 133
Uriah 27, 65
BLITH (see Blyth)
William 89
BLOOMFIELD
Joseph 4, 87
Mary 4, 37
BLUE (see Blew & Belew)
Abraham 4(2), 29(2), 65, 89, 109(3)
Barnet 26
Benjamin 109
Catherine 4, 65
Cattron 109
Charity 109
Charles 108(2), 112(2), 133, 134
Cornelius 2
David 109
Eleanor 108
Elizabeth 4, 109, 114, 126
Ezekinl 2
Fanny 122
Frances Lawson 120
Garret (Garrat) 89, 108, 109(4), 111
Garret I. 110
Garrett J. 108, 120
Garret W. 108, 109, 111, 120, 122
Hannah 108, 109(3)
Isabella 118
Ivea 109
Jacob 109, 126
James 12, 15, 89, 109
Jesse 109
John 4, 19(2), 35, 39, 42, 60, 63, 65(2), 89, 109(5), 122
John ,Capt. 26, 65
John L. 126
John, Jr. 26, 89
John, Sr. 89, 109
Lawson 109
Louisa 109
M. 113
Margaret 109(2)
Mary 108

Mary Ann, Mrs. 99
Mich. 44
Mical 109
Micheal 11, 65(2), 89, 108, 109(3), 122
Misheal ?
Nancy 108, 138
Peter 109
Phoebe ?
Rebecca 120(2)
Rebecca Susan 120
Richard 63, 108, 109, 128, 136
Samuel 108
Sarah 108
Sarah A. 128
Scioto 120
Susannah 109
Thomas 109(2), 126, 135
Uriah 27, 58, 63, 65, 89, 108(2), 109(3), 114, 120 (3)
William 109
William Inskeep 120
Zachariah 99, 108, 109
BLY
Isaac 113
William 89
BLYTH (see Blith)
William 28
BOARDMAN (Bordman)
Elizabeth 4
Joseph 4, 89
BOATH (Booth)
Susannah 131
BOBO
Rebecca 99, 104
William 104
BODINE
John 106
BODKIN
Richard 89, 140
BODLEY (Bodly)
Samuel D. 122
BOFT
Jacob 55, 65
BOGARD (Bogart - Boggardt)
Charity 109
Cornelius 109(2)
Elizabeth 4, 109
Ezekiel 89, 109
Gaisbert (Gysbert 109
Grizene 109
Gysbert (Gaisbert) 109
Hannah 109
Jacob 4(2), 28, 39, 61(2), 65(2), 89
John H. 8
Mary 4(2)
Phoebe 109
Warner 109
BOGLE (Boggrell)
Andrew 4, 86
Andrew, Jr. 109
James 1, 8, 89
Mary 4(3), 4, 8
Thomas 65
BOLEY (see Bailey)
BOMAN (see Bowman and Dowman)
BOMGARDNER (see Bumgarneror & Baumgardner)
Rudy 63, 65
BON (Bond?)
Thomas 4
BOND
Anne 109
Elizabeth 109, 132
John 109
Mary 109
Spelman 109
Thomas 12, 65, 89, 109, 132
Walter 4
Winifred 109
William 120
BONNFIELD (Bornfeald)
Sam 89
BONHAM
Benjamin 109
Hezekiah 89
Jeremiah 109
John 109
Maude, Mrs. 99
Samuel 99, 102(2), 109(2)
Sarah 109
Wesley 109
BONNER
William 89, 140
BONNET (Bennet-Barrett?)
Elizabeth 4
Henry 89
Samuel 4, 89
BOOK (Buck)
Anthony 89
Robert 89
BOOKER
Phil 89
BOOKLESS
David 60, 65, 86
BOOTH (see Boath)

William 8
BOOTS
George 89
BORAH (may be Borer oor Borrer)
Charles 89, 121
BORD
John 26
BORER (Borrer - Borah)
Barbary 109(2)
Charles 89, 109
Charles C. 137
Elizabeth 109
Jacob 89, 109, 121
Martin 109
Mary 109
Rosanna 109
Thomas 89, 109
Widow 89
BORN
John 4
BONNFEALD
Samuel 135
BOSLER
John 2, 54, 89
BOSLEY
Alice 99(2)
Anna 109(2)
Anna Bella 109
Arabella 109(3)
Betsy 109
Eleanor 109(2)
Elizabeth 109(2)
Hannah 109(2)
Henry 109(8)
Jacob 109(3)
James 48, 65, 109(4)
Jemima 109, 121
John 109(8)
John C. 99(2)
Joseph 109(2)
Levin 109
Nelly 109
Mary 109(5)
Mary, Mrs. 99(2)
Polly 109
Priscilla 109(4)
Robert 109(3)
William 109(6)
BOULGER
Michael 140
Thomas 89
BOURK (Bourke - Burke)
Elizabeth 109(2)
Micheal 109
BOWEL (Bowels - Bowles)
Bazil 4, 11(2), 65
S. J. 121
Thos. 11(2), 13(2), 33, 122
William 4(3), 26, 65
William, Sr. 15(2), 65(2)
BOWEN
Lucy Ann 112
Peter 112
T. B. 33
Thomas Barth 124
Uriah 112
BOWER (see Borrer and Borer)
Charles 109
BOWES
Jacob 86
BOWLER
Thomas 112
BOWLES - Bowels
Charles 9
S. J. 124
BOWMAN (see Boman and Dowman - Bauman-Baughman)
Adam 126
Andrew 99, 102, 130
Benjamin 10
Charles 89
Eleanor 107
George 86, 99, 103
John 57, 65
Margaret, Mrs. 99
Nelly 109
Rachel, Mrs. 99
Samuel 45
BOXELL (Boxwell)
John 15, 65
BOYCE (Boice)
Ann 5, 109
James 109(2)
John 109(2)
Nicholas 5(3), 19, 40(3), 54, 65, 109
Micheal 86
Richard 3, 4(2), 5, 39, 40 (2), 45, 52, 65(4), 89, 109
Robert 109(2)
Sarah 5, 109
BOYD
Alexander 5(2)
Andrew 113
Elisha 38, 59, 60
John 9
Thomas 21

Sam 85(2)
Sarah 5(2), 14
BOYDSTON
Thomas 5
BOYKIN
William 8, 56
BOYLE
Andrew 136
Patrick 57
BOYTON (see Baynton)
John 21(2), 30, 65(3)
BR——
Isaac 110
BRADFORD
John 89
BRADRUCK
Ralph 54
BRADY
James M. 116
John 106, 110(2), 114, 116, 119(2), 122, 126, 130, 135
John J. 130
Micheal 1, 8, 65
Samuel 122, 128
Samuel D. 109, 112, 122, 126
Samuel H. 130
Samuel W. 132
BRAHAN
John 5, 8, 65
BRAKE (Break)
Jacob 80, 65
Jacob, Jr. 89
Jacob, Sr. 89
John 89
BRALL
Basil 33, 65
BRAMAN
Thomas 52, 53, 129
BRANDENBURG(en) Branninburg(er) - Brandenbaugh - Brandenberg)
Aaron 5, 9, 26
Ann 5
Esther 5
Matthias 5(3), 9, 21, 27, 45, 65
William 18, 65
BRANDT (Brat)
Catherine, Mrs. 99
John 99, 100
BRANNINBURG (see Brandenburg)
William 18
BRANSON
Amos 89
Barbary 109
Cathron 109
Fredrick 109
John 109
Joseph 109
Susan 109
BRAY
Henry 5
Samuel 107(5)
BRAYFALL
Christopher 134
BRAXTON
Mary 136
BREAK (Brake)
Catherine 5
Jacob 5
BRFCHEN
William 89
BRECHTEL
Jacob 24, 65
BREEZE
Margaret 109
BRELSFORD (see Bellford & Belsford & Brelesford)
Ann 109
Bernard 5(2), 15, 65, 109
Daniel 26
David 109
Elizabeth 109
Eve 109, 119
Jesse 109(2), 122
John 109(2)
Leah 109
Mahaly 109
Margaret 109, 124
Marjoram 23, 26, 65(2)
Mary 109
Naomi 5(2)
Nathan B. 115
Phoebe 109
Rachel 109
Sarah 109
Thomas 109, 122
BREMEGEN
William 89
BRENT
Charity 50
George 2, 39(7), 47, 50
BRESST (see Best)
Hannah 109
BREWSTER
Ebenezer 5
BRIAN (see Bryan)
Daniel 6
BRIANT (see Bryant)

James 25, 65
BRIGGS
Abigail 5
Ann 100
Joseph 3, 5, 33(3), 47, 65 (4), 110
Thomas 110
Villetta 110
Walter 110
BRIGHT
Hensom 26
John 89
BRILL (Breill - Briel)
Alfred A. 129
Alfred 129
Catherine, Mrs. 99
Henry 5, 101, 122, 129, 133
Isaac 99(2), 101, 103
Jane, Mrs. 99
Jane 101
John 122
Micheal 5(2), 65, 101, 122, 124
BRINK
Huselty 110(2)
Hybert 45, 65, 109, 110
Isaac 110
John 110
Mary 110
Phillip 110
Samuel 115, 123
Ursulla 89
BRINKER
Henry 32, 52, 65, 110
Henry, Lieut. 98
BRISCOE (Brico)
Hanson 22
BRITAIN (Brittin or Brittain)
John 21
Nathaniel 48
Joseph 5
BROADHEAD
Richard 27
BROCK
Thomas 5
BRODY (Brady)
James 89
BROMSEY
Joshua 5
Mary 5(2)
Thomas 5, 63
BROOKE (Brookes)
Abraham 29
Elizabeth Ann 135
James 89
Mary Ellen 135
Nancy 135
Thomas D. 135
Thomas T. 135
Richard 89
BROOKHART (Brookhard)
Abraham 53
Catherine 5
Jacob 5(5), 20(2), 23, 81, 65(8)
John 5, 56
Micheal 20(2), 65(2), 138
Phillip 31, 65
Rhody 99, 104
BROOM
John 140
BROUGH
Charles M. 125
Franklin 125
James 125
Jane 125
John 125
Maria 125
BROUGHTON
W. 47
William 13, 89
BROWN
A. 27, 29, 61
Adam 1, 110(2), 118
Alexander 34, 56(2), 65, 110
Ann M. 99, 101, 110
Ann 110
Catherine 5
Clothem 23
Daniel 5(2), 23, 33, 40, 89, 110
David 110, 118
Elizabeth 5, 110
Frances 5, 110
Hetty 117
Isaac 110, 112, 124
James 89
Jane 110
John 5(3), 7, 9, 18, 19, 22 (3), 21, 31, 35, 37(2), 38 (3), 42, 46, 47, 51, 55, 62, 65(8), 89(2), 98, 110, 118, 130
John, Jr. 22(8), 99, 104
Matthew 110
Mary 110, 118
Nancy 110
Nathan 5
Parthenia 136
Parthenia, Mrs. 99

Polly 110
Richard 118
Samuel 30, 110
Sarah 110, 128
Solomon 118
Stacy 61
Thos. 5, 89(3), 110(2), 137
William 129
BROWNING
Elias 35, 65, 121(2)
BRUCE
Andrew 110(3), 114
Bruce 110 error
Charles 110(2), 89
Daniel 110
Dan. C. 111
George 110(3)
Helen 110(2)
John J. 138
Joseph 89, 139
Margaret 111
Norman 86
Norman Murdock 110
Susannah 110
William 110, 135
BRUEN (Bruin)
Bryan 5(9), 6(11), 9, 10, 10, 22(3), 23, 26(2), 28, 30, 32, 34(3), 35(2), 36 (3), 37, 39(2), 42, 45, 46, 47, 50, 51, 52(2), 54(7), 56, 58(2), 59, 60, 65(10), 66(5), 110
Charles 6
Elizabeth 5(7)
Margaret 6
Peter Bryan 6
Peter 54
Colo. Peter 6, 66
BRUNER
George 92, 103
Henry 57, 66
Maria, Mrs. 99
Peter 3, 28(2), 57, 66, 87, 120, 136, 138
BRYAN (see Brian - Byrn)
James 6, 32, 66
John 61, 66
Mary 6, 137
Thomas 110
Richard 47
BUBBERS (see Buzzard) may be Bupora)
Catherine 110
Sambred 210
BUCK (see Book)
Anthony 6(3), 23, 47, 58 (2), 66(2), 89, 124
John 6, 42
Micheal 54, 66
Robert 6(3), 23, 38, 55, 58, 63(3), 89, 116
Thomas 123
Wm. 6(3), 66, 89, 114
BUCKINGHAM
Fanny 134
BUCKNER
Anthony 3
BUCKRIDGE
James 89
BUCKWALTER
Anthony 110(2)
David 110(2)
Jacob 110(2)
John 110
Magdelene 110
Mary 110
Sarah 110
Sarah B. 110
BUFF
John 44
BUFFENBERRY
Peter 140
BUFFINGTON
Abraham 110
David 6, 89, 110(3)
Elizabeth 6(3)
Joel 6(3), 19, 89, 110(2)
John 110
Johathan 110
Joseph 110
Magdelene 6
Mary 6, 89, 110(5)
Peter 89, 110, 140
Phillip 110
Rebecca 110
Richard 110(3)
Ruth 110
Susannah 110(2)
Thomas 7(2), 10, 29, 42, 45, 66(2), 89, 110 (3)
William 5, 6(3), 9, 11(3), 16, 18(2), 21, 22, 23, 29, 32, 43, 44, 45, 51, 53, 66(3), 86, 88, 89, 110(9), 122, 128, 129, 132, 139
William Sr. 210
BULL
Henry 122

John 104
Mary 99, 104
Thos. 7, 22, 57, 137
BULLETT (Bullitt)
Cuthbert 3, 9, 14, 15(2), 16, 27, 39, 61
Sarah 6
William 8, 41(5), 42, 53, 60, 66, 89
William, Jr. 25
BUMGARDNER see Baumgardner - Bomgardner - Gartner
Ann 99, 104
Agnes 6, 110
Eleanor 110
Hannah 110
Jemima 110
Rachel 110
Rebecca 110
Reuben 110, 124, 125
Rudolph 6, 63, 65, 89, 110, 119
Rudy 26(2), 63, 65, 89
Samuel 110, 115, 118, 122, 124
Susan 110
BUMEROTZ (Borncrotz - Bornerotz - Bumrotz)
Catherine 110
Ellinor 110(2)
Elizabeth Ann 110
George 110(2)
George 110(2)
John 110(2)
Julian 110
Landrum 110
Leonard 103, 110
Leonard, Jr. 110
Mary 110
Mortimore 110
Sarah Ann 110
William 110
BUNN (Dunn?)
Henry 121
Mary 6
Peter 6, 40, 66
BURACK
Ann 6
William 6
BURBRIDGE (Burridge)
John 14, 126
Mary 3, 66
BURGESS
Anna 109(2)
Elizabeth, Mrs. 99
James 99(2)
Isabel 6(2)
Priscilla 100
Thomas 109
William 6(2)
BURGIT
Jacob 89
BURHAM - Burnham
Augustine 130
John 130
BURK (Birk - Bourk)
Benjamin 6
Elizabeth 6
John 6
Jonathan 89
Margaret 6
BURKIT (Burket - Burkett - Birket)
Fred 89
Henry 89, 109
Jacob 6, 29, 66
John 99, 104
Maria, Mrs. 99
Rachel 99, 100
Rhoda 128
Simon 6
Thomas 41, 46, 66(2), 100, 106, 109
Thomas A. 109
Valentine 50, 66
William 128
BURNS (Byrns - Byrnee - Byrne)
Christine 11
John 5, 6, 22, 25, 41, 51, 66, 89, 41
Morgan 99, 104
Ruth 99, 104
Samuel 19
Sarah, Mrs. 99
William 14, 18, 28, 66
William H 40, 66
BURNFIELD
John 16, 66
BURNGAME
Samuel 122
BURNETT
Alex. 34
James 115
BURNILL
John 14(3), 29, 37
BURRELL
Charles 132
Francis 46, 63
BURRIDGE (Burbridge)
John 119

BURRIS (Burress)
Henry 6, 11, 66
Nathan 130
Rebecca 6
BURROUGHS
Jeremiah 6
BURTON
Abendego 110
BUSBEE (Busby - Busbey)
Samuel 133(2)
BUSBY (Bushey - Busbee)
Ann 99, 104
Benjamin 110
Elizabeth 110
Elizabeth 110
Hamilton 110
James 104, 127
John 6(2), 7(3), 40, 53, 66 (2), 89, 110, 125
John, Jr. 6
Margaret 6(2), 7(3), 110
Matthew 25, 110
Meredith 110
Samuel 110(2), 125, 133(2)
William 110
BUSH
Catherine 7
Elizabeth 124
Henry 89, 124
James McAlester 124
John 89
Lewis 89
Matthias 35, 36(2), 66(3)
Phillip 7(2), 11, 66
BUSSY (Bussey)
Eleanor 7(2), 52, 66
BUTCHER
Eve 89
James 29
John 10, 12, 29, 66, 86, 89, 112(2)
Paulsen 89
BUTE
Joseph 85
BUTLER (Buttler)
Elizabeth 137
John 137
Laurence 125
Richard 89
BUZBY see Busby & Busbey
John 89
BUZZARD (see Bubbers - Bupora)
Barbary 110
Elizabeth 110
Eliza 110
Esther 110
Eva 110
Everline 110
Fredrick 21, 66, 87, 110(2), 130
Fred, Sr. 121
Henry 89
Humel 110
Jacob 102, 110
John 89, 110(2)
Juda 110
Lucinda 117
Magdelene (Molly) 110
Mary Jenkins 121
Rudolph 26, 66, 89
Susan 110
Susannah 110
BYERLY
A. 31
BYRN (see Byrnes)
Barnet 89
Eleanor 7
John 89
Phillip 89
Richard 7, 5, 47, 53, 60(2), 128
BYZER (see Biser-Bizer)
Elizabeth 110
Jacob 110
CACKLEY
Abraham 104
Margaret 99, 104
CADE
Major 25, 66, 89
CADY
James 3
C'ID
Ephraim 114
CAIN
Catherine 113
Levi 113, 114
Micheal 28
CALAHAM (Callahan)
Charles 89
CALDWELL
Charles 111
I. 47
Joseph 59
Samuel 111(2)
CALE (may be Cole)
George 30 62
CALERMAN (Caterman)
Dan 89, 140
CALF (Metcalf)
James M. 89

CALHOUN
James, Jr. 52
CALLEHAN (Calahan)
Cassandra 111(2)
Charity 111
Jenny 111
John 111
CALMES 131
Catherine 111
F. 50
Fielding 12, 13, 19(2), 66, 111, 131(2)
George 111
Isabella (Isabelle) 111(2)
Lucy 111
Marquis 88, 89
Mary 111
William 8(2), 66
CALOS
Josiah 117
CALVIN (see Colvin) 140
Ann 19
John 134
Joshua 15, 42, 66(2), 85, 112(3)
Luther 134
Luther, Jr. 121
Robert 19(2), 66, 116, 140
Samuel 112
Stephen (Steven) 7(3), 44, 46, 52, 61, 66, 89, 109, 124(2), 129
Vincent 7, 124
CAMEL (Campbell)
Elizabeth 47
CAMPBELL
Andrew 48
Archable 45, 66
Eliz. 7(4), 45, 47, 111, 140
George 50
John 7(2), 11, 22, 32, 45 (2), 66, 89(2), 110, 122
John, Jr. 89
Patrick 115
Robert 7, 52, 66(2)
Rosanna 7
Rune (Runa-Runey) 7(2), 28, 51, 66(2)
Sarah 7, 45
Susanner 7(2)
Thomas 34, 47(2), 54, 66
Widow 186
William 5, 5, 6(3), 7(2), 23, 33(2), 34, 36, 37, 42, 45, 46, 47(3), 50, 54(2), 55(3), 66(2), 89
CANADA (see Kanada and Kennedy)
CANBY
Samuel 49, 66
CANDIFF (Caniff)
John 30
CANDY error for Caudy 140
David 89, 114
James 15(2), 33, 37
John 7, 30, 60, 66(2), 110
Martha 89
CANE (see Cain)
Gabriel 114
Mary 114
William 48
CANFIELD
Edgar W. 116
CANN (Caun)
Elizabeth 118
Jacob 100()
Jane, Mrs. 100
John 29, 39, 41, 66
Micheal 89
CANNON
John 7, 11, 66
Thomas 89
CANTER (Carter)
Henry 89
CANTIEN
Abraham 27, 66
CANTRELL
Christopher 89
CANTWELL
John 53
CAPELL
Littleton 89
CAPLENOR
Jacob 121
CAPLINGER
Jacob 89
John 7, 89
Lydia 7
C'PPER
Charles 103, 125, 130
Elizabeth 118, 122
Micheal 122
Priscilla 131
CAR (Carr - Kerr)
Henry, Sr. 89
CARABAUGH
Peter 89
C'RDER (see Carter)
Abbott 7, 66, 103

Ann 99, 192
Charlotte 99, 100
Elizabeth 7, 99, 105
George 99, 100, 101, 102, 105, 130
Jackson 129
John 7
Maria, Mrs. 99
Mary 99, 103
Sarah 7
Thomas 34
William 7(2), 26, 89, 110
CAREY (see Carrey)
CARLIN (Carline-Carlon)
Andrew 8(2), 89(2)
CARLISLE (Carlyle) 125
Ann 7, 89
Charles 27, 125
Elizabeth 99
Isaac 108
John 84, 66
Joseph 108
J. W. 119
Rebecca, Mrs. 99
Sally 119
William 3(2), 7, 25, 27, 35, 36, 47, 48, 66, 86, 89, 114, 121
William, Jr. 99, 102
William, Sr. 99
CARMAN
Joseph 33
CARELL (Carnell)
John 123
CARMICHEAL
Ann 111
Daniel 48, 110(3), 125(2), 134
Franklin 111
Hannah 100(2)
John 111, 125
Richard 100
Robert 109, 124, 127(2), 133, 134(2)
CARN (Corn)
Andrew 140
CARNELL (Carmell)
Thomas 113, 114
CARNEND
Leonard 26(2), 66(2)
CARPENTER (Carpender)
Ann 7
Conrod 90
Hannah, Mrs. 99
Jacob 90
John 7, 52, 66
Nicholas 12
Sudrah 120
William 99, 102
CARR (see Car & Cann or Kerr)
Conrod 99, 140
Henry, Sr. 140
James 138
John 90
Joseph 140
Jude 138
Margaret 138
Micheal 17, 66, 90
T. 5
Walter 99
William 90, 138
CARREY (Carey & Cary)
Catherine 107
Joseph 37, 66
Lydia 107
Micheal 107
Virginia 115
CARROLL (Carrole)
John 90
Joseph 37, 137
Pat 38
William 116
CARRUTHERS
George 16, 19, 25, 51, 68, 66, 90, 107, 121
George, Jr. 25
James 1, 3(2), 6, 7(2), 12 (3), 13(3), 26, 27, 41, 42, 46, 47(2), 49(2), 53(2), 66, 86, 90, 111, 120, 130, 134
Mary 7(2), 101, 111
Mary Ann 111
Ulary 120
CARSKADON (Carzkahadon - Carichadon - Cascadin)
Catherine 111
Elizabeth I. 111
Isaac H. 111
James 111, 114, 128
John Robert 111
Thomas 86, 107, 108(2), 111, 113(2), 114, 115, 117 (3), 110, 122(3), 124, 128(3), 131, 135, 136, 137(2)
Thomas R. 111
William 111
CARSON

INDEX

Barclay & Mitchell 6, 66
Thomas 23, 66
CARSWELL (Caswell)
Abigail 111
John 111
CARTER (Carder)
Albert 99(2), 104, 136
Benjamin 111
Betsy 111
Eleanor 111
Elizabeth 111
George 111
Grayson 111
Hannah 111
Henry 90, 135
James W. 108
John Tasker 111
Joseph 123
Judith 113
Mary, Mrs. 99, 112, 136
Robert 100, 103
Sophia, Mrs. 100
William 90
CARTRIGHT (Wright)
Henry 50
Peter 7(2)
Samuel 7(2), 11
Richard 7
CARY (see Carrey)
Joseph 37, 66
CASE
Sarah 99, 100
CASEY
Benjamin 7, 66, 139(2)
Grace 7
John 7, 66
Mary 7
Nicholas 2(2), 7(6), 11, 13
 (2), 19(2), 22, 35, 49
 (2), 63, 66(5), 90, 124,
 135
N. 19, 42
Patrick 137
Peter 7(5), 9, 17(5), 26, 27
 (2), 46, 49, 52, 61, 63,
 66(2), 90
Peter, Jr. 7, 48, 139(2)
William F. 132
CASLER
John 7(2), 66(2), 111(2)
James 111(2)
Micheal 7(2), 90, 111, 134
Sarah 111
CASNER
John 90
CASPER
John 66, 89
W. 120
CASSELMAN(N) (Castle-
man - Cassalman)
David 7, 8(2), 66, 110
Jacob 7, 8(3), 46, 61, 62,
 66(2), 90, 121, 129
Jemima 8
Lewis (Louis) 8(3), 24, 29,
 66, 90(2)
Ludwick 7(2)
Margaret 8(3)
William 8, 63
CASWELL (see Carswell)
John 8, 66
CATERMAN
Dan 140
CATHER
Hannah 116
Elizabeth 116
James 122(3)
John, Sr. 8
Jasper (Tasper) 4, 8(2), 66(2
Sarah 8
Thomas 8, 116
CATLITT
William 113
CAUDY (Candy-Canby)
Ann 111
David 89, 104, 111, 114, 125
 139
Evan 118
James 15(2), 33, 37, 86,
 110, 111, 118(2), 125
 (2), 130, 133, 139(2)
John 7, 30, 60, 66(2), 110
Joseph 118
Margaret 100, 104, 111
Martha 89, 111
Mary 111
Mary Eliz. 125
Micheal 125
Rebecca 111(3)
Sarah 100, 108, 111
CAUFMAN (Coffman see)
Adam 90
CAUGHNEY
Charlotte 129
CAULSON (see Cann)
Margaret 140
CAVENDER
Garrett 8, 41, 66
Janey 8
CENAS
Blaise 28

CESSNA
Margaret H., Mrs. 100
Samuel 100, 101
CHADWICK
J. F. 119
Jacob 2, 127
CHAMBERLIN
Nancy 108
Joseph B. 108
CHAMBERS
Benjamin 57
Christopher 49, 66
George 86
John 124
Nancy 108
Mary 124
CHAMP
Chris 8
John 8
Thomas 90
William 90
CHANDLER
Ellis 24, 66
Elizabeth 24, 66
Sarah 24, 66
CHAPLINE
Moses 49
CHAPMAN
Cattran 111
Dorety 111
Elizabeth 111, 125
Luke 90
Phoebe (Feby) 111
William 6, 24(2), 29, 52,
 56, 66(5), 85, 90,
 111, 139
CHASE
Samuel, Jr. 52
CHEESE (see Cheses)
Job 125
CHENEY
John 112
CHENOWITH (weth) (see
Chinoth, also Chinoweth)
Absolom 111, 121, 130
Arthur 90
Eleanor 111(2)
Elias 111(2)
Elijah 2
Elizabeth 111
James 111
Jane 8
John 3, 6, 8(7), 10(2), 24
 (4), 33(2), 37, 50, 56
 (2), 66(5), 85, 90, 111,
 121, 127(2), 128, 130,
 131, 134
John, Jr. 4, 6, 8(3), 66(2),
 90
John, Sr. 90
Jonathan 32, 90
Joseph 37
Mary 8(5), 111
Rachel 111
Richard 118
Sarah 124(2)
William 8, 111, 118
CHERRY
Andrew 41, 66, 90
Eveline 117
Jane 131
CHESE (see Cheese)
Samuel 136, 139
CHESHIRE
Ann 90
Axhsa 111
Barbary 111((2)
Benjamin 123
Catherine Ann 111
Delilah 100, 104, 111
Delila, Mrs. 100
Elias 111
Franklin 111
James 111
Joel 111(2), 114
John 15, 66, 100(2), 104,
 111, 129
Juliet Ann 111
Margaret 111
Maria 111
Maris 111
Mary 111
Mary, Mrs. 111
Mary Ann 111
Nancy 111(2)
Obadiah 111(2)
Perry 111
Rachel 111
Rebecca 111
Samuel 39, 86, 90, 100, 108,
 111(4)
Sarah 111(2)
Uriah 111(2), 129, 130, 132
William 111(2)
CHESTER
Thomas 56
CHESTERTON
John 90
CHESTNUT
Alexander 8, 56
James 8(2), 19, 56(2), 66

John 8(2), 56(2), 66, 135
CHEW
Benjamin 8(2), 38, 21(2)
Colby 12, 66, 114
H. 133
James 4, 59
Robert 39(2)
CHILCOTT
Aaron 124
Eber 90
Eli 90
Jesse 122
Joel 90
Mary 90
CHILDERS
William 90
CHINN
Helen 137
Samuel 137
Susan 137
CHINOWETH (Chenowith)
John 90
John, Sr. 90
John, Jr. 90
Jonathan 90
CHINOTH
John 15, 66
CHISHOLM (Chrisholm)
Alexander 8(8), 134
John 8, 66
Mary 8(8)
William 1(2)
CHISLER
Eleanor 106
CHISWELL
Mary 128
CHITTON (Critton)
John 90
CHOPPER
Jacob 99
CHRISHOLM (see Chis-
holm)
CHRISMAN (Crisman)
Adam 90
Conrad 90
Issac 8(2), 36, 66
Jacob 8(5), 56, 57, 90(2)
Jacob, Jr. 8, 14
Jane 8(2), 125
Magdelena 8
Mary 8(3), 57
Phillip 90
Phillip, Jr. 90
Phillip, Sr. 90
Rebecca 8(2)
CHRISTIAN
Edward 52
CHRISTIE
James 90
CHURCH
Baptist Church 50, 78
Pres. 50, 78
CHURCHILL
H. 27(3), 30, 39, 50, 60(2)
CINNAMON
Martha 132
CLANCY
William 54
CLARK (Clarke)
Abraham 8(2), 13, 18, 35,
 50, 90
Abraham, Jr. 8, 90
Ambrose 38, 66
Bazilla 12
Catherine 123
Charles H. 101
Daniel 118(2), 140
Esther 8, 133
Henry 8, 9, 66, 90
Jas. 1, 8(2), 16(3), 20, 30
 (2), 31(6), 48, 66(4), 116,
 121
Jean 133
John 9, 16, 41, 66, 90, 140
Jonathan 26, 66
Mary 107
Massey 9
Robert 9, 17, 66, 90, 140
Ruby 9
Samuel 10
Stephen 9, 90
Thomas 9, 27, 42, 44
Watson 9, 60, 66, 90
William 102
CLARKSON
Thomas 107
CLATON (see Clayton)
John 35, 66
Polly Brown 110
CLAWSON
Israel 53
CLAY
James M. 118
CLAYPOOL (Claypoole -
Claypole)
Abraham 90
Abigail 9(2)
Blondius 9
Fanny (Tramey) 139
Fredrick 33
George 90, 113, 139

James 13, 22, 67(2), 90
James, Jr. 36, 44, 67
James, Sr. 9, 57, 67(2), 90
Jeremiah 9(2), 33, 90, 122
 (2)
Jesse 90
John 13, 36, 54, 67(2), 90,
 123
Joseph 8, 9(2), 67
Nathaniel 122
CLAYTON (see Claton)
John 123
Mary 9(2)
Polly B. 110
Thomas 9(2), 38, 56(2), 90
Tow 115
Townsend 109
William C. 111
CLEAVER
Ellis 9
Ezekiel 9(2)
John 138
Peter 9(2), 67
Sarah 9
CLEIZER - Clisher-Cliesher
Christian 115
Eliz 9
Jacob 9
Joseph 9(3), 62
CLIFFORD
James 90
CLIFT
Mahala 115
CLINE (see Kline-Clyne)
Abraham 111
Anthony 111
Elizabeth 111
Jacob 10, 67, 111
James 111
John 111
Joseph 111(2)
Katy 138
Mary 111, 138
Mary Jane 111
Micheal 111
Phillip 7, 111(2), 121, 138
 (2)
Rebecca 111
Sarah 111
Stephen 111
CLING (Clung-McClung)
William 108
CLINTOCK (see Lintock &
McClintock)
Robert M. 90
CLINTON
Charles 9(2), 27, 53, 67(2)
John 2, 27
Mary 27
CLISER see Cleiser-Clisher
Joseph 9
CLISHER (see Cliser)
Elizabeth 9
Joseph 9, 35, 67
CLOUD
Isaac 36
CLURLAND
Eli 9
CLUTTER
Ann 111
Caroline 111
Eliza F. 111
Harriet Rozanne 111
Jacob 90, 124, 133(2)
John 125
Jos. 102, 111, 127, 128, 131
Joseph C. 131
Joseph P. 111, 128
Margaret J. 111
Mary 111
Nancy 111
Peggy Ann 111
Rebecca C. 111
Sarah 111
CLYNE see Cline & Kline
Jacob 10, 67
COAKLEY
Benjamin 125
COATES
Edward 6, 67
Joseph S. 49
COBERLY
James Stell 8, 27, 28, 44, 67
Mary 8
COBUN (Coban)
Catherine 9(2)
Jonathan 9(2), 31, 57, 60
 (2), 67
COBURN
Jonathan 138
COCHRAN (Cochrane-Coc-
krane - Conchron - Cockh-
rane)
Edward 56, 67
Elizabeth 14
James 9(3), 14, 18, 21, 32,
 44, 49, 53(2), 62, 67(3)
John 9
Mary 9
Simon 9, 90
Susanna 9, 90

Thrusby and Cochran 25, 67
William 3, 32, 67
COCKBURN
Robert 6, 37
COCKE (Cox - Cook)
Christopher 9, 63
Moses 32, 67
COCKENOW
Catherine, Mrs. 100
Henry 100, 104
COCKERILL see Cockswell
Samuel 108, 117(3), 121,
 124, 133, 136
COCKEWELL see Cockswell
William S. 111
Samuel 113, 119, 133
COCKSWELL see Cockerell
 & Cockewell-Cockwell
Jane 111, 119
Samuel 111, 119, 133(2), 136
Spencer 111
Susan 111
Thomas 111
William S. 111
COCKWILL
Jan 122
CODY (Cady-Caid)
James 107
COE
James, Mrs. 100
Sarah 128
Wesley 100, 101
COFFMAN
Abraham 119
John 136
COHOON
John 48
COKELEY (Cackley)
David 137
COL (Colvin)
Margaret 106
S. 106
COLENS (see Collins)
COLES (Cale)
Frances 90
George 30, 62, 67, 111
John 63(2)
COLLENS see Collins
Eben 106
Elisha 90
COLLIER (Collyer)
Isaac 10
John 9
Mary 10
Micheal 20, 67, 133
COLLINS (Collins - Col-
lings-Cullins-Colens) 127
Ann 127
Catherine 10
Cassandra 111
Daniel 7, 9(4), 13, 15, 27,
 49, 67, 111(2), 130, 135
 (2), 139
David 25(2), 50
Eben 106
Ebenezer 99, 102
Elizabeth 10, 111
Elisha 9, 18, 23, 85, 90
Guy M. 100
Hannah 9
Jean 9
Jenny 111
Jno. 5, 9(4), 27, 30(2), 42(2)
 48, 50, 52, 62, 67, 111, 131
John I. 23
Luke 5(2), 9(11), 10, 14,
 22, 24, 26, 27, 29(3), 30,
 36(2), 46(3), 47, 56, 63
 (2), 67(4), 127, 130
Margaret, Mrs. 100
Mary 7, 125
Moses 100, 104
Nancy 127
Ruth 10, 110
Samuel 2, 67
Sarah 9(7), 10
Thomas 6(2), 7, 9(3), 10
 (5), 11, 12(2), 15(2), 16,
 21(2), 22, 23, 26, 44,
 46, 47, 49, 56, 67(5), 85,
 90, 109, 110, 116, 120,
 121, 124(2)
Thomas Jr. 111
Thomas, Sr. 111
T. 29, 57
Timothy 10
COLLIS (Collins)
Daniel 130
COLLONS
Mary 125
COLLYER (Colyer-Collier)
COLSON see Colston-Coul-
son-Caulson
John 10
Margaret 10
COLSTON (Colstone-Coul-
son-Colson)
Jacob 111
John 10, 111
Margaret 10, 111, 140
Rawleigh 1, 15, 40, 67(2)

COLVIN see Calvin - Col
Barbara 33
James 33
Joshus 19, 67
Luther 86
Margaret 106
Robert 90
Samuel 86, 134
S. 106
COLYER see Collier
Isaac 10
Mary 10
COMBS
Arthur 106
Billy or Bilby 130
Daniel 1, 54, 67, 112
David 10, 112
Frances 55, 67, 90, 112
Jacob 5
James 104
John 10, 37, 67, 110, 112, 138
Jonas 10, 67, 112, 116
Jonathan 112
Joseph 10
Margaret 110
Martha 10, 112
Mary 112
Moses 112
Rosannah 123
Sarah 100, 104
Thomas 6(2), 10, 41, 56, 67 (2), 90, 112
COMLINSON (Tomilison)
Jesse 27
COMPSTON
Henry 61, 67
CONKENOW (Cokenow - Cockenow)
Catherine 100
Henry 100, 104
CONKLIN
Ann 3
Annanias 10, 51, 67
Jacob 10, 43, 57, 59, 67
Susanna 10
CONLEY (Connley)
Margaret 112
CONLON
Anna 127
James 127
CONNARD(S) (Cunnard - Cunard - Cunnrad)
Hester 10
James 10, 12, 13, 112
James, Jr. 10, 11, 13, 90
James, Sr. 90
CONNELLY (See Conley)
Catherine 112
John 110
John Patrick 112
Margaret 112
CONNER (Connor)
Baldwin 118
Cornelius 1, 10(2), 51, 58, 67
Daniel 90
Elizabeth 123
Ephraim 114
Margaret 10
Susan 90
Thomas 90
CONOWAY
Thomas 188
CONRAD (Conrod - see Connards)
Daniel 38(2)
Edward 38
Fredrick 5, 10, 30, 37, 67
Hester 10(2)
James 10, 30(2), 67
James Jr. 10, 67
James, Sr. 10
Jean 10
John 38, 49, 67, 90
CONSTABLE
Caty 113
Josiah 137, 138
CONSTANT (Constent - Constart)
John 10(4), 33(2), 39, 41, 43, 67, 90, 113, 123, 138, 139
Elizabeth 10(2)
CONSTART see Constant
John 67
COOKE (Cookes)
Alice 10(2)
Henry 184
L. 50
William 7, 10(2), 23, 32, 47, 49, 51(2), 67(3)
COOKER (see Cooper)
Thomas 10(2)
COOKLEY (Cokley - Cookley)
David (Cavid) 118
COOKSEY
William 130
COOL
Ann 132

Catherine 10, 100, 101, 112 (3)
Elizabeth 132
Harbut (Herbert) 10, 43, 67(2), 101, 112(4), 132
Jacob 112(2), 132(2)
Lydia 112
Nancy 112
Paul 112
Phillip 2(2), 10, 11, 67(3), 112(3)
Polly 112
Rebecca 112
William 112
COON (Coone-Coones)
David 32, 46, 90
Joseph 90
Lorey 90, 140
Peter 90
COOPER (Cowper)
Adam 112(2), 123
Andrew 10(2), 20, 23, 31 67(2), 85
Ann, Mrs. 100, 127
Catherine 100, 101, 112(2)
Caty (Katy) 112
Charles 112(2)
Christian 112(2)
David 10
Elender 112
Elizabeth 112(2)
E. P. 108
George 10, 32, 48, 67(2)
Jacob 100, 102, 112
Jacob Rutman 112(2)
Job 90
Joel 10, 90, 112
John 112, 119
Joseph 10
Joul 112
Kety 112
Margaret 112(3)
Mary 112(6)
Martin 101
Rachel (Reachel) 112
Rebecca(y) 10(3), 112(2), 114
Sally 112
Samuel 108, 112
Sarah 112
Solomon 112
Stephen 54
Thomas 7, 10(3), 23, 39, 67, 90, 112, 126
Thomas, Jr. 10, 67
Thomas, Sr. 10
Valentine 48, 67, 90
COPSEY
Ann D. 112
John Vanburen 46, 112
John 1, 4, 6, 7, 8(2), 10 (5), 12, 18, 33, 41, 46(2), 60(2), 61, 112, 119, 127, 131, 138, 139
Lucindy M. 112
Martin 112
Mary (see Mary Rector) 112
Sarah 10(4)
Sally 112
CORBAN (Coban)
David 116
CORBIN (Corban see Cobun)
Amelia 112
Anderson 3, 10, 67
Ann 90
Alsy 112(2)
Bathsheba (Bersheba) 11 (8), 112
Benjamin 100(2), 104
Catherine, Mrs. 100, 135
Charles 90
Cornelius 100, 104
Daniel 10, 11, 38, 67, 112
David 8, 10, 11(10), 67(2), 90, 100, 107, 112, 116
Elizabeth 112
Humphrey 112
Israel 112
Jane 10, 11
John 39, 100
John, Sr. 43
Jonah 129
Mildred 112
Nancy 116
Parthenia, Mrs. 100
Susannah 11(2)
William 11(3), 13(3), 15, 41, 42(2), 43, 67(3), 90 (2), 112
Winney 100(2)
CORBLY (Corbley)
John 11, 15(2)
CORBUS
Richard 14
CORCHRANE see Cochrane Cochran
CORDER
Ann 112
Betsy (or Lety) 112
Charlotty 112

George, Jr. 112
Judith 112
Lety 112
Mary Ann 112
William 112
CORE (Cox)
George 11(2)
COREY (Cary)
Joseph 29(2), 67
CORN (Carn)
Andrew 11, 39, 67(2), 90
Edward E. 52
Hannah 11
Timothy 10, 22, 36, 49(2) 47, 67, 126
William 11
CORNET (Cornnet)
Nancy 134
CORNMAN
John 5, 52, 67
CORNWELL
Enoch 1, 9, 11, 12, 67
CORY (Corey - Carey)
Joseph 11, 29, 90
COSSY (Casey - Cossey)
Peter 127
COSGROVE (see Posgrove)
COTRALL (Cotrel)
David 49
Elizabeth 90
COTTELL
David 28
COUCHMAN (Cushman)
Adam 133
COUCHRON (Cochran)
Elizabeth 14
COUDEN (Coudin)
James 55, 67
James, Sr. 90
James, Jr. 90
COULSHINE
Ernest 18
COULSHIRE (Coulshine)
Ernest 18, 112
Elizabeth 112
Henry 112
John 112
Lottie 112
COULSON Colston - Coulson
John 90, 140
Margaret 90
COULTER
Thomas 61
COUTHER
Thomas 42
COUTZMAN
Adam 90
COVERT
Bergen 11
Chirche 11
COWAN (Cowens)
Lydia 4, 112
Robert 4, 10, 28, 67, 112
William 112
COWENS (Cowan)
Robert 28, 67
COWERDEN
Susan 112
COWFELT
Henry 90
Phillip 90
COWGER
David 90
George 12, 67
COWGILL (Cowgile)
Catherine 122
Elisha 13(2), 24, 67
Frances 118
Susan 110
COWPER (see Cooper)
Edward 25
Job 90
COWICK (Cowhick)
Thomas 123
COX(E) (Core - Cocke)
David 11, 21, 35
Eleanor 11
Friend 11(2)
Gabriel 11(4)
George 11, 48
Hannah 112
Isaac 11, 12, 21(2), 22, 35, 67(2), 112
John 3(2), 11
John A. 112, 121
John Abbe 124
Mary 11(2)
Sarah 11(2)
Susannah 11
Thomas 112
William, Jr. 4, 37(2)
CRABBE
Anna 120
Abigail 110
Isaac 110
Jonathan 110
Joseph 110
Nancy 110
CRABTREE
Micheal 136

CRACKEY
Ruth 123
CRACRAFT (Creacraft - Craycraft)
Joseph 11
Thomas 90
William 11(2)
CRAGE (Craig - Craike)
David 123
Dr. 108
CRAIG (Crage - Craik(e)- Creagh - Craige) 118
David 90, 123
George 11, 18, 60
James 2, 11(2), 13, 31, 40, 57, 67(2)
James, Dr. 7, 67
John 8, 13
Doctor 107
Mary Ann 11
Marianne 11
Samuel 40(3), 60, 67
CRAM
Eleanor 11
John 11, 111
CRAMER (see Creamer)
CRAMPTON
Jane 100, 102
CRAVINE
Joseph 53, 67
CRAWFORD
Jane 11
Rachel 128
Val. 21
William 90, 119, 133
CRAWLES (IS)
Nicholas 14, 67
CRAY (see Gray)
Simon 7
CRAYCRAFT (Cracraft - Crecraft - Crecroft)
Joseph 90
Thomas 90
William 11(2), 67
CREAGH (see Craig)
John 13
CREAGUR
Jacob 18, 59(2), 67
CREAMER (Creamour)
G. 60
George 6, 134
Mary 1, 11(3), 67
CRECRAFT see Craycraft - Cracraft
Charles 39
Eunice 11(2)
Joseph 4, 11(3), 12, 67, 138
Margaret 4, 67
Sarah 4, 67
Thomas 90
William 4, 11, 15(2), 67
CREEGAN (Crogan)
James 112
CREETCHFIELD see Crutchfield - Cretchfield)
Benjamin 11
Joseph 11
Mary 11
CRESAP (Crisip)
Daniel 11, 35, 61, 67(2), 120, 124
Daniel, Jr. 28
James 56, 112
Joseph 111, 135
Elizabeth 12(2)
Margaret 12(2)
Mary 11(2), 112(2)
Mary Elizabeth 112
Mr. 6
Micheal 11(4), 12(6), 19, 22, 28, 44, 51, 54(2), 56, 63, 67(5), 88, 90, 112
Micheal Col. 6, 67
Micheal, Sr. 11(2), 12(2)
Micheal, Jr. 54
P. 120
Rebecca 124
Ruth 11
Sarah 112
Thomas 11(4), 12(3), 19, 26, 28, 42, 44, 46, 56, 63, 67(2), 112
Thomas, Col. 12(2), 139
CRESSWELL
Abraham 107(2), 111, 129
Adam 126
James 128, 130
John 128
Samuel 130
CREYMOUR (Creamour)
Mary 1, 67
CRIM
Rosannah 138
CRISHOLM see Chisholm
CRISMAN (Christman - Cristman)
Conrad 28
Jacob, Jr. 14
Phillip 55, 67
CRIST
Hannah 12

Jacob 12
CRITCHELOW see Crutchlow
CRITCHFIELD (Creelchfield and Crutchfield)
Amos 139
CRITES
Jacob 90
Phillip, Sr. 90
Phillip, Jr. 90
CRITTON
Barbara 12
Elizabeth, Mrs. 99
Isaac 99, 100
John 10, 12, 22, 36, 55(2), 56, 67, 90, 113
John, Jr. 12(3), 53, 56
John, Sr. 12, 90
Tatiska 12
William 12, 14, 53, 67(2), 90, 101, 116(2)
CROCK
Ann Elizabeth 112
Barbara 12(2), 112
David 52
George 10, 12(2), 35, 52(2), 67(2), 68, 90, 112
John 12, 49, 52, 68
CROMPTON (Crampton)
Henry 32
CROMWELL
Thomas 31
CRONFIN
Nancy 123
CROOK
John 21
CROOKHART Brookhart
Abraham 115
CROSS (Croose)
Christian 29, 68, 90
Eliza 128
Gassaway 128
Nancy 111
Washington 111
CROS(S)LEY
Abel 32, 33, 90, 112
Henry 7
Johanna 7, 12, 112
John 28, 68, 112, 113(2) 116
Joseph 116
CROW
David 90
John 118
CRUMPTON see Crompton and Crampton
Jane 128(2)
CRUMRINE
Christian 12, 68
CRUTCHLOW Critchelow
John 12, 21, 68
William 90
CRUTCHFIELD see Creetchfield - Cretchfield
CRYDER (Crider)
John 42, 68
CUBBERLY
James 90, 140
CUDDING
John 90
CUISCO
Fredrick 14(3), 29, 37
CULL
William 106
CULLINS (Collins)
John 42, 61, 90
CULP
Amos 113(2), 136
Ann 113
Clara Isabel 113
Dennis 113(2)
Edward 113
Elizabeth 113(2)
Elijah 113
Garrett 113
George 113
James 113(2)
John 103, 113(2)
John, Jr. 99, 100
John, Sr. 113
Maria 100, 103, 113
Nancy 113
Rachel, Mrs. 100
Randle 113
Sally 113
Sally 113
CUMP (Klump)
Henry 98
Juliet 133
CUNDIFF (Cuniff)
Alley (Allender) 113
Alex 113
Anna 114
Benjamin 113
Catherine Nash 100, 102
Elizabeth 100, 101
Hannah 113
Henry 100(2), 101
James 102
John 12, 48(3), 68, 98, 101, 102, 104, 113

INDEX

John, Jr. 117
John, Sr. 126, 137
Layton S. 113
Milly 100(2)
Nancy 100, 104
Oliver 101
Sally 12, 137
Wesley 137
CUNNARD (Cunard - Connard)
James 12, 90
James, Jr. 11
CUNNINGHAM
Alexe 9
Catty 129
David 137
Deborah 12
Derna 126
Elizabeth 122
Eliz. J. 137(2)
Harress 123
Isaac 137
Israel 10, 106
James 48, 49, 68, 90, 113, 121, 122, 134
Jessee 34, 137, 139
John 12, 16, 63, 68, 90(2) 116, 133, 134
Mary 106, 116
Pheby 12
Rebecca 139
Robert 8, 13, 17, 34, 68(3), 90, 128
Sally 137
Sarah 122
Wm. 9(2), 12(2), 59, 68(2), 90(2), 115, 119, 122, 128
William, Jr. 12, 68, 90
William, Sr. 12, 90
CUPPY
Elizabeth 122
John 12(2), 26, 45, 68(2), 90(2), 126
John, Jr. 12(2), 22, 68
Margaret 12(2)
CURLATT (Curlett)
Catherine 113(2)
Christiana 100, 102, 113
Eliz. 113(2)
John 113(2)
Margaret 113
Mary 100, 102, 113(2), 128
Marey 113
Walter 102
William 102(2), 113, 128
CURLE
Jeremiah 12, 90
Mary 12
William 90
James 128
Jean 100, 101
Jane 132
CURTIS
Job 27, 41, 106
CURTRIGHT (see Cutright)
Samuel C. 17, 26, 119
CUTHBERT
William 33
CUTRACK
Henry 90
John 90
Sam 90
CUTRIGHT (Curtright)
Peter 1
Samuel 17, 68, 90
Samuel C. 17, 26, 119
CUTTER
Cornelius 118
Eleanor 118
DAILY (see Dailey - Daley Dayley)
Betsy 117
Comfort 135
Elizabeth 12, 138
Hugh 118
Jacob 106, 118
James 2, 6, 7(2), 9(2), 10, 12(5), 14, 15, 21, 23, 26, 27, 29, 34, 38(3), 42, 44(2), 45, 46, 47, 48, 51, 54, 57(6), 58, 61(2), 62, 68(7), 110(3), 114(2), 118 (2), 127, 132(3), 133, 134, 138(2)
Jane 113
John 12, 36, 68, 113, 127
Rhoda 127
Robert W. 119, 128
Samuel 57, 113
Thomas (see Hailey) 86
Widow 128
William see Daily 90
DALE
James 11
DALIS
James 124
DALL (see Doll - Dull)
James 36(3), 68(3)
DALTON (see Daulton and Dolton)
John 34, 68

DANGERFIELD
Henry 87
DANFORD
Peter 12, 30, 68
DANHAM
John 85
Stephen 16
DANIELS
Catherine 106, 113
Dennis 5, 32, 56, 68(2), 106 (2), 113, 130, 136
Jacob 122
Jacob P. 113, 122, 123
John 113
Mary 90
Rachel 113
Thos. 113(3), 121, 130, 136 (2)
William 90
DANLEY (see Don(n)elly)
Elizabeth 111
DANMETERE (Van?)
Henry 58, 82
DANSON (Dawson?)
John 85
DARBY
Jacob 114
John, Jr. 112
DARLING
Robert 121(2)
Sarah 121(2)
Sophia 127
William 83, 90, 127
William, Jr. 90
DARLINGTON (Darlinton)
J. 27(2)
Joseph 43
Meredith 139
DASHER
Christian 12(2), 90
Elizabeth 12(2)
DATON (see Dayton - Deaton)
Isaac 85, 109, 139
Jean 45
John 34, 45, 49, 61, 68, 132
Roland S. 122
William 57, 60, 132
DAUGHERTY (see Dougherty and Dorety)
E. E. 112(2)
James 28, 31, 33, 68, 139
James Vance 111(2)
Sally 112
DAULTON (Dalton)
Mary 112
DAVEY
William 37, 68
DAVID
Elijah 128
DAVIDSON (Davison)
Hezakiah 130
James, Jr. 136
DAVIS
Absolem 113
Alfred 113
Alice 12
Anna 12, 113(3)
Attelia 113
Augustus 90
Catherine 113
David 113
Ebenezer 2
Eleanor, Mrs. 100
Eli 12, 19, 21, 29, 35(2), 42, 44, 46(2), 61, 68
Elijah 1(2), 2(2), 24, 68, 90, 111, 113(2)
Eliza Ann 113
Elizabeth 7, 113
Enos 38
Feliz 100, 104
George 5
Granville 113
Gustan 1, 68
Henry 36, 68
Jane 113
James 44, 68, 100, 105, 133, 136
Jared 33
Jesse 109
Jethrow 113
John 12, 44, 48, 68, 90, 113
Joseph 114, 137, 140
Joseph Warters 113
Mary 12, 113, 114
Merian 113
Nancy 113(2), 128
Nancy Baker 113
Peter 131
R. 118
Rachel 12
Richard 117
Ruben(in) 107(3), 113(2), 114, 117(2), 121, 136
Sam 12, 50, 57, 60(2), 68, 90, 107, 108(2), 122(4), 133(2)
Sam B. 98, 120
Sam B., Sr. 113

Sarah 107, 113
Sarah C., Mrs. 100
Sarah Matilda 113
Spencer 98
Susan M. 131, 133
Susan Virginia 138
Theophilus 90
Thomas 12, 90, 108(2), 113 (2), 117, 140
Walter 57, 68
William 5, 12, 115, 120, 135
DAVISON (error Dawson) 140
Abraham 90, 140
David 90, 140
Edith 12(2)
Isaac 90, 140
Jacob 90
James 12
Josiah 12
DAWSON (see Davison & Davidson)
Abraham 12, 28, 68, 113(2), 138, 139, 140
Ann 109
Ary 113
Betsy 118
David 12(3), 68, 140
Elizabeth 8, 12(2), 138
Isaac 10, 12, 68, 113(3), 138, 140
Israel 113(2)
Jacob 12, 68, 138
James 12
Mary 12, 68
Ruth 126
Sally 113
Sibyl 12
Teeny 113
Thomas 13, 16(3), 109, 125, 138
William 138
DAVY
Catherine 110
Stephen 110
DAY
Amat (Armat) 104
Amy 1, 106
Amey 118
Amery 7
Ann, Mrs. 100, 106
John 118
Larkin 118(2)
Leonard 90
Lewis 13(2), 14
Nancy 118
Nancy Brown 110
Wheny 29
Winny 13
William 10, 38, 47, 56, 118
DAYLEY (see Dailey)
Samuel 57
DAYTON (see Daton-Deaton)
Isaac 13, 42, 68
John 13(2), 14
Mary 42
Rebecca 124
Roland 118
Susannah 90
DEADRICK (Dedrick and Dietrich)
David 7, 26
George Micheal 13(3)
John 13(3)
DEAKINS
Francis 3, 10, 13, 22, 26, 29, 40, 49, 62, 68(8), 86, 113 (2)
Leonard 113
Leonard M. 113
William 10, 12, 22, 26, 29, 40, 62, 68(8), 86, 113
William Francis 113
William, Jr. 1, 13, 49, 62
DEALE (Dale - Beale?)
James 11, 68
DEAN (Deane)
Anne 100(2), 113
Dan 90, 113
Elinor 118
Elizabeth 113
Henry 113
Jane 13, 118
John 113(2)
Joshua 90
Margaret 113
Mary 113
Nathan 113
Ruth 114
Sarah Ann 114
Susannah 90
Thomas 5, 6, 25, 68(2), 90, 113(2), 139
Thomas, Jr. 13, 68
Thomas, Sr. 13(3)
William 113
DEAT (Dent)
Thomas 36
DEATON (see Daton - Day-

ton)
Isaac 13, 90
Mary 13
DEAVER (see Deever - Devore - Duver) 101
Aley 102
George 13, 15, 48, 68(2)
John 13, 127
Jonathan 13
Lucinda 118
Mary 13
DE BAUFRE (Debaufre)
James 28
DE BUTTS
Joshua 7
Samuel 40
DECKER (Deckar)
Barbara 33, 68
Cathran 13
Diana 13(2)
Garret 13, 137
Hannah 13(2)
Isaac 126
John 9, 13(5), 24, 32(3), 33, 63, 68(6), 90, 108, 110, 117, 122, 126
Luke 9(2), 13, 68
Nicholas 21
Sam 127
Sarah 13
DEDRICK see Deadrich
DEER
George 56
DEEVEER see Deaver
Loyd 125
Richard 129
DEEWALD
Nicholas 6, 68
DEITRICH see Deatrich
David 26
DELANO
Samuel 114
DELANY
Emaly 118
Patrick 28, 38, 68
DELHAM
James 126
DELM
John 90
DELONGA
John 90
DELOZEA
John 90
DEMONNER (Le Monnier)
J. I. 23
DEMOSE see Demoss
William 7, 13(2), 39
DEMOSS (Demose)
Catherine 13
John 13(5), 90
Lewis 13(2)
Martha 13(2)
Mary 90
Rachel 13(2)
Thomas 90
Wm. 13(7), 90
DEMSOE (likely Demose)
William 39
DENANNA
Mary 112
Patrick 112
DENHAM
Guin 13
John 13(2), 35, 68, 90, 91
DENNON
William 24
DENOZE
John 133
DENT
Thomas 13, 22(2), 24, 36 (2)
DENTON
Elizabeth 13(3)
Jacob 13(5), 50, 68, 91, 113 (3)
Jane 13(5), 91, 113
John 13(2), 68, 89, 91, 113
Robert 13(6), 35, 52, 68, 113(2)
Thomas 13(6), 34, 68(2), 91, 113
DERMOT (Dermott)
James R. 32
DEVAULT (Devolt)
Andrew 139
DEVEAR (see Deever - Devore)
John 91
DEVER
E. P. 140
John 13
William 139
DEVENCMUN (see Evecmon - Devrecmon)
Hannah 16(2)
P. 43
Peter 16(2)
DEVOE
John 91
E. P. 140
DEVOLT

ton)
Isaac 13, 90
Mary 13
DEAVER (see Deever - Devore - Duver) 101
Aley 102
George 13, 15, 48, 68(2)
John 13, 127
Jonathan 13
Lucinda 118
Mary 13
DE BAUFRE (Debaufre)
James 28
DE BUTTS
Joshua 7
Samuel 40
DECKER (Deckar)
Barbara 33, 68
Cathran 13
Diana 13(2)
Garret 13, 137
Hannah 13(2)
Isaac 126
John 9, 13(5), 24, 32(3), 33, 63, 68(6), 90, 108, 110, 117, 122, 126
Luke 9(2), 13, 68
Nicholas 21
Sam 127
Sarah 13
DEDRICK see Deadrich
DEER
George 56
DEEVEER see Deaver
Loyd 125
Richard 129
DEEWALD
Nicholas 6, 68
DEITRICH see Deatrich
David 26
DELANO
Samuel 114
DELANY
Emaly 118
Patrick 28, 38, 68
DELHAM
James 126
DELM
John 90
DELONGA
John 90
DELOZEA
John 90
DEMONNER (Le Monnier)
J. I. 23
DEMOSE see Demoss
William 7, 13(2), 39
DEMOSS (Demose)
Catherine 13
John 13(5), 90
Lewis 13(2)
Martha 13(2)
Mary 90
Rachel 13(2)
Thomas 90
Wm. 13(7), 90
DEMSOE (likely Demose)
William 39
DENANNA
Mary 112
Patrick 112
DENHAM
Guin 13
John 13(2), 35, 68, 90, 91
DENNON
William 24
DENOZE
John 133
DENT
Thomas 13, 22(2), 24, 36(2)
DENTON
Elizabeth 13(3)
Jacob 13(5), 50, 68, 91, 113(3)
Jane 13(5), 91, 113
John 13(2), 68, 89, 91, 113
Robert 13(6), 35, 52, 68, 113(2)
Thomas 13(6), 34, 68(2), 91, 113
DERMOT (Dermott)
James R. 32
DEVAULT (Devolt)
Andrew 139
DEVEAR (see Deever - Devore)
John 91
DEVER
E. P. 140
John 13
William 139
DEVENCMUN (see Evecmon - Devrecmon)
Hannah 16(2)
P. 43
Peter 16(2)
DEVOE
John 91
E. P. 140
DEVOLT

Andrew 113
Caty 113
Eliza 113
Elizabeth 113
Rebecca 113
DEVRECMON (see Evecmon - Devecmon)
Leon W. 121
DEVORE see Duver
Cornelius 26
DEW
Anna 114
Betty 5, 6, 9, 13, 23, 28, 30, 33, 44, 58
Betty Ann 113
Betsy Ann 113
Eam (Sam) 43
Joanna 128
John L. 114
Sam 1(2), 2(4), 3, 4(5), 5 (3), 6(2), 8(6), 9(5), 10 (3), 11(4), 12(2), 13(4), 14(3), 15(3), 19(2), 21 (5), 22(3), 23(2), 24(2), 25(2), 26(3), 27(2), 28(3), 29(2), 30(6), 31(2), 32 (5), 33(3), 34(2), 35, 36 (2), 37, 40(2), 41(3), 42, 43(2), 44(9), 45(5), 46 (4), 47, 48, 49, 50, 51, 52, 54, 55, 56, 58, 60, 63, 110, 121, 128
Sam, Jr. 4, 14, 25
Sarah 113(2)
Susan 113, 122
Susannah 113, 122
Wm. Harrison 113
DEWIT (see D'Witt)
Charles 27
Peter 91
DEYEA
Charles, Jr. 91
Charles, Sr. 91
D'WITT (see Dewitt)
Charles 27
DICK (Dicks)
Elisha 59
Elisha C. 29, 37, 68, 86
Elisha Cullen 14(4), 29, 37, 68(2)
Hannah 14(3)
Mary 100(2)
Nicholas 20, 68, 108
Peter 100
DICKEN
Amos 6, 68
DICKENSON (Dickinson)
Jacob 91
John 91
DICKSON (see Dixon)
George 91
DIE (Dye)
Rachel 127
DIETRICH (see Deadrick)
DILLY (see Ditty)
DIM(M)IT(T)
Ezekiel 60(2)
John 60(2), 68(2)
Moses 28(2), 49, 60(2), 61, 68(3)
DINNETT
Samuel 38, 54, 57, 58, 68
DISCON (Dixon)
Jno 28
DITTY (Dilly)
Sam 120
DIXON (Discon - Dickson)
Garret V. 138
John 4, 8, 14, 16(5), 32, 37(2), 39, 55, 60, 61, 120, 121
Jonathan 138
Joseph 133, 137
Maddelene 120
Rachel 135
Thomas 16(2), 91, 124
Thomas Jr. 124
William 109
DOBBINS (Dobins)
Ann 113
Esabel 113(2)
Elizabeth 14, 113
Jackson 113
John 113(3)
Johnson 113(2)
July 113
Martin 113
Mary 118
Nancy 113(2)
Samuel 86, 113(5)
Sarah 113, 126
Sarah Ann 113
Thomas 14, 91, 113(3)
Thomas, Jr. 113(3)
Thomas, Sr. 113
Vance 113(2)
William 113(2)
DOBINS (Dobbins
Elizabeth 14
Thomas 14
DOBSON (see Dopson)

Thos. 129
William 14, 91
DODD
Edward 44
DOE
John 91
DOLAHAN (Dolohan)
Daniel 14(2), 26, 43(3)
Eleanor 14
Michael 7
DOLBY
Elijah 128
DOLL (see Dall & Dull)
Abraham 100(2), 104, 113(2), 114, 120
Anna 113
Catherine 113(2)
Conrad 43, 68
Daniel 113(2)
George 113(2)
George W. 113
Jacob 43, 48, 100, 113(2), 117
Jane, Mrs. 100
Margaret 113
Mary 113
Phillip 113, 117(2)
Sarah 113
Susanna 113
DOLLSON
Mary 122
DOLON
Pat. 48, 137
DOMAN
Catherine 99, 100
Jacob 19, 43, 50, 68
William 99, 116
DOMAR
John M. 187
DONALDSON see Donelson1
Anthony 114
Charles 14
Jacob 114
James 6(2), 68(2), 91, 114, 132
John 23, 55, 58, 68, 109, 114, 116, 137
Margaret 114
Mary 14, 114(2)
Peggy 114
Richard 114
Robert 114(2)
William 10, 23, 35, 106, 108(2), 112(2), 114(5), 116, 124, 125(2), 130, 132(2), 135, 137
DONELSOL (Donaldson)
James 91
DONNALSON (Donnelson - Donaldson)
James 6, 68
William 120
DONNELY (Danley)
Elizabeth 91
DOOLEY
William 138
DOPSON (see Dobson)
Margaret 114(2)
Martha 114
William 9(3), 10, 28, 47, 68, 91, 114, 139
DORAN
Alex 102, 114
Evadne 114
Elizabeth 114(2)
Felix 91
Hannah, Mrs. 100
James 114
James Alexander 114
Jessie 114
John 114
Joseph 100(2), 114, 116
Lucy I. 116
Lucy G., Mrs. 100
Mary Ann 114
Peter 114
Sarah 100, 114
Sarah Jane 114
William 100(2), 111, 114(3), 131, 134, 136
DOSTEN
James 55
Thomas 55
DOSTLEHWAIT
William 14
DOUDALL
John 2
DOUGHERTY (may be Doughty or Doughtie)
James 20, 68, 91, 118
DOUGHTIE (Doughty - Dougherty)
Thomas 53(2), 68
DOUGLAS
James 50, 68
Jonas 125
DOUTHAIT
John 91
Thomas 91
DOUTHER

Thomas 14
DOUTHIT (Douthitt - see Douthwars)
Caleb 114
Catherine 114
Christena 114
Daniel 114
David 114
Jacob 25
John 9, 14, 39, 68(2), 112(2), 114, 127
John, Sr. 14(3), 68(2)
John, Jr. 14, 68
Margaret 14(2), 114
Mary 14(2), 109, 114
Rebecca 114
Sarah 114
Silas 114
Solomon 14(2), 68, 114
Thomas 41, 109, 114
DOUTHWARS (Douthit)
John 14
Margaret 14
DOVERIDGE
John 14
Margaret 14
DOWDEN
Jane 14(2)
Jean 14
John 8, 14(4), 20, 25(4), 29(2), 33, 122
John B. 14, 131
John Briggs 14, 69
John, Jr. 37, 69
Sarah 14, 42, 69
Thomas 14, 16, 25, 31, 37, 46, 53, 55, 69
Thomas S. 131
DOWELL
Thomas 58
DOWELS (Bowels)
Charles 86
DOWEN
John 14
DOWMAN (see Bowman)
Anna 114
Catherine 114
Jacob 114
John 114
Margaret 114(2)
Mary 114
Rachel 114
Sarah 114
William 114
DOWNING
Dillon 91
John 12, 14, 69
DOWSMAN
Henry 99, 100
Rachel, Mrs. 100
DOYAL (Doyle)
Frances 91
DOYLE (Doyal)
Elizabeth 14(2)
Ference 14(2)
James 100
Jane 100(2)
John 100
Matthew 100(2)
Torrence 91
Simon 4, 14(2), 34, 39, 46, 69(2)
Winney 100
DREW
D. 39
Elizabeth 114
Mary 14(4), 28, 114
Perez 7, 8, 9, 10, 11, 13, 39, 114
Priz 8
Sylvanus 114(2)
William 39(2)
DUCKOOD
John 127
DUDLEY (Dutley)
Elizabeth 135
William 91
DUDWICK (Ludwick)
Thomas 118
DUFFIL
William 91
DOUGAN (Duggan)
Alex 91
Dan 86
Thomas 14, 33, 63
William 91
DUGING
Pat. 91
DULAIN
Ann 211
DULING
Achilles 108, 114(4)
Anna 114
Anne, Mrs. 100
Catherine 114
David Gibson 114
David 114
Edmond 113, 114
Elijah 100(2), 114
Eliza 114

Elizabeth 114
Harriett R. 114
James 114
Margaret 114
Margaret Maranda 114
Mary 114
Nancy 100, 101
Philadelphia 114
Rebecca Frances 114
Ruth 114
Sarah Ann 114
Sarah Jane 114
Virginia 114
William 28, 44, 60(2), 69, 100, 108(2), 114, 132
William A. 117
William Collin 114
William, Sr. 114(2)
Zachariah 114
DULL (see Dall-Doll)
Christian 94
Jacob 113
DUNBAR
John 14, 36, 49, 91
Sarah 14
DUNCAN
Fr. 14(2)
William 14(2)
DUNHAM
John 91
DUNKLE
Jacob 33
DUNLAP
Ann 130
Ferdinand I. 130
James 13
John 18, 69
Mary 130
Mary Ann 130
William 115
DUNLAVY
Aaron 122
DUNMORE
Lord 130
DUNN
Alex 101
Dan 14
Davis 106
Drusilla 114
Ephraim 14(2), 18, 43, 46, 69, 101, 114, 115, 125, 129, 137
Ephraim Jefferson 114
Ezekiel 1(2)
Jane 106
Jacob 5, 114
Lewis 20, 22, 31(3), 46, 53, 55, 69, 129, 130
Lewis T. 113, 114
Louisa 114
Mary 114
Rebecca 114
Rosanna 14(3), 114
Sophiean 114
Thomas 14(8), 18(3), 21, 29, 30(2), 43, 46(2), 55, 59, 69(5), 106, 113, 114, 139
Thomas, Sr. 125
Vance 124
William 114
DUNOHAW
James 82
DURBIN
Nicholas 135
DURGAN
John 91
DUTLEY (Dudley)
Thomas 91
DUTTON
Kingman 15, 24(2), 69
Mary 15, 24
DUTTY
Thomas 21
DUVAL
Isaac 118
James 118
Thomas 118
William 118
DUVER (Devore-Deever)
Richard 100
Susan 100
DYE (Die)
Anna 114(2)
Anna Maria 114
George 114(2)
Hannah 113, 114
James 114
John 100(2), 114(2), 119(2), 133
Mary Evline 114
Rachel 127
Rebecca 114
Thomas 113, 114
Thomas, Sr. 114
William 114(2)
DYER
(E.) Edward 23, 57, 11(2)
El. 23

Nathan 19, 22, 33(2)
Nathaniel 11(2), 15, 19, 22, 28, 33(2), 37(2), 44, 51, 52, 53
Roger 11, 69
Susanna 15
William L. 136
EAKMAN (Aikman)
Adam Boyd 106
Eleanor 57
EARL (Earle)
Eliz. 15
Sam 15, 63
EALY (Eli - Ely)
Isaac 91
EARLY
Thos. 91
EARHART
John W. 117
EARSAM
Catherine 1
Jacob 1, 22
Mary 1
Simon 1
Susanna 1
EARSOM (also Earson, Earsam, Earsham, Ahrsam, Ihresam)
Ann 114
Barbara 114
Catherine 114
Christiana 114
Harriet Ann 114
EARSOM
Jacob 53(2), 91, 114(3), 123
James 114(2)
Jane 114
John 15, 69, 91, 109, 113, 114(2)
Margaret 131
Mary 114(2)
Mary M. 114
Nancy 114(2)
Samuel 114
Sarah 114(2)
Sidney 114(2)
Susannah 114(2)
Wm. 114(3)
EARSON
Catherine 1(2)
Jacob 1(2), 55
John 1
EASTER
Henry 100(2)
John 56, 69
Nancy, Mrs. 100
EASTON
John 56, 69
EATON
B. F. 122
Benj. 91
Joseph 91
Thos. 91
EBERY
Eliz. 15
Wm. 15
EBROD
Peter 11
ECKART (Eckhart)
A. 44
Henry 43, 52, 69
Henry, Jr. 14, 33
ECKSTINE (see Extine - Eckstine)
Eliz. 114
Lenord 29, 30(2), 41, 69, 114
Magdilene 114
Margaret 114
Mary 114
Rosanna 114
EDINGTON
Geo. 12, 15, 69
Mary 15
EDMONS(T)ON (Edmondston, Edmindston, Edmiston, Edmondson)
Elizabeth 100, 101
Mary Pruchet 120
Thos. 22, 54, 63, 101
Wm. 101, 120
EDWARDS
Abigal 15
Andrew 115
Ann 100, 103, 115
Catherine 15(3)
David 15, 114(2), 115(2)
Eve, Mrs. 100
Hannah 115
Jesse 15(2), 33, 69, 115
Joseph 15(3), 47, 114
Margaret 115
Martha 15, 100, 103
Mary 15, 25, 114
Naomi 115
Richard 5
Robert 100, 101
Sam 15(5), 31, 48, 69, 91, 111, 114
Sarah 91

Sarah Ann 115
Thos. 3, 15(4), 18, 25, 30(2), 69(3), 91, 103, 114(2), 124
Wm. 100
EGAN
Eliz. 114
James 114
EGGLESTON
Frances 107
EICHELBERGER
Eleanore 132
Henrietta 132
Julianna 132
Maria 132
Martin 132
ELDRIDGE
David 91
ELEFRITZ
Sarah 100, 102
ELI (Ely - Ealy)
Benjamin 15
Mary 15
ELLIOT (Elliott)
Annabell 15
John 1, 2, 15, 22, 40, 53, 69(2)
Samuel 15
ELLIS
David 106(2), 104, 115(2), 122, 132
Dudley Brown 115
Eliza 100, 104
Ira 115
James 115
Joel 130
John 115
(Morris) 22(3), 24(2), 127
Nelson 115
Phillip 91
Sarah 115
Sarah Jane, Mrs. 100
ELLOR
Daniel 25(2), 54, 69
ELMORE
Charity 15
Martha 15
Mathias 15
Stephen 15
Wm. 15
ELSEY
Thomazier 15
ELSWICK (WISK) (Esswick)
John 15, 44, 115
Rachel 15(2), 44, 115(2)
Thos. 15(2), 27, 69, 91, 115
Thos., Sr. 91
Thos., Jr. 15
ELY (Eli or Elay)
Benjamin 3(2), 15, 91, 100(2), 103, 115
Charlotte, Mrs. 100
Elizabeth 115(3)
Isaac 91, 115(2), 130, 132
Janie 115
Jean 15
James 115(2)
Joshua 115(3)
Margaret 115(2)
Mary 15
Rosanna, Mrs. 100
Sarah 115
Wm. 14(2), 99, 100, 103, 114, 115(3), 116
Wm., Jr. 112(2)
EMBERSON (Emerson - Emmerson)
Able 91
Thos. 30, 37, 69, 91
EMERESON
Abel 1, 23, 69
Thos. 31
EMERY (see Amory and Emmery)
Edward 91, 112
EMIT Emmet - Emmitt)
Eliz. 15
Geo. 15
EMMARTS
Henry 111
Geo. 104
Jacob 100
John 111
Nancy 111
Rebecca 111
Jacob, Sr. 100
EMMERSON
Hannah, Mrs. 100, 128(2)
James 128
Mary 15(2)
Thos. 12, 15(2), 16, 30, 32(2), 49, 69(5)
EMMERY
John 91
EMMET(T) (Emmitt)
Andrew 108
EMMITT
Eliz. 129
Jacob 2

INDEX

EMMERT(T) (Emmarts - Emmitt - Emmart)
Abraham 134
Andrew 115(3)
Benjamin 115
Catherine 115(2)
Christina 115
Eliza 115
Eliza Jane 115
Elizabeth 115(2), 129
Hannah 115
Henry 111(2)
Isaac N. 115
Isaac Newton 115
George 104
Geo. Washington 115
Jacob 2, 38, 46, 69, 115(3), 130
John 111
John Henry 115
Marianna 115
Mary 115
Nancy 115
Phillip 115
Rebecca 111
Washington 115
ENGLAND (see English)
Henry 137
ENGLE
Amelia, Mrs. 100
Charlotte 115
Christian 120
Eliz. 115
Hannah 15
Hiram 100, 101
John 133
Joseph 15(2), 69
Justinius 115(2)
Martin 13
Mary Ann 108
Peter 15, 18, 43(2), 54(2), 69, 115
Sarah 112
Wm. 15(2), 46, 91
Wm., Sr. 91
Wm., Jr. 91
ENGLISH (see England)
Henry 137
Wm. 91
ENNIS (Innes)
Enoch 112
ENOCH
Eliz. 15(6), 16(2), 91, 132
Enoch 3, 14, 15(3), 16, 69 (2), 91, 122
Henry 8, 15(7), 16(2), 69, 91, 122, 132
Henry, Jr. 15(2), 25
Henry, Sr. 15(8), 16, 25, 69
Rebecca 15
Sarah 16(3)
ENTLER
Henry 115
Jeptha 115
John 104, 115
Margaret 115
Nancy 100, 104
Sally, Mrs. 100
Wm. 100, 103, 115
Wm., Sr. 115
ERHART
Jacob 40
ERMINTRANT (Hermintrant and Armintrant)
Christopher 56(2), 67, 69, 91, 109, 133(2)
ERNEST (see Harness)
ERRETT (Arrett)
Christopher 121(2), 139
ESSEX
Thos. 27
ESSWICK (see Elswick)
John 15, 44
Rachel 15, 44
ESTRAU (see Antrau)
Andrew 18
ETCHASON (see Atchison)
Sam 91
ETTITCHELL
John 20
EULDY
Thos. 91
EVANS
Abel 115
Alexander 100, 104
Ann 136
Ann, Mrs. 100
Benjamin 119
Caleb 16(2), 57, 69, 100(2), 113
Cabel 119
Ellenor 109
Eliz. 115
Emily 136
Eve 16(2)
Evelilner 115
Garet 115
James 115
Jemima 136
John 111(2), 136

Nancy 109
Nath 58, 60, 61
Pricilla 109(4)
Oliver 115
Peter 128
Rhoda 136
Sarah 115
Wm. 115, 136
EVERMAN
Micheal 91
EVERCMON (see D'evercmon)
Hannah 16(2)
Peter 16(2)
EVERSAL (Eversol - Eversole - Eversold)
Abraham 5, 14(2), 16, 18, 48, 59
Mary 16, 53(2), 59
Peter 18(2), 53, 59, 69
EVERETT
Asa 115
Dan 115
Darius 115
Ezekiel 115
Eliz. 115
Enos. 115
Fanny 115
Moses 115
Sarah 115(2), 132
Sarah, Mrs. 100
EVHANT (Erhart)
Jacob 40
EWAIN
John 48
EWEL(L)
Bertrain 16, 63, 69
Jeremiah 63, 69
Tristram 20, 69
EWING
Susannah 16
Tristram 16(2)
EXTINE (Eckstine - Exstine)
Leonard 41, 91, 115

F——
Ludwig 131
FAHS
John 124
Joseph 100, 102, 104
Leah, Mrs. 100, 102
Maria, Mrs. 100
Phil 120, 130(2), 138
Phil, Jr. 125
FAIRDAIN
Thos. N. 125
FAIRDOWN 125
FAIRFAX 125
Buckner 128
Denny 16(11)
Rev. Denny 16(3)
Eliza C. 115
Louisa W. 100, 104
Mary Martin 115
Thos. Lord 6, 9, 16(12), 17(27), 18(6), 37, 39(4), 69(6)
FAIRLEY (see Farley and Fearley)
Andrew 4, 18
David 91
Eliz. 18(2)
James 125
John 4, 18(3), 91
Thos. 18
FAIRTAIRN 125
FAKE
Adam 18
FARCE (see Ferree Fence)
Cornelius 91
FARILY (Fear - Fair)
Thos. 23, 69
FARLEY (Fear - Fair)
Andrew 23, 115
David 115
Elinor 115
Jane 91, 115
John 18, 23, 115
Margaret 115
Mary 115
Eleanor 115
Thos. 23, 72, 115
FARMER
Alice 115
Ann 124
Frances 100, 115
Frankey 132
Sarah 115
Sarah Jane 100(2)
Sam 100, 115, 132
FARPLEY (Tarpley)
James 140
FARRAND
Nathan 4(2)
FARRELL
Chas. 47
FARROW
Alex 58
Joanna 24

FASH
Phillip 111
FAW
Abraham 31, 69
FAWCETT
Joseph 37, 52
FAWVER
Henry 60, 69
FEAREND (Ferrand)
Isaac 91
FEARIS
James 140
FEARLY (Fair and Far-)
Thos. 23, 69
FEARON
Robert 18
FEARSON
Robert 18(2)
FEATER
John 28, 69
FEATHER
Stephen 18, 50, 69
FEATTER
Stephen 55
FELEY
Wm. S. 108
FENCE (Farce)
Cornelius 119
FENS
Mary 124
FENTON
John 108
Josiah I. 138
FEREBEE 108
FERGUSON
Frances 18
Geo. 59(2)
James 91
Robert 7, 9, 18, 30, 32(2)
FERMAN (Forman)
Catherine 106, 131
FERRAND
Nathaniel 8, 18, 69
FERRALL
James 18(2), 42, 69
Pat. 91
Robert 59
FERREE (see Farce)
Cornelius 6, 11, 18(2), 25, 54, 60(2), 61(2), 69, 119
Helene 18
Isaac 11, 18, 54, 61
Joshua 11, 18, 61
FERRELL (Ferree)
Cornelius 12, 55, 60
FERREW
Cornelius 12
FERRY
Geo., Sr. 18
Rachel 18
Stephen 18, 69
FERRYMAN
Francis 100, 103
Henry 102
Lydia (Mrs.) 100
Rebecca 100, 102
Stephen 102
FETTER (see Feather)
Daniel 10, 50, 69(2)
George 50
FENT (Fout?)
Geo. 91
FICHENAL (see Tichenal)
Margaret 18
Moses 18
FIDDLER (Fidler)
Edw. 9, 91
Eliz. 18(2), 69
George 44, 61, 69, 91
Jacob 18(3), 91
Magdalene 18
Mary 138
Molly 25, 69
FIELDS
J. Fred. 63
Joseph 38
Simon 87, 91, 135
FIFE
John 18, 58
Margaret 18
FILINK
John 14, 69
FILLING
Barbara 115
Catherine 115
Eliz. 115
Nancy 115
FINGLE
Wm. 27
FINK
Andrew 20, 69
Dan. 115, 124, 135
Catherine 115
Esther 18(6)
Esto (Eston) 18
Fred 18(7), 24, 53, 59(3), 69, 126, 135(2)
Henry 18, 59(2), 69
John 128
Sam 115, 135

FINLEY
Patrick 140
FINNY
M. 132
FISHEL(L)
Jacob 129, 133(2)
FISHALL
Phillip 135
FISHER
Adam 34(2), 59(2), 69(20), 91, 115
Adam, Jr. 91, 115
Adam, Sr. 91
Catherine 115
Christiana 91, 115
Eliz. 115
Dan 91
Geo. 7, 38, 91, 115, 121
Jacob 14, 91, 115
John 91, 115
Meirs 49
Micheal 115
Nancy 87, 69
Solomon 115
Thos. Jr. 19
FITZGERALD
Ann 115, 137
Cahterine 110
Edward 110, 115
Eliza 110
Job (Tob) 110
John 108
Maria(h) 100, 105, 115
Mary 110
Mary Elen 110
Nancy 100, 103
Rebecca 110
Richard 110
Thomas 21, 29, 51, 69, 110(2), 137
Tob (Job) 110
FITZMILLER
Casper 113
FITZPATRICK
Anthony 91
FLANAGAN (Flanigan)
Daniel 107
John 122
Susan 107
FLARTY (Flaharty - Florty - Flaughery)
James 22, 44, 51, 91
FLECK (Flick - Fleek)
Catherine 18(2)
Henry 10, 15, 69(2)
Jacob 11, 18(2), 69, 130
FLEEK (see Flick and Fleck)
Arthur 106
Eliz. 134
Henry 115
Henry, Sr. 115
Jacob 110
John 115(2)
Mary 134
Nancy 134
Peter 100, 104
Rachel, Mrs. 100
Rachel 115
Solomon 115
Susannah 115(2)
FLESON (Fleeson)
Plun 22
FLEMING
Ann 18(2), 100, 104, 115
Catherine 115
Christina 115
Edward 115
Elizabeth 115
James 3, 18(5), 25, 34, 41, 52, 54(2), 59, 60, 69(7), 85(2), 91(2), 115(2), 140
John 115, 130
Nancy 100(2)
Patrick 104, 115
Thos. 115
FLETCHER
Alice 115
Harriet 115
Elijah 100, 103
Eliz., Mrs. 100
Frances 115
Geo. W. 100, 115
Joseph 91
Thos. 10, 28
FLICH
Henry 29, 69
FLICK (see Fleck - Fleek)
Adam 103
Henry 134
Isaac 107
Magdalene 100, 103
FLINT
Jane 124
FLOOD
Ann 115
Chas. O. 115(2)
Eliz. 115
Eloner 115

PAGE 149

James 4
John 115(3))
Mary 115
Mary Rachen 115
Phoby 115
Sarah 115
Sarah Eliz. 115
Washington 115
FLORA
Abyah 91
Archibald 21, 36
Jacob 57
Joseph 21(2), 36
Margaret 21, 36
Thos. 21, 57, 69
William 61, 91
FLORENCE
Wm. 87
FLORANE
Wm. 69
FLORY
John 134(2)
FLOYD
Enoch 26
FLOUGHERTY see Flarty
James 91
FLURY
Sarah Jane 136
FLYE (see Frye)
John, Sr. 121
FOCSH (see Fox)
James 123
FOGEL
Charlotte 100, 101
Henry 101
FOLEY
John 25(3), 57, 86, 91
John, Jr. 25(3)
Milly 100, 102
Sarah 123
Wm. 57
FOLLERY
James 108
FOLLIS
Geo. 2
FOLKIMER
John Martin 15, 69
FOOLE (Foote)
Ann W. 116
Rev. Wm. Henry 116(2)
FORD
Jacob, Jr. 47
FORECRAFT see Foxcraft
John 18
Judith 18(3)
FORMAN or Foreman see Foxman
Aaron 18(2), 61, 62, 69(2)
Ann 58
Anna 116
Benjamin 16, 18(2), 19(4), 28, 63(2), 80, 106
Catherine 19(4), 139
Christine 116
D. 127
David 22, 69, 91, 109, 131
Elizabeth 19(2), 58
Farm 127
Henry 116
James 19, 85, 116
James W. 118
John 2(2), 3, 4, 7(2), 8(2), 10(2), 18, 19(6), 22, 23, 28(2), 33(3), 43, 45, 46, 52, 56(2), 63(2), 69(3), 139
John, Sr. 19
John, Jr. 19(4), 91
Joseph 19(5), 56, 70(4), 125
Margaret 19(2), 116
Mary 19(4)
Moses 116
Nancy 139
Samuel 116
Sarah 116
Sarah Jane 116
Susan 116
Wm. 12, 18, 19(13), 22, 23, 28, 45, 46, 61, 62, 63, 70(3), 91, 118, 128
Wm., Jr. 19, 70
FORRENCE (Torrence - Florance)
John 110
Wm. 110
FORSHEY
John 91
FORST (Post?)
Valentine 56, 70
FORTE
Henry 114
FOSTE
Benj. 28
FOSTER
Ach 59
Archibald 5, 34
Isaac 19
Jane 19
John 11, 19(2), 27, 61, 70(4)

Ezekiel 40(3)
FOULKE (Fouke)
Mary 19
Nathaniel 19, 53, 112
Sarah 19
Thos. 55
FOTTEN (see Totten)
Caleb 23, 70
FOUGHTY (see Fouty)
FOUKE
George 133
FOUT
Ann 100, 101
Charlotte 19, 70
Jacob 70
Mary 100, 101
Micheal 1, 4, 19, 70, 112
Wm. 101, 109, 117
Wm. Jacob 19, 70
FOUTLEY (Fouthley)
Fredrick 108
FOUTY (Foughty)
George 85
Jacob 109
Sarah 109
FOWLER
John 91
Wm. 55, 60, 70
FOX
Abcolom 19
Christian 19
Elizabeth 120(2)
Ivea 116
Gabriel 8, 19(2), 91, 116, 120
John I. 120
Sarah 25, 70
Susan 120
Vance 120
Vanse (Vause) 119, 122
Col. Wm. 184
Wm. 4, 7, 8, 10, 19(4), 28, 31, 38, 37(2), 38(5), 40(2), 41, 48, 54, 58, 70(5), 85, 116, 118, 129(2)
FOXCRAFT (see Forcraft)
John 19(5), 21, 26, 37, 45, 47, 57(4), 59
Thomas 59(2)
FOXMAN (see Forman)
Catherine 87
John 27
Wm. 37
FOY (Fox)
Gabriel 140
FRANCE
Mary 130
Frances V. 136
FRANK (2)
Chas. 122
George 19
Henry 19, 49, 59, 70
FRANKFORT TRUSTEES
12, 20(46), 21(2), 70
FAZEE
Henry 111, 126
FRAZER (also Frazier)
Alex 128
Catherine 117
Dan 91, 132
Eliz. 119
James 109
John 128
Joseph 43, 70, 108
Thos. 117
FRAZIN
Eleanor 100, 108
Eliz. 119
Joseph 117, 119
FREE (Ferree)
Cornelius 10, 70
FREMAN (also Freeman)
Nancy 130
Rosanna 91
FRENCH
Ann Eliz. 116
Alevander 32
Eleanor 116
Eliza Maria 116
Hetty 118
Katherine 116
Marie 116
Mary 116
Matthew 21
Nancy 116
James 116, 127
John 116
Robert 21(3), 31, 42, 43, 85, 112, 116(2), 138
Sarah 21, 116
Susan, Mrs. 112
Thos. 112, 126
Wm. 21(2), 23, 29, 42, 44, 46, 47, 70(6), 100, 104
Wm. Jr. 114, 116(2), 119, 121, 132, 135, 138
FREY (Frye)
Henry 120
FRIBACS (see Fryback)
Geo. 91

FRIDDLE
Betsy Ann, Mrs. 100
Henry 100, 101, 119
John 100, 116
John, Jr. 100, 103
Lydia, Mrs. 100
Mary 116
FRIEND
Andrew 21
Carenhapech 21
Gabriel 21(2)
Jane 21
John 21(4))
Karumhapspuck 21
Nicholas 21
FRINKLE (Trinkle and Tunkle)
Christopher 32, 70
FRIZEL
Chas. 122
Janet 122
FROGG
Margaret 1
FRONS
Thos. 132
FRY (or Frye - Frey)
Abraham 8, 21, 49(2), 70
Abr. W. 116
Benjamin 9(2), 21, 27, 28, 70(2), 100(2), 110, 126, 131
Benjamine P. 116
Catherine 80, 70
Christopher 33, 70, 88
Fanny 116
Geo. Washington 126
Henry 1(2), 21(2), 27(5), 28, 52(2), 106, 110, 129, 139
Isaac L. 118
Jacob 126
James H. 100(3)
James Madison 126
Jane Eliz. 116
Jesse P. 100
Jackson 116
John 9
Joseph 21, 117, 134
Lucy G. 100(2)
Lucy I. 116
Mary 100, 116
Mary Ann 116
Nancy 100(2), 116
Nancy A. 116
Nany T., Mrs. 100
Peter 41, 70
Phoeby 21, 134
Rhody 134(2)
Samuel 116
Sarah Ann 126
Sarah M. 116
Susan 116
Susannah 41
Thos. 86, 100
Wm. 2, 21, 70, 134
FRYBACK (Friback)
John 91
FRYER
Jesse 107
FUGATE
Jean 133
FULKAMORE Folkimore
Asa 116
John 116
Joseph 116
John Martin 116
Martin 123
Tasey 116
Unity 116
FULLER
Rebecca 104
Robert 12
FULLERTON
Humphrey 110
FULTZ
Philip 91
FUNK (Fink)
Adam 91
FUNKHOUSER
Solo. 118
FURST (Forst)
Valentine 91
GADDIS
John 116(2)
Persila 116
Priscilla 21
Sarah Ann 121
Wm. 116
GAITHER
E. 6, 13, 23, 25, 37, 38(5), 41, 43, 44, 45, 46, 47
Elijah 4, 5, 21(4), 61, 62(3), 70(2)
Harriot 21
Henry 46, 70
GAL(L)ASPY (Gillespie)
Catherine 116
Henry 116(2)
James 116

Mary 116
Micheal 18, 70, 116
GALE
George 12(2), 63, 70
GALLAGHER
Wm. 49
GALLANT (Gallent)
James 21(2), 45, 70
Mary 21(2)
GALLOWAY
James 30, 31, 70(2)
Mrs. 127
Wm. 138
GAMMAGE
John 134
GANNO (Ganoe)
Stephen 50, 70
GANOE (Ganno)
Elizabeth 100, 104
Isaac 100
Jane 106(2), 116
Margaret 100, 101
Stephen 50, 70, 106, 116(2)
GANTHROP
John D. 138
GARD (Guard)
Cornelius 14, 24, 56, 91, 114
John 127
Nathan 21
Samuel 15, 70, 103, 118
Sarah 101, 108
Wm. 180
GARDNER
Richard 23
GARRART
Benj. 2, 70
GARRETT
Eliz. 138
Wm. 118
GARRIGUES
Edw. 21, 31, 37, 70
GARRISON
Charity 21
Jacob 11
John 91
Joseph 11, 21, 33, 70(3), 107
GARRITT (Garrett)
Benj. 2, 70
Eliz. 138
Wm. 118
GARVINS
Samuel 122
GARVIS
Robert 91
GASSAWAY (Gazaway)
Benj. 116
Liddy 116
Miriam 116
Nance 116
Nelly 116
Nicholas 116
Robert 116(3)
Sally 116
Sarah 116
GATES
David 115
GATEWOOD
John 21
GATHORP (see Ganthorp)
James 31, 70
GAW
James 21, 31
GAZAWAY (Gassaway)
Robert 12, 70
GEIGER
Jacob 18
GELISON (Gelleson)
James 3, 9, 33, 70
GEMNETZ (Gennitz)
John Wm. 21
GENEY (Janny)
Daniel 135
GEORGE
Ellis 5, 35, 70(2), 116
Evan 116
George 116
Henry 108, 116(2), 128
James 35(2), 116(2), 123(2)
Joel 131
John 116, 119
Joseph 91
King 116
Lydia 116
Lydia, Jr. 116
Mary 116
Mary Ann 113
Mary Lydia 116
Matthew 49, 53, 70, 116, 139
Nancy, Mrs. 100
Rachel 116
Rebecca 116
Richard 108, 116(3), 123(2), 133
Ruth 116

Sarah 116(6)
Silas 100, 104, 116
Susannah 91, 116
GEPHART
Wm. 131
GIBBONS
G. 119
GIBBONY (Gibony)
Alexander 21, 22, 33(2), 70, 132
Alex., Sr. 91, 132
Alex., Jr. 91, 132
Ann 21, 182
Robert 91
GIBBS
Samuel 6, 26, 42, 61
GIBSON
Andrew, Jr. 116
Anna M. 137
Dan 119, 120(2)
David 101, 106(8), 116, 120(2), 127, 131, 133, 185, 186, 138
James 2, 21, 25(2), 42, 46, 61, 70, 110(2), 127, 135, 136
John 8(2), 21(2), 38, 129(2)
Wm. 9, 21
GIDDENS
James 91
GILBERT
Geo. 125, 134
GILCHRIST
Andrew 58
Robert 21(3), 54(3)
GILE (Gill)
John 1, 70
Joseph 89, 70
GILING
John 133
GILKINSON
Samuel 21
GILL
Chas. 109
Esther 116
John 1, 21, 70
Moses 3, 70
GILLETT
Wheeler 128
GILLIPSY (Gallaspy)
Micheal 18, 70
GILIMER (Gilmore - Gillmer - (mour)
Elinor (Eleanor) 44, 116(2)
Eliz. 116
John 3, 21, 45, 70, 116
Henry 116
Margart 21, 27, 116(2)
GILMORE (Gillmor)
Ann 21
Elizabeth 21
Jane 21, 116
John 10, 89
Mary 21
Matthew 139
Micheal 139
Sarah 91
GILMOUR
Matthew 17, 70, 139
GILPIN (Gilfin)
Edward 125
George 11, 27, 29, 40, 59, 70(6), 86
GINNES
James W. 15
GINNER (Janny)
Wm. 185
GITHENS
Henr. (Henry) 132
GIVEN
Adam 133
GLASS
Ann McAllister 116
Eliza 116
Emaline 116
Hester Sophia 116
Rev. Joseph 116
Joseph 124
Mary 116
Samuel 91, 124
Sarah 21
Sarah Ann 116
Sidney 116
Susan Emily 116
Robert 21
GLASSELL
Wm. 7, 70
GLAZE
Andrew 22, 35, 70, 91, 116
Christeny 130
Conrad 36(2), 70(2), 91, 116
E. 63
Earhart 5, 22, 30, 70(2), 91
Eliz. 22(2)
Eve 22
Geore 22(2), 24, 70, 91
Geo. W. 130
Hannah 116
John 22(2), 32, 70, 91

Laurence 22(3)
Mary 22, 126
Nancy 116
Peggy 116
Polly 116
Sally 116
GLOID (Gloyd)
James 112
John 112
Sam 134
GLOVER
Richard 21, 70
GODLIN
Hannah 110
GODFREY
Edward 91
John 57, 70
Wm. 91
GOFF
John 22, 85
Salathiel 13
Thos. 91
GOFFICK (Gossick)
Richard 1, 22, 70
GOINGS
Louisa 133
GOLDSBERRY
Widow 136
GOOD
Abraham 22, 26, 70, 116
Eliz. 22, 116(2)
Eliz., Mrs. 100
Isaac 5, 22(3), 48, 70(2), 91, 116
Isaac, Jr. 6, 52
Jacob 22, 48, 70
John 116
Mary 116
Nancy 135
Peter 26, 86, 91, 116(2)
Phillip 99, 100, 116
Sarah 116, 137
Susannah 216
GOODMAN
Ignatious 91
GOODWILL
Sarah 4(2)
GOODWINE
John 54
Solomon 91
GOOSET
Eve 22
Peter 22, 29, 70
GORDON
George 91
Moreses 119
GORE
Geo. W. 132, 133
Wm. 99
GOSSETT
Wm. 24
GOSSICK (Goffick)
Richard 22, 70
GOUGE (George)
Chas. 91
GOYAS
Harrison 117
GRACE
Christeny 130
Ephraim M. 114(4)
Jacob 108, 114(2), 130(2)
John 114
Nancy 122
Phillip 111(2), 124
Sidney 114(3)
Stephen 114
GRAFF
Andrew 22, 38
GRAGG (Gregg - Craig?)
Lydia 127
Robert 22
GRAHAME
Daniel 27
John 4, 6, 22, 25, 41
R. 48
GRAND
Sam 130
GRANT (see Henderson 118)
Hannah 117
James 20, 70
James M. 112
John G. 109
Wm. 10, 70, 107, 116
GRAPES
Catherine 99, 100
Jacob 99, 100, 129
John 5, 70
Maria, Mrs. 100
GRAY (Cray)
Friend 3, 21, 22, 47, 70(2), 91, 116
Isaac 15, 22, 70
James 124, 128
Mary 22
Sarah 22
Spencer 108
Spencer R. 117
Vincent 29, 37
Wm. 86

INDEX

GRAYBILL
Virgel 86
GRAYSON
Ambrose 117
Benj. 80, 101, 111, 117(5)
Benj., Jr. 118
Betsy 111
Catherine 117(2)
Clary 117
Eliz. 111, 117(2)
Felix 117
John 117
Lydia (Lidday) 117
Margaret A. 117
Mariah 117(2)
Mary, Mrs. 101
Nancy 117
Reuben (Rhubin) 117(2)
Richard 111
Sanford 117
Sarah 117
Tomazen 117, 118
Thomas 101
Wm. 117(3), 121
GREATHOUSE
Harman 22
Mary 22
GREATWATER
Polly 126
GREGG (see Gragg)
B. J. 113
David 28
Margaret 22
Nathan 36, 70
Robert 9, 15, 22(2), 28(2), 37, 45, 52, 56, 71(2)
Thos. 36, 71
GREEN
Eliz. 108
Isaac 35, 127
John 109, 117, 124
Henry 91, 138
Lewis 91, 138
Thos. 57, 71
GREENFIELD
John 6, 16(2), 22(5), 26, 28, 29(2), 30, 35(2), 36 (2), 42, 47, 60, 71
Mary 22(2)
GREENVILLE
Thos. 41
GREENWADE
Rhona 106
GREENWALT
Mary 135
GREENWELL (Greene)
Ann (Anna) 22(3)
Catherine 117
Elizabeth 117
Elijah 14, 22(2), 41, 49, 71 (2), 117
Thos. 22(6), 25(2), 29(2), 63, 71(6)
GREENWOOD
Thos. 22, 42, 71
GRIFFIN
Barton 119
John 86
Wm. 119
GRIFFITH
David 46, 120
Eliz. 132
Susan 131
GRIM
Arthur F. 126
Balsar 91
GRITTON (Critton)
John 124
GRISCOM
James 128
GROOMIS (Grooms)
John 136, 140
GROVES
Amelia 100, 101
Anna 111
Barbara, Mrs. 101
Catherine 117
Charlotte 22(3)
Charles 24(3)
Elizabeth 117
Elizabeth Ann 117
Eliza 117
Henry 22(3), 24(6), 71(2)
Jackson 117
Jacob 99, 117
James 101
John 117
Margaret H. 100, 101
Mary, Mrs. 101
Mary 91, 100, 116, 122
Peter 100
Phillip 38, 71, 101, 117, 122
Phoebe 107
Polly 117
Sam H. 100
Wm. 99, 100, 101(3)
Wm. J. 119
GRUBB
Ben 54
GRUNDY
Thos. 132
GRYMMS
Eliz. 101
George 104
John H. 101
John W. 104
GSINER
Deliah 123
GUARD (Gard)
Sarah 101
Samuel 103
GUFFICK (Goffick)
Richard 114
GULICK
Amos 117
Elisha 117
Fardanand (Ferdinand) 11, 71
Fred 86, 117
Ivea 109
Jane 111
Polly 117
Richard B. 111
Stephen 117
Wm. 109
GUM
Jacob 22, 36, 71
Sarah 22
GUPHILL
Eliz. 19, 22
Edward 19, 22
GUSLER
John 47, 71
GUSSET
Peter 91
GUSTIN
Alpheus, Jr. 6, 22, 71
John 22
GWYNNE
Evan 107
HAAUVER (Hoover)
Jacob 53
HAAS (Hass - Huff)
Christian 98
Peter 24
HACKNEY
W. 14(2), 32
Wm. 49
HACOCK
Sarah 99, 101
HAEL
Peter 140
HAAF (Hass undoutedly) - (see Hass - Haas)
Abraham 23(2), 71, 117
Andrew 117
Catherine 101, 102, 117
Cornelius 71(2), 91, 117(5)
Elizabeth 117(3)
Hannah 117
Jacob 117
John 117(2)
Lawrence 24(3), 71(3), 63, 91, 117
Luke 84, 71, 91, 117
Paul 117
Peter 24(2), 91, 102
Rachel 117
Richard 91, 117, 123
Sarah 23, 24(2), 71, 117(2)
HAGARTY (Haggerty)
John 91
HAGGARD
Wm. 11, 71
HAGGERTY
Geo. 130
James 134
Paul 53
HAGLER
Bastoin 91
Wm. 91
HAGUE (Hogue maybe Hoge) 12, 23, 26, 29, 43
Samuel 71(4)
HAHN (see Haun)
John 91
Micheal 17, 22, 34, 71(2)
HAIL (Dailey)
Thos. 86
HAINES (see Haynes)
A. J. 118, 124
Andrew 55(2), 112(2)
David 108
Eliza 101, 103
Elizabeth 129(2)
Everline 101
Henry 107
Isaac 101
Isrel 101
John 117, 140
Joseph 91
Josiah 3
Lenah 22
Leweza 117
Mary 133
Peter 11, 22(2), 71
Rudolph 91, 140
Rachel 101, 117
Samuel 117
Sarah 117
Thomas 29
Wm. 129
HAIRE (see Heare)
Adam 106
HAIZE (see Haise - Hase - Hays)
Adam 8, 71
Susan 134
HALDEMAN
Peter 23
HALDERMAN (see Holterman - Holderman)
Abr. 58, 71
Peter 23
HALE
James 140
HALL (Hill - Halle)
Adam 12(2), 19, 40, 52, 54, 71, 85, 109
Amanda 117
Beales 117
Boales 117
Boolys 117
Catherine 117
Dan 92
Eleanor 129
Elyali 117
James 117
Janeny 117
John 39, 112
Emily 117
Elijah 117
Joseph 91, 110, 117, 121
Lucy 117
Mary 117
Micheal 18, 23, 71
Norman 117
Peter 91
Richard 117
Sydner 117
Thos. 91
William 53, 117(3)
Winney 117
HALLE
Wm. 53
HALLOWELL
Thos. 23
HAM
A. J. 124
Jeremiah 25
Wm. 91
HAMBLER (see Humbler)
HAMBLETON (see Hamilton - Hamil)
ames 126
Mary 126
Nancy 126
Patrick 126
HAMILTON
Catherine, Mrs. 101, 112
Eliz. 112
Elisha 100, 101(2)
Hanah, Mrs. 101
Harry 139
Henry 17, 23(3), 53, 71(2), 91
Jacob 2
James 4, 71, 55, 99
John 108, 112, 128
John A. 138
Mary 23, 112
Samuel 101, 103
Sarah, Mrs. 101
Thos. 91
HAMLIN
Joseph 23
HAMMACK (Hammock)
Abraham 117(2)
Catherine 117(2)
Harriet Ann 117
Jacob 117, 129
Jane 117
John A. 71, 135
John 44, 128
John, Jr. 128
John, Sr. 128
Mary 117
Rebecca 117
Samuel 7, 117
Sarah 117
Wm. Thornton 117
HAMMAR (Hammer)
John 121
Jonathan 11, 35
John, Jr. 132
HAMMIL
Henry 133
HAMMON
Hutson 132
HAMMOND see Haymond
Absolom 7, 135
Charles 52(2)
Thos. 44
Wm. 23, 30, 62, 71
HAMMORY
John 91
HAMPSHIRE CO. 71
Trustees 18, 23, 71
Commissioners 23
HAMPTON
Geo. 111
Thos. 111
HAMRICK
Siras 98, 117
HAMSON
James 42
HANCHER
Eliz., Mrs. 101
James 100, 101
John 111(2)
Sarah 111
W. 1, 12(2), 35, 60
HANDY (Hardy)
Thos. 11
HANES
Joseph 91
HANKLE (see Hinkle - Henkle - Hinckle)
Jacob 109, 123
HANKS (Hawks)
Joseph 23, 91, 140
HANNAN
John N. 107
HANNAS (Harris?)
Charity 101, 103
Daniel 117
Isabelle, Mrs. 101
John 117
Stephen 99, 101, 116, 117
Wm. 101
HANSBOROUGH (Hans)
Ann, Mrs. 101
Eveline 117
Fanny 118
James 101
John 6, 9, 11, 12, 14, 18, 19 (2), 23(2), 27, 34, 36, 38, 42, 46, 61, 99, 117, 118, 119
John, Jr. 99, 101
Maria 99, 101
Mary 23
HAMSHIRE
James 14
HANSON
Geo. Y. 115
John 38
Thos. 91, 140
HARD (see Head - Heard)
HARBUS
Mary 133
HARDIN (Harden - Harding?)
Ann 23, 118
Catherine 23(2)
Evanglist 91
John 22, 23(4), 36(2), 52 (3), 63(2), 71(3)
John, Sr. 23
Mark 23(2), 71, 91
Vanglist 92
Wm. 34, 92
HARDING
Sam 34
Wm. 34, 71
HARDIE
Peter 113
HARDY (Hardee)
Ann 117
Co. Trustees and Commissioners 71
Henry 1, 35
John I. 123
John J. 130
Martin 112, 115
Peter 113
HARE (see Haire - Heare - Harre)
Adam 111
Margaret, Mrs. 101
Matilda 133
Matthew 101, 108, 115
HARFORD (see Hurford)
Joseph 2, 9, 71
HARGIS
Wm. 92, 114, 140
HARLAND
Jesse 111
HARLMAN (Hartman)
Mary 126
HARLOW
Jesse 18, 71
HARMAN (Harmon)
Betsy 132
Fredrisk 49(2)
Joseph 12, 55, 71
M. F. 129
Thos. 23, 30, 72
HARNESS (see Hurness - Ernest)
Adam 13, 23(2), 32(2), 33 (2), 38, 71(2), 92, 121, 122, 140
Adam, Jr. 23(2), 71(2)
Barbara 117
Elizabeth 117(3)
George 14, 23, 33, 34, 71(2), 92, 117, 137
George, Jr. 23, 32
Isaac 122
Jacob 23(2), 71(2), 117
John 92(2), 110, 115, 117
Capt. John 109
Leonard 23(3), 71, 92(2), 117
Margaret 117
Michail 117
Micheal, Jr. 92
Micheal, Sr. 23, 92
Peter 58, 71, 92, 117
Rebecca 23(2)
Sarah 23(2), 122
Wm. 116
HAROD
Ephram 92
HARPER
Adam 92
Mary 109
Wm. 120
HARPOLE
Adam 92, 140
Adam, Jr. 92
HARRE
John 23
Phoebe 23
HARRESS (Harris)
Mary 110
HARRIS
Daniel 54(2)
Eliz. 117, 138
John 92(3), 127, 133
Lawson 119
Margaret 23
Mary 119
Nehemiah 23
Nicholas 133
Sarah 121, 138
Sharloty (?) 117
Solomon 127
Tempa 136
Thomas 92
William 54(2)
HARRISON
Amy 118
Ann 118
Betsy 118
Caroline 121
Elinore 121
Eliza 121
Elizabeth 108, 121
George D. 117, 118
Henry 118
James 118
Joe 114
John 92, 118
Lucy 121
M. 117
Margaret 118
Mary 117
Matthew 4, 23(2)
Orpha 101
Percy 118
Percy J. 121
Richard 43
Robert 109, 117, 118
Sarah N. 121
Simeon 93
Theodore 117, 118
Wm. 121
HARROW
Arthur 140
HARSEL (Horsel - Hasel)
Peter 4, 25, 112
HARSHER
Thos. 92
HARSMAN (see Hearsman - Horsman - Hiersman)
Agnes 24
Barbara 24
Casper 24(4)
Eve 24
Gasper 24
Hannah 24
Jacob 140
Matthias Ulrick 24
Mary 24
Stephen 92
HART (see Harte - Heard)
George 13, 41, 56, 57, 138
Jasow 119
Magdaline 26, 71
Sarah 107
HARTLEY
Ann 118
Betsy 138
Eleanore 118
Eliz. 108, 118
Hannah 118
Hugh 92
Margaret 118
Mary 118
John 21, 23(2), 43, 46, 63, 92, 108, 136
Rebecca 108
Roger 26
Susan 108
Thos. 92, 108
HARTMAN
Anthony 118

Caty 118
Daniel 118
Henry 118, 140
Margaret 101, 103, 118
Mary 118, 126
Peter 21, 92, 103, 118, 140
Phillip 118
HARTSHORN
Susannah 23
Wm. 28
HARVEY (Harvy)
Francis 6, 60
Mary 9
HASE (see Haise - Hays)
Thos. 92
HASEL (see Harsel - Hazell)
Peter 112
HASS (Haff, one and same also see Haas)
Abraham 21, 23(2), 24, 71, 118, 127
Catherine 101, 102, 117
Cornelius 18(2), 71(2)
Cornelius, Jr. 13
Eliz. 117(3), 178
Lawrence 9, 12, 18, 21, 24 (3), 48, 52, 71(3)
Lawrence, Jr. 48
Leonard 71
Luke 21, 24, 71
Mary 32
Nancy 118
Peter 24(2), 102, 118
Sarah 9, 23, 24(2), 71, 118
Susan 118
Wm. 118
HASTINGS
Joseph 5
Robert 13
HATHAWAY
Eliezer 92
HATTEN
Henry 3, 71
Sam 61, 113
HAUN
Micheal 92
HAUSER (Houser)
Chas. 2, 56, 71
HAVER (see O'Haver)
HAWK (Hank)
Catherine 92
Christian 24
Eliza Jane 119
Henry 5, 25(2), 26(2), 44, 53, 71(2), 92, 107
Henry, Jr. 107
Isaac 10, 24, 92, 101, 118
Jane, Mrs. 101
John 24, 92
Joseph 23, 118
Mary 24
Sarah 118 (see Sarah Arrent)
HAWKINS
David 101
Eve 100, 101
Jacob 121
John 31, 33, 47, 71, 92
John, Jr. 81
Mary 101
Sam 111
HAYDON (Hayton - Dayton)
Belimus 24, 71
Enoch 25, 28, 48, 58, 71
John 3, 10, 15, 30
Louisa 136
Lydia 24(2)
Wm. 24(10), 61, 71, 92
HAYES (see Hase - Haise)
John 11
HAYMOND see Hammond
Wm. 48
Thos. 48
HAYNES
Dan 120
John 28, 71, 101
Joseph 28
Nancy, Mrs. 101, 104
HAYS
Carter John 126
John 92
Rebecca 101
HAYTON
John 8, 10, 15, 30
HAZEL (Hazell - Hasel; see Hoesel)
Henry 2, 24(3), 92
Power 22, 71
Sarah 24(3)
HEAD (Hard - Heard)
Eliz. 1 111
James 5
Jonathan 135
John 101
Henry 133
Nathan 135
Orpha 101
Sarra Eliz. 117

HEALE (Neale?)
Benj. 1
HEALY (Healey)
P. H. 138
Thos. 12, 24(3), 71
HEARD (see Hard)
Nath. 137
HEARE (see Hare -Harre- Hearn)
Adam 106, 129
James 129
John L. 101, 106, 115, 130
Matthew 101, 115
HEARN
Eliza 101
John H. 101
Matthew 101
HEARSMAN (see Hersman - Hiersman)
Abraham 118
Agnes 24
Ann 24
Barbara 24
Christopher 24, 71, 118
Eve 24, 25, 118
Gasper 24
George 24, 71, 118
Gilbert 48
Hannah 24
Jacob 8
Jemez 118
Margaret 118
Mary 24(2)
Marguerite 118
Mark 118(2)
Matthias Ulrich 24(4), 50 (2), 71(2)
Phillip 24, 50, 71, 92
Stephen 92
Susannah 118
HEASEL
Henry 50
HEATH (Heathe)
Azakel 92, 140
Agnes 24(4)
Jonathan 1, 4, 5, 7(3), 8, 13, 17, 19, 24(4), 25, 26, 28, 35, 41(2), 48, 58, 61, 63, 71, 92, 109, 120, 136 137
Wm. 24, 39, 62, 71
HEATHERINGTON
John 124
HEATOR
Barbara 115
Marget 118
Marey 118
Micheal 92, 118
Phillip 118
Solomon 137
HEAVILL (Neavill or Nevell?)
Joseph 7, 23, 44, 61, 63
HEAW
Peter 39, 71
HEDGER (Hedgers)
John 53, 92
HEDGES
Silas 7, 11, 25, 50
Solomon 25(2), 46, 52
Stephen 132
Rebecca 25
HEERMAN
Thos. 27
HEFFELBON (see Heffelbower)
Dan F. 120
Eseers 120
HEFFELBOWER (see Heffelbon)
Daniel F. 118
David 118
Edward 118
Eliz. 118
Mary Eliza 118
Sarah Jane 118
HEISKELL
Adam 131
Catherine 106, 109, 118, 130, 131
Christopher 110, 118, 126, 127, 133, 138
Felix 119
Fred W. 133
Isaac 118, 127
Isaac N. 126
Jacob 118
James P. 127
John C. 119, 124, 127, 128
John 118, 137
Peter 127
Rickey 131
Susanna 118
Samuel 118
Wm. 109, 134
Wm. P. 126
HEINSMAN (Heinzman)
Andrew F. 111
Barbara 25(2)
Catherine 25(2)
Charles 43
Eliz. 4, 25, 117, 128

Henry 4, 5, 6, 7, 14, 15, 21, 28, 25(3), 33(2), 35(2), 51(4), 53, 55, 61(2), 62 (3), 71(10)
Dr. Henry 128
H. 44
Henry, Jr. 111
George 25(2)
Jacob 25(2)
John 55, 111
Samuel 111
HEITH (Keith?)
Henry 3
Jonathan 41
HEITT (see Hiett)
HEIZER
Jean, Mrs. 100, 101
John L. 101
Leonard John 100, 101
Mary Ann 101
HELLYER
Elizabeth 113
HELPENSTINE
Andrew 128
HELMICK (Hellmick)
Jacob 17, 71, 92, 109
John 92
HELM
Joseph 9(2), 71(2)
Meredith, Jr. 111
Wm. 111
HENDERSON
Andrew 45
Cornes 45
David 55, 71, 116, 184
Henry 3
John 12, 52(2), 111, 112, 118, 132
John K. 121
John Grant 118
Larkin ???
Moses 55, 71, 116
Nancy 118
Sampson 3, 71, 92
Sophia 137
Thos. 27, 47, 71
Wm. 106, 118
HENDRICKS
Abraham 9, 92
Dan 121
Heirs 107
Maria 117
HENDRICKSON (Hendrixon)
John 111
Amaria 113
HENDRY (Hendery) see Henry and Hennery
Alix 25, 71, 92
Daniel (Henry) 71
Eliz. 25
John 25, 92
Micheal 92
Scythe 25
Wm. M. 122
HENNERY
John 92
HENKLE (see Hinkle)
Barbara 92
Widow 92
HENNING
Eliz. 137
HENRY (Hendry)
Alex 38, 92
Dan 43
Eliz. 25
John 25
Micheal 92
N. 37, 38, 48(4)
HENSHAW
Wm. 55
HENWOOD
Wm. 25, 92
HERGOT
John 128
Joseph 128
HERMAN
Richard 40
Thos. 25
HERMANBRANT (Erm-intrant) 17, 71
HERNDON
John 7, 18, 19(2), 21, 22, 27(2), 32, 33, 34, 38, 39, 42, 49, 58(2), 59
HERON
Wm. 108
HERRIN
George 118
Isaac 118
Wm. 118
HERRIOS
Wm. 117
HERRIOTT
Anna 138
Eliza, Mrs. 101
Ephriam 19, 71, 92, 101, 118
Ephriam, Sr. 118
Isabella 118
John 118

Sarah 118
Ursela 118
Wm. 117, 118
HERRSMAN
Christopher 24, 92
HERSHMAN
Christopher 37, 59
HERSMAN (see Harsman - Horsman - Hiersman)
Barbara 24
Casper 24
Christopher 24
George 24, 92
Mary 24
Matthias 24, 92
Wm. 136
HESS
Henry 92
James 1
Johanes 3
HETER
Micheal 28, 71
HETH
Andrew Thos. 118
Eliz. 118
John Thaddens 118
Henry 5, 15, 22, 28, 51, 63
Sam Pleasants 118
Wm. Henry 118
Wm. 118
HEW (seeHeaw)
Peter 25
HEWES
Caleb 25
HEWS
Ellis 180
Josiah 34(2)
Wm. 130
HEWLINGS
F. W. 7(2)
Joseph H. 134
HIATT (see Hiett)
Geo. 25, 71
John 124
John, Sr. 25, 72
HICKLE (Hinkle - Henkle)
Elizabeth 101, 102
Jonathan 118
Joseph 102
Henry 113
Stephen 125, 138
Stevin 102
Timothy 102
HICKMAN
John 120
Major 135
HICKS
Moses 6, 22, 25(2), 41
Samuel 6, 22, 25(2), 41
Thos. 92
HICKSON
George 8
HIDE
Isaac 109, 110
Scythe 25
HIDER (Hidner)
Adam 34, 37, 44, 71(2), 92, 115, 131
Micheal 137
HIDNER
Adam 115
Jacob 140
John 92
Leonard, Sr. 92
Lems 92
HIERONIMUS
Andrew S. 132
HIERSMAN see Hearsman
Casper 24
HIETT (Hiatt -Haitt - Heitt - see Hite)
Ann 118
Arthur 118
Arthur Melanchton ???
Asa 118
Elias 2
Eliza 118
Elizabeth 118(2)
Emily 127
Evan 3, 25(3), 71, 92, 108, 111, 115, 118(2), 34
Frances 118
George 25, 124
Hannah 118
Harriet Ann 127
James 15, 25(4), 33, 45, 48, 71(2), 118
James S. 118
James W. 124
Jane 118
John 101, 118(2), 122, 124 (2), 126, 130
Johanathen 118
Jonathan T. 111, 118(3), 125, 130, 135
Jeremiah T. 118(3)
Joseph 25, 47, 118(2)
Joseph B. 118
Julia Ann 135
Lucinda 118(2)

Lucresia 25
Lucretia 25
Lucy 25(2)
Lydia Ann 118
Margaret 118(2)
Marjery 124
Martha 118
Mary 118
Mary Virginia 137
Robert 118
Sam 118
Sarah 25, 101, 118(3), 124 (2)
Susannah 118
Susan 118
Timothy 114
Wm. 118, 137
HIGGING
John 106
John, Jr. 25, 71
Sarah 25
HIGGINS (often confused with Wiggins...see Wiggins)
Ann 118
Archibald 119
Bustired 118
Edy 119
Eliz. 109
Hannah 25(2)
Hetty 118
Ione 118
James T. 10, 60, 71, 112, 119(2), 125, 131, 137
James, Jr. 112
Jane 25, 118
Major John 119
John 3, 4, 12, 25(3), 36, 37, 38, 42, 46, 71(4), 92(2), 104, 107(2), 108, 118, 119, 126, 127, 134
John, Jr. 7, 71
John, Sr. 119
John Copsey 118
John M. 118
Jonathan 118
Joseph T. 118, 119
Joseph C. 118, 131
Joshua 119
Judiah 25, 37, 119
Justinian ???
Kewsiah 119
Maria N. 119
Maria 119
Martha 118
Martha Ellen 118
Martha V. 118
Matilda 119
Mary 118, 119
Matty 118
Metilda 25
Morttgomery P. 112, 131
Morttgomery Pike 118
Patsy 101, 104, 119, 127
Peter 7(2), 36(2), 35(2), 39, 92
Rachel 118, 119
Robert 6, 25(8), 39, 41(3), 71, 92
Sally 25, 127
Sarah 119
Sarah Y.
Thos. 118, 119
Wm.
HIGH (see Hile...High and Hile are sometimes confused)
Anna 119
Ann Maria 119
Catherine 119(2)
Christiania 119
Elijah 107, 118, 119(2)
Eliz. 25(4), 119(2)
Emily 118, 34
Fred 118, 119(2)
Geo. 101, 19(2), 120
Henry 25(2), 72, 101, 107, 118, 119, 120
Henry M. 107, 118, 119
Jane 101
Jacob 26, 57, 72, 119
John 25(7), 26, 53, 72(3), 92, 119, 120, 130
John, Jr. 25, 72
Jonathan 119(2)
Luke 109, 110
Margaret 119
Mary 101, 109, 110, 119, 136
Nancy 119
Sarah Ann 119
Susannah 119
Thos. 1
Warner T. 118
HIGHLEY
Charlotta 25, 72
Rubin 25, 72
Sarah 25, 72
HITE (also see Hart-Hiett-Hiatt)
Abraham 2, 3, 4, 5, 7(2), 8,

INDEX — PAGE 153

HILEY
Rudolph 92
HILES
Sarah 137
HILKEY (Hilky)
Christian 59, 72
Eliz. 107
HILL (Hall or Hull)
Ann 11, 26
Betty 7
Daniel 25(2), 72, 92
Elinor 72(2), 129
Fredrick 15
Gasper 92
Geo. 2, 5, 9, 12, 22, 25(2), 28, 34, 35, 40, 48(2), 72(2), 117, 138
John 38
John W. 117
Jos. 25(2), 54, 72, 92, 137
Joshua 40, 72
Kesiah 129
Le Roy 7, 11, 25, 26, 28, 47(2), 48(2), 72(4), 48(2), 72(4)
Mrs. 135
Robert 7
Thos. 37
Rev. Wm. 135
Wm. 7, 72, 92
Wm., Jr. 125
HILLERY
Wm. 16(3), 72
HILLEY
Fredrick 51(2), 72(2)
Wm. 16
HILLS
Wm. N. 125
HILTON
F. N. 136
Francis 136
HIMELVRIGHT
John H. 129
Joseph 26(2)
HINES (Hinds)
Henry 26, 37, 61(2), 114
Jacob 44, 72
Jacobas 42
Joseph 26, 44, 112
Nancy, Mrs. 101
Susan 112
Thos. 101, 106
HINKINS
HINKLE (see Henkle)
Catherine, Mrs. 101
John 100, 101
HIRE
Rudolph 26
HIRSMAN (see Hiersman - Hearsman or Hersman)
John 98
Casper 3, 72
Stephen 92
HIRT
HISS
Henry 140
HITE (also see Hart-Hiett-Hiatt)
Abraham 2, 3, 4, 5, 7(2), 8, 9, 13, 17(2), 18(2), 19, 21, 22, 23, 25, 26(6), 27, 30, 33, 35(3), 41, 44, 46, 49, 52(2), 53(2), 55, 56, 57, 58, 60, 68, 88, 92, 125, 133, 136, 137
Maj. Abraham 26
Abraham, Sr. 125
Abraham, Jr. 26, 33, 41, 56, 125
Casper 2, 133
Eleanor 26
I. 2nd 25
I. 23, 33, 46, 68
Isaac 21(3), 26, 41, 62, 72(5)
Jacob 125
Col. John 26, 72
Joseph 57
John, Jr. 26
John 26(3)
Matthias 22, 26, 39, 72(2), 92
M. W. 26(2)
Rebecca 26(6), 137
Sarah 26(3)
Thos. 125
T. 33
Jonathan 111
HITFE
Henry 48, 72
HOAGLAND (Houghland - Hogelang)
Cornelius 68, 129
HOAK (Hoke - Hock - Houck - Hawk)
Enos, Esq. 116
Stephen 92
HOBBS (see Hubs - Hubbs)

John 24, 72
HOBSON
Jane 101, 102
HOCK (Hoak - Hawk)
Catherine 92
HODGER
Reuben 92
HODDY
Mary 26
Richard 26
Wm. 34
HOFF (Huff - Hess - Haff - Hase)
Peter 92
HOFFMAN (Hof) (Huffman)
Aaron 104
Agnes 26
Benj. 18(2), 26, 27, 72, 126
Charity 5
Catherine 26, 41
Christiana 123
Christopher 17
Conrad 5, 16, 58, 72(3), 92
Conrath 9(3)
Eliz. 101, 104
George 41, 72
Henry 26, 41, 72, 108
H. K. 119
Henry K. 127, 128, 135
John 26, 32, 72
Joseph 104, 123
Juliana 41
Sarah 26, 101, 104
HOFFORD (Huford - Stafford)
Richard 31
HOG Hoge - Hogg - Hogge
Aaron 92
George 132
Pet & Peter 3, 5(6), 6(2), 7(2), 9, 11, 12(2), 15(2), 16(6), 17(88), 18, 22, 23(2), 24(8), 26(8), 27(2), 30, 32, 34(4), 36(4), 39, 16), 44(2), 47(2), 50, 52, 54, 55(2), 58, 59(5), 60, 62, 72(8), 117.
HOGAN(S)
Thos. 53
HOGAN
Mary 119
Susannah 117, 119
Thos. 3, 80, 87, 72(2), 109, 117
Wm. 57, 60
HOGBINE
John 92, 137
HOGE 63, 125
Ann 119
Asa 119
Eliza 119
Elizabeth 26, 119
Esther 119
Geo. 22, 26(2), 30, 51, 72, G. Wilson 119
John 113
Maria 119
Mary 121
Major 129
Moses 92, 119, 122, 125
Paul 113
Ruth 119
Solomon 86
Sarah 119
Wm. 26, 119
Wm., Jr. 119
HOGELAND (Hoa - Hough)
Cornelius 26, 92
HOGERTY (Hagerty)
John 92
HOGG
John 57
HOGANS
Thos. 117
HOGELAND (Houghlan)
Cornelius 11, 17, 72
HOGUE (Hague - Hoge)
Eleanor 26(4)
Samuel 26(4)
HOKE (Hoek - Hawk - Houck)
Elliner 110
George 110
HOLDERMAN (see Halterman)
Abraham 58
Abram 26
Noney 26
HOLE (Hall) 140
Daniel 17, 92
HOLLAND
Amanda 117
Norrie 117
Thos. 2, 61, 92
Thos. 2, 4, 61, 92
HOLLAS
Daniel 72

HOLLENBACK (-beck)
Amee 116
Catherine 116
Caroline 119
Dan. 31, 72, 116, 119, 126
Isaac 119, 122
John 106
Sarah 116
Susan 116
Thos. 3, 20, 49, 62, 72, 92
HOLLEBACK
Thos. 7, 72, 92
Thos., Sr. 23, 72
HOLLIDAY
Angus M.D. 101, 104
Eliz. 137
Jane 26
John 16, 24, 26(2), 30, 72
Richard 21, 113, 114, 120
Rub. 56
Ruth 118
Susan, Mrs. 101
Wm. 8, 21, 72
HOLMES
David 85(2)
Ebenezer 137
Hugh 30, 85
John 14, 72
HOLOBACK see Hollenback
HOLT
Absolom 180
Martha 130
Samuel 135
HOLTERMAN (Holderman)
Abram 26
Noney 26
HOLTZ
Martin 127
Reuben 127
HOMAN
Almona K. 117
German C. 117
Henry 117
Henry 117
Jacob 92
HONORE (see Howard p. 27, 46)
HOOE
Robert 59, 72
HOOFMAN (Hoffman - Huffman)
Christopher 119
Joseph 119
Mary 119
HOOK
Catherine 132 (Kool)
David S. 125
Eliz. 119
Hetty 119
Jane 100, 101
Josiah 119
Joseph 119, 127
Mary 119(2)
Matthias 59, 72
Priscilla Ann 131
Robert 119(2), 122
Samuel 119, 121, 125, 127
Thos. 130
Wm. 2, 24, 72, 98, 107, 119, 131
Wm. W. 131
HOOKER
John 53(3)
Phillip 185
Susanna 119
HOOPER
Thos. J. 125, 133
HOORNBECK
Abr. 53
HOOVER (Hauver - Haauver)
Henry 26
Jacob 26, 27(4), 53, 72(4), 86, 92
Iseak 60
John 104, 124
Sarah 101, 104
HOPESELL MONTHLY MEETING 116
HOPKINS
John 26
Lambeth 26
HOPPY
David 26, 72
Christopher John 26
HOPWOOD
Dan 38, 40, 86
John 30
HORD (Hard)
Phillip (???(
HOREN
Richard 109
HORN
Andrew 26(3), 39, 47(2), 72, 119
Catherine 26, 112(2), 115
Eve 119

Eliz. 26, 101(4)
George 2, 8, 40, 44, 72, 92, 119, 127, 129
Geo., Sr. 26, 119
Geo., Jr. 26, 27, 39, 47, 72
Hannah 180
Henry 26, 39, 47(2), 50, 72 (2), 119
John 101, 111
Mary 26, 119
Phillip 25, 26(2), 47(2), 112, 119(2)
HORNBECK (Hornback) (Hoornbach)
Abraham 26, 53, 92, 119
Anthony 140(2)
Benjamin 119
Daniel 119
Dorothy 117
Eleanor 119
Eliz. 26
Hussethy 119
Isaac 26(2), 60, 92, 109, 119(2)
James 26, 119, 140
John 7, 72
Magdelene 92, 119
Micheal 17, 119, 137
Richard 119
Samuel 2, 11, 26(2), 72(3), 92, 117, 119, 138
Simon 11, 92, 119
Solomon 119
Wm. 119
HORNER
Eliz. 26
Geo. 26(2), 44
Stephen 27(2)
HORSAL
Peter, Jr. 136
HORSK
Peter 92, 140
HORSEMAN (Hier - Hers(h)
Lydia 128
Wm. 123
HORSMAN (see Harsman)
Christian 119
Christopher 119
Casper 119
Geo. 119
Eve 119
Jacob 92, 119
Joseph 125
Martha 119
Matthies U. (Ulrich) 72, 119
Matthies V. (Ulrich) 72, 119
Phillip 119
HORST
Geo. 92
Wm. 92
HOSKINSON
And. 123
HOSNAN
Patsy 112
HATTEN
Isabella 126
Rebecca 126
HOTTINGHAM Nothing-
Stephen, Jr. 27
Susannah 27
Thos. 27
HOTSENBELLA Hotzenbeler - Hotzendiller - Hotzenpoller - Hotzindiller - Hotzenbeler)
Ann 119
Abraham 119
Eliz. 27(3)
Jacob 27(5), 72, 110
John 119
Henery 119
Peter 119
Stephen 27(4), 50, 72
HOTZINPELER
Christinia 119
Henry 119
Levi 119
HOUGH
Hannah 27
John 27, 113
Malon 31, 72
Wm. 5, 27, 28, 58, 62
HOUGHLAND (see Houghland - Hogeland)
Ann 118
Cornelius 26, 92, 118
Eleanore 118
Eliz. 27
Hannah 118
Henry 118
John 119
Macey 118
Mary 118
Margaret 118
Richard 27(3), 36, 45, 52
HOUGLAN
Henry 1, 72

HOUGHTY (Foughty)
Fredrick 21
HOUSE
Amous 101
Andrew 27
Catherine 27(3)
Catherine, Mrs. 101
Eliz. 27
Jacob 92
John 9, 18, 20(2), 56, 92(2), 107
Jos. 28, 27(2), 46, 72, 92, 118
Mary 121
Samuel 101(3), 123
Wm. 22, 27
HOUSEHOLDER
Easter 102
Mary 101
HOUSER (see Howzar - Howzar)
Chas. D. 61(2)
HOUSEMAN
Martin 132
HOW (Howe)
Edward 2
Eleanore 27
Joseph 15(2), 27, 44(2), 52(2), 57, 72, 120
HOWARD (Honore)
Elizabeth 119, 137
Evelina 119
Esther 27(5)
Frances Maurice 27(2), 84, 38, 46
Jane Eliz. 119
John 27, 44, 47, 72
Jonathan 111
Lucy 119, 137
Lucy Fenevra 27
Parson 92
Margaret 119
Mary Frances 119
Mary P. 119
Mary 111, 137
Risin 92
Reason 27(5), 30, 41, 56, 72
Sarah M. 119
Susan 119
Talifero S. 118
Widow (nee Ashbrook) 139
W. James 137
Wm. 119
HOWELL
Anna 120
George 27
Hannah 120
Jemmina 27, 72
Isaac 22
Jonathan 92
Lucreasy 120
Sarah 119
Wm. 2, 14, 27, 28, 57, 72, 92, 116
HOWLAND
Richard 63
HOWMAN
John 106
Stithman 92
HOWZAR (Houser?)
Charlotte 120
Cassandra 120
Jacob 120
Jacob 120
Lewis 120
Lysander 120
Mary Pritchet 120
Thomas Offielt 120
HOYE
John 111, 113
Mary 111
Paul 27, 72
Wm. 27
"HRINSARDT" 119
HUBBARD (Hubbert)
Catherine 27(2)
Jacob 2, 27(2), 36, 40, 72(2), 92
John, Sr. 92
John, Jr. 92
HUBBERT
Jacob 92
HUBBS (Hubs)
Thos. 92
Thos., Sr. 92, 140
HUBER
Jacob 92
HUBS (Hobbs)
Thos. 92, 140
HUDDLERTON
Nathan 50(2), 72
HUDDLESTON
Mary 133
Naiti. 133, 134
HUDSON
David 92
John 92, 140
HUES (Hewes - Hugbee)
Thos. 11

HUFF
Leonard 135
Richard 85
HUFFMAN (see Hoffman)
Anna 119
Amos 136
Benjamin 27, 92
Catherine 92
Christian 115, 120
Christopher 72, 92, 140
Conrad 7, 27, 72, 92, 126
Dan 119, 120(2)
Elisa 113
Elizabeth 120(2)
Geo. 138
Henry 92(2)
John 33, 35, 72
Joseph 113, 136
Phillip 92
HUGH(S) (Huges - Hewes-Hewe)
Aaron 127
Caleb 27
David 27
Ellis (Elis) 27(2), 106, 120
Evan 120(2)
Hugh 27(2), 28, 120(2)
James 35, 92, 120
Jane 27(2)
John 1, 85, 92
Jonathan 92, 120
Josiah 35, 55, 61, 72(3)
Mary 28, 120
Sarah 120
Sudrah 120
Susanna 27(4), 28, 92, 120
Thos. 15, 27(5), 35, 41, 72 (2), 92, 120
Wm. 1, 28(2), 72, 106, 120 (4)
HULICK (Gulick?)
Milly 125
HULL
Ann 120
Benj. 120, 125(2)
Eliz., Mrs. 101
Elizabeth 120
Isaac 104, 120
Jacob 100, 101, 120
Jemma 120
Mary 120
Martin 109, 120
Mary Virginia 137
Silas 120
Stephen 120
Wm. 120, 137
HULS (Hulse)
Richard 28(2)
HUMBLER
Adam 92
HUMES
Andrew 38, 92, 114, 139
Herbert 31, 72
Margaret 41
Nancy 101, 103, 131
Peace 114
Samuel 103
HUMPHREYS Humphries
Agnes 27(2)
Jacob 41
Ralph 2, 6, 7, 21, 22, 28 (3), 32, 37, 42, 56, 72 (3), 92
Thos. 54, 112, 139
T. 12
HUNIMAN
Ellinor 110
HUNSMAN
Eliz. 101
Henry 103
HUNTER
David 6, 37, 59, 85
John 22
Moses 23, 40(3)
Richard 27, 29(2), 62, 72(2)
Thos. 92
Wm. 92
HURFORD
Joseph 28, 38, 72
HURNE
Andrew 28
HURNESS (Harness)
John 115
HUROMOUS
Henry 125
HURST
Moses R. 131
HUTCHINGS
Richard 33
HUTCHINSON
James 52
HUTSON (Hudson)
David 92
John 92
Mary 113
HUTTA
Catherine 120
Christian 120
Eliz. 120
HUTTON
Gideon 136
Isaac 92
Jacob 92
Moses 1, 7(3), 8, 17, 21, 25 (2), 26(2), 27, 28, 30, 85 (2), 38, 39, 41(3), 44, 48, 58, 72(5), 92, 138
HYE
Fredrick 5, 44
HYETT (Hiett or Hiatt)
James 92
Evan 92

IAAC
Addom 28
ICE
Eleanor 28(2)
Fredrick 28(3)
IHRESOM(ON) Ahrsom - Earson
Simon 32, 73
IMART (Stuart)
John Black 47
INGLE (see Engle)
Christian 120
Elizabeth 120
Eve 120
Margaret 120
Matthias 120(2)
Rachel 120
INGMAN
James 126
Jane (Jen) 126
Nancy 126
INGRAM
Anna 48
Sam 28, 44
INNIS (Ennis)
Enoch 3(2), 11(3), 12(2), 16, 26, 28(3), 35(2), 36, 43, 46, 63, 72(2), 112, 120
James 15, 120
Sarah 11(2), 28, 120
INSKEEP
Abraham 19, 28, 33, 40, 72 (2), 92, 120(2), 136, 139
Abraham W. 120
Anna T. 120
Catherine 120(2)
David 120
Elizabeth T. 120(6), 137
Foreman 120(5)
Hannah 109
Hannah Eliz. 120
Henry M. (Mackin) 120
Isaac 120
"A" 101(2)
James 120, 121, 137
James Goldsmith 120
James H. (Henry) 111, 120
Jeremiah 120
John 119, 120(3), 132, 134
John Foreman 109, 120
Joseph 11, 50, 63, 73, 118, 120, 121, 139
Joseph, Jr. 120
Margaret V., Mrs. 101
Mary Ann 120
Rachel 120
Rebecca 120(2)
Rebecca Susan 120
Sally 120
Samuel 120(2)
Sarah 120(6)
Sarah W. 120
Susan Vance 120(2)
Wm. 19(8), 28, 73(5), 120 (8), 134, 136(2)
Wm. C. 121
Wm. Foreman 120(2), 136
Wm. Vance 120
Wm., Jr. 120
IRESON (Earson)
James 27(2), 55
IRESHAM (Earsom - Ahrsom)
Simon 32, 73
IRONTON
Lydia 28, 120
Richard 28, 120
Thomas 120
IRVINE
William 54
IRWIN
I. 58
Jared 137
John 189
Margaret 28
Robert 22, 28, 73
Thos. 18
IUART (Stuart) 47
JACK (see Jacques)
Edward Wilson 120(2)
Carter T. 120
Frances Rebecca 120
John 2, 5, 7(3), 9(2), 10, 12(2), 16, 18, 19(2), 21, 25(2), 27(2), 28(5), 29, 35, 36, 38(5), 41, 42(5), 44, 45, 48, 51(3), 59, 61 (2), 62, 110, 116, 127
John G. 120
John J. 25
Judith 120
Mary 120
Rebecca 28, 120
Rebecca 28, 120
Rebecca B., Mrs. 120
Robert Y. 120
JACKSON
Abraham 120
Benjamin 120
Ebenezar 120
Eliz. 28(3), 120
James 132, 137
Laser 132
Margaret 129
Nancy 130
Samuel A. 220(2)
Thos. 92
Wm. 10(4), 13, 28(3), 33, 39, 41, 43, 57, 73(3), 86, 92, 120, 123, 124
JACO
Thos. 35, 73
JACOB(S)
Elizabeth 28
Ezekiel 14, 73
G. 131
Gabriel 14, 33, 36
J. J. 25
Jeremiah 28
John 121
John, Jr. 36, 73
John J. 3, 12(4), 14, 16, 18(2), 19, 33, 38(2), 50, 56, 73, 85, 92, 107, 116
John J. Jr. 25(2), 57, 73
John Jeremiah 28(4), 58, 73 (4), 109, 113, 124
Joseph 12, 28, 30, 57, 60, 73
Julia Ann 120
Mary 28, 113
R. 128
Samuel 32, 92
Susan 120, 131
Wm. 7(2), 19, 21, 26, 27(2), 28, 32, 36, 37, 42(2), 44, 53, 58
JACQUES (see Jack)
Benton 124
Mrs. Anna 131
JAMES
Eliza 114
Elizabeth 28, 113, 121
Elizabeth Ann 121
Evan 61
George C. 121
Huldah 120, 125
Isaac 59, 92, 113, 121, 125(2)
Isaac N. 121
James Lanson 121
Jemima 121
John 130
John Culp 121
Joseph 130
Lewis 51, 73
Martha 121
Mary 121
Rebecca 123
Rodham (Rod) Rd. 5, 10, 12, 13, 18(2), 22, 38, 59, 125, 137
Sarah 119, 121, 124
Thornton Bosley 121, 126
Wm. 28, 43, 60, 73, 112, 132
Wm. C. 121
JAMESON
James 86
Robert 12
JANE (Zane and Bane)
Joseph 92
JANNEY (Jenney)
Amos 119
Catherine 135
Edward 119
Wm. 1, 32(2), 33, 43, 73(2), 93
JARBOE
Sarah 126
JARVIS(S)
Milly 135
Robert 14, 73
JARY
Wm. 48
JEFFERSON
Luke 92
JENKES
Jacob 87
JENKING
Richard 116
JENKINS (Junkan - Jenking)
Abraham 6
Ann 92, 121
Betsy Ann 121
Benjamin 121
Eliz. 121(2)
Evan 92, 108, 115, 121(2)
Fred B. 123
Fredrick 121
George 121
Isaac 21
Israel 121
Jacob 8, 28, 73, 93, 103, 116, 119, 121(2)
Jacob, Sr. 108
James 121(2)
John 104, 106, 108, 109, 121(3), 133, 135
Jonathan 121, 139
Joseph 121
Mary 101, 103, 104, 121(3)
Mary Eveline 121
Micheal 121(2)
Rachel 121
Richard 116
Ruth 121
Sarah Ann 121
Sussanna 121
Susan Mariah 121
Wm. 109, 121(2)
JENNY see Janney - Janey
Catherine 135
Wm. 32(2), 85, 73(3), 93
JENNINGS
Ann 28, 32, 121
Mary 121
Wm. 32, 121
JERKINS
Jacob 86
JETT
Daniel 130
JEWEL
Patrick 112(2)
JOHNS
Aquila 35, 73
Isaac 2, 15, 93
JOHNSON (Johnston) 93, 53
Abigail 28(3), 121
Abigail, Mrs. 101
Abraham 1(2), 2(2), 4(3), 7, 8(2), 10, 12(2), 13, 14, 20(3), 24(3), 25(2), 27 (2), 28(3), 29(3), 31(4), 35, 38(2), 45, 49, 50(3), 51, 52(2), 56, 57(2), 58, 61, 62(3), 63, 73(4), 85 (2), 88, 119, 120
Abraham, Sr. 4, 28, 61, 73, 93
Abraham, Jr. 4, 5, 8(2), 24 (2), 28(3), 34, 38, 39, 62, 73, 93
Abraham Okey 134
Amos 99, 101
Anna 120
B. 9
Barnet 50, 73, 121
Benjamin 123
Bazel 101, 102
Catreen 128
Catherine 29(4)
Charity 29(4), 124
Cornelius 108
Deborah 121
Deborah Jane 132
Deborah Hood 132
Debra 121
Dinah 29, 121
Eleanor 29(3)
Elisha 93
Elizabeth 29, 108, 109, 121 (2), 128(2), 133
Elijah 33
Ephraim 1, 29, 39, 40, 73, 85
Geo. W. 133
Hannah 29(2)
Isaac 2
Jacob 128
James 121(2), 126, 128
Jane 123
Jane, Mrs. 101
John 4, 14, 21, 29(6), 49, 52, 53, 56, 73(3), 106, 109, 121(4), 132, 133
John, Sr. 93, 111, 121
John, Jr. 111, 116
Jonathan 121
Joseph 29(3), 47, 52, 73, 93, 108, 121(2), 123, 129
Joshua 25(2), 73(2), 124, 133
Margaret 29, 133
Mary 12, 121, 123, 128(2), 133
Mary Jane 133
Mary, Mrs. 101
Mary Ann 133
Minard 46, 63
Money 133
Nance 121
Nancy 121(2), 133
Nathaniel 121
Okey 4(6), 5(2), 6(2), 7, 8, 9, 12, 24, 25(4), 26(2), 29 (11), 31, 34, 48(2), 45, 46, 48, 50, 52(2), 53, 57, 73(10), 88, 93(2), 115(2)
Okey Greenville 134
Peter 118
Rachel 28(2), 29, 108
Rebecca 128
Robert 53
Sarah 109, 111, 136
Sofia 127
Susan Harriett 133
Susannah 121, 125
Thornton 137
Thos. 29, 41
Thos., Jr. 33, 73
Wm. 10, 19, 22, 24, 28(2), 29(8), 39, 40, 42, 45(3), 49, 50(2), 52(2), 53, 57 (2), 58, 61, 62(4), 73(6), 93(2), 101, 104, 121, 125, 131, 134
Wm., Jr. 4, 13, 14, 28, 39, 73(3), 93
Wm., Sr. 93
JOHNSTON (Johnstone - Johnson)
Abraham 2, 28, 29, 59
Abraham, Jr. 2
Ephraim 29(2), 39(2)
John 6(2), 73(2), 93
John, Jr. 93
Minard 46, 63
Okey 4, 22
Robert 53
Thornton 137
Wm. 30(2)
Wm., Jr. 2, 30(2), 73(2)
JONES
Aaron (Aron) 1, 2, 21, 30, 32, 37, 73, 121(3)
Abel 121
Abraham 20(36), 29(2), 30, 37, 55, 73(2), 121
Benjamin 16, 29(3), 73
Babiel (Gabriel) 27
Carlton S. 121
Catherine 30, 121
Daniel 1, 23, 29(8), 30(4), 31, 32, 34, 37(3), 38, 48, 55(2), 62, 73(5), 121(3)
David 4, 12, 29(2), 30(3), 35, 37, 50, 62, 73(4), 93, 121(5)
David, Jr. 30, 45, 73
Eleanor 30
Elias 121
Elizabeth 30(2), 137
Esther 30
Gabriel (G.-Ga.-Gab.) 1, 3 (2), 5(5), 6, 8, 9(4), 11, 12(2), 15(3), 16(7), 17 (36), 18(6), 19, 21, 24(3), 25, 26, 27(4), 30(3), 32 (2), 34(4), 35, 36(5), 39 (10), 44(2), 45(2), 47, 48, 50(2), 52, 54, 55, 58, 59 (4), 60, 63
Isabella 30, 73
Isaac 29, 30, 73, 121(2)
Jacob 121
James 30
Jenny 111
John 1, 12, 14, 16, 21, 23(2), 37, 29, 30(5), 31, 35, 45, 50, 56, 59, 73(4), 85, 86, 93, 121(5), 138, 139
John, Jr. 13(2), 20, 42, 45, 50, 53, 73
John, Sr. 1(2), 14(2), 18, 27, 30(2), 31, 32, 43, 58, 114
Joseph 30, 73, 116
Joshua 21, 40, 55, 73(2), 121
Kesiah 121
Louise E. 121
Lucy 121(2)
Margaret 30(2)
Mary Ann 101, 140
Mary 29(2)
Matthias 37, 73
Moses 27, 29, 30(2), 73, 101 (2), 121
Moses, Sr. 101
Nancy 121(2)
Owen 5, 30, 73
Peter 23, 30, 31, 50(2), 73 (3), 93, 121
Peter, Jr. 20, 73
Peter W. 100
Richard 28
Robert 87, 117, 121, 137
Capt. Robert 121
Rosanna 29(5), 30(3)
Ruth 121
Samuel 30, 36, 37, 43, 53(4),

73(2), 93, 121
Sarah 80, 121(3)
Solomon 2, 18, 20(37), 55 (2), 73, 93, 121(2)
Susannah 80, 121
Thos. 3, 8, 37, 56, 113, 121
Walter, Jr. 63
Wm. 2, 37, 121
JONLEY (Yonley or Tonley)
Chas. A. 111
JOONES (Jones)
Gab. 19
JORDAN
Katherine 93
John 54
Julius 93
Mark 93
JUDY
Elizabeth 121
Henry 93, 109, 121
Jacob 121
John 121
Margaret 93, 121
Martin 93, 121(8)
Nicholas 93, 121(2)
Rosanna 121
JUNKAN (see Jenkins)
Richard 10, 73
Wm. 10, 73

K.
John J. 111
KABUCK
Peter 121
Sarah 121
KACKLEY (Keck - Kark - Ca)
C. 131
Cephas 121
Elias 121
James Addison 121
Joseph 121
Joseph Ira 121
Lydia 121
Mary 121
KALE (Kail)
Anna 117
Jacob 101
Peter 127
KAIL (Kale)
Christina 101, 104
Eliz. 101, 104, 121
Geo. 92, 104(2), 121
John 93, 104(2), 121
Peter 93, 121
KANADA (Kennedy - see Canada)
Thos. 93
KARKLEY (Heckley and Kackley)
Joseph 180
KARNES
Elishia 101
Patrick, Sr. 80
KAY
John 30(2)
KAYSER (Kaiser)
Joseph 58, 93
KEADSY
Nathan 132
KEAREN
Barnard 93
KEARFOOT
Anna 229
Amee 129
John Piersall 129
KEARNS
Elisha 100, 101
John 188
Margaret, Mrs. 101
KEATING
Jane 30(5)
Joan 30
John 5, 9(3), 10, 19, 30(7), 35, 56, 63(2), 73
Mary 30, 73
KEATS (Yeats)
Mary 124
KEAVILLE (Neville)
Joseph 83
KECKLEY (Kackley)
Jacob 119
KEEDER
Jemima 30
Wm. 30, 85
KEELE
Geo. 10
James 10
KEENAN
Edward 119
KEENER (Kenner - Kennear - Kinnear)
Caty 121
Eliz. 121(4)
Geo. 121, 140
John 73, 121, 140, 174
Katy 121
Mary 121(2)

KEERAN (Kearns)
Thos. 27
KEISER
Joseph 7
KEITER
Esther 110
Geo. 110
Geo., Jr. 129
John 125
KEITH (Heith)
Alex 30, 61, 63
Eliz. 30
James (Ja) 3, 5(4), 6, 9, 15 (3), 16, 19, 21(2), 22, 24 (3), 26(2), 27(5), 30(4), 34(4), 35, 36(6), 39, 46, 50, 51, 52, 54, 55, 57, 59 (3), 60, 61, 62, 73(3)
John 11, 21, 30(2), 73(2)
Mary 30(2)
Thos. 30, 41
KEIZNER (Kis)
Hannah 82
Jacob 10, 30(2), 32, 73
John 30
Judy 30
Martha 30
KELLAR (Keller)
Ann 31(13)
Catherine 117
Charles 101, 103, 124, 130
Elmera 101
George 93
John 2, 18(2), 26(2), 27, 29, 30(8), 31(29), 32, 37 (3), 43(3), 46, 53(2)
Mary Ann 120
Thos. 120
KELLEY
Eleanor, Mrs. 101
Frances 107(2)
Hannah 129
Henry 118
Isabelle 101, 103
John 99, 101, 102, 103, 107 (4), 133
John D. 136
Josh. 189
Larkun C. 102
Patrick 93
Sam 93
Thos. 6
KELSO (Relse)
Anna 122
Ellen 122
Elise 122
Eliza 122
Ephram 114
Isaac Bull 122
James 80, 39, 58, 62, 73(2), 99, 119, 122, 138
James F. 122(2)
Jane 99, 101
John, Wesley 122(2)
Joseph A. 122(2)
Mary 122
Robert 122
Rosanna 114
Wm. 122
KEMPS (Kumps)
Jacob 135
KENNEDY (see Kannady and Canada)
David 49
Eliz. 31
Jane 31
Lillian 125
Samuel 31, 137
Thos. 31(2), 47, 73, 93
Wm. 21, 31, 37, 125
KENNY (Kenney)
Sarah Ann 129
KENNER (Kiener)
John 42(3), 73
KENNISON
Edward 31, 52, 73
Matilda 31
KENT
Isabelle 93
Jesse 4, 22, 31, 73
John 4, 61, 73, 93
Joseph 186
KENYON
John 129
KEPLINGER
John 15, 44, 73(2)
KER (Carr)
Fred 117
KERAN (Kern) - (Kee)
Baryn (Bryan) 30, 32, 37
Edward 3, 6, 82
Patrick 6, 31(6), 32, 56, 74 (2), 93
Peter 93
Rebecca 81
Sarah 31(2)
Thos. 27
Wm. 31, 74
KERCHEVAL

Andrew Woodrow 122
Jean 122
John B. 122
John Bellfield 122
Mary Susan 122
Robert 222, 180
Robert C. 122, 130
Sam 120
Sam, Jr. 120, 122, 128, 136
Wm. 136
KERKBRIDE (Kirkbride)
John 125
KERN (Kerns - see Keran)
Barney (Bryan) 132(2)
Catherine 122
Elias 122
Elisha 122
Eliz. 122(2)
Fredrick 122
Hannah 122
Henry 122
Isaac 122
Jacob 39, 74, 119
John 116, 122, 126
John, Jr. 102, 109, 113, 115 (2), 120, 127, 128, 129
John W. 120
Lewis 122
Mary 122
Patrick 31(6), 32, 56, 75(2)
Philip 122
Rebecca 31
Sarah 31(2), 122
Wm. 122
KERSHAM (Kerfam)
Josheph 8, 56
KERSMAN 93
KESLER
John 3, 75
John S. 101
KESTER
Fredrick 31
Hanner 31
KERVEY (Harvey)
Benjamin 100, 101
Charlotte, Mrs. 101
KEYS (Keyes)
Alex 122
Ann 32, 122
Anna P. 122
Chas. (Clem) 122
LABES (Sabes error)
James 33(2)
John 14(2), 74(2)
LACEFIELD
Elias 93
LACEWELL   E
Elias 93
LACK
William 111
LACOCK (see Leacock-Lay-
David 33, 41, 74
Rachel 33
LAFFERTY
Catherine 127
LA FOLLETTE (Lafolet - Lefolet)
Amos 122(2)
Anna 122
Bartholomew 99, 100, 107, 122
Eleanor 107, 122
Mrs. Eleanor 101
Elias 107
Elizabeth 107, 131, 123
Faney 129
H. W. 107, 122(2), 131
Henry W. 107, 131
James 107, 122, 124
Jane 123
John 122
Margaret 122
Mary 101(2), 122
Silas 101
William 198, 122
LAGABEDE
John 36
LAGARDE
John 39(2)
LAIN
Sam 111
LAIRD (Lard-Leard)
Micheal 93
LAING
Daniel 19
LAKUE (Larue)
Isaac 33(2)
Phoebe 33(2)
LAMASTER
Isaac 93
Joseph 93
LAMBERT
Barnabas 93
John 103, 122, 136
Joseph 21
Keziah 122
William 122
LAME
Daniel 33

Eliz. 33
Jacob 27
LANAHAM (see Lanham)
LANBERGER (Laubenger)
George M. 47
LANCASTER
Sarah 124
T. 19
LANCISCUS (Lansiscus & Lansisko)
Henry 16, 33, 52, 74, 93
LADEN (Lander)
Charles 93, 140
LANDER
Barbara 136
Charles 7
Christina 136
Felix 136
Frederick 136
Hannah 33(2)
Henry 33(2), 47, 93
Jacob 93
Jane 33(3)
John 1, 33, 42, 52(2)
Joseph 136
Mary 136
Michael 33(3), 93
Samuel 119
Sarah 33
LANDIS
Henry 5, 74
John 127
LANE (Lain)
Anna 33
Wm. 21, 33, 74
LANFORD (Samford)
William 35, 74
LANGE
Godfrey 2, 33
LANGLEY
John 12
LANGSTOO
Ann 123
LANEHAM
Dennis 101, 102
Nancy, Mrs. 101
LANSISCUS (Lanciscus)
Henry 83
LANSISKO (Lanciscus)
Henry 93, 140
LAPP
Christina 33
George 33
LARD (Laird - Leard)
Micheal 93
LAREN (Larue)
Peter 27
LARGENT (Sargent)
Abe 14
Benjamin F. 109(2), 134
Betsy 122
Ellender 122
James 3(4), 15, 16(2), 22, 25(3), 33(5), 47, 52, 56, 74(8), 86, 99, 122, 123
Jane 122
John 15, 23, 41, 49, 74, 112, 116(2), 122(2), 123
John, Jr. 93
John, Sr. 93
John Washington 122
Lewis 122
Margrate 122
Margaret 33(5)
Margery 122
Mary 122(2)
Milly 122
Nancy 122
Peggy 122
Randle 122
Samuel 122
Sarah 122(2)
Susan 100, 122
Thos. 100, 122
William 3, 93, 122(2)
LAREN (Larue)
Peter 33
LARGENT
Margaret 33(5)
Margery 122
Margrate 122
Mary 122(2)
Milly 122
Nancy 122
Peggy 122
Randle 122
Samuel 122
Sarah 122(2)
Susan 122
Thomas 122
William 93, 122(2)
LARGIN
John 93
LARNER
Amy 112(2)
LARRIMORE (Larramore - Laremore - Larremore - Laurimore)

Eliz. 99, 101
James 86, 106, 109, 121
John 101
Nancy 101(2)
Naomi 106
Rachel 99, 101
Mrs. Rachel 101
Sam 99, 106, 138
Thos. 101(2)
Wm. 99(2)
Wm. E. 109, 123
LARUE (La Rue - Larew - Loren see Lakue)
Abigail 122
Abraham 10, 27, 33
Ann 122
Cornelius 132
Hannah 33(2), 122, 139
Isaac 33(2)
Jacob 21, 27, 33, 55, 74(2), 93, 122(2), 132
Jesse 132
John 10, 33(3), 55, 93, 122
Noah 10, 23, 33, 74(3), 93, 122
Peter 10, 13, 27, 33, 74, 85, 122(3)
Rachel 122(2)
Mrs. Rachel 101
Samuel 33
Sarah 122
LASH
James G. 122
LASHER
William 93
LASSON (Lawson)
Thos. 115
LATIMORE (see Larrimore)
James 106
LAUBINGER (Lob - Law)
Barbara 33
G. 37
George 4, 110
G. Micheal 5, 30, 54, 59
George Michael 33
George M. 47, 52
Hannah 110
LAUGHAN
E. 37, 38(3)
LAUGHLIN (see McLaughlin)
James 93
William 3
LAURENCE (Lawrence)
Edy 119
John 93, 140
Micheal 33, 93
LAURENER (Larrimore)
Eliz. 106
Jane 106
LAURIMORE
Nancy 101(2)
John 101
LAVENDER
Jacob 23
LAWBINGER
G. Micheal 5
LAWLER
James 53(2)
LAWRENCE (Laurence)
Micheal 33, 93
LAWSON (see Lasson and Lawton)
Ann 122, 123
Catherine 101(2), 121, 123
Eliz. 123
Fanny 122, 123(2)
Hannah 109, 122, 123(2)
Halloras 122
Jacob 93, 123
James 33(2), 93, 123, 137
John 123(2)
Jane 123
Margaret 123
Mary 123
Moses 93, 140
Nancy 101(2), 121
Peggy 123
Samuel 123
Sarah 123
Septimus 121
Sophia 33(2)
Richard 93, 140
Thos. 33, 51, 68, 74, 93, 122(2)
Wm. 123
LAY
John 86
LAYCOCK
David 41, 74
LAYFOLLET
William 45(2), 74(2)
LAYMAN
George 126
Sarah 124
LEA (Sea - Lee)
Adam 101
Mrs. Eliz. 101, 103

Micheal 115
LEACH
James 3
LEAMAN
Jonah 13, 74
LEAPHART
Augustine 98
LEAPLEY
Mrs. Elizabeth 101
John 101(2)
LEARD (see Lard)
Jean 48
Micheal 29, 45(2), 48, 50(2), 52, 93, 116(3), 139
LEARY
Dennis 93
LEASE
July Ann 124
LEASON (Leeson)
Margaret 34
Richard 34, 93
Thomas 34
LEATHERMAN 107
Ann 123(2)
Benjamin 101, 103, 107
Chritiana 123
Daniel 102
Elizabeth 135
Mrs. Eliz. 101
Fredrick 123
John 123, 134
John, Jr. 123
Joseph 103, 120
Margaret 118
Nicholas 29, 110
Nicholas, Jr. 123
Peter 121
Polly 101, 103
Susannah 101, 102
LEATZFRITZ
Babruck 127
LEAVER (Seaver)
Elizabeth 34
Nicholas 34
Nicholas, Sr. 34
LEAZENBY
Elizabeth 34(3)
Thomas 18(2), 24(2), 30, 34(3), 74(2)
William 25(2), 74(2)
LEE (Lea - See)
Adam 53
Andrew 123
Barbara 123
Catherine 123
Charles 12
Elizabeth 123
Fredrick 123
George 60, 74, 93, 109, 123, 127, 138
Grizena 109
Henry 29(2), 37(2), 74(2)
Jacob 123(3)
John 112
Letty 123
Madline 123
Margaret 123(2)
Mary 123(2)
Micheal 93, 123(2), 138
Nancy 34
Peter 93
Rebecca 135
Richard Bland 34
Solomon 34(2)
Stephen 9, 74, 112
Susan 106
William 93, 123
LEEK
Catrika 123
Christopher 44, 74, 123
Sofia 123
LEEKINS
Jesse 138
LEEPER
Eliza 123
Ellaner 123
Martha 123
Rebecca 123
LEESON (Leason)
Elizabeth 34
Richard 34
LEFEVRE
John 5
LEFOLET (Lafollette)
Faney 129
LEG
Ambrose 93
LEGATE (Liggate)
Frances 17, 140
John 3, 17(3), 74
George 17, 74
LEGLER
Jacob 126
LEHOW (Sehow an error)
John 23(4), 33(2), 62(2)
John S. 10, 13, 74
LEICHTER (Lighter - Liter - Lichteter)
Andrew G. 123

Ann 123
Catherine 123
Daniel 123
Delilah 123
Elizabeth 123
Elmira 123
Emma 123
George 123
John Corbin 123
Margaret 123
Nancy 123
Rebecca 123
Susan 123
LEIGH
Stephen 27, 40
LEITER
Henry 45
LEITH
James 102
Mary 129
Sarah 101, 102
LEIZE
Thos. 99
LELLER (Lillar)
Susan 116
LEMMES (is)
Thos. 14(3), 29, 37
LEMMON
Abr. 107
Le Monnier L. I. 14(2)
LEMMONIER
Alex. Lewis 27, 34
James 51, 74
Lewis James 51, 74
Lewis Victor 27, 34
Valentine Louisa 27(2), 34
LENDORA
Ann 132
Prudence 132
LENOSA
James 122
LEONARD
Enoch 34
Martin 26, 93
Phoebe 34
LEOPARD
Jacob 87
Nelle 34
Patrick 55
Patsy 13
LINDSAY
Geo. W. 82
LINDSEY
Alice 34(2)
Edmond 34
James 34
John 19, 34(3)
LINEGER
Hester 84
LINN
William 24, 45, 74(2)
LINORE
John 92
LINTHICUM
Ann 123
Archibald 13, 74, 100, 102, 108, 125, 126, 128, 139
Charles Masterson 128
Edw. 128
Charles Parrel 128
Hezekiah 123
Jane. 128
Mrs. Jane 102
Joseph 123
Mary 123
Sarah 123
Sarah Ann 136
William 128
LINTON
Mary 34(3), 35(1)
Wm. 16(2), 19, 34(4), 35, 36, 44, 46, 51(5), 74(8), 109
Zachariah 56
LINZIE (Lindsay)
Charles 7
LION(S) see Lyons
John 14, 93
Mary 93
LITER (Lighter)
Henry 93
LITLER (Littler)
Henry 21, 74
LITNER
Catherine 35(2)
Henry 35(2)
LITTEL
William 3
LITTLE
Daniel C. 108
Elizabeth 118
George 98
Job 17, 35, 74, 140
Josiah 93
Micheal 35
Thomas 93
William 34
LITTLAR

LICHTETER (Lighter)
Ann 135
LIG(G)ETT (Liggate - Legate)
Alex 34(2)
John 17(2), 93
LIGHTER (Liter - Lichter)
Catherine 34(2)
Henry 3, 7, 34(4), 57, 74(3), 93
LIGHTOR
Henry 34
LIGHTNER
Henry 116
LIGHTHOLSE
John 93
LIGNER
Jacob 122
LIKENS
John 93
LIKINGS
Richard 93
LILLARD see Lillard - Sulard 8
LILLAS
Mrs. Ann 101
Isaac 100, 101
LILLER
Betsy 119
Elizabeth 117, 123, 136
Eve 119
George 138
Henry 25, 48(2), 74, 100, 102
Nancy 117
Noah 107
S. 48
Samuel 126
Sarah, Mrs. 102
LILLY
David 93
LIMKINS
Dickeson 16, 74
LINCH (Lynch)
Charles 21, 39(2), 34(2), 36, 42, 55
Milly 34
LESER
Adam 21
LESSE
Lydia 112
LESSMAN
Joseph 123
LEVIL (Nevil - Sevil)
Joseph 8, 74
LEVIN
Jane 34
John 34
LEVINGS
Caleb 101(2)
Mrs. Mary Ann 101
LEWCAS (Lucas)
Phillip 16, 74
LEWIS
Alfred 123
Aney 123
Amos 93
Daniel 123
David 93, 123
Elinore 123
Elizabeth 123(2)
Evan 123
Fielding 34
George 25(2), 37, 59, 74, 93, 137, 140
Hannah 84(2)
Henry 123
Henry, Jr. 4
Isabel 111
James 24, 51
John 14, 21, 33(2), 34(10), 39(3), 40(3), 53, 59, 74(4), 93(2), 121, 123
John, Jr. 34, 39
Joseph S. 49
Louisa 109
Malen 116
Mahlon 111
Mary 111, 128(2)
Oliver 123
Patsy 123
Robert 49
Rosannah 123
Sam 4, 34(2), 59, 74, 93, 123
Sam Harding 34
Sidney 123
Silas 109, 123
Stephen 35, 74
Thos. 7, 21, 34(4), 74, 110
William Barber 14, 21, 34(3), 40(3), 59, 74(2)

Thos. 52
LITTLER (lar)
John 21, 126
Henry 54
Magdeline 35
Thomas 1, 21, 35, 52, 54, 74(8), 93, 106, 110
LITTLEJOHN
John 55, 74
LITTLEMAYER
Casper 15
LIVINGSTON
James 5, 11, 35(2)
Mayor James 22, 35, 36, 60
John 22, 35(2)
William 120
LNICK (Linch or Lynch)
Benjamin 35
Monaca 35
LOAN
Isaac 138
LOCHMILLER
Isaac 123
LOCK(S) (Locke)
Abraham 35, 123
Jacob 33, 74, 93, 123
Thos. 123
LOCKHARD
Josiah 130
LOCKHART(D)
Bird 93
Elizabeth 102, 103
John 35
General Josiah 130
Robert 35(4), 43, 74
Robert T. 122
William 3, 10, 74, 103
LOCKWOOD
William 11, 35, 74, 93
LODGE
Matthew 1, 15, 16, 24, 35 (2), 38(2), 58, 62
LOGAN
David 93
Elizabeth 35
John 1, 35, 55, 75
William 8, 16(8), 75
LONG
Ann 123
Christinia, Mrs. 102
Christian 35(3), 58, 93
David 14, 43(2), 51, 52, 75, 93, 100, 102(2), 109, 113, 114(2), 122, 123(4), 136
David, Jr. 131
Eliza Ann 123(2)
Eliza Jane 102(2)
Elizabeth 35(3), 123(3)
George 123
George W. 30
Jacob 2, 35, 75, 93, 123
James 101, 102, 135
John 14, 75, 116, 123(2), 131
Joseph 52, 115, 123(3), 128, 131
Margaret 123
Mary 123
Mary Ann 123
Nancy 123
Polly 116
Pompey 35, 51, 75
Rebecca 123(2), 128(2)
Rosanna 93
Ruth 123
Sam 123(2)
Sarah 123(2)
Sarah Ann 113
Stansbury 24(3), 75, 102
Stansbury 24(3), 75
Thomas 122, 123(2), 131, 186
William 113, 123(3)
LONGBERRY
Charles 9
LONGSTRACH
Catherine 125
LONGSTRETH
Phillip 108
Salome 108
LONGWITH
Thos. 133
LONGWORTH
Thos. 93
LOOPRY
Hannah 125
LOOS (Luce)
Nathan 105
Sarah 102, 105
William 115
LORANCE (Laurence)
John 124
Mary Ann 119
LORRENTZ (Laurence)
William 93
LOUBINGER (Laubinger)
George Micheal 50, 75
LOUGHAN
E. 48(4)

LOUR
William 138
LOUTHER
George 93
Walker 126
LOVE
Isabel 35, 43
Neilson 35(3), 43
LOVETT
Jonathan 123
LOWRIE
John Adam 93
LOWRY
John 55
Sam 93
LOY
Adam 138
Christina 35(2)
Daniel 33, 35(2), 75
David (error) 75 (Daniel)
George 133
Hiett 112
John 35(2), 75(2)
Lea, Mrs. 102
Peter 112
Samuel 102(2)
William 102
LUCAS (see Lewcas)
Basil 23, 53(2), 75(2)
John 53
John D. 23, 53(2)
LUCKETT
William 46
LUDWICH(K) (Ludwig)
Ailsa C. 118
Andrew 119, 123
Ann 107, 136
Mrs. Ann 102
Catherine 119, 123
Daniel 119, 123(2)
Elizabeth 123
Esdras 118
Fredrick 123
George 101, 102, 123
Henry 107, 118
Henry M. 118
Isaac 123
Jacob 75, 123
James W. 132
John 119, 123, 130
Joseph 102, 104, 107
Katherine Ann 107
Leonard 12(2)
Margaret A. 123
Mary, Mrs. 102, 119
Mary A. 118
Mary Ann 107
Mary E. 123
Nancy 123
Polly 123
Sarah Jane 107, 118
Susannah 118
Thos. 130
William 123
William B. 132
William H. 113
LUDWIG (Ludwick)
Leonard 77
Jacob 49
LUEARENGER
Joseph 37, 38(3), 48(4)
LUFBOROUGH
James 111
LULARD (Sulard)
Elias 75
LUNNSFORD
Catherine 123
Catherine P. 123
Elizabeth 123
Lewis 123, 135
Martha 123
Mary Susannah 123
Nancy 123(2)
Simon P. 123
William 123
LUNT
Jacob 112
LUPTON
Ann 35, 123(3)
Asa 35, 75, 123
Daniel 123
David 123(4)
Edith 123(2)
Elias 112
Ellis 123(2), 132
Elizabeth 35
Hannah 123(3)
Harriet 137
Isaac 35, 54, 75, 86, 93, 123(3)
Jacob 111, 116(2), 123, 134, (75 error for Jesse
Jesse 47, 75, 100
Jesse, Jr. 132, 137
John 35, 116
Jonah 123
Joshua 85
Lydia 123
Margaret 123(2)

INDEX

Rachel 123
Rebecca 116, 123
Ruth 123(2)
Samuel 134
Sarah 123, 134
William 123, 127, 137(2)
LURKE (Turke)
Andrew 120
LUSE (Loos)
Sibble 102
Thomas 102, 104
LUTTRELL
Barbary 110
LUTTS (Lutz)
Agnes 124
Barbara 124
Conrad 124
LUTZ
Daniel 86
LYAL (see Lyle)
LYLE (Lyal)
Abigail 107(2)
Daniel 124
Eliza 124
Jane 124
John 32, 47, 61, 111(2), 124, 138
John Newton 124
Joseph Glass 124
Robert 8, 75
Sarah 124(2)
Wilberforce 124
LYMES
John 93
LYNCH (see Lnick - Linch)
Cornelius 61
Chas. 3, 21, 25, 30, 35(6), 36, 53, 75, 93, 126, 131, 133, 137
Margaret 128
Milly (Mille Milley) 85(5)
Pat 15, 61, 75, 93, 126
LYNE
John 1, 11, 22(2), 27, 28, 30(3), 32, 35, 42, 47
LYNN(E)
David 131
James Galloway 135
Rebecca 133
LYON(S) (Lions)
Archibald 124
Bruce 124
Dan P. 134
Charles 93
Eleanor 124(2), 129(2)
Ellen 124
Elijah 124
Ezakiel 93
Greenwell 124
John 42, 62, 75(2), 102, 104, 124(2), 132
Joseph 85, 42, 75
Joseph F. 124
July Ann 124
Margaret Ann 124, 134
Mary 35(2), 75, 134
Mary, Mrs. 102
Micheal 93
Noah 124, 134
Richard 24, 124
William 85
Peter 36, 85
Phoebe 124
Rebecca, Mrs. 102
Sarah 124, 139
Sarenah 106
Susan 102, 103
Sydnor 108
Thompson 101, 132
William 102
McALESTER (McAllester - MacAllister - McAlster)
Dan 26
Elizabeth 124
Jas. 10(2), 35, 38, 54, 55, 57, 58, 75, 124
John 32, 124
Mary 124(2)
Sarah 35, 124
McATESTER
James 55, 75
McATTEE
Sam 114
McBRIDE
Abigail 116
Adonorim 124
Alexander 11, 61, 62, 75(2), 99, 124, 129
Alex, Jr. 42, 75, 124
Archibald 139
Eleanor 124(2)
Elijah 124
Eliza 124
Elzabeth 36, 107, 124
Frances 13, 35, 36(5), 75, 93
Gelpha R. 124
Hannah 99, 102, 124
Jackson 131(2)
James 3, 5(2), 15(3), 18, 26, 36(2), 47, 56, 60, 75(3), 93, 124(3), 125, 129, 130, 134
Jean 124
John 1, 3, 11(4), 14, 23, 33(2), 34, 36(2), 41, 42, 55(2), 75(5), 93(3), 106, 107, 116(2), 117, 121(2), 124(3), 129, 132, 136
Louise 102, 104
Lydia 102, 108
Margaret 99, 102, 124
Maria 124
Marjery 124
Martha 102, 103
Mary 36(5), 124(4)
Matilda 102, 104, 124
Nance 124
Nancy 101, 102(4), 103
Nancy, Mrs. 102
Peter 124
Rachel 124
Rhoda 124
Robert 11, 75, 99, 101, 102 (2), 124
Samuel 124, 130
Sarah 36, 124(3)
Stephen 124(2)
Sylvester 136
Thos. 21, 102, 103, 124(3), 129
Thos. M. 104
McCABE
Daniel 106(2)
Eva 106
Terrance (Terrence) 93
McCARNY
James 93
McCARROLL
Thos. 36
McCANLEY (McCauley)
Elias 112
McCARTNEY 36
John 36(2)
Mary 110, 139(2)
McCARTY (McCartie)
Aquila Brown 124
B. 57
Charles 93
Elizabeth 36
Elizabeth Susan 124
Edward 2(2), 5, 14, 19, 21, 33(2), 34, 36(4), 37, 40, 41, 43, 45, 49, 52(2), 53 (2), 56, 59, 60, 61, 62(3), 75(10), 125, 132, 134
Isaac 111, 124
Jacob 111
James 124
John 124
Joseph 50, 124
Mary 111
Mary Cynthia 132
Patrick 127, 137
Rebecca 124
Ruth 124
Sally 124
Susan 138
Thos. 2, 3, 23, 61, 75, 93
McCAULEY (McCanley)
Addison 114
Eliz. 134
George 102, 103
Jacob 110, 111
John 117
Juliana, Mrs. 102
Lavinia 134
Mary 111
Parthinia 99, 124
Rebecca 102, 104
Sarah 134
McCAVE (McKave)
Ross 93, 140
McCHISNEY
Wm. 112
McCLARY (See Maclary)
John 43
McCLEERY
Isabel 9(2)
William 9(2)
McCLELLEN
William 28, 75
McCLINIC see McLintic - Clintic - McLintock-McLluntuck)
Moses 117, 120, 130
Robert 93
Susan 120
McCLUNG 108
McCLURE
Sarah 124
Rebecca 124
McCLUTUCK
Sammuel 12
McCOLLOCH (lough-ogh)
John 9, 12, 29(2), 36, 87, 40, 53, 58, 59
McCONLEY
George 112
McCOOLE
Elinor 22, 123
Jacob 121

John 22, 121, 130, 132
Lewis 113
McCORD
John 93
McCORMAC (McCormick - McCormack)
Ailsy 124
George 124
James 116, 124, 135
John 93, 124, 135
John, Sr. 56, 75
Nancy 124
Rebecca 124
McCOULL
Nell 23, 75
McCOY
Dunkin 50
McCRACKEN (Mecrackin - Merackin - McCrackin) 127
Catherine 139
Charles 56
Frank 36, 75, 76
Isaac 124
Jane 36, 52, 63, 124
Margaret 36(2), 52(2), 63(2)
Ovid 25, 36, 75, 93, 124
Sarah 124(2)
Senca 33, 36, 124
Virgil 25(3), 36(2), 61, 86
Wm. 5, 44, 46, 75(2), 61(2), 124
McCULLOGH (McColloch)
George 36
John 12, 36(2)
McCULLY
James 16(7)
McCUNE
Micheal 134
McDADE
James 93
McDANIEL
Arch 93
Mary 117
Sarah 117
McDANYEL
James 4
McDAVID
James 93
McDEVIT see Mackdevit
James 4, 36
Mary 36
McDEWGAL 140
McDONALD (McDonal)
Ann(e) (Annie) 86, 124, 125, 139
Alex 132
Amy 127
Angus 5(2), 8, 21(2), 22(2), 23, 24, 26, 35, 36(3), 42, (2), 47, 54, 55, 60(2), 62, 74(4), 105, 111, 124(3), 135
Angus, Jr. 106
A. W. 133
Angus W. 36, 124, 125
Archibald 11(3), 21, 23, 75 (5), 93, 124
Benjamin 15, 119, 124
Catherine 124
Charles 101
Daniel 22, 24, 36, 75, 93, 124, 126
Donald 36, 139
Edward C. 138
Eliz. 36(3), 101, 102, 124
Evan 119, 124
George 36, 75, 102(2), 124
Hannah 36, 122
James 100, 102, 105, 111, 117, 119, 124(2)
Jemima 36, 101
John 36(3), 46, 52, 58, 59, 75, 101, 110(2), 132
Lucy Ann, Mrs. 102
Margaret 124
Mary 124
Mary, Mrs. 102
Millicent S. 102, 103
Nancy 103
Neil 93
McDOUGAL (McDougle - McDugle - McDewga)
Alexander 124
James 93, 140
Peter 124
McDOWELL
Andrew 120
H. C. 124
Jane 124
John 124, 138
Mary 124
Matilda 124, 138
Matilda Wodrow 124
Sarah Matilda 124
Sidney O. 116
William 124
McDUGLE
Margaret 124
Mary 124
McELWEE

David 124
McENALLY
Dan 114(2)
McFADIN (McFadden)
James 61
William 47, 130
McFARLAND
Catherine 102, 104
John 104
Robert 85
McFARLANE
Thos. 93
McFARLING
Thos. 93
McFERON
Daniel 128
McFERSON (McPherson)
William 98
McGARRETY
James 36
McGLATHERTY
Alen 108
McGINNIS
Edward 24
John 125
Samuel 24
McGLAUGHLIN
Daniel 52, 75
McGLOUGHLAN (LIN) see McLaughlin
Ann 36
Daniel 36, 40
Daniel, Jr. 94
McGLOLIN (McGloughlan - McLaughlin)
Daniel 29, 40, 75
McGLUMPHY
John 31
McGOWAN
Anthony 138
William 30
McGRAW
Margaret, Mrs. 102
Marion 85
Morris 94
Samuel 102, 103
McGRUDER
Lorenzen 138
Sam 134
McGUIRE 63
Anna 124
Dowdell 31, 37
Edward 5(5), 6(2), 10, 15 (2), 16, 22, 26, 30, 31, 35, 36(8), 37(9), 39(2), 42, 46, 47, 52, 54(3), 55, 59 (2)
Eliz. 37, 124
Frances 124(2)
Hannah 37
James 37, 124(2)
John 37
Margaret 124
Mary 124
Millicent 36(2), 37(5), 124
Rachel 124
Robert 124(2)
Sam 111
Susan 124
Susannah 36(3)
Thomas 21, 37(2), 45, 124 (2), 128, 134
Wm. 1, 2, 7, 21, 29(3), 30, 32(2), 37(2), 42(2), 56, 60, 75, 94, 115, 124, 128
McHEAL (McNeal)
Daniel 68
McHEILL (McNeill)
Daniel 61
McHENDRY (McHenry)
Eliz. 137
Hannah 43
John 37, 59
Joseph 48, 75
Sam 34, 37, 40(2)
Susannah 37, 137
Wm. 94
McILHENNY (McIlhanny)
Felix 94
James 45, 75
John 48
McILVANE
Mary 4, 37(2)
Wm. 4, 37(2)
McINSKEEP
Mary E. 137
Susan 137
Walter 137
McINTYRE (McIntire)
Abigail 37
Nicholas 5, 37, 75
McIVER (McKeever)
Paul 94
McKEAN
Samuel 36(3), 75(3)
McKAIG
Thomas I. or J. 135
McKAVE 140
McKEE
A. A. 122
Aaron 110

Anna 122
Amos A. 107
Eliz. 131
Robert 1
Wm. 122
McKEEVER (McKever - McIver - McKiver)
Christena 125
Derby 133
Eleanor 125
Elizabeth 125
Hugh 3(2), 116, 124, 125(2)
Jacob 107
John 133
John W. 125
Julian 125
Margaret 125(2)
Moses 125
Paul 6, 15, 37(3), 94, 125, 128, 133
Rachel 15
Sally 125
McKENNARD
Thos. 88
McKENNY (McKinny)
John 94
McKEWN
Micheal 6, 37, 75
McKIERNAN
Micheal 37, 120
Patrick 37, 75
McKINN
John, Jr. 32, 75
McKINNEY (McKenny)
Ayese 134
McKINLEY
Ebenezer 14, 37, 85
Hugh 14, 37, 75
McKIVER see McKeever & McIver
Hugh 116
McLAMORE
John 94
Phil 94
McLARN
Thos. 39
McLARY see Maclary
McLAUGHLIN (McLoughlin - McGloghlin - O'Laughlin - McGla(o)laughlin)
Anner 125
Benjamin 125
Daniel 13, 29, 82, 36, 37(2), 40, 75, 107, 108, 121
Daniel, Sr. 37
David 125
Eliz. 125
Hannah 108
Mary 125
Rachel 32, 87
Rachel, Mrs. 87
Wm. 125(2)
McLEERY
William 23
McLENE
John 110
McLINTOCK (see McClintock and Clintock)
Alex 15, 37, 75, 94
John 94
Mary 37
Robert 94
McMACHAN
Christian 87
John 3, 13, 75
Lucy 135
William 87
McMAHAN
Barnard 94
Elizabeth 131
Isabella 87
John 87
Wm. 62, 75, 94, 111
McMARRO
Henry 50
McMECHEN (McMeekin)
David 23, 75
John 23
Wm. 23
McMEEKIN (McMechin)
Ann 37(2)
John 5, 7, 16, 19, 20, 29, 31 (2), 34, 35(2), 37(5), 38, 40, 46, 48, 53, 55, 75(5)
J. 19
Nancy 87
McMICKLIN
John 114
McMONGLE
Barney 124
McMURY
Sam 127
McNALLY
Wm. 138
McNAMARR
Joseph 93
McNARY
Ami 129
Ebenezer 46, 75, 125, 129(2)
Naomi 129

INDEX

Nimrod 119, 125(2)
Susan 125
Wm. 125(3)
McNEAL (McNeil - Mc-
Neel)
Daniel 5, 35, 48, 75(2), 94
John 37(2), 94
Isaac 125
McNEES
John 94, 113
McNEIL(L) (Neel)
Arch 131
Dan 3, 5(2), 9, 26, 35, 37, 41, 44, 57, 75, 117, 133, 137
Dan, Jr. 57
John 44, 57, 75
Sydney 102(2)
McNEMAR (Nemer) error McMemar
Ann Maria 114
Elias 118
Wesley B. 117, 118, 129
Wesley M. 131
McNEMASON
Febe 100
McPHERESON (McPherson - McFerson)
Angus 125(2)
David 125
James 125
John ???
Wm. 10, 35(2), 37, 52, 75, 98, 125
McQUAD
Joseph 108
McQUEEN
Minor 125
McQUILLEN
Hannah 123
James 123
McQUILLING
James 20, 75
McTHIERNAN (McKier-
Micheal, Sr. 61
Micheal 61, 75
McVICKERS
Archibald 101
Betsy 129
Diania 125
Duncan 3, 75
Isabel 102, 103
Jane 101, 102
Mary 102, 103
William 125
McWILLIAMS
MABRY (Mayberry)
Ellonder 107
MACBERRY
John 42
MACALISTOR (McAllister)
Daniel 32
MACDEVITT (see Mc)
James 46
MACE (Mase) 123
Anne 94
Isaac 94, 140
John 94
Nicholas 34(2), 75, 94(2)
MACHAN
James 85
MACHIE 119
Eliz. 125
Jas. 15, 18, 38, 45, 62, 75(4)
Jane 125
John 125(2)
Maria 125
Rachel 125
MACKEY
Robert 88
MACLARY
John 43
MADE (Maid)
John 94
MADDEN
Joseph 16, 37(2), 75
Micheal 37, 38(3), 48(4)
MADDOX
G. W. 123
MADERIA
Chas. 52
MAGAW see Mc
John 48
MAGILL
Alfred T. 104
Arch. 10(2), 15, 35, 38(3), 46, 60(2), 85
Charles 1(2), 2, 3, 5, 7, 15 (2), 19, 24(2), 25(2), 31 (2), 37, 38(7), 40, 46 (2), 49(2), 53, 54(2), 57(2), 58(3), 59, 60(2), 75(2), 124, 134
Elia 38
James 6
John 2, 3(2), 6(3), 7(2), 8 (2), 11, 12, 15, 21, 22, 23, 26(2), 27, 30(3), 32, 33(2), 34, 36(2), 37(2), 38(2), 39(9), 47(2), 50, 52(2), 54(3), 58(4), 59

(2)
John S. 133
Mary 88(2)
MAGLAULIN McLaughlin
Daniel 108
Hannah 108
MAGRAW (see Megraw & McGraw)
Morris 94
Thos. 2
MAGRUDER
Mary 120
MAGUIRE (Meguire and McGuire)
Nancy 118
Thomas 111
MAHAN (Mahen or McMahan?)
James 94
William 94, 139
MAHONEY
Dan 115
Flor 115
Jeremmiah 28, 38, 115
Micheal 132
Thos. 115
MAHUREN
Ebenezer 95
MAIL (Male)
MAIRHEAD
Geo. 38
Geo., Jr. 38
Martha 38
MAJORS
John 94
MALCOLM
Catherine 124, 125
Jane 125
Mrs. Jane 102
James 32, 46, 75(2), 94, 99, 102, 104, 124, 125
Jean 137
Jennet 124
Maude 99, 102
Peter 124, 125(2), 133
Wm. 99, 124, 125
Wm., Jr. 125, 133
MALE (see Mail)
Wilmore 24, 75, 94
Wilmor, Sr. 94
MALEE
Geo. 108
MALICK
Aaron 107, 110, 111, 125 (2), 132
David 125
John 98, 110, 111, 112, 125
John, Sr. 129
Margarate 125
Martha 125
Mary 125
Phillip 111, 112, 125
Uriah 125
MALIN
Isaac 38
Susannah 38
MALLO (Mallow)
Geo. 1
MALLOW (Mallo)
Adam 94
Henry 94
MALONE
Geo. 102(2)
Hugh 85
MALONEY
Dan. 115
MALOPEAN
Alix. Joseph 27, 38
MALOY
James 94
MANEAR
Abraham 94
MANN
Christopher 94
MANNIN
Wm. 6, 38
MANNING
Hathel 23
Mary 38, 41, 75, 125
Rev. Nathaniel 125
MANTILL (Mantell)
John 26, 38, 75
Mary 38
MARANDA (Miranda)
Margaret 114
MARBY
John 36
MARCH (Marsh-Martch)
Henry 94
MARIGE
Henry 117
MARKWOOD
Henry 126
MARLEY (Morley)
John 2, 57
MARLINE
John 133
MARQUIS
Andrew 94
Ann 38(3)
Christopher 94
Richard 38(4), 94

MARRS (Meyers)
Barnabas 94
Henry 35(2)
Henry M. 94
MASE (Mace) 123
MARSH (March - Martch - Mash)
Cyrus 125
Eliz. 125
Ezekiel 125(2)
Hannah 125
Henry 38(3), 42, 63, 75, 110, 131
Lemwel 1, 125
R. M. 68
Vincent 125
MARSHALL
Ann 99, 102
Benjamin 54, 75, 94, 136
Chas. 38, 54, 75
Christopher 38(2), 54, 61, 75
Emaline 116
Hatty (Hetty) 38(2)
Hester 38(5)
James 38(6), 45, 75
James M. 38(3)
John 63, 99(2), 108
Rachel 99, 102
MARTCH (March - Martch Mash)
Christina 135(3)
Henry 125
Mary 125
MARTIN
Ann 38(3), 125
B. 112
Benjamin 116
Catherine 125
Charles 29
Charolette 39
Christopher 38, 43, 75, 113
Copsey D. 112
David 94
Dodd 112
Edmund 94
Edward 38, 75, 125
Ellen, Mrs. 102
Eli 27, 125
Eliz. 38, 45
Euria 94
Frances 125(2)
George 7(2), 10, 11, 38, 41 (2), 47, 76(5), 94, 100, 102, 125
Geo., Sr. 38(2), 76
Geo., Jr. 27, 38, 76
Geo. Esquire 7
Hannah 125
Jas. 10(2), 19, 22, 24, 32, 36, 37, 38(3), 56, 58, 76(3), 94, 133
Janes 94
Jesse 125
Job 125
John 94(2), 99, 102, 104, 106(2), 110, 125(8), 126 (2), 130(2), 133, 135
John, Sr. 125
John, Jr. 125(2)
Joseph 110(2), 113, 125(4)
Joshua 125
Lea 102(2)
Leah, Mrs. 102
Lenox 28, 45, 76(2)
Levy 125
Lucindy 112
Luther 12(2), 28, 45
Luther, Jr. 38(2), 76
Margaret 38, 137
Maria 38, 76
Mary 17, 45, 63, 76, 99, 102, 125(2), 137
Nehemiah 38
Phillip 39(14)
Sam 2(2), 94(2)
Sarah 102, 103
Thos. 2, 39, 76, 94
Thos. Bryan 39(7), 47, 85
Uriah 94
Urias 125
Wm. 56(2), 76(2), 125
MASH (Marsh)
Edw. 136
Eliz. 136
Ezekiel 136
Magdeline 136
Nancy 136
Scibi 136
Susanna 136
MASON
Ann 39(2)
Heirs 125
James 13
John 32, 39(4), 43, 53, 76
Phillip 39, 124
Sam 39
Susan Ann 138
Thos. 11, 76, 107
Wm. 121
MASTORS (Masters)
Josiah 10, 39, 43, 59, 76

Lucy 39
MATOR
Phil. 94
MATLOCK (Mattock)
Rebecca 39(2)
Thos. 39(2)
MATTOCK (Maddox)
Thos. 32
MATTHEWS
Catherine 123
Huldah 39
James 29, 113
Jonathan 39, 94
John 3, 13, 28(2), 29(3), 39, 57, 76(2), 113
Levi 13(8), 23(3), 28(2), 29 (3), 39, 57, 76(3), 113, 117
Lewis 94
Wm. G. 123
MAURICE
Frances 46
MAUZEY (Mauzee or Mauzy)
Eliz., Mrs. 102
Eliz. 125, 129
Henry 125(3)
Geo. 125
John 125(3)
John, Jr. 102, 103
Nance 125
Peter 125(4)
Peter, Sr. 125
Polly 125
Sarah, Mrs. 102
Susan 125, 129
Wm. 101, 102, 125
MAXWELL
Absolom 125
H., Mrs. 113
John 35(2)
John H. 125
John, Jr. 35(2)
R. 34(3), 109, 110
Robert 17, 59(2), 76, 94, 109, 110, 115
MAY
Jacob 34(2), 39, 76
John 94
MAYBERRY (Mabbry)
Catherine, Mrs. 102
Ellinore 109
Frances 118
Israel 101, 102
Peter 118
Sarah 118
Thos. 118
MAYHALL
Ellender 125
Stephen 125
MAYER (Marr)
Bernhart 126
MEADE
Geo. 24, 76
MEANS
Ann 39(2)
Betsy 125
Ephraim 125
Isable 113
Maj. Isaac 123
Isaac 4, 12, 18, 19(3), 28, 30, 34, 39(3), 40, 43, 44, 60, 76, 94, 124, 125, 131
Jane 125
Margaret 125
Mariah 101, 102
Mary Ann 123
Nancy 125
Robert 125(2)
Sally 125
Thomas 113
MECRAKIN see McCrackin(en)
Ann 94
Ovid 25, 94, 127
Virgil 38, 76, 127
Wm. 5, 125
MEDCALF (Metcalf)
Asa 102
Fenton 102, 105
James 102
Lucy Ann, Mrs. 102
MEDLEY
John, Jr. 39
MEEKINS
James 18, 37, 76, 125
James, Sr. 135
John 18
Joseph 125
Milley 125
Tamer 125
MEENTNER
Jacob 111
John 111
MEESBY
John 22, 76
MEGRAW (Magraw - McGraw)
Thomas 2
MEGUIRE see McGuire -
Nancy 118

Thos. 111
MELICK (Malich)
John 8, 76
MELLOC
Henry 121
MELONE
John 94
MELTON (Milton)
Ann D. 112
John 112
John Wm. 112
J. W. 112
MENEAR (Minniear)
John 94
MENIFEE (Minnifee)
Eliz. 39
Henry 39
MENSER
Conrad 126
MENTHENY (Metheny or Mentheany)
Fredrick 132
MERCER
Aaron 81, 76
James 34, 39(4), 40
Hon. James 39
John 39(2), 40
Robert 39(2), 40
MERIMAN
Rebecca 137
MERRIDITH
Eliz. 40
John 76
John W. 6, 30, 40, 51(2), 76
MERRITT
Wm. 130
MESHIA (Meshy)
Christian 40
John 40
MESHY
Benj. 54, 76
METCALF (see Medcalf - Calf)
James 94
Wm. H. 128
METHEANY
Luke 2
METHENY
Fred 85
METHODIST CHURCH 109 (2)
METTS
John 54
MEYERS (Miars - Miers - Myers)
Chas. 110, 124, 138
Eliz. 102, 104
Geo. 138
Henry 108
Jacob 102, 104
John 108, 112(2), 137
MIARS
Geo. 94
MICHEL
John 114
MICHAEL
Eliz. 126
Fred. 126(2)
George 44, 76, 94
Jacob 44, 76
Mary Ann 126
Michial 134
Phillip 126
MICHLSCHLEGEL
Andreas 22
MICHALL (see Mitchell)
John 62
MIERS (Mears - Meyers - Myers)
Frances 118
John 40, 94
John, Sr. 94
Mary 123
Michial 27
Peter 118
MILASON (see Millison)
MILAW
James 94
MILBOWER (Milbrowen)
Wm. 2, 76
MILDRUM
Robert 109
MILER (Miler - Milar)
Christiana 107
Margaret 115
MILES
David 94, 137
James 94
MILLAT
Ephram 114
MILISHAGLE see Millslagle
MILLBURN
Andrew 94
Joseph 94
Wm. 2, 56, 57, 94
Wm. Jr. 94
MILLER (Millar - Miler)
Abraham 94
Absolom 102(2)

INDEX

Adam 126(3)
Ann 127
Anthony 94
Catherine 94, 125, 126(2)
Christina 107
Cornelius 132(3)
Daniel 30, 40(2), 42, 76(3)
David 38, 40
Eliz. 126(4), 133
Feaby 129
George 4, 22, 26, 34, 39(2), 46, 48, 49, 76(3), 94 (2), 126, 139
Hannah 40(2), 132
Hanse Michial 3, 76
Henry 3(2), 18, 40, 49, 56, 76, 94, 126, 139
Isaac 5, 6(2), 7, 10, 14, 31, 33(3), 41, 43, 45, 50, 53, 76, 94, 108, 109, 110, 121, 126(2)
Jacob 9, 21, 76(2), 94, 104, 126, 136
James 102(2)
John 9, 20, 40(2), 41, 49, 76(2), 94(2), 121, 126, 132(2)
John, Jr. 94
John D. 126
John B. 122
John Henry 94, 126
Julia Ann, Mrs. 102
Juliann 134
Leonard 94
Margaret 126
Mary 102(2), 104, 126
Michial 22(2), 29, 33, 37, 40(2), 45, 49(2), 62, 94(3), 112, 116, 126(6)
Nicholas 10
Rev. Peter 110
Peter 102, 104(2), 126
Phoebe (Feaby) 129
Phillip 94
Polly 126
Reuben 126
Robert 133
Sarah 102 (Susannah error)
Susannah, Mrs. 126
Sinthy 40
Stephen 54, 76, 116, 127
Thomas 94, 139
Wendel 126
Wm. 5, 14, 16, 27, 37, 40, 50, 56, 76, 94, 126(7), 127, 128(2), 138
Wm., Jr. 14
MILLET (Millat)
John 14, 38
MILLASON (Millison)
John 106
MILLISON (Milleson or Millason)
Benj. 126
Geo. 126, 130, 134(2)
Hannah 126(2)
Harriet, Mrs. 102, 126
Mary 132
Martha 102, 105
Isaac 105, 126
John 30, 49, 76, 106, 126(4)
Phoebe 124, 126
Silas 102, 104, 126(3, 124
MILLS
Eliz. Mary 118
Jacob 40
James H. 118
Joseph 118
Sarah Y. 118
Thos. Wilson 138
Hamilton 108
MILLSLAGLE (Mishlagle - Milslager)
Abraham 112
Andreas 22
Andrew 33, 48, 76(2), 94, 119
94, 119
Axaha 111
Eady Ann 129
Elias 129, 131
Eliz. 112
Hannah 102, 103, 129
Jacob 2, 86, 115
Geo. 2, 32(3), 94, 111
John 103
Sam 103, 107, 122, 129
Uriah 108
MILLSLAGER
Sam 129
MILTON (Nelton)
Ann D. 112
MINHUR
John 16, 76
MINIFEE (Menifee)
Agnes 40
Garrard 40
MINNEAR
Abraham 126
Isaac 126(2)

John 126
Mary 126(2)
Wm. 126
MINOR
John 11, 60
MITCHAR
Nicholas 94
MITCHELL (Mich-)
Abraham 21(2), 30
Ann 126
Carson & Barclay 76(6)
Daniel 22, 76
David 11(2), 19, 29, 76(2), 88, 94, 112
Eliza 40(4)
Eliz. 40(3), 126
George 23, 76
Henry 23, 76
Izabella 126
James 62, 76, 126
James, Jr. 126
J. M. 124
John 1(2), 3, 4, 5(2), 9, 10 (2), 11, 14, 16(3), 18, 19 (4), 20, 22, 23(6), 24, 26(2), 27(2), 28, 29(4), 30 (3), 31(13), 32, 33(2), 34, 35(2), 37(2), 38(6), 40 (13), 41, 43(4), 44, 45(2), 46, 48, 49(2), 53(4), 54 (3), 55(4), 56, 58, 60(3), 61(2), 62(5), 76(16), 94, 124, 126
John, Jr.13, 14, 32, 40, 43, 55, 60, 61, 62, 108, 109
John, Sr. 108
Mr. John 124
Joseph 23, 37, 40(5), 58
Maria 2
Martha 40(5)
Sarah 126
Thos. 108
MITSCAW (see Mitchar)
Eve 40
Nicholas 40
Valentine 40
MITTS
Adam 94
MIXER
Phin. 51
MOAK
Henry 94
MOALE
Sam 52
MOELT
Sylvester 113
MOFFETT
John 28, 40(3)
Lydia 40
MOLLISON
John 36, 76
MOLLOY
James 1, 40, 76
Rachel 40
MONKS
John 94
MONEY (Mooney)
Bryan 94
MONET(T) (Monnett or Monett)
Abraham 16(7), 37, 40, 76 (2)
Jeremiah 131
MONNIER
L. I. 44
MONROE (Munroe)
A. 107, 133, 134
Alex 37(2), 39, 56, 77(2), 86, 94, 102, 126, 133
Ann 126
Christena 40
Eleanore 108, 126
Eliza 126
Elizabeth 111, 126(2)
George 126
Jacob 40, 60, 75
Jacob, Jr. 40
James 1(4), 2(2), 3, 10, 33, 39, 40(2), 49(3), 53, 66, 76 (4), 102, 103, 119, 126(2), 130
Jane, Mrs. 102
John 27, 40, 76, 111, 126 (2)
John G. 126
Jesse (Isse) 108(3), 109(2), 126, 136
Lucy 118, 126
Lydia Ann 118
Marcus 126
Margaret, Mrs. 102
Marquis 126
Molley 126(2)
Robert 19, 54(2), 76(3), 129 137
Sarah 114
Sidney 126
Siney 40
Sylvester 101, 102
Wm. 126

William J. 136
MONTGOMERY
Eliz. 40
Matthew 40, 42, 51(2), 76 (2)
MOOBER (Mouser)
Jacob, Sr. 110
MOODY
Wm. 123
MOON
J. 109
Jacob 120(2)
Jeremiah 109
Mary 120
MOONEY (Money-Moonee)
Bryan 94
David 129
Edmund 129
Isaac 129
Rachel 129(2)
MOONIE
Bryan 94
MOOR (Moore - More)
Jamie 134
Joseph 94
Ruth 134
MOORE (More Moores - Moor)
Abraham 7, 76, 102, 104, 135
Aley B. 99
Ann 126
Anthony 94, 126
Benj. 126(3), 136
Betsy 135
Catherine 116, 126(2)
Conrad 94
Edward 20(4), 37, 40, 43, 46, 53, 76
Eneas 41, 76
Eliz., Mrs. 102, 126(4)
Frances 126
Fanny 116
Henry 41
Isaac 101, 102
Jacob 126
Jackson Fry 116
James 12, 76, 94, 126(2), 129(2), 134
James, Jr. 126
James, Sr. 126
Jeremiah 109, 126
John 12, 41(2), 58, 76, 86, 94, 126(2), 135
Joseph 41(8), 94
Katherine 41
Lydia 41, 58
Margaret 126
Mary 51, 76, 126(3)
Mary Ann 116
Micheal 41(2), 76, 126
Milly, Mrs. 102
Nancy 116
Peggy 126
Phillip 26, 41, 57(2), 126, 139
Phillip, Sr. 41
Phoebe 109
Rebecca 41(7), 99, 126(2)
Reese 126
Samuel 126
Sary 126(2)
Sarah, Mrs. 102(2), 114
Solomon 100, 102
Susannah 126
Thomas 100, 102(2), 126(3)
MOOREFIELD TRUSTEES 41(6)
MORCTON
Messers Smith & Moreton 6, 76
MORED (Morehead)
Rebecca 99, 102
MOREHEAD
Geo. 94
Susannah 102, 140
MORELAND
Basil (Bazil) 111, 126
Eliz. 126
George 100, 112, 117, 126
Jacob 126
James 116, 126
John 126
John Z. 120
Margaret 126
Mary 102(2), 103(2), 126
Richard 103, 126
Wm. 126
MORELL (Morrell)
John 19, 41, 57, 76
Martha 41
MORGAN (Morgain)
Eliz. 41(2)
Gerad 120
Jacob B. 110
John 10, 13, 39(2), 41(3), 94, 110, 128, 138
Jonathan 41(3), 76, 94
Martha 41(3)
Mary 41, 110
Mordecai 4, 6, 25(2), 41,

76(2)
Thos. 33, 85, 94, 122, 138(2)
Wm. 4, 15, 23, 41(2), 76(2)
94
MORRIS
Bushrod 118
David H. 118
Esac(k) 2, 41, 76
Esram 118
Frances C. 118
Henry 88
John David 118
John 94
Cuthbert 6, 25
Luis 57
Mary Ann 118
Pythagoras 118
Robert 41
Sam H. 134
MORRISON
Agnes 126
James 122, 126
James, Jr. 126
Jen (Jane) 126
John 41, 126(2)
Mary 126(2)
Nancy 126
Ruth 126
MORROW
Adam 29
James 94
John 57, 76
Ralph 94
MORSE
Henry 2, 76, 133
MOSER (Moses)
Jacob 136
Magdeline 136
MOSES (Moser)
Adam 32, 76, 94, 121
Ruth 128
MOSLEY (Moxley)
Abr. 41(2)
Jesse 127
Lary 41
Washington 133
MOTT
Jemima 137
Lucy 137
Mary 137
Randolph 126
Sarah 137
Sylvester 137
MOUNTS
Asa 1, 46, 133
Jesse 133
Joseph 1, 46
MOUSE
Dan 94
MOUSER (Mouzer(ey)
Catherine 41(3), 126
Christina 41, 42
Eliz. 110
Jacob 29, 41(4), 51, 76(3), 110, 126
Jacob, Sr. 7, 41, 76, 126
Jacob, Jr. 21, 41, 42, 58, 76
Katherine 41
Peter 110(2)
Susanna 110
MOWATT
Alex 10
MOXLEY (see Mosley)
Ann 42
John 42
MOYER (Moyers)
John 42
John, Jr. 3, 76
MUDEY
Mary 135
MUELLY see McCully 16
MULLADY (Mulledy)
Alfred 126(2)
Mary 42, 126
Mildred 126
Milly 102
Robert 126(2)
Sarah 126
Samuel 126
Thos. 3, 4, 10, 21, 23(4), 25, 42(4), 46(2), 50, 51, 76(2), 77, 102, 114, 125, 126, 131, 134, 135
Thos. F. 126
Wm. 134
MULLINS (Mullen)
Charles 42(2)
John 6
Wm. 47
MUMA (Mumma) 9
Christian 42(3), 77
Conrad 16(2), 77
Nancy 42
MUNCHEN
Jane 119
MUNDEN
Jesse 119
MUNISE
John 132
MUNROE (see Monroe)
Alex 2

MURDOCK 22
MURPHEW (Murphy)
Hugh 42, 94
MURPHY
Edmond 119
Eliza 38
Francis 4, 10, 42(3), 77, 112, 119(2), 127(2), 131, 139(2)
Gabriel 94
Hiram 113
Hugh 30, 41, 42(14), 56, 77 (2), 85
Hugh, Sr. 42
Hugh, Jr. 42(5), 77
James 2, 4(2), 6, 8, 12, 15, 21, 24, 27, 28(3), 31, 32(3) 37, 42(12), 43, 45, 51(2), 56, 57, 58, 77(6), 94, 99, 115, 127, 131, 139
John 4, 5, 13, 22, 23(3), 42 (3), 56, 76(3), 131, 189
Joseph 124
Lender 42(3)
Mary 28(2), 42(7), 112, 127, 131
Phoebe 119
Sally 112, 127
Sally Ann 127
Samuel 4, 21, 24, 41
Sarah 126, 131
Susannah 129
Thos. Newton 119
Walter 129
William 32(3), 42, 53, 76 (2), 94(2)
MURRAY
Alley 132
Charles 84
Daniel 130
G. 16(4)
George 16
Patrick 49, 76
Reuben 132
MUSE
Edward 122
MUSGROVE
Edward 61
MUSSELMAN
Christian 5, 12, 14, 16, 18, 26, 31(2), 32, 33, 43(4), 48, 77(5)
Susanna 43(3)
MUSSELTER
Michial 121
MUTTE
Archibald 102, 105
Susanna, Mrs. 102
MYER (Meyer - Miar - Miers - Myre)
Anna 43(2)
Betsy 125
Charles 26, 110, 119, 131
Conrad 42, 77
Eliz. 43, 128
Florence 127
Frances 43, 77, 94(2), 127
Geo. 94, 116, 135
Harry 61, 77
Henry 61(2), 108
Jacob 128
John 35, 43, 77, 94, 102, 108, 119, 120(2), 127, 131
Joseph 12, 43(2), 77
Margaret 137
Mary 133
Peter 127
Sally 117, 125
Samuel 137
Sarrah 127
Sarah M. 127, 131
Susan 127
Wm. 48, 77, 130
MYRE (Myres)
Conrad 42, 43, 77
Eliz. 43
Frances 32, 43, 77
Frances 43, 77
MYLES
David 4, 77
MYTLINGER (Mylinger)
Daniel 104, 120, 128(2)
David 128
Sarah 120
MYNATT
Richard (R.) 1, 12, 27, 47, 52, 106, 129
NAAF (Naff - Nafe-Nave- Neiff)
George 94, 127
Henry 6, 77, 94, 127
Leonard 57, 77(2), 127
Micheal 94, 127
NAIL (see Nall)
Bery 136
Eliz. 136
Ellen 136
John 37, 136
Lucinda 136
NAILOR (Nailer - see Naylor)

Robert 6
William 94
NALL (see Nail)
Eliz. 37
John 57, 77
William 53(4), 77
William, Jr. 53(2)
NALLEY
Hezekiah 135
NAUSE (Vauce - Vause)
William 4
NASH
Martha 106
NAVE (see Naaf - Knave)
Geo. 127, 140
Henry 94, 127
Jacob 127
John 127, 140
Leonard 127
Mary 131
Micheal 127, 140
NAYLOR (see Nailor)
Edward 124
James 124
Jane 102, 104
John 124
Millicent 124
Lucy Ann 102(2)
Robert 6
Samuel 124
Susan 124
William 24, 25, 33, 43, 62
(2), 86, 102, 104, 108, 110,
118, 120, 127, 131, 134,
138
W. J. 120
NEACE
Peter 43
NEAL (Neale - see Neel -
O'Neal - O'Neil - Neell)
Benjamin 15, 44, 52, 62, 94,
112, 114
Dan. 121
Dan D. 1, 121
Edward 94
Jacob 33, 43, 77, 94
John 140
Nancy 33, 43, 121(2)
Robert 121(2)
Thos. 94, 107
William 34, 94
NEAVIL (see Nevill)
NEAW (New)
Jacob 48, 45, 61, 77
Mary 43
NEEL (Neal - Neale)
Benjamin 94
Jacob 94
Thos. 107
NEELAND
John 15
NEELEY
William 28, 138
NEES
John M. 94
NEFF (see Naaf and Neef
and Nave)
Adam 5, 43(2), 54
Abraham 4(2), 43, 77(2),
86
Catherine 43, 54
Christina 43(2), 54
Elizabeth 43
Esther 43, 54
Henry 43(2)
Sylvester 43, 54, 77
NEIFF (see Neff - Naaf -
Nave)
Henry 94
Micheal 49, 77
NEIL (Niel - Niell)
Benjamin 15, 44, 52, 77
John 94
William 34
NEILSON (Nelson)
Isabel 35(2), 43
Richard 12, 43, 85
William 47
Neilson & Wodrow 17, 24
NELSON (Neilson)
Eliz. 43
George 57
Jacob 112
James 48, 136
Richard 12
NESBIT
Eliz. 127
John 127
Nathaniel 127
NESON (likely Nelson)
James 42
NETON
William 50
NEVILL (Neavill - Newell)
Agnes 43
Jacob 57
Jane 137
Jethrow 120

John 37, 47, 77
John, Jr. 1
Joseph 3, 4, 5, 6(2), 9, 12,
17(4), 19, 23(2), 26, 32,
41(3), 42, 44, 49, 50, 51,
53, 55, 60(2), 77, 94, 109,
110, 117, 189
Joseph, Jr. 21, 37, 47, 94
Winnifred 107(2)
NEW (Neaw)
Henry 60, 61
Jacob 48, 45
Peter 43, 94
NEWBANKS 127
Eliz. 119, 127
John 127
NEWCOMB
Dan 10(2), 15, 23, 43, 53,
56(2), 85, 94
Jean 43
Sarah 32
William 10, 43, 77
NEWELL (Nevill)
Jane 137
John 94
Joseph 94
Joseph, Gent. 94
William 55, 77
NEWILL
Joseph, Sr. 140
NEWMAN
Anna 48
Catsby 102, 103
Christopher 33, 43(2)
David 48, 94
Eliz. 127(3)
Elijah 42
George 12(2), 15(2), 19, 42,
43(2), 53, 57, 59, 74(4),
94
Hannah 43(3)
Isaac 15, 19, 33, 43(4), 50,
53, 57, 61, 77(6), 94, 112,
130
James 14
James Meekins 127
John 32, 33, 36(2), 43(3),
52(2), 77, 94(2), 114, 123,
124, 127(2), 130
John C. 123, 128, 135
Margaret 33, 43(2), 113
Mary Ann 127
Micheal 127
Ralph 127
R. 115, 127, 134
Robert D. 123
Robert 116, 118
Robert, Dr. 124
Sally 127(2)
Sarah, Mrs. 102
Solomon 18, 94, 121
William 42
Wm. C. 127
NEWTON
John 118
William 50, 77
NICHOLAS (Nichols)
Amos 43, 56
John 11, 35, 43
Joseph 28
Margaret 43
NICHOLSON
Eliz. 102, 105
Thomas 15, 77, 105, 138
NICKSON (Nixon)
Eliz. 48
George 26(2), 46, 48
Rachel 127
NISEMANGER
Mary 62
NIXON (Nickson)
Catherine 129
Eliz. 48, 107, 127
George 1, 2, 57, 77(2), 94,
101, 107, 127(2), 129
Hannah 127
John 10, 16, 17, 43, 59, 77
Jonathan 120, 127(2)
Jonathan, Jr. 6, 77
Joseph 111(2), 125, 127
Levi 127
Marey 94
Molly 127
Nancy 101, 102, 127
Rachel 127
Thomas 10
William 14, 103, 108, 122,
127(2), 139
William C. 134
NOBLE
George 2(2), 47(2)
Noah 135
Thomas 2, 43(4), 60, 77
NOEL
Peter 43, 94
NOLAND (see Neeland)
Andrew 16, 52

NORMAN
Benjamin 26, 38, 43(4), 77,
94
George 94
John 39, 43, 77(2), 94
Lucy 101, 102
Margaret 43(3)
Mary 43
Sarah 94
William 14, 17, 26(3), 43
(2), 77(2), 94, 112
NORRIS
Joseph 2(2)
NOLMAN (Noleman)
James 94
Jane 94
NOTTINGHAM
Thomas 137
NOURSE
Ann 44
Gabriel 44
NUFF (see Neff)
Henry 23
NUT
John 94, 140
NUTTER
Elizabeth 113
Thomas C. 113
OARE
Thomas 120
OATES
Catherine 127
Christopher 127(2)
Daniel 108
Everline 118
George 127
Jeremiah 118
Johatnan 127
Lorenzo 107
Margaret 127
Micheal 127
Peter 127(2)
O'BANNION
John 26
Joseph 94
O'BAR
Peter 127
William V., Capt. 127
O'BRIAN
John 124
O'BRYAN
Adam 11, 44
Tallent 94
O'CANNON
Joseph 39
O'CONNER
Dan 94
O'DANNIEL
Hugh 41, 77
O'DELL
Abigail 24
ODDLE (Odle)
John 133
William 33(2), 77(2), 94,
125
O'DONNELL
Elizabeth 44
Hugh 44
OFFORD
John 32, 37, 112, 132
Thomas 29
OFFUTT (Ofutt - Offet -
Affut)
Ann 102, 103
Elizabeth 127
Harriet 127
Hester 227
Jesse 121
J. M. 52
John J. 129
Joseph 103, 127(2)
Nancy 127
Nash 109
Nathan 112
Nathaniel 127
Owen 127, 132
Rachel 127
Sam 53, 118
Sarah 102, 103, 127
Sarah Jane 118
Solomon 103(2), 127, 130
Thornton 127
Zephiniah 127
OGDEN
David 125
Isaac 125
Joseph 34(2), 35, 55, 77(4)
Joseph, Mrs. 61, 77
O'GIN (Ongan)
Peter 95
O'HARA
Arthur 16(3), 17, 107(2)
Daniel 127
James 1, 35
John 52, 133
Patrick 57
Susan 127
Susanna 118

O'HAVER
Christopher 44, 95
Cornelius 95
Mary 44
OHRSAN (see Ohrsain &
Earsam)
"OIBOROSRON" 119
O'LAUGHLIN
Dan 121
OLDAKERS ((Oldacres)
Eleanore 44(2)
Elenore 44(2)
Helenore 44
Henry 44(3)
John 57, 77
Isaac 95(2)
William 54, 77
OLDERTON
William 45
OLDHAM
Abigail 107(2)
Ann 107
Ann Conway 132
John 132
Mary Ann 107(2)
Nancy 107
Samuel 107(2)
Susannah 107(2)
Wineford 107
William 16(2), 63, 77
OLLEY (Alley)
Chas. 138
OLLER (Aller)
Ann 127
Arthur 127, 182
PPter 182
O'NEAL (O'Neale see Neal)
Barton 16, 37, 44, 77(2)
Benjamin 40, 95
Daniel 127, 182
Edward 95, 140
John 16
Lawrence 43
William 30(2), 77(2)
ONGAN (Ogin)
Peter 125
O'NTANG
Joseph Phernica 119
O'QUEEN
James 139
O'QUINN
James 44, 77, 139
ORAHOOD
Alex 95, 140
ORCHARD
Nancy 127
ORD
John 5(2), 77(2)
ORENDORF
William 128
ORR
James 95
John 133
ORTON (Urton)
Robert 95
OSBORNE (Osburn - Oz-
born - Ozboren)
Betty 44
Charles 119
Frances 127
George 40(2), 44, 60, 77, 95,
237
Hannah 44, 127
Jeremiah 44, 95
John 40(2), 44, 77
Josiah 95, 127(2), 140
Kewsiah 119
Solomon 127
OSMUN (Osman - Ozman -
Ozmund)
Catherine 127
Charles 25, 44, 77(2), 119,
127(2)
Comfort 44
Elizabeth 127
Isaac 48, 77, 95, 124, 127
JabesJabes 95, 124(2)
Rebecca 127
Rodey 127
Sam 44(2), 95, 127(2)
OTTO
Henry 124
OURS (Orr)
Stithinman 95
OUTS
George 95
OVERLY
Peter 44
OWENS
Ann 26, 44
John 26, 44, 77
Robert. 44, 58, 77
M. W. 125
OZBURN (see Osburn)
George 95
Isaac 95
OZMUN(D) (see Osmun)
PACK (Park)

Joseph 4, 25
Sarah 5, 44
PAGE
Catherine, Mrs. 102
Elizabeth 117
Hannibal 102(2)
John 101, 102
Sydney, Mrs. 102
Thomas 117
PAIN (Payne)
Evan 95
PAINTER (Panter)
Benjamin 44, 95, 140
Israel 138
Juliana 131
Sarah 188
Susanna 14, 114
PAISLEY (Pursley - Pars-
ley)
Benjamin 117
Robert 117
PALMER
Ann 126, 127
Andrew Sadowski 127
Joseph 186
Mary 127
Sofia Johnson 127
PANABAKER
William 2
PANCAKE
Abraham 127
Agnes 127
Andrew 11(2), 44(5), 77(3),
95, 127
Catherine 44, 95
Eliz. 127(2)
George 14, 127
Hannah 127
Harbart (Herbert) 128
Isaac 127, 128
James 139
John 33(2), 37, 44(11), 52,
55(3), 63, 77(3), 86, 95,
114, 127, 128
John M. 114, 128, 135
John, Jr., 34, 44(2), 63(3),
77
John, Sr. 63, 127
John McNeil 102(2)
Joseph 55, 77, 95, 126, 127
(2)
Mary 127
Parthenia, Mrs. 102
Samuel 127, 128(2)
Sarah 128
Susan 114, 118
Susannah 44(6)
Simon 44, 114
PANILL
John 6
PANTER (Painter)
Benj. 140
PARELL (Parrell - Perrill)
Edward 44
John 95
Rachel 44
PARGITT (Pargit - Pargit-
Purgitt)
Jacob 26
PARISH
Adam 102, 103
John 44
Joseph 95
Mary, Mrs. 102
Wm. 102
PARK (Parks - Parke)
Alfred 128
Amos 13, 77, 100, 127(2),
128(2), 131
Amos, Sr. 137
Amos, Jr. 137
Amos Harvey 127
Amy 127
Andrew 44, 77, 95(2), 127
Anne 100, 102, 127, 128
Anne, Mrs. 102
Daniel 139
Elizabeth 120(2), 128
Elizabeth, Mrs. 102
Emily 127
Enoch 102, 136
Evan 127
George 44, 47, 50, 99, 102
(4), 113, 128(2)
Griffith 127
Hannah 127, 128(2)
Harbert (Herbert) 128, 129,
131
Jefferson 128(2)
Joanna 128
Job 95
John 44(2), 47, 50, 77, 95
(2), 99, 102, 127(3), 128
(2)
Lawrence 112
Lydia 44, 127
Malinda 128
Mary, Mrs. 102
Rachel 127
Rebecca 112
Rhoda 128

INDEX

Roger 107, 128
Robert 45
Ruth 127
Sam 50, 62, 77, 95, 113, 125, 127(3), 128(2),131, 134, 135
Sam J. 102(2)
Sarah 44, 127, 128
Solomon 128
Solomon, Jr. 128
Susannah 44, 128
Timothy 128
Washington 128(2)
Westley 128(2)
Wina 128
Wm. 35, 116
PARKER
A. V. 68
Aaron 37, 77
Abraham 45, 77, 109, 128(2)
Absolom 24, 128
Ann 44, 45, 77, 128(2)
Ashford 100, 128(2), 137
Benj. 4, 20, 22, 24, 35, 44, 45(9), 56, 77(3), 95(2), 102(2), 128(4), 137, 139
Catreen 128
David 128(2), 137
Elijah 15
Elizabeth 4, 37, 45, 78, 128 (3), 133, 136, 138
Elizabeth A. 131
Eliza 128
Eliza Jane, Mrs. 102, 128
George 48, 95, 128(8)
Grace 128
Hannah 45, 128(2), 129
Harriet 128
Isaias 45
Isaac 128
Isabella 128(2)
Jacob 26, 125, 128
James 14, 24, 45(3), 78, 98, 115, 122, 128(6)
James T. 128
James H. 118
James S. 133
Jeremiah 23, 78
Job 4, 43, 95
John 37, 39, 45(5), 48, 78, 95, 102, 104, 105, 116, 117, 118, 128(4), 129, 135
John M. 128
Johnathan 41, 50
Joseph 15, 128
Margaret 45(5), 128(3)
Martha R. 128
Mary Ann, Mrs. 102
Mary Jane 128
Mary 45(4), 128(4), 135
Mary I. 128
Mary E. 128
Nath. 28, 37, 45(4), 50, 78 (2), 85, 95, 114, 139
Nath, Sr. 95
Noble 128
Peter 2, 123, 128
Polly 123
Rebecca 128(2)
Richard 36, 37, 78(2)
Robert 7, 8, 35, 37, 44, 45 (7), 46, 48, 51, 61, 63, 78 (3), 95, 128(2), 129(2), 139
Robert, Jr. 114
Robert, Sr. 114(2)
Robert W. 128(2)
Samuel 22
Sarah 7, 45(2), 128(2)
Solomon 125(2), 128(3), 135
Susanna 128
Thornton 128(3), 136
Thomas 45, 47, 78(2), 86, 95, 114, 128(2), 140
Wm. 23, 45, 110, 114, 128 (2), 131
Wm. P. 118(2)
PARKINS (see Perkins)
Isaac 45, 78
Mary 45
PARKINSON
Christopher 128
Eliza 128
PARR
Will 60
PARRELL (see Parrill-Perrill - Peril - Paril)
Ann 128
Christine 45(2)
Edward 44, 128(3), 135
Eliz. 128
Hugh 114, 117
Jane 128
Jane C. 128
John 3(2), 7, 15, 19, 36, 45 (2), 55, 78(2), 95, 117, 127, 128 ,131, 135
John, Sr. 108
Joseph 128(2), 135
Rachel 44, 128
William 124, 128(2), 135
PARROTT

Christopher 37, 48, 78, 128
Dennis 128, 135
Dennis M. 102, 103
Joseph 126, 128(2)
Louisa, Mrs. 102
Margaret 128
Martha 128
Nancy 128
PARSLEY (Pursley)
Daniel 21
Dennis 21, 108
PARSONS
Agnes 128
Alex 95
Baulden 7, 45
Baldwin 45, 128
Catherine 45
Dana 128
David 37, 38, 45(2), 54, 63, 78(2), 86, 102(2), 110
Elizabeth 128(2)
Isaac 4, 7(2), 11, 12(2), 15, 16, 19(4), 21(2), 22, 28, 30, 32(4), 33, 34, 37, 39, 42(2), 45(3), 47, 49(2), 58
Jas. 7, 17(4), 18, 25, 38, 44, 45(8), 54, 60, 68, 78(3), 95, 102, 110, 113, 117, 120 (2), 124(4)
James, Jr. 128, 129
James G. 100, 102
Jona 15
John 25, 78
Jonathan 130
Margaret (Rebeca) 128
Mary 45, 78, 118, 128
Mary E. 128
Mary ,Mrs. 102
Milly, Mrs. 102
Mildred 126
Parthenia 102(2)
Prudence 128
Rachel 45
Rebecca 128(2)
Robert 137
Sam 116
Sally 124
Sarah A. 128, 140
Susan 114
Thomas 4, 10, 17, 19, 31, 44, 45(4), 47, 50, 128(2), 137(2), 140
William 124, 128, 140
PARVIANCE (Purvance)
Henry 49
Robert 55, 78
PASCALL
David 133(2)
PATTEN (Paton - Patton)
James 45
John 45
Rd. 53(2)
Richard 53
Ruth 127
Sam 118
Wm., Jr. 19
PATRICK
Lucien 123
PATTERSON
Alex 129
Anna 129
Betsy 129
Eliz. 106
Isabel 129
James 14(2), 84, 45, 61, 78 (2), 124, 129(4), 136
James Henry 129(2)
Jane 129(2)
Jean 45
Jennet 129
John 129(4), 132
Joseph 129
Margaret 129(2)
Martha Jane 129
Mary 129
Mary Ann 129
Nancy 129
Nancy, Mrs. 103
P. 7
Peggy 129
Richard 129
Robert 115, 129(4)
Samuel 102, 103, 129(2)
Sarah 129(2)
Thomas 102, 129(3)
William 129
PAUGH
John 95
Micheal 139
Nicholas 139
PAULSGROVE
Jaob 32
PAYNE (see Pain)
David 95
John 95
William 122
PAYTON
John 85
PEACEMAKER
Adam 119, 129
Catherine 119
David 129

Jacob, Jr. 129
Jacob W. 129(2)
William 129
PEAR
Joseph 129
Sarah 129
PEARCE (Pierce)
Andrew 134
Henry 46, 49
Henry Ward 46, 49
Henry W. 46
PEARCEALL (Pearsal(l) - Purcell)
Hannah 46
John 43(2), 46, 56, 78(2)
PEARPOINT (Pierpont - Pe(e)rpont)
Frances 14, 35
PEARSAL (Pearsall - see Purcoll - Piersall - Pearceall)
Ann 127
Bethia 46
Daniel 46
Hannah 46, 118
Job 7, 15, 26(2), 36, 46(8), 50, 62, 63, 78(2), 137
Daniel 46
John 4, 6(2), 7, 18(2), 20, 46, 48(2), 49, 56, 57, 61 (2), 78, 86, 95
Jonathan 131
Kesiah 46
PEAR(R)SON (Pearson - Persons - Parsons)
David 95
PEATT
Rachel 99, 103
PECK
George 95, 140
PEERPONT (Pear - Per - Pierpont)
Frances 14, 28, 35, 46, 78
PEGG
Thompson 18, 55, 62, 78(2)
PEIRCE (see Pearce and Pierce)
Ronnie 46
PELLET 112
PELLY
E. 56
PELTON
Incretia 123
PEMBROOK
John 7
PENCE
Jacob 109
PENCEOR
Jacob 109
PENDLETON
John 95
Phillip 7, 11, 12, 21, 23, 26, 39(8), 40(3), 44, 54, 55, 58 (2), 78, 86(2)
Richard 95
PENNINGTON
Abraham 2, 121
Adam 129(2)
Catherine V. 122
Charlotte 129
Elijah 129, 133
Elizabeth 129, 133
Enoch 124, 129, 135
Faney 129
Feaby 129
Hannah, Mrs. 103
Hannah 129
Henry 129
Isaac 129
Isaac J. 129
James 102, 103, 129
John 129
Julius G. 129
Levy 129
Mary Catherine 129
Nancy 129
Sarah 129
Thomas 124, 129
Wm. 124, 129
William Paul 129
PENNISTON (Pennington)
Phillip 59, 78
Phillip C. 59
PENNYPACKER
Elizabeth 110
Matthey 110
Matthies 120
PEPPE 115
PEPPER(S) (Peppe)
Deborah Mrs. 103
Fredrick 103, 104, 125
Henry 102, 130
Jacob 114, 115, 134
John 46, 48, 78, 100, 130
John, Jr. 46, 78
Joshua, Jr. 95
Joshua, Sr. 95
Juliana 102, 103
Sophiah 100, 103
PERKINS (Parkins)

Isaac 47(2), 78
PERPONT (Peerpont)
Frances 25, 35, 78
PERREL (Perrell - Parrill-Parrill)
John 55, 78, 95
John, Jr. 55
Joseph, Jr. 55
PERRIN
Chas. Westly 127
Hannah 127
Ralph 127
Sally 127(2)
Thomas 95
Upton 127
PERRY
Daniel 46
Mandlen 46
Lucy 111
Roger 119, 131
Samuel 46
Susan 119
Thos. 8, 35, 78(2)
William 137
PERSEL (Pear-Pur)
Daniel 46
Keziah 46
PERSONS (Parsons - see Pearsons - Pearson)
Alex 95
Catherine 126
David 126
PETERS (Petters)
Abraham 18, 20, 46(2), 78 (2)
Asenath 129
Branson 131, 132
Catherine 46
Caty 129
Cherese 129
Edward 46, 78, 129
Hannah 129
Hester Ann 129
James 129
John 31, 32, 33, 43, 46, 49, 78(2), 95, 98, 129, 132, 136
Joshua 62, 78
Lydia 100, 103
Marian 46(2)
Maria B. 128
Mary 129
Permelia Ann 129
Peter 46(3), 61, 78, 100, 103, 129, 139
Phillip 62, 78
Samuel 2
Susannah 129
Tunis 27, 40, 120
PETERSON
Jacob 26, 95
Jacob, Jr. 95
Jacob, Sr. 95(2)
Margaret 95
Martin 95
Micheal 95
Pter 5, 78, 95, 139
Tunis 9, 78
PETRID
Christian 54
PETRO
Leonard 95
PETERS (see Peters)
PETTIT (Pettet)
Eliz. 46(2)
John 129
Moses 100
Rebecca 112, 129(2)
Sarah 100, 103
Thos. 9, 19, 42, 46(2), 78(3)
PETTY
Joseph 4, 78, 95, 110(2), 117
PEYAT
Cornelius 24, 46, 78
Eliz. 46
PEYROURET (Peyrouet)
Adelaid Louisa 27, 46
John Baptist 27, 46
PEYTON
Francis 50
F. Jr. 3, 45
G. Jr. 6
J. 33
John 7, 46, 78, 85(2)
Thomas 13
PHEBUS
George 86
PHILLIPS 111
Ann 46
Henry 57, 78
John 46, 78, 136
P. 109
Plunkett 57, 78
William 132
Wm. J. 107
PHIPPS
Benjamin 46
PICKERING
Benjamin 108
Hiram 103(2)
Massey 123

Sarah Ann, Mrs. 103
Wm. 123
PICKLE
Jacob 95
PIERSALL (Pursall - Purcell - Pearsall)
Benjamin 129(2)
Eleanore 129
Hannah 46, 129
John 46, 95, 129(2)
Margaret 129
Rachel 129(2)
PIERCE(SE) (Pearce - Peirce)
Benoni 35, 55
Benjamin 95
John 49
Dan 95
Frances Ann 46(2)
George 6, 24, 40, 46, 78(2)
George C. 46, 78
Henry 46(2)
Henry Ward 46, 49
James 46(2), 51(3), 78(3)
John 24, 32, 35, 46(2), 49, 51, 78(3)
John Thompson 137
Rachel 46(3)
PIERCEAL (see Pearsall - Hannah 46
John 13, 46, 61(2), 78(2), 125, 139
PIERPONT (Pear - Per - Peerpont)
John 35
PIERCE
Benjamin 95
PIGGOT
James 23
PIGMAN (Pigmaer)
Bean 2
Margaret 46
Matthew 6, 9, 18, 40, 78
Moses 15, 30, 46(2), 78, 95, 137
M. 6
PILCHER (see Pitcher)
Stephen 4, 22, 78, 114
PILES
Elizabeth 103, 105
Elizabeth, Mrs. 103
John H. 103(2)
Zachariah 103
PILLMAN
Peter 95
PIPER
John 102, 104, 127, 130
Micheal 127
R. G. 110
PISER
Jacob 18, 54
John 18, 54(2)
PITCHER (see Pilcher)
Stephen 22, 78
R. G. 110
PLACE
Thomas 6, 78
PLANK
Fredrick 95
PLEASANTS
John 36(3), 78(3)
PLOUGH
Jacob 46, 95
Lydia 46
PLOW
Alders 95
PLUMB
Abraham 118
Elizabeth 46
John 3, 26, 35, 62, 78(2) 86, 95, 100, 103
Nancy, Mrs. 103
Sam 46
PLUMMER
Ann 118
PLUMSOME
John 138
POAGUE
Robert 95
POE
Samuel 22
POELZER 115
POISER
Jacob 18, 78
POLAND (Polin)
John 86, 99, 103, 126
Mary, Mrs. 103
Nancy 129, 132
POLIN (Poland)
Lewiza 132
POLING
Joseph 127
POLLOCK (Polock)
Isaac 16(2), 78(2)
Joseph W. 138
Pompey 23
PONEMUS (Ronemus)
Christopher 117
POOL
Ann 129

George 48
Ashby 129
Benjamin 129
Deborah 121
Easter 129
Eliz. 129
George 129
Haner 129
Henry 129
John 129
Mary 129
Robert 109, 129
Rhoda 129
Sarah 129
Sufier 129
Susannah 129
William 2, 126, 129
William H. 121, 126
POPE
Andrew 16
Lidia 47
Robert 47
POPEJOY
John 95
Terrance 95
PORTER
Anson V. 131
Eli 95
Elias 95
Phillip 95
Robert 95, 123
William 95
POSEY
Sarah Ann 103(2)
William 103
POSSILMAN
Lookey 40, 78
POSTELWAIT
William 22
POST (Forst)
Valentine 56, 78, 95
POSTIN (Posten)
Alexander 100, 134
Ashford 102, 103(2)
Rranson 100
Catherine 129
Deliah 100, 103
Deliha 129
Elias 1(2), 2(2), 3(2), 8, 14, 15(8), 22, 24, 27, 31, 33, 37, 39, 46(2), 47(2), 53, 54, 63, 78(6), 88, 95, 111, 114, 129, 130, 134, 135, 137, 138
Isabelle, Mrs. 103
John 102, 103(2)
Mary, Mrs. 103
Polly 112
Rebecca 15, 129
Richard 112(2)
Sam 15(2), 112, 129, 134
William 100, 129
POTT(A)INGER
John 57
POULSON (Powelson)
Anderson 47
POWELL
Abraham 47, 54, 59, 78, 95, 129, 131, 134
Amery C. 112
Ann 47, 115, 134
Ann, Mrs. 103
Caleb 95(2)
Christian 27, 129
Clark 108, 112
Clark D. 112
Dade 103, 129
Elisha 102, 103, 129
Eliz. 102, 103, 115(2), 129
Eliz. T. (Heth) 118
Eliz. B. 129
Horatic N. 103
Isaac J. 109
Isaiah 106, 109
James 31, 78, 118, 129, 134
James L. 101, 103
James R. 103, 135
Joanna W. 103(2)
John J. 136
John 100, 102, 103(2), 115, 129
Joseph 47, 112, 120, 129(2)
Joseph, Jr. 129
Juliah D. 112, 115, 129
Lazarus 118
Mary 129
Mrs. 103(2)
Nancy 129
Robert 121(2), 129
Robert M. 102(2), 103, 129
Samuel 95, 129
Sarah 129
Sarah Ann 129
Sarah B. 129
Stephen 129
Susanna 129
Susanna, Mrs. 103
Thornton F. 103(2), 129, 130
Thos. 131
William 95, 103, 108, 130

William M. 112
POWELSON (Poulson)
Abraham 3, 47, 107, 108
Anderson 47
Byansa 57, 78
Catherine Ann 111
Charles 47, 78, 101, 103, 129
Cloe (Cloann) 129, 130
Conrad 129
Cornelius 106, 129
Delilah, Mrs. 103
Eliza 101, 103, 129, 130
Elizabeth 112, 129
Eve 129
Henry 3, 19, 43, 78(2), 98, 129, 130
James 111, 129
John 19(2), 47, 78, 106, 129 (3)
John, J. 107
John R. 130
Joseph J. 129
Margaret 101, 103
Mary 3, 47, 107, 108
Paul 15, 78, 129(2)
Powel 130
Robert 99, 103
Rosannah 100, 103, 130
Rinare (Riner) 130
Rynear(Ryneay) 100, 101
S. I. 130
Thomas 129, 130
POWER
John 45
Martin 95
Stephen C. 132
Valentine 35, 78, 95
POWITT
Abraham 54
POWNALL (Powell - Pownell)
Abigail 130(2)
Elisha 118, 130
Elizabeth 107
Isaiah 109
Isaac 138, 139
Isaac J. 107
John 109
John A. 107
John J. 102, 103, 107, 117
Jonathan 106, 117, 130
Joshua 107
Levinia 130
Mahala 107
Martha 130
Sarah 130, 133
Sarah, Mrs. 103
Rachel 130
Robert 117
Ruben 130
William 103, 107
PRAGE
Robert 121
PRATER (Prathr)
James 33, 136
Joseph 52
PRATHER (Prater)
Ann H. 130
Ann M. 130
Basil 130
Caty 130
Charles 10, 47, 53, 78, 130 (2)
Eliz. 130
James 28, 33, 38, 58, 78, 120, 130(2), 136
John 53
Joseph 52
Laban A. 130
Martha M. 130(2)
Mary 130
Ruth 47, 130
Silas 122, 130
Socratoris 130
Theodocis W. 130
Van 130
William B. 130
PRATT
Foster 120
PRATZMAN see Protzman
John 121
PRESBYTERIAN and Baptist Church 50, 78
PRICE
Arjalon (Arsalon) 5, 9, 10 (2), 11, 22, 24(2), 26, 29, 30, 33(2), 34(2), 47(3), 48, 49, 78(4), 95, 102, 119, 131
Arjalon, Jr. 112
Arajalon, Sr. 112
Elmira 101, 103
Caty 47(2)
Frances 47
Keorge 114
George W. 30, 131
G. W. 29
I. 10
Ignatius 138
John 7(2), 9, 40, 47

John A. 22
John H. (Hill) 3, 5, 11, 22, 28, 34(2), 37
Kate 47
Lewellen 95
Louisa 102, 103
Mary 5, 47
Mary Ellen 135
Nathan 9, 21, 54, 57, 78
Phillip 47
Silas 30, 139
Smith T. 99
Thomas 47
William 28, 95, 139
PRICKETT
Lewis 99, 103
Eleanor, Mrs. 103
PRIEST
Sally Ann 137
PRIM (Primm)
Betty 56
John 14, 56(2), 56, 79(2)
PRINGLE
Adaiah 130
Andrew 14
David 14
Eliz. 130
George W. 130
Henry 130
Jedidiah 130
John 130
Margaret 130
Malinda 130
Mary 130(2)
William 98, 130
PRITCHARD (Pilcher - Pitcher - Prichard)
Alice 47, 78
Alse 130
Barthama 27, 47(8)
Barthamy 47(3)
Catherine 134
Hannah 130
Jacob 134
John 35, 139
Joseph 28, 47(2), 78, 130
Margaret 47(2)
Rees (Reese) 1, 3(3), 22(3), 27, 29, 30, 31, 32, 34, 36 (2), 45, 47(11), 48, 62, 78(2), 85, 95(2), 130
Robert 47(2)
Ross 47
Samuel 3(2), 9, 12, 15(3), 25, 26, 27, 29(2), 34(4), 37, 46, 47(9), 56, 59, 63, 78(3) 79(2), 130
Stephen 47, 130
PRIZER
Henry 48
PROBASCO
Elijah 103(2)
Eleanor, Mrs. 103
Francis 103, 130
Jacob 100, 103(2)
Margaret 103(2)
Margaret, Mrs. 103
Samuel 101, 103
PROTZMAN (Pratzman)
Henry 4, 5, 14, 16(2), 18, 24, 27, 29(2), 31, 32, 34, 40, 43(3), 48, 49, 53, 79
John 121
PRUNTY
John 2, 12, 15, 27(2), 32, 41, 47(4), 48, 79, 95, 130
Mary 47(2)
PUGH
Abraham 61, 79
Alfred 130
Amos 130
Amy 130
Ann(e) 100, 103, 130(3), 137
Ann, Mrs. 103
Arthur 130
Arthur T. 116
Azariah 107, 130(2)
Benjamin 130(2), 137
Betheul 27(2), 47, 48, 79, 95, 125
Bethel 130
Catherine 107
Daniel 47, 85, 95, 130
Darius 103
David 46, 74, 48, 107(3), 122, 124, 128, 130(5), 131 137
Edward 137
Eli 48
Eleanore 130
Eliz. 119, 130
Mrs. Elizabeth 103
Evan 48
Evan, Jr. 48
Evelina 119(2), 137
Ezra 100, 102, 103(2)
Hannibal 130
Hannah 107, 130, 130(2)
Harriet 130

Hetty 119
Jacob 38, 42, 47, 48, 58, 95, 100, 103, 128, 130, 138, 140
Jas. 79, 102, 111, 115, 130, 137
James B. 137
James Brown 110
Jane 47, 111
Jesse 1(2), 15, 48(5), 79, 85, 95, 103, 107(3), 114(2), 130(3)
Jesse S. 131
Jessie 103
John 48, 101, 102(3), 103 (4), 112, 130(4)
Jonathan 27(2), 41, 46, 48 (4), 53, 63, 79(3), 95, 116 (2), 125, 126, 130(5)
Jonathan, Jr. 102, 103, 130
Joseph 48(3), 79, 112, 130 (4)
Juliana 130
Leonard 127
Lucy 130(2)
Lydia, Mrs. 103
Mahlon 130
Malign 28
Malign 48
Malachi 100, 119, 130(3)
Maragaret 48(3), 102, 103, 130(3)
Martha 125
Maria 130
Mary 15, 48(2), 107, 114, 130
Micheal 107(2), 108, 119(2), 130
Mishack 130
Mishall 130
Monroe 130(2)
Nancy 127
Phoebe 127
Rebecca 47, 130
Robert 2, 15(2), 47, 48, 95, 102(2), 103, 111, 114, 128, 130(3), 137
Robert J. 119
Sally 47
Sarah 48(3), 107, 127, 130
Sarah, Mrs. 103(3)
Samuel 15, 48(2), 79, 95, 114, 130
Solomon 130
Susan 119
Thomas 1, 48, 79, 95
William 137
William E. 119
PULTZ (Putze)
Eliz. 130
Jacob 130, 132
John G. 132
Katherine 130
Mary 130
Micheal 130, 132
Nancy 130
PURCELL (Pear - Pier - sall - celi - ceall)
Andrew 88
Ann 127
Benjamin 129
Bethia 46
Cathrine 48(3)
Daniel 46, 48(2), 124
Dennis 48
Edward 95, 133, 139
Hannah 46, 118, 129
John 4, 13(2), 20, 43(2), 46(2), 49, 56, 57, 61(2), 79, 95, 125, 129, 133
Jonathan 7, 13, 14, 21, 37, 48(3), 50, 60, 62, 79(3), 95, 117, 133, 138
Job 7, 15, 26, 27, 36, 46, 50, 62, 63, 137
Keziah 48
Margaret 129
Rachel 129
Susanna 48
William 21, 22, 95
PURGET(T)
PURGITT (Purgatt)
Elizabeth 130(2)
Fetty 47
Fredrick 29, 79, 130
George 130
Henry 18(2), 79, 95, 98, 130
Henry, Sr. 98, 130
Jacob 26, 48(2), 79, 86
Madelana 48
Magdaline 48(2)
Mary 48, 130
Rachel 103(2), 130
Simon 29
Valentine 12, 48(4), 79(3)
William 130
PURSLEY (see Parsley)
Daniel 21
Dennis 21, 79, 108

PURVIANCE (Perviance - Parviance)
Henry 49
PUSINGER
Conrad 53, 79, 130
PUTMAN (Puttman)
Jacob 37, 100, 108, 130
Magdalene, Mrs. 103
Mary 32, 46, 48(4), 49, 79
Peter 3, 5, 23, 32, 38, 45, 46 48(6), 49, 57, 79(5), 86, 95, 116
Rachel 103(2), 130
PUTZE
Micheal 133
QUEEN (O'Queen)
Absolom 130
Charles 42, 95
Chloe 126
Elizabeth 100, 108
John 98, 100, 103, 130
John, Jr. 130(2)
Martha 130
Mary, Mrs. 103, 126
Sarah 103
Stephen 102, 103, 126(2)
Stevan 103
QUENLLY
Patrick 6
QUEHAN
Paul 95
QUINN (see O'Quinn)
William 44, 57
QUIRK
John 30(2)
RACE
Sally 103
RACEY
Harriet 131
John 108, 129, 130
Lewis 122
Lydia 132
Margaret 130
Rebecca 130
Sarah 108, 130
Thomas 130
William 130(3), 131(2), 137
RACHEN
Mary 115
RADCLIFF (see Ratcliff)
Benjamin 95
Richard 95
Stephen 95
RAFLIN
W. H. 126
RAGAN (Ragun)
Jacob 48, 50, 123
Mary 48
Magdelene (Molly) 110
RAGLAND
Eliza C. 115
Louisa Craig 115
Thomas 104
Virgina Carey 115
RALFE (see Rolfe)
John 46(2), 59(3)
Richard 46
RALSTON
Robert 48
RAMBO
Ezikiel 48
Mary 129
Peter 48, 129
RAMSEVIL (Rounsevill)
Richard 48
RAMSEY
Andrew 32, 48
Dennis 37, 38(3), 48(4), 79 (4)
Eve 32, 48, 79
John 39, 48(2), 79
Margaret 48
Richard 8
William 9(2), 48, 55, 79(4)
RANDELL (Randall)
Abel 2, 4(2), 6, 7(4), 9, 17 (6), 18, 21, 23, 25(2), 26 (4), 28, 35(3), 37, 41(2), 42(2), 45, 48(2), 49(3), 53, 58, 60(3), 62, 79(3), 88, 95, 125, 137(3), 138, 139
Alex 29, 35, 48, 79
Catherine 48
Felix 48
James 102
Linda 48
Priscilla, Mrs. 103
Thos. 103, 104
William 134
RANDOLPH
Eliz. 49
John 48, 49(2), 62, 79, 86
RANKIN
Eleanor 115
John 115, 124
RANNELS
Christina (Christiny) 130 (2)
David 130, 131

INDEX

Eliz. 101, 103
Jas. 12, 101, 114, 130(2), 131, 139
Jan 180
Jane 131
Jeremiah 95
John 20, 22, 23, 24, 52, 79, 95, 106, 123, 125, 127, 180 (4)
John Robert 131
Margaret 130, 131
Mary 103, 104, 123, 130(2)
Nancy 130, 131
Nancy, Mrs. 103
Peggy 130
Samuel 130, 131
Sarah 52
Sally 125
Samuel 130, 131
Robert 1, 15, 55(2), 114(3), 123, 130, 131, 138
William 1, 27, 101, 103, 104, 130, 131
RASNER
Gideon 95
RATC(H)LIFF(E) (see Radcliff)
Benj. 131
David 189
Stephen 8, 9
RATCLIFF (see Radcliff - Ratchliff)
Benjamin 131
Stephen 8, 9
RATHELL
Thomas 47
RATIEN
C. 33, 79
RAVENILL 99
Frances 3
RAVENSCRAFT (Ravenscroft)
C. S. 125
Francis 37
James 108, 109, 125
John 6, 34, 35, 45, 49, 79, 95, 107, 117, 132
John D. 100, 103
John N. 125
Maria 113
Maria, Mrs. 103
Nicholas 125
Pricilla)Priscilla) 49(2)
Sam 6, 45, 49(3), 52, 59, 62, 79, 95
Solomon 35
William 37, 45, 95
RAWLES
John 7(2), 49(4), 60, 95
RAWLINGS
Ann 131
Benjamin 139
Elijah 123
Elizabeth 131
Lloyd 131
Moses, Col. 133
Moses (Mose) 16, 79, 131, 133
Nancy 131
Richard 131
RAY
Joseph 95
Sarah 184
RAYER (Roger)
Mary Ann 111
RAYMOND
Isabella 137
Moses 114
Sally 137
Sam 137
Susan 137
READ (se Reed - Reid)
Ann 131
Eliz. 95, 131(2)
George 95, 131
I. I. 122
Jane 131
Jeremiah 131
John 95, 131
John M. 131
Mary Anne 131
Mrs. 95
Rikey 131
READER (Reeder)
Daniel 47, 79
Hannah 49(2)
Jemima 49(2)
Joseph 41, 49, 79(20)
Joseph, Jr. 49
Sarah 49
William 47(2), 49(4), 79 (3), 86
William, Sr. 11, 49(2), 79
William, Jr. 49, 79
REAGER (see Regar)
Anthony 49, 95
Jacob 49, 95
REAM
David 128, 139

RENNICK (see Renick - Rennock)
REASNER (Reasener)
Abraham 139
David 189
Frances 139
Garret 29, 49(3), 50(2), 79, 109
Jacob 4, 49, 57, 79(2), 131, 139
Jemima 49
Jerimiah 49
John 21, 37, 41, 109, 112, 131(2)
Kesiah 49
Mary 49(2), 117, 131
Peter 41, 49(2), 117, 131
Rebecca 131
Susannah 131
William 22, 49, 79, 131
REASUM (Reasun)
Garrett 109
John 109
REAVES (see Reeves)
Austin 95
Benjamin 95
Richard 95
RECER
Mary 180
RECTOR
Areline 131
Caleb 132
Charles 95, 132
Conway 107(3), 131, 132, 139
Dan 95, 132
Harriet Ann 131
James Nelson 131
Mary 112, 127, 131
Maria 131
Nancy 107(2)
Presley 120, 125
Winifred 132
REDBURN
William 120
REDDICK
Margaret 49
William 49
REDDING (Reding - Reddick)
Amy 137
John 32(2)
Joseph 137
Margaret 49
William 18, 20, 49, 79
REDMAN
Henry 60
William 95
REDSLEEVES
Jacob 95
REDTRUCK
Andrew 2, 41, 79
REED (see Read - Reid)
Ann 131
Charles 4, 37(2), 131(3)
Christopher 43
David 128
Eleanor 49
Eliz. 49(2), 95, 131
George 8, 16, 18, 62, 79(3), 95, 102, 126, 131(4)
Grace 79
Hannah 131
Jaob, Capt. 126
Jacob 41, 44, 57(2), 79
James 131(3), 136, 138
Jeremiah 131, 133
John 12, 20(2), 27(2), 31, 37, 45(3), 47, 49(3), 52, 55, 56
John, Capt. 126
Joshua 79
Maria 99, 103
Mary 131(2)
Nancy 131
Samuel 9, 79
Sarah 102, 103, 114
Solomon 49, 131(2)
Thomas 108
William 26, 151
REEDER (see Reader)
REEL (Rule)
David 49, 95(2)
Margaret 49
Nicholas 95
REES (Reese - Rheas)
Ashford 125, 131(2)
Catherine, Mrs. 103
David 18, 79
Eleanor Naomi 131
Ellen 131
Eliza 101, 103, 119
Elizabeth 131
George 18, 49, 131
Hannah 100, 103
Harriet Ann 131
John 101, 131
John McNary 131
Lydia 103(2)
Margaret 131(2)
Martha 131

Morris 27(2)
Samuel 131
Sidney 123
Silas 114(2), 117
Susan 125
Susanna 131
Susan Matilda 131
Thomas 131
Thomas, Jr. 131
Thomas, Sen. 103, 104
William 28, 45(2), 48, 79 (2), 100, 101, 103, 107, 117, 131(3)
William Davis 131
William D. 106, 116, 133, 137
REEVE (Reeves - see Reaves)
Austin 95
Austin Smith 132, 135
Benjamin 29, 49(2), 51, 79, 132
Mary 49
Nancy 132
Peter 15, 49(2), 60, 79(2)
Richard 95
Sibbey (Libby) 49(2)
REGAR (see Reager)
Anthony 95, 131
Antony 131
Jacob 95
John 95
Maddenline 131
Martin 131
REID (see Reed and Read)
Amilda 131
Austin P. 131
Azariah 131
Dorcy 131
Eliz. Ann 131
Eliz. R. 131
Francis U. A. 131
George 95, 131
Harriet 131
James 3, 95, 131
Jeremiah 95, 131(2), 133
John 33, 35, 131
Josiah 131
Joseph 47
Lavinia 131
Margaret Jane 131(2)
Martin V. 131
Mary Ann 131(2)
Morgan 131
Nancy 131
Priscilla Ann 131
Rhuan 131
Sarah Malinda 131
Smith 131
Theophelos P. 131
Tillberry 131
William 131
REIDT
Andrew 26(2), 79(2)
REILLY (see Rilley and Riley)
Patrick 95
REINHART (see Rienhart-Rhinehart - Renehart)
Abner 131
Abraham 86, 116, 119, 123, 126, 131(2)
Andrew 131
Anthony 131
Catherine 131
David 131(3)
Elijah 116
Frances C. 118, 119
George 123, 131(2))
Hannah 131
James 131(2)
Joel 131
John 131
John W. 118, 119, 131
Margaret 131
Mary 131
Rachel 131
Sarah 131
Sary 131
Susan 131
Susannah 131
RELFE (Rolfe - Relse - Ralfe)
John 46(2), 49(3), 58, 59 (3), 79(3)
Richard 46(2), 49(2)
RELSE (see Relfe)
John 49(2)
Richard 49
RENDING
Reuben 95
RENICK (see Rennick - Rennock)
George 41, 49, 50(3), 53, 79
John 21, 25, 54, 79
Mary 50(3)
Thos. 49
William 17, 50, 57, 79
RENNELS (see Rannels - Reynolds)

James 31, 79
Rennock)
Elizabeth 95
George 50(3), 52(2), 131, 139
John 95
Jermy 131
Mary 50(3), 131
Millia 131
William 95, 131(2), 138(2)
RENNOCK (see Rennick - Renick)
George 50(3)
John 54, 79
Mary 50(3)
RENO
D. 36
John 35(2), 50(3), 56, 59 (2), 79(2)
John, Sr. 50
Susannah 50
William 35
RESE (see Rees and Reid)
Thos. 108
RESONNER (see Reasoner)
Jacob 52
REVNALS (Reynolds)
William 95
REYNOLDS (see Rennels and Rannels)
Cornelius 131
Elizabeth 131
John 131, 134
Robert 20, 79
REYNALDS (Reynolds)
William 51, 79
RHEAS (see Reese)
David 22(2), 30, 79(5)
John 21(2), 30, 79(3)
RHINEHART (see Reinhart - Rhineheart)
Abraham 131
Elisha 136
Mary 137
RHODES (see Roads)
Henry 95
John 4(2), 95
Tholemnish 50, 53, 79
Thomas 50, 95
RICE (Rise)
John 11, 79
RICHARDS (see Ritchard and Pritchard)
Benjamin F. 117, 128
Benjamin Fry 131
George 3
Henry 131
Henry Secris 131
Isaac 95
John W. 131
Rachel Ann 131
Samuel 104
Sarah B. 110
Sarah Jane 131
William 3, 79, 95
RICHARDSON (see Richison)
Abraham 50(2)
Amos 19
Arthur 44, 46, 61, 79
Dan 3, 8(2), 33, 45, 50(2), 56, 79(3), 95
Jonathan 95
Joseph 95
Richard 95
William 124
RICHISON (see Richardson)
William 95
RICHE (see Richie-Richey)
Charity 109
RICHIE (see Riche-Richey)
Nancy 125
RICHY (Richie-Riche)
David N. 125
William 7
RICHMOND
Wm. 6, 8, 10, 12, 49, 79(2), 120
RICKETTS (Rickets)
John 27, 61, 79(2)
John Thomas 19, 50, 79
Mary 50, 118
Thomas 11, 79
RIDGER
John E. 114
RIDGELY
Charles 5, 6, 79(2)
Charles, Jr. 5, 6, 79(2)
Edward 132
Eliza 132
Elizabeth 132
John 5, 6, 79(2)
Malinda 132
Nicholas G. 132
Richard 132
Sarah 132
RIDGEWAY
Richard Hews 125
RIDING

Joseph 95
RIDOUT
Thomas 50
RIGGLE
Catherine 99, 103
Elijah 99
RIGGS
John 132
Matilda 137
Rebecky 132
Simeon 132
RIGHT (see Wright)
John 50
RILEY (see Reilly and (Rilley)
Alex. 101, 103, 104, 134
Edward. 130
George 134
Isabelle, Mrs. 103
Jane 161, 104, 134(3)
Mary Ann 123
Samuel 134
Sarah Jane 134
William 134
RILLEY (see Riley and Reilly - Rilley)
Patrick 16(2)
RINEHART (see Rhinehart Reinhart)
Abraham 106, 119, 131
Elijah 116
Lepah 106
Rachel 24, 79, 131, 134
Sarah 131
RINKER
Casper 50
Lew 131
Mary 50
Mary Jane 131
RIORDAN (Riorden)
Robert 118
RISE (see Rice)
Aaron 56
RISER (see Rizer)
RISLEY
Dan 95
RITCHARDS (see Richards)
John 95
RITCHART (see Ritchards and Richards)
John 117
RIZER (Riser)
Nancy 114
ROADS (see Rhodes)
Henry 95
ROBERSON (Robertson)
Asenath 128
Roberson A. 134
ROBESON
Christina 123
Juliet Ann 111
ROBERTS
A. W. 117
Benjamin 101, 103
David 13, 59, 79(2), 95
David, Sr. 95
David, Jr. 95
Eliz. 50
John 86, 79, 99
Kisey 132
Louden 7, 40, 79(2), 132
Martha 104
Mary 109(3)
Mary Elender 132
Polly 109
Polly, Mrs. 103
Sary 132
Thomas 95, 109
William 14, 18(2), 50, 79 (3)
ROBERTSON (Roberson)
Elsa 107
Richard 107(2)
Roberson A. 134
Thomas 111
ROBINSON
Benjamin 17, 50, 79(2), 111
Elizabeth 117
Hannah, Mrs. 108
James 132
Joel 13, 50, 62, 79(2), 95, 113(2)
John 17, 39, 49, 50, 80, 96 (2), 116, 132
Joseph 50
Lot 2
Lydia 132
McKenney 23, 50(2), 80
Margaret 50
Nicholas 27, 50
Phoebe 132
Richard 132
Roger 96
Solomon 103(2), 123
ROBEY (Roby)
Notley 86
ROBY (Robey)
Benjamin 96
David, Sr. 96

Peter 96
Prior 96
Thomas 96
William 96(2)
ROCK
Fridel 132
Henry 132
John 132
Katherine 132
RODEBAUGH
Adam 96
RODGERS (Rogers - Roogers)
David 58, 80
James 50(2)
Jonathan 50
Martha 50(2)
Owen 59
Sarah 50
William 50, 52, 96
RODRICK (Rodrock)
Abraham 134
Daniel 16, 50, 80
Elizabeth 50
RODROCK (Rodrick)
Andrew 50
Eave 50
ROE (Row)
Walter 44, 80
ROGERS (see Rodgers - Roogers)
Aaron 129(2)
Barnabas 129
Calvin 129
Catherine 132
Cherise 229, 132
Deiadanna (Diedamia) 50 (2)
David 189
Ezekiel 50(7), 132(2)
George 50, 126, 127
Isabella 111
James 50, 80
John 19, 41, 42, 50(5), 53, 55, 80(2), 103(2), 104, 111, 132
Lewiza 132
Lydia 128 132
Lydia, Mrs. 103
Margaret 121
Martha 103, 104
Mary 50(4), 132
Mary Ann 111
Matthew 80
Matty 121
Owen 59, 116, 132
Patrick 48, 50, 55, 80
Rhodon 131
Robert 57, 58, 80(2), 86, 108, 116, 121, 132(2)
Sarah 50
Thomas 55, 80
William 50, 121(2)
ROLFE (see Relfe - Relse - Ralfe)
John 46(2), 59(3), 80(3)
Richard 46
ROLLER
Martin 30, 33, 50, 80(2)
Priscilla 50
ROLLINS (Rollings)
Benj. 54, 80
George 55, 80, 131
ROLLS
John 113
ROMAIN (Ronomus - Romney)
Jonathan 112
ROMNEY (Romain - Rnoomus)
Romney Trustee Deeds 50 (2), 51(44)
RONOMUS (Romain - Romney)
Conrod (Conrad) 117
ROOGERS (see Rodgrs - Rogers)
Jonathan 51, 80
Matthew 51, 80
William 51(2)
ROOTES
George 2, 3, 6(2), 12(2), 23, 27, 32, 33, 36, 37, 39(8), 45, 50, 52, 54, 55
ROREBAUGH (see Rodebaugh)
Henry 96
John 96
ROSE (see Ross)
Jacob 96
John 96
Robert 61, 80
ROSEBOROUGH (Rosenbrough)
John 98
ROSEBURGH (Rosenbough)
Jamse 126
Jessie L. 126
John 5(2)
Solomon 126

ROSEBOOM
Fredrick 80
Hendrick 14, 37, 43(2), 53, 128
Henry 53, 80
ROSENCRANTZ
Henry 96
ROSENBRICK (see Rosen-Moses 126
ROSENBROUGH (see Rosenborough)
John 5(2), 138
Mary 138
Moses 138
ROSENBERGER
Asamus 132
Eliz. 132(2)
John 132
ROSS (Roff - Rose)
Aphia, Mrs. 132
Arminilla 51, 132(2)
Barbary (Barbara) 51(3)
Charlie 118
Elizabeth 51, 52, 132(3)
Deborah Jane, Mrs. 132
Francis 51
Hannah (Hanna) 132(2)
Jaco 109
John 51(6), 63(2), 96(2), 128, 132(2)
John J. 132
Laurence 132
Lawrence 51, 63, 80, 96, 132
Letty 52
Lettice 52
Margaret 136
Nancy, Mrs. 132
Phillip 9, 27, 30, 36, 51, 52, 55
Robert 6, 20(3), 52(3), 55, 63, 80(2), 85, 96, 132(2)
Robert, Sr. 96
Stephen 96, 138
Susannah 107(2)
Susannah, Mrs. 132
Tavener 132
Winnyfrite 51
Winnifred 132
William 4, 11, 51(3), 63(2), 118, 132(3)
ROSSAU
John 42
ROSSAU
John 63, 120, 128
ROSSEAW (-sau)
John 4, 5, 52, 59
ROTH
Noah 59
ROTTLE 115
ROUNSOSER (Rounsover)
Richard 50
ROUNSOVEL (Rounsovelle - Rousevell)
Benjamin 96
Richard 19, 50, 53, 80
ROUNSOVER (Rounsoser)
Richard 80
ROUSSAW (Rousaw)
John 1, 2(2), 4, 5, 6, 7, 8, 11, 17, 19, 28, 42, 44, 52, 61, 63(2)
ROUSEVELL (see Rounsovell)
Benjamin 96
ROW (see Roe)
William 49, 53, 80, 96
ROWLES (see Rawles - Rolls)
John 117
ROY
Abraham 96
James 96
Joseph 96
Ronald 34
Thomas 96
ROYCE (see Royse)
ROYENER
Eve 52
Gedion 52
ROYSE (Royce)
Aaron 33, 35, 41, 80, 96
Daniel 29, 51, 47, 52, 80, 132
David 80
Fred 52, 132
Hannah 52(2)
Jacob 132
John 15, 22, 29, 36, 52(3), 80, 96
John, Sr. 52
Nicholas 44
Solomon 41
RUCHMAN
Thomas 14
RUCKMAN (Rukman)
Catherine 132
Charity, Mrs. 103
Charles 112
Eli 117
Elijah 113, 114, 117

Elizabeth 103(3)
Elizabeth, Mrs. 103
Eliza 103, 104
Gibson 132(2)
Hannah 103, 132
Jane 133
John 102, 113, 132(2)
Joseph 103
Mary 102, 103, 132
Mary Ann 99, 103
Nancy 111
Richard 99, 104, 132(2)
Sam C. 136
Samuel 7, 19, 38, 80(2), 103, 104, 112, 132, 136
Sarah 132, 137
Solomon 103
Survey 115
Thomas 14, 19, 56, 62, 80(3), 136, 139
Watson 132
Wilson 101, 103(2), 132
RUDDLE (Ruddles -Riddle)
Mary 52(2)
Stephen 8(2), 9, 13(5), 21, 23, 87, 52(2), 54, 80(2), 88, 96, 122, 136
Stevin 113
RUDER
Joseph 96
RUDOLPH
Jacob 133
Laurence 132
Rachel 112(2)
Silvester 131
RUDYBAUGH
Adam 96
RUKMAN (Ruckman)
Henry 49, 80, 96
Henry, Sr. 96
Henry, Jr. 96
RULE
RUNGELS (Rumels)
Stephen 188
RUNNELS (Rannels)
Jacob 103, 105
Sarah, Mrs. 103
RUSE
Thomas 106
RUSH
John 52, 59, 60, 80, 137
Leah 52
Lewis 96
RUSSELL
Emilia 31
Joseph 53
Margaret 31
Rebecca 52
Thomas 37, 52, 80
RUST
Jacob 96
RUSUM
Garrett 109
RUTAN
Catherine 52(2)
John 49(2), 52(2), 102, 109
RUTHERFORD
Benjamin 16, 36(2), 52(4), 63(2), 80
Drusilla 52
Eliz. 36(2), 52(2)
Mary 52(2)
R. 32
Reuben 82
Robert 4, 5, 52(2), 54, 80 (3)
Thomas 22(2), 32, 52(2), 54, 57, 135
Van 52
RUTHVEN
Alex 4, 27(2), 43, 53, 56
RUTLEDGE
James 16(2), 52, 80(2)
RUTMAN
Davis 127
RUTTER
Christian 112
Jacob 112
RUYNON
John 112
RYAN
Edward 19, 116
James 14, 52(4), 80(3), 96
John 7, 52, 80, 96, 127
Mary 52
Sarah 52
Timothy 9
SABARETT (may be Sarrett or Barrett)
Comfort 138
SABES (see Labes - may be LeBes)
James 14(2)
SADOWSKI
Andrew 57, 127, 138
Jacob 96
Sam 96
SAGE
William 96
Samuel 7
SALTS

Thomas 96
SALZWEDEL
John J. 135
SAMPLE (Semple)
Lew 131
Rhuan 187
SANDERS (see Saunders)
Chas. 96
Henry 96
Joseph 15
SANDERSON
John 12
Othoniel 52
Alex 122
SANFORD
William 5, 40, 44, 80(2)
SARGENT (see Largent)
John 110
SARRETT (Sterrett)
William 40, 80
SASOLLET (may be LaFollett)
George 2
SATURLY
Samuel 96
SAULTERS
John 116
SAUNDERS (Sanders)
Joseph 15, 80
SAVAGE
Ann 132
Eliz. 58, 80, 132
Ester 132
James 108, 139
Jane 132
Jean 132(2)
John 87, 52, 96, 132(4)
John, Capt. 110
Lydia 132(2)
Nicholas 182
Patrick 132
Sary 132
SAVELLE (Seville)
Abraham 101, 103, 132
Catherine 132
Eliza, Mrs. 103
Elizabeth 80, 132
George 132
Isaac 107, 132
Jacob 132
John 114, 132(2)
Joseph 132, 134
Lydia 132
Martha 132
Mary 132
Peter 132
Phillip 182(2)
Oliver 132(3)
Susannah 135
SAVOUR
Prudence 137
SCARDON
Thomas 18(2), 80(2)
SCHARF (Sharff - Sharp)
George 47
George Heirs 118
Line 118
SCHART
Henry, Jr. 26
SCHELHOM
John 7
SCHLAGLE (Slagle)
Jacob 123, 133
SCHOONHAVEN
Thomas 122
SCHOONOVER
Benjamin 96
SCRAFF (Sharff)
James 123, 132
Tacey 132
SCHRIED (see Shried)
Adam 31, 52, 8
Charity 96
SCHROCK
Betsy 125
Jane 125
Rachel 120
William 6, 18, 37, 40, 42, 46, 51, 80
SCHROEDER
Henry 33, 80
SCHULLAR
Benj. 52
Katherine 52
SCHUMAN
John 139
SCOALS
John 96
SCOTT (Scoot)
Aaron 9, 52
Adonijah 52
Alex 96
Benj. 17, 60, 80, 96
Benj., Jr. 96
Benj. Sr. 96
David 52, 60(2), 80, 100, 103
Edward 52
Eliz. 52(2)

George 3, 19
Isaih 59
James 8(2), 15, 28, 36, 52 (4), 59, 80, 96, 113, 115, 117, 135
Jane 52
John 96
Joseph 96, 121, 129
Mary 117(2)
Marey 132
Patrick 52
Robert 58(7)
Sarah 132
Susannah 52
William 7, 23, 30, 89(2), 54, 55, 59, 87
SCREACHFIELD
Joseph 52
Joshua 97
SEA (See and Lee - Lea)
Adam 101, 108
Eliz., Mrs. 103
George 96
Micheal 96, 115
SEABURN
John 86
SEACHRIST (see Secrist or Secrest)
SEARS (Seers)
Abraham 101
Catherine 132
James 58, 96, 116, 120, 127 (2), 181
John 96, 132
Mary 132
Sarah 96
William 96, 132
SEATON
Alley 132
Alice 100
Frankey 132
George 132
Hiram 132
James 132
John 132
Lydia 132
Nancy 129
William 132
SEAVERS (Leaver)
Ann 132
Charles 35
Eliz. 132
James 63
John 132
Lydia 132
Nicholas 30, 62, 96, 125, 127(2), 128, 132
Nicholas, Jr. 96, 107, 132
Nicholas, Sr. 107, 132
Prudence 132
Susan 103
SEAVNY
Truman 120
SEBASTIAN
Nicholas 4(2)
SEBRING
Ann 132
Catherine 132
Eliz. 132, 139
John 8, 19, 53, 65
Peter Oller 132
SECRIST (Seachrist - Secrest - Seacrist)
Abraham 122, 129, 133, 135
Fred 133, 135
Henry 125
James 131(2)
John 181
Mary 126
Meriam 113
Rebecca 133
Sarah 117
Valentine 122, 135(2)
SEE (see Lee - Sea - Lea)
Adam 23, 84, 108
Eliz., Mrs. 103
George 60, 116, 138
Micheal 138
SEERS (Sears)
James 31, 53, 80
Sarah 53
SEELY
John 113
SEEVER (see Duver)
SEGULL
Thomas 108
SEHOW (Lehow) 23
SELBY
John 87
SELLARS
Barbarry 109
Cathran 109
Fredrick 96, 109(2)
John 96
Susan 109
SEMORE (see Seymour - Symore)
Carroll, Col. 138
Felix 138

INDEX

SEMPLE
Steel 55
SETLER
Susan 116
SEVIL (Savelle -Levil)
Joseph 8, 80
SEVILLE (Sevil - Saville)
John 114
SEYMOUR (Simore - Symore - Semore)
Abel 8, 9, 13, 29, 35, 40, 44, 80(3), 96
Felix 13, 31, 36, 44, 50(2), 52, 53(2), 59, 60(2), 60(2), 80(5), 96, 109, 135, 136, 138
George 96
Richard 8, 9, 80(2), 96
Thomas 9, 96
SHACKLEFORD
Henry 118
SHADD (Shaff - Shade)
George 96
SHADE (Shadd)
George 96
SHAFFER (Shafer - Shaver)
Christopher 18, 80
David 122, 125, 132
Genima 133
George 101
Hannah 101, 103
Jacob 133
Mary 125
Ptter 99, 120
William 133
SHANKLIN
Richard 96
Robert 96
SHANK (Shanks)
Ann 133
Christian 22
Elizabeth 133
George 117, 133
Hannah 133
Jacob 117(2), 133
Joseph 96
Louisa I. 133
Margaret 133
Mary 133
Sarah 133
William G. 133
William 117
SHAMHOLTZER
Peter 53
SHANNON
Andrew 103, 104
Benjamin 135, 137
Daniel 112
Esther 132
Hannah 133, 137
Hugh 96, 133, 137
James C. 137
John 81
Rachel 133
Rebecca, Mrs. 103
Ruth 96, 133
Thomas 124, 139
SHANTON
Abraham 53(2)
Joseph 53, 80
Raymond 96
SHARES (Shores)
Micheal 96
SHARFF (Sharfe - Sharp - Searff)
George 80, 80(2), 110, 118, 121, 126
SHARKER
George 123
SHARP
Anna 63
Andrew 96
SHARPLESS
Joseph 96
SHARPLER
Jeose 1, 80
SHANE
William G. 129
SHANGAN
Daniel 53
Darby 53, 80
SHAVER
Martin 60, 80
SHEARER
John 135
Mary, Mrs. 103
William 99, 103, 133
SHEARWOOD
John 135
SHEETS (Sheats - Sheetz - Streets)
Ann 15, 80
Eliz. 133
Fredrick 15, 20, 31, 80(2), 106, 108, 111, 117, 124, 131, 136(2)
Fredrick, Jr. 133
Fredrick, Sr. 133
Henry T. 133

Henry 20, 80
George F. 133
Isabella 128
James 108(2), 133(2)
John 128
Margaret 133
Mary Ann 133
Micheal 106
Nancy 133
Phillip B. 111
Robert 124
Robert K. 124, 133(2)
Sam 111
Susan M. 133
Zebulon 115, 122, 129, 188
SHELBY
Aaron 136
John 28
SHELLHORN
Balser - Balson 7, 53(3), 80
John 47, 80
Mary 58(3)
SHELTON
William 89
SHEPARD (Sheppard - Shepherd)
Benjamin 18, 20, 53, 80
Berry 20, 80
Catherine 53
David 49
James 96
Job 31, 60, 61, 86, 138
John 20, 80, 96, 124, 127
Jonathan 46, 53, 80
Joseph 124
Rachel 53
Robert 88, 80
Samuel 18
SHEPLAR (Shipler - Shepler)
Catherine 53
Elizabeth 49, 53(2), 96, 133(4)
Henry 53, 133
John 133
SHERIDAN
Paul 13, 60, 80
SHERILL
John 124
SHERRARD (Sherard)
Aaron 100
Eliz. Morton 133
Frank Dixon 133
John B. 129, 133
Joseph H. 103, 133(2)
Mary 133
Mary, Mrs. 133
Mary W. 133
Millicent 133
Millicent S., Mrs. 103
Moses 100
Robert 110, 119, 122(3), 125, 132, 133
Robert B. 103, 133(2)
Robert W. 133
William 102, 103, 133(2), 135
SHEVELEAR
Anthony 94
SHIBLER
Henry 57(2)
SHIELDS
Peter 96
SHILLS
George 96
SHINEAR
George 96
SHINERS
John 131
SHINLEY (see Shirley)
SHIN (Shinn - Chinn)
David 9, 80, 133
Elizabeth 134
Levi 134
Lydia 133
Mary 133
SHIPLER (see Shepler)
Henry 53(2), 119
John 53
SHIPLEY
Richard 96
SHIPWITH
Peyton 33, 80
SHIRE
Sarah 127
SHIRLEY (Shinley)
Ann 115
Eliz. 115
Thomas 115
SHIVENS
John 99, 103
Rhoda, Mrs. 103
SHIVERS
John 127
Samuel 56
SHOBE (see Swobe-Schobe)
Abraham 138
Barbara 133(2)
Eliz. 128, 133
Eve 133

Flore 133
Jacob 22(2), 80(2), 96, 133
John 35, 80
Martin 26, 56(2), 80, 96, 121, 123, 133(2)
Ridley 96
Rudy 96
Rudolph 96, 133
SHOCKEY (Shokey)
Joseph 100, 101, 103
Lydia 100, 103
Margaret, Mrs. 103
SHOEMAKER
Abraham 60
Eliz. 130
Peter 96
SHOFF (see Shaff)
George 115
Ruth 184
SHOKEY (Schokey)
Abraham 128
SHOLDER
Conrad 96
SHOMAD (Thomad)
Daniel 129
SHOOK (Shuck)
Catherine 132
David 96, 116
Herman 83, 127(2)
Harman 49, 96
Harman, Jr. 96
Hermanous 132
Jacob 96
John 96
Jonas 96
Laurence 96
Peter 96
William 96
SHOPE
Elias 108, 104
Margaret, Mrs. 103
SHORES
Lander 100
Margaret 102, 103
Thomas 10, 28, 102
SHOREBAUGH (Rorebaugh)
David 96
SHORT
Benjamin 124
George 102, 103, 106
Isaac 6(2), 32, 56, 80(2), 96, 103, 104, 125, 133
Jacob 53, 85, 96
John 133
Lucy, Mrs. 103
Martha, Mrs. 103, 133
Mary 53
Mary, Mrs. 103
Richard 103, 116, 121, 125 (2), 129, 133(2)
William 99, 103, 133(2))
SHOWP
John 31, 80
SHRIDE (Schreid)
Adam 133
Charity 96, 126, 133
Eliz. 133
SHRIVER
Peter 61
SHROCK
Nancy 123
SHRODES
John 96
SHROTE
Peter 96
SHROUT
Samuel 96
SHUCK (Shook)
Herman 96, 131(2)
Laurence 17, 80, 96
SHULTZ
Andrew 96
SHULTZER
Henry 103(2)
Rachl, Mrs. 103
SHUMATE
James 96
SHUMAN
George 133
John 133
SHUNHOLTZ (Shanholtz)
Sarah Jane 116
SHURLEY (Shirley)
Anne, Mrs. 104
Lazarus 100, 104
SHUTEN
Ann, Mrs. 104
John N. 99, 104
SHUTZ
Catherine 111
Fred 111
Isabella 128
James 111
Sam 111
SIBERT (Seibert)
Jacob 58, 80
SIBLEY
John 33, 55, 66, 96
SIDWELL

Hugh 27(2), 53, 80
SIGAPOS (Sickaposs) (-foss)
Catherine, Mrs. 104
John, Jr. 102, 104
SILKWOOD
Solomon 39, 43, 80
SIMS (Simms)
SIMCOCK
Elizabeth 53
Sam 12, 53
SIMKINS (Simpkons-Limpkins)
Dickeson 16
Gassedg 53, 80
Silas 16(2)
SIMON (see Simmons - Simond)
SIMOND (Simmonds - Simonds - Simon)
Christian 12, 80
George 12, 80, 96
Henry 96(2)
John 96
Joseph 133
Leonard 96
Mary 112(2)
Phillip 96
Simon 133
Susannah 133
William 133
SIMMOND (Simmonds)
Agnes 53
Thomas 53
SIMMONS (Simmond - Simmonds)
Asa 98
Henry 96
Mary 112
Simon 133
SIMMS (Sims)
Barnet 110
Charles 12
John Jr. 96
Thomas 108
William 96
SIMPKONS (Simpson)
Gassedgin 139
Silas 16(2)
SIMPSON (Simpkons)
Alex 26, 96
David 25
James 81, 48, 53(3)
Jane 104(2)
John 102, 104(2)
Jonathan 96, 133
Lidy 106
Lucy 106
Rebecca, Mrs. 104
SINCLAIR
Alex 133
Daniel 133
Hector 133
Hugh 133
Jane 133
Nancy 133
Marjarh 133
Robert 37, 80, 133
SINE
Christy 99, 104, 130
Margaret, Mrs. 104
SINGLETON
Aaron 133(2)
Gracy 133
James 133(2)
John 53, 103, 110, 127, 130, 131, 133
John F. 133
John T. 133(2)
Jonathan 133
Martha 133
Mary 133
Mary Ann 133
Rebecca 133
Susan 133
Tobe 133
Thomas 12, 60, 80, 139
SINKS
Jacob 96, 125
SIRAMONS
Ann 113
SISLER
William 96
SISTON
Joseph 44
SITES
George 96
SIX (Sixe)
Conrad 133
Eliz. 133
George 133
John 133
Mary 133
Phillip 133
William 133(2)
SIXE (Six)
George 139
Henry 139
SKELDING
J. 47

SKIDMER (Skidmore)
Mary 96
SKIDMORE (Skidmer)
William 139
SKIPLOE
Henry 124
SKIPWITH (Shipwith)
Peyton 38, 80
SLACK
Abraham 133
Betsy 133
George 133
Henry 133
James 41, 50, 60, 80(3), 86, 138
James, Jr. 126
Jane 133
John 133
Jonathan 133(2)
Mary 133
SLAGLE (Schlagle)
Christiana 133
Conrad 133
Elizabeth 133
Jacob 7, 9, 11(2), 27, 80(3), 96, 118(2), 131, 133
John 133
Joseph 131
SLAGER
Ales 133
Amy 133
Elenore 133
Hannah 133
Jacob 133
John 133
Joseph 133(2)
Statia 133
SLAIN (see Slane)
Dan 85
SLANE (Slone - Sloan - Stone or Stane)
Anne 33, 130, 134
Benjamin 33, 80, 100, 104, 115, 129, 184(2)
Catherine 134
Delilah, Mrs. 104, 134
Daniel 33, 85, 184(2)
Elias 134
Elizabeth 99, 104
Hugh 111, 118, 122, 134(2)
James 38, 80(2), 100(2), 122(4), 134(4)
John 25(3), 33(2), 45, 46, 49, 80, 99, 115, 134(4)
Mariah 100, 104
Mary 122, 184
Nancy 104, 105
Rebecca 134
Richard 99
Thomas 33, 81, 100, 103, 128, 134(2)
SLATEN
Thomas 54
SLATER
Richard 96
Thomas 50, 81
SLAUGHTER
James 53
John 80
Mary 124
SLEAGLE
John 187
Joseph 137
SLEITH
Alex. 96
SLOAN (Sloane)
Ann 134
Benjamin 134(2))
Charlotte 134
Daniel 134
Eliz. 99, 104, 134
George 102, 128, 134(3)
Harriet 102, 104
James 101, 122, 134
John 96, 99, 107, 108, 110 (2), 111, 115, 118, 119, 127, 134
John, Esq. 134, 135
Magdalenia 107
Mary 134
Rebecca 99, 104
Richard 7, 14, 26, 27, 46, 99 (2), 107, 110, 134(3)
Sarah 99, 104
Thomas 99, 102(2), 118, 119, 123(2), 128, 134(4), 136
SLOCUM (Slocumb)
Ann 125
Deborate 103, 104
Isaac 125, 134
John 111
Robert 111(2)
SLONAKER
Christian 89, 53, 81
Eleanor, Mrs. 104
Mary 53
Micheal 99, 104, 127
Nancy 132
SLONE (Stone - Sloan)
Daniel 96

Elizabeth High 118
James 96, 122
Milly 99, 104
SLUMP (Stump)
William P. 108, 123
SLY
David 96
George 52, 81, 96
SMALL
Jacob 52, 132
SMALLEY
Agariah (Azariah) 53, 56, 81
Andrew 1, 7, 10, 22(2), 26(2), 41(2), 53(7), 60(2), 81(6), 96, 112
Christina (Christana) 23(2), Christian 23, 53
Ezekiel 26, 53, 81
Jacob 52
Rebecca 53
SMALTZ
George W. 128
SMART
Thos. 4(2), 18
SMILEY
Elizabeth 84
Thomas 54, 81
SMITH
Aaron 134(2)
Abraham 104, 134
Abraham I. 104
Adam 134
Anne (Anna) 54, 116, 134(3)
Charles 26, 54(4), 96
Christopher 45, 81, 110, 139
Clement 96(2)
Dan. 119
David 96(2)
Dorcas 137
Edward 1, 5, 19(4), 38(2), 54(3), 57(2), 58(2), 62(2), 81(2)
Elijah 123, 134(2)
Elizabeth 54
Elizabeth, Mrs. 104
Fanny 134
George 23, 33(2), 54(2), 114, 123, 139
George A. 115
Henry 107
Hugh 121
Isaac 134
Jacob 96, 100, 104, 123, 130
James 2(2), 27, 54(4), 96, 108, 136(4), 137, 138
James, Jr. 81
James, Sr. 47, 54
Jemima 137
John 3(2), 23(3), 54, 96(3), 100, 101, 103, 129, 134
John, 1st. 100, 104
John, 2nd. 104
John C. 129
Joseph 109, 114(2), 117, 123, 127, 131, 132, 134(5)
Joseph L. 129
Joseph P. 127
Jr. A. 113
Lewis 123, 124(2), 131(2), 134(4), 138
Margaret 134
Martha, Mrs. 104
Mary 54(5)), 102, 104, 118, 125, 134(4), 139
Micheal 7, 54(2), 84, 96, 134
Milburn 124
Nancy 137
Nathan 20, 81
Nathaniel 54(3), 96
Paul 127
Phebe 134
Rachel 54, 134
Rebecca 54(3), 103, 104
Reuben 63(2), 137
Rhody 134
Richard 54, 96, 109, 134
Richard, Jr. 134
Richard, Sr. 134
Robert 96
Rub. 42
Ruth 134
Sam D. 134
Sam P., Dr. 138
Sam P. 120
Sarah 123, 134(2)
Sarah C. 100, 134
Sarah, Mrs. 104
Simon 124, 134
Solomon 103, 104, 119
Stephen 129, 134(3)
Thomas 2(2), 54, 59, 81, 96, 136
Timothy 81, 102, 123(2), 124, 134
William 3, 8, 16, 18(5), 22, 27, 36, 40(3), 47, 54(3), 81(3), 85, 96(2), 121, 128, 134, 137, 139
Yokle 96
SMOCK
Jacob 96
SMOOT
Ann 107
Bartin (Barton) 56, 81, 99, 133, 134
Catherine 54(2)
Charity 134
Eliz., Mrs. 104
Jacob 180, 134(2)
James 134
Jane 134
Jane, Mrs. 104
Jonas 43, 81, 137
John 47(2), 53, 81(3), 139
Josiah 103, 104, 115
Joseph 134
Joshua 134
Lucinda 117
Lucrecy 134
Margaret, Mrs. 104
Maria 99, 104
Martha 137
Nancy 134
Norman 109
Priscilla 134
Samuel 101, 104, 134
Sarah Queen 180
Solomon 134
Susan 134
Thomas 18, 29, 43, 54(2), 81, 134
Thomas Barton 43, 54
Thomas Norman 99, 104
William 81, 117, 134
SMALL
William 96
SNAPP
Cynthia 134
Cynthia Jane 184
Diana 134
Hannah 126(2)
James C. (Cravins) 134(2)
John 126, 134
Joseph 105, 134(3)
Joseph, Jr. 126
Margaret 134
Margarette 126
Maria (Mariah) 104, 105, 134
Robert 134
Rhoda 134
William C. 134
SNEATHEN
Sam 106
SNICKERS
Edward 44, 54(3), 81
SNYDER
Adam 39, 81
Charles 134
Christopher 25, 96
Eliz. 134
Harriet 104(2), 134
Henry 115
Jacob 138
John 4, 5(2), 10(2), 14(2), 24, 28(2), 29(6), 31, 40, 45, 56, 61, 81(5), 101, 110, 126, 128, 129, 131, 134, 136
John M. 129
John, Dr. 134
Letitia 54
Samuel 134
William 134
SOMMERS
Paul 118
SOMMERVILLE (see Soverville)
Eliz. 125
James 21(3), 23, 24, 39, 54(4), 55, 81
Richard 12
William 119
SOMMETT
Jacob 96
SONNEN
David 115
SOOGE
Matthew 6
SOUTHAN (Louthan)
George 139
SOUTHWARD
James 114
SOVERVELLE (see Sommerville)
James 7
SOWERS
Jacob 47
Land 111
SPADE (see Spaid)
George 2, 108, 121
SPAID (see Spade)
Elizabeth 101, 104
Fredrick 99, 101, 117, 127
George 81, 101, 107, 129
Hiram 122(2), 124
John 107, 117, 127, 130
Joseph 129
Margaret 122
SPARKS
Humphrey 12, 80
SPEAKE
Thomas 34, 81
SPEALMAN (Spelman - Spillman)
William 96
SPELMAN (Spellman - Spillman)
Robert 96
SPENCER (Spenser)
Alex 134
Arthur M. 184
Kyese 184
Ellen 124
Eliz. 113, 184
John 42, 54, 81, 96, 102, 104, 115, 134
John, Jr. 54, 81, 134
John, Sr. 54, 100
Joice 54
Joseph 134
Mary, Mrs. 104
Mary 134
Nancy 134
Othio H. 134
Rachel 100, 104, 134
Ruth 134
Sarah 54, 134
Susanna 134
Thomas 35
William 184
SPERRY
Nicholas 108
Peter 96
SPICER (Spiker)
Henry 126, 134(2)
Luezer 134
Luizer 134
Maria 134
Thomas 56, 126, 134
William 132
SPIKER (see Spicer)
Jacob 54
SPILLMAN (see Spellman-Spelman)
Charles 135(2)
Eliz. 185
James 96, 135
John 96(2), 135
Polly 135
Rebekah 135
Sarah 135(2)
William 96, 135
SPODE (see Spade)
George 2
SPONE (Spore)
John 5
SPORE (Spone - Spohr)
John 5, 54(2), 81(2)
John W. 96
Mary 54(2)
SPOHR (Spohre)
John 41, 54
John Ulrick 54
Judith 54
Mary 54
SPOTZ
Jane, Mrs. 104
Joseph 104(2)
SPRIGG (Spriggs)
Azburn 81(2)
Joseph 12
Osborn 19, 54, 63
Osburn (Ozburn) 28(2), 45, 63, 81(2)
Sarah 45
SPRINGER
Anne 55
Rachel 118
Zadick 55
SPRINGFIELD
Trustees of 55(15)
SQUIRE
Micheal 139
STACEY
Thomas 96
STACKHOUSE
Isaac 96(2)
John 37
STACKSLAGER (Stockslager)
Jacob 106
STADDLER
Jacob 20, 81
STADLOR
Hannah 55
Jacob 55
STAFFORD
Catherine 55, 135
Eliz. 123
John F. 55
Joseph S. 185
Richard 16(2), 20, 30, 81(2), 55, 81(4), 85, 144, 188, 139
Sarah 135
Washington 135
STAFLER (Stafter - see Stip) 114
STAGG (Stag)
Abraham 135
Catherine 135
Christopher 135
Eve 118
Elizabeth 135
Franklin 127
Franklin G. 135(2)
George 25, 127, 135
George, Jr. 135(2)
James H. 135
John 25, 55, 81, 96, 135(2)
Margaret 135
Martha 135
Mary 135
Mary, Mrs. 104
William 99, 104(2), 135
STALECUP (see Stallcup - Stallcop - Stattecop)
Ann 123
Eliz. 135
Emma, Sr. 123
Emma, Jr. 123
Israel 12, 29, 81, 135
STALER
Isaac 116
STALKER (Stolker)
Peter 21, 22, 81
STALLCUP (see Stalecup)
Anne 135
Eliz. 135
Ennor 135
Enner, Jr. 135
John 96
John Quincy 135
John Q. 135
Israil 4, 12, 20, 84, 35, 81, 102, 135
STALLMAN
Lews 55, 85
Mary 55
STALNAKER
Sam 21, 81, 138
STALLOP (see Stallcup)
Israel 12, 55
STAMBAUGH
Phil 96
STAMBERRY
Job 123
STARKEY
Catiren 135
Edward 135
Eliz. 135
Fredrick 8, 81, 96, 135
Fredrick, Jr. 100, 104, 135, 139
Fred., Sr. 104, 139
George 135
Mary 135(2)
Sarah, Mrs. 104
William 60, 81
STARN
Catherine 55(2)
Fredrick 135(2), 138
Jacob 18, 19, 33(2), 34, 55(3), 61(2), 115, 124(2)
John 33, 84, 55, 61, 81, 134, 135
Joseph 18, 33(8), 34, 44, 55, 81, 135
Katheryn 135
Ruth, Mrs. 104
Thomas 99, 104
STARR
Catherine 96
James 55, 57, 81
John 55
Margaret 119
Moses 85
Nancy 55
STATER
Isaac 119
STATLER
Jacob 119
Peter 60
STATLIN (see Statler)
STATLECOP (Stallcop)
Israel 55
STEARMAN
Alice 107
STEATHER
John 55
STEED
Aaron 55(2), 86, 96
Eleanor 55
STEEL (Steele)
Henry 96
John 55(2), 59, 81, 96
Joseph 55(2), 81
Sam 37
STEER (Steers)
Isaac 19, 56(3), 79, 81(2)
Joseph 85
STEENBARGER
Peter 44, 52
STEENBERGER (Steengergon - see Steenbergen)
Peter 4, 15, 25, 30(2), 44(2), 55(2), 60(2), 61, 62, 81(2), 122
Will 57
STEENBURGIN (Steenbarger - Steenberger - Steenbergen)
Peter 58
STEERMAN (Stearman)
John 5
STEINBECK
Anna Dorothea 135
Fredrick 99, 111
John C. 135
Sarah 99, 104
STEINBERGER (Steenberger - Steengarger)
Pet 7
STEM
Isabella 139
STEMMELL (Stirmel)
Joseph 43, 81
STEMMELT
William 86
STEPHENS (Stevins - Stevens)
Adam 55
Christian 30, 32, 55(2), 60, 62(2), 81, 138
Dan 86
Eliz. 55
Leah 109
Mary 55(2)
Peter 55
Robert 7, 14, 17(36), 18(6), 23, 32, 39(8), 55, 60
William 55
STEPHENSON
Catherine 132
Edward 96
Hugh 21
J. 21
James 96
Marcus 21
Sam 50, 55(2), 81, 96, 132
STERMAN (Sturman)
Ann 135
Alice 107
Hannah Christener 135
James 135
John 5, 135
Rachel 135
Rebecca 135
Richard 135
STERN
George 101, 104
Sarah, Mrs. 104
STERNBERGER (see Steenberger)
Peter 123
STERRET
Will 4, 81
William, Col. 135
STETTLER
John 96
STEVINS (see Stephens)
Christian 82, 61
James 104
James N. 102
Leah 109
STEVINSON (Stephenson)
Edward 96
STEWARD
James 96
Joseph 97
STEWART (Stuart - Steward)
Catherine 111
James 8, 41(2), 96, 99 104
Jasper 96
John 103, 130(2), 133
John N. 133
Mary 109
Mary, Mrs. 104
Mary W. 133
Perry A. 188
Priscilla 103, 104
William 85, 81
STIBBS
Joseph 54
STIFF
Margaret 103, 104
Stephen 103
STILEY
Elen, Mrs. 104
Jacob 104, 105
STIMMEL (Stemmil)
Ann 135
Catherine 135
Daniel 135
Elizabeth 135
Hannah Magdalanah 135(2)
Jacob 135
Jost 18, 135
Mary 135
Micheal 135
Peter 135
STINGLEE
Jacob 96
SLIP (Slipp)
Margaret 114
Peter 114

INDEX

STITH
Baldwin 12
STOCKDALE
Elizabeth 123
Bolser 96
STOCKSLAGER
Jacob 99, 104
Mary, Mrs. 104
STODDARD (Storddart)
Charlotte 12(2)
James 96
STOKER (see Stocker)
Balser 55, 56, 96
Eve. 56
John 6(2), 23, 53, 56(2), 81, 96
John, Sr. 121
Paltzer 11, 81
STOKES
John 86, 125
STOLLENBERGER
Matthew 101, 104
Rebecca, Mrs. 104
STOLLMAN (see Stallman)
Lewis 55
Mary 55
STOLKER (see Stalker)
STOLKNAR (see Stalnaker)
STONE (see Slone - Sloan)
Ann (Anna) 56(6)
Benjamin 38, 56(6), 81, 85
James 25(2), 81
Joseph 56, 138
Rhoda 186
STONSMAN
Lydia 186
STOOKEY
Abraham 97
Magdalen 97
STORDDART (Stoddart)
Charlotte 12(2)
STORM
Joseph 107
STOTTS
Abraham 97
John 52, 81
STOUT
Ann 108
James 137
St. Ledger 108
STOVER
Christopher 135
Daniel 58, 59, 81(2), 135
Daniel, Jr. 135
Eliz. 135(2)
Mary 135
Nancy 135
STOTTER
Jacob 31, 81
STOTTLER
Jacob 27
STRADER (Straider)
Christopher 97
STRADDLER
Jacob 59
Straddler's Meadow 124
STRAIDER (see Streiter)
Frances 56
STRATLEY
Christian 97
STRATTER (Streatter)
Christopher 21
Francis 56, 81
John 56
STRATTON
John 109, 110
STRAW
John 14, 81
STRADERS
Rachel 108
STREATHER
John 55, 56
STRECHFIELD (Strichfield)
Sibble 102, 104
STREET
H. 133
STREETZ (see Sheets)
John 56
STREITHER (Strellier)
Frances 56, 81
STRETT (Street)
John 97
STRICHFIELD (see Strechfield)
Joshua 97
Joseph 52
STRICKER
George 56
STRISCHKA
Jos. A. 135
STRODE
Edward 56, 81
John 56
Margaret 58, 61, 81
STROTHER
James 40, 56, 81
Jane 56
Reuben 40

William 40
STROUD
Adam 97
Thomas 2(2)
STUARDT
James 6, 41(2)
John 55
STUCKSLAGLE
Jacob 87
STUMP
A. J. 135
Adam 128
Benj. D. 124, 135(2)
B. S. 135
Benjamin 135(2), 137
Betsy 135
Catherine 56, 97, 135(2)
Eliz. D. W. 99, 104
Eliz. 111
George 97, 116, 122, 135
Harriet Ann 135
John 99, 102, 135
Joseph 102, 127, 135
Julia Ann 135
Leonard 97, 135
Lucy 135
Margaret 111
Margaret, Mrs. 104
Mary 135
Micheal 31, 35, 44, 49, 59, 63(8), 88, 97, 135
Micheal, Jr. 56, 81
Micheal, Sr. 56
Nancy 118
Peter 100, 104(2), 135
Rebecca 104(2), 111(2), 135
Rebecca, Mrs. 104
Samuel J. 124, 135(2)
Sam P. 133
S. J. 124(2)
S. S. 134
Sam 111
Sarah 102, 104
Sarah Jane 111
Susannah 126
T. J. 118
W. P. 137
William 104(2), 127(2)
W. B. 68
William P. 108, 114, 119, 128, 128, 135(2)
STURMAN (Stearman - Sterman)
Alice 107
Christina 109
James 107
John 14, 40(3), 52, 81, 97
Richard 3, 40(3), 109
STUTEMAN
John 32, 56, 81
Mary 56
SUBER (Subers)
Rachel 130
SUGWICK (Ludwick) 50
SUFFOLK
John 97
SULARD (Lulard)
Elias 8
SULLIVAN (Sullavan)
Giles 56
James 33
Jermiah 6(2), 56, 81, 97, 114, 130
Susannah 110
William 110
SUMMERS
John 99, 104
Rebecca, Mrs. 104
SUMMERSON
John 138
SUMMERVILLE (see Sommerville)
James 125
SUMWALT
James 38
SUTEN
Benjamin 44, 81
SUTHERLAND
Alexander 25
W. 97
SUTTLE (Suttles)
Henry 32, 97
SUTTON (see Suten)
Benjamin 44, 56, 81
Isaac 56
Jasper 56(2)
John 14(3), 81(3)
Joshua 18(2)
Nathan 87
Richard 8, 56
SWAIN
John 10, 13, 41
SWAMLEY
Jacob 108
SWAN
John 86, 123
Joseph 86
Robert 131
SWANEY

Elloner 123
Isaac 123(2)
SWANK (Swanke)
David 16, 81
Phillip 17, 26, 56(2), 81, 97
SWARTZ
Delilah 111
John 111
SWEANINGER
Thomas 5
SWEARINGER
Thomas 54
SWEARINGON
Charles 135
Eli 135
Franklin 135
Sarah 135
SWEIR (Sweirs)
Barbary 135
Catherine 100, 104, 135
David (Davis) 100, 102, 104, 135
Eliz. 135
George 135(2)
Jacob 100, 107, 135
John 100, 133, 135
Louisa, Mrs. 104
Martin 135
Mary Ann 135(2)
Peter 107
Samuel 135
Sarah 135
Susan Maria 135
SWIM
John 28, 81, 97
Lasler 97
Mattbias 119
William 119
SWISHER
Adam 135
Anthony 135
Catherine 100, 104, 135
Christina 135
David 109, 135
Eliz. 122, 135(2)
Henry 101, 104
Henry F. 135
Isaac 135
Jacob 135
John 87, 97, 100, 124, 125 (2), 135
Maria 135
Micheal 119, 135
Nicholas 36, 81, 97
Rebecca 135
Sarah, Mrs. 104
Stephen 119(2), 135
Valentine 27, 81(2), 85, 97, 133
SWITZER
Abraham 135
Catherine 135
Henry 135
Jacob 2, 81
John 86, 122, 133, 135(2)
Nicholas 81, 135
Peter 125, 135
Phillip 135
Valentine 27, 36, 42, 50, 56, 119(2), 135
SWOBE
Barbara 5, 56(2)
John 31, 56
SYMOR (Seymour)
Felix 109
TAAF (see Taass)
Eliz. 97
James 8(2), 10, 58, 97, 139
TABS
Phillip 5
TAFT (Tafte)
Peter 59, 81
TAGGART (see Tygart)
Daniel 42(2), 81(3)
Eliz. 108
Francis 2, 7, 11, 21, 23(4), 26, 37, 41, 42(3), 47, 56 (3), 62, 81(6), 130(8)
Fras 21, 27
Lucy 56(3), 130
TALBOT (Talbott)
Thomas 97, 127
TALLMAN
Peter 108
TANEY (see Tamney)
Wm. 60, 81
Wm. M. 107
TARPLEY
Eliz. 56(2)
James 11(2), 29, 56(3), 97, 136, 139
TAPISCOTT (Tappiscott)
Baker 135(2)
Caroline 135
Chichester 102, 104, 135
Jane 135
Jane, Mrs. 104
John B. 109
Louisa, Mrs. 104
Newton 100, 104, 135

TARVIN
George 13, 24, 83, 56(3), 97, 122
Sarah 56
TASKER
Benjamin 106, 108, 135
Christina 135
George R. 116
Geo. G. 116, 135
Katherine 135
Marium 108
Mary, Mrs. 108
W. 124
TASSEE
James 58
TAVENER
Christina 120
TAYLOR
Alfred (Alf) 113, 128, 133, 135
Ann 102, 104, 114, 136
Ann Brooks 135
Benjamin 117
Catherine 124
Charles 135
Charles S. 101, 104, 106, 119, 127
Daniel 45, 103, 104, 136
Edward 125(2), 128, 130, 135
Eliza 135
Elizabeth 123, 135, 139(2)
Elizabeth, Mrs. 104
Geo. 45, 81, 97, 135, 136
Griffin 5, 63(2)
Hannah 136
Henry 1, 56, 81
Hoge & Taylor 63
Isaac 135
Isaac, Jr. 135
Jacob 135(2)
James 123, 125(2), 135(2)
John 16, 21, 55, 56, 57, 81, 82, 97, 131, 135(2), 136, 139(3)
John, Jr. 38, 82, 123
John M. 126
John William 119
Joseph 56, 82, 136, 139
Leacy Ann 135
Lettie 56
Libra (Sibia) 136
Libby 97
Margaret 97, 125, 135, 136
Margaret A. 97, 118
Martha Ann, Mrs. 104
Mary 56, 135, 136, 139
Mary Ann 135
Mary E. 126
Matty 119
Nancy 135, 136
Parsons 135
Parthenia 99, 104, 136
Patsy, Mrs. 104, 119
Rebecca 135, 139
Richard 56, 61(2), 62(2), 97, 135
Robert 97, 101, 104
Sarah 136
Sallie 116
Septimus 139
Sibia (Libia) 136
Simon 8, 16, 24, 26, 42, 55, 56, 63, 82(3), 86, 88, 97 (2), 114, 123(2), 125, 135 (2), 136(2), 139(2)
Simon, Jr. 16
Simon, Sr. 136
Simon D. 135
Simon, son of George 135
Susan 100, 104, 135
Susanna 139
Tarpley (Tapley) 17, 63, 82, 97, 136
Tarpley, Jr. 136
Thomas 98, 102, 104, 198, 136
Warner 135
William 25, 107, 117, 125, 135(2), 136(2), 139
William F. 63(2)
William F. J. 63
Wm. F. 63, 100, 125
Zulemma 136
TEAD
Abraham 120
TEBOLT (Tepelt - Tepolt)
Micheal 30, 80, 56
TEGARDEN
Abraham 56
TEMPLE
Jane 136
John 110, 120, 136
Mary E. 136
Solomon J. 136
Wm. F. 136
TEMPLETON
John 86, 110
TERNAY (Tierman)
Matthew 56
Phoebe 56

TERRY
George 56
George, Jr. 97
George, Sr. 97
Mary Ann 56
Stephen 56, 82
TERVIN (see Tarvin)
George 97
TESKIN
John Peter 32, 82
TEVAULT (see Tebolt - Terbaugh)
Adam 97
John 97
John, Sr. 97
Nicholas 57, 97, 117
TEVERBAUGH
Daniel 133
TEWALT
Nicholas 117(2)
THICKSON
William 47, 82
THICKSTONE (see Thixton)
Thomas 97
THIERMAN
P. 132
THIENLEN
Thomas 137
THILLER
John 121
THISTLE
Thomas 132
THIXTON (see Thickstone)
Thomas 97
THOM (see Thorn)
Benjamin 131
Micheal 57(2), 82, 124, 138
Peter 131
THOMAKER
Abraham 57
THOMAS
Aaron 100, 113
Anna 57
Barbary 136
Benjamin 46, 82
Christian 136
David 97
Enoch David 97
Enoch, Sr. 57, 82
Enoch, Jr. 57, 82
Enoch 57(2), 136
Eliz. 136
Eliz. R. 131
Ezekiel 41, 57, 97
Hannah 127
Hiram 131
Hugh 57(3)
Jacob 136, 137
James 36, 57, 97, 130
James Fillet 57, 82
Jane 100, 104
John 25, 26, 33, 35(2), 57
Johannah 57(2)
Jinney 136
Joseph 136
Magdeline 57, 136
Margaret 113
Mary 136(2)
Morris 12, 82, 97, 137
Moses 57(2), 60, 82, 85, 112, 136
Samuel 34(4), 57(2), 82(4), 136
Sarah 57
Sophia 57, 136
Sophria 100
Stephen 57(2), 82
Susannah 136
THOMPSON (sin)
A. 82
Abraham 57(2), 111, 136
Ann (Anna) 57, 108
Betty 57
Benjamin 102
Christina, Mrs. 104
Cornelius 26
Charles 19(3), 21, 26, 37, 57 (4), 59(4), 82(7)
Dan 113, 119
David 57, 97, 139
Eder 14, 82
Ellen 102, 104
Elisha 57, 136
Emily 117
Elijah 101, 104
Elizabeth 57, 136(2)
Esther 44, 57(2), 136
Frances 97
Geo. 57, 115, 129, 136
Isaac 136
Isaac H. 136
Isaac N. 136
Isaac Newton 136
James 57, 99, 102, 136
James, Sr. 99
Jeremiah 3, 10, 29, 43, 44, 57(2), 58, 82(2), 97, 113, 136, 139
Jethro 97
John 14, 15, 16, 26, 42, 52,

57(4), 62(2), 97(2), 108, 109, 111, 115, 117, 121, 130, 136, 139(2)
John A. 136
John G. 99, 104
Joseph 57, 97, 117, 129
Jonah 1, 10, 32(2)
Louisa 136
Margaret 136
Martha 57, 108(2), 121
Mary 57, 99, 104, 136(2), 139
Mrs. 112
Moses 57
Peggy 136
Peter 136
Peter Sperry 136
Rebecca 136
Samuel 57, 97, 112(2)
Sarah 136(2)
Sarah Jane 136
Thomas 18, 81, 82, 113
William 57(3), 97, 109, 136
Zulemme 136
THOMSON (see Thompson)
Jethro 97
John 97
Joseph 97
Sam 97
Sam 97
William 97
William, Jr. 97
William, Sr. 97
THORN
Catherine 57(2)
Fred 97
Micheal 1, 57(2), 82, 124, 138
Peter 97, 131
Valentine 97, 133
THORNTON
B. B. 136
Benjamin B. 102
Hannah 136
Jane 111(2)
John 57
THORP (Thorpe)
Ann 100, 104, 137
Elizabeth 137
Elizabeth Ann 136
Isaac 137
John 100
John, Jr. 136
Mary 137
Nancy 137
Solomon 137
William 97
THRASH
John 104
Margaret 99, 104
Mary 104(2)
THRASHER
Benj. 52, 57
Ephraim 114
Peter 125
P. I. 138
Thomas 15
THROCKMORTON
Catherine 120, 136
Daniel 57
Gabriel 86, 110, 133
Lewis 13(2), 56, 57
Mary 57
Warner 99, 118, 130, 134, 136
Warren 120
William 121
Wiliam Inskeep 136
THROGMORTON
Drousilla 108
Lewis 57(2), 97
Rachel 57(2)
THROUSH
Margaret 126
THRUSBY (Thursby)
Hannah 57
Cockran and Thursby 25
THRUSH
Catherine, Mrs. 104
Micheal 104(2)
THRUSTON
Buckner 2
Charles Mynn 38(2), 54(2), 57(2), 58(2)
John 49
THYGER (Kyger)
George 22, 82
TICHENAL (Tichenall - see Ticheval)
Margaret 57
Margaret 57
Moses 2, 43, 57, 82
TICHEVAL (see Tichenal)
TIDBAL (Tidbale)
Joseph 56, 82
Mrs. 135
Thomas Allen 135
TIERMAN (Thierman)
Margaret 57
Micheal, Jr. 57, 82
Patrick 57

TIEVERBAUGH (see Teverbaugh - Fever-)
Dan 117, 138
David 137
TILFORD (may be Titzford)
Isaac 97
TILGMAN
Andrew 58, 97
Tench 49
TILLYER
Thomas 59
TIMBERLAKE
Eppa 2
George 131
TIMBROOK
Elis 134
John 33, 103
William 103
TIMKINS
John 133
TIMMONS
John 97
Sam 97
TIPSORD (Titzord - Tipsord)
Isaac 97
Leonard 46, 57, 82
Pashinah 57
TIPTON
Sylvester 16(4), 82
TITUS (see Tytus)
TITZORD (see Tipsord)
Isaac 97
TIVAULT (see Tevault)
Andrew 24, 97
John 97
TIVEBAUGH
Dan. 138
David 137
Dean 97
TODD (see Tood)
Eliz. 57
John 8, 44, 57, 82
Rebeckah 44
Samuel 8, 44, 57, 82
TOMBINSON
Joseph, Jr. 85
TOMLINSON
Jesse 32, 82
TOMS (see Thom)
Abraham 57
TOOD (see Todd)
Elizabeth 57
TOOPES
John 97
TOPPER
Sam A. 134
William H. 115
TORRENCE
John 47, 82
William 120, 126, 129, 132 (2)
TOSELWRIGHT
William 97
TOTTEN (122)
James 136
John 136
Ezekiel 29, 34, 57(2), 82, 97
Ezek 116
Sam 136
TRACE (Traise)
Jacob 97
TRACY
Archibald 57, 97
TRAISE
Jacob 97
TRAVIS
Robert 9, 57, 82
TREABLE (Teable)
Edward 29
TREAKLE
Sam 28(2)
TRENTON
John 109
TRENTOR
Eliza, Mrs. 104
William L. 103, 104
TREVETT
Joseph 99, 104
Rhody, Mrs. 104
TRICKLE
Edward 105
TRIMBLE
Jane 124
TRINKLE (see Frinkle))
Christopher 32, 58
Eliz. 58
TRIPLEMAN
Jere 126
TRIPLETT
Betsy Hodgeman 58
Eliz 58
Thomas 58(2)
TRIPP
Nichlas 134
TROTTER
James 25
TROUT
Betsy 137
James H. 137

Henry 113, 126, 137(3)
Sarah 137
William 108
William B. 137
TROUTTEN
Richard 45, 82, 97
TRUMBO
Andrew 58, 97
George (Georgie) 12, 82, 97
Margaret 58, 117
TROWBRIDGE
Catherine 136
Eliz. 136
John 136
Mary 136
Sarah 107
TUCKER
Abraham 136
Asa 97
Dan 118
Erasmus 58, 82, 136
George G. 108
Jacob 97
John 136
Josephus 136
Josephine 136
Joseph 13, 57, 58, 82(2),)136
Lucey 58, 136
Mary 136
Milly 136
Nathan 136
Phoebe 58, 128
Ruth 136
Thomas 58, 136
Thomas, Jr. 54, 82
Thomas A. 119
William 97
TUCKWELL
Israel 136
James 13, 136(2)
John 119, 136
TUDOR
Joseph 47
TULY
Abraham 14
TUNCLE
Catherine 114
TURK(E)
Andrew 3, 6, 20(5), 36, 37, 46, 53, 58, 136(2)
Betsy 136
Isaac 136
Jean 58
Mary 136
Samuel 136
TURNER
Charles 12, 136
Daniel 136
Evan 23
Evin 136
James 136
John 2, 136
Lydia 121
Peggy 136
Plummer 136
Solomon 97, 136
Thomas 38(3), 48(3), 82(3)
William 26, 58(3), 62, 82 (2), 136
TUTT
Ben 11, 13, 25, 50, 61, 138
Richard, Jr. 50
TUTWILER
Martin 133
TURVEY
John 14
TWEEY (Tuohy?)
Dan 97
John 97
TWIG (Twigg)
Amanda 136
Ann Virginia 136
Catherine 136
Eli 136
Evelina 136
James 136
James Ross 136
Luvinia 136
Margaret 136
Oviiere 136
Pearce 136
Rebecca 136
William 136
TWILLY
William 24, 97
TYGART (see Taggert)
Taggart)
Francis 97
TYLER
Charles 7, 58, 82
Henry 1
TYTUS (see Titus)
Margaret 100, 104
Tunis 100
UHAM
William 113
UMSTOTT (Umpstott)
Catherine 58(2), 104(3)
Jacob 1, 28, 42, 58(2), 82 103, 104

John 5, 134
Peter 18, 24, 25, 46, 59(2), 82(3), 97 (3), 97
Simon 106
UNCE
George 115
UNGE
John 53
UNGLESBY
Rebecca 99, 104
UNGLESLY
Erassmus 116
UNTIS
George 15, 82
UPP
Fred 58
URIES
Charles 136
URTON
Norman 117(2)
Phoebe 136
Sam 136
Susanna 134
UTT (Ut)
Catherine 58
George 24, 58, 82
VALENTINE
Rebecca 116
VALLANDGHOM
William 84, 82
VANARSDAL (see Vanorsdal)
Abraham 34, 82
Cornelius 84, 82
Martha 57
VANBUSKIRK (Vanboskirk)
John 46, 63(2), 82(2), 118
Micheal 39, 58, 82
VANCE (Vanse - Vause)
Catherine, Mrs. 101, 104
George 118
James 104, 125
Jemima 33
John 101, 107, 113, 133
Joseph 58
Rachel 33
Sarah 58
Theodosia 33
Thomas 114
William A. 106, 111, 117
Wm. 1, 3, 4(2), 5, 6, 14, 25, 26, 29, 32, 33, 39 43, 49, 53, 82(3), 88, 97, 106, 107, 111, 112(2), 114, 118, 119, 122, 125, 126, 127, 128(2), 130(2)
VANCHOCK
John 97
VANCOUVER
Charles 18, 49, 82
VANDAGRIFT (Vandergrift)
Anna 106
Christopher 103, 106, 138
John 138
Mary 103, 104
VANDEVAUTER (Vantervuter - Vandevander)
Cornelous 54, 82, 136
Jacob 97
Jametee 136
Janetty 97
John 97, 136
Molly 136
Nicholas 136
Nicholas 136
Peter 97, 136(2)
VANDIVEH (Vandivear - Vandimere)
Archibald 122, 133
Eliz. 137
Elmira Jane 137
Jacob 128, 135, 187
George 97
John 59, 97, 109, 117, 125, 126, 131, 137(2)
John William 137
Lewis 6, 35, 82, 114, 124
Mary Eliz. 137
Matilda 137
Nancy 137
Sally Ann 137
Samuel 101, 107, 117, 128
Sophia 137
Susan 101, 104
Vincent 119
William 4, 6, 14, 19, 27, 28, 29, 39, 49, 82(9), 97, 98, 109, 113, 124, 135, 137(2)
William, Jr. 137
VANDISOL (see Vanorsdel)
Cornelius 137
Jerimiah 137
VANMETER (see Danmeter)
Abraham 13, 21, 82(2), 97, 107, 137
Anna M. 137

Annah 18
Betsy Ann 137
Catherine 187
David 120, 137
Elizabeth 137
Eliz. J. 187
Garret 4, 7(2), 12, 17(17), 18(2), 23, 25, 28, 35, 36, 37(3), 46, 48(2), 53, 56, 57, 58, 61, 120, 137(3), 138(2)
Hellita 137
Henry 16, 45, 50, 58, 82(2), 120, 133, 137
Isaac 5, 7, 13, 14, 17, 25, 29, 33, 39, 40, 44, 51, 53, 56, 58, 82(2), 97, 137
Islac 97
Jacob 18(4), 23, 58, 61, 82 (3), 97, 137(3)
Jacob, Sr. 45, 82
John J. 187
John, Sr. 18, 58, 82
Joseph 9, 82, 97, 137
Rebecca 137(2)
Sally 137
Sarah 137
Solomon 23, 49, 127, 137
William C. 137
VANORSDEL (Vanarsdale) see Vandosal)
Abraham 34, 121
Cornelius 84
Martha 57
Peter 112
VANPELT
Jacob 2, 58
Sarah 58
VAN SHAICK
John 6
VANTEVENTER (see Vandaventer)
Cornelius 54, 82
Janely 97
VARDEN (see Verdon-Virden)
R. M. 128
William 5, 6
VARM
George 118
VAUSE (Vanse - Vance)
Jemima 33
John 113
Rachel 33
TThedosia 33
Thomas 114
William 3, 4, 5, 14, 18(3), 23, 29, 32, 33, 39, 43, 49, 53, 82(3), 88, 97, 124, 124, 127, 129 (see Vance)
William, Capt. 127
VERDEN (see Varden-Virden)
William 5, 6
VESTALL (Westfall)
Hannah 58
William 58
VINEY
Andrew 6, 58, 62, 137
Ann 137
Drusilla 137
Eliz. 137
Margaret 137
Mary 132
John 136
Stephen 97, 137
Susan 57, 97, 137
Susannah 137(2)
VIRDEN (see Verdon-Vardin)
William 5, 6
VISER (Biser)
Mary 137
Micheal 137
VOSS (see Vause)
Wm. 118
VOWLES (Bowles)
Charles 9
WADDLE
Julius 118(2)
WAGER
Archd. 47
WAGGONER (Waggener - Wagner)
A. 54, 59
Andrew 38(2), 54(2), 57(2), 58(3), 59
Agnes 124
Barbara 124
Catherine 137
Christopher 35
Eliz. 124, 137
Fred. 114, 137
Hannah 137
Henry L. 137
Jacob 114, 137
John 33(2), 82(2), 97, 124
John M. 137
Joseph 137
Mary 137
Nancy 137

INDEX

Peter 124
Rachel 137
Rosanna 137
Sally 137
Thomas 53, 82
WAGNER (see Waggoner)
Christopher 35
WAITE (Waites)
Ann 58
John 130
John, Sr. 58
William 130
WALIS (Walles - Wallace)
Thomas 108
WALKER
Andrew 58(2), 82, 114, 137
Ann 122, 137
David 8
Hannah 137
Hugh 24, 82
Isabella 137
James 7, 8, 26(2), 27, 36 (2), 46, 52, 58(3), 82, 97, 137
Jane 137
Jean 58
John 21, 58(2), 82, 97, 109
John, Sr. 58(2), 83
Margaret 137
Martha 128
Mary 58
Phoebe 58
Peter 20, 46, 58(2), 83(2)
Rebecca 137
Robert 6, 24, 40(5), 58(6), 83(7), 97, 114, 123, 137(3)
Sally 137
Samuel 58, 83
Sarah 137
Thomas 58(2), 83, 97, 108, 109, 123, 137
William 114, 137
William W. 114, 137
WALL
Amelia 107
WALLACE
John 108, 104
Mary, Mrs. 104
Peggy 116
Robert 58
Thomas 116
WALLES
John 86, 123
WALLIS (Walis)
John 43, 45, 61, 83(2), 123
WALTERS (see Watters - Waller)
Ephraim 59
John 59
Mary 59(2)
Peter 4
WAMSLEY
David 140
WANAMAKER
George 115
WARD (Wart)
Abigail 101, 104, 125
Alex 113
Aphia 132
Cassey 125
Cornelius 9, 17, 23, 52, 59 (2), 83(4)
David 59, 137
Edward 137
Eliz. 137(3)
Eliz., Mrs. 104
George 97
Hannah 137
Hester 137
Henry 101, 125
Israil 97, 137
Jesse 125, 137
Joel 131(2), 137(2)
John 101, 104, 109, 113, 114, 117(2), 121, 137(4)
John, Sr. 137
John W. 109
Joseph 46, 59, 83, 97
Lydia 137
Mary 59, 137(2)
Mrs. 127
Rachel 113
Ruth 137
Sarah 125, 137(2)
Simon 122, 137(2)
Stephen 97
Susannah 139
Sylvester (Syl.) 17(2), 50 (2), 97, 137, 140
WARDELL
John 10, 43, 57, 59, 83
Robert 10
WARDEN
Eliz. 59
James 97
William 97, 137
WARFIELD
Elijah 100
George, Col. 110
George 120, 130
Jesse 120

WARNER
Abigail 27
Dennis 52(2)
John 9
John Nicholas 115
WARREN
John 116
WARRING
P. 112
WART (Ward)
John 114
Joseph 59
Mary 59
WASHINGTON
G. 25
George 63
George W. 106, 108, 113, 128 (2), 135
Lund 52, 59, 83
Susanna 59
William 11, 60
WASSER
Adam 115
WASSON
Ann 137
Catherine 137
Dorcas 137
Elizabeth 137
Hannah 137
Isabella 137
James 137
Jane 137
Martha 137
Mary 137
Nancy 137
Polly 137
Sally 137
WASTEL (see Wostel)
Humphrey 28
WATATS (Watts)
Archibald 18(2)
WATERS (Watters - see Walters)
Ann 59
Catherine 59
John 20, 31, 59, 83(3)
Nancy 134
Philemon 59
William 134
WATERHOUSE
John 115
WATERMAN (Watterman)
James 59(2), 97
John 97, 137
Leah 59(2)
Mary 137
WATHEY
John 124
WATKINS
Ann 129
Catherine, Mrs. 104
Catherine 104, 107
Elizabeth 103, 104
Harrison 99, 104, 107
James 107
Jane 107
John A. 107
Moses 59
Mrs. 120(2)
Rebecca 129
William 107
WATSON
J. 6, 21, 39(5)
James 3, 59(3), 83, 102, 137
Jane 102, 104
Jean 137
John 137
Joseph 7, 9, 24(2), 29(2), 50, 59, 59(13)
Margaret 137
Martha 137
Mary 59, 137(2)
Rebecca 137
Robert 137
Thomas 42
William 59, 63, 137
WATTERS (Waters - Walters)
John 97
Peter 4, 83
WATTS
Archibald 18(2), 34(3), 50, 55, 59, 83(5), 116
Isabella 137
James 18(3), 24(2), 59(5), 83, 137
Jonathan 97
Susannah 59(5), 137(2)
Thomas 97, 137
WAXLER
Micheal 58, 59, 83
WAYLER
Micheal 97
WAYUNG
Daniel 125
WEALE
Peter 139
WEARSHALL
James 3
WEASE (Weaze)

Adam, Jr. 97
Adam, Sr. 97
Henry 137(2)
Jacob 97, 137
Jacob 97, 137
John 97
Mafgaret 137(2)
Mary 137
Micheal 97(2), 137
Solomon 137(2)
WEATHERINGTON (Worthington)
Ann 36(2)
Robert 36(2)
John 36, 97
Ann 36(2)
WEAVER
Abraham 110
Eliza, Mrs. 104
Franklin 100, 104
George 97, 139
WEB
Elizabeth 127
WEEMS
Frances 118
WEES
Thomas 54
WEIDENER
Jacob 97
WEIDNAR
Jacob 59
Sally 59
WEITMILLER
John 97, 139
WELCH
Benjamin 137
B. 109
Betsy 137
Denny (Dency) 18(2), 49, 83, 101, 119, 135, 137
Demsey 59, 104
Dempsy, Jr. 119(2)
Dorcas 137
Eliz. 101, 104, 137(2), 138
Eliz., Mrs. 104
Isaac 26, 43, 48(2), 83, 137
James 16, 83
Jemma 137
John 118, 137
Joseph 100
Lucy 137
Mary 137
Nancy 137
Randolph S. 119
Sarah 137
Sarah Jane 114
Susan 137
Susanna 137
Sylvester 18(2), 43, 53, 83, 102, 104, 137(2)
Thomas 108, 109, 110, 116, 119, 120
Wm. 14, 83, 100, 107, 108, 114, 117(2), 119, 137
WELLER
Daniel 42, 83
WELLS
Andrew 59
Humphrey 19, 34, 59, 83
Joseph 57
Phineas 97, 138
Samuel 111
Thomas 12, 132
WELTON (see Wetton)
Alanzo 104(2)
Ann 60(2)
Welton and Blue 63
David 1, 14, 38(2), 48, 52, 53, 60, 63, 83(7), 97, 131 (), 138(2)
Harriet, Mrs. 104
Jan 138
Jane 59
Jesse 17, 97, 138, 140
John 6, 53, 59(3), 60(2), 63, 138
Job 15, 17(7), 21, 23, 26(2), 45, 50, 53, 56(2), 57, 59, 60(2), 63, 83(3), 88, 97, 109, 124, 131, 138(2)
John, Capt. 55, 83
John, Jr. 60, 83
Jonathan 138
Mary 60
Mary Jane 138
Mary Msgdeline 138
Martha 138
Micheal 138
Rachel 138
Randle 133
Solo. 60, 131, 138
Susannah 60
William 15, 33, 60(3), 126, 128, 131, 133(2), 138(3)
WERBLE
John 60(2)
WERMAN
Nancy, Mrs. 104
Thomas 104
William 100, 104

WERTMILLER (see Weitmiller)
Jacob 97
WESS
Thomas 54
WESTABERGER
Barbara 138
George 138
Katy 138
Mary 138
WESTELL (see Wostell)
Humphrey 60
WESTFALL (see Vestall)
Abel 1, 6
Cornelius 60, 97, 138(2)
Daniel 97
Eleanor 97, 138
Eliza 60
Elizabeth 60
Hannah (Vestall) 58
Henry 97
Isaac 97, 138
Jacob 60, 97, 138
John 35, 48, 59, ,60, 117, 138(2)
John, Sr. 97, 110
John, Jr. 97
Judith 60
Mary 138
William 58, 59, 60(2), 83
Zachariah 138
WETTON (see Welton)
David 60
Job 60
Mary 60
WHALEY
Catherine 111
George 111
WHARTON
Isaac 49
John 60
Joseph 14, 30, 59(3), 83(5)
Joseph, Jr. 60
Rachel 49
Samuel 21(2), 30, 83(3)
Thomas 14, 15, 30, 49, 59 (8), 60(2), 83(7)
WHEAT
Joseph S. 131
WHEATLEY
Thomas 138
WHEELER
I. 34
Ignatius 43, 57, 60(4), 83, 97
J. 4, 25, 39, 43, 52, 59
J. G. 4, 35
Stephen B. 112
WHEELEY
William 24
WHELAN (Whelen)
Thomas 132
William 132
WHELEN (Whelan)
Mary 112(2)
WHETEBARY (Whiteberry)
George 41, 83
WHETSTONE
George 97
WHIGHT (White)
Adam 6
WHIP
Elizabeth 99, 104
WHITE
Abraham 36, 38, 83(2)
Adam 6, 53, 83
Alex exec. 23(2), 35, 42
Alex 1(2), 2, 3, 4, 5(5), 6, 7(6), 9, 10(2), 16(2), 20 (2), 23(4), 26(3), 27(2), 30(3), 32, 33, 35, 36(4), 37, 38, 39, 42(2), 44, 45, 46, 47(3), 50, 51, 52, 54 (2), 55, 58, 60(6), 63, 117, 138(2)
Alex 3rd 60(2)
Betsy 99, 104
Charles 97
C. S. 133
Ebenezer 97
Elizabeth 60, 136
F. 12, 21
F. Fr Frances 1, 4, 5, 6(3), 7, 8, 9, 10(3), 11, 12, 15, 19, 21, 25, 36, 38, 41, 42, 46, 48, 51, 60(5), 83(12), 86, 111, 122(3), 127, 128, 129, 134, 138
Frances M. 138
Fred. 7, 25
J. B. 119, 135
J. B., Jr. 133
James 41, 83, 99, 104
John 3, 123, 138(2)
John A. 138
John B. 103(2), 104(2), 109, 110, 113, 115, 116, 118, 120(3), 122(2), 124(2), 126, 127(2), 132, 133, 135

(2)
John M. 112
Joseph 112(3)
Margaret 60(4)
Mary 112, 137
Matilda, Mrs. 104, 124
Nowell 102, 104
Obed 88
Parthenia 100, 104
Robert 119, 122, 129
Robert, Jr. 23, 32, 33, 46, 47, 131
Robert N. 112, 138
Samuel P. 99, 122, 138
Sarah 104(2), 111
Thomas 14, 37, 52, 83, 112, 128
Thomas B. 99, 100, 101(2), 104, 112, 126, 134, 138
WHITEBERRY (see Whetebary)
George 31, 33, 41, 47, 60(3), 83
Mary 60
Nancy 60
WHITECOTTON
James 97
WHITEFIELD
Martin 102, 105
Sarah, Mrs. 105
WHITEHEAD
Benjamin 28, 111
R. 31
WHITEMAN
Dorcas 60, 138
Ezekiel 2, 23, 31(6), 60, 83, 85(2), 138
George 17(2), 83(2), 97, 140
John 60, 97, 132
Mary Ann 102, 105
Richard 12, 43, 58, 123
Sarah 132
WHOOP
Daniel 5, 83
WIATT
James 138
Leander 138
Mary 138
WICK
Mary 2(2), 61
Moses 2
WICKHAM
Matthew 97
WICKINS (see Wiggins)
John 25
WICUFF
Ursula
WIDMEYER (Widmire)
Micheal 35, 87, 113, 136
WIDMER
J. B. 138
WIGG (see Wiggins)
Archibald 41, 83
WIGGING (see Wiggins)
Archibald 60
Mary 60
WIGGINS (see Wigg - Wigging - Wickins)
Archibald 41, 60(3), 61(3), 98, 138, 139
Comfort 138
Joseph 60(2))
Metilda 60
Mary 60(2), 61
Sabarett 138
Phillip 60(3), 61, 83(3), 98 (2), 138
Thomas 60(4), 61, 83, 138
Thomas, Jr. 6, 60, 83
Thomas, Sr. 60(2)
WILBERFORCE
Jane 131
WILEY (see Willey)
Able 9, 18
Ann 61
Asahel 138
Benjamin 9, 18, 61, 83(2), 138
Betsy 138
Edward 138
Eliza Jane 138
Eliza Ann 138
Fanny 138
Jane 138
John 138
Joseph 4, 54
Laban 138(2)
Laura 138
Margaret 8
Sarah Jane 138
Zail 138
WILFRED
David 137
WILLEYS (Wiley)
Ann 61
Benjamin 61
Margaret 3
WILKEY
Eliza 107
Godfrey 83

John 83, 107, 139
WILKINS
George 97
Godfrey 45, 83, 97
John 46, 51, 83, 85, 139
Matthias 97
WILKINSON
John 40(2), 83, 134
Lucrelia 40
William 134
WILLETT
Benj. 6, 22, 25, 41, 83
WILLIAMS
Ann 61(2)
Barbary 119
Benjamin 38, 61, 138(2)
Bu. 38
Burnet 61
Catherine 61
Charles 38, 61
Daniel 38, 54, 61, 83
David 13, 32, 37, 61, 62, 83, 85, 113
Ebenezer 2, 8, 20, 61, 83(2), 97
Edward 26(3)
Edward, Jr. 53
Elizabeth 61(3), 138(2)
Elisabeth, Mrs. 105
Ephraim 138
Even 85
George 97
George S. 133
G. Washington 25
Hannah 122
Isaac 53, 85, 138(2)
James 61, 97, 138
Jane Thornton 111
Jared J. 116
John 2, 20, 25, 31, 34, 37, 45(2), 48, 60, 61(10), 83 (5), 103(2), 105, 113, 125, 138(5)
John, Jr. 20, 31, 38(2), 83 (2)
John, Sr. 31, 83
John H. 105
John R. 125
Joseph 2(2), 28, 31, 55, 61 (3), 83(4), 138
Lucy 111
Martha 61(2)
Martin, Dr. 111
Mary 61, 138(2)
McGuire 124
Moses 61(2), 83, 97
Nathaniel 61(2), 97
Noah 61
Owen 134
Peter 2, 10, 19, 34(2), 35, 36, 42, 46, 51, 57(3), 61 (5)
Phillip 138
Providence 61(2)
Prudence 61
Remembrance 97
Rhoda 128
Richard 5, 46, 61(2)
Richard, Sr. 97
Robert 58
Ruth 61
S. H. 63
Sabinah 61
Sam 61(2)
Sarah 61, 128, 138(2)
Susannah 129, 139
Thomas 11, 12, 18, 25, 28, 37, 60
Venson 138
Vincent 12 ,23, 26, 53, 61 (2), 84, 88, 98, 129, 138
William 30, 33, 61(2), 98, 116, 138(2)
Zedekiah 138
WILLIAMSON
Benjamin 102, 105
Cornelius 56, 61(2), 64, 99
Elizabeth 62
John 1, 5, 19(2), 49, 55, 61, 84(5), 98
Martha, Mrs. 105
Mary 99, 105
Rodey 61
Sam 56, 61(2), 84, 98, 107, 132
Thomas 61(2), 85, 98
William 1, 26, 33(2), 36, 43, 54, 55, 61, 62(2), 84 (4), 98
WILLIS
Maryan 131
WILLOWBY
Benjamin 98
WILSON
Abraham 138
Alex 105(2), 138
Ann 131
Aquilla P. 129
Benjamin 100, 134
Charles 98, 131

Dan 118(2)
David 15, 98(2)
Elen 104, 105
Elizabeth 120, 135, 138(3)
Eliza Jane 138
G. 21(2), 58, 63, 119
George 24, 30, 36, 58, 59 (2), 84(3), 128
Henry L. 98, 128
Hester Ann 138
Isaac Newton 134, 136, 138
James F. 123
James 30, 39, 58, 62(2), 84 (2), 118
Jim 109
John 17(4), 23, 35, 48, 62, 84, 88, 98(3), 104, 109, 137
John O. 129
Jonathan 138
Joseph D. 100, 105
Julianna 138
Lucinnda 138
Margaret, Mrs. 105
Maria 119
Maria L., Mrs. 105
Mary 98, 118(2)
P. P. 6, 7, 10(2), 25, 52
Phil P. 2, 37, 44, 62
Phil 6, 12, 24, 28, 31, 38(2), 62
Priscilla 62
Rachel 138(2)
Ralph 22
Ruth 118
Robert 12, 98
S. S. 129
Sarah 32, 138
Susanna 30
Susan V. 138
Susan Ann 138
Tacey Ann 138
Thomas 134, 138
Willinda 138
William 18, 52, 58, 61, 84 (2), 98, 108, 118, 120, 138
William, Sr. 98
William, Jr. 98
WILT (see Witt)
John M. 108
Jonathan 138
Rebecca 108
WILTZ
Fred 115
WINCKELBECK
Phillip 104, 105
Nancy, Mrs. 105
WIND
Moses 40, 84
WINE
Catherine 107
WINEOW
Adelaide Caroline Missouri 114
Catherine 114
Margaret Catherine 114
WINGFIELD
Elijah 102
Susannah 102, 105
WINGAT
William 35(2)
WINTERTON
John 27, 84, 98, 110(2), 138
John W. 100
Mary 138(2)
William 86
WIREMILLER
Jacob 50
WIREY
Robert 98
WISE
Abraham 4, 11, 20, 62(3), 84(3), 139
Adam 50, 62, 98
Bastian 98
Catherine 62
Christopher 98
Fredrick 57, 84
Jacob 98
John, Sr. 98
John, Jr. 98
Margaret 62
Martin 98
WISER
Henry 32, 58, 84(2)
WISTER
Daniel 30
WITHERS
A. G. 135
WITT (see Wilt)
Jonathan 138
Rebecca 108
WITTECHER
Thomas 85
WOODROW
And. (nearly every page) from 1 to 63, also 84(36), 98, 104, 114, 115, 116, 117 (2), 124, 127, 131, 135, 138
Andrew J. 138
Andrew, Jr. 117, 138
Andrew, Col. 111, 124

Craig 117
Elizabeth 138
Emily 117, 138
Mary Ann 6, 40, 62, 106
Mary 28, 62(8), 117, 131, 138
M. A. 20, 37
Matilda 138
Morgan 20
Tett 19
Woodrow and Neilson 24, 84
William 138
WOLF (Woolf)
Ann 113
David 22, 45, 49, 84, 98
George 62, 98, 129, 134
H. B. 124
Jacob 4, 23
John 5, 84, 86, 98
Lucy Ann 102, 105
Mary 62
Micheal 62
Nancy 113(2)
Phillip 31
Thomas 5
WOLFORD
Adam 111, 138
Ann 138
Eliz. 138
Henry 125, 138(2)
Isabella 99, 103, 105, 138
Jacob 102, 138
James M. 102
John 38, 84, 87, 99, 103, 111, 112, 126, 134, 138
Josiah 134
Lucy Ann 102, 105
Martin 138(2)
Mary 134
Micheal C. 115
Mitchell C. 111
Phoebe 138
Rosanna 138
WOLLESTON
John 85(2)
WOLVERTON
Elizabeth 63, 104, 105
Elizabeth, Mrs. 105
Isaac 62, 104, 105, 126, 137
Jacob 105
Joel 48, 84, 99, 105
Margaret 134
Mariah 105
WOOD
Arminella 132
B. W. 125
Bettia 98
Daniel 44, 52, 62(2), 84(2), 111
David 128
Elias 126
Ebenezer 98
Elizabeth 126, 128
Gabriel 40, 84
James 7, 55, 59
John 17, 34(2), 37, 52, 59, 63, 84(2)
Jonathan 138
Joseph 19, 98
Margaret 62(2)
Mary 63, 138
Peter 98
Richard 98
Robert 7, 84, 54
Thomas 28, 32, 34, 35, 47, 63, 98
William 108
WOODCOCK
John 16(8)
John S. 16
WOODFORD
William 53
WOODSON
Betty 63, 84
Eliz. 63
John 26, 63(2), 84(2)
Mary 63, 84
Nicholas 63, 84
Samuel 63(2), 56, 84
Thomas 63, 84
William C. 113, 135
WOOLF (Wolf)
John 140
WORKMAN
John 110
WORLEY
John 138
Jude 138
Margaret 138
Micheal 98, 138
WORTHINGTON (see Weatherington)
Ann 36(2)
Eliz. 63
John 36, 98
Robert 36(2), 52(2), 63(2)
Sam, Jr. 46, 63(2), 84
WORSTEL

Humphrey 46, 61, 63
WOSTELL
Humphrey 10, 63
WRENN
Angeline 138
Eliz. 113, 138
Hannah 138
James 138
John 138
Lucinda 138
Margaret 138
Turner 138
William 138
WRIGHT
Anna 138
Benjamin 48, 58
Eliz. 138
Fanny 138
Gabriel 28, 29, 61, 98
George 119
John 63, 138
Joseph 138
Margaret 138
Pegga 138
Robert 46, 84, 138
William 138
WULFF (see Wolfe -Woolf)
John Hurd 135, 140
WYECOFF (Wycoff - see Wicuf)
Jeter 98
Peter 63
Urusla 118
WYNKOOP
Benjamin 22, 84
WYNN
Robert 108, 128
WYTHE
B. 15
YAGAR
Catherine 63
Joseph 40, 63, 84
YAKEHAN
Letty 123
Jacob 128
YANGLING
Abraham 115
YANCY
Richard 53
YATES (Yeats)
Charles 36
Eleanor 100, 105
Gabriel 100
Joseph 15(2), 38
Robert 38
YAZLE (see Yeazle)
YEATYRATER
Peter 98
YEATS (Keats - see Yates)
Margery 124
Mary 124
YEATER
Peter 98
YEAZLE (Hazle - see Yazle)
David 140
Jacob 98
YEIDER
Elizabeth 108(2)
John 108
YEIZER (Yeiser)
Eliz. 63
John 44, 63, 84
YETTER
Eliz. 63
Peter 63
YOAKAM (Yoakim - Yoakum)
Eliz. 98, 117, 138(2)
George 98, 138
Isaac 138
Jacob 35(2), 98, 117, 138
John 17, 84, 98, 138
Mathias 138
Michael 98, 138
Millia 138
Phillip Paul 98
Solomon 138
YOAKMAN
Jacob 7(2)
YOKAM (Yokum)
YONLEY
Rebecca 117, 123
Thomas 117
YORK
Ammen 116
Jeremiah 15(2)
YOST
Catherine 132
Charles 35
John 105
Matthew 110
Margaret 105(2)
YOTHER
Malichi 31, 84
YOUNG
Andrew 124
Chas., Jr. 37
Edwin 3
Eliz., Mrs. 105

Eliz. 120
George 37, 53, 63, 102, 105
Hannah 12
Henry 98
James 128
J. B. 135
Jacob 46, 49
John 98
Robert 26, 63, 121
Sarah 103, 105
William 1, 12, 22(2), 24, 36, 63, 84(3), 85, 98, 107
William B. 108
YOUNGLEY
Thos. 87
YOUNT
Elizabeth 135
ZAILOR (see Zilor)
Jacob 35, 84
ZANE
Isaac 3, 32, 52, 84(3)
Joseph 98
ZEE (see Lee)
Barbara 117(2)
ZILOR (see Zailor)
Jacob, Jr. 136
Jacob, Sr. 136
ZIMMERMON (man)
Jacob 131, 136
William 48